admirador *m*, **admiradora** *f* admirer
campeón *m*, **-ona** *f* champion
salvapantallas *m inv* INFOR screensaver
ronquido *m* snore; ***ronquidos*** *pl* snoring *sg*
enemigo 1 *adj* enemy *atr* **2** *m* enemy; ***ser enemigo de*** *fig* be opposed to, be against
lleno *adj* full (***de*** of); *pared* covered (***de*** with)

Grammatical information

debatir ⟨3a⟩ **1** *v/t* debate, discuss **2** *v/i* struggle **3** *v/r* **debatirse**: ***debatirse entre la vida y la muerte*** fight for one's life

Entries divided into grammatical categories

uva *f* BOT grape; ***estar de mala uva*** F be in a foul mood; ***tener mala uva*** F be a nasty piece of work F
fiambre *m* cold cut, *Br* cold meat; P (*cadáver*) stiff P
profiláctico 1 *adj* preventive, prophylactic *fml* **2** *m* condom

Register labels

acomedido *adj* *L.Am.* obliging, helpful
acomedirse ⟨3l⟩ *v/r* *Méx* offer to help
residencial 1 *adj* residential **2** *f* *Arg, Chi* boarding house
sablear ⟨1a⟩ *v/t & v/i* *L.Am.* F scrounge (***a*** from)

Latin American Spanish

riñonera *f* fanny pack, *Br* bum bag
rotonda *f* traffic circle, *Br* roundabout

British variants

C D E F G H I J K L M N Ñ O P Q R S T U V W XY Z

Spanish Concise Dictionary

Spanish – English
Inglés – Español

Berlitz Publishing
New York · Munich · Singapore

Edited by the Langenscheidt editorial staff

Based on a dictionary compiled by LEXUS

Activity section by Heather Bonikowski

Book in cover photo: © Punchstock/Medioimages

Berlitz Publishing
193 Morris Avenue
Springfield, NJ 07081
USA

Printed in Germany
ISBN-13: 978-981-268-018-1
ISBN-10: 981-268-018-7

1. 2. 3. 4. 5. 11 10 09 08 07

Preface

This new dictionary of English and Spanish is a tool with 50,000 references for learners of the Spanish language at beginner's or intermediate level.

Thousands of colloquial and idiomatic expressions have been included. The user-friendly layout with all headwords in blue allows the user to have quick access to all the words, expressions and their translations.

Clarity of presentation has been a major objective. Is the *mouse* you need for your computer, for example, the same in Spanish as the *mouse* you don't want in the house? This dictionary is rich in sense distinctions like this - and in translation options tied to specific, identified senses.

Vocabulary needs grammar to back it up. In this dictionary you will find extra grammar information on Spanish conjugation and on irregular verb forms.

The additional activity section provides the user with an opportunity to develop language skills with a selection of engaging word puzzles. The games are designed specifically to improve vocabulary, spelling, grammar and comprehension in an enjoyable style.

Designed for a wide variety of uses, this dictionary will be of great value to those who wish to learn Spanish and have fun at the same time.

Contents

Preface 3
Contents 4
How to use the dictionary 5
Abbreviations 10
The pronunciation of Spanish 12
Written Spanish 15
English pronunciation 16
Spanish-English dictionary 17
Activity section 239
English-Spanish dictionary 287
Spanish verb conjugations 595
Notas sobre el verbo inglés 616
Numbers 621

How to use the dictionary

To get the most out of your dictionary you should understand how and where to find the information you need. Whether you are yourself writing text in a foreign language or wanting to understand text that has been written in a foreign language, the following pages should help.

1. How and where do I find a word?

1.1 Spanish and English headwords. The word list for each language is arranged in alphabetical order and also gives irregular forms of verbs and nouns in their correct alphabetical order.

Sometimes you might want to look up terms made up of two separate words, for example **shooting star**, or hyphenated words, for example **absent-minded**. These words are treated as though they were a single word and their alphabetical ordering reflects this.

The only exception to this strict alphabetical ordering is made for English phrasal verbs - words like **go off**, **go out**, **go up**. These are positioned in a block directly after their main verb (in this case **go**), rather than being scattered around in alphabetical positions.

Spanish words beginning with **ch** and **ll** are positioned in their alphabetical position in letters C and L. Words beginning with **ñ** are listed after N.

1.2 Spanish feminine headwords are shown as follows:

> **abogado** *m*, **-a** *f* lawyer
> **fumador** *m*, **fumadora** *f* smoker
> **bailarín** *m*, **-ina** *f* dancer
> **pibe** *m*, **-a** *f Rpl* F kid F
> **edil** *m*, **edila** *f* council(l)or

The feminine forms of these headwords are: **abogada**, **fumadora**, **bailarina**, **piba** and **edila**.

When a Spanish headword has a feminine form which translates differently from the masculine form, the feminine is entered as a separate headword in alphabetical order:

> **empresaria** *f* businesswoman; **empresario** *m* businessman

1.3 Running heads

If you are looking for a Spanish or English word you can use the **running heads** printed in bold in the top corner of each page. The running head on the left tells you the *first* headword on the left-hand page and the one on the right tells you the *last* headword on the right-hand page.

1.4 How is the word spelt?

You can look up the spelling of a word in your dictionary in the same way as you would in a spelling dictionary. British spelling variants are marked *Br.* If just a single letter is omitted in the American spelling, this is put between round brackets:

colo(u)r – hono(u)r – travel(l)er

2. How do I split a word?

Spanish speakers find English hyphenation very difficult. All you have to do with this dictionary is look for the bold dots between syllables. These dots show you where you can split a word at the end of a line but you should avoid having just one letter before or after the hyphen as in **a·mend** or **thirst·y**. In such cases it is better to take the entire word over to the next line.

3. Long dashes

In the Spanish-English part of the dictionary, when a headword is repeated in a phrase or compound with an altered form, a long dash is used:

escaso *adj* … ***-as posibilidades de*** not much chance of, little chance of

Here ***-as posibilidades*** means ***escasas posibilidades***.

4. What do the different typefaces mean?

4.1 All Spanish and English headwords and the Arabic numerals differentiating between parts of speech appear in **bold**:

neoyorquino 1 *adj* New York *atr* **2** *m*, **-a** New Yorker
splin·ter ['splɪntər] **1** *n* astilla *f* **2** *v/i* astillarse

4.2 Italics are used for:

a) abbreviated grammatical labels: *adj*, *adv*, *v/i*, *v/t* etc

b) gender labels: *m*, *f*, *mpl* etc

c) all the indicating words which are the signposts pointing to the correct translation for your needs:

sport·y ['spɔːrtɪ] *adj person* deportista; *clothes* deportivo
◆**work out 1** *v/t problem*, *puzzle* resolver; *solution* encontrar, hallar **2** *v/i at gym* hacer ejercicios; *of relationship etc* funcionar, ir bien
completo *adj* complete; *autobús*, *teatro* full
grano *m* grain; *de café* bean; *en la piel* pimple, spot

4.3 All phrases (examples and idioms) are given in ***secondary bold italics***:

> **sym·pa·thet·ic** [sɪmpə'θetɪk] *adj* (*showing pity*) compasivo; (*understanding*) comprensivo; ***be sympathetic toward a person / an idea*** simpatizar con una persona / idea
> **salsa** *f* GASTR sauce; *baile* salsa; ***en su salsa*** *fig* in one's element

4.4 The normal typeface is used for the translations.

4.5 If a translation is given in italics, and not in the normal typeface, this means that the translation is more of an *explanation* in the other language and that an explanation has to be given because there just is no real equivalent:

> **'walk-up** *n apartamento en un edificio sin ascensor*
> **adobera** *f Méx type of mature cheese*

5. Stress

To indicate where to put the **stress** in English words, the stress marker appears before the syllable on which the main stress falls:

> **mo·tif** [moʊ'tiːf] motivo *m*
> **rec·ord**[1] ['rekɔːrd] *n* MUS disco *m*; SP *etc* récord *m*
> **re·cord**[2] [rɪ'kɔːrd] *v/t electronically* grabar; *in writing* anotar

Stress is shown either in the pronunciation or, if there is no pronunciation given, in the actual headword or compound itself:

> **'rec·ord hold·er** plusmarquista *m/f*

6. What do the various symbols and abbreviations tell you?

6.1 A solid blue diamond is used to indicate a phrasal verb:

> ◆**call off** *v/t* (*cancel*) cancelar; *strike* desconvocar

6.2 A white diamond is used to divide up longer entries into more easily digested chunks of related bits of text:

> **de** *prp* ◇ *origen* from; ***de Nueva York*** from New York; ***de a*** from to ◇ *posesión* of; ***el coche de mi amigo*** my friend's car ◇ *material* (made) of; ***un anillo de oro*** a gold ring ◇ *contenido* of; ***un vaso de agua*** a glass of water ◇ *cualidad*: ***una mujer de 20 años*** a 20 year old woman ◇ *causa* with; ***temblaba de miedo*** she was shaking with fear …

6.3 The abbreviation F tells you that the word or phrase is used colloquially rather than in formal contexts. The abbreviation V warns you that a word or phrase is vulgar or taboo.Words or phrases labeled P are slang. Be careful how you use these words.

These abbreviations, F, V and P, are used both for headwords and phrases (placed after) and for the translations of headwords and phrases (placed after). If there is no such label given, then the word or phrase is neutral.

6.4 A colon before an English or Spanish word or phrase means that usage is restricted to this specific example (at least as far as this dictionary's translation is concerned):

catch-22 [kætʃtwentɪ'tuː]: ***it's a catch-22 situation*** es como la pescadilla que se muerde la cola
co-au·thor [koʊɒθər] ... **2** *v/t*: ***co-author a book*** escribir un libro conjuntamente
decantarse ⟨1a⟩ *v/r*: ***decantarse por*** opt for

7. Does the dictionary deal with grammar too?

7.1 All English headwords are given a part of speech label:

tooth·less ['tuːθlɪs] *adj* desdentado
top·ple ['tɑːpl] **1** *v/i* derrumbarse **2** *v/t* *government* derrocar

But if a headword can only be used as a noun (in ordinary English) then no part of speech is given, since none is needed:

'tooth·paste pasta *f* de dientes, dentífrico *m*

7.2 Spanish headwords have part of speech labels. Spanish gender markers are given:

barbacoa *f* barbecue
bocazas *m/f inv* F *loudmouth* F
budista *m/f & adj* Buddhist

7.3 If an English translation of a Spanish adjective can only be used in front of a noun, and not after it, this is marked with *atr*:

bursátil *adj* stock market *atr*
campestre *adj* rural, country *atr*

7.4 If the Spanish, unlike the English, doesn't change form if used in the plural, this is marked with *inv*:

cortacircuitos *m inv* circuit breaker
metrópolis *f inv* metropolis

7.5 If the English, in spite of appearances, is not a plural form, this is marked with *nsg*:

> **bil·li·ards** ['bɪljərdz] *nsg* billar *m*
> **mea·sles** ['miːzlz] *nsg* sarampión *m*

English translations are given a *pl* or *sg* label (for plural or singular) in cases where this does not match the Spanish:

> **acciones** *pl* COM stock *sg*, *Br* shares
> **entarimado** *m* (*suelo*) floorboards *pl*

7.6 Irregular English plurals are identified:

> **the·sis** ['θiːsɪs] (*pl* ***theses*** ['θiːsiːz]) tesis *f inv*
> **thief** [θiːf] (*pl* ***thieves*** [θiːvz]) ladrón (-ona) *m*(*f*)
> **trout** [traʊt] (*pl* ***trout***) trucha *f*

7.7 Words like **physics** or **media studies** have not been given a label to say if they are singular or plural for the simple reason that they can be either, depending on how they are used.

7.8 Irregular and semi-irregular verb forms are identified:

> **sim·pli·fy** ['sɪmplɪfaɪ] *v/t* (*pret & pp* ***-ied***) simplificar
> **sing** [sɪŋ] *v/t & v/i* (*pret* ***sang***, *pp* ***sung***) cantar
> **la·bel** ['leɪbl] **1** *n* etiqueta *f* **2** *v/t* (*pret & pp* ***-ed***, *Br* ***-led***) *bags* etiquetar

7.9 Cross-references are given to tables of Spanish conjugations:

> **gemir** ⟨3l⟩ *v/i* moan, groan
> **esconder** ⟨2a⟩ **1** *v/t* hide, conceal …

7.10 Grammatical information is provided on the prepositions you'll need in order to create complete sentences:

> **'switch·o·ver** *to new system* cambio *m* (***to*** a)
> **sneer** [sniːr] **1** *n* mueca *f* desdeñosa **2** *v/i* burlarse (***at*** de)
> **escindirse** ⟨3a⟩ *v/r* (*fragmentarse*) split (***en*** into); (*segregarse*) break away (***de*** from)
> **enviciarse** ⟨1b⟩ *v/r* get addicted (***con*** to)

Abbreviations

and	&	y
see	→	véase
registered trademark	®	marca registrada
abbreviation	*abbr*	abreviatura
abbreviation	*abr*	abreviatura
adjective	*adj*	adjetivo
adverb	*adv*	adverbio
agriculture	AGR	agricultura
anatomy	ANAT	anatomía
architecture	ARCHI	arquitectura
Argentina	*Arg*	Argentina
architecture	ARQUI	arquitectura
article	*art*	artículo
astronomy	AST	astronomía
astrology	ASTR	astrología
attributive	*atr*	atributivo
motoring	AUTO	automóvil
civil aviation	AVIA	aviación
biology	BIO	biología
Bolivia	*Bol*	Bolivia
botany	BOT	botánica
British English	*Br*	inglés británico
Central America	*C.Am.*	América Central
chemistry	CHEM	química
Chile	*Chi*	Chile
Colombia	*Col*	Colombia
commerce, business	COM	comercio
comparative	*comp*	comparativo
computers, IT term	COMPUT	informática
conjunction	*conj*	conjunción
Southern Cone	*CSur*	Cono Sur
sports	DEP	deporte
contemptuous	*desp*	despectivo
determiner	*det*	determinante
Ecuador	*Ecuad*	Ecuador
education (schools, universities)	EDU	educación, enseñanza (sistema escolar y universitario)
electronics, electronic engineering	EL	electrónica, electrotecnia
electronics, electronic engineering	ELEC	electrónica, electrotecnia
Spain	*Esp*	España
especially	*esp*	especialmente
euphemistic	*euph*	eufemismo
familiar, colloquial	F	familiar
feminine	*f*	femenino
feminine noun and adjective	*f/adj*	sustantivo femenino y adjetivo
railroad	FERR	ferrocarriles
figurative	*fig*	figurativo
financial	FIN	finanzas
physics	FÍS	física
formal	*fml*	formal
photography	FOT	fotografía
feminine plural	*fpl*	femenino plural
feminine singular	*fsg*	femenino singular
gastronomy	GASTR	gastronomía
geography	GEOG	geografía
geology	GEOL	geología
geometry	GEOM	geometría
grammatical	GRAM	gramática
historical	HIST	histórico
humorous	*hum*	humorístico
IT term	INFOR	informática
interjection	*int*	interjección
interrogative	*interr*	interrogativo
invariable	*inv*	invariable
ironic	*iron*	irónico
ironic	*irón*	irónico
law	JUR	jurisprudencia
Latin America	*L.Am.*	América Latina
law	LAW	jurisprudencia
linguistics	LING	lingüística
literary	*lit*	literario
masculine	*m*	masculino
masculine noun and adjective	*m/adj*	sustantivo masculino y adjetivo
nautical	MAR	navegación, marina
mathematics	MAT	matemáticas

mathematics	MATH	matemáticas
medicine	MED	medicina
meteorology	METEO	meteorología
Mexico	*Mex*	México
Mexico	*Méx*	México
masculine and feminine	*m/f*	masculino y femenino
masculine and feminine plural	*m/fpl*	masculino y femenino plural
military	MIL	militar
mineralogy	MIN	mineralogía
motoring	MOT	automóvil
masculine plural	*mpl*	masculino plural
music	MUS	música
music	MÚS	música
mythology	MYTH	mitología
noun	*n*	sustantivo
nautical	NAUT	navegación, náutica
negative	*neg*	negativo
noun plural	*npl*	sustantivo plural
noun singular	*nsg*	sustantivo singular
ornithology	ORN	ornitología
oneself	O.S.	sí mismo
popular, slang	P	popular
painting	PAINT	pintura
Paraguay	Parag	Paraguay
past participle	*part*	participio pasado
Peru	*Pe*	Perú
pejorative	*pej*	peyorativo
photography	PHOT	fotografía
physics	PHYS	física
painting	PINT	pintura
plural	*pl*	plural
politics	POL	política
possessive	*pos*	posesivo
possessive	*poss*	posesivo
past participle	*pp*	participio pasado
predicative usage	*pred*	predicativo
prefix	*pref*	prefijo
preposition	*prep*	preposición
preterite (past tense)	*pret*	pretérito
pronoun	*pron*	pronombre
preposition	*prp*	preposición
psychology	PSI	psicología
psychology	PSYCH	psicología
chemistry	QUÍM	química
radio	RAD	radio
railroad	RAIL	ferrocarriles
relative	*rel*	relativo
religion	REL	religión
River Plate	*Rpl*	Río de la Plata
South America	*S.Am.*	América del Sur
singular	*sg*	singular
someone	s.o.	alguien
sports	SP	deporte
Spain	*Span*	España
something	*sth*	algo, alguna cosa
subjunctive	*subj*	subjuntivo
superlative	*sup*	superlativo
bullfighting	TAUR	tauromaquia
also	*tb*	también
theater, theatre	TEA	teatro
technology	TÉC	técnica
technology	TECH	técnica
telecommunications	TELEC	telecomunicaciones
theater	THEA	teatro
typography, typesetting	TIP	tipografía
transportation	TRANSP	transportes
television	TV	televisión
vulgar	V	vulgar
auxiliary verb	*v/aux*	verbo auxiliar
verb	*vb*	verbo
Venezuela	*Ven*	Venezuela
intransitive verb	*v/i*	verbo intransitivo
impersonal verb	*v/impers*	verbo impersonal
reflexive verb	*v/r*	verbo reflexivo
transitive verb	*v/t*	verbo transitivo
West Indies	*W.I.*	Antillas
zoology	ZO	zoología

The pronunciation of Spanish

Stress

1. If a word ends in a vowel, or in *n* or *s*, the penultimate syllable is stressed: **espada**, **biblioteca**, **hablan**, **telefonean**, **edificios**.
2. If a word ends in a consonant other than *n* or *s*, the last syllable is stressed: **dificultad**, **hablar**, **laurel**, **niñez**.
3. If a word is to be stressed in any way contrary to rules 1 and 2, an acute accent is written over the stressed vowel: **rubí**, **máquina**, **crímenes**, **carácter**, **continúa**, **autobús**.
4. **Diphthongs and syllable division**. Of the 5 vowels *a*, *e*, *o* are considered "strong" and *i* and *u* "weak":

   a) A combination of weak + strong forms a diphthong, the stress falling on the stronger element: **reina**, **baile**, **cosmonauta**, **tiene**, **bueno**.
   b) A combination of weak + weak forms a diphthong, the stress falling on the second element: **viuda**, **ruido**.
   c) Two strong vowels together remain two distinct syllables, the stress falling according to rules 1 and 2: **ma/estro**, **atra/er**.
   d) Any word having a vowel combination not stressed according to these rules has an accent: **traído**, **oído**, **baúl**, **río**.

Sounds

Since the pronunciation of Spanish is (unlike English) adequately represented by the spelling of words, Spanish headwords have not been given a phonetic transcription. The sounds of Spanish are described below.

The pronunciation described is primarily that of the educated Spaniard. But the main features of Latin American pronunciation are also covered.

Vowels

a As in English *father*: **paz**, **pata**.

e Like *e* in English *they* (but without the following sound of *y*): **grande**, **pelo**. A shorter sound when followed by a consonant in the same syllable, like *e* in English *get*: **España**, **renta**.

i Like *i* in English *machine*, though somewhat shorter: **pila**, **rubí**.

o As in English *November*, *token*: **solo**, **esposa**. A shorter sound when followed by a consonant in the same syllable, like *au* in English *fault* or the *a* in *fall*: **costra**, **omba**.

u Like *oo* in English *food*: **pura**, **luna**. Silent after **q** and in **gue**, **gui**, unless marked with a dieresis (**antigüedad**, **argüir**).

y When occurring as a vowel (in the conjunction **y** or at the end of a word), is pronounced like *i*.

Diphthongs

ai like *i* in English *right*: **baile**, **vaina**.

ei like *ey* in English *they*: **reina**, **peine**.

oi like *oy* in English *boy*: **boina**, **oigo**.

au like *ou* in English *bout*: **causa**, **audacia**.

eu like the vowel sounds in English *may-you*, without the sound of the *y*: **deuda**, **reuma**.

Semiconsonants

i, y like *y* in English *yes*: **yerno**, **tiene**; in some cases in *L.Am.* this *y* is pronounced like the *s* in English *measure*: **mayo**, **yo**.

u like *w* in English *water*: **huevo**, **agua**.

Consonants

b, v These two letters represent the same value in Spanish. There are two distinct pronunciations:

1. At the start of a word and after *m* and *n* the sound is like English *b*: **batalla**, **ventaja**; **tromba**, **invierno**.
2. In all other positions the sound is what is technically a "bilabial fricative". This sound does not exist in English. Go to say a *b* but do not quite bring your lips together: **estaba**, **cueva**, **de Vigo**.

c
1. *c* before *a*, *o*, *u* or a consonant is like English *k*: **café**, **cobre**.
2. *c* before *e*, *i* is like English *th* in *thin*: **cédula**, **cinco**. In *L.Am.* this is pronounced like an English *s* in *chase*.

ch like English ch in church: **mucho**, **chocho**.

d Three distinct pronunciations:

1. At the start of a word and after *l* and *n*, the sound is like English *d*: **doy**, **aldea**, **conde**.
2. Between vowels and after consonants other than *l* and *n* the sound is relaxed and approaches English *th* in *this*: **codo**, **guardar**; in parts of Spain it is further relaxed and even disappears, particularly in the **-ado** ending.
3. In final position, this type 2 is further relaxed or omitted altogether: **usted**, **Madrid**.

f like English *f*: **fuero**, **flor**.

g Three distinct pronunciations:

1. Before *e* and *i* it is the same as the Spanish **j** (below): **coger, general.**
2. At the start of a word and after *n*, the sound is that of English *g* in *get*: **granada**, **rango**.
3. In other positions the sound is like 2 above, but much softer, the *g* almost disappearing: **agua**, **guerra**. N.B. In the group **gue**, **gui** the **u** is silent (**guerra**, **guindar**) unless marked with a dieresis (**antigüedad**, **argüir**). In the group **gua** all letters are sounded.

h always silent: **honor**, **búho**.

j A strong guttural sound not found in English, but like the *ch* in Scots *loch*, German *Achtung*: **jota**, **ejercer**.

k like English *k*: **kilogramo**, **ketchup**.

l like English *l*: **león**, **pala**.

ll approximating to English *lli* in *million*: **millón**, **calle**. In *L.Am.* like the *s* in English *measure*.

m like English *m*: **mano**, **como**.

n like English *n*: **nono**, **pan**; except before **v**, when the group is pronounced like *mb*: **enviar**, **invadir**.

ñ approximating to English *ni* in *onion*: **paño**, **ñoño**.

p like English *p*: **Pepe**, **copa**.

q like English *k*; always in combination with *u* , which is silent: **que**, **quiosco**.

r a single trill stronger than any *r* in English, but like Scots *r*: **caro**, **querer**. Somewhat relaxed in final position. Pronounced like **rr** at the start of a word and after **l**, **n**, **s**: **rata**.

rr strongly trilled: **carro**, **hierro**.

s like *s* in English *chase*: **rosa**, **soso**. But before **b**, **d**, hard **g**, **l**, **m** and **n** it is like English *s* in *rose*: **desde**, **mismo**, **asno**. Before "impure **s**" in recent loan-words, an extra *e*-sound is inserted in pronunciation: **e-sprint**, **e-stand**.

t like English *t*: **patata**, **tope**.

v see *b*.

w found in a few recent loan-words only and pronounced pretty much as the English *w*, but sometimes with a very slight *g* sound before it: **whisky**, **windsurf**. In one exceptional case it is pronounced like an English *v* or like Spanish **b** and **v**: **wáter**.

x like English *gs* in *big sock*: **máximo**, **examen**. Before a consonant like English *s* in *chase*: **extraño**, **mixto**.

z like English *th* in *thin*: **zote**, **zumbar**. In *L.Am.* like English *s* in *chase*.

The Spanish Alphabet

a [ah]	g [Heh]	m ['emeh]	rr ['erreh]	x ['ekees]
b [beh]	h ['acheh]	n ['eneh]	s ['eseh]	y [eegree-eh-ga]
c [theh]	i [ee]	ñ ['en-yeh]	t [teh]	z ['theh-ta]
ch [cheh]	j ['ɧota]	o [oh]	u [oo]	
d [deh]	k [ka]	p [peh]	v ['ooveh]	H *is pronounced*
e [eh]	l ['eleh]	q [koo]	w ['ooveh	*as in the Scottish*
f ['ef-feh]	ll ['el-yeh]	r ['ereh]	doh-bleh]	*way of saying loch*

Written Spanish

I. Capitalization

The rules for capitalization in Spanish largely correspond to those for the English language. In contrast to English, however, adjectives derived from proper nouns are not capitalized (*americano* American, *español* Spanish).

II. Word division

Spanish words are divided according to the following rules:

1. If there is a **single consonant** between two vowels, the division is made between the first vowel and the consonant (*di-ne-ro*, *Gra-na-da*).
2. **Two consecutive consonants** may be divided (*miér-co-les*, *dis-cur-so*). If the second consonant is an *l* or *r*, however, the division comes before the two consonants (*re-gla*, *nie-bla*; *po-bre*, *ca-bra*). This also goes for *ch*, *ll* and *rr* (*te-cho*, *ca-lle*, *pe-rro*).
3. In the case of **three consecutive consonants** (usually including an *l* or *r*), the division comes after the first consonant (*ejem-plo*, *siem-pre*). If the second consonant is an *s*, however, the division comes after the *s* (*cons-tan-te*, *ins-ti-tu-to*).
4. In the case of **four consecutive consonants** (the second of these is usually an *s*), the division is made between the second and third consonants (*ins-tru-men-to*).
5. **Diphthongs** and **triphthongs** may not be divided (*bien*, *buey*). Vowels which are part of different syllables, however, may be divided (*frí-o*, *acre-e-dor*).
6. **Compounds**, including those formed with prefixes, are divided morphologically (*nos-otros*, *des-ali-ño*, *dis-cul-pa*).

III. Punctuation

In Spanish a comma is often placed after an adverbial phrase introducing a sentence (*sin embargo, todos los esfuerzos fueron inútiles* however, all efforts were in vain). A subsidiary clause beginning a sentence is also followed by a comma (*si tengo tiempo, lo haré* if I have time, I'll do it, **but**: *lo haré si tengo tiempo* I'll do it if I have time).

Questions and exclamations are introduced by an inverted question mark and exclamation point respectively, which immediately precedes the question or exclamation (*Dispense usted, ¿está en casa el señor Pérez?* Excuse me, is Mr. Pérez at home?; *¡Que lástima!* What a shame!).

English pronunciation

Vowels

[ɑː]	*father* ['fɑːðər]
[æ]	*man* [mæn]
[e]	*get* [get]
[ə]	*about* [ə'baʊt]
[ɜ]	*absurd* [əb'sɜːrd]
[ɪ]	*stick* [stɪk]
[iː]	*need* [niːd]
[ɒː]	*in-laws* ['ɪnlɒːz]
[ɔː]	*more* [mɔːr]
[ʌ]	*mother* ['mʌðər]
[ʊ]	*book* [bʊk]
[uː]	*fruit* [fruːt]

Diphthongs

[aɪ]	*time* [taɪm]
[aʊ]	*cloud* [klaʊd]
[eɪ]	*name* [neɪm]
[ɔɪ]	*point* [pɔɪnt]
[oʊ]	*oath* [oʊθ]

Consonants

[b]	*bag* [b] [æ]
[d]	*dear* [dɪr]
[f]	*fall* [fɒːl]
[g]	*give* [gɪv]
[h]	*hole* [hoʊl]
[j]	*yes* [jes]
[k]	*come* [kʌm]
[l]	*land* [lænd]
[m]	*mean* [miːn]
[n]	*night* [naɪt]
[p]	*pot* [pɑːt]
[r]	*right* [raɪt]
[s]	*sun* [sʌn]
[t]	*take* [teɪk]
[v]	*vain* [veɪn]
[w]	*wait* [weɪt]
[z]	*rose* [roʊz]
[ŋ]	*bring* [brɪŋ]
[ʃ]	*she* [ʃiː]
[ʧ]	*chair* [ʧer]
[dʒ]	*join* [dʒɔɪn]
[ʒ]	*leisure* ['liːʒər]
[θ]	*think* [θɪŋk]
[ð]	*the* [ðə]
[']	means that the following syllable is stressed: *ability* [ə'bɪlətɪ]

Part 1

Spanish-English Dictionary

A

a *prp* ◇ *dirección* to; ***al este de*** to the east of; ***a casa*** home; ***ir a la cama / al cine*** go to bed / to the movies; ***vamos a Bolivia*** we're going to Bolivia; ***voy a casa de Marta*** I'm going to Marta's (house)
◇ *situación* at; ***a la mesa*** at the table; ***al lado de*** next to; ***a la derecha*** on the right; ***al sol*** in the sun; ***a treinta kilómetros de Quito*** thirty kilometers (*Br* kilometres) from Quito; ***está a cinco kilómetros*** it is five kilometers (*Br* kilometres) away
◇ *tiempo*: ***¿a qué hora llegas?*** what time do you arrive?; ***a las tres*** at three o'clock; ***estamos a quince de febrero*** it's February fifteenth; ***a los treinta años*** at the age of thirty
◇ *modo*: ***a la española*** the Spanish way; ***a mano*** by hand; ***a pie*** on foot; ***a 50 kilómetros por hora*** at fifty kilometers (*Br* kilometres) an hour
◇ *precio*: ***¿a cómo*** *or* ***cuánto está?*** how much is it?
◇ *objeto indirecto*: ***dáselo a tu hermano*** give it to your brother
◇ *objeto directo*: ***vi a mi padre*** I saw my father
◇ *en perífrasis verbal*: ***empezar a*** begin to; ***jugar a las cartas*** play cards; ***a decir verdad*** to tell the truth
◇ *para introducir pregunta*: ***¿a que no lo sabes?*** I bet you don't know; ***a ver ...*** OK ..., right ...

ábaco *m* abacus

abadía *f* abbey

abajo 1 *adv situación* below, underneath; *en edificio* downstairs; ***ponlo ahí abajo*** put it down there; ***el cajón de abajo*** *siguiente* the drawer below; *último* the bottom drawer ◇ *dirección* down; *en edificio* downstairs; ***cuesta abajo*** downhill; ***empuja hacia abajo*** push down
◇ *con cantidades*: ***de diez para abajo*** ten or under, ten or below **2** *int*: ***¡abajo los traidores!*** down with the traitors!

abalanzarse ⟨1f⟩ *v/i* rush *o* surge forward; ***abalanzarse sobre algo / alguien*** leap *o* pounce on sth/s.o.

abalear ⟨1a⟩ *v/t S. Am.* shoot

abandonar ⟨1a⟩ **1** *v/t lugar* leave; *objeto, a alguien* abandon; *a esposa, hijos* desert; *idea* give up, abandon; *actividad* give up **2** *v/r* **abandonarse** let o.s. go; ***abandonarse a*** abandon o.s. to

abanicar ⟨1g⟩ **1** *v/t* fan **2** *v/r* **abanicarse** *v/r* fan o.s.

abanico *m* fan; *fig* range; ***abanico eléctrico*** *Méx* electric fan

abaratar ⟨1a⟩ *v/t* reduce or lower the price of; *precio* reduce, lower

abarcar ⟨1g⟩ *v/t territorio* cover; *fig* comprise, cover; *L.Am.* (*acaparar*) hoard, stockpile; ***el libro abarca desde ... hasta ...*** the book covers the period from ... to ...; ***abarcar con la vista*** take in

abarrotado *adj* packed

abarrotar ⟨1a⟩ **1** *v/t lugar* pack; *L.Am.* COM buy up, stockpile **2** *v/r* **abarrotarse** *L.Am. del mercado* become glutted

abarrotes *mpl L.Am.* (*mercancías*) groceries; (***tienda de***) ***abarrotes*** grocery store, *Br* grocer's

abarrotería *f Méx, C.Am.* grocery store, *Br* grocer's

abarrotero *m*, **-a** *f Méx, C.Am.* storekeeper, shopkeeper

abastecer ⟨2d⟩ **1** *v/t* supply (***de*** with) **2** *v/r* **abastecerse** stock up (***de*** on *o* with)

abastecimiento *m* supply

abasto *m*: ***no dan abasto*** they can't cope (***con*** with)

abatí *m Rpl* corn, *Br* maize; *Parag*: *fermented maize drink*

abatible *adj* collapsible, folding *atr*

abatido *adj* depressed

abatimiento *m* gloom

abatir ⟨3a⟩ *v/t edificio* knock *o* pull down; *árbol* cut down, fell; AVIA shoot *o* bring down; *fig* kill; (*deprimir*) depress

abdicación *f* abdication

abdicar ⟨1g⟩ *v/t* abdicate

abdomen *m* abdomen

abdominal *adj* abdominal

abdominales *mpl* sit-ups

abecedario *m* alphabet

abedul *m* birch

abeja *f* zo bee

abejorro *m* bumblebee

aberración *f* aberration

abertura *f* opening

abeto *m* fir (tree)

abiertamente *adv* openly

abierto 1 *part* → **abrir 2** *adj tb persona* open; ***está abierto a nuevas ideas*** *fig* he's open to new ideas

abigarrado *adj* multicolo(u)red

abismo *m* abyss; *fig* gulf

ablandar ⟨1a⟩ **1** *v/t tb fig* soften **2** *v/r*

ablandarse soften, get softer; *fig* relent
ablande *m Arg* AUTO running in
abnegación *f* self-denial
abnegado *adj* selfless
abocado *adj* doomed; ***abocado al fracaso*** doomed to failure, destined to fail
abochornar ⟨1a⟩ **1** *v/t* embarrass **2** *v/r* **abochornarse** feel embarrassed
abogacía *f* law
abogaderas *fpl L.Am.* F (*discusiones*) arguments
abogado *m*, **-a** *f* lawyer; *en tribunal superior* attorney, *Br* barrister; ***no le faltaron abogados*** *fig* there were plenty of people who defended him
abogar ⟨1h⟩ *v/i*: ***abogar por*** *alguien* defend; *algo* advocate
abolición *f* abolition
abolir ⟨3a⟩ *v/t* abolish
abollado *adj* dented
abolladura *f* dent
abollar ⟨1a⟩ *v/t* dent
abombado *adj S. Am.* F *comida* rotten, bad; F (*tonto*) dopey F
abombarse *S. Am. de comida* go off, go bad
abominable *adj* abominable
abominar ⟨1a⟩ *v/t* detest, loathe
abonado *m*, **-a** *f* subscriber; *a teléfono, gas, electricidad* customer; *a ópera, teatro* season-ticket holder
abonar ⟨1a⟩ **1** *v/t* COM pay; AGR fertilize; *Méx* pay on account; ***abonar el terreno*** *fig* sow the seeds **2** *v/r* **abonarse** *a espectáculo* buy a season ticket (***a*** for); *a revista* take out a subscription (***a*** to)
abono *m* COM payment; AGR fertilizer; *para espectáculo, transporte* season ticket
abordar ⟨1a⟩ *v/t* MAR board; *tema, asunto* broach, raise; *problema* tackle, deal with; *a una persona* approach
aborigen **1** *adj* native, indigenous **2** *m/f* native
aborrecer ⟨2d⟩ *v/t* loathe, detest
abortar ⟨1a⟩ **1** *v/i* MED *espontáneamente* miscarry; *de forma provocada* have an abortion **2** *v/t plan* foil
abortivo *adj* abortion *atr*; ***píldora -a*** abortion pill
aborto *m espontáneo* miscarriage; *provocado* abortion; *fig* F freak F; ***tener un aborto*** have a miscarriage
abotonar ⟨1a⟩ *v/t* button up
abra *f L.Am.* clearing
abrasador *adj* scorching (hot)
abrasar ⟨1a⟩ **1** *v/t* burn **2** *v/i del sol* burn, scorch; *de bebida, comida* be boiling hot **3** *v/r* **abrasarse**: ***abrasarse de sed*** F be parched F; ***abrasarse de calor*** F be sweltering F; ***abrasarse de pasión*** *lit* be aflame with passion *lit*
abrazar ⟨1f⟩ **1** *v/t* hug **2** *v/r* **abrazarse** embrace
abrazo *m* hug; ***dar un abrazo a alguien*** hug s.o., give s.o. a hug; ***un abrazo*** *en carta* best wishes; *más íntimo* love
abrebotellas *m inv* bottle opener
abrelatas *m inv* can opener, *Br tb* tin opener
abreviar ⟨1b⟩ *v/t* shorten; *palabra* abbreviate; *texto* abridge
abreviatura *f* abbreviation
abridor *m* bottle opener
abrigado *adj* warmly dressed
abrigar ⟨1h⟩ **1** *v/t* wrap up; *esperanzas* hold out; *duda* entertain **2** *v/r* **abrigarse** wrap up warm; ***abrigarse del frío*** (take) shelter from the cold
abrigo *m* coat; (*protección*) shelter; ***ropa de abrigo*** warm clothes; ***al abrigo de*** in the shelter of
abril *m* April
abrir ⟨3a; *part* **abierto**⟩ **1** *v/t* open; *túnel* dig; *grifo* turn on; ***le abrió el apetito*** it gave him an appetite **2** *v/i de persona* open up; *de ventana, puerta* open; ***en un abrir y cerrar de ojos*** in the twinkling of an eye **3** *v/r* **abrirse** open; ***abrirse a algo*** *fig* open up to sth; ***abrirse paso entre*** make one's way through
abrochar ⟨1a⟩ **1** *v/t* do up; *cinturón de seguridad* fasten **2** *v/r* **abrocharse** do up; *cinturón de seguridad* fasten; ***tendremos que abrocharnos el cinturón*** we'll have to tighten our belts
abrumador *adj* overwhelming
abrumar ⟨1a⟩ *v/t* overwhelm (***con*** *or* ***de*** with); ***abrumado de*** *or* ***con trabajo*** snowed under with work
abrupto *adj terreno* rough; *pendiente* steep; *tono, respuesta* abrupt; *cambio* sudden
absentismo *m* absenteeism; ***absentismo escolar*** truancy
absolución *f* absolution
absolutamente *adv* absolutely; ***no entendió absolutamente nada*** he didn't understand a thing
absolutismo *m* absolutism
absoluto *adj* absolute; ***en absoluto*** not at all
absolver ⟨2h; *part* **absuelto**⟩ *v/t* JUR acquit; REL absolve
absorbente *adj* absorbent
absorber ⟨2a⟩ *v/t* absorb; (*consumir*) take; (*cautivar*) absorb
absorto *adj* absorbed (***en*** in), engrossed (***en*** in)

abstemio 1 *adj* teetotal **2** *m*, **-a** *f* teetotal(l)er
abstención *f* abstention
abstenerse ⟨2l⟩ *v/r* refrain (**de** from); POL abstain
abstinencia *f* abstinence; ***síndrome de abstinencia*** MED withdrawal symptoms *pl*
abstracto *adj* abstract
abstraerse ⟨2p; *part* **abstraido** ⟩ *v/r* shut o.s. off (**de** from)
abstraído 1 *adj* preoccupied; ***abstraído en algo*** engrossed in sth **2** *part* → ***abstraerse***
absuelto *part* → ***absolver***
absurdo 1 *adj* absurd **2** *m*: ***es un absurdo que*** it's absurd that
abuchear ⟨1a⟩ *v/t* boo
abucheo(s) *m* (*pl*) booing *sg*, boos *pl*
abuela *f* grandmother; F *persona mayor* old lady; ***¡cuéntaselo a tu abuela!*** F don't try to put one over on me! F, *Br* pull the other one! F
abuelo *m* grandfather; F *persona mayor* old man; ***abuelos*** grandparents
abultado *adj* bulging; *derrota* heavy
abultamiento *m* bulge
abultar ⟨1a⟩ *v/i* be bulky; ***no abulta casi nada*** it takes up almost no room at all
abundancia *f* abundance; ***había comida en abundancia*** there was plenty of food
abundante *adj* plentiful, abundant
abundar ⟨1a⟩ *v/i* be plentiful *o* abundant
aburguesarse ⟨1a⟩ *v/r desp* become bourgeois *o* middle class
aburrido *adj* (*que aburre*) boring; (*que se aburre*) bored; ***aburrido de algo*** bored *o* fed up F with sth
aburrimiento *m* boredom
aburrir ⟨3a⟩ **1** *v/t* bore **2** *v/r* **aburrirse** get bored; ***aburrirse de algo*** get bored *o* fed up F with sth; ***aburrirse como una ostra*** F get bored stiff F
abusado *adj Méx* F smart, clever; ***¡abusado!*** look out!
abusar ⟨1a⟩ *v/i*: ***abusar de*** *poder, confianza* abuse; *persona* take advantage of; ***abusar del alcohol*** drink too much; ***abusar sexualmente de alguien*** sexually abuse s.o.
abusivo *adj* JUR unfair
abuso *m* abuse; ***abusos*** *pl* ***deshonestos*** indecent assault *sg*
A.C. *abr* (***= antes de Cristo***) BC (= before Christ)
acá *adv* here; ***de acá para allá*** from here to there; ***de entonces para acá*** since then
acabado *m* finish
acabar ⟨1a⟩ **1** *v/t* finish **2** *v/i de persona* finish; *de función, acontecimiento* finish, end; ***acabé haciéndolo yo*** I ended up doing it myself; ***acabar con*** put an end to; *caramelos* finish off; *persona* destroy; ***acabar de hacer algo*** have just done sth; ***va a acabar mal*** F *persona* he'll come to no good; ***esto va a acabar mal*** F this is going to end badly **3** *v/r* **acabarse** *de actividad* finish, end; *de pan, dinero* run out; ***se nos ha acabado el azúcar*** we've run out of sugar; ***¡se acabó!*** that's that!
acacia *f* acacia
academia *f* academy; ***academia de idiomas*** language school; ***academia militar*** military academy
académico 1 *adj* academic **2** *m*, **-a** *f* academician
acalenturarse ⟨1a⟩ *v/r L.Am.* (*afiebrarse*) get a temperature *o* fever
acallar ⟨1a⟩ *v/t tb fig* silence
acalorarse ⟨1a⟩ *v/r* (*enfadarse*) get worked up; (*sofocarse*) get embarrassed
acampada *f* camp; ***ir de acampada*** go camping
acampar ⟨1a⟩ *v/i* camp
acantilado *m* cliff
acaparar ⟨1a⟩ *v/t* hoard, stockpile; *tiempo* take up; *interés* capture; (*monopolizar*) monopolize
acápite *m L.Am.* section; (*párrafo*) paragraph
acaramelado *adj fig* F lovey-dovey F
acariciar ⟨1b⟩ *v/t* caress; *perro* stroke; ***acariciar una idea*** *fig* contemplate an idea
acarrear ⟨1a⟩ *v/t* carry; *fig* give rise to, cause
acaso *adv* perhaps; ***por si acaso*** just in case
acatar ⟨1a⟩ *v/t* comply with, obey
acatarrarse ⟨1a⟩ *v/r* catch a cold
acaudalado *adj* wealthy, well-off
acceder ⟨2a⟩ *v/i* (*ceder*) agree (**a** to), accede (**a** to) *fml*; ***acceder a*** *lugar* gain access to; *cargo* accede to *fml*
accesible *adj* accessible
acceso *m tb* INFOR access; *de fiebre* attack, bout; *de tos* fit; ***de difícil acceso*** inaccessible
accesorio 1 *adj* incidental **2** *m* accessory
accidentado 1 *adj terreno, camino* rough; *viaje* eventful **2** *m*, **-a** *f* casualty
accidental *adj* (*no esencial*) incidental; (*casual*) chance *atr*
accidente *m* accident; (*casualidad*) chance; GEOG feature; ***accidente de tráfico*** *or* ***de circulación*** road traffic ac-

cident, RTA; ***accidente laboral*** industrial accident
acción *f* action; ***acciones*** *pl* COM stock *sg*, *Br* shares; ***poner en acción*** put into action
accionar ⟨1a⟩ *v/t* activate
accionista *m/f* stockholder, *Br* shareholder
acebo *m* holly
acechar ⟨1a⟩ *v/t* lie in wait for
acecho *m*: ***al acecho*** lying in wait
aceite *m* oil; ***aceite de girasol / oliva*** sunflower / olive oil; ***aceite lubricante*** lubricating oil
aceitera *f* TÉC oilcan; GASTR cruet
aceitoso *adj* oily
aceituna *f* olive
aceleración *f* acceleration
acelerador *m* accelerator
acelerar ⟨1a⟩ **1** *v/t motor* rev up; *fig* speed up; ***aceleró el coche*** she accelerated **2** *v/i* accelerate **3** *v/r* **acelerarse** *L.Am.* F (*enojarse*) lose one's cool
acelgas *fpl* BOT Swiss chard *sg*
acento *m en ortografía, pronunciación* accent; (*énfasis*) stress, emphasis; ***poner el acento en*** *fig* stress, emphasize
acentuar ⟨1e⟩ **1** *v/t* stress; *fig* accentuate, emphasize **2** *v/r* **acentuarse** become more pronounced
acepción *f* sense, meaning
aceptable *adj* acceptable
aceptación *f* acceptance; (*éxito*) success
aceptar ⟨1a⟩ *v/t* accept
acequia *f* irrigation ditch
acera *f* sidewalk, *Br* pavement; ***ser de la otra acera, ser de la acera de enfrente*** F be gay
acerca *adv*: ***acerca de*** about
acercar ⟨1g⟩ **1** *v/t* bring closer; ***acercar a alguien a un lugar*** give s.o. a ride (*Br* lift) somewhere **2** *v/r* **acercarse** approach; (*ir*) go; *de grupos, países* come closer together; *de fecha* draw near; ***se acercó a mí*** she came up to me *o* approached me; ***acércate*** come closer; ***no te acerques a la pared*** don't get close to the wall
acero *m* steel; ***acero inoxidable*** stainless steel
acertado *adj comentario* apt; *elección* good, wise; ***estar muy acertado*** be dead right
acertar ⟨1k⟩ **1** *v/t respuesta* get right; *al hacer una conjetura* guess **2** *v/i* be right; ***acertar con algo*** get sth right
acertijo *m* riddle, puzzle
achacar ⟨1g⟩ *v/t* attribute (***a*** to)
achantarse ⟨1a⟩ *v/r* F keep quiet, keep one's mouth shut F
achaque *m* ailment
achatado *adj* flattened
achatarse ⟨1a⟩ *v/r* be flattened
achicharrar ⟨1a⟩ *v/t* **1** burn **2** *v/r* **achicharrarse** *fig* F roast F
achinado *adj L.Am.* oriental-looking
achinero *m C.Am. vendedor* peddler
achiquitarse ⟨1a⟩ *v/r L.Am.* become frightened *o* scared
achisparse ⟨1a⟩ *v/r* F get tipsy F
acholar ⟨1a⟩ *v/t S. Am.* embarrass
achuchar ⟨1a⟩ *v/t fig* F pester, nag
achuchón *m* F squeeze, hug; (*empujón*) push; ***le dio un achuchón*** *desmayo* she felt faint
achuras *fpl S. Am.* variety meat *sg*, *Br* offal *sg*
aciago *adj* fateful
acicalarse ⟨1a⟩ *v/r* get dressed up
acidez *f* acidity; ***acidez de estómago*** heartburn
ácido **1** *adj tb fig* sour, acid **2** *m* acid
acierto *m idea* good idea; *respuesta* correct answer; *habilidad* skill
aclamación *f* acclaim
aclamar ⟨1a⟩ *v/t* acclaim
aclaración *f* clarification
aclarar ⟨1a⟩ **1** *v/t duda, problema* clarify, clear up; *ropa, vajilla* rinse **2** *v/i de día* break, dawn; *del tiempo* clear up **3** *v/r* **aclararse**: ***aclararse la voz*** clear one's throat; ***no me aclaro*** F I don't understand; *por cansancio, ruido etc* I can't think straight
aclimatarse ⟨1a⟩ *v/r* acclimatize, become acclimatized
acné *m* acne
ACNUR *abr* (**= *Alto Comisionado de las Naciones Unidas para los Refugiados***) UNHCR (= United Nations High Commission for Refugees)
acobardar ⟨1a⟩ **1** *v/t* daunt **2** *v/r* **acobardarse** get frightened, lose one's nerve
acodarse ⟨1a⟩ *v/r* lean (one's elbows) (***en*** on)
acogedor *adj* welcoming; *lugar* cozy, *Br* cosy
acoger ⟨2c⟩ **1** *v/t* receive; *en casa* take in; ***acoger con satisfacción*** welcome, greet with satisfaction **2** *v/r* **acogerse**: ***acogerse a algo*** have recourse to sth
acogida *f* reception; ***tener buena acogida*** get a good reception, be well received
acojonar ⟨1a⟩ **1** *v/t* V (*asustar*) scare the shit out of P; (*asombrar*) knock out F, blow away P **2** *v/r* **acojonarse** V be shit scared P
acolchado *adj Rpl* quilted

acolchonar ⟨1a⟩ *v/t Rpl* quilt
acomedido *adj L.Am.* obliging, helpful
acomedirse ⟨3l⟩ *v/r Méx* offer to help
acometer ⟨2a⟩ **1** *v/t* attack; *tarea, proyecto* undertake, tackle **2** *v/i* attack; ***acometer contra algo*** attack sth
acomodado *adj* well-off
acomodador *m* usher
acomodadora *f* usherette
acomodar ⟨1a⟩ **1** *v/t* (*adaptar*) adapt; *a alguien* accommodate **2** *v/r* **acomodarse** make o.s. comfortable; (*adaptarse*) adapt (***a*** to)
acompañamiento *m* accompaniment
acompañante *m/f* companion; MÚS accompanist
acompañar ⟨1a⟩ *v/t* (*ir con*) go with, accompany *fml*; (*permanecer con*) keep company; MÚS, GASTR accompany
acompaño *m C.Am.* (*reunión*) meeting
acomplejar ⟨1a⟩ **1** *v/t*: ***acomplejar a alguien*** give s.o. a complex **2** *v/r* **acomplejarse** get a complex
acondicionar ⟨1a⟩ *v/t un lugar* equip, fit out; *pelo* condition
acongojar ⟨1a⟩ *v/t lit* grieve *lit*, distress
aconsejable *adj* advisable
aconsejar ⟨1a⟩ *v/t* advise
acontecer ⟨2d⟩ *v/i* take place, occur
acontecimiento *m* event
acopio *m*: ***hacer acopio de*** gather, muster
acoplar ⟨1a⟩ **1** *v/t piezas* fit together **2** *v/r* **acoplarse** *de persona* fit in (***a*** with); *de nave espacial* dock (***a*** with); *de piezas* fit together
acorazado *adj* armo(u)red
acordar ⟨1m⟩ **1** *v/t* agree **2** **acordarse** *v/r* remember; ***¿te acuerdas de él?*** do you remember him?
acorde **1** *adj*: ***acorde con*** appropriate to, in keeping with **2** *m* MÚS chord
acordeón *m* accordion
acordeonista *m/f* accordionist
acordonar ⟨1a⟩ *v/t* cordon off
acorralar ⟨1a⟩ *v/t tb fig* corner
acortar ⟨1a⟩ **1** *v/t* shorten **2** *v/i* take a short cut **3** *v/r* **acortarse** get shorter
acosar ⟨1a⟩ *v/t* hound, pursue; *con preguntas* bombard (***con*** with)
acosijar ⟨1a⟩ *v/t Méx* badger, pester
acoso *m fig* hounding, harrassment; ***acoso sexual*** sexual harrassment
acostar ⟨1m⟩ **1** *v/t* put to bed **2** *v/r* **acostarse** go to bed; (*tumbarse*) lie down; ***acostarse con alguien*** go to bed with s.o., sleep with s.o.
acostumbrado *adj* (*habitual*) usual; ***estar acostumbrado a algo*** be used to sth
acostumbrar ⟨1a⟩ **1** *v/t* get used (***a*** to) **2** *v/i*: ***acostumbraba a venir a este café todas las mañanas*** he used to come to this café every morning **3** *v/r* **acostumbrarse** get used (***a*** to); ***se acostumbró a levantarse temprano*** he got used to getting up early
ácrata *m/f & adj* anarchist
acre *adj olor* acrid; *crítica* biting
acrecentar ⟨1k⟩ **1** *v/t* increase **2** *v/r* **acrecentarse** increase, grow
acreditar ⟨1a⟩ **1** *v/t diplomático etc* accredit (***como*** as); (*avalar*) prove; ***un documento que lo acredita como el propietario*** a document that is proof of his ownership **2** *v/r* **acreditarse** acquire a good reputation
acreedor *m*, **acreedora** *f* creditor
acreencia *f L.Am.* credit
acribillar ⟨1a⟩ *v/t*: ***acribillar a alguien a balazos*** riddle s.o. with bullets; ***acribillar a alguien a preguntas*** bombard s.o. with questions
acrílico *m/adj* acrylic
acristalar ⟨1a⟩ *v/t* glaze
acróbata *m/f* acrobat
acrobático *adj* acrobatic; ***vuelo acrobático*** stunt flight
acta(s) *f* (*pl*) minutes *pl*
actitud *f* (*disposición*) attitude; (*posición*) position
activar ⟨1a⟩ *v/t* activate; (*estimular*) stimulate
actividad *f* activity
activista *m/f* POL activist
activo **1** *adj* active; ***en activo*** on active service; ***población -a*** labo(u)r force **2** *m* COM assets *pl*
acto *m* (*acción*), TEA act; *ceremonia* ceremony; ***acto sexual*** sexual intercourse; ***acto seguido*** immediately afterward(s); ***en el acto*** instantly, there and then
actor *m* actor
actriz *f* actress
actuación *f* TEA performance; (*intervención*) intervention
actual *adj* present, current; ***un tema muy actual*** a very topical issue
actualidad *f* current situation; ***en la actualidad*** at present, presently; (*hoy en día*) nowadays; ***actualidades*** current affairs
actualizar ⟨1f⟩ *v/t* bring up to date, update
actualmente *adv* currently
actuar ⟨1e⟩ *v/i* (*obrar, ejercer*), TEA act; MED work, act
acuarela *f* watercolo(u)r
acuario *m* aquarium

Acuario *m/f inv* ASTR Aquarius
acuático *adj* aquatic; ***deporte acuático*** water sport
acuchillar ⟨1a⟩ *v/t* stab
acuciante *adj* pressing, urgent
acudir ⟨3a⟩ *v/i* come; ***acudir a alguien*** turn to s.o.; ***acudir a las urnas*** go to the polls
acueducto *m* aqueduct
acuerdo *m* agreement; ***estar de acuerdo con*** agree with; ***llegar a un acuerdo, ponerse de acuerdo*** come to *o* reach an agreement (***con*** with); ***de acuerdo con algo*** in accordance with sth; ***¡de acuerdo!*** all right!, OK!
acumulación *f* accumulation
acumular ⟨1a⟩ **1** *v/t* accumulate **2** *v/r* **acumularse** accumulate
acunar ⟨1a⟩ *v/t* rock
acuñar ⟨1a⟩ *v/t monedas* mint; *término, expresión* coin
acuoso *adj* watery
acupuntura *f* acupuncture
acurrucarse ⟨1g⟩ *v/r* curl up
acusación *f* accusation
acusado *m*, **-a** *f* defendant
acusar ⟨1a⟩ *v/t* accuse (***de*** of); JUR charge (***de*** with); (*manifestar*) show; ***acusar recibo de*** acknowledge receipt of
acuse *m*: ***acuse de recibo*** acknowledg(e)ment
acusetas *m/f inv S. Am.* F tattletale F, *Br* tell-tale F
acusica *m/f* F tattletale F, *Br* tell-tale F
acústica *f* acoustics
adaptable *adj* adaptable
adaptación *f* adaptation; ***adaptación cinematográfica*** screen *o* movie version
adaptador *m* adaptor
adaptar ⟨1a⟩ **1** *v/t* adapt **2** **adaptarse** *v/r* adapt (***a*** to)
A. de C. *abr* (= ***año de Cristo***) AD (= Anno Domini)
adecentar ⟨1a⟩ *v/t* straighten up, tidy up
adecuadamente *adv* properly
adecuado *adj* suitable, appropriate
adecuar ⟨1d⟩ **1** *v/t* adapt (***a*** to) **2** *v/r* **adecuarse** fit in (***a*** with)
adefesio *m fig* F monstrosity F; *persona* freak F; ***estar hecho un adefesio*** look a sight
a. de J.C. *abr* (= ***antes de Jesucristo***) BC (= before Christ)
adelantado *adj* advanced; ***por adelantado*** in advance; ***ir adelantado*** *de un reloj* be fast
adelantamiento *m* AUTO passing maneuver, *Br* overtaking manoeuvre
adelantar ⟨1a⟩ **1** *v/t mover* move forward; *reloj* put forward; AUTO pass, *Br* overtake; *dinero* advance; (*conseguir*) achieve, gain **2** *v/i de un reloj* be fast; (*avanzar*) make progress; AUTO pass, *Br* overtake **3** *v/r* **adelantarse** *mover* move forward; (*ir delante*) go on ahead; *de estación, cosecha* be early; *de un reloj* gain; ***se me adelantó*** she beat me to it, she got there first
adelante *adv en espacio* forward; ***seguir adelante*** carry on, keep going; ***¡adelante!*** come in; ***más adelante*** *en tiempo* later on; ***de ahora*** *or* ***de aquí en adelante*** from now on; ***salir adelante*** *fig*: *de persona* succeed; *de proyecto* go ahead
adelanto *m tb* COM advance
adelfa *f* BOT oleander
adelgazante *adj* weight-reducing, slimming *atr*
adelgazar ⟨1f⟩ **1** *v/t* lose **2** *v/i* lose weight
ademán *m* gesture; ***hacer ademán de*** make as if to
además **1** *adv* as well, besides **2** *prp*: ***además de*** as well as
adentrarse ⟨1a⟩ *v/r*: ***adentrarse en*** *territorio* penetrate; *tema* go into
adentro **1** *adv* inside; ***¡adentro!*** get inside!; ***mar adentro*** out to sea; ***adentro de*** *L.Am.* inside **2** *mpl*: ***para sus adentros*** to oneself
adepto *m* follower; *fig* supporter
aderezar ⟨1f⟩ *v/t con especias* season; *ensalada* dress; *fig* liven up
adeudar ⟨1a⟩ *v/t* owe
adherente *adj* adhesive
adherir ⟨3i⟩ **1** *v/i* stick, adhere *fml* **2** *v/t* stick **3** *v/r* **adherirse** *a superficie* stick (***a*** to), adhere (***a*** to) *fml*; ***adherirse a una organización*** become a member of *o* join an organization; ***adherirse a una idea*** support an idea
adhesivo *m/adj* adhesive
adicción *f* addiction; ***adicción a las drogas*** drug addiction
adicional *adj* additional
adictivo *adj* addictive
adicto **1** *adj* addicted (***a*** to); ***ser adicto al régimen*** be a supporter of the regime **2** *m*, **-a** *f* addict
adiestrar ⟨1a⟩ *v/t* train
adinerado *adj* wealthy
adiós **1** *int* goodbye, bye; *al cruzarse* hello **2** *m* goodbye; ***decir adiós*** say goodbye (***a*** to)
aditivo *m* additive
adivinanza *f* riddle
adivinar ⟨1a⟩ *v/t* guess; *de adivino* foretell
adjetivo *m* adjective
adjudicar ⟨1g⟩ **1** *v/t* award **2** *v/r* **adjudi-**

carse win
adjuntar ⟨1a⟩ *v/t* enclose
adm. *abr* (= ***administración***) admin (= administration)
administración *f* administration; *de empresa etc* management; (*gobierno*) administration, government; ***administración púiblica*** civil service
administrador *m*, **administradora** *f* administrator; *de empresa etc* manager
administrar ⟨1a⟩ *v/t medicamento, sacramentos* administer, give; *empresa* run, manage; *bienes* manage
administrativo 1 *adj* administrative **2** *m*, **-a** *f* administrative assistant
admirable *adj* admirable
admiración *f* admiration; ***signo de admiración*** exclamation mark
admirador *m*, **admiradora** *f* admirer
admirar ⟨1a⟩ **1** *v/t* admire; (*asombrar*) amaze **2** *v/r* **admirarse** be amazed (***de*** at *o* by)
admisible *adj* admissible
admisión *f* admission; ***derecho de admisión*** right of admission
admitir ⟨3a⟩ *v/t* (*aceptar*) accept; (*reconocer*) admit
admón. *abr* (= ***administración***) admin (= administration)
ADN *abr* (= ***ácido desoxirribonucleico***) DNA (= deoxyribonucleic acid)
adobar ⟨1a⟩ *v/t* GASTR marinate
adobera *f Méx type of mature cheese*
adobo *m* GASTR marinade
adoctrinar ⟨1a⟩ *v/t* indoctrinate
adolecer ⟨2d⟩ *v/t* suffer (***de*** from)
adolescencia *f* adolescence
adolescente *m/f* adolescent
adonde *adv* where
adónde *interr* where
adopción *f* adoption
adoptar ⟨1a⟩ *v/t* adopt
adoptivo *adj padres* adoptive; *hijo* adopted
adoquín *m* paving stone
adorable *adj* lovable, adorable
adoración *f* adoration
adorar ⟨1a⟩ *v/t* love, adore; REL worship
adormecer ⟨2d⟩ **1** *v/t* make sleepy **2** *v/r* **adormecerse** doze off
adormidera *f* BOT poppy
adormilado *adj* sleepy
adormilarse ⟨1a⟩ *v/r* doze off
adornar ⟨1a⟩ *v/t* decorate
adorno *m* ornament; *de Navidad* decoration
adosar ⟨1a⟩ *v/t*: ***adosar algo a algo*** put sth (up) against sth
adquirir ⟨3i⟩ *v/t* acquire; (*comprar*) buy
adquisición *f* acquisition; ***hacer una buena adquisición*** make a good purchase
adquisitivo *adj*: ***poder adquisitivo*** purchasing power
adrede *adv* on purpose, deliberately
adrenalina *f* adrenaline
aduana *f* customs
aduanero 1 *adj* customs *atr* **2** *m*, **-a** *f* customs officer
aducir ⟨3o⟩ *v/t razones, argumentos* give, put forward; (*alegar*) claim
adueñarse ⟨1a⟩ *v/r*: ***adueñarse de*** take possession of
adulación *f* flattery
adular ⟨1a⟩ *v/t* flatter
adulón 1 *adj S. Am.* fawning **2** *m*, **-ona** *f* flatterer
adultera *f* adulteress
adulterar ⟨1a⟩ *v/t* adulterate
adulterio *m* adultery; ***cometer adulterio*** commit adultery
adúltero 1 *adj* adulterous **2** *m* adulterer
adultez *f* adulthood
adulto 1 *adj* adult; ***edad -a*** adulthood **2** *m*, **-a** *f* adult
adusto *adj paisaje* harsh; *persona* stern, severe; *L.Am.* (*inflexible*) stubborn
adverbio *m* adverb
adversario *m*, **-a** *f* adversary, opponent
adverso *adj* adverse
advertencia *f* warning
advertir ⟨3i⟩ *v/t* warn (***de*** about, of); (*notar*) notice
adyacente *adj* adjacent
aéreo *adj* air *atr*; *vista, fotografía* aerial; ***compañía -a*** airline
aerobic, **aeróbic** *m* aerobics
aerodinámico *adj* aerodynamic
aeroespacial *adj* aerospace *atr*
aerolínea *f* airline
aeromozo *m*, **-a** *f L.Am.* flight attendant
aeronáutico *adj* aeronautical
aeropuerto *m* airport
aerosol *m* aerosol
afable *adj* pleasant, affable
afamado *adj* famous
afán *m* (*esfuerzo*) effort; (*deseo*) eagerness; ***sin afán de lucro*** *organización* not-for-profit, non-profit (making)
afanar ⟨1a⟩ **1** *v/i C.Am.* (*ganar dinero*) make money **2** *v/t C.Am. dinero* make; *Rpl* F (*robar*) pinch F **3** *v/r* **afanarse** make an effort
afección *f* MED complaint, condition
afectado *adj* (*afligido*) upset (***por*** by); (*amanerado*) affected
afectar ⟨1a⟩ *v/t* (*producir efecto en*) affect; (*conmover*) upset, affect; (*fingir*)

feign
afectivo *adj* emotional
afecto *m* affection; ***tener afecto a alguien*** be fond of s.o.
afectuoso *adj* affectionate
afeitada *f* shave
afeitado *m* shave
afeitadora *f* electric razor
afeitar ⟨1a⟩ **1** *v/t* shave; *barba* shave off **2** *v/r* **afeitarse** shave, have a shave
afeminado *adj* effeminate
aferrarse ⟨1k⟩ *v/r fig* cling (***a*** to)
Afganistán Afghanistan
afianzar ⟨1f⟩ **1** *v/t fig* strengthen **2** *v/r* **afianzarse** become consolidated
afición *f* love (***por*** of); (*pasatiempo*) pastime, hobby; ***la afición*** DEP the fans
aficionado 1 *adj*: ***ser aficionado a*** be interested in, *Br tb* be keen on **2** *m*, **-a** *f* enthusiast; *no profesional* amateur; ***un partido de aficionados*** an amateur game
aficionarse ⟨1a⟩ *v/r* become interested (***a*** in)
afiebrarse ⟨1a⟩ *v/r L.Am.* develop a fever
afilado *adj* sharp
afilador *m* sharpener
afilalápices *m inv* pencil sharpener
afilar ⟨1a⟩ **1** *v/t* sharpen; *L.Am.* F (*halagar*) flatter, butter up F; *S. Am.* (*seducir*) seduce **2** *v/r* **afilarse** *S. Am.* F (*prepararse*) get ready
afiliarse ⟨1a⟩ *v/r*: ***afiliarse a un partido*** become a member of a party, join a party
afinar ⟨1a⟩ *v/t* MÚS tune; *punta* sharpen; *fig* perfect, fine-tune
afincarse ⟨1g⟩ *v/r* settle
afinidad *f* affinity
afirmación *f* statement; *declaración positiva* affirmation
afirmar ⟨1a⟩ *v/t* state, declare
afirmativo *adj* affirmative
afligido *adj* upset
afligir ⟨3c⟩ **1** *v/t* afflict; (*apenar*) upset; *L.Am.* F (*golpear*) beat up **2** *v/r* **afligirse** get upset
aflojar ⟨1a⟩ **1** *v/t nudo, tornillo* loosen; F *dinero* hand over **2** *v/i de tormenta* abate; *de viento, fiebre* drop **3** *v/r* **aflojarse** come *o* work loose
afluente *m* tributary
afmo. *abr* (= ***afectísimo***): ***su afmo*** Yours truly
afónico *adj*: ***está afónico*** he has lost his voice
aforo *m* capacity
afortunado *adj* lucky, fortunate
afrecho *f Arg* bran
África Africa; ***África del Sur*** South Africa
africano 1 *adj* African **2** *m*, **-a** *f* African
afrodisíaco *m* aphrodisiac
afrontar ⟨1a⟩ *v/t* face (up to)
afuera *adv* outside
afueras *fpl* outskirts
agachar ⟨1a⟩ **1** *v/i* duck **2** *v/r* **agacharse** bend down; (*acuclillarse*) crouch down; *L.Am.* (*rendirse*) give in
agalla *f* ZO gill; ***tener agallas*** F have guts F
agarrado *adj fig* F mean, stingy F
agarrar ⟨1a⟩ **1** *v/t* (*asir*) grab; *L.Am.* (*tomar*) take; *L.Am.* (*atrapar, pescar*), *resfriado* catch; *L.Am. velocidad* gather, pick up; ***agarrar una calle*** *L.Am.* go up *o* along a street **2** *v/i* (*asirse*) hold on; *de planta* take root; *L.Am. por un lugar* go; ***agarró y se fue*** he upped and went **3** *v/r* **agarrarse** (*asirse*) hold on; *L.Am. a golpes* get into a fight
agarrón *m Rpl* P (*pleito*) fight, argument; *L.Am.* (*tirón*) pull, tug
agarrotado *adj* stiff
agarrotarse ⟨1a⟩ *v/r de músculo* stiffen up; TÉC seize up
agasajar ⟨1a⟩ *v/t* fête
agazaparse ⟨1a⟩ *v/r* crouch (down); (*ocultarse*) hide
agencia *f* agency; ***agencia inmobiliaria*** real estate office, *Br* estate agency; ***agencia de viajes*** travel agency
agenciarse ⟨1b⟩ *v/r* F get hold of
agenda *f diario* diary; *programa* schedule; *de mitin* agenda
agente 1 *m* agent **2** *m/f* agent; ***agente de cambio y bolsa*** stockbroker; ***agente de policía*** police officer
ágil *adj* agile
agilidad *f* agility
agilizar ⟨1f⟩ *v/t* speed up
agitación *f* POL unrest
agitar ⟨1a⟩ **1** *v/t* shake; *brazos, pañuelo* wave; *fig* stir up **2** *v/r* **agitarse** become agitated *o* worked up
aglomeración *f de gente* crowd
aglomerar ⟨1a⟩ *v/t* pile up
aglutinar ⟨1a⟩ *v/t fig* bring together
agobiante *adj* oppresssive
agobiar ⟨1b⟩ **1** *v/t de calor* oppress; *de problemas* get on top of, overwhelm **2** *v/r* **agobiarse** F feel overwhelmed
agobio *m*: ***es un agobio*** it's unbearable, it's a nightmare F
agolparse ⟨1a⟩ *v/r* crowd together
agonía *f* agony; ***la espera fue una agonía*** the wait was unbearable
agonizante *adj* dying
agonizar ⟨1f⟩ *v/i de persona* be dying; *de régimen* be crumbling

agorero *adj* ominous
agosto *m* August; ***hacer su agosto*** F make a fortune
agotado *adj* (*cansado*) exhausted, worn out; (*terminado*) exhausted; (*vendido*) sold out
agotador *adj* exhausting
agotar ⟨1a⟩ **1** *v/t* (*cansar*) wear out, exhaust; (*terminar*) use up, exhaust **2** *v/r* **agotarse** (*cansarse*) get worn out, exhaust o.s.; (*terminarse*) run out, become exhausted; (*venderse*) sell out
agraciado *adj persona* attractive
agradable *adj* pleasant, nice
agradar ⟨1a⟩ *v/i*: ***me agrada la idea*** *fml* I like the idea; ***nos agradaría mucho que ...*** *fml* we would be delighted *o* very pleased if ...
agradecer ⟨2d⟩ *v/t*: ***agradecer algo a alguien*** thank s.o. for sth; ***te lo agradezco*** I appreciate it
agradecimiento *m* appreciation
agrado *m*: ***ser del agrado de alguien*** be to s.o.'s liking
agrandar ⟨1a⟩ **1** *v/t* make bigger **2** *v/r* **agrandarse** get bigger
agrario *adj* land *atr*, agrarian; *política* agricultural
agravar ⟨1a⟩ **1** *v/t* make worse, aggravate **2** *v/r* **agravarse** get worse, deteriorate
agravio *m* offense, *Br* offence
agredir ⟨3a⟩ *v/t* attack, assault
agregado *m*, **-a** *f en universidad* senior lecturer; *en colegio* senior teacher; POL attaché; ***agregado cultural*** cultural attaché
agregar ⟨1h⟩ *v/t* add
agresión *f* aggression
agresividad *f* aggression
agresivo *adj* aggressive
agresor *m*, **agresora** *f* aggressor
agreste *adj terreno* rough; *paisaje* wild
agriarse ⟨1b *or* 1c⟩ *v/r de vino* go sour; *de carácter* become bitter
agrícola *adj* agricultural, farming *atr*
agricultor *m*, **agricultora** *f* farmer
agricultura *f* agriculture
agridulce *adj* bittersweet
agriera *f L.Am.* heartburn
agrietarse ⟨1a⟩ *v/r* crack; *de manos, labios* chap
agringarse ⟨1h⟩ *v/r L.Am.* become Americanized
agrio *adj fruta* sour; *disputa, carácter* bitter
agrios *mpl* BOT citrus fruit *sg*
agropecuario *adj* farming *atr*, agricultural
agrupar ⟨1a⟩ **1** *v/t* group, put into groups **2** *v/r* **agruparse** gather
agua *f* water; ***agua corriente*** running water; ***agua dulce*** fresh water; ***agua mineral*** mineral water; ***agua oxigenada*** (hydrogen) peroxide; ***agua potable*** drinking water; ***es agua pasada*** it's water under the bridge; ***está con el agua al cuello*** *con problemas* he's up to his neck in problems F; *con deudas* he's up to his neck in debt F; ***se me hace la boca agua*** it makes my mouth water
aguas waters; ***aguas*** *pl* ***residuales*** effluent *sg*, sewage *sg*
aguacate *m* BOT avocado
aguacero *m* downpour
aguachento *adj CSur* watery
aguafiestas *m/f inv* partypooper F, killjoy
aguaitar ⟨1a⟩ *v/t S. Am.* spy on
aguamala *f S. Am.* jellyfish
aguamiel *f L.Am. mixture of water and honey*; *Méx* (*jugo de maguey*) agave sap
aguanieve *f* sleet
aguantar ⟨1a⟩ **1** *v/t un peso* bear, support; *respiración* hold; (*soportar*) put up with; ***no lo puedo aguantar*** I can't stand *o* bear it **2** *v/i* hang on, hold out **3** *v/r* **aguantarse** *contenerse* keep quiet; ***me tuve que aguantar*** *conformarme* I had to put up with it
aguante *m* patience; *física* stamina, endurance
aguar ⟨1a⟩ *v/t fiesta* spoil
aguardar ⟨1a⟩ **1** *v/t* wait for, await **2** *v/i* wait
aguardiente *m fruit-based alcoholic spirit*
aguarrás *m* turpentine, turps F
aguatero *m*, **-a** *f S. Am.* water-seller
agudeza *f de voz, sonido* high pitch; MED intensity; (*perspicacia*) sharpness; ***agudeza visual*** sharp-sightedness
agudizar ⟨1f⟩ **1** *v/t un sentido* sharpen; ***agudizar un problema*** make a problem worse **2** *v/r* **agudizarse** MED get worse; *de un sentido* become sharper
agudo *adj* acute; (*afilado*) sharp; *sonido* high-pitched; (*perspicaz*) sharp
agüero *m* omen; ***ser de mal agüero*** be an ill omen
aguijón *m* ZO sting; *fig* spur
águila *f* eagle; ***¿águila o sol?*** *Méx* heads or tails?; ***ser un águila*** *fig* be very sharp
aguilucho *m* eaglet
agüita *f L.Am.* F (*agua*) water; (*infusión*) infusion
aguja *f* needle; *de reloj* hand; ***buscar una aguja en un pajar*** *fig* look for a needle in a haystack
agujerear ⟨1a⟩ **1** *v/t* make holes in **2** *v/r* **agujerearse** develop holes

agujero *m* hole
agujetas *fpl* stiffness *sg*; ***tener agujetas*** be stiff
aguzar ⟨1f⟩ *v/t* sharpen; ***aguzar el ingenio*** sharpen one's wits; ***aguzar el oído*** prick up one's ears
ah *int* ah!
ahí *adv* there; ***está por ahí*** it's (somewhere) over there; *dando direcciones* it's that way
ahijada *f* goddaughter
ahijado *m* godson
ahínco *m* effort; ***trabajar con ahínco*** work hard
ahogado *adj en agua* drowned
ahogar ⟨1h⟩ **1** *v/t* (*asfixiar*) suffocate; *en agua* drown; AUTO flood; *protestas* stifle **2** *v/r* **ahogarse** choke; (*asfixiarse*) suffocate; *en agua* drown; AUTO flood; ***ahogarse en un vaso de agua*** *fig* F get in a state over nothing
ahondar ⟨1a⟩ *v/i*: ***ahondar en algo*** go into sth in depth
ahora *adv* (*en este momento*) now; (*pronto*) in a moment; ***ahora mismo*** right now; ***por ahora*** for the present, for the time being; ***ahora bien*** however; ***desde ahora, de ahora en adelante*** from now on; ***¡hasta ahora!*** see you soon
ahorcar ⟨1g⟩ **1** *v/t* hang **2** *v/r* **ahorcarse** hang o.s.
ahorita *adv L.Am.* (*en este momento*) (right) now; *Méx, C.Am.* (*pronto*) in a moment; *Méx, C.Am.* (*hace poco*) just now
ahorrar ⟨1a⟩ **1** *v/t* save; ***ahorrar algo a alguien*** save s.o. (from) sth **2** *v/i* save (up) **3** *v/r* **ahorrarse** *dinero* save; *fig* spare o.s., save o.s.
ahorro *m* saving; ***ahorros*** *pl* savings; ***caja de ahorros*** savings bank
ahulado *m C.Am., Méx* oilskin
ahumar ⟨1a⟩ *v/t* smoke
ahuyentar ⟨1a⟩ **1** *v/t* scare off *o* away **2** *v/r* **ahuyentarse** *L.Am.* run away
AI *abr* (***= Amnistía Internacional***) AI (= Amnesty International)
airado *adj* angry
airbag *m* AUTO airbag
aire *m* air; ***aire acondicionado*** air-conditioning; ***al aire libre*** in the open air; ***a mi aire*** in my own way; ***estar en el aire*** *fig* F be up in the air F; ***hace mucho aire*** it is very windy
airear ⟨1a⟩ *v/t tb fig* air
airoso *adj*: ***salir airoso de algo*** do well in sth
aislado *adj* isolated
aislante **1** *adj* insulating, insulation *atr* **2** *m* insulator
aislar ⟨1a⟩ **1** *v/t* isolate; EL insulate **2** *v/r* **aislarse** cut o.s. off
ajardinado *adj* landscaped; ***zona -a*** area with parks and gardens
a. J.C. *abr* (***= antes de Jesucristo***) BC (= before Christ)
ajedrez *m* chess
ajeno *adj propiedad, problemas etc* someone else's; ***me era totalmente ajeno*** it was completely alien to me; ***estar ajeno a*** be unaware of, be oblivious to; ***por razones -as a nuestra voluntad*** for reasons beyond our control
ajete *m* BOT young garlic
ajetreo *m* bustle
ají *m S. Am.* chili, *Br* chilli
ajiaco *m Col spicy potato stew*
ajillo *m*: ***al ajillo*** with garlic
ajo *m* BOT garlic; ***estar*** *or* ***andar en el ajo*** F be in the know F
ajuar *m de novia* trousseau
ajustar ⟨1a⟩ **1** *v/t máquina etc* adjust; *tornillo* tighten; *precio* set; ***ajustar cuentas*** *fig* settle a score **2** *v/i* fit **3** *v/r* **ajustarse** *el cinturón* tighten; ***ajustarse a algo*** *fig* keep within sth; ***ajustarse a la ley*** comply with the law
ajuste *m*: ***ajuste de cuentas*** settling of scores
ajusticiar ⟨1b⟩ *v/t* execute
al *prp* ***a*** *y art* ***el***; ***al entrar*** on coming in, when we / they *etc* came in
ala *f* wing; MIL flank; ***ala delta*** hang glider; ***cortar las alas a alguien*** clip s.o.'s wings
alabanza *f* acclaim
alabar ⟨1a⟩ *v/t* praise, acclaim
alacena *f* larder
alacrán *m* ZO scorpion
alambrada *f* wire fence
alambrar ⟨1a⟩ *v/t* fence
alambre *m* wire; ***alambre de espino*** *or* ***de púías*** barbed wire
álamo *m* BOT poplar; ***álamo temblón*** aspen
alarde *m* show, display; ***hacer alarde de*** make a show of
alardear ⟨1a⟩ *v/i* show off (***de*** about)
alargador *m* TÉC extension cord, *Br* extension lead
alargar ⟨1h⟩ **1** *v/t* lengthen; *prenda* let down; *en tiempo* prolong; *mano, brazo* stretch out **2** *v/r* **alargarse** *de sombra, día* get longer, lengthen
alarido *m* shriek; ***dar alaridos*** shriek
alarma *f* (*mecanismo, miedo*) alarm; ***dar la voz de alarma*** raise the alarm
alarmante *adj* alarming

alarmar ⟨1a⟩ **1** *v/t* alarm **2** *v/r* **alarmarse** become alarmed
alba *f* dawn
albahaca *f* BOT basil
Albania Albania
albañil *m* bricklayer
albaricoque *m* BOT apricot
albatros *m inv* ZO albatross
albedrío *m*: ***libre albedrío*** free will
alberca *f* reservoir; *Méx* (swimming) pool
albergar ⟨1h⟩ *v/t* (*hospedar*) put up; (*contener*) house; *esperanzas* hold out
albergue *m* refuge, shelter; ***albergue juvenil*** youth hostel
albino *m*, **-a** *f* albino
albóndiga *f* meatball
albornoz *m* bathrobe
alborotador *m*, **alborotadora** *f* rioter
alborotar ⟨1a⟩ **1** *v/t* stir up; (*desordenar*) disturb **2** *v/i* make a racket **3** *v/r* **alborotarse** get excited; (*inquietarse*) get worked up
alboroto *m* commotion
álbum *m* album
alcachofa *f* BOT artichoke; *de ducha* shower head
alcalde *m*, **-esa** *f* mayor
alcalino *adj* alkaline
alcance *m* reach; *de arma etc* range; *de medida* scope; *de tragedia* extent, scale; ***al alcance de la mano*** within reach; ***¿está al alcance de tu bolsillo?*** can you afford it?; ***dar alcance a alguien*** catch up with s.o.; ***poner al alcance de alguien*** put within s.o.'s reach
alcancía *f L.Am.* piggy bank
alcantarilla *f* sewer; (*sumidero*) drain
alcanzar ⟨1f⟩ **1** *v/t a alguien* catch up with; *lugar* reach, get to; *en nivel* reach; *cantidad* amount to; *objetivo* achieve **2** *v/i en altura* reach; *en cantidad* be enough; ***alcanzar a oír / ver*** manage to hear / see
alcaparra *f* BOT caper
alcayata *f* hook
alcázar *m* fortress
alce *m* ZO elk
alcista *adj en bolsa* rising, bull *atr*; ***tendencia alcista*** upward trend
alcoba *f S. Am.* bedroom
alcohol *m* alcohol; MED rubbing alcohol, *Br* surgical spirit; ***alcohol de quemar*** denatured alcohol, *Br* methylated spirits *sg*
alcoholemia *f* blood alcohol level; ***prueba de alcoholemia*** drunkometer test, *Br* Breathalyzer® test
alcohólico **1** *adj* alcoholic **2** *m*, **-a** *f* alcoholic
alcoholismo *m* alcoholism
alcornoque *m* BOT cork oak; ***pedazo de alcornoque*** F blockhead F
alcurnia *f* ancestry
aldea *f* (small) village
aleación *f* alloy
aleatorio *adj* random
aleccionar ⟨1a⟩ *v/t* instruct; (*regañar*) lecture
aledaños *mpl* surrounding area *sg*; *de ciudad* outskirts
alegador *adj L.Am.* argumentative
alegar ⟨1h⟩ **1** *v/t motivo, razón* cite; ***alegar que*** claim *o* allege that **2** *v/i L.Am.* (*discutir*) argue; (*quejarse*) moan, gripe
alegrar ⟨1a⟩ **1** *v/t* make happy; (*animar*) cheer up **2** *v/r* **alegrarse** cheer up; F *bebiendo* get tipsy; ***alegrarse por alguien*** be pleased for s.o. (**de** about)
alegre *adj* (*contento*) happy; *por naturaleza* happy, cheerful; F *bebido* tipsy
alegría *f* happiness
alejar ⟨1a⟩ **1** *v/t* move away **2** *v/r* **alejarse** move away (**de** from); *de situación, ámbito* get away (**de** from); ***¡no te alejes mucho!*** don't go too far away!
alelar ⟨1a⟩ *v/t* stupefy
aleluya *m & int* hallelujah
alemán **1** *m/adj* German **2** *m*, **-ana** *f persona* German
Alemania Germany
alentado *adj L.Am.* encouraged
alentar ⟨1k⟩ **1** *v/t* (*animar*) encourage; *esperanzas* cherish **2** *v/r* **alentarse** *L.Am.* get better
alergia *f* allergy
alérgico *adj* allergic (**a** to)
alerta **1** *adv*: ***estar alerta*** be on the alert **2** *f* alert; ***dar la alerta*** raise the alarm; ***poner en alerta*** alert
alertar ⟨1a⟩ *v/t* alert (**de** to)
aleta *f* ZO fin; *de buzo* flipper; *de la nariz* wing
aletargarse ⟨1h⟩ *v/r* feel lethargic
aletear ⟨1a⟩ *v/i* flap one's wings
alevosía *f* treachery
alfabético *adj* alphabetical
alfabetizar ⟨1f⟩ *v/t lista etc* put into alphabetical order; ***alfabetizar a alguien*** teach s.o. to read and write
alfabeto *m* alphabet
alfalfa *f* BOT alfalfa
alfanumérico *adj* alphanumeric
alfarero *m*, **-a** *f* potter
alfil *m* bishop
alfiler *m* pin; ***alfiler de gancho*** *Arg* safety pin; ***no cabe un alfiler*** *fig* F there's no room for anything else
alfiletero *m* (*cojín*) pincushion; (*estuche*) needlecase

alfombra *f* carpet; *más pequeña* rug
alfombrado *m* *L.Am.* carpeting, carpets *pl*
alfombrar ⟨1a⟩ *v/t* carpet
alfombrilla *f* mouse mat
alga *f* BOT alga; *marina* seaweed
álgebra *f* algebra
álgido *adj fig* decisive
algo **1** *pron en frases afirmativas* something; *en frases interrogativas o condicionales* anything; ***algo es algo*** it's something, it's better than nothing **2** *adv* rather, somewhat
algodón *m* cotton; ***criado entre algodones*** F mollycoddled, pampered
alguacil *m*, **alguacilesa** *f* bailiff
alguien *pron en frases afirmativas* somebody, someone; *en frases interrogativas o condicionales* anybody, anyone
algúín *adj en frases afirmativas* some; *en frases interrogativas o condicionales* any; ***algúín día*** some day
alguno **1** *adj en frases afirmativas* some; *en frases interrogativas o condicionales* any; ***no la influyó de modo alguno*** it didn't influence her in any way; ***¿has estado alguna vez en …?*** have you ever been to …? **2** *pron*: *persona* someone, somebody; ***algunos opinan que …*** some people think that …; ***alguno se podrá usar*** *objeto* we'll be able to use some of them
alhaja *f* piece of jewel(le)ry; *fig* gem; ***alhajas*** jewelry *sg*
alhelí *m* BOT wallflower
aliado *m*, **-a** *f* ally
alianza *f* POL alliance; (*anillo*) wedding ring
aliarse ⟨1c⟩ *v/r* form an alliance (***con*** with)
alias *m inv* alias
alicaído *adj* F down F
alicatar ⟨1a⟩ *v/t* tile
alicates *mpl* pliers
aliciente *m* (*estímulo*) incentive; (*atractivo*) attraction
alienar ⟨1a⟩ *v/t* alienate
alienígena *m/f* alien
aliento *m* breath; *fig* encouragement
aligerar ⟨1a⟩ *v/t carga* lighten; ***aligerar el paso*** quicken one's pace
alijo *m* MAR consignment
alimentación *f* (*dieta*) diet; *acción* feeding; EL power supply
alimentar ⟨1a⟩ **1** *v/t tb* TÉC, *fig* feed; EL power **2** *v/i* be nourishing **3** *v/r* **alimentarse** feed o.s.; ***alimentarse de algo*** *de persona*, *animal* live on sth; *de máquina* run on sth
alimento *m* (*comida*) food; ***tiene poco alimento*** it has little nutritional value; ***alimentos dietéticos*** (***de régimen***) slimming aids
alineación *f* DEP line-up
alinear ⟨1a⟩ **1** *v/t* align **2** *v/r* **alinearse** (*ponerse en fila*) line up; POL align o.s. (***con*** with)
aliñar ⟨1a⟩ *v/t* dress
aliño *m* dressing
alioli *m* GASTR garlic mayonnaise
alisar ⟨1a⟩ *v/t* smooth
alistarse ⟨1a⟩ *v/r* MIL enlist
aliviar ⟨1b⟩ *v/t* alleviate, relieve
alivio *m* relief
allá *adv de lugar* (over) there; ***allá por los años veinte*** back in the twenties; ***más allá*** further on; ***más allá de*** beyond; ***el más allá*** the hereafter; ***allá él / ella*** F that's up to him / her
allanamiento *m*: ***allanamiento de morada*** JUR breaking and entering
allanar ⟨1a⟩ *v/t* (*alisar*) smooth; (*aplanar*) level (out); *obstáculos* overcome
allegado *m*, **-a** *f* relation, relative
allí *adv* there; ***por allí*** over there; *dando direcciones* that way; ***¡allí está!*** there it is!
alma *f* soul; ***se me cayó el alma a los pies*** F my heart sank; ***llegar al alma*** *conmover* move deeply; *herir* hurt deeply; ***no se ve un alma*** there isn't a soul to be seen; ***lo siento en el alma*** I am truly sorry
almacén *m* warehouse; (*tienda*) store, shop; ***grandes almacenes*** *pl* department store *sg*
almacenamiento *m* storage; ***almacenamiento de datos*** data storage
almacenar ⟨1a⟩ *v/t tb* INFOR store
almacenero *m*, **-a** *f* storekeeper, shopkeeper
almanaque *m* almanac
almeja *f* ZO clam
almenas *fpl* battlements
almendra *f* almond
almendro *m* almond tree
almíbar *m* syrup; ***en almíbar*** in syrup
almibarado *adj fig* syrupy
almidón *m* starch
almirante *m* admiral
almirez *m* mortar
almohada *f* pillow; ***consultarlo con la almohada*** sleep on it
almohadilla *f* small cushion; TÉC pad
almohadón *m* large cushion
almorranas *fpl* piles
almorzada *f Méx* lunch
almorzar ⟨1f & 1m⟩ **1** *v/i al mediodía* have

lunch; *a media mañana* have a mid-morning snack **2** *v/t*: ***almorzar algo*** *al mediodía* have sth for lunch; *a media mañana* have sth as a mid-morning snack

almuerzo *m al mediodía* lunch; *a media mañana* mid-morning snack; ***almuerzo de trabajo*** working lunch

¿ alo? *L.Am.* hello?

alocado 1 *adj* crazy **2** *m*, **-a** *f* crazy fool

áloe *m* BOT aloe

alojamiento *m* accommodations *pl*, *Br* accommodation

alojar ⟨1a⟩ **1** *v/t* accommodate **2** *v/r* **alojarse** stay (***en*** in)

alojo *m L.Am.* → ***alojamiento***

alondra *f* ZO lark

alopecia *f* MED alopecia

alpaca *f animal, lana* alpaca

alpargata *f Esp* espadrille

alpinismo *m* mountaineering

alpinista *m/f* mountaineer, climber

alpiste *m* birdseed

alquilar ⟨1a⟩ *v/t de usuario* rent; *de dueño* rent out

alquiler *m acción*: *de coche etc* rental; *de casa* renting; *dinero* rental, *Br tb* rent; ***alquiler de coches*** car rental, *Br tb* car hire

alquitrán *m* tar

alrededor 1 *adv* around **2** *prp*: ***alrededor de*** around

alrededores *mpl* surrounding area *sg*

alta *f* MED discharge; ***dar de alta*** MED discharge; ***darse de alta*** *en organismo* register

altanero *adj* arrogant

altar *m* altar; ***llevar al altar*** marry

altavoz *m* loudspeaker

alteración *f* alteration

alterar ⟨1a⟩ **1** *v/t* (*cambiar*) alter; *a alguien* upset; ***alterar el orden púíblico*** cause a breach of the peace **2** *v/r* **alterarse** get upset (***por*** because of)

altercado *m* argument, altercation *fml*

alternar ⟨1a⟩ **1** *v/t* alternate; ***alternar el trabajo con el descanso*** alternate work and study **2** *v/i* mix **3** *v/r* **alternarse** alternate, take turns

alternativa *f* alternative

alternativo *adj* alternative

alterno *adj* alternate; ***corriente -a*** EL alternating current; ***en días alternos*** on alternate days

Alteza *f título* Highness

altibajos *mpl* ups and downs

altillo *m* (*desván*) attic; *en armario* top (part of the) closet

altiplano *m* high plateau

altisonante *adj* high-flown

altitud *f* altitude

altivo *adj* haughty

alto[1] **1** *adj persona* tall; *precio, núímero, montaña* high; ***-as presiones*** high pressure; ***alto horno*** blast furnace; ***clase -a*** high class; ***en -a mar*** on the high seas; ***en voz -a*** out loud **2** *adv volar, saltar* high; ***hablar alto*** speak loudly; ***pasar por alto*** overlook; ***poner más alto*** TV, RAD turn up; ***por todo lo alto*** F lavishly **3** *m* (*altura*) height; *Chi* pile

alto[2] *m* halt; (*pausa*) pause; ***hacer un alto*** stop; ***alto el fuego*** ceasefire; ***¡alto!*** halt!

altoparlante *m L.Am.* loudspeaker

altozano *m* hillock

altramuz *m planta* lupin; *semilla* lupin seed

altruismo *m* altruism

altruista *adj* altruistic

altura *f* MAT height; MÚS pitch; AVIA altitude, height; GEOG latitude; ***a estas alturas*** by this time, by now; ***estar a la altura de algo*** be up to sth F

alubia *f* BOT kidney bean

alucinación *f* hallucination

alucinado *adj* F gobsmacked F

alucinante *adj* F incredible

alucinar ⟨1a⟩ **1** *v/i* hallucinate **2** *v/t* F amaze

alucine *m*: ***de alucine*** F amazing

alucinógeno *m* hallucinogen

alud *m* avalanche

aludir ⟨3a⟩ *v/i*: ***aludir a algo*** allude to sth

aludido: ***darse por aludido*** take it personally

alumbrar ⟨1a⟩ **1** *v/t* (*dar luz a*) light (up) **2** *v/i* give off light

aluminio *m* aluminum, *Br* aluminium; ***papel de aluminio*** aluminum (*Br* aluminium) foil

alumno *m*, **-a** *f* student

alusión *f* allusion (***a*** to); ***hacer alusión a*** refer to, allude to

aluvión *m* barrage

alza *f* rise; ***en alza*** *en bolsa* rising

alzado *m*, **-a** *f L.Am.* insurgent

alzar ⟨1f⟩ **1** *v/t barrera, brazo* lift, raise; *precios* raise **2** *v/r* **alzarse** rise; *en armas* rise up

alzo *m C.Am.* theft

a. m. *abr* (***= ante meridiem***) a. m. (= ante meridiem)

ama *f* (*dueña*) owner; ***ama de casa*** housewife, homemaker; ***ama de llaves*** housekeeper; ***ama de leche*** *or* ***cría*** *L.Am.* wetnurse

amabilidad *f* kindness

amable *adj* kind (***con*** to)

amaestrar ⟨1a⟩ *v/t* train

amago *m* threat; ***hizo amago de levantarse*** she made as if to get up; ***amago de infarto*** minor heart attack

amainar ⟨1a⟩ *v/i de lluvia, viento* ease up, slacken off

amalgamar ⟨1a⟩ **1** *v/t fig* combine **2** *v/r* **amalgamarse** amalgamate

amamantar ⟨1a⟩ *v/t bebé* breastfeed; *cría* feed

amanecer 1 ⟨2d⟩ *v/i* get light; *de persona* wake up **2** *m* dawn

amanerado *adj* affected

amante 1 *adj* loving; ***es amante de la buena vida*** he's fond of good living **2** *m/f en una relación* lover; ***los amantes de la naturaleza*** nature lovers

amañar ⟨1a⟩ *v/t* F rig F; *partido* fix F

amapola *f* BOT poppy

amar ⟨1a⟩ *v/t* love

amargar ⟨1h⟩ **1** *v/t día, ocasión* spoil; ***amargar a alguien*** make s.o. bitter **2** *v/r* **amargarse** get bitter; ***amargarse la vida*** get upset

amargo *adj tb fig* bitter

amargura *f tb fig* bitterness

amarillento *adj* yellowish

amarillo *m/adj* yellow

amarrar ⟨1a⟩ *v/t L.Am.* (*atar*) tie

amasar ⟨1a⟩ *v/t pan* knead; *fortuna* amass

amatista *f* amethyst

amazona *f* horsewoman

amazónico *adj* GEOG Amazonian

Amazonas: ***el Amazonas*** the Amazon

ambages *mpl*: ***decirlo sin ambages*** say it straight out

ámbar *m* amber; ***el semáforo está en ámbar*** the lights are yellow, *Br* the lights are at amber

ambición *f* ambition

ambicioso *adj* ambitious

ambidextro, **ambidiestro** *adj* ambidextrous

ambientador *m* air freshener

ambiental *adj* environmental

ambientar ⟨1a⟩ **1** *v/t película, novela* set **2** *v/r* **ambientarse** be set

ambiente 1 *adj*: ***medio ambiente*** environment; ***temperatura ambiente*** room temperature **2** *m* (*entorno*) environment; (*situación*) atmosphere

ambigüedad *f* ambiguity

ambiguo *adj* ambiguous

ámbito *m* area; (*límite*) scope

ambo *m Arg* two-piece suit

ambos, **ambas 1** *adj* both **2** *pron* both (of us / you / them)

ambulancia *f* ambulance

ambulante 1 *adj* travel(l)ing; ***venta ambulante*** peddling, hawking **2** *m/f L.Am.* (*vendedor*) street seller

ambulatorio 1 *adj* MED out-patient *atr* **2** *m* out-patient clinic

amedrentar ⟨1a⟩ *v/t* terrify

amén 1 *m* amen **2** *prp*: ***amén de*** as well as

amenaza *f* threat; ***amenaza de bomba*** bomb scare

amenazador *adj* threatening

amenazante *adj* threatening

amenazar ⟨1f⟩ **1** *v/t* threaten (***con, de*** with) **2** *v/i*: ***amenazar con*** threaten to; ***amenaza tempestad*** there's a storm brewing

amenizar ⟨1f⟩ *v/t*: ***amenizar algo*** make sth more entertaining *o* enjoyable

ameno *adj* enjoyable

América America; ***América del Norte*** North America; ***América del Sur*** South America

americana *f* American (woman); *prenda* jacket

americano *m/adj* American

amerizar ⟨1f⟩ *v/i de nave espacial* splash down

ametralladora *f* machine gun

amianto *m* MIN asbestos

amígdala *f* ANAT tonsil

amigdalitis *f* MED tonsillitis

amigo 1 *adj* friendly; ***ser amigo de algo*** be fond of sth **2** *m*, **-a** *f* friend; ***hacerse amigos*** make friends

aminorar ⟨1a⟩ *v/t* reduce; ***aminorar la marcha*** slow down

amistad *f* friendship; ***amistades*** friends

amistosamente *adv* amicably

amistoso *adj* friendly; ***partido amistoso*** DEP friendly (game)

amnesia *f* amnesia

amnistía *f* amnesty

amo *m* (*dueño*) owner; HIST master

amoblado *S. Am.* **1** *adj* furnished **2** *m* furniture

amodorrarse ⟨1a⟩ *v/r* feel sleepy

amoldarse ⟨1a⟩ *v/r* adapt (***a*** to)

amonestación *f* warning; DEP caution

amonestar ⟨1a⟩ *v/t reñir* reprimand; DEP caution

amoníaco, **amoniaco** *m* ammonia

amontonar ⟨1a⟩ **1** *v/t* pile up **2** *v/r* **amontonarse** *de objetos, problemas* pile up; *de gente* crowd together

amor *m* love; ***amor mío*** my love, darling; ***amor propio*** self-respect; ***por amor al arte*** *fig* just for the fun of it; ***por amor de Dios*** for God's sake; ***hacer el amor*** make love

amoral *adj* amoral

amoratado *adj* bruised

amordazar ⟨1f⟩ *v/t* gag; *animal, la prensa*

muzzle
amorfo *adj* shapeless
amoroso *adj* amorous
amortajar ⟨1a⟩ *v/t* shroud
amortiguador *m* AUTO shock absorber
amortiguar ⟨1i⟩ *v/t impacto* cushion; *sonido* muffle
amortizar ⟨1f⟩ *v/t* pay off; COM *bienes* charge off, *Br* write off
amotinarse ⟨1a⟩ *v/r* rebel
amp. *abr* (= ***amperios***) amp (= amperes)
amparar ⟨1a⟩ **1** *v/t* protect; (*ayudar*) help **2** *v/r* **ampararse** seek shelter (***de*** from); ***ampararse en algo*** seek protection in sth
amparo *m* protection; (*cobijo*) shelter; ***al amparo de*** under the protection of
ampliación *f de casa, carretera* extension; FOT enlargement; ***ampliación de capital*** COM increase in capital
ampliadora *f* FOT enlarger
ampliamente *adv* widely
ampliar ⟨1c⟩ **1** *v/t plantilla* increase; *negocio* expand; *plazo, edificio* extend; FOT enlarge **2** *v/r* **ampliarse** broaden
amplificador *m* amplifier
amplificar ⟨1g⟩ *v/t* amplify
amplio *adj casa* spacious; *gama, margen* wide; *falda* full
amplitud *f* breadth
ampolla *f* MED blister; (*botellita*) vial, *Br* phial
ampolleta *f Arg, Chi* light bulb
ampuloso *adj* pompous
amputación *f* amputation
amputar ⟨1a⟩ *v/t brazo, pierna* amputate
amueblar ⟨1a⟩ *v/t* furnish
amuermar ⟨1a⟩ *v/t* F bore
amuleto *m* charm
anabolizante *m* anabolic steroid
anacardo *m* BOT cashew
anaconda *f* ZO anaconda
anacoreta *m/f* hermit
anacrónico *adj* anachronistic
ánade *m* ZO duck
anagrama *m* anagram
anal *adj* anal
anales *mpl* annals
analfabeto **1** *adj* illiterate **2** *m*, **-a** *f* illiterate
analgésico **1** *adj* painkilling, analgesic **2** *m* painkiller, analgesic
análisis *m inv* analysis; ***análisis de mercado*** market research; ***análisis de sangre*** blood test; ***análisis de sistemas*** INFOR systems analysis
analista *m/f* analyst
analizar ⟨1f⟩ *v/t* analyze
analogía *f* analogy
analógico *adj* analog, *Br* analogue
análogo *adj* analogous
ananá(s) *m S. Am.* BOT pineapple
anarquía *f* anarchy
anárquico *adj* anarchic
anarquista **1** *adj* anarchist *atr* **2** *m/f* anarchist
anatema *m* anathema
anatomía *f* anatomy
anatómico *adj* anatomical; ***asiento anatómico*** AUTO anatomically designed seat
anca *f* haunch; ***ancas*** *pl* ***de rana*** GASTR frogs' legs
ancestral *adj* ancestral
ancho **1** *adj* wide, broad; ***a sus -as*** at ease, relaxed; ***quedarse tan ancho*** F carry on as if nothing had happened **2** *m* width; ***ancho de vía*** FERR gauge; ***dos metros de ancho*** two meters (*Br* metres) wide
anchoa *f* anchovy
anchura *f* width
anciana *f* old woman
anciano **1** *adj* old **2** *m* old man
ancla *f* MAR anchor
anclar ⟨1a⟩ *v/i* MAR anchor
andadas *fpl*: ***volver a las andadas*** F fall back into one's old ways
andador *m para bebé* baby walker; *para anciano* walker, Zimmer®
andamio *m* scaffolding
andanzas *fpl* adventures
andar ⟨1q⟩ **1** *v/i* (*caminar*) walk; (*funcionar*) work; ***andando*** on foot; ***andar bien / mal*** *fig* go well / badly; ***andar con cuidado*** be careful; ***andar en algo*** (*buscar*) rummage in sth; ***andar tras algo*** be after sth F; ***andar haciendo algo*** be doing sth; ***¡anda!*** come on! **2** *v/t* walk **3** *v/r* **andarse**: ***andarse con bromas*** kid around F
andas *fpl*: ***llevar en andas*** carry on one's shoulders
andén *m* platform; *L.Am.* sidewalk, *Br* pavement
Andes *mpl* Andes
andinismo *m L.Am.* mountaineering, climbing
andinista *m/f L.Am.* mountaineer, climber
andino *adj* Andean
Andorra Andorra
andrajoso *adj* ragged
andurriales *mpl*: ***por estos andurriales*** F around here
anécdota *f* anecdote
anegar ⟨1h⟩ **1** *v/t* flood **2** *v/r* **anegarse** *de campo, terreno* be flooded; ***anegarse en llanto*** dissolve into tears

anemia *f* MED an(a)emia
anémico *adj* an(a)emic
anestesia *f* MED an(a)esthesia
anestesiado *adj* an(a)esthetized, under F
anestesiar ⟨1b⟩ *v/t* an(a)esthetize
anexión *f* POL annexation
anexionar ⟨1a⟩ *v/t* POL annex
anexo 1 *adj* attached **2** *m edificio* annex, *Br* annex(e)
anfeta F, **anfetamina** *f* MED amphetamine
anfibio *m/adj* amphibian
anfiteatro *m* TEA amphitheater, *Br* amphitheatre; *de teatro* dress circle
anfitrión *m* host
anfitriona *f* hostess
ánfora *f L.Am.* POL ballot box; HIST amphora
ángel *m* angel; ***ángel custodio** or **de la guarda*** guardian angel
angelical *adj* angelic
angina *f* MED: ***anginas*** *pl* sore throat *sg*, strep throat *sg*; ***angina de pecho*** angina
anglicano 1 *adj* Anglican **2** *m*, **-a** *f* Anglican
anglicismo *m* Anglicism
anglófono *adj* English-speaking
anglosajón 1 *adj* Anglo-Saxon **2** *m*, **-ona** *f* Anglo-Saxon
angora *f* angora
angosto *adj* narrow
anguila *f* ZO eel
angula *f* ZO, GASTR elver
ángulo *m* MAT, *fig* angle
angustia *f* anguish
angustiado *adj* distraught
angustiante *adj* distressing
angustiar ⟨1b⟩ **1** *v/t* distress **2** *v/r* **angustiarse** agonize (***por*** over)
angustioso *adj* agonizing
anhelar ⟨1a⟩ *v/t* long for
anhelo *m* longing, desire (***de*** for)
anhídrido *m* QUÍM anhydride; ***anhídrido carbónico*** carbon dioxide
anidar ⟨1a⟩ *v/i* nest
anilla *f* ring; ***cuaderno de anillas*** ring binder; ***anillas*** *pl* DEP rings
anillo *m* ring; ***te viene como anillo al dedo*** F it suits you perfectly
animación *f* liveliness; *en películas* animation; ***hay mucha animación*** it's very lively
animado *adj* lively
animador *m* host; ***animador turístico*** events organizer
animadora *f* hostess; DEP cheerleader
animal 1 *adj* animal *atr*; *fig* stupid **2** *m tb fig* animal; ***animal doméstico*** *mascota* pet; *de granja* domestic animal
animalada *f*: ***decir / hacer una animalada*** F say / do something nasty
animar ⟨1a⟩ **1** *v/t* cheer up; (*alentar*) encourage **2** *v/r* **animarse** cheer up
anímico *adj* mental; ***estado anímico*** state of mind
ánimo *m* spirit; (*coraje*) encouragement; ***estado de ánimo*** state of mind; ***con ánimo de*** with the intention of; ***¡ánimo!*** cheer up!
animosidad *f* animosity
aniquilar ⟨1a⟩ *v/t* annihilate
anís *m* BOT aniseed; *bebida* anisette
aniversario *m* anniversary
ano *m* ANAT anus
anoche *adv* last night; ***antes de anoche*** the night before last
anochecer ⟨2d⟩ **1** *v/i* get dark; ***anocheció*** night fell, it got dark **2** *m* dusk
anodino *adj* anodyne; *fig* bland
anómalo *adj* anomalous
anonadar ⟨1a⟩ *v/t*: ***anonadar a alguien*** take s.o. aback
anónimo 1 *adj* anonymous **2** *m* poison pen letter
anorak *m* anorak
anorexia *f* MED anorexia
anoréxico *adj* anorexic
anormal *adj* abnormal
anotar ⟨1a⟩ *v/t* note down
anquilosarse ⟨1a⟩ *v/r* get stiff
ansia *f* yearning; (*inquietud*) anxiousness
ansiar ⟨1b⟩ *v/t* yearn for, long for
ansiedad *f* anxiety
ansioso *adj* anxious; ***está ansioso por verlos*** he's longing to see them
anta *f L.Am.* ZO tapir
antagonista *m/f* antagonist
antaño *adv* long ago
antártico *adj* Antarctic
Antártida Antarctica
ante[1] *m* suede; ZO moose; *Méx* (*postre*) *egg and coconut dessert*
ante[2] *prp posición* before; *dificultad* faced with; ***ante todo*** above all
anteayer *adv* the day before yesterday
antebrazo *m* forearm
antecedente *m* precedent; ***antecedentes penales*** previous convictions; ***poner a alguien en antecedentes*** put s.o. in the picture
antecesor *m*, **antecesora** *f* predecessor
antediluviano *adj* prehistoric *hum*
antelación *f*: ***con antelación*** in advance
antemano: ***de antemano*** beforehand
antena *f de radio, televisión* antenna, *Br* aerial; ZO antenna; ***antena parabólica*** satellite dish
anteojos *mpl* binoculars
antepasado *m*, **-a** *f* ancestor

antepenúltimo *adj* third last
anteponer ⟨2r⟩ *v/t*: ***anteponer algo a algo*** put sth before sth
anteproyecto *m* draft
anterior *adj* previous, former
antes 1 *adv* before; ***cuanto antes, lo antes posible*** as soon as possible; ***poco antes*** shortly before; ***antes que nada*** first of all **2** *prp*: ***antes de*** before
antesala *f* lobby
antiadherente *adj* non-stick
antiaéreo *adj* anti-aircraft *atr*
antibala(s) *adj* bulletproof
antibelicista *adj* anti-war
antibiótico *m* antibiotic
anticiclón *m* anticyclone
anticipado *adj pago* advance *atr*; *elecciones* early; ***por anticipado*** in advance
anticipar ⟨1a⟩ **1** *v/t sueldo* advance; *fecha, viaje* move up, *Br* bring forward; *información, noticias* give a preview of **2** *v/r* **anticiparse** *de suceso* come early; ***anticiparse a alguien*** get there ahead of s.o.
anticonceptivo 1 *adj* contraceptive *atr* **2** *m* contraceptive
anticongelante *m* antifreeze
anticonstitucional *adj* unconstitutional
anticuado *adj* antiquated
anticuario *m* antique dealer
anticuerpo *m* BIO antibody
antideslizante *adj* non-slip
antidisturbios *adj*: ***policía antidisturbios*** riot police
antidoping *adj*: ***control antidoping*** dope test, drug test
antídoto *m* MED antidote; *fig* cure
antifaz *m* mask
antiguamente *adv* in the past
antigüedad *f* age; *en el trabajo* length of service; ***antigüedades*** antiques
antiguo *adj* old; *del pasado remoto* ancient; ***su antiguo novio*** her old *o* former boyfriend
antiinflamatorio *adj* MED anti-inflammatory
Antillas *fpl* West Indies
antílope *m* ZO antelope
antinatural *adj* unnatural
antinuclear *adj* anti-nuclear
antioxidante *m/adj* antioxidant
antipatía *f* antipathy, dislike
antipático *adj* disagreeable, unpleasant
antípodas *mpl* antipodes
antirreglamentario *adj* DEP *posición* offside; ***una jugada -a*** a foul
antirrobo *m* AUTO antitheft device
antisemitismo *m* anti-Semitism
antiséptico *m/adj* antiseptic
antisocial *adj* antisocial
antiterrorista *adj brigada* antiterrorist; ***la lucha antiterrorista*** the fight against terrorism
antítesis *f inv* antithesis
antojarse ⟨1a⟩ *v/r*: ***se le antojó salir*** he felt like going out; ***se me antoja que ...*** it seems to me that ...
antojo *m* whim; *de embarazada* craving; ***a mi antojo*** as I please
antología *f* anthology; ***de antología*** *fig* F fantastic, incredible F
antonomasia *f*: ***por antonomasia*** par excellence
antorcha *f* torch
antro *m* F dive F, dump F
antropófago *m*, **-a** *f* cannibal
antropología *f* anthropology
anual *adj* annual
anualidad *f* annual payment
anualmente *adv* yearly
anudar ⟨1a⟩ *v/t* knot
anular[1] ⟨1a⟩ *v/t* cancel; *matrimonio* annul; *gol* disallow
anular[2] *adj* ring-shaped; ***dedo anular*** ring finger
anunciante *m* COM advertiser
anunciar ⟨1b⟩ *v/t* announce; COM advertise
anuncio *m* announcement; (*presagio*) sign; COM advertisement; ***anuncio luminoso*** illuminated sign; ***anuncios por palabras, pequeños anuncios*** classified advertisements
anzuelo *m* (fish) hook; ***morder*** *or* ***tragar el anzuelo*** *fig* F take the bait
añadidura *f*: ***por añadidura*** in addition
añadir ⟨3a⟩ *v/t* add
añejo *adj* mature
añicos *mpl*: ***hacer añicos*** F smash to smithereens F
año *m* year; ***año bisiesto*** leap year; ***año fiscal*** fiscal year, *Br* financial year; ***año luz*** light year; ***año nuevo*** New Year; ***¿cuándo cumples años?*** when's your birthday?; ***¿cuántos años tienes?*** how old are you?; ***a los diez años*** at the age of ten; ***los años veinte*** the twenties
añorar ⟨1a⟩ *v/t* miss
aorta *f* ANAT aorta
apabullante *adj* overwhelming
apabullar ⟨1a⟩ *v/t* overwhelm
apacible *adj* mild-mannered
apaciguar ⟨1i⟩ **1** *v/t* pacify, calm down **2** *v/r* **apaciguarse** calm down
apadrinar ⟨1a⟩ *v/t* be godparent to; *político* support, back; *artista etc* sponsor; ***apadrinar a la novia*** give the bride away
apagado *adj fuego* out; *luz* off; *persona*

dull; *color* subdued
apagar ⟨1h⟩ **1** *v/t televisor, luz* turn off; *fuego* put out **2** *v/r* **apagarse** *de luz* go off; *de fuego* go out
apagón *m* blackout
apaisado *adj* landscape *atr*
apalabrar ⟨1a⟩ *v/t* agree (verbally)
apalancar ⟨1g⟩ **1** *v/t* lever **2** *v/r* **apalancarse** F settle
apalear ⟨1a⟩ *v/t* beat
apañar ⟨1a⟩ **1** *v/t* tidy up; *aparato* repair; *resultado* rig F, fix F; ***estamos apañados*** F we've had it F **2** *v/r* **apañarse** manage; ***apañárselas*** manage, get by
apaño *m fig* F makeshift repair
aparador *m* sideboard; *Méx* (*escaparate*) shop window
aparato *m* piece of equipment; *doméstico* appliance; BIO, ANAT system; *de partido político* machine; ***aparato respiratorio*** respiratory system; ***al aparato*** TELEC speaking
aparatoso *adj* spectacular
aparcacoches *m inv* valet
aparcamiento *m* parking lot, *Br* car park; ***aparcamiento subterráneo*** underground parking garage, *Br* underground car park
aparcar ⟨1g⟩ **1** *v/t* park; *tema, proyecto* shelve **2** *v/i* park
aparearse ⟨1a⟩ *v/r* ZO mate
aparecer ⟨2d⟩ **1** *v/i* appear **2** *v/r* **aparecerse** turn up
aparejador *m*, **aparejadora** *f architectural technician, Br* quantity surveyor
aparejo *m*: ***aparejos*** *pl* ***de pesca*** fishing gear *sg*
aparentar ⟨1a⟩ *v/t* pretend; ***no aparenta la edad que tiene*** she doesn't look her age
aparente *adj* (*evidente*) apparent; *L.Am.* (*fingido*) feigned
aparentemente *adv* apparently
aparición *f* appearance; (*fantasma*) apparition; ***hacer su aparición*** make one's appearance
apariencia *f* appearance; ***en apariencia*** outwardly; ***las apariencias engañan*** appearances can be deceptive
apartado *m* section; ***apartado de correos*** PO box
apartamento *m* apartment, *Br* flat
apartamiento *m* separation; *L.Am.* (*apartamento*) apartment, *Br* flat
apartar ⟨1a⟩ **1** *v/t* separate; *para después* set *o* put aside; *de un sitio* move away (***de*** from); ***apartar a alguien de hacer algo*** dissuade s.o. from doing sth **2** *v/r* **apartarse** move aside (***de*** from); ***apartarse del tema*** stray from the subject
aparte *adv* to one side; (*por separado*) separately; ***aparte de*** aside from, *Br* apart from; ***punto y aparte*** new paragraph
apasionado 1 *adj* passionate **2** *m/f* enthusiast
apasionante *adj* fascinating
apasionar ⟨1a⟩ *v/t* fascinate
apatía *f* apathy
apático *adj* apathetic
apdo. *abr* (= ***apartado*** (***de correos***)) PO Box (= Post Office Box)
apearse ⟨1a⟩ *v/r* get off, alight *fml*; ***apearse de algo*** get off sth, alight from sth *fml*
apechugar ⟨1h⟩ *v/i*: ***apechugar con algo*** cope with sth
apego *m* attachment
apelación *f* JUR appeal
apelar ⟨1a⟩ *v/t tb* JUR appeal (***a*** to)
apellidarse ⟨1a⟩ *v/r*: ***¿cómo se apellida?*** what's your / his / her surname?; ***se apellida Ocaña*** his / her surname is Ocaña
apellido *m* surname; ***apellido de soltera*** maiden name
apelmazarse ⟨1f⟩ *v/r de lana* get matted; *de arroz* stick together
apelotonarse ⟨1a⟩ *v/r* crowd together
apenado *adj* sad; *L.Am.* (*avergonzado*) ashamed; *L.Am.* (*incómodo*) embarrassed; *L.Am.* (*tímido*) shy
apenar ⟨1a⟩ **1** *v/t* sadden **2** *v/r* **apenarse** be upset *o* distressed; *L.Am.* (*avergonzarse*) be ashamed; *L.Am.* (*sentir incómodo*) be embarrassed; *L.Am.* (*ser tímido*) be shy
apenas 1 *adv* hardly, scarcely **2** *conj* as soon as
apéndice *m* appendix
apendicitis *f* MED appendicitis
apercibirse ⟨3a⟩ *v/r*: ***apercibirse de algo*** notice sth
apergaminado *adj fig* wrinkled
aperitivo *m comida* appetizer; *bebida* aperitif
apero *m utensilio* implement; *L.Am.* (*arneses*) harness; ***aperos de labranza*** farming implements
apertura *f* opening; FOT aperture; POL opening up
apesadumbrado *adj* heavy-hearted
apestar ⟨1a⟩ **1** *v/t* stink out F **2** *v/i* reek (***a*** of); ***huele que apesta*** it reeks
apestoso *adj* smelly
apetecer ⟨2d⟩ *v/i*: ***me apetece ir a dar un paseo*** I feel like going for a walk; ***¿qué te apetece?*** what do you feel like?
apetito *m* appetite

apetitoso *adj* appetizing
apiadarse ⟨1a⟩ *v/r* take pity (***de*** on)
ápice *m*: ***ni un ápice*** *fig* not an ounce; ***no ceder ni un ápice*** *fig* not give an inch
apicultura *f* beekeeping
apilar ⟨1a⟩ *v/t* pile up
apiñarse ⟨1a⟩ *v/r* crowd together
apio *m* BOT celery
apisonadora *f* steamroller
aplacar ⟨1g⟩ *v/t hambre* satisfy; *sed* quench; *a alguien* calm down, placate *fml*
aplanar ⟨1a⟩ **1** *v/t* level, flatten; ***aplanar las calles*** *C.Am., Pe* hang around the streets **2** *v/r* **aplanarse** *fig* (*descorazonarse*) lose heart
aplastante *adj* overwhelming; *calor* suffocating
aplastar ⟨1a⟩ *v/t tb fig* crush
aplaudida *f L.Am.* applause
aplaudir ⟨3a⟩ **1** *v/i* applaud, clap **2** *v/t tb fig* applaud
aplauso *m* round of applause
aplazamiento *m de visita, viaje* postponement
aplazar ⟨1f⟩ *v/t visita, viaje* put off, postpone; *Arg* fail
aplicación *f* application
aplicar ⟨1g⟩ **1** *v/t* apply; *sanciones* impose **2** *v/r* **aplicarse** apply o.s.
aplomo *m* composure, aplomb *fml*
apocalíptico *adj* apocalyptic
apócrifo *adj* apocryphal
apodar ⟨1a⟩ *v/t* nickname, call
apoderado *m* COM agent
apoderar ⟨1a⟩ **1** *v/t* authorize **2** *v/r* **apoderarse** take possession *o* control (***de*** of)
apodo *m* nickname
apogeo *m fig* height, peak; ***estar en su apogeo*** be at its height
apolillarse ⟨1a⟩ *v/r* get moth-eaten
apolítico *adj* apolitical
apología *f* defense, *Br* defence
apoltronarse ⟨1a⟩ *v/r en asiento* settle down; *en trabajo, rutina* get into a rut
apoplejía *f* MED apoplexy; ***ataque de apoplejía*** MED stroke
aporrear ⟨1a⟩ *v/t* pound on
aportación *f* contribution; COM investment
aportar ⟨1a⟩ *v/t* contribute; ***aportar pruebas*** JUR provide evidence
apósito *m* dressing
aposta *adv* on purpose, deliberately
apostar ⟨1m⟩ **1** *v/t* bet (***por*** on) **2** *v/i* bet; ***apostar por algo*** opt for sth **3** *v/r* **apostarse** bet; MIL position o.s.
apóstata *m/f* apostate
apóstol *m* apostle
apóstrofe, **apóstrofo** *m* apostrophe
apoteosis *f fig* climax
apoyar ⟨1a⟩ **1** *v/t* lean (***en*** against), rest (***en*** against); (*respaldar, confirmar*) support **2** *v/r* **apoyarse** lean (***en*** on; ***contra*** against); *en persona* rely (***en*** on); ***¿en qué te apoyas para decir eso?*** what are you basing that comment on?
apoyo *m fig* support
apreciable *adj* (*visible*) appreciable, noticeable; (*considerable*) considerable, substantial
apreciar ⟨1b⟩ *v/t* appreciate; (*sentir afecto por*) be fond of, think highly of
aprecio *m* respect
apremiar ⟨1b⟩ **1** *v/t* pressure, put pressure on **2** *v/i*: ***el tiempo apremia*** time is pressing
aprender ⟨2a⟩ **1** *v/t* learn **2** *v/r* **aprenderse** learn; ***aprenderse algo de memoria*** learn sth (off) by heart
aprendiz *m*, **aprendiza** *f* apprentice, trainee
aprendizaje *m* apprenticeship
aprensión *f* (*miedo*) apprehension; (*asco*) squeamishness
apresar ⟨1a⟩ *v/t nave* seize; *ladrón, animal* catch, capture
aprestarse ⟨1a⟩ *v/r*: ***aprestarse a*** get ready to
apresurar ⟨1a⟩ **1** *v/t* hurry **2** *v/r* **apresurarse** hurry up; ***apresurarse a hacer algo*** hurry *o* rush to do sth
apretado *adj* tight; ***iban muy apretados en el coche*** they were very cramped *o* squashed in the car
apretar ⟨1k⟩ **1** *v/t botón* press; (*pellizcar, pinzar*) squeeze; *tuerca* tighten; ***apretar el paso*** quicken one's pace; ***apretar los puños*** clench one's fists **2** *v/i de ropa, zapato* be too tight **3** *v/r* **apretarse** squeeze *o* squash together; ***apretarse el cinturón*** *fig* tighten one's belt
apretón *m* squeeze; ***apretón de manos*** handshake
apretujar ⟨1a⟩ **1** *v/t* F squeeze, squash **2** *v/r* **apretujarse** F squash *o* squeeze together
aprieto *m* predicament
aprisa *adv* quickly
aprisionar ⟨1a⟩ *v/t fig* trap
aprobación *f* approval; *de ley* passing
aprobado *m* EDU pass
aprobar ⟨1m⟩ *v/t* approve; *comportamiento, idea* approve of; *examen* pass
apropiado *adj* appropriate, suitable
apropiarse ⟨1b⟩ *v/r*: ***apropiarse de algo*** take sth
aprovechado **1** *adj desp* opportunistic **2** *m*, **-a** *f desp* opportunist

aprovechar ⟨1a⟩ **1** *v/t* take advantage of; *tiempo*, *espacio* make good use of; ***quiero aprovechar la ocasión para ...*** I would like to take this opportunity to ... **2** *v/i* take the opportunity (***para*** to); ***¡que aproveche!*** enjoy your meal! **3** *v/r* **aprovecharse** take advantage (***de*** of)
aprovisionarse ⟨1a⟩ *v/r* stock up (***de*** on)
aproximadamente *adv* approximately
aproximado *adj* approximate
aproximar ⟨1a⟩ **1** *v/t* bring closer **2** *v/r* **aproximarse** approach
aptitud *f* aptitude (***para*** for), flair (***para*** for)
apto *adj* suitable (***para*** for); *para servicio militar* fit; EDU pass
apuesta *f* bet
apuesto *adj* handsome
apunado *adj Pe, Bol* suffering from altitude sickness
apunarse ⟨1a⟩ *v/r S. Am.* get altitude sickness
apuntador *m*, **apuntadora** *f* TEA prompter
apuntalar ⟨1a⟩ *v/t edificio* shore up; *fig* prop up
apuntar ⟨1a⟩ **1** *v/t* (*escribir*) note down, make a note of; TEA prompt; *en curso*, *para viaje etc* put down (***en, a*** on; ***para*** for); ***apuntar con el dedo*** point at *o* to **2** *v/i con arma* aim **3** *v/r* **apuntarse** put one's name down (***para, en*** *or* ***a*** for); ***¡me apunto!*** count me in!
apunte *m* note
apuñalar ⟨1a⟩ *v/t* stab
apurado *adj L.Am.* (*con prisa*) in a hurry; (*pobre*) short (of cash)
apurar ⟨1a⟩ **1** *v/t vaso* finish off; *a alguien* pressure, put pressure on **2** *v/i Chi*: ***no me apura*** I'm not in a hurry for it **3** *v/r* **apurarse** worry; *L.Am.* (*darse prisa*) hurry (up)
apuro *m* predicament, tight spot F; *vergüenza* embarrassment; *L.Am.* rush; ***me da apuro*** I'm embarrassed
aquejado *adj*: ***estar aquejado de*** be suffering from
aquel, **aquella**, **aquellos**, **aquellas** *det singular* that; *plural* those
aquél, **aquélla**, **aquéllos**, **aquéllas** *pron singular* that (one); *plural* those (ones)
aquello *pron* that
aquí *adv en el espacio* here; *en el tiempo* now; ***desde aquí*** from here; ***por aquí*** here
árabe **1** *m/f & adj* Arab **2** *m idioma* Arabic
Arabia Saudí Saudi Arabia
arado *m* plow, *Br* plough
arancel *m* tariff
arancelario *adj* tariff *atr*
arándano *m* blueberry
arandela *f* washer
araña *f* ZO spider; *lámpara* chandelier
arañar ⟨1a⟩ *v/t* scratch
arañazo *m* scratch
arar ⟨1a⟩ *v/t* plow, *Br* plough
arbitraje *m* arbitration
arbitrar ⟨1a⟩ *v/t en fútbol, boxeo* referee; *en tenis, béisbol* umpire; *en conflicto* arbitrate
arbitrario *adj* arbitrary
árbitro *m en fútbol, boxeo* referee; *en tenis, béisbol* umpire; *en conflicto* arbitrator
árbol *m* tree; ***árbol genealógico*** family tree
arboleda *f* grove
arbusto *m* shrub, bush
arca *f* chest; ***arca de Noé*** Noah's Ark
arcada *f* MED: ***me provocó arcadas*** it made me retch *o* heave F
arcaico *adj* archaic
arce *m* BOT maple
arcén *m* shoulder, *Br* hard shoulder
archidiócesis *f inv* archdiocese
archipiélago *m* archipelago
archivador *m* filing cabinet
archivar ⟨1a⟩ *v/t papeles, documentos* file; *asunto* shelve
archivo *m* archive; INFOR file
arcilla *f* clay
arco *m* ARQUI arch; MÚS bow; *L.Am.* DEP goal; ***arco iris*** rainbow
arder ⟨2a⟩ *v/i* burn; *estar muy caliente* be exceedingly hot; ***la reunión está que arde*** F the meeting is about to erupt F
ardilla *f* ZO squirrel
ardor *m entusiasmo* fervo(u)r; ***ardor de estómago*** heartburn
arduo *adj* arduous
área *f* area; DEP ***área de castigo*** *or* ***de penalty*** penalty area; ***área de descanso*** pull-in (at the side of the road); ***área de servicio*** service area
arena *f* sand; ***arenas*** *pl* ***movedizas*** quicksand *sg*
arenga *f* morale-boosting speech; (*sermõn*) harangue
arenque *m* herring
arepa *f C.Am., Ven cornmeal roll*
arete *m L.Am. joya* earring
Argelia Algeria
Argentina Argentina
argentino **1** *adj* Argentinian **2** *m*, **-a** *f* Argentinian
argolla *f L.Am.* ring
argot *m* slang
argucia *f* clever argument
argüir ⟨3g⟩ *v/t & v/i* argue

argumentar ⟨1a⟩ *v/t* argue

argumento *m razón* argument; *de libro, película etc* plot

árido *adj* arid, dry; *fig* dry

Aries *m/f inv* ASTR Aries

arisco *adj* unfriendly

aristocracia *f* aristocracy

aristócrata *m/f* aristocrat

aristocrático *adj* aristocratic

aritmética *f* arithmetic

arma *f* weapon; ***arma blanca*** knife; ***arma de doble filo*** *or* ***de dos filos*** *fig* two-edged sword; ***arma de fuego*** firearm; ***alzarse en armas*** rise up in arms

armada *f* navy

armadillo *m* ZO armadillo

armado *adj* armed

armadura *f* armo(u)r

armamento *m* armaments *pl*

armar ⟨1a⟩ **1** *v/t* MIL arm; TÉC assemble, put together; ***armar un escándalo*** F kick up a fuss F, make a scene F **2** *v/r* **armarse** arm o.s.; ***la que se va a armar*** F all hell will break loose F; ***armarse de valor*** pluck up courage

armario *m* closet, *Br* wardrobe; *de cocina* cabinet, *Br* cupboard

armazón *f* skeleton, framework

armisticio *m* armistice

armonía *f* harmony

armónica *f* harmonica, mouth organ

armonioso *adj* harmonious

armonizar ⟨1f⟩ **1** *v/t* harmonize; *diferencias* reconcile **2** *v/i de color, estilo* blend (***con*** with); *de persona* get on (***con*** with)

arnés *m* harness; *para niños* leading strings *pl*, *Br* leading reins *pl*

aro *m* hoop; *L.Am.* (*pendiente*) earring; ***entrar*** *or* ***pasar por el aro*** *fig* F bite the bullet, take the plunge

aroma *m* aroma; *de flor* scent

arpa *f* harp

arpía *f* harpy

arpón *m* harpoon

arquear ⟨1a⟩ *v/t espalda* arch; *cejas* raise

arqueología *f* arch(a)eology

arqueológico *adj* arch(a)eological

arqueólogo *m*, **-a** *f* arch(a)eologist

arquero *m* archer; *L.Am. en fútbol* goalkeeper

arquetipo *m* archetype

arquitectónico *adj* architectural

arquitecto *m*, **-a** *f* architect

arquitectura *f* architecture

arrabal *m* poor outlying area

arraigado *adj* entrenched

arraigar ⟨1h⟩ **1** *v/i* take root **2** *v/r* **arraigarse** *de persona* settle (***en*** in); *de costumbre, idea* take root

arramblar ⟨1a⟩ *v/t* (*destruir*) destroy

arrancar ⟨1g⟩ **1** *v/t planta, página* pull out; *vehículo* start (up); (*quitar*) snatch **2** *v/i de vehículo, máquina* start (up); INFOR boot (up); *Chi* (*huir*) run away **3** *v/r* **arrancarse** *Chi* run away

arranque *m* AUTO starting mechanism; (*energía*) drive; (*ataque*) fit

arrasar ⟨1a⟩ **1** *v/t* devastate **2** *v/i* F be a big hit

arrastrar ⟨1a⟩ **1** *v/t por el suelo*, INFOR drag (***por*** along); (*llevarse*) carry away **2** *v/i por el suelo* trail on the ground **3** *v/r* **arrastrarse** crawl; *fig* (*humillarse*) grovel (***delante de*** to)

arrastre *m*: ***estar para el arrastre*** *fig* F be fit to drop F

arreada *f Rpl* round-up

arrebatar ⟨1a⟩ *v/t* snatch (***a*** from)

arrebato *m* fit

arrebujarse ⟨1a⟩ *v/r* F wrap o.s. up; *en cama* snuggle up

arreciar ⟨1b⟩ *v/i* get worse; *de viento* get stronger

arrecife *m* reef

arredrarse ⟨1a⟩ *v/r* be intimidated (***ante*** by)

arreglar ⟨1a⟩ **1** *v/t* (*reparar*) fix, repair; (*ordenar*) tidy (up); (*solucionar*) sort out; MÚS arrange; ***arreglar cuentas*** settle up; *fig* settle scores **2** *v/r* **arreglarse** get (o.s.) ready; *de problema* get sorted out; (*apañarse*) manage; ***arreglárselas*** manage

arreglo *m* (*reparación*) repair; (*solución*) solution; (*acuerdo*) arrangement, agreement; MÚS arrangement; ***arreglo de cuentas*** settling of scores; ***con arreglo a*** in accordance with; ***esto no tiene arreglo*** there's nothing to be done

arrellanarse ⟨1a⟩ *v/r* settle

arremangarse ⟨1h⟩ *v/r* roll up one's sleeves

arremeter ⟨2a⟩ *v/i*: ***arremeter contra*** charge (at); *fig* (*criticar*) attack

arremolinarse ⟨1a⟩ *v/r* mill around

arrendamiento *m* renting

arrendar ⟨1k⟩ *v/t L.Am.* (*dar en alquiler*) rent (out), let; (*tomar en alquiler*) rent; ***se arrenda*** for rent

arreo *m Rpl* driving, herding; (*manada*) herd

arrepentimiento *m* repentance; (*cambio de opinión*) change of heart

arrepentirse ⟨3i⟩ *v/r* be sorry; (*cambiar de opinión*) change one's mind; ***arrepentirse de algo*** regret sth

arrestar ⟨1a⟩ *v/t* arrest

arresto *m* arrest

arriba 1 *adv* ◇ *situación* up; *en edificio* upstairs; ***ponlo ahí arriba*** put it up there; ***el cajón de arriba*** *siguiente* the next drawer up, the drawer above; *úúltimo* the top drawer; ***arriba del todo*** right at the top
◇ *dirección* up; *en edificio* upstairs; ***sigan hacia arriba*** keep going up; ***me miró de arriba abajo*** *fig* she looked me up and down
◇ *con cantidades*: ***de diez para arriba*** ten or above **2** *int* long live
arribeño *m*, **-a** *f L.Am.* uplander, highlander
arribista *m/f* social climber
arriesgado *adj* adventurous
arriesgar ⟨1h⟩ **1** *v/t* risk **2** *v/r* **arriesgarse** take a risk; ***arriesgarse a hacer algo*** risk doing sth
arrimar ⟨1a⟩ **1** *v/t* move closer; ***arrimar el hombro*** F pull one's weight **2** *v/r* **arrimarse** move closer (***a*** to)
arrinconar ⟨1a⟩ *v/t* (*acorralar*) corner; *libros etc* put away; *persona* cold-shoulder
arroba *f* INFOR 'at' symbol, @
arrodillarse ⟨1a⟩ *v/r* kneel (down)
arrogancia *f* arrogance
arrogante *adj* arrogant
arrojar ⟨1a⟩ **1** *v/t* (*lanzar*) throw; *resultado* produce; (*vomitar*) throw up **2** *v/r* **arrojarse** throw o.s.
arrollador *adj* overwhelming
arropar ⟨1a⟩ *v/t* wrap up; *fig* protect
arrope *m Rpl, Chi, Pe* fruit syrup
arroyo *m* stream; ***sacar a alguien del arroyo*** *fig* lift s.o. out of the gutter
arroz *m* rice; ***arroz con leche*** rice pudding
arruga *f* wrinkle
arrugar ⟨1h⟩ **1** *v/t* wrinkle; **2** *v/r* **arrugarse** *de piel, ropa* get wrinkled
arruinado *adj* ruined, broke F
arruinar ⟨1a⟩ **1** *v/t* ruin **2** *v/r* **arruinarse** be ruined
arrullo *m de paloma* cooing; *para niño* lullaby
arsenal *m* arsenal
arsénico *m* arsenic
art *abr* (= ***artículo***) art. (= article)
art.° *abr* (= ***artículo***) art. (= article)
arte *m* (*pl f*) art; ***arte dramático*** dramatic art; ***bellas artes*** *pl* fine art *sg*; ***malas artes*** *pl* guile *sg*
artefacto *m* (*dispositivo*) device
arteria *f* artery
arterio(e)sclerosis *f* arteriosclerosis
artesana *f* craftswoman
artesanía *f* (handi)crafts *pl*
artesano *m* craftsman
Ártico *zona, océano* Arctic
articulación *f* ANAT, TÉC joint; *de sonidos* articulation
artículo *m de periódico*, GRAM, JUR article; COM product, item
artificial *adj* artificial
artillería *f* artillery; ***artillería ligera / pesada*** light / heavy artillery
artilugio *m aparato* gadget
artimaña *f* trick
artista *m/f* artist
artístico *adj* artistic
artritis *f* MED arthritis
arveja *f Rpl, Chi, Pe* BOT pea
arzobispo *m* archbishop
as *m tb fig* ace
asa *f* handle
asado **1** *adj* roast *atr* **2** *m* roast
asalariado *m*,**-a** *f* wage earner; *de empresa* employee
asaltante *m/f* assailant
asaltar ⟨1a⟩ *v/t persona* attack; *banco* rob
asalto *m a persona* attack (***a*** on); *robo* robbery, raid; *en boxeo* round
asamblea *f reunión* meeting; *ente* assembly
asar ⟨1a⟩ **1** *v/t* roast; ***asar a la parrilla*** broil, *Br* grill **2** *v/r* **asarse** *fig* F be roasting F
ascender ⟨2g⟩ **1** *v/t a empleado* promote **2** *v/i de precios, temperatura etc* rise; *de montañero* climb; DEP, *en trabajo* be promoted (***a*** to)
ascensión *f* ascent
ascenso *m de temperatura, precios* rise (***de*** in); *de montaña* ascent; DEP, *en trabajo* promotion
ascensor *m* elevator, *Br* lift
ascético *adj* ascetic
asco *m* disgust; ***me da asco*** I find it disgusting; ***¡qué asco!*** how revolting *o* disgusting!
ascua *f* ember; ***estar en*** *or* ***sobre ascuas*** be on tenterhooks
asearse ⟨1a⟩ *v/r* wash up, *Br* have a wash
asediar ⟨1b⟩ *v/t tb fig* besiege
asedio *m* MIL siege, blockade; *a alguien* hounding
aseguradora *f* insurance company
asegurar ⟨1a⟩ **1** *v/t* (*afianzar*) secure; (*prometer*) assure; (*garantizar*) guarantee; COM insure **2** *v/r* **asegurarse** make sure
asentamiento *m* settlement
asentarse ⟨1k⟩ *v/r* settle
asentir ⟨3i⟩ *v/i* agree (***a*** to), consent (***a*** to); *con la cabeza* nod
aseo *m* cleanliness; (*baño*) restroom, toilet

aséptico *adj* aseptic
asequible *adj precio* affordable; *obra* accessible
aserrar ⟨1k⟩ *v/t* saw
aserrín *m L.Am.* sawdust
asesinar ⟨1a⟩ *v/t* murder; POL assassinate
asesinato *m* murder; POL assassination
asesino *m*, **-a** *f* murderer; POL assassin
asesor *m*, **asesora** *f* consultant, advisor, *Br* adviser; ***asesor fiscal*** financial advisor (*Br* adviser); ***asesor de imagen*** public relations consultant
asesorar ⟨1a⟩ *v/t* advise
asesoría *f* consultancy
asestar ⟨1a⟩ *v/t golpe* deal (***a*** to); ***me asestó una puñalada*** he stabbed me
asfaltar ⟨1a⟩ *v/t* asphalt
asfalto *m* asphalt
asfixia *f* asphyxiation
asfixiante *adj* asphyxiating, suffocating
asfixiar ⟨1b⟩ **1** *v/t* asphyxiate, suffocate **2** *v/r* **asfixiarse** asphyxiate, suffocate
así 1 *adv* (*de este modo*) like this; (*de ese modo*) like that; ***así no más*** *S. Am.* just like that; ***así pues*** so; ***así que*** so; ***así de grande*** this big **2** *conj*: ***así como*** *al igual que* while, whereas
Asia Asia
asiático 1 *adj* Asian **2** *m*, **-a** *f* Asian
asiduidad *f* frequency; ***con asiduidad*** *con frecuencia* regularly
asiduo *adj* regular
asiento *m* seat; ***tomar asiento*** take a seat
asignación *f acción* allocation; *dinero* allowance
asignar ⟨1a⟩ *v/t* allocate; *persona*, *papel* assign
asignatura *f* subject
asilarse ⟨1a⟩ *v/r* take refuge, seek asylum
asilo *m* home, institution; POL asylum; ***asilo de ancianos*** old people's home
asimétrico *adj* asymmetrical
asimilar ⟨1a⟩ *v/t* assimilate
asimismo *adv* (*también*) also; (*igualmente*) in the same way, likewise
asistencia *f* (*ayuda*) assistance; *a lugar* attendance (***a*** at); ***asistencia en carretera*** AUTO roadside assistance; ***asistencia médica*** medical care
asistenta *f* cleaner, cleaning woman
asistente *m/f* (*ayudante*) assistant; ***asistente social*** social worker; ***los asistentes*** those present
asistir ⟨3a⟩ **1** *v/t* help, assist **2** *v/i* be present; ***asistir a una boda*** attend a wedding
asma *f* asthma
asmático *adj* asthmatic
asno *m* ZO donkey; *persona* idiot
asociación *f* association
asociar ⟨1b⟩ **1** *v/t* associate; ***asociar a alguien con algo*** associate s.o. with sth **2** *v/r* **asociarse** team up (***con*** with), go into partnership (***con*** with); ***asociarse a*** *grupo*, *club* become a member of
asolar ⟨1m⟩ *v/t* devastate
asoleada *f*: ***pegarse una asoleada*** *Bol*, *Pe* sunbathe
asomar ⟨1a⟩ **1** *v/t* put *o* stick out **2** *v/i* show **3** *v/r* **asomarse** lean out; ***asomarse a*** *or* ***por la ventana*** lean out of the window
asombrado *adj* amazed
asombrar ⟨1a⟩ **1** *v/t* amaze, astonish **2** *v/r* **asombrarse** be amazed *o* astonished
asombro *m* amazement, astonishment
asombroso *adj* amazing
asomo *m*: ***ni por asomo*** no way
asorocharse ⟨1a⟩ *v/r Pe*, *Bol* get altitude sickness
aspecto *m de persona*, *cosa* look, appearance; (*faceta*) aspect; ***tener buen aspecto*** look good
áspero *adj superficie* rough; *sonido* harsh; *persona* abrupt
aspersor *m* sprinkler
aspiraciones *fpl* aspirations
aspirador *m*, **aspiradora** *f* vacuum cleaner
aspirante *m/f a cargo* candidate (***a*** for); *a título* contender (***a*** for)
aspirar ⟨1a⟩ **1** *v/t* suck up; *al respirar* inhale, breathe in **2** *v/i*: ***aspirar a*** aspire to
aspirina *f* aspirin
asqueado *adj* disgusted
asquear ⟨1a⟩ *v/t* disgust
asqueroso 1 *adj* (*sucio*) filthy; (*repugnante*) revolting, disgusting **2** *m*, **-a** *f* creep
asterisco *m* asterisk
astigmatismo *m* astigmatism
astilla *f* splinter; ***astillas*** *pl para fuego* kindling *sg*; ***hacer astillas algo*** *fig* smash sth to pieces
astillero *m* shipyard
astral *adj* astral
astringente *m/adj* astringent
astro *m* AST, *fig* star
astrología *f* astrology
astrólogo *m*, **-a** *f* astrologer
astronauta *m/f* astronaut
astronave *f* spaceship
astronomía *f* astronomy
astronómico *adj* astronomical
astrónomo *m*, **-a** *f* astronomer
astucia *f* shrewdness, astuteness
astuto *adj* shrewd, astute
asumir ⟨3a⟩ *v/t* assume; (*aceptar*) accept, come to terms with

asunto *m* matter; F (*relación*) affair; ***asuntos exteriores*** foreign affairs; ***no es asunto tuyo*** it's none of your business
asustar ⟨1a⟩ **1** *v/t* frighten, scare **2** *v/r* **asustarse** be frightened *o* scared
atacar ⟨1g⟩ *v/t* attack
atajar ⟨1a⟩ **1** *v/t* check the spread of, contain; *L.Am. pelota* catch **2** *v/i* take a short cut
atajo *m L.Am.* short cut
atañer ⟨2f⟩ *v/i* concern
ataque *m* (*agresión*) attack; (*acceso*) fit; ***ataque cardíaco*** *or* ***al corazón*** MED heart attack; ***le dio un ataque de risa*** she burst out laughing
atar ⟨1a⟩ *v/t* tie (up); *fig* tie down
atardecer ⟨2d⟩ **1** *v/i* get dark **2** *m* dusk
atareado *adj* busy
atascar ⟨1g⟩ **1** *v/t* block **2** *v/r* **atascarse** *de cañería* get blocked; *de mecanismo* jam, stick; *al hablar* dry up
atasco *m* traffic jam
ataúíd *m* coffin, casket
atemorizar ⟨1f⟩ *v/t* frighten
atención *f* attention; (*cortesía*) courtesy; ***¡atención!*** your attention, please!; ***llamar la atención a alguien*** *reñir* tell s.o. off; *por ser llamativo* attract s.o.'s attention; ***prestar atención*** pay attention (***a*** to)
atender ⟨2g⟩ **1** *v/t a enfermo* look after; *en tienda* attend to, serve **2** *v/i* pay attention (***a*** to)
atenerse ⟨2l⟩ *v/r*: ***atenerse a*** *normas* abide by; *consecuencias* face, accept; ***saber a qué atenerse*** know where one stands
atentado *m* attack (***contra, a*** on); ***atentado terrorista*** terrorist attack
atentamente *adv* attentively; *en carta* sincerely, *Br* Yours sincerely
atentar ⟨1k⟩ *v/i*: ***atentar contra*** *vida* make an attempt on; *moral etc* be contrary to
atento *adj* attentive; ***estar atento a algo*** pay attention to sth
atenuante *adj* JUR extenuating; ***circunstancia atenuante*** JUR extenuating circumstance
atenuar ⟨1e⟩ *v/t* lessen, reduce
ateo **1** *adj* atheistic **2** *m*, **-a** *f* atheist
aterciopelado *adj tb fig* velvety
aterido *adj* frozen
aterrador *adj* frightening
aterrar ⟨1a⟩ *v/t* terrify
aterrizaje *m* AVIA landing; ***aterrizaje forzoso*** *or* ***de emergencia*** emergency landing
aterrizar ⟨1f⟩ *v/i* land
aterrorizado *adj* terrified, petrified F
aterrorizar ⟨1f⟩ *v/t* terrify; (*amenazar*) terrorize
atestado *adj* overcrowded
atestiguar ⟨1i⟩ *v/t* JUR testify; *fig* bear witness to
atiborrarse ⟨1a⟩ *v/r* F stuff o.s. F (***de*** with)
ático *m piso* top floor; *apartamento* top floor apartment (*Br* flat); (*desván*) attic
atinar ⟨1a⟩ *v/i* manage (***a*** to); ***no atinó con la respuesta correcta*** she couldn't come up with the right answer
atípico *adj* atypical
atisbo *m* sign
atizar ⟨1f⟩ *v/t fuego* poke; *pasiones* stir up; ***le atizó un golpe*** she hit him
Atlántico *m/adj*: ***el*** (***océano***) ***Atlántico*** the Atlantic (Ocean)
atlas *m inv* atlas
atleta *m/f* athlete
atlético *adj* athletic
atletismo *m* athletics
atmo. *abr* (***= atentísimo***): ***su atmo*** Yours truly
atmósfera *f* atmosphere
atole *m Méx flavored hot drink made with maize flour*
atolladero *m*: ***sacar a alguien del atolladero*** *fig* F get s.o. out of a tight spot
atolondrado *adj* scatterbrained
atómico *adj* atomic
átomo *m* atom; ***ni un átomo de*** *fig* not an iota of
atónito *adj* astonished, amazed
atontar ⟨1a⟩ *v/t* make groggy *o* dopey; *de golpe* stun, daze; (*volver tonto*) turn into a zombie
atorar ⟨1a⟩ *L.Am.* **1** *v/t cañeria etc* block (up) **2** *v/r* **atorarse** choke; *de cañeria etc* get blocked (up)
atormentar ⟨1a⟩ *v/t* torment
atornillar ⟨1a⟩ *v/t* screw on
atorrante *m Rpl*, *Chi* F bum F, *Br* tramp; (*holgazán*) layabout
atosigar ⟨1h⟩ *v/t* pester
atrabancado *adj Méx* clumsy
atracar ⟨1g⟩ **1** *v/t banco*, *tienda* hold up; *a alguien* mug; *Chi* F make out with F, neck with *Br* F **2** *v/i* MAR dock
atracción *f* attraction
atraco *m de banco*, *tienda* robbery; *de persona* mugging
atracón *m*: ***darse un atracón de*** stuff o.s. with F
atractivo **1** *adj* attractive **2** *m* appeal, attraction
atraer ⟨2p⟩ *v/t* attract
atragantarse ⟨1a⟩ *v/r* choke (***con*** on); ***se***

le ha atragantado *fig* she can't stand *o* stomach him
atrancar ⟨1g⟩ **1** *v/t puerta* barricade **2** *v/r* **atrancarse** *fig* get stuck
atrapar ⟨1a⟩ *v/t* catch, trap
atrás *adv para indicar posición* at the back, behind; *para indicar movimiento* back; ***años atrás*** years ago *o* back; ***hacia atrás*** back, backwards; ***quedarse atrás*** get left behind
atrasado *adj en estudios, pago* behind (***en*** in *o* with); *reloj* slow; *pueblo* backward; ***ir atrasado*** *de un reloj* be slow
atrasar ⟨1a⟩ **1** *v/t reloj* put back; *fecha* postpone, put back **2** *v/i de reloj* lose time
atraso *m* backwardness; COM ***atrasos*** arrears
atravesar ⟨1k⟩ *v/t* cross; (*perforar*) go through, pierce; *crisis* go through
atrevido *adj* daring
atreverse ⟨2a⟩ *v/r* dare
atribuir ⟨3g⟩ **1** *v/t* attribute (***a*** to) **2** *v/r* **atribuirse** claim
atrincherarse ⟨1a⟩ *v/r* MIL dig o.s. in, entrench o.s.; ***se atrincheró en su postura*** *fig* he dug his heels in
atrocidad *f* atrocity
atrofiado *adj* atrophied
atrofiarse ⟨1b⟩ *v/r* atrophy
atropellar ⟨1a⟩ *v/t* knock down
atroz *adj* appalling, atrocious
ATS *abr* (= ***ayudante técnico sanitario***) registered nurse
atte. *abr* (= ***atentamente***) sincerely (yours)
atuendo *m* outfit
atufar ⟨1a⟩ *v/t* F stink out F
atúín *m* tuna (fish)
aturdido *adj* in a daze
aturdir ⟨3a⟩ **1** *v/t de golpe, noticia* stun, daze; (*confundir*) bewilder, confuse **2** *v/r* **aturdirse** be stunned *o* dazed; (*confundirse*) be bewildered *o* confused
aturullar ⟨1a⟩ **1** *v/t* confuse **2** *v/r* **aturullarse** get confused
audacia *f* audacity
audaz *adj* daring, bold, audacious
audición *f* TEA audition; JUR hearing
audiencia *f* audience; JUR court; ***índice de audiencia*** TV ratings *pl*
audífono *m para sordos* hearing aid
audiovisual *adj* audiovisual
auditivo *adj* auditory; *problema* hearing *atr*
auditor *m*, **auditora** *f* auditor
auditoría *f* audit
auditorio *m* (*púíblico*) audience; *sala* auditorium
auge *m* peak; ***estar en auge*** *aumento* be enjoying a boom
augurar ⟨1a⟩ *v/t de persona* predict, foretell; *de indicio* augur
augurio *m* omen, sign; ***un buen / mal augurio*** a good / bad omen
aula *f* classroom; *en universidad* lecture hall, *Br* lecture theatre
aullido *m* howl
aumentar ⟨1a⟩ **1** *v/t* increase; *precio* increase, raise, put up **2** *v/i de precio, temperatura* rise, increase, go up
aumento *m de precios, temperaturas etc* rise (***de*** in), increase (***de*** in); *de sueldo* raise, *Br* rise; ***ir en aumento*** be increasing
aun *adv* even; ***aun así*** even so
aúín *adv en oraciones no negativas* still; *en oraciones negativas* yet; *en comparaciones* even; ***aúín no*** not yet
aunar ⟨1a⟩ *v/t* combine
aunque *conj* although, even though; + *subj* even if
auricular *m de teléfono* receiver; ***auriculares*** headphones, earphones
aurora *f* dawn; ***aurora boreal*** northern lights *pl*
auscultar ⟨1a⟩ *v/t*: ***auscultar a alguien*** listen to s.o.'s chest
ausencia *f de persona* absence; *no existencia* lack (***de*** of); ***brillaba por su ausencia*** he was conspicuous by his absence
ausente *adj* absent
auspicio *m* sponsorship; ***bajo los auspicios de*** under the auspices of
austeridad *f* austerity
austero *adj* austere
austral *adj* southern
Australia Australia
australiano **1** *adj* Australian **2** *m*, **-a** *f* Australian
Austria Austria
austriano **1** *adj* Austrian **2** *m*, **-a** *f* Austrian
auténtico *adj* authentic
autentificar ⟨1g⟩ *v/t* authenticate
autismo *m* autism
auto *m* JUR order; *L.Am.* AUTO car
autoadhesivo *adj* self-adhesive
autoayuda *f* self-help
autobiografía *f* autobiography
autobombo *m* F self-glorification
autobúís *m* bus
autocar *m* bus
autocaravana *f* camper van
autocontrol *m* self-control
autocrítica *f* self-criticism
autóctono *adj* indigenous, native
autodefensa *f* self-defense, *Br* self-de-

fence
autodeterminación *f* self-determination
autodidacta 1 *adj* self-taught **2** *m/f* self-taught person
autoedición *f* desktop publishing, DTP
autoescuela *f* driving school
autoestima *f* self-esteem
autoestop *m* hitchhiking
autoestopista *m/f* hitchhiker
autógrafo *m* autograph
automático *adj* automatic
automatizar ⟨1f⟩ *v/t* automate
automedicación *f* self-medication
automóvil *m* car, automobile
automovilismo *m* driving
automovilista *m/f* motorist
autonomía *f* autonomy; *en España* automous region
autónomo *adj* autonomous
autopista *f* freeway, *Br* motorway; ***autopista de la información*** *or* ***de la comunicación*** INFOR information (super)highway
autopsia *f* post mortem, autopsy
autor *m*, **autora** *f* author; *de crimen* perpetrator
autoridad *f* authority
autoritario *adj* authoritarian
autorización *f* authority
autorizar ⟨1f⟩ *v/t* authorize
autorradio *m* car radio
autorretrato *m* self-portrait
autoservicio *m* supermarket; *restaurante* self-service restaurant
autostop *m* hitchhiking; ***hacer autostop*** hitch(hike)
autosuficiencia *f* self-sufficiency; *desp* smugness
autosuficiente *adj* self-sufficient; *desp* smug
autovía *f* divided highway, *Br* dual carriageway
auxiliar 1 *adj* auxiliary; *profesor* assistant **2** *m/f* assistant; ***auxiliar*** *f* ***de vuelo*** stewardess, flight attendant **3** ⟨1b⟩ *v/t* help
auxilio *m* help; ***primeros auxilios*** *pl* first aid *sg*
Av. *abr* (= ***Avenida***) Ave (= Avenue)
aval *m* guarantee; ***aval bancario*** bank guarantee
avalancha *f* avalanche
avalar ⟨1a⟩ *v/t* guarantee; *fig* back
avance *m* advance
avanzado *adj* advanced
avanzar ⟨1f⟩ **1** *v/t* move forward, advance **2** *v/i* advance, move forward; MIL advance (***hacia*** on); *en trabajo* make progress
avaricia *f* avarice
avaro 1 *adj* miserly **2** *m*, **-a** *f* miser
avasallar ⟨1a⟩ *v/t* subjugate; ***no dejes que te avasallen*** *fig* don't let them push you around
Av.[da] *abr* (= ***Avenida***) Ave (= Avenue)
ave *f* bird; *S. Am.* (*pollo*) chicken; ***ave de presa*** *or* ***de rapiña*** bird of prey
avecinarse ⟨1a⟩ *v/r* approach
avejentar ⟨1a⟩ *v/t* age
avellana *f* BOT hazelnut
avellano *m* BOT hazel
avena *f* oats *pl*
avenida *f* avenue
avenirse ⟨3s⟩ *v/r* agree (***a*** to)
aventajar ⟨1a⟩ *v/t* be ahead of
aventura *f* adventure; *riesgo* venture; *amorosa* affair
aventurar ⟨1a⟩ **1** *v/t* risk; *opinión* venture **2** *v/r* **aventurarse** venture; ***aventurarse a hacer algo*** dare to do sth
aventurero *adj* adventurous
avergonzar ⟨1n & 1f⟩ **1** *v/t* (*aborchornar*) embarrass; ***le avergüenza*** *algo reprensible* she's ashamed of it **2** *v/r* **avergonzarse** be ashamed (***de*** of)
avería *f* TÉC fault; AUTO breakdown
averiarse ⟨1c⟩ *v/r* break down
averiguar ⟨1i⟩ *v/t* find out
aversión *f* aversion
avestruz *m* ZO ostrich; ***del avestruz*** *política, táctica* head-in-the-sand
aviación *f* aviation; MIL air force
avicultor *m*, **avicultora** *f* poultry farmer
avidez *f* eagerness
ávido *adj* eager (***de*** for), avid (***de*** for)
avinagrarse ⟨1a⟩ *v/r de vino* turn vinegary; *fig* become bitter *o* sour
avión *m* plane; ***por avión*** *mandar una carta* (by) airmail
avioneta *f* light aircraft
avisar ⟨1a⟩ *v/t notificar* let know, tell; *de peligro* warn; (*llamar*) call, send for
aviso *m comunicación* notice; (*advertencia*) warning; *L.Am.* (*anuncio*) advertisement; ***hasta nuevo aviso*** until further notice; ***sin previo aviso*** unexpectedly, without any warning
avispa *f* ZO wasp
avivar ⟨1a⟩ *v/t fuego* revive; *interés* arouse
avizor *adj*: ***estar ojo avizor*** be alert
axila *f* armpit
axioma *m* axiom
ay *int de dolor* ow!, ouch!; *de susto* oh!
ayer *adv* yesterday; ***ayer por la mañana*** yesterday morning
ayuda *f* help; ***ayuda al desarrollo*** development aid *o* assistance
ayudante *m/f* assistant
ayudar ⟨1a⟩ *v/t* help

ayunas: ***estoy en ayunas*** I haven't eaten anything
ayuno *m* fast
ayuntamiento *m* city council, town council; *edificio* city hall
azabache *m* MIN jet
azadón *m* mattock
azafata *f* flight attendant; ***azafata de congresos*** hostess
azafrán *m* BOT saffron
azalea *f* BOT azalea
azar *m* fate, chance; ***al azar*** at random
azorarse ⟨1a⟩ *v/r* be embarrassed
azotar ⟨1a⟩ *v/t con látigo* whip, flog; *con mano* smack; *de enfermedad, hambre* grip; *Méx puerta* slam
azote *m con látigo* lash; *con mano* smack; *fig* scourge; ***dar un azote a alguien*** F smack s.o.
azotea *f* flat roof; ***estar mal de la azotea*** *fig* F be crazy F
azteca *m/f & adj* Aztec
azúcar *m* (*also f*) sugar; ***azúcar glas*** confectioner's sugar, *Br* icing sugar; ***azúcar moreno*** brown sugar
azucarero *m* sugar bowl
azucena *f* BOT Madonna lily
azufre *m* sulfur, *Br* sulphur
azul 1 *adj* blue; ***azul celeste*** sky-blue; ***azul marino*** navy(-blue) **2** *m* blue
azulejo *m* tile
azuzar ⟨1f⟩ *v/t*: ***azuzar los perros a alguien*** set the dogs on s.o.; *fig* egg s.o. on

B

B.A. *abr* (**= *Buenos Aires***) Buenos Aires
baba *f* drool, dribble; ***se le caía la baba*** F he was drooling F (***con*** over)
babear ⟨1a⟩ *v/i* dribble
babero *m* bib
Babia *f*: ***estar en Babia*** be miles away
babor *m* MAR port
babosa *f* ZO slug
babosada *f L.Am.* F stupid thing to do / say
baboso *adj L.Am.* F stupid
baca *f* AUTO roof rack
bacalao *m* cod; ***cortar el bacalao*** F call the shots F
bache *m* pothole; *fig* rough patch
bachicha 1 *m/f Rpl, Chi desp* wop *desp* **2** *f Méx* cigarette stub
bachillerato *m Esp high school leaver's certificate*
bacón *m* bacon
bacteria *f* bacteria
bádminton *m* badminton
bafle *m* loudspeaker
bahía *f* bay
bailaor *m*, **bailaora** *f* flamenco dancer
bailar ⟨1a⟩ **1** *v/i* dance; *de zapato* be loose **2** *v/t* dance; ***se lo bailó*** *Méx* F he pinched F *o* swiped F it
bailarín *m*, **-ina** *f* dancer
baile *m* dance; *fiesta formal* ball; ***baile de salón*** ballroom dancing; ***baile de San Vito*** *fig* St. Vitus's dance
baja *f descenso* fall, drop; ***estar de baja*** (***por enfermedad***) be off sick; ***bajas*** MIL casualties
bajada *f* fall
bajar ⟨1a⟩ **1** *v/t voz, precio* lower; *escalera* go down; ***bajar algo*** *de arriba* get sth down **2** *v/i* go down; *de intereses* fall, drop **3** *v/r* **bajarse** get down; *de automóvil* get out (***de*** of); *de tren, autobús* get off (***de*** sth)
bajío *m L.Am.* lowland
bajo 1 *adj* low; *persona* short; ***por lo bajo*** at least **2** *m* MÚS bass; *piso* first floor, *Br* ground floor **3** *adv cantar, hablar* quietly, softly; *volar* low **4** *prp* under; ***tres grados bajo cero*** three degrees below zero
bajón *m* sharp decline; ***dar un bajón*** decline sharply, slump
bala *f* bullet; ***como una bala*** like lightning; ***ni a bala*** *L.Am.* F no way
balaceo *m L.Am.*, **balacera** *f L.Am.* shooting
balada *f* ballad
balance *m* COM balance
balancearse ⟨1a⟩ *v/r* swing, sway
balanza *f* scales *pl*; ***balanza comercial*** balance of trade; ***balanza de pagos*** balance of payments
balaustrada *f* balustrade
balazo *m* shot
balbucear ⟨1a⟩, **balbucir** ⟨3f; *defective* ⟩ **1** *v/i* stammer; *de niño* babble **2** *v/t* stam-

mer
Balcanes *mpl* Balkans
balcánico *adj* Balkan
balcón *m* balcony
baldado *adj fig* F bushed F
balde *adv*: ***de balde*** for nothing; ***en balde*** in vain
baldosa *f* floor tile
balear ⟨1a⟩ *v/t L.Am.* shoot
baleo *m L.Am.* shooting
Baleares *fpl* Balearic Islands
baleárico *adj* Balearic
baliza *f* MAR buoy
ballena *f* ZO whale
ballet *m* ballet
balneario *m* spa
balón *m* ball
baloncesto *m* basketball
balonmano *m* handball
balonvolea *m* volleyball
balsa *f* raft; ***como una balsa de aceite*** *fig* like a mill pond
bálsamo *m* balsam
baluarte *m* stronghold; *persona* pillar, stalwart
balumba *f L.Am.* F heap, pile; F (*ruido*) noise, racket F
bambolearse ⟨1a⟩ *v/r* sway
bambolla *f L.Am.* F fuss
bambúí *m* BOT bamboo
banal *adj* banal
banana *f L.Am., Rpl, Pe, Bol* banana
banca *f actividad* banking; *conjunto de bancos* banks *pl*; *en juego* bank; DEP, *Méx* (*asiento*) bench
bancal *m* terrace; *división de terreno* plot
bancario *adj* bank *atr*
bancarrota *f* bankruptcy; ***estar en bancarrota*** be bankrupt
banco *m* COM bank; *para sentarse* bench; ***banco de arena*** sand bank; ***banco de datos*** data bank
banda *f* MÚS, (*grupo*) band; *de delincuentes* gang; (*cinta*) sash; *en fúútbol* touchline; ***banda sonora*** soundtrack
bandada *f de pájaros* flock
bandazo *m*: ***dar bandazos*** *de coche* swerve
bandeja *f* tray; ***servir en bandeja*** hand on a plate
bandera *f* flag; (***lleno***) ***hasta la bandera*** packed (out); ***bajar la bandera*** *de taxi* start the meter running
banderilla *f* TAUR banderilla (*dart stuck into bull's neck during bullfight*)
bandido *m*, **-a** *f* bandit
bando *m* edict; *en disputa* side
bandolero *m*, **-a** *f* bandit
banjo *m* MÚS banjo
banquero *m*, **-a** *f* banker
banqueta *f L.Am.* stool; *L.Am.* (*acera*) sidewalk, *Br* pavement; ***banqueta trasera*** AUTO back seat
banquete *m* banquet; ***banquete de bodas*** wedding reception
banquillo *m* JUR dock; DEP bench
bañadera *f Rpl* (*baño*) bath
bañador *m* swimsuit
bañar ⟨1a⟩ **1** *v/t de sol, mar* bathe; *a un niño, un enfermo* bathe, *Br* bath; GASTR coat (***con*** with, ***en*** in) **2** *v/r* **bañarse** have a bath; *en el mar* go for a swim
bañera *f* (bath)tub, bath
bañista *m/f* swimmer
baño *m* bath; *en el mar* swim; *esp L.Am.* bathroom; TÉC plating; ***baño de sangre*** blood bath; ***baño María*** bain-marie
baptisterio *m* baptistry
baquiano *L.Am.* **1** *adj* expert *atr* **2** *m*, **-a** *f* guide
bar *m* bar
baraja *f* deck of cards
barandilla *f* handrail, banister
barata *f Méx* bargain counter; (*saldo*) sale
baratero *m*, **-a** *f Chi tendero* junk-shop owner
baratija *f* trinket
barato *adj* cheap
barba *f tb* BOT beard; ***por barba*** F a head, per person
barbacoa *f* barbecue
barbaridad *f* barbarity; ***costar una barbaridad*** cost a fortune; ***decir barbaridades*** say outrageous things; ***¡qué barbaridad!*** what a thing to say / do!
bárbaro 1 *adj* F tremendous, awesome F; ***¡qué bárbaro!*** amazing!, wicked! F **2** *m*, **-a** *f* F punk F
barbería *f* barber's shop
barbero *m* barber
barbilla *f* chin
barbitúírico *m* barbiturate
barbo *m pescado* barbel
barca *f* boat
barcaza *f* MAR barge
barco *m* boat; *más grande* ship; ***barco de vela*** sailing ship
baremo *m* scale
barniz *m para madera* varnish
barnizar ⟨1f⟩ *v/t* varnish
barómetro *m* barometer
barquero *m* boatman
barquillo *m* wafer; *Méx, C.Am.* ice-cream cone
barra *f de metal, en bar* bar; *de cortinas* rod; ***barra de labios*** lipstick; ***barra de pan*** baguette; ***barra espaciadora*** space-bar; ***barra de herramientas*** INFOR

tool bar; ***barra invertida*** backslash
barraca *f* (*chabola*) shack; *de tiro* stand; *de feria* stall; *L.Am.* (*deposito*) shed; ***barracas*** *pl L.Am.* shanty town *sg*
barracón *f* MIL barrack room
barranco *m* ravine
barrenar ⟨1a⟩ *v/t* drill
barrendero *m*, **-a** *f* street sweeper
barreno *m* drill hole
barreño *m* washing up bowl
barrer ⟨2a⟩ *v/t* sweep
barrera *f* barrier; ***barrera del sonido*** sound barrier
barriada *f C.Am.* (*barrio marginal*) slum, shanty town
barrial *m L.Am.* bog
barricada *f* barricade
barrida *f L.Am.* sweep; *L.Am.* (*redada*) police raid
barriga *f* belly; ***rascarse la barriga*** *fig* F sit on one's butt F
barrigón *adj* F pudgy F
barril *m* barrel
barrio *m* neighbo(u)rhood, area; ***barrio de chabolas*** *Esp* shanty town; ***irse al otro barrio*** F kick the bucket P
barro *m* mud
barroco *m*/*adj* baroque
barrote *m* bar
bártulos *mpl* F things, gear *sg* F
barullo *m* uproar, racket
basar ⟨1a⟩ **1** *v/t* base (***en*** on) **2** *v/r* **basarse** be based (***en*** on)
báscula *f* scales
base *f* QUÍM, MAT, MIL base; ***base de datos*** INFOR database; ***bases*** *de concurso etc* conditions; ***a base de*** by dint of
básico *adj* basic
basílica *f* basilica
básquetbol *m L.Am.* basketball
bastante 1 *adj* enough; *número o cantidad considerable* plenty of; ***quedan bastantes plazas*** there are plenty of seats left **2** *adv* quite, fairly; ***bebe bastante*** she drinks quite a lot
bastar ⟨1a⟩ *v/i* be enough; ***basta con uno*** one is enough; ***¡basta!*** that's enough!
bastardo 1 *adj* bastard *atr* **2** *m* bastard
bastidor *m*: ***entre bastidores*** F behind the scenes
bastión *m* bastion
basto 1 *adj* rough, coarse **2** *mpl*: **bastos** (*en naipes*) *suit in Spanish deck of cards*
bastón *m* stick
basura *f tb fig* trash, *Br* rubbish; ***cubo de la basura*** trash can, *Br* rubbish bin
basural *m L.Am.* dump, *Br* tip
basurero *m* garbage collector, *Br* dustman
bata *f* robe, *Br* dressing gown; MED (white) coat; TÉC lab coat
batacazo *m* F bump
batalla *f* battle
batallón *m* battalion
batata *f* BOT sweet potato
bate *m* DEP bat
batería *f* MIL, EL, AUTO battery; MÚS drums, drum kit; ***batería de cocina*** set of pans; ***aparcar en batería*** AUTO parallel park
batido 1 *adj camino* well-trodden **2** *m* GASTR milkshake
batidora *f* mixer
batir ⟨3a⟩ *v/t* beat; *nata* whip; *récord* break
baúl *m* chest, trunk; *L.Am.* AUTO trunk, *Br* boot
bautismo *m* baptism, christening; ***bautismo de fuego*** baptism of fire
bautizar ⟨1f⟩ *v/t* baptize, christen; *barco* name; *vino* F water down
bautizo *m* baptism, christening
baya *f* berry
bayeta *f* cloth
bayoneta *f* bayonet
bayunco *adj C.Am.* P silly, stupid
baza *f en naipes* trick; *fig* trump card; ***meter baza*** F interfere
bazar *m* hardware and fancy goods store; *mercado* bazaar
bazo *m* ANAT spleen
bazofia *f fig* F load of trash F
beatífico *adj* beatific
beatitud *f* beatitude
beato 1 *adj desp* overpious **2** *m*, **-a** *f desp* over-pious person
bebé *m* baby
bebedor *m*, **bebedora** *f* drinker
beber ⟨2a⟩ **1** *v/i* & *v/t* drink **2** *v/r* **beberse** drink up
bebida *f* drink
beca *f* scholarship; (*del estado*) grant
becerro *m* calf
béchamel *f* GASTR béchamel (sauce)
bedel *m* porter
beige *adj* beige
béisbol *m* baseball
belén *m* nativity scene
belga *m*/*f* & *adj* Belgian
Bélgica Belgium
Belice Belize
belicista *m*/*f* warmonger
bélico *adj* war *atr*
beligerante *adj* belligerent
bellaco *m*, **-a** *f Arg* rascal
belleza *f* beauty
bello *adj* beautiful
bellota *f* BOT acorn
bemol *m* MÚS flat; ***mi bemol*** E flat; ***tener***

bemoles *fig* F be tricky F
bencina *f* benzine; *Pe, Bol* (*gasolina*) gas, *Br* petrol
bendecir ⟨3p⟩ *v/t* bless
bendición *f* blessing
bendito *adj* blessed
benefactor *adj* charitable
beneficencia *f* charity
beneficiar ⟨1b⟩ **1** *v/t* benefit; *Rpl ganado* slaughter **2** *v/r* **beneficiarse** benefit (***de, con*** from)
beneficio *m* benefit; COM profit; *Rpl* slaughterhouse; *C.Am.* coffee-processing plant; ***en beneficio de*** in aid of
beneficioso *adj* beneficial
benéfico *adj* charity *atr*; ***función -a*** charity function *o* event
beneplácito *m* approval
benévolo *adj* benevolent, kind; (*indulgente*) lenient
bengala *f* flare
benigno *adj* MED benign
benjamín *m* youngest son
benjamina *f* youngest daughter
beodo *adj* drunk
berberecho *m* ZO cockle
berenjena *f* BOT egg plant, *Br* aubergine
berenjenal *m*: ***meterse en un berenjenal*** *fig* F get o.s. into a jam F
bermudas *mpl, fpl* Bermuda shorts
berrear ⟨1a⟩ *v/i* bellow; *de niño* bawl, yell
berrido *m* bellow; *de niño* yell
berrinche *m* F tantrum; ***coger un berrinche*** F throw a tantrum
berro *m* BOT watercress
berza *f* BOT cabbage
besamel *f* GASTR béchamel (sauce)
besar ⟨1a⟩ **1** *v/t* kiss **2** *v/r* **besarse** kiss
beso *m* kiss
bestia **1** *f* beast **2** *m/f fig* F brute F, swine F; *mujer* bitch F; ***conducir a lo bestia*** F drive like a madman
besugo *m* ZO bream; *fig* F idiot
betúin *m* shoe polish
biberón *m* baby's bottle
Biblia *f* Bible
bibliografía *f* bibliography
biblioteca *f* library; *mueble* bookcase
bibliotecario *m*, **-a** *f* librarian
bicarbonato *m*: ***bicarbonato*** (***de sodio***) bicarbonate of soda, bicarb F
bíceps *mpl* biceps
bicho *m* bug, *Br tb* creepy-crawly; (*animal*) creature; *fig* F *persona* nasty piece of work; ***¿qué bicho te ha picado?*** what's eating you?
bici *f* F bike
bicicleta *f* bicycle; ***ir*** *or* ***montar en bicicleta*** go cycling; ***bicicleta de montaña*** mountain bike
BID *abr* (***= Banco Interamericano de Desarollo***) IADB (= Inter-American Development Bank)
bidé *m* bidet
bidón *m* drum
bien **1** *m* good; ***por tu bien*** for your own good; ***bienes*** *pl* goods, property *sg*; ***bienes de consumo*** consumer goods *o* durables; ***bienes inmuebles*** real estate *sg* **2** *adv* well; (*muy*) very; ***más bien*** rather; ***o bien … o …*** either … or …; ***¡está bien!*** it's OK!, it's alright!; ***estoy bien*** I'm fine, I'm OK; ***¿estás bien aquí?*** are you comfortable here?; ***¡bien hecho!*** well done!
bienestar *m* well-being
bienvenida *f* welcome; ***dar la bienvenida a alguien*** welcome s.o.
bienvenido *adj* welcome
bife *m Rpl* steak
bifocal *adj* bifocal
bifurcación *f* fork; *de línea férrea* junction
bifurcarse ⟨1g⟩ *v/r* fork
bigamia *f* bigamy
bigote *m* m(o)ustache; ***bigotes*** *de gato etc* whiskers
bikini *m* bikini
bilateral *adj* bilateral
bilingüe *adj* bilingual
bilis *f* bile; *fig* F bad mood
billar *m* billiards; ***billar americano*** pool
billete *m* ticket; ***billete abierto*** open ticket; ***billete de autobúís*** bus ticket; ***billete de banco*** bill, *Br* banknote; ***billete de ida, billete sencillo*** one-way ticket, *Br* single (ticket); ***billete de ida y vuelta*** round-trip ticket, *Br* return (ticket)
billetera *f L.Am.*, **billetero** *m* billfold, *Br* wallet
billón *m* trillion
binario *adj* binary
bingo *m* bingo; *lugar* bingo hall
biodegradable *adj* biodegradable
biodiversidad *f* biodiversity
biografía *f* biography
biología *f* biology
biológico *adj* biological; AGR organic
biólogo *m*, **-a** *f* biologist
biombo *m* folding screen
biopsia *f* MED biopsy
bioquímica *f* biochemistry
bipartidismo *m* POL two-party system
biquini *m* bikini
birlar ⟨1a⟩ *v/t* F lift F, swipe F
birome *m Rpl* ballpoint (pen)
birria *f* F piece of junk F; ***va hecha una birria*** F she looks a real mess
bis *m* encore; ***9 bis*** 9A
bisabuela *f* great-grandmother

bisabuelo *m* great-grandfather
bisagra *f* hinge
biscote *m* rusk
bisexual *adj* bisexual
bisiesto *adj*: ***año bisiesto*** leap year
bisnieta *f* great-granddaughter
bisnieto *m* great-grandson
bisonte *m* ZO bison
bisoñé *m* hairpiece, toupee
bisté, **bistec** *m* steak
bisturí *m* MED scalpel
bisutería *f* costume jewel(le)ry
bit *m* INFOR bit
bizco *adj* cross-eyed
bizcocho *m* sponge (cake)
blanca *f persona* white; MÚS half-note, *Br* minim; ***estar sin blanca*** *fig* F be broke F
blanco **1** *adj* white; (*sin escrito*) blank; ***arma -a*** knife **2** *m persona* white; (*diana*), *fig* target; ***dar en el blanco*** hit the nail on the head; ***ser el blanco de todas las miradas*** be the center (*Br* centre) of attention
blando *adj* soft
blanquear ⟨1a⟩ *v/t* whiten; *pared* whitewash; *dinero* launder
blanqueo *m* whitewashing; ***blanqueo de dinero*** money laundering
blanquillo *m Méx* egg
blasfemar ⟨1a⟩ *v/i* curse, swear; REL blaspheme
blasfemia *f* REL blasphemy
blindado *adj* armo(u)red; *puerta* reinforced; EL shielded
bloc *m* pad
blof *m L.Am.* bluff
bloque *m* block; POL bloc; ***bloque de apartamentos*** apartment building, *Br* block of flats; ***en bloque*** en masse
bloquear ⟨1a⟩ *v/t* block; DEP obstruct; (*atascar*) jam; MIL blockade; COM freeze
bloqueo *m* blockade
blusa *f* blouse
boa *f* ZO boa constrictor
bobada *f* piece of nonsense
bobina *f* bobbin; FOT reel, spool; EL coil
bobo **1** *adj* silly, foolish **2** *m*, **-a** *f* fool
boca *f* mouth; ***boca a boca*** mouth to mouth; ***boca de metro*** subway entrance; ***boca abajo*** face down; ***boca arriba*** face up; ***dejar con la boca abierta*** leave open-mouthed; ***se me hace la boca agua*** my mouth is watering
bocacalle *f* side street
bocadillo *m* sandwich
bocado *m* mouthful, bite
bocana *f* river mouth
bocanada *f* mouthful; *de viento* gust
bocata *m* F → ***bocadillo***
bocazas *m/f inv* F loudmouth F
boceto *m* sketch
bochar ⟨1a⟩ *v/t Rpl* F *en examen* fail, flunk F; *Méx* cold-shoulder, rebuff
bochinche *m Méx* uproar
bochorno *m* sultry weather; *fig* embarrassment
bocina *f* MAR, AUTO horn
bocio *m* MED goiter, *Br* goitre
boda *f* wedding
bodega *f* wine cellar; MAR, AVIA hold; *L.Am.* bar; *C.Am.*, *Pe*, *Bol* grocery store
bodeguero *m*, **-a** *f C.Am.*, *Pe*, *Ven* storekeeper
body *m prenda* body
bofetada *f* slap
bofetear ⟨1a⟩ *v/t L.Am.* slap
bofia *f* F cops *pl* F
boga *f*: ***estar en boga*** *fig* be in fashion
bogavante *m* ZO lobster
bohemio **1** *adj* bohemian **2** *m*, **-a** *f* bohemian
bohío *m Cuba*, *Ven* hut
boicot *m* boycott
boicotear ⟨1a⟩ *v/t* boycott
boicoteo *m* boycotting
boina *f* beret
bojote *m L.Am. fig* bundle
bol *m* bowl
bola *f* ball; TÉC ball bearing; *de helado* scoop; F (*mentira*) fib F; ***bola de nieve*** snowball; ***no dar pie con bola*** get everything wrong
bolada *f L.Am.* throw; (*suerte*) piece of luck
bolado *m S. Am.* deal; *L.Am.* F (*mentira*) fib F
boleada *f Arg* hunt
boleador *m*, **boleadora** *f Méx* bootblack
boleadoras *fpl L.Am.* bolas
bolear ⟨1a⟩ **1** *v/i L.Am.* DEP have a knockabout **2** *v/t L.Am.* DEP bowl; *Rpl con boleadoras* bring down; *Méx zapatos* shine **3** *v/r* **bolearse** *Rpl* fall; (*aperarse*) get embarrassed
bolera *f* bowling alley
bolero **1** *m* MÚS bolero **2** *m/f Méx* F bootblack
boleta *f L.Am.* ticket; *L.Am.* (*pase*) pass, permit; *L.Am.* (*voto*) ballot paper
boletería *f L.Am.* ticket office; *en cine*, *teatro* box office
boletero *m*, **-a** *f L.Am.* ticket clerk; *en cine*, *teatro* box office employee
boletín *m* bulletin, report; ***boletín de evaluación*** report card; ***boletín meteorológico*** weather report
boleto *m L.Am.* ticket; ***boleto de autobúís*** *L.Am.* bus ticket; ***boleto de ida y***

vuelta *L.Am.*, ***boleto redondo*** *Méx* round-trip ticket, *Br* return
boliche *m* AUTO jack; *CSur* grocery store, *Br* grocer's
bólido *m fig* racing car
bolígrafo *m* ball-point pen
bolillo *m* bobbin; *Méx* bread roll; ***encaje de bolillos*** handmade lace
Bolivia Bolivia
boliviano 1 *adj* Bolivian **2** *m*, **-a** *f* Bolivian
bollo *m* bun; (*abolladura*) bump
bolo *m* pin; *C.Am.*, *Méx* christening present
bolos *mpl* bowling *sg*
bolsa *f* bag; COM stock exchange; *L.Am.* (*bolsillo*) pocket; ***bolsa de agua caliente*** hot-water bottle
bolsero *m*, **-a** *f Méx* F scrounger
bolsillo *m* pocket; ***meterse a alguien en el bolsillo*** F win s.o. over
bolso *m* purse, *Br* handbag
bolsón *m Arg*, *Pe* traveling bag, *Br* holdall
bomba *f* bomb; TÉC pump; *S. Am.* gas station; ***bomba de relojería*** time bomb; ***caer como una bomba*** *fig* F come as a bombshell; ***pasarlo bomba*** F have a great time
bombacha *f Arg* panties *pl*, *Br tb* knickers *pl*
bombacho *m*: ***bombachos*** *pl*, ***pantalón bombacho*** baggy pants *pl*
bombardear ⟨1a⟩ *v/t* bomb
bombero *m*, **-a** *f* firefighter; ***llamar a los bomberos*** call the fire department
bombilla *f* light bulb; *Rpl metal straw for the mate gourd*
bombillo *m C.Am.*, *Pe*, *Bol* light bulb
bombita *f Arg* light bulb
bombo *m* MÚS bass drum; TÉC drum
bombón *m* chocolate; *fig* F babe F
bombona *f* cylinder
bonaerense 1 *adj* of Buenos Aires, Buenos Aires *atr* **2** *m/f* native of Buenos Aires
bonanza *f fig* boom, bonanza
bondad *f* goodness, kindness; ***tenga la bondad de*** please be so kind as to
bondadoso *adj* caring
bongo *m L.Am.* bongo
boniato *m* BOT sweet potato
bonito 1 *adj* pretty **2** *m* ZO tuna
bono *m* voucher; COM bond
bonsái *m* bonsai
boñiga *f* dung
boom *m* boom
boquerón *m* ZO anchovy
boquete *m* hole
boquiabierto *adj fig* F speechless
borbotón *m*: ***salir a borbotones*** *de agua* gush out; ***hablaba a borbotones*** *fig* it all came out in a rush; ***hablar borbotón*** burble, splutter
borda *f* MAR gunwale; ***echar*** *or* ***tirar por la borda*** throw overboard
bordado 1 *adj* embroidered **2** *m* embroidery
bordar ⟨1a⟩ *v/t* embroider; ***bordar algo*** *fig* do sth brilliantly
borde[1] *adj* F rude, uncouth
borde[2] *m* edge; ***al borde de*** *fig* on the verge *o* brink of
bordear ⟨1a⟩ *v/t* border
bordillo *m* curb, *Br* kerb
bordo *m*: ***a bordo*** MAR, AVIA on board
borona *f* corn, *Br* maize
borrachera *f* drunkenness; ***agarrar una borrachera*** get drunk
borrachería *f Méx*, *Rpl* → ***borrachera***
borracho 1 *adj* drunk **2** *m*, **-a** *f* drunk
borrador *m* eraser; *de texto* draft; (*boceto*) sketch
borrar ⟨1a⟩ *v/t* erase; INFOR delete; *pizarra* clean; *recuerdo* blot out
borrasca *f* area of low pressure
borrego *m* ZO lamb; *fig*: *persona* sheep
borrico *m*, **-a** *f* donkey; *fig* dummy
borrón *m* blot; *mancha extendida* smudge; ***hacer borrón y cuenta nueva*** *fig* wipe the slate clean
borroso *adj* blurred, fuzzy
Bosnia Bosnia
bosque *m* wood; *grande* forest
bosquejo *m* sketch; *fig* outline
bostezar ⟨1f⟩ *v/i* yawn
bostezo *m* yawn
bota *f* boot; ***bota de montar*** riding boot; ***ponerse las botas*** *fig* F coin it F, rake it in F; (*comer mucho*) make a pig of o.s. F
botado *L.Am.* F **1** *adj* (*barato*) dirt cheap **2** *m*, **-a** *f* abandoned child
botana *f Méx* snack
botánica *f* botany
botar ⟨1a⟩ **1** *v/t* MAR launch; *pelota* bounce; *L.Am.* (*echar*) throw; *L.Am.* (*desechar*) throw out; *L.Am.* (*despedir*) fire **2** *v/i de pelota* bounce
bote *m* (*barco*) boat; *L.Am.* (*lata*) can, *Br tb* tin; (*tarro*) jar; ***pegar un bote*** jump; ***bote de la basura*** *Méx* trash can, *Br* rubbish bin; ***bote salvavidas*** lifeboat; ***chupar del bote*** *fig* F line one's pockets F; ***tener a alguien en el bote*** F have s.o. in one's pocket F; ***de bote en bote*** packed out
botella *f* bottle
botijo *m container with a spout for drinking from*
botín *m* loot; *calzado* ankle boot

botiquín *m* medicine chest; *estuche* first--aid kit
botón *m en prenda*, TÉC button; BOT bud
botones *m inv en hotel* bellhop, bellboy
boutique *f* boutique
bóveda *f* vault
bovino *adj* bovine
boxeador *m*, **boxeadora** *f* boxer
boxear ⟨1a⟩ *v/i* box
boxeo *m* boxing
boya *f* buoy; *de caña* float
boyante *adj fig* buoyant
bragas *fpl* panties, *Br tb* knickers
bragueta *f* fly
bramido *m* roar, bellow
brandy *m* brandy
branquia *f* zo gill
brasa *f* ember; ***a la brasa*** GASTR charbroiled, *Br* char-grilled
brasero *m* brazier; *eléctrico* electric heater
Brasil Brazil
brasileño 1 *adj* Brazilian **2** *m*, **-a** *f* Brazilian
bravata *f* boast; (*amenaza*) threat
bravo *adj animal* fierce; *mar* rough, choppy; *persona* brave; *L.Am.* (*furioso*) angry; ***¡bravo!*** well done!; *en concierto etc* bravo!
bravucón *m*, **-ona** *f* F boaster, blowhard F
braza *f* breaststroke
brazalete *m* bracelet; (*banda*) armband
brazo *m* arm; ***brazo de gitano*** GASTR jelly roll, *Br* Swiss roll; ***con los brazos abiertos*** with open arms; ***dar su brazo a torcer*** give in
brebaje *m desp* concoction
brecha *f* breach; *fig* F gap; MED gash; ***seguir en la brecha*** F hang on in there F
brécol *m* broccoli
breva *f* BOT early fig; ***no caerá esa breva*** *fig* F no such luck!
breve *adj* brief; ***en breve*** shortly
brevedad *f* briefness, shortness
brevemente *adv* briefly
brezo *m* BOT heather
bribón *m*, **-ona** *f* rascal
bricolaje *m* do-it-yourself, DIY
brigada *f* MIL brigade; *en policía* squad
brillante 1 *adj* bright; *fig* brilliant **2** *m* diamond
brillar ⟨1a⟩ *v/i fig* shine
brillo *m* shine; *de estrella, luz* brightness; ***dar*** *or* ***sacar brillo a algo*** polish sth
brincar ⟨1g⟩ *v/i* jump up and down
brinco *m* F leap, bound; ***dar brincos*** jump
brindar ⟨1a⟩ **1** *v/t* offer **2** *v/i* drink a toast (***por*** to)
brindis *m inv* toast
brío *m fig* F verve, spirit
brisa *f* MAR breeze
brisera *f L.Am.* windshield, *Br* windscreen
británico 1 *adj* British **2** *m*, **-a** *f* Briton, Brit F
broca *f* TÉC drill bit
brocha *f* brush
broche *m* brooch; (*cierre*) fastener; *L.Am.* (*pinza*) clothes pin
brocheta *f* skewer
brócoli *m* broccoli
broma *f* joke; ***en broma*** as a joke; ***gastar bromas*** play jokes; ***tomar algo a broma*** take sth as a joke
bromear ⟨1a⟩ *v/i* joke
bromista *m/f* joker
bronca *f* F telling off F; *Méx* P fight; ***armar una bronca*** *Méx* get into a fight; ***echar bronca a alguien*** F give s.o. a telling off, tell s.o. off
bronce *m* bronze
bronceado 1 *adj* tanned **2** *m* suntan
bronceador *m* suntan lotion
broncearse ⟨1a⟩ *v/r* get a tan
bronquitis *f* MED bronchitis
brotar ⟨1a⟩ *v/i* BOT sprout, bud; *fig* appear, arise
brote *m* BOT shoot; MED, *fig* outbreak; ***brotes de bambúi*** bamboo shoots; ***brotes de soja*** beansprouts
bruces: ***caer de bruces*** F fall flat on one's face
bruja *f* witch
brujo *m* wizard
brújula *f* compass
bruma *f* mist
bruñir ⟨3h⟩ *v/t* burnish, polish; *C.Am.* F (*molestar*) annoy
brusco *adj* sharp, abrupt; *respuesta, tono* brusque, curt
Bruselas Brussels
brutalidad *f* brutality
bruto 1 *adj* brutish; (*inculto*) ignorant; (*torpe*) clumsy; COM gross **2** *m*, **-a** *f* brute, animal
buceador *m*, **buceadora** *f* diver
bucear ⟨1a⟩ *v/i* dive; *fig* delve (***en*** into)
bucólico *adj* bucolic
budista *m/f & adj* Buddhist
buen *adj* → ***bueno***
buenaventura *f* fortune
bueno *adj* good; (*bondadoso*) kind; (*sabroso*) nice; ***por las -as*** willingly; ***de -as a primeras*** without warning; ***ponerse bueno*** get well; ***¡bueno!*** well!; ***¿bueno?*** *Méx* hello; ***-a voluntad*** goodwill; ***¡-as!*** hello!; ***buenos días*** good morning;

-as noches good evening; ***-as tardes*** good evening
buey *m* zo ox
búfalo *m* zo buffalo
bufanda *f* scarf; *fig* F perk
bufete *m* lawyer's office
buffet *m* GASTR buffet
bufón *m* buffoon, fool
buganvilla *f* BOT bougainvillea
buhardilla *f* attic, loft
búho *m* zo owl
buitre *m* zo vulture
bulbo *m* BOT bulb
bulevar *m* boulevard
Bulgaria Bulgaria
bulimia *f* MED bulimia
bulla *f* din, racket
bullicio *m* hubbub, din; (*actividad*) bustle
bullir ⟨3h⟩ *v/i fig*: *de sangre* boil; *de lugar* swarm, teem (***de*** with)
bulo *m* F rumo(u)r
bulto *m* package; MED lump; *en superficie* bulge; (*silueta*) vague shape; (*pieza de equipaje*) piece of baggage
bumerán *m* boomerang
buque *m* ship; ***buque de guerra*** warship
burbuja *f* bubble
burdel *m* brothel
burdo *adj* rough
burgués 1 *adj* middle-class, bourgeois **2** *m*, **-esa** *f* middle-class person, member of the bourgeoisie
burguesía *f* middle class, bourgeoisie
burla *f* joke; (*engaño*) trick; ***hacer burla de alguien*** F make fun of s.o.
burlar ⟨1a⟩ **1** *v/t* F get round **2** *v/r* **burlarse** make fun (***de*** of)
burlete *m L.Am.* draft excluder, *Br* draught excluder
buró *m* bureau
burocracia *f* bureaucracy
burócrata *m/f* bureaucrat
burocrático *adj* bureaucratic
burrada *f fig* F piece of nonsense; ***hay una burrada*** there's loads F; ***costar una burrada*** cost a packet F
burro *m* zo donkey; ***no ver tres en un burro*** be as blind as a bat
bursátil *adj* stock market *atr*
bus *m* bus
busca 1 *f* search; ***en busca de*** in search of **2** *m* F pager
buscador *m* searcher; INFOR search engine
buscapersonas *m inv* pager
buscapleitos *m/f inv* F troublemaker
buscar ⟨1a⟩ *v/t* search for, look for
búsqueda *f* search
busto *m* bust
butaca *f* armchair; TEA seat
butano *m* butane
butifarra *f type of sausage*
buzo *m* diver
buzón *m* mailbox, *Br* postbox; ***buzón de voz*** TELEC voicemail
byte *m* INFOR byte

C

C *abr* (***= Centígrado***) C (= Centigrade); (***= compañía***) Co. (= Company); c (***= calle***) St. (= Street); (***= capítulo***) ch. (= chapter)
cabal *adj*: ***no estar en sus cabales*** not be in one's right mind
cabalgar ⟨1h⟩ *v/i* ride
cabalgata *f* procession
caballa *f* zo mackerel
caballada *f Rpl*: ***decir / hacer una caballada*** say / do sth stupid
caballería *f* MIL cavalry; (*caballo*) horse
caballero 1 *adj* gentlemanly, chivalrous **2** *m hombre* gentleman, man; *hombre educado* gentleman; HIST knight; *trato* sir; (***servicio de***) ***caballeros*** *pl* men's room, gents; *en tienda de ropa* menswear
caballeroso *adj* gentlemanly, chivalrous
caballito *m*: ***caballito del diablo*** zo dragonfly; ***caballito de mar*** zo seahorse; ***caballitos*** *pl* carousel *sg*, merry-go-round *sg*
caballo *m* horse; *en ajedrez* knight; ***caballo balancín*** rocking horse; ***a caballo entre*** halfway between; ***montar*** *or* ***andar*** *Rpl* ***a caballo*** ride (a horse); ***me gusta montar a caballo*** I like riding; ***ir a caballo*** go on horseback
cabaña *f* cabin
cabaret *m* cabaret
cabecear ⟨1a⟩ **1** *v/i* nod **2** *v/t el balón* head
cabecera *f de mesa, cama* head; *de periódico* masthead; *de texto* top

cabecero *m de cama* headboard
cabecilla *m/f* ringleader
cabello *m* hair
caber ⟨2m⟩ *v/i* fit; ***caben tres litros*** it holds three liters *o Br* litres; ***cabemos todos*** there's room for all of us; ***no cabe duda*** *fig* there's no doubt; ***no me cabe en la cabeza*** I just don't understand
cabestrillo *m* MED sling
cabeza 1 *f* ANAT head; ***cabeza de ajo*** bulb of garlic; ***cabeza (de ganado)*** head (of cattle); ***cabeza nuclear*** nuclear warhead; ***el equipo a la cabeza*** *or* ***en cabeza*** the team at the top; ***por cabeza*** per head, per person; ***estar mal*** *or* ***no estar bien de la cabeza*** F not be right in the head F **2** *m/f*: ***cabeza de familia*** head of the family; ***cabeza de turco*** scapegoat; ***cabeza rapada*** skinhead
cabezada *f*: ***echar una cabezada*** have a nap
cabezonería *f* pigheadedness
cabezota 1 *adj* pig-headed **2** *m/f* pig-headed person
cabida *f* capacity; ***dar cabida a*** hold
cabildo *m* POL council
cabina *f* cabin; ***cabina telefónica*** phone booth
cabizbajo *adj* dejected, downhearted
cable *m* EL cable; MAR line, rope; ***echar un cable a alguien*** give s.o. a hand
cabo *m* end; GEOG cape; MAR rope; MIL corporal; ***al cabo de*** after; ***de cabo a rabo*** F from start to finish; ***atar cabos*** F put two and two together F; ***llevar a cabo*** carry out
cabra *f* ZO goat; ***estar como una cabra*** F be nuts F
cabrear ⟨1a⟩ **1** *v/t* P bug F **2** *v/r* **cabrearse** P get mad F
cabriola *f*: ***hacer cabriolas*** *de niño* jump around
cabro *m Chi* boy; ***cabro chico*** *Chi* baby
cabrón *m* V bastard P, son of a bitch V
caca *f* F poop F, *Br* pooh F; *cosa mala* piece of trash F; ***hacer caca*** F poop F, *Br* do a pooh F
cacahuate *m Méx* peanut
cacahuete *m* peanut
cacalote *m C.Am., Cuba, Méx* crow
cacao *m* cocoa; *de labios* lip salve; ***no valer un cacao*** *L.Am. fig* F not be worth a bean F
cacatúía *f* ZO cockatoo
cacería *f* hunt
cacerola *f* pan
cachar ⟨1a⟩ *v/t L.Am.* (*engañar*) trick; *L.Am.* (*sorprender*) catch out; ***¿me cachas?*** *Chi* get it?
cacharro *m* pot; *Méx, C.Am.* F (*trasto*) piece of junk; *Méx, C.Am.* F *coche* junkheap; ***lavar los cacharros*** *Méx, C.Am.* wash the dishes
cachas *adj*: ***estar cachas*** F be a real hunk F
cachear ⟨1a⟩ *v/t* frisk
cachemira *f* cashmere
cachetada *f L.Am.* slap
cachete *m* cheek
cachetear ⟨1a⟩ *v/t L.Am.* slap
cachimba *f* pipe
cachivache *m* thing; ***cachivaches*** *pl* (*cosas*) things, stuff *sg* F; (*basura*) junk *sg*
cacho *m* F bit; *Rpl* (*cuerno*) horn; *Ven, Col* F (*marijuana*) joint F; ***jugar al cacho*** *Bol, Pe* play dice; ***ponerle cachos a alguien*** cheat on sb
cachondeo *m*: ***estar de cachondeo*** F be joking; ***tomar a cachondeo*** F take as a joke; ***¡vaya cachondeo!*** F what a laugh! F
cachondo *adj* F (*caliente*) horny F; (*gracioso*) funny
cachorro *m* ZO pup
cacique *m* chief; POL *local political boss*; *fig* F tyrant
cacle *m Méx* shoe
caco *m* F thief
cactus *m inv* BOT cactus
cada *adj considerado por separado* each; *con énfasis en la totalidad* every; ***cada cosa en su sitio*** everything in its place; ***cada uno, cada cual*** each one; ***cada vez*** every time, each time; ***cada vez más*** more and more, increasingly; ***cada tres días*** every three days; ***uno de cada tres*** one out of every three
cadáver *m* (dead) body, corpse
cadena *f* chain; *de perro* leash, *Br* lead; TV channel; ***cadena perpetua*** life sentence
cadencia *f* MÚS rhythm, cadence
cadera *f* hip
caducado *adj* out of date
caducar ⟨1g⟩ *v/i* expire
caducidad *f*: ***fecha de caducidad*** expiry date; *de alimentos, medicinas* use-by date
caer ⟨2o⟩ **1** *v/i* fall; ***me cae bien / mal*** *fig* I like / don't like him; ***dejar caer algo*** drop sth; ***estar al caer*** be about to arrive; ***caer enfermo*** fall ill; ***caer en lunes*** fall on a Monday; ***¡ahora caigo!*** *fig* now I get it! **2** *v/r* **caerse** fall (down)
café *m* coffee; (*bar*) café; ***café con leche*** white coffee; ***café descafeinado*** decaffeinated coffee; ***café instantáneo*** instant coffee; ***café solo*** black coffee
cafeína *f* caffeine

C

cafetera *f* coffee maker; *para servir* coffee pot
cafetería *f* coffee shop
cagar ⟨1h⟩ V **1** *v/i* have a shit P **2** *v/r* **cagarse** shit o.s. P; ***cagarse de miedo*** shit o.s. P
caguama *f Méx* (*tortuga*) turtle
caída *f* fall
caigo *vb* → ***caer***
caimán *m* ZO alligator; *Méx*, *C.Am.* *úútil* monkey wrench
Cairo: ***El Cairo*** Cairo
caja *f* box; *de reloj*, *ordenador* case, casing; COM cash desk; *en supermercado* checkout; ***caja de ahorros*** savings bank; ***caja de cambios*** gearbox; ***caja de caudales, caja fuerte*** safe, strongbox; ***caja de cerillas*** matchbox; ***caja de múísica*** music box; ***caja postal*** post office savings bank; ***caja registradora*** cash register; ***echar a alguien con cajas destempladas*** F send s.o. packing
cajero *m*, **-a** *f* cashier; *de banco* teller; ***cajero automático*** ATM, *Br tb* cash point
cajeta *f Méx* caramel spread
cajón *m* drawer; *L.Am.* casket, coffin
cajuele *f Méx* AUTO trunk, *Br* boot
cal *f* lime
cala *f* cove
calabacín *m* BOT zucchini, *Br* courgette
calabaza *f* pumpkin; ***dar calabazas a alguien*** F *en examen* fail s.o., flunk s.o. F; *en relación* give s.o. the brush off F
calabozo *m* cell
calada *f* puff
calado *adj* soaked; ***calado hasta los huesos*** soaked to the skin
calamar *m* ZO squid
calambre *m* EL shock; MED cramp
calamidad *f* calamity
calaña *f desp* sort, type
calar ⟨1a⟩ **1** *v/t* (*mojar*) soak; *techo*, *tela* soak through; *persona*, *conjura* see through **2** *v/i de zapato* leak; *de ideas*, *costumbres* take root; ***calar hondo en*** make a big impression on **3** *v/r* **calarse** *de motor* stall; ***calarse hasta los huesos*** get soaked to the skin
calato *adj Chi*, *Pe* naked
calavera *f* skull
calcar ⟨1g⟩ *v/t* trace
calceta *f*: ***hacer calceta*** knit
calcetín *m* sock
calcinado *adj* burnt
calcio *m* calcium
calcomanía *f* decal, *Br* transfer
calculador *adj fig* calculating
calculadora *f* calculator
calcular ⟨1a⟩ *v/t tb fig* calculate
cálculo *m* calculation; MED stone; ***cálculo biliar*** gallstone; ***cálculo renal*** kidney stone
caldear ⟨1a⟩ *v/t* warm up; *ánimos* inflame
caldera *f* boiler; *Rpl*, *Chi* kettle
calderilla *f* small change
caldero *m* (small) boiler
caldillo *m Méx* GASTR stock
caldo *m* GASTR stock; ***caldo de cultivo*** *fig* breeding ground
caldoso *adj* watery
calefacción *f* heating; ***calefacción central*** central heating
calefactor *m* heater
calendario *m* calendar; (*programa*) schedule
caléndula *f* BOT marigold
calentador *m* heater; ***calentador de agua*** water heater
calentamiento *m*: ***calentamiento global*** global warming
calentar ⟨1k⟩ **1** *v/t* heat (up); ***calentar a alguien*** *fig* provoke s.o. **2** *v/i* DEP warm up **3** *v/r* **calentarse** warm up; *fig*: *de discusión*, *disputa* become heated
calentura *f* fever
calibrar ⟨1a⟩ *v/t* gauge; *fig* weigh up
calibre *m tb fig* caliber, *Br* calibre
calidad *f* quality; ***calidad de vida*** quality of life; ***en calidad de médico*** as a doctor
cálido *adj tb fig* warm
caliente *adj* hot; F (*cachondo*) horny F; ***en caliente*** in the heat of the moment
calificable *adj* gradable
calificación *f* description; EDU grade, *Br* mark
calificar ⟨1g⟩ *v/t* describe, label (**de** as); EDU grade, *Br* mark
caligrafía *f* calligraphy
caliza *f* limestone
callado *adj* quiet
callar ⟨1a⟩ **1** *v/i* (*dejar de hablar*) go quiet; (*guardar silencio*) be quiet, keep quiet; ***¡calla!*** be quiet!, shut up! **2** *v/t* silence **3** *v/r* **callarse** (*dejar de hablar*) go quiet; (*guardar silencio*) be quiet, keep quiet; ***callarse algo*** keep sth quiet
calle *f* street; DEP lane; ***echar a alguien a la calle*** *fig* throw s.o out onto the street
callejón *m* alley; ***callejón sin salida*** blind alley; *fig* dead end
callo *m* callus; ***callos*** *pl* GASTR tripe *sg*
calma *f* calm
calmante **1** *adj* soothing **2** *m* MED sedative
calmar ⟨1a⟩ **1** *v/t* calm (down) **2** *v/r* **calmarse** calm down
calor *m* heat; *fig* warmth; ***hace mucho calor*** it's very hot; ***tengo calor*** I'm hot
caloría *f* calorie

calumnia *f oral* slander; *por escrito* libel
calumniar ⟨1b⟩ *v/t oralmente* slander; *por escrito* libel
caluroso *adj* hot; *fig* warm
calva *f* bald patch
calvario *m fig* calvary
calvicie *f* baldness
calvo 1 *adj* bald **2** *m* bald man
calzada *f* road (surface)
calzado *m* footwear
calzador *m* shoe horn
calzar ⟨1f⟩ **1** *v/t zapato, bota etc* put on; *mueble, rueda* wedge **2** *v/r* **calzarse** *zapato, bota etc* put on
calzón *m* DEP shorts *pl*; *L.Am. de hombre* shorts *pl*, *Br* (under)pants *pl*; *L.Am. de mujer* panties *pl*, *Br tb* knickers *pl*; ***calzones*** *L.Am.* shorts, *Br* (under)pants
calzoncillos *mpl* shorts, *Br* (under)pants
cama *f* bed; ***cama de matrimonio*** double bed; ***hacer la cama*** make the bed; ***irse a la cama*** go to bed
camaleón *m* chameleon
cámara *f* FOT, TV camera; (*sala*) chamber; ***cámara de comercio e industria*** chamber of commerce and industry; ***a cámara lenta*** in slow motion; ***cámara de vídeo*** video camera
camarada *m/f* comrade; *de trabajo* colleague, co-worker
camaradería *f* camaraderie, comradeship
camarera *f* waitress
camarero *m* waiter
camarógrafo *m*, **-a** *f L.Am.* camera operator
camarón *m L.Am.* ZO shrimp, *Br* prawn
camarote *m* MAR cabin
camarotero *m L.Am.* steward
cambalache *m Arg* F second-hand shop
cambiar ⟨1b⟩ **1** *v/t* change (***por*** for); *compra* exchange (***por*** for) **2** *v/i* change; ***cambiar de lugar*** change places; ***cambiar de marcha*** AUTO shift gear, *Br* change gear **3** *v/r* **cambiarse** change; ***cambiarse de ropa*** change (one's clothes)
cambio *m* change; COM exchange rate; ***cambio climático*** climate change; ***cambio de marchas*** AUTO gear shift, *Br* gear change; ***cambio de sentido*** U-turn; ***a cambio de*** in exchange for; ***en cambio*** on the other hand
camelia *f* BOT camellia
camello 1 *m* ZO camel **2** *m/f* F (*vendedor de drogas*) pusher F, dealer
camelo *m* F con F; (*broma*) joke
camilla *f* stretcher
caminar ⟨1a⟩ **1** *v/i* walk; *fig* move; ***caminando*** on foot **2** *v/t* walk
camino *m* (*senda*) path; (*ruta*) way; ***a medio camino*** halfway; ***de camino a*** on the way to; ***por el camino*** on the way; ***abrirse camino*** *fig* make one's way; ***ir por buen / mal camino*** *fig* be on the right / wrong track; ***ponerse en camino*** set out
camión *m* truck, *Br tb* lorry; *Méx* bus
camionero *m*, **-a** *f* truck driver, *Br tb* lorry driver; *Méx* bus driver
camioneta *f* van
camisa *f* shirt
camiseta *f* T-shirt
camisón *m* nightdress
camorra *f* F fight; ***armar camorra*** F cause trouble
campal *adj*: ***batalla campal*** pitched battle
campamento *m* camp
campana *f* bell; ***campana extractora*** extractor hood
campanada *f* chime; ***dar la campanada*** cause a stir
campanario *m* bell tower
campanazo *m L.Am.* warning
campanilla *f* small bell; ANAT uvula
campante *adj*: ***tan campante*** F as calm as anything F
campaña *f* campaign; ***campaña electoral*** election campaign
campechano *adj* down-to-earth
campeón *m*, **-ona** *f* champion
campeonato *m* championship; ***de campeonato*** F terrific F
campera *f L.Am.* jacket
campesino 1 *adj* peasant *atr* **2** *m*, **-a** *f* peasant
campestre *adj* rural, country *atr*
camping *m* campground, *Br tb* campsite
campo *m* field; DEP field, *Br tb* pitch; (*estadio*) stadium, *Br tb* ground; ***el campo*** (*área rural*) the country; ***campo de batalla*** battlefield; ***campo de concentración*** concentration camp; ***campo de golf*** golf course; ***campo visual*** MED field of vision; ***a campo traviesa, campo a través*** cross-country
campus *m inv*: ***campus universitario*** university campus
camuflaje *m* camouflage
camuflar ⟨1a⟩ *v/t* camouflage
cana *f* gray (*Br* grey) hair
Canadá Canada
canadiense *m/f & adj* Canadian
canal *m* channel; TRANSP canal
canalete *m* paddle
canalizar ⟨1f⟩ *v/t* channel
canalla *m* swine F, rat F
canalón *m* gutter

C

canapé *m* (*sofá*) couch; *para cama* base; GASTR canapé
Canarias *fpl* Canaries
canario 1 *adj* Canary *atr* **2** *m* ZO canary
canasta *f* basket; *juego* canasta
cancela *f* (wrought-iron) gate
cancelación *f* cancellation
cancelar ⟨1a⟩ *v/t* cancel; *deuda, cuenta* settle, pay
cáncer *m* MED, *fig* cancer; ***Cáncer*** *m/f inv* ASTR Cancer
cancerígeno *adj* carcinogenic
canceroso *adj* cancerous
cancha *f* DEP court; *L.Am. de fútbol* field, *Br tb* pitch; ***cancha de tenis*** tennis court; ***¡cancha!*** *Rpl* F gangway! F; ***abrir*** *or* ***hacer cancha*** *Rpl* make room
canchear ⟨1a⟩ *v/i L.Am.* climb
canciller *m* Chancellor; *S.Am. de asuntos exteriores* Secretary of State, *Br* Foreign Minister
canción *f* song; ***siempre la misma canción*** F the same old story F
candado *m* padlock
candela *f L.Am.* fire; ***¿me das candela?*** have you got a light?
candelabro *m* candelabra
candelero *m*: ***estar en el candelero*** *de persona* be in the limelight
candente *adj* red-hot; *tema* topical
candidato *m*, **-a** *f* candidate
candidatura *f* candidacy
cándido *adj* naive
candor *m* innocence; (*franqueza*) cando(u)r
canela *f* cinnamon
canelones *mpl* GASTR cannelloni *sg*
cangrejo *m* ZO crab
canguro 1 *m* ZO kangaroo **2** *m/f* F baby-sitter
caníbal 1 *adj* cannibal *atr* **2** *m/f* cannibal
canica *f* marble
caniche *m* poodle
canícula *f* dog days *pl*
canijo *adj* F puny
canilla *f L.Am.* faucet, *Br* tap
canillita *m/f Arg* newspaper vendor
canjear ⟨1a⟩ *v/t* exchange (***por*** for)
canoa *f* canoe
canónico *adj* canonical
canónigo *m* canon
canonizar ⟨1f⟩ *v/t* canonize
cansado *adj* tired
cansancio *m* tiredness
cansar ⟨1a⟩ **1** *v/t* tire; (*aburrir*) bore **2** *v/r* **cansarse** get tired; (*aburrirse*) get bored; ***cansarse de algo*** get tired of sth
cantante *m/f* singer
cantar ⟨1a⟩ **1** *v/i* sing; *de delincuente* squeal P **2** *v/t* sing **3** *m*: ***ése es otro cantar*** *fig* F that's a different story
cántaro *m* pitcher; ***llover a cántaros*** F pour (down)
cantautor *m*, **cantautora** *f* singer-songwriter
cante *m*: ***cante hondo*** *or* ***jondo*** flamenco singing
cantera *f* quarry
cantidad *f* quantity, amount; ***había cantidad de*** there was (*pl* were) a lot of
cantimplora *f* water bottle
cantina *f* canteen
canto¹ *m* singing; *de pájaro* song
canto² *m* edge; (*roca*) stone; ***canto rodado*** boulder; ***darse con un canto en los dientes*** count o.s. lucky
canturrear ⟨1a⟩ *v/t* sing softly
canutas: ***las pasé canutas*** F it was really tough F
caña *f* BOT reed; (*tallo*) stalk; *cerveza* small glass of beer; *L.Am.* straw; ***muebles de caña*** cane furniture; ***caña de azúícar*** sugar cane; ***caña de pescar*** fishing rod; ***dar*** *or* ***meter caña a alguien*** F wind s.o. up F; ***¡dale caña!*** F get off your butt! F
cañada *f* ravine; *L.Am.* (*arroyo*) stream
cáñamo *m* hemp; *L.Am.* marijuana plant
cañería *f* pipe
cañero *adj L.Am.* sugar-cane *atr*
caño *m* pipe; *de fuente* spout
cañón 1 *m* HIST cannon; *antiaéreo, antitanque etc* gun; *de fusil* barrel; GEOG canyon **2** *adj* F great, fantastic F
cañonazo *m* gunshot
caoba *f* mahogany
caos *m* chaos
caótico *adj* chaotic
cap *abr* (**= *capítulo***) ch. (= chapter)
capa *f* layer; *prenda* cloak; ***capa de ozono*** ozone layer; ***capa de pintura*** coat of paint
capacidad *f* capacity; (*aptitud*) competence; ***capacidad de memoria / de almacenamiento*** INFOR memory / storage capacity
capacitar ⟨1a⟩ *v/t* prepare; ***capacitar alguien para hacer algo*** qualify s.o. to do sth
capar ⟨1a⟩ *v/t* castrate
caparazón *m* ZO shell
capataz *m* foreman
capataza *f* forewoman
capaz *adj* able (***de*** to); ***ser capaz de*** be capable of
capcioso *adj*: ***pregunta -a*** trick question
capear ⟨1a⟩ *v/t temporal* weather
capellán *m* chaplain

capicúa *adj*: ***número capicúa*** reversible number
capilar 1 *adj* capillary *atr*; *loción* hair *atr* **2** *m* capillary
capilla *f* chapel; ***capilla ardiente*** chapel of rest
capirotada *f Méx type of French toast with honey, cheese, raisins etc*
capital 1 *adj importancia* prime; ***pena capital*** capital punishment **2** *f de país* capital **3** *m* COM capital
capitalismo *m* capitalism
capitalista 1 *adj* capitalist *atr* **2** *m/f* capitalist
capitán *m* captain
capitanear ⟨1a⟩ *v/t* captain
capitel *m* ARQUI capital
Capitolio *m* Capitol
capitulación *f* capitulation, surrender; (*pacto*) agreement
capitular ⟨1a⟩ *v/i* surrender, capitulate
capítulo *m* chapter
capó *m* AUTO hood, *Br* bonnet
capón *m Rpl* mutton
capota *f* AUTO top, *Br* hood
capote *m* cloak; MIL greatcoat
capotera *f L.Am.* coat stand
capricho *m* whim
caprichoso *adj* capricious
Capricornio *m/f inv* ASTR Capricorn
cápsula *f* capsule; ***cápsula espacial*** space capsule
captar ⟨1a⟩ *v/t* understand; RAD pick up; *negocio* take
capturar ⟨1a⟩ *v/t* capture
capucha *f* hood
capuchino *m* cappuccino
capullo *m* ZO cocoon; BOT bud
caqui 1 *adj* khaki **2** *m* BOT persimmon
cara *f* face; (*expresión*) look; *fig* nerve; ***cara a algo*** facing sth; ***cara a cara*** face to face; ***de cara a*** facing; *fig* with regard to; ***dar la cara*** face the consequences; ***echar algo en cara a alguien*** remind s.o. of sth; ***tener cara dura*** have a nerve; ***tener buena / mala cara*** *de comida* look good / bad; *de persona* look well / sick; ***cara o cruz*** heads or tails
carabinero *m* GASTR (large) shrimp, *Br* prawn; (*agente de aduana*) border guard
caracol *m* snail; ***¡caracoles!*** wow! F; *enfado* damn! F
caracola *f* ZO conch
carácter *m* character; (*naturaleza*) nature
característica *f* characteristic
característico *adj* characteristic (***de*** of)
caracterizar ⟨1f⟩ **1** *v/t* characterize; TEA play (the part of) **2** *v/r* ***caracterizarse*** be characterized (***por*** by)
caradura *m/f* F guy / woman with a nerve, *Br* cheeky devil F
carajillo *m coffee with a shot of liquor*
carajo *m*: ***irse al carajo*** F go down the tubes F
caramba *int* wow!; *enfado* damn! F
carambola *f billar* carom, *Br* cannon; ***por*** *or* ***de carambola*** F by sheer chance
caramelo *m dulce* candy, *Br* sweet; (*azúcar derretida*) caramel
carantoña *f* caress
caraqueño 1 *adj* of / from Caracas, Caracas *atr* **2** *m*, **-a** *f* native of Caracas
carátula *f de disco* jacket, *Br tb* sleeve; *L.Am. de reloj* face
caravana *f* (*remolque*) trailer, *Br* caravan; *de tráfico* queue of traffic, traffic jam; *Méx* (*reverencia*) bow
caray *int* F wow! F; *enfado* damn! F
carbón *m* coal
carboncillo *m* charcoal
carbonizar ⟨1f⟩ *v/t* char
carbono *m* QUÍM carbon
carburador *m* AUTO carburet(t)or
carburante *m* fuel
carca *m/f & adj* F reactionary
carcajada *f* laugh, guffaw; ***reír a carcajadas*** roar with laughter
carcajearse ⟨1a⟩ *v/r* have a good laugh (***de*** at)
cárcel *f* prison
carcelero *m*, **-a** *f* warder, jailer
carcinoma *f* MED carcinoma
carcoma *f* ZO woodworm
carcomer ⟨2a⟩ **1** *v/t* eat away; *fig*: *de envidia* eat away at, consume **2** *v/r* ***carcomerse*** be eaten away; ***carcomerse de*** *fig* be consumed with
cardamomo *m* BOT cardamom
cardenal *m* REL cardinal; (*hematoma*) bruise
cardíaco, **cardiaco** *adj* cardiac
cardinal *adj* cardinal; ***número cardinal*** cardinal number; ***puntos cardinales*** points of the compass, cardinal points
cardiólogo *m*, **-a** *f* cardiologist
cardo *m* BOT thistle
carecer ⟨2d⟩ *v/i*: ***carecer de algo*** lack sth
carencia *f* lack (***de*** of)
carente *adj*: ***carente de*** lacking in
careta *f* mask
carga *f* load; *de buque* cargo; MIL, EL charge; (*responsabilidad*) burden; ***carga explosiva*** explosive charge; ***carga fiscal*** *or* ***impositiva*** tax burden; ***ser una carga para alguien*** be a burden to s.o.; ***volver a la carga*** return to the attack
cargado *adj* loaded (***de*** with); *aire* stuffy; *ambiente* tense; *café* strong

C

cargamento *m* load
cargante *adj* F annoying
cargar ⟨1h⟩ **1** *v/t arma, camión* load; *batería, acusado* charge; COM charge (**en** to); *L.Am.* (*traer*) carry; ***esto me carga*** *L.Am.* P I can't stand this **2** *v/i* (*apoyarse*) rest (***sobre*** on); (*fastidiar*) be annoying; ***cargar con algo*** carry sth; ***cargar con la culpa*** *fig* shoulder the blame; ***cargar contra alguien*** MIL, DEP charge (at) s.o. **3** *v/r* **cargarse** *con peso, responsabilidad* weigh o.s. down; F (*matar*) bump off F; F (*romper*) wreck F
cargo *m* position; JUR charge; ***alto cargo*** high-ranking position; *persona* high-ranking official; ***a cargo de la madre*** in the mother's care; ***está a cargo de Gómez*** Gómez is in charge of it; ***hacerse cargo de algo*** take charge of sth
cariarse ⟨1b⟩ *v/r* decay
Caribe *m* Caribbean
caribeño *adj* Caribbean
caricatura *f* caricature
caricaturizar ⟨1f⟩ *v/t* caricature
caricia *f* caress
caridad *f* charity
caries *f* MED caries
cariño *m* affection, fondness; ***hacer cariño a alguien*** *L.Am.* (*acariciar*) caress s.o.; (*abrazar*) hug s.o.; ***¡cariño!*** darling!; ***con cariño*** with love
cariñoso *adj* affectionate
carisma *m* charisma
carismático *adj* charismatic
caritativo *adj* charitable
cariz *m* look; ***tomar mal cariz*** start to look bad
carmín *m de labios* lipstick
carnaval *m* carnival
carne *f* meat; *de persona* flesh; ***carne de gallina*** *fig* goose bumps *pl*, *Br* goose-flesh; ***carne picada*** ground meat, *Br* mince; ***de carne y hueso*** flesh and blood; ***sufrir algo en sus propias carnes*** *fig* go through sth oneself
carné *m* → ***carnet***
carnear ⟨1a⟩ *v/t L.Am.* slaughter
carnero *m* ram
carnet *m* card; ***carnet de conducir*** driver's license, *Br* driving licence; ***carnet de identidad*** identity card
carnicería *f* butcher's; *fig* carnage
carnicero *m*, **-a** *f* butcher
carnívoro *adj* carnivorous
carnoso *adj* fleshy
caro *adj* expensive, dear; ***costar caro*** *fig* cost dear
carozo *m Chi, Rpl* pit
carpa *f de circo* big top; ZO carp; *L.Am. para acampar* tent; *L.Am. de mercado* stall
carpeta *f* file
carpintero *m* carpenter; *de obra* joiner; ***pájaro carpintero*** woodpecker
carpir ⟨3a⟩ *v/t L.Am.* hoe
carraspear ⟨1a⟩ *v/i* clear one's throat
carraspera *f* hoarseness
carrera *f* race; EDU degree course; *profesional* career; ***carrera de armamento*** arms race; ***a las carreras*** at top speed; *con prisas* in a rush; ***hacer la carrera*** F *de prostituta* turn tricks F; ***carreras*** *pl* ***de coches*** motor racing *sg*
carrerilla *f*: ***tomar carrerilla*** take a run up; ***decir algo de carrerilla*** reel sth off
carreta *f* cart
carrete *m* FOT (roll of) film; ***carrete de hilo*** reel of thread
carretera *f* highway, (main) road; ***carretera de circunvalación*** ring road
carretilla *f* wheelbarrow
carril *m* lane; ***carril-bici*** cycle lane; ***carril-bus*** bus lane
carrillo *m* cheek; ***comer a dos carrillos*** F stuff oneself F
carrito *m* cart, *Br* trolley; ***carrito de bebé*** buggy, *Br* pushchair
carro *m* cart; *L.Am.* car; *L.Am.* (*taxi*) taxi, cab; ***carro de combate*** tank; ***carro-patrulla*** *L.Am.* F patrol car
carrocería *f* AUTO bodywork
carroña *f* carrion
carruaje *m* carriage
carta *f* letter; GASTR menu; (*naipe*) playing card; (*mapa*) chart; ***carta certificada*** *or* ***registrada*** registered letter; ***carta urgente*** special-delivery letter; ***a la carta*** a la carte; ***dar carta blanca a alguien*** give s.o. carte blanche *o* a free hand; ***poner las cartas boca arriba*** *fig* put one's cards on the table; ***tomar cartas en el asunto*** intervene in the matter
cartearse ⟨1a⟩ *v/r* write to each other
cartel *m* poster; ***estar en cartel*** *de película, espectáculo* be on
cártel *m* cartel
cartelera *f* billboard; *de periódico* listings, entertainments section
cartera *f* wallet; (*maletín*) briefcase; COM, POL portfolio; *de colegio* knapsack, *Br* satchel; *L.Am.* purse, *Br* handbag; *mujer* mailwoman, *Br* postwoman
carterista *m/f* pickpocket
cartero *m* mailman, *Br* postman
cartílago *m* cartilage
cartilla *f* reader; *Méx* identity card; ***cartilla de ahorros*** savings book; ***leerle a alguien la cartilla*** F give s.o. a telling off F

C

cartógrafo *m*, **-a** *f* cartographer
cartón *m* cardboard; *de tabaco* carton; ***cartón piedra*** pap(i)er- mâché
cartuchera *f* cartridge belt
cartucho *m de arma* cartridge
cartulina *f* sheet of card; ***cartulina roja*** DEP red card
casa *f* house; (*hogar*) home; ***en casa*** at home; ***como una casa*** F huge F; ***casa cuna*** children's home; ***casa de huéspedes*** rooming house, *Br* boarding house; ***casa matriz*** head office; ***casa de socorro*** first aid post; ***casa adosada, casa pareada*** → ***chalet***
casaca *f* cassock
casado *adj* married; ***recién casado*** newly-wed
casamentero *m*, **-a** *f* matchmaker
casar 〈1a〉 **1** *v/i fig* match (up); ***casar con*** go with **2** *v/r* ***casarse*** get married; ***casarse con alguien*** marry s.o.; ***no casarse con nadie*** *fig* refuse to compromise
cascabel *m* small bell
cascada *f* waterfall
cascado *adj voz* hoarse; F *persona* worn out F
cascanueces *m inv* nutcracker
cascar 〈1g〉 *v/t* crack; *algo quebradizo* break; *fig* F whack F; ***cascarla*** peg out F
cáscara *f de huevo* shell; *de naranja, limón* peel
cascarón *m* shell; ***salir del cascarón*** hatch (out)
cascarrabias *m inv* F grouch F
casco *m* helmet; *de barco* hull; (*botella vacía*) empty (bottle); *edificio* empty building; *de caballo* hoof; *de vasija* fragment; ***casco urbano*** urban area; ***cascos azules*** MIL blue berets, UN peace-keeping troops
cascote *m* piece of rubble
casera *f* landlady
casero 1 *adj* home-made; ***comida -a*** home cooking **2** *m* landlord
caseta *f* hut; *de feria* stall
casete *m* (*also f*) cassette
casi *adv* almost, nearly; *en frases negativas* hardly
casilla *f en formulario* box; *en tablero* square; *de correspondencia* pigeon hole; *S. Am.* post office box; ***sacar a alguien de sus casillas*** drive s.o. crazy
casino *m* casino
caso *m* case; ***en caso de que, caso de*** in the event that, in case of; ***hacer caso*** take notice; ***ser un caso*** F be a real case F; ***no venir al caso*** be irrelevant; ***en todo caso*** in any case, in any event; ***en el peor de los casos*** if the worst comes to the worst; ***en úiltimo caso*** as a last resort
caspa *f* dandruff
caspiroleta *f S. Am.* eggnog
casquillo *m de cartucho* case; EL bulb holder; *L.Am.* horseshoe
cassette *m* (*also f*) cassette; ***cassette virgen*** blank cassette
casta *f* caste
castaña *f* chestnut; ***sacar las castañas del fuego a alguien*** *fig* F pull s.o.'s chestnuts out of the fire F
castaño 1 *adj color* chestnut, brown **2** *m* chestnut (tree); *color* chestnut, brown; ***ya pasa de castaño oscuro*** F it's gone too far, it's beyond a joke
castañuela *f* castanet; ***estar como unas castañuelas*** F be over the moon F
castellano *m* (Castilian) Spanish
castidad *f* chastity
castigar 〈1h〉 *v/t* punish
castigo *m* punishment
castillo *m* castle; ***castillo de fuegos artificiales*** firework display
castizo *adj* pure
casto *adj* chaste
castor *m* ZO beaver
castrar 〈1a〉 *v/t* castrate; *fig* emasculate
castrense *adj* army *atr*
casual *adj* chance *atr*
casualidad *f* chance, coincidence; ***por*** *or* ***de casualidad*** by chance
cataclismo *m* cataclysm, catastrophe
catalán 1 *adj* Catalan **2** *m*, **-ana** *f* Catalan
catalejo *m* telescope
catalizador *m* catalyst; AUTO catalytic converter
catalizar 〈1f〉 *v/t* catalyze
catalogar 〈1h〉 *v/t* catalog(ue); *fig* class
catálogo *m* catalog(ue)
catamarán *m* MAR catamaran
cataplasma *f* MED poultice; *fig*: *persona* bore
catapulta *f* slingshot, *Br* catapult
catapultar 〈1a〉 *v/t* catapult
catar 〈1a〉 *v/t* taste
catarata *f* GEOG waterfall; MED cataract
catarro *m* cold; *inflamación* catarrh
catástrofe *f* catastrophe
catastrófico *adj* catastrophic
cate *m* EDU F fail
catear 〈1a〉 *v/t* F flunk F
catecismo *m* catechism
catedral *f* cathedral; ***una mentira como una catedral*** F a whopping great lie F
catedrático *m*, **-a** *f* EDU head of department
categoría *f* category; *social* class; *fig*: *de local*, *restaurante* class; (*estatus*) standing;

C

actor de primera categoría first-rate actor
categórico *adj* categorical
catequesis *f* catechism
catéter *m* MED catheter
catolicismo *m* (Roman) Catholicism
católico 1 *adj* (Roman) Catholic **2** *m*, **-a** *f* (Roman) Catholic
catorce *adj* fourteen
catre *m* bed
cauce *m* riverbed; *fig* channel; ***volver a su cauce*** *fig* get back to normal
caucho *m* rubber; *L.Am.* (*neumático*) tire, *Br* tyre
caudal *m de río* volume of flow; *fig* wealth
caudillo *m* leader
causa *f* cause; (*motivo*) reason; JUR lawsuit; ***a causa de*** because of
causante *m* cause
causar ⟨1a⟩ *v/t* cause
cáustico *adj tb fig* caustic
cautela *f* caution
cauteloso *adj* cautious
cauterizar ⟨1f⟩ *v/t* cauterize
cautivar ⟨1a⟩ *v/t fig* captivate
cautiverio *m*, **cautividad** *f* captivity
cautivo 1 *adj* captive **2** *m*, **-a** *f* captive
cauto *adj* cautious
cava *m* cava, sparkling wine
cavar ⟨1a⟩ *v/t* dig
caverna *f* cavern
cavernícola *m/f* caveman; *mujer* cavewoman
caviar *m* caviar
cavidad *f* cavity
cavilar ⟨1a⟩ *v/t* meditate on
cayó *vb* → ***caer***
caza 1 *f* hunt; *actividad* hunting; ***caza mayor / menor*** big / small game; ***andar a la caza de algo / alguien*** be after sth/s.o. **2** *m* AVIA fighter
cazador *m* hunter
cazadora *f* hunter; *prenda* jacket
cazar ⟨1f⟩ **1** *v/t animal* hunt; *fig*: *información* track down; (*pillar*, *captar*) catch; ***cazar un buen trabajo*** get o.s. a good job **2** *v/i* hunt; ***ir a cazar*** go hunting
cazo *m* saucepan
cazuela *f* pan; *de barro*, *vidrio* casserole
cazurro *adj* stubborn; (*basto*) coarse; (*lento de entender*) dense F, thick F
c.c. *abr* (= ***centímetro cúibico***) c.c. (= cubic centimeter)
c/c *abr* (= ***cuenta corriente***) C/A(= checking account)
CD *m* (= ***disco compacto***) CD (= compact disc); *reproductor* CD-player
CD-ROM *m* CD-ROM
cebada *f* barley
cebar ⟨1a⟩ **1** *v/t* fatten; *anzuelo* bait; TÉC prime; *L.Am. mate* prepare **2** *v/r* **cebarse** feed (***en*** on); ***cebar con alguien*** vent one's fury on s.o.
cebo *m* bait
cebolla *f* onion
cebra *f* zebra; ***paso de cebra*** crosswalk, *Br* zebra crossing
ceceo *m pronunciation of 's' with 'th' sound*
cecina *f* cured meat
cedazo *m* sieve
ceder ⟨2a⟩ **1** *v/t* give up; (*traspasar*) transfer, cede; ***ceder el paso*** AUTO yield, *Br* give way **2** *v/i* give way, yield; *de viento, lluvia* ease off
cedro *m* BOT cedar
cédula *f L.Am.* identity document
cegar ⟨1h & 1k⟩ *v/t* blind; *tubería* block
ceguera *f tb fig* blindness
ceja *f* eyebrow; ***lo tiene entre ceja y ceja*** F she can't stand him F
cejar ⟨1a⟩ *v/i* give up; ***no cejar en*** not let up in
celador *m*, **celadora** *f* orderly; *de cárcel* guard; *de museo* attendant
celda *f* cell
celebración *f* celebration
celebrar ⟨1a⟩ *v/t misa* celebrate; *reunión, acto oficial* hold; *fiesta* have, hold
célebre *adj* famous
celeste *adj* light blue, sky blue
celestial *adj* celestial; *fig* heavenly
celibato *m* celibacy
celo *m* zeal; (*cinta adhesiva*) Scotch® tape, *Br* Sellotape®; ***en celo*** zo in heat; ***celos*** *pl* jealousy *sg*; ***tener celos de*** be jealous of
celofán *m* cellophane
celoso *adj* jealous (***de*** of)
célula *f* cell
celular *adj* cellular
celulitis *f* cellulite
celulosa *f* cellulose
cementerio *m* cemetery
cemento *m* cement
cena *f* dinner; *más tarde* supper
cenagoso *adj* boggy
cenar ⟨1a⟩ **1** *v/t*: ***cenar algo*** have sth for dinner **2** *v/i* have dinner
cencerro *m* cowbell
cenicero *m* ashtray
cenit *m* AST zenith; *fig* peak
ceniza *f* ash; ***cenizas*** ashes
censo *m* census; ***censo electoral*** voting register, electoral roll
censura *f* censorship
censurar ⟨1a⟩ *v/t* censor; *tratamiento* condemn

cent *abr* (= ***céntimo***) cent
centavo *m* cent
centellear ⟨1a⟩ *v/i* sparkle; *de estrella* twinkle
centena *f* hundred
centenar *m* hundred; ***regalos a centenares*** hundreds of gifts
centenario 1 *adj* hundred-year-old *atr* **2** *m* centennial, *Br* centenary
centeno *m* BOT rye
centígrado *adj* centigrade; ***dos grados centígrados*** two degrees centigrade
centímetro *m* centimeter, *Br* centimetre
céntimo *m* cent; ***estar sin un céntimo*** not have a red cent F
centinela *m/f* sentry; *de banda criminal* lookout
central 1 *adj* central; (*principal*) main, central **2** *f* head office; ***central atómica*** *or* ***nuclear*** nuclear power station; ***central eléctrica*** power station; ***central telefónica*** telephone exchange; ***central térmica*** thermal power station
centralismo *m* POL centralism
centralita *f* TELEC switchboard
centralizar ⟨1f⟩ *v/t* centralize
centrar ⟨1a⟩ **1** *v/t tb* DEP center, *Br* centre; *esfuerzos* focus (***en*** on) **2** *v/r* **centrarse** concentrate (***en*** on)
céntrico *adj* central
centrifugar ⟨1h⟩ *v/t* spin
centro *m* center, *Br* centre; ***centro comercial*** (shopping) mall, *Br* shopping centre; ***centro urbano*** *en señal* town center (*Br* centre)
Centroamérica Central America
centroamericano *adj* Central American
ceñido *adj* tight
ceñirse ⟨3h & 3l⟩ *v/r*: ***ceñirse a algo*** *fig* stick to sth
ceño *m*: ***fruncir el ceño*** frown
cepa *f de vid* stock
cepillar ⟨1a⟩ **1** *v/t* brush **2** *v/r* **cepillarse** brush; F (*comerse*) polish off F; F (*matar*) kill, knock off F
cepillo *m* brush; ***cepillo de dientes*** toothbrush
cera *f* wax
cerámica *f* ceramics
cerca[1] *f* fence
cerca[2] *adv* near, close; ***de cerca*** close up; ***cerca de*** near, close to; (*casi*) nearly
cercanía *f*: ***tren de cercanías*** suburban train
cercano *adj* nearby; ***cercano a*** close to, near to
cercar ⟨1g⟩ *v/t* surround; *con valla* fence in
cerciorarse ⟨1a⟩ *v/r* make sure (***de*** of)
cerco *m* ring; *de puerta* frame; *L.Am.* fence; ***poner cerco a*** lay siege to
cerda *f animal* sow; *fig* F *persona* pig F; *de brocha* bristle
cerdo *m* hog, *Br* pig; *fig* F *persona* pig F
cereal *m* cereal; ***cereales*** *pl* (breakfast) cereal *sg*
cerebro *m* ANAT brain; *fig*: *persona* brains *sg*
ceremonia *f* ceremony
cereza *f* cherry
cerezo *m* cherry (tree)
cerilla *f* match
cernerse ⟨2g⟩ *v/r*: ***cernerse sobre*** *fig* hang over
cernícalo *m* ZO kestrel
cero *m* EDU zero, *Br tb* nought; *en fútbol etc* zero, *Br* nil; *en tenis* love; ***bajo / sobre cero*** below / above zero; ***empezar desde cero*** *fig* start from scratch; ***vencer por tres a cero*** win three-zero (*Br* nil)
cerrado *adj* closed; *persona* narrow-minded; (*tímido*) introverted; *cielo* overcast; ***curva -a*** tight curve
cerradura *f* lock; ***ojo de la cerradura*** keyhole
cerrajero *m*, **-a** *f* locksmith
cerrar ⟨1k⟩ **1** *v/t* close; *para siempre* close down; *tubería* block; *grifo* turn off; ***cerrar con llave*** lock **2** *v/i* close; *para siempre* close down **3** *v/r* **cerrarse** close; *de cielo* cloud over; *de persona* shut o.s. off (***a*** from); ***cerrarse de golpe*** slam shut
cerrazón *f fig* narrow-mindedness
cerrero *adj L.Am. persona* rough
cerril *adj animal* wild; (*terco*) stubborn, pig-headed F; (*torpe*) F dense F
cerro *m* hill
cerrojo *m* bolt; ***echar el cerrojo*** bolt the door
certamen *m* competition
certeza *f* certainty
certidumbre *f* certainty
certificado 1 *adj carta* registered **2** *m* certificate
certificar ⟨1g⟩ *v/t* certify; *carta* register
cerval *adj*: ***miedo cerval*** terrible fear
cervecería *f* bar
cerveza *f* beer; ***cerveza de barril*** *or* ***de presión*** draft, *Br* draught (beer); ***cerveza negra*** stout; ***cerveza rubia*** lager; ***fábrica de cerveza*** brewery
cesante *adj Chi* unemployed, jobless; ***dejar cesante a alguien*** let s.o. go
cesar ⟨1a⟩ *v/i* stop; ***no cesar de hacer algo*** keep on doing sth; ***sin cesar*** non-stop
cesárea *f* MED C(a)esarean
cese *m* cessation

C

cesión *f* transfer
césped *m* lawn
cesta *f* basket; ***cesta de la compra*** shopping basket
cesto *m* large basket
C.F. *abr* (= ***Club de Fúítbol***) FC (= Football Club)
cfc *abr* (= ***clorofluorocarbono***) CFC (= chlorofluorocarbon)
cg. *abr* (= ***centigramo***) centigram
ch/ *abr* (= ***cheque***) check
chabacano *adj* vulgar, tacky F
chabola *f* shack; ***barrio de chabolas*** shanty town
chacal *m* ZO jackal
chacarero *m*, **-a** *f Rpl*, *Chi* smallholder, farmer
chacha *f* F maid
cháchara *fpl L.Am.* junk *sg*, bits and pieces
chachi *adj* F great F
chacra *f L.Am.* AGR smallholding
chafar ⟨1a⟩ *v/t* squash; *cosa erguida* flatten; F *planes etc* ruin F
chaflán *m* corner
chal *m* shawl
chalado *adj* F crazy F (***por*** about)
chalé *m* → ***chalet***
chaleco *m de traje* waistcoat; *de sport* gilet, bodywarmer; ***chaleco salvavidas*** life vest; ***chaleco antibalas*** bulletproof vest
chalet *m* chalet; ***chalet adosado*** *house sharing one or more walls with other houses*; ***chalet pareado*** semi-detached house
chalupa *f* MAR small boat; *Méx* stuffed tortilla
chamaca *f C.Am.*, *Méx* girl
chamaco *m C.Am.*, *Méx* boy
chamarra *f Méx* (*saco*) (short) jacket
chamba *f Méx* F job
chambón *m*, **-ona** *f Méx* F clumsy idiot F
champán *m*, **champaña** *m* champagne
champiñón *m* BOT mushroom
champúí *m* shampoo
chamuscar ⟨1g⟩ *v/t* scorch; *pelo* singe
chamusquina *f*: ***oler a chamusquina*** F smell fishy F
chance 1 *m L.Am.* chance; ***dame chance*** let me have a go **2** *conj Méx* perhaps, maybe
chanchería *f L.Am.* pork butcher's shop
chancho *m L.Am.* hog, *Br* pig; *carne* pork
chanchullo *m* F trick, scam F
chancla *f* thong, *Br* flip-flop; *Méx*, *C.Am.* (*zapato*) slipper
chancleta *f* thong, *Br* flip-flop; *S. Am.* F baby girl
chándal *m* tracksuit
changa *f Rpl* odd job
chango 1 *adj Méx* F sharp, smart **2** *m*, **-a** *f Méx* monkey
chanquetes *mpl* GASTR whitebait *sg*
chantaje *m* blackmail; ***hacer chantaje a alguien*** blackmail s.o.
chantajear ⟨1a⟩ *v/t* blackmail
chantajista *m/f* blackmailer
chanza *f* wisecrack
chao *int* bye
chapa *f* (*tapón*) cap; (*plancha*) sheet (of metal); (*insignia*) badge; AUTO bodywork
chapado *adj* plated; ***chapado a la antigua*** old-fashioned; ***chapado en oro*** gold-plated
chapar ⟨1a⟩ *v/t* plate; *Arg*, *Pe* catch
chaparro *adj Méx* small
chaparrón *m* downpour; *fig* F *de insultos* barrage
chapotear ⟨1a⟩ *v/i* splash
chapucero 1 *adj* shoddy, slapdash **2** *m*, **-a** *f* shoddy worker
chapurrear ⟨1a⟩ *v/t*: ***chapurrear el francés*** speak poor French
chapuza *f* (*trabajo mal hecho*) shoddy piece of work; (*trabajo menor*) odd job
chapuzón *m* dip; ***darse un chapuzón*** go for a dip
chaqué *m* morning coat
chaqueta *f* jacket; ***chaqueta de punto*** cardigan
chaquetero *m*, **-a** *f* F turncoat
chaquetón *m* three-quarter length coat
charango *m Pe*, *Bol* five string guitar
charca *f* pond
charco *m* puddle
charcutería *f* delicatessen
charla *f* chat; *organizada* talk
charlar ⟨1a⟩ *v/i* chat
charlatán 1 *adj* talkative **2** *m*, **-ana** *f* chatterbox
charol *m* patent leather; ***zapatos de charol*** patent leather shoes
charqui *m L.Am.* beef jerky
charro 1 *adj desp* garish, gaudy **2** *m Méx* (Mexican) cowboy
chasco *m* joke; ***llevarse un chasco*** be disappointed
chasis *m inv* AUTO chassis
chasquear ⟨1a⟩ *v/t* click; *látigo* crack
chasquido *m* click; *de látigo* crack
chatarra *f* scrap
chato *adj nariz* snub; *L.Am. nivel* low
chau *int Rpl* bye
chaucha *f Rpl* French bean
chaval *m* F kid F, boy
chavala *f* F kid F, girl
chavalo *m C.Am.* F kid F, boy
che *int Rpl* hey!, look!

checar ⟨1g⟩ *v/t Méx* check
checo 1 *adj* Czech **2** *m*, **-a** *f* Czech
chef *m* chef
chelo *m* MÚS cello
chepa *f* F hump; ***subírsele a la chepa*** get too familiar
cheque *m* check, *Br* cheque; ***cheque cruzado*** crossed check (*Br* cheque); ***cheque sin fondos*** bad check (*Br* cheque); ***cheque de viaje*** traveler's check, *Br* traveller's cheque
chequear ⟨1a⟩ *v/t* check; *C.Am. equipaje* check (in)
chequeo *m* MED check-up
chequera *f* checkbook, *Br* chequebook
chica *f* girl
chicha *f L.Am.* corn liquor; ***no ser ni chicha ni limonada*** F be neither one thing nor the other
chícharo *m Méx* pea
chiche 1 *adj C.Am.* F (*fácil*) easy **2** *m S. Am.* (*juguete*) toy; (*adorno*) trinket
chichera *f C.Am.* jail
chichería *f L.Am. bar selling corn liquor*
chichón *m* bump
chicle *m* chewing gum
chico 1 *adj* small, little **2** *m* boy
chifa *m Pe* Chinese restaurant; (*comida china*) Chinese food
chifla *f Méx* whistling
chiflado *adj* F crazy F (***por*** about), nuts F (***por*** about)
chiflar ⟨1a⟩ **1** *v/t* boo **2** *v/i* whistle; ***me chifla …*** F I'm crazy about … F
chile *m* chilli (pepper)
Chile Chile
chileno 1 *adj* Chilean **2** *m*, **-a** *f* Chilean
chillar ⟨1a⟩ *v/i* scream, shriek; *de cerdo* squeal
chillido *m* scream, shriek; *de cerdo* squeal
chillón 1 *adj voz* shrill; *color* loud **2** *m*, **-ona** *f* loudmouth
chilote *m C.Am.* baby corn
chimenea *f* chimney; *de salón* fireplace
chimichurri *m Rpl* hot sauce
chimpancé *m* ZO chimpanzee
China China
china[1] *f* Chinese woman
china[2] *f piedra* small stone
chincheta *f* thumbtack, *Br* drawing pin
chinchorro *m* hammock
chinear ⟨1a⟩ *v/t C.Am. niños* look after
chingar ⟨1h⟩ *v/t Méx* V screw V, fuck V; ***¡chinga tu madre!*** screw you! V, fuck you! V; ***no chingues*** don't screw me around V
chino 1 *adj* Chinese **2** *m* Chinese man; *idioma* Chinese; *L.Am. desp* half-breed *desp*; ***trabajo de chinos*** F hard work; ***me suena a chino*** F it's all Chinese *o* double Dutch to me F
chip *m* INFOR chip
chipirón *m* baby squid
chiquilla *f* girl, kid
chiquillo *m* boy, kid
chirimoya *f* BOT custard apple
chiringuito *m* beach bar
chiripa *f*: ***de chiripa*** F by sheer luck
chirona *f*: ***en chirona*** F in the can F, inside F
chirriar ⟨1c⟩ *v/i* squeak
chirrido *m* squeak
chisme *m* F bit of gossip; *objeto* doodad F, *Br* doodah F
chismografía *f* F gossip
chismorrear ⟨1a⟩ *v/i* F gossip
chismoso 1 *adj* gossipy **2** *m*, **-a** *f* F gossip
chispa *f* spark; (*cantidad pequeña*) spot; *fig* F wit
chispear ⟨1a⟩ *v/i* spark; *fig* sparkle; *de lluvia* spit
chistar ⟨1a⟩ *v/i*: ***sin chistar*** without saying a word
chiste *m* joke
chiva *f L.Am.* goat; *C.Am.*, *Col* bus
chivarse ⟨1a⟩ *v/r* F rat F (***a*** to)
chivato *m*, **-a** *f* F stool pigeon F
chivo *m* ZO kid; *C.Am.*, *Méx* wages *pl*
chocante *adj* (*sorprendente*) startling; *que ofende* shocking; (*extraño*) odd; *L.Am.* (*antipático*) unpleasant
chocar ⟨1g⟩ **1** *v/t*: ***¡choca esos cinco!*** P give me five! P, put it there! P **2** *v/i* crash (***con, contra*** into), collide (***con*** with); ***chocarle a alguien*** (*sorprender*) surprise s.o.; (*ofender*) shock s.o.; ***me choca ese hombre*** F that guy disgusts me; ***chocar con un problema*** come up against a problem
chocho *adj* F senile; ***estar chocho con*** dote on
choclo *m Rpl* corn, *Br* corn on the cob
chocolate *m* chocolate; F (*hachís*) hashish, hash F
chocolatina *f* chocolate bar
chófer, *L.Am.* **chofer** *m* driver
chollo *m* F bargain
cholo *m L.Am.* half-caste *desp*
chompa *f S. Am.* jumper, sweater
chop *m L.Am.* large beer
chopo *m* BOT poplar
choque *m* collision, crash; DEP, MIL clash; MED shock
chorizo *m* chorizo (*spicy cured sausage*); F thief; *Rpl* (*filete*) rump steak
chorlito *m*: ***cabeza de chorlito*** F featherbrain F
chorrada *f* F piece of junk; ***decir chorra-***

C

das F talk garbage, *Br* talk rubbish
chorrear ⟨1a⟩ *v/i* gush out, stream; (*gotear*) drip
chorro *m líquido* jet, stream; *fig* stream; *C.Am.* faucet, *Br* tap
chovinista *m/f* chauvinist
choza *f* hut
chubasco *m* shower
chubasquero *m* raincoat
chuchería *f* knick-knack; (*golosina*) candy, *Br* sweet
chucho 1 *adj C.Am.* mean **2** *m* F (*perro*) mutt F, mongrel; *Chi* (*cárcel*) can F, prison
chueco *adj L.Am.* (*torcido*) twisted
chulería *f* bragging
chuleta *f* GASTR chop
chulo F **1** *adj* fantastic F, great F; *Méx* (*guapo*) attractive; (*presuntuoso*) cocky F **2** *m* pimp F
chumbera *f C.Am.* prickly pear
chumpipe *m C.Am.* turkey
chupa *f* jacket
chupado *adj* F (*delgado*) skinny F; F (*fácil*) dead easy F; *L.Am.* F drunk
chupar ⟨1a⟩ **1** *v/t* suck; (*absorber*) soak up **2** *v/r* **chuparse**: ***chuparse algo*** suck sth; *fig* F put up with sth; ***chuparse los dedos*** F lick one's fingers
chupete *m de bebé* pacifier, *Br* dummy; (*sorbete*) Popsicle®, *Br* ice lolly
chupi *adj* F great F, fantastic F
churrasco *m Rpl* steak
churro *m* fritter; (*chapuza*) botched job
chusma *f desp* rabble *desp*
chutar ⟨1a⟩ *v/i* DEP shoot; ***esto va que chuta*** F this is working out fine; ***y vas que chutas*** F and that's your lot! F
chuzo *m Chi* F *persona* dead loss F; ***caer chuzos de punta*** F pelt down F
Cía. *abr* (**= *Compañía***) Co. (= Company)
ciberespacio *m* cyberspace
cibernauta *m/f* Internet surfer
cibernética *f* cybernetics
cicatriz *f* scar
cicatrizar ⟨1f⟩ scar
cíclico *adj* cyclical
ciclismo *m* cycling
ciclista *m/f* cyclist
ciclo *m* cycle; *de cine* season
ciclomotor *m* moped
ciclón *m* cyclone
cicloturismo *m* bicycle touring
ciega *f* blind woman
ciego 1 *adj* blind; ***a -as*** blindly **2** *m* blind man
cielito *m Rpl folk dance*
cielo *m* sky; REL heaven; ***ser un cielo*** F be an angel F; ***cielo raso*** ceiling
ciempiés *m inv* ZO centipede
cien *adj* a *o* one hundred
ciencia *f* science; ***ciencia ficción*** science fiction; ***a ciencia cierta*** for certain, for sure
científico 1 *adj* scientific **2** *m*, **-a** *f* scientist
ciento *pron* a *o* one hundred; ***cientos de*** hundreds of; ***el cinco por ciento*** five percent
ciernes: ***en ciernes*** *fig* potential, in the making
cierre *m* fastener; *de negocio* closure; ***cierre centralizado*** AUTO central locking; ***cierre relámpago*** *L.Am.* zipper, *Br* zip
cierto *adj* certain; ***hasta cierto punto*** up to a point; ***un cierto encanto*** a certain charm; ***es cierto*** it's true; ***cierto día*** one day; ***por cierto*** incidentally; ***estar en lo cierto*** be right
ciervo *m* ZO deer; ***ciervo volante*** ZO stag beetle
c.i.f. *abr* (**= *costo, seguro y flete***) cif (= cost, insurance, freight)
cifra *f* figure
cigala *f* ZO crayfish
cigarra *f* ZO cicada
cigarrería *f L.Am. shop selling cigarettes etc*
cigarrillo *m* cigarette
cigarro *m* cigar; *L.Am.* cigarette
cigüeña *f* ZO stork
cigüeñal *m* AUTO crankshaft
cilantro *m* BOT coriander
cilindrada *f* AUTO cubic capacity
cilíndrico *adj* cylindrical
cilindro *m* cylinder
cima *f* summit; *fig* peak
cimarrón *adj L.Am. animal* wild; *esclavo* runaway; ***mate cimarrón*** *Arg* unsweetened maté
cimentar ⟨1k⟩ *v/t* lay the foundations of; *fig* base (***en*** on)
cimientos *mpl* foundations
cinc *m* zinc
cincel *m* chisel
cinco 1 *adj* five **2** *m* five; ***no tener ni cinco*** F not have a red cent F
cincuenta *adj* fifty
cincuentón *m* man in his fifties
cincuentona *f* woman in her fifties
cine *m* movies *pl*, cinema
cineasta *m/f* film-maker
cinéfilo *m*, **-a** *f* movie buff
cinematográfico *adj* movie *atr*
cinético *adj* kinetic
cínico 1 *adj* cynical **2** *m*, **-a** *f* cynic
cinismo *m* cynicism
cinta *f* ribbon; *de música, vídeo* tape; ***cinta adhesiva*** adhesive tape; ***cinta aislan-***

te electrical tape, friction tape, *Br* insulating tape; ***cinta métrica*** tape measure; ***cinta de vídeo*** video tape
cintura *f* waist
cinturón *m* belt; ***cinturón de seguridad*** AUTO seatbelt
cíper *m Méx* zipper, *Br* zip
ciprés *m* BOT cypress
circo *m* circus
circuito *m* circuit; ***corto circuito*** EL short circuit
circulación *f* movement; FIN, MED circulation; AUTO traffic; ***poner en circulación*** put into circulation
circular 1 *adj* circular **2** ⟨1a⟩ *v/i* circulate; AUTO drive, travel; *de persona* move (along)
círculo *m* circle; ***círculo vicioso*** vicious circle
circuncisión *f* circumcision
circundante *adj* surrounding
circunferencia *f* circumference
circunscribir ⟨3a; *part* ***circunscrito*** ⟩ *v/t* limit (***a*** to)
circunscripción *f* POL electoral district, *Br* constituency
circunspecto *adj* circumspect, cautious
circunstancia *f* circumstance
circunstancial *adj* circumstantial
circunvalación *f*: (***carretera de***) ***circunvalación*** beltway, *Br* ring-road
cirio *m* candle; ***armar*** *or* ***montar un cirio*** F kick up a fuss F
ciruela *f* plum; ***ciruela pasa*** prune
cirugía *f* surgery; ***cirugía estética*** cosmetic surgery
cirujano *m*, **-a** *f* surgeon
cisco *m*: ***hacer cisco*** smash
cisne *m* ZO swan
cisterna *f de WC* cistern
cistitis *f* MED cystitis
cita *f* appointment; *de texto* quote, quotation
citar ⟨1a⟩ **1** *v/t a reunión* arrange to meet; *a juicio* summon; (*mencionar*) mention; *de texto* quote **2** *v/r* **citarse** arrange to meet
citología *f* smear test
cítrico *m* citrus fruit
ciudad *f* town; *más grande* city; ***ciudad universitaria*** university campus
ciudadano *m*, **-a** *f* citizen
cívico *adj* civic
civil *adj* civil; ***casarse por lo civil*** have a civil wedding
civilización *f* civilization
civismo *m* civility
cizaña *f*: ***sembrar*** *or* ***meter cizaña*** cause trouble

cl. *abr* (**= *centilitro***) cl. (= centiliter)
clamar ⟨1a⟩ *v/i*: ***clamar por algo*** clamo(u)r for sth, cry out for sth
clamor *m* roar; *fig* clamo(u)r
clan *m* clan
clandestino *adj* POL clandestine, underground
claqué *m* tap-dancing
clara *f de huevo* white; *bebida* beer with lemonade, *Br* shandy
claraboya *f* skylight
claridad *f* light; *fig* clarity
clarificar ⟨1g⟩ *v/t* clarify
clarinete *m* clarinet
clarividente *m/f* clairvoyant
claro *adj tb fig* clear; *color* light; (*luminoso*) bright; *salsa* thin; ***¡claro!*** of course!; ***hablar claro*** speak plainly
clase *f* class; (*variedad*) kind, sort; ***clase particular*** private class; ***dar clase*** (***s***) teach
clásico *adj* classical
clasificación *f* DEP league table
clasificar ⟨1g⟩ **1** *v/t* classify **2** *v/r* **clasificarse** DEP qualify
claudicar ⟨1g⟩ *v/i* give in
claustro *m* ARQUI cloister
claustrofobia *f* claustrophobia
cláusula *f* clause
clausurar ⟨1a⟩ *v/t acto oficial* close; *por orden oficial* close down
clavadiste *m/f Méx* diver
clavado *adj*: ***ser clavado a alguien*** be the spitting image of s.o. F
clavar ⟨1a⟩ **1** *v/t* stick (***en*** into); *clavos, estaca* drive (***en*** into); *uñas* sink (***en*** into); ***clavar los ojos en alguien*** fix one's eyes on s.o.; ***clavar a alguien por algo*** F overcharge s.o. for sth **2** *v/r* **clavarse**: ***clavarse un cuchillo en la mano*** stick a knife into one's hand
clave 1 *f* key; ***en clave*** in code **2** *adj* (*importante*) key
clavel *m* BOT carnation
clavícula *f* ANAT collarbone
clavija *f* EL pin
clavo *m de metal* nail; GASTR clove; *CSur* F *persona* dead loss F; ***dar en el clavo*** hit the nail on the head
claxon *m* AUTO horn
clemencia *f* clemency, mercy
clementina *f* BOT clementine
clérigo *m* priest, clergyman
clero *m* clergy
clic *m* INFOR click; ***hacer clic en*** click on
cliché *m* cliché
clienta, cliente *m/f de tienda* customer; *de empresa* client
clientela *f* clientele, customers *pl*

C

clima *m* climate
climatizado *adj* air-conditioned
climatizar ⟨1f⟩ *v/t* air-condition
clímax *m fig* climax
clínica *f* clinic
clínico *adj* clinical
clip *m para papeles* paperclip; *para el pelo* bobby pin, *Br* hairgrip
cloaca *f tb fig* sewer
clon *m* BIO clone
clonación *f* BIO cloning
clonar ⟨1a⟩ *v/t* clone
cloro *m* QUÍM chlorine
clóset *m L.Am.* closet, *Br* wardrobe
club *m* club; ***club náutico*** yacht club
cm *abr* (**= *centímetro***) cm (= centimeter)
coacción *f* coercion
coaccionar ⟨1a⟩ *v/t* coerce
coagular ⟨1a⟩ **1** *v/t* coagulate; *sangre* clot **2** *v/r* **coagularse** coagulate; *de sangre* clot
coágulo *m* clot
coala *m* ZO koala
coalición *f* coalition
coaligarse ⟨1h⟩ *v/r tb* POL work together, join forces
coartada *f* JUR alibi
coba *f*: ***dar coba a alguien*** F soft-soap s.o. F
cobarde 1 *adj* cowardly **2** *m/f* coward
cobaya *m/f* guinea pig
cobertizo *m* shed
cobertor *m* (*manta*) blanket
cobertura *f* cover; TV *etc* coverage
cobija *f L.Am.* blanket
cobijar ⟨1a⟩ **1** *v/t* give shelter to; (*acoger*) take in **2** *v/r* **cobijarse** take shelter
cobijo *m* shelter, refuge
cobra *f* ZO cobra
cobrador *m*, **cobradora** *f a domicilio* collector
cobrar ⟨1a⟩ **1** *v/t* charge; *subsidio*, *pensión* receive; *deuda* collect; *cheque* cash; *salud*, *fuerzas* recover; *importancia* acquire **2** *v/i* be paid, get paid; ***vas a cobrar*** F (*recibir un palo*) you're going to get it! F
cobre *m* copper
cobro *m* charging; *de subsidio* receipt; *de deuda* collection; *de cheque* cashing
coca *f* F *droga* coke F; ***de coca*** *Méx* free
cocacho *m S. Am.* F whack on the head F
cocada *f L.Am.* coconut cookie
cocaína *f* cocaine
cocainómano *m*, **-a** *f* cocaine addict
cocción *f* cooking; *en agua* boiling; *al horno* baking
cocer ⟨2b & 2h⟩ **1** *v/t* cook; *en agua* boil; *al horno* bake **2** *v/r* **cocerse** cook; *en agua* boil; *al horno* bake; *fig* F *de persona* be roasting F
cochambroso *adj* F filthy
coche *m* car; *Méx* (*taxi*) cab, taxi; ***coche de caballos*** horse-drawn carriage; ***coche cama*** sleeping car; ***coche comedor*** *L.Am.* dining car; ***coche de línea*** (long-distance) bus
cochecito *m*: ***cochecito de niño*** stroller, *Br* pushchair
cochera *f* garage; *de trenes* locomotive shed
cochina *f* sow; F *persona* pig F
cochino 1 *adj fig* filthy, dirty; (*asqueroso*) disgusting **2** *m* hog, *Br* pig; F *persona* pig F
cocido 1 *adj* boiled **2** *m* stew
cociente *m* quotient
cocina *f habitación* kitchen; *aparato* cooker, stove; *actividad* cooking; ***cocina de gas*** gas cooker *o* stove
cocinar ⟨1a⟩ **1** *v/t* cook; *fig* F plot **2** *v/i* cook
cocinero *m*, **-a** *f* cook
coco *m* BOT coconut; *monstruo* bogeyman F; ***comer el coco a alguien*** F softsoap s.o.; *más fuerte* brainwash s.o.
cocodrilo *m* crocodile
cocoliche *m Arg* pidgin Spanish
cocotazo *m L.Am.* F whack on the head F
cocotero *m* coconut palm
cóctel *m* cocktail; ***cóctel Molotov*** Molotov cocktail
cód *abr* (**= *código***) code
codazo *m*: ***darle a alguien un codazo*** elbow s.o.
codearse ⟨1a⟩ *v/r*: ***codearse con alguien*** rub shoulders with s.o.
codicia *f* greed
codiciar ⟨1b⟩ *v/t* covet
codicioso *adj* greedy
codificado *adj* TV encrypted
código *m* code; ***código de barras*** COM barcode; ***código postal*** zip code, *Br* postcode
codo *m* ANAT elbow; ***codo con codo*** *fig* F side by side; ***hablar por los codos*** F talk nineteen to the dozen F
codorniz *f* ZO quail
coeficiente *m* coefficient
coetáneo *m*, **-a** *f* contemporary
coexistir ⟨3a⟩ *v/i* coexist (***con*** with)
cofradía *f* fraternity; (*gremio*) guild
cofre *m de tesoro* chest; *para alhajas* jewel(le)ry box
coger ⟨2c⟩ **1** *v/t* (*asir*) take (hold of); *del suelo* pick up; *ladrón*, *enfermedad* catch; TRANSP catch, take; (*entender*) get; *L.Am.* V screw V **2** *v/i en un espacio*

fit; *L.Am.* V screw V; ***coger por la primera a la derecha*** take the first right **3** *v/r* **cogerse** hold on (tight); ***cogerse de algo*** hold on to sth
cogorza *f*: ***agarrar una cogorza*** F get plastered F
cogote *m* F nape of the neck
cohabitar ⟨1a⟩ *v/i* live together, cohabit
cohecho *m* JUR bribery
coherencia *f* coherence
coherente *adj* coherent; ***ser coherente con*** be consistent with
cohesión *f* cohesion
cohete *m* rocket
cohibir ⟨3a⟩ *v/t* inhibit
COI *abr* (***= Comité Olímpico Internacional***) IOC (= International Olympic Committee)
coima *f L.Am.* bribe
coincidencia *f* coincidence
coincidir ⟨3a⟩ *v/i* coincide
coito *m* intercourse
cojear ⟨1a⟩ *v/i de persona* limp, hobble; *de mesa, silla* wobble
cojera *f* limp
cojín *m* cushion
cojo *adj persona* lame; *mesa, silla* wobbly
cojón *m* V ball V
cojonudo *adj* P awesome F, brilliant
col. *abr* (***= columna***) col. (= column)
col *f* cabbage; ***col de Bruselas*** Brussels sprout
cola[1] *f* (*pegamento*) glue
cola[2] *f* (*de animal*) tail; *de gente* line, *Br* queue; *L.Am.* F *de persona* butt F, *Br* bum F; ***hacer cola*** stand in line, *Br* queue; ***estar a la cola*** be in last place
colaboración *f* collaboration
colaborador *m*, **colaboradora** *f* collaborator; *en periódico* contributor
colaborar ⟨1a⟩ *v/i* collaborate
colación *f*: ***traer*** *or* ***sacar a colación*** bring up
colada *f*: ***hacer la colada*** do thc laundry *o* washing
colado *adj*: ***estar colado por alguien*** F be nuts about s.o. F
colador *m* colander; *para té etc* strainer
colapsar ⟨1a⟩ **1** *v/t* paralyze; ***colapsar el tráfico*** bring traffic to a standstill **2** *v/r* **colapsarse** grind to a halt
colapso *m* collapse; ***provocar un colapso en la ciudad*** bring the city to a standstill
colar ⟨1m⟩ **1** *v/t líquido* strain; *billete falso* pass; ***colar algo por la aduana*** F smuggle sth through customs **2** *v/i fig* F: ***no cuela*** I'm not buying it F **3** *v/r* **colarse** F *en un lugar* get in; *en una fiesta* gatecrash; *en una cola* cut in line, *Br* push in
colcha *f L.Am.* bedspread
colchón *m* mattress; *fig* buffer
colchoneta *f* DEP mat; *hinchable* air bed
cole *m* F school
colección *f* collection
coleccionar ⟨1a⟩ *v/t* collect
coleccionista *m/f* collector
colecta *f* collection
colectivero *m*, **-a** *f Arg* bus driver
colectivo **1** *adj* collective **2** *m L.Am.* bus; *Méx, C.Am.* taxi
colega *m/f* colleague; F pal
colegiado *m*, **-a** *f* DEP referee
colegial *m* student, schoolboy
colegiala *f* student, schoolgirl
colegio *m* school; ***colegio electoral*** electoral college; ***colegio profesional*** professional institute
cólera **1** *f* anger; ***montar en cólera*** get in a rage **2** *m* MED cholera
colesterol *m* cholesterol
coleta *f* ponytail; ***coletas*** *de pelo* bunches
colgado *adj*: ***dejar colgado a alguien*** F let s.o. down
colgador *m L.Am.* hanger
colgante **1** *adj* hanging **2** *m* pendant
colgar ⟨1h & 1m⟩ **1** *v/t* hang; TELEC put down **2** *v/i* hang (***de*** from); TELEC hang up **3** *v/r* **colgarse** hang o.s.; INFOR F lock up; ***colgarse de algo*** hang from sth; ***colgarse de alguien*** hang onto s.o.
colibrí *m* ZO hummingbird
cólico *m* MED colic
coliflor *f* cauliflower
colilla *f* cigarette end
colina *f* hill
colindante *adj* adjoining
colirio *m* MED eye drops *pl*
colisión *f* collision; *fig* clash
colisionar ⟨1a⟩ *v/i* collide (***con*** with)
colitis *f* MED colitis
collar *m* necklace; *para animal* collar
colleras *fpl Chi* cuff links
colmar ⟨1a⟩ *v/t deseos, ambición etc* fulfill; ***colmar un vaso*** fill a glass to the brim; ***colmar a alguien de elogios*** heap praise on s.o.
colmena *f* beehive
colmillo *m* ANAT eye tooth; *de perro* fang; *de elefante, rinoceronte* tusk
colmo *m*: ***¡es el colmo!*** this is the last straw!; ***para colmo*** to cap it all
colocación *f* positioning, placing; (*trabajo*) position
colocar ⟨1g⟩ **1** *v/t* put, place; ***colocar a alguien en un trabajo*** get s.o. a job **2** *v/r* **colocarse** *de persona* position o.s.; ***se colocó a mi lado*** he stood next to

C

me; ***se colocaron en primer lugar*** they moved into first place
colofón *m fig* culmination
Colombia Colombia
colombiano 1 *adj* Colombian **2** *m*, **-a** *f* Colombian
Colón Columbus
colonia *f* colony; *de viviendas* subdivision, *Br* estate; *perfume* cologne; ***colonia de verano*** summer camp
colonial *adj* colonial
colonización *f* colonization
colonizar ⟨1f⟩ *v/t* colonize
coloquial *adj* colloquial
coloquio *m* talk
color *m* colo(u)r; ***color café*** coffee-colo(u)red; *L.Am.* brown
colorado *adj* red
colorante *m* colo(u)ring
colorear ⟨1a⟩ *v/t* colo(u)r
colorete *m* blusher
colorido *m* colo(u)rs *pl*
colosal *adj* colossal
columna *f* column; ***columna vertebral*** ANAT spinal column
columnista *m/f* columnist
columpiar ⟨1b⟩ **1** *v/t* swing **2** *v/r* **columpiarse** swing
columpio *m* swing
colza *f* BOT rape
coma 1 *f* GRAM comma **2** *m* MED coma
comadre *f L.Am.* godmother
comadrear ⟨1a⟩ *v/i* F gossip
comadrona *f* midwife
comandante *m* MIL commander; *rango* major; AVIA captain
comarca *f* area
comba *f* jump rope, *Br* skipping rope; ***jugar*** *or* ***saltar a la comba*** jump rope, *Br* skip
combate *m acción* combat; MIL engagement; DEP fight; ***fuera de combate*** out of action
combatir ⟨3a⟩ *v/t & v/i* fight
combi *m Méx* minibus
combinación *f* combination; *prenda* slip; ***hacer combinación*** TRANSP change
combinar ⟨1a⟩ *v/t* combine
combustible *m* fuel
combustión *f* combustion
comedia *f* comedy
comedianta *f* actress
comediante *m* actor
comedido *adj* moderate
comedor *m* dining room
comején *m* termite
comensal *m/f* diner
comentar ⟨1a⟩ *v/t* comment on
comentario *m* comment; ***comentario de texto*** textual analysis; ***comentarios*** *pl* gossip *sg*
comentarista *m/f* commentator
comenzar ⟨1f & 1k⟩ *v/t* begin
comer ⟨2a⟩ **1** *v/t* eat; *a mediodía* have for lunch **2** *v/i* eat; *a mediodía* have lunch; ***dar de comer a alguien*** feed s.o. **3** *v/r* **comerse** *tb fig* eat up; ***se comió una palabra*** she missed out a word; ***está para comértela*** F she's really tasty F
comercial 1 *adj* commercial; *de negocios* business *atr*; ***el déficit comercial*** the trade deficit **2** *m/f* representative
comercializar ⟨1f⟩ *v/t* market, sell; *desp* commercialize
comerciante *m/f* trader; ***comerciante al por menor*** retailer
comercio *m actividad* trade; *local* store, shop; ***comercio exterior*** foreign trade
comestible 1 *adj* eatable, edible **2** *m* foodstuff; ***comestibles*** *pl* food *sg*
cometa 1 *m* comet **2** *f* kite
cometer ⟨2a⟩ *v/t* commit; *error* make
cometido *m* task
comezón *f* itch
cómic *m* comic
comicios *mpl* elections *pl*
cómico 1 *adj* comical **2** *m*, **-a** *f* comedian
comida *f* (*comestibles*) food; *ocasión* meal
comienzo *m* beginning
comillas *fpl* quotation marks, inverted commas
comino *m* BOT cumin; ***me importa un comino*** F I don't give a damn F
comisaría *f* precinct, *Br* police station
comisario *m* commissioner; *de policía* captain, *Br* superintendent
comisión *f* committee; *de gobierno* commission; (*recompensa*) commission
comité *m* committee
comitiva *f* retinue
como 1 *adv* as; ***así como*** as well as; ***había como cincuenta*** there were about fifty **2** *conj* if; ***como si*** as if; ***como no bebas vas a enfermar*** if you don't drink you'll get sick; ***como no llegó, me fui solo*** as *o* since she didn't arrive, I went by myself
cómo *adv* how; ***¿cómo estás?*** how are you?; ***¡cómo me gusta!*** I really like it; ***me gusta cómo habla*** I like the way he talks; ***¿cómo dice?*** what did you say?; ***¡cómo no!*** *Méx* of course!
cómoda *f* chest of drawers
comodidad *f* comfort
comodín *m en naipes* joker
cómodo *adj* comfortable
comp. *abr* (***= compárese***) cf (= confer)
compacto *adj* compact

compadecer ⟨2d⟩ **1** *v/t* feel sorry for **2** *v/r* **compadecerse** feel sorry (***de*** for)
compadre *m L.Am.* F buddy F
compadrear ⟨1a⟩ *v/i Arg* F brag
compadrito *m Arg* F show-off
compaginar ⟨1a⟩ *v/t fig* combine
compañero *m*, **-a** *f* companion; *en una relación, un juego* partner; ***compañero de trabajo*** coworker, colleague; ***compañero de clase*** classmate
compañía *f* company; ***hacer compañía a alguien*** keep s.o. company
comparación *f* comparison; ***en comparación con*** in comparison with
comparado *adj*: ***comparado con*** compared with
comparar ⟨1a⟩ *v/t* compare
comparecencia *f* JUR appearance
comparecer ⟨2d⟩ *v/i* appear
compartir ⟨3a⟩ *v/t* share (***con*** with)
compás *m* MAT compass; MÚS rhythm; ***al compás*** to the beat
compasión *f* compassion
compatibilidad *f* compatibility
compatible *adj* INFOR compatible
compatriota *m/f* compatriot
compendio *m* summary
compenetrado *adj*: ***están muy compenetrados*** they are very much in tune with each other
compenetrarse ⟨1a⟩ *v/r*: ***compenetrarse con alguien*** reach a good understanding with s.o.
compensación *f* compensation
compensar ⟨1a⟩ **1** *v/t* compensate (***por*** for) **2** *v/i fig* be worthwhile
competencia *f* (*habilidad*) competence; *entre rivales* competition; (*incumbencia*) area of responsibility, competency; ***competencia desleal*** unfair competition
competente *adj* competent
competición *f* DEP competition
competir ⟨3l⟩ *v/i* compete (***con*** with)
competitivo *adj* competitive
compilar ⟨1a⟩ *v/t* compile
compinche *m/f* F buddy F; *desp* crony F
complacencia *f* (*placer*) pleasure; (*tolerancia*) indulgence
complacer ⟨2x⟩ *v/t* please
complaciente *adj* obliging, helpful
complejidad *f* complexity
complejo **1** *adj* complex **2** *m* PSI complex; ***complejo de inferioridad*** inferiority complex
complementar ⟨1a⟩ *v/t* complement
complemento *m* complement; GRAM complement, object; ***complementos de moda*** fashion accessories
completar ⟨1a⟩ *v/t* complete
completo *adj* complete; *autobús, teatro* full; ***por completo*** completely
complicación *f* complication
complicado *adj* complicated
complicar ⟨1g⟩ **1** *v/t* complicate **2** *v/r* **complicarse** get complicated; ***complicarse la vida*** make things difficult for o.s.
cómplice *m/f* accomplice
complot *m* plot
componente *m* component
componer ⟨2r; *part* **compuesto** ⟩**1** *v/t* make up, comprise; *sinfonía, poema etc* compose; *algo roto* fix, mend **2** *v/r* **componerse** be made up (***de*** of); *L.Am.* MED get better
comportamiento *m* behavio(u)r
comportarse ⟨1a⟩ *v/r* behave
composición *f* composition
compositor *m*, **compositora** *f* composer
compostura *f fig* composure
compota *f* compote
compra *f acción* purchase; (*cosa comprada*) purchase, buy; ***ir de compras*** go shopping
comprar ⟨1a⟩ *v/t* buy, purchase
compraventa *f* buying and selling
comprender ⟨2a⟩ *v/t* understand; (*abarcar*) include
comprensión *f* understanding; *de texto, auditiva* comprehension
comprensivo *adj* understanding
compresa *f* sanitary napkin, *Br* sanitary towel
compresión *f tb* INFOR compression
comprimido *m* MED pill
comprimir ⟨3a⟩ *v/t* compress
comprobación *f* check
comprobar ⟨1m⟩ *v/t* check; (*darse cuenta de*) realize
comprometer ⟨2a⟩ **1** *v/t* compromise; (*obligar*) commit **2** *v/r* **comprometerse** promise (***a*** to); *a una causa* commit o.s.; *de novios* get engaged
comprometido *adj* committed; ***estar comprometido en algo*** be implicated in sth; ***estar comprometido*** *de novios* be engaged
compromiso *m* commitment; (*obligación*) obligation; (*acuerdo*) agreement; (*apuro*) awkward situation; ***sin compromiso*** COM without commitment; ***soltero y sin compromiso*** F footloose and fancy-free
compuesto **1** *part* → ***componer*** **2** *adj* composed; ***estar compuesto de*** be composed of
compulsar ⟨1a⟩ *v/t* certify
compulsivo *adj* PSI compulsive

C

computación *f L.Am.* computer science
computadora *f L.Am.* computer; ***computadora de escritorio*** desktop (computer); ***computadora personal*** personal computer; ***computadora portátil*** laptop
computarizar ⟨1f⟩ *v/t* computerize
comulgar ⟨1h⟩ *v/i* take communion; ***comulgar con alguien*** (***en algo***) *fig* F think the same way as s.o. (on sth)
comúín *adj* common; ***por lo comúín*** generally
comuna *f* commune; *L.Am.* (*población*) town
comunicación *f* communication; TRANSP link
comunicado 1 *adj* connected; ***el lugar está bien comunicado*** the place has good transport links **2** *m* POL press release, communiqué
comunicar ⟨1g⟩ **1** *v/t* TRANSP connect, link; ***comunicar algo a alguien*** inform s.o. of sth **2** *v/i* communicate; TELEC be busy, *Br tb* be engaged **3** *v/r* **comunicarse** communicate
comunidad *f* community; ***comunidad autónoma*** autonomous region
comunión *f* REL communion
comunismo *m* Communism
comunista *m/f & adj* Communist
comunitario *adj* POL EU *atr*, Community *atr*
con *prp* with; ***voy con ellos*** I'm going with them; ***pan con mantequilla*** bread and butter; ***con todo eso*** in spite of all that; ***con tal de que*** provided that, as long as; ***con hacer eso*** by doing that
conato *m*: ***conato de violencia*** minor outbreak of violence; ***conato de incendio*** small fire
cóncavo *adj* concave
concebir ⟨3l⟩ *v/t* conceive
conceder ⟨2a⟩ *v/t* concede; *entrevista, permiso* give; *premio* award
concejal *m*, **concejala** *f* council(l)or
concentración *f* concentration; *de personas* gathering
concentrar ⟨1a⟩ **1** *v/t* concentrate **2** *v/r* **concentrarse** concentrate (***en*** on); *de gente* gather
concepto *m* concept; ***en concepto de algo*** COM (in payment) for sth; ***bajo ningúín concepto*** on no account
concernir ⟨3i⟩ *v/i* concern; ***en lo que concierne a X*** as far as X is concerned
concertar ⟨1k⟩ *v/t cita* arrange; *precio* agree; *esfuerzos* coordinate
concesión *f* concession; COM dealership; ***hacer concesiones*** make concessions
concesionario *m* dealer
concha *f* ZO shell
conchabar ⟨1a⟩ **1** *v/t L.Am. trabajador* hire **2** *v/r* **conchabarse** F plot
conciencia *f* conscience; ***a conciencia*** conscientiously; ***con plena conciencia de*** fully conscious of
concienciar ⟨1b⟩ **1** *v/t*: ***concienciar a alguien de algo*** make s.o. aware of sth **2** *v/r* **concienciarse** realize (***de*** sth)
concienzudo *adj* conscientious
concierto *m* MÚS concert; *fig* agreement
conciliador *adj* conciliatory
conciliar ⟨1b⟩ *v/t* reconcile; ***conciliar el sueño*** get to sleep
conciso *adj* concise
concluir ⟨3g⟩ *v/t & v/i* conclude
conclusión *f* conclusion; ***en conclusión*** in short
concretar ⟨1a⟩ **1** *v/t* specify; (*hacer concreto*) realize **2** *v/r* **concretarse** materialize; *de esperanzas* be fulfilled
concreto 1 *adj* specific; (*no abstracto*) concrete; ***en concreto*** specifically **2** *m L.Am.* concrete
concurrencia *f* audience; *de circunstancias* combination
concurrido *adj* crowded
concursante *m/f* competitor
concursar ⟨1a⟩ *v/i* compete
concurso *m* competition; COM tender
conde *m* count
condecoración *f* decoration
condecorar ⟨1a⟩ decorate
condena *f* JUR sentence; (*desaprobación*) condemnation
condenar ⟨1a⟩ *v/t* JUR sentence (***a*** to); (*desaprobar*) condemn
condensación *f* condensation
condensado *adj* condensed
condensar ⟨1a⟩ **1** *v/t* condense; *libro* abridge **2** *v/r* **condensarse** condense
condesa *f* countess
condescendiente *adj actitud* accommodating; *desp* condescending
condición *f* condition; ***a condición de que*** on condition that; ***estar en condiciones de*** be in a position to
condimentar ⟨1a⟩ flavo(u)r
condimento *m* seasoning
condón *m* condom
cóndor *m* ZO condor
conducir ⟨3o⟩ **1** *v/t vehículo* drive; (*dirigir*) lead (***a*** to); EL, TÉC conduct **2** *v/i* drive; *de camino* lead (***a*** to)
conducta *f* conduct, behavio(u)r
conducto *m* pipe; *fig* channel; ***por conducto de*** through
conductor *m*, **conductora** *f* driver; ***conductor de orquesta*** *L.Am.* conductor

condujo *vb* → ***conducir***
conectar ⟨1a⟩ *v/t* connect, link; EL connect
conejillo *m*: ***conejillo de Indias*** *tb fig* guinea pig
conejo *m* rabbit
conexión *f tb* EL connection
confabularse ⟨1a⟩ *v/r* plot
confección *f* making; *de vestidos* dressmaking; *de trajes* tailoring
confeccionar ⟨1a⟩ *v/t* make
confederación *f* confederation
conferencia *f* lecture; (*reunión*) conference; TELEC long-distance call
conferenciante *m/f* lecturer
conferencista *m/f L.Am.* lecturer
conferir ⟨3i⟩ *v/t* award
confesar ⟨1k⟩ **1** *v/t* REL confess; *delito* confess to, admit **2** *v/i* JUR confess **3** *v/r* **confesarse** confess; (*declararse*) admit to being
confesión *f* confession
confeti *m* confetti
confiado *adj* trusting
confianza *f* confidence; ***confianza en sí mismo*** self-confidence; ***de confianza*** *persona* trustworthy; ***amigo de confianza*** good friend
confiar ⟨1c⟩ **1** *v/t secreto* confide (***a*** to); ***confiar algo a alguien*** entrust s.o. with sth, entrust sth to s.o. **2** *v/i* trust (***en*** in); (*estar seguro*) be confident (***en*** of)
confidencia *f* confidence
confidencial *adj* confidential
configuración *f* configuration; INFOR set-up, configuration
configurar ⟨1a⟩ *v/t* shape; INFOR set up, configure
confinar ⟨1a⟩ *v/t* confine
confirmación *f* confirmation
confirmar ⟨1a⟩ *v/t* confirm
confiscar ⟨1g⟩ *v/t* confiscate
confitería *f* confectioner's
confitura *f* preserve
conflagración *f* conflagration; (*guerra*) war
conflicto *m* conflict
conformarse ⟨1a⟩ *v/r* make do (***con*** with)
conforme **1** *adj* satisfied (***con*** with) **2** *prp*: ***conforme a*** in accordance with
confortable *adj* comfortable
confrontación *f* confrontation
confundir ⟨3a⟩ **1** *v/t* confuse; (*equivocar*) mistake (***con*** for) **2** *v/r* **confundirse** make a mistake; ***confundirse de calle*** get the wrong street
confusión *f* confusion
confuso *adj* confused
congelación *f* freezing; ***congelación de precios / de salarios*** price / wage freeze
congelado *adj* frozen
congelador *m* freezer
congelar ⟨1a⟩ **1** *v/t* freeze **2** *v/r* **congelarse** freeze
congeniar ⟨1b⟩ *v/i* get on well (***con*** with)
congénito *adj* congenital
congestión *f* MED congestion; ***congestión del tráfico*** traffic congestion
congestionar ⟨1a⟩ *v/t* congest
congoja *f* anguish
congregar ⟨1h⟩ *v/t* bring together
congresal *m/f L.Am.*, **congresista** *m/f* conference *o* convention delegate, conventioneer
congreso *m* conference, convention; ***Congreso*** *en EE.UU* Congress; ***congreso de los diputados*** *lower house of Spanish parliament*
congrio *m* ZO conger eel
conjetura *f* conjecture
conjugar ⟨1h⟩ *v/t* GRAM conjugate; *fig* combine
conjunción *f* GRAM conjunction
conjuntivitis *f* MED conjunctivitis
conjunto **1** *adj* joint **2** *m de personas*, *objetos* collection; *de prendas* outfit; MAT set; ***en conjunto*** as a whole
conllevar ⟨1a⟩ *v/t* entail
conmemorar ⟨1a⟩ *v/t* commemorate
conmigo *pron* with me
conmoción *f* shock; (*agitación*) upheaval
conmocionar ⟨1a⟩ *v/t* shock
conmovedor *adj* moving
conmover ⟨2h⟩ **1** *v/t* move **2** *v/r* **conmoverse** be moved
conmutador *m* EL switch; *L.Am.* TELEC switchboard
connotación *f* connotation
cono *m* cone
conocer ⟨2d⟩ **1** *v/t* know; *por primera vez* meet; *tristeza*, *amor etc* experience, know; (*reconocer*) recognize; ***dar a conocer*** make known **2** *v/r* **conocerse** know one another; *por primera vez* meet one another; *a sí mismo* know o.s.; ***se conoce que*** it seems that
conocido **1** *adj* well-known **2** *m*, **-a** *f* acquaintance
conocimiento *m* knowledge; MED consciousness; ***perder el conocimiento*** lose consciousness
conquista *f* conquest
conquistar ⟨1a⟩ *v/t* conquer; *persona* win over
consabido *adj* usual
consagrar ⟨1a⟩ **1** *v/t* REL consecrate; (*hacer famoso*) make famous; *vida* devote **2** *v/r* **consagrarse** devote o.s. (***a*** to)

C

consciente *adj* MED conscious; ***consciente de*** aware of, conscious of
consecuencia *f* consequence; ***a consecuencia de*** as a result of; ***en consecuencia*** consequently
consecuente *adj* consistent
consecutivo *adj* consecutive; ***tres años consecutivos*** three years in a row
conseguir ⟨3l & 3d⟩ *v/t* get; *objetivo* achieve
consejero *m*, **-a** *f* adviser; COM director
consejo *m* piece of advice; ***consejo de administración*** board of directors; ***consejo de ministros*** *grupo* cabinet; *reunión* cabinet meeting
consenso *m* consensus
consentido *adj* spoilt
consentimiento *m* consent
consentir ⟨3i⟩ **1** *v/t* allow; *a niño* indulge **2** *v/i*: ***consentir en algo*** agree to sth
conserje *m/f* superintendent, *Br* caretaker
conserva *f*: ***en conserva*** canned, *Br* tinned; ***conservas*** *pl* canned (*Br* tinned) food *sg*
conservación *f de alimentos* preservation; *de edificios, especies* conservation
conservador *adj* conservative
conservante *m* preservative
conservar ⟨1a⟩ **1** *v/t* conserve; *alimento* preserve **2** *v/r* **conservarse** survive
conservatorio *m* conservatory
considerable *adj* considerable
consideración *f* consideration
considerar ⟨1a⟩ *v/t* consider
consigna *f* order; *de equipaje* baggage room, *Br* left-luggage
consigo *pron* with him / her; (*con usted, con ustedes*) with you; (*con uno*) with you, with one *fml*
consiguiente *adj* consequent; ***por consiguiente*** and so, therefore
consistencia *f* consistency
consistente *adj* consistent; (*sólido*) solid
consistir ⟨3a⟩ *v/i* consist (***en*** of)
consola *f* INFOR console
consolar ⟨1m⟩ *v/t* console
consolidar ⟨1a⟩ **1** *v/t* consolidate **2** *v/r* **consolidarse** strengthen
consomé *m* GASTR consommé
consonancia *f*: ***en consonancia con*** in keeping with
consonante *f* consonant
consorte *m/f* spouse
conspiración *f* conspiracy
conspirar ⟨1a⟩ *v/i* conspire
constancia *f* constancy; ***dejar constancia de*** leave a record of
constante *adj* constant
constar ⟨1a⟩ *v/i* be recorded; ***constar de*** consist of
constatación *f* verification
constatar ⟨1a⟩ *v/t* verify
constelación *f* AST constellation
consternar ⟨1a⟩ *v/t* dismay
constipado 1 *adj*: ***estar constipado*** have a cold **2** *m* cold
constiparse ⟨1a⟩ *v/r* get a cold
constitución *f* constitution
constituir ⟨3g⟩ *v/t* constitute, make up; *empresa, organismo* set up
construcción *f* construction; (*edificio*) building
construir ⟨3g⟩ *v/t* build, construct
consuelo *m* consolation
cónsul *m/f* consul
consulado *m* consulate
consulta *f* consultation; MED *local* office, *Br* surgery
consultar ⟨1a⟩ *v/t* consult
consultor *m*, **consultora** *f* consultant
consultoría *f* consultancy
consultorio *m* MED office, *Br* surgery
consumidor *m*, **consumidora** *f* COM consumer
consumir ⟨3a⟩ **1** *v/t* consume **2** *v/r* **consumirse** waste away
consumo *m* consumption; ***de bajo consumo*** economical
contabilidad *f* accountancy; ***llevar la contabilidad*** do the accounts
contable *m/f* accountant
contactar ⟨1a⟩ *v/i*: ***contactar con alguien*** contact s.o.
contacto *m* contact; AUTO ignition; ***ponerse en contacto*** get in touch (***con*** with)
contado *adj*: ***al contado*** in cash
contador 1 *m* meter **2** *m*, **contadora** *f L.Am.* accountant
contagiar ⟨1b⟩ **1** *v/t*: ***contagiar la gripe a alguien*** give s.o. the flu; ***nos contagió su entusiasmo*** he infected us with his enthusiasm **2** *v/r* **contagiarse** become infected
contagioso *adj* contagious
contaminación *f de agua etc* contamination; *de río, medio ambiente* pollution
contaminar ⟨1a⟩ *v/t* contaminate; *río, medio ambiente* pollute
contar ⟨1m⟩ **1** *v/t* count; (*narrar*) tell **2** *v/i* count; ***contar con*** count on
contemplación *f*: ***sin contemplaciones*** without ceremony
contemplar ⟨1a⟩ *v/t* (*mirar*) look at, contemplate; *posibilidad* consider
contemporáneo 1 *adj* contemporary **2** *m*, **-a** *f* contemporary

C

contenedor *m* TRANSP container; ***contenedor de basura*** dumpster, *Br* skip; ***contenedor de vidrio*** bottle bank
contener ⟨2l⟩ **1** *v/t* contain; *respiración* hold; *muchedumbre* hold back **2** *v/r* **contenerse** control o.s.
contenido *m* content
contentarse ⟨1a⟩ *v/r* be satisfied (***con*** with)
contento *adj* (*satisfecho*) pleased; (*feliz*) happy
contestación *f* answer
contestador *m*: ***contestador automático*** TELEC answer machine
contestar ⟨1a⟩ **1** *v/t* answer, reply to **2** *v/i* reply (***a*** to), answer (***a*** sth); *de forma insolente* answer back
contexto *m* context
contigo *pron* with you
contiguo *adj* adjoining, adjacent
continental *adj* continental
continente *m* continent
continuación *f* continuation; ***a continuación*** (*ahora*) now; (*después*) then
continuar ⟨1e⟩ **1** *v/t* continue **2** *v/i* continue; ***continuar haciendo algo*** continue *o* carry on doing sth
continuidad *f* continuity
continuo *adj* (*sin parar*) continuous; (*frecuente*) continual
contorno *m* outline
contra *prp* against; ***en contra de*** against
contraataque *m* counterattack
contrabajo *m* double bass
contrabandista *m/f* smuggler
contrabando *m* contraband, smuggled goods *pl*; *acción* smuggling; ***hacer contrabando*** smuggle; ***pasar algo de contrabando*** smuggle sth in
contracción *f* contraction
contraceptivo *m/adj* contraceptive
contradecir ⟨3p⟩ *v/t* contradict
contradicción *f* contradiction
contradictorio *adj* contradictory
contraer ⟨2p; *part* ***contraido*** ⟩ **1** *v/t* contract; *músculo* tighten; ***contraer matrimonio*** marry **2** *v/r* **contraerse** contract
contraindicación *f* MED contraindication
contraluz *f*: ***a contraluz*** against the light
contrapartida *f* COM balancing entry; ***como contrapartida*** *fig* in contrast
contrapeso *m* counterweight
contraposición *f*: ***en contraposición a*** in comparison to
contraproducente *adj* counterproductive
contrariedad *f* setback; (*disgusto*) annoyance
contrario **1** *adj* contrary; *sentido* opposite; *equipo* opposing; ***al contrario, por el contrario*** on the contrary; ***de lo contrario*** otherwise; ***ser contrario a algo*** be opposed to sth; ***llevar la -a a alguien*** contradict s.o. **2** *m*, **-a** *f* adversary, opponent
contrarreloj *f* DEP time trial
contrarrestar ⟨1a⟩ *v/t* counteract
contraseña *f* password
contrastar ⟨1a⟩ *v/t & v/i* contrast (***con*** with)
contraste *m* contrast
contratar ⟨1a⟩ *v/t* contract; *trabajadores* hire
contratiempo *m* setback
contrato *m* contract
contravenir ⟨3s⟩ *v/i* contravene
contribución *f* contribution; (*impuesto*) tax
contribuir ⟨3g⟩ *v/t* contribute (***a*** to)
contribuyente *m/f* taxpayer
contrincante *m/f* opponent
control *m* control; (*inspección*) check; ***control remoto*** remote control
controlador *m*, **controladora** *f*: ***controlador aéreo*** air traffic controller
controlar ⟨1a⟩ **1** *v/t* control; (*vigilar*) check **2** *v/r* **controlarse** control o.s.
controversia *f* controversy
contundente *adj arma* blunt; *fig*: *derrota* overwhelming
contusión *f* MED bruise
convalecencia *f* convalescence
convaleciente *m/f* convalescent
convalidar ⟨1a⟩ *v/t* recognize
convencer ⟨2b⟩ *v/t* convince
convención *f* convention
convencional *adj* conventional
conveniencia *f de hacer algo* advisability; ***hacer algo por conveniencia*** do sth in one's own interest
conveniente *adj* convenient; (*útil*) useful; (*aconsejable*) advisable
convenio *m* agreement
convenir ⟨3s⟩ **1** *v/t* agree **2** *v/i* be advisable; ***no te conviene*** it's not in your interest; ***convenir a alguien hacer algo*** be in s.o.'s interests to do sth
conventillo *m CSur* tenement
convento *m de monjes* monastery; *de monjas* convent
converger ⟨2c⟩ *v/i* converge
conversación *f* conversation
conversar ⟨1a⟩ *v/i* make conversation
conversión *f* conversion
convertible **1** *adj* COM convertible **2** *m L.Am.* convertible
convertir ⟨3i⟩ **1** *v/t* convert **2** *v/r* **convertirse**: ***convertirse en algo*** turn into sth

C

convexo *adj* convex
convicción *f* conviction
convidar ⟨1a⟩ *v/t* invite (***a*** to)
convincente *adj* convincing
convivencia *f* living together
convivir ⟨3a⟩ *v/i* live together
convocar ⟨1g⟩ *v/t* summon; *huelga* call; *oposiciones* organize
convocatoria *f* announcement; *de huelga* call
convoy *m* convoy
convulsión *f* convulsion; *fig* upheaval
conyugal *adj* conjugal
cónyuge *m/f* spouse
coña *f*: ***decir algo de coña*** F say sth as a joke; ***darle la coña a alguien*** F bug s.o. F; ***¡ni de coña!*** F no way! F
coñac *m* (*pl* ~s) brandy, cognac
coño *m* V cunt V
cooperación *f* cooperation
cooperar ⟨1a⟩ *v/i* cooperate
cooperativa *f* cooperative
coordinación *f* coordination
coordinar ⟨1a⟩ *v/t* coordinate
copa *f de vino etc* glass; DEP cup; ***tomar una copa*** have a drink; ***copas*** *pl* (*en naipes*) *suit in Spanish deck of cards*
copia *f* copy; ***copia pirata*** pirate copy
copiar ⟨1b⟩ *v/t* copy
copiloto *m/f* copilot
copioso *adj* copious
copla *f* verse; (*canción*) popular song
copo *m* flake; ***copo de nieve*** snowflake; ***copos de maíz*** cornflakes
copropietario *m*, **-a** *f* co-owner, joint owner
coquetear ⟨1a⟩ *v/i* flirt
coquetería *f* flirtatiousness
coqueto *adj* flirtatious; *lugar* pretty
coraje *m* courage; ***me da coraje*** *fig* F it makes me mad F
corajudo *adj L.Am.* brave
coral[1] *m* ZO coral
coral[2] *f* MÚS choir
Corán *m* Koran
coraza *f* cuirasse; ZO shell; *fig* shield
corazón *m* heart; *de fruta* core
corazonada *f* hunch
corbata *f* tie
corcho *m* cork
cordel *m* string
cordero *m* lamb
cordial *adj* cordial
cordillera *f* mountain range
cordón *m* cord; *de zapato* shoelace; ***cordón umbilical*** ANAT umbilical cord
cordura *f* sanity; (*prudencia*) good sense
Corea Korea
coreano **1** *adj* Korean **2** *m*, **-a** *f* Korean
coreografía *f* choreography
cormorán *m* ZO cormorant
cornada *f* TAUR goring
corneja *f* ZO crow
córner *m en fútbol* corner (kick)
corneta *f* MIL bugle
cornisa *f* ARQUI cornice
cornudo **1** *adj* horned **2** *m* cuckold
coro *m* MÚS choir; *de espectáculo, pieza musical* chorus; ***a coro*** together, in chorus
corona *f* crown; ***corona de flores*** garland
coronar ⟨1a⟩ *v/t* crown
coronario *adj* MED coronary
coronel *m* MIL colonel
coronilla *f* ANAT crown; ***estoy hasta la coronilla*** F I've had it up to here F
corotos *mpl L.Am.* F bits and pieces
corporación *f* corporation
corporal *adj placer, estética* physical; *fluido* body *atr*
corpulento *adj* solidly built
corral *m* farmyard
correa *f* lead; *de reloj* strap
corrección *f* correction; *en el trato* correctness
correcto *adj* correct; (*educado*) polite
corredizo *adj* sliding
corredor **1** *m*, **corredora** *f* DEP runner; COM agent; ***corredor de bolsa*** stockbroker **2** *m* ARQUI corridor
corregir ⟨3c & 3l⟩ *v/t* correct
correlación *f* correlation
correligionario *m*, **-a** *f*: ***sus correligionarios republicanos*** his fellow republicans
correntada *f L.Am.* current
correntoso *adj L.Am.* fast-flowing
correo *m* mail, *Br tb* post; ***correos*** *pl* post office *sg*; ***correo aéreo*** airmail; ***correo electrónico*** e-mail; ***por correo*** by mail; ***echar al correo*** mail, *Br tb* post
correr ⟨2a⟩ **1** *v/i* run; (*apresurarse*) rush; *de tiempo* pass; *de agua* run, flow; ***correr con los gastos*** pay the expenses; ***a todo correr*** at top speed **2** *v/t* run; *cortinas* draw; *mueble* slide, move; ***correr la misma suerte*** suffer the same fate **3** *v/r* **correrse** move; *de tinta* run
correspondencia *f* correspondence; FERR connection (***con*** with)
corresponder ⟨2a⟩ *v/i*: ***corresponder a alguien*** *de bienes* be for s.o., be due to s.o.; *de responsabilidad* be up to s.o.; *de asunto* concern s.o.; *a un favor* repay s.o. (***con*** with); ***actuar como corresponde*** do the right thing
correspondiente *adj* corresponding
corresponsal *m/f* correspondent

corretear ⟨1a⟩ *v/i* run around
corrida *f*: ***corrida de toros*** bullfight
corrido *adj*: ***decir algo de corrido*** *fig* say sth parrot-fashion
corriente 1 *adj* (*actual*) current; (*común*) ordinary; ***corriente y moliente*** F run-of--the-mill; ***estar al corriente*** be up to date **2** *f* EL, *de agua* current; ***corriente de aire*** draft, *Br* draught
corro *m* ring
corroborar ⟨1a⟩ *v/t* corroborate
corroer ⟨2za⟩ *v/t* corrode; *fig* eat up
corromper ⟨2a⟩ **1** *v/t* corrupt **2** *v/r* ***corromperse*** become corrupted
corrosión *f* corrosion
corrosivo *adj* corrosive; *fig* caustic
corrupción *f* decay; *fig* corruption; ***corrupción de menores*** corruption of minors
corrupto *adj* corrupt
corsetería *f* lingerie store
cortacésped *m* lawnmower
cortacircuitos *m inv* circuit breaker
cortada *f L.Am.* cut
cortado 1 *adj* cut; *calle* closed; *leche* curdled; *persona* shy; ***quedarse cortado*** be embarrassed **2** *m* coffee with a dash of milk
cortar ⟨1a⟩ **1** *v/t* cut; *electricidad* cut off; *calle* close **2** *v/i* cut **3** *v/r* ***cortarse*** cut o.s.; *fig* F get embarrassed; ***cortarse el pelo*** have one's hair cut
cortaúñas *m inv* nail clippers *pl*
corte[1] *m* cut; ***corte de luz*** power outage; ***corte de pelo*** haircut; ***corte de tráfico*** F road closure; ***me da corte*** F I'm embarrassed
corte[2] *f* court; *L.Am.* JUR (law) court; ***las Cortes*** *Spanish parliament*
cortejar ⟨1a⟩ *v/t* court
cortés *adj* courteous
cortesía *f* courtesy
corteza *f de árbol* bark; *de pan* crust; *de queso* rind
cortina *f* curtain
corto *adj* short; ***corto de vista*** nearsighted; ***ni corto ni perezoso*** as bold as brass; ***quedarse corto*** fall short
cortocircuito *m* EL short circuit
corzo *m* ZO roe deer
cosa *f* thing; ***como si tal cosa*** as if nothing had happened; ***decir a alguien cuatro cosas*** give s.o. a piece of one's mind; ***eso es otra cosa*** that's another matter; ***¿qué pasa? – poca cosa*** what's new? - nothing much
coscorrón *m* bump on the head
cosecha *f* harvest
cosechar ⟨1a⟩ *v/t* harvest; *fig* gain, win
coser ⟨2a⟩ *v/t* sew; ***ser coser y cantar*** F be dead easy F
cosmético *m/adj* cosmetic
cósmico *adj* cosmic
cosmonauta *m/f* cosmonaut
cosmopolita *adj* cosmopolitan
cosmos *m* cosmos
cosmovisión *f L.Am.* world view
cosquillas *fpl*: ***hacer cosquillas a alguien*** tickle s.o.; ***tener cosquillas*** be ticklish
cosquilleo *m* tickle
costa[1] *f*: ***a costa de*** at the expense of; ***a toda costa*** at all costs
costa[2] *f* GEOG coast
costado *m* side; ***por los cuatro costados*** *fig* throughout, through and through
costar ⟨1m⟩ **1** *v/t en dinero* cost; *trabajo, esfuerzo etc* take; ***¿cuánto cuesta?*** how much does it cost? **2** *v/i en dinero* cost; ***me costó*** it was hard work; ***cueste lo que cueste*** at all costs; ***costar caro*** *fig* cost dear
Costa Rica Costa Rica
costarricense *m/f & adj* Costa Rican
coste *m* → ***costo***
costear ⟨1a⟩ *v/t* pay for
costero *adj* coastal
costilla *f* ANAT rib; GASTR sparerib
costo *m* cost; ***costo de la vida*** cost of living
costoso *adj* costly
costra *f* MED scab
costumbre *f* custom; *de una persona* habit; ***de costumbre*** usual
costura *f* sewing
costurear ⟨1a⟩ *v/t L.Am.* sew
cotarro *m*: ***manejar el cotarro*** F be the boss F
cotejar ⟨1a⟩ *v/t* compare
cotidiano *adj* daily
cotilla *m/f* F gossip
cotillear ⟨1a⟩ *v/i* F gossip
cotizado *adj* COM quoted; *fig* sought-after
cotizar ⟨1f⟩ *v/i de trabajador* pay social security, *Br* pay National Insurance; *de acciones, bonos* be listed (***a*** at); ***cotizar en bolsa*** be listed on the stock exchange
coto[1] *m*: ***coto de caza*** hunting reserve; ***poner coto a algo*** *fig* put a stop to sth
coto[2] *m S. Am.* MED goiter, *Br* goitre
cotorra *f* ZO parrot; F *persona* motormouth F
coyote *m* ZO coyote
coyuntura *f* situation; ANAT joint
C.P. *abr* (**= *código postal***) zip code, *Br* post code
cráneo *m* ANAT skull, cranium
cráter *m* crater

C

creación *f* creation
creador *m*, **creadora** *f* creator
crear ⟨1a⟩ *v/t* create; *empresa* set up
creativo *adj* creative
crecer ⟨2d⟩ *v/i* grow
creces *fpl*: ***con creces*** *superar* by a comfortable margin; *pagar* with interest
creciente *adj* growing; *luna* waxing
crecimiento *m* growth
credencial *f* document
credibilidad *f* credibility
crédito *m* COM credit; ***a crédito*** on credit; ***no dar crédito a sus oídos / ojos*** F not believe one's ears / eyes
credo *m* REL, *fig* creed
crédulo *adj* credulous
creencia *f* belief
creer ⟨2e⟩ **1** *v/i* believe (***en*** in) **2** *v/t* think; (*dar por cierto*) believe; ***no creo que esté aquí*** I don't think he's here; ***¡ya lo creo!*** F you bet! F **3** *v/r* **creerse**: ***creerse que ...*** believe that ...; ***se cree muy lista*** she thinks she's very clever
crema *f* GASTR cream
cremallera *f* zipper, *Br* zip; TÉC rack
crematorio *m* crematorium
cremoso *adj* creamy
crepe *f* GASTR crêpe, pancake
crepitar ⟨1a⟩ *v/i* crackle
crepúsculo *m tb fig* twilight
cresta *f* crest
cretino *m*, **-a** *f* F cretin F, moron F
creyente 1 *adj*: ***ser creyente*** REL believe in God **2** *m* REL believer
creyó *vb* → ***creer***
cría *f acción* breeding; *de zorro, león* cub; *de perro* puppy; *de gato* kitten; *de oveja* lamb; ***sus crías*** her young
criada *f* maid
criado *m* servant
criar ⟨1c⟩ **1** *v/t niños* raise, bring up; *animales* breed **2** *v/r* **criarse** grow up
criatura *f* creature; F (*niño*) baby, child
crimen *m* crime
criminal *m/f & adj* criminal
crío *m*, **-a** *f* F kid F
criollo 1 *adj* Creole **2** *m*, **-a** *f* Creole
cripta *f* crypt
crisantemo *m* BOT chrysanthemum
crisis *f inv* crisis
crismas *m inv* Christmas card
crispar ⟨1a⟩ *v/t* irritate; ***crisparle a alguien los nervios*** get on s.o.'s nerves
cristal *m* crystal; (*vidrio*) glass; (*lente*) lens; *de ventana* pane; ***cristal líquido*** liquid crystal
cristalizar ⟨1f⟩ *v/i* crystallize; *de idea, proyecto* jell
cristianismo *m* Christianity
cristiano 1 *adj* Christian **2** *m*, **-a** *f* Christian
Cristo Christ
criterio *m* criterion; (*juicio*) judg(e)ment
crítica *f* criticism; ***muchas críticas*** a lot of criticism
criticar ⟨1g⟩ *v/t* criticize
crítico 1 *adj* critical **2** *m*, **-a** *f* critic
Croacia Croatia
crol *m* crawl
cromo *m* QUÍM chrome; (*estampa*) picture card, trading card
crónica *f* chronicle; *en periódico* report
crónico *adj* MED chronic
cronológico *adj* chronological
cronometrar ⟨1a⟩ *v/t* DEP time
cronómetro *m* stopwatch
croqueta *f* GASTR croquette
croquis *m inv* sketch
cross *m* DEP cross-country (running); *con motocicletas* motocross
cruce *m* cross; *de carreteras* crossroads *sg*; ***cruce en las lineas*** TELEC crossed line
crucero *m* cruise
crucial *adj* crucial
crucificar ⟨1g⟩ *v/t* crucify
crucifijo *m* crucifix
crucigrama *m* crossword
crudo 1 *adj alimento* raw; *fig* harsh **2** *m* crude (oil)
cruel *adj* cruel
cruento *adj* bloody
crujiente *adj* GASTR crunchy
crujir ⟨3a⟩ *v/i* creak; *al arder* crackle; *de grava* crunch
cruz *f* cross; ***Cruz Roja*** Red Cross
cruzar ⟨1f⟩ **1** *v/t* cross **2** *v/r* **cruzarse** pass one another; ***cruzarse de brazos*** cross one's arms; ***cruzarse con alguien*** pass s.o.
c.s.f. *abr* (= ***costo, seguro, flete***) cif (= cost, insurance, freight)
cta, **c.ta** *abr* (= ***cuenta***) A/C (= account)
cuaderno *m* notebook; EDU exercise book
cuadra *f* stable; *L.Am.* (*manzana*) block
cuadrado 1 *adj* square **2** *m* square; ***al cuadrado*** squared
cuadrilla *f* squad, team
cuadro *m* painting; (*grabado*) picture; (*tabla*) table; DEP team; ***cuadro de mandos*** *or* ***de instrumentos*** AUTO dashboard; ***de*** *or* ***a cuadros*** checked
cuádruple, **cuadruplo** *m* quadruple
cuajada *f* GASTR curd
cuajar ⟨1a⟩ *v/i de nieve* settle; *fig*: *de idea, proyecto etc* come together, jell F
cuajo *m*: ***de cuajo*** by the roots
cual 1 *pron rel*: ***el cual, la cual*** *etc cosa*

which; *persona* who; ***por lo cual*** (and) so **2** *adv* like
cuál *interr* which (one)
cualidad *f* quality
cualificar ⟨1g⟩ *v/t* qualify
cualquier *adj* any; ***cualquier día*** any day; ***cualquier cosa*** anything; ***de cualquier modo*** *or* ***forma*** anyway
cualquiera *pron persona* anyone, anybody; *cosa* any (one); ***un cualquiera*** a nobody; ***¡cualquiera lo comprende!*** nobody can understand it!
cuando 1 *conj* when; *condicional* if; ***cuando quieras*** whenever you want **2** *adv* when; ***de cuando en cuando*** from time to time; ***cuando menos*** at least
cuándo *interr* when
cuantía *f* amount, quantity; *fig* importance
cuantificar ⟨1g⟩ *v/t* quantify
cuantioso *adj* substantial
cuanto 1 *adj*: ***cuanto dinero quieras*** as much money as you want; ***unos cuantos chavales*** a few boys **2** *pron* all, everything; ***se llevó cuanto podía*** she took all *o* everything she could; ***le dio cuanto necesitaba*** he gave her everything she needed; ***unas -as*** a few; ***todo cuanto*** everything **3** *adv*: ***cuanto antes, mejor*** the sooner the better; ***en cuanto*** as soon as; ***en cuanto a*** as for
cuánto 1 *interr adj* how much; *pl* how many; ***¿cuánto café?*** how much coffee?; ***¿cuántos huevos?*** how many eggs? **2** *pron* how much; *pl* how many; ***¿cuánto necesita Vd.?*** how much do you need?; ***¿cuántos ha dicho?*** how many did you say?; ***¿a cuánto están?*** how much are they?; ***¿a cuántos estamos?*** what's the date today? **3** *exclamaciones*: ***¡cuánta gente había!*** there were so many people!; ***¡cuánto me alegro!*** I'm so pleased!
cuarenta *adj* forty
Cuaresma *f* Lent
cuartear ⟨1a⟩ **1** *v/t* cut up, quarter **2** *v/r* **cuartearse** crack
cuartel *m* barracks *pl*; ***cuartel general*** headquarters *pl*
cuartelazo *m L.Am.* military uprising
cuartilla *f* sheet of paper
cuarto 1 *adj* fourth **2** *m* (*habitación*) room; (*parte*) quarter; ***cuarto de baño*** bathroom; ***cuarto de estar*** living room; ***cuarto de hora*** quarter of an hour; ***cuarto de kilo*** quarter of a kilo; ***de tres al cuarto*** F third-rate; ***las diez y cuarto*** quarter past ten, quarter after ten; ***las tres menos cuarto*** a quarter to *o* of three
cuarzo *m* quartz
cuatro *adj* four; ***cuatro gotas*** F a few drops
cuatrocientos *adj* four hundred
cuba *f*: ***estar como una cuba*** F be plastered F
Cuba Cuba
cubano 1 *adj* Cuban **2** *m*, **-a** *f* Cuban
cubierta *f* MAR deck; AUTO tire, *Br* tyre
cubierto 1 *part* → ***cubrir*** **2** *m* piece of cutlery; *en la mesa* place setting; ***cubiertos*** *pl* cutlery *sg*
cubito *m*: ***cubito de hielo*** ice cube
cubo *m* cube; *recipiente* bucket; ***cubo de la basura*** *dentro* garbage can, *Br* rubbish bin; *fuera* garbage can, *Br* dustbin
cubrir ⟨3a; *part* ***cubierto***⟩ **1** *v/t* cover (***de*** with) **2** *v/r* **cubrirse** cover o.s.
cucaracha *f* ZO cockroach
cuchara *f* spoon; ***meter su cuchara*** *L.Am.* F stick one's oar in F
cucharada *f* spoonful
cucharilla *f* teaspoon
cucharón *m* ladle
cuchichear ⟨1a⟩ *v/i* whisper
cuchilla *f* razor blade
cuchillo *m* knife
cuclillas: ***en cuclillas*** squatting
cuco 1 *m* ZO cuckoo; ***reloj de cuco*** cuckoo clock **2** *adj* (*astuto*) sharp
cucurucho *m de papel etc* cone; *sombrero* pointed hat
cuece *vb* → ***cocer***
cuelgo *vb* → ***colgar***
cuello *m* ANAT neck; *de camisa etc* collar
cuelo *vb* → ***colar***
cuenca *f* GEOG basin
cuenco *m* bowl
cuenta *f* (*cálculo*) sum; *de restaurante* check, *Br* bill; COM account; ***cuenta atrás*** countdown; ***cuenta bancaria*** bank account; ***cuenta corriente*** checking account, *Br* current account; ***más de la cuenta*** too much; ***caer en la cuenta*** realize; ***darse cuenta de algo*** realize sth; ***pedir cuentas a alguien*** ask s.o. for an explanation; ***perder la cuenta*** lose count; ***tener*** *or* ***tomar en cuenta*** take into account; ***corre por mi / su cuenta*** I'll / he'll pay for it
cuentagotas *m inv* dropper
cuentakilómetros *m inv* odometer, *Br* mileometer
cuentista *m/f* story-teller; F (*mentiroso*) fibber F
cuento *m* (short) story; (*pretexto*) excuse; ***cuento chino*** F tall story F; ***venir a cuento*** be relevant

C

cuerda *f* rope; *de guitarra, violín* string; ***dar cuerda al reloj*** wind the clock up; ***dar cuerda a algo*** *fig* F string sth out F; ***cuerdas vocales*** ANAT vocal chords
cuerdo *adj* sane; (*sensato*) sensible
cuerno *m* horn; *de caracol* feeler; ***irse al cuerno*** F fall through, be wrecked; ***poner los cuernos a alguien*** F be unfaithful to s.o.
cuero *m* leather; *Rpl* (*fuete*) whip; ***en cueros*** F naked
cuerpo *m* body; *de policía* force; ***cuerpo diplomático*** diplomatic corps *sg*; ***a cuerpo de rey*** like a king; ***en cuerpo y alma*** body and soul
cuervo *m* ZO raven, crow
cuesta *f* slope; ***cuesta abajo*** downhill; ***cuesta arriba*** uphill; ***a cuestas*** on one's back
cuestión *f* question; (*asunto*) matter, question; ***en cuestión de …*** in a matter of …
cuestionar ⟨1a⟩ *v/t* question
cuestionario *m* questionnaire
cueva *f* cave
cuidado *m* care; ***¡cuidado!*** look out!; ***andar con cuidado*** tread carefully; ***me tiene sin cuidado*** I could *o Br* couldn't care less; ***tener cuidado*** be careful
cuidadora *f Méx* nursemaid
cuidadoso *adj* careful
cuidar ⟨1a⟩ **1** *v/t* look after, take care of **2** *v/i*: ***cuidar de*** look after, take care of **3** *v/r* **cuidarse** look after o.s., take care of o.s.; ***cuidarse de hacer algo*** take care to do sth
culebra *f* ZO snake
culebrón *m* TV soap
culinario *adj* cooking *atr*, culinary
culminación *f* culmination
culminante *adj*: ***punto culminante*** peak, climax
culminar ⟨1a⟩ **1** *v/i* culminate (**en** in); *fig* reach a peak *o* climax **2** *v/t* finish
culo *m* V ass V, *Br* arse V; F butt F, *Br* bum F; ***ser culo de mal asiento*** *fig* F be restless, have ants in one's pants F
culpa *f* fault; ***echar la culpa de algo a alguien*** blame s.o. for sth; ***ser por culpa de alguien*** be s.o.'s fault; ***tener la culpa*** be to blame (***de*** for)
culpabilidad *f* guilt
culpable **1** *adj* guilty **2** *m/f* culprit
culpar ⟨1a⟩ *v/t*: ***culpar a alguien de algo*** blame s.o. for sth
cultivar ⟨1a⟩ *v/t* AGR grow; *tierra* farm; *fig* cultivate
cultivo *m* AGR crop; BIO culture
culto **1** *adj* educated **2** *m* worship
cultura *f* culture
cultural *adj* cultural; ***un nivel cultural muy pobre*** a very poor standard of education
cumbre *f tb* POL summit
cumpleaños *m inv* birthday
cumplido *m* compliment; ***no andarse con cumplidos*** not stand on ceremony
cumplimentar ⟨1k⟩ *v/t trámite* carry out
cumplir ⟨3a⟩ **1** *v/t orden* carry out; *promesa* fulfill; *condena* serve; ***cumplir diez años*** reach the age of ten, turn ten **2** *v/i*: ***cumplir con algo*** carry sth out; ***cumplir con su deber*** do one's duty; ***te invita sólo por cumplir*** he's only inviting you out of politeness **3** *v/r* **cumplirse** *de plazo* expire
cúmulo *m* (*montón*) pile, heap
cuna *f tb fig* cradle
cundir ⟨3a⟩ *v/i* spread; (*dar mucho de sí*) go a long way
cuneta *f* ditch
cuñada *f* sister-in-law
cuñado *m* brother-in-law
cuota *f* share; *de club, asociación* fee
cupón *m* coupon
cúpula *f* dome; *esp* POL leadership
cura **1** *m* priest **2** *f* cure; (*tratamiento*) treatment; *Méx, C.Am.* F hangover; ***tener cura*** be curable
curado *adj Méx, C.Am.* F drunk
curandero *m*, **-a** *f* faith healer
curar ⟨1a⟩ **1** *v/t tb* GASTR cure; (*tratar*) treat; *herida* dress; *pieles* tan **2** *v/i* MED recover (**de** from) **3** *v/r* **curarse** MED recover; *Méx, C.Am.* F get drunk
curda *f*: ***agarrarse una curda*** F get plastered F
curiosidad *f* curiosity
curioso **1** *adj* curious; (*raro*) curious, odd, strange **2** *m*, **-a** *f* onlooker
curita *f L.Am.* Band-Aid®, *Br* Elastoplast®
currar ⟨1a⟩ *v/i* F work
currículum vitae *m* résumé, *Br* CV, *Br* curriculum vitae
curry *m* GASTR curry
cursi *adj* F *persona* affected
cursillo *m* short course
cursiva *f* italics *pl*
curso *m* course; ***curso a distancia*** *or* ***por correspondencia*** correspondence course; ***en el curso de*** in the course of
cursor *m* INFOR cursor
curtir ⟨3a⟩ *v/t* tan; *fig* harden
curva *f* curve
curvo *adj* curved
cúspide *f de montaña* summit; *de fama etc* height

custodia *f* JUR custody
custodiar ⟨1b⟩ *v/t* guard
cususa *f C.Am.* corn liquor
cutre *adj* F shabby, dingy
cuyo, -a *adj* whose
CV *m* resumé, *Br* CV

D

D. *abr* (= ***Don***) Mr
Dª. *abr* (= ***Doña***) Mrs
dactilar *adj* finger *atr*
dadivoso *adj* generous
dado[1] *m* dice
dado[2] **1** *part* → ***dar*** **2** *adj* given; ***ser dado a algo*** be given to sth **3** *conj*: ***dado que*** since, given that
dalia *f* BOT dahlia
daltónico *adj* colo(u)r-blind
daltonismo *m* colo(u)r-blindness
dama *f* lady; ***dama de honor*** bridesmaid; (***juego de***) ***damas*** checkers *sg*, *Br* draughts *sg*
damasco *m* damask; *L.Am. fruta* apricot
damnificado 1 *adj* affected **2** *m*, **-a** *f* victim
danés 1 *adj* Danish **2** *m*, **-esa** *f* Dane
danza *f* dance
danzar ⟨1f⟩ *v/i* dance
dañar ⟨1a⟩ **1** *v/t* harm; *cosa* damage **2** *v/r* **dañarse** harm o.s.; *de un objeto* get damaged
dañino *adj* harmful; *fig* malicious
daño *m* harm; *a un objeto* damage; ***hacer daño*** hurt; ***daños*** *pl* damage *sg*; ***daños y perjuicios*** damages
dar ⟨1r; *part* ***dado*** ⟩ **1** *v/t* give; *beneficio* yield; *luz* give off; *fiesta* give, have; ***dar un golpe a*** hit; ***dar un salto / una patada / miedo*** jump / kick / frighten; ***el jamón me dió sed*** the ham made me thirsty **2** *v/i*: ***dame*** give it to me, give me it; ***dar a*** *de ventana* look onto; ***dar con algo*** come across sth; ***dar de comer a alguien*** feed s.o.; ***dar de beber a alguien*** give s.o. something to drink; ***dar de sí*** *de material* stretch, give; ***le dio por insultar a su madre*** F she started insulting her mother; ***¡qué más da!*** what does it matter!; ***da igual*** it doesn't matter **3** *v/r* **darse** *de una situación* arise; ***darse a algo*** take to sth; ***esto se me da bien*** I'm good at this; ***dárselas de algo*** make o.s. out to be sth, claim to be sth
dardo *m* dart
datar ⟨1a⟩ *v/i*: ***datar de*** date from
dátil *m* BOT date
dato *m* piece of information; ***datos*** *pl* information *sg*, data *sg*; ***datos personales*** personal details
D.C. *abr* (= ***después de Cristo***) AD (= Anno Domini)
dcho, dcha *abr* (= ***derecho, derecha***) r (= right)
d. de J.C. *abr* (= ***después de Jesucristo***) AD (= Anno Domini)
de *prp* ◇ *origen* from; ***de Nueva York*** from New York; ***de … a*** from … to
◇ *posesión* of; ***el coche de mi amigo*** my friend's car
◇ *material* (made) of; ***un anillo de oro*** a gold ring
◇ *contenido* of; ***un vaso de agua*** a glass of water
◇ *cualidad*: ***una mujer de 20 años*** a 20 year old woman
◇ *causa* with; ***temblaba de miedo*** she was shaking with fear
◇ *hora*: ***de noche*** at night, by night; ***de día*** by day
◇ *en calidad de* as; ***trabajar de albañil*** work as a bricklayer
◇ *agente* by; ***de Goya*** by Goya
◇ *condición* if; ***de haberlo sabido*** if I'd known
dé *vb* → ***dar***
deambular ⟨1a⟩ *v/i* wander around
debajo 1 *adv* underneath **2** *prp*: (***por***) ***debajo de*** under; ***un grado por debajo de lo normal*** one degree below normal
debate *m* debate, discussion
debatir ⟨3a⟩ **1** *v/t* debate, discuss **2** *v/i* struggle **3** *v/r* **debatirse**: ***debatirse entre la vida y la muerte*** fight for one's life
deber 1 *m* duty; ***deberes*** *pl* homework *sg* **2** ⟨2a⟩ *v/t* owe **3** *v/i en presente* must, have to; *en pretérito* should have; *en futuro* (will) have to; *en condicional* should; ***debe de tener quince años*** he must be about 15 **4** *v/r* **deberse**: ***deberse a*** be due to, be caused by

D

debido 1 *part* → ***deber* 2** *adj*: ***como es debido*** properly; ***debido a*** owing to, on account of
débil *adj* weak
debilitar ⟨1a⟩ **1** *v/t* weaken **2** *v/r* **debilitarse** weaken, become weak; *de salud* deteriorate
debut *m* debut
década *f* decade
decadencia *f* decadence; *de un imperio* decline
decaer ⟨2o; *part* ***decaido*** ⟩ *v/i tb fig* decline; *de rendimiento* fall off, decline; *de salud* deteriorate
decaído 1 *part* → ***decaer* 2** *adj fig* depressed, down F
decantarse ⟨1a⟩ *v/r*: ***decantarse por*** opt for
decapitar ⟨1a⟩ *v/t* behead, decapitate
decenio *m* decade
decente *adj* decent
decepción *f* disappointment
decepcionado *adj* disappointed
decepcionante *adj* disappointing
decepcionar ⟨1a⟩ *v/t* disappoint
decidido 1 *part* → ***decidir* 2** *adj* decisive; ***estar decidido*** be determined (***a*** to)
decidir ⟨3a⟩ **1** *v/t* decide **2** *v/r* **decidirse** make up one's mind, decide
decimal *adj* decimal *atr*
décimo 1 *adj* tenth **2** *m de lotería share of a lottery ticket*
decir ⟨3p; *part* ***dicho*** ⟩ **1** *v/t* say; (*contar*) tell; ***querer decir*** mean; ***decir que sí*** say yes; ***decir que no*** say no; ***es decir*** in other words; ***no es rico, que digamos*** let's say he's not rich; ***¡no me digas!*** you're kidding!; ***¡quién lo diría!*** who would believe it!; ***se dice que …*** they say that …, it's said that … **2** *v/i*: ***¡diga!, ¡dígame!*** *Esp* TELEC hello
decisión *f* decision; *fig* decisiveness
decisivo *adj* critical, decisive
declaración *f* declaration; ***declaración de la renta*** *or* ***de impuestos*** tax return; ***prestar declaración*** JUR testify, give evidence
declarar ⟨1a⟩ **1** *v/t* state; *bienes* declare; ***declarar culpable*** find guilty **2** *v/i* JUR give evidence **3** *v/r* **declararse** declare o.s.; *de incendio* break out; ***declararse a alguien*** declare one's love for s.o.
declinar ⟨1a⟩ *v/t & v/i* decline
declive *m fig* decline; ***en declive*** in decline
decodificador *m* → ***descodificador***
decodificar ⟨1g⟩ *v/t* → ***descodificar***
decolaje *m L.Am.* takeoff
decolar ⟨1a⟩ *v/i L.Am.* take off
decolorar ⟨1a⟩ *v/t* bleach
decoración *f* decoration
decorado *m* TEA set
decorador *m*, **decoradora** *f*: ***decorador*** (***de interiores***) interior decorator
decorar ⟨1a⟩ *v/t* decorate
decorativo *adj* decorative
decreciente *adj* decreasing, diminishing
decrépito *adj* decrepit
decretar ⟨1a⟩ *v/t* order, decree
decreto *m* decree
dedicación *f* dedication
dedicar ⟨1g⟩ **1** *v/t* dedicate; *esfuerzo* devote **2** *v/r* **dedicarse** devote o.s. (***a*** to); ***¿a qué se dedica?*** what do you do (for a living)?
dedicatoria *f* dedication
dedillo *m*: ***conocer algo al dedillo*** F know sth like the back of one's hand; ***saber algo al dedillo*** F know sth off by heart
dedo *m* finger; ***dedo del pie*** toe; ***dedo gordo*** thumb; ***dedo índice*** forefinger; ***no tiene dos dedos de frente*** F he doesn't have much commonsense
deducción *f* deduction
deducir ⟨3o⟩ *v/t* deduce; COM deduct
defecar ⟨1g⟩ *v/i* defecate
defecto *m* defect; *moral* fault; INFOR default
defectuoso *adj* defective, faulty
defender ⟨2g⟩ **1** *v/t* defend **2** *v/r* **defenderse** defend o.s. (***de*** against); *fig* F manage, get by; ***defenderse del frío*** ward off the cold
defenestrar ⟨1a⟩ *v/t fig* F oust
defensa 1 *f* JUR, DEP defense, *Br* defence; *L.Am.* AUTO fender, *Br* bumper; ***defensas*** MED defenses, *Br* defences **2** *m/f* DEP defender
defensivo *adj* defensive
defensor *m*, **defensora** *f* defender, champion; JUR defense counsel, *Br* defending counsel; ***defensor del pueblo*** *en España* ombudsman
deficiente 1 *adj* deficient; (*insatisfactorio*) inadequate **2** *m/f* handicapped person
déficit *m* deficit
definición *f* definition; ***de alta definición*** TV high definition
definir ⟨3a⟩ **1** *v/t* define **2** *v/r* **definirse** come down (***por*** in favor of)
definitivo *adj* definitive; *respuesta* definite; ***en -a*** all in all
deforestación *f* deforestation
deformar ⟨1a⟩ *v/t* distort; MED deform
deforme *adj* deformed
defraudar ⟨1a⟩ *v/t* disappoint; (*estafar*)

defraud; ***defraudar a Hacienda*** evade taxes
defunción *f* death, demise *fml*
degenerar ⟨1a⟩ *v/i* degenerate (***en*** into)
degollar ⟨1n⟩ *v/t* cut the throat of
degradante *adj* degrading
degradar ⟨1a⟩ **1** *v/t* degrade; MIL demote; PINT gradate **2** *v/r* **degradarse** demean o.s.
degustar ⟨1a⟩ *v/t* taste
dejadez *f* slovenliness; (*negligencia*) neglect
dejar ⟨1a⟩ **1** *v/t* leave; (*permitir*) let, allow; (*prestar*) lend; *beneficios* yield; ***déjame en la esquina*** drop me at the corner; ***dejar para mañana*** leave until tomorrow; ***dejar caer algo*** drop sth **2** *v/i*: ***dejar de hacer algo*** (*parar*) stop doing sth; ***no deja de fastidiarme*** he keeps (on) annoying me **3** *v/r* **dejarse** let o.s. go; ***dejarse llevar*** let o.s. be carried along
del *prp* ***de*** *y art* ***el***
delantal *m* apron
delante *adv* in front; (*más avanzado*) ahead; (*enfrente*) opposite; ***por delante*** ahead; ***se abrocha por delante*** it does up at the front; ***tener algo por delante*** have sth ahead of *o* in front of one; ***delante de*** in front of; ***el asiento de delante*** the front seat
delantera *f* DEP forward line; ***llevar la delantera*** be ahead of, lead
delantero *m*, **-a** *f* DEP forward
delatar ⟨1a⟩ *v/t*: ***delatar a alguien*** inform on s.o.; *fig* give s.o. away
delegación *f* delegation; (*oficina*) local office; ***delegación de Hacienda*** tax office
delegado *m*, **-a** *f* delegate; COM representative
delegar ⟨1h⟩ *v/t* delegate
deleitar ⟨1a⟩ **1** *v/t* delight **2** *v/r* **deleitarse** take delight
deletrear ⟨1a⟩ *v/t* spell
delfín *m* ZO dolphin
delgado *adj* slim; *lámina*, *placa* thin
deliberado *adj* deliberate
deliberar ⟨1a⟩ *v/i* deliberate (***sobre*** on)
delicadeza *f* gentleness; *de acabado*, *tallado* delicacy; (*tacto*) tact
delicado *adj* delicate
delicia *f* delight; ***hacer las delicias de alguien*** delight s.o.
delicioso *adj* delightful; *comida* delicious
delimitar ⟨1a⟩ *v/t* delimit
delincuente *m/f* criminal
delineante *m/f* draftsman, *Br* draughtsman; *mujer* draftswoman, *Br* draughtswoman
delinear ⟨1a⟩ *v/t* draft; *fig* draw up
delirar ⟨1a⟩ *v/i* be delirious; ***¡tú deliras!*** *fig* you must be crazy!
delirio *m* MED delirium; ***tener delirio por el fútbol*** *fig* be mad about soccer; ***delirios de grandeza*** delusions of grandeur
delito *m* offense, *Br* offence
demacrado *adj* haggard
demagógico *adj* demagogic
demanda *f* demand (***de*** for); JUR lawsuit, claim
demandar ⟨1a⟩ *v/t* JUR sue
demás **1** *adj* remaining **2** *adv*: ***lo demás*** the rest; ***los demás*** the rest, the others; ***por lo demás*** apart from that
demasiado **1** *adj* too much; *antes de pl* too many; ***demasiada gente*** too many people; ***hace demasiado calor*** it's too hot **2** *adv antes de adj*, *adv* too; *con verbo* too much
demencia *f* MED dementia; *fig* madness; ***demencia senil*** MED senile dementia
demencial *adj fig* crazy, mad
demente **1** *adj* demented, crazy **2** *m/f* mad person
democracia *f* democracy
demócrata **1** *adj* democratic **2** *m/f* democrat
democrático *adj* democratic
demografía *f* demographics
demoler ⟨2h⟩ *v/t* demolish
demoniaco, **demoníaco** *adj* demonic
demonio *m* demon; ***¡demonios!*** F hell! F, damn! F
demora *f* delay; ***sin demora*** without delay
demorar ⟨1a⟩ **1** *v/i* stay on; *L.Am.* (*tardar*) be late; ***no demores*** don't be long **2** *v/t* delay **3** *v/r* **demorarse** be delayed; ***¿cuánto se demora de Concepción a Santiago?*** how long does it take to get from Concepción to Santiago?
demostración *f* proof; *de método* demonstration; *de fuerza*, *sentimiento* show
demostrar ⟨1m⟩ *v/t* prove; (*enseñar*) demonstrate; (*mostrar*) show
denegar ⟨1h & 1k⟩ *v/t* refuse
denigrante *adj* degrading; *artículo* denigrating
denigrar ⟨1a⟩ *v/t* degrade; (*criticar*) denigrate
denominación *f* name; ***denominación de origen*** *guarantee of quality of a wine*
denominador *m*: ***denominador común*** *fig* common denominator
denominar ⟨1a⟩ **1** *v/t* designate **2** *v/r* **denominarse** be called
denotar ⟨1a⟩ *v/t* show, indicate
densidad *f* density

D

D

denso *adj bosque* dense; *fig* weighty
dentadura *f*: ***dentadura postiza*** false teeth *pl*, dentures *pl*
dental *adj* dental
dentera *f*: ***darle dentera a alguien*** set s.o.'s teeth on edge
dentífrico *m* toothpaste
dentista *m/f* dentist
dentro 1 *adv* inside; ***por dentro*** inside; ***de dentro*** from inside **2 *dentro de*** *en espacio* in, inside; *en tiempo* in, within
denuncia *f* report; ***poner una denuncia*** make a formal complaint
denunciar ⟨1b⟩ *v/t* report; *fig* condemn, denounce
departamento *m* department; *L.Am.* (*apartamento*) apartment, *Br* flat
depender ⟨2a⟩ *v/i* depend (***de*** on); ***depender de alguien*** *en una jerarquía* report to s.o.; ***eso depende*** that all depends
dependiente 1 *adj* dependent **2** *m*, **-a** *f* sales clerk, *Br* shop assistant
depilación *f* hair removal; *con cera* waxing; *con pinzas* plucking
depilar ⟨1a⟩ *v/t con cera* wax; *con pinzas* pluck
deplorar ⟨1a⟩ *v/t* deplore
deportar ⟨1a⟩ *v/t* deport
deporte *m* sport
deportista *m/f* sportsman; *mujer* sportswoman
depositar ⟨1a⟩ *v/t tb fig* put, place; *dinero* deposit (***en*** in)
depósito *m* COM deposit; (*almacén*) store; *de agua*, AUTO tank; ***depósito de cadáveres*** morgue, *Br* mortuary
depravado *adj* depraved
depravar ⟨1a⟩ *v/t* deprave
depreciación *f* depreciation
depreciar ⟨1b⟩ **1** *v/t* lower the value of **2** *v/r* **depreciarse** depreciate, lose value
depredador 1 *adj* predatory **2** *m* ZO predator
depresión *f* MED depression
deprimente *adj* depressing
deprimir ⟨3a⟩ **1** *v/t* depress **2** *v/r* **deprimirse** get depressed
depuradora *f* purifier
depurar ⟨1a⟩ *v/t* purify; *agua* treat; POL purge
derecha *f tb* POL right; ***la derecha*** the right(-hand); ***a la derecha*** *posición* on the right; *dirección* to the right
derecho 1 *adj lado* right; (*recto*) straight; *C.Am. fig* straight, honest **2** *adv* straight **3** *m* (*privilegio*) right; JUR law; ***del derecho*** on the right side; ***derecho de asilo*** right to asylum; ***derechos de autor*** royalties; ***derechos humanos*** human rights; ***derecho de voto*** right to vote; ***no hay derecho*** it's not fair, it's not right; ***tener derecho a*** have a right to **4** *mpl*: ***derechos*** fees; ***derechos de inscripción*** registration fee *sg*
derechura *f* straightness; *C.Am.*, *Pe* (*suerte*) luck; ***en derechura*** straight away
deriva *f*: ***ir a la deriva*** MAR, *fig* drift
derivar ⟨1a⟩ **1** *v/i* derive (***de*** from); *de barco* drift **2** *v/r* **derivarse** be derived (***de*** from)
dermatólogo *m*, **-a** *f* dermatologist
derogar ⟨1h⟩ *v/t* repeal
derramar ⟨1a⟩ **1** *v/t* spill; *luz*, *sangre* shed; (*esparcir*) scatter **2** *v/r* **derramarse** spill; *de gente* scatter
derrame *m* MED: ***derrame cerebral*** stroke
derrapar ⟨1a⟩ *v/i* AUTO skid
derrengado *adj* exhausted
derretir ⟨3l⟩ **1** *v/t* melt **2** *v/r* **derretirse** melt; *fig* be besotted (***por*** with)
derribar ⟨1a⟩ *v/t edificio*, *persona* knock down; *avión* shoot down; POL bring down
derrocar ⟨1g⟩ *v/t* POL overthrow
derrochador *m*, **derrochadora** *f* spendthrift
derrochar ⟨1a⟩ *v/t* waste; *salud*, *felicidad* exude, burst with
derroche *m* waste
derrota *f* defeat
derrotar ⟨1a⟩ *v/t* MIL defeat; DEP beat, defeat
derruir ⟨3g⟩ *v/t edificio* demolish
derrumbar ⟨1a⟩ **1** *v/t* knock down **2** *v/r* **derrumbarse** collapse, fall down; *de una persona* go to pieces
desabrido *adj* (*soso*) tasteless; *persona* surly; *tiempo* unpleasant
desabrochar ⟨1a⟩ *v/t* undo, unfasten
desacato *m* JUR contempt
desaceleración *f* deceleration
desacertado *adj* misguided
desaconsejar ⟨1a⟩ *v/t* advise against
desacreditado *adj* discredited
desacreditar ⟨1a⟩ *v/t* discredit
desactivar ⟨1a⟩ *v/t bomba etc* deactivate
desacuerdo *m* disagreement; ***estar en desacuerdo con*** disagree with
desafiar ⟨1c⟩ *v/t* challenge; *peligro* defy
desafinar ⟨1a⟩ *v/i* MÚS be out of tune
desafío *m* challenge; *al peligro* defiance
desafortunado *adj* unfortunate, unlucky
desagradable *adj* unpleasant, disagreeable
desagradar ⟨1a⟩ *v/i*: ***me desagrada tener que …*** I dislike having to …
desagradecido *adj* ungrateful; ***una tarea -a*** a thankless task

desagrado *m* displeasure
desagravio *m* apology
desagüe *m* drain; *acción* drainage; (*cañería*) drainpipe
desahogar ⟨1h⟩ **1** *v/t sentimiento* vent **2** *v/r* **desahogarse** *fig* F let off steam F, get it out of one's system F
desahogo *m* comfort; ***con desahogo*** comfortably
desahuciar ⟨1b⟩ *v/t*: ***desahuciar a alguien*** declare s.o. terminally ill; (*inquilino*) evict s.o.
desairar ⟨1a⟩ *v/t* snub
desajustar ⟨1a⟩ *v/t tornillo, pieza* loosen; *mecanismo, instrumento* affect, throw out of balance
desajuste *m* disruption; COM imbalance
desalentar ⟨1k⟩ *v/t* discourage
desaliento *m* discouragement
desalinización *f* desalination
desaliñado *adj* slovenly
desalojar ⟨1a⟩ *v/t ante peligro* evacuate; (*desahuciar*) evict; (*vaciar*) vacate
desamparar ⟨1a⟩ *v/t*: ***desamparar a alguien*** abandon s.o.
desangelado *adj lugar* soulless
desangrarse ⟨1a⟩ *v/r* bleed to death
desanimar ⟨1a⟩ **1** *v/t* discourage, dishearten **2** *v/r* **desanimarse** become discouraged *o* disheartened
desánimo *m* discouragement
desapacible *adj* nasty, unpleasant
desaparecer ⟨2d⟩ **1** *v/i* disappear, vanish **2** *v/t L.Am.* disappear F
desaparecido *m*, **-a** *f L.Am.*: ***un desaparecido*** one of the disappeared
desaparición *f* disappearance
desapego *m* indifference; (*distancia*) distance, coolness
desapercibido *adj* unnoticed; ***pasar desapercibido*** go unnoticed
desaprensivo *adj* unscrupulous
desaprobar ⟨1m⟩ *v/t* disapprove of
desaprovechar ⟨1a⟩ *v/t oportunidad* waste
desarmado *adj* unarmed
desarmar ⟨1a⟩ *v/t* MIL disarm; TÉC take to pieces, dismantle
desarme *m* MIL disarmament
desarraigo *m fig* rootlessness
desarreglar ⟨1a⟩ *v/t* make untidy; *horario* disrupt
desarrollar ⟨1a⟩ **1** *v/t* develop; *tema* explain; *trabajo* carry out **2** *v/r* **desarrollarse** develop, evolve; (*ocurrir*) take place
desarrollo *m* development
desarticular ⟨1a⟩ *v/t banda criminal* break up; MED dislocate
desaseado *adj* F scruffy
desasirse ⟨3a⟩ *v/r* get free, free o.s.
desasosiego *m* disquiet, unease
desastre *m tb fig* disaster
desastroso *adj* disastrous
desatar ⟨1a⟩ **1** *v/t* untie; *fig* unleash **2** *v/r* **desatarse** *de animal, persona* get free; *de cordón* come undone; *fig* be unleashed, break out
desatascar ⟨1g⟩ *v/t* unblock
desatender ⟨2g⟩ *v/t* neglect; (*ignorar*) ignore
desatino *m* mistake
desatornillador *m esp L.Am.* screwdriver
desatornillar ⟨1a⟩ *v/t* unscrew
desatrancar ⟨1g⟩ *v/t cañería* unblock
desavenencia *f* disagreement
desaventajado *adj* unfavo(u)rable
desayunar ⟨1a⟩ **1** *v/i* have breakfast **2** *v/t*: ***desayunar algo*** have sth for breakfast
desayuno *m* breakfast
desazón *f* (*ansiedad*) uneasiness, anxiety
desazonar ⟨1a⟩ *v/t* worry, make anxious
desbancar ⟨1g⟩ *v/t fig* displace, take the place of
desbandarse ⟨1a⟩ *v/r* disband; *de un grupo de personas* scatter
desbarajuste *m* mess
desbaratar ⟨1a⟩ *planes* ruin; *organización* disrupt
desbarrancar ⟨1g⟩ *L.Am.* **1** *v/t* push over the edge of a cliff **2** *v/r* **desbarrancarse** go over the edge of a cliff
desbocarse ⟨1g⟩ *v/r de un caballo* bolt
desbordante *adj energía, entusiasmo etc* boundless; ***desbordante de*** bursting with, overflowing with
desbordar ⟨1a⟩ **1** *v/t de un río* overflow, burst; *de un multitud* break through; *de un acontecimiento* overwhelm; *fig* exceed **2** *v/i* overflow **3** *v/r* **desbordarse** *de un río* burst its banks, overflow; *fig* get out of control
descabellado *adj*: ***idea -a*** F hare-brained idea F
descabellar ⟨1a⟩ *v/t* TAUR *kill with a knife-thrust in the neck*
descabello *m fatal knife thrust*
descafeinado *adj* decaffeinated; *fig* watered-down
descalabro *m* calamity, disaster
descalificar ⟨1g⟩ *v/t* disqualify
descalzarse ⟨1f⟩ *v/r* take one's shoes off
descalzo *adj* barefoot
descaminado *adj fig* misguided; ***andar*** *or* ***ir descaminado*** be on the wrong track
descamisado *adj* shirtless; *fig* ragged
descampado *m* open ground
descansar ⟨1a⟩ *v/i* rest, have a rest; ***¡que descanses!*** sleep well

D

descansillo *m* landing
descanso *m* rest; DEP half-time; TEA interval; ***sin descanso*** without a break
descapotable *m* AUTO convertible
descarado *adj* rude, impertinent
descarga *f* EL, MIL discharge; *de mercancías* unloading
descargar ⟨1h⟩ *v/t arma*, EL discharge; *fig*: *ira etc* take out (***en, sobre*** on); *mercancías* unload; *de responsabilidad, culpa* clear (***de*** of)
descaro *m* nerve
descarriado *adj*: ***ir descarriado*** go astray
descarrilar ⟨1a⟩ *v/t* derail
descartar ⟨1a⟩ *v/t* rule out
descastado *adj* cold, uncaring
descender ⟨2g⟩ **1** *v/i para indicar alejamiento* go down, descend; *para indicar acercamiento* come down, descend; *fig* go down, decrease, diminish; ***descender de*** descend from **2** *v/t escalera* go down; *para indicar acercamiento* come down
descendiente **1** *adj* descended **2** *m/f* descendant
descenso *m de precio etc* drop; *de montaña*, AVIA descent; DEP relegation; ***la prueba de descenso*** *en esquí* the downhill (race *o* competition)
descentralizar ⟨1f⟩ *v/t* decentralize
descentrar ⟨1a⟩ *v/t fig* shake
descifrar ⟨1a⟩ *v/t* decipher; *fig* work out
descodificación *f* decoding
descodificador *m* decoder
descodificar ⟨1g⟩ *v/t* decode
descolgar ⟨1h & 1m⟩ **1** *v/t* take down; *teléfono* pick up **2** *v/r* **descolgarse** *por una cuerda* lower o.s.; *de un grupo* break away
descollar ⟨1m⟩ *v/i* stand out (***sobre*** among)
descolonización *f* decolonization
descolorido *adj* faded; *fig* colo(u)rless
descomponer ⟨2r; *part* ***descompuesto***⟩ **1** *v/t* (*dividir*) break down; (*pudrir*) cause to decompose; *L.Am.* (*romper*) break **2** *v/r* **descomponerse** (*pudrirse*) decompose, rot; TÉC break down; *Rpl* (*emocionarse*) break down (in tears); ***se le descompuso la cara*** he turned pale
descomposición *f* breaking down; *putrefacción* decomposition; (*diarrea*) diarrh(o)ea
descompuesto **1** *part* → ***descomponer*** **2** *adj alimento* rotten; *cadáver* decomposed; *persona* upset; *L.Am.* tipsy; *L.Am. máquina* broken down
descomunal *adj* huge, enormous
desconcertar ⟨1k⟩ *v/t a persona* disconcert
desconchado, **desconchón** *m place where the paint is peeling*; *en porcelana* chip
desconcierto *m* uncertainty
desconectar ⟨1a⟩ **1** *v/t* EL disconnect **2** *v/i fig* switch off **3** *v/r* **desconectarse** *fig* lose touch (***de*** with)
desconfiar ⟨1c⟩ *v/i* be mistrustful (***de*** of), be suspicious (***de*** of)
descongelar ⟨1a⟩ *v/t comida* thaw, defrost; *refrigerador* defrost; *precios* unfreeze
descongestionar ⟨1a⟩ *v/t* MED clear; ***descongestionar el tráfico*** relieve traffic congestion
desconocer ⟨2d⟩ *v/t* not know
desconocido **1** *adj* unknown **2** *m*, **-a** *f* stranger
desconsiderado *adj* inconsiderate
desconsolado *adj* inconsolable
desconsuelo *m* grief
descontado **1** *part* → ***descontar*** **2** *adj*: ***dar por descontado*** take for granted; ***por descontado*** certainly
descontaminar ⟨1a⟩ *v/t* decontaminate
descontar ⟨1m⟩ *v/t* COM deduct, take off; *fig* exclude
descontento **1** *adj* dissatisfied **2** *m* dissatisfaction
descontrol *m* chaos
descontrolarse ⟨1a⟩ *v/r* get out of control
desconvocar ⟨1g⟩ *v/t* call off
descorazonar ⟨1a⟩ **1** *v/t* discourage **2** *v/r* **descorazonarse** get discouraged
descorchar ⟨1a⟩ *v/t botella* uncork
descortés *adj* impolite, rude
descoserse ⟨2a⟩ *v/r de costura, dobladillo etc* come unstitched; *de prenda* come apart at the seams
descosido *m*: ***como un descosido*** F like mad F
descoyuntar ⟨1a⟩ *v/t* dislocate
descremado *adj* skimmed
describir ⟨3a; *part* ***descrito***⟩ *v/t* describe
descripción *f* description
descrito *part* → ***describir***
descuajaringarse ⟨1h⟩ *v/r* F fall apart, fall to bits
descuartizar ⟨1f⟩ *v/t* quarter
descubierto **1** *part* → ***descubrir*** **2** *adj* uncovered; *persona* bareheaded; *cielos* clear; *piscina* open-air; ***al descubierto*** in the open; ***quedar al descubierto*** be exposed **3** *m* COM overdraft
descubrimiento *m* discovery; (*revelación*) revelation
descubrir ⟨3a; *part* ***descubierto***⟩ **1** *v/t* discover; *poner de manifiesto* uncover, reveal; *estatua* unveil **2** *v/r* **descubrirse**

take one's hat off; *fig* give o.s. away
descuento *m* discount; DEP stoppage time
descuerar ⟨1a⟩ *v/t L.Am.* skin; ***descuerar a alguien*** *fig* tear s.o. to pieces
descuidado *adj* careless
descuidar ⟨1a⟩ **1** *v/t* neglect **2** *v/i*: ***¡descuida!*** don't worry! **3** *v/r* **descuidarse** get careless; *en cuanto al aseo* let o.s. go; (*despistarse*) let one's concentration drop
descuido *m* carelessness; (*error*) mistake; (*omisión*) oversight; ***en un descuido*** *L.Am.* in a moment of carelessness
desde 1 *prp en el tiempo* since; *en el espacio* from; *en escala* from; ***desde 1993*** since 1993; ***desde hace tres días*** for three days; ***desde ... hasta ...*** from ... to ... **2** *adv*: ***desde luego*** of course; ***desde ya*** *Rpl* right away
desdén *m* disdain, contempt
desdeñable *adj* contemptible; ***nada desdeñable*** far from insignificant
desdeñar ⟨1a⟩ *v/t* scorn
desdibujado *adj* blurred
desdichado 1 *adj* unhappy; (*sin suerte*) unlucky **2** *m*, **-a** *f* poor soul
desdoblar ⟨1a⟩ *v/t* unfold; (*dividir*) split
desear ⟨1a⟩ *v/t* wish for; *suerte etc* wish; ***¿qué desea?*** what would you like?
desecar ⟨1g⟩ *v/t* dry
desechable *adj* disposable
desechar ⟨1a⟩ *v/t* (*tirar*) throw away; (*rechazar*) reject
desechos *mpl* waste *sg*
desembalar ⟨1a⟩ *v/t* unpack
desembarazarse ⟨1f⟩ *v/r*: ***desembarazarse de*** get rid of
desembarazo *m* ease
desembarcadero *m* MAR landing stage
desembarcar ⟨1g⟩ *v/i* disembark
desembocadura *f* mouth
desembocar ⟨1g⟩ *v/i* flow (***en*** into); *de calle* come out (***en*** into); *de situación* end (***en*** in)
desembolsar ⟨1a⟩ *v/t* pay out
desembuchar ⟨1a⟩ *v/i fig* F spill the beans F, come out with it F
desempacar ⟨1g⟩ *v/t* unpack
desempaquetar ⟨1a⟩ *v/t* unwrap
desempatar ⟨1a⟩ *v/i* DEP, POL decide the winner
desempeñar ⟨1a⟩ *v/t deber*, *tarea* carry out; *cargo* hold; *papel* play
desempleado 1 *adj* unemployed **2** *m*, **-a** *f* unemployed person
desempleo *m* unemployment
desencadenar ⟨1a⟩ **1** *v/t fig* trigger **2** *v/r* **desencadenarse** *fig* be triggered
desencajarse ⟨1a⟩ *v/r de una pieza* come out; ***se me ha desencajado la mandíbula*** I dislocated my jaw
desencantado *adj fig* disenchanted (***con*** with)
desencanto *m fig* disillusionment
desenchufar ⟨1a⟩ *v/t* EL unplug
desenfadado *adj* self-assured; *programa* light, undemanding
desenfocado *adj* FOT out of focus
desenfrenado *adj* frenzied, hectic
desenfreno *m* frenzy
desenfundar ⟨1a⟩ *v/t arma* take out, draw
desengañarse ⟨1a⟩ *v/r* become disillusioned (***de*** with); (*dejar de engañarse*) stop kidding o.s.
desengaño *m* disappointment
desenlace *m* outcome, ending
desenmascarar ⟨1a⟩ *v/t fig* unmask, expose
desenredar ⟨1a⟩ *v/t* untangle; *situación confusa* straighten out, sort out
desenrollar ⟨1a⟩ *v/t* unroll
desenroscar ⟨1g⟩ *v/t* unscrew
desentenderse ⟨2g⟩ *v/r* not want to know (***de*** about)
desentendido *adj*: ***hacerse el desentendido*** F pretend not to notice
desentonar ⟨1a⟩ *v/i* MÚS go off key; ***desentonar con*** *fig* clash with; ***decir algo que desentona*** say sth out of place
desentrañar ⟨1a⟩ *v/t fig* unravel
desenvoltura *f* ease
desenvolverse ⟨2h; *part* **desenvuelto** ⟩ *v/r fig* cope
desenvuelto 1 *part* → ***desenvolverse*** **2** *adj* self-confident
deseo *m* wish
desequilibrar ⟨1a⟩ *v/t* unbalance; ***desequilibrar a alguien*** throw s.o. off balance
desequilibrio *m* imbalance; ***desequilibrio mental*** mental instability
desertar ⟨1a⟩ *v/i* MIL desert
desertor *m*, **desertora** *f* deserter
desértico *adj* desert *atr*
desertización *f* desertification
desesperación *f* despair
desesperado *adj* in despair
desesperante *adj* infuriating, exasperating
desesperar ⟨1a⟩ **1** *v/t* infuriate, exasperate **2** *v/i* give up hope (***de*** of), despair (***de*** of) **3** *v/r* **desesperarse** get exasperated
desestabilizar ⟨1f⟩ *v/t* POL destabilize
desfachatez *f* impertinence
desfalco *m* embezzlement
desfallecer ⟨2d⟩ *v/i* faint
desfase *m fig* gap

D

desfavorable *adj* unfavo(u)rable
desfavorecer ⟨2d⟩ *v/t* (*no ser favorable*) not favo(u)r, be disadvantageous to; *de ropa etc* not suit
desfigurar ⟨1a⟩ *v/t* disfigure
desfiladero *m* ravine
desfilar ⟨1a⟩ *v/i* parade
desfile *m* parade; ***desfile de modelos*** *or* ***de modas*** fashion show
desfogarse ⟨1h⟩ *v/r fig* vent one's emotions
desforestación *f* deforestation
desgana *f* loss of appetite; ***con desgana*** *fig* reluctantly, half-heartedly
desgañitarse ⟨1a⟩ *v/r* F shout one's head off F
desgarbado *adj* F ungainly
desgarrador *adj* heartrending
desgarrar ⟨1a⟩ *v/t* tear up; *fig*: *corazón* break
desgastar ⟨1a⟩ *v/t* wear out; *defensas* wear down
desgaste *m* wear (and tear)
desglose *m* breakdown, itemization
desgracia *f* misfortune; *suceso* accident; ***por desgracia*** unfortunately
desgraciadamente *adv* unfortunately
desgraciado **1** *adj* unfortunate; (*miserable*) wretched **2** *m*, **-a** *f* wretch; (*sinvergüenza*) swine F
desgravar ⟨1a⟩ **1** *v/t* deduct **2** *v/i* be tax-deductible
desguazar ⟨1f⟩ *v/t* scrap
deshabitado *adj* uninhabited
deshacer ⟨2s; *part* ***deshecho*** ⟩ **1** *v/t* undo; *maleta* unpack; *planes* wreck, ruin; ***eso los obligó a deshacer todos sus planes*** this forced them to cancel their plans **2** *v/r* **deshacerse** *de nudo de corbata, lazo etc* come undone; *de hielo* melt; ***deshacerse de*** get rid of
deshecho **1** *part* → ***deshacer*** **2** *adj* F *anímicamente* devastated F; *de cansancio* beat F, exhausted
desheredar ⟨1a⟩ *v/t* disinherit
deshice *vb* → ***deshacer***
deshidratar ⟨1a⟩ *v/t* dehydrate
deshielo *m* thaw
deshinchar ⟨1a⟩ **1** *v/t globo* deflate, let down **2** *v/r* **deshincharse** deflate, go down; *fig* lose heart
deshonesto *adj* dishonest
deshonra *f* dishono(u)r
deshonroso *adj* dishono(u)rable
deshora *f*: ***a deshora*** (***s***) at the wrong time
desidia *f* apathy, lethargy
desierto **1** *adj lugar* empty, deserted; ***isla -a*** desert island **2** *m* desert
designar ⟨1a⟩ *v/t* appoint, name; *lugar* select
designio *m* plan
desigual *adj* unequal; *terreno* uneven, irregular
desigualdad *f* inequality
desilusión *f* disappointment
desilusionado *adj* disappointed
desilusionar ⟨1a⟩ **1** *v/t* disappoint; (*quitar la ilusión*) disillusion **2** *v/r* **desilusionarse** be disappointed; (*perder la ilusión*) become disillusioned
desinfectante *m* disinfectant
desinfectar ⟨1a⟩ *v/t* disinfect
desinflar ⟨1a⟩ **1** *v/t globo, neumático* let the air out of, deflate **2** *v/r* **desinflarse** *de neumático* deflate; *fig* lose heart
desinformación *f* disinformation
desinhibir ⟨3a⟩ **1** *v/t*: ***desinhibir alguien*** get rid of s.o.'s inhibitions **2** *v/r* **desinhibirse** lose one's inhibitions
desintegrar ⟨1a⟩ **1** *v/t* cause to disintegrate; *grupo de gente* break up **2** *v/r* **desintegrarse** disintegrate; *de grupo de gente* break up
desinterés *m* lack of interest; (*generosidad*) unselfishness
desinteresado *adj* unselfish
desintoxicación *f* detoxification; ***hacer una cura de desintoxicación*** go into detox F, have treatment for drug / alcohol abuse
desistir ⟨3a⟩ *v/i* give up; ***tuvo que desistir de hacerlo*** I had to stop doing it
deslealtad *f* disloyalty
desligar ⟨1h⟩ **1** *v/t* separate (***de*** from); *fig persona* cut off (***de*** from) **2** *v/r* **desligarse** *fig* cut o.s. off (***de*** from)
desliz *m fig* F slip-up F
deslizar ⟨1f⟩ **1** *v/t* slide, run (***por*** along); *idea, frase* slip in **2** *v/i* slide **3** *v/r* **deslizarse** slide
deslomarse ⟨1a⟩ *v/r fig* kill o.s.
deslucido *adj* tarnished; *colores* dull, drab
deslucir ⟨3f⟩ *v/t* tarnish; *fig* spoil
deslumbrante *adj* dazzling
deslumbrar ⟨1a⟩ **1** *v/t fig* dazzle **2** *v/r* **deslumbrarse** *fig* be dazzled
desmadre *m* F chaos
desmandarse ⟨1a⟩ *v/r de animal* break loose
desmantelar ⟨1a⟩ *v/t fortificación, organización* dismantle
desmañado *adj* clumsy
desmaquillar ⟨1a⟩ **1** *v/t* remove makeup from **2** *v/r* **desmaquillarse** remove one's makeup
desmarcarse ⟨1g⟩ *v/r* DEP lose one's

marker; ***desmarcarse de*** distance o.s. from
desmayarse ⟨1a⟩ *v/r* faint
desmayo *m* fainting fit; ***sin desmayo*** without flagging
desmedido *adj* excessive
desmelenarse ⟨1a⟩ *v/r fig* F let one's hair down F; (*enfurecerse*) hit the roof F
desmembrar ⟨1k⟩ *v/t* dismember
desmemoriado *adj* forgetful
desmentido *m* denial
desmentir ⟨3i⟩ *v/t* deny; *a alguien* contradict
desmenuzar ⟨1f⟩ *v/t* crumble up; *fig* break down
desmerecer ⟨2d⟩ **1** *v/t* not do justice to **2** *v/i* be unworthy (***con*** of); ***desmerecer de*** not stand comparison with; ***no desmerecer de*** be in no way inferior to
desmesurado *adj* excessive
desmilitarización *f* demilitarization
desmitificar ⟨1g⟩ *v/t* demystify, demythologize
desmontar ⟨1a⟩ **1** *v/t* dismantle, take apart; *tienda de campaña* take down **2** *v/i* dismount
desmoralizado *adj* demoralized
desmoralizar ⟨1f⟩ *v/t* demoralize
desmoronamiento *m tb fig* collapse
desmoronarse ⟨1a⟩ *v/r tb fig* collapse
desnatado *adj* skimmed
desnaturalizado *adj* QUÍM denatured
desnivel *m* unevenness; *entre personas* disparity
desnivelar ⟨1a⟩ *v/t* upset the balance of
desnucarse ⟨1g⟩ *v/r* break one's neck
desnudar ⟨1a⟩ **1** *v/t* undress; *fig* fleece **2** *v/r* **desnudarse** undress
desnudo **1** *adj* naked; (*sin decoración*) bare **2** *m* PINT nude
desnutrición *f* undernourishment
desobedecer ⟨2d⟩ *v/t* disobey
desobediencia *f* disobedience
desobediente *adj* disobedient
desocupación *f L.Am.* unemployment
desocupado **1** *adj apartamento* vacant, empty; *L.Am. sin trabajo* unemployed **2** *mpl*: ***los desocupados*** the unemployed
desocupar ⟨1a⟩ *v/t* vacate
desodorante *m* deodorant
desoído *part* → ***desoír***
desoír ⟨3q; *part* ***desoído***⟩ *v/t* ignore, turn a deaf ear to
desolado *adj* desolate; *fig* griefstricken, devastated
desolar ⟨1m⟩ *v/t tb fig* devastate
desollar ⟨1m⟩ *v/t* skin
desorbitado *adj* astronomical; ***con ojos desorbitados*** pop-eyed
desorden *m* disorder
desordenado *adj* untidy, messy F; *fig* disorganized
desordenar ⟨1a⟩ *v/t* make untidy
desorganización *f* lack of organization
desorganizado *adj* disorganized
desorientar ⟨1a⟩ **1** *v/t* disorient; (*confundir*) confuse **2** *v/r* **desorientarse** get disoriented, lose one's bearings; *fig* get confused
despabilado *adj fig* bright
despabilar ⟨1a⟩ **1** *v/t* wake up; ***¡despabila!*** get your act together! **2** *v/r* **despabilarse** *fig* get one's act together
despachar ⟨1a⟩ **1** *v/t a persona, cliente* attend to; *problema* sort out; (*vender*) sell; (*enviar*) send, dispatch **2** *v/i* meet (***con*** with) **3** *v/r* **despacharse** F polish off F; ***despacharse a su gusto*** speak one's mind
despacho *m* office; *diplomático* dispatch; ***despacho de billetes*** ticket office
despacio *adv* slowly; *L.Am.* (*en voz baja*) in a low voice
desparpajo *m* self-confidence
desparramar ⟨1a⟩ **1** *v/t* scatter; *líquido* spill; *dinero* squander **2** *v/r* **desparramarse** spill; *fig* scatter
despavorido *adj* terrified
despecho *m* spite; ***a despecho de*** in spite of
despectivo *adj* contemptuous; GRAM pejorative
despedazar ⟨1f⟩ *v/t* tear apart
despedida *f* farewell; ***despedida de soltero*** stag party; ***despedida de soltera*** hen party
despedir ⟨3l⟩ **1** *v/t* see off; *empleado* dismiss; *perfume* give off; *de jinete* throw **2** *v/r* **despedirse** say goodbye (***de*** to)
despegar ⟨1h⟩ **1** *v/t* remove, peel off **2** *v/i* AVIA, *fig* take off **3** *v/r* **despegarse** come unstuck (***de*** from), come off (***de*** sth); *de persona* distance o.s. (***de*** from)
despegue *m* AVIA, *fig* take-off
despeinar ⟨1a⟩ *v/t*: ***despeinar a alguien*** muss s.o.'s hair
despejado *adj cielo, cabeza* clear
despejar ⟨1a⟩ **1** *v/t* clear; *persona* wake up **2** *v/r* **despejarse** *de cielo* clear up; *fig* wake o.s. up
despellejar ⟨1a⟩ *v/t* skin; ***despellejar a alguien*** *fig* tear s.o. to pieces
despenalizar ⟨1f⟩ *v/t* decriminalize
despensa *f* larder
despeñarse ⟨1a⟩ *v/r* throw o.s. off a cliff
desperdiciar ⟨1b⟩ *v/t oportunidad* waste

D

desperdicio *m* waste; ***desperdicios*** *pl* waste *sg*; ***no tener desperdicio*** be worthwhile
desperdigar ⟨1h⟩ *v/t* scatter
despertador *m* alarm (clock)
despertar ⟨1k⟩ **1** *v/t* wake, waken; *apetito* whet; *sospecha* arouse; *recuerdo* reawaken, trigger **2** *v/i* wake up **3** *v/r* **despertarse** wake (up)
despiadado *adj* ruthless
despido *m* dismissal
despierto *adj* awake; *fig* bright
despilfarrar ⟨1a⟩ *v/t* squander
despistado *adj* scatterbrained
despistarse ⟨1a⟩ *v/r* get distracted
despiste *m* distraction; ***tener un despiste*** become distracted
desplante *m*: ***hacer un desplante a alguien*** *fig* be rude to s.o.
desplazar ⟨1f⟩ **1** *v/t* move; (*suplantar*) take over from **2** *v/r* **desplazarse** travel
desplegar ⟨1h & 1k⟩ *v/t* unfold, open out; MIL deploy
despliegue *m* MIL deployment; ***con gran despliegue de*** *fig* with a great show of
desplomarse ⟨1a⟩ *v/r* collapse
desplome *m* collapse
despojar ⟨1a⟩ **1** *v/t* strip (***de*** of) **2** *v/r* **despojarse**: ***despojarse de*** *prenda* take off
despojos *mpl* (*restos*) left-overs; (*desperdicios*) waste *sg*; *fig* spoils; *de animal* offal *sg*
desposeídos *mpl*: ***los desposeídos*** the dispossessed
déspota *m/f* despot
despotricar ⟨1g⟩ *v/i* F rant and rave F (***contra*** about)
despreciar ⟨1b⟩ *v/t* look down on; *propuesta* reject
desprecio *m* contempt; (*indiferencia*) disregard; *acto* slight
desprender ⟨2a⟩ **1** *v/t* detach, separate; *olor* give off **2** *v/r* **desprenderse** come off; ***desprenderse de*** *fig* part with; ***de este estudio se desprende que ...*** what emerges from the study is that ...
despreocupación *f* indifference
despreocuparse ⟨1a⟩ *v/r* not worry (***de*** about)
desprestigio *m* loss of prestige
desprevenido *adj* unprepared; ***pillar*** *or L.Am.* ***agarrar desprevenido*** catch unawares
desproporcionado *adj* disproportionate
despropósito *m* stupid thing
desprotegido *adj* unprotected
desprovisto *adj*: ***desprovisto de*** lacking in
después *adv* (*más tarde*) afterward, later; *seguido en orden* next; *en el espacio* after; ***yo voy después*** I'm next; ***después de*** after; ***después de todo*** after all; ***después de que se vaya*** after he's gone
desquiciar ⟨1b⟩ **1** *v/t fig* drive crazy **2** *v/r* **desquiciarse** *fig* lose one's mind
desquitarse ⟨1a⟩ *v/r* get one's own back (***de*** for)
desrielar ⟨1a⟩ *v/t Chi* derail
destacado *adj* outstanding
destacar ⟨1g⟩ **1** *v/i* stand out **2** *v/r* **destacarse** stand out (***por*** because of); (*ser excelente*) be outstanding (***por*** because of)
destajo *m*: ***a destajo*** piecework
destapar ⟨1a⟩ **1** *v/t* open, take the lid off; *fig* uncover **2** *v/r* **destaparse** take one's coat off; *en cama* kick off the bedcovers; *fig* strip (off)
destartalado *adj vehículo, casa* dilapidated
destello *m de estrella* twinkling; *de faros* gleam; *fig* brief period, moment
destemplarse ⟨1a⟩ *v/r fig* become unwell
desteñir ⟨3h & 3l⟩ **1** *v/t* discolo(u)r, fade **2** *v/r* **desteñirse** fade
desternillante *adj* F hilarious
desterrar ⟨1k⟩ *v/t* exile
destiempo *m*: ***a destiempo*** at the wrong moment
destierro *m* exile
destilar ⟨1a⟩ *v/t* distill; *fig* exude
destinar ⟨1a⟩ *v/t fondos* allocate (***para*** for); *a persona* post (***a*** to)
destino *m* fate; *de viaje etc* destination; *en el ejército etc* posting
destituir ⟨3g⟩ *v/t* dismiss
destornillador *m* screwdriver
destornillar ⟨1a⟩ *v/t* unscrew
destreza *f* skill
destrozar ⟨1f⟩ *v/t* destroy; *emocionalmente* shatter, devastate
destrozos *mpl* damage *sg*
destrucción *f* destruction
destruir ⟨3g⟩ *v/t* destroy; (*estropear*) ruin, wreck
desunir ⟨3a⟩ *v/t* divide
desuso *m* disuse; ***caer en desuso*** fall into disuse
desvaído *adj color, pintura* faded
desvalido *adj* helpless
desvalijar ⟨1a⟩ *v/t* rob; *apartamento* burglarize, burgle
desván *m* attic
desvanecimiento *m* MED fainting fit
desvarío *m* delirium; ***desvaríos*** ravings
desvelar ⟨1a⟩ **1** *v/t* keep awake; *secreto* reveal **2** *v/r* **desvelarse** stay awake; *fig* do one's best (***por*** for)
desvelo *m* sleeplessness; ***desvelos*** ef-

forts
desventaja *f* disadvantage
desventura *f* misfortune
desvergonzado *adj* shameless
desvergüenza *f* shamelessness
desvestir ⟨3l⟩ **1** *v/t* undress **2** *v/r* **desvestirse** get undressed, undress
desviar ⟨1c⟩ **1** *v/t golpe* deflect, parry; *tráfico* divert; *río* alter the course of; ***desviar la conversación*** change the subject; ***desviar la mirada*** look away; ***desviar a alguien del buen camino*** lead s.o. astray **2** *v/r* **desviarse** (*girar*) turn off; (*bifurcarse*) branch off; (*apartarse*) stray (***de*** from)
desvincular ⟨1a⟩ **1** *v/t* dissociate (***de*** from) **2** *v/r* **desvincularse** dissociate o.s. (***de*** from)
desvío *m* diversion
detallar ⟨1a⟩ *v/t* explain in detail, give details of; COM itemize
detalle *m* detail; *fig* thoughtful gesture; ***al detalle*** retail
detección *f* detection
detectar ⟨1a⟩ *v/t* detect
detective *m/f* detective; ***detective privado*** private detective
detector *m* detector; ***detector de mentiras*** lie detector
detención *f* detention; ***orden de detención*** arrest warrant
detener ⟨2l⟩ **1** *v/t* stop; *de policía* arrest, detain **2** *v/r* **detenerse** stop
detenido **1** *adj* held up; (*minucioso*) detailed **2** *m*, **-a** *f* person under arrest
detenimiento *m*: ***con detenimiento*** thoroughly
detentar ⟨1a⟩ *v/t* hold
detergente *m* detergent
deteriorar ⟨1a⟩ **1** *v/t* damage **2** *v/r* **deteriorarse** deteriorate
deterioro *m* deterioration
determinado *adj* certain
determinar ⟨1a⟩ **1** *v/t* determine **2** *v/r* **determinarse** decide (***a*** to)
detestar ⟨1a⟩ *v/t* detest
detonación *f* detonation
detonante *m* explosive; *fig* trigger
detonar ⟨1a⟩ **1** *v/i* detonate, go off **2** *v/t* detonate, set off
detractor *m*, **detractora** *f* detractor, critic
detrás *adv* behind; ***por detrás*** at the back; *fig* behind your / his etc back; ***detrás de*** behind; ***uno detrás de otro*** one after the other; ***estar detrás de algo*** *fig* be behind sth
detrimento *m*: ***en detrimento de*** to the detriment of
detritus *m* detritus
detuvo *vb* → ***detener***
deuda *f* debt; ***estar en deuda con alguien*** *fig* be in s.o.'s debt, be indebted to s.o.
deudor *m*, **deudora** *f* debtor
devaluación *f* devaluation
devaluar ⟨1e⟩ *v/t* devalue
devanarse ⟨1a⟩ *v/r*: ***devanarse los sesos*** F rack one's brains F
devaneo *m* affair
devastar ⟨1a⟩ *v/t* devastate
devoción *f tb fig* devotion
devolver ⟨2h; *part* ***devuelto*** ⟩ **1** *v/t* give back, return; *fig*: *visita*, *saludo* return; F (*vomitar*) throw up F **2** *v/r* **devolverse** *L.Am.* go back, return
devorar ⟨1a⟩ *v/t* devour
devuelto *part* → ***devolver***
D.F. *abr Méx* (= ***Distrito Federal***) Mexico City
dg. *abr* (= ***decigramo***) decigram
di *vb* → ***dar***
día *m* day; ***día de fiesta*** holiday; ***día festivo*** holiday; ***día hábil*** *or* ***laborable*** work day; ***poner al día*** update, bring up to date; ***a los pocos días*** a few days later; ***algúín día, un día*** some day, one day; ***de día*** by day, during the day; ***de un día a*** *or* ***para otro*** from one day to the next; ***el día menos pensado*** when you least expect it; ***hace mal día*** *tiempo* it's a nasty day; ***hoy en día*** nowadays; ***todo el santo día*** all day long; ***todos los días*** every day; ***un día sí y otro no*** every other day; ***ya es de día*** it's light already; ***¡buenos días!*** good morning
diabetes *f* diabetes
diabético **1** *adj* diabetic **2** *m*, **-a** *f* diabetic
diablesa *f* F she-devil
diablo *m* devil; ***un pobre diablo*** *fig* a poor devil; ***mandar a alguien al diablo*** tell s.o. to go to hell
diablura *f* prank, lark
diabólico *adj* diabolical
diadema *f* tiara; *para el pelo* hair-band
diáfano *adj* clear
diafragma *m* diaphragm
diagnosticar ⟨1g⟩ diagnose
diagnóstico **1** *adj* diagnostic **2** *m* diagnosis
diagonal **1** *adj* diagonal **2** *f* diagonal (line)
diagrama *m* diagram
dialecto *m* dialect
dialogar ⟨1h⟩ *v/i* talk (***sobre*** about), discuss (***sobre*** sth); (*negociar*) hold talks (***con*** with)
diálogo *m* dialog(ue)
diamante *m* diamond
diametralmente *adv*: ***diametralmente***

opuesto diametrically opposed
diámetro *m* diameter
diana *f* MIL reveille; (*blanco*) target; *para jugar a los dardos* dartboard; (*centro de blanco*) bull's eye; ***dar en la diana*** *fig* hit the nail on the head
diantre *int* F hell! F
diapositiva *f* FOT slide, transparency
diariero *m*, **-a** *f Arg* newspaper vendor
diario 1 *adj* daily **2** *m* diary; (*periódico*) newspaper; ***a diario*** daily
diarrea *f* MED diarrh(o)ea
dibujante *m/f* draftsman, *Br* draughtsman; *mujer* draftswoman, *Br* draughtswoman; *de viñetas* cartoonist
dibujar ⟨1a⟩ **1** *v/t* draw; *fig* describe **2** *v/r* **dibujarse** *fig* appear
dibujo *m arte* drawing; *ilustración* drawing, sketch; *estampado* pattern; ***dibujos animados*** cartoons; ***película de dibujos animados*** animation
diccionario *m* dictionary
dic.[e] *abr* (**= *diciembre***) Dec. (= December)
dice *vb* → ***decir***
díceres *mpl L.Am.* sayings
dicharachero *adj* chatty; (*gracioso*) witty
dicho 1 *part* → ***decir*** **2** *adj* said; ***dicho y hecho*** no sooner said than done; ***mejor dicho*** or rather **3** *m* saying
dichoso *adj* happy; F (*maldito*) damn F
diciembre *m* December
diciendo *vb* → ***decir***
dictado *m* dictation
dictador *m*, **dictadora** *f* dictator
dictadura *f* dictatorship
dictaminar ⟨1a⟩ *v/t* state
dictar ⟨1a⟩ *v/t lección*, *texto* dictate; *ley* announce; ***dictar sentencia*** JUR pass sentence
didáctico *adj* educational
diecinueve *adj* nineteen
dieciocho *adj* eighteen
dieciséis *adj* sixteen
diecisiete *adj* seventeen
diente *m* tooth; ***diente de ajo*** clove of garlic; ***diente de león*** BOT dandelion; ***poner los dientes largos a alguien*** make s.o. jealous
diesel *m* diesel
diestro 1 *adj*: ***a diestro y siniestro*** *fig* F left and right **2** *m* TAUR bullfighter
dieta *f* diet; ***estar a dieta*** be on a diet; ***dietas*** travel(l)ing expenses
dietético *adj* dietary
diez *adj* ten
diezmar ⟨1a⟩ *v/t* decimate
difamar ⟨1a⟩ *v/t* slander, defame; *por escrito* libel, defame
difamatorio *adj* defamatory
diferencia *f* difference; ***a diferencia de*** unlike; ***con diferencia*** *fig* by a long way
diferenciar ⟨1b⟩ **1** *v/t* differentiate **2** *v/r* **diferenciarse** differ (***de*** from); ***no se diferencian en nada*** there's no difference at all between them
diferente *adj* different
diferido *adj* TV: ***en diferido*** prerecorded
difícil *adj* difficult
dificultad *f* difficulty; ***poner dificultades*** make it difficult
dificultar ⟨1a⟩ *v/t* hinder
difundir ⟨3a⟩ **1** *v/t* spread; (*programa*) broadcast **2** *v/r* **difundirse** spread
difunto 1 *adj* late **2** *m*, **-a** *f* deceased
difuso *adj idea*, *conocimientos* vague, sketchy
digerir ⟨3i⟩ *v/t* digest; F *noticia* take in
digestión *f* digestion
digital *adj* digital
digitalizar ⟨1f⟩ *v/t* INFOR digitalize
dígito *m* digit
dignarse ⟨1a⟩ *v/r* deign
dignidad *f* dignity
digno *adj* worthy; *trabajo* decent; ***digno de mención*** worth mentioning
digo *vb* → ***decir***
digresión *f* digression
dije *vb* → ***decir***
dilación *f*: ***sin dilación*** without delay
dilapidar ⟨1a⟩ *v/t* waste
dilatar ⟨1a⟩ **1** *v/t* dilate; (*prolongar*) prolong; (*aplazar*) postpone **2** *v/i Méx* (*tardar*) be late; ***no me dilato*** I won't be long
dilema *m* dilemma
diligencia *f* diligence; *vehículo* stagecoach; ***diligencias*** JUR procedures, formalities
diligente *adj* diligent
dilucidar ⟨1a⟩ *v/t* clarify
diluir ⟨3g⟩ *v/t* dilute
diluviar ⟨1b⟩ *v/i* pour down
diluvio *m* downpour; *fig* deluge
dimensión *f* dimension; *fig* size, scale; ***dimensiones*** measurements
diminutivo *m* diminutive
diminuto *adj* tiny, diminutive
dimisión *f* resignation
dimitir ⟨3a⟩ *v/t* resign
Dinamarca Denmark
dinámico *adj fig* dynamic
dinamita *f* dynamite
dinastía *f* dynasty
dinero *m* money; ***dinero en efectivo, dinero en metálico*** cash
dinosaurio *m* dinosaur
dio *vb* → ***dar***
Dios *m* God; ***hazlo como Dios manda*** do

it properly; ***¡Dios mío!*** my God!; ***¡por Dios!*** for God's sake!; ***sabe Dios lo que dijo*** God knows what he said
dios *m tb fig* god
diosa *f* goddess
diploma *m* diploma
diplomacia *f* diplomacy
diplomático 1 *adj* diplomatic **2** *m*, **-a** *f* diplomat
diputado *m*, **-a** *f* representative, *Br* Member of Parliament
dique *m* dike, *Br* dyke
dirá *vb* → ***decir***
diré *vb* → ***decir***
dirección *f tb* TEA, *de película* direction; COM management; POL leadership; *de coche* steering; *en carta* address; ***en aquella dirección*** that way; ***dirección asistida*** AUTO power steering; ***dirección de correo electrónico*** e-mail address
directiva *f* board of directors; POL executive committee
directivo 1 *adj* governing; COM managing **2** *m*, **-a** *f* COM manager
directo *adj* direct; ***en directo*** TV, RAD live
director 1 *adj* leading **2** *m*, **directora** *f* manager; EDU principal, *Br* head (teacher); TEA, *de película* director; ***director de orquesta*** conductor
directriz *f* guideline
dirigir ⟨3c⟩ **1** *v/t* TEA, *película* direct; COM manage, run; MÚS conduct; ***dirigir una carta a*** address a letter to; ***dirigir una pregunta a*** direct a question to **2** *v/r* **dirigirse** make, head (***a, hacia*** for)
discapacidad *f* disability
discapacitado 1 *adj* disabled **2** *m*, **-a** *f* disabled person
discar ⟨1g⟩ *v/t L.Am.* TELEC dial
discernir ⟨3i⟩ *v/t* distinguish, discern
disciplina *f* discipline
disciplinar ⟨1a⟩ *v/t* discipline
discípulo *m*, **-a** *f* REL, *fig* disciple
disco *m* disk, *Br* disc; MÚS record; (*discoteca*) disco; DEP discus; ***disco compacto*** compact disc; ***disco duro***, *L.Am.* ***disco rígido*** INFOR hard disk
discordante *adj* discordant
discordia *f* discord; (*colección de discos*) record collection
discreción *f* discretion; ***a discreción*** *disparar* at will; ***a discreción de*** at the discretion of
discrepancia *f* discrepancy; (*desacuerdo*) disagreement
discrepar ⟨1a⟩ *v/i* disagree
discreto *adj* discreet
discriminación *f* discrimination
discriminar ⟨1a⟩ *v/t* discriminate against; (*diferenciar*) differentiate
disculpa *f* apology
disculpar ⟨1a⟩ **1** *v/t* excuse **2** *v/r* **disculparse** apologize
discurrir ⟨3a⟩ *v/i de tiempo* pass; *de acontecimiento* pass off; (*reflexionar*) reflect (***sobre*** on)
discurso *m* speech; *de tiempo* passage, passing
discusión *f* discussion; (*disputa*) argument
discutir ⟨3a⟩ **1** *v/t* discuss **2** *v/i* argue (***sobre*** about)
diseminar ⟨1a⟩ *v/t* scatter; *fig* spread
disentir ⟨3i⟩ *v/i* disagree (***de*** with)
diseñador *m*, **diseñadora** *f* designer
diseñar ⟨1a⟩ *v/t* design
diseño *m* design; ***diseño gráfico*** graphic design
disfraz *m para ocultar* disguise; *para fiestas* costume, fancy dress
disfrazarse ⟨1f⟩ *v/r para ocultarse* disguise o.s. (***de*** as); *para divertirse* dress up (***de*** as)
disfrutar ⟨1a⟩ **1** *v/t* enjoy **2** *v/i* have fun, enjoy o.s.; ***disfrutar de buena salud*** be in *o* enjoy good health
disgregarse ⟨1h⟩ *v/r* disintegrate
disgustar ⟨1a⟩ **1** *v/t* upset **2** *v/r* **disgustarse** get upset
disgusto *m*: ***me causó un gran disgusto*** I was very upset; ***llevarse un disgusto*** get upset; ***a disgusto*** unwillingly
disidente *m/f* dissident
disimular ⟨1a⟩ **1** *v/t* disguise **2** *v/i* pretend
disimulo *m*: ***con disimulo*** unobtrusively
disipar ⟨1a⟩ **1** *v/t duda* dispel **2** *v/r* **disiparse** *de niebla* clear; *de duda* vanish
diskette *m* diskette, floppy (disk)
dislexia *f* dyslexia
dislocar ⟨1g⟩ *v/t* dislocate
disminución *f* decrease
disminuido 1 *adj* handicapped **2** *m*, **-a** *f* handicapped person; ***disminuido físico*** physically handicapped person
disminuir ⟨3g⟩ **1** *v/t gastos, costos* reduce, cut; *velocidad* reduce **2** *v/i* decrease, diminish
disociar ⟨1b⟩ *v/t* separate
disolvente *m* solvent
disolver ⟨1h; *part* **disuelto** ⟩ *v/t* dissolve; *manifestación* break up
disparada *f L.Am.*: ***a la disparada*** in a rush
disparar ⟨1a⟩ **1** *v/t tiro, arma* fire; *foto* take; *precios* send up **2** *v/i* shoot, fire **3** *v/r* **dispararse** *de arma, alarma* go off; *de precios* rise dramatically, rocket F
disparatado *adj* absurd

D

disparate *m* F piece of nonsense; ***es un disparate hacer eso*** it's crazy to do that
disparo *m* shot
dispendio *m* waste
dispensar ⟨1a⟩ *v/t* dispense; *recibimiento* give; (*eximir*) excuse (***de*** from)
dispensario *m* MED clinic
dispersar ⟨1a⟩ **1** *v/t* disperse **2** *v/r* **dispersarse** disperse
disperso *adj* scattered
displicente *adj* disdainful
disponer ⟨2r; *part* ***dispuesto***⟩ **1** *v/t* (*arreglar*) arrange; (*preparar*) prepare; (*ordenar*) stipulate **2** *v/i*: ***disponer de algo*** have sth at one's disposal **3** *v/r* **disponerse** get ready (***a*** to)
disponibilidad *f* COM availability
disponible *adj* available
disposición *f* disposition; *de objetos* arrangement; ***disposición de ánimo*** state of mind; ***estar a disposición de alguien*** be at s.o.'s disposal
dispositivo *m* device
dispuesto 1 *part* → ***disponer*** **2** *adj* ready (***a*** to)
disputa *f* dispute
disputar ⟨1a⟩ **1** *v/t* dispute; *partido* play **2** *v/i* argue (***sobre*** about) **3** *v/r* **disputarse** compete for
disquería *f L.Am.* record store
disquete *m* INFOR diskette, floppy (disk)
disquetera *f* disk drive
distancia *f tb fig* distance
distanciarse ⟨1b⟩ *v/r* distance o.s. (***de*** from)
distante *adj tb fig* distant
distar ⟨1a⟩ *v/i* be far (***de*** from)
distinción *f* distinction; ***a distinción de*** unlike
distinguido *adj* distinguished
distinguir ⟨3d⟩ *v/t* distinguish (***de*** from); (*divisar*) make out; *con un premio* hono(u)r
distintivo *m* emblem; MIL insignia
distinto *adj* different; ***distintos*** (*varios*) several
distorsión *f* distortion
distracción *f* distraction; (*descuido*) absent-mindedness; (*diversión*) entertainment; (*pasatiempo*) pastime; ***por distracción*** out of absent-mindedness
distraer ⟨2p; *part* ***distraído***⟩ **1** *v/t* distract; ***la radio la distrae*** she enjoys listening to the radio **2** *v/r* **distraerse** get distracted; (*disfrutar*) enjoy o.s.
distraído 1 *part* → ***distraer*** **2** *adj* absent-minded; *temporalmente* distracted
distribución *f* COM, *de película* distribution
distribuir ⟨3g⟩ *v/t* distribute; *beneficio* share out
distrito *m* district
disturbio *m* disturbance
disuadir ⟨3a⟩ *v/t* dissuade; POL deter; ***disuadir a alguien de hacer algo*** dissuade s.o. from doing sth
disuelto *part* → ***disolver***
disyuntiva *f* dilemma
diurético *adj* diuretic
diurno *adj* day *atr*
divagar ⟨1h⟩ *v/i* digress
diván *m* couch
diversidad *f* diversity
diversión *f* fun; (*pasatiempo*) pastime; ***aquí no hay muchas diversiones*** there's not much to do around here
diverso *adj* diverse; ***diversos*** several, various
divertido *adj* funny; (*entretenido*) entertaining
divertir ⟨3i⟩ **1** *v/t* entertain **2** *v/r* **divertirse** have fun, enjoy o.s.
dividendo *m* dividend
dividir ⟨3a⟩ *v/t* divide
divinamente *adv fig* wonderfully
divinidad *f* divinity
divino *adj tb fig* divine
divisa *f* currency; ***divisas*** *pl* foreign currency *sg*
divisar ⟨1a⟩ *v/t* make out
división *f* MAT, MIL, DEP division; ***hubo división de opiniones*** there were differences of opinion
divorciado 1 *adj* divorced **2** *m*, **-a** *f* divorcee
divorciarse ⟨1b⟩ *v/r* get divorced
divorcio *m* divorce
divulgación *f* spread
divulgar ⟨1h⟩ **1** *v/t* spread **2** *v/r* **divulgarse** spread
d. J.C. *abr* (***= después de Jesucristo***) A.D. (= Anno Domini)
dl. *abr* (***= decilitro***) deciliter
dm. *abr* (***= decímetro***) decimeter
dobladillo *m* hem
doblado *adj película* dubbed
doblaje *m de película* dubbing
doblar ⟨1a⟩ **1** *v/t* fold; *cantidad* double; *película* dub; MAR round; *pierna, brazo* bend; *en una carrera* pass, *Br* overtake; ***doblar la esquina*** go round *o* turn the corner **2** *v/i* turn; ***doblar a la derecha*** turn right **3** *v/r* **doblarse** bend; *fig* give in
doble 1 *adj* double; *nacionalidad* dual; ***doble clic*** *m* double click **2** *m*: ***el doble*** twice as much (***de*** as); ***el doble de gente*** twice as many people; ***dobles*** *tenis* doubles **3** *m/f en película* double

D

doblegar ⟨1h⟩ *v/t fig*: *voluntad* break; *orgullo* humble
doblez 1 *m* fold **2** *f fig* deceit
doce *adj* twelve
docena *f* dozen
docente *adj* teaching *atr*
dócil *adj* docile
doctor *m*, **doctora** *f* doctor; ***doctor honoris causa*** honorary doctor
doctorado *m* doctorate
doctrina *f* doctrine
documentación *f* documentation; *de una persona* papers
documental *m* documentary
documento *m* document; ***documento nacional de identidad*** national identity card
dogma *m* dogma
dogo *m* zo mastiff
dólar *m* dollar
dolencia *f* ailment
doler ⟨2h⟩ *v/t tb fig* hurt; ***me duele el brazo*** my arm hurts; ***le dolió que le mintieran*** *fig* she was hurt that they had lied to her
dolor *m tb fig* pain; ***dolor de cabeza*** headache; ***dolor de estómago*** stomach-ache; ***dolor de muelas*** toothache
dolorido *adj* sore, aching; *fig* hurt
doloroso *adj tb fig* painful
domador *m*, **domadora** *f* tamer
domesticar ⟨1g⟩ *v/t* domesticate
doméstico 1 *adj* domestic, household *atr* **2** *m*, **-a** *f* servant
domiciliación *f de sueldo* credit transfer; *de pagos* direct billing, *Br* direct debit
domicilio *m* address; ***repartir a domicilio*** do home deliveries
dominante *adj* dominant; *desp* domineering
dominar ⟨1a⟩ **1** *v/t* dominate; *idioma* have a good command of **2** *v/i* dominate **3** *v/r* **dominarse** control o.s.
domingo *m* Sunday; ***domingo de Ramos*** Palm Sunday
dominguero *m*, **-a** *f* F weekender, Sunday tripper
dominical *adj* Sunday *atr*
dominicano GEOG **1** *adj* Dominican **2** *m*, **-a** *f* Dominican
dominio *m* control; *fig* command; ***ser del dominio púiblico*** be in the public domain
dominó *m* dominoes *pl*
don[1] *m* gift; ***don de gentes*** way with people
don[2] *m* Mr; ***don Enrique*** Mr Sanchez *English uses the surname while Spanish uses the first name*
donación *f* donation; ***donación de sangre*** blood donation; ***donación de órganos*** organ donation
donante *m/f* donor; ***donante de sangre*** blood donor
donar ⟨1a⟩ *v/t sangre, órgano, dinero* donate
donativo *m* donation
doncella *f* maid
donde 1 *adv* where **2** *prp esp L.Am.*: ***fui donde el médico*** I went to the doctor's
dónde *interr* where; ***¿de dónde eres?*** where are you from?; ***¿hacia dónde vas?*** where are you going?
dondequiera *adv* wherever
doña *f* Mrs; ***doña Estela*** Mrs Sanchez *English uses the surname while Spanish uses the first name*
dopaje, **doping** *m* doping
dorada *f* zo gilthead
dorado *adj* gold; *montura* gilt
dormido *adj* asleep; ***quedarse dormido*** fall asleep
dormir ⟨3k⟩ **1** *v/i* sleep; (*estar dormido*) be asleep **2** *v/t* put to sleep; ***dormir a alguien*** MED give s.o. a general an(a)esthetic **3** *v/r* **dormirse** go to sleep; (*quedarse dormido*) fall asleep; (*no despertarse*) oversleep; ***no podía dormirme*** I couldn't get to sleep
dormitorio *m* bedroom
dorso *m* back
dos *adj* two; ***de dos en dos*** in twos; ***los dos*** both; ***anda con ojo con los dos*** watch out for the pair of them; ***cada dos por tres*** all the time, continually
doscientos *adj* two hundred
dosificar ⟨1g⟩ *v/t* cut down on
dosis *f inv* dose
dotar ⟨1a⟩ *v/t* equip (***de*** with); *fondos* provide (***de*** with); *cualidades* endow (***de*** with)
dote *f a novia* dowry; ***tener dotes para algo*** have a gift for sth
doy *vb* → ***dar***
dpto. *abr* (**= *departamento***) dept (= department)
Dr. *abr* (**= *Doctor***) Dr (= Doctor)
Dra. *abr* (**= *Doctora***) Dr (= Doctor)
dragar ⟨1h⟩ *v/t* dredge
dragón *m* dragon; MIL dragoon
drama *m* drama
dramático *adj* dramatic; ***arte dramático*** dramatic art
dramatizar ⟨1f⟩ *v/t* dramatize
drástico *adj* drastic
drenaje *m* drainage
droga *f* drug; ***droga de diseño*** designer drug

drogadicto 1 *adj*: ***una mujer -a*** a woman addicted to drugs **2** *m*, **-a** *f* drug addict
drogarse ⟨1h⟩ *v/r* take drugs
drogodependencia *f* drug dependency
droguería *f store selling cleaning and household products*
dromedario *m* zo dromedary
d.[to] *abr* (= ***descuento***) discount
ducha *f* shower; ***ser una ducha de agua fría*** *fig* come as a shock
ducharse ⟨1a⟩ *v/r* have a shower, shower
duda *f* doubt; ***sin duda*** without doubt; ***poner en duda*** call into question
dudar ⟨1a⟩ **1** *v/t* doubt **2** *v/i* hesitate (***en*** to)
dudoso *adj* doubtful; (*indeciso*) hesitant
duele *vb* → ***doler***
duelo *m* grief; (*combate*) duel
duende *m* imp
dueño *m*, **-a** *f* owner
duermo *vb* → ***dormir***
dulce 1 *adj* sweet; *fig* gentle **2** *m* candy, *Br* sweet
dulzura *f tb fig* sweetness
dumping *m* dumping
duna *f* dune
duo *m* MÚS duo
duodécimo *adj* twelfth
dúíplex *m* duplex (apartment)
duplicado 1 *adj* duplicate; ***por duplicado*** in duplicate **2** *m* duplicate
duplicar ⟨1g⟩ *v/t* duplicate
duque *m* duke
duquesa *f* duchess
duración *f* duration
duradero *adj* lasting; *ropa*, *calzado* hard-wearing
durante *prp indicando duración* during; *indicando período* for; ***durante seis meses*** for six months
durar ⟨1a⟩ *v/i* last
duraznero *m L.Am.* BOT peach (tree)
durazno *m L.Am.* BOT peach
Durex® *m Méx* Scotch tape®, *Br* Sellotape®
duro 1 *adj* hard; *carne* tough; *clima*, *fig* harsh; ***duro de oído*** F hard of hearing; ***ser duro de pelar*** be a tough nut to crack **2** *adv* hard **3** *m* five peseta coin
DVD *abr* (= ***Disco de Vídeo Digital***) DVD (= Digital Versatile *o* Video Disc)

E

E *abr* (= ***este***) E (= East(ern))
e *conj* (*instead of* ***y*** *before words starting with* ***i, hi***) and
ebanista *m* cabinetmaker
ébano *m* ebony
ebrio *adj* drunk
ebullición *f*: ***punto de ebullición*** boiling point
eccema *m* eczema
echar ⟨1a⟩ **1** *v/t* (*lanzar*) throw; (*poner*) put; *de un lugar* throw out; *humo* give off; *carta* mail, *Br tb* post; ***lo han echado del trabajo*** he's been fired; ***echar abajo*** pull down, destroy; ***echar la culpa a alguien*** blame s.o., put the blame on s.o.; ***me echó 40 años*** he thought I was 40 **2** *v/i*: ***echar a*** start to, begin to; ***echar a correr*** start *o* begin to run, start running **3** *v/r* **echarse** (*tirarse*) throw o.s.; (*tumbarse*) lie down; (*ponerse*) put on; ***echarse a llorar*** start *o* begin to cry, start crying
eclesiástico *adj* ecclesiastical, church *atr*
eclipsar ⟨1a⟩ *v/t* eclipse
eclipse *m* eclipse
eco *m* echo; ***tener eco*** *fig* make an impact
ecografía *f* (ultrasound) scan
ecología *f* ecology
ecológico *adj* ecological; *alimentos* organic
ecologista *m/f* ecologist
economato *m* co-operative store
economía *f* economy; *ciencia* economics; ***economía de mercado*** market economy; ***economía sumergida*** black economy
económico *adj* economic; (*barato*) economical
economista *m/f* economist
economizar ⟨1f⟩ *v/t* economize on, save
ecosistema *m* ecosystem
ecoturismo *m* ecotourism
ecuación *f* equation
ecuador *m* equator
Ecuador Ecuador
ecuánime *adj* (*sereno*) even-tempered; (*imparcial*) impartial

ecuatorial *adj* equatorial
ecuatoriano 1 *adj* Ecuadorean **2** *m*, **-a** *f* Ecuadorean
eczema *m* eczema
ed. *abr* (**= edición**) ed (= edition)
edad *f* age; ***la Edad Media*** the Middle Ages *pl*; ***la tercera edad*** the over 60s; ***estar en la edad del pavo*** be at that awkward age; ***a la edad de*** at the age of; ***¿qué edad tienes?*** how old are you?
edición *f* edition
edificar ⟨1g⟩ *v/t* construct, build
edificio *m* building
edil *m*, **edila** *f* council(l)or
editar ⟨1a⟩ *v/t* edit; (*publicar*) publish
editor *m*, **editora** *f* editor
editorial 1 *m* editorial, leading article **2** *f* publishing company *o* house, publisher
edredón *m* eiderdown
educación *f* (*crianza*) upbringing; (*modales*) manners; ***educación física*** physical education, PE
educado *adj* polite, well-mannered; ***mal educado*** rude, ill-mannered
educar ⟨1g⟩ *v/t* educate; (*criar*) bring up; *voz* train
educativo *adj* educational
edulcorante *m* sweetener
EE. UU. *abr* (***= Estados Unidos***) US(A) (= United States (of America))
efectista *adj* theatrical, dramatic
efectivamente *adv* indeed
efectivo 1 *adj* effective; ***hacer efectivo*** COM cash **2** *m*: ***en efectivo*** (in) cash
efecto *m* effect; ***efecto invernadero*** greenhouse effect; ***efectos secundarios*** side effects; ***en efecto*** indeed; ***surtir efecto*** take effect, work
efectuar ⟨1e⟩ *v/t* carry out
efervescente *adj* effervescent; *bebida* carbonated, sparkling
eficacia *f* efficiency
eficaz *adj* (*efectivo*) effective; (*eficiente*) efficient
eficiencia *f* efficiency
eficiente *adj* efficient
efímero *adj* ephemeral, short-lived
efusivo *adj* effusive
egipcio 1 *adj* Egyptian **2** *m*, **-a** *f* Egyptian
Egipto Egypt
ego *m* ego
egocéntrico *adj* egocentric, self-centered (*Br* -centred)
egoísmo *m* selfishness, egoism
egoísta 1 *adj* selfish, egoistic **2** *m/f* egoist
egresar ⟨1a⟩ *v/i L.Am. de universidad* graduate; *de colegio* graduate from high school, *Br* leave school
egreso *m L.Am.* graduation
eh *int para llamar atención* hey!; ***¿eh?*** eh?
eje *m* axis; *de auto* axle; *fig* linchpin
ejecución *f* (*realización*) implementation, carrying out; *de condenado* execution; MÚS performance
ejecutar ⟨1a⟩ *v/t* (*realizar*) carry out, implement; *condenado* execute; INFOR run, execute; MÚS play, perform
ejecutiva *f* executive
ejecutivo 1 *adj* executive; ***el poder ejecutivo*** POL the executive **2** *m* executive; ***el Ejecutivo*** the government
ejemplar 1 *adj alumno, padre etc* model *atr*, exemplary **2** *m de libro* copy; *de revista* issue; *animal, planta* specimen
ejemplo *m* example; ***dar buen ejemplo*** set a good example; ***por ejemplo*** for example
ejercer ⟨2b⟩ **1** *v/t cargo* practice, *Br* practise; *influencia* exert **2** *v/i de profesional* practice, *Br* practise; ***ejerce de médico*** he's a practicing (*Br* practising) doctor
ejercicio *m* exercise; COM fiscal year, *Br* financial year; ***hacer ejercicio*** exercise
ejercitar ⟨1a⟩ **1** *v/t múísculo, derecho* exercise **2** *v/r* **ejercitarse** train; ***ejercitarse en*** practice, *Br* practise
ejército *m* army
ejido *m Méx traditional rural communal farming unit*
ejote *m L.Am.* green bean
el 1 *art* the **2** *pron*: ***el de …*** that of …; ***el de Juan*** Juan's; ***el más grande*** the biggest (one); ***el que está …*** the one who is …
él *pron sujeto* he; *cosa* it; *complemento* him; *cosa* it; ***de él*** his
elaborar ⟨1a⟩ *v/t* produce, make; *metal etc* work; *plan* devise, draw up
elasticidad *f* elasticity
elástico 1 *adj* elastic **2** *m* elastic; (*goma*) elastic band, *Br* rubber band
elección *f* choice
eleccionario *adj L.Am.* election *atr*, electoral
elecciones *fpl* election *sg*
elector *m* voter
electorado *m* electorate
electoral *adj* election *atr*, electoral
electricidad *f* electricity
electricista *m/f* electrician
eléctrico *adj luz, motor* electric; *aparato* electrical
electrocutar ⟨1a⟩ **1** *v/t* electrocute **2** *v/r* **electrocutarse** be electrocuted, electrocute o.s.
electrodo *m* electrode
electrodoméstico *m* electrical appliance
electrón *m* electron
electrónica *f* electronics

electrónico *adj* electronic

elefante *m* zo elephant; ***elefante marino*** elephant seal, sea elephant

elegancia *f* elegance, stylishness

elegante *adj* elegant, stylish

elegantoso *adj L.Am.* F stylish, classy F

elegía *f* elegy

elegible *adj* eligible

elegir ⟨3c & 3l⟩ *v/t* choose; *por votación* elect

elemental *adj* (*esencial*) fundamental, essential; (*básico*) elementary, basic

elemento *m* element

elevado *adj* high; *fig* elevated

elevador *m* hoist; *L.Am.* elevator, *Br* lift

elevar ⟨1a⟩ **1** *v/t* raise **2** *v/r* **elevarse** rise; *de monumento* stand

eliminación *f* elimination; *de desperdicios* disposal

eliminar ⟨1a⟩ *v/t* eliminate; *desperdicios* dispose of

eliminatoria *f* DEP qualifying round, heat

élite *f* elite

elitista *adj* elitist

elixir *m* elixir; ***elixir bucal*** mouthwash

ella *pron sujeto* she; *cosa* it; *complemento* her; *cosa* it; ***de ella*** her; ***es de ella*** it's hers

ellas *pron sujeto* they; *complemento* them; ***de ellas*** their; ***es de ellas*** it's theirs

ello *pron* it

ellos *pron sujeto* they; *complemento* them; ***de ellos*** their; ***es de ellos*** it's theirs

elocuente *adj* eloquent

elogiar ⟨1b⟩ *v/t* praise

elogio *m* praise

elote *m L.Am.* corncob; *granos* corn, *Br* sweetcorn

El Salvador El Salvador

eludir ⟨3a⟩ *v/t* evade, avoid

emanar ⟨1a⟩ **1** *v/i fml* emanate (***de*** from) *fml*; *fig* stem (***de*** from), derive (***de*** from) **2** *v/t* exude, emit

emancipación *f* emancipation

emanciparse ⟨1a⟩ *v/r* become emancipated

embadurnar ⟨1a⟩ *v/t* smear (***de*** with)

embajada *f* embassy

embajador *m*, **embajadora** *f* ambassador

embalaje *m* packing

embalar ⟨1a⟩ **1** *v/t* pack **2** *v/r* **embalarse** *de persona* get excited; ***el coche se embaló*** the car went faster and faster; ***no te embales*** don't go so fast

embalse *m* reservoir

embarazada **1** *adj* pregnant **2** *f* pregnant woman

embarazo *m* pregnancy; ***interrupción del embarazo*** termination, abortion

embarazoso *adj* awkward, embarrassing

embarcación *f* vessel, craft

embarcadero *m* wharf

embarcar ⟨1g⟩ **1** *v/t pasajeros* board, embark; *mercancías* load **2** *v/i* board, embark **3** *v/r* **embarcarse** *en barco* board, embark; *en avión* board; ***embarcarse en*** *fig* embark on

embargo *m* embargo; JUR seizure; ***sin embargo*** however

embarque *m* boarding; *de mercancías* loading

embarrancar ⟨1g⟩ **1** *v/i* MAR run aground **2** *v/r* **embarrancarse** MAR run aground

embaucador **1** *adj* deceitful **2** *m*, **embaucadora** *f* trickster

embeberse ⟨2a⟩ *v/r* get absorbed *o* engrossed (***en*** in)

embelesar ⟨1a⟩ *v/t* captivate

embestir ⟨3l⟩ **1** *v/t* charge **2** *v/i* charge (***contra*** at)

emblema *m* emblem

embobar ⟨1a⟩ *v/t* fascinate

embolarse ⟨1a⟩ *v/r C.Am.*, *Méx* F get plastered F

émbolo *m* TÉC piston

embolsar ⟨1a⟩ **1** *v/t* pocket **2** *v/r* **embolsarse** pocket

emborrachar ⟨1a⟩ **1** *v/t* make drunk, get drunk **2** *v/r* **emborracharse** get drunk

emborronar ⟨1a⟩ *v/t* blot, smudge

emboscada *f* ambush

embotar ⟨1a⟩ *v/t* blunt

embotellamiento *m* traffic jam

embotellar ⟨1a⟩ *v/t* bottle

embrague *m* AUTO clutch

embriagar ⟨1h⟩ *v/t fig* intoxicate

embriaguez *f* intoxication

embrión *m* embryo; ***en embrión*** in an embryonic state, in embryo

embrollo *m* tangle; *fig* mess, muddle

embromar ⟨1a⟩ *v/t Rpl* F (*molestar*) annoy

embrujar ⟨1a⟩ *v/t tb fig* bewitch

embrutecer ⟨2d⟩ **1** *v/t* brutalize **2** *v/r* **embrutecerse** become brutalized

embudo *m* funnel

embustero **1** *adj* deceitful **2** *m*, **-a** *f* liar

embutido *m* GASTR *type of dried sausage*

emergencia *f* emergency

emerger ⟨2c⟩ *v/i* emerge

emigración *f* emigration

emigrante *m* emigrant

emigrar ⟨1a⟩ *v/i* emigrate; zo migrate

eminente *adj* eminent

emirato *m* emirate

emisario *m* emissary

emisión *f* emission; COM issue; RAD, TV broadcast
emisora *f* radio station
emitir ⟨3a⟩ *v/t calor, sonido* give out, emit; *moneda* issue; *opinión* express, give; *veredicto* deliver; RAD, TV broadcast; *voto* cast
emoción *f* emotion; ***¡qué emoción!*** how exciting!
emocionado *adj* excited
emocionante *adj* (*excitante*) exciting; (*conmovedor*) moving
emocionarse ⟨1a⟩ *v/r* get excited; (*conmoverse*) be moved
emotivo *adj* emotional; (*conmovedor*) moving
empacar ⟨1g⟩ **1** *v/t & v/i L.Am.* pack **2** *v/r* **empacarse** *L.Am.* (*ponerse tozudo*) dig one's heels in; *tragar* devour
empacharse ⟨1a⟩ *v/r* F get an upset stomach (***de*** from); ***empacharse de*** *fig* overdose on
empacho *m* F upset stomach; *fig* bellyful F; ***sin empacho*** unashamedly
empadronar ⟨1a⟩ **1** *v/t* register **2** *v/r* **empadronarse** register
empalagoso *adj* sickly; *fig* sickly sweet, cloying
empalizada *f* palisade
empalmar ⟨1a⟩ **1** *v/t* connect, join **2** *v/i* connect (***con*** with), join up (***con*** with); *de idea, conversación* run *o* follow on (***con*** from)
empanada *f* pie
empanadilla *f* pasty
empanar ⟨1a⟩ *v/t* coat in breadcrumbs
empantanarse ⟨1a⟩ *v/r* become swamped *o* waterlogged; *fig* get bogged down
empañado *adj* misty
empañar ⟨1a⟩ **1** *v/t* steam up, mist up; *fig* tarnish, sully **2** *v/r* **empañarse** *de vidrio* steam up, mist up
empapado *adj* soaked, dripping wet
empapar ⟨1a⟩ **1** *v/t* soak; (*absorber*) soak up; **2** *v/r* **empaparse** get soaked *o* drenched; ***empaparse de algo*** immerse o.s. in sth
empapelar ⟨1a⟩ *v/t* wallpaper
empaque *m* presence; (*seriedad*) solemnity
empaquetar ⟨1a⟩ *v/t* pack
emparedado *m* sandwich
emparejar ⟨1a⟩ *v/t personas* pair off; *calcetines* match up
emparentado *adj* related
empastador *m*, **empastadora** *f L.Am.* bookbinder
empastar ⟨1a⟩ *v/t muela* fill; *libro* bind
empaste *m* filling
empatar ⟨1a⟩ *v/i* tie, *Br* draw; (*igualar*) tie the game, *Br* equalize
empate *m* tie, draw; ***gol del empate*** *en fútbol* equalizer
empecinarse ⟨1a⟩ *v/r* get an idea into one's head; ***empecinarse en algo*** insist on sth
empedernido *adj* inveterate, confirmed
empedrado *m* paving
empeine *m* instep
empellón *m* shove; ***entró a empellones*** he shoved his way in
empelotarse ⟨1a⟩ *v/r L.Am. P* take one's clothes off, strip off
empeñado *adj* (*endeudado*) in debt; ***estar empeñado en hacer algo*** be determined to do sth
empeñar ⟨1a⟩ **1** *v/t* pawn **2** *v/r* **empeñarse** (*endeudarse*) get into debt; (*esforzarse*) strive (***en*** to), make an effort (***en*** to); ***empeñarse en hacer*** *obstinarse* insist on doing, be determined to do
empeñero *Méx* **1** *adj* determined **2** *m*, **-a** *f* determined person
empeño *m* (*obstinación*) determination; (*esfuerzo*) effort; *Méx fig* pawn shop
empeñoso *adj L.Am.* hard-working
empeorar ⟨1a⟩ **1** *v/t* make worse **2** *v/i* deteriorate, get worse
empequeñecer ⟨2d⟩ *v/t fig* diminish
emperador *m* emperor; *pez* swordfish
emperatriz *f* empress
emperrarse ⟨1a⟩ *v/r* F: ***emperrarse en hacer algo*** have one's heart set on doing sth; ***emperrarse con algo*** set one's heart on sth
empezar ⟨1f & 1k⟩ **1** *v/t* start, begin **2** *v/i* start, begin; ***empezar a hacer algo*** start to do sth, start doing sth; ***empezar por hacer algo*** start *o* begin by doing sth
empiezo *m S. Am.* start, beginning
empinado *adj* steep
empinar ⟨1a⟩ *v/t* raise; ***empinar el codo*** F raise one's elbow F
empírico *adj* empirical
emplazamiento *m* site, location; JUR subpoena, summons
empleado **1** *adj*: ***le está bien empleado*** it serves him right **2** *m*, **-a** *f* employee; ***-a de hogar*** maid
emplear ⟨1a⟩ *v/t* (*usar*) use; *persona* employ
empleo *m* employment; (*puesto*) job; (*uso*) use; ***modo de empleo*** instructions for use *pl*, directions *pl*
emplomar ⟨1a⟩ *v/t S. Am.* fill
empobrecer ⟨2d⟩ **1** *v/t* impoverish, make poor **2** *v/i* become impoverished, become poor **3** *v/r* **empobrecerse** become

impoverished, become poor
empobrecimiento *m* impoverishment
empollar ⟨1a⟩ *v/i* F cram F, *Br* swot F
empollón *m* F grind F, *Br* swot F
emporio *m L.Am. almacén* department store
empotrado *adj* built-in, fitted
empotrarse ⟨1a⟩ *v/r* crash (***contra*** into)
emprendedor *adj* enterprising
emprender ⟨2a⟩ *v/t* embark on, undertake; ***emprenderla con alguien*** F take it out on s.o.
empresa *f* company; *fig* venture, undertaking; ***empresa de trabajo temporal*** temping agency
empresaria *f* businesswoman
empresarial *adj* business *atr*; ***ciencias empresariales*** business studies
empresario *m* businessman
empujar ⟨1a⟩ *v/t* push; *fig* urge on, spur on
empujón *m* push, shove; ***salían a empujones*** F they were pushing and shoving their way out
empuñar ⟨1a⟩ *v/t* grasp
emular ⟨1a⟩ *v/t* emulate
emulsión *f* emulsion
en *prp* (*dentro de*) in; (*sobre*) on; ***en un mes*** in a month; ***en la mesa*** on the table; ***en inglés*** in English; ***en la calle*** on the street, *Br tb* in the street; ***en casa*** at home; ***en coche / tren*** by car / train
enajenación *f* JUR transfer; ***enajenación mental*** insanity
enajenar ⟨1a⟩ *v/t* JUR transfer; (*trastornar*) drive insane
enamorado *adj* in love (***de*** with)
enamorar ⟨1a⟩ **1** *v/t*: ***lo enamoró*** she captivated him **2** *v/r* **enamorarse** fall in love (***de*** with)
enano **1** *adj* tiny; *perro*, *árbol* miniature, dwarf *atr* **2** *m* dwarf; ***trabajar como un enano*** *fig* F work like a dog F
enarbolar ⟨1a⟩ *v/t* hoist, raise
encabezamiento *m* heading
encabezar ⟨1f⟩ *v/t* head; *movimiento*, *revolución* lead
encabritarse ⟨1a⟩ *v/r de caballo* rear up
encadenar ⟨1a⟩ **1** *v/t* chain (up); *fig* link *o* put together **2** *v/r* **encadenarse** chain oneself (***a*** to)
encajar ⟨1a⟩ **1** *v/t piezas* fit; *golpe* take **2** *v/i* fit (***en*** in; ***con*** with)
encaje *m* lace
encalado *m* whitewashing
encalar ⟨1a⟩ *v/t* whitewash
encallar ⟨1a⟩ *v/i* MAR run aground
encaminarse ⟨1a⟩ *v/r* set off (***a*** for), head (***a*** for); *fig* be aimed *o* directed (***a*** at)
encandilar ⟨1a⟩ *v/t* dazzle
encantado *adj* (*contento*) delighted; *castillo* enchanted; ***¡encantado!*** nice to meet you
encantador *adj* charming
encantar ⟨1a⟩ *v/t*: ***me / le encanta*** I love / he loves it
encanto *m* (*atractivo*) charm; ***como por encanto*** as if by magic; ***eres un encanto*** you're an angel
encapricharse ⟨1a⟩ *v/r* fall in love (***de*** with)
encapuchado *adj* hooded
encaramarse ⟨1a⟩ *v/r* climb
encarar ⟨1a⟩ *v/t* approach; *desgracia etc* face up to
encarcelar ⟨1a⟩ *v/t* put in prison, imprison
encarecer ⟨2d⟩ **1** *v/t* put up the price of, make more expensive **2** *v/r* **encarecerse** become more expensive; *de precios* increase, rise
encarecidamente *adv*: ***le ruego encarecidamente que …*** I beg *o* urge you to …
encargado *m*, **-a** *f* person in charge; *de un negocio* manager
encargar ⟨1h⟩ **1** *v/t* (*pedir*) order; ***le encargué que me trajera …*** I asked him to bring me … **2** *v/r* **encargarse** (*tener responsibilidad*) be in charge; ***yo me encargo de la comida*** I'll take care of *o* see to the food
encargo *m* job, errand; COM order; ***¿te puedo hacer un encargo?*** can I ask you to do something for me?; ***hecho por encargo*** made to order
encariñarse ⟨1a⟩ *v/r*: ***encariñarse con alguien / algo*** grow fond of s.o/sth, become attached to s.o./sth
encarnado *adj* red
encarnar ⟨1a⟩ *v/t cualidad etc* embody; TEA play
encarnizado *adj* bitter, fierce
encarrilar ⟨1a⟩ *v/t fig* direct, guide
encasillar ⟨1a⟩ *v/t* class, classify; (*estereotipar*) pigeonhole
encasquetar ⟨1a⟩ *v/t gorro* etc pull down; ***me lo encasquetó*** F he landed me with it F
encasquillarse ⟨1a⟩ *v/r de arma* jam
encauzar ⟨1f⟩ *v/t tb fig* channel
encefalopatía *f*: ***encefalopatía espongiforme bovina*** bovine spongiform encephalitis, BSE
encendedor *m* lighter
encender ⟨2g⟩ **1** *v/t fuego* light; *luz*, *televisión* switch on, turn on; *fig* inflame, arouse, stir up **2** *v/r* **encenderse** *de luz*, *televisión* come on

encendido 1 *adj luz, televisión* (switched) on; *fuego* lit; *cara* red **2** *m* AUTO ignition
encerado *m* blackboard
encerar ⟨1a⟩ *v/t* polish, wax
encerrar ⟨1k⟩ **1** *v/t* lock up, shut up; (*contener*) contain **2** *v/r* **encerrarse** shut o.s. up
encerrona *f tb fig* trap
encestar ⟨1a⟩ *v/i* score
encharcado *adj* flooded, waterlogged
enchicharse ⟨1a⟩ *v/r L.Am.* (*emborracharse*) get drunk; *Rpl* P (*enojarse*) get angry, get mad F
enchilada *f Méx* GASTR enchilada (*tortilla with a meat or cheese filling*)
enchiloso *adj C.Am., Méx* hot
enchufado *m*: ***es un enchufado*** F he has connections, he has friends in high places
enchufar ⟨1a⟩ *v/t* EL plug in
enchufe *m* EL *macho* plug; *hembra* socket; ***tener enchufe*** *fig* F have pull F, have connections F
enchufismo *m* string-pulling
encía *f* gum
enciclopedia *f* encyclop(a)edia
encierro *m protesta* sit-in; *de toros* bull running
encima *adv* on top; ***encima de*** on top of, on; ***por encima de*** over, above; ***por encima de todo*** above all; ***lo ayudo, y encima se queja*** I help him and then he goes and complains; ***hacer algo muy por encima*** do sth very quickly; ***no lo llevo encima*** I haven't got it on me; ***ponerse algo encima*** put sth on
encimera *f sábana* top sheet; *Esp mostrador* worktop
encina *f* BOT holm oak
encinta *adj* pregnant
enclaustrarse ⟨1a⟩ *v/r fig* shut o.s. away
enclave *m* enclave
enclenque 1 *adj* sickly, weak **2** *m/f* weakling
encoger ⟨2c⟩ **1** *v/t* shrink; *las piernas* tuck in **2** *v/i de material* shrink **3** *v/r* **encogerse** *de material* shrink; *fig*: *de persona* be intimidated, cower; ***encogerse de hombros*** shrug (one's shoulders)
encolar ⟨1a⟩ *v/t* glue, stick
encolerizarse ⟨1f⟩ *v/r* get angry
encomienda *f L.Am.* HIST *grant of land and labor by colonial authorities after the Conquest*
enconado *adj* fierce, heated
encontrar ⟨1m⟩ **1** *v/t* find **2** *v/r* **encontrarse** (*reunirse*) meet; (*estar*) be; ***encontrarse con alguien*** meet s.o., run into s.o.; ***me encuentro bien*** I'm fine, I feel fine
encontronazo *m* smash, crash
encorvar ⟨1a⟩ *v/t* hunch; *estantería* cause to buckle
encrespar ⟨1a⟩ **1** *v/t pelo* curl; *mar* make rough *o* choppy; *fig* arouse, inflame **2** *v/r* **encresparse** *del mar* turn choppy; *fig* become inflamed
encrucijada *f* crossroads; *fig* dilemma
encuadernar ⟨1a⟩ *v/t* bind
encuadrar ⟨1a⟩ *v/t en marco* frame; *en grupo* include, place
encuartelar ⟨1a⟩ *v/t L.Am.* billet
encubierto *part* → ***encubrir***
encubrir ⟨3a; *part* ***encubierto***⟩ *v/t delincuente* harbo(u)r; *delito* cover up, conceal
encuentro *m* meeting, encounter; DEP game; ***salir*** *or* ***ir al encuentro de alguien*** meet s.o., greet s.o.
encuerado *adj L.Am.* naked
encuesta *f* survey; (*sondeo*) (opinion) poll
encuestar ⟨1a⟩ *v/t* poll
encumbrarse ⟨1a⟩ *v/r fig* rise to the top
encurtidos *mpl* pickles
ende *adv*: ***por ende*** therefore, consequently
endeble *adj* weak, feeble
endémico *adj* endemic
endemoniado *adj* possessed; *fig* F terrible, awful
enderezar ⟨1f⟩ **1** *v/t* straighten out **2** *v/r* **enderezarse** straighten up, stand up straight; *fig* straighten o.s. out, sort o.s out
endeudarse ⟨1a⟩ *v/r* get (o.s.) into debt
endiablado *adj fig* (*malo*) terrible, awful; (*difícil*) tough
endibia *f* BOT endive
endilgar ⟨1h⟩ *v/t*: ***me lo endilgó a mí*** F he landed me with it F; ***endilgar un sermón a alguien*** F lecture s.o., give s.o. a lecture
endosar ⟨1a⟩ *v/t* COM endorse; ***me lo endosó a mí*** F she landed me with it F
endrina *f* BOT sloe
endrogarse ⟨1h⟩ *v/r Méx, C.Am.* get into debt
endulzar ⟨1f⟩ *v/t* sweeten; (*suavizar*) soften
endurecer ⟨2d⟩ **1** *v/t* harden; *fig* toughen up **2** *v/r* **endurecerse** harden, become harder; *fig* become harder, toughen up
enebro *m* BOT juniper
enema *m* MED enema
enemigo 1 *adj* enemy *atr* **2** *m* enemy; ***ser enemigo de*** *fig* be opposed to, be against
enemistarse ⟨1a⟩ *v/r* fall out

energético *adj crisis* energy *atr*; *alimento* energy-giving
energía *f* energy; ***energía eólica*** wind power; ***energía nuclear*** nuclear power, nuclear energy; ***energía solar*** solar power, solar energy
enérgico *adj* energetic; *fig* forceful, strong
energúmeno *m* lunatic; ***ponerse hecho un energúmeno*** go crazy F, blow a fuse F
ene. *abr* (= ***enero***) Jan. (= January)
enero *m* January
enervar ⟨1a⟩ *v/t* irritate, get on the nerves of
enésimo *adj* nth; ***por -a vez*** for the umpteenth time
enfadado *adj* annoyed (**con** with); (*encolerizado*) angry (**con** with)
enfadar ⟨1a⟩ **1** *v/t* (*molestar*) annoy; (*encolerizar*) make angry, anger **2** *v/r* **enfadarse** (*molestarse*) get annoyed (**con** with); (*encolerizarse*) get angry (**con** with)
enfado *m* (*molestia*) annoyance; (*cólera*) anger
enfangarse ⟨1h⟩ *v/r* get muddy; ***enfangarse en*** *fig* get (o.s.) mixed up in
énfasis *m* emphasis; ***poner énfasis en*** emphasize, stress
enfático *adj* emphatic
enfermar ⟨1a⟩ **1** *v/t* drive crazy **2** *v/i* get sick, *Br tb* get ill
enfermedad *f* illness, disease
enfermería *f sala* infirmary, sickbay; *carrera* nursing
enfermero *m*, **-a** *f* nurse
enfermizo *adj* unhealthy
enfermo 1 *adj* sick, ill **2** *m*, **-a** *f* sick person
enfermoso *adj L.Am.* sickly, unhealthy
enfiestarse ⟨1a⟩ *v/r L.Am.* F party F, live it up F
enfocar ⟨1g⟩ *v/t cámara* focus; *imagen* get in focus; *fig*: *asunto* look at, consider
enfoque *m fig* approach
enfrentamiento *m* clash, confrontation
enfrentar ⟨1a⟩ **1** *v/t* confront, face up to **2** *v/r* **enfrentarse** DEP meet; ***enfrentarse con alguien*** confront s.o.; ***enfrentarse a algo*** face (up to) sth
enfrente *adv* opposite; ***enfrente del colegio*** opposite the school, across (the street) from the school
enfriar ⟨1c⟩ **1** *v/t vino* chill; *algo caliente* cool (down); *fig* cool **2** *v/r* **enfriarse** (*perder calor*) cool down; (*perder demasiado calor*) get cold, go cold; *fig* cool, cool off; MED catch a cold, catch a chill
enfurecer ⟨2d⟩ **1** *v/t* infuriate, make furious **2** *v/r* **enfurecerse** get furious, get into a rage **enfurecido** *adj* furious, enraged
enfurruñado *adj* F sulky
enfurruñarse ⟨1a⟩ *v/r* F go into a huff F
engalanar ⟨1a⟩ *v/t* decorate, deck
enganchar ⟨1a⟩ **1** *v/t* hook; F *novia, trabajo* land F **2** *v/r* **engancharse** get caught (**en** on); MIL sign up, enlist; ***engancharse a la droga*** F get hooked on drugs F
engañar ⟨1a⟩ **1** *v/t* deceive, cheat; (*ser infiel a*) cheat on, be unfaithful to; ***te han engañado*** you've been had **2** *v/r* **engañarse** (*mentirse*) deceive o.s., kid o.s. F; (*equivocarse*) be wrong
engaño *m* (*mentira*) deception, deceit; (*ardid*) trick
engarzar ⟨1f⟩ *v/t joya* set
engatusar ⟨1a⟩ *v/t* F sweet-talk F
engendrar ⟨1a⟩ *v/t* father; *fig* breed, engender *fml*
engendro *m fig* eyesore
englobar ⟨1a⟩ *v/t* include, embrace *fml*
engordar ⟨1a⟩ **1** *v/t* put on, gain **2** *v/i de persona* put on weight, gain weight; *de comida* be fattening
engorrar ⟨1a⟩ *v/t Méx, W.I.* F annoy
engorroso *adj* tricky
engranaje *m* TÉC gears *pl*; *fig* machinery
engrasar ⟨1a⟩ *v/t* grease, lubricate
engrase *m* greasing, lubrication
engreído *adj* conceited
engrosar ⟨1m⟩ **1** *v/t* swell, increase **2** *v/i* put on weight, gain weight
engrudo *m* (flour and water) paste
engullir ⟨3h⟩ *v/t* bolt (down)
enhebrar ⟨1a⟩ *v/t* thread, string
enhiesto *adj lit persona* erect, upright; *torre, árbol* lofty
enhorabuena *f* congratulations *pl*; ***dar la enhorabuena*** congratulate (**por** on)
enigma *m* enigma
enigmático *adj* enigmatic
enjabonar ⟨1a⟩ *v/t* soap
enjambre *m tb fig* swarm
enjoyado *adj* bejewel(l)ed
enjuagar ⟨1h⟩ *v/t* rinse
enjugar ⟨1h⟩ *v/t deuda etc* wipe out; *líquido* mop up; *lágrimas* wipe away
enjuiciar ⟨1b⟩ *v/t* JUR institute proceedings against; *fig* judge
enlace *m* link, connection; ***enlace matrimonial*** marriage
enlatar ⟨1a⟩ *v/t* can, *Br tb* tin
enlazar ⟨1f⟩ **1** *v/t* link (up), connect; *L.Am. con cuerda* rope, lasso **2** *v/i de carretera* link up (**con** with); AVIA, FERR connect (**con** with)
enloquecer ⟨2d⟩ **1** *v/t* drive crazy *o* mad **2** *v/i* go crazy *o* mad

enmarañar ⟨1a⟩ **1** *v/t pelo* tangle; *asunto* complicate, muddle **2** *v/r* **enmarañarse** *de pelo* get tangled; ***enmarañarse en algo*** get entangled *o* embroiled in sth
enmarcar ⟨1g⟩ *v/t* frame
enmascarar ⟨1a⟩ *v/t* hide, disguise
enmendar ⟨1k⟩ **1** *v/t asunto* rectify, put right; JUR, POL amend; ***enmendarle la plana a alguien*** find fault with what s.o. has done **2** *v/r* **enmendarse** mend one's ways
enmienda *f* POL amendment
enmicar ⟨1g⟩ *v/t L.Am.* laminate
enmudecer ⟨2d⟩ **1** *v/t* silence **2** *v/i* fall silent
ennoblecer ⟨2d⟩ *v/t* ennoble
enojado *adj L.Am.* angry
enojar ⟨1a⟩ **1** *v/t* (*molestar*) annoy; *L.Am.* (*encolerizar*) make angry **2** *v/r* **enojarse** *L.Am.* (*molestarse*) get annoyed; (*encolerizarse*) get angry
enojo *m L.Am.* anger
enojón *adj L.Am.* F irritable, touchy
enojoso *adj* (*delicado*) awkward; (*aburrido*) tedious, tiresome
enorgullecer ⟨2d⟩ **1** *v/t* make proud, fill with pride **2** *v/r* **enorgullecerse** be proud (***de*** of)
enorme *adj* enormous, huge
enrarecido *adj aire* rarefied; *relaciones* strained
enredadera *f* BOT creeper, climbing plant
enredar ⟨1a⟩ **1** *v/t* tangle, get tangled; *fig* complicate, make complicated **2** *v/i* make trouble **3** *v/r* **enredarse** get tangled; *fig* get complicated; ***enredarse en algo*** get mixed up *o* involved in sth
enredo *m* tangle; (*confusión*) mess, confusion; (*intriga*) intrigue; *amoroso* affair
enrevesado *adj* complicated, involved
enriquecer ⟨2d⟩ **1** *v/t* make rich; *fig* enrich **2** *v/r* **enriquecerse** get rich; *fig* be enriched
enrojecer ⟨2d⟩ **1** *v/t* turn red **2** *v/i* blush, go red
enrolarse ⟨1a⟩ *v/r* MIL enlist
enrollar ⟨1a⟩ **1** *v/t* roll up; *cable* coil; *hilo* wind; ***me enrolla*** F I like it, I think it's great **2** *v/r* **enrollarse** F *hablar* go on and on F; ***se enrolló mucho con nosotros*** (*se portó bien*) he was great to us; ***¡no te enrolles!*** F get to the point!; ***enrollarse con alguien*** *fig* F neck with s.o.
enroscar ⟨1g⟩ **1** *v/t tornillo* screw in; *cable, cuerda* coil **2** *v/r* **enroscarse** coil up
ensaimada *f* GASTR *pastry in the form of a spiral*
ensalada *f* GASTR salad
ensaladera *f* salad bowl
ensaladilla *f*: ***ensaladilla rusa*** GASTR Russian salad
ensalmo *m*: ***como por ensalmo*** as if by magic
ensalzar ⟨1f⟩ *v/t* extol, praise
ensamblar ⟨1a⟩ *v/t* assemble
ensanchar ⟨1a⟩ **1** *v/t* widen; *prenda* let out **2** *v/r* **ensancharse** widen, get wider; *de prenda* stretch
ensangrentar ⟨1k⟩ *v/t* stain with blood, cover with blood
ensañarse ⟨1a⟩ *v/r* show no mercy (***con*** to)
ensartar ⟨1a⟩ **1** *v/t en hilo* string; *aguja* thread; *L.Am.* (*engañar*) trick, trap **2** *v/r* **ensartarse** *L.Am. en discusión* get involved, get caught up
ensayar ⟨1a⟩ *v/t* test, try (out); TEA rehearse
ensayo *m* TEA rehearsal; *escrito* essay; ***ensayo general*** dress rehearsal
enseguida *adv* immediately, right away
ensenada *f* inlet, cove
enseñanza *f* teaching; ***enseñanza primaria*** elementary education, *Br* primary education; ***enseñanza secundaria*** *or* ***media*** secondary education; ***enseñanza superior*** higher education
enseñar ⟨1a⟩ *v/t* (*dar clases*) teach; (*mostrar*) show
ensillar ⟨1a⟩ *v/t* saddle
ensimismarse ⟨1a⟩ *v/r* become lost in thought; *L.Am.* F get conceited *o* big-headed F
ensombrecer ⟨2d⟩ *v/t* cast a shadow over
ensordecedor *adj* deafening
ensuciar ⟨1b⟩ **1** *v/t* (get) dirty; *fig* sully, tarnish **2** *v/r* **ensuciarse** get dirty; *fig* get one's hands dirty
ensueño *m*: ***de ensueño*** *fig* fairy-tale *atr*, dream *atr*
entablar ⟨1a⟩ *v/t* strike up, start
entablillar ⟨1a⟩ *v/t* splint, put in a splint
entarimado *m* (*suelo*) floorboards *pl*; (*plataforma*) stage, platform
ente *m* (*ser*) being, entity; F (*persona rara*) oddball F; (*organización*) body
entejar ⟨1a⟩ *v/t L.Am.* tile
entender ⟨2g⟩ **1** *v/t* understand; ***dar a entender a alguien*** give s.o. to understand **2** *v/i* understand; ***entender de algo*** know about sth **3** *v/r* **entenderse** communicate; ***a ver si nos entendemos*** let's get this straight; ***yo me entiendo*** I know what I'm doing; ***entenderse con alguien*** get along with s.o., get on with s.o. **4** *m*: ***a mi entender*** in my opinion, to my mind
entendido **1** *adj* understood; ***¿entendi-***

E

do? do you understand?, understood?; ***tengo entendido que*** I gather *o* understand that **2** *m*, **-a** *f* expert, authority

entendimiento *m* understanding; (*inteligencia*) mind

enterado *adj* knowledgeable, well-informed; ***estar enterado de*** know about, have heard about; ***darse por enterado*** get the message, take the hint

enterarse ⟨1a⟩ *v/r* find out, hear (***de*** about); ***¡para que te enteres!*** F so there! F; ***¡se va a enterar!*** F he's in for it! F

entereza *f* fortitude

enternecer ⟨2d⟩ *v/t* move, touch

entero 1 *adj* (*completo*) whole, entire; (*no roto*) intact, undamaged; ***por entero*** completely, entirely **2** *m* (*punto*) point

enterrar ⟨1k⟩ *v/t* bury; ***enterrar a todos*** *fig* outlive everybody

entidad *f* entity, body

entierro *m* burial; (*funeral*) funeral

entonar ⟨1a⟩ **1** *v/t* intone, sing; *fig* F perk up **2** *v/i* sing in tune **3** *v/r* **entonarse** *con bebida* get tipsy

entonces *adv* then; ***desde entonces*** since, since then; ***por entonces, en aquel entonces*** in those days, at that time

entornar ⟨1a⟩ *v/t puerta* leave ajar; *ojos* half close

entorno *m* environment

entorpecer ⟨2d⟩ *v/t* hold up, hinder; *paso* obstruct; *entendimiento* dull

entrada *f acción* entry; *lugar* entrance; *localidad* ticket; *pago* deposit, down payment; *de comida* starter; ***de entrada*** from the outset, from the start

entrañable *adj amistad* close, deep; *amigo* close, dear; *recuerdo* fond

entrañar ⟨1a⟩ *v/t* entail, involve

entrañas *fpl* entrails

entrar ⟨1a⟩ **1** *v/i para indicar acercamiento* come in, enter; *para indicar alejamiento* go in, enter; *caber* fit; ***me entró frío / sueño*** I got cold / sleepy, I began to feel cold / sleepy; ***no me entra en la cabeza*** I can't understand it **2** *v/t para indicar acercamiento* bring in; *para indicar alejamiento* take in

entre *prp dos cosas, personas* between; *más de dos* among(st); *expresando cooperación* between; ***la relación entre ellos*** the relationship between them; ***entre nosotros*** among us; ***lo pagamos entre todos*** we paid for it among *o* between us

entreabierto 1 *part* → ***entreabrir* 2** *adj* half-open; *puerta* ajar

entreabrir ⟨3a; *part* ***entreabierto*** ⟩ *v/t* half-open

entreacto *m* TEA interval

entrecejo *m*: ***fruncir el entrecejo*** frown

entrecomillar ⟨1a⟩ *v/t* put in quotation marks

entrecortado *adj habla* halting; *respiración* difficult, labo(u)red

entrecot *m* entrecote

entredicho *m*: ***poner en entredicho*** call into question, question

entrega *f* handing over; *de mercancías* delivery; (*dedicación*) dedication, devotion; ***entrega a domicilio*** (home) delivery; ***entrega de premios*** prize-giving, presentation; ***hacer entrega de algo a alguien*** present s.o. with sth

entregar ⟨1h⟩ **1** *v/t* give, hand over; *trabajo, deberes* hand in; *mercancías* deliver; *premio* present **2** *v/r* **entregarse** give o.s. up; ***entregarse a*** *fig* devote o.s. to, dedicate o.s. to

entrelazar ⟨1f⟩ *v/t* interweave, intertwine

entremeses *mpl* GASTR appetizers, hors d'oeuvres

entremezclar ⟨1a⟩ **1** *v/t* intermingle, mix **2** *v/r* **entremezclarse** intermingle, mix

entrenador *m*, **entrenadora** *f* coach

entrenamiento *m* coaching

entrenar ⟨1a⟩ **1** *v/t* train **2** *v/r* **entrenarse** train

entrepierna *f* ANAT crotch

entresacar ⟨1g⟩ *v/t* extract, select

entresijos *mpl fig* details, ins and outs F

entresuelo *m* mezzanine; TEA dress circle

entretanto *adv* meanwhile, in the meantime

entretecho *m Arg, Chi* attic

entretener ⟨2l⟩ **1** *v/t* (*divertir*) entertain, amuse; (*retrasar*) keep, detain; (*distraer*) distract **2** *v/i* be entertaining **3** *v/r* **entretenerse** (*divertirse*) amuse o.s.; (*distraerse*) keep o.s. busy; (*retrasarse*) linger

entretenido *adj* (*divertido*) entertaining, enjoyable; ***estar entretenido*** *ocupado* be busy

entretenimiento *m* entertainment, amusement

entrevero *m S. Am.* (*lío*) mix-up, mess; *Chi* (*discusión*) argument

entrevista *f* interview

entrevistar ⟨1a⟩ **1** *v/t* interview **2** *v/r* **entrevistarse**: ***entrevistarse con alguien*** meet (with) s.o.

entristecer ⟨2d⟩ **1** *v/t* sadden **2** *v/r* **entristecerse** grow sad

entrometerse ⟨2a⟩ *v/r* meddle (***en*** in)

entrometido 1 *part* → ***entrometerse* 2** *adj* meddling *atr*, interfering **3** *m* meddler, busybody

entronizar ⟨1f⟩ *v/t fig* instal(l)
entumecer ⟨2d⟩ **1** *v/t* numb **2** *v/r* **entumecerse** go numb, get stiff
enturbiar ⟨1b⟩ *v/t tb fig* cloud
entusiasmado *adj* excited, delirious
entusiasmar ⟨1a⟩ *v/t* excite, make enthusiastic
entusiasmo *m* enthusiasm
entusiasta 1 *adj* enthusiastic **2** *m/f* enthusiast
enumerar ⟨1a⟩ *v/t* list, enumerate
enunciar ⟨1b⟩ *v/t* state
envalentonarse ⟨1a⟩ *v/r* become bolder *o* more daring; (*insolentarse*) become defiant
envanecerse ⟨2d⟩ *v/r* become conceited *o* vain
envasar ⟨1a⟩ *v/t en botella* bottle; *en lata* can; *en paquete* pack
envase *m* container; *botella* (empty) bottle; ***envase de cartón*** carton; ***envase no retornable*** nonreturnable bottle
envejecer ⟨2d⟩ **1** *v/t* age, make look older **2** *v/i* age, grow old
envejecimiento *m* aging, ageing
envenenar ⟨1a⟩ *v/t tb fig* poison
envergadura *f* AVIA wingspan; MAR breadth; *fig* magnitude, importance; ***de gran*** *or* ***mucha envergadura*** *fig* of great importance
enviado *m*, **-a** *f* POL envoy; *de un periódico* reporter, correspondent; ***enviado especial*** POL special envoy; *de un periódico* special correspondent
enviar ⟨1c⟩ *v/t* send
enviciarse ⟨1b⟩ *v/r* get addicted (***con*** to)
envidia *f* envy, jealousy; ***me da envidia*** I'm envious *o* jealous; ***tener envidia a alguien de algo*** envy s.o. sth
envidiar ⟨1b⟩ *v/t* envy; ***envidiar a alguien por algo*** envy s.o. sth
envidioso *adj* envious, jealous
envilecer ⟨2d⟩ **1** *v/t* degrade, debase **2** *v/r* **envilecerse** degrade o.s., debase o.s.
envío *m* shipment
enviudar ⟨1a⟩ *v/i* be widowed
envoltorio *m* wrapper
envoltura *f* cover, covering; *de regalo* wrapping; *de caramelo* wrapper
envolver ⟨2h; *part* ***envuelto***⟩ **1** *v/t* wrap (up); (*rodear*) surround, envelop; (*involucrar*) involve; ***envolver a alguien en algo*** involve s.o. in sth **2** *v/r* **envolverse** wrap o.s. up; ***envolverse en*** *fig* become involved in
envuelto *part* → ***envolver***
enyesado *m* plastering
enzarzarse ⟨1f⟩ *v/r* get involved (***en*** in)
eólico *adj* wind *atr*
épico *adj* epic
epidemia *f* epidemic
epilepsia *f* MED epilepsy
epílogo *m* epilog(ue)
episcopal *adj* episcopal
episodio *m* episode
epistolar *adj* epistolary
epitafio *m* epitaph
época *f* time, period; *parte del año* time of year; GEOL epoch; ***hacer época*** be epoch-making
epopeya *f* epic, epic poem
equidad *f* fairness
equidistante *adj* equidistant
equilibrado *adj* well-balanced
equilibrar ⟨1a⟩ *v/t* balance
equilibrio *m* balance; FÍS equilibrium
equino *adj* equine
equinoccio *m* equinox
equipaje *m* baggage; ***equipaje de mano*** hand baggage
equipamiento *m*: ***equipamiento de serie*** AUTO standard features *pl*
equipar ⟨1a⟩ *v/t* equip (***con*** with)
equiparar ⟨1a⟩ *v/t* put on a level (***a*** *or* ***con*** with); ***equiparar algo con algo*** *fig* compare *o* liken sth to sth
equipo *m* DEP team; *accesorios* equipment; ***equipo de múísica*** *or* ***de sonido*** sound system
equitación *f* riding
equitativo *adj* fair, equitable
equivalente *m/adj* equivalent
equivaler ⟨2q⟩ *v/i* be equivalent (***a*** to)
equivocación *f* mistake; ***por equivocación*** by mistake
equivocado *adj* wrong; ***estar equivocado*** be wrong, be mistaken
equivocar ⟨1g⟩ **1** *v/t*: ***equivocar a alguien*** make s.o. make a mistake **2** *v/r* **equivocarse** make a mistake; ***te has equivocado*** you are wrong *o* mistaken; ***equivocarse de núímero*** TELEC get the wrong number
equívoco 1 *adj* ambiguous, equivocal **2** *m* misunderstanding; (*error*) mistake
era *f* era
erección *f* erection
eres *vb* → ***ser***
ergonómico *adj* ergonomic
erguir ⟨3n⟩ **1** *v/t* raise, lift; (*poner derecho*) straighten **2** *v/r* **erguirse** *de persona* stand up, rise; *de edificio* rise
erial *m* uncultivated land
erigir ⟨3c⟩ **1** *v/t* erect **2** *v/r* **erigirse**: ***erigirse en*** set o.s. up as
erizarse ⟨1f⟩ *v/r de pelo* stand on end
erizo *m* ZO hedgehog; ***erizo de mar*** ZO sea urchin

E

ermita *f* chapel
ermitaño **1** *m* zo hermit crab **2** *m*, **-a** *f* hermit
erogación *f Méx, S. Am.* expenditure, outlay
erógeno *adj* erogenous
erosión *f* erosion
erosionar ⟨1a⟩ *v/t* GEOL erode
erótico *adj* erotic
erotismo *m* eroticism
erradicar ⟨1g⟩ *v/t* eradicate, wipe out
errante *adj* wandering
errar ⟨1l⟩ **1** *v/t* miss; ***errar el tiro*** miss **2** *v/i* miss; ***errar es humano*** to err is human
equivocarse be wrong, be mistaken
errata *f* mistake, error; *de imprenta* misprint
erre *f*: ***erre que erre*** F doggedly, stubbornly
erróneo *adj* wrong, erroneous *fml*
error *m* mistake, error; ***error de cálculo*** error of judg(e)ment
eructar ⟨1a⟩ *v/i* belch F, burp F
eructo *m* belch F, burp F
erudito **1** *adj* learned, erudite **2** *m* scholar
erupción *f* GEOL eruption; MED rash
esbelto *adj* slim, slender
esbozar ⟨1f⟩ *v/t* sketch; *idea, proyecto etc* outline
esbozo *m* sketch; *de idea, proyecto etc* outline
escabeche *m type of marinade*
escabroso *adj* rough; *problema* tricky; *relato* indecent
escabullirse ⟨3h⟩ *v/r* escape, slip away
escala *f tb* MÚS scale; AVIA stopover; ***escala de cuerda*** rope ladder; ***escala de valores*** scale of values; ***a escala*** to scale, life-sized
escalada *f* DEP climb, ascent; ***escalada de los precios*** increase in prices, escalation of prices
escalador *m*, **escaladora** *f* climber
escalafón *m fig* ladder
escalar ⟨1a⟩ **1** *v/t* climb, scale **2** *v/i* climb
escaldar ⟨1a⟩ *v/t* GASTR blanch; *manos* scald
escalera *f* stairs *pl*, staircase; ***escalera de caracol*** spiral staircase; ***escalera de incendios*** fire escape; ***escalera de mano*** ladder; ***escalera mecánica*** escalator
escalfar ⟨1a⟩ *v/t* poach
escalofriante *adj* horrifying
escalofrío *m* shiver
escalón *m* step; *de escalera de mano* rung
escalonar ⟨1a⟩ *v/t en tiempo* stagger; *terreno* terrace
escalope *m* escalope
escama *f* zo scale; *de jabón, piel* flake
escamar ⟨1a⟩ **1** *v/t* scale, remove the scales from; *fig* make suspicious **2** *v/r* **escamarse** become suspicious
escamotear ⟨1a⟩ *v/t* (*ocultar*) hide, conceal; (*negar*) withhold
escampar ⟨1a⟩ *v/i* clear up, stop raining
escanciar ⟨1b⟩ *v/t fml* pour
escandalizar ⟨1f⟩ **1** *v/t* shock, scandalize **2** *v/r* **escandalizarse** be shocked
escándalo *m* (*asunto vergonzoso*) scandal; (*jaleo*) racket, ruckus; ***armar un escándalo*** make a scene
escandaloso *adj* (*vergonzoso*) scandalous, shocking; (*ruidoso*) noisy, rowdy
Escandinavia Scandinavia
escanear ⟨1a⟩ *v/t* scan
escáner *m* scanner
escaño *m* POL seat
escapar ⟨1a⟩ **1** *v/t* escape (**de** from); ***dejar escapar*** *oportunidad* pass up, let slip; *suspiro* let out, give **2** *v/r* **escaparse** (*huir*) escape (**de** from); *de casa* run away (**de** from); ***escaparse de*** *situación* get out of
escaparate *m* store window
escapatoria *f*: ***no tener escapatoria*** have no way out
escape *m de gas* leak; AUTO exhaust; ***salir a escape*** rush out
escarabajo *m* zo beetle
escaramuza *f* skirmish
escarbadientes *m inv* toothpick
escarbar ⟨1a⟩ **1** *v/i tb fig* dig around (**en** in) **2** *v/t* dig around in
escarceos *mpl* forays, dabbling *sg*; ***escarceos amorosos*** romantic *o* amorous adventures
escarcha *f* frost
escardar ⟨1a⟩ *v/t* hoe
escarmentar ⟨1k⟩ **1** *v/t* teach a lesson to **2** *v/i* learn one's lesson; ***escarmentar en cabeza ajena*** learn from other people's mistakes
escarmiento *m* lesson; ***le sirvió de escarmiento*** it taught him a lesson
escarnio *m* ridicule, derision
escarola *f* endive, escarole
escarpado *adj* sheer, steep
escarpia *f* hook
escasear ⟨1a⟩ *v/i* be scarce, be in short supply
escasez *f* shortage, scarcity
escaso *adj recursos* limited; ***andar escaso de algo*** *falto* be short of sth; ***-as posibilidades de*** not much chance of, little chance of; ***falta un mes escaso*** it's barely a month away
escatimar ⟨1a⟩ *v/t* be mean with, be very sparing with; ***no escatimar esfuerzos***

be unstinting in one's efforts, spare no effort

escayola *f* (plaster) cast

escayolar ⟨1a⟩ *v/t* put in a (plaster) cast

escena *f* scene; *escenario* stage; ***entrar en escena*** come on stage; ***hacer una escena*** *fig* make a scene

escenario *m* stage; *fig* scene

escénico *adj* stage *atr*

escenificar ⟨1g⟩ *v/t* stage

escepticismo *m* skepticism, *Br* scepticism

escéptico 1 *adj* skeptical, *Br* sceptical **2** *m*, **-a** *f* skeptic, *Br* sceptic

escindirse ⟨3a⟩ *v/r* (*fragmentarse*) split (**en** into); (*segregarse*) break away (**de** from)

escisión *f* (*fragmentación*) split; (*segregación*) break

esclarecer ⟨2d⟩ *v/t* throw *o* shed light on; *misterio* clear up

esclarecimiento *m* clarification; *de misterio* solving

esclavitud *f* slavery

esclavizar ⟨1f⟩ *v/t* enslave; *fig* tie down

esclavo *m* slave

esclerosis *f* MED: ***esclerosis múíltiple*** multiple sclerosis

escoba *f* broom

escobilla *f* small brush; AUTO wiper blade

escocer ⟨2b & 2h⟩ *v/i* sting, smart; ***todavía escuece la derrota*** he's still smarting from the defeat

escocés 1 *adj* Scottish **2** *m* Scot, Scotsman

escocesa *f* Scot, Scotswoman

Escocia Scotland

escoger ⟨2c⟩ *v/t* choose, select

escogido *adj* select

escolar 1 *adj* school *atr* **2** *m/f* student

escolarización *f* education, schooling; ***escolarización obligatoria*** compulsory education

escolarizar ⟨1f⟩ *v/t* educate, provide schooling for

escolástico *adj* scholarly

escollera *f* breakwater

escollo *m* MAR reef; (*obstáculo*) hurdle, obstacle

escolta 1 *f* escort **2** *m/f motorista* outrider; (*guardaespaldas*) bodyguard

escoltar ⟨1a⟩ *v/t* escort

escombros *mpl* rubble *sg*

esconder ⟨2a⟩ **1** *v/t* hide, conceal **2** *v/r* **esconderse** hide

escondidas *fpl S. Am.* hide-and-seek *sg*; ***a escondidas*** in secret, secretly

escondite *m lugar* hiding place; *juego* hide-and-seek

escondrijo *m* hiding place

escopeta *f* shotgun; ***escopeta de aire comprimido*** air gun, air rifle

escopetado *adj*: ***salir escopetado*** F shoot *o* dash off F

escopetazo *m* gunshot

escorbuto *m* scurvy

escoria *f* slag; *desp* dregs *pl*

Escorpio *m/f inv* ASTR Scorpio

escorpión *m* ZO scorpion

escotado *adj* low-cut

escote *m* neckline; *de mujer* cleavage

escotilla *f* MAR hatch

escozor *m* burning sensation, stinging; *fig* bitterness

escribir ⟨3a; *part* ***escrito*** ⟩ *v/t* write; (*deletrear*) spell; ***escribir a mano*** hand-write, write by hand; ***escribir a máquina*** type

escrito 1 *part* → ***escribir*** **2** *adj* written; ***por escrito*** in writing **3** *m* document; ***escritos*** writings

escritor *m*, **escritora** *f* writer, author

escritorio *m* desk; ***artículos de escritorio*** stationery

escritura *f* writing; JUR deed; ***Sagradas Escrituras*** Holy Scripture

escrúípulo *m* scruple; ***sin escrúípulos*** unscrupulous

escrupuloso *adj* (*cuidadoso*) meticulous; (*honrado*) scrupulous; (*aprensivo*) fastidious

escrutar ⟨1a⟩ *v/t* scrutinize; *votos* count

escrutinio *m de votos* count; (*inspección*) scrutiny

escuadrón *m* squadron

escuálido *adj* skinny, emaciated

escucha *f*: ***estar a la escucha*** be listening out; ***escuchas*** *pl* ***telefónicas*** wire-tapping *sg*, *Br tb* phone-tapping *sg*

escuchar ⟨1a⟩ **1** *v/t* listen to; *L.Am.* (*oír*) hear **2** *v/i* listen

escuchimizado *adj* F puny F, scrawny F

escudarse ⟨1a⟩ *v/r fig* hide (**en** behind)

escudería *f* stable

escudilla *f* bowl

escudo *m arma* shield; *insignia* badge; *moneda* escudo; ***escudo de armas*** coat of arms

escudriñar ⟨1a⟩ *v/t* (*mirar de lejos*) scan; (*examinar*) scrutinize

escuela *f* school; ***escuela de comercio*** business school; ***escuela de idiomas*** language school; ***escuela primaria*** elementary school, *Br* primary school

escuelero 1 *adj L.Am.* school *atr* **2** *m*, **-a** *f L.Am.* (*maestro*) teacher; *Pe, Bol* (*alumno*) student

escueto *adj* succinct, concise

escuincle *m/f Méx, C.Am.* F kid
esculpir ⟨3a⟩ *v/t* sculpt
escultor *m*, **escultora** *f* sculptor
escultura *f* sculpture
escupidera *f* spitoon; *L.Am.* chamber pot
escupir ⟨3a⟩ **1** *v/i* spit **2** *v/t* spit out
escupitajo *m* F gob of spit F
escurreplatos *m inv* plate rack
escurridizo *adj* slippery; *fig* evasive
escurridor *m* (*colador*) colander; (*escurreplatos*) plate rack
escurrir ⟨3a⟩ **1** *v/t ropa* wring out; *platos, verduras* drain **2** *v/i de platos* drain; *de ropa* drip-dry **3** *v/r* **escurrirse** *de líquido* drain away; (*deslizarse*) slip; (*escaparse*) slip away
escusado *m* bathroom
ese, **esa**, **esos**, **esas** *det singular* that; *plural* those
ése, **ésa**, **ésos**, **ésas** *pron singular* that (one); *plural* those (ones); ***le ofrecí dinero pero ni por ésas*** I offered him money but even that wasn't enough; ***no soy de ésos que*** I'm not one of those who
esencia *f* essence
esencial *adj* essential
esfera *f* sphere; ***esfera de actividad*** *fig* field *o* sphere (of activity)
esférico **1** *adj* spherical **2** *m* DEP F ball
esfinge *f* sphinx
esforzarse ⟨1f & 1m⟩ *v/r* make an effort, try hard
esfuerzo *m* effort; ***hacer un esfuerzo*** make an effort; ***sin esfuerzo*** effortlessly
esfumarse ⟨1a⟩ *v/r* F *tb fig* disappear
esgrima *f* fencing
esgrimir ⟨3a⟩ *v/t arma* wield; *fig: argumento* put forward, use
esguince *m* sprain
eslabón *m* link; ***el eslabón perdido*** the missing link
eslavo **1** *adj* Slavic, Slavonic **2** *m*, **-a** *f* Slav
eslogan *m* slogan
eslora *f* length
Eslovaquia Slovakia
Eslovenia Slovenia
esmalte *m* enamel; ***esmalte de uñas*** nail polish, nail varnish
esmerado *adj* meticulous
esmeralda *f* emerald
esmerarse ⟨1a⟩ *v/r* take great care (**en** over)
esmerilado *adj*: ***cristal esmerilado*** frosted glass
esmero *m* care; ***con esmero*** carefully
esmirriado *adj* F skinny F, scrawny F
esmoquin *m* tuxedo, *Br* dinner jacket
esnifar ⟨1a⟩ *v/t* F *pegamento* sniff F; *cocaína* snort F
esnob **1** *adj* snobbish **2** *m* snob
esnobismo *m* snobbishness
eso *pron* that; ***en eso*** just then, just at that moment; ***eso mismo, eso es*** that's it, that's the way; ***a eso de las dos*** at around two; ***por eso*** that's why; ***¿y eso?*** why's that?; ***y eso que le dije que no se lo contara*** and after I told him not to tell her
esotérico *adj* esoteric
espabilado *adj* (*listo*) bright, smart; (*vivo*) sharp, on the ball F
espabilar ⟨1a⟩ **1** *v/t* (*quitar el sueño*) wake up, revive; ***lo ha espabilado*** (*avivado*) she's got him to wise up **2** *v/i* (*darse prisa*) hurry up, get a move on; (*avivarse*) wise up **3** *v/r* **espabilarse** *del sueño* wake oneself up; (*darse prisa*) hurry up, get a move on; (*avivarse*) wise up
espacial *adj cohete, viaje* space *atr*; FÍS, MAT spatial
espaciarse ⟨1a⟩ *v/r* become more (and more) infrequent
espacio *m* space; TV program, *Br* programme; ***espacios verdes*** green spaces; ***espacio de tiempo*** space of time; ***espacio vital*** living space
espacioso *adj* spacious, roomy
espada *f* sword; ***espadas*** *pl* (*en naipes*) *suit in Spanish deck of cards*; ***estar entre la espada y la pared*** be between a rock and a hard place
espadachín *m* skilled swordsman
espaguetis *mpl* spaghetti *sg*
espalda *f* back; ***a espaldas de alguien*** behind s.o.'s back; ***de espaldas a*** with one's back to; ***por la espalda*** from behind; ***caerse de espaldas*** fall flat on one's back; ***no me des la espalda*** don't sit with your back to me; ***nadar a espalda*** swim backstroke; ***tener cubiertas las espaldas*** *fig* keep one' s back covered; ***volver la espalda a alguien*** *fig* turn one's back on s.o.
espaldarazo *m* slap on the back; (*reconocimiento*) recognition
espalderas *fpl* wall bars
espantajo *m* scarecrow; *fig* sight
espantapájaros *m inv* scarecrow
espantar ⟨1a⟩ **1** *v/t* (*asustar*) frighten, scare; (*ahuyentar*) frighten away, shoo away; F (*horrorizar*) horrify, appal(l) **2** *v/r* **espantarse** get frightened, get scared; F (*horrorizarse*) be horrified, be appal(l)ed
espanto *m* (*susto*) fright; *L.Am.* (*fantasma*) ghost; ***nos llenó de espanto*** *desagrado* we were horrified; ***¡qué espanto!*** how awful!; ***de espanto*** terrible

espantoso *adj* horrific, appalling; *para enfatizar* terrible, dreadful; ***hace un calor espantoso*** it's terribly hot, it's incredibly hot
España Spain
español 1 *adj* Spanish **2** *m idioma* Spanish **3** *m*, **-a** *f* Spaniard; ***los españoles*** the Spanish
esparadrapo *m* Band-Aid®, *Br* plaster
esparcimiento *m* relaxation
esparcir ⟨3b⟩ **1** *v/t papeles* scatter; *rumor* spread **2** *v/r* **esparcirse** *de papeles* be scattered; *de rumor* spread
espárrago *m* BOT asparagus; ***espárrago triguero*** wild asparagus; ***¡vete a freír espárragos!*** F get lost! F
espartano *adj* spartan
esparto *m* BOT esparto grass
espasmo *m* spasm
espátula *f* spatula; *en pintura* palette knife
especia *f* spice
especial *adj* special; (*difícil*) fussy; ***en especial*** especially
especialidad *f* specialty, *Br* speciality
especialista *m/f* specialist, expert; *en cine* stuntman; *mujer* stuntwoman
especializarse ⟨1f⟩ *v/r* specialize (**en** in)
especie *f* BIO species; (*tipo*) kind, sort
especiero *m* spice rack
especificar ⟨1g⟩ *v/t* specify
específico *adj* specific
espectacular *adj* spectacular
espectáculo *m* TEA show; (*escena*) sight; ***dar el espectáculo*** *fig* make a spectacle of o.s.
espectador *m*, **espectadora** *f en cine etc* member of the audience; DEP spectator; (*observador*) on-looker, observer
espectro *m* FÍS spectrum; (*fantasma*) ghost
especulación *f* speculation
especular ⟨1a⟩ *v/i* speculate
especulativo *adj* speculative
espejismo *m* mirage
espejo *m* mirror; ***espejo retrovisor*** rear-view mirror
espeleólogo *m* spelunker, *Br* pot-holer
espeluznante *adj* horrific, horrifying
espera *f* wait; ***sala de espera*** waiting room; ***en espera de*** pending; ***estar a la espera de*** be waiting for
esperanza *f* hope; ***esperanza de vida*** life expectancy
esperar ⟨1a⟩ **1** *v/t* (*aguardar*) wait for; *con esperanza* hope; (*suponer, confiar en*) expect **2** *v/i* (*aguardar*) wait
esperma *f* sperm
espesar ⟨1a⟩ **1** *v/t* thicken **2** *v/r* **espesarse** thicken, become thick
espeso *adj* thick; *vegetación, niebla* thick, dense
espesor *m* thickness
espesura *f* dense vegetation
espía *m/f* spy
espiar ⟨1c⟩ **1** *v/t* spy on **2** *v/i* spy
espiga *f* BOT ear, spike
espina *f de planta* thorn; *de pez* bone; ***espina dorsal*** spine, backbone; ***dar mala espina a alguien*** F make s.o. feel uneasy
espinacas *fpl* BOT spinach *sg*
espinazo *m* spine, backbone; ***doblar el espinazo*** *fig* (*trabajar mucho*) work o.s. into the ground; (*humillarse*) kowtow (***ante*** to)
espinilla *f de la pierna* shin; *en la piel* pimple, spot
espinoso *adj* thorny, prickly; *fig* thorny, knotty
espionaje *m* spying, espionage
espiral 1 *adj* spiral *atr* **2** *f* spiral
espirar ⟨1a⟩ *v/t & v/i* exhale
espiritismo *m* spiritualism
espíritu *m* spirit
espiritual *adj* spiritual
espléndido *adj* splendid, magnificent; (*generoso*) generous
esplendor *m* splendo(u)r
espliego *m* lavender
espolear ⟨1a⟩ *v/t tb fig* spur on
espolvorear ⟨1a⟩ *v/t* sprinkle
esponja *f* sponge
esponjoso *adj bizcocho* spongy; *toalla* soft, fluffy
espónsor *m/f* sponsor
esponsorizar ⟨1f⟩ *v/t* sponsor
espontáneo *adj* spontaneous
esporádico *adj* sporadic
esposa *f* wife
esposas *fpl* (*manillas*) handcuffs *pl*
esposar ⟨1a⟩ *v/t* handcuff
esposo *m* husband
esprint *m* sprint
espuela *f* spur
espuerta *f*: ***ganar dinero a espuertas*** F make money hand over fist F
espuma *f* foam; *de jabón* lather; *de cerveza* froth; ***espuma de afeitar*** shaving foam; ***espuma moldeadora*** styling mousse
espumadera *f* slotted spoon, skimmer
espumarajo *m* froth, foam
espumilla *f C.Am.* GASTR meringue
espumoso *adj* frothy, foamy; *caldo* sparkling
esqueje *m* cutting
esquela *f aviso* death notice, obituary
esquelético *adj* skeletal

E

esqueleto *m* skeleton; *Méx*, *C.Am.*, *Pe*, *Bol fig* blank form; ***mover*** *or* ***menear el esqueleto*** F dance
esquema *m* (*croquis*) sketch, diagram; (*sinopsis*) outline, summary
esquemático *adj dibujo* schematic, diagrammatic; *resumen* simplified
esquí *m tabla* ski; *deporte* skiing; ***esquí de fondo*** cross-country skiing; ***esquí náutico*** o ***acuático*** waterskiing
esquiador *m*, **esquiadora** *f* skier
esquiar ⟨1a⟩ *v/i* ski
esquilar ⟨1a⟩ *v/t* shear
esquilmar ⟨1a⟩ *v/t* overexploit; *a alguien* suck dry
esquina *f* corner
esquinazo *m Arg*, *Chi* serenade; ***dar esquinazo a alguien*** F give s.o. the slip F
esquirol *m/f* strikebreaker, scab F
esquite *m C.Am.*, *Méx* popcorn
esquivar ⟨1a⟩ *v/t* avoid, dodge F
esquivo *adj* (*huraño*) unsociable; (*evasivo*) shifty, evasive
esquizofrenia *f* schizophrenia
esquizofrénico *adj* schizophrenic
esta *det* this
está *vb* → ***estar***
estabilidad *f* stability
estabilizante *m* stabilizer
estabilizar ⟨1f⟩ *v/t* stabilize
estable *adj* stable
establecer ⟨2d⟩ **1** *v/t* establish; *negocio* set up **2** *v/r* **establecerse** *en lugar* settle; *en profesión* set up
establecimiento *m* establishment
establo *m* stable
estaca *f* stake
estacada *f*: ***dejar a alguien en la estacada*** F leave s.o. in the lurch
estación *f* station; *del año* season; ***estación espacial*** *or* ***orbital*** space station; ***estación de invierno*** *or* ***invernal*** winter resort; ***estación de servicio*** service station; ***estación de trabajo*** INFOR work station
estacional *adj* seasonal
estacionamiento *m* AUTO parking; *L.Am.* parking lot, *Br* car park
estacionar ⟨1a⟩ **1** *v/t* AUTO park **2** *v/r* **estacionarse** stabilize
estacionómetro *m Méx* parking meter
estadio *m* DEP stadium
estadística *f cifra* statistic; *ciencia* statistics
estado *m* state; MED condition; ***estado civil*** marital status; ***estado de guerra*** state of war; ***en buen estado*** in good condition; ***el Estado*** the State; ***estado del bienestar*** welfare state; ***los Estados Unidos*** (***de América***) the United States (of America)
estadounidense **1** *adj* American, US *atr* **2** *m/f* American
estafa *f* swindle, cheat
estafador *m*, **estafadora** *f* con artist F, fraudster
estafar ⟨1a⟩ *v/t* swindle, cheat (***a*** out of), defraud (***a*** of)
estalactita *f* stalactite
estalagmita *f* stalagmite
estallar ⟨1a⟩ *v/i* explode; *de guerra* break out; *de escándalo* break; ***estalló en llanto*** she burst into tears
estallido *m* explosion; *de guerra* outbreak
estamento *m* stratum, class
estampa *f de libro* illustration; (*aspecto*) appearance; REL prayer card
estampado *adj tejido* patterned
estampar ⟨1a⟩ *v/t sello* put; *tejido* print; *pasaporte* stamp; ***le estampó una bofetada en la cara*** F she smacked him one F
estampido *m* bang
estampilla *f L.Am.* stamp
estancado *adj agua* stagnant; *fig* at a standstill
estancar ⟨1g⟩ **1** *v/t río* dam up, block; *fig* bring to a standstill **2** *v/r* **estancarse** stagnate; *fig* come to a standstill
estancia *f* stay; *Rpl* farm, ranch
estanciero *m*, **-a** *f Rpl* farmer, rancher
estanco **1** *adj* watertight **2** *m shop selling cigarettes etc*
estándar *m* standard
estandarizar ⟨1f⟩ *v/t* standardize
estandarte *m* standard, banner
estanque *m* pond
estante *m* shelf
estantería *f* shelves *pl*; *para libros* bookcase
estaño *m* tin
estar ⟨1p⟩ **1** *v/i* be; ***¿está Javier?*** is Javier in?; ***estar haciendo algo*** be doing sth; ***estamos a 3 de enero*** it's January 3rd; ***el kilo está a cien pesetas*** they're a hundred pesetas a kilo; ***te está grande*** it's too big for you; ***estar con alguien*** agree with s.o.; (*apoyar*) support s.o.; ***ahora estoy con Vd.*** I'll be with you in just a moment; ***estar a bien / mal con alguien*** be on good / bad terms with s.o.; ***estar de*** *ocupación* work as, be; ***estar en algo*** be working on sth; ***estar para hacer algo*** be about to do sth; ***no estar para algo*** not be in a mood for sth; ***estar por algo*** be in favo(u)r of sth; ***está por hacer*** it hasn't been done yet; ***estar sin dinero*** have no money; ***¿cómo está Vd.?*** how are you?; ***estoy mejor*** I'm

(feeling) better; ***¡ya estoy!*** I'm ready!; ***¡ya está!*** that's it! **2** *v/r* **estarse** stay; ***estarse quieto*** keep still
estárter *m* choke
estatal *adj* state *atr*
estático *adj* static
estatua *f* statue
estatura *f* height
estatutario *adj* statutory
estatuto *m* statute; ***estatutos*** articles of association
estatus *m* status
este[1] *m* east
este[2], **esta**, **estos**, **estas** *det singular* this; *plural* these
éste, **ésta**, **éstos**, **éstas** *pron singular* this (one); *plural* these (ones)
estela *f* MAR wake; AVIA, *fig* trail
estelar *adj* star *atr*
estepa *f* steppe
estera *f* mat
estercolero *m* dunghill, dung heap
estéreo *adj* stereo
estereofónico *adj* stereophonic
estereotipo *m* stereotype
estéril *adj* MED sterile; *trabajo*, *esfuerzo etc* futile
esterilidad *f* sterility
esterilizar ⟨1f⟩ *v/t tb persona* sterilize
esterilla *f* mat
esterlina *adj*: ***libra esterlina*** pound sterling
esternón *m* breast bone, sternum
estero *m Rpl* marsh
estertor *m* death rattle
esteticista *m/f* beautician
estético *adj* esthetic, *Br* aesthetic
estetoscopio *m* MED stethoscope
estibador *m* stevedore
estiércol *m* dung; (*abono*) manure
estilarse ⟨1a⟩ *v/r* be fashionable
estilista *m/f* stylist; *de modas* designer
estilo *m* style; ***al estilo de*** in the style of; ***algo por el estilo*** something like that; ***son todos por el estilo*** they're all the same
estilográfica *f* fountain pen
estima *f* esteem, respect; ***tener a alguien en mucha estima*** hold s.o. in high regard *o* esteem
estimación *f* (*cálculo*) estimate; (*estima*) esteem, respect
estimar ⟨1a⟩ *v/t* respect, hold in high regard; ***estimo conveniente que*** I consider it advisable to
estimulante 1 *adj* stimulating **2** *m* stimulant
estimular ⟨1a⟩ *v/t* stimulate; (*animar*) encourage
estímulo *m* stimulus; (*incentivo*) incentive
estío *m lit* summertime
estipular ⟨1a⟩ *v/t* stipulate
estirado *adj* snooty F, stuck-up F
estirar ⟨1a⟩ *v/t* stretch; (*alisar*) smooth out; *dinero* stretch, make go further; ***estirar la pata*** F kick the bucket F; ***estirar las piernas*** stretch one's legs
estirpe *f* stock
estival *adj* summer *atr*
esto *pron* this; ***esto es*** that is to say; ***por esto*** this is why; ***a todo esto*** (*mientras tanto*) meanwhile; (*a propósito*) incidentally
estofa *f*: ***de baja estofa*** *desp* low-class *desp*
estofado *adj* stewed
estofar ⟨1a⟩ *v/t* stew
estoico 1 *adj* stoic(al) **2** *m*, **-a** *f* stoic
estómago *m* stomach
estor *m* blind
estorbar ⟨1a⟩ **1** *v/t* (*dificultar*) hinder; ***nos estorbaba*** he was in our way **2** *v/i* get in the way
estorbo *m* hindrance, nuisance
estornino *m* zo starling
estornudar ⟨1a⟩ *v/i* sneeze
estornudo *m* sneeze
estoy *vb* → ***estar***
estrado *m* platform
estrafalario *adj* F eccentric; *ropa* outlandish
estragón *m* BOT tarragon
estragos *mpl* devastation *sg*; ***causar estragos entre*** wreak havoc among
estrambótico *adj* F eccentric; *ropa* outlandish
estrangular ⟨1a⟩ *v/t* strangle
estraperlo *m* black market; ***de estraperlo*** on the black market
estratagema *f* stratagem
estrategia *f* strategy
estratégico *adj* strategic
estrato *m fig* stratum
estrechar ⟨1a⟩ **1** *v/t ropa* take in; *mano* shake; ***estrechar entre los brazos*** hug, embrace **2** *v/r* **estrecharse** narrow, get narrower
estrechez *f fig* hardship; ***estrechez de miras*** narrow-mindedness; ***pasar estrechezes*** suffer hardship
estrecho 1 *adj* narrow; (*apretado*) tight; *amistad* close; ***estrecho de miras*** narrow-minded **2** *m* strait, straits *pl*
estrella *f tb de cine etc* star; ***estrella fugaz*** falling star, shooting star; ***estrella de mar*** zo starfish; ***estrella polar*** Pole star
estrellar ⟨1a⟩ **1** *v/t* smash; ***estrellar algo***

E

contra algo smash sth against sth; ***estrelló el coche contra un muro*** he smashed the car into a wall **2** *v/r* **estrellarse** crash (***contra*** into)
estrellón *m Pe, Bol* crash
estremecer ⟨2d⟩ **1** *v/t* shock, shake F **2** *v/r* **estremecerse** shake, tremble; *de frío* shiver; *de horror* shudder
estrenar ⟨1a⟩ **1** *v/t ropa* wear for the first time, christen F; *objeto* try out, christen F; TEA, *película* premiere; ***a estrenar*** brand new **2** *v/r* **estrenarse** make one's debut
estreno *m* TEA, *de película* premiere; *de persona* debut; ***estar de estreno*** be wearing new clothes
estreñimiento *m* constipation
estrépito *m* noise, racket
estrés *m* stress
estresar ⟨1a⟩ *v/t*: ***estresar alguien*** cause s.o. stress, subject s.o. to stress
estría *f en piel* stretch mark
estribar ⟨1a⟩ *v/i*: ***estribar en*** stem from, lie in
estribillo *m* chorus, refrain
estribo *m* stirrup; ***perder los estribos*** *fig* fly off the handle F
estrictez *f S. Am.* strictness
estricto *adj* strict
estridente *adj* shrill, strident
estrofa *f* stanza, verse
estropajo *m* scourer
estropajoso *adj persona* wiry; *boca* dry; *camisa* scruffy
estropeado *adj* (*averiado*) broken
estropear ⟨1a⟩ **1** *v/t aparato* break; *plan* ruin, spoil **2** *v/r* **estropearse** break down; *de comida* go off, go bad; *de plan* go wrong
estructura *f* structure
estructurar ⟨1a⟩ *v/t* structure, organize
estruendo *m* racket, din
estrujar ⟨1a⟩ *v/t* F crumple up, scrunch up F; *trapo* wring out; *persona* squeeze, hold tightly
estuario *m* estuary
estuche *m* case, box
estuco *m* stuccowork
estudiante *m/f* student
estudiantil *adj* student *atr*
estudiar ⟨1b⟩ *v/t & v/i* study
estudio *m disciplina* study; *apartamento* studio, *Br* studio flat; *de cine, música* studio
estudioso *adj* studious
estufa *f* heater
estupefaciente *m* narcotic (drug)
estupefacto *adj* stupefied, speechless
estupendo *adj* fantastic, wonderful
estupidez *f cualidad* stupidity; *acción* stupid thing
estúpido **1** *adj* stupid **2** *m*, **-a** *f* idiot
estupor *m* astonishment, amazement; MED stupor
esturión *m* ZO sturgeon
estuve *vb* → ***estar***
estuvo *vb* → ***estar***
etapa *f* stage; ***por etapas*** in stages
etarra *m/f* member of ETA
etc *abr* (= ***etcétera***) etc (= etcetera)
etcétera *m* etcetera, and so on; ***y un largo etcétera de …*** and a long list of …, and many other …
etéreo *adj* ethereal
eternidad *f* eternity
eterno *adj* eternal; ***la película se me hizo -a*** the movie seemed to go on for ever
ética *f en filosofía* ethics; *comportamiento* principles *pl*
ético *adj* ethical
etimología *f* etymology
Etiopía Ethiopia
etiqueta *f* label; (*protocolo*) etiquette
etiquetar ⟨1a⟩ *v/t tb fig* label
étnico *adj* ethnic
eucalipto *m* BOT eucalyptus
eucaristía *f* Eucharist
eufemismo *m* euphemism
euforia *f* euphoria
eufórico *adj* euphoric
euro *m* euro
eurodiputado *m*, **-a** *f* MEP, member of the European Parliament
Europa Europe
europeísta *m/f* pro-European
europeo **1** *adj* European **2** *m*, **-a** *f* European
eusquera *m/adj* Basque
eutanasia *f* euthanasia
evacuación *f* evacuation
evacuar ⟨1d⟩ *v/t* evacuate
evadir ⟨3a⟩ **1** *v/t* avoid; *impuestos* evade **2** *v/r* **evadirse** *tb fig* escape
evaluación *f* evaluation, assessment; (*prueba*) test
evaluar ⟨1e⟩ *v/t* assess, evaluate
evangelio *m* gospel
evangelizar ⟨1f⟩ *v/t* evangelize
evaporación *f* evaporation
evaporarse ⟨1a⟩ *v/r* evaporate; *fig* F vanish into thin air
evasión *f tb fig* escape; ***evasión de capitales*** flight of capital; ***evasión fiscal*** tax evasion
evasiva *f* evasive reply
evento *m* event
eventual *adj* possible; *trabajo* casual, temporary; ***en el caso eventual de*** in the

event of
eventualidad *f* eventuality
evidencia *f* evidence, proof; ***poner en evidencia*** demonstrate; ***poner a alguien en evidencia*** show s.o. up
evidente *adj* evident, clear
evitar ⟨1a⟩ *v/t* avoid; (*impedir*) prevent; *molestias* save; ***no puedo evitarlo*** I can't help it
evocar ⟨1g⟩ *v/t* evoke
evolución *f* BIO evolution; (*desarrollo*) development
evolucionar ⟨1a⟩ *v/t* BIO evolve; (*desarrollar*) develop
ex **1** *pref* ex- **2** *m/f* F ex F
exabrupto *m* sharp remark
exacerbar ⟨1a⟩ *v/t* exacerbate, make worse; (*irritar*) exasperate
exacto *adj medida* exact, precise; *informe* accurate; ***¡exacto!*** exactly!, precisely!
exageración *f* exaggeration
exagerado *adj* exaggerated
exagerar ⟨1a⟩ *v/t* exaggerate
exaltación *f* (*alabanza*) exaltation; (*entusiasmo*) agitation, excitement
exaltar ⟨1a⟩ *v/t* excite, get worked up
examen *m* test, exam; MED examination; (*análisis*) study; ***examen de conducir*** driving test
examinar ⟨1a⟩ **1** *v/t* examine **2** *v/r* **examinarse** take an exam
exasperar ⟨1a⟩ **1** *v/t* exasperate **2** *v/r* **exasperarse** get exasperated
excarcelar ⟨1a⟩ *v/t* release (from prison)
excavación *f* excavation
excavadora *f* digger
excavar ⟨1a⟩ *v/t* excavate; *túnel* dig
excedencia *f* extended leave of absence
excedente **1** *adj* surplus; *empleado* on extended leave of absence **2** *m* surplus
exceder ⟨2a⟩ **1** *v/t* exceed **2** *v/r* **excederse** go too far, get carried away
excelencia *f* excellence; ***Su Excelencia la señora embajadora*** Her Excellency the Ambassador; ***por excelencia*** par excellence
excelente *adj* excellent
excéntrico **1** *adj* eccentric **2** *m*, **-a** *f* eccentric
excepción *f* exception; ***a excepción de*** except for; ***sin excepción*** without exception
excepcional *adj* exceptional
excepto *prp* except
exceptuar ⟨1e⟩ *v/t* except; ***exceptuando*** with the exception of, except for
excesivo *adj* excessive
exceso *m* excess; ***exceso de equipaje*** excess baggage; ***exceso de velocidad*** speeding; ***en exceso*** in excess, too much
excitación *f* excitement, agitation
excitante **1** *adj* exciting; ***una bebida excitante*** a stimulant **2** *m* stimulant
excitar ⟨1a⟩ **1** *v/t* excite; *sentimientos*, *sexualmente* arouse **2** *v/r* **excitarse** get excited; *sexualmente* become aroused
exclamación *f* exclamation
exclamar ⟨1a⟩ *v/t* exclaim
excluir ⟨3g⟩ *v/t* leave out (**de** of), exclude (**de** from); *posibilidad* rule out
exclusiva *f privilegio* exclusive rights *pl* (**de** to); *reportaje* exclusive
exclusivo *adj* exclusive
excomunión *f* excommunication
excremento *m* excrement
exculpar ⟨1a⟩ *v/t* exonerate
excursión *f* trip, excursion
excursionista *m/f* excursionist
excusa *f* excuse; ***excusas*** apologies
excusado *m* bathroom
excusar ⟨1a⟩ *v/t* excuse
execrable *adj* abominable, execrable *fml*
exención *f* exemption; ***exención fiscal*** tax exemption
exento *adj* exempt (**de** from); ***exento de impuestos*** tax-exempt, tax-free
exhalación *f*: ***salir como una exhalación*** *fig* rush *o* dash out
exhaustivo *adj* exhaustive
exhausto *adj* exhausted
exhibición *f* display, demonstration; *de película* screening, showing
exhibicionista *m/f* exhibitionist
exhibir ⟨3a⟩ **1** *v/t* show, display; *película* screen, show; *cuadro* exhibit **2** *v/r* **exhibirse** show o.s., let o.s. be seen
exhumar ⟨1a⟩ *v/t* exhume
exigencia *f* demand
exigente *adj* demanding
exigir ⟨3c⟩ *v/t* demand; (*requirir*) call for, demand; ***le exigen mucho*** they ask a lot of him
exiguo *adj* meager, *Br* meagre
exiliado **1** *adj* exiled, in exile *pred* **2** *m*, **-a** *f* exile
exiliar ⟨1a⟩ **1** *v/t* exile **2** *v/r* **exiliarse** go into exile
exilio *m* exile; ***en el exilio*** in exile
eximir ⟨3a⟩ *v/t* exempt (**de** from)
existencia *f* existence; (*vida*) life; ***existencias*** COM supplies, stocks
existencialista *m/f & adj* existentialist
existir ⟨3a⟩ *v/i* exist; ***existen muchos problemas*** there are a lot of problems
éxito *m* success; ***éxito de taquilla*** box office hit; ***tener éxito*** be successful, be a success
exitoso *adj* successful

Exmo. *abr* (= ***Excelentísimo***) Your / His Excellency
exonerar ⟨1a⟩ *v/t* exonerate; ***exonerar a alguien de algo*** exempt s.o. from sth
exorbitante *adj* exorbitant
exorcista *m/f* exorcist
exótico *adj* exotic
expandir ⟨3a⟩ **1** *v/t* expand **2** *v/r* **expandirse** expand; *de noticia* spread
expansión *f* expansion; (*recreo*) recreation
expatriarse ⟨1b⟩ *v/r* leave one's country
expectación *f* sense of anticipation
expectativa *f* (*esperanza*) expectation; ***estar a la expectativa de algo*** be waiting for sth; ***expectativas*** (*perspectivas*) prospects
expedición *f* expedition
expediente *m* file, dossier; (*investigación*) investigation, inquiry; ***expediente académico*** student record; ***expediente disciplinario*** disciplinary proceedings *pl*; ***abrir un expediente a alguien*** take disciplinary action against s.o.
expedir ⟨3l⟩ *v/t documento* issue; *mercancías* send, dispatch
expeditar ⟨1a⟩ *v/t L.Am.* (*apresurar*) hurry; (*concluir*) finish, conclude
expeditivo *adj* expeditious
expendedor *adj*: ***máquina expendedora*** vending machine
expendio *m L.Am.* store, shop
expensas *fpl*: ***a expensas de*** at the expense of
experiencia *f* experience
experimentado *adj* experienced
experimentar ⟨1a⟩ **1** *v/t* try out, experiment with **2** *v/i* experiment (***con*** on)
experimento *m* experiment
experto 1 *adj* expert; ***experto en hacer algo*** expert *o* very good at doing sth **2** *m* expert (***en*** on)
expiar ⟨1c⟩ *v/t* expiate, atone for
expirar ⟨1a⟩ *v/i* expire
explanada *f* open area; *junto al mar* esplanade
explayarse ⟨1a⟩ *v/r* speak at length; (*desahogarse*) unburden o.s.; (*distraerse*) relax, unwind; ***explayarse sobre algo*** expound on sth
explicación *f* explanation
explicar ⟨1g⟩ **1** *v/t* explain **2** *v/r* **explicarse** (*comprender*) understand; (*hacerse comprender*) express o.s.; ***no me lo explico*** I can't understand it, I don't get it F
explícito *adj* explicit
explorador *m*, **exploradora** *f* explorer; MIL scout
explorar ⟨1a⟩ *v/t* explore
explosión *f* explosion; ***explosión demográfica*** population explosion; ***hacer explosión*** go off, explode
explosionar ⟨1a⟩ *v/t & v/i* explode
explosivo *m/adj* explosive
explotación *f de mina, tierra* exploitation, working; *de negocio* running, operation; *de trabajador* exploitation
explotar ⟨1a⟩ **1** *v/t tierra, mina* work, exploit; *situación* take advantage of, exploit; *trabajador* exploit **2** *v/i* go off, explode; *fig* explode, blow a fuse F
expoliar ⟨1b⟩ *v/t* plunder, pillage
exponente *m* exponent
exponer ⟨2r; *part* ***expuesto*** ⟩ **1** *v/t idea, teoría* set out, put forward; (*revelar*) expose; *pintura, escultura* exhibit, show; (*arriesgar*) risk **2** *v/r* **exponerse**: ***exponerse a algo*** (*arriesgarse*) lay o.s. open to sth
exportación *f* export
exportar ⟨1a⟩ *v/t* export
exposición *f* exhibition
expresar ⟨1a⟩ **1** *v/t* express **2** *v/r* **expresarse** express o.s.
expresión *f* expression
expresivo *adj* expressive
expreso 1 *adj* express *atr*; ***tren expreso*** express (train) **2** *m tren* express (train); *café* espresso
exprimidor *m* lemon squeezer; *eléctrico* juicer
exprimir ⟨3a⟩ *v/t* squeeze; (*explotar*) exploit
ex profeso *adv* (*especialmente*) expressly; (*a propósito*) deliberately
expropiar ⟨1b⟩ *v/t* expropriate
expuesto *part* → ***exponer***
expugnar ⟨1a⟩ *v/t* take by storm
expulsar ⟨1a⟩ *v/t* expel, throw out F; DEP expel from the game, *Br* send off
expulsión *f* expulsion; DEP sending off
exquisito *adj comida* delicious; (*bello*) exquisite; (*refinado*) refined
extasiarse ⟨1c⟩ *v/r* be enraptured, go into raptures
éxtasis *m tb droga* ecstasy
extender ⟨2g⟩ **1** *v/t brazos* stretch out; (*untar*) spread; *tela, papel* spread out; (*ampliar*) extend; ***me extendió la mano*** she held out her hand to me **2** *v/r* **extenderse** *de campos* stretch; *de influencia* extend; (*difundirse*) spread; (*durar*) last; *explayarse* go into detail
extendido 1 *part* → ***extender*** **2** *adj costumbre* widespread; *brazos* outstretched; *mapa* spread out
extensión *f tb* TELEC extension; *superficie* expanse, area; ***por extensión*** by exten-

sion
extenso *adj* extensive, vast; *informe* lengthy, long
extenuar ⟨1e⟩ **1** *v/t* exhaust, tire out **2** *v/r* **extenuarse** exhaust o.s., tire o.s. out
exterior 1 *adj aspecto* external, outward; *capa* outer; *apartamento* overlooking the street; POL foreign; ***la parte exterior del edificio*** the exterior *o* the outside of the building **2** *m* (*fachada*) exterior, outside; *aspecto* exterior, outward appearance; ***viajar al exterior*** (*al extranjero*) travel abroad
exteriorizar ⟨1f⟩ *v/t* externalize
exterminar ⟨1a⟩ *v/t* exterminate, wipe out
externo 1 *adj aspecto* external, outward; *influencia* external, outside; *capa* outer; *deuda* foreign **2** *m*, **-a** *f* EDU *student who attends a boarding school but returns home each evening*, *Br* day boy / girl
extinción *f*: ***en peligro de extinción*** in danger of extinction
extinguidor *m L.Am.*: ***extinguidor (de incendios)*** (fire) extinguisher
extinguir ⟨3d⟩ **1** *v/t* BIO, ZO wipe out; *fuego* extinguish, put out **2** *v/r* **extinguirse** BIO, ZO become extinct, die out; *de fuego* go out; *de plazo* expire
extintor *m* fire extinguisher
extirpar ⟨1a⟩ *v/t* MED remove; *vicio* eradicate, stamp out
extorsión *f* extortion
extorsionar ⟨1a⟩ *v/t* extort money from
extra 1 *adj excelente* top quality; *adicional* extra; ***horas extra*** overtime; ***paga extra*** extra month's pay **2** *m/f de cine* extra **3** *m gasto* additional expense
extracto *m* extract; (*resumen*) summary; GASTR, QUÍM extract, essence; ***extracto de cuenta*** bank statement
extractor *m* extractor; ***extractor de humos*** extractor fan
extradición *f* extradition
extraditar ⟨1a⟩ *v/t* extradite
extraer ⟨2p⟩ *v/t* extract, pull out; *conclusión* draw
extrajudicial *adj* out-of-court
extralimitarse ⟨1a⟩ *v/r* go too far, exceed one's authority
extramatrimonial *adj* extramarital
extranjería *f*: ***ley de extranjería*** immigration laws *pl*
extranjero 1 *adj* foreign **2** *m*, **-a** *f* foreigner; ***en el extranjero*** abroad
extranjis: ***de extranjis*** F on the quiet F, on the sly F
extrañar ⟨1a⟩ **1** *v/t L.Am.* miss **2** *v/r* **extrañarse** be surprised (***de*** at)
extraño 1 *adj* strange, odd **2** *m*, **-a** *f* stranger
extraordinario *adj* extraordinary
extrapolar ⟨1a⟩ *v/t* extrapolate
extrarradio *m* outlying districts *pl*, outskirts *pl*
extraterrestre *adj* extraterrestial, alien
extravagante *adj* outrageous
extravertido *adj* extrovert
extraviar ⟨1c⟩ **1** *v/t* lose, mislay **2** *v/r* **extraviarse** get lost, lose one's way
extremadamente *adv* extremely
extremado *adj* extreme
extremar ⟨1a⟩ *v/t* maximize
extremidad *f* end; ***extremidades*** extremities
extremista 1 *adj* extreme **2** *m/f* POL extremist
extremo 1 *adj* extreme **2** *m* extreme; *parte primera o último* end; *punto* point; ***llegar al extremo de*** reach the point of **3** *m/f*: ***extremo derecho / izquierdo*** DEP right / left wing; ***en extremo*** in the extreme
extrovertido *adj* extrovert
exuberante *adj* exuberant; *vegetación* lush
exultante *adj* elated
eyacular ⟨1a⟩ *v/t* ejaculate

F

fabada *f* GASTR *Asturian stew with pork sausage, bacon and beans*
fábrica *f* plant, factory
fabricación *f* manufacturing
fabricante *m* manufacturer, maker
fabricar ⟨1g⟩ *v/t* manufacture
fábula *f* fable; (*mentira*) lie
fabuloso *adj* fabulous, marvel(l)ous
facción *f* POL faction; ***facciones*** *pl* (*rasgos*) features

faceta *f fig* facet
facha 1 *f* look; (*cara*) face **2** *m/f desp* fascist
fachada *f tb fig* façade
facial *adj* facial
fácil *adj* easy; ***es fácil que*** it's likely that
facilidad *f* ease; ***con facilidad*** easily; ***tener facilidad para algo*** have a gift for sth; ***facilidades de pago*** credit facilities, credit terms

F

facilitar ⟨1a⟩ *v/t* facilitate, make easier; (*hacer factible*) make possible; *medios, dinero etc* provide
factible *adj* feasible
factor *m* factor
factoría *f esp L.Am.* plant, factory
factura *f* COM invoice; *de luz, gas etc* bill
facturación *f* COM invoicing; (*volumen de negocio*) turnover; AVIA check-in
facturar ⟨1a⟩ *v/t* COM invoice, bill; *volumen de negocio* turn over; AVIA check in
facultad *f* faculty; (*autoridad*) authority
faena *f* task, job; ***hacer una faena a alguien*** play a dirty trick on s.o.
fagot *m* MÚS bassoon
faisán *m* ZO pheasant
faja *f prenda interior* girdle
fajarse ⟨1a⟩ *v/r Méx, Ven* F get into a fight
fajo *m* wad; *de periódicos* bundle
falacia *f* fallacy; (*engaño*) fraud
falange *f* ANAT phalange; MIL phalanx
falda *f* skirt; *de montaña* side
faldero *adj*: ***perro faldero*** lap dog
falla *f* fault; *de fabricación* flaw
fallar ⟨1a⟩ **1** *v/i* fail; (*no acertar*) miss; *de sistema etc* go wrong; JUR find (***en favor de*** for; ***en contra de*** against); ***fallar a alguien*** let s.o. down **2** *v/t* JUR pronounce judg(e)ment in; *pregunta* get wrong; ***fallar el tiro*** miss
fallecer ⟨2d⟩ *v/i* pass away
fallecimiento *m* demise
fallo *m* mistake; TÉC fault; JUR judg(e)ment; ***fallo cardiaco*** heart failure
falsedad *f* falseness; (*mentira*) lie
falsificación *f de moneda* counterfeiting; *de documentos, firma* forgery
falsificar ⟨1g⟩ *v/t moneda* counterfeit; *documento, firma* forge, falsify
falso *adj* false; *joyas* fake; *documento, firma* forged; ***jurar en falso*** commit perjury
falta *f* (*escasez*) lack, want; (*error*) mistake; (*ausencia*) absence; *en tenis* fault; *en fútbol* foul; (*tiro libre*) free kick; ***hacerle falta a alguien*** foul s.o.; ***falta de*** lack of, shortage of; ***sin falta*** without fail; ***buena falta le hace*** it's about time; ***echar en falta a alguien*** miss s.o.; ***hacer falta*** be necessary
faltar ⟨1a⟩ *v/i* be missing; ***falta una hora*** there's an hour to go; ***faltan 10 kilómetros*** there are 10 kilometers to go; ***sólo falta hacer la salsa*** there's only the sauce to do; ***faltar a*** be absent from; ***faltar a clase*** miss class, be absent from class; ***faltar a alguien*** be disrespectful to s.o.; ***faltar a su palabra*** not keep one's word
falto *adj*: ***falto de*** lacking in, devoid of; ***falto de recursos*** short of resources
fama *f* fame; (*reputación*) reputation; ***tener mala fama*** have a bad reputation
familia *f* family; ***sentirse como en familia*** feel at home
familiar 1 *adj* family *atr*; (*conocido*) familiar; LING colloquial **2** *m/f* relation, relative
familiaridad *f* familiarity
familiarizarse ⟨1f⟩ *v/r* familiarize o.s. (***con*** with)
famoso 1 *adj* famous **2** *m*, **-a** *f* celebrity
fan *m/f* fan
fanático 1 *adj* fanatical **2** *m*, **-a** *f* fanatic
fanatismo *m* fanaticism
fanfarrón 1 *adj* boastful **2** *m*, **-ona** *f* boaster
fanfarronear ⟨1a⟩ *v/i* boast, brag
fango *m tb fig* mud
fantasear ⟨1a⟩ *v/i* fantasize
fantasía *f* fantasy; (*imaginación*) imagination; ***joyas de fantasía*** costume jewel(l)ery
fantasma *m* ghost
fantástico *adj* fantastic
farándula *f* show business
fardar ⟨1a⟩ *v/i*: ***fardar de algo*** F boast about sth, show off about sth
fardo *m* bundle
faringitis *f* MED inflammation of the pharynx, pharyngitis
fariña *f S. Am.* manioc flour, cassava
farmacéutico 1 *adj* pharmaceutical **2** *m*, **-a** *f* pharmacist, *Br* chemist
farmacia *f* pharmacy, *Br* chemist's; *estudios* pharmacy; ***farmacia de guardia*** *24-hour pharmacist, Br* emergency chemist
fármaco *m* medicine
farmacología *f* pharmacology
faro *m* MAR lighthouse; AUTO headlight, headlamp; ***faro antiniebla*** fog light
farol *m* lantern; (*farola*) streetlight, streetlamp; *en juegos de cartas* bluff
farola *f* streetlight, streetlamp
farolillo *m*: ***ser el farolillo rojo*** *fig* F be bottom of the league
farragoso *adj texto* dense

farrear ⟨1a⟩ *v/i L.Am.* F go out on the town F
farrista *adj L.Am.* F hard-drinking
farsa *f tb fig* farce
farsante *m/f* fraud, fake
fascículo *m* TIP instal(l)ment
fascinación *f* fascination
fascinante *adj* fascinating
fascinar ⟨1a⟩ *v/t* fascinate
fascismo *m* fascism
fascista *m/f & adj* fascist
fase *f* phase
fastidiar ⟨1b⟩ **1** *v/t* annoy; F (*estropear*) spoil **2** *v/r* **fastidiarse** grin and bear it
fastidio *m* annoyance; ***¡qué fastidio!*** what a nuisance!
fastuoso *adj* lavish
fatal 1 *adj* fatal; (*muy malo*) dreadful, awful **2** *adv* very badly
fatídico *adj* fateful
fatiga *f* tiredness, fatigue
fatigar ⟨1h⟩ **1** *v/t* tire **2** *v/r* **fatigarse** get tired
fatuo *adj* conceited; (*necio*) fatuous
fauces *fpl* ZO jaws
fauna *f* fauna
favor *m* favo(u)r; ***a favor de*** in favo(u)r of; ***por favor*** please; ***hacer un favor*** do a favo(u)r
favorecer ⟨2d⟩ *v/t* favo(u)r; *de ropa, color* suit
favoritismo *m* favo(u)ritism
favorito 1 *adj* favo(u)rite **2** *m*, **-a** *f* favo(u)rite
fax *m* fax; ***enviar un fax a alguien*** send s.o. a fax, fax s.o.
fayuca *f Méx* smuggling
fayuquero *m*, **-a** *f Méx* dealer in smuggled goods
F.C. *abr* (= ***Fúítbol Club***) FC (= Football Club)
fdo. *abr* (= ***firmado***) signed
fe *f* faith (***en*** in); ***fe de erratas*** errata
fealdad *f* ugliness
feb. *abr* (= ***febrero***) Feb. (= February)
febrero *m* February
fecal *adj* f(a)ecal
fecha *f* date; ***fecha límite de consumo*** best before date; ***fecha de nacimiento*** date of birth
fechador *m Chi, Méx* postmark
fécula *f* starch
fecundación *f* fertilization; ***fecundación in vitro*** MED in vitro fertilization
fecundar ⟨1a⟩ *v/t* fertilize
fecundo *adj* fertile
federación *f* federation
federal *adj* federal
felicidad *f* happiness; ***¡felicidades!*** congratulations!
felicitación *f* letter of congratulations; ***¡felicitaciones!*** congratulations!
felicitar ⟨1a⟩ *v/t* congratulate (***por*** on)
felino *adj tb fig* feline
feliz *adj* happy; ***¡feliz Navidad!*** Merry Christmas!
felpa *f* towel(l)ing
felpudo *m* doormat
femenino 1 *adj* feminine; *moda, equipo* women's **2** GRAM feminine
femin(e)idad *f* femininity
feminismo *m* feminism
feminista *m/f & adj* feminist
fenomenal 1 *adj* F fantastic F, phenomenal F **2** *adv*: ***lo pasé fenomenal*** F I had a fantastic time F
fenómeno 1 *m* phenomenon; *persona* genius **2** *adj* F fantastic F, great F
feo 1 *adj* ugly; *fig* nasty **2** *m*: ***hacer un feo a alguien*** F snub s.o.
féretro *m* casket, coffin
feria *f* COM fair; *L.Am.* (*mercado*) market; *Méx* (*calderilla*) small change; ***feria de muestras*** trade fair
feriado 1 *adj L.Am.*: ***día feriado*** (public) holiday **2** *m L.Am.* (public) holiday; ***abierto feriados*** open on public holidays
ferial 1 *adj*: ***recinto ferial*** fairground **2** *m* fair
fermentación *f* fermentation
fermentar ⟨1a⟩ *v/t* ferment
fermento *m* ferment
ferocidad *f* ferocity
feroz *adj* fierce; (*cruel*) cruel
férreo *adj tb fig* iron *atr*; *del ferrocarril* rail *atr*
ferretería *f* hardware store
ferrocarril *m* railroad, *Br* railway
ferrocarrilero *m L.Am.* railroad *o Br* railway worker
ferroviario *adj* rail *atr*
ferry *m* ferry
fértil *adj* fertile
fertilidad *f* fertility
fertilizante *m* fertilizer
ferviente *adj fig* fervent
fervor *m* fervo(u)r
festejar ⟨1a⟩ *v/t persona* wine and dine; *L.Am.* celebrate
festejo *m* celebration; ***festejos*** festivities
festín *m* banquet
festival *m* festival; ***festival cinematográfico*** film festival
festividad *f* feast; ***festividades*** festivities
festivo *adj* festive
fetal *adj* fetal
fetiche *m* fetish

F

fétido *adj* fetid
feto *m* fetus
feudal *adj* feudal
feudo *m fig* domain
FF. AA. *abr* (= ***fuerzas armadas***) armed forces
FF. CC. *abr* (= ***ferrocarriles***) railroads
fiable *adj* trustworthy; *datos*, *máquina* etc reliable
fiambre *m* cold cut, *Br* cold meat; P (*cadáver*) stiff P
fiambrera *f* lunch pail, *Br* lunch box
fiambrería *f L.Am.* delicatessen
fianza *f* deposit; JUR bail; ***bajo fianza*** on bail
fiar ⟨1c⟩ **1** *v/i* give credit **2** *v/r* **fiarse**: ***fiarse de alguien*** trust s.o.; ***no me fío*** I don't trust him / them *etc*
fiasco *m* fiasco
fibra *f en tejido*, *alimento* fiber, *Br* fibre; ***fibra óptica*** optical fiber (*Br* fibre); ***fibra de vidrio*** fiberglass, *Br* fibreglass
fibroso *adj* fibrous
ficción *f* fiction
ficha *f* file card, index card; *en juegos de mesa* counter; *en un casino* chip; *en damas* checker, *Br* draught; *en ajedrez* man, piece; TELEC token
fichar ⟨1a⟩ **1** *v/t* DEP sign; JUR open a file on **2** *v/i* DEP sign (***por*** for)
fichero *m* file cabinet, *Br* filing cabinet; INFOR file
ficticio *adj* fictitious
fidedigno *adj* reliable
fidelidad *f* fidelity
fideo *m* noodle
fiebre *f* fever; (*temperatura*) temperature; ***fiebre del heno*** hay fever
fiel **1** *adj* faithful; (*leal*) loyal **2** *mpl*: ***los fieles*** REL the faithful *pl*
fieltro *m* felt
fiera *f* wild animal; ***ponerse hecho una fiera*** F go wild F
fiero *adj* fierce
fierro *m L.Am.* iron
fiesta *f* festival; (*reunión social*) party; (*día festivo*) public holiday; ***estar de fiesta*** be in a party mood
fifí *m L.Am.* P *afeminado* sissy F
figura *f* figure; (*estatuilla*) figurine; (*forma*) shape; *naipes* face card, *Br* picture card; ***tener buena figura*** have a good figure
figurado *adj* figurative; ***sentido figurado*** figurative sense
figurar ⟨1a⟩ **1** *v/i* appear (***en*** in); ***aquí figura como …*** she appears *o* is down here as … **2** *v/r* **figurarse** imagine; ***¡figúrate!*** just imagine!
fijar ⟨1a⟩ **1** *v/t* fix; *cartel* stick; *fecha*, *objetivo* set; *residencia* establish; *atención* focus **2** *v/r* **fijarse** (*establecerse*) settle; (*prestar atención*) pay attention (***en*** to); ***fijarse en algo*** (*darse cuenta*) notice sth
fijo *adj* fixed; *trabajo* permanent; *fecha* definite
fila *f* line, *Br* queue; *de asientos* row; ***en fila india*** in single file; ***filas*** MIL ranks
filatelia *f* philately, stamp collecting
filete *m* GASTR fillet
filial **1** *adj* filial **2** *f* COM subsidiary
Filipinas *fpl* Philippines
film(e) *m* movie, film
filmación *f* filming, shooting
filmar ⟨1a⟩ *v/t* film, shoot
filo *m* edge; *de navaja* cutting edge; ***al filo de las siete*** *fig* around 7 o'clock
filología *f* philology; ***filología hispánica*** EDU Spanish language and literature
filólogo *m*, **-a** *f* philologist
filón *m* vein, seam; *fig* goldmine
filoso *adj L.Am.* sharp
filosofía *f* philosophy
filosófico *adj* philosophical
filósofo *m*, **-a** *f* philosopher
filtración *f* leak
filtrar ⟨1a⟩ **1** *v/t* filter; *información* leak **2** *v/r* **filtrarse** filter (***por*** through); *de agua*, *información* leak
filtro *m* filter
fin *m* end; (*objetivo*) aim, purpose; ***fin de semana*** weekend; ***a fines de mayo*** at the end of May; ***al fin y al cabo*** at the end of the day, after all; ***en fin*** anyway
final *f/adj* final
finalidad *f* purpose, aim
finalista **1** *adj*: ***las dos selecciones finalistas*** the two teams that reached the final **2** *m/f* finalist
finalización *f* completion
finalizado *adj* complete
finalizar ⟨1f⟩ *v/t & v/i* end, finish
finalmente *adv* eventually
financiación *f* funding
financiar ⟨1b⟩ *v/t* finance, fund
financista *m/f L.Am.* financier
finanzas *fpl* finances
finca *f* (*bien inmueble*) property; *L.Am.* (*granja*) farm
fingido *adj* false
fingir ⟨3c⟩ **1** *v/t* feign *fml*; ***fingió no haberlo oído*** I pretended I hadn't heard **2** *v/r* **fingirse**: ***fingirse enfermo*** pretend to be ill, feign illness *fml*
finlandés **1** *adj* Finnish **2** *m*, **-esa** *f* Finn
Finlandia Finland
fino *adj calidad* fine; *libro*, *tela* thin; (*esbelto*) slim; *modales*, *gusto* refined; *sen-*

tido de humor subtle
firma *f* signature; *acto* signing; COM firm
firmamento *m* firmament
firmar ⟨1a⟩ *v/t* sign
firme *adj* firm; (*estable*) steady; ***en firme*** COM firm
fiscal 1 *adj* tax *atr*, fiscal **2** *m/f* district attorney, *Br* public prosecutor
fisgar ⟨1h⟩ *v/i* F snoop F; ***fisgar en algo*** snoop around in sth
fisgón *m*, **-ona** *f* snoop
fisgonear ⟨1a⟩ *v/i* F snoop around F (***en*** in)
física *f* physics
físico 1 *adj* physical **2** *m*, **-a** *f* physicist **3** *m de una persona* physique
fisiología *f* physiology
fisión *f* fission
fisioterapeuta *m/f* physical therapist, *Br* physiotherapist
fisioterapia *f* physical therapy, *Br* physiotherapy
fisonomía *f* features *pl*
fisura *f* crack; MED fracture
flác(c)ido *adj* flabby
flaco *adj* thin; ***punto flaco*** weak point
flacuchento *adj L.Am.* F skinny
flagelar ⟨1a⟩ *v/t* flagellate
flagrante *adj* flagrant; ***en flagrante delito*** red-handed, in flagrante delicto
flamante *adj* (*nuevo*) brand-new
flamenco 1 *adj* MÚS flamenco **2** *m* MÚS flamenco; ZO flamingo
flan *m* crème caramel
flanco *m* flank
flaquear ⟨1a⟩ *v/i* weaken; *de entusiasmo* flag
flaqueza *f fig* weakness
flash *m* FOT flash
flato *m* MED stitch
flatulencia *f* MED flatulence
flauta *f* flute; *Méx* fried taco; ***flauta dulce*** recorder; ***flauta travesera*** (transverse) flute
flautista *m/f* flautist
flecha *f* arrow
flechazo *m fig* love at first sight
flecos *mpl* fringe *sg*
flema *f fig* phlegm
flemático *adj* phlegmatic
flemón *m* MED gumboil
flequillo *m del pelo* fringe
fletar ⟨1a⟩ *v/t* charter; (*embarcar*) load
flete *m L.Am.* freight, cost of transport
fletero *adj L.Am.* hire *atr*, charter *atr*
flexibilidad *f* flexibility
flexible *adj* flexible
flexión *f en gimnasia* push-up, *Br* press-up; *de piernas* squat; *de la voz* inflection
flexionar ⟨1a⟩ **1** *v/t* flex **2** *v/r* **flexionarse** bend
flexo *m* desk lamp
flipar ⟨1a⟩ *v/i*: ***le flipa el cine*** P he's mad about the movies F
flirtear ⟨1a⟩ *v/i* flirt (***con*** with)
flojo *adj* loose; *café, argumento* weak; COM *actividad* slack; *novela, redación* poor; *L.Am.* lazy
flojera *f L.Am.* laziness; ***me da flojera*** I can't be bothered
flor *f* flower
flora *f* flora
florear ⟨1a⟩ **1** *v/t* decorate with flowers; *Méx* (*halagar*) flatter, compliment **2** *v/i* flower, bloom
florecer ⟨2d⟩ *v/i* BOT flower. bloom; *de negocio, civilización* etc flourish
floreciente *adj* flourishing
florero *m* vase
florista *m/f* florist
floristería *f* florist's, flower shop
flota *f* fleet
flotación *f* flotation
flotador *m* float
flotar ⟨1a⟩ *v/i* float
flote MAR: ***a flote*** afloat
fluctuación *f* fluctuation
fluctuar ⟨1e⟩ *v/i* fluctuate
fluidez *f* fluidity
fluido 1 *adj* fluid; *tráfico* free-flowing; *lenguaje* fluent **2** *m* fluid
fluir ⟨3g⟩ *v/i* flow
flujo *m* flow
fluorescente 1 *adj* fluorescent **2** *m* strip light
fluvial *adj* river *atr*
FM *abr* (= ***frecuencia modulada***) FM (= frequency modulation)
FMI *abr* (= ***Fondo Monetario Internacional***) IMF (= International Monetary Fund)
fobia *f* phobia
foca *f* ZO seal
foco *m* focus; TEA, TV spotlight; *de infección* center, *Br* centre; *de incendio* seat; *L.Am.* (*bombilla*) lightbulb; *de auto* headlight; *de calle* streetlight
fofo *adj* flabby
fogata *f* bonfire
fogoso *adj* fiery, ardent
foie-gras *m* foie gras
folclore *m* folklore
fólico *adj*: ***ácido fólico*** folic acid
folio *m* sheet (of paper)
folklore *m* folklore
follaje *m* foliage
folleto *m* pamphlet
follón *m* argument; (*lío*) mess; ***armar un***

follón kick up a fuss
fomentar ⟨1a⟩ *v/t* foster; COM promote; *rebelión* foment, incite
fomento *m* COM promotion
fonda *f L.Am.* cheap restaurant; (*pensión*) boarding house
fondear ⟨1a⟩ **1** *v/t* MAR anchor **2** *v/r* **fondearse** *L.Am.* get rich
fondero *m*, **-a** *f L.Am.* restaurant owner
fondista *m/f* DEP long-distance runner
fondo *m* bottom; *de sala, cuarto* etc back; *de pasillo* end; (*profundidad*) depth; PINT, FOT background; *de un museo* etc collection; COM fund; ***fondo de inversión*** investment fund; ***fondo de pensiones*** pension fund; ***Fondo Monetario Internacional*** International Monetary Fund; ***fondos*** *pl* money *sg*, funds; ***tiene buen fondo*** he's got a good heart; ***en el fondo*** deep down; ***tocar fondo*** *fig* reach bottom
fonética *f* phonetics
fontanería *f* plumbing
fontanero *m* plumber
footing *m* DEP jogging; ***hacer footing*** go jogging, jog
forastero 1 *adj* foreign **2** *m*, **-a** *f* outsider, stranger
forcejear ⟨1a⟩ *v/i* struggle
forcejeo *m* struggle
forense 1 *adj* forensic **2** *m/f* forensic scientist
forestación *f* afforestation
forestal *adj* forest *atr*
forestar ⟨1a⟩ *v/t L.Am.* afforest
forjar ⟨1a⟩ *v/t metal* forge
forma *f* form; (*apariencia*) shape; (*manera*) way; ***de todas formas*** in any case, anyway; ***estar en forma*** be fit
formación *f* formation; (*entrenamiento*) training; ***formación profesional*** vocational training
formal *adj* formal; *niño* well-behaved; (*responsable*) responsible
formalizar ⟨1f⟩ *v/t* formalize; *relación* make official
formar ⟨1a⟩ **1** *v/t* form; (*educar*) educate **2** *v/r* **formarse** form
formatear ⟨1a⟩ *v/t* INFOR format
formato *m* format
formidable *adj* huge; (*estupendo*) tremendous
fórmula *f* formula
formular ⟨1a⟩ *v/t teoría* formulate; *queja* make, lodge
formulario *m* form
fornicar ⟨1g⟩ *v/i* fornicate
fornido *adj* well-built
foro *m* forum
forofo *m*, **-a** *f* F fan
forrado *adj prenda* lined; *libro* covered; *fig* F loaded F
forraje *m* fodder
forrar ⟨1a⟩ **1** *v/t prenda* line; *libro, silla* cover **2** *v/r* **forrarse** F make a fortune F
forro *m de prenda* lining; *de libro* cover
fortalecer ⟨2d⟩ **1** *v/t tb fig* strengthen **2** *v/r* **fortalecerse** strengthen
fortaleza *f* strength of character; MIL fortress
fortificar ⟨1g⟩ *v/t* MIL fortify
fortuito *adj* chance *atr*, accidental
fortuna *f* fortune; (*suerte*) luck; ***por fortuna*** fortunately, luckily
forzar ⟨1f & 1m⟩ *v/t* force; (*violar*) rape
forzoso *adj aterrizaje* forced
forzudo *adj* brawny
fosa *f* pit; (*tumba*) grave; ***fosa comúín*** common grave; ***fosas nasales*** nostrils
fósforo *m* QUÍM phosphorus; *L.Am.* (*cerilla*) match
fósil 1 *adj* fossilized **2** *m* fossil
foso *m* ditch; TEA, MÚS pit; *de castillo* moat
foto *f* photo
fotocopia *f* photocopy
fotocopiadora *f* photocopier
fotocopiar ⟨1a⟩ *v/t* photocopy
fotogénico *adj* photogenic
fotografía *f* photography
fotografiar ⟨1c⟩ *v/t* photograph
fotógrafo *m*, **-a** *f* photographer
FP *f* (= ***formación profesional***) vocational training
frac *m* tail coat
fracasado 1 *adj* unsuccessful **2** *m*, **-a** *f* loser
fracasar ⟨1a⟩ *v/i* fail
fracaso *m* failure
fracción *f* fraction; POL faction
fraccionamiento *m L.Am.* (housing) project, *Br* estate
fraccionar ⟨1a⟩ *v/t* break up; FIN pay in instal(l)ments
fractura *f* MED fracture
fracturar ⟨1a⟩ *v/t* MED fracture
fragancia *f* fragrance
frágil *adj* fragile
fragmentar ⟨1a⟩ *v/t* fragment
fragmento *m* fragment; *de novela, poema* excerpt, extract
fraguar ⟨1i⟩ *v/t* forge; *plan* devise; *complot* hatch
fraile *m* friar, monk
frambuesa *f* raspberry
francés 1 *adj* French **2** *m* Frenchman; *idioma* French
francesa *f* Frenchwoman

Francia France
franco *adj* (*sincero*) frank; (*evidente*) distinct, marked; COM free
francotirador *m* sniper
franela *f* flannel
franja *f* fringe; *de tierra* strip
franquear ⟨1a⟩ *v/t carta* pay the postage on; *camino*, *obstáculo* clear
franqueo *m* postage
franqueza *f* frankness
franquicia *f* (*exención*) exemption; COM franchise
frasco *m* bottle
frase *f* phrase; (*oración*) sentence; ***frase hecha*** set phrase
fraternal *adj* brotherly
fraternidad *f* brotherhood, fraternity
fraternizar ⟨1f⟩ *v/i* POL fraternize
fraude *m* fraud
fraudulento *adj* fraudulent
frazada *f L.Am.* blanket
frecuencia *f* frequency; ***frecuencia modulada*** RAD frequency modulation; ***con frecuencia*** frequently
frecuentar ⟨1a⟩ *v/t* frequent
frecuente *adj* frequent; (*común*) common
frecuentemente *adv* often, frequently
fregadero *m* sink
fregar ⟨1h & 1k⟩ *v/t platos* wash; *el suelo* mop; *L.Am.* F bug F
fregón 1 *adj* annoying **2** *m L.Am.* F nuisance, pain in the neck F
fregona *f* mop; *L.Am.* F nuisance, pain in the neck F
freidora *f* deep fryer
freidura *f* frying
freír ⟨3m; *part* ***frito*** ⟩ *v/t* fry; F (*matar*) waste P
frenada *f esp L.Am.*: ***dar una frenada*** F slam the brakes on, hit the brakes F
frenar ⟨1a⟩ **1** *v/i* AUTO brake **2** *v/t fig* slow down; *impulsos* check
frenazo *m*: ***pegar*** *or* ***dar un frenazo*** F slam the brakes on, hit the brakes F
frenesí *m* frenzy
frenético *adj* frenetic
freno *m* brake; ***freno de mano*** parking brake, *Br* handbrake
frente 1 *f* forehead **2** *m* MIL, METEO front; ***de frente*** *colisión* head-on; ***de frente al grupo*** *L.Am.* facing the group; ***hacer frente a*** face up to **3** *prp*: ***frente a*** opposite
fresa *f* strawberry
fresco 1 *adj* cool; *pescado etc* fresh; *persona* F fresh F, *Br* cheeky F **2** *m*, **-a** *f*: ***¡eres un fresco!*** F you've got nerve! F, *Br* you've got a cheek! F **3** *m* fresh air; *C.Am.* fruit drink
frescor *m* freshness
frescura *f* freshness; (*frío*) coolness; *fig* nerve
fresno *m* BOT ash tree
fresón *m* strawberry
frialdad *f tb fig* coldness
fricción *f* TÉC, *fig* friction
friccionar ⟨1a⟩ *v/t* rub
friega *f L.Am.* F hassle F, drag F
frígido *adj* MED frigid
frigorífico 1 *adj* refrigerated **2** *m* fridge
fríjol *m*, **frijol** *m L.Am.* bean
frío 1 *adj tb fig* cold **2** *m* cold; ***tener frío*** be cold
friolento *L.Am.*, **friolero** *adj*: ***es friolento*** he feels the cold
fritar ⟨1a⟩ *v/t L.Am.* fry
frito 1 *part* → ***freír*** **2** *adj* fried **3** *mpl*: ***fritos*** fried food *sg*
fritura *f* fried food
frívolo *adj* frivolous
frondoso *adj* leafy
frontal *adj* frontal; *ataque etc* head-on; (*delantero*) front *atr*
frontera *f* border
fronterizo *adj* border *atr*
frontón *m* DEP pelota; *cancha* pelota court
frotar ⟨1a⟩ *v/t* rub
fructífero *adj* fruitful, productive
frugal *adj persona* frugal
fruncir ⟨3b⟩ *v/t material* gather; ***fruncir el ceño*** frown
frustración *f* frustration
frustrante *adj* frustrating
frustrar ⟨1a⟩ **1** *v/t* frustrate; *plan* thwart **2** *v/r* **frustrarse** fail
fruta *f* fruit
frutal 1 *adj* fruit *atr* **2** *m* fruit tree
frutería *f* fruit store, *Br* greengrocer's
frutilla *f S. Am.* strawberry
fruto *m tb fig* fruit; *nuez*, *almendra etc* nut; ***frutos secos*** nuts
fucsia *adj* fuchsia
fue *vb* → ***ir***, ***ser***
fuego *m* fire; ***¿tienes fuego?*** do you have a light?; ***fuegos artificiales*** fireworks; ***pegar*** *or* ***prender fuego a*** set fire to
fuel(-oil) *m* fuel oil
fuelle *m* bellows *pl*
fuente *f* fountain; *recipiente* dish; *fig* source
fuera 1 *vb* → ***ir***, ***ser*** **2** *adv* outside; (*en otro lugar*) away; (*en otro país*) abroad; ***por fuera*** on the outside; ***¡fuera!*** get out! **3** *prp*: ***fuera de*** outside; ***¡sal fuera de aquí!*** get out of here!; ***está fuera del país*** he's abroad, he's out of the country
fuero *m*: ***en el fuero interno*** deep down

F

fuerte 1 *adj* strong; *dolor* intense; *lluvia* heavy; *aumento* sharp; *ruido* loud; *fig* P incredible F **2** *adv* hard **3** *m* MIL fort
fuerza *f* strength; (*violencia*) force; EL power; ***fuerza aérea*** air force; ***fuerza de voluntad*** willpower; ***fuerzas armadas*** armed forces; ***fuerzas de seguridad*** security forces; ***a fuerza de …*** by (dint of)
fuese *vb* → ***ir***, ***ser***
fuete *m L.Am.* whip
fuga *f* escape; *de gas*, *agua* leak; ***darse a la fuga*** flee
fugarse ⟨1h⟩ *v/r* run away; *de la cárcel* escape
fugaz *adj fig* fleeting
fugitivo 1 *adj* runaway *atr* **2** *m*, **-a** *f* fugitive
fui *vb* → ***ir***, ***ser***
fuimos *vb* → ***ir***, ***ser***
fulano *m* so-and-so
fulgor *m* brightness
fulgurante *adj fig* dazzling
fulminante *adj* sudden
fulminar ⟨1a⟩ *v/t*: ***lo fulminó un rayo*** he was killed by lightning; ***fulminar a alguien con la mirada*** look daggers at s.o. F
fumador *m*, **fumadora** *f* smoker
fumar ⟨1a⟩ **1** *v/t* smoke **2** *v/i* smoke; ***prohibido fumar*** no smoking **3** *v/r* **fumarse** smoke; ***fumarse una clase*** F skip a class F
fumigar ⟨1h⟩ *v/t* fumigate
función *f* purpose, function; *en el trabajo* duty; TEA performance; ***en función de*** according to
funcional *adj* functional
funcionamiento *m* working
funcionar ⟨1a⟩ *v/i* work; ***no funciona*** out of order
funcionario *m*, **-a** *f* government employee, civil servant
funda *f* cover; *de gafas* case; *de almohada* pillowcase
fundación *f* foundation
fundador *m*, **fundadora** *f* founder
fundamental *adj* fundamental
fundamentalismo *m* fundamentalism
fundamentalista *m/f* fundamentalist
fundamentalmente *adv* essentially
fundamento *m* foundation; ***fundamentos*** (*nociones*) fundamentals
fundar ⟨1a⟩ **1** *v/t fig* base (***en*** on) **2** *v/r* **fundarse** be based (***en*** on)
fundición *f* smelting; (*fábrica*) foundry
fundir ⟨3a⟩ **1** *v/t hielo* melt; *metal* smelt; COM merge **2** *v/r* **fundirse** melt; *de bombilla* fuse; *de plomos* blow; COM merge; *L.Am. fig*: *de empresa* go under
fúinebre *adj* funeral *atr*; *fig*: *ambiente* gloomy
funeral *m* funeral
funeraria *f* funeral parlo(u)r, *Br* undertaker's
funesto *adj* disastrous
funicular *m* funicular; (*teleférico*) cable car
furcia *f* P whore P
furgón *m* van; FERR boxcar, *Br* goods van; ***furgón de equipajes*** baggage car, *Br* luggage van
furgoneta *f* van
furia *f* fury; ***ponerse hecho una furia*** go into a fury *o* rage
furibundo *adj* furious
furioso *adj* furious
furor *m*: ***hacer furor*** *fig* be all the rage F
furtivo *adj* furtive
fuselaje *m* fuselage
fusible *m* EL fuse
fusil *m* rifle
fusilar ⟨1a⟩ *v/t* shoot; *fig* F (*plagiar*) lift F
fusión *f* FÍS fusion; COM merger
fusionar ⟨1a⟩ **1** *v/t* COM merge **2** *v/r* **fusionarse** merge
fusta *f* riding crop
fúitbol *m* soccer, *Br* football; ***fúitbol americano*** football, *Br* American football; ***fúitbol sala*** five-a-side soccer (*Br* football)
futbolín *m* Foosball®, table football
futbolista *m/f* soccer player, *Br* footballer, *Br* football player
fúitil *adj* trivial
futre *m Chi* dandy
futuro 1 *adj* future *atr* **2** *m* future
futurólogo *m*, **-a** *f* futurologist

G

g. *abr* (= ***gramo*** (***s***)) gr(s) (= gram(s))
gabardina *f prenda* raincoat; *material* gabardine
gabinete *m* (*despacho*) office; *en una casa* study; POL cabinet; *L.Am. de médico* office, *Br* surgery
gacela *f* ZO gazelle
gaceta *f* gazette
gachas *fpl* porridge *sg*
gachupín *m Méx desp* Spaniard
gacilla *f C.Am.* safety pin
gafas *fpl* glasses; ***gafas de sol*** sunglasses
gafe 1 *adj* jinxed **2** *m* jinx **3** *m/f*: ***es un gafe*** he's jinxed
gaita *f* MÚS bagpipes *pl*
gajes *mpl*: ***gajes del oficio*** *iron* occupational hazard
gajo *m* segment
gala *f* gala; ***traje de gala*** formal dress
galante *adj* gallant
galápago *m* ZO turtle
galardonar ⟨1a⟩ *v/t*: ***fue galardonado con …*** he was awarded …
galaxia *f* galaxy
galería *f* gallery; ***galería de arte*** art gallery
Gales Wales
galés Welsh
galgo *m* grayhound
gallera *f L.Am.* cockpit
galleta *f* cookie, *Br* biscuit
gallina 1 *f* hen **2** *m* F chicken
gallinazo *m L.Am.* turkey buzzard
gallo *m* rooster, *Br* cock
galón *m adorno* braid; MIL stripe; *medida* gallon
galope *m* gallop
galpón *m L.Am.* large shed; *W.I.* HIST slave quarters *pl*
gama *f* range
gamba *f* ZO GASTR shrimp, *Br* prawn
gamberro *m*, **-a** *f* troublemaker
gamín *m*, **-ina** *f Col* street kid
gamo *m* ZO fallow deer
gamonal *m Pe*, *Bol desp* chief
gamuza *f* chamois
gana *f*: ***de mala gana*** unwillingly, grudgingly; ***no me da la gana*** I don't want to; ***… me da ganas de*** … makes me want to; ***tener ganas de*** (***hacer***) ***algo*** feel like (doing) sth
ganadería *f* stockbreeding
ganadero *m*, **-a** *f* stockbreeder
ganado *m* cattle *pl*
ganador *m* winner
ganancia *f* profit
ganar ⟨1a⟩ **1** win; *mediante el trabajo* earn **2** *v/i mediante el trabajo* earn; (*vencer*) win; (*mejorar*) improve **3** *v/r* **ganarse** earn; *a alguien* win over; ***ganarse la vida*** earn one's living
ganchillo *m* crochet
gancho *m* hook; *L.Am.*, *Arg fig* F sex-appeal; ***hacer gancho*** *L.Am.* (*ayudar*) lend a hand; ***tener gancho*** F *de un grupo, una campaña* be popular; *de una persona* have that certain something
gandul *m* lazybones *sg*
gandulear ⟨1a⟩ *v/i* F loaf around F
ganga *f* bargain
gangrena *f* MED gangrene
gángster *m* gangster
ganso *m* goose; *macho* gander
garabatear ⟨1a⟩ *v/i & v/t* doodle
garabato *m* doodle
garaje *m* garage
garantía *f* guarantee
garantizar ⟨1f⟩ *v/t* guarantee
garapiña *f Cuba*, *Méx* pineapple squash
garbanzo *m* BOT chickpea
garbo *m al moverse* grace
gardenia *f* BOT gardenia
garete *m*: ***irse al garete*** *fig* F go to pot F
garfio *m* hook
gargajo *m* piece of phlegm
garganta *f* ANAT throat; GEOG gorge
gargantilla *f* choker
gárgaras *fpl*: ***hacer gárgaras*** gargle
garito *m* gambling den
garra *f* claw; *de ave* talon; ***caer en las garras de alguien*** *fig* fall into s.o.'s clutches; ***tener garra*** F be compelling
garrafa *f* carafe
garrafal *adj error etc* terrible
garrapata *f* ZO tick
garrote *m palo* club, stick; *tipo de ejecución* garrotte
garúia *f L.Am.* drizzle
garuar ⟨1e⟩ *v/i L.Am.* drizzle
garzón *m Rpl* (*mesero*) waiter
garza *f* ZO heron
gas *m* gas; ***gas natural*** natural gas; ***gases*** *pl* MED gas *sg*, wind *sg*; ***con gas*** sparkling, carbonated; ***sin gas*** still
gasa *f* gauze
gaseosa *f* lemonade
gasfitero *m Pe*, *Bol* plumber
gasoducto *m* gas pipeline

gasoil, gasóleo *m* oil; *para motores* diesel
gasolina *f* gas, *Br* petrol
gasolinera *f* gas station, *Br* petrol station
gastar ⟨1a⟩ **1** *v/t dinero* spend; *energía, electricidad etc* use; (*llevar*) wear; (*desperdiciar*) waste; (*desgastar*) wear out; ***¿qué núimero gastas?*** what size do you take?, what size are you? **2** *v/r* **gastarse** *dinero* spend; *gasolina, agua* run out of; *pila* run down; *ropa, zapatos* wear out
gasto *m* expense
gastronomía *f* gastronomy
gata *f* (female) cat; *Méx* servant, maid; ***a gatas*** F on all fours; ***andar a gatas*** F crawl
gatear ⟨1a⟩ *v/i* crawl
gatillo *m* trigger
gato *m* cat; AUTO jack; ***aquí hay gato encerrado*** F there's something fishy going on here F; ***cuatro gatos*** a handful of people
gaucho *m Rpl* gaucho
gaviota *f* (sea)gull
gay 1 *adj* gay **2** *m* gay (man)
gazpacho *m* gazpacho (*cold soup made with tomatoes, peppers, garlic etc*)
gel *m* gel
gelatina *f* gelatin(e); GASTR Jell-O®, *Br* jelly
gélido *adj* icy
gema *f* gem
gemelo 1 *adj* twin *atr*; ***hermano gemelo*** twin brother **2** *mpl*: ***gemelos*** twins; *de camisa* cuff links; (*prismáticos*) binoculars
gemido *m* moan, groan
Géminis *m/f inv* ASTR Gemini
gemir ⟨3l⟩ *v/i* moan, groan
gen *m* gene
genealógico *adj*: ***árbol genealógico*** family tree
generación *f* generation
generador *m* EL generator
general 1 *adj* general; ***en general*** in general; ***por lo general*** usually, generally **2** *m* general
generalización *f* generalization
generalizar ⟨1f⟩ **1** *v/t* spread **2** *v/i* generalize **3** *v/r* **generalizarse** spread
generalmente *adv* generally
generar ⟨1a⟩ *v/t* generate
género *m* (*tipo*) type; *de literatura* genre; GRAM gender; COM goods *pl*, merchandise
generosidad *f* generosity
generoso *adj* generous
genética *f* genetics
genético *adj* genetic
genial *adj* brilliant; F (*estupendo*) fantastic F, great F
genialidad *f* brilliance
genio *m talento, persona* genius; (*carácter*) temper; ***tener mal genio*** be bad-tempered
genital *adj* genital
genitales *mpl* genitals
genocidio *m* genocide
gente *f* people *pl*; *L.Am.* (*persona*) person
gentileza *f* kindness; ***por gentileza de*** by courtesy of
gentío *m* crowd
genuino *adj* genuine, real
geografía *f* geography
geográfico *adj* geographical
geología *f* geology
geológico *adj* geological
geólogo *m*, **-a** *f* geologist
geometría *f* geometry
geométrico *adj* geometric(al)
geranio *m* BOT geranium
gerente *m/f* manager
geriatría *f* geriatrics *sg*
germen *m* germ
germinar ⟨1a⟩ *v/i tb fig* germinate
gerundio *m* GRAM gerund
gestación *f* gestation
gesticular ⟨1a⟩ *v/i* gesticulate
gestión *f* management; ***gestiones*** *pl* (*trámites*) formalities, procedure *sg*
gestionar ⟨1a⟩ *v/t trámites* take care of; *negocio* manage
gesto *m movimiento* gesture; (*expresión*) expression
gestoría *f Esp agency offering clients help with official documents*
gigante 1 *adj* giant *atr* **2** *m* giant
gilipollas *m/f inv* P jerk P
gilipollez *f Esp* V bullshit V
gimnasia *f* gymnastics; ***hacer gimnasia*** do exercises
gimnasio *m* gym
gimnasta *m/f* gymnast
gimotear ⟨1a⟩ *v/i* whine, whimper
ginebra *f* gin
ginecólogo *m*, **-a** *f* gyn(a)ecologist
gin-tonic *m* gin and tonic, G and T F
gira *f* tour
girar ⟨1a⟩ **1** *v/i* (*dar vueltas, torcer*) turn; *alrededor de algo* revolve; *fig* (*tratar*) revolve (***en torno a*** around) **2** *v/t* COM transfer
girasol *m* BOT sunflower
giro *m* turn; GRAM idiom; ***giro postal*** COM money order
gis *m L.Am.* chalk
gitano 1 *adj* gypsy *atr* **2** *m*, **-a** *f* gypsy
glacial *adj* icy

glaciar *m* glacier
glándula *f* ANAT gland
global *adj* (*de todo el mundo*) global; *visión, resultado* overall; *cantidad* total
globo *m aerostático, de niño* balloon; *terrestre* globe; ***globo terráqueo*** globe
gloria *f* glory; (*delicia*) delight; ***estar en la gloria*** F be in seventh heaven
gloriado *m Pe, Bol, Ecuad type of punch*
glorieta *f* traffic circle, *Br* roundabout
glorioso *adj* glorious
glosario *m* glossary
glotón 1 *adj* greedy **2** *m*, **-ona** *f* glutton
glucosa *f* glucose
gnomo *m* gnome
gobernador *m* governor
gobernante *m* leader
gobernar ⟨1k⟩ *v/t & v/i* rule, govern
gobierno *m* government
goce *m* pleasure, enjoyment
gofre *m* waffle
gol *m* DEP goal
goleador *m* DEP (goal-)scorer
golf *m* DEP golf
golfista *m/f* golfer
golfo 1 *m* GEOG gulf **2** *m*, **-a** *f* good-for--nothing; *niño* little devil
Golfo de México *m* Gulf of Mexico
golondrina *f* ZO swallow
golosina *f* candy, *Br* sweet
goloso *adj* sweet-toothed
golpe *m* knock, blow; ***golpe de Estado*** coup d'état; ***de golpe*** suddenly; ***no da golpe*** F she doesn't do a thing
golpear ⟨1a⟩ *v/t cosa* bang, hit; *persona* hit
goma *f* (*caucho*) rubber; (*pegamento*) glue; (*banda elástica*) rubber band; F (*preservativo*) condom, rubber P; *C.Am.* F (*resaca*) hangover; ***goma*** (***de borrar***) eraser; ***goma espuma*** foam rubber
gomina *f* hair gel
gominola *f* jelly bean
góndola *f Chi* bus
gong *m* gong
gordinflón *m*, **-ona** *f* F fatso F
gordo 1 *adj* fat; ***me cae gordo*** F I can't stand him; ***se va a armar la -a*** all hell will break loose F **2** *m*, **-a** *f* fat person **3** *m premio* jackpot
gorila *m* ZO gorilla
gorjeo *m de pájaro* chirping, warbling; *de niño* gurgling
gorra *f* cap; ***de gorra*** F for free F
gorrino *m fig* pig
gorrión *m* ZO sparrow
gorro *m* cap; ***estar hasta el gorro de algo*** F be fed up to the back teeth with sth F
gorrón *m*, **-ona** *f* F scrounger
gorronear ⟨1a⟩ *v/t & v/i* F scrounge F
gota *f* drop; ***ni gota*** F *de cerveza, leche etc* not a drop; *de pan* not a scrap
gotear ⟨1a⟩ *v/i* drip; *filtrarse* leak
gotera *f* leak; (*mancha*) stain
gotero *m* MED drip; *L.Am.* (eye)dropper
gozar ⟨1f⟩ *v/i* (*disfrutar*) enjoy o.s.; ***gozar de*** (*disfrutar de*) enjoy; (*poseer*) have, enjoy
gozo *m* (*alegría*) joy; (*placer*) pleasure
grabación *f* recording
grabado *m* engraving
grabadora *f* tape recorder
grabar ⟨1a⟩ *v/t record, video etc* record; PINT, *fig* engrave
gracia *f*: ***tener gracia*** (*ser divertido*) be funny; (*tener encanto*) be graceful; ***me hace gracia*** I think it's funny, it makes me laugh; ***no le veo la gracia*** I don't think it's funny; ***dar las gracias a alguien*** thank s.o.; ***gracias*** thank you
grácil *adj* dainty
gracioso *adj* funny
gradas *fpl* DEP stands, grandstand *sg*
graderío *m* stands *pl*
grado *m* degree; ***de buen grado*** with good grace, readily
graduación *f* TÉC *etc* adjustment; *de alcohol* alcohol content; EDU graduation; MIL rank
gradual *adj* gradual
gradualmente *adv* gradually
graduarse ⟨1e⟩ *v/r* graduate, get one's degree
gráfica *f* graph
gráfico 1 *adj* graphic; ***artes -as*** graphic arts **2** *m* MAT graph; INFOR graphic
gragea *f* tablet, pill
grajo *m* ZO rook
Gral. *abr* (**= *General***) Gen (= General)
gramática *f* grammar
gramatical *adj* grammatical
gramo *m* gram
gran *short form of* **grande** *before a noun*
granada *f* BOT pomegranate; ***granada de mano*** MIL hand grenade
granangular *m* wide-angle lens
granate *adj* dark crimson
Gran Bretaña Great Britain
grande 1 *adj* big; ***a lo grande*** in style **2** *m/f L.Am.* (*adulto*) grown-up, adult; (*mayor*) eldest; ***pasarlo en grande*** F have a great time
grandeza *f* greatness
grandiosidad *f* grandeur
grandioso *adj* impressive, magnificent
granel *m*: ***vender a granel*** COM sell in bulk; ***había comida a granel*** F there

G

was loads of food F
granero *m* granary
granito *m* granite
granizada *f* hailstorm
granizado *m type of soft drink made with crushed ice*
granizar ⟨1f⟩ *v/i* hail
granizo *m* hail
granja *f* farm
granjearse ⟨1a⟩ *v/r* win, earn
granjero *m*, **-a** *f* farmer
grano *m* grain; *de café* bean; *en la piel* pimple, spot; ***ir al grano*** get (straight) to the point
granuja *m* rascal
grapa *f* staple
grapadora *f* stapler
grapar ⟨1a⟩ staple
grasa *f* BIO, GASTR fat; *lubricante, suciedad* grease
grasiento *adj* greasy, oily
graso *adj* greasy; *carne* fatty
gratificación *f* gratification
gratificar ⟨1g⟩ *v/t* reward
gratinar ⟨1a⟩ *v/t* cook au gratin
gratis *adj & adv* free
gratitud *f* gratitude
gratuito *adj* free
grava *f* gravel
gravar ⟨1a⟩ *v/t* tax
grave *adj* serious; *tono* grave, solemn; *nota* low; *voz* deep; ***estar grave*** be seriously ill
gravedad *f* seriousness, gravity; FÍS gravity
gravemente *adv* seriously
gravilla *f* grave
Grecia Greece
gremio *m* HIST guild; *fig* F (*oficio manual*) trade; (*profesión*) profession
griego 1 *adj* Greek **2** *m*, **-a** *f* Greek
grieta *f* crack
grifo 1 *adj Méx* F high **2** *m* faucet, *Br* tap; *Pe* (*gasolinera*) gas station, *Br* petrol station
grillo *m* ZO cricket
grima *f*: ***me da grima*** *Esp de ruido, material etc* it sets my teeth on edge; *de algo asqueroso* it gives me the creeps F; ***en grima*** *Pe* alone
gringo *m L.Am. desp* gringo *desp*, foreigner
gripe *f* flu, influenza
gris *adj* gray, *Br* grey
gritar ⟨1a⟩ *v/t & v/i* shout, yell
griterío *m* shouting
grito *m* cry, shout; ***a grito pelado*** at the top of one's voice; ***pedir algo a gritos*** F be crying out for sth
grosella *f* redcurrant
grosero 1 *adj* rude **2** *m*, **-a** *f* rude person
grosor *m* thickness
grotesco *adj* grotesque
grúía *f* crane; AUTO wrecker, *Br* breakdown truck
grueso *adj* thick; *persona* stout
grulla *f* ZO crane
grumo *m* lump
gruñido *m* grunt; *de perro* growl
gruñir ⟨3h⟩ *v/i* (*quejarse*) grumble, moan F; *de perro* growl; *de cerdo* grunt
gruñón 1 *adj* F grumpy **2** *m*, **-ona** *f* F grouch F
grupo *m* group
gruta *f* cave; *artificial* grotto
guacamol, **guacamole** *m* guacamole
guachimán *m Chi* watchman
guacho 1 *adj S. Am.* (*sin casa*) homeless; (*huérfano*) orphaned **2** *m*, **-a** *f S. Am. sin casa* homeless person; (*huérfano*) orphan
guadaño *m Cuba, Méx* small boat
guagua *f W.I., Ven, Canaries* bus; *Pe, Bol, Chi* (*niño*) baby
guajolote *m Méx, C.Am.* turkey
guanaco 1 *adj L.Am.* F dumb F, stupid **2** *m* ZO guanaco **3** *m*, **-a** *f persona* idiot
guantazo *m* slap
guante *m* glove
guantera *f* AUTO glove compartment
guapo *adj hombre* handsome, good-looking; *mujer* beautiful; *S. Am.* gutsy
guaracha *f W.I.* street band
guarache → ***huarache***
guarapo *m L.Am. alcoholic drink made from sugar cane and herbs*
guarda *m/f* keeper; ***guarda jurado*** security guard
guardabosques *m/f inv* forest ranger
guardacostas *m inv* coastguard vessel
guardaespaldas *m/f inv* bodyguard
guardameta *m/f* DEP goalkeeper
guardar ⟨1a⟩ **1** *v/t* keep; *poner en un lugar* put (away); *recuerdo* have; *apariencias* keep up; INFOR save; ***guardar silencio*** remain silent, keep silent **2** *v/r* **guardarse** keep; ***guardarse de*** refrain from
guardarropa *m* checkroom, *Br* cloakroom; (*ropa, armario*) wardrobe
guardería *f* nursery
guardia 1 *f* guard; ***de guardia*** on duty; ***bajar la guardia*** *fig* lower one's guard **2** *m/f* MIL guard; (*policía*) police officer; ***guardia civil*** *Esp* civil guard; ***guardia de seguridad*** security guard; ***guardia de tráfico*** traffic warden
guardián 1 *adj*: ***perro guardián*** guard dog **2** *m*, **-ana** *f* guard; *fig* guardian

guarecer ⟨2d⟩ **1** *v/t* shelter **2** *v/r* **guarecerse** shelter, take shelter (***de*** from)
guarida *f* zo den; *de personas* hideout
guarnición *f* GASTR accompaniment; MIL garrison
guaro *m C.Am.* sugar-cane liquor
guarro 1 *adj* F *sucio* filthy **2** *m tb fig* F pig
guarura *m Méx* (*guardaespaldas*) bodyguard; F (*gamberro*) thug
guasa *f L.Am.* joke; ***de guasa*** as a joke
guaso 1 *adj S. Am.* rude **2** *m Chi* peasant
guata *f L.Am.* F paunch
Guatemala Guatemala
guatemalteco 1 *adj* Guatemalan **2** *m*, **-a** *f* Guatemalan
guatón *adj L.Am.* F pot-bellied, big-bellied
guay *int Esp* F cool F, neat F
guayaba *f L.Am.* BOT guava
guayabera *f Méx, C.Am., W.I. loose embroidered shirt*
gubernamental *adj* governmental, government *atr*
guepardo *m* zo cheetah
güero 1 *adj Méx, C.Am.* fair, light-skinned **2** *m*, **-a** *f Méx, C.Am.* blond(e)
guerra *f* war; ***guerra civil*** civil war; ***guerra fría*** cold war; ***guerra mundial*** world war; ***dar guerra a alguien*** F give s.o. trouble
guerrero 1 *adj* warlike **2** *m* warrior
guerrilla *f* guerillas *pl*
guerrillero *m* guerilla
gueto *m* ghetto
guevear *v/i* → ***huevear***
guevón → ***huevón***
guía 1 *m/f* guide; ***guía turístico*** tourist guide **2** *f libro* guide (book); ***guía telefónica*** *or* ***de teléfonos*** phone book
guiar ⟨1c⟩ **1** *v/t* guide **2** *v/r* **guiarse**: ***guiarse por*** follow
guijarro *m* pebble
guillotina *f* guillotine
güinche *m L.Am.* winch, pulley
guinda 1 *adj L.Am.* purple **2** *f fresca* morello cherry; *en dulce* glacé cherry
guindilla *f* GASTR chil(l)i
guiñar ⟨1a⟩ *v/t*: ***le guiñó un ojo*** she winked at him
guiño *m* wink
guión *m de película* script; GRAM *corto* hyphen; *largo* dash
guionista *m/f* scriptwriter
guiri *m Esp* P (light-skinned) foreigner
guirnalda *f* garland
guisante *m* pea
guisar ⟨1a⟩ *v/t* GASTR stew, casserole
guiso *m* GASTR stew, casserole
guitarra *f* guitar
guitarrista *m/f* guitarist
gula *f* gluttony
gusano *m* worm
gustar ⟨1a⟩ *v/i*: ***me gusta viajar*** I like to travel, I like travelling; ***¿te gusta el ajo?*** do you like garlic?; ***no me gusta*** I don't like it
gusto *m* taste; (*placer*) pleasure; ***a gusto*** at ease; ***con mucho gusto*** with pleasure; ***de buen gusto*** in good taste, tasteful; ***de mal gusto*** in bad taste, tasteless; ***da gusto …*** it's a pleasure …; ***mucho*** *or* ***tanto gusto*** how do you do
gutural *adj* guttural

H

ha *vb* → ***haber***
haba *f* broad bean; ***en todas partes se cuecen habas*** it's the same the world over
Habana: ***La Habana*** Havana
habanero *m*, **-a** *f* citizen of Havana
habano *m* Havana (cigar)
haber ⟨2k⟩ **1** *v/aux* have; ***hemos llegado*** we've arrived; ***he de levantarme pronto*** I have to *o* I've got to get up early; ***de haberlo sabido*** if I'd known; ***has de ver*** *Méx* you ought to see it **2** *v/impers*: ***hay*** there is *sg*, there are *pl*; ***hubo un incendio*** there was a fire; ***¿qué hay?***, *Méx* ***¿qué hubo?*** how's it going?, what's happening?; ***hay que hacerlo*** it has to be done; ***no hay de qué*** not at all, don't mention it; ***no hay más que decir*** there's nothing more to be said **3** *m* asset; *pago* fee; ***tiene en su haber 50.000 ptas*** she's 50,000 pesetas in credit
habichuela *f* kidney bean
hábil *adj* skilled; (*capaz*) capable; (*astuto*) clever, smart

habilidad *f* skill; (*capacidad*) ability; (*astucia*) cleverness
habilitar ⟨1a⟩ *v/t lugar* fit out; *persona* authorize
habitación *f* room; (*dormitorio*) bedroom; ***habitación doble / individual*** double / single room
habitante *m/f* inhabitant
habitar ⟨1a⟩ *v/i* live (***en*** in)
hábitat *m* habitat
hábito *m tb* REL habit; (*práctica*) knack; ***colgar los hábitos*** *fig de sacerdote* give up the priesthood
habitual 1 *adj* usual, regular **2** *m/f* regular
habituar ⟨1e⟩ **1** *v/t*: ***habituar a alguien a algo*** get s.o. used to sth **2** *v/r* **habituarse**: ***habituarse a algo*** get used to sth
habla *f* speech; ***¡al habla!*** TELEC speaking; ***quedarse sin habla*** *fig* be speechless
hablada *f L.Am.* piece of gossip; ***habladas*** *pl* gossip *sg*
hablador *adj* talkative; *Méx* boastful
habladurías *fpl* gossip *sg*
hablante *m/f* speaker
hablar ⟨1a⟩ **1** *v/i* speak; (*conversar*) talk; ***hablar claro*** *fig* say what one means; ***hablar con alguien*** talk to s.o., talk with s.o.; ***hablar de*** *de libro etc* be about, deal with; ***hablar por hablar*** talk for the sake of it; ***¡ni hablar!*** no way! **2** *v/r* **hablarse** speak to one another; ***no se hablan*** they're not speaking (to each other)
hacendado 1 *adj* land-owing **2** *m*, **-a** *f* land-owner
hacendoso *adj* hardworking
hacer ⟨2s; *part* **hecho**⟩ **1** *v/t* (*realizar*) do; (*elaborar*, *crear*) make; ***¡haz algo!*** do something!; ***hacer una pregunta*** ask a question; ***¡qué le vamos a hacer!*** that's life; ***no hace más que quejarse*** all he does is complain; ***le hicieron ir*** they made him go; ***tengo que hacer los deberes*** I have to do my homework **2** *v/i*: ***haces bien / mal en ir*** you are doing the right / wrong thing by going; ***me hace mal*** it's making me ill; ***esto hará de mesa*** *de objeto* this will do as a table; ***hacer como que*** *or* ***como si*** act as if; ***no le hace*** *L.Am.* it doesn't matter; ***se me hace qué*** *L.Am.* it seems to me that **3** *v/impers*: ***hace calor / frío*** it's hot / cold; ***hace tres días*** three days ago; ***hace mucho (tiempo)*** a long time ago; ***desde hace un año*** for a year **4** *v/r* **hacerse** *traje* make; *casa* build o.s.; (*cocinarse*) cook; (*convertirse*, *volverse*) get, become; ***hacerse viejo*** get old; ***hacerse de noche*** get dark; ***se hace tarde*** it's getting late; ***hacerse el sordo / el tonto*** pretend to be deaf / stupid; ***hacerse a algo*** get used to sth; ***hacerse con algo*** get hold of sth
hacha *f* ax, *Br* axe; ***ser un hacha para algo*** F be brilliant at sth
hachís *m* hashish
hacia *prp* toward; ***hacia adelante*** forward; ***hacia abajo*** down; ***hacia arriba*** up; ***hacia atrás*** back(ward); ***hacia las cuatro*** about four (o'clock)
Hacienda *f ministerio* Treasury Department, *Br* Treasury; *oficina* Internal Revenue Service, *Br* Inland Revenue
hacienda *f L.Am.* (*granja*) ranch, estate
hacinar ⟨1a⟩ *v/t* stack
hada *f* fairy
haga *vb* → ***hacer***
hago *vb* → ***hacer***
Haití Haiti
hala *int* come on!; *sorpresa* wow!
halagar ⟨1h⟩ *v/t* flatter
halago *m* flattery
halar ⟨1a⟩ *v/t L.Am.* haul, pull
halcón *m* ZO falcon
halitosis *f* MED halitosis, bad breath
hall *m* hall
hallar ⟨1a⟩ **1** *v/t* find; (*descubrir*) discover; *muerte*, *destino* meet **2** *v/r* **hallarse** be; (*sentirse*) feel
hallazgo *m* find; (*descubrimiento*) discovery
halógeno *adj* halogen
halterofilia *f* DEP weight-lifting
hamaca *f* hammock; (*tumbona*) deck chair; *L.Am.* (*mecedora*) rocking chair
hamacar ⟨1g⟩ *v/t L.Am.* swing
hamaquear ⟨1a⟩ *v/t L.Am.* swing
hambre *f* hunger; ***morirse de hambre*** *fig* be starving; ***pasar hambre*** be starving
hambriento *adj tb fig* hungry (***de*** for)
hambruna *f* famine
hamburguesa *f* GASTR hamburger
hamburguesería *f* hamburger bar
hampa *f* underworld
hámster *m* ZO hamster
hangar *m* hangar
haragán *m*, **-ana** *f* shirker
harapo *m* rag
hardware *m* INFOR hardware
haré *vb* → ***hacer***
harina *f* flour
harinoso *adj* floury
hartar ⟨1a⟩ **1** *v/t*: ***hartar a alguien con algo*** tire s.o. with sth; ***hartar a alguien de algo*** give s.o. too much of sth **2** *v/r* **hartarse** get sick (***de*** of) F, get tired (***de*** of); (*llenarse*) stuff o.s. (***de*** with)
harto 1 *adj* fed up F; (*lleno*) full (up); ***había hartos pasteles*** there were cakes in abundance; ***hace harto frío*** *L.Am.* it's

H

very cold; ***estar harto de algo*** be sick of sth F, be fed up with sth F **2** *adv* very much; *delante del adjetivo* extremely; ***me gusta harto*** *L.Am.* F I like it a lot
hartón 1 *adj L.Am.* greedy **2** *m*: ***darse un hartón de algo*** overdose on sth
has *vb* → ***haber***
hasta 1 *prp* until, till; ***llegó hasta Bilbao*** he went as far as Bilbao; ***hasta ahora*** so far; ***hasta aquí*** up to here; ***¿hasta cuándo?*** how long?; ***hasta que*** until; ***¡hasta luego!*** see you (later); ***¡hasta la vista!*** see you (later) **2** *adv* even
hastiar ⟨1c⟩ *v/t* tire; (*aburrir*) bore
hastío *m* boredom
hatajo *m* bunch
hato *m L.Am.* bundle
hay *vb* → ***haber***
haya 1 *vb* → ***haber*** **2** *f* BOT beech
haz 1 *m* bundle; *de luz* beam **2** *vb* → ***hacer***
hazaña *f* achievement
hazmerreír *m fig* F laughing stock
he *vb* → ***haber***
hebilla *f* buckle
hechicero 1 *adj* bewitching, captivating **2** *m* sorcerer; *de tribu* witch-doctor
hechizado *adj* spellbound
hechizar ⟨1f⟩ *v/t fig* bewitch, captivate
hechizo *m* spell, charm
hecho 1 *part* → ***hacer***; ***hecho a mano*** hand-made; ***¡bien hecho!*** well done!; ***muy hecho*** *carne* well-done **2** *adj* finished; ***un hombre hecho y derecho*** a fully grown man **3** *m* fact; ***de hecho*** in fact
hectárea *f* hectare (*10,000 sq m*)
hedor *m* stink, stench
helada *f* frost
heladera *f Rpl* fridge
heladería *f* ice-cream parlo(u)r
helado 1 *adj* frozen; *fig* icy; ***quedarse helado*** be stunned **2** *m* ice cream
helar ⟨1k⟩ **1** *v/t* freeze **2** *v/i* freeze; ***anoche heló*** there was a frost last night **3** *v/r* **helarse** *tb fig* freeze
helecho *m* BOT fern
hélice *f* propeller
helicóptero *m* helicopter
hematoma *m* bruise
hembra *f* ZO, TÉC female
hemiplejía *f* MED hemiplegia
hemisferio *m* hemisphere
hemofilia *f* MED h(a)emophilia
hemorragia *f* MED h(a)emorrhage, bleeding
hemorroides *fpl* MED h(a)emorrhoids, piles
hendidura *f* crack
heno *m* hay
hepatitis *f* MED hepatitis
herbicida *m* herbicide, weed-killer
herboristería *f* herbalist
hercúleo *adj* Herculean
heredar ⟨1a⟩ *v/t* inherit (**de** from)
heredera *f* heiress
heredero *m* heir
hereditario *adj* hereditary
hereje *m* heretic
herencia *f* inheritance
herida *f de arma* wound; (*lesión*) injury; *mujer* wounded woman; *mujer lesionada* injured woman
herido 1 *adj de arma* wounded; (*lesionado*) injured **2** *m de bala* wounded man; (*lesionado*) injured man
herir ⟨3i⟩ *v/t con arma* wound; (*lesionar*) injure; *fig* (*ofender*) hurt
hermana *f* sister
hermanastra *f* stepsister
hermanastro *m* stepbrother
hermano *m* brother
hermético *adj* airtight, hermetic; *fig*: *persona* inscrutable
hermoso *adj* beautiful
hernia *f* MED hernia
héroe *m* hero
heroico *adj* heroic
heroína *f mujer* heroine; *droga* heroin
heroinómano *m*, **-a** *f* heroin addict
herpes *m* MED herpes
herradura *f* horseshoe
herramienta *f* tool
hervidero *m fig* hotbed
hervido *m S. Am.* stew
hervir ⟨3i⟩ **1** *v/i* boil; *fig* swarm, seethe (**de** with) **2** *v/t* boil
heterodoxo *adj* unorthodox
heterogéneo *adj* heterogeneous
hez *f* scum, dregs *pl*
hibernar ⟨1a⟩ *v/i* hibernate
híbrido 1 *adj* hybrid *atr* **2** *m* hybrid
hice *vb* → ***hacer***
hicimos *vb* → ***hacer***
hidratante *adj* moisturizing; ***crema hidratante*** moisturizing cream
hidratar ⟨1a⟩ *v/t* hydrate; *piel* moisturize
hidrato *m*: ***hidrato de carbono*** carbohydrate
hidráulico *adj* hydraulic
hidroavión *m* seaplane
hidroeléctrico *adj* hydroelectric
hidrógeno *m* hydrogen
hiedra *f* BOT ivy
hielo *m* ice; ***romper el hielo*** *fig* break the ice
hiena *f* ZO hyena
hierba *f* grass; ***mala hierba*** weed
hiere *vb* → ***herir***

H

hierro *m* iron
hierve *vb* → ***hervir***
hígado *m* liver; ***ser un hígado*** *C.Am.*, *Méx* F be a pain in the butt F
higiene *f* hygiene
higiénico *adj* hygienic
higo *m* BOT fig
higuera *f* BOT fig tree
hija *f* daughter
hijastra *f* stepdaughter
hijastro *m* stepson
hijo *m* son; ***hijos*** children *pl*; ***hijo de puta*** P son of a bitch V, bastard P; ***hijo úinico*** only child
hilachos *mpl Méx* rags
hilera *f* row, line
hilo *m* thread; ***hilo dental*** dental floss; ***sin hilos*** TELEC cordless; ***colgar*** *or* ***pender de un hilo*** *fig* hang by a thread; ***perder el hilo*** *fig* lose the thread
himno *m* hymn; ***himno nacional*** national anthem
hincapié *m*: ***hacer hincapié*** put special emphasis (***en*** on)
hincar ⟨1g⟩ **1** *v/t* thrust, stick (***en*** into); ***hincar el diente*** F sink one's teeth (***en*** into) **2** *v/r* **hincarse**: ***hincarse de rodillas*** kneel down
hincha *m* F fan, supporter
hinchado *adj* swollen
hinchar ⟨1a⟩ **1** *v/t* inflate, blow up; *Rpl* P annoy **2** *v/r* **hincharse** MED swell; *fig* stuff o.s (***de*** with); (*mostrarse orgulloso*) swell with pride
hinchazón *f* swelling
hiperactivo *adj* hyperactive
hipermercado *m* hypermarket
hipertensión *f* MED high blood pressure, hypertension
hipertexto *m* hypertext
hípico *adj* equestrian; ***concurso hípico*** show-jumping event; ***carrera -a*** horse race
hipnosis *f* hypnosis
hipnotizar ⟨1f⟩ *v/t* hypnotize
hipo *m* hiccups *pl*, hiccoughs *pl*; ***quitar el hipo*** F take one's breath away
hipocondríaco **1** *adj* hypochondriac **2** *m*, **-a** *f* hypochondriac
hipocresía *f* hypocrisy
hipócrita **1** *adj* hypocritical **2** *m/f* hypocrite
hipódromo *m* racetrack
hipopótamo *m* ZO hippopotamus
hipoteca *f* COM mortgage
hipotecar ⟨1g⟩ *v/t* COM mortgage; *fig* compromise
hipótesis *f* hypothesis
hipotético *adj* hypothetical
hispánico *adj* Hispanic
hispano **1** *adj* (*español*) Spanish; (*hispanohablante*) Spanish-speaking; *en EE.UU.* Hispanic **2** *m*, **-a** *f* (*español*) Spaniard; (*hispanohablante*) Spanish speaker; *en EE.UU.* Hispanic
hispanohablante *adj* Spanish-speaking
histeria *f* hysteria
histérico *adj* hysterical
historia *f* history; (*cuento*) story; ***una historia de drogas*** F some drugs business; ***déjate de historias*** F stop making excuses
historiador *m*, **historiadora** *f* historian
historial *m* record
histórico *adj* historical; (*importante*) historic
historieta *f* anecdote; (*viñetas*) comic strip
hito *m tb fig* milestone
hizo *vb* → ***hacer***
Hnos. *abr* (= ***Hermanos***) Bros (= Brothers)
hobby *m* hobby
hocico *m* snout; *de perro* muzzle
hockey *m* field hockey, *Br* hockey; ***hockey sobre hielo*** hockey, *Br* ice hockey
hogar *m fig* home
hogareño *adj* home *atr*; *persona* home-loving
hoguera *f* bonfire
hoja *f* BOT leaf; *de papel* sheet; *de libro* page; *de cuchillo* blade; ***hoja de afeitar*** razor blade; ***hoja de cálculo*** INFOR spreadsheet
hojalata *f* tin
hojaldre *m* GASTR puff pastry
hojear ⟨1a⟩ *v/t* leaf through, flip through
hola *int* hello, hi F
Holanda Holland
holandés **1** *adj* Dutch **2** *m* Dutchman
holandesa *f* Dutchwoman
holding *m* holding company
holgado *adj* loose, comfortable; ***estar holgado de tiempo*** have time to spare
holgazán *m* idler
holgazanear ⟨1a⟩ *v/i* laze around
holgura *f* ease; *de ropa* looseness; TÉC play; ***vivir con holgura*** live comfortably
hollín *m* soot
holocausto *m* holocaust
hombre *m* man; ***el hombre*** (*la humanidad*) man, mankind; ***hombre lobo*** werewolf; ***hombre de negocios*** businessman; ***hombre rana*** frogman; ***¡claro, hombre!*** you bet!, sure thing!; ***¡hombre, qué alegría!*** that's great!
hombro *m* shoulder; ***hombro con hombro*** shoulder to shoulder; ***encogerse***

de hombros shrug (one's shoulders)
homenaje *m* homage; ***rendir homenaje a alguien*** pay tribute to s.o.
homeopatía *f* hom(o)eopathy
homicidio *m* homicide
homogéneo *adj* homogenous
homologación *f* approval; *de título, diploma* official recognition
homólogo *m*, **-a** *f* counterpart, opposite number
homosexual *m/f & adj* homosexual
hondo *adj* deep
Honduras Honduras
hondureño 1 *adj* Honduran **2** *m*, **-a** *f* Honduran
honesto *adj* hono(u)rable, decent
hongo *m* fungus
honor *m* hono(u)r; ***en honor a*** in hono(u)r of; ***hacer honor a*** live up to; ***palabra de honor*** word of hono(u)r
honorarios *mpl* fees
honra *f* hono(u)r; ***¡a mucha honra!*** I'm hono(u)red
honradez *f* honesty
honrado *adj* honest
hora *f* hour; ***horas*** *pl* ***extraordinarias*** overtime *sg*; ***hora local*** local time; ***hora punta*** rush hour; ***a la hora de …*** *fig* when it comes to …; ***a úiltima hora*** at the last minute; ***¡ya era hora!*** about time too!; ***tengo hora con el dentista*** I have an appointment with the dentist; ***¿qué hora es?*** what time is it?
horario *m* schedule, *Br* timetable; ***horario comercial*** business hours *pl*; ***horario flexible*** flextime, *Br* flexitime; ***horario de trabajo*** (working) hours *pl*
horca *f* gallows *pl*
horcajadas *fpl*: ***a horcajadas*** astride
horchata *f drink made from tiger-nuts*
horda *f* horde
horizontal *adj* horizontal
horizonte *m* horizon
hormiga *f* ant
hormigón *m* concrete; ***hormigón armado*** reinforced concrete
hormigueo *m* pins and needles *pl*
hormiguero *m* ant hill; ***la sala era un hormiguero de gente*** the hall was swarming with people
hormona *f* hormone
hornilla *f* ring
horno *m* oven; *de cerámica* kiln; ***alto horno*** blast furnace
horóscopo *m* horoscope
horqueta *f L.Am. de camino* fork
horquilla *f para pelo* hairpin
horrendo *adj* horrendous
horrible *adj* horrible, dreadful
horripilante *adj* horrible
horror *m* horror (***a*** of); ***tener horror a*** be terrified of; ***me gusta horrores*** F I like it a lot; ***¡qué horror!*** how awful!
horrorizar ⟨1f⟩ *v/t* horrify
horroroso *adj* terrible; (*de mala calidad*) dreadful; (*feo*) hideous
hortaliza *f* vegetable
hortensia *f* BOT hydrangea
hortera 1 F *adj* tacky F **2** *m/f* F tacky person F
horterada *f* F tacky thing F; ***es una horterada*** it's tacky F
horticultor *m*, **horticultora** *f* horticulturist
horticultura *f* horticulture
hosco *adj* sullen
hospedaje *m* accommodations *pl*, *Br* accommodation; ***dar hospedaje a alguien*** put s.o. up
hospedarse ⟨1a⟩ *v/r* stay (***en*** at)
hospital *m* hospital
hospitalario *adj* hospitable; MED hospital *atr*
hospitalidad *f* hospitality
hospitalizar ⟨1f⟩ *v/t* hospitalize
hostal *m* hostel
hostelera *f* landlady
hostelería *f* hotel industry
hostelero 1 *adj* hotel *atr* **2** *m* landlord
hostia *f* REL host; P (*golpe*) sock F, wallop F; ***¡hostias!*** P Christ! P
hostigar ⟨1h⟩ *v/t* pester; MIL harass; *caballo* whip
hostil *adj* hostile
hostilidad *f* hostility
hotel *m* hotel
hotelero *m*, **-a** *f* hotelier
hoy *adv* today; ***de hoy*** of today; ***los padres de hoy*** today's parents, parents today; ***de hoy en adelante*** from now on; ***por hoy*** for today; ***hoy por hoy*** at the present time; ***hoy en día*** nowadays
hoya *f* hole; *de tumba* grave; GEOG plain; *S. Am.* river basin
hoyo *m* hole; (*depresión*) hollow
hoyuelo *m* dimple
hoz *f* sickle
huachafo *adj Pe* (*cursi*) affected, pretentious
huarache *m Méx rough sandal*
huayno *m Pe, Bol Andean dance rhythm*
hubo *vb* → ***haber***
hucha *f* money box
hueco 1 *adj* hollow; (*vacío*) empty; *fig: persona* shallow **2** *m* gap; (*agujero*) hole; *de ascensor* shaft
huele *vb* → ***oler***
huelga *f* strike; ***huelga de celo*** work-to-

rule; ***huelga general*** general strike; ***huelga de hambre*** hunger strike; ***declararse en huelga, ir a la huelga*** go on strike
huelguista *m/f* striker
huella *f* mark; *de animal* track; ***huellas dactilares*** finger prints
huelo *vb* → ***oler***
huérfano 1 *adj* orphan *atr* **2** *m*, **-a** *f* orphan
huero *adj fig* empty; *L.Am.* blond
huerta *f* truck farm, *Br* market garden
huerto *m* kitchen garden; ***llevar a alguien al huerto*** F put one over on s.o. F
huesear ⟨1a⟩ *v/t C.Am.* beg
huesillo *m S. Am.* sun-dried peach
hueso *m* bone; *de fruta* pit, stone; *persona* tough nut; *Méx* F cushy number F; *Méx* F (*influencia*) influence, pull F; ***hueso duro de roer*** *fig* F hard nut to crack F; ***estar en los huesos*** be all skin and bone
huésped *m/f* guest
huesudo *adj* bony
huevas *fpl* roe *sg*
huevear ⟨1a⟩ *v/i Chi* P mess around F
huevo *m* egg; P (*testículo*) ball V; ***huevo duro*** hard-boiled egg; ***huevo escalfado*** poached egg; ***huevo frito*** fried egg; ***huevo pasado por agua*** soft-boiled egg; ***huevos revueltos*** scrambled eggs; ***un huevo de*** P a load of F
huevón *m*, **-ona** *f Chi* P idiot; *L.Am.* F (*flojo*) idler F
huida *f* flight, escape
huir ⟨3g⟩ *v/i* flee, escape (***de*** from); ***huir de algo*** avoid sth
hulado *m C.Am., Méx* rubberized cloth
hule *m* oilcloth; *L.Am.* (*caucho*) rubber
humanidad *f* humanity; ***humanidades*** humanities
humanismo *m* humanism
humanitario *adj* humanitarian
humanizar ⟨1f⟩ *v/t* humanize
humano *adj* human
humareda *f* cloud of smoke
humear ⟨1a⟩ *v/i con humo* smoke; *con vapor* steam
humedad *f* humidity; *de una casa* damp (-ness)
humedecer ⟨2d⟩ *v/t* dampen
húmedo *adj* humid; *toalla* damp
humildad *f* humility
humilde *adj* humble; (*sin orgullo*) modest; *clase social* lowly
humillación *f* humiliation
humillante *adj* humiliating
humillar ⟨1a⟩ *v/t* humiliate
humita *f S. Am. meat and corn paste wrapped in leaves*
humo *m* smoke; (*vapor*) steam; ***tener muchos humos*** F be a real bighead F
humor *m* humo(u)r; ***estar de buen / mal humor*** be in a good / bad mood; ***sentido del humor*** sense of humo(u)r
humorista *m/f* humo(u)rist; (*cómico*) comedian
humus *m* GASTR hummus
hundido *adj fig*: *persona* depressed
hundir ⟨3a⟩ **1** *v/t* sink; *fig*: *empresa* ruin, bring down; *persona* devastate **2** *v/r* **hundirse** sink; *fig*: *de empresa* collapse; *de persona* go to pieces
húngaro 1 *adj* Hungarian **2** *m*, **-a** *f* Hungarian
Hungría Hungary
huracán *m* hurricane
huraño *adj* unsociable
hurgar ⟨1h⟩ **1** *v/i* rummage (***en*** in) **2** *v/r* **hurgarse**: ***hurgarse la nariz*** pick one's nose
hurón *m* zo ferret
hurtadillas *fpl*: ***a hurtadillas*** furtively
hurtar ⟨1a⟩ *v/t* steal
hurto *m* theft
husmear ⟨1a⟩ *v/i* F nose around F (***en*** in)
huy *int sorpresa* wow!; *dolor* ouch!
huyo *vb* → ***huir***

I

I+D *abr* (= ***investigación y desarrollo***) R&D (= research and development)
iba *vb* → ***ir***
ibérico *adj* Iberian
iberoamericano *adj* Latin American
iceberg *m* iceberg
icono *m tb* INFOR icon
ida *f* outward journey; (***billete de***) ***ida y vuelta*** round trip (ticket), *Br* return (ticket)
idea *f* idea; ***hacerse a la idea de que ...*** get used to the idea that ...; ***no tener ni***

idea not have a clue
ideal *m/adj* ideal
idealista 1 *adj* idealistic **2** *m/f* idealist
idear *v/t* ⟨1a⟩ think up, come up with
idéntico *adj* identical
identidad *f* identity
identificación *f* identification
identificar ⟨1g⟩ **1** *v/t* identify **2** *v/r* **identificarse** identify o.s.
ideología *f* ideology
idílico *adj* idyllic
idilio *m* idyll; (*relación amorosa*) romance
idioma *m* language
idiota 1 *adj* idiotic **2** *m/f* idiot
idiotez *f* stupid thing to say / do
ido 1 *part* → ***ir*** **2** *adj* (*chiflado*) nuts F; ***estar ido*** be miles away F
idolatrar ⟨1a⟩ *v/t tb fig* worship
ídolo *m tb fig* idol
idóneo *adj* suitable
iglesia *f* church
ignominioso *adj* ignominious
ignorancia *f* ignorance
ignorante *adj* ignorant
ignorar ⟨1a⟩ *v/t* not know, not be aware of; ***ignoro cómo sucedió*** I don't know how it happened
igual 1 *adj* (*idéntico*) same (***a, que*** as); (*proporcionado*) equal (***a*** to); (*constante*) constant; ***al igual que*** like, the same as; ***me da igual*** I don't mind **2** *m/f* equal; ***no tener igual*** have no equal
igualado *adj* even
igualar ⟨1a⟩ **1** *v/t precio, marca* equal, match; (*nivelar*) level off; ***igualar algo*** MAT make sth equal (***con, a*** to) **2** *v/i* DEP tie the game, *Br* equalize
igualdad *f* equality; ***igualdad de oportunidades*** equal opportunities
igualitario *adj* egalitarian
igualmente *adv* equally
iguana *f* ZO iguana
ilegal *adj* illegal
ilegible *adj* illegible
ilegítimo *adj* unlawful; *hijo* illegitimate
ileso *adj* unhurt
ilícito *adj* illicit
ilimitado *adj* unlimited
Ilmo. *abr* (= ***ilustrísimo***) His / Your Excellency
ilógico *adj* illogical
iluminación *f* illumination
iluminar ⟨1a⟩ *v/t edificio, calle etc* light, illuminate; *monumento* light up, illuminate; *fig* light up
ilusión *f* illusion; (*deseo, esperanza*) hope
ilusionarse ⟨1a⟩ *v/r* get one's hopes up; (*entusiasmarse*) get excited (***con*** about)
ilustración *f* illustration
ilustrar ⟨1a⟩ *v/t* illustrate; (*aclarar*) explain
ilustre *adj* illustrious
imagen *f tb fig* image; ***ser la viva imagen de*** be the spitting image of
imaginable *adj* imaginable
imaginación *f* imagination
imaginar ⟨1a⟩ **1** *v/t* imagine **2** *v/r* **imaginarse** imagine; ***¡ya me lo imagino!*** I can just imagine it!
imaginativo *adj* imaginative
imán *m* magnet
imbatible *adj* unbeatable
imbécil 1 *adj* stupid **2** *m/f* idiot, imbecile
imbecilidad *f* stupidity; ***¡qué imbecilidad decir eso!*** what a stupid thing to say!
imitación *f* imitation
imitar ⟨1a⟩ *v/t* imitate
impaciencia *f* impatience
impacientar ⟨1a⟩ **1** *v/t* make impatient **2** *v/r* **impacientarse** lose (one's) patience
impaciente *adj* impatient
impactar ⟨1a⟩ *v/t* hit; (*impresionar*) have an impact on
impacto *m tb fig* impact; ***impacto de bala*** bullet wound; ***impacto ecológico*** ecological
impar *adj número* odd
imparcial *adj* impartial
imparcialidad *f* impartiality
impasible *adj* impassive
impávido *adj* fearless, undaunted
impecable *adj* impeccable
impedimento *m* impediment
impedir ⟨3l⟩ *v/t* prevent; (*estorbar*) impede
imperante *adj* ruling; *fig* prevailing
imperar ⟨1a⟩ *v/i* rule; *fig* prevail
imperativo 1 *adj* GRAM imperative; *obligación* pressing **2** *m* GRAM imperative
imperdible *m* safety pin
imperdonable *adj* unpardonable, unforgivable
imperfecto *m/adj* imperfect
imperial *adj* imperial
imperio *m* empire
imperioso *adj necesidad* pressing; *persona* imperious
impermeable 1 *adj* waterproof **2** *m* raincoat
impersonal *adj* impersonal
impertérrito *adj* unperturbed, unmoved
impertinente 1 *adj* impertinent **2** *m/f*: ***¡eres un impertinente!*** you've got nerve! F, *Br* you've got a cheek! F
ímpetu *m* impetus
impetuoso *adj* impetuous
implacable *adj* implacable

I

implemento *m* implement
implicar ⟨1g⟩ *v/t* mean, imply; (*involucrar*) involve; *en un delito* implicate (***en*** in)
implícito *adj* implicit
implorar ⟨1a⟩ *v/t* beg for
imponente *adj* impressive, imposing; F terrific
imponer ⟨2r⟩ **1** *v/t* impose; *miedo, respeto* inspire; *impuesto* impose, levy **2** *v/i* be imposing *o* impressive **3** *v/r* **imponerse** (*hacerse respetar*) assert o.s.; DEP win; (*prevalecer*) prevail; (*ser necesario*) be imperative; ***imponerse una tarea*** set o.s. a task
importación *f* import, importation; *artículo* import
importancia *f* importance; ***dar importancia a*** attach importance to; ***darse importancia*** give o.s. airs; ***tener importancia*** be important
importante *adj* important
importar ⟨1a⟩ *v/i* matter; ***no importa*** it doesn't matter; ***eso a ti no te importa*** that's none of your business; ***¿qué importa?*** what does it matter?; ***¿le importa …?*** do you mind …?
importe *m* amount; (*coste*) cost
importuno *adj* inopportune;
imposibilitar ⟨1a⟩ *v/t*: ***imposibilitar algo*** make sth impossible, prevent sth
imposible *adj* impossible
impostor *m*, **impostora** *f* impostor
impotencia *f* impotence, helplessness; MED impotence
impotente *adj* helpless, powerless, impotent; MED impotent
impreciso *adj* imprecise
impredecible *adj* unpredictable
impregnar ⟨1a⟩ *v/t* saturate (***de*** with); TÉC impregnate (***de*** with)
imprenta *f taller* printer's; *arte, técnica* printing; *máquina* printing press
imprescindible *adj* essential; *persona* indispensable
impresión *f* impression; *acto* printing; (*tirada*) print run; ***la sangre le da impresión*** he can't stand the sight of blood
impresionante *adj* impressive
impresionar ⟨1a⟩ *v/t*: ***impresionarle a alguien*** impress s.o.; (*conmover*) move s.o.; (*alterar*) shock s.o.
impresionismo *m* impressionism
impreso *m* form; ***impresos*** *pl* printed matter *sg*
impresora *f* INFOR printer; ***impresora de chorro de tinta*** inkjet (printer); ***impresora de inyección de tinta*** inkjet (printer); ***impresora láser*** laser (printer)
imprevisible *adj* unpredictable
imprevisto **1** *adj* unforeseen, unexpected **2** *m* unexpected event
imprimir ⟨3a⟩ *v/t tb* INFOR print; *fig* transmit
improbable *adj* unlikely, improbable
improcedente *adj* improper
improductivo *adj* unproductive
impropio *adj* inappropriate
improvisar ⟨1a⟩ *v/t* improvise
improviso *adj*: ***de improviso*** unexpectedly
imprudencia *f* recklessness, rashness
imprudente *adj* reckless, rash
impuesto *m* tax; ***impuesto sobre el valor añadido*** *sales tax, Br* value-added tax; ***impuesto sobre la renta*** income tax
impugnar ⟨1a⟩ *v/t* challenge
impulsar ⟨1a⟩ *v/t* TÉC propel; COM boost
impulsivo *adj* impulsive
impulso *m* impulse; (*empuje*) impetus; COM boost; *fig* urge, impulse; ***tomar impulso*** take a run up
impunidad *f* impunity
impureza *f* impurity
imputar ⟨1a⟩ *v/t* attribute
inacabable *adj* endless, never-ending
inaccesible *adj* inaccessible
inaceptable *adj* unacceptable
inactivo *adj* inactive
inadaptado *adj* maladjusted
inadecuado *adj* inadequate
inadmisible *adj* inadmissible
inadvertido *adj*: ***pasar inadvertido*** go unnoticed
inagotable *adj* inexhaustible
inaguantable *adj* unbearable
inalámbrico **1** *adj* TELEC cordless **2** *m* TELEC cordless telephone
inamovible *adj* immovable
inanición *f* starvation
inapreciable *adj* (*valioso*) priceless; (*insignificante*) negligible
inasequible *adj objetivo* unattainable; *precio* prohibitive;
inaudito *adj* unprecedented
inauguración *f* official opening, inauguration
inaugurar ⟨1a⟩ *v/t* (officially) open, inaugurate
inca *m/f & adj* HIST Inca
incalculable *adj* incalculable
incalificable *adj* indescribable
incandescente *adj* incandescent
incansable *adj* tireless
incapacidad *f* disability; (*falta de capacidad*) inability; (*ineptitud*) incompetence
incapacitar ⟨1a⟩ *v/t* JUR disqualify
incapaz *adj* incapable (***de*** of)

incautarse ⟨1a⟩ *v/r*: ***incautarse de*** seize
incauto *adj* unwary
incendiar ⟨1b⟩ **1** *v/t* set fire to **2** *v/r* **incendiarse** burn
incendio *m* fire; ***incendio forestal*** forest fire
incentivo *m* incentive
incertidumbre *f* uncertainty
incesante *adj* incessant
incesto *m* incest
incidencia *f* (*efecto*) effect; (*frecuencia*) incidence; (*incidente*) incident
incidente *m* incident
incidir ⟨3a⟩ *v/i*: ***incidir en*** (*afectar*) have an effect on, affect; (*recalcar*) stress; ***incidir en un error*** make a mistake
incienso *m* incense
incierto *m* uncertain
incineración *f de cadáver* cremation
incinerador *adj* incinerator
incinerar ⟨1a⟩ *v/t* incinerate; *cadáver* cremate
incipiente *adj* incipient
incitante *adj* provocative
incitar ⟨1a⟩ *v/t* incite
inclemencia *f del tiempo* inclemency
inclinación *f* inclination; *de un terreno* slope; *muestra de respeto* bow; *fig* tendency
inclinar ⟨1a⟩ **1** *v/t* tilt; ***inclinar la cabeza*** nod (one's head); ***me inclina a creer que ...*** it makes me think that ... **2** *v/r* **inclinarse** bend (down); *de un terreno* slope; *desde la vertical* lean; *en señal de respeto* bow; ***inclinarse a*** *fig* tend to, be inclined to
incluido *prp* inclusive
incluir ⟨3g⟩ *v/t* include
inclusive *adv* inclusive
incluso *adv, prp & conj* even
incógnita *f* unknown factor; MAT unknown (quantity)
incógnito *adj*: ***de incógnito*** incognito
incoherente *adj* incoherent
incombustible *adj* fireproof
incomodidad *f* uncomfortableness; (*fastidio*) inconvenience
incómodo *adj* uncomfortable; (*fastidioso*) inconvenient
incomparable *adj* incomparable
incompatibilidad *f* incompatibility
incompatible *adj tb* INFOR incompatible
incompetencia *f* incompetence
incompetente *adj* incompetent
incompleto *adj* incomplete
incomprendido *adj* misunderstood
incomprensible *adj* incomprehensible
incomunicado *adj* isolated, cut off; JUR in solitary confinement
inconcebible *adj* inconceivable
incondicional *adj* unconditional;
inconexo *adj* unconnected
inconfesable *adj* shameful
inconformista *m/f* nonconformist
inconfundible *adj* unmistakable
incongruente *adj* incongruous
inconsciencia *f* MED unconsciousness; (*desconocimiento*) lack of awareness, unawareness; (*irreflexión*) thoughtlessness
inconsciente *adj* MED unconscious; (*ignorante*) unaware; (*irreflexivo*) thoughtless
inconsecuente *adj* inconsistent
inconsistente *adj* flimsy, weak
inconsolable *adj* inconsolable
inconstante *adj* fickle
incontable *adj* uncountable
incontinencia *f* MED incontinence
incontrolable *adj* uncontrollable
inconveniente 1 *adj* (*inoportuno*) inconvenient; (*impropio*) inappropriate **2** *m* (*desventaja*) drawback, disadvantage; (*estorbo*) problem; ***no tengo inconveniente*** I don't mind
incordiar ⟨1b⟩ *v/t* annoy
incordio *m* nuisance
incorporar ⟨1a⟩ **1** *v/t* incorporate **2** *v/r* **incorporarse** sit up; ***incorporarse a*** MIL join
incorrecto *adj* incorrect, wrong; *comportamiento* impolite
incorregible *adj* incorrigible
incorruptible *adj* incorruptible
incredulidad *f* disbelief, incredulity
incrédulo *adj* incredulous
increíble *adj* incredible
incrementar ⟨1a⟩ **1** *v/t* increase **2** *v/r* **incrementarse** increase
incremento *m* growth
incriminar ⟨1a⟩ *v/t* incriminate
incruento *adj* bloodless
incrustar ⟨1a⟩ **1** *v/t* incrust (***de*** with) **2** *v/r* **incrustarse** *de la suciedad* become ingrained
incubación *f* incubation
incubadora *f* incubator
incubar ⟨1a⟩ *v/t* incubate
incuestionable *adj* unquestionable
inculcar ⟨1g⟩ *v/t* instil(l) (***en*** in)
inculpar ⟨1a⟩ *v/t* JUR accuse;
inculto *adj* ignorant, uneducated
incultura *f* ignorance, lack of education
incumbencia *f* responsibility, duty; ***no es de mi incumbencia*** it's not my responsibility
incumplimiento *m* non-fulfillment (***de*** of), non-compliance (***de*** with)
incumplir ⟨3a⟩ *v/t* break
incurable *adj* incurable

incurrir ⟨3a⟩ *v/i*: ***incurrir en un error*** make a mistake; ***incurrir en gastos*** incur costs
incursión *f* MIL raid; *fig* foray
indagar ⟨1h⟩ *v/i* investigate
indecente *adj* indecent; *película* obscene
indecisión *f* indecisiveness
indeciso *adj* undecided; *por naturaleza* indecisive
indefenso *adj* defenseless, *Br* defenceless
indefinidamente *adv* indefinitely
indefinido *adj* (*impreciso*) vague; (*ilimitado*) indefinite
indemnización *f* compensation
indemnizar ⟨1f⟩ *v/t* compensate (***por*** for)
independencia *f* independence
independentismo *m* POL pro-independence movement
independiente *adj* independent
independizarse ⟨1f⟩ *v/r* become independent
indescriptible *adj* indescribable
indeseable *adj* undesirable
indestructible *adj* indestructible
indeterminado *adj* indeterminate; (*indefinido*) indefinite
India: ***la India*** India
indiada *f L.Am.* group of Indians
indicación *f* indication; (*señal*) sign; ***indicaciones*** *para llegar* directions; (*instrucciones*) instructions
indicado *adj* (*adecuado*) suitable; ***lo más / menos indicado*** the best / worst thing; ***hora -a*** specified time
indicador *m* indicator
indicar ⟨1g⟩ *v/t* show, indicate; (*señalar*) point out; (*sugerir*) suggest
índice *m* index; ***dedo índice*** index finger; ***índice de precios al consumo*** consumer price index, *Br* retail price index
indicio *m* indication, sign; (*vestigio*) trace
indiferencia *f* indifference
indiferente *adj* indifferent; (*irrelevante*) immaterial
indígena 1 *adj* indigenous, native **2** *m/f* native
indigente *adj* destitute
indigestión *f* indigestion
indigesto *adj* indigestible
indignación *f* indignation
indignado *adj* indignant
indignar ⟨1a⟩ **1** *v/t*: ***indignar a alguien*** make s.o. indignant **2** *v/r* **indignarse** become indignant
indigno *adj* unworthy (***de*** of)
indio 1 *adj* Indian **2** *m*, **-a** *f* Indian; ***hacer el indio*** F clown around F, play the fool F
indirecta *f* insinuation; (*sugerencia*) hint
indirecto *adj* indirect
indiscreción *f* indiscretion, lack of discretion; (*declaración*) indiscreet remark
indiscreto *adj* indiscreet
indiscriminado *adj* indiscriminate
indiscutible *adj* indisputable
indispensable *adj* indispensable
indisponerse ⟨2r⟩ *v/r* become unwell; ***indisponerse con alguien*** fall out with s.o.
indisposición *f* indisposition
indispuesto *adj* indisposed, unwell
indistinto *adj forma* indistinct, vague; *noción* vague; *sonido* faint
individual *adj* individual; *cama, habitación* single
individualismo *m* individualism
individualista *m/f* individualist
individuo *m* individual
indivisible *adj* indivisible
indocumentado *adj*: ***un hombre indocumentado*** a man with no identity papers
índole *f* nature
indolente *adj* lazy
indoloro *adj* painless
indómito *adj* indomitable
Indonesia Indonesia
inducir ⟨3o⟩ *v/t* (*persuadir*) lead, induce (***a*** to); EL induce
indudable *adj* undoubted
indudablemente *adv* undoubtedly
indulgente *adj* indulgent
indultar ⟨1a⟩ *v/t* pardon
indulto *m* pardon
indumentaria *f* clothing
industria *f* industry; (*esfuerzo*) industriousness, industry
industrial 1 *adj* industrial **2** *m/f* industrialist
industrializar ⟨1f⟩ **1** *v/t* industrialize **2** *v/r* **industrializarse** industrialize
inédito *adj* unpublished; *fig* unprecedented
ineficacia *f* inefficiency; *de un procedimiento* ineffectiveness
ineficaz *adj* inefficient; *procedimiento* ineffective
ineficiencia *f* inefficiency
ineficiente *adj* inefficient
ineludible *adj* unavoidable
inepto 1 *adj* inept, incompetent **2** *m*, **-a** *f* incompetent fool
inequívoco *adj* unequivocal
inercia *f* inertia
inerte *adj fig* lifeless; FÍS inert
inesperado *adj* unexpected
inestabilidad *f* instability
inestable *adj* unstable; *tiempo* unsettled
inestimable *adj* invaluable
inevitable *adj* inevitable

inexacto *adj* inaccurate
inexcusable *adj* inexcusable
inexistente *adj* non-existent
inexperto *adj* inexperienced
inexplicable *adj* inexplicable
infalible *adj* infallible
infame *adj* vile, loathsome; (*terrible*) dreadful
infancia *f* infancy
infantería *f* MIL infantry
infantil *adj* children's *atr*; *naturaleza* childlike; *desp* infantile, childish
infarto *m* MED heart attack
infección *f* MED infection
infeccioso *adj* infectious
infectar ⟨1a⟩ **1** *v/t* infect **2** *v/r* **infectarse** become infected
infecundo *adj* infertile
infeliz 1 *adj* unhappy, miserable **2** *m/f* poor devil
inferior 1 *adj* inferior (***a*** to); *en el espacio* lower (***a*** than) **2** *m/f* inferior
inferioridad *f* inferiority
inferir ⟨3i⟩ *v/t* infer (***de*** from); *daño* do, cause (***a*** to)
infernal *adj ruido* infernal; (*muy malo*) diabolical
infertilidad *f* infertility
infestar ⟨1a⟩ *v/t* infest; (*invadir*) overrun
infidelidad *f* infidelity
infiel 1 *adj* unfaithful **2** *m/f* unbeliever
infierno *m* hell
infiltrarse ⟨1a⟩ *v/r*: ***infiltrarse en*** infiltrate; *de agua* seep into
infinidad *f*: ***infinidad de*** countless
infinitivo *m* GRAM infinitive
infinito 1 *adj* infinite **2** *m* infinity
inflación *f* COM inflation; ***tasa de inflación*** inflation rate
inflacionista *adj* inflationary
inflamable *adj* flammable
inflamación *f* MED inflammation
inflamar ⟨1a⟩ **1** *v/t tb fig* inflame **2** *v/r* **inflamarse** MED become inflamed
inflar ⟨1a⟩ **1** *v/t* inflate **2** *v/r* **inflarse** swell (up); *fig* F get conceited
infligir ⟨3c⟩ *v/t* inflict
inflexible *adj fig* inflexible
influencia *f* influence; ***tener influencias*** have contacts
influenciar ⟨1b⟩ *v/t* influence
influir ⟨3g⟩ *v/i*: ***influir en alguien / algo*** influence s.o./sth, have an influence on s.o./sth
influjo *m* influence
influyente *adj* influential
infografía *f* computer graphics *pl*
información *f* information; (*noticias*) news *sg*
informal *adj* informal; *persona* unreliable
informar ⟨1a⟩ **1** *v/t* inform (***de, sobre*** about) **2** *v/r* **informarse** find out (***de, sobre*** about)
informática *f* information technology
informático 1 *adj* computer *atr* **2** *m*, **-a** *f* IT specialist
informativo 1 *adj* informative; *programa* news *atr* **2** *m* TV, RAD news *sg*
informatizar ⟨1f⟩ *v/t* computerize
informe 1 *adj* shapeless **2** *m* report; ***informes*** (*referencias*) references
infracción *f* offense, *Br* offence
infraestructura *f* infrastructure
in fraganti *adv* F in the act F
infrahumano *adj* subhuman
infrarrojo *adj* infra-red
infravalorar ⟨1a⟩ *v/t* undervalue
infrecuente *adj* infrequent
infringir ⟨3c⟩ *v/t* JUR infringe, violate
infructuoso *adj* fruitless
infundado *adj* unfounded, groundless
infundir ⟨3a⟩ *v/t* inspire; *terror* instil(l); *sospechas* arouse
infusión *f* infusion; *de tila, manzanilla* tea
ingeniarse ⟨1b⟩ *v/r*: ***ingeniárselas para*** manage to
ingeniería *f* engineering
ingeniero *m*, **-a** *f* engineer
ingenio *m* ingenuity; (*aparato*) device; ***ingenio azucarero*** *L.Am.* sugar refinery
ingenioso *adj* ingenious
ingenuidad *f* naivety
ingenuo 1 *adj* naive **2** *m*, **-a** *f* naive person, sucker F
ingerir ⟨3i⟩ *v/t* swallow
Inglaterra England
ingle *f* groin
inglés 1 *adj* English **2** *m* Englishman; *idioma* English
inglesa *f* Englishwoman
ingrato *adj* ungrateful; *tarea* thankless
ingrediente *m* ingredient
ingresar ⟨1a⟩ **1** *v/i*: ***ingresar en*** *en universidad* go to; *en asociación, cuerpo* join; *en hospital* be admitted to **2** *v/t cheque* pay in, deposit
ingreso *m* entry; *en una asociación* joining; *en hospital* admission; COM deposit; ***ingresos*** *pl* income *sg*; ***examen de ingreso*** entrance exam
inhabitable *adj* uninhabitable
inhalar ⟨1a⟩ *v/t* inhale
inherente *adj* inherent
inhibición *f* inhibition; JUR disqualification
inhibir ⟨3a⟩ *v/t* inhibit
inhóspito *adj* inhospitable
inhumano *adj* inhuman

iniciación *f* initiation
inicial *f/adj* initial
iniciar ⟨1b⟩ *v/t* initiate; *curso* start, begin
iniciativa *f* initiative; ***tomar la iniciativa*** take the initiative
inicio *m* start, beginning
inigualable *adj* incomparable; *precio* unbeatable
inimaginable *adj* unimaginable
inimitable *adj* inimitable
ininteligible *adj* unintelligible
ininterrumpido *adj* uninterrupted
injerencia *f* interference
injertar ⟨1a⟩ *v/t* graft
injerto *m* graft
injuriar ⟨1b⟩ *v/t* insult
injusticia *f* injustice
injustificado *adj* unjustified
injusto *adj* unjust
inmaculado *adj* immaculate
inmaduro *adj* immature
inmediaciones *fpl* immediate area *sg* (***de*** of), vicinity *sg* (***de*** of)
inmediatamente *adv* immediately
inmediato *adj* immediate; ***de inmediato*** immediately
inmejorable *adj* unbeatable
inmenso *adj* immense
inmersión *f* immersion; *de submarino* dive
inmerso *adj fig* immersed (***en*** in)
inmigración *f* immigration
inmigrante *m/f* immigrant
inmigrar ⟨1a⟩ *v/i* immigrate
inminente *adj* imminent
inmiscuirse ⟨3g⟩ *v/r* meddle
inmobiliaria *f* realtor's office, *Br* estate agency
inmoderado *adj* excessive, immoderate
inmoral *adj* immoral
inmoralidad *f* immorality
inmortal *adj* immortal
inmóvil *adj persona* motionless; *vehículo* stationary
inmovilizar ⟨1f⟩ *v/t* immobilize
inmueble *m* building
inmundo *adj* filthy
inmune *adj* immune
inmunidad *f* MED, POL immunity
inmunizar ⟨1f⟩ *v/t* immunize
inmutarse ⟨1a⟩ *v/r*: ***no inmutarse*** not bat an eyelid; ***sin inmutarse*** without batting an eyelid
innato *adj* innate, inborn
innecesario *adj* unnecessary
innegable *adj* undeniable
innovación *f* innovation
innumerable *adj* innumerable, countless
inocencia *f* innocence
inocente *adj* innocent
inocuo *adj* harmless, innocuous; *película* bland
inodoro *m* toilet
inofensivo *adj* inoffensive, harmless
inoficioso *adj L.Am.* (*inútil*) useless
inolvidable *adj* unforgettable
inopia *f*: ***estar en la inopia*** F (*distraído*) be miles away F; (*alejado de la realidad*) be on another planet F
inoportuno *adj* inopportune; (*molesto*) inconvenient
inorgánico *adj* inorganic
inoxidable *adj*: ***acero inoxidable*** stainless steel
inquietar ⟨1a⟩ **1** *v/t* worry **2** *v/r* **inquietarse** worry, get worried *o* anxious
inquietud *f* worry, anxiety; *intelectual* interest
inquilino *m* tenant
inquisitivo *adj* inquisitive
insaciable *adj* insatiable
insatisfacción *f* dissatisfaction
insatisfactorio *adj* unsatisfactory
insatisfecho *adj* dissatisfied
inscribir ⟨3a⟩ **1** *v/t* (*grabar*) inscribe; *en lista, registro* register, enter; *en curso, concurso* enrol(l), register **2** *v/r* **inscribirse** *en un curso* enrol(l), register; *en un concurso* enter
inscripción *f* inscription; *en lista, registro* registration, entry; *en curso, concurso* enrol(l)ment, registration;
insecticida *m* insecticide
insecto *m* insect
inseguro *adj* insecure; *estructura* unsteady; (*peligroso*) dangerous, unsafe
inseminación *f* insemination; ***inseminación artificial*** artificial insemination
insensato *adj* foolish
insensible *adj* insensitive (***a*** to)
inseparable *adj* inseparable
insertar ⟨1a⟩ *v/t* insert
inservible *adj* useless
insidia *f* treachery; ***actuar con insidia*** act treacherously
insignia *f* insignia
insignificante *adj* insignificant
insinuante *adj* suggestive
insinuar ⟨1e⟩ **1** *v/t* insinuate **2** *v/r* **insinuarse**: ***insinuarse a alguien*** make advances to s.o.
insípido *adj* insipid
insistencia *f* insistence
insistir ⟨3a⟩ *v/i* insist; ***insistir en hacer algo*** insist on doing sth; ***insistir en algo*** stress sth
insociable *adj* unsociable
insolación *f* MED sunstroke

insolente *adj* insolent
insólito *adj* unusual
insolvente *adj* insolvent
insomnio *m* insomnia
insondable *adj* unfathomable
insonorizar ⟨1f⟩ *v/t* soundproof
insoportable *adj* unbearable, intolerable
insospechado *adj* unexpected
inspección *f* inspection
inspeccionar ⟨1a⟩ *v/t* inspect
inspector *m*, **inspectora** *f* inspector
inspiración *f* inspiration; MED inhalation
inspirar ⟨1a⟩ *v/t* inspire; MED inhale
instalación *f acto* installation; ***instalaciones deportivas*** sports facilities
instalar ⟨1a⟩ **1** *v/t* instal(l); (*colocar*) put; *un negocio* set up **2** *v/r* **instalarse** *en un sitio* instal(l) o.s.
instancia *f* JUR petition; (*petición por escrito*) application; ***a instancias de*** at the request of
instantáneo *adj* immediate, instantaneous
instante *m* moment, instant; ***al instante*** right away, immediately
instar ⟨1a⟩ *v/t* urge, press
instaurar ⟨1a⟩ *v/t* establish
instigar ⟨1h⟩ *v/t* incite (***a*** to)
instinto *m* instinct
institución *f* institution
instituto *m* institute; *Esp* high school, *Br* secondary school; ***instituto de belleza*** beauty salon; ***instituto de educación secundaria*** high school, *Br* secondary school
instrucción *f* education; (*formación*) training; MIL drill; INFOR instruction, statement; JUR hearing; ***instrucciones de uso*** instructions, directions (for use)
instructor *m*, **instructora** *f* instructor
instruido *adj* educated
instruir ⟨3g⟩ *v/t* educate; (*formar*) train; JUR *pleito* hear
instrumental **1** *adj* instrumental **2** *m* MED instruments *pl*
instrumento *m* instrument; (*herramienta*) tool, instrument; *fig* tool; ***instrumento musical*** musical instrument
insubordinación *f* insubordination
insubordinarse ⟨1a⟩ *v/r con un superior* be insubordinate; (*rebelarse*) rebel
insuficiente **1** *adj* insufficient, inadequate **2** *m* EDU *nota* fail
insufrible *adj* insufferable
insulina *f* insulin
insulso *adj* bland, insipid
insultada *f L.Am.* (*insultos*) string of insults
insultar ⟨1a⟩ *v/t* insult
insulto *m* insult
insumiso *m person who refuses to do military service*
insuperable *adj* insurmountable
insurrección *f* insurrection
insustancial *adj conferencia* lightweight; *estructura* flimsy
intachable *adj* faultless
intacto *adj* intact; (*sin tocar*) untouched
integración *f* integration
integral *adj* complete; *alimento* whole
integrar ⟨1a⟩ *v/t* integrate; *equipo* make up
íntegro *adj* whole, entire; ***un hombre íntegro*** *fig* a man of integrity
intelectual *m/f & adj* intellectual
inteligencia *f* intelligence
inteligente *adj* intelligent
inteligible *adj* intelligible
intemperie *f*: ***a la intemperie*** in the open air
intempestivo *adj* untimely
intención *f* intention; ***doble*** *or* ***segunda intención*** ulterior motive
intencionado *adj* deliberate
intendente *m Rpl* military governor; (*alcalde*) mayor
intensidad *f* intensity; (*fuerza*) strength
intensificar ⟨1g⟩ **1** *v/t* intensify **2** *v/r* **intensificarse** intensify
intensivo *adj* intensive
intenso *adj* intense; (*fuerte*) strong
intentar ⟨1a⟩ *v/t* try, attempt
intento *m* attempt, try; *Méx* (*intención*) aim
interacción *f* interaction
interactivo *adj* interactive
intercalar ⟨1a⟩ *v/t* insert
intercambiar ⟨1a⟩ *v/t* exchange, swap
intercambio *m* exchange, swap
interceder ⟨2a⟩ *v/i* intercede (***por*** for)
interceptar ⟨1a⟩ *v/t tb* DEP intercept
intercesión *f* intercession
interés *m tb* COM interest; *desp* self-interest; ***sin interés*** interest free; ***intereses*** (*bienes*) interests
interesante *adj* interesting
interesar ⟨1a⟩ **1** *v/t* interest **2** *v/r* **interesarse**: ***interesarse por*** take an interest in
interface *m*, **interfaz** *f* INFOR interface
interferencia *f* interference
interferir ⟨3i⟩ **1** *v/t* interfere with **2** *v/i* interfere (***en*** in)
interino *adj* substitute *atr*, replacement *atr*; (*provisional*) provisional, acting *atr*
interior **1** *adj* interior; *bolsillo* inside *atr*; COM, POL domestic **2** *m* interior; DEP inside-forward; ***en su interior*** *fig* inwardly
interiorista *m/f* interior designer

interjección *f* GRAM interjection
interlocutor *m*, **interlocutora** *f* speaker; ***mi interlocutor*** the person I was talking to
intermediario *m* COM intermediary, middle-man
intermedio 1 *adj nivel* intermediate; *tamaño* medium; *calidad* average, medium **2** *m* intermission
interminable *adj* interminable, endless
intermitente 1 *adj* intermittent **2** *m* AUTO turn signal, *Br* indicator
internacional *adj* international
internado *m* boarding school
internarse ⟨1a⟩ *v/r*: ***internarse en*** go into
internauta *m/f* INFOR Internet user, Net surfer
Internet *f* INFOR Internet
interno 1 *adj* internal; POL domestic, internal **2** *m*, **-a** *f* EDU boarder; (*preso*) inmate; MED intern, *Br* houseman
interpelar ⟨1a⟩ *v/t* question
interplanetario *adj* interplanetary
interpolar ⟨1a⟩ *v/t* insert, interpolate *fml*
interponerse ⟨2r⟩ *v/r* intervene
interpretación *f* interpretation; TEA performance (***de*** as)
interpretar ⟨1a⟩ *v/t* interpret; TEA play
intérprete *m/f* interpreter
interrogación *f* interrogation; ***signo de interrogación*** question mark
interrogante 1 *adj* questioning **2** *m* (*also f*) question; *fig* question mark, doubt
interrogar ⟨1h⟩ *v/t* question; *de policía* interrogate, question
interrogatorio *m* questioning, interrogation
interrumpir ⟨3a⟩ **1** *v/t* interrupt; *servicio* suspend; *reunión*, *vacaciones* cut short, curtail **2** *v/i* interrupt
interrupción *f* interruption; *de servicio* suspension; *de reunión*, *vacaciones* curtailment; ***sin interrupción*** non-stop
interruptor *m* EL switch
intersección *f* intersection
intervalo *m tb* MÚS interval; (*espacio*) gap
intervención *f* intervention; *en debate*, *congreso* participation; *en película*, *espectáculo* appearance; MED operation
intervenir ⟨3s⟩ **1** *v/i* intervene; *en debate*, *congreso* take part, participate; *en película*, *espectáculo* appear **2** *v/t* TELEC tap; *contrabando* seize; MED operate on
intestino *m* intestine
intimar ⟨1a⟩ *v/i* (*hacerse amigos*) become friendly (***con*** with); (*tratar*) mix (***con*** with)
intimidad *f* intimacy; (*lo privado*) privacy; ***en la intimidad*** in private
intimidar ⟨1a⟩ *v/t* intimidate
íntimo *adj* intimate; (*privado*) private; ***somos íntimos amigos*** we're close friends
intolerable *adj* intolerable, unbearable
intolerante *adj* intolerant
intoxicación *f* poisoning
intranquilidad *f* unease; (*nerviosismo*) restlessness
intranquilo *adj* uneasy; (*nervioso*) restless
intransferible *adj* non-transferable
intransigente *adj* intransigent
intransitable *adj* impassable
intransitivo *adj* GRAM intransitive
intrascendente *adj* unimportant
intravenoso *adj* MED intravenous
intrépido *adj* intrepid
intriga *f* intrigue; *de novela* plot
intrigante 1 *adj* scheming; (*curioso*) intriguing **2** *m/f* schemer
intrigar ⟨1h⟩ **1** *v/t* (*interesar*) intrigue **2** *v/i* plot, scheme
intrincado *adj* intricate
intrínseco *adj* intrinsic
introducción *f* introduction; *acción de meter* insertion; INFOR input
introducir ⟨3o⟩ **1** *v/t* introduce; (*meter*) insert; INFOR input **2** *v/r*: **introducirse**: ***introducirse en*** get into; ***introducirse en un mercado*** gain access to *o* break into a market
intromisión *f* interference
introvertido *adj* introverted
intruso *m* intruder
intuición *f* intuition
intuir ⟨3g⟩ *v/t* sense
intuitivo *adj* intuitive
inundación *f* flood
inundadizo *adj L.Am.* prone to flooding
inundar ⟨1a⟩ *v/t* flood
inusitado *adj* unusual, uncommon
inusual *adj* unusual
inútil 1 *adj* useless; MIL unfit **2** *m/f*: ***es un inútil*** he's useless
inutilidad *f* uselessness
inutilizar ⟨1f⟩ *v/t*: ***inutilizar algo*** render sth useless
inútilmente *adv* uselessly
invadir ⟨3a⟩ *v/t* invade; *de un sentimiento* overcome
invalidar ⟨1a⟩ *v/t* invalidate
invalidez *f* disability
inválido 1 *adj persona* disabled; *documento*, *billete* invalid **2** *m*, **-a** *f* disabled person
invasión *f* MIL invasion
invasor *m*, **invasora** *f* invader
invencible *adj* invincible; *miedo* insur-

mountable
invención *f* invention
inventar ⟨1a⟩ *v/t* invent
inventario *m* inventory
invento *m* invention
inventor *m* inventor
invernada *f Rpl* winter pasture
invernadero *m* greenhouse
invernal *adj* winter *atr*
inverosímil *adj* unlikely
inversión *f* reversal; COM investment
inverso *adj* opposite; *orden* reverse; ***a la -a*** the other way round
inversor *m*, **inversora** *f* investor
invertir ⟨3i⟩ *v/t* reverse; COM invest (***en*** in)
invertebrado *m* invertebrate
investigación *f* investigation; EDU, TÉC research; ***investigación y desarrollo*** research and development
investigador *m*, **investigadora** *f* researcher
investigar ⟨1h⟩ *v/t* investigate; EDU, TÉC research
inviable *adj* nonviable
invidente *m/f* blind person
invierno *m* winter
inviolable *adj* inviolable
invisible *adj* invisible
invitación *f* invitation
invitado *m*, **-a** *f* guest
invitar ⟨1a⟩ *v/t* invite (***a*** to); (*convidar*) treat (***a*** to)
invocar ⟨1g⟩ *v/t* invoke
involucrar ⟨1a⟩ *v/t* involve (***en*** in)
involuntario *adj* involuntary
invulnerable *adj* invulnerable
inyección *f* MED, AUTO injection
inyectar ⟨1a⟩ *v/t tb* TÉC inject
IPC *abr* (= ***índice de precios al consumo***) CPI (= consumer price index), *Br* RPI (= retail price index)
ir ⟨3t⟩ **1** *v/i* go (***a*** to); ***ir a pie*** walk, go on foot; ***ir en avión*** fly; ***¡ya voy!*** I'm coming!; ***ir a por algo*** go and fetch sth; ***ir bien / mal*** go well / badly; ***iba de amarillo / de uniforme*** she was wearing yellow/a uniform; ***van dos a dos*** DEP the score is two all; ***¿de qué va la película?*** what's the movie about?; ***¡qué va!*** you must be joking! F; ***¡vamos!*** come on!; ***¡vaya!*** well! **2** *v/aux*: ***va a llover*** it's going to rain; ***ya voy comprendiendo*** I'm beginning to understand; ***ir para viejo*** be getting old **3** *v/r* **irse** go (away), leave; ***¡vete!*** go away!; ***¡vámonos!*** let's go
ira *f* anger
Irak Iraq, Irak
Irán Iran
iraní *m/f & adj* Iranian
iraquí *m/f & adj* Iraqi, Iraki
iris *m inv* ANAT iris; ***arco iris*** rainbow
Irlanda Ireland
irlandés 1 *adj* Irish **2** *m* Irishman
irlandesa *f* Irishwoman
ironía *f* irony
irónico *adj* ironic
irracional *adj tb* MAT irrational
irradiar ⟨1b⟩ *v/t* radiate; MED irradiate
irreal *adj* unreal
irrealizable *adj* unattainable; *proyecto* unfeasible
irreconciliable *adj* irreconcilable
irrecuperable *adj* irretrievable
irrefutable *adj* irrefutable
irregular *adj* irregular; *superficie* uneven
irregularidad *f* irregularity; *de superficie* unevenness
irrelevante *adj* irrelevant
irremediable *adj fig* irremediable
irreparable *adj* irreparable
irreprochable *adj* irreproachable
irresistible *adj* irresistible
irrespetuoso *adj* disrespectful
irresponsable *adj* irresponsible
irreverente *adj* irreverent
irreversible *adj* irreversible
irrevocable *adj* irrevocable
irrigar ⟨1h⟩ *v/t* MED, AGR irrigate
irrisorio *adj* laughable, derisory
irritación *f tb* MED irritation
irritante *adj tb* MED irritating
irritar ⟨1a⟩ **1** *v/t tb* MED irritate **2** *v/r* **irritarse** get irritated
irrompible *adj* unbreakable
irrumpir ⟨3a⟩ *v/i* burst in
irrupción *f*: ***hacer irrupción en*** burst into
isla *f* island
islám *m* Islam
islámico *adj* Islamic
islamismo *m* Islam
isleño 1 *adj* island *atr* **2** *m*, **-a** *f* islander
Israel Israel
israelí *m/f & adj* Israeli
Italia Italy
italiano 1 *adj* Italian **2** *m*, **-a** *f* Italian
itinerario *m* itinerary
ITV *abr Esp* (= ***inspección técnica de vehículos***) *compulsory annual test of motor vehicles of a certain age*, *Br* MOT
IVA *abr* (= ***impuesto sobre el valor añadido***) *sales tax*, *Br* VAT (= value-added tax)
izar ⟨1f⟩ *v/t* hoist
izdo., **izda** *abr* (= ***izquierdo, izquierda***) l (= left)
izquierda *f tb* POL left; ***por la izquierda*** on the left
izquierdo *adj* left

J

jabalí *m* ZO wild boar
jabalina *f* javelin
jabón *m* soap; ***jabón de afeitar*** shaving soap
jabonera *f* soap dish
jabonoso *adj* soapy
jacinto *m* hyacinth
jactancia *f* boasting
jactancioso *adj* boastful
jactarse ⟨1a⟩ *v/r* boast (***de*** about), brag (***de*** about)
jacuzzi *m* jacuzzi®
jade *m* MIN jade
jadear ⟨1a⟩ *v/i* pant
jadeo *m* panting
jaguar *m* ZO jaguar
jalar ⟨1a⟩ **1** *v/t L.Am.* pull; *con esfuerza* haul; (*atraer*) attract; *Méx* F (*dar aventón*) give a ride *o Br* a lift to; ***¿te jala el arte?*** *Méx* do you feel drawn to art? **2** *v/i L.Am.* pull; (*trabajar mucho*) work hard; *Méx* F (*tener influencia*) have pull F; ***jalar hacia*** F head toward; ***jalar para la casa*** F clear off home F **3** *v/r* **jalarse** *Méx* (*irse*) go, leave; F (*emborracharse*) get plastered F
jalea *f* jelly; ***jalea real*** royal jelly
jaleo *m* (*ruido*) racket, uproar; (*lío*) mess, muddle; ***armar jaleo*** F kick up a fuss F
jalón *m* pull; ***dar un jalón a algo*** pull sth; ***de un jalón*** *Méx fig* in one go
jalonar ⟨1a⟩ *v/t fig* mark out
Jamaica Jamaica
jamás *adv* never; ***jamás te olvidaré*** I'll never forget you; ***¿viste jamás algo así?*** did you ever see anything like it?; ***nunca jamás*** never ever; ***por siempre jamás*** for ever and ever
jamón *m* ham; ***jamón de York*** cooked ham; ***jamón serrano*** cured ham; ***¡y un jamón!*** F (*¡no!*) no way! F; (*¡bromeas!*) come off it! F
jangada *f S. Am.* F dirty trick
Japón Japan
japonés **1** *adj* Japanese **2** *m*, **-esa** *f* Japanese
jaque *m* check; ***jaque mate*** checkmate; ***dar jaque a*** checkmate
jaqueca *f* MED migraine
jarabe *m* syrup; *Méx type of folk dance*
jardín *m* garden; ***jardín botánico*** botanic(al) gardens; ***jardín de infancia*** kindergarten
jardinería *f* gardening
jardinero *m*, **-a** *f* gardener
jarra *f* pitcher, *Br* jug; ***en jarras*** with hands on hips
jarro *m* pitcher, *Br* jug; ***un jarro de agua fría*** *fig* a total shock, a bombshell
jarrón *m* vase
jauja *f*: ***¡esto es jauja!*** this is the life!
jaula *f* cage
jauría *f* pack
jazmín *m* BOT jasmine
J.C. *abr* (= ***Jesucristo***) J.C. (= Jesus Christ)
jefatura *f* headquarters; (*dirección*) leadership; ***jefatura de policía*** police headquarters
jefe *m*, **-a** *f de departamento*, *organización* head; (*superior*) boss; POL leader; *de tribu* chief; ***jefe de cocina*** (head) chef; ***jefe de estado*** head of state
jengibre *m* BOT ginger
jeque *m* sheik
jerarquía *f* hierarchy
jerez *m* sherry
jerga *f* jargon; (*argot*) slang
jeringa *f* MED syringe
jeringuilla *f* MED syringe; ***jeringuilla desechable*** *or* ***de un solo uso*** disposable syringe
jeroglífico *m* hieroglyphic; *rompecabezas* puzzle
jersey *m* sweater
Jesucristo *m* Jesus Christ
Jesúís *m* Jesus; ***¡Jesúís!*** good grief!; *por estornudo* bless you!
jet **1** *m* AVIA jet **2** *f*: ***jet*** (***set***) jet set
jeta *f* F face, mug F; ***¡qué jeta tiene!*** F he's got nerve! F, *Br* what a cheek! F
jibia *f* ZO cuttlefish
jícara *f Méx* drinking bowl
jícaro *m L.Am.* BOT calabash
jilguero *m* ZO goldfinch
jilote *m C.Am.*, *Méx* young corn
jineta *f* ZO civet
jinete *m* rider; *en carrera* jockey
jirafa *f* ZO giraffe
jitomate *m Méx* tomato
JJ.OO *abr* (= ***Juegos Olímpicos***) Olympic Games
jocoso *adj* humorous, joking
joder ⟨2a⟩ **1** *v/i* V screw V, fuck V **2** *v/t* V (*follar*) screw V, fuck V; (*estropear*) screw up V, fuck up V; *L.Am.* F (*fastidiar*) annoy, irritate; ***¡joder!*** V fuck! V; ***me jode***

un montón V it really pisses me off P
jolgorio *m* F partying F
jolín *int* wow! F, jeez! F
jornada *f* (working) day; *distancia* day's journey; ***media jornada*** half-day; ***jornada laboral*** work day; ***jornada partida*** split shift
jornal *m* day's wage
jornalero *m*, **-a** *f* day labo(u)rer
joroba *f* hump; *fig* pain F, drag F
jorobado *adj* hump-backed; *fig* F in a bad way F
jorobar ⟨1a⟩ *v/t* F (*molestar*) bug F; *planes* ruin
jorongo *m Méx* poncho
jota *f letter 'j'*; ***no saber ni jota*** F not have a clue F
joven 1 *adj* young **2** *m/f* young man; *mujer* young woman; ***los jóvenes*** young people
jovial *adj* cheerful
joya *f* jewel; *persona* gem; ***joyas*** *pl* jewelry *sg*, *Br* jewellery *sg*
joyería *f* jewelry store, *Br* jeweller's
joyero 1 *m*, **-a** *f* jewel(l)er **2** *m* jewelry (*Br* jewellery) box
juanete *m* MED bunion
jubilación *f* retirement; ***jubilación anticipada*** early retirement
jubilado 1 *adj* retired **2** *m*, **-a** *f* retiree, *Br* pensioner
jubilar ⟨1a⟩ **1** *v/t* retire; (*desechar*) get rid of **2** *v/r* **jubilarse** retire; *C.Am.* play hooky F, play truant
júbilo *m* jubilation
jubiloso *adj* jubilant
judaísmo *m* Judaism
judía *f* BOT bean; ***judía verde*** green bean, runner bean
judicial *adj* judicial
judío 1 *adj* Jewish **2** *m*, **-a** *f* Jew
judo *m* DEP judo
juego *m* game; *acción* play; *por dinero* gambling; (*conjunto de objetos*) set; ***juego de azar*** game of chance; ***juego de café*** coffee set; ***juego de manos*** conjuring trick; ***juego de mesa*** board game; ***juego de rol*** role-playing game; ***juego de sociedad*** game; ***Juegos Olímpicos*** Olympic Games; ***estar en juego*** *fig* be at stake; ***fuera de juego*** DEP offside; ***hacer juego con*** go with, match
juerga *f* F partying F; ***irse de juerga*** F go out on the town F, go out partying F
jueves *m inv* Thursday
juez *m/f* judge; ***juez de línea*** *en fútbol* assistant referee; *en fútbol americano* line judge
jueza *f* → ***juez***
jugada *f* play, *Br* move; *en ajedrez* move; ***hacerle una mala jugada a alguien*** play a dirty trick on s.o.
jugador *m*, **jugadora** *f* player
jugar ⟨1o⟩ **1** *v/t* play **2** *v/i* play; *con dinero* gamble; ***jugar al baloncesto*** play basketball **3** *v/r* **jugarse** risk; ***jugarse la vida*** risk one's life; ***jugársela a alguien*** F do the dirty on s.o. F
jugarreta *f* F dirty trick F
jugo *m* juice; ***sacar jugo a algo*** get the most out of sth
jugoso *adj tb fig* juicy
juguete *m* toy
juguetear ⟨1a⟩ *v/i* play
juicio *m* judg(e)ment; JUR trial; (*sensatez*) sense; (*cordura*) sanity; ***a mi juicio*** in my opinion; ***estar en su juicio*** be in one's right mind; ***perder el juicio*** lose one's mind
julio *m* July
junco *m* BOT reed
jungla *f* jungle
junio *m* June
júnior *adj tb* DEP junior
junta *f* POL (regional) government; *militar* junta; COM board; (*sesión*) meeting; TÉC joint; ***junta directiva*** board of directors; ***junta general anual*** annual general meeting
juntar ⟨1a⟩ **1** *v/t* put together; *gente* gather together; *bienes* collect, accumulate **2** *v/r* **juntarse** (*reunirse*) meet, assemble; *de pareja: empezar a salir* start going out; *empezar a vivir juntos* move in together; *de caminos, ríos* meet, join; ***juntarse con alguien*** *socialmente* mix with s.o.
junto 1 *adj* together **2** *prp*: ***junto a*** next to, near; ***junto con*** together with
juntura *f* TÉC joint
jupa *f C.Am., Méx fig* F head, nut F
jurado *m* JUR jury
juramento *m* oath; ***bajo juramento*** under oath
jurar ⟨1a⟩ *v/i* swear
jurídico *adj* legal
jurisdicción *f* jurisdiction
jurisprudencia *f* jurisprudence
justamente *adv* fairly; (*precisamente*) precisely
justicia *f* justice; ***la justicia*** (*la ley*) the law; ***hacer justicia a*** do justice to
justificable *adj* justifiable
justificación *f tb* TIP justification
justificante *m de pago* receipt; *de ausencia, propiedad* certificate
justificar ⟨1g⟩ *v/t tb* TIP justify; *mala conducta* justify, excuse
justo *adj* just, fair; (*exacto*) right, exact;

lo justo just enough; ***¡justo!*** right!, exactly!
juvenil *adj* youthful
juventud *f* youth
juzgado 1 *part* → ***juzgar*** **2** *m* court
juzgar ⟨1h⟩ *v/t* JUR try; (*valorar*) judge; *considerar* consider, judge; ***a juzgar por*** to judge by, judging by

K

kárate *m* DEP karate
kayak *m* DEP kayak
ketchup *m* ketchup
kg. *abr* (= ***kilogramo***) kg (= kilogram)
kilo *m* kilo; *fig* F million
kilogramo *m* kilogram, *Br* kilogramme
kilómetro *m* kilometer, *Br* kilometre
kiosco *m* kiosk
kiwi *m* BOT kiwi (fruit)
kleenex® *m* kleenex, tissue
km. *abr* (= ***kilómetro***) km (= kilometer)
km./h. *abr* (= ***kilómetros por hora***) kph (= kilometers per hour)
kv. *abr* (= ***kilovatio***) kw (= kilowatt)

L

L

la 1 *art* the **2** *pron complemento directo sg* her; *a usted* you; *algo* it; ***la que está embarazada*** the one who is pregnant; ***la más grande*** the biggest (one); ***dame la roja*** give me the red one
laberinto *m* labyrinth, maze
labia *f*: ***tener mucha labia*** have the gift of the gab
labio *m* lip
labor *f* work; (*tarea*) task, job; ***hacer labores*** do needlework; ***no estar por la labor*** F not be enthusiastic about the idea
laborable *adj*: ***día laborable*** workday
laboral *adj* labo(u)r *atr*
laboratorio *m* laboratory, lab F
laborioso *adj* laborious; *persona* hard-working
labrador *m* farm labo(u)rer, farm worker
labranza *f de la tierra* cultivation
labrar ⟨1a⟩ *v/t tierra* work; *piedra* carve
labriego *m* farm labo(u)rer, farm worker
laca *f* lacquer; *para el cabello* hairspray; ***laca de uñas*** nail varnish *o* polish
lacear ⟨1a⟩ *v/t Rpl* lasso
lacio *adj* limp; *pelo* lank
lacónico *adj* laconic
lacra *f* scar; *L.Am.* (*llaga*) sore; ***la corrupción es una lacra social*** corruption is a blot on society
lacre *m* sealing wax
lacrimógeno *adj fig* tear-jerking
lactancia *f* lactation
lácteo *adj*: ***Vía Láctea*** Milky Way; ***productos lácteos*** dairy products
ladear ⟨1a⟩ *v/t* tilt
ladera *f* slope
ladino 1 *adj* cunning, sly **2** *m C.Am. Indian who has become absorbed into white culture*
lado *m* side; (*lugar*) place; ***al lado*** nearby; ***al lado de*** beside, next to; ***de lado*** sideways; ***ir por otro lado*** go another way; ***por un lado … por otro lado*** on the one hand … on the other hand; ***hacerse a un lado*** *tb fig* stand aside
ladrar ⟨1a⟩ *v/i* bark
ladrillo *m* brick
ladrón *m* thief
lagartija *f* ZO small lizard
lagarto *m* ZO lizard
lago *m* lake
lágrima *f* tear
laguna *f* lagoon; *fig* gap
laico *adj* lay
lamentable *adj* deplorable
lamentablemente *adv* regretfully

lamentar ⟨1a⟩ **1** *v/t* regret, be sorry about; *muerte* mourn **2** *v/r* **lamentarse** complain (***de*** about)
lamento *m* whimper; *por dolor* groan
lamer ⟨2a⟩ *v/t* lick
lámina *f* sheet
lámpara *f* lamp; ***lámpara halógena*** halogen lamp; ***lámpara de pie*** floor lamp, *Br* standard lamp
lamparón *m* F grease mark
lana *f* wool; *Méx* P dough F; ***pura lana virgen*** pure new wool
lancha *f* launch; ***lancha fueraborda*** outboard
langosta *f* ZO *insecto* locust; *crustáceo* spiny lobster
langostino *m* ZO king prawn
languidecer ⟨2d⟩ *v/i* languish
lánguido *adj* languid
lanza *f* lance
lanzadera *f* shuttle; ***lanzadera espacial*** space shuttle
lanzado 1 *adj fig* go-ahead; ***es muy lanzado con las chicas*** he's not shy with girls **2** *part* → ***lanzar***
lanzamiento *m* MIL, COM launch; ***lanzamiento de disco / de martillo*** discus / hammer (throw); ***lanzamiento de peso*** shot put
lanzar ⟨1f⟩ **1** *v/t* throw; *cohete, producto* launch; *bomba* drop **2** *v/r* **lanzarse** throw o.s. (***en*** into); (*precipitarse*) pounce (***sobre*** on); ***lanzarse a hacer algo*** rush into doing sth
lapa *f* ZO limpet
lapicera *f Rpl, Chi* (ballpoint) pen; ***lapicera fuente*** *L.Am.* fountain pen
lapicero *m* automatic pencil, *Br* propelling pencil
lápida *f* memorial stone
lapidario *adj* memorable
lápiz *m* pencil; ***lápiz de ojos*** eyeliner; ***lápiz labial*** *or* ***de labios*** lipstick; ***lápiz óptico*** light pen
lapso *m de tiempo* space, period
lapsus *m inv* slip; ***tener un lapsus*** have a momentary lapse
larga *f*: ***poner la (s) larga (s)*** put the headlights on full beam; ***dar largas a alguien*** F put s.o. off
largar ⟨1h⟩ **1** *v/t* drive away **2** *v/r* **largarse** F clear off *o* out F
largo 1 *adj* long; *persona* tall; ***a la -a*** in the long run; ***a lo largo del día*** throughout the day; ***a lo largo de la calle*** along the street; ***¡largo!*** F scram! F; ***esto va para largo*** this will take some time; ***pasar de largo*** go (straight) past **2** *m* length
largometraje *m* feature film
larguero *m* DEP crossbar
laringe *f* larynx
laringitis *f* MED laryngitis
larva *f* ZO larva
las 1 *art fpl* the **2** *pron complemento directo pl* them; *a ustedes* you; ***llévate las que quieras*** take whichever ones you want; ***las de …*** those of …; ***las de Juan*** Juan's; ***las que llevan falda*** the ones *o* those that are wearing dresses
lasaña *f* GASTR lasagne
lascivo *adj* lewd
láser *m* laser; ***rayo láser*** laser beam
lástima *f* pity, shame; ***me da lástima no usarlo*** it's a shame *o* pity not to use it; ***¡qué lástima!*** what a pity *o* shame!
lastimar ⟨1a⟩ **1** *v/t* (*herir*) hurt **2** *v/r* **lastimarse** hurt o.s.
lastimoso *adj* pitiful; (*deplorable*) shameful
lastre *m* ballast; *fig* burden
lata *f* can, *Br tb* tin; *fig* F drag F, pain F; ***dar la lata*** F be a drag F *o* a pain F
latente *adj* latent
lateral 1 *adj* side *atr*; ***cuestiones laterales*** side issues **2** *m* DEP: ***lateral derecho / izquierdo*** right / left back
latería *f L.Am.* tin works
latero *m*,**-a** *f L.Am.* tinsmith
latido *m* beat
latifundio *m* large estate
latigazo *m* lash; (*chasquido*) crack
látigo *m* whip
latín *m* Latin
latino *adj* Latin
Latinoamérica Latin America
latinoamericano 1 *adj* Latin American **2** *m*, **-a** *f* Latin American
latir ⟨3a⟩ *v/i* beat
latitud *f* GEOG latitude
latón *m* brass
laucha *f S. Am.* mouse
laurel *m* BOT laurel; ***dormirse en los laureles*** *fig* rest on one's laurels
lava *f* lava
lavable *adj* washable
lavabo *m* washbowl
lavada *f L.Am.* wash
lavado *m* washing; ***lavado de cerebro*** *fig* brainwashing
lavadora *f* washing machine
lavamanos *m inv L.Am.* → ***lavabo***
lavanda *f* BOT lavender
lavandería *f* laundry
lavaplatos *m inv* dishwasher; *L.Am.* sink
lavar ⟨1a⟩ **1** *v/t* wash; ***lavar los platos*** wash the dishes; ***lavar la ropa*** do the laundry, *Br tb* do the washing; ***lavar en seco*** dry-clean **2** *v/i* (*lavar los platos*)

L

do the dishes; *de detergente* clean **3** *v/r* **lavarse** wash up, *Br* have a wash; ***lavarse los dientes*** brush one's teeth; ***lavarse las manos*** wash one's hands; ***yo me lavo las manos*** *fig* I wash my hands of it
lavarropas *m inv L.Am.* washing machine
lavavajillas *m inv líquido* dishwashing liquid, *Br* washing-up liquid; *electrodoméstico* dishwasher
laxante *m/adj* MED laxative
laxo *adj* relaxed; (*poco estricto*) lax
lazada *f* bow
lazarillo *m* guide; ***perro lazarillo*** seeing eye dog, *Br* guide dog
lazo *m* knot; *de adorno* bow; *para atrapar animales* lasso
le *pron sg complemento indirecto* (to) him; (*a ella*) (to) her; (*a usted*) (to) you; (*a algo*) (to) it; *complemento directo* him; (*a usted*) you
leal *adj* loyal
lealtad *f* loyalty
lección *f* lesson; ***esto le servirá de lección*** that will teach him a lesson
lechar ⟨1a⟩ *v/t L.Am.* (*ordeñar*) milk
leche *f* milk; ***leche condensada*** condensed milk; ***leche entera*** whole milk; ***leche en polvo*** powdered milk; ***estar de mala leche*** P be in a foul mood; ***tener mala leche*** P be out to make trouble
lechería *f* dairy
lechero 1 *adj* dairy *atr* **2** *m* milkman
lecho *m tb de río* bed
lechón *m* suckling pig
lechuga *f* lettuce; ***ser más fresco que una lechuga*** F have a lot of nerve
lechuza *f* ZO barn-owl; *Cuba, Méx* P hooker F
lectivo *adj*: ***día lectivo*** school day
lector *m*, **~a** *f* reader
lectura *f* reading
leer ⟨2e⟩ *v/t* read
legado *m* legacy; *persona* legate
legal *adj* legal; *fig* F *persona* great F, terrific F
legalidad *f* legality
legalizar ⟨1f⟩ *v/t* legalize
legaña *f*: ***tener legañas en los ojos*** have sleep in one's eyes
legar ⟨1h⟩ *v/t* leave
legendario *adj* legendary
legible *adj* legible
legión *f* legion
legislación *f* legislation
legislar ⟨1a⟩ *v/i* legislate
legislativo *adj* legislative
legislatura *f cuerpo* legislature; *periodo* term of office
legitimar ⟨1a⟩ *v/t* justify; *documento* authenticate
legítimo *adj* legitimate; (*verdadero*) authentic
lego *adj* lay *atr*; *fig* ignorant
legua *f*: ***se ve a la legua*** *fig* F you can see it a mile off F; *hecho* it's blindingly obvious F
legumbre *f* BOT pulse
leída *f L.Am.* reading
lejanía *f* distance; ***en la lejanía*** in the distance
lejano *adj* distant
lejía *f* bleach
lejos 1 *adv* far, far away; ***Navidad queda lejos*** Christmas is a long way off; ***a lo lejos*** in the distance; ***ir demasiado lejos*** *fig* go too far, overstep the mark; ***llegar lejos*** *fig* go far **2** *prp*: ***lejos de*** far from
lele *adj C.Am.* stupid
lema *m* slogan
lencería *f* lingerie
lengua *f* tongue; ***lengua materna*** mother tongue; ***con la lengua fuera*** *fig* with one's tongue hanging out; ***irse de la lengua*** let the cat out of the bag; ***sacar la lengua a alguien*** stick one's tongue out at s.o.; ***lo tengo en la punta de la lengua*** it's on the tip of my tongue
lenguado *m* ZO sole
lenguaje *m* language; ***lenguaje de programación*** INFOR programming language
lenguaraz *adj* foul-mouthed
lengüeta 1 *f de zapato* tongue **2** *adj*: ***ser lengüeta*** *S. Am.* F be a gossip
lenitivo *m* balm
lente *f* lens; ***lentes de contacto*** contact lenses, contacts
lentes *mpl L.Am.* glasses
lenteja *f* BOT lentil
lentejuela *f* sequin
lentillas *fpl* contact lenses
lentitud *f* slowness
lento *adj* slow; ***a fuego lento*** on a low heat
leña *f* (fire)wood; ***echar leña al fuego*** *fig* add fuel to the fire
leñador *m* woodcutter
leño *m* log
Leo *m/f inv* ASTR Leo
león *m* ZO lion; *L.Am.* puma; ***león marino*** sealion
leona *f* lioness
leonera *f* lion's den; *jaula* lion's cage; *Rpl, Chi fig* F *habitación desordenada etc* pigsty F; *L.Am.* F *para prisioneros* bullpen F, *Br communal cell for holding prisoners temporarily*

leopardo *m* ZO leopard
leotardo *m de gimnasta* leotard; ***leotardos*** tights, *Br* heavy tights
lépero *adj C.Am., Méx* coarse
lerdo *adj* (*torpe*) slow(-witted)
les *pron pl complemento indirecto* (to) them; (*a ustedes*) (to) you; *complemento directo* them; (*a ustedes*) you
lesbiana *f* lesbian
lesión *f* injury
lesionado *adj* injured
lesionar ⟨1a⟩ *v/t* injure
letal *adj* lethal
letanía *f* litany
letárgico *adj* lethargic
letra *f* letter; *de canción* lyrics *pl*; ***letra de cambio*** COM bill of exchange; ***letra de imprenta*** block capital; ***letra mayúscula*** capital letter; ***al pie de la letra*** word for word
letrero *m* sign
letrina *f* latrine
leucemia *f* MED leuk(a)emia
levadura *f* yeast
levantamiento *m* raising; (*rebelión*) rising; *de embargo* lifting
levantar ⟨1a⟩ **1** *v/t* raise; *bulto* lift (up); *del suelo* pick up; *edificio*, *estatua* put up, erect; *embargo* lift; ***levantar sospechas*** arouse suspicion; ***¡levanta los ánimos!*** cheer up!; ***levantar la voz*** raise one's voice **2** *v/r* **levantarse** get up; (*ponerse de pie*) stand up; *de un edificio*, *una montaña* rise; *en rebelión* rise up
levante *m* east
levar ⟨1a⟩ *v/t*: ***levar anclas*** weigh anchor
leve *adj* slight; *sonrisa* faint
levedad *f* lightness
levitar ⟨1a⟩ *v/i* levitate
léxico *m* lexicon
ley *f* law; ***con todas las de la ley*** fairly and squarely
leyenda *f* legend
leyendo *vb* → ***leer***
leyó *vb* → ***leer***
liana *f* BOT liana, creeper
liar ⟨1c⟩ **1** *v/t* tie (up); *en papel* wrap (up); *cigarillo* roll; *persona* confuse **2** *v/r* **liarse** *de una persona* get confused; ***liarse a hacer algo*** get tied up doing sth; ***liarse con alguien*** F get involved with s.o.
Líbano Lebanon
libélula *f* ZO dragonfly
liberación *f* release; *de un país* liberation
liberal *adj* liberal
liberalización *f* liberalization
liberalizar ⟨1f⟩ *v/t* liberalize
liberar ⟨1a⟩ **1** *v/t* (set) free, release; *país* liberate; *energía* release **2** *v/r* **liberarse**: ***liberarse de algo*** free o.s. of sth
libertad *f* freedom, liberty; ***libertad bajo fianza*** JUR bail; ***libertad condicional*** JUR probation; ***dejar a alguien en libertad*** release s.o., let s.o. go
libertinaje *m* licentiousness
Libia Libya
líbido *f* libido
libio(-a) *m/f & adj* Libyan
libra *f* pound; ***libra esterlina*** pound (sterling)
Libra *m/f inv* ASTR Libra
librar ⟨1a⟩ **1** *v/t* free (**de** from); *cheque* draw; *batalla* fight **2** *v/i*: ***libro los lunes*** I have Mondays off **3** *v/r* **librarse**: ***librarse de algo*** get out of sth; ***de buena nos hemos librado*** F that was lucky
libre *adj* free; *tiempo* spare, free; ***eres libre de*** you're free to
librecambio *m* free trade
librera *f* bookseller
librería *f* book store
librero *m* bookseller; *L.Am. mueble* bookcase
libreta *f* notebook; ***libreta de ahorros*** bankbook, passbook
libro *m* book; ***libro de bolsillo*** paperback (book); ***libro de cocina*** cookbook, cookery book; ***libro de familia*** *booklet recording family births, marriages and deaths*; ***libro de reclamaciones*** complaints book
licencia *f* permit, license, *Br* licence; (*permiso*) permission; MIL leave; ***licencia*** (***de manejar*** *or* ***conducir***) *L.Am.* driver's license, *Br* driving licence; ***tomarse demasiadas licencias*** take liberties
licenciado *m*, **-a** *f* graduate
licenciar ⟨1b⟩ **1** *v/t* MIL discharge **2** *v/r* **licenciarse** graduate; MIL be discharged
licenciatura *f* EDU degree
liceo *m L.Am.* high school, *Br* secondary school
licitación *f L.Am.* bidding
licitador *m*, **licitadora** *f L.Am.* bidder
licitar ⟨1a⟩ *v/t L.Am. en subasta* bid for
lícito *adj* legal; (*razonable*) fair, reasonable
licor *m* liquor, *Br* spirits *pl*
licuado *m Méx* fruit milkshake
licuadora *f* blender
licuar ⟨1d⟩ *v/t* blend, liquidize
líder **1** *m/f* leader **2** *adj* leading
liderar ⟨1a⟩ *v/t* lead
liderazgo *m* leadership
lidia *f* bullfighting
lidiar ⟨1b⟩ **1** *v/i fig* do battle, struggle **2** *v/t toro* fight
liebre *f* ZO hare

lienzo *m* canvas
liga *f* POL, DEP league; *de medias* garter
ligamento *m* ANAT ligament
ligar ⟨1h⟩ **1** *v/t* bind; (*atar*) tie **2** *v/i*: ***ligar con*** F pick up F
ligereza *f* lightness; (*rapidez*) speed; *de movimiento* agility; *de carácter* shallowness, superficiality
ligero 1 *adj* (*de poco peso*) light; (*rápido*) rapid, quick; *movimiento* agile, nimble; (*leve*) slight; ***ligero de ropa*** scantily clad; ***a la -a*** (*sin pensar*) lightly, casually; ***tomar algo a la -a*** not take sth seriously **2** *adv* quickly
ligón *m* F: ***es un ligón*** he's a real Don Juan F
ligue *m* F: ***estar de ligue*** be on the pick-up F, *Br* be on the pull F
liguero *m* garter belt, *Br* suspender belt
lija *f*: ***papel de lija*** sandpaper
lijar ⟨1a⟩ *v/t* sand
lila *f* BOT lilac
lima *f* file; BOT lime; ***lima de uñas*** nail file
limar ⟨1a⟩ *v/t* file; *fig* polish
limitado 1 *adj* limited **2** *part* → ***limitar***
limitar ⟨1a⟩ **1** *v/t* limit **2** *v/i*: ***limitar con*** border on **3** *v/r* **limitarse** limit *o* restrict o.s. (***a*** to)
límite 1 *m* limit; (*linea de separación*) boundary; ***límite de velocidad*** speed limit **2** *adj*: ***situación límite*** life-threatening situation
limítrofe *adj* neighbo(u)ring
limón *m* lemon
limonada *f* lemonade
limosna *f*: ***una limosna, por favor*** can you spare some change?
limpiabotas *m/f inv* bootblack
limpiacristales *m inv* window cleaner
limpiada *f L.Am.* clean
limpiamanos *m inv L.Am.* hand towel
limpiaparabrisas *m inv* AUTO windshield wiper, *Br* windscreen wiper
limpiar ⟨1b⟩ *v/t* clean; *con un trapo* wipe; *fig* clean up; ***limpiar a alguien*** F clean s.o. out F
limpieza *f estado* cleanliness; *acto* cleaning; ***limpieza general*** spring cleaning; ***limpieza en seco*** dry-cleaning; ***hacer la limpieza*** do the cleaning
limpio *adj* clean; (*ordenado*) neat, tidy; *político* honest; ***gana $5.000 limpios al mes*** he takes home $5,000 a month; ***quedarse limpio*** *S. Am.* F be broke F; ***sacar algo en limpio*** *fig* make sense of sth
limusina *f* limousine
linaje *m* lineage
lince *m* ZO lynx; ***ojos*** *or* ***vista de lince*** *fig* eyes like a hawk
linchar ⟨1a⟩ *v/t* lynch
lindar ⟨1a⟩ *v/i*: ***lindar con algo*** adjoin sth; *fig* border on sth
lindo *adj* lovely; ***de lo lindo*** a lot, a great deal
línea *f* line; ***línea aérea*** airline; ***mantener la línea*** watch one's figure; ***de primera línea*** *fig* first-rate; ***tecnología de primera línea*** state-of-the art technology; ***entre líneas*** *fig* between the lines
lineal *adj* linear
linfático *adj* lymphatic
lingote *m* ingot; ***lingote de oro*** gold bar
lingüista *m/f* linguist
lingüística *f* linguistics
lingüístico *adj* linguistic
linier *m* DEP assistant referee, linesman
lino *m* linen; BOT flax
linterna *f* flashlight, *Br* torch
lío *m* bundle; F (*desorden*) mess; F (*jaleo*) fuss; ***lío amoroso*** F affair; ***estar hecho un lío*** be all confused; ***hacerse un lío*** get into a muddle; ***meterse en líos*** get into trouble
liposucción *f* MED liposuction
lipotimia *f* MED blackout
liquen *m* BOT lichen
liquidación *f* COM *de cuenta*, *deuda* settlement; *de negocio* liquidation; ***liquidación total*** clearance sale
liquidar ⟨1a⟩ *v/t cuenta*, *deuda* settle; COM *negocio* wind up, liquidate; *existencias* sell off; F (*matar*) liquidate F, bump off F
liquidez *f* COM liquidity
líquido 1 *adj* liquid; COM net **2** *m* liquid
lira *f* lira
lírico *adj* lyrical
lirio *m* BOT lily
lirón *m* ZO dormouse; ***dormir como un lirón*** *fig* F sleep like a log
lisiado 1 *adj* crippled **2** *m* cripple
liso *adj* smooth; *terreno* flat; *pelo* straight; (*sin adornos*) plain; ***-a y llanamente*** plainly and simply
lisonja *f* flattery
lista *f* list; ***lista de boda*** wedding list; ***lista de espera*** waiting list; ***pasar lista*** take the roll call, *Br* call the register
listado *m* INFOR printout
listín *m*: ***listín*** (***telefónico***) phone book
listo *adj* (*inteligente*) clever; (*preparado*) ready; ***pasarse de listo*** F try to be too smart F
listón *m de madera* strip; DEP bar; ***poner el listón muy alto*** *fig* set very high standards
lisura *f Rpl*, *Pe* curse, swearword

litera *f* bunk; *de tren* couchette
literal *adj* literal
literario *adj* literary
literatura *f* literature
litigante *m/f & adj* JUR litigant
litigar ⟨1h⟩ *v/i* JUR go to litigation
litigio *m* lawsuit
litografía *f* lithography
litoral 1 *adj* coastal **2** *m* coast
litro *m* liter, *Br* litre
liturgia *f* REL liturgy
liviano *adj* light; (*de poca importancia*) trivial
lívido *adj* pale
llaga *f* ulcer; ***poner*** *or* ***meter el dedo en la llaga*** *fig* put one's finger on it
llama *f* flame; zo llama
llamada *f* call; *en una puerta* knock; *en timbre* ring; ***llamada a cobro revertido*** collect call; ***llamada de auxilio*** distress call
llamado *m L.Am.* call
llamador *m* (door) knocker
llamamiento *m* call; ***hacer un llamamiento a algo*** call for sth
llamar ⟨1a⟩ **1** *v/t* call; TELEC call, *Br tb* ring **2** *v/i* TELEC call, *Br tb* ring; ***llamar a la puerta*** knock at the door; *con timbre* ring the bell; ***el fúítbol no me llama nada*** football doesn't appeal to me in the slightest **3** *v/r* **llamarse** be called; ***¿cómo te llamas?*** what's your name?
llamarada *f* flare-up
llamativo *adj* eyecatching; *color* loud
llamón *adj Méx* moaning
llano 1 *adj terreno* level; *trato* natural; *persona* unassuming **2** *m* flat ground
llanta *f* wheel rim; *C.Am., Méx* (*neumático*) tire, *Br* tyre
llanto *m* sobbing
llanura *f* plain
llave *f* key; *para tuerca* wrench, *Br tb* spanner; ***llave de contacto*** AUTO ignition key; ***llave inglesa*** TÉC monkey wrench; ***llave de paso*** stop cock; ***llave en mano*** available for immediate occupancy; ***bajo llave*** under lock and key; ***cerrar con llave*** lock
llavero *m* key ring
llegada *f* arrival
llegar ⟨1h⟩ **1** *v/i* arrive; (*alcanzar*) reach; ***la comida no llegó para todos*** there wasn't enough food for everyone; ***me llega hasta las rodillas*** it comes down to my knees; ***el agua me llegaba a la cintura*** the water came up to my waist; ***llegar a saber*** find out; ***llegar a ser*** get to be; ***llegar a viejo*** live to a ripe old age **2** *v/r* **llegarse**: ***llégate al vecino*** F run over to the neighbo(u)r's
llenar ⟨1a⟩ **1** *v/t* fill; *impreso* fill out *o* in **2** *v/i* be filling **3** *v/r* **llenarse** fill up; ***me he llenado*** I have had enough (to eat)
lleno *adj* full (***de*** of); *pared* covered (***de*** with); ***de lleno*** fully
llevadero *adj* bearable
llevar ⟨1a⟩ **1** *v/t* take; *ropa, gafas* wear; *ritmo* keep up; ***llevar a alguien en coche*** drive s.o., take s.o. in the car; ***llevar dinero encima*** carry money; ***llevar las de perder*** be likely to lose; ***me lleva dos años*** he's two years older than me; ***llevo ocho días aquí*** I've been here a week; ***llevo una hora esperando*** I've been waiting for an hour **2** *v/i* lead (***a*** to) **3** *v/r* **llevarse** take; *susto, sorpresa* get; ***llevarse bien / mal*** get on well / badly; ***se lleva el color rojo*** red is fashionable
llorar ⟨1a⟩ *v/i* cry, weep
lloriquear ⟨1a⟩ *v/i* snivel, whine
lloro *m* weeping, crying
llorón 1 *adj*: ***ser llorón*** be a crybaby F **2** *m* F crybaby F
llovedera *f L.Am.*, **llovedero** *m L.Am.* rainy season
llover ⟨2h⟩ *v/i* rain; ***llueve*** it is raining
llovizna *f* drizzle
lloviznar ⟨1a⟩ *v/i* drizzle
llueve *vb* → ***llover***
lluvia *f* rain; *Rpl* (*ducha*) shower; ***lluvia ácida*** acid rain
lluvioso *adj* rainy
lo 1 *art sg* the; ***lo bueno*** the good thing; ***no sabes lo difícil que es*** you don't know how difficult it is **2** *pron sg*: *a él* him; *a usted* you; *algo* it; ***lo sé*** I know **3** *pron rel sg*: ***lo que*** what; ***lo cual*** which
loable *adj* praiseworthy, laudable
lobo *m* wolf; ***lobo marino*** seal; ***lobo de mar*** *fig* sea dog
lóbrego *adj* gloomy
lóbulo *m* lobe; ***lóbulo de la oreja*** earlobe
loca *f* madwoman
locador *m S. Am.* landlord
local 1 *adj* local **2** *m* premises *pl*; ***local comercial*** commercial premises *pl*
localidad *f* town; TEA seat
localización *f* location
localizar ⟨1f⟩ *v/t* locate; *incendio* contain, bring under control
loción *f* lotion
loco 1 *adj* mad, crazy; ***a lo loco*** F (*sin pensar*) hastily; ***es para volverse loco*** it's enough to drive you mad *o* crazy **2** *m* madman
locomoción *f* locomotion; ***medio de locomoción*** means of transport
locomotora *f* locomotive

L

locro *m S. Am. stew of meat, corn and potatoes*
locuaz *adj* talkative, loquacious *fml*
locución *f* phrase
locura *f* madness; ***es una locura*** it's madness
locutor *m*, **locutora** *f* RAD, TV presenter
locutorio *m* TELEC phone booth
lodazal *m* quagmire
lodo *m* mud
lógica *f* logic
lógico *adj* logical
logística *f* logistics
logopeda *m/f* speech therapist
logotipo *m* logo
logrado *adj* excellent
lograr ⟨1a⟩ *v/t* achieve; (*obtener*) obtain; ***lograr hacer algo*** manage to do sth; ***lograr que alguien haga algo*** (manage to) get s.o. to do sth
logrero *m L.Am.* F profiteer
logro *m* achievement
loma *f L.Am.* small hill
lombriz *f*: ***lombriz de tierra*** earthworm
lomo *m* back; GASTR loin; ***a lomos de burro*** on a donkey
lona *f* canvas
loncha *f* slice
lonche *m L.Am.* afternoon snack
lonchería *f L.Am.* diner, luncheonette
londinense **1** *adj* London *atr* **2** *m/f* Londoner
Londres London
longaniza *f type of dried sausage*
longevidad *f* longevity
longevo *adj* long-lived
longitud *f* longitude; (*largo*) length
longitudinal *adj* longitudinal
lonja *f de pescado* fish market; (*loncha*) slice
loquera *f L.Am.* F shrink F; *enfermera* psychiatric nurse
loquero *m L.Am.* F *persona* shrink F; *enfermero* psychiatric nurse; (*manicomio*) mental hospital, funny farm F
loro *m* parrot; ***estar al loro*** F (*enterado*) be clued up F, be on the ball F
los *mpl* **1** *art* the **2** *pron complemento directo pl* them; *a ustedes* you; ***llévate los que quieras*** take whichever ones you want; ***los de …*** those of …; ***los de Juan*** Juan's; ***los que juegan*** the ones *o* those that are playing
losa *f* flagstone
lote *m en reparto* share, part; *L.Am.* (*solar*) lot
lotería *f* lottery
loto **1** *m* BOT lotus **2** *f* F lottery
loza *f* china
lozano *adj* healthy-looking
lubina *f* ZO sea bass
lubri(fi)cación *f* lubrication
lubri(fi)cante **1** *adj* lubricating **2** *m* lubricant
lubri(fi)car ⟨1g⟩ *v/t* lubricate
lucero *m* bright star; (*Venus*) Venus
lucha *f* fight, struggle; DEP wrestling; ***lucha libre*** DEP all-in wrestling
luchador **1** *adj espíritu* fighting **2** *m*, **luchadora** *f* fighter
luchar ⟨1a⟩ *v/i* fight (***por*** for)
lúícido *adj* lucid, clear
luciérnaga *f* ZO glow-worm
lucimiento *m* (*brillo*) splendo(u)r; ***le ofrece oportunidades de lucimiento*** it gives him a chance to shine
lucio *m* ZO pike
lucir ⟨3f⟩ **1** *v/i* shine; *L.Am.* (*verse bien*) look good **2** *v/t ropa, joya* wear **3** *v/r* **lucirse** *tb irón* excel o.s., surpass o.s.
lucrativo *adj* lucrative
lucro *m* profit; ***afán de lucro*** profit-making; ***sin ánimo de lucro*** non-profit (making), not-for-profit
ludopatía *f* compulsive gambling
luego **1** *adv* (*después*) later; *en orden, espacio* then; *L.Am.* (*en seguida*) right now; ***luego luego*** *Méx* straight away; ***¡desde luego!*** of course!; ***¡hasta luego!*** see you (later) **2** *conj* therefore; ***luego que*** *L.Am.* after
lugar *m* place; ***lugar comúín*** cliché; ***en lugar de*** instead of; ***en primer lugar*** in the first place, first(ly); ***fuera de lugar*** out of place; ***yo en tu lugar*** if I were you, (if I were) in your place; ***dar lugar a*** give rise to; ***tener lugar*** take place
lúígubre *adj* gloomy
lujo *m* luxury
lujoso *adj* luxurious
lujuria *f* lust
lujurioso *adj* lecherous
lumbago *m* MED lumbago
lumbre *f* fire
lumbrera *f* genius
luminoso *adj* luminous; *lámpara, habitación* bright
luna *f* moon; *de tienda* window; *de vehículo* windshield, *Br* windscreen; ***luna de miel*** honeymoon; ***luna llena / nueva*** full / new moon; ***media luna*** *L.Am.* GASTR croissant; ***estar en la luna*** F have one's head in the clouds F
lunar **1** *adj* lunar **2** *m en la piel* mole; ***de lunares*** spotted, polka-dot
lunático *adj* lunatic
lunes *m inv* Monday
luneta *f*: ***luneta térmica*** AUTO heated

windshield, *Br* heated windscreen
lunfardo *m Arg slang used in Buenos Aires*
lupa *f* magnifying glass; ***mirar algo con lupa*** *fig* go through sth with a fine tooth-comb
lustrabotas *m/f inv L.Am.* bootblack
lustrador *m*, **lustradora** *f L.Am.* bootblack
lustrar ⟨1a⟩ *v/t* polish
lustre *m* shine; *fig* luster, *Br* lustre; ***dar lustre a*** *fig* give added luster (*Br* lustre) to
lustro *m* period of five years
lustroso *adj* shiny
luto *m* mourning; ***estar de luto por alguien*** be in mourning for s.o.
luxación *f* MED dislocation
luz *f* light; ***luz trasera*** AUTO rear light; ***luces de carretera*** *or* ***largas*** AUTO full *o* main beam headlights; ***luces de cruce*** *or* ***cortas*** AUTO dipped headlights; ***luz verde*** *tb fig* green light; ***arrojar luz sobre algo*** *fig* shed light on s.th.; ***dar a luz*** give birth to; ***salir a la luz*** *fig* come to light; ***a todas luces*** evidently, clearly; ***de pocas luces*** *fig* F dim F, not very bright

M

m *abr* (***= metro***) m (= meter); (***= minuto***) m (= minute)
macabro 1 *adj* macabre **2** *m*, **-a** *f* ghoul
macaco *m* ZO macaque
macana *f L.Am.* billyclub, *Br* truncheon; F (*mentira*) lie, fib F; ***hizo / dijo una macana*** he did / said something stupid; ***¡qué macana!*** *Rpl* P what a drag!
macanear ⟨1a⟩ *v/t L.Am.* (*aporrear*) beat
macanudo *S. Am.* F great F, fantastic F
macarra 1 *m* P pimp **2** *adj* F: ***ser macarra*** be a bastard P
macarrones *mpl* macaroni *sg*
macedonia *f*: ***macedonia de frutas*** fruit salad
macerar ⟨1a⟩ *v/t* GASTR soak
maceta *f* flowerpot
macetero *m* flowerpot holder; *L.Am.* flowerpot
machacar ⟨1g⟩ *v/t* crush; *fig* thrash
machete *m* machete
machismo *m* male chauvinism
machista 1 *adj* sexist **2** *m* sexist, male chauvinist
macho 1 *adj* male; (*varonil*) tough; *desp* macho **2** *m* male; *apelativo* F man F, *Br* mate F; *L.Am.* (*plátano*) banana
macizo 1 *adj* solid; ***estar macizo*** F be a dish F **2** *m* GEOG massif; ***macizo de flores*** flower bed
macuto *m* backpack
madeja *f* hank
madera *f* wood; ***tener madera de*** have the makings of
maderera *f* timber merchant
madero *m* P cop P
madrastra *f* step-mother
madre 1 *f* mother; ***madre soltera*** single mother; ***dar en la madre a alguien*** F hit s..o. where it hurts; ***¡me vale madre!*** *Méx* V I don't give a fuck! V **2** *adj Méx, C.Am.* F great F, fantastic
madreselva *f* BOT honeysuckle
Madrid Madrid
madriguera *f* (*agujero*) burrow; (*guarida*) *tb fig* den
madrileño 1 *adj* of / from Madrid, Madrid *atr* **2** *m*, **-a** *f* native of Madrid
madrina *f* godmother
madrugada *f* early morning; (*amanecer*) dawn; ***de madrugada*** in the small hours
madrugador *m*, **madrugadora** *f* early riser
madrugar ⟨1h⟩ *v/i L.Am.* (*quedar despierto*) stay up till the small hours; (*levantarse temprano*) get up early
madurar ⟨1a⟩ **1** *v/t fig*: *idea* think through **2** *v/i de persona* mature; *de fruta* ripen
madurez *f mental* maturity; *edad* middle age; *de fruta* ripeness
maduro *adj mentalmente* mature; *de edad* middle-aged; *fruta* ripe
maestría *f* mastery; *Méx* EDU master's (degree)
maestro 1 *adj* master *atr* **2** *m*, **-a** *f* EDU teacher; MÚS maestro
mafia *f* mafia
mafioso 1 *adj* mafia *atr* **2** *m* mafioso, gangster
magdalena *f* cupcake, *Br tb* fairy cake

magia *f tb fig* magic
mágico *adj* magic
magisterio *m* teaching profession
magistrado *m* judge
magistral *adj* masterly
magnanimidad *f* magnanimity
magnánimo *adj* magnanimous
magnate *m* magnate, tycoon
magnesio *m* magnesium
magnético *adj* magnetic
magnetofón *m* tape recorder
magnífico *adj* wonderful, magnificent
magnitud *f* magnitude
magnolia *f* BOT magnolia
mago *m tb fig* magician; ***los Reyes Magos*** the Three Wise Men, the Three Kings
magrear ⟨1a⟩ *v/t* F feel up F
Magreb Maghreb
magro *adj carne* lean
magulladura *f* bruise
magullar ⟨1a⟩ *v/t* bruise
magullón *m L.Am.* bruise
mahometano 1 *adj* Muslim **2** *m*, **-a** *f* Muslim
mahonesa *f* mayonnaise
maillot *m* DEP jersey
maíz *m* corn
majada *f CSur* flock of sheep
majaderear ⟨1a⟩ *L.Am.* F **1** *v/t* bug F **2** *v/i* keep going on F
majadería *f*: ***decir / hacer una majadería*** say / do something stupid
majadero F **1** *adj* idiotic, stupid **2** *m*, **-a** *f* idiot
majareta *adj* F nutty F, screwy F
majestad *f* majesty
majestuoso *adj* majestic
majo *adj* F nice; (*bonito*) pretty
mal 1 *adj* → ***malo*** **2** *adv* badly; ***mal que bien*** one way or the other; ***¡menos mal!*** thank goodness!; ***ponerse a mal con alguien*** fall out with s.o.; ***tomarse algo a mal*** take sth badly **3** *m* MED illness; ***el mal menor*** the lesser of two evils
malabar *m/adj*: **(*juegos*) *-es*** *pl* juggling *sg*
malabarista *m/f* juggler
malacrianza *f L.Am.* rudeness
malaria *f* MED malaria
malcriadez *f L.Am.* bad upbringing
malcriado *adj* spoilt
malcrianza *f L.Am.* rudeness
malcriar ⟨1c⟩ *v/t* spoil
maldad *f* evil; ***es una maldad hacer eso*** it's a wicked thing to do
maldecir ⟨3p⟩ **1** *v/i* curse; ***maldecir de alguien*** speak ill of s.o. **2** *v/t* curse
maldición *f* curse
maldito *adj* F damn F; ***¡-a sea!*** (god)damn it!
maleante *m/f & adj* criminal
malecón *m* breakwater
maleducado *adj* rude, bad-mannered
maleficio *m* curse
maléfico *adj* evil
malentendido *m* misunderstanding
malestar *m* MED discomfort; *social* unrest
maleta *f* bag, suitcase; *L.Am.* AUTO trunk, *Br* boot; ***hacer la maleta*** pack one's bags
maletero *m* trunk, *Br* boot
maletín *m* briefcase
malévolo *adj* malevolent
maleza *f* undergrowth
malformación *f* MED malformation
malgastar ⟨1a⟩ *v/t* waste
malgenioso *adj Méx* bad-tempered
malhablado *adj* foul-mouthed
malhechor *m*, **malhechora** *f* criminal
malherir ⟨3i⟩ *v/t* hurt badly
malhumorado *adj* bad-tempered
malicia *f* (*mala intención*) malice; (*astucia*) cunning, slyness; ***no tener malicia*** F be very naive
malicioso *adj* (*malintencionado*) malicious; (*astuto*) cunning, sly
maligno *adj* harmful; MED malignant
malinchismo *m Méx* treason
malla *f* mesh; *Rpl* swimsuit
malo 1 *adj* bad; *calidad* poor; (*enfermo*) sick, ill; ***por las buenas o por las -as*** whether he / she etc likes it or not; ***por las -as*** by force; ***lo malo es que*** unfortunately; ***ponerse malo*** fall ill **2** *m hum* bad guy, baddy F
malogrado *adj muerto* dead before one's time
malograr ⟨1a⟩ **1** *v/t* waste; *trabajo* spoil, ruin **2** *v/r* **malograrse** fail; *de plan* come to nothing; *fallecer* die before one's time; *S. Am.* (*descomponerse*) break down; (*funcionar mal*) go wrong
maloliente *adj* stinking
malparado *adj*: ***quedar*** *or* ***salir malparado de algo*** come out badly from sth
malpensado *adj*: ***ser malpensado*** have a nasty mind
malsano *adj* unhealthy
malsonante *adj* rude
malta *f* malt
maltratar ⟨1a⟩ *v/t* mistreat
maltrato *m* abuse, harsh words *pl*
maltrecho *adj* weakened, diminished; *cosa* damaged
malva *adj* mauve
malvado *adj* evil
malversación *f*: ***malversación de fondos*** embezzlement

malversar ⟨1a⟩ *v/t* embezzle
Malvinas: ***las Malvinas*** the Falklands, the Falkland Islands
malvivir ⟨3a⟩ *v/i* scrape by
mamá *f* mom, *Br* mum
mama *f* breast
mamadera *f L.Am.* feeding bottle
mamar ⟨1a⟩ *v/i* suck; ***dar de mamar*** (breast)feed
mamarracho *m*: ***vas hecho un mamarracho*** F you look a mess F
mamífero *m* mammal
mamila *f Méx* feeding bottle
mamografía *f* MED mammography
mamón 1 *adj Méx* P cocky **2** *m* P bastard P
mamona *f* P bitch P
mamotreto *m* F *libro* hefty tome
mampara *f* screen
mamporro *m* F punch
mampostería *f* masonry
maná *m fig* manna
manada *f* herd; *de lobos* pack
manantial *m* spring
manar ⟨1a⟩ *v/i* flow
manatí *m* ZO manatee
manaza *f*: ***ser un manazas*** F be ham-handed F
mancebo *m* youth
Mancha: ***Canal de la Mancha*** English Channel
mancha *f* (dirty) mark; *de grasa, sangre etc* stain
manchar ⟨1a⟩ **1** *v/t* get dirty; *de grasa, sangre etc* stain **2** *v/r* **mancharse** get dirty
mancillar ⟨1a⟩ *v/t fig* sully
manco *adj de mano* one-handed; *de brazo* one-armed
mancornas *fpl Pe, Bol* cufflinks
mancuernas *fpl C.Am.* cufflinks
mandamás *m inv* F big shot F
mandado *m Méx, C.Am.*: ***los mandados*** *pl* the shopping *sg*
mandamiento *m* order; JUR warrant; REL commandment
mandar ⟨1a⟩ **1** *v/t* order; (*enviar*) send; ***a mí no me manda nadie*** nobody tells me what to do; ***mandar hacer algo*** have sth done **2** *v/i* be in charge; ***¿mande?*** *Méx* can I help you?; *Méx* TELEC hallo?; (*¿cómo?*) what did you say?, excuse me?
mandarina *f* mandarin (orange)
mandatario *m* leader; ***primer mandatario*** *Méx* President
mandato *m* order; POL mandate
mandíbula *f* ANAT jaw; ***reírse a mandíbula batiente*** F laugh one's head off F
mandioca *f* cassava
mando *m* command; ***alto mando*** high command; ***mando a distancia*** TV remote control; ***tablero de mandos*** AUTO dashboard
mandolina *f* MÚS mandolin
mandón *adj* F bossy F
manecilla *f* hand
manejable *adj* easy to handle; *automovil* maneuverable, *Br* manoeuvrable
manejar ⟨1a⟩ **1** *v/t* handle; *máquina* operate; *L.Am.* AUTO drive **2** *v/i L.Am.* AUTO drive **3** *v/r* **manejarse** manage, get by
manejo *m* handling; *de una máquina* operation
manera *f* way; ***esa es su manera de ser*** that's the way he is; ***maneras*** manners; ***lo hace a su manera*** he does it his way; ***de manera que*** so (that); ***de ninguna manera*** certainly not; ***no hay manera de*** it is impossible to; ***de todas maneras*** anyway, in any case
manga *f* sleeve; ***manga de riego*** hosepipe; ***en mangas de camisa*** in shirtsleeves; ***sin mangas*** sleeveless; ***sacarse algo de la manga*** *fig* make sth up; ***traer algo en la manga*** F have sth up one's sleeve
manganeso *m* manganese
mangar ⟨1h⟩ *v/t* P swipe F, pinch F
mangle *m* BOT mangrove
mango *m* BOT mango; *CSur* F (*dinero*) dough F, cash; ***estoy sin un mango*** *CSur* F I'm broke F, I don't have a bean F
mangonear ⟨1a⟩ **1** *v/i* F boss people around; (*entrometerse*) meddle **2** *v/t* F: ***mangonear a alguien*** boss s.o. around
manguera *f* hose(pipe)
maní *m S. Am.* peanut
manía *f* (*costumbre*) habit, mania; (*antipatía*) dislike; (*obsesión*) obsession; ***manía persecutoria*** persecution complex; ***tiene sus -s*** she has her little ways; ***tener manía a alguien*** F have it in for s.o. F
maniaco *m* maniac
maniatar ⟨1a⟩ *v/t*: ***maniatar a alguien*** tie s.o.'s hands
maniático *adj* F fussy
manicomio *m* lunatic asylum
manicura *f* manicure; ***hacerse la manicura*** have a manicure
manido *adj fig* clichéd, done to death F
manifestación *f de gente* demonstration; (*muestra*) show; (*declaración*) statement
manifestante *m/f* demonstrator
manifestar ⟨1k⟩ **1** *v/t* (*demostrar*) show; (*declarar*) declare, state **2** *v/r* **manifestarse** demonstrate
manifiesto 1 *adj* clear, manifest; ***poner***

de manifiesto make clear **2** *m* manifesto
manigua *f W.I.* thicket, bush
manija *f L.Am.* (*asa*) handle
manillar *m* handlebars *pl*
maniobra *f* maneuver, *Br* manoeuvre; ***hacer maniobras*** maneuver, *Br* manoeuvre
maniobrar ⟨1a⟩ *v/i* maneuver, *Br* manoeuvre
manipulación *f* manipulation; (*manejo*) handling
manipular ⟨1a⟩ *v/t* manipulate; (*manejar*) handle
maniquí 1 *m* dummy **2** *m/f* model
manirroto 1 *adj* extravagant **2** *m*, **-a** *f* spendthrift
manisero *m*, **-a** *f W.I., S. Am.* peanut seller
manitas *fpl*: ***ser un manitas*** be handy
manito *m Méx* pal, buddy
manivela *f* handle
manjar *m* delicacy
mano 1 *f* hand; ***mano de obra*** labo(u)r, manpower; ***mano de pintura*** coat of paint; ***¡manos arriba!*** hands up!; ***a mano derecha / izquierda*** on the right/left; ***atar las manos a alguien*** *fig* tie s.o.'s hands; ***de segunda mano*** second-hand; ***echar una mano a alguien*** give s.o. a hand; ***estar a manos*** *L.Am.* F be even, be quits; ***hecho a mano*** handmade; ***poner la mano en el fuego*** *fig* swear to it; ***poner manos a la obra*** get down to work; ***se le fue la mano con*** *fig* he overdid it with; ***tener a mano*** have to hand; ***traerse algo entre manos*** be plotting sth **2** *m Méx* F pal F, buddy F
manojo *m* handful; ***manojo de llaves*** bunch of keys; ***manojo de nervios*** *fig* bundle of nerves
manopla *f* mitten
manosear ⟨1a⟩ *v/t fruta* handle; *persona* F grope F
manotazo *m* slap
manotear ⟨1a⟩ **1** *v/t Arg, Méx* grab **2** *v/i Arg, Méx* wave one's hands around
mansalva *f*: ***a mansalva*** in vast numbers; *bebida, comida* in vast amounts
mansedumbre *f* docility; *de persona* mildness
mansión *f* mansion
manso *adj* docile; *persona* mild
manta *f* blanket; ***tirar de la manta*** *fig* uncover the truth
manteca *f* fat; *Rpl* butter; ***manteca de cacao*** cocoa butter; ***manteca de cerdo*** lard
mantel *m* tablecloth; ***mantel individual*** table mat
mantelería *f* table linen; ***una mantelería*** a set of table linen
mantención *f L.Am.* → ***manutención***
mantener ⟨2l⟩ **1** *v/t* (*sujetar*) hold; *techo etc* hold up; (*preservar*) keep; *conversación, relación* have; *económicamente* support; (*afirmar*) maintain **2** *v/r* **mantenerse** (*sujetarse*) be held; *económicamente* support o.s.; *en forma* keep
mantenimiento *m* maintenance; *económico* support; ***gimnasia de mantenimiento*** gym
mantequilla *f* butter
mantequillera *f L.Am.* butter dish
mantilla *f de bebé* shawl; ***estar en mantillas*** *fig* F be in its infancy
mantuvo *vb* → ***mantener***
manual *m/adj* manual
manualidades *fpl* handicrafts
manubrio *m* handle; *S. Am.* handlebars *pl*
manufacturar ⟨1a⟩ *v/t* manufacture
manuscrito 1 *adj* handwritten **2** *m* manuscript
manutención *f* maintenance
manzana *f* apple; *de casas* block; ***manzana de la discordia*** *fig* bone of contention
manzanilla *f* camomile tea
manzano *m* apple tree
maña *f* skill; ***darse*** *or* ***tener maña para*** be good at; ***tiene muchas mañas*** *L.Am.* she's got lots of tricks up her sleeve F
mañana 1 *f* morning; ***por la mañana*** in the morning; ***mañana por la mañana*** tomorrow morning; ***de la mañana a la noche*** from morning until night; ***de la noche a la mañana*** *fig* overnight; ***esta mañana*** this morning; ***muy de mañana*** very early (in the morning) **2** *adv* tomorrow; ***pasado mañana*** the day after tomorrow
mañanita *f* shawl
mañero *adj Rpl* (*animal*: *terco*) stubborn; (*nervioso*) skittish, nervous
mañoso *adj* skil(l)ful; *L.Am. animal* stubborn
mapa *m* map; ***mapa de carreteras*** road map
mapache *m* raccoon
mapamundi *m* map of the world
maqueta *f* model
maquillador *m*, **maquilladora** *f* make-up artist
maquillaje *m* make-up
maquillar ⟨1a⟩ **1** *v/t* make up **2** *v/r* **maquillarse** put on one's make-up
máquina *f* machine; FERR locomotive; *C.Am., W.I.* car; ***máquina de afeitar*** (electric) shaver; ***máquina de coser***

sewing machine; ***máquina de fotos*** camera; ***máquina recreativa*** arcade game; ***pasar algo a máquina*** type sth; ***a toda máquina*** at top speed
maquinaciones *fpl* scheming *sg*
maquinador 1 *adj* scheming **2** *m*, **maquinadora** *f* schemer
maquinal *adj fig* mechanical
maquinar ⟨1a⟩ *v/t* plot
maquinaria *f* machinery
maquinilla *f*: ***maquinilla de afeitar*** razor; ***maquinilla eléctrica*** electric razor
maquinista *m/f* FERR engineer, *Br* train driver
mar *m* (*also f*) GEOG sea; ***sudaba a mares*** *fig* F the sweat was pouring off him F; ***llover a mares*** *fig* F pour, bucket down F; ***alta mar*** high seas *pl*; ***la mar de bien*** (*muy bien*) really well
maraca *f* MÚS maraca
maraña *f de hilos* tangle; (*lío*) jumble
marasmo *m fig* stagnation
maratón *m* (*also f*) marathon
maratoniano *adj* marathon *atr*
maravilla *f* marvel, wonder; BOT marigold; ***de maravilla*** marvellously, wonderfully; ***a las mil maravillas*** marvellously, wonderfully
maravillar ⟨1a⟩ **1** *v/t* amaze, astonish **2** *v/r* **maravillarse** be amazed *o* astonished (**de** at)
maravilloso *adj* marvellous, wonderful
marca *f* mark; COM brand; ***marca registrada*** registered trademark; ***de marca*** brand-name *atr*
marcador *m* DEP scoreboard
marcaje *m* DEP marking
marcapasos *m inv* MED pacemaker
marcar ⟨1g⟩ *v/t* mark; *núimero de teléfono* dial; *gol* score; *res* brand; *de termómetro, contador etc* read, register
marcha *f* (*salida*) departure; (*velocidad*) speed; (*avance*) progress; MIL march; AUTO gear; DEP walk; ***marcha atrás*** AUTO reverse (gear); ***a marchas forzadas*** *fig* flat out; ***a toda marcha*** at top speed; ***hacer algo sobre la marcha*** do sth as one goes along; ***ponerse en marcha*** get started, get going; ***tener mucha marcha*** F be very lively
marchante *m L.Am.* regular customer
marchar ⟨1a⟩ **1** *v/i* (*progresar*) go; (*funcionar*) work; (*caminar*) walk; MIL march **2** *v/r* **marcharse** leave, go
marchitarse ⟨1a⟩ *v/r* wilt
marcial *adj* martial; ***artes marciales*** martial arts
marciano *m* Martian
marco *m moneda* mark; *de cuadro, puerta* frame; *fig* framework
marea *f* tide; ***marea alta*** high tide; ***marea baja*** low tide; ***marea negra*** oil slick
mareado *adj* dizzy
marear ⟨1a⟩ **1** *v/t* make feel nauseous, *Br* make feel sick; *fig* (*confundir*) confuse **2** *v/r* **marearse** feel nauseous, *Br* feel sick
marejada *f* heavy sea
maremoto *m* tidal wave
mareo *m* seasickness
marfil *m* ivory
margarina *f* margarine
margarita *f* BOT daisy
margen *m tb fig* margin; ***al margen de eso*** apart from that; ***mantenerse al margen*** keep out
marginación *f* marginalization
marginal *adj* marginal
marginar ⟨1a⟩ *v/t* marginalize
mariachi 1 *m* mariachi band **2** *m/f* mariachi player
marica *m* F fag P, *Br* poof P
maricón *m* P fag P, *Br* poof P
marido *m* husband
marihuana *f* marijuana
marimacho *m* F butch woman
marimba *f Rpl* MÚS marimba
marina *f* navy; ***marina mercante*** merchant navy
marinar ⟨1a⟩ *v/t* GASTR marinade
marinero 1 *adj* sea *atr* **2** *m* sailor
marino 1 *adj brisa* sea *atr*; *planta, animal* marine; ***azul marino*** navy blue **2** *m* sailor
marioneta *f tb fig* puppet
mariposa *f* butterfly
mariquita *f* ladybug, *Br* ladybird
marisco *m* seafood
marisma *f* salt marsh
marítimo *adj* maritime
marketing *m* marketing
marmita *f* pot, pan
mármol *m* marble
marmota *f*: ***dormir como una marmota*** F sleep like a log
marqués *m* marquis
marquesa *f* marchioness
marquesina *f* marquee, *Br* canopy
marranada *f* F dirty trick
marrano 1 *adj* filthy **2** *m* hog, *Br* pig; F *persona* pig F
marras *adv*: ***el ordenador de marras*** the darned computer F
marrón *m/adj* brown
marroquinería *f* leather goods
Marruecos Morocco
marta *f* ZO marten
Marte *m* AST Mars
martes *m inv* Tuesday

martillero *m S. Am.* auctioneer
martillo *m* hammer; ***martillo neumático*** pneumatic drill
martín *m*: ***martín pescador*** zo kingfisher
mártir *m/f* martyr
martirio *m tb fig* martyrdom
martirizar ⟨1f⟩ *v/t tb fig* martyr
marzo *m* March
mas *conj* but
más 1 *adj* more **2** *adv comp* more; *sup* most; MAT plus; ***más grande / pequeño*** bigger / smaller; ***el más grande / pequeño*** the largest / smallest; ***trabajar más*** work harder; ***más bien*** rather; ***más que, más de lo que*** more than; ***más o menos*** more or less; ***¿qué más?*** what else?; ***no más*** *L.Am.* → ***nomás***; ***por más que*** however much; ***sin más*** without more ado; ***más lejos*** further
masa *f* mass; GASTR dough; ***pillar a alguien con las manos en la masa*** F catch s.o. red-handed
masacrar ⟨1a⟩ *v/t* massacre
masacre *f* massacre
masaje *m* massage
masajista *m/f* masseur; *mujer* masseuse
mascar ⟨1g⟩ **1** *v/t* chew **2** *v/i L.Am.* chew tobacco
máscara *f* mask
mascarilla *f* mask; *cosmética* face pack
mascota *f* mascot; *animal doméstico* pet
masculino *adj* masculine
mascullar ⟨1a⟩ *v/t* mutter
masificación *f* overcrowding
masilla *f* putty
masita *f L.Am. small sweet cake or bun*
masivo *adj* massive
masón *m* mason
masoquismo *m* masochism
masoquista 1 *adj* masochistic **2** *m/f* masochist
máster *m* master's (degree)
masticación *f* chewing
masticar ⟨1g⟩ *v/t* chew
mástil *m* mast; *de tienda* pole
mastín *m* zo mastiff
mastodóntico *adj* colossal, enormous
mastuerzo *m* BOT cress
masturbarse ⟨1a⟩ *v/r* masturbate
mata *f* bush
matadero *m* slaughterhouse
matador *m* TAUR matador
matanza *f de animales* slaughter; *de gente* slaughter, massacre
matar ⟨1a⟩ **1** *v/t* kill; *ganado* slaughter **2** *v/r* **matarse** kill o.s.; *morir* be killed; ***matarse a trabajar*** work o.s. to death
matarratas *m* rat poison
matasanos *m/f inv* F quack F
matasellos *m inv* postmark
mate 1 *adj* matt **2** *m en ajedrez* mate; *L.Am.* (*infusión*) maté
matear ⟨1a⟩ **1** *v/t CSur* checkmate **2** *v/i L.Am.* drink maté
matemáticas *fpl* mathematics
matemático 1 *adj* mathematical **2** *m*, **-a** *f* mathematician
materia *f* matter; (*material*) material; (*tema*) subject; ***materia prima*** raw material; ***en materia de*** as regards
material *m/adj* material
materialismo *m* materialism
materializar ⟨1f⟩ *v/t*: ***materializar algo*** make sth a reality
maternal *adj* maternal
matero *m*, **-a** *f L.Am.* maté drinker
matinal *adj* morning *atr*
matiz *m de ironía* touch; *de color* shade
matizar ⟨1f⟩ *v/t comentarios* qualify
matón *m* bully; (*criminal*) thug
matorral *m* thicket
matrícula *f* AUTO license plate, *Br* numberplate; EDU enrol(l)ment, registration
matricular ⟨1a⟩ **1** *v/t* register **2** *v/r* **matricularse** EDU enrol(l), register
matrimonial *adj* marriage *atr*, marital
matrimonio *m* marriage; *boda* wedding
matriz *f* matrix; ANAT womb
matrona *f* (*comadrona*) midwife
matutino *adj* morning *atr*
maullar ⟨1a⟩ *v/i* miaow
maullido *m* miaow
mausoleo *m* mausoleum
máxima *f* maxim
máxime *adv* especially
máximo *adj* maximum
mayo *m* May
mayonesa *f* GASTR mayonnaise
mayor 1 *adj comp*: *en tamaño* larger, bigger; *en edad* older; *en importancia* greater; ***ser mayor de edad*** be an adult; ***al por mayor*** COM wholesale **2** *adj sup*: ***el mayor*** *en edad* the oldest *o* eldest; *en tamaño* the largest *o* biggest; *en importancia* the greatest; ***los mayores*** adults; ***la mayor parte*** the majority
mayordomo *m* butler
mayoreo *m*: ***vender al mayoreo*** *Méx* sell wholesale
mayoría *f* majority; ***alcanzar la mayoría de edad*** come of age; ***la mayoría de*** the majority of, most (of); ***en la mayoría de los casos*** in the majority of cases, in most cases
mayorista *m/f* wholesaler
mayoritario *adj* majority *atr*
mayúscula *f* capital (letter), upper case letter

M

mazamorra *f S. Am. kind of porridge made from corn*
mazapán *m* marzipan
mazmorra *f* dungeon
mazo *m* mallet
mazorca *f* cob
me *pron pers complemento directo* me; *complemento indirecto* (to) me; *reflexivo* myself; ***me dio el libro*** he gave me the book, he gave the book to me
mear ⟨1a⟩ F **1** *v/i* pee F **2** *v/r* **mearse** pee o.s. F; ***mearse de risa*** wet o.s. (laughing) F
meca *f fig* mecca
mecachis *int* F blast! F
mecánica *f* mechanics
mecánico 1 *adj* mechanical **2** *m*, **-a** *f* mechanic
mecanismo *m* mechanism
mecanizar ⟨1f⟩ *v/t* mechanize
mecanógrafo *m*, **-a** *f* typist
mecanografiar ⟨1c⟩ *v/t* type
mecate *m Méx* string, cord
mecedora *f* rocking chair
mecenas *m inv* patron, sponsor
mecer ⟨2b⟩ **1** *v/t* rock **2** *v/r* **mecerse** rock
mecha *f* wick; *de explosivo* fuse; *del pelo* highlight; *Méx* F fear
mechero *m* cigarette lighter
mechón *m de pelo* lock
medalla *f* medal
medallista *m/f* medal(l)list
media *f* stocking; ***medias*** *pl* pantyhose *pl*, *Br* tights *pl*
mediación *f* mediation
mediado *adj*: ***a mediados de junio*** in mid-June, halfway through June
mediador *m*, **mediadora** *f* mediator
mediana *f* AUTO median strip, *Br* central reservation
mediano *adj* medium, average
medianoche *f* midnight
mediante *prp* by means of
mediar ⟨1b⟩ *v/i* mediate
mediático *adj* media *atr*
medicación *f* medication
medicamento *m* medicine, drug
medicina *f* medicine
medicinal *adj* medicinal
médico 1 *adj* medical **2** *m/f* doctor; ***médico de cabecera*** *or* ***de familia*** family physician, *Br* GP, *Br* general practitioner; ***médico de urgencia*** emergency doctor
medida *f* measure; *acto* measurement; (*grado*) extent; ***hecho a medida*** made to measure; ***a medida que*** as; ***tomar medidas*** *fig* take measures *o* steps
medidor *m S. Am.* meter
medieval *adj* medi(a)eval
medio 1 *adj* half; *tamaño* medium; (*de promedio*) average; ***las tres y -a*** half past three, three-thirty **2** *m* environment; (*centro*) middle; (*manera*) means; ***medio ambiente*** environment; ***por medio de*** by means of; ***en medio de*** in the middle of; ***medios*** *dinero* means, resources; ***medios de comunicación*** *or* ***de información*** (mass) media; ***medios de transporte*** means of transport **3** *adv* half; ***hacer algo a -as*** half do sth; ***ir a -as*** go halves; ***día por medio*** *L.Am.* every other day; ***quitar de en medio algo*** F move sth out of the way
medioambiental *adj* environmental
mediocre *adj* mediocre
mediodía *m* midday; ***a mediodía*** (*a las doce*) at noon, at twelve o'clock; (*a la hora de comer*) at lunchtime
medir ⟨3l⟩ **1** *v/t* measure **2** *v/i*: ***mide 2 metros de ancho / largo / alto*** it's 2 meters (*o Br* metres) wide / long / tall
meditación *f* meditation
meditar ⟨1a⟩ **1** *v/t* ponder **2** *v/i* meditate
Mediterráneo *m/adj*: (***mar***) ***Mediterráneo*** Mediterranean (Sea)
médium *m/f* medium
médula *f* marrow; ***médula espinal*** spinal cord; ***hasta la médula*** *fig* through and through, to the core
medusa *f* ZO jellyfish
megafonía *f* public-address *o* PA system
megáfono *m* bullhorn, *Br* loud-hailer
megalomanía *f* megalomania
mejicano 1 *adj* Mexican **2** *m*, **-a** *f* Mexican
Méjico Mexico; *Méx DF* Mexico City
mejilla *f* cheek
mejillón *m* ZO mussel
mejor *adj comp* better; ***el mejor*** *sup* the best; ***lo mejor*** the best thing; ***lo mejor posible*** as well as possible; ***a lo mejor*** perhaps, maybe; ***tanto mejor*** all the better
mejora *f* improvement
mejorana *f* BOT marjoram
mejorar ⟨1a⟩ **1** *v/t* improve **2** *v/i* improve; ***¡que te mejores!*** get well soon!
mejoría *f* improvement
mejunje *m desp* concoction
melancolía *f* melancholy
melancólico *adj* gloomy, melancholic
melena *f* long hair; *de león* mane
melindroso *adj* affected
mella *f*: ***hacer mella en alguien*** have an effect on s.o., affect s.o.
mellado *adj* gap-toothed
mellizo 1 *adj* twin *atr* **2** *m*, **-a** *f* twin
melocotón *m* peach

melocotonero *m* peach tree
melodía *f* melody
melodrama *m* melodrama
melón *m* melon
membrana *f* membrane
membrillo *m* quince; ***dulce de membrillo*** quince jelly
memela *f Méx* corn tortilla
memo 1 *adj* F dumb F **2** *m*, **-a** *f* F idiot
memorable *adj* memorable
memoria *f tb* INFOR memory; (*informe*) report; ***de memoria*** by heart; ***memorias*** (*biografía*) memoirs
memorizar ⟨1f⟩ *v/t* memorize
mención *f*: ***hacer mención de*** mention
mencionar ⟨1a⟩ *v/t* mention
mendigar ⟨1h⟩ *v/t* beg for
mendigo *m* beggar
menear ⟨1a⟩ **1** *v/t* shake; *las caderas* sway; ***menear la cola*** wag its tail **2** *v/r* **menearse** fidget
menestra *f* vegetable stew
mengano *m*, **-a** *f* F so-and-so F
menguante *adj* decreasing, diminishing; *luna* waning
menguar ⟨1i⟩ *v/i* decrease, diminish; *de la luna* wane
meningitis *f* MED meningitis
menopausia *f* MED menopause
menor *adj comp* less; *en tamaño* smaller; *en edad* younger; ***ser menor de edad*** be a minor; ***al por menor*** COM retail; ***el menor*** *sup*: *en tamaño* the smallest; *en edad* the youngest; ***el número menor*** the lowest number
menos 1 *adj en cantidad* less; *en número* fewer **2** *adv comp en cantidad* less; *sup en cantidad* least; MAT minus; ***es menos guapa que Ana*** she is not as pretty as Ana; ***tres menos dos*** three minus two; ***a menos que*** unless; ***al menos, por lo menos*** at least; ***echar de menos*** miss; ***eso es lo de menos*** that's the least of it; ***ni mucho menos*** far from it; ***son las dos menos diez*** it's ten of two, it's ten to two
menoscabar ⟨1a⟩ *v/t autoridad* diminish; (*dañar*) harm
menospreciar ⟨1b⟩ *v/t* underestimate; (*desdeñar*) look down on
mensaje *m* message
mensajero *m* courrier
menstruación *f* menstruation
menstruar ⟨1h⟩ *v/i* menstruate
mensual *adj* monthly
mensualidad *f* monthly instal(l)ment, monthly payment
mensualmente *adv* monthly
menta *f* BOT mint
mental *adj* mental
mentalidad *f* mentality
mentalizar ⟨1f⟩ **1** *v/t*: ***mentalizar a alguien*** make s.o. aware **2** *v/r* **mentalizarse** mentally prepare o.s.
mente *f* mind
mentecato 1 *adj* F dim F **2** *m* F fool
mentir ⟨3i⟩ *v/i* lie
mentira *f* lie
mentiroso 1 *adj*: ***ser muy mentiroso*** tell a lot of lies **2** *m*, **-a** *f* liar
mentón *m* chin
mentor *m* mentor
menú *m tb* INFOR menu; ***menú de ayuda*** help menu
menudencias *fpl Méx* giblets
menudeo *m L.Am.* retail trade
menudo 1 *adj* small; ***¡-a suerte!*** *fig* F lucky devil!; ***¡-as vacaciones!*** *irón* F some vacation!; ***a menudo*** often **2** *m L.Am.* small change; ***menudos*** GASTR giblets
meñique *m/adj*: (***dedo***) ***meñique*** little finger
meollo *m fig* heart
mercader *m* trader
mercadería *f L.Am.* merchandise
mercadillo *m* street market
mercado *m* market; ***Mercado Común*** Common Market; ***mercado negro*** black market
mercadotecnia *f* marketing
mercancía *f* merchandise
mercantil *adj* commercial
merced *f*: ***estar a merced de alguien*** be at s.o.'s mercy
mercenario *m/adj* mercenary
mercería *f* notions *pl*, *Br* haberdashery
MERCOSUR *abr* (***= Mercado Común del Sur***) *Common Market including Argentina, Brazil, Paraguay and Uruguay*
mercurio *m* mercury
merecer ⟨2d⟩ *v/t* deserve; ***no merecer la pena*** it's not worth it
merecido *m* just deserts *pl*
merendar ⟨1k⟩ **1** *v/t*: ***merendar algo*** have sth as an afternoon snack **2** *v/i* have an afternoon snack
merengue *m* GASTR meringue
meridiano *m/f* meridian
meridional 1 *adj* southern **2** *m* southerner
merienda *f* afternoon snack
mérito *m* merit
merluza *f* ZO hake; ***agarrar una merluza*** *fig* F get plastered F
mermar ⟨1a⟩ **1** *v/t* reduce **2** *v/i* diminish
mermelada *f* jam
mero 1 *adj* mere; ***el mero jefe*** *Méx* F the big boss **2** *m* ZO grouper

merodear ⟨1a⟩ *v/i* loiter
mes *m* month
mesa *f* table; ***mesa redonda*** *fig* round table; ***poner / quitar la mesa*** set / clear the table
mesera *f L.Am.* waitress
mesero *m L.Am.* waiter
meseta *f* plateau
mesilla, **mesita** *f*: ***mesilla*** (***de noche***) night stand, *Br* bedside table
mesón *m traditional restaurant decorated in rustic style*
mestizo *m* person of mixed race
mesura *f*: ***con mesura*** in moderation
meta *f en fúítbol* goal; *en carrera* finishing line; *fig* (*objetivo*) goal, objective
metabolismo *m* metabolism
metafísica *f* metaphysics
metáfora *f* metaphor
metal *m* metal
metálico 1 *adj* metallic **2** *m*: ***en metálico*** (in) cash
metalúírgico *adj* metallurgical
metamorfosis *f inv* transformation, metamorphosis
metedura *f*: ***metedura de pata*** F blunder
meteorito *m* meteorite
meteorológico *adj* weather *atr*, meteorological; ***pronóstico meteorológico*** weather forecast
meteorólogo *m*, **-a** *f* meteorologist
meter ⟨2a⟩ **1** *v/t gen* put (***en*** in, into); (*involucrar*) involve (***en*** in); ***meter a alguien en un lío*** get s.o. into a mess **2** *v/r* **meterse**: ***meterse en algo*** get into sth; (*involucrarse*) get involved in sth, get mixed up in sth; ***meterse con alguien*** pick on s.o.; ***meterse de administrativo*** get a job in admin; ***¿dónde se ha metido?*** where has he got to?
meticuloso *adj* meticulous
metido *adj* involved; *L.Am.* F nosy F; ***estar muy metido en algo*** be very involved in sth
metódico *adj* methodical
método *m* method
metomentodo *m/f* F busybody F
metralleta *f* sub-machine gun
métrico *adj* metric
metro *m medida* meter, *Br* metre; *para medir* rule; *transporte* subway, *Br* underground
metrópolis *f inv* metropolis
metropolitano *adj* metropolitan
mexicano 1 *adj* Mexican **2** *m*, **-a** Mexican
México Mexico; *Méx DF* Mexico City
mezcal *m Méx* mescal
mezcla *f sustancia* mixture; *de tabaco, café etc* blend; *acto* mixing; *de tabaco, café etc* blending
mezclar ⟨1a⟩ **1** *v/t* mix; *tabaco, café etc* blend; ***mezclar a alguien en algo*** get s.o. mixed up *o* involved in sth **2** *v/r* **mezclarse** mix; ***mezclarse en algo*** get mixed up *o* involved in sth
mezquinar ⟨1a⟩ *v/t L.Am.* skimp on
mezquino *adj* mean
mezquita *f* mosque
mg. *abr* (***= miligramo***) mg (= milligram)
mi, **mis** *adj pos* my
mí *pron* me; *reflexivo* myself; ***¿y a mí qué?*** so what?, what's it to me?
michelín *m* F spare tire, *Br* spare tyre
mico *m* zo monkey
micro *m or f Chi* bus
microbio *m* microbe
microbúís *m* minibus
microchip *m* (micro)chip
microfilm(e) *m* microfilm
micrófono *m* microphone; ***micrófono oculto*** bug
microondas *m inv* microwave
microordenador *m* microcomputer
microprocesador *m* microprocessor
microscópico *adj* microscopic
microscopio *m* microscope
mide *vb* → ***medir***
miedo *m* fear (***a*** of); ***dar miedo*** be frightening; ***me da miedo la oscuridad*** I'm frightened of the dark; ***tener miedo de que*** be afraid that; ***por miedo a*** for fear of; ***de miedo*** F great F, awesome F
miedoso *adj* timid; ***¡no seas tan miedoso!*** don't be scared!
miel *f* honey
miembro *m* member; (*extremidad*) limb, member *fml*
mientras 1 *conj* while; ***mientras que*** whereas **2** *adv*: ***mientras tanto*** in the meantime, meanwhile
miércoles *m inv* Wednesday
mierda *f* P shit P, crap P; ***una mierda de película*** a crap movie P; ***¡una mierda!*** no way! F
miga *f de pan* crumb; ***migas*** crumbs; ***hacer buenas / malas migas*** *fig* F get on well / badly
migraña *f* MED migraine
migratorio *adj* migratory
mijo *m* BOT millet
mil *adj* thousand
milagro *m* miracle; ***de milagro*** miraculously, by a miracle
milagroso *adj* miraculous
milano *m* zo kite
milenio *m* millennium
mili *f* F military service
milicia *f* militia

M

milico *m S. Am. desp* soldier
milímetro *m* millimeter, *Br* millimetre
militante *m/f & adj* militant
militar 1 *adj* military **2** *m* soldier; ***los militares*** the military **3** ⟨1a⟩ *v/i* POL: ***militar en*** be a member of
milla *f* mile
millar *m* thousand
millón *m* million; (*mil millones*) billion
millonario *m* millionaire
milpa *f Méx, C.Am.* corn, *Br* maize; *terreno* cornfield, *Br* field of maize
mimar ⟨1a⟩ *v/t* spoil, pamper
mimbre *m* BOT willow; ***muebles*** *pl* ***de mimbre*** wicker furniture *sg*
mímica *f* mime
mimo *m* TEA mime
mimosa *f* BOT mimosa
mimoso *adj*: ***ser mimoso*** be cuddly
mina *f* MIN mine; *Rpl* F broad F, *Br* bird F; ***mina antipersonal*** MIL antipersonnel mine
minar ⟨1a⟩ *v/t* mine; *fig* undermine
mineral *m/adj* mineral
minería *f* mining
minero 1 *adj* mining **2** *m* miner
miniatura *f* miniature
minifalda *f* miniskirt
minimizar ⟨1f⟩ *v/t* minimize
mínimo 1 *adj* minimum; ***como mínimo*** at the very least **2** *m* minimum
minino *m* F puss F, pussy (cat) F
ministerio *m* POL department; ***ministerio de Asuntos Exteriores***, *L.Am.* ***ministerio de Relaciones Exteriores*** State Department, *Br* Foreign Office; ***ministerio de Hacienda*** Treasury Department, *Br* Treasury; ***ministerio del Interior*** Department of the Interior, *Br* Home Office
ministro *m*, **-a** *f* minister; ***ministro del Interior*** Secretary of the Interior, *Br* Home Secretary; ***primer ministro*** Prime Minister
minoría *f* minority
minorista COM **1** *adj* retail *atr* **2** *m/f* retailer
minoritario *adj* minority *atr*
mintió *vb* → ***mentir***
minucia *f* minor detail
minucioso *adj* meticulous, thorough
minúíscula *f* small letter, lower case letter
minúísculo *adj* tiny, minute
minusvalía *f* disability
minusválido 1 *adj* disabled **2** *m*, **-a** *f* disabled person; ***los minusválidos*** the disabled
minutero *m* minute hand
minuto *m* minute
mío, mía *pron* mine; ***el mío / la -a*** mine
miope *adj* near-sighted, short-sighted
miopía *f* near-sightedness, short-sightedness
mira *f*: ***con miras a*** with a view to
mirada *f* look; ***echar una mirada*** take a look (***a*** at)
mirador *m* viewpoint
mirar ⟨1a⟩ **1** *v/t* look at; (*observar*) watch; *L.Am.* (*ver*) see; ***¿qué miras desde aquí?*** what can you see from here? **2** *v/i* look; ***mirar al norte*** *de una ventana etc* face north; ***mirar por la ventana*** look out of the window
mirilla *f* spyhole
mirlo *m* ZO blackbird
misa *f* REL mass
misántropo *m* misanthropist
miserable *adj* wretched
miseria *f* poverty; *fig* misery
misericordia *f* mercy, compassion
mísero *adj* wretched; *sueldo* miserable
misil *m* missile
misión *f* mission
misionero *m*, **-a** *f* missionary
mismo 1 *adj* same; ***lo mismo que*** the same as; ***yo mismo*** I myself; ***da lo mismo*** it doesn't matter, it's all the same; ***me da lo mismo*** I don't care, it's all the same to me **2** *adv*: ***aquí mismo*** right here; ***ahora mismo*** right now, this very minute
misógino *adj* misogynistic
misterio *m* mystery
misterioso *adj* mysterious
místico *adj* mystic(al)
mitad *f* half; ***a mitad del camino*** halfway; ***a mitad de la película*** halfway through the movie; ***a mitad de precio*** half-price
mítico *adj* mythical
mitigar ⟨1h⟩ *v/t* mitigate; *ansiedad, dolor etc* ease
mitin *m* POL meeting
mito *m* myth
mitología *f* mythology
mixto *adj* mixed; *comisión* joint
mm. *abr* (***= milímetro***) mm (= millimeter)
mobiliario *m* furniture
mochila *f* backpack
mochilero *m*, **-a** *f* backpacker
mochuelo *m* ZO little owl
moción *f* POL motion; ***moción de confianza / censura*** vote of confidence / no confidence
moco *m*: ***tener mocos*** have a runny nose
mocoso *m*, **-a** *f* F snotty-nosed kid F
moda *f* fashion; ***de moda*** fashionable, in fashion; ***estar pasado de moda*** be out of fashion
modales *mpl* manners

M

modalidad *f* form; DEP discipline; ***modalidad de pago*** method of payment
modelar ⟨1a⟩ *v/t* model
modelismo *m* model making
modelo 1 *m* model **2** *m/f persona* model
módem *m* INFOR modem
moderado 1 *adj* moderate **2** *m*, **-a** *f* moderate
moderador *m*, **moderadora** *f* TV presenter
moderar ⟨1a⟩ **1** *v/t* moderate; *impulsos* control, restrain; *velocidad, gastos* reduce; *debate* chair **2** *v/r* **moderarse** control o.s., restrain o.s.
modernización *f* modernization
modernizar ⟨1f⟩ *v/t* modernize
moderno *adj* modern
modestia *f* modesty; ***modestia aparte*** though I say so myself
modesto *adj* modest
módico *adj precio* reasonable
modificación *f* modification
modificar ⟨1g⟩ *v/t* modify
modista *m/f* dressmaker; *diseñador* fashion designer
modo *m* way; ***a modo de*** as; ***de modo que*** so that; ***de ningúín modo*** not at all; ***en cierto modo*** in a way *o* sense; ***de todos modos*** anyway
modorra *f* drowsiness
módulo *m* module
mofarse ⟨1a⟩ *v/r*: ***mofarse de*** make fun of
mofeta *f* ZO skunk
mofletes *mpl* chubby cheeks
mogollón *m* F (*discusión*) argument; ***mogollón de*** F loads of F
moho *m* mo(u)ld
moisés *m inv* Moses basket
mojado *adj* (*húímedo*) damp, moist; (*empapado*) wet
mojar ⟨1a⟩ **1** *v/t* (*humedecer*) dampen, moisten; (*empapar*) wet; *galleta* dunk, dip **2** *v/r* **mojarse** get wet
mojigato 1 *adj* prudish **2** *m*, **-a** *f* prude
mojón *m tb fig* milestone
molar ⟨2h⟩ **1** *v/t*: ***me mola ese tío*** P I like the guy a lot **2** *v/i* P be cool F
molcajete *m Méx, C.Am.* (*mortero*) grinding stone
molde *m* mo(u)ld; *para bizcocho* (cake) tin; ***romper moldes*** *fig* break the mo(u)ld
moldear ⟨1a⟩ *v/t* mo(u)ld
moldura *f* ARQUI mo(u)lding
mole 1 *f* mass **2** *m Méx* mole (*spicy sauce made with chilies and tomatoes*)
molécula *f* molecule
moler ⟨2h⟩ *v/t* grind; *fruta* mash; ***carne molida*** ground meat, *Br* mince; ***moler a alguien a palos*** *fig* beat s.o. to a pulp
molestar ⟨1a⟩ **1** *v/t* bother, annoy; (*doler*) trouble; ***no molestar*** do not disturb **2** *v/r* **molestarse** get upset; (*ofenderse*) take offense (*Br* offence); (*enojarse*) get annoyed; ***molestar en hacer algo*** take the trouble to do sth
molestia *f* nuisance; ***molestias*** *pl* MED discomfort *sg*
molesto *adj* annoying; (*incómodo*) inconvenient
molestoso *adj L.Am.* annoying
molido *adj* F bushed F
molinillo *m*: ***molinillo de café*** coffee grinder *o* mill
molino *m* mill; ***molino de viento*** windmill
mollera *f* F head; ***duro de mollera*** F pigheaded F
molusco *m* ZO mollusk, *Br* mollusc
momento *m* moment; ***al momento*** at once; ***por el momento, de momento*** for the moment
momia *f* mummy
momificar ⟨1g⟩ *v/t* mummify
monada *f*: ***su hija es una monada*** her daughter is lovely; ***¡qué monada!*** how lovely!
monaguillo *m* altar boy
monarca *m* monarch
monarquía *f* monarchy
monasterio *m* monastery
mondadientes *m inv* toothpick
mondar ⟨1a⟩ **1** *v/t* peel; *árbol* prune **2** *v/r* **mondarse**: ***mondarse de risa*** F split one's sides laughing
mondongo *m* tripe
moneda *f* coin; (*divisa*) currency
monedero *m* change purse, *Br* purse
monetario *adj* monetary
monigote *m* rag doll; F (*tonto*) idiot
monitor[1] *m* TV, INFOR monitor
monitor[2] *m*, **monitora** *f* (*profesor*) instructor
monja *f* nun
monje *m* monk
mono 1 *m* ZO monkey; *prenda* coveralls *pl*, *Br* boilersuit **2** *adj* pretty, cute
monógamo *adj* monogamous
monólogo *m* monolog(ue)
monopatín *m* skateboard
monopolio *m* monopoly
monopolizar ⟨1f⟩ *v/t tb fig* monopolize
monosílabo *adj* monosyllabic
monotonía *f* monotony
monótono *adj* monotonous
monovolumen *m* AUTO minivan, *Br* people carrier, MPV

monsergas *fpl*: ***déjate de monsergas*** F stop going on F
monstruo *m* monster; (*fenómeno*) phenomenon
monstruosidad *f* eyesore, monstrosity
monstruoso *adj* monstrous
monta *f*: ***de poca monta*** unimportant
montacargas *m inv* hoist
montada *f L.Am.* mounted police
montaje *m* TÉC assembly; *de película* editing; TEA staging; *fig* F con F
montante *m* COM total
montaña *f* mountain; ***montaña rusa*** rollercoaster
montañero *m*, **-a** *f* mountaineer
montañismo *m* mountaineering
montañoso *adj* mountainous
montaplatos *m inv* dumb waiter
montar ⟨1a⟩ **1** *v/t* TÉC assemble; *tienda* put up; *negocio* set up; *película* edit; *caballo* mount; ***montar la guardia*** mount guard **2** *v/i*: ***montar en bicicleta*** ride a bicycle; ***montar a caballo*** ride a horse
monte *m* mountain; (*bosque*) woodland
montículo *m* mound
montón *m* pile, heap; ***ser del montón*** *fig* be average, not stand out; ***montones de*** F piles of F, loads of F

M

montura *f de gafas* frame
monumento *m* monument
moño *m* bun
moqueta *f* (wall-to-wall) carpet
mora *f* BOT *de zarza* blackberry; *de morera* mulberry
morada *f* dwelling
morado *adj* purple; ***pasarlas -as*** F have a rough time
moral 1 *adj* moral **2** *f* (*moralidad*) morals *pl*; (*ánimo*) morale
moraleja *f* moral
moralidad *f* morality
moralista *m/f* moralist
moratón *m* bruise
moratoria *f* moratorium
morbo *m* F perverted kind of pleasure
morboso *adj* perverted
morcilla *f* blood sausage, *Br* black pudding
mordaz *adj* biting
mordaza *f* gag
morder ⟨2h⟩ *v/t* bite
mordida *f Méx* F bribe
mordisco *m* bite
mordisquear ⟨1a⟩ *v/t* nibble
morena *f* ZO moray eel
moreno *adj pelo*, *piel* dark; (*bronceado*) tanned
morera *f* BOT white mulberry tree
moretón *m L.Am.* bruise
morfina *f* morphine
morfología *f* morphology
moribundo *adj* dying
morir ⟨3k; *part* ***muerto***⟩ **1** *v/i* die (***de*** of); ***morir de hambre*** die of hunger, starve to death **2** *v/r* **morirse** die; ***morirse de*** *fig* die of; ***morirse por*** *fig* be dying for
morisco *adj* Moorish
mormón *m* Mormon
moro 1 *adj* North African **2** *m* North African; ***no hay moros en la costa*** F the coast is clear
morocho *adj S. Am. persona* dark
moronga *f C.Am.*, *Méx* blood sausage, *Br* black pudding
morralla *f Méx* small change
morriña *f* homesickness
morro *m* ZO snout; ***tener mucho morro*** F have a real nerve
morrongo *m* F pussycat F
morsa *f* ZO walrus
mortaja *f* shroud; *L.Am.* cigarette paper
mortal 1 *adj* mortal; *accidente*, *herida* fatal; *dosis* lethal **2** *m/f* mortal
mortalidad *f* mortality
mortalmente *adv* fatally
mortero *m tb* MIL mortar
mortífero *adj* lethal
mortificar ⟨1g⟩ **1** *v/t* torment **2** *v/r* **mortificarse** *fig* distress o.s.; *Méx* (*apenarse*) be embarrassed *o* ashamed
mosaico *m* mosaic
mosca *f* fly; ***por si las moscas*** F just to be on the safe side
moscada *adj*: ***nuez moscada*** nutmeg
moscardón *m* hornet
Moscúí Moscow
mosquear ⟨1a⟩ **1** *v/t Esp* F rile **2** *v/r* **mosquearse** F get hot under the collar F; (*sentir recelo*) smell a rat F
mosquitero *m* mosquito net
mosquito *m* mosquito
mostaza *f* mustard
mosto *m* grape juice
mostrador *m* counter; *en bar* bar; ***mostrador de facturación*** check-in desk
mostrar ⟨1m⟩ **1** *v/t* show **2** *v/r* **mostrarse**: ***mostrarse contento*** seem happy
mota *f* speck; *en diseño* dot
mote *m* nickname; *S. Am.* boiled corn *o Br* maize
motel *m* motel
motín *m* mutiny; *en una cárcel* riot
motivación *f* motivation
motivar ⟨1a⟩ *v/t* motivate
motivo *m* motive, reason; MÚS, PINT motif; ***con motivo de*** because of
moto *f* motorcycle, motorbike; ***moto acuática*** *or* ***de agua*** jet ski

motocicleta *f* motorcycle
motociclismo *m* motorcycle racing
motociclista *m/f* motorcyclist
motocross *m* motocross
motor *m* engine; *eléctrico* motor
motora *f* motorboat
motorista *m/f* motorcyclist
motosierra *f* chain saw
motriz *adj* motor
mover ⟨2h⟩ **1** *v/t* move; (*agitar*) shake; (*impulsar, incitar*) drive **2** *v/r* **moverse** move; ***¡muévete!*** get a move on! F, hurry up!
movida *f* F scene
móvil 1 *adj* mobile **2** *m* TELEC cellphone, *Br* mobile (phone)
movilidad *f* mobility
movilizar ⟨1f⟩ *v/t* mobilize
movimiento *m* movement; COM, *fig* activity
moza *f* girl; *camarera* waitress
mozo 1 *adj*: ***en mis años mozos*** in my youth **2** *m* boy; *camarero* waiter
mucama *f Rpl* maid
mucamo *m Rpl* servant
muchacha *f* girl
muchachada *f Arg* group of youngsters
muchacho *m* boy
muchedumbre *f* crowd
mucho 1 *adj cantidad* a lot of, lots of; *esp neg* much; ***no tengo mucho dinero*** I don't have much money; ***muchos*** a lot of, lots of, many; *esp neg* many; ***no tengo muchos amigos*** I don't have many friends; ***tengo mucho frío*** I am very cold; ***es mucho coche para mí*** it's too big a car for me **2** *adv* a lot; *esp neg* much; ***no me gustó mucho*** I didn't like it very much; ***¿dura / tarda mucho?*** does it last / take long?; ***como mucho*** at the most; ***ni mucho menos*** far from it; ***por mucho que*** however much **3** *pron* a lot, much; ***muchos*** a lot of people, many people
muda *f de ropa* change of clothes
mudanza *f de casa* move
mudarse ⟨1a⟩ *v/r*: ***mudarse de casa*** move house; ***mudarse de ropa*** change (one's clothes)
mudo *adj* mute; *letra* silent
mueble *m* piece of furniture
mueca *f de dolor* grimace; ***hacer muecas*** make faces
muela *f* tooth; ANAT molar; ***muela del juicio*** wisdom tooth
muelle *m* TÉC spring; MAR wharf
muérdago *m* BOT mistletoe
muerde *vb* → ***morder***
muere *vb* → ***morir***
muermo *m fig* F boredom; ***ser un muermo*** *fig* F be a drag F
muerte *f* death; ***de mala muerte*** *fig* F lousy F, awful F
muerto 1 *part* → ***morir*** **2** *adj* dead **3** *m*, **-a** *f* dead person
muestra *f* sample; (*señal*) sign; (*exposición*) show
muestrario *m* collection of samples
mueve *vb* → ***mover***
mugir ⟨3c⟩ *v/i* moo
mugre *f* filth
mugriento *adj* filthy
mugroso *adj* dirty
mujer *f* woman; (*esposa*) wife
mujeriego *m* womanizer
múíjol *m* ZO gray *o Br* grey mullet
mula *f* mule; *Méx* trash, *Br* rubbish
mulato *m* mulatto
muleta *f* crutch; TAUR cape
mullido *adj* soft
mullir ⟨3h⟩ *v/t almohada* plump up
multa *f* fine
multar ⟨1a⟩ *v/t* fine
multicine *m* multiscreen
multicolor *adj* multicolo(u)red
multilateral *adj* multilateral
multimedia *f/adj* multimedia
multimillonario *m* multimillionaire
multinacional *f* multinational
múíltiple *adj* multiple
multiplicación *f* multiplication
multiplicar ⟨1g⟩ **1** *v/t* multiply **2** *v/r* **multiplicarse** multiply
múíltiplo *m* MAT multiple
multipropiedad *f* timeshare
multitud *f* crowd; ***multitud de*** thousands of
multitudinario *adj* mass *atr*
multiuso *adj* multipurpose
mundano *adj* society *atr*; REL wordly
mundial 1 *adj* world *atr* **2** *m*: ***el mundial de fúítbol*** the World Cup
mundo *m* world; ***el otro mundo*** the next world; ***nada del otro mundo*** nothing out of the ordinary; ***todo el mundo*** everybody, everyone
munición *f* ammunition
municipal *adj* municipal
municipio *m* municipality
muñeca *f* doll; ANAT wrist
muñeco *m* doll; *fig* puppet; ***muñeco de nieve*** snowman
muñón *m* MED stump
mural 1 *adj* wall *atr* **2** *m* mural
muralla *f de ciudad* wall
murciélago *m* ZO bat
murga *f*: ***dar la murga a alguien*** F bug s.o. F

M

murió *vb* → ***morir***
murmullo *m* murmur
murmurar ⟨1a⟩ *v/i hablar* murmur; *criticar* gossip
muro *m* wall
musa *f* muse
musaraña *f* ZO shrew; ***pensar en las musarañas*** F daydream
muscular *adj* muscular
múísculo *m* muscle
musculoso *adj* muscular
museo *m* museum; *de pintura* art gallery
musgo *m* BOT moss
múísica *f* music
musical *m/adj* musical
múísico *m*, **-a** *f* musician
musitar ⟨1a⟩ *v/i* mumble
muslo *m* thigh
mustio *adj* withered; *fig* down F
musulmán 1 *adj* Muslim **2** *m*, **-ana** *f* Muslim
mutilado *m*, **-a** *f* disabled person
mutilar ⟨1a⟩ *v/t* mutilate
mutualidad *f* benefit society, *Br* friendly society
mutuo *adj* mutual
muy *adv* very; (*demasiado*) too; ***muy valorado*** highly valued

N, Ñ

N *abr* (= ***norte***) N (North(ern))
nabo *m* **1** *adj Arg* F dumb F **2** *m* turnip
nácar *m* mother-of-pearl
nacatamal *m C.Am.*, *Méx meat, rice and corn in a banana leaf*
nacer ⟨2d⟩ *v/i* be born; *de un huevo* hatch; *de una planta* sprout; *de un río*, *del sol* rise; (*surgir*) arise (***de*** from)
naciente *adj país*, *gobierno* newly formed; *sol* rising
nacimiento *m* birth; *de Navidad* crèche, nativity scene
nación *f* nation
nacional *adj* national
nacionalidad *f* nationality
nacionalismo *m* nationalism
nacionalización *f* COM nationalization
nacionalizar ⟨1f⟩ **1** *v/t* COM nationalize; *persona* naturalize **2** *v/r* **nacionalizarse** become naturalized
naco *m Col* purée
nada 1 *pron* nothing; ***no hay nada*** there isn't anything; ***¡nada de eso!*** F you can put that idea out of your head; ***nada más*** nothing else; ***nada menos que*** no less than; ***lo dices como si nada*** you talk about it as if it was nothing; ***¡de nada!*** you're welcome, not at all; ***no es nada*** it's nothing **2** *adv* not at all; ***no ha llovido nada*** it hasn't rained **3** *f* nothingness
nadador *m*, **nadadora** *f* swimmer
nadar ⟨1a⟩ *v/i* swim
nadería *f* trifle
nadie *pron* nobody, no-one; ***no había nadie*** there was nobody there, there wasn't anyone there
nado: ***atravesar a nado*** swim across
nafta *f Arg* gas(oline), *Br* petrol
naftalina *f* naphthalene
nailon *m* nylon
naipe *m* (playing) card
nalga *f* buttock
nana *f* lullaby; *Rpl* F (*abuela*) grandma
napias *fpl* F schnozzle *sg* F, *Br* hooter *sg* F
naranja 1 *f* orange; ***media naranja*** F (*pareja*) other half **2** *adj* orange
naranjada *f* orangeade
naranjo *m* orange tree
narciso *m* BOT daffodil
narcótico *m/adj* narcotic
narcotráfico *m* drug trafficking
nariz *f* nose; ***¡narices!*** F nonsense!; ***estar hasta las narices de algo*** F be sick of sth F, be up to here with sth F; ***meter las narices en algo*** F stick one's nose in sth F
narración *f* narration
narrador *m*, **narradora** *f* narrator
narrar ⟨1a⟩ *v/t*: ***narrar algo*** tell the story of sth
nasal *adj* nasal
nata *f* cream; ***nata montada*** whipped cream
natación *f* swimming
natal *adj* native; ***ciudad natal*** city of one's birth, home town
natalidad *f* birthrate
natillas *fpl* custard *sg*
nativo *m*, **-a** *f* native
nato *adj* born
natural 1 *adj* natural; ***ser natural de*** come

from; ***es natural*** it's only natural **2** *m*: ***fruta al natural*** fruit in its own juice
naturaleza *f* nature
naturalidad *f* naturalness
naturalmente *adv* naturally
naturista 1 *adj* nudist, naturist; *medicina* natural **2** *m/f* nudist, naturist
naufragar ⟨1h⟩ *v/i* be shipwrecked; *fig* fail
naufragio *m* shipwreck
náufrago 1 *adj* shipwrecked **2** *m*, **-a** *f* shipwrecked person
náuseas *fpl* nausea *sg*
nauseabundo *adj* nauseating
náutico *adj* nautical
navaja *f* knife
navajazo *m* knife wound, slash
navajero *m*: ***le asaltó un navajero*** he was attacked by a man with a knife
naval *adj* naval
nave *f* ship; *de iglesia* nave; ***nave espacial*** spacecraft
navegación *f* navigation; ***navegación a vela*** sailing
navegador *m* INFOR browser
navegante *m/f* navigator
navegar ⟨1h⟩ **1** *v/i* sail; *por el aire, espacio* fly; ***navegar por la red*** *or* ***por Internet*** INFOR surf the Net **2** *v/t* sail
Navidad *f* Christmas
navideño *adj* Christmas *atr*
navío *m* ship
nazi *m/f* & *adj* Nazi
nazismo *m* Nazi(i)sm
N. B. *abr* (= ***nótese bien***) NB (= nota bene)
neblina *f* mist
nebuloso *adj fig* hazy, nebulous
necesario *adj* necessary
neceser *m* toilet kit, *Br* toilet bag
necesidad *f* need; (*cosa esencial*) necessity; ***de primera necesidad*** essential; ***en caso de necesidad*** if necessary; ***hacer sus -es*** F relieve o.s.
necesitado *adj* needy
necesitar ⟨1a⟩ *v/t* need
necio *adj* brainless
necrológica *f* obituary
nefasto *adj* harmful
negación *f* negation; *de acusación* denial
negar ⟨1h & 1k⟩ **1** *v/t acusación* deny; (*no conceder*) refuse **2** *v/r* **negarse** refuse (***a*** to)
negativa *f* refusal; *de acusación* denial
negativo 1 *adj* negative **2** *m* FOT negative
negligencia *f* JUR negligence
negociable *adj* negotiable
negociación *f* negotiation; ***negociaciones*** talks
negociador *m*, **negociadora** *f* negotiator
negociante *m/f* businessman; *mujer* businesswoman; *desp* money-grubber
negociar ⟨1b⟩ *v/t* negotiate
negocio *m* business; (*trato*) deal
negra *f* black woman; MÚS quarter note, *Br* crotchet; *L.Am.* (*querida*) honey, dear
negrita *f* bold
negro 1 *adj* black; ***estar negro*** F be furious **2** *m* black man; *L.Am.* (*querido*) honey, dear
nena *f* F little girl, kid F
nene *m* F little boy, kid F
nenúfar *m* BOT water lily
neocelandés *m*, **-esa** *f* New Zealander
neón *m* neon
neoyorquino 1 *adj* New York *atr* **2** *m*, **-a** *f* New Yorker
nepotismo *m* nepotism
nervio *m* ANAT nerve
nerviosismo *m* nervousness
nervioso *adj* nervous; ***ponerse nervioso*** get nervous; (*agitado*) get agitated; ***poner a alguien nervioso*** get on s.o.'s nerves
neto *adj* COM net
neumático 1 *adj* pneumatic **2** *m* AUTO tire, *Br* tyre
neumonía *f* MED pneumonia
neurocirujano *m*, **-a** *f* brain surgeon
neurólogo *m*, **-a** *f* neurologist
neurosis *f inv* neurosis
neurótico *adj* neurotic
neutral *adj* neutral
neutralidad *f* neutrality
neutralizar ⟨1f⟩ *v/t* neutralize
neutro *adj* neutral
nevada *f* snowfall
nevar ⟨1k⟩ *v/i* snow
nevazón *f Arg*, *Chi* snowstorm
nevera *f* refrigerator, fridge; ***nevera portátil*** cooler
nevería *f Méx*, *C.Am.* ice-cream parlo(u)r
nevero *m* snowdrift
nexo *m* link; GRAM connective
ni *conj* neither; ***ni … ni*** neither … nor; ***ni siquiera*** not even; ***no di ni una*** I made a real mess of things
Nicaragua Nicaragua
nicaragüense *m/f* & *adj* Nicaraguan
nicho *m* niche
nicotina *f* nicotine; ***bajo en nicotina*** low in nicotine
nido *m* nest
niebla *f* fog
nieta *f* granddaughter
nieto *m* grandson; ***nietos*** grandchildren
nieva *vb* → ***nevar***
nieve *f* snow; *Méx* water ice, sorbet

N Ñ

nihilismo *m* nihilism
nimiedad *f* triviality
nimio *adj* trivial
ningúin *adj* → ***ninguno***
ninguno *adj* no; ***no hay -a razón*** there's no reason why, there isn't any reason why
niña *f* girl; *forma de cortesía* young lady
niñato *m*, **-a** *f* brat
niñera *f* nanny
niñería *f*: ***una niñería*** a childish thing
niñez *f* childhood
niño 1 *adj* young; *desp* childish **2** *m* boy; *forma de cortesía* young man; ***niños*** children *pl*; ***niño de pecho*** infant
níquel *m* nickel
níspero *m* BOT loquat
nítido *adj* clear; *imagen* sharp
nitrógeno *m* nitrogen
nitroglicerina *f* nitroglycerin
nivel *m* level; (*altura*) height; ***nivel del mar*** sea level; ***nivel de vida*** standard of living
nivelar ⟨1a⟩ *v/t* level
nixtamal *m Méx, C.Am. dough from which corn tortillas are made*
n.° *abr* (= ***núímero***) No. (= number)
no *adv* no; *para negar verbo* not; ***no entiendo*** I don't understand, I do not understand; ***no te vayas*** don't go; ***no bien*** as soon as; ***no del todo*** not entirely; ***ya no*** not any more; ***no más*** *L.Am.* → ***nomás***; ***así no más*** *L.Am.* just like that; ***te gusta, ¿no?*** you like it, don't you?; ***te ha llamado, ¿no?*** he called you, didn't he?; ***¿a que no?*** I bet you don't/can't etc
nobiliario *adj* noble
noble *m/f & adj* noble
nobleza *f* nobility
noche *f* night; ***de noche, por la noche*** at night; ***de la noche a la mañana*** *fig* overnight; ***¡buenas noches!*** *saludo* good evening; *despedida* good night
Nochebuena *f* Christmas Eve
nochecita *f L.Am.* evening
nochero *m L.Am.* night watchman
Nochevieja *f* New Year's Eve
noción *f* notion
nocivo *adj* harmful
noctámbulo *m*, **-a** *f* sleepwalker
nocturno *adj* night *atr*; ZO nocturnal; ***clase -a*** evening class
nogal *m* BOT walnut
nómada 1 *adj* nomadic **2** *m/f* nomad
nomás *adv L.Am.* just, only; ***llévaselo nomás*** just take it away; ***nomás llegue, te avisaré*** as soon as he arrives, I'll let you know; ***siga nomás*** just carry on; ***nomás lo vio, echó a llorar*** as soon as she saw him she started to cry
nombramiento *m* appointment
nombrar ⟨1a⟩ *v/t* mention; *para un cargo* appoint
nombre *m* name; GRAM noun; ***nombre de pila*** first name; ***no tener nombre*** *fig* be inexcusable
nomenclatura *f* nomenclature
nomeolvides *f inv* BOT forget-me-not
nómina *f* pay slip
nominal *adj* nominal
nominar ⟨1a⟩ *v/t* nominate
non *adj* odd
nono *adj* ninth
nopal *m L.Am.* BOT prickly pear
nor(d)este *m* northeast
noria *f de agua* waterwheel; *en feria* ferris wheel
norma *f* standard; (*regla*) rule, regulation
normal *adj* normal
normalidad *f* normality
normalizar ⟨1f⟩ *v/t* standardize
normativa *f* rules *pl*, regulations *pl*
noroeste *m* northwest
norte *m* north
Norteamérica North America
norteamericano 1 *adj* North American **2** *m*, **-a** *f* North American
norteño 1 *adj* northern **2** *m*, **-a** *f* northerner
Noruega Norway
noruego 1 *adj* Norwegian **2** *m*, **-a** *f* Norwegian
nos *pron complemento directo* us; *complemento indirecto* (to) us; *reflexivo* ourselves; ***nos dio el dinero*** he gave us the money, he gave the money to us
nosotros, **nosotras** *pron* we; *complemento* us; ***ven con nosotros*** come with us; ***somos nosotros*** it's us
nostalgia *f* nostalgia; *por la patria* homesickness
nostálgico *adj* nostalgic
nota *f tb* MÚS note; EDU grade, mark; ***nota a pie de página*** footnote; ***tomar nota de algo*** make a note of sth
notable *adj* remarkable, notable
notar ⟨1a⟩ *v/t* notice; (*sentir*) feel; ***hacer notar algo a alguien*** point sth out to s.o.; ***se nota que*** you can tell that; ***hacerse notar*** draw attention to o.s.
notaría *f* notary's office
notario *m*, **-a** *f* notary
noticia *f* piece of news; *en noticiario* news story, item of news; ***noticias*** *pl* news *sg*
noticiario *m* RAD, TV news *sg*
notificación *f* notification
notificar ⟨1g⟩ *v/t* notify
notorio *adj* famous, well-known
novatada *f* practical joke

novato *m*, **-a** *f* beginner, rookie F
novecientos *adj* nine hundred
novedad *f* novelty; *cosa* new thing; (*noticia*) piece of news; *acontecimiento* new development; ***llegar sin novedad*** arrive safely
novedoso *adj* novel, new; *invento* innovative
novela *f* novel; ***novela negra*** crime novel; ***novela rosa*** romantic novel
novelista *m/f* novelist
noveno *adj* ninth
noventa *adj* ninety
novia *f* girlfriend; *el día de la boda* bride
noviazgo *m* engagement
noviembre *m* November
novillada *f bullfight featuring novice bulls*
novillero *m* novice (bullfighter)
novillo *m* zo young bull; *vaca* heifer; ***hacer novillos*** F play hooky F, play truant
novio *m* boyfriend; *el día de la boda* bridegroom; ***los novios*** the bride and groom; (*recién casados*) the newly-weds
nube *f* cloud; ***estar en las nubes*** *fig* be miles away; ***estar por las nubes*** *fig* F be incredibly expensive
nublado 1 *adj* cloudy, overcast **2** *m* storm cloud
nublarse ⟨1a⟩ *v/r* cloud over
nuboso *adj* cloudy
nuca *f* nape of the neck
nuclear *adj* nuclear
núcleo *m* nucleus; *de problema* heart
nudillo *m* knuckle
nudista *m/f* nudist; ***playa nudista*** nudist beach
nudo *m* knot; ***se me hace un nudo en la garganta*** F I get a lump in my throat
nuera *f* daughter-in-law
nuestro 1 *adj pos* our **2** *pron* ours
nueva *f lit* piece of news
nuevamente *adv* again
Nueva York New York
Nueva Zelanda New Zealand
nueve *adj* nine
nuevo *adj* new; (*otro*) another; ***de nuevo*** again
nuez *f* BOT walnut; ANAT Adam's apple
nulidad *f* nullity; *fig* F dead loss F
nulo *adj* null and void; F *persona* hopeless; (*inexistente*) non-existent, zero
núm. *abr* (**= *número***) No. (= number)
numerar ⟨1a⟩ *v/t* number
numérico *adj* numerical; ***teclado numérico*** numeric keypad, number pad
número *m* number; *de publicación* issue; *de zapato* size; ***número complementario*** *en lotería* bonus number; ***número secreto*** PIN (number); ***en números rojos*** *fig* in the red; ***montar un número*** F make a scene
numeroso *adj* numerous
numismática *f* numismatics
nunca *adv* never; ***nunca jamás*** *or* ***más*** never again; ***más que nunca*** more than ever
nupcial *adj* wedding *atr*
nutria *f* zo otter
nutrición *f* nutrition
nutrido *adj fig* large
nutriente *m* nutrient
nutrir ⟨3a⟩ *v/t* nourish; *fig*: *esperanzas* cherish
nutritivo *adj* nutritious, nourishing
nylon *m* nylon
ñandú *m* zo rhea
ñandutí *m Parag type of lace*
ñapa *f S. Am.* extra, bonus; ***le di dos de ñapa*** I threw in an extra two
ñato *adj Rpl* snub-nosed
ñeque *m S. Am.* strength; ***de ñeque*** F gutsy F; ***tener mucho ñeque*** F have a lot of guts F
ñoñería *f* feebleness F, wimpish behavio(u)r F
ñoño 1 *adj* feeble F, wimpish F **2** *m*, **-a** *f* drip F, wimp F
ñu *m* zo gnu

O

O *abr* (**= *oeste***) W (= West(ern))
o *conj* or; ***o … o*** either … or; ***o sea*** in other words
oasis *m inv* oasis
obcecación *f* obstinacy
obcecarse ⟨1g⟩ *v/r* stubbornly insist
obedecer ⟨2d⟩ **1** *v/t* obey **2** *v/i* obey; *de una máquina* respond; ***obedecer a*** *fig* be due to
obediencia *f* obedience

obediente *adj* obedient
obelisco *m* obelisk
obesidad *f* obesity
obeso *adj* obese
obispo *m* bishop
objeción *f* objection; ***objeción de conciencia*** conscientious objection
objetar ⟨1a⟩ **1** *v/t* object; ***tener algo que objetar*** have any objection **2** *v/i* become a conscientious objector
objetividad *f* objectivity
objetivo 1 *adj* objective **2** *m* objective; MIL target; FOT lens
objeto *m* object; ***con objeto de*** with the aim of
objetor *m*, **objetora** *f* objector; ***objetor de conciencia*** conscientious objector
oblícuo *adj* oblique, slanted
obligación *f* obligation, duty; COM bond
obligar ⟨1h⟩ *v/t*: ***obligar a alguien*** oblige *o* force s.o. (***a*** to); *de una ley* apply to s.o.
obligatorio *adj* obligatory, compulsory
obnubilar ⟨1a⟩ *v/t* cloud
oboe *m* MÚS oboe
obra *f* work; ***obras*** *pl de construcción* building work *sg*; *en la vía púíblica* road works; ***obra de arte*** work of art; ***obra maestra*** masterpiece; ***obra de teatro*** play
obraje *m Méx* butcher's
obrar ⟨1a⟩ *v/i* act
obrero 1 *adj* working **2** *m*, **-a** *f* worker
obsceno *adj* obscene
obsequiar ⟨1b⟩ *v/t*: ***obsequiar a alguien con algo*** present s.o. with sth
obsequio *m* gift
obsequioso *adj* attentive
observación *f* observation; JUR observance
observador 1 *adj* observant **2** *m*, **observadora** *f* observer
observar ⟨1a⟩ *v/t* observe; (*advertir*) notice, observe; (*comentar*) remark, observe
observatorio *m* observatory
obsesión *f* obsession
obsesionar ⟨1a⟩ **1** *v/t* obsess **2** *v/r* **obsesionarse** become obsessed (***con*** with)
obsesivo *adj* obsessive
obsoleto *adj* obsolete
obstaculizar ⟨1f⟩ *v/t* hinder, hamper
obstáculo *m* obstacle
obstante: ***no obstante*** nevertheless
obstetra *m/f* obstetrician
obstetricia *f* obstetrics
obstinación *f* obstinacy
obstinado *adj* obstinate
obstinarse ⟨1a⟩ *v/r* insist (***en*** on)
obstrucción *f* obstruction, blockage
obstruir ⟨3g⟩ *v/t* obstruct, block
obtener ⟨2l; *part* ***obtuvo*** ⟩ *v/t* get, obtain *fml*
obturador *m* shutter
obtuvo *vb* → ***obtener***
obvio *adj* obvious
oca *f* goose
ocasión *f* occasion; (*oportunidad*) chance, opportunity; ***con ocasión de*** on the occasion of; ***de ocasión*** COM cut-price, bargain *atr*; *de segunda mano* second-hand, used
ocasional *adj* occasional
ocasionar ⟨1a⟩ *v/t* cause
ocaso *m del sol* setting; *de un imperio*, *un poder* decline
occidental 1 *adj* western **2** *m/f* Westerner
occidente *m* west
OCDE *abr* (***= Organizacíon de Cooperación y Desarrollo Económico***) OECD (= Organization for Economic Cooperation and Development)
océano *m* ocean
oceanógrafo *m*, **-a** *f* oceanographer
ocelote *m* ZO ocelot
ochenta *adj* eighty
ocho *adj* eight
ochocientos *adj* eight hundred
ocio *m* leisure time, free time; *desp* idleness
ociosear ⟨1a⟩ *v/i S. Am.* laze around
ocioso *adj* idle
ocre *m/adj* ocher, *Br* ochre
oct.ᵉ *abr* (***= octubre***) Oct. (= October)
octavilla *f* leaflet
octavo 1 *adj* eighth **2** *m* eighth; DEP ***octavos de final*** last 16
octógono *m* octagon
octubre *m* October
ocular *adj* eye *atr*
oculista *m/f* ophthalmologist
ocultación *f* concealment
ocultar ⟨1a⟩ *v/t* hide, conceal
ocultismo *m* occult
oculto *adj* hidden; (*sobrenatural*) occult
ocupación *f tb* MIL occupation; (*actividad*) activity
ocupado *adj* busy; *asiento* taken
ocupante *m/f* occupant
ocupar ⟨1a⟩ **1** *v/t espacio* take up, occupy; (*habitar*) live in, occupy; *obreros* employ; *periodo de tiempo* spend, occupy; MIL occupy **2** *v/r* **ocuparse**: ***ocuparse de*** deal with; (*cuidar de*) look after
ocurrencia *f* occurrence; (*chiste*) quip, funny remark
ocurrir ⟨3a⟩ *v/i* happen, occur; ***se me ocurrió*** it occurred to me, it struck me
odiar ⟨1b⟩ *v/t* hate

O

odio *m* hatred, hate
odioso *adj* odious, hateful
odisea *f fig* odyssey
odontólogo *m* odontologist
OEA *abr* (= ***Organizacíon de los Estados Americanos***) OAS (= Organization of American States)
oeste *m* west
ofender ⟨2a⟩ **1** *v/t* offend **2** *v/r* **ofenderse** take offense (***por*** at)
ofensa *f* insult
ofensiva *f* offensive
ofensivo *adj* offensive
oferta *f* offer; ***oferta púiblica de adquisición*** takeover bid
oficial 1 *adj* official **2** *m/f* MIL officer
oficialista *adj L.Am.* pro-government
oficina *f* office; ***oficina de correos*** post office; ***oficina de empleo*** employment office; ***oficina de turismo*** tourist office
oficinista *m/f* office worker
oficio *m trabajo* trade
oficioso *adj* unofficial
ofimática *f* INFOR office automation
ofrecer ⟨2d⟩ **1** *v/t* offer **2** *v/r* **ofrecerse** volunteer, offer one's services (***de*** as); (*presentarse*) appear; ***¿qué se le ofrece?*** what can I do for you?
ofrecimiento *m* offer
ofrenda *f* offering
oftalmólogo *m*, **-a** *f* ophthalmologist
ofuscar ⟨1g⟩ *v/t tb fig* blind
ogro *m tb fig* ogre
oída *f*: ***conocer algo de oídas*** have heard of sth
oído *m* hearing; ***hacer oídos sordos*** turn a deaf ear; ***ser todo oídos*** *fig* be all ears
oigo *vb* → ***oír***
oír ⟨3q⟩ *v/t tb* JUR hear; (*escuchar*) listen to; ***¡oye!*** listen!, hey! F; ***como quien oye llover, salió sin él*** F he turned a deaf ear and went off without it
OIT *abr* (= ***Organizacíon Internacional de Trabajo***) ILO (= International Labor Organization)
ojal *m* buttonhole
ojalá *int*: ***¡ojalá!*** let's hope so; ***¡ojalá venga!*** I hope he comes; ***¡ojalá tuvieras razón!*** I only hope you're right
ojeada *f* glance; ***echar una ojeada a alguien*** glance at s.o.
ojeras *fpl* bags under the eyes
ojo *m* ANAT eye; ***¡ojo!*** F watch out!, mind! F; ***ojo de la cerradura*** keyhole; ***a ojo*** roughly; ***andar con ojo*** F keep one's eyes open F; ***costar un ojo de la cara*** F cost an arm and a leg F; ***no pegar ojo*** F not sleep a wink F
ojota *f C.Am., Méx* sandal
okupa *m/f Esp* F squatter
ola *f* wave; ***ola de calor*** heat wave; ***ola de frío*** cold spell
oleada *f fig* wave, flood
oleaje *m* swell
óleo *m* oil
oleoducto *m* (oil) pipeline
oler ⟨2i⟩ **1** *v/i* smell (***a*** of) **2** *v/t* smell **3** *v/r*: ***me huelo algo*** *fig* there's something fishy going on, I smell a rat
olfatear ⟨1a⟩ *v/t* sniff
olfato *m* sense of smell; *fig* nose
olimpíada, olimpiada *f* Olympics *pl*
olímpico *adj* Olympic
olisquear ⟨1a⟩ *v/t* sniff
oliva *f* BOT olive
olivo *m* olive tree
olla *f* pot; ***olla exprés*** *or* ***a presión*** pressure cooker
olmo *m* BOT elm
olor *m* smell; *agradable* scent; ***olor corporal*** body odo(u)r, BO
oloroso *adj* scented
OLP *abr* (= ***Organizacíon para la Liberación de Palestina***) PLO (= Palestine Liberation Organization)
olvidadizo *adj* forgetful
olvidar ⟨1a⟩ **1** *v/t* forget **2** *v/r* **olvidarse**: ***olvidarse de algo*** forget sth
olvido *m* oblivion
ombligo *m* ANAT navel
OMC *abr* (= ***Organización Mundial de Comercio***) WTO (= World Trade Organization)
omisión *f* omission
omiso *adj*: ***hacer caso omiso de algo*** ignore sth
omitir ⟨3a⟩ *v/t* omit, leave out
omnipotente *adj* omnipotent
omóplato, **omoplato** *m* ANAT shoulder blade
OMS *abr* (= ***Organizacíon Mundial de la Salud***) WHO (= World Health Organization)
once *adj* eleven
oncología *f* MED oncology
onda *f* wave; ***estar en la onda*** F be with it F; ***¿qué onda?*** *Méx* F what's happening? F
ondulado *adj* wavy; *cartón* corrugated
ONG *abr* (= ***Organización no Gubernamental***) NGO (= non-governmental organization)
onomatopeya *f* onomatopœia
ONU *abr* (= ***Organización de las Naciones Unidas***) UN (= United Nations)
onza *f* ounce
OPA *abr* (= ***oferta púiblica de adquisición***) takeover bid

O

opaco *adj* opaque
opción *f* option, choice; (*posibilidad*) chance
opcional *adj* optional
OPEP *abr* (= ***Organización de Países Exportadores de Petróleo***) OPEC (= Organization of Petroleum Exporting Countries)
ópera *f* MÚS opera; ***ópera prima*** first work
operación *f* operation
operador *m*, **operadora** *f* TELEC, INFOR operator; ***operador turístico*** tour operator
operar ⟨1a⟩ **1** *v/t* MED operate on; *cambio* bring about **2** *v/i* operate; COM do business (***con*** with) **3** *v/r* **operarse** MED have an operation (***de*** on); *de un cambio* occur
operario *m*, **-a** *f* operator, operative
operativo 1 *adj* operational; ***sistema operativo*** INFOR operating system **2** *m L.Am.* operation
opereta *f* MÚS operetta
opinar ⟨1a⟩ **1** *v/t* think (***de*** about) **2** *v/i* express an opinion
opinión *f* opinion; ***la opinión púiblica*** public opinion; ***en mi opinión*** in my opinion
opio *m* opium
opíparo *adj* sumptuous
oponente *m/f* opponent
oponer ⟨2r; *part* ***opuesto*** ⟩ **1** *v/t resistencia* put up (***a*** to), offer (***a*** to); *razón, argumento* put forward (***a*** against) **2** *v/r* **oponerse** be opposed (***a*** to); (*manifestar oposición*) object (***a*** to)
oporto *m* port
oportunidad *f* opportunity
oportunista 1 *adj* opportunistic **2** *m/f* opportunist
oportuno *adj* timely; *momento* opportune; *respuesta, medida* suitable, appropriate
oposición *f* POL opposition; ***oposiciones*** official entrance exams
opresión *f* oppression
opresor 1 *adj* oppressive **2** *m*, **opresora** *f* oppressor
oprimir ⟨3a⟩ *v/t* oppress; *botón* press; *de zapatos* be too tight for
optar ⟨1a⟩ *v/i* (*elegir*) opt (***por*** for); ***optar a*** be in the running for; ***optar por hacer algo*** opt to do sth
optativo *adj* optional
óptica *f* optician's; FÍS optics; *fig* point of view
óptico 1 *adj* optical **2** *m*, **-a** *f* optician
optimismo *m* optimism
optimista 1 *adj* optimistic **2** *m/f* optimist
optimizar ⟨1f⟩ *v/t* optimize
óptimo *adj* ideal
opuesto 1 *part* → ***oponer*** **2** *adj* opposite; *opinión* contrary
opulencia *f* opulence
opuso *vb* → ***oponer***
oquedad *f* cavity
oración *f* REL prayer; GRAM sentence
orador *m*, **oradora** *f* orator
oral *adj* oral; ***prueba de inglés oral*** English oral (exam)
orangután *m* ZO orangutan
orar ⟨1a⟩ *v/i* pray (***por*** for)
oratoria *f* oratory
órbita *f* orbit; ***colocar*** *or* ***poner en órbita*** put into orbit
orca *m* ZO killer whale
órdago *m*: ***de órdago*** F terrific F
orden 1 *m* order; ***orden del día*** agenda; ***por orden alfabético*** in alphabetical order; ***poner en orden*** tidy up **2** *f* (*mandamiento*) order; ***¡a la orden!*** yes, sir; ***por orden de*** by order of, on the orders of
ordenado *adj* tidy
ordenador *m* INFOR computer; ***ordenador de escritorio*** desktop (computer); ***ordenador personal*** personal computer; ***ordenador portátil*** portable (computer), laptop; ***asistido por ordenador*** computer aided
ordenanza 1 *f* by-law **2** *m* office junior, gofer F; MIL orderly
ordenar ⟨1a⟩ *v/t habitación* tidy up; *alfabéticamente* arrange; (*mandar*) order
ordeñar ⟨1a⟩ *v/t* milk
ordinario *adj* ordinary; *desp* vulgar; ***de ordinario*** usually, ordinarily
orégano *m* BOT oregano
oreja *f* ear; ***aguzar las orejas*** *L.Am.* prick one's ears up; ***ver las orejas al lobo*** *fig* F wake up to the danger
orejeras *fpl* earmuffs
orfanato *m* orphanage
orfebrería *f* goldsmith / silversmith work
orfelinato *m* orphanage
orgánico *adj* organic
organigrama *m* flow chart; *de empresa* organization chart, tree diagram
organillo *m* barrel organ
organismo *m* organism; POL agency, organization; ***organismo modificado genéticamente*** genetically modified organism
organización *f* organization; ***Organizacíon de Cooperación y Desarrollo Económico*** Organization for Economic Cooperation and Development; ***Organización de las Naciones Unidas*** United Nations; ***Organizacíon de los Estados Americanos*** Organization of American

States; ***Organización del Tratado del Atlántico Norte*** North Atlantic Treaty Organization; ***Organización de Países Exportadores de Petróleo*** Organization of Petroleum Exporting Countries; ***Organizacíon Internacional de Trabajo*** International Labor Organization; ***Organización Mundial de Comercio*** World Trade Organization; ***Organizacíon Mundial de la Salud*** World Health Organization; ***Organizacíon para la Liberación de Palestina*** Palestine Liberation Organization

organizador 1 *adj* organizing **2** *m*, **organizadora** *f* organizer; ***organizador personal*** personal organizer

organizar ⟨1f⟩ **1** *v/t* organize **2** *v/r* **organizarse** *de persona* organize one's time

órgano *m* MÚS, ANAT, *fig* organ

orgasmo *m* orgasm

orgía *f* orgy

orgullo *m* pride

orgulloso *adj* proud (***de*** of)

orientación *f* orientation; (*ayuda*) guidance; ***sentido de la orientación*** sense of direction

orientador *m*, **orientadora** *f* counsel(l)or

oriental 1 *adj* oriental, eastern **2** *m/f* Oriental

orientar ⟨1a⟩ **1** *v/t* (*aconsejar*) advise; ***orientar algo hacia algo*** turn sth toward sth **2** *v/r* **orientarse** get one's bearings; *de una planta* turn (***hacía*** toward)

oriente *m* east; ***Oriente*** Orient; ***Oriente Medio*** Middle East; ***Extremo*** *or* ***Lejano Oriente*** Far East

orificio *m* hole; *en cuerpo* orifice

origen *m* origin; ***dar origen a*** give rise to

original *m/adj* original

originalidad *f* originality

originar ⟨1a⟩ **1** *v/t* give rise to **2** *v/r* **originarse** originate; *de un incendio* start

originario *adj* original; (*nativo*) native (***de*** of)

orilla *f* shore; *de un río* bank

orina *f* urine

orinal *m* urinal

orinar ⟨1a⟩ *v/i* urinate

oriundo *adj* native (***de*** to)

ornamental *adj* ornamental

ornitología *f* ornithology

ornitólogo *m*, **-a** *f* ornithologist

oro *m* gold; ***guardar como oro en paño*** *con mucho cariño* treasure sth; *con mucho cuidado* guard sth with one's life; ***prometer el oro y el moro*** promise the earth; ***oros*** (*en naipes*) *suit in Spanish deck of cards*

orondo *adj* fat; *fig* smug

oropéndola *f* ZO golden oriole

orquesta *f* orchestra

orquestar ⟨1a⟩ *v/t fig* orchestrate

orquídea *f* BOT orchid

ortiga *f* BOT nettle

ortodoncia *f* MED orthodontics

ortodoxo *adj* orthodox

ortografía *f* spelling

ortopédico 1 *adj* orthop(a)edic **2** *m*, **-a** *f* orthop(a)edist

oruga *f* ZO caterpillar; TÉC (caterpillar) track

orujo *m liquor made from the remains of grapes*

orzuelo *m* MED stye

os *pron complemento directo* you; *complemento indirecto* (to) you; *reflexivo* yourselves; ***os lo devolveré*** I'll give you it back, I'll give it back to you

osa *f* AST: ***Osa Mayor*** Great Bear; ***Osa Menor*** Little Bear

osadía *f* daring; (*descaro*) audacity

osamenta *f* bones *pl*

osar ⟨1a⟩ *v/i* dare

oscilación *f* oscillation; *de precios* fluctuation

oscilar ⟨1a⟩ *v/i* oscillate; *de precios* fluctuate

oscurecer ⟨2d⟩ **1** *v/t* darken; *logro*, *triunfo* overshadow **2** *v/i* get dark **3** *v/r* **oscurecerse** darken

oscuridad *f* darkness

oscuro *adj* dark; *fig* obscure; ***a -as*** in the dark

óseo *adj* bone *atr*

osezno *m* cub

osito *m*: ***osito de peluche*** teddy bear

oso *m* bear; ***oso hormiguero*** anteater; ***oso panda*** panda; ***oso polar*** polar bear

ostensible *adj* obvious

ostentación *f* ostentation; ***hacer ostentación de*** flaunt

ostentar ⟨1a⟩ *v/t* flaunt; *cargo* hold

ostentoso *adj* ostentatious

osteoporosis *f* MED osteoporosis

ostra *f* ZO oyster; ***¡ostras!*** F hell! F

ostrero *m* ZO oyster-catcher

OTAN *abr* (= ***Organización del Tratado del Atlántico Norte***) NATO (= North Atlantic Treaty Organization)

otitis *f* MED earache

otoño *m* fall, *Br* autumn

otorgar ⟨1h⟩ *v/t* award; *favor* grant

otorrino F, **otorrinolaringólogo** *m* MED ear, nose and throat *o* ENT specialist

otro 1 *adj* (*diferente*) another; *con el*, *la* other; ***otros*** other; ***otros dos libros*** another two books **2** *pron* (*adicional*) another (one); (*persona distinta*) someone

o somebody else; (*cosa distinta*) another one, a different one; ***otros*** others; ***entre otros*** among others **3** *siguiente*: ***¡hasta -a!*** see you soon **4** *pron recíproco*: ***amar el uno al otro*** love one another
ovación *f* ovation
ovacionar ⟨1a⟩ *v/t* cheer, give an ovation to
ovalado *adj* oval
óvalo *m* oval
ovario *m* ANAT ovary
oveja *f* sheep; ***oveja negra*** *fig* black sheep
overol *m Méx* overalls *pl*, *Br* dungarees *pl*
ovillo *m* ball; ***hacerse un ovillo*** *fig* curl up (into a ball)
ovino 1 *adj* sheep *atr* **2** *m* sheep; ***ovinos*** sheep *pl*
OVNI *abr* (= ***objeto volante no identificado***) UFO (= unidentified flying object)
ovulación *f* ovulation
óvulo *m* egg
oxidado *adj* rusty
oxidar ⟨1a⟩ **1** *v/t* rust **2** *v/r* **oxidarse** rust, go rusty
óxido *m* QUÍM oxide; (*herrumbre*) rust
oxigenarse ⟨1a⟩ *v/r fig* get some fresh air
oxígeno *m* oxygen
oye *vb* → ***oír***
oyendo *vb* → ***oír***
oyente *m/f* listener
oyó *vb* → ***oír***
ozono *m* ozone; ***capa de ozono*** ozone layer

P

pabellón *m* pavilion; *edificio* block; MÚS bell; MAR flag
pachanga *f*: ***ir de pachanga*** *Méx*, *W.I.*, *C.Am.* F go on a spree F
pachocha *L.Am.*, **pachorra** *f* F slowness
pachucho *adj* MED F poorly
paciencia *f* patience
paciente *m/f & adj* patient
pacificador *m*, **pacificadora** *f* peace-maker
pacificar ⟨1g⟩ *v/t* pacify
pacífico 1 *adj* peaceful; *persona* peaceable; ***el océano Pacífico*** the Pacific Ocean **2** *m*: ***el Pacífico*** the Pacific
pacifista 1 *adj* pacifist *atr* **2** *m/f* pacifist
paco *m*, **-a** *f L.Am.* F (*policía*) cop F
pacotilla *f*: ***de pacotilla*** third-rate, lousy F
pacotillero *m*, **-a** *f L.Am.* street vendor
pactar ⟨1a⟩ **1** *v/t* agree; ***pactar un acuerdo*** reach (an) agreement **2** *v/i* reach (an) agreement
pacto *m* agreement, pact
padecer ⟨2d⟩ **1** *v/t* suffer **2** *v/i* suffer; ***padecer de*** have trouble with
padrastro *m* step-father
padre *m* father; REL Father; ***de padre y muy señor mío*** terrible; ***padres*** parents; ***¡qué padre!*** *Méx* F brilliant!
padrenuestro *m* Lord's Prayer
padrillo *m Rpl* stallion
padrino *m en bautizo* godfather; (*en boda*) *man who gives away the bride*
padrón *m register of local inhabitants*
paella *f* GASTR paella
pág. *abr* (= ***página***) p. (= page)
paga *f* pay; *de niño* allowance, *Br* pocket money
pagado *adj* paid
pagano *adj* pagan
pagar ⟨1h⟩ **1** *v/t* pay; *compra*, *gastos*, *crimen* pay for; *favor* repay; ***¡me las pagarás!*** you'll pay for this! **2** *v/i* pay; ***pagar a escote*** F go Dutch F
pagaré *m* IOU
página *f* page; ***página web*** web page; ***páginas amarillas*** yellow pages
pago *m* payment; *Rpl* (*quinta*) piece of land; ***pago al contado*** *or* ***en efectivo*** payment in cash; ***en pago de*** in payment for; ***por estos pagos*** F in this neck of the woods F
país *m* country; ***país en vías de desarrollo*** developing country; ***los Países Bajos*** the Netherlands
paisaje *m* landscape
paisano *m*: ***de paisano*** MIL in civilian clothes; *policía* in plain clothes
paja *f* straw; ***hacerse una paja*** V jerk off V
pajar *m* hayloft
pajarería *f* pet shop
pajarita *f corbata* bow tie; *de papel* paper bird
pájaro *m* bird; *fig* ugly customer F, nasty piece of work F; ***pájaro carpintero***

woodpecker; ***matar dos pájaros de un tiro*** kill two birds with one stone
Pakistán Pakistan
pakistaní *m/f & adj* Pakistani
pala *f* spade; *raqueta* paddle; *para servir* slice; *para recoger* dustpan
palabra *f tb fig* word; ***palabra de honor*** word of hono(u)r; ***bajo palabra*** on parole; ***en una palabra*** in a word; ***tomar la palabra*** speak
palabrota *f* swearword
palacete *m* small palace
palaciego *adj* palace *atr*
palacio *m* palace; ***palacio de deportes*** sports center (*Br* centre); ***palacio de justicia*** law courts
paladar *m* palate
palanca *f* lever; ***palanca de cambios*** AUTO gearshift, *Br* gear lever; ***tener palanca*** *Méx fig* F have pull F *o* clout F
palangana *f plastic bowl for washing dishes*, *Br* washing-up bowl
palanganear ⟨1a⟩ *v/i S. Am.* show off
palanqueta *f* crowbar
palco *m* TEA box
palenque *m L.Am. cockpit (in cock fighting)*
Palestina Palestine
palestino 1 *adj* Palestinian **2** *m*, **-a** *f* Palestinian
palestra *f* arena; ***salir*** *or* ***saltar a la palestra*** *fig* hit the headlines
paleta *f* PINT palette; TÉC trowel
paletilla *f* GASTR shoulder
paleto F **1** *adj* hick *atr* F, provincial **2** *m*, **-a** *f* hick F, *Br* yokel F
paliar ⟨1b⟩ *v/t* alleviate; *dolor* relieve
paliativo *m/adj* palliative
palidecer ⟨2d⟩ *v/i de persona* turn pale
palidez *f* paleness
pálido *adj* pale
palillo *m para dientes* toothpick; *para comer* chopstick
palique *m*: ***estar de palique*** F have a chat
paliza 1 *f* beating; (*derrota*) thrashing F, drubbing F; (*pesadez*) drag F **2** *m/f* F drag F
palma *f* palm; ***dar palmas*** clap (one's hands)
palmada *f* pat; (*manotazo*) slap
palmar ⟨1a⟩ *v/t*: ***palmarla*** P kick the bucket F
palmera *f* BOT palm tree; (*dulce*) *heart-shaped pastry*
palmito *m* BOT palmetto; GASTR palm heart; *fig* F attractiveness
palmo *m* hand's breadth; ***palmo a palmo*** inch by inch
palo *m de madera etc* stick; MAR mast; *de portería* post, upright; ***palo de golf*** golf club; ***palo mayor*** MAR mainmast; ***a medio palo*** *L.Am.* F half-drunk; ***a palo seco*** *whisky* straight up; ***ser un palo*** *L.Am.* F be fantastic; ***de tal palo tal astilla*** a chip off the old block F
paloma *f* pigeon; *blanca* dove; ***paloma mensajera*** carrier pigeon
palomar *m* pigeon loft
palometa *f* ZO *pez* pompano
palomilla *f C.Am., Méx* F gang
palomita *f Méx* checkmark, *Br* tick; ***palomitas*** *pl* ***de maíz*** popcorn *sg*
palpable *adj fig* palpable
palpar ⟨1a⟩ *v/t con las manos* feel, touch; *fig* feel
palpitación *f* palpitation
palpitante *adj corazón* pounding; *cuestión* burning
palpitar ⟨1a⟩ *v/i del corazón* pound; *Rpl fig* have a hunch F, have a feeling
palta *f S. Am.* BOT avocado
palto *m S. Am.* jacket
paludismo *m* MED malaria
palurdo 1 *adj* F hick *atr* F, provincial **2** *m*, **-a** *f* F hick F, *Br* yokel F
pamela *f* picture hat
pampa *f* GEOG pampa, prairie; ***a la pampa*** *Rpl* in the open
pamplinas *fpl* nonsense *sg*
pan *m* bread; ***un pan*** a loaf; ***pan francés*** *L.Am.* French bread; ***pan integral*** wholemeal bread; ***pan de molde*** sliced bread; ***pan de barra*** French bread; ***pan rallado*** breadcrumbs *pl*; ***pan tostado*** toast; ***ser pan comido*** F be easy as pie F
pana *f* corduroy
panacea *f* panacea
panadería *f* baker's shop
panadero *m*, **-a** *f* baker
panal *m* honeycomb
Panamá Panama; ***el Canal de Panamá*** the Panama Canal; ***Ciudad de Panamá*** Panama city
panameño 1 *adj* Panamanian **2** *m*, **-a** *f* Panamanian
pancarta *f* placard
panceta *f* belly pork
páncreas *m inv* ANAT
panda *m* ZO panda
pandereta *f* tambourine
pandilla *f* group; *de delincuentes* gang
panecillo *m* (bread) roll
panel *m tb grupo de personas* panel; ***panel solar*** solar panel
panela *f L.Am.* brown sugar loaf
panera *f* bread basket
panfleto *m* pamphlet

pánico *m* panic; ***sembrar el pánico*** spread panic
panocha, **panoja** *f* ear
panoli *adj* F dopey F
panorama *m* panorama
panorámico *adj*: ***vista -a*** panoramic view
panqueque *m L.Am.* pancake
pantalla *f* TV, INFOR screen; *de lámpara* shade; ***pequeña pantalla*** *fig* small screen
pantalón *m*, **pantalones** *mpl* pants *pl*, *Br* trousers *pl*; ***llevar los pantalones*** *fig* F wear the pants (*Br* trousers) F
pantano *m* reservoir
panteón *m* pantheon
pantera *f* ZO panther
pantomima *f* pantomime
pantorrilla *f* ANAT calf
pantufla *f* slipper
panty *m* pantyhose *pl*, *Br* tights *pl*
panza *f de persona* belly
pañal *m* diaper, *Br* nappy
paño *m* cloth; ***paño de cocina*** dishtowel
pañuelo *m* handkerchief; ***el mundo es un pañuelo*** *fig* F it's a small world
papa 1 *m* Pope **2** *f L.Am.* potato
papá *m* F pop F, dad F; ***papás*** *L.Am.* parents; ***Papá Noel*** Santa Claus
papada *f* double chin
papagayo *m* ZO parrot
papal 1 *adj* papal **2** *m L.Am.* potato field
papalote *m Méx* kite
papanatas *m/f inv* F dope F, dimwit F
paparruchas *fpl* F baloney *sg* F
papaya *f* BOT papaya
papel *m* paper; *trozo* piece of paper; TEA, *fig* role; ***papel de aluminio*** foil; ***papel de envolver*** wrapping paper; ***papel de regalo*** giftwrap; ***papel higiénico*** toilet paper *o* tissue; ***papel reciclado*** recycled paper; ***perder los papeles*** lose control; ***ser papel mojado*** *fig* not be worth the paper it's written on
papelada *f L.Am.* farce
papeleo *m* paperwork
papelera *f* wastepaper basket
papelería *f* stationer's shop
papelerío *m L.Am.* F muddle, mess
papeleta *f de rifa* raffle ticket; *fig* chore; ***papeleta de voto*** ballot paper
paperas *fpl* MED mumps
papilla *f para bebés* baby food; *para enfermos* puree; ***hacer papilla a alguien*** F beat s.o. to a pulp F
papista *adj*: ***ser más papista que el papa*** hold extreme views
paquete *m* package, parcel; *de cigarrillos* packet; F *en moto* (pillion) passenger
Paquistán Pakistan
paquistaní *m/f & adj* Pakistani
par 1 *f* par; ***es bella a la par que inteligente*** she is beautiful as well as intelligent, she is both beautiful and intelligent **2** *m* pair; ***abierto de par en par*** wide open; ***un par de*** a pair of
para *prp* for ◇ *dirección* toward(s); ***ir para*** head for; ***va para directora*** she's going to end up as manager
◇ *tiempo* for; ***listo para mañana*** ready for tomorrow; ***para siempre*** forever; ***diez para las ocho*** *L.Am.* ten of eight, ten to eight
◇ *finalidad*: ***lo hace para ayudarte*** he does it (in order) to help you; ***para que*** so that; ***¿para qué te marchas?*** what are you leaving for?; ***para mí*** for me; ***lo heredó todo para morir a los 30*** he inherited it all, only to die at 30
parabólica *f* satellite dish
parabrisas *m inv* AUTO windshield, *Br* windscreen
paracaídas *m inv* parachute
paracaidista *m/f* parachutist; MIL paratrooper
parachoques *m inv* AUTO fender, *Br* bumper
parada *f* stop; ***parada de autobúís*** bus stop; ***parada de taxis*** taxi rank
paradero *m* whereabouts *sg*; *L.Am.* → ***parada***
parado 1 *adj* unemployed; *L.Am.* (*de pie*) standing (up); ***salir bien / mal parado*** come off well / badly **2** *m*, **-a** *f* unemployed person
paradoja *f* paradox
paradójico *adj* paradoxical
parador *m Esp* parador (*state-run luxury hotel*)
parafernalia *f* F paraphernalia
parafina *f* kerosene, *Br* paraffin
paraguas *m inv* umbrella
Paraguay Paraguay
paraguayo 1 *adj* Paraguayan **2** *m*, **-a** *f* Paraguayan
paraíso *m* paradise; ***paraíso fiscal*** tax haven
paralelismo *m* parallel
paralelo *m/adj* parallel
parálisis *f tb fig* paralysis
paralítico 1 *adj* paralytic **2** *m*, **-a** *f* person who is paralyzed
paralización *f tb fig* paralysis
paralizar ⟨1f⟩ *v/t* MED paralyze; *actividad* bring to a halt; *país*, *economía* paralyze, bring to a standstill
parámetro *m* parameter
paramilitar *adj* paramilitary
parangón *m*: ***sin parangón*** incompara-

ble
paranoia *f* paranoia
paranoico **1** *adj* MED paranoid **2** *m*, **-a** *f* MED person suffering from paranoia
paranormal *adj* paranormal
parapente *m* hang glider; *actividad* hang gliding
parapeto *m* parapet
parapléjico **1** *adj* MED paraplegic **2** *m*, **-a** *f* paraplegic
parar ⟨1a⟩ **1** *v/t* stop; *L.Am.* (*poner de pie*) stand up **2** *v/i* stop; *en alojamiento* stay; ***parar de llover*** stop raining; ***ir a parar*** end up **3** *v/r* **pararse** stop; *L.Am.* (*ponerse de pie*) stand up
pararrayos *m inv* lightning rod
parásito *m* parasite
parcela *f* lot, *Br* plot
parchar ⟨1a⟩ *v/t L.Am.* patch; (*arreglar*) repair
parche *m* patch
parcial *adj* (*partidario*) bias(s)ed
pardo **1** *adj color* dun; *L.Am. desp* half-breed *desp*, *Br tb* half-caste *desp* **2** *m color* dun; *L.Am. desp* half-breed *desp*
parecer **1** *m* opinion, view; ***al parecer*** apparently **2** ⟨2d⟩ *v/i* seem, look; ***me parece que*** I think (that), it seems to me that; ***me parece bien*** it seems fine to me; ***¿qué te parece?*** what do you think? **3** *v/r* **parecerse** resemble each other; ***parecerse a alguien*** resemble s.o.
parecido **1** *adj* similar **2** *m* similarity
pared *f* wall; ***subirse por las paredes*** F hit the roof F
pareja *f* (*conjunto de dos*) pair; *en una relación* couple; *de una persona* partner; *de un objeto* other one
parejo *adj L.Am. suelo* level, even; ***andar parejos*** be neck and neck; ***llegaron parejos*** they arrived at the same time
paréntesis *m inv* parenthesis; *fig* break; ***entre paréntesis*** *fig* by the way
pareo *m* wrap-around skirt
parida *f* P stupid thing to say / do
pariente *m/f* relative
paripé *m*: ***hacer el paripé*** F put on an act F
parir ⟨3a⟩ **1** *v/i* give birth **2** *v/t* give birth to
París Paris
parisino **1** *adj* Parisian **2** *m*, **-a** *f* Parisian
parka *f* parka
parking *m* parking lot, *Br* car park
parlamentario **1** *adj* parliamentary **2** *m*, **-a** *f* member of parliament
parlamento *m* parliament
parlanchín *adj* chatty
parlante *m L.Am.* loudspeaker
parlotear ⟨1a⟩ *v/i* chatter
parmesano *m/adj* Parmesan
paro *m* unemployment; ***estar en paro*** be unemployed; ***paro cardíaco*** cardiac arrest
parodia *f* parody
parpadear ⟨1a⟩ *v/i* blink
parpadeo *m* blinking
párpado *m* eye lid
parque *m* park; *para bebé* playpen; ***parque de atracciones*** amusement park; ***parque de bomberos*** fire station; ***parque nacional*** national park; ***parque natural*** nature reserve; ***parque temático*** theme park
parqué *m* → ***parquet***
parquear ⟨1a⟩ *v/t L.Am.* park
parquet *m* parquet
parquímetro *m* parking meter
parra *f* (grape) vine
párrafo *m* paragraph
parranda *f*: ***andar*** *or* ***irse de parranda*** F go out on the town F
parricidio *m* parricide
parrilla *f* broiler, *Br* grill; ***a la parrilla*** broiled, *Br* grilled
parrillada *f L.Am.* barbecue
párroco *m* parish priest
parroquia *f* REL parish; COM clientele, customers *pl*
parsimonia *f* parsimony
parte **1** *m* report; ***parte meteorológico*** weather report; ***dar parte a alguien*** inform s.o. **2** *f trozo* part; JUR party; ***alguna parte*** somewhere; ***ninguna parte*** nowhere; ***otra parte*** somewhere else; ***de parte de*** on behalf of; ***en parte*** partly; ***en*** *or* ***por todas partes*** everywhere; ***la mayor parte de*** the majority of, most of; ***por otra parte*** moreover; ***estar de parte de alguien*** be on s.o.'s side; ***formar parte de*** form part of; ***tomar parte en*** take part in
participación *f* participation
participante *m/f* participant
participar ⟨1a⟩ **1** *v/t una noticia* announce **2** *v/i* take part (***en*** in), participate (***en*** in)
participio *m* GRAM participle
partícula *f* particle
particular **1** *adj clase*, *propiedad* private; *asunto* personal; (*específico*) particular; (*especial*) peculiar; ***en particular*** in particular **2** *m* (*persona*) individual; ***particulares*** particulars
particularidad *f* peculiarity
partida *f en juego* game; (*remesa*) consignment; *documento* certificate; ***partida de nacimiento*** birth certificate
partidario **1** *adj*: ***ser partidario de*** be in favo(u)r of **2** *m*, **-a** *f* supporter

partidismo *m* partisanship
partido *m* POL party; DEP game; ***sacar partido de*** take advantage of; ***tomar partido*** take sides
partir ⟨3a⟩ **1** *v/t* (*dividir, repartir*) split; (*romper*) break open, split open; (*cortar*) cut **2** *v/i* (*irse*) leave; ***a partir de hoy*** (starting) from today; ***a partir de ahora*** from now on; ***partir de*** *fig* start from **3** *v/r* **partirse** (*romperse*) break; ***partirse de risa*** F split one's sides laughing F
partitura *f* MÚS score
parto *m* birth; *fig* creation
parvulario *m* kindergarten
pasa *f* raisin
pasable *adj* passable
pasada *f con trapo* wipe; *de pintura* coat; ***de pasada*** in passing; ***¡qué pasada!*** F that's incredible! F
pasadizo *m* passage
pasado 1 *adj tiempo* last; ***el lunes pasado*** last Monday; ***pasado de moda*** old-fashioned **2** *m* past
pasaje *m* (*billete*) ticket; MÚS, *de texto* passage
pasajero 1 *adj* temporary; *relación* brief **2** *m*, **-a** *f* passenger
pasamano(s) *m* handrail
pasamontañas *m inv* balaclava (helmet)
pasaporte *m* passport
pasar ⟨1a⟩ **1** *v/t* pass; *el tiempo* spend; *un lugar* go past; *frontera* cross; *problemas, dificultades* experience; AUTO (*adelantar*) pass, *Br* overtake; *una película* show; ***para pasar el tiempo*** (in order) to pass the time; ***pasar la mano por*** run one's hand through; ***pasarlo bien*** have a good time **2** *v/i* (*suceder*) happen; *en juegos* pass; ***pasar de alguien*** F not want anything to do with s.o.; ***paso de coger el teléfono*** F I can't be bothered to pick up the phone; ***pasé a visitarla*** I dropped by to see her; ***pasar de moda*** go out of fashion; ***pasar por*** go by; ***pasé por la tienda*** I stopped off at the shop; ***pasa por aquí*** come this way; ***dejar pasar*** *oportunidad* miss; ***hacerse pasar por*** pass o.s. off as; ***pasaré por tu casa*** I'll drop by your house; ***¡pasa!*** come in; ***¿qué pasa?*** what's happening?, what's going on?; ***¿qué te pasa?*** what's the matter?; ***pase lo que pase*** whatever happens, come what may **3** *v/r* **pasarse** *tb fig* go too far; *del tiempo* pass, go by; (*usar el tiempo*) spend; *de molestia, dolor* go away; ***pasarse al enemigo*** go over to the enemy; ***se le pasó llamar*** he forgot to call
pasarela *f* catwalk
pasatiempo *m* pastime
Pascua *f* Easter; ***¡felices Pascuas!*** Merry Christmas!
pase *m tb* DEP, TAUR pass; *en el cine* showing; ***pase de modelos*** fashion show
pasear ⟨1a⟩ **1** *v/t* take for a walk; (*exhibir*) show off **2** *v/i* walk **3** *v/r* **pasearse** walk
paseo *m* walk; ***paseo marítimo*** seafront; ***dar un paseo*** go for a walk; ***mandar a alguien a paseo*** *fig* F tell s.o. to get lost
pasillo *m* corridor; *en avión, cine* aisle
pasión *f* passion
pasividad *f* passivity
pasivo *adj* passive
pasmar ⟨1a⟩ *v/t* amaze, astonish
paso *m* step; (*manera de andar*) walk; (*ritmo*) pace, rate; *de agua* flow; *de tráfico* movement; (*cruce*) crossing; *de tiempo* passing; (*huella*) footprint; ***paso a nivel*** grade crossing, *Br* level crossing; ***paso de peatones*** crosswalk, pedestrian crossing; ***a este paso*** *fig* at this rate; ***de paso*** on the way; ***estar de paso*** be passing through
pasta *f sustancia* paste; GASTR pasta; P (*dinero*) dough P; ***pasta de dientes*** toothpaste; ***pastas de té*** *type of cookie* (*Br biscuit*)
pastel *m* GASTR cake; *pintura, color* pastel
pastelería *f* cake shop
pastelero *m*, **-a** *f* pastry cook
paste(u)rizar ⟨1f⟩ *v/t* pasteurize
pastilla *f* tablet; *de jabón* bar; ***a toda pastilla*** F at top speed F, flat out F
pasto *m* (*hierba*) grass; ***a todo pasto*** F for all one is worth F
pastor *m* shepherd; REL pastor; ***pastor alemán*** German shepherd
pata¹ *m/f Pe* F pal F, buddy F
pata² *f* leg; ***a cuatro patas*** on all fours; ***meter la pata*** F put one's foot in it F; ***tener mala pata*** F be unlucky
patada *f* kick; ***dar una patada*** kick
patalear ⟨1a⟩ *v/i* stamp one's feet; *fig* kick and scream
patata *f* potato; ***patatas fritas*** *de sartén* French fries, *Br* chips; *de bolsa* chips, *Br* crisps
patatús *m*: ***le dio un patatús*** F he had a fit F
paté *m* paté
patear ⟨1a⟩ *v/t & v/i L.Am. de animal* kick
patentar ⟨1a⟩ *v/t* patent
patente 1 *adj* clear, obvious **2** *f* patent; *L.Am.* AUTO license plate, *Br* numberplate
paternidad *f* paternity, fatherhood
paterno *adj* paternal
patético *adj* pitiful

patíbulo *m* scaffold
patilla *f de gafas* arm; ***patillas*** *barba* sideburns
patín *m* skate; ***patín (de ruedas) en línea*** rollerblade®, in-line skate
patinador *m*, **patinadora** *f* skater
patinaje *m* skating; ***patinaje artístico*** figure skating; ***patinaje sobre hielo*** ice-skating; ***patinaje sobre ruedas*** roller-skating
patinar ⟨1a⟩ *v/i* skate
patinazo *m* skid; *fig* F blunder; ***dar un patinazo*** skid
patinete *m* scooter
patio *m* courtyard, patio; ***patio de butacas*** TEA orchestra, *Br* stalls *pl*
pato *m* ZO duck; ***pagar el pato*** F take the rap F, *Br* carry the can F
patojo *adj Chi* F squat
patológico *adj* pathological
patoso *adj* clumsy
patraña *f* tall story
patria *f* homeland
patriarca *m* patriarch
patrimonio *m* heritage; ***patrimonio artístico*** artistic heritage
patriota *m/f* patriot
patriótico *adj* patriotic
patriotismo *m* patriotism
patrocinador *m*, **patrocinadora** *f* sponsor
patrocinar ⟨1a⟩ *v/t* sponsor
patrocinio *m* sponsorship
patrón *m* (*jefe*) boss; REL patron saint; *para costura* pattern; (*modelo*) standard; MAR skipper
patrona *f* (*jefa*) boss; REL patron saint
patronal employers *pl*
patrulla *f* patrol
patrullar ⟨1a⟩ *v/t* patrol
patrullero *m* patrolman
paulatino *adj* gradual
pausa *f* pause; *en una actividad* break; MÚS rest; ***pausa publicitaria*** commercial break
pausado *adj* slow, deliberate
pauta *f* guideline; ***marcar la pauta*** set the guidelines
pavimento *m* pavement, *Br* road surface
pavo 1 *adj L.Am.* F stupid **2** *m* ZO turkey; ***pavo real*** peacock
pavonearse ⟨1a⟩ *v/r* boast (***de*** about)
pavor *m* terror; ***me da pavor*** it terrifies me
payada *f Rpl improvized ballad*
payador *m Rpl* gaucho singer
payasadas *fpl* antics; ***hacer payasadas*** fool *o* clown around
payaso *m* clown
paz *f* peace; ***dejar en paz*** leave alone
pe: ***de pe a pa*** F from start to finish
PC *abr* (= ***Partido Comunista***) CP (= Communist Party)
P.D. *abr* (= ***posdata***) PS (= postscript)
peaje *m dinero, lugar* toll
peatón *m* pedestrian
peatonal *adj* pedestrian *atr*
pebete *m*, **-a** *f Rpl* F kid F
peca *f* freckle
pecado *m* sin
pecador *m*, **pecadora** *f* sinner
pecaminoso *adj* sinful
pecar ⟨1g⟩ *v/i* sin; ***pecar de ingenuo / generoso*** be very naive / generous
pecera *f* fish tank, aquarium
pecho *m* (*caja torácica*) chest; (*mama*) breast; ***tomar algo a pecho*** take sth to heart
pechuga *f* GASTR breast; *L.Am. fig* F (*caradura*) nerve F
pecoso *adj* freckled
pectoral *adj* ANAT pectoral
peculiar *adj* peculiar, odd; (*característico*) typical
peculiaridad *f* (*característica*) peculiarity
pedagogía *f* education
pedagogo *m*, **-a** *f* teacher
pedal *m* pedal
pedalear ⟨1a⟩ *v/i* pedal
pedante 1 *adj* pedantic; (*presuntuoso*) pretentious **2** *m/f* pedant; (*presuntuoso*) pretentious individual
pedantería *f* pedantry; (*presunción*) pretentiousness
pedazo *m* piece, bit; ***pedazo de bruto*** F blockhead F; ***hacer pedazos*** F smash to bits F
pederasta *m* pederast
pedestal *m* pedestal
pediatra *m/f* p(a)ediatrician
pedicura *f* pedicure
pedicuro *m*, **-a** *f* pedicurist, *Br* chiropodist
pedido *m* order
pedigrí *m* pedigree
pedigüeño *m*, **-a** *f person who is always asking to borrow things*, moocher F
pedir ⟨3l⟩ **1** *v/t* ask for; (*necesitar*) need; *en bar, restaurante* order; ***me pidió que no fuera*** he asked me not to go **2** *v/i mendigar* beg; *en bar, restaurante* order
pedo 1 *adj* drunk **2** *m* F fart F; ***agarrarse un pedo*** F get plastered F; ***tirarse*** *or* ***echar un pedo*** F fart F
pedorreta *f* F Bronx cheer F, *Br* raspberry F
pedrada *f* blow with a stone; ***me dio una pedrada en la cabeza*** he hit me over the

head with a stone
pedregal *m* stony ground
pedregoso *adj* stony
Pedro *m*: ***como Pedro por su casa*** *fig* F as if he / she owned the place
pega *f* F snag F, hitch F; ***poner pegas*** raise objections
pegadizo *adj* catchy
pegado *adj* (*adherido*) stuck (***a*** to); ***estar pegado a*** (*cerca de*) be right up against; ***estar pegado a alguien*** *fig* follow s.o. around, be s.o.'s shadow
pegajoso *adj* sticky; *fig*: *persona* clingy
pegamento *m* glue
pegar ⟨1h⟩ **1** *v/t* (*golpear*) hit; (*adherir*) stick, glue; *bofetada*, *susto*, *resfriado* give; ***pegar un grito*** shout; ***no me pega la gana*** *Méx* F I don't feel like it **2** *v/i* (*golpear*) hit; (*adherir*) stick; *del sol* beat down; (*armonizar*) go (together) **3** *v/r* **pegarse** *resfriado* catch; *acento* pick up; *susto* give o.s.; ***pegarse un golpo / un tiro*** hit / shoot o.s.; ***pegársela a alguien*** F con s.o. F
pegatina *f* sticker
pegote *m* F (*cosa fea*) eyesore
peinado *m* hairstyle
peinador *m*, **peinadora** *f L.Am.* hairdresser
peinar ⟨1a⟩ **1** *v/t tb fig* comb; ***peinar a alguien*** comb s.o.'s hair **2** *v/r* **peinarse** comb one's hair
peine *m* comb
p. ej. *abr* (***= por ejemplo***) e.g. (= exempli gratia, for example)
Pekín Beijing
pela *f* F peseta
peladero *m L.Am.* vacant lot
peladilla *f* sugared almond
pelado *adj* peeled; *fig* bare; F (*sin dinero*) broke F
pelar ⟨1a⟩ **1** *v/t manzana*, *patata etc* peel; ***hace un frío que pela*** F it's freezing **2** *v/r* **pelarse** (*cortarse el pelo*) have a haircut; *Rpl* F (*chismear*) gossip
pelazón *f C.Am.* backbiting
peldaño *m* step
pelea *f* fight
pelear ⟨1a⟩ **1** *v/i* fight **2** *v/r* **pelearse** fight
pelele *m* puppet
peleón *adj* argumentative; ***vino peleón*** F jug wine, *Br* plonk F
peletería *f* furrier's
peliagudo *adj* tricky
pelícano *m* ZO pelican
película *f* movie, film; FOT film; ***película del Oeste*** Western; ***de película*** F awesome F, fantastic F
peligrar ⟨1a⟩ *v/i* be at risk
peligro *m* danger; ***correr peligro*** be in danger; ***poner en peligro*** endanger, put at risk
peligroso *adj* dangerous
pelillo *m*: ***¡pelillos a la mar*** *fig* F let's bury the hatchet
pelín: ***un pelín*** F a (little) bit
pelirrojo *adj* red-haired, red-headed
pellejo *m de animal* skin, hide; ***salvar el pellejo*** *fig* F save one's (own) skin F
pellizcar ⟨1g⟩ *v/t* pinch
pellizco *m* pinch; ***un buen pellizco*** F a tidy sum F
pelma **1** *adj* annoying **2** *m/f* pain F
pelmazo *m*, **-a** *f* F pain F
pelo *m de persona*, *de perro* hair; *de animal* fur; ***tiene el pelo muy largo*** he has very long hair; ***a pelo*** F (*sin preparación*) unprepared; ***montar a pelo*** ride bareback; ***por los pelos*** F by a whisker F, by the skin of one's teeth F; ***tomar el pelo a alguien*** F pull s.o.'s leg F
pelota **1** *f* ball; ***pelotas*** F nuts F, balls F; ***en pelotas*** P stark naked; ***hacer la pelota a alguien*** suck up to s.o. F **2** *m/f* F creep F
pelotazo *m*: ***rompió el cristal de un pelotazo*** he smashed the window with a ball
pelotero *m*, **-a** *f L.Am.* (base)ball player
pelotón *m* MIL squad; DEP bunch, pack
peluca *f* wig
peluche *m* soft toy; ***oso de peluche*** teddy bear
peludo *adj persona* hairy; *animal* furry
peluquearse ⟨1a⟩ *v/r L.Am.* get one's hair cut
peluquería *f* hairdresser's
peluquero *m*, **-a** *f* hairdresser
peluquín *m* toupee, hairpiece
pelusa *f* fluff
pelvis *f inv* ANAT pelvis
pena *f* (*tristeza*) sadness, sorrow; (*congoja*) grief, distress; (*lástima*) pity; JUR sentence; ***pena capital*** death penalty,capital punishment; ***pena de muerte*** death penalty; ***no vale*** *or* ***no merece la pena*** it's not worth it; ***¡qué pena!*** what a shame *o* pity!; ***a duras penas*** with great difficulty; ***me da pena*** *L.Am.* I'm ashamed
penal *adj* penal; ***derecho penal*** criminal law
penalidad *f fig* hardship
penalización *f acción* penalization; DEP penalty
penalizar ⟨1f⟩ *v/t* penalize
penalty *m* DEP penalty
penca **1** *adj Chi* soft, weak **2** *f L.Am.* (*nopal*) leaf of the prickly pear plant

pendejada *f L.Am.* stupid thing to do
pendejo 1 *m* (*pelea*) fight **2** *m*, **-a** *f L.Am.* F dummy F
pendenciero *adj* troublemaker
pendiente 1 *adj* unresolved, unfinished; *cuenta* unpaid **2** *m* earring **3** *f* slope
pendón 1 *adj* swinging F **2** *m*, **-ona** *f* F swinger F
péndulo *m* pendulum
pene *m* ANAT penis
penetración *f* penetration
penetrante *adj mirada* penetrating; *sonido* piercing; *frío* bitter; *herida* deep; *análisis* incisive
penetrar ⟨1a⟩ *v/i* penetrate; (*entrar*) enter; *de un líquido* seep in
penicilina *f* penicillin
península *f* peninsula; ***península Ibérica*** Iberian Peninsula
penique *m* penny
penitencia *f* penitence
penitenciado *m L.Am.* prisoner, convict
penitenciario *adj* penitentiary *atr*, prison *atr*
penoso *adj* distressing; *trabajo* laborious
pensamiento *m* thought; BOT pansy
pensar ⟨1k⟩ **1** *v/t* think about; (*opinar*) think; ***¡ni pensarlo!*** don't even think about it **2** *v/i* think (***en*** about)
pensativo *adj* thoughtful
pensión *f hotel* rooming house, *Br* guesthouse; *dinero* pension; ***pensión alimenticia*** child support, *Br* maintenance; ***pensión completa*** American plan, *Br* full board
pensionista *m/f* pensioner
pentagrama *m* MÚS stave
pentatlón *m* DEP pentathlon
penúltimo *adj* penultimate
penumbra *f* half-light
penuria *f* shortage (***de*** of); (*pobreza*) poverty
peña *f* crag, cliff; (*roca*) rock; F *de amigos* group, circle
peñasco *m* boulder
peñón *m*: ***el Peñon de Gibraltar*** the Rock of Gibraltar
peón *m en ajedrez* pawn; *trabajador* labo(u)rer
peor *adj comp* worse; ***de mal en peor*** from bad to worse
pepa *f L.Am.* (*semilla*) seed; ***soltar la pepa*** F spill the beans
pepinillo *m* gherkin
pepino *m* cucumber; ***me importa un pepino*** F I don't give a damn F
pepita *f* pip
pequeño 1 *adj* small, little; ***de pequeño*** when I was small *o* little **2** *m*, **-a** *f* little one
pequinés *m* ZO Pekinese, Peke F
pera *f* pear
peral *m* pear tree
perca *f pez* perch
percance *m* mishap
percatarse ⟨1a⟩ *v/r* notice; ***percatarse de algo*** notice sth
percebe *m* ZO barnacle
percepción *f* perception; COM *acto* receipt
percha *f* coat hanger; *gancho* coat hook
perchero *m* coat rack
percibir ⟨3a⟩ *v/t* perceive; COM *sueldo* receive
percusión *f* MÚS percussion
perdedor *m*, **perdedora** *f* loser
perder ⟨2g⟩ **1** *v/t objeto* lose; *tren, avión etc* miss; *el tiempo* waste **2** *v/i* lose; ***echar a perder*** ruin; ***echarse a perder*** *de alimento* go bad **3** *v/r* **perderse** get lost
perdición *f* downfall
pérdida *f* loss
perdido *adj* lost; ***ponerse perdido*** get filthy
perdigón *m* pellet
perdiz *f* ZO partridge
perdón *m* pardon; REL forgiveness; ***pedir perdón*** say sorry, apologize; ***¡perdón!*** sorry
perdonar ⟨1a⟩ *v/t* forgive; JUR pardon; ***perdonar algo a alguien*** forgive s.o. sth; ***¡perdone!*** sorry; ***perdone, ¿tiene hora?*** excuse me, do you have the time?
perdurar ⟨1a⟩ *v/i* endure
perecedero *adj* perishable
perecer ⟨2d⟩ *v/i* perish
peregrinación *f* pilgrimage
peregrinar ⟨1a⟩ *v/i* go on a pilgrimage
peregrino *m*, **-a** *f* pilgrim
perejil *m* BOT parsley
perenne *adj* BOT perennial
perentorio *adj* (*urgente*) urgent, pressing; (*apremiante*) peremptory
pereza *f* laziness
perezoso 1 *adj* lazy **2** *m* ZO sloth
perfección *f* perfection; ***a la perfección*** perfectly, to perfection
perfeccionamiento *m* perfecting
perfeccionar ⟨1a⟩ *v/t* perfect
perfeccionista *m/f* perfectionist
perfecto *adj* perfect
pérfido *adj* treacherous
perfil *m* profile; ***de perfil*** in profile, from the side
perforación *f* puncture
perforadora *f* punch
perforar ⟨1a⟩ *v/t* pierce; *calle* dig up
perfumar ⟨1a⟩ *v/t* perfume
perfume *m* perfume

perfumería *f* perfume shop
pergamino *m* parchment
pergenio *m*, **-a** *f Rpl* F kid F
pericia *f* expertise
pericote *m Chi, Pe* zo large rat
periferia *f* periphery; *de ciudad* outskirts *pl*
perilla *f* goatee; ***me viene de perilla*** F that'll be very useful; ***tu visita me viene de perilla*** F you've come at just the right time
perímetro *m* perimeter
periódico 1 *adj* periodic **2** *m* newspaper
periodismo *m* journalism
periodista *m/f* journalist
período, **periodo** *m* period
peripecia *f* adventure
periquete *m*: ***en un periquete*** F in a second, in no time F
periquito *m* zo budgerigar
periscopio *m* periscope
perito 1 *adj* expert **2** *m*, **-a** *f* expert; COM *en seguros* loss adjuster
perjudicar ⟨1g⟩ *v/t* harm, damage
perjudicial *adj* harmful, damaging
perjuicio *m* harm, damage; ***sin perjuicio de*** without affecting
perjurio *m* perjury
perla *f* pearl; ***nos vino de perlas*** F it suited us fine F
permanecer ⟨2d⟩ *v/i* remain, stay
permanente 1 *adj* permanent **2** *f* perm
permeable *adj* permeable
permisible *adj* permissible
permisivo *adj* permissive
permiso *m* permission; *documento* permit; ***permiso de conducir*** driver's license, *Br* driving licence; ***permiso de residencia*** residence permit; ***con permiso*** excuse me; ***estar de permiso*** be on leave
permitir ⟨3a⟩ **1** *v/t* permit, allow **2** *v/r* **permitirse** afford; ***permitirse el lujo de*** permit o.s. the luxury of
pernicioso *adj* harmful
pernoctar ⟨1a⟩ *v/i* spend the night
pero 1 *conj* but **2** *m* flaw, defect; ***no hay peros que valgan*** no excuses
perogrullada *f* platitude
peronismo *m* Peronism
peronista *m/f* Peronist
perorata *f* F lecture
perpendicular *adj* perpendicular
perpetrar ⟨1a⟩ *v/t crimen* perpetrate, commit
perpetuar ⟨1e⟩ *v/t* perpetuate
perpetuidad *f*: ***a perpetuidad*** in perpetuity
perpetuo *adj fig* perpetual
perplejidad *f* perplexity
perplejo *adj* puzzled, perplexed
perra *f* dog; ***el perro y la perra*** the dog and the bitch; ***perras*** F pesetas
perrera *f* kennels *pl*
perrería *f* F dirty trick
perrito *m*: ***perrito caliente*** GASTR hot dog
perro *m* dog; ***perro callejero*** stray; ***perro guardián*** guard dog; ***perro lazarillo*** seeing eye dog, *Br* guide dog; ***perro pastor*** sheepdog; ***llevarse como el perro y el gato*** *fig* fight like cat and dog; ***hace un tiempo de perros*** F the weather is lousy F
persecución *f* pursuit; (*acoso*) persecution
perseguidor *m*, **perseguidora** *f* persecutor
perseguir ⟨3l & 3d⟩ *v/t* pursue; *delincuente* look for; (*molestar*) pester; (*acosar*) persecute
perseverancia *f* perseverance
perseverar ⟨1a⟩ *v/i* persevere (***en*** with)
persiana *f* blind
pérsico *adj* Persian
persignarse ⟨1a⟩ *v/r* cross o.s.
persistente *adj* persistent
persistir ⟨3a⟩ *v/i* persist
persona *f* person; ***quince personas*** fifteen people
personaje *m* TEA character; *famoso* celebrity
personal 1 *adj* personal **2** *m* personnel, staff
personalidad *f* personality
personalizar ⟨1f⟩ *v/t* personalize
personificar ⟨1g⟩ *v/t* personify, embody
perspectiva *f* perspective; *fig* point of view; ***perspectivas*** *pl* outlook *sg*, prospects
perspicacia *f* shrewdness, perspicacity
persuadir ⟨3a⟩ *v/t* persuade
persuasión *f* persuasion
persuasivo *adj* persuasive
pertenecer ⟨2d⟩ *v/i* belong (***a*** to)
pertenencias *fpl* belongings
pértiga *f* pole; ***salto con pértiga*** DEP pole vault
pertinaz *adj* persistent; (*terco*) obstinate
pertinente *adj* relevant, pertinent
pertrechos *mpl* MIL equipment *sg*
perturbar ⟨1a⟩ *v/t* disturb; *reunión* disrupt
Perú*m* Peru
peruano 1 *adj* Peruvian **2** *m*, **-a** *f* Peruvian
perversión *f* perversion
perverso *adj* perverted
pervertido *m*, **-a** *f* pervert
pervertir ⟨3i⟩ *v/t* pervert

P

pesa *f para balanza* weight; DEP shot; *C.Am., W.I.* butcher's shop
pesadez *f fig* drag F
pesadilla *f* nightmare
pesado 1 *adj objeto* heavy; *libro, clase etc* tedious, boring; *trabajo* tough **2** *m*, **-a** *f* bore; ***¡qué pesado es!*** F he's a real pain F
pésame *m* condolences *pl*
pesar ⟨1a⟩ **1** *v/t* weigh **2** *v/i* be heavy; (*influir*) carry weight; *fig* weigh heavily (***sobre*** on); ***me pesa tener que informarle ...*** I regret to have to inform you ... **3** *m* sorrow; ***a pesar de*** in spite of, despite
pesca *f actividad* fishing; (*peces*) fish *pl*
pescadería *f* fish shop
pescadero *m*, **-a** *f* fishmonger
pescadilla *f pez* whiting
pescado *m* GASTR fish
pescador *m* fisherman
pescar ⟨1g⟩ **1** *v/t un pez, resfriado etc* catch; (*intentar tomar*) fish for; *trabajo, marido etc* land F **2** *v/i* fish
pescuezo *m* neck
pese: ***pese a*** despite
pesero *m L.Am.* minibus; *Méx* (collective) taxi
peseta *f* peseta
pesetero *adj* F money-grubbing F
pesimismo *m* pessimism
pesimista 1 *adj* pessimistic **2** *m/f* pessimist
pésimo *adj sup* awful, terrible
peso *m* weight; *moneda* peso; ***de peso*** *fig* weighty
pesquero 1 *adj* fishing *atr* **2** *m* fishing boat
pesquisa *f* investigation
pestaña *f* eyelash
pestañear ⟨1a⟩ *v/i* flutter one's eyelashes; ***sin pestañear*** *fig* without batting an eyelid
peste *f* MED plague; F *olor* stink F; ***echar pestes*** F curse and swear
pesticida *m* pesticide
pestilente *adj* foul-smelling
pestillo *m* (*picaporte*) door handle; (*cerradura*) bolt
petaca *f para tabaco* tobacco pouch; *para bebida* hip flask; *C.Am.* F *insecto* ladybug, *Br* ladybird
pétalo *m* petal
petanca *f type of bowls*
petardo 1 *m* firecracker **2** *m*, **-a** *f* F nerd F
petate *m* kit bag; *L.Am.* F *en el suelo* mat
petición *f* request; ***a petición de*** at the request of
petirrojo *m* ZO robin
petiso *L.Am.* **1** *m*, **-a** *f* F shorty F **2** *m* pony
peto *m* bib; ***pantalón de peto*** overalls *pl*, *Br* dungarees *pl*
petrificado *adj* petrified
petróleo *m* oil, petroleum
petrolero 1 *adj* oil *atr* **2** *m* MAR oil tanker
petrolífero *adj* oil *atr*
petroquímica *f* petrochemical
petulante *adj* smug
peyorativo *adj* pejorative
pez *m* ZO fish; ***pez espada*** swordfish; ***pez gordo*** F big shot F; ***estar pez en algo*** F be clueless about sth F
pezón *m* nipple
pezuña *f* ZO hoof
piadoso *adj* pious
pianista *m/f* pianist
piano *m* piano; ***piano de cola*** grand piano
piar ⟨1c⟩ *v/i* tweet, chirrup
PIB *abr* (***= producto interior bruto***) GDP (= gross domestic product)
pibe *m*, **-a** *f Rpl* F kid F
picada *f de serpiente* bite; *de abeja* sting; *L.Am. para comer* snacks *pl*, nibbles *pl*; *Rpl* (*camino*) path
picadero *m escuela* riding school
picado 1 *adj diente* decayed; *mar* rough, choppy; *carne* ground, *Br* minced; *verdura* minced, *Br* finely chopped; *fig* offended **2** *m L.Am.* dive; ***caer en picado*** *de precios* nosedive, plummet
picadora *f en cocina* mincer
picadura *f de reptil, mosquito* bite; *de avispa* sting; *tabaco* cut tobacco
picaflor *m L.Am.* ZO hummingbird; *fig* womanizer
picante 1 *adj* hot, spicy; *chiste* risqué **2** *m* hot spice
picaporte *m* door handle
picar ⟨1g⟩ **1** *v/t de mosquito, serpiente* bite; *de avispa* sting; *de ave* peck; *carne* grind, *Br* mince; *verdura* mince, *Br* finely chop; TAUR jab with a lance; (*molestar*) annoy; *la curiosidad* pique **2** *v/i tb fig* take the bait; *L.Am. de la comida* be hot; (*producir picor*) itch; *del sol* burn
picardía *f* (*astucia*) craftiness, slyness; (*travesura*) mischievousness; *Méx* (*taco, palabrota*) swearing, swearwords *pl*
pícaro *adj persona* crafty, sly; *comentario* mischievous
picarón *m Méx, Chi, Pe* (*buñuelo*) fritter
picatoste *m* piece of fried bread
picha *f* V prick V
pichicato *m Pe, Bol* P coke P
pichincha *f L.Am.* bargain
pichón *m L.Am.* ORN chick; F (*novato*) rookie F
Picio: ***más feo que Picio*** F as ugly as sin F

P

picnic *m* (*pl* ~s) picnic
pico *m* ZO beak; F (*boca*) mouth; *de montaña* peak; *herramienta* pickax(e); ***a las tres y pico*** some time after three o'clock; ***cerrar el pico*** F shut one's mouth F
picor *m* itch
picota *f* bigarreau (*type of sweet cherry*)
picotazo *m* peck
picotear ⟨1a⟩ *v/t* peck
pido *vb* → ***pedir***
pie *m* foot; *de estatua, lámpara* base; ***a pie*** on foot; ***de pie*** standing; ***no tiene ni pies ni cabeza*** it doesn't make any sense at all, I can't make head nor tail of it
piedad *f* pity; (*clemencia*) mercy
piedra *f tb* MED stone; ***piedra preciosa*** precious stone; ***quedarse de piedra*** *fig* F be stunned
piel *f de persona, fruta* skin; *de animal* hide, skin; (*cuero*) leather; ***abrigo de pieles*** fur coat
pienso[1] *vb* → ***pensar***
pienso[2] *m* animal feed
pierdo *vb* → ***perder***
pierna *f* leg; ***dormir a pierna suelta*** sleep like a log
pieza *f de un conjunto*, MÚS piece; *de aparato* part; TEA play; (*habitación*) room; ***pieza de recambio*** spare (part); ***quedarse de una pieza*** F be amazed
pifia *f* F (*error*) booboo F; *Chi, Pe, Rpl* defect
pigmento *m* pigment
pigmeo *m*, **-a** *f* pigmy
pijama *m* pajamas *pl*, *Br* pyjamas *pl*
pijo **1** *adj* posh **2** *m* V (*pene*) prick V **3** *m*, **-a** *f* F *persona* rich kid F
pila *f* EL battery; (*montón*) pile; (*fregadero*) sink
pilar *m tb fig* pillar
píldora *f* pill
pileta *f Rpl* sink; (*alberca*) swimming pool
pillaje *m* pillage
pillar ⟨1a⟩ *v/t* (*tomar*) seize; (*atrapar*) catch; (*atropellar*) hit; *chiste* get
pillo **1** *adj* mischievous **2** *m*, **-a** *f* rascal
pilón *m Méx*: ***me dio dos de pilón*** he gave me two extra
pilotar ⟨1a⟩ *v/t* AVIA fly, pilot; AUTO drive; MAR steer
piloto *m* AVIA, MAR pilot; AUTO driver; EL pilot light; ***piloto automático*** autopilot
piltrafa *f*: ***piltrafas*** rags; ***estar hecho una piltrafa*** *fig* be a total wreck F
pimentón *m* paprika
pimienta *f* pepper
pimiento *m* pepper; ***me importa un pimiento*** F I couldn't care less F
pimpón *m* ping-pong
PIN *m* PIN
pinar *m* pine forest
pincel *m* paintbrush
pinchadiscos *m/f* F disc jockey, DJ
pinchar ⟨1a⟩ **1** *v/t* prick; AUTO puncture; TELEC tap; F (*molestar*) bug F, needle F; ***pincharle a alguien*** MED give s.o. a shot **2** *v/i* prick; AUTO get a flat tire, *Br* get a puncture **3** *v/r* **pincharse** *con aguja etc* prick o.s.; F (*inyectarse*) shoot up P; ***se nos pinchó una rueda*** we got a flat (tire) *o Br* a puncture
pinchazo *m herida* prick; *dolor* sharp pain; AUTO flat (tire), *Br* puncture; F flop F
pinche[1] *m* cook's assistant
pinche[2] *adj Méx* F rotten F; *C.Am., Méx* (*tacaño*) tight-fisted
pincho *m* GASTR bar snack
pingajo *m* F rag
ping-pong *m* ping-pong
pingüino *m* ZO penguin
pino *m* BOT pine; ***hacer el pino*** do a handstand
pinol(e) *m C.Am., Méx* cornstarch, *Br* cornflour; *L.Am.* roasted corn
pinta *f* pint; *aspecto* looks *pl*; ***tener buena pinta*** *fig* look inviting
pintalabios *m* lipstick
pintar ⟨1a⟩ **1** *v/t* paint; ***no pintar nada*** *fig* F not count **2** *v/r* **pintarse** put on one's makeup
pintor *m*, **pintora** *f* painter; ***pintor (de brocha gorda)*** (house) painter
pintoresco *adj* picturesque
pintura *f sustancia* paint; *obra* painting
pinza *f* clothes pin, *Br* clothes peg; ZO claw; ***pinzas*** tweezers; *L.Am.* (*alicates*) pliers
piña *f del pino* pine cone; *fruta* pineapple
piñón *m* BOT pine nut; TÉC pinion
piojo *m* ZO louse; ***piojos*** *pl* lice *pl*
piola *f L.Am.* cord, twine
piolín *m Arg* cord, twine
pionero **1** *adj* pioneering **2** *m*, **-a** *f tb fig* pioneer
pipa *f* pipe; ***pipas*** *semillas* sunflower seeds; ***pasarlo pipa*** F have a great time
pipí *m* F pee F; ***hacer pipí*** F pee F
pipiolo *m C.Am., Méx* F kid F; ***pipiolos*** *pl C.Am.* F (*dinero*) cash *sg*
pique *m* resentment; (*rivalidad*) rivalry; ***irse a pique*** *fig* go under, go to the wall
piqueta *f herramienta* pickax(e); *en cámping* tentpeg
piquete *m* POL picket
pirado *adj* F crazy F
piragua *f* canoe

P

piragüista *m/f* DEP canoeist
pirámide *f* pyramid
piraña *f* ZO piranha
pirarse ⟨1a⟩ *v/r* F (*marcharse*) clear off F; ***pirarse por alguien*** F lose one's head over s.o. F
pirata *m/f* pirate; ***pirata informático*** hacker
piratear ⟨1a⟩ *v/t* INFOR pirate
pirenaico *adj* Pyrenean
Pirineos *mpl* Pyrenees
pirómano *m*, **-a** *f* pyromaniac; JUR arsonist
piropo *m* compliment
pirotécnico *adj* fireworks *atr*
piruleta *f*, **pirulí** *m* lollipop
pis *m* F pee F; ***hacer pis*** F have a pee F
pisada *f* footstep; *huella* footprint
pisapapeles *m* paperweight
pisar ⟨1a⟩ *v/t* step on; *uvas* tread; *fig* (*maltratar*) walk all over; *idea* steal; ***pisar a alguien*** step on s.o.'s foot
piscifactoría *f* fish farm
piscina *f* swimming pool
Piscis *m/f inv* ASTR Pisces
piso *m* apartment, *Br* flat; (*planta*) floor
pisotear ⟨1a⟩ *v/t* trample
pista *f* track, trail; (*indicio*) clue; *de atletismo* track; ***pista de aterrizaje*** AVIA runway; ***pista de baile*** dance floor; ***pista de tenis / squash*** tennis / squash court; ***seguir la pista a alguien*** be on the trail of s.o.
pistacho *m* BOT pistachio
pisto *m* GASTR *mixture of tomatoes, peppers etc cooked in oil*; *C.Am., Méx* F (*dinero*) cash, dough F
pistola *f* pistol
pistón *m* piston
pitada *f* (*abucheo*) whistle; *S. Am. de cigarillo* puff
pitar ⟨1a⟩ **1** *v/i* whistle; *con bocina* beep, hoot; *L.Am.* (*fumar*) smoke; ***salir pitando*** F dash off F **2** *v/t* (*abuchear*) whistle at; *penalti, falta etc* call, *Br* blow for; *silbato* blow
pitazo *m L.Am.* whistle
pitear ⟨1a⟩ *v/i L.Am.* blow a whistle
pitido *m* whistle; *con bocina* beep, hoot
pitillo *m* cigarette; *hecho a mano* roll-up
pito *m* whistle; (*bocina*) horn; ***me importa un pito*** F I don't give a hoot F
pitón *m* ZO python
pitonisa *f* fortune-teller
pitorrearse ⟨1a⟩ *v/r*: ***pitorrearse de alguien*** F make fun of s.o.
pívot *m en baloncesto* center, *Br* centre
piyama *m L.Am.* pajamas *pl*, *Br* pyjamas *pl*
pizarra *f* blackboard; *piedra* slate
pizca *f* pinch; *Méx* AGR harvest; ***ni pizca de*** not a bit of
pizza *f* pizza
placa *f* (*lámina*) sheet; (*plancha*) plate; (*letrero*) plaque; *Méx* AUTO license plate, *Br* number plate; ***placa madre*** INFOR motherboard; ***placa*** (***dental***) plaque; ***placa de matrícula*** AUTO license plate, *Br* number plate
placer ⟨2x⟩ **1** *v/i* please; ***siempre hace lo que le place*** he always does as he pleases **2** *m* pleasure
plácido *adj* placid
plaga *f* AGR pest; MED plague; *fig* scourge; (*abundancia*) glut
plagado *adj* infested; (*lleno*) full; ***plagado de gente*** swarming with people
plagiar ⟨1b⟩ *v/t* plagiarize; *L.Am.* (*secuestrar*) kidnap
plagio *m* plagiarism
plan *m* plan
plana *f*: ***primera plana*** front page
plancha *f para planchar* iron; *en cocina* broiler, *Br* grill; *de metal* sheet; F (*metedura de pata*) goof F; ***a la plancha*** GASTR broiled, *Br* grilled
planchar ⟨1a⟩ *v/t* iron; *Méx* F (*dar plantón*) stand up F; *L.Am.* (*lisonjear*) flatter
planeador *m* glider
planear ⟨1a⟩ **1** *v/t* plan **2** *v/i* AVIA glide
planeta *m* planet
planetario *m* planetarium
planificación *f* planning; ***planificación familiar*** family planning
planificar ⟨1g⟩ *v/t* plan
plano **1** *adj* flat **2** *m* ARQUI plan; *de ciudad* map; *en cine* shot; MAT plane; *fig* level
planta *f* BOT plant; (*piso*) floor; ***planta del pie*** sole of the foot
plantación *f* plantation
plantado *adj*: ***dejar a alguien plantado*** F stand s.o. up F
plantar ⟨1a⟩ **1** *v/t árbol etc* plant; *tienda de campaña* put up; ***plantar a alguien*** F stand s.o. up F **2** *v/r* **plantarse** put one's foot down
planteamiento *m de problema* posing; (*perspectiva*) approach
plantear ⟨1a⟩ *v/t dificultad, problema* pose, create; *cuestión* raise
plantel *m* (*equipo*) team; *L.Am.* staff
plantilla *f para zapato* insole; (*personal*) staff; DEP squad; *para cortar*, INFOR template
plantón *m*: ***dar un plantón a alguien*** F stand s.o. up F
plasma *m* plasma
plasmar ⟨1a⟩ *v/t* (*modelar*) shape; *fig* (*representar*) express

plasta 1 *m/f* F pain F, drag F **2** *adj*: ***ser plasta*** F be a pain *o* drag F
plástica *f* EDU *handicrafts*
plástico *m* plastic
plastificado *adj* laminated
plastificar ⟨1g⟩ *v/t documento* laminate
plastilina *f* Plasticine®
plata *f* silver; *L.Am.* F (*dinero*) cash, dough F
plataforma *f tb* POL platform; ***plataforma petrolífera*** oil rig
platal *m L.Am.* fortune
plátano *m* banana
plateado *adj Méx* wealthy
plática *f Méx* chat, talk
platicar ⟨1g⟩ **1** *v/t L.Am.* tell **2** *v/i Méx* chat, talk
platillo *m*: ***platillo volante*** flying saucer; ***platillos*** MÚS cymbals
platino *m* platinum
plato *m* plate; GASTR dish; ***plato principal*** main course; ***plato preparado / precocinado*** ready meal; ***plato sopero / hondo*** soup dish; ***pagar los platos rotos*** F carry the can F
plató *m de película* set; TV studio
platónico *adj* platonic
platudo *adj Chi* rich
plausible *adj* plausible
playa *f* beach; ***playa de estacionamiento*** *L.Am.* parking lot, *Br* car park
playeras *fpl* canvas shoes
playo *adj Rpl* shallow
plaza *f* square; (*vacante*) job opening, *Br* vacancy; *en vehículo* seat; *de trabajo* position; ***plaza de toros*** bull ring
plazo *f* period; (*pago*) instal(l)ment; ***a corto / largo plazo*** in the short / long term; ***a plazos*** in instal(l)ments
plebiscito *m* plebiscite
plegable *adj* collapsible, folding
plegar ⟨1h & 1k⟩ **1** *v/t* fold (up) **2** *v/r* **plegarse** *fig* submit (***a*** to)
plegaria *f* prayer
pleito *m* JUR lawsuit; *fig* dispute; ***poner un pleito a alguien*** sue s.o.
pleno 1 *adj* full; ***en pleno día*** in broad daylight **2** *m* plenary session
pliego 1 *vb* → ***plegar*** **2** *m* (*hoja de papel*) sheet (of paper); (*carta*) sealed letter *o* document
pliegue *m* fold, crease
plomería *f Méx* plumbing
plomero *m Méx* plumber
plomo *m* lead; EL fuse; *fig* F drag F; ***sin plomo*** AUTO unleaded
pluma *f* feather; *para escribir* fountain pen
plumaje *m* plumage
plumero *m para limpiar* feather duster; *CSur para maquillaje* powder puff; ***vérsele el plumero a alguien*** *fig* F see what s.o. is up to F
plumífero *m* F down jacket
plural 1 *adj* plural **2** *m* GRAM plural
pluralismo *m* POL pluralism
pluriempleo *m* having more than one job
plus *m* bonus
plusmarquista *m/f* record holder
plusvalía *f* COM capital gain
plutonio *m* QUÍM plutonium
pluviosidad *f* rainfall
PNB *abr* (**= *producto nacional bruto***) GNP (= gross national product)
P.° *abr* (**= *Paseo***) Ave (= Avenue)
p.o. *abr* (**= *por orden***) p. p. (per procurationem, by proxy)
población *f gente* population; (*ciudad*) city, town; (*pueblo*) village; *Chi* shanty town
poblado 1 *adj* populated; *barba* bushy; ***poblado de*** *fig* full of **2** *m* (*pueblo*) settlement
poblador *m*, **pobladora** *f Chi* shanty town dweller
poblar ⟨1m⟩ *v/t* populate
pobre 1 *adj económicamente*, *en calidad* poor **2** *m/f* poor person; ***los pobres*** the poor
pobreza *f* poverty
pocilga *f* pigpen
pócima *f* concoction
poción *f* potion
poco 1 *adj sg* little, not much; *pl* few, not many; ***un poco de*** a little; ***unos pocos*** a few **2** *adv* little; ***trabaja poco*** he doesn't work much; ***ahora se ve muy poco*** it's seldom seen now; ***estuvo poco por aquí*** he wasn't around much; ***poco conocido*** little known; ***poco a poco*** little by little; ***dentro de poco*** soon, shortly; ***hace poco*** a short time ago, not long ago; ***por poco*** nearly, almost; ***¡a poco no lo hacemos!*** *Méx* don't tell me we're not doing it; ***de a poco me fui tranquilizando*** *Rpl* little by little I calmed down **3** *m*: ***un poco*** a little, a bit
podar ⟨1a⟩ *v/t* AGR prune
poder ⟨2t⟩ **1** *v/aux capacidad* can, be able to; *permiso* can, be allowed to; *posibilidad* may, might; ***no pude hablar con ella*** I wasn't able to talk to her; ***¿puedo ir contigo?*** can *o* may I come with you?; ***¡podías habérselo dicho!*** you could have *o* you might have told him **2** *v/i*: ***poder con*** (*sobreponerse a*) manage, cope with; ***me puede*** he can beat me; ***es franco a más no poder*** F he's as frank as

they come F; ***comimos a más no poder*** F we ate to bursting point F; ***no puedo más*** I can't take any more, I've had enough; ***puede ser*** perhaps, maybe; ***puede que*** perhaps, maybe; ***¿se puede?*** can I come in?, do you mind if I come in? **3** *m tb* POL power; ***en poder de alguien*** in s.o.'s hands
poderoso *adj* powerful
podio *m* podium
podólogo *m*, **-a** *f* MED podiatrist, *Br* chiropodist
podrido *adj tb fig* rotten
poema *m* poem
poesía *f género* poetry; (*poema*) poem
poeta *m/f* poet
poético *adj* poetic
poetisa *f* poet
polaco 1 *adj* Polish **2** *m*, **-a** *f* Pole
polar *adj* polar
polea *f* TÉC pulley
polémica *f* controversy
polémico *adj* controversial
polen *m* BOT pollen
poleo *m* BOT pennyroyal
polera *f Chi* turtle neck (sweater)
poli *m/f* F cop F; ***la poli*** F the cops *pl* F
policía 1 *f* police **2** *m/f* police officer, policeman; *mujer* police officer, policewoman
policíaco, policiaco *adj* detective *atr*
policial *adj* police *atr*
polideportivo *m* sports center, *Br* sports centre
poliéster *m* polyester
polifacético *adj* versatile, multifaceted
poligamia *f* polygamy
políglota *m/f* polyglot
polígono *m* MAT polygon; ***polígono industrial*** industrial zone, *Br* industrial estate
polilla *f* ZO moth
polio *f* MED polio
poliomielitis *f* MED poliomyelitis
política *f* politics
políticamente *adv*: **políticamente correcto** politically correct
político 1 *adj* political **2** *m*, **-a** *f* politician
póliza *f* policy; ***póliza de seguros*** insurance policy
polizón *m/f* stowaway
polla *f* V prick V, cock V
pollera *f L.Am.* skirt
pollería *f* poulterer's
pollito *m* chick
pollo *m* ZO, GASTR chicken
polluelo *m* ZO chick
polo *m* GEOG, EL pole; *prenda* polo shirt; DEP polo; ***Polo Norte*** North Pole; ***Polo Sur*** South Pole
polola *f Chi* girlfriend
pololear ⟨1a⟩ *v/i Chi* be going steady
pololo *m Chi* boyfriend
Polonia Poland
poltrona *f* easy chair
polución *f* pollution; ***polución atmosférica*** air pollution, atmospheric pollution
polucionar ⟨1a⟩ *v/t* pollute
polvo *m* dust; *en química, medicina etc* powder; ***polvos*** *pl* ***de talco*** talcum powder *sg*; ***echar un polvo*** V have a screw V; ***estar hecho polvo*** F be all in F
pólvora *f* gunpowder
polvorín *m almacén* magazine; *fig* powder keg
polvorón *m* GASTR *type of small cake*
pomada *f* cream
pomelo *m* BOT grapefruit
pómez *f*: ***piedra pómez*** pumice stone
pomo *m* doorknob
pompa *f* pomp; ***pompa de jabón*** bubble; ***pompas*** *pl* ***fúnebres*** *ceremonia* funeral ceremony *sg*; *establecimiento* funeral parlo(u)r *sg*
pomposo *adj* pompous
pómulo *m* ANAT cheekbone
pon *vb* → ***poner***
ponchadura *f Méx* flat, *Br* puncture
ponchar ⟨1a⟩ **1** *v/t L.Am.* puncture **2** *v/r* **poncharse** *Méx* get a flat *o Br* puncture
ponche *m* punch
poncho *m* poncho; ***pisarse el poncho*** *S. Am.* be mistaken
ponderación *f mesura* deliberation; *en estadísticas* weighting
ponencia *f* presentation; EDU paper
poner ⟨2r; *part* ***puesto*** ⟩ **1** *v/t* put; (*añadir*) put in; RAD, TV turn on, switch on; *la mesa* set; *ropa* put on; *telegrama* send; (*escribir*) put down; *en periódico, libro etc* say; *negocio* set up; *huevos* lay; ***poner a alguien furioso*** make s.o. angry; ***ponerle a alguien con alguien*** TELEC put s.o. through to s.o.; ***ponerle una multa a alguien*** fine s.o.; ***pongamos que*** let's suppose *o* assume that **2** *v/r* **ponerse** *ropa* put on; ***ponte en el banco*** go and sit on the bench; ***se puso ahí*** she stood over there; ***dile que se ponga*** TELEC tell her to come to the phone; ***ponerse palido*** turn pale; ***ponerse furioso*** get angry; ***ponerse enfermo*** become *o* fall ill; ***ponerse a*** start to
pongo[1] *vb* → ***poner***
pongo[2] *m Pe* indentured Indian laborer
poni *m* ZO pony
poniente *m* west
pontífice *m* pontiff; ***sumo pontífice***

Pope
ponzoñoso *adj* poisonous
pop 1 *adj* pop; ***música pop*** pop music **2** *m* pop
popa *f* MAR stern
popular *adj* popular; (*del pueblo*) folk *atr*; *barrio* lower-class
popularidad *f* popularity
popularizar ⟨1f⟩ *v/t* popularize
póquer *m* poker
por *prp* ◇ *motivo* for, because of; ***lo hizo por amor*** she did it out of love; ***luchó por sus ideales*** he fought for his ideals
◇ *medio* by; ***por avión*** by air; ***por correo*** by mail, *Br tb* by post
◇ *tiempo*: ***por un segundo*** *L.Am.* for a second; ***por la mañana*** in the morning
◇ *movimiento*: ***por la calle*** down the street; ***por un tunel*** through a tunnel; ***por aquí*** this way
◇ *posición aproximada* around, about; ***está por aquí*** it's around here (somewhere)
◇ *cambio*: ***por cincuenta pesos*** for fifty pesos
◇ *otros usos*: ***por hora*** an *o* per hour; ***dos por dos*** two times two; ***¿por qué?*** why?; ***el motivo por el cual*** *or* ***por el que …*** the reason why …
porcelana *f* porcelain, china; ***de porcelana*** porcelain *atr*, china *atr*
porcentaje *m* percentage
porche *f* porch
porción *f* portion
pordiosero *m*, **-a** *f* beggar
porfiar ⟨1c⟩ *v/i* insist (***en*** on)
pormenor *m* detail
porno 1 *adj* porn *atr* **2** *m* porn
pornografía *f* pornography
pornográfico *adj* pornographic
poro *m* pore
poroso *adj* porous
poroto *m Rpl*, *Chi* bean; ***porotos verdes*** *L.Am.* green beans
porque *conj* because; ***porque sí*** just because
porqué *m* reason
porquería *f* (*suciedad*) filth; F *cosa de poca calidad* piece of trash F
porra *f* baton; (*palo*) club; ***¡vete a la porra!*** F go to hell! F
porrazo *m*: ***darle un porrazo a alguien*** F hit s.o.; ***darse*** *or* ***pegarse un porrazo*** crash (***contra*** into)
porro *m* F joint F
porrón *m container from which wine is poured straight into the mouth*
portaaviones *m inv* aircraft carrier
portada *f* TIP front page; *de revista* cover; ARQUI front
portafolios *m inv* briefcase
portal *m* foyer; (*entrada*) doorway
portaligas *m inv Arg*, *Chi* garter belt, *Br* suspender belt
portarse ⟨1a⟩ *v/r* behave
portátil *adj* portable
portavoz *m/f* spokesman; *mujer* spokeswoman
portazo *m*: ***dar un portazo*** F slam the door
porte *m* (*aspecto*) appearance, air; (*gasto de correo*) postage
portento *m* wonder; *persona* genius
porteño *Arg* **1** *adj* of Buenos Aires, Buenos Aires *atr* **2** *m*, **-a** *f* native of Buenos Aires
portería *f* reception; *casa* superintendent's apartment, *Br* caretaker's flat; DEP goal
portero *m* doorman; *de edificio* superintendent, *Br* caretaker; DEP goalkeeper; ***portero automático*** intercom, *Br* entryphone
portón *m* large door
Portugal Portugal
portugués 1 *m/adj* Portuguese **2** *m*, **-esa** *f persona* Portuguese
porvenir *m* future
posada *f C.Am.*, *Méx* Christmas party; (*fonda*) inn
posar ⟨1a⟩ **1** *v/t mano* lay, place (***sobre*** on); ***posar la mirada en*** gaze at **2** *v/r* **posarse** *de ave*, *insecto*, AVIA land
posavasos *m inv* coaster
posdata *f* postscript
poseer ⟨2e⟩ *v/t* possess; (*ser dueño de*) own, possess
posesión *f* possession; ***tomar posesión*** (***de un cargo***) POL take up office
posguerra *f* postwar period
posibilidad *f* possibility
posibilitar ⟨1a⟩ *v/t* make possible
posible *adj* possible; ***en lo posible*** as far as possible; ***hacer todo lo posible*** do everything possible; ***es posible que …*** perhaps …
posición *f tb* MIL, *fig* position; *social* standing, status
positivo *adj* positive
posmoderno *adj* postmodern
poso *m* dregs *pl*
posología *f* dosage
posponer ⟨2r; *part* ***pospuesto*** ⟩ *v/t* postpone
pospuesto *part* → ***posponer***
posta *f*: ***a posta*** on purpose
postal 1 *adj* mail *atr*, postal **2** *f* postcard
poste *m* post

P

póster *m* poster
postergar ⟨1a⟩ *v/t* postpone
posteridad *f* posterity
posterior *adj* later, subsequent; (*trasero*) rear *atr*, back *atr*
postizo 1 *adj* false **2** *m* hairpiece
postor *m* bidder; ***al mejor postor*** to the highest bidder
postrar ⟨1a⟩ **1** *v/t*: ***la gripe lo postró*** he was laid up with flu **2** *v/r* **postrarse** prostrate o.s.
postre *m* dessert; ***a la postre*** in the end
postular ⟨1a⟩ *v/t hipótesis* put forward, advance
póstumo *adj* posthumous
postura *f tb fig* position
pos(t)venta *adj inv* after-sales *atr*
potable *adj* drinkable; *fig* F passable; ***agua potable*** drinking water
potaje *m* GASTR stew
potasio *m* potassium
potencia *f* power; ***en potencia*** potential
potencial *m/adj* potential
potenciar ⟨1b⟩ *v/t fig* foster, promote
potentado *m*, **-a** *f* tycoon
potente *adj* powerful
potestad *f* authority; ***patria potestad*** parental authority
potingue *m* F *desp* lotion, cream
potro *m* zo colt
pozo *m* well; MIN shaft; *Rpl* pothole; ***un pozo sin fondo*** *fig* a bottomless pit
pozol *m C.Am.* corn liquor
pozole *m Méx* corn stew
práctica *f* practice
practicar ⟨1g⟩ *v/t* practice, *Br* practise; *deporte* play; ***practicar la equitación / la esgrima*** ride / fence
práctico *adj* practical
pradera *f* prairie, grassland
prado *m* meadow
pragmático *adj* pragmatic
pragmatismo *m* pragmatism
pral. *abr* (= ***principal***) first
preámbulo *m* preamble
prebenda *f* sinecure
precalentamiento *m* DEP warm-up
precario *adj* precarious
precaución *f* precaution; ***tomar precauciones*** take precautions
precavido *adj* cautious
precedente 1 *adj* previous **2** *m* precedent
preceder ⟨2a⟩ *v/t* precede
preceptivo *adj* compulsory, mandatory
preciado *adj* precious
preciarse ⟨1b⟩ *v/r*: ***cualquier fontanero que se precie …*** any self-respecting plumber …
precinto *m* seal
precio *m* price; ***precio de venta al púiblico*** recommended retail price
preciosidad *f*: ***esa casa / chica es una preciosidad*** that house / girl is gorgeous *o* beautiful
precioso *adj* (*de valor*) precious; (*hermoso*) beautiful
preciosura *f L.Am.* F → ***preciosidad***
precipicio *m* precipice
precipitación *f* (*prisa*) hurry, haste; ***precipitaciones*** rain *sg*
precipitado *adj* hasty, sudden
precipitarse ⟨1a⟩ *v/r* rush; *fig* be hasty
precisamente *adv* precisely
precisión *f* precision
preciso *adj* precise, accurate; ***ser preciso*** be necessary
preconcebido *adj* preconceived
precoz *adj* early; *niño* precocious
precursor *m*, **precursora** *f* precursor, forerunner
predecesor *m*, **predecesora** *f* predecessor
predecir ⟨3p; *part* ***predicho*** ⟩ *v/t* predict
predestinar ⟨1a⟩ *v/t* predestine
predicado *m* predicate
predicador *m*, **predicadora** *f* preacher
predicar ⟨1g⟩ *v/t* preach; ***predicar con el ejemplo*** F practice (*Br* practise) what one preaches
predicción *f* prediction, forecast
predicho *part* → ***predecir***
predilecto *adj* favo(u)rite
predisponer ⟨2r⟩ *v/t* prejudice
predisposición *f tb* MED predisposition; (*tendencia*) tendency; ***una predisposición en contra de*** a prejudice against
predispuesto *adj* predisposed (***a*** to)
predominante *adj* predominant
predominar ⟨1a⟩ *v/t* predominate
preeminente *adj* preeminent
preescolar *adj* preschool
preestreno *m* preview
preexistente *adj* pre-existing
prefabricado *adj* prefabricated
prefacio *m* preface, foreword
preferencia *f* preference
preferente *adj* preferential
preferible *adj* preferable (***a*** to); ***es preferible que …*** it's better if …
preferido 1 *part* → ***preferir*** **2** *adj* favo(u)rite
preferir ⟨3i⟩ *v/t* prefer
prefijo *m* prefix; TELEC area code, *Br* dialling code
pregonar ⟨1a⟩ *v/t* proclaim, make public
pregunta *f* question
preguntar ⟨1a⟩ **1** *v/t* ask **2** *v/i* ask; ***preguntar por algo*** ask about sth; ***preguntar***

P

por alguien *paradero* ask for s.o.; *salud etc* ask about s.o. **3** *v/r* **preguntarse** wonder

prehistoria *f* prehistory

prehistórico *adj* prehistoric

prejuicio *m* prejudice

prelado *m* prelate

prelavado *m* prewash

preliminar 1 *adj* preliminary; DEP qualifying **2** *m L.Am.* qualifier

preludio *m* prelude

premamá *adj* maternity *atr*

prematrimonial *adj* premarital

prematuro 1 *adj* premature **2** *m*, **-a** *f* premature baby

premeditado *adj* premeditated

premeditación *f* premeditation; ***con premeditación*** deliberately

premiado 1 *adj* prizewinning **2** *m*, **-a** *f* prizewinner

premiar ⟨1b⟩ *v/t* award a prize to

premio *m* prize

premisa *f* premise

premonición *f* premonition

premura *f* haste

prenatal *adj* prenatal

prenda *f* item of clothing, garment; *garantía* security; *en juegos* forfeit; ***no soltar prenda*** not say a word (***sobre*** about)

prender ⟨2a; *part* ***preso*** ⟩ **1** *v/t a fugitivo* capture; *sujetar* pin up; *L.Am. fuego* light; *L.Am. luz* switch on, turn on; ***prender fuego a*** set fire to **2** *v/i de planta* take; (*empezar a arder*) catch; *de moda* catch on

prendería *f Esp* pawnbroker's, pawn shop

prensa *f* press; ***prensa amarilla*** gutter press

prensar ⟨1a⟩ *v/t* press

preñado *adj* pregnant

preocupación *f* worry, concern

preocupado *adj* worried (***por*** about), concerned (***por*** about)

preocupante *adj* worrying

preocupar ⟨1a⟩ **1** *v/t* worry, concern **2** *v/r* **preocuparse** worry (***por*** about); ***preocuparse de*** (*encargarse*) look after, take care of

preparación *f* preparation; (*educación*) education; *para trabajo* training

preparado *adj* ready, prepared

preparador *m*, **preparadora** *f*: ***preparador físico*** trainer

preparar ⟨1a⟩ **1** *v/t* prepare, get ready **2** *v/r* **prepararse** get ready (***para*** for), prepare o.s. (***para*** for); *de tormenta, crisis* be brewing

preparativos *mpl* preparations

preponderante *adj* predominant

preposición *f* preposition

prepotente *adj* arrogant

prerrogativa *f* prerogative

presa *f* (*dique*) dam; (*embalse*) reservoir; (*víctima*) prey; *L.Am. para comer* bite to eat

presagio *m* omen, sign; (*premonición*) premonition

prescindir ⟨3a⟩ *v/i*: ***prescindir de*** (*privarse de*) do without; (*omitir*) leave out, dispense with; (*no tener en cuenta*) disregard

prescribir ⟨3a; *part* ***prescrito*** ⟩ *v/i* JUR prescribe

prescrito *part* → ***prescribir***

presencia *f* presence; ***buena presencia*** smart appearance

presenciar ⟨1b⟩ *v/t* witness; (*estar presente a*) attend, be present at

presentación *f* presentation; COM launch; *entre personas* introduction

presentador *m*, **presentadora** *f* TV presenter

presentar ⟨1a⟩ **1** *v/t* present; *a alguien* introduce; *producto* launch; *solicitud* submit **2** *v/r* **presentarse** *en sitio* show up; (*darse a conocer*) introduce o.s.; *a examen* take; *de problema, dificultad* arise; *a elecciones* run

presente 1 *adj* present; ***tener algo presente*** bear sth in mind; ***¡presente!*** here! **2** *m tiempo* present **3** *m/fpl*: ***los presentes*** those present

presentimiento *m* premonition

presentir ⟨3i⟩ *v/t* foresee; ***presiento que vendrá*** I have a feeling he'll come

preservar ⟨1a⟩ *v/t* protect

preservativo *m* condom

presidencia *f* presidency; *de compañía* presidency, *Br* chairmanship; *de comité* chairmanship

presidencial *adj* presidential

presidente *m*, **-a** *f* president; *de gobierno* premier, prime minister; *de compañía* president, *Br* chairman, *Br mujer* chairwoman; *de comité* chair

presidiario *m*, **-a** *f* prisoner

presidir ⟨3a⟩ *v/t* be president of; *reunión* chair, preside over

presión *f* pressure; ***presión sanguínea*** blood pressure

presionar ⟨1a⟩ *v/t botón* press; *fig* put pressure on, pressure

preso 1 *part* → ***prender*** **2** *m*, **-a** *f* prisoner

prestación *f* provision; ***prestación social sustitutoria*** MIL community service in lieu of military service

prestado *adj*: ***dejar prestado algo*** lend sth; ***pedir prestado algo*** borrow sth

prestamista *m/f* moneylender
préstamo *m* loan; ***préstamo bancario*** bank loan
prestar ⟨1a⟩ *v/t dinero* lend; *ayuda* give; *L.Am.* borrow; ***prestar atencíon*** pay attention
prestidigitador *m*, **prestidigitadora** *f* conjurer
prestigio *m* prestige
prestigioso *adj* prestigious
presumido *adj* conceited; (*coqueto*) vain
presumir ⟨3a⟩ **1** *v/t* presume **2** *v/i* show off; ***presumir de algo*** boast *o* brag about sth; ***presume de listo*** he thinks he's very clever
presuntamente *adv* allegedly
presunto *adj* alleged, suspected
presuntuoso *adj* conceited
presuponer ⟨2r; *part* ***presupuesto*** ⟩ *v/t* assume
presupuesto 1 *part* → ***presuponer*** **2** *m* POL budget
presuroso *adj* hurried
pretencioso *adj* pretentious
pretender ⟨2a⟩ *v/t*: ***pretendía convencerlos*** he was trying to persuade them
pretendiente *m de mujer* suitor
pretensión *f L.Am.* (*arrogancia*) vanity; ***sin pretensiones*** unpretentious
pretérito *m* GRAM preterite
pretextar ⟨1a⟩ *v/t* claim
pretexto *m* pretext
prevalecer ⟨2d⟩ *v/t* prevail (***sobre*** over)
prevaricación *f* corruption
prevención *f* prevention
prevenido 1 *part* → ***prevenir*** **2** *adj* well-prepared
prevenir ⟨3s⟩ *v/t* prevent; (*avisar*) warn (***contra*** against)
preventivo *adj* preventive, preventative
prever ⟨2v; *part* ***previsto*** ⟩ *v/t* foresee
previo *adj* previous; ***sin previo aviso*** without (prior) warning
previsible *adj* foreseeable
previsión *f* (*predicción*) forecast; (*preparación*) foresight
previsor *adj* farsighted
previsto 1 *part* → ***prever*** **2** *adj* foreseen, expected; ***tener previsto*** have planned
prieto *adj L.Am.* dark-skinned
prima *f de seguro* premium; (*pago extra*) bonus
primacía *f* supremacy, primacy; (*prioridad*) priority
primario *adj* primary
primavera *f* spring; BOT primrose
primer *adj* first
primera *f* first class; AUTO first gear; ***a la primera*** first-time; ***de primera*** F first-class, first-rate
primerizo *adj* inexperienced, green F; *madre* new, first-time
primero 1 *adj* first; ***primeros auxilios*** *pl* first aid *sg* **2** *m*, **-a** *f* first (one) **3** *adv* first
primitivo *adj* primitive; (*original*) original
primo *m*, **-a** *f* cousin
primogénito 1 *adj* first **2** *m*, **-a** *f* first child
primordial *adj* fundamental
primoroso *adj* exquisite
princesa *f* princess
principal *adj* main, principal; ***lo principal*** the main *o* most important thing
príncipe *m* prince
principiante 1 *adj* inexperienced **2** *m/f* beginner
principio *m* principle; *en tiempo* beginning; ***a principios de abril*** at the beginning of April; ***en principio*** in principle
pringar ⟨1h⟩ **1** *v/t ensuciar* get greasy; *fig* F get involved (***en*** in) **2** *v/r* **pringarse** get greasy; *fig* F get mixed up (***en*** in)
pringoso *adj* greasy
prioridad *f* priority
prioritario *adj* priority *atr*
prisa *f* hurry, rush; ***darse prisa*** hurry (up); ***tener prisa*** be in a hurry *o* rush
prisión *f* prison, jail
prisionero 1 *adj* captive **2** *m*, **-a** *f* prisoner
prismáticos *mpl* binoculars
priva *f Esp* F booze F
privacidad *f* privacy
privación *f acción* deprivation; ***sufrir privaciones*** sufffer privation(s) *o* hardship
privado 1 *part* → ***privar*** **2** *adj* private
privar ⟨1a⟩ **1** *v/t*: ***privar a alguien de algo*** deprive s.o. of sth **2** *v/r* **privarse** deprive o.s.; ***privarse de algo*** deprive o.s. of sth, go without sth
privatización *f* privatization
privatizar ⟨1f⟩ *v/t* privatize
privilegiado *adj* privileged; (*excelente*) exceptional
privilegio *m* privilege
pro 1 *prp* for, in aid of; ***en pro de*** for **2** *m* pro; ***los pros y los contras*** the pros and cons
proa *f* MAR bow
probabilidad *f* probability
probable *adj* probable, likely; ***es probable que venga*** she'll probably come
probador *m* fitting room
probar ⟨1m⟩ **1** *v/t teoría* test, try out; (*comer un poco de*) taste, try; (*comer por primera vez*) try **2** *v/i* try; ***probar a hacer*** try doing **3** *v/r* **probarse** try on
probeta *f* test tube
problema *m* problem
problemático *adj* problematic

P

procedencia *f* origin, provenance
proceder ⟨2a⟩ **1** *v/i* come (***de*** from); (*actuar*) proceed; (*ser conveniente*) be fitting; ***proceder a*** proceed to; ***proceder contra alguien*** initiate proceedings against s.o. **2** *m* conduct
procedimiento *m* procedure, method; JUR proceedings *pl*
procesado *m*, **-a** *f* accused, defendant
procesador *m* INFOR processor; ***procesador de textos*** word processor
procesamiento *m*: ***procesamiento de textos*** word processing
procesar ⟨1a⟩ *v/t* INFOR process; JUR prosecute
procesión *f* procession
proceso *m* process; JUR trial; ***proceso de datos / textos*** INFOR data / word processing
proclamar ⟨1a⟩ *v/t* proclaim
proclive *adj* given (***a*** to)
procrear ⟨1a⟩ *v/i* breed, procreate *fml*
procurar ⟨1a⟩ *v/t* try; ***procura no llegar tarde*** try not to be late
prodigar ⟨1h⟩ **1** *v/t* be generous with **2** *v/r* **prodigarse** (*aparecer*) be seen in public
prodigio *m* wonder, miracle; *persona* prodigy
prodigioso *adj* prodigious
pródigo *adj* (*generoso*) generous; (*derrochador*) extravagant
producción *f* production
producir ⟨3o⟩ **1** *v/t* produce; (*causar*) cause **2** *v/r* **producirse** happen, occur; ***se produjo un ruido tremendo*** there was a tremendous noise
productividad *f* productivity
productivo *adj* productive; *empresa* profitable
producto *m* product; ***producto interior bruto*** gross domestic product; ***producto nacional bruto*** gross national product
productor *m*, **productora** *f* producer
produjo *vb* → ***producir***
produzco *vb* → ***producir***
proeza *f* feat, exploit
profana *f* laywoman
profanar ⟨1a⟩ *v/t* defile, desecrate
profano **1** *adj fig* lay *atr* **2** *m* layman
profecía *f* prophecy
profesar ⟨1a⟩ *v/t* REL profess; *fig* feel, have
profesión *f* profession
profesional *m/f & adj* professional
profesor *m*, **profesora** *f* teacher; *de universidad* professor, *Br* lecturer
profesorado *m* faculty, *Br* staff *pl*
profeta *m* prophet
profetizar ⟨1f⟩ *v/t* prophesy
profiláctico **1** *adj* preventive, prophylactic *fml* **2** *m* condom
prófugo *m*, **-a** *f* JUR fugitive
profundidad *f* depth
profundizar ⟨1f⟩ *v/i*: ***profundizar en algo*** go into sth in depth
profundo *adj* deep; *pensamiento, persona* profound
profuso *adj* abundant, plentiful
programa *m* program, *Br* programme; INFOR program; EDU syllabus; ***programa de estudios*** curriculum
programación *f* RAD, TV programs *pl*, *Br* programmes; INFOR programming
programador *m*, **programadora** *f* programmer
programar ⟨1a⟩ *v/t aparato* program, *Br* programme; INFOR program; (*planear*) schedule
progresar ⟨1a⟩ *v/i* progress, make progress
progresista *m/f & adj* progressive
progresivo *adj* progressive
progreso *m* progress
prohibición *f* ban (***de*** on)
prohibido *adj* forbidden
prohibir ⟨3a⟩ *v/t* forbid; *oficialmente* ban
prohibitivo *adj precio* prohibitive
prójimo *m* fellow human being
prole *f* offspring
proletario **1** *adj* proletarian **2** *m*, **-a** *f* proletarian
proliferación *f* proliferation
proliferar ⟨1a⟩ *v/t* proliferate
prolífico *adj* prolific
prolijo *adj* long-winded; (*minucioso*) detailed
prólogo *m* preface
prolongado *adj* prolonged, lengthy
prolongar ⟨1h⟩ **1** *v/t* extend, prolong **2** *v/r* **prolongarse** go *o* carry on; *en espacio* extend
promedio *m* average
promesa *f* promise
prometedor *adj* bright, promising
prometer ⟨2a⟩ **1** *v/t* promise **2** *v/r* **prometerse** get engaged
prometida *f* fiancée
prometido **1** *part* → ***prometer*** **2** *adj* engaged **3** *m* fiancé
prominente *adj* prominent
promiscuidad *f* promiscuity
promiscuo *adj* promiscuous
promoción *f* promotion; EDU year
promocionar ⟨1a⟩ *v/t* promote
promotor *m*, **promotora** *f* promoter; ***promotor inmobiliario*** developer
promover ⟨2h⟩ *v/t* promote; (*causar*) provoke, cause

promulgar ⟨1h⟩ *v/t ley* promulgate
pronombre *m* GRAM pronoun
pronosticar ⟨1g⟩ *v/t* forecast
pronóstico *m* MED prognosis; ***pronóstico del tiempo*** weather forecast
pronto 1 *adj* prompt **2** *adv* (*dentro de poco*) soon; (*temprano*) early; ***de pronto*** suddenly; ***tan pronto como*** as soon as
pronunciación *f* pronunciation
pronunciar ⟨1b⟩ *v/t* pronounce; (*decir*) say; ***pronunciar un discurso*** give a speech
propaganda *f* advertising; POL propaganda
propagar ⟨1h⟩ **1** *v/t* spread **2** *v/r* **propagarse** spread
propano *m* propane
propasarse ⟨1a⟩ *v/r* go too far
propenso *adj* prone (***a*** to); ***ser propenso a hacer*** be prone to do, have a tendency to do
propiciar ⟨1b⟩ *v/t* (*favorecer*) promote; (*causar*) bring about
propicio *adj* favo(u)rable
propiedad *f* property
propietario *m*, **-a** *f* owner
propina *f* tip
propinar ⟨1a⟩ *v/t golpe, paliza* give
propio *adj* own; (*característico*) characteristic (***de*** of), typical (***de*** of); (*adecuado*) suitable (***para*** for); ***la -a directora*** the director herself
proponer ⟨2r; *part* ***propuesto*** ⟩ *v/t* propose, suggest
proporción *f* proportion
proporcional *adj* proportional
proporcionar ⟨1a⟩ *v/t* provide, supply; *satisfacción* give
proposición *f* proposal, suggestion
propósito *m* (*intención*) intention; (*objetivo*) purpose; ***a propósito*** on purpose; (*por cierto*) by the way
propuesto *part* → ***proponer***
propuesta *f* proposal
propugnar ⟨1a⟩ *v/t* advocate
propulsar ⟨1a⟩ *v/t* TÉC propel; *fig* promote
propulsor *m* (*motor*) engine
prórroga *f* DEP overtime, *Br* extra time
prorrogar ⟨1h⟩ *v/t plazo* extend
prorrumpir ⟨3a⟩ *v/i* burst (***en*** into)
prosa *f* prose
prosaico *adj* mundane, prosaic
proseguir ⟨3d & 3l⟩ **1** *v/t* carry on, continue **2** *v/i* continue (***con*** with)
proselitismo *m* proselytism
prospecto *m* directions for use *pl*; *de propaganda* leaflet
prosperar ⟨1a⟩ *v/i* prosper, thrive
prosperidad *f* prosperity
próspero *adj* prosperous, thriving
próstata *f* prostate
prostíbulo *m* brothel
prostitución *f* prostitution
prostituirse ⟨3g⟩ *v/r* prostitute o.s.
prostituta *f* prostitute
prostituto *m* male prostitute
protagonista *m/f personaje* main character; *actor, actriz* star; *de una hazaña* hero; *mujer* heroine
protagonizar ⟨1f⟩ *v/t* star in, play the lead in; *incidente* play a leading role in
protección *f* protection
proteger ⟨2c⟩ *v/t* protect (***de*** from)
proteína *f* protein
protésico *m*, **-a** *f*: ***protésico dental*** dental technician
prótesis *f* prosthesis
protesta *f* protest
protestante *m/f* Protestant
protestar ⟨1a⟩ **1** *v/t* protest **2** *v/i* (*quejarse*) complain (***por, de*** about); (*expresar oposición*) protest (***contra, por*** about, against)
protocolo *m* protocol
prototipo *m* TÉC prototype
protuberancia *f* protuberance
prov. *abr* (= ***provincia***) province
provecho *m* benefit; ***¡buen provecho!*** enjoy (your meal); ***sacar provecho de*** benefit from
proveedor *m*, **proveedora** *f* supplier; ***proveedor de*** (***acceso a***) ***Internet*** Internet Service Provider, ISP
proveer ⟨2e; *part* ***provisto*** ⟩ *v/t* supply; ***proveer a alguien de algo*** supply s.o. with sth
provenir ⟨3s⟩ *v/i* come (***de*** from)
proverbio *m* proverb
providencia *f* providence
provincia *f* province
provincial *adj* provincial
provinciano 1 *adj* provincial **2** *m*, **-a** *f* provincial
provisional *adj* provisional
provisiones *fpl* provisions
provisto 1 *part* → ***proveer*** **2** *adj*: ***provisto de*** equipped with
provocación *f* provocation
provocador *adj* provocative
provocar ⟨1g⟩ *v/t* cause; *al enfado* provoke; *sexualmente* lead on; ***¿te provoca un café?*** *S. Am.* how about a coffee?
provocativo *adj* provocative
proxeneta *m* pimp
proxenetismo *m* procuring
proximidad *f* proximity
próximo *adj* (*siguiente*) next; (*cercano*) near, close

P

proyección *f* MAT, PSI projection; *de película* showing
proyectar ⟨1a⟩ *v/t* project; (*planear*) plan; *película* show; *sombra* cast
proyectil *m* missile
proyecto *m* plan; *trabajo* project; ***proyecto de ley*** bill; ***tenir en proyecto hacer algo*** plan to do sth
proyector *m* projector
prudencia *f* caution, prudence
prudente *adj* careful, cautious
prueba *f tb* TIP proof; JUR piece of evidence; DEP event; EDU test; ***a prueba de bala*** bulletproof; ***poner algo a prueba*** put sth to the test
P.S. *abr* (**= *postscriptum*** (***posdata***)) PS (= postscript)
pseudo... *pref* pseudo-
pseudónimo *m* pseudonym
psicoanálisis *f* (psycho)analysis
psicoanalista *m/f* (psycho)analyst
psicodélico *adj* psychedelic
psicología *f* psychology
psicológico *adj* psychological
psicólogo *m*, **-a** *f* psychologist
psicópata *m/f* psychopath
psicosis *f inv* psychosis
psicoterapia *f* psychotherapy
psiquiatra *m/f* psychiatrist
psiquiatría *f* psychiatry
psiquiátrico *adj* psychiatric
psíquico *adj* psychic
pta *abr* (**= *peseta***) peseta
ptas *abr* (**= *pesetas***) pesetas
púía *f* ZO spine, quill; MÚS plectrum, pick
pub *m* bar
pubertad *f* puberty
publicación *f* publication
publicar ⟨1g⟩ **1** *v/t* publish **2** *v/r* **publicarse** come out, be published
publicidad *f* (*divulgación*) publicity; COM advertising; (*anuncios*) advertisements *pl*
publicista *m/f* advertising executive
publicitario 1 *adj* advertising *atr* **2** *m*, **-a** *f* advertising executive
púíblico 1 *adj* public; *escuela* public, *Br* state **2** *m* public; TEA audience; DEP spectators *pl*, crowd
pucho *m S. Am.* P cigarette butt, *Br* fag end F; ***no valer un pucho*** be completely worthless
pude *vb* → ***poder***
púídico *adj* modest
pudín *m* pudding
pudo *vb* → ***poder***
pudor *m* modesty
pudrir ⟨3a⟩ **1** *v/t* rot **2** *v/r* **pudrirse** rot; ***pudrirse de envidia*** be green with envy
pueblerino *m*, **-a** *f* hick *desp*
pueblero *m*, **-a** *f L.Am.* villager; *de pueblo más grande* townsman; *mujer* townswoman
pueblo *m* village; *más grande* town
puedo *vb* → ***poder***
puente *m* bridge; ***hacer puente*** *have a day off between a weekend and a public holiday*
puenting *m* bungee jumping
puerco 1 *adj* dirty; *fig* filthy F **2** *m* ZO pig; ***puerco espín*** porcupine
puericultura *f* childcare
puerro *m* BOT leek
puerta *f* door; *en valla* gate; DEP goal; ***puerta de embarque*** gate
puerto *m* MAR port; GEOG pass
Puerto Rico Puerto Rico
puertorriqueño 1 *adj* Puerto Rican **2** *m*, **-a** *f* Puerto Rican
pues *conj* well; *fml* (*porque*) as, since; ***pues bien*** well; ***¡pues sí!*** of course!
puesta *f*: ***puesta a punto*** tune-up; ***puesta de sol*** sunset
puestero *m*, **-a** *f L.Am.* stall holder
puesto 1 *part* → ***poner* 2** *m lugar* place; *en mercado* stand, stall; MIL post; ***puesto*** (***de trabajo***) job **3** *conj*: ***puesto que*** since, given that
pugnar ⟨1a⟩ *v/i* fight (***por*** for; ***por hacer*** to do)
puja *f* (*lucha*) struggle; *en subasta* bid
pujar ⟨1a⟩ *v/i* (*luchar*) struggle; *en subasta* bid
pulcro *adj* immaculate
pulga *f* ZO flea; ***tener malas pulgas*** *fig* F be bad-tempered
pulgada *f* inch
pulgar *m* thumb
pulimentar ⟨1a⟩ *v/t* polish
pulir ⟨3a⟩ *v/t* polish
pulla *f* gibe
pulmón *m* lung
pulmonía *f* MED pneumonia
pulpa *f* pulp
pulpería *f L.Am.* mom-and-pop store, *Br* corner shop
pulpero *m*, **-a** *f S. Am.* storekeeper, shopkeeper
púílpito *m* pulpit
pulpo *m* ZO octopus
pulque *m Méx* pulque (*alcoholic drink made from cactus*)
pulquería *f Méx* pulque bar
pulsación *f* beat; *al escribir a máquina* key stroke
pulsar ⟨1a⟩ *v/t botón*, *tecla* press
pulsera *f* bracelet
pulso *m* pulse; *fig* steady hand; ***tomar el pulso a alguien*** take s.o.'s pulse; ***tomar***

el pulso a algo *fig* take the pulse of sth
pulular ⟨1a⟩ *v/i* mill around
pulverizador *m* spray
pulverizar ⟨1f⟩ *v/t* spray; (*convertir en polvo*) pulverize, crush
puma *m* ZO puma, mountain lion
puna *f L.Am.* GEOG high Andean plateau; MED altitude sickness
pundonor *m* pride
punitivo *adj* punitive
punta *f* tip; (*extremo*) end; *de lápiz*, GEOG point; *L.Am.* (*grupo*) group; ***sacar punta a*** sharpen
puntada *f* stitch
puntapié *m* kick
puntera *f* toe
puntería *f* aim
puntero 1 *adj* leading **2** *m* pointer
puntiagudo *adj* pointed, sharp
puntilla *f*: ***de puntillas*** on tippy-toe, *Br* on tiptoe
puntilloso *adj* particular, punctilious *fml*
punto *m* point; *señal* dot; *signo de puntuación* period, *Br* full stop; *en costura, sutura* stitch; ***dos puntos*** colon; ***punto muerto*** AUTO neutral; ***punto de vista*** point of view; ***punto y coma*** semicolon; ***a punto*** (*listo*) ready; (*a tiempo*) in time; ***de punto*** knitted; ***en punto*** on the dot; ***estar a punto de*** be about to; ***hacer punto*** knit; ***hasta cierto punto*** up to a point; ***empresa** f **punto.com*** dot.com (company)
puntuación *f* punctuation; DEP score; EDU grade, mark
puntual *adj* punctual
puntualidad *f* punctuality
puntualizar ⟨1f⟩ *v/t* (*señalar*) point out; (*aclarar*) clarify
punzada *f* sharp *o* stabbing pain
punzante *adj* stinging
puñado *m* handful
puñal *m* dagger
puñalada *f* stab wound
puñeta *f*: ***puñeta(s)!*** F for heaven's sake! F; ***hacer la puñeta a alguien*** F give s.o. a hard time F
puñetazo *m* punch; ***dar un puñetazo*** punch
puño *m* fist; *de camisa* cuff; *de bastón, paraguas* handle
pupa *f en labio* cold sore; ***hacerse pupa*** *lenguaje infantil* hurt o.s.
pupila *f* pupil
pupitre *m* desk
pupusa *f L.Am.* filled dumpling
purasangre *m* thoroughbred
puré *m* purée; *sopa* cream; ***puré de patatas** or **papas*** *L.Am.* mashed potatoes
pureza *f* purity
purga *f* POL purge
purgante *m/adj* laxative, purgative
purgatorio *m* REL purgatory
purificación *f* purification
purificar ⟨1g⟩ *v/t* purify
purista *m/f* purist
puritano 1 *adj* puritanical **2** *m*, **-a** *f* puritan
puro 1 *adj* pure; *casualidad, coincidencia* sheer; *Méx* (*úínico*) sole, only; ***la -a verdad*** the honest truth; ***te sirven la -a comida*** *Méx* they just serve food **2** *m* cigar
púírpura *f* purple
pus *m* pus
puse *vb* → ***poder***
pusilánime *adj* fainthearted
puso *vb* → ***poder***
puta *f* P whore P
putada *f* P dirty trick; ***¡qué putada!*** shit! P
putear ⟨1a⟩ *v/t L.Am.* P swear at; ***putear alguien*** *Esp* give s.o. a hard time, make life difficult for s.o.
puto *adj* P goddamn F, *Br* bloody F; ***de puta madre*** P great F, fantastic F
putrefacción *f* putrefaction
puzzle *m* jigsaw (puzzle)
PVC *abr* (***= cloruro de polivinilo***) PVC (= polyvinyl chloride)
P.V.P. *abr* (***= precio de venta al púíblico***) RRP (= recommended retail price)
pza. *abr* (***= plaza***) sq (= square)

Q

q.e.p. d. *abr* (= ***que en paz descanse***) RIP (= requiescat in pace)
que 1 *pron rel sujeto*: *persona* who, that; *cosa* which, that; *complemento*: *persona* that, whom *fml*; *cosa* that, which; ***el coche que ves*** the car you can see, the car that *o* which you can see; ***el que*** the one that **2** *conj* that; ***lo mismo que tú*** the same as you; ***¡que entre!*** tell him to come in; ***¡que descanses!*** sleep well; ***¡que sí!*** I said yes; ***¡que no!*** I said no; ***es que …*** the thing is …; ***yo que tú*** if I were you
qué 1 *adj & pron interr* what; ***¿qué pasó?*** what happened?; ***¿qué día es?*** what day is it?; ***¿qué vestido prefieres?*** which dress do you prefer? **2** *adj & pron int*: ***¡qué moto!*** what a motorbike!; ***¡qué de flores!*** what a lot of flowers! **3** *adv*: ***¡qué alto es!*** he's so tall!; ***¡qué bien!*** great!
quebrada *f L.Am.* stream
quebradero *m*: ***quebraderos de cabeza*** F headaches
quebradizo *adj* brittle
quebrado 1 *adj* broken **2** *m* MAT fraction
quebrantahuesos *m inv* ZO lammergeier
quebrantar ⟨1a⟩ *v/t ley*, *contrato* break
quebrar ⟨1k⟩ **1** *v/t* break **2** *v/i* COM go bankrupt **3** *v/r* **quebrarse** break
quedar ⟨1a⟩ **1** *v/i* (*permanecer*) stay; *en un estado* be; (*sobrar*) be left; ***quedó sin resolver*** it remained unresolved, it wasn't sorted out; ***te queda bien / mal*** *de estilo* it suits you / doesn't suit you; *de talla* it fits you / doesn't fit you; ***quedar cerca*** be nearby; ***quedar con alguien*** F arrange to meet (with) s.o.; ***quedar en algo*** agree to sth; ***¿queda mucho tiempo?*** is there much time left? **2** *v/r* **quedarse** stay; ***quedarse ciego*** go blind; ***quedarse con algo*** keep sth; ***me quedé sin comer*** I ended up not eating
quehaceres *mpl* tasks
queja *f* complaint
quejarse ⟨1a⟩ *v/r* complain (***a*** to; ***de*** about)
quejica *adj* F whining F
quejido *m* moan, groan
quejumbroso *adj* moaning
quemado *adj* burnt; *Méx* (*desvirtuado*) discredited; ***quemado por el sol*** sunburnt; ***oler a quemado*** smell of burning
quemadura *f* burn
quemar ⟨1a⟩ **1** *v/t* burn; *con agua* scald; F *recursos* use up; F *dinero* blow F **2** *v/i* be very hot **3** *v/r* **quemarse** burn o.s.; *de tostada*, *papeles* burn; *fig* burn o.s. out; *Méx* (*desvirtuarse*) become discredited
quena *f S. Am.* Indian flute
quepo *vb* → ***caber***
queque *m L.Am.* cake
querella *f* JUR lawsuit
querellarse ⟨1a⟩ *v/r* JUR bring a lawsuit (***contra*** against)
querer ⟨2u⟩ *v/t* (*desear*) want; (*amar*) love; ***querer decir*** mean; ***sin querer*** unintentionally; ***quisiera …*** I would like …
querido 1 *part* → ***querer* 2** *adj* dear **3** *m*, **-a** *f* darling
queroseno *m* kerosene
querrá *vb* → ***querer***
querría *vb* → ***querer***
quesadilla *f* quesadilla (*folded tortilla*)
queso *m* cheese; ***queso para untar*** cheese spread; ***queso rallado*** grated cheese
quicio *m*: ***sacar de quicio a alguien*** F drive s.o. crazy F
quid *m*: ***el quid de la cuestión*** the nub of the question
quiebra *f* COM bankruptcy
quien *pron rel sujeto* who, that; *objeto* who, whom *fml*, that; ***no soy quien para hacerlo*** I'm not the right person to do it
quién *pron* who; ***¿quién es?*** who is it?; ***¿de quién es este libro?*** whose is this book?, who does this book belong to?
quienquiera *pron* whoever
quiero *vb* → ***querer***
quieto *adj* still; ***¡estáte quieto!*** keep still!
quijotesco *adj* quixotic
quilate *m* carat
quilla *f* keel
quimera *f* pipe dream
química *f* chemistry
químico 1 *adj* chemical **2** *m*, **-a** *f* chemist
quimioterapia *f* MED chemotherapy
quimono *m* kimono
quincalla *f* junk
quince *adj* fifteen
quincena *f* two weeks, *Br* fortnight
quiniela *f lottery where the winners are decided by soccer results*
quinientos *adj* five hundred
quinina *f* quinine
quinquenio *m* five-year period

quinta *f* MIL draft, *Br* call-up; ***es de mi quinta*** he's my age
quinteto *m* MÚS quintet
quinto 1 *adj* fifth **2** *m* MIL conscript
quiosco *m* kiosk; ***quiosco de prensa*** newsstand, *Br* newsagent's
quiosquero *m*, **-a** *f* newspaper vendor
quirófano *m* operating room, *Br* operating theatre
quiromancia, quiromancía *f* palmistry
quirúrgico *adj* surgical
quise *vb* → ***querer***
quisiera *vb* → ***querer***
quiso *vb* → ***querer***
quisque F: ***todo quisque*** everyone and his brother F, *Br* the world and his wife F
quisquilla *f* ZO shrimp
quisquilloso *adj* touchy
quiste *m* MED cyst
quitaesmalte *m* nail varnish remover
quitamanchas *m inv* stain remover
quitar ⟨1a⟩ **1** *v/t ropa* take off, remove; *obstáculos* remove; ***quitar algo a alguien*** take sth (away) from s.o.; ***quitar la mesa*** clear the table **2** *v/i*: ***¡quita!*** get out of the way! **3** *v/r* **quitarse** *ropa, gafas* take off; (*apartarse*) get out of the way; ***quitarse algo/a alguien de encima*** get rid of s.o./sth; ***¡quítate de en medio!*** F get out of the way!
quizá(s) *adv* perhaps, maybe
quórum *m* quorum

R

rabadilla *f* ANAT coccyx
rábano *m* BOT radish; ***me importa un rábano*** F I don't give a damn F
rabia *f* MED rabies *sg*; ***dar rabia a alguien*** make s.o. mad; ***tener rabia a alguien*** have it in for s.o.
rabiar ⟨1b⟩ *v/i*: ***rabiar de dolor*** be in agony; ***hacer rabiar a alguien*** *fig* F jerk s.o.'s chain F, pull s.o.'s leg F; ***rabiar por*** be dying for
rabieta *f* tantrum
rabino *m* rabbi
rabioso *adj* MED rabid; *fig* furious
rabo *m* tail
rabón *adj L.Am. animal* short-tailed
rácano *adj* F stingy F, mean
racha *f* spell
racial *adj* racial
racimo *m* bunch
ración *f* share; (*porción*) serving, portion
racional *adj* rational
racionalizar ⟨1f⟩ *v/t* rationalize
racionamiento *m* rationing
racionar ⟨1a⟩ *v/t* ration
racismo *m* racism
racista *m/f & adj* racist
radar *m* radar
radiación *f* radiation
radiactividad *f* radioactivity
radiactivo *adj* radioactive
radiador *m* radiator
radiante *adj* radiant
radiar ⟨1b⟩ *v/t* radiate
radical *m/f & adj* radical
radicalismo *m* radicalism
radicar ⟨1g⟩ *v/i* stem (***en*** from), lie (***en*** in)
radio 1 *m* MAT radius; QUÍM radium; *L.Am.* radio; ***en un radio de*** within a radius of; ***radio de acción*** range **2** *f* radio; ***radio despertador*** clock radio
radioaficionado *m* radio ham
radiocasete *m* radio cassette player
radiodifusión *f* broadcasting
radiofónico *adj* radio *atr*
radiografía *f* X-ray
radiografiar ⟨1c⟩ *v/t* X-ray
radiología *f* radiology
radiólogo *m*, **-a** *f* radiologist
radiotaxi *m* radio taxi
radiotelegrafista *m/f* radio operator
radioyente *m/f* listener
ráfaga *f* gust; *de balas* burst
rafia *f* raffia
rafting *m* rafting
ragúí *m* GASTR ragout
raído *adj* threadbare
rail, raíl *m* rail
raíz *f* root; ***raíz cuadrada / cúbica*** MAT square / cube root; ***a raíz de*** as a result of; ***echar raíces*** *de persona* put down roots
raja *f* (*rodaja*) slice; (*corte*) cut; (*grieta*) crack
rajar ⟨1a⟩ **1** *v/t fruta* cut, slice; *cerámica* crack; *neumático* slash **2** *v/i* F gossip **3** *v/r* **rajarse** *fig* F back out F

rajatabla: ***a rajatabla*** strictly, to the letter
ralentí *m*: ***al ralentí*** AUTO idling; FOT in slow motion
ralentizar ⟨1f⟩ *v/t* slow down
rallador *m* grater
rallar ⟨1a⟩ *v/t* GASTR grate
rally(e) *m* rally
rama *f* branch; POL wing; ***andarse por las ramas*** beat about the bush
ramificación *f* ramification
ramo *m* COM sector; ***ramo de flores*** bunch of flowers
rampa *f* ramp; ***rampa de lanzamiento*** launch pad
ramplón *adj* vulgar
rana *f* ZO frog
ranchera *f typical Mexican song*
ranchero 1 *adj*: ***canción -a*** romantic ballad; ***múísica -a*** *music of northern Mexico* **2** *m L.Am.* rancher
rancho *m Méx* small farm; *L.Am.* (*barrio de chabolas*) shanty town
rancio *adj* rancid; *fig* ancient
rango *m* rank; ***de alto rango*** high-ranking
ranking *m* ranking
ranura *f* slot
rapapolvo *m* F telling-off F
rapar ⟨1a⟩ *v/t pelo* crop
rapaz 1 *adj* predatory; ***ave rapaz*** bird of prey **2** *m*, **-a** *f* F kid F
rape *m pescado* anglerfish; ***al rape*** *pelo* cropped
rapidez *f* speed, rapidity
rápido 1 *adj* quick, fast **2** *m* rapids *pl*
rapiña *f* pillage
raptar ⟨1a⟩ *v/t* kidnap
rapto *m* kidnap
raptor *m*, **raptora** *f* kidnapper
raqueta *f* racket
raquítico *adj fig* rickety
rareza *f* scarcity, rarity
raro *adj* rare
ras *m*: ***a ras de tierra*** at ground level
rasante *adj vuelo* low
rasca *f L.Am.*: ***pegarse una rasca*** F get plastered F
rascacielos *m inv* skyscraper
rascado *adj L.Am.* F plastered F
rascar ⟨1g⟩ *v/t* scratch; *superficie* scrape, scratch
rasero *m*: ***medir por el mismo rasero*** treat equally
rasgado *adj boca* wide; ***ojos rasgados*** almond-shaped eyes
rasgar ⟨1h⟩ *v/t* tear (up)
rasgo *m* feature; ***a grandes rasgos*** broadly speaking
rasguño *m* MED scratch
raso 1 *adj* flat, level; ***soldado raso*** private **2** *m material* satin; ***al raso*** in the open air
raspa *f* fishbone; *L.Am.* F (*reprimanda*) telling-off
raspado *m Méx* water ice
raspadura *f* scrape
raspar ⟨1a⟩ **1** *v/t* scrape; *con lija* sand **2** *v/i* be rough
rastra *f*: ***entrar a rastras*** drag o.s. in, crawl in
rastreador *adj*: ***perro rastreador*** tracker dog
rastrear ⟨1a⟩ **1** *v/t persona* track; *bosque, zona* comb **2** *v/i* rake
rastrero *adj* mean, low
rastrillo *m* rake
rastro *m* flea market; (*huella*) trace; ***desaparecer sin dejar rastro*** vanish without trace
rastrojo *m* stubble
rasurar ⟨1a⟩ *v/t* shave
rata *f* ZO rat
ratero *m*, **-a** *f* petty thief
raticida *m* rat poison
ratificar ⟨1g⟩ *v/t* POL ratify
rato *m* time, while; ***ratos libres*** spare time *sg*; ***al poco rato*** after a short time *o* while; ***todo el rato*** all the time; ***un buen rato*** a good while, a pretty long time; ***pasar el rato*** pass the time; ***he pasado un buen / mal rato*** I've had a great / an awful time
ratón *m* ZO, INFOR mouse
ratonera *f* mouse trap
raudal *m*: ***tienen dinero a raudales*** they've got loads of money F
raudo *adj* swift
raya *f* GRAM dash; ZO ray; *de pelo* part, *Br* parting; ***a*** *or* ***de rayas*** striped; ***pasarse de la raya*** overstep the mark, go too far
rayado *adj disco, superficie* scratched
rayano *adj* bordering (***en*** on)
rayar ⟨1a⟩ **1** *v/t* scratch; (*tachar*) cross out **2** *v/i* border (***en*** on), verge (***en*** on)
rayo *m* FÍS ray; METEO (bolt of) lightning; ***rayo láser*** laser beam; ***rayo X*** X-ray; ***rayos ultravioleta*** ultraviolet rays
raza *f* race; *de animal* breed
razón *f* reason; ***a razón de*** *precio* at; ***dar la razón a alguien*** admit that s.o. is right; ***entrar en razón*** see sense; ***perder la razón*** lose one's mind; ***tener razón*** be right
razonable *adj precio* reasonable
razonamiento *m* reasoning
razonar ⟨1a⟩ *v/i* reason
RDSI *abr* (= ***Red Digital de Servicios Integrados***) ISDN (= Integrated Services Digital Network)

reacción *f* reaction (***a*** to); ***avión a reacción*** jet (aircraft)
reaccionar ⟨1a⟩ *v/i* react (***a*** to)
reaccionario **1** *adj* reactionary **2** *m*, **-a** *f* reactionary
reacio *adj* reluctant (***a*** to)
reactivación *f* COM revival, upturn
reactivar ⟨1a⟩ *v/t* COM revive
reactor *m* reactor; (*motor*) jet engine
reafirmar ⟨1a⟩ **1** *v/t* reaffirm **2** *v/r* **reafirmarse**: ***reafirmarse en*** *idea* reassert
reajuste *m* adjustment; ***reajuste ministerial*** POL cabinet reshuffle
real *adj* (*regio*) royal; (*verdadero*) real
realeza *f* royalty
realidad *f* reality; ***en realidad*** in fact, in reality
realismo *m* realism
realista **1** *adj* realistic **2** *m/f* realist
realización *f* fulfil(l)ment; RAD, TV production
realizador *m*, **realizadora** *f de película* director; RAD, TV producer
realizar ⟨1f⟩ **1** *v/t tarea* carry out; RAD, TV produce; COM realize **2** *v/r* **realizarse** *de persona* fulfil(l) o.s.
realquilar ⟨1a⟩ *v/t* sublet
realzar ⟨1f⟩ *v/t* highlight
reanimación *f* revival
reanimar ⟨1a⟩ *v/t* revive
reanudación *f* resumption
reanudar ⟨1a⟩ *v/t* resume
reaparecer ⟨2d⟩ *v/i* reappear
reaparición *f* reappearance
reaseguro *m* reinsurance
rebaja *f* reduction; ***rebajas de verano / invierno*** summer / winter sale
rebajar ⟨1a⟩ **1** *v/t precio* lower, reduce; *mercancías* reduce **2** *v/r* **rebajarse** lower o.s., humble o.s.
rebanada *f* slice
rebanar ⟨1a⟩ *v/t* slice
rebañar ⟨1a⟩ *v/t*: ***rebañar algo*** wipe sth clean
rebaño *m* flock
rebasar ⟨1a⟩ *v/t Méx* AUTO pass, *Br* overtake
rebatir ⟨3a⟩ *v/t razones* rebut, refute
rebeca *f* cardigan
rebeco *m* ZO chamois
rebelarse ⟨1a⟩ *v/r* rebel
rebelde **1** *adj* rebel *atr* **2** *m/f* rebel
rebeldía *f* rebelliousness
rebelión *f* rebellion
reblandecer ⟨2d⟩ *v/t* soften
rebobinar ⟨1a⟩ *v/t* rewind
rebosar ⟨1a⟩ *v/i* overflow
rebotar ⟨1a⟩ **1** *v/t* bounce; (*disgustar*) annoy **2** *v/i* bounce, rebound
rebote *m* bounce; ***de rebote*** on the rebound
rebozar ⟨1f⟩ *v/t* GASTR coat
rebuscado *adj* over-elaborate
rebuznar ⟨1a⟩ *v/i* bray
recado *m* errand; *Rpl* (*arnés*) harness; ***dejar un recado*** leave a message
recaída *f* MED relapse
recalar ⟨1a⟩ *v/i* MAR put in (***en*** at), call (***en*** at)
recalcar ⟨1g⟩ *v/t* stress, emphasize
recalcitrante *adj* recalcitrant
recalentar ⟨1k⟩ *v/t comida* warm *o* heat up
recámara *f de arma de fuego* chamber; *L.Am.* (*dormitorio*) bedroom
recambio *m* COM spare part
recapacitar ⟨1a⟩ *v/t* think over, reflect on
recapitular ⟨1a⟩ *v/t* recap
recargar ⟨1h⟩ *v/t batería* recharge; *recipiente* refill; ***recargar un 5%*** charge 5% extra
recargo *m* surcharge
recatado *adj* modest; (*cauto*) cautious
recato *m* modesty; (*prudencia*) caution
recauchutar ⟨1a⟩ *v/t neumáticos* retread
recaudación *f acción* collection; *cantidad* takings *pl*
recaudar ⟨1a⟩ *v/t impuestos, dinero* collect
recaudo *m*: ***poner a buen recaudo*** put in a safe place
recelo *m* mistrust
recepción *f en hotel* reception
recepcionista *m/f* receptionist
receptivo *adj* receptive
receptor *m* receiver
recesión *f* recession
receta *f* GASTR recipe; ***receta médica*** prescription
recetar ⟨1a⟩ *v/t* MED prescribe
recetario *m* recipe book
rechazar ⟨1f⟩ *v/t* reject; MIL repel
rechazo *m* rejection
rechinar ⟨1a⟩ *v/i* creak, squeak
rechistar ⟨1a⟩ *v/i* protest; ***sin rechistar*** F without a murmur, without complaining
rechoncho *adj* F dumpy F
rechupete: ***de rechupete*** F delicious
recibidor *m* entrance hall
recibimiento *m* reception
recibir ⟨3a⟩ *v/t* receive
recibo *m* (sales) receipt
reciclable *adj* recyclable
reciclado, reciclaje *m* recycling
reciclar ⟨1a⟩ *v/t* recycle
recién *adv* newly; *L.Am.* (*hace poco*) just; ***recién casados*** newly-weds; ***recién nacido*** newborn; ***recién pintado*** wet

paint; ***recién llegamos*** we've only just arrived
reciente *adj* recent
recinto *m* premises *pl*; *área* grounds *pl*
recio *adj* sturdy, tough
recipiente *m* container
recíproco *adj* reciprocal
recital *m* recital
recitar ⟨1a⟩ *v/t* recite
reclamación *f* complaint; POL claim, demand
reclamar ⟨1a⟩ **1** *v/t* claim, demand **2** *v/i* complain
reclame *m L.Am.* advertisement
reclamo *m* lure
reclinable *adj*: ***asiento reclinable*** reclining seat
reclinar ⟨1a⟩ **1** *v/t* rest **2** *v/r* **reclinarse** lean, recline (***contra*** against)
recluir ⟨3g⟩ *v/t* imprison, confine
reclusión *f* JUR imprisonment, confinement
recluso *m*, **-a** *f* prisoner
recluta *m/f* recruit
reclutar ⟨1a⟩ *v/t tb* COM recruit
recobrar ⟨1a⟩ **1** *v/t* recover **2** *v/r* **recobrarse** recover (***de*** from)
recogedor *m* dustpan
recogepelotas *m/f inv* ball boy; *niña* ball girl
recoger ⟨2c⟩ **1** *v/t* pick up, collect; *habitación* tidy up; AGR harvest; (*mostrar*) show **2** *v/r* **recogerse** go home
recogida *f* collection; ***recogida de basuras*** garbage collection, *Br* refuse collection; ***recogida de equipajes*** baggage reclaim
recolectar ⟨1a⟩ *v/t* AGR harvest, bring in
recomendación *f* recommendation
recomendar ⟨1k⟩ *v/t* recommend
recompensa *f* reward
recompensar ⟨1a⟩ *v/t* reward
recomponer ⟨2r; *part* ***recompuesto*** ⟩ *v/t* mend
reconciliación *f* reconciliation
reconciliar ⟨1b⟩ **1** *v/t* reconcile **2** *v/r* **reconciliarse** make up (***con*** with), be reconciled (***con*** with)
recóndito *adj* remote
reconfortar ⟨1a⟩ *v/t* comfort
reconocer ⟨2d⟩ *v/t* recognize; *errores* admit, acknowledge; *area* reconnoiter, *Br* reconnoitre; MED examine
reconocimiento *m* recognition; *de error* acknowledg(e)ment; MED examination, check-up; MIL reconnaissance
reconquista *f* reconquest
reconquistar ⟨1a⟩ *v/t* reconquer
reconsiderar ⟨1a⟩ *v/t* reconsider
reconstrucción *f* reconstruction
reconstruir ⟨3g⟩ *v/t fig* reconstruct
reconvenir ⟨3s⟩ *v/i* JUR counterclaim
reconversión *f* COM restructuring
recopilación *f* compilation
recopilar ⟨1a⟩ *v/t* compile
récord 1 *adj* record(-breaking) **2** *m* record
recordar ⟨1m⟩ *v/t* remember, recall; ***recordar algo a alguien*** remind s.o. of sth
recordatorio *m* reminder
recorrer ⟨2a⟩ *v/t distancia* cover, do; *a pie* walk; *territorio*, *país* go around, travel around; *camino* go along, travel along
recorrido *m* route; DEP round
recortar ⟨1a⟩ *v/t* cut out; *fig* cut
recorte *m fig* cutback; ***recorte de periódico*** cutting, clipping; ***recorte salarial*** salary cut
recostarse ⟨1m⟩ *v/r* lie down
recoveco *m* nook, cranny; *en camino* bend
recrearse ⟨1a⟩ *v/r* amuse o.s.
recreativo *adj* recreational; ***juegos recreativos*** amusements
recreo *m* recreation; EDU recess, *Br* break
recriminar ⟨1a⟩ *v/t* reproach
recrudecerse ⟨2d⟩ *v/r* intensify
recta *f* DEP straight; ***recta final*** *tb fig* home straight
rectángulo *m* rectangle
rectificar ⟨1g⟩ *v/t* correct, rectify; *camino* straighten
rectitud *f* rectitude, probity
recto *adj* straight; (*honesto*) honest
rector *m* rector, *Br* vice-chancellor
rectorado *m* rector's office, *Br* vice-chancellor's office
recuadro *m* TIP inset, box
recubierto *part* → ***recubrir***
recubrir ⟨3a; *part* ***recubierto*** ⟩ *v/t* cover (***de*** with)
recuento *m* count; ***recuento de votos*** recount
recuerdo *m* memory; ***da recuerdos a Luís*** give my regards to Luís
recuperación *f tb fig* recovery
recuperar ⟨1a⟩ **1** *v/t tiempo* make up; *algo perdido* recover **2** *v/r* **recuperarse** recover (***de*** from)
recurrir ⟨3a⟩ **1** *v/t* JUR appeal against **2** *v/i*: ***recurrir a*** resort to, turn to
recurso *m* JUR appeal; *material* resource; ***recursos humanos*** human resources; ***recursos naturales*** natural resources
red *f* net; INFOR, *fig* network; ***caer en las redes de*** *fig* fall into the clutches of; ***Red Digital de Servicios Integrados*** Integrated Services Digital Network
redacción *f* writing; *de editorial* editorial

R

department; EDU essay
redactar ⟨1a⟩ *v/t* write, compose
redactor *m*, **redactora** *f* editor
redada *f* raid
redentor *m*, **redentora** *f* COM redeemer; ***el Redentor*** REL the Savio(u)r
redoble *m* MÚS (drum)roll
redomado *adj* F total, out-and-out
redonda *f*: ***a la redonda*** around, round about
redondear ⟨1a⟩ *v/t para más* round up; *para menos* round down; (*rematar*) round off
redondo *adj* round; *negocio* excellent; ***caer redondo*** flop down
reducción *f* reduction; MED setting
reducido *adj precio* reduced; *espacio* small, confined
reducir ⟨3o⟩ **1** *v/t* reduce (***a*** to); MIL overcome **2** *v/r* **reducirse** come down (***a*** to)
reducto *m* redoubt
redujo *vb* → ***reducir***
redundancia *f* tautology
redundar ⟨1a⟩ *v/i* have an impact (***en*** on)
reeditar ⟨1a⟩ *v/t* republish, reissue
reelegir ⟨3c & 3l⟩ *v/t* re-elect
reembolsar ⟨1a⟩ *v/t* refund
reembolso *m* refund; ***contra reembolso*** collect on delivery, *Br* cash on delivery, COD
reemplazar ⟨1f⟩ *v/t* replace
reencarnación *f* REL reincarnation
reestructurar ⟨1a⟩ *v/t* restructure
refacción *f L.Am. de edificio* refurbishment; AUTO spare part
referencia *f* reference; ***hacer referencia a*** refer to, make reference to; ***referencias*** COM references
referéndum *m* referendum
referente *adj*: ***referente a*** referring to, relating to
referirse ⟨3i⟩ *v/r* refer (***a*** to)
refilón *m*: ***mirar de refilón*** glance at
refinado *adj tb fig* refined
refinar ⟨1a⟩ *v/t* TÉC refine
refinería *f* TÉC refinery
reflector *m* reflector; EL spotlight
reflejar ⟨1a⟩ **1** *v/t tb fig* reflect **2** *v/r* **reflejarse** be reflected
reflejo *m* reflex; *imagen* reflection
reflexión *f fig* reflection, thought
reflexionar ⟨1a⟩ *v/t* reflect on, ponder
reflexivo *adj* GRAM reflexive
reflotar ⟨1a⟩ *v/t* COM refloat
reforestar ⟨1a⟩ *v/t* reforest
reforma *f* reform; ***reformas*** *pl* (*obras*) refurbishment *sg*; (*reparaciones*) repairs
reformador *m*, **reformadora** *f* reformer
reformar ⟨1a⟩ **1** *v/t* reform; *edificio* refurbish; (*reparar*) repair **2** *v/r* **reformarse** mend one's ways, reform
reformatorio *m* reform school, reformatory
reformista **1** *adj* reformist, reform *atr* **2** *m/f* reformer
reforzar ⟨1f & 1m⟩ *v/t* reinforce; *vigilancia* increase, step up
refrán *m* saying
refrenar ⟨1a⟩ *v/t* restrain, contain
refrescante *adj* refreshing
refrescar ⟨1g⟩ **1** *v/t tb fig* refresh; *conocimientos* brush up **2** *v/i* cool down **3** *v/r* **refrescarse** cool down
refresco *m* soda, *Br* soft drink
refriega *f* MIL clash, skirmish
refrigerador *m* refrigerator
refrigerar ⟨1a⟩ *v/t* refrigerate
refrigerio *m* snack
refuerzo *m* reinforcement; ***refuerzos*** MIL reinforcements
refugiado *m*, **-a** *f* refugee
refugiarse ⟨1b⟩ *v/r* take refuge
refugio *m* refuge
refulgente *adj* dazzling
refunfuñar ⟨1a⟩ *v/i* grumble
refutar ⟨1a⟩ *v/t* refute
regadera *f* watering can; *Méx* (*ducha*) shower; ***estar como una regadera*** F be nuts F
regadío *m*: ***tierra de regadío*** irrigated land
regalar ⟨1a⟩ *v/t*: ***regalar algo a alguien*** give sth to s.o., give s.o. sth
regaliz *m* BOT licorice, *Br* liquorice
regalo *m* gift, present
regañadientes: ***a regañadientes*** reluctantly
regañar ⟨1a⟩ **1** *v/t* tell off **2** *v/i* quarrel
regañina *f* F telling off
regar ⟨1h & 1k⟩ *v/t* water; AGR irrigate
regata *f* regatta
regatear ⟨1a⟩ *v/t* DEP get past, dodge; ***no regatear esfuerzos*** spare no effort
regazo *m* lap
regenerar ⟨1a⟩ *v/t* regenerate
regente *m/f* regent
regidor **1** *adj* governing, ruling **2** *m*, **regidora** *f* TEA stage manager
régimen *m* POL regime; MED diet; ***estar a régimen*** be on a diet
regimiento *m* MIL regiment
regio *adj* regal, majestic; *S. Am.* F (*estupendo*) great F, fantastic F
región *f* region
regional *adj* regional
regionalismo *m* regionalism
regir ⟨3l & 3c⟩ **1** *v/t* rule, govern **2** *v/i* apply, be in force **3** *v/r* **regirse** be guided

(***por*** by)
registrar ⟨1a⟩ **1** *v/t* register; *casa* search **2** *v/r* **registrarse** be recorded; ***se registró un máximo de 45°C*** a high of 45°C was recorded
registro *m* register; *de casa* search; ***registro civil*** register of births, marriages and deaths
regla *f* (*norma*) rule; *para medir* ruler; MED period; ***por regla general*** as a rule
reglamentar ⟨1a⟩ *v/t* regulate
reglamentario *adj* regulation *atr*
reglamento *m* regulation
regocijarse ⟨1a⟩ *v/r* rejoice (***de*** at), take delight (***de*** in)
regocijo *m* delight
regodearse ⟨1a⟩ *v/r* gloat (***con*** over), delight (***en*** in)
regresar ⟨1a⟩ **1** *v/i* return **2** *v/t Méx* return, give back **3** *v/r* **regresarse** *L.Am.* return
regreso *m* return
regüeldo *m* F belch
reguero *m* trail; ***como un reguero de pólvora*** *fig* like wildfire
regulación *f* regulation; *de temperatura* control
regular 1 *adj sin variar* regular; (*común*) ordinary; (*habitual*) regular, normal; (*no muy bien*) so-so **2** ⟨1a⟩ *v/t* TÉC regulate; *temperatura* control
regularidad *f* regularity
regularizar ⟨1f⟩ *v/t* regularize
regusto *m* aftertaste
rehabilitación *f* MED, *fig* rehabilitation; ARQUI restoration
rehabilitar ⟨1a⟩ *v/t* ARQUI restore
rehacer ⟨2s; *part* ***rehecho*** ⟩ *v/t película, ropa, cama* remake; *trabajo, ejercicio* redo; *casa, vida* rebuild
rehén *m* hostage
rehice *vb* → ***rehacer***
rehizo *vb* → ***rehacer***
rehogar ⟨1h⟩ *v/t* GASTR fry
rehuir ⟨3g⟩ *v/t* shy away from
rehusar ⟨1a⟩ *v/t* refuse, decline
reimprimir ⟨3a⟩ *v/t* reprint
reina *f* queen
reinado *m* reign
reinante *adj tb fig* reigning
reinar ⟨1a⟩ *v/i tb fig* reign
reincidente 1 *adj* repeat **2** *m/f* repeat offender
reincidir ⟨3a⟩ *v/i* reoffend
reincorporarse ⟨1a⟩ *v/r* return (***a*** to)
reino *m tb fig* kingdom; ***el Reino Unido*** the United Kingdom
reinserción *f*: ***reinserción social*** social rehabilitation
reinsertar ⟨1a⟩ *v/t* rehabilitate
reinstaurar ⟨1a⟩ *v/t* bring back
reintegrarse ⟨1a⟩ *v/r* return (***a*** to)
reintegro *m* (*en lotería*) *prize in the form of a refund of the stake money*
reír ⟨3m⟩ **1** *v/i* laugh **2** *v/r* **reírse** laugh (***de*** at)
reiterar ⟨1a⟩ *v/t* repeat, reiterate
reivindicación *f* claim
reivindicar ⟨1g⟩ *v/t* claim; ***reivindicar un atentado*** claim responsibility for an attack
reja *f* AGR plowshare, *Br* ploughshare; (*barrote*) bar, railing; ***meter entre rejas*** *fig* F put behind bars
rejilla *f* FERR luggage rack
rejuvenecer ⟨2d⟩ *v/t* rejuvenate
relación *f* relationship; ***relaciones púiblicas*** *pl* public relations, PR *sg*
relacionado *adj* related (***con*** to)
relacionarse ⟨1a⟩ *v/r* be connected (***con*** to), be related (***con*** to)
relajación *f* relaxation
relajante *adj* relaxing
relajar ⟨1a⟩ **1** *v/t* relax **2** *v/r* **relajarse** relax
relajo *m C.Am., Méx* uproar
relamerse ⟨2a⟩ *v/r* lick one's lips
relámpago *m* flash of lightning; ***viaje relámpago*** flying visit
relatar ⟨1a⟩ *v/t* tell, relate
relatividad *f* relativity
relativo *adj* relative; ***relativo a*** regarding, about
relato *m* short story
relax *m* relaxation
releer ⟨2e⟩ *v/t* reread
relegar ⟨1h⟩ *v/t* relegate
relevante *adj* relevant
relevar ⟨1a⟩ *v/t* MIL relieve; ***relevar a alguien de algo*** relieve s.o. of sth
relevo *m* MIL change; (*sustituto*) relief, replacement; ***carrera de relevos*** relay (race); ***tomar el relevo de alguien*** take over from s.o., relieve s.o.
relicario *m* shrine
relieve *m* relief; ***poner de relieve*** highlight
religión *f* religion
religiosa *f* nun
religioso 1 *adj* religious **2** *m* monk
relinchar ⟨1a⟩ *v/i* neigh
reliquia *f* relic
rellano *m* landing
rellenar ⟨1a⟩ *v/t* fill; GASTR *pollo, pimientos* stuff; *formulario* fill out, fill in
relleno 1 *adj* GASTR *pollo, pimientos* stuffed; *pastel* filled **2** *m tb en cojín* stuffing; *en pastel* filling
reloj *m* clock; *de pulsera* watch, wrist-

watch; ***reloj de pared*** wall clock; ***reloj de sol*** sundial
relojería *f* watchmaker's
relojero *m*, **-a** *f* watchmaker
reluciente *adj* sparkling, glittering
remanso *m* backwater; ***remanso de paz*** *fig* haven of peace
remar ⟨1a⟩ *v/i* row
remarcar ⟨1g⟩ *v/t* stress, emphasize
rematar ⟨1a⟩ **1** *v/t* finish off; *L.Am.* COM auction **2** *v/i en fútbol* shoot
remate *m L.Am.* COM auction, sale; *en fútbol* shot; ***ser tonto de remate*** be a complete idiot
remediar ⟨1b⟩ *v/t* remedy; ***no puedo remediarlo*** I can't do anything about it
remedio *m* remedy; ***sin remedio*** hopeless; ***no hay más remedio que …*** there's no alternative but to …
rememorar ⟨1a⟩ *v/t* remember
remendar ⟨1k⟩ *v/t con parche* patch; (*zurcir*) darn
remesa *f* (*envío*) shipment, consignment; *L.Am. dinero* remittance
remezón *m L.Am.* earth tremor
remiendo *m* (*parche*) patch; (*zurcido*) darn
remilgado *adj* fussy, finicky
reminiscencia *f* reminiscence
remiso *adj* reluctant (***a*** to)
remite *m en carta* return address
remitente *m/f* sender
remitir ⟨3a⟩ **1** *v/t* send, ship; *en texto* refer (***a*** to) **2** *v/i* MED go into remission; *de crisis* ease (off)
remo *m pala* oar; *deporte* rowing
remodelar ⟨1a⟩ *v/t* redesign, remodel
remojar ⟨1a⟩ *v/t* soak; *L.Am.* F *acontecimiento* celebrate
remojo *m*: ***poner a*** *or* ***en remojo*** leave to soak
remojón *m* drenching, soaking; ***darse un remojón*** go for a dip
remolacha *f* beet, *Br* beetroot; ***remolacha azucarera*** sugar beet
remolcador *m* tug
remolcar ⟨1g⟩ *v/t* AUTO, MAR tow
remolino *m de aire* eddy; *de agua* whirlpool
remolón *m*, **-ona** *f* F slacker; ***hacerse el remolón*** slack (off)
remolque *m* AUTO trailer
remontarse ⟨1a⟩ *v/r en el tiempo* go back (***a*** to)
remonte *m* ski lift
remorder ⟨2h⟩ *v/t*: ***me remuerde la conciencia*** I have a guilty conscience
remordimiento *m* remorse
remoto *adj* remote; ***no tengo ni la más -a idea*** I haven't the faintest idea
remover ⟨2h⟩ *v/t* (*agitar*) stir; *L.Am.* (*destituir*) dismiss; *C.Am.*, *Méx* (*quitar*) remove
remplazar *v/t* → ***reemplazar***
remuneración *f* remuneration
remunerar ⟨1a⟩ *v/t* pay
renacentista *adj* Renaissance *atr*
renacer ⟨2d⟩ *v/i fig* be reborn
Renacimiento *m* Renaissance
renacuajo *m* ZO tadpole; F *persona* shrimp F
renal *adj* ANAT renal, kidney *atr*
rencilla *f* fight, argument
rencor *m* resentment; ***guardar rencor a alguien*** bear s.o. a grudge
rencoroso *adj* resentful
rendición *f* surrender
rendija *f* crack; (*hueco*) gap
rendimiento *m* performance; FIN yield; (*producción*) output
rendir ⟨3l⟩ **1** *v/t honores* pay, do; *beneficio* produce, yield **2** *v/i* perform **3** *v/r* **rendirse** surrender
renegado **1** *adj* renegade *atr* **2** *m* renegade
renegar ⟨1h & 1k⟩ *v/i*: ***renegar de alguien*** disown s.o.; ***renegar de algo*** renounce sth
renegrido *adj* blackened
RENFE *abr* (***= Red Nacional de Ferrocarriles Españoles***) *Spanish rail operator*
renglón *m* line; ***a renglón seguido*** immediately after
rengo *adj CSur* lame
renguear ⟨1a⟩ *v/i CSur* limp, walk with a limp
reno *m* ZO reindeer
renombre *m*: ***de renombre*** famous, renowned
renovación *f* renewal
renovador *adj*: ***las fuerzas renovadores*** the forces of renewal
renovar ⟨1m⟩ *v/t* renew
renta *f* income; *de casa* rent; ***renta per cápita*** income per capita
rentabilidad *f* profitability
rentable *adj* profitable
rentar ⟨1a⟩ *v/t* (*arrendar*) rent out; (*alquiler*) rent; *carro* hire
renuente *adj* reluctant, unwilling
renunciar ⟨1b⟩ *v/i*: ***renunciar a*** *tabaco, alcohol etc* give up; *puesto* resign; *demanda* drop
reñir ⟨3h & 3l⟩ **1** *v/t* tell off **2** *v/i* quarrel, fight F
reo *m*, **-a** *f* accused
reojo: ***de reojo*** out of the corner of one's eye

R

repantigarse ⟨1h⟩ *v/r* lounge, sprawl
reparación *f* repair; *fig* reparation
reparar ⟨1a⟩ **1** *v/t* repair **2** *v/i*: ***reparar en algo*** notice sth
reparo *m*: ***poner reparos a*** find problems with; ***no tener reparos en*** have no reservations about
repartición *f S. Am.* department
repartidor *m* delivery man
repartir ⟨3a⟩ *v/t* (*dividir*) share out, divide up; *productos* deliver
reparto *m* (*división*) share-out, distribution; TEA cast; ***reparto a domicilio*** home delivery
repasar ⟨1a⟩ *v/t trabajo* go over again; EDU revise
repecho *m* steep slope
repelente **1** *adj fig* repellent, repulsive; F *niño* horrible **2** *m* repellent
repelúís *m*: ***dar repelúís a alguien*** F give s.o. the creeps F
repente: ***de repente*** suddenly
repentino *adj* sudden
repercusión *f fig* repercussion
repercutir ⟨3a⟩ *v/i* have repercussions (***en*** on)
repertorio *m* TEA, MÚS repertoire
repetición *f* repetition
repetido *adj* repeated
repetir ⟨3l⟩ **1** *v/t* repeat **2** *v/i de comida* repeat **3** *v/r* **repetirse** happen again
repetitivo *adj* repetitive
repipi *adj* F (*afectado*) affected; ***es tan repipi*** *niño* he's such a know-it-all F
repisa *f* shelf
replantear ⟨1a⟩ *v/t pregunta, problema* bring up again
replegarse ⟨1h & 1k⟩ *v/r* MIL withdraw
repleto *adj* full (***de*** of)
réplica *f* replica
replicar ⟨1g⟩ *v/t* reply
repoblar ⟨1m⟩ *v/t* repopulate
repollo *m* BOT cabbage
reponerse ⟨2r; *part* ***repuesto*** ⟩ *v/r* recover (***de*** from)
reportaje *m* story, report
reportero *m*, **-a** *f* reporter; ***reportero gráfico*** press photographer
reposacabezas *m inv* AUTO headrest
reposar ⟨1a⟩ *v/i* rest; *de vino* settle
reposera *f L.Am.* lounger
reposición *f* TEA revival; TV repeat
reposo *m* rest
repostar ⟨1a⟩ *v/i* refuel
repostería *f* pastries *pl*
reprender ⟨2a⟩ *v/t* scold, tell off
represa *f* dam; (*embalse*) reservoir
represalia *f* reprisal
representación *f* representation; TEA performance; ***en representación de*** on behalf of
representante *m/f tb* COM representative
representar ⟨1a⟩ *v/t* represent; *obra* put on, perform; *papel* play; ***representar menos años*** look younger
represión *f* repression
reprimenda *f* reprimand
reprimir ⟨3a⟩ *v/t tb* PSI repress
reprobar ⟨1m⟩ *v/t* condemn; *L.Am.* EDU fail
reprochar ⟨1a⟩ *v/t* reproach
reproche *m* reproach
reproducción *f* BIO reproduction
reproducir ⟨3o⟩ **1** *v/t* reproduce **2** *v/r* **reproducirse** BIO reproduce, breed
reptil *m* ZO reptile
repúíblica *f* republic
republicano **1** *adj* republican **2** *m*, **-a** *f* republican
repudiar ⟨1b⟩ *v/t fml* repudiate; *herencia* renounce
repuesto **1** *part* → ***reponerse*** **2** *m* spare part, replacement; ***de repuesto*** spare
repugnancia *f* disgust, repugnance
repugnante *adj* disgusting, repugnant
repugnar ⟨1a⟩ *v/t* disgust, repel
repulsión *f* repulsion
repulsivo *adj* repulsive
repuse *vb* → ***reponerse***
reputación *f* reputation
requerir ⟨3i⟩ *v/t* require; JUR summons
requesón *m* cottage cheese
requetebién *adv* F really well, brilliantly F
réquiem *m* requiem
requisar ⟨1a⟩ *v/t Arg, Chi* MIL requisition
requisito *m* requirement
res *f L.Am.* bull; ***carne f de res*** beef; ***reses*** *pl* cattle *pl*
resaca *f* MAR undertow, undercurrent; *de beber* hangover
resaltar ⟨1a⟩ **1** *v/t* highlight, stress **2** *v/i* ARQUI jut out; *fig* stand out
resarcirse ⟨3b⟩ *v/r* make up (***de*** for)
resbaladizo *adj* slippery; *fig* tricky
resbalar ⟨1a⟩ *v/i* slide; *fig* slip (up)
resbalón *m* slip; *fig* F slip-up
resbaloso *adj L.Am.* slippery
rescatar ⟨1a⟩ *v/t persona, animal* rescue, save; *bienes* save
rescate *m de peligro* rescue; *en secuestro* ransom
rescindir ⟨3a⟩ *v/t* cancel; *contrato* terminate
rescisión *f* cancellation; *de contrato* termination
reseco *adj* (*seco*) parched; (*flaco*) skinny
resentimiento *m* resentment
resentirse ⟨3i⟩ *v/r* get upset; *de rendi-*

miento, calidad suffer; ***resentirse de algo*** suffer from the effects of sth
reseña *f de libro etc* review
reseñar ⟨1a⟩ *v/t* review
reserva 1 *f* reservation; ***reserva natural*** nature reserve; ***sin reservas*** without reservation **2** *m/f* DEP reserve
reservar ⟨1a⟩ **1** *v/t* (*guardar*) set aside, put by; *billete* reserve **2** *v/r* **reservarse** save o.s. (***para*** for)
resfriado 1 *adj*: ***estar resfriado*** have a cold **2** *m* cold
resfriarse ⟨1c⟩ *v/r* catch cold
resfrío *m L.Am.* cold
resguardar ⟨1a⟩ **1** *v/t* protect (***de*** from) **2** *v/r* **resguardarse** protect o.s. (***de*** from)
resguardo *m* COM counterfoil
residencia *f* residence; ***residencia de ancianos*** *or* ***para la tercera edad*** retirement home
residencial 1 *adj* residential **2** *f Arg, Chi* boarding house
residente 1 *adj* resident **2** *m/f* resident
residir ⟨3a⟩ *v/i* reside; ***residir en*** *fig* lie in
residual *adj* residual; (*de desecho*) waste *atr*
residuo *m* residue; ***residuos*** waste *sg*
resignación *f actitud* resignation
resignarse ⟨1a⟩ *v/r* resign o.s. (***a*** to)
resina *f* resin
resistencia *f* resistance; EL, TÉC resistor
resistir ⟨3a⟩ **1** *v/i* resist; (*aguantar*) hold out **2** *v/t tentación* resist; *frío, dolor etc* stand, bear **3** *v/r* **resistirse** be reluctant (***a*** to)
resolución *f actitud* determination, decisiveness; *de problema* solution (***de*** to); JUR ruling
resolver ⟨2h; *part* ***resuelto***⟩ **1** *v/t problema* solve **2** *v/r* **resolverse** decide (***a*** to; ***por*** on)
resonar ⟨1m⟩ *v/i* echo
resoplar ⟨1a⟩ *v/i* snort
resorte *m* spring
respaldar ⟨1a⟩ *v/t* back, support
respaldo *m de silla* back; *fig* backing, support
respectar ⟨1a⟩ *v/i*: ***por lo que respecta a ...*** as regards ..., as far as ... is concerned
respectivo *adj* respective
respecto *m*: ***al respecto*** on the matter; ***con respecto a*** regarding, as regards
respetable *adj* respectable
respetar ⟨1a⟩ *v/t* respect
respeto *m* respect
respetuoso *adj* respectful
respiración *f* breathing; ***estar con respiración asistida*** MED be on a respirator
respirar ⟨1a⟩ *v/t & v/i* breathe
respiratorio *adj* respiratory
respiro *m fig* breather, break
resplandeciente *adj* shining
resplandor *m* shine, gleam
responder ⟨2a⟩ **1** *v/t* answer **2** *v/i*: ***responder a*** answer, reply to; MED respond to; *descripción* fit, match; (*ser debido a*) be due to
responsabilidad *f* responsibility
responsabilizarse ⟨1f⟩ *v/r* take responsibility (***de*** for)
responsable 1 *adj* responsible (***de*** for) **2** *m/f* person responsible (***de*** for); ***los responsables del crimen*** those responsible for the crime
respuesta *f* (*contestación*) reply, answer; *fig* response
resquebrajar ⟨1a⟩ **1** *v/t* crack **2** *v/r* **resquebrajarse** crack
resquicio *m* gap
resta *f* MAT subtraction
restablecer ⟨2d⟩ **1** *v/t* re-establish **2** *v/r* **restablecerse** recover
restablecimiento *m* re-establishment; *de enfermo* recovery
restante 1 *adj* remaining **2** *m/fpl*: ***los / las restantes*** *pl* the rest *pl*, the remainder *pl*
restar ⟨1a⟩ **1** *v/t* subtract; ***restar importancia a*** play down the importance of **2** *v/i* remain, be left
restauración *f* restoration
restaurante *m* restaurant
restaurar ⟨1a⟩ *v/t* restore
restituir ⟨3g⟩ *v/t* restore; *en cargo* reinstate
resto *m* rest, remainder; ***los restos mortales*** the (mortal) remains
restregar ⟨1h & 1k⟩ *v/t* scrub
restricción *f* restriction
restringir ⟨3c⟩ *v/t* restrict, limit
resucitar ⟨1a⟩ **1** *v/t* resuscitate; *fig* revive **2** *v/i de persona* rise from *o* come back from the dead
resuello *m* puffing, heavy breathing
resuelto 1 *part* → ***resolver*** **2** *adj* decisive, resolute
resultado *m* result; ***sin resultado*** without success
resultar ⟨1a⟩ *v/i* turn out; ***resultar caro*** prove expensive, turn out to be expensive; ***resulta que ...*** it turns out that ...
resumen *m* summary; ***en resumen*** in short
resumir ⟨3a⟩ *v/t* summarize
resurgir ⟨3c⟩ *v/i* reappear, come back
resurrección *f* REL resurrection
retaguardia *f* MIL rearguard
retahíla *f* string
retar ⟨1a⟩ *v/t* challenge; *Rpl* (*regañar*)

scold, tell off
retardar ⟨1a⟩ *v/t* delay
retazo *m fig* snippet, fragment
retención *f* MED retention; *de persona* detention; ***retención fiscal*** tax deduction
retener ⟨2l⟩ *v/t dinero etc* withhold, deduct; *persona* detain, hold
reticencia *f* reticence
reticente *adj* reticent
retintín *m*: ***con retintín*** F sarcastically
retirada *f* MIL retreat, withdrawal
retirado *adj* (*jubilado*) retired; (*alejado*) remote, out-of-the-way
retirar ⟨1a⟩ **1** *v/t* take away, remove; *acusación, dinero* withdraw **2** *v/r* **retirarse** MIL withdraw
retiro *m lugar* retreat
reto *m* challenge; *Rpl* (*regañina*) scolding, telling-off
retobado *adj L.Am.* unruly
retocar ⟨1g⟩ *v/t* FOT retouch, touch up; (*acabar*) put the finishing touches to
retomar ⟨1a⟩ *v/t*: ***retomar algo*** *fig* take sth up again
retoque *m* FOT touching-up; (*acabado*) finishing touch
retorcer ⟨2b & 2h⟩ *v/t* twist
retorcido *adj fig* twisted
retorcijón *m* stomach cramp
retórica *f* rhetoric
retornar ⟨1a⟩ *v/i* return
retorno *m* return
retortijón *m* cramps *pl*, *Br* stomach cramp
retozar ⟨1f⟩ *v/i* frolic, romp
retractar ⟨1a⟩ *v/t* retract, withdraw
retraer ⟨2p; *part* ***retraido***⟩ **1** *v/t* retract **2** *v/r* **retraerse** withdraw
retraído **1** *part* → ***retraer*** **2** *adj* withdrawn
retransmisión *f* RAD, TV transmission, broadcast
retransmitir ⟨3a⟩ *v/t* transmit, broadcast
retrasado **1** *part* → ***retrasar*** **2** *adj tren, entrega* late; *con trabajo, pagos* behind; ***está retrasado en clase*** he's lagging behind in class; ***retrasado mental*** mentally handicapped
retrasar ⟨1a⟩ **1** *v/t* hold up; *reloj* put back; *reunión* postpone, put back **2** *v/i de reloj* lose time; *en los estudios* be behind **3** *v/r* **retrasarse** (*atrasarse*) be late; *de reloj* lose time; *con trabajo, pagos* get behind
retraso *m* delay; ***ir con retraso*** be late
retratar ⟨1a⟩ *v/t* FOT take a picture of; *fig* depict
retrato *m* picture; ***retrato-robot*** composite photo, E-Fit®
retrete *m* bathroom
retribución *f* salary
retroactivo *adj* retroactive
retroceder ⟨2a⟩ *v/i* go back, move back; *fig* back down
retroceso *m fig* backward step
retrógrado *adj* retrograde
retroproyector *m* overhead projector
retrospectiva *f* retrospective
retrovisor *m* AUTO rear-view mirror; ***retrovisor exterior*** wing mirror
retumbar ⟨1a⟩ *v/i* boom
retuve *vb* → ***retener***
reuma, **reúma** *m* MED rheumatism
reunificación *f* POL reunification
reunión *f* meeting; *de amigos* get-together
reunir ⟨3a⟩ **1** *v/t personas* bring together; *requisitos* meet, fulfil(l); *datos* gather (together) **2** *v/r* **reunirse** meet up, get together; COM meet
reutilizar ⟨1f⟩ *v/t* re-use
revalorizar ⟨1f⟩ **1** *v/t* revalue **2** *v/r* **revalorizarse** appreciate (***en*** by), increase in value (***en*** by)
revaluar *vb* → ***revalorizar***
revancha *f* revenge
revelación *f* revelation
revelado *m* development
revelar ⟨1a⟩ *v/t* FOT develop
reventa *f* resale
reventar ⟨1k⟩ **1** *v/i* burst; ***lleno a reventar*** full to bursting **2** *v/t puerta etc* break down **3** *v/r* **reventarse** burst; ***se reventó a trabajar*** *fig* he worked his butt off F
reventón *m* AUTO blowout
reverberar ⟨1a⟩ *v/i de sonido* reverberate
reverencia *f* reverence; *saludo*: *de hombre* bow; *de mujer* curtsy
reverendo *m* REL reverend
reversible *adj ropa* reversible
reverso *m* reverse, back
revés *m* setback; *tenis* backhand; ***al*** *or* ***del revés*** back to front; *con el interior fuera* inside out
revestir ⟨3l⟩ *v/t* TÉC cover (***de*** with); ***revestir gravedad*** be serious
revisación *f L.Am.* check-up
revisada *f L.Am.* → ***revisión***
revisar ⟨1a⟩ *v/t* check, inspect
revisión *f* check, inspection; AUTO service; ***revisión técnica*** roadworthiness test, *Br* MOT (test); ***revisión médica*** check-up
revisor *m*, **revisora** *f* FERR (ticket) inspector
revista *f* magazine; ***pasar revista a*** MIL inspect, review; *fig* review
revivir ⟨3a⟩ **1** *v/i* revive **2** *v/t* relive
revocar ⟨1g & 1m⟩ *v/t pared* render; JUR revoke
revolcarse ⟨1g & 1m⟩ *v/r* roll around
revolcón *m* tumble; F *de amantes* roll in the hay F

R

revolotear ⟨1a⟩ *v/t* flutter
revoltijo, **revoltillo** *m* mess, jumble
revoltoso *adj niño* naughty
revolución *f* revolution
revolucionario 1 *adj* revolutionary **2** *m*, **-a** *f* revolutionary
revólver *m* revolver
revolver ⟨2h; *part* ***revuelto***⟩ **1** *v/t* GASTR stir; *estómago* turn; (*desordenar*) mess up **2** *v/i* rummage (***en*** in) **3** *v/r* **revolverse** *del tiempo* worsen
revuelo *m* stir
revuelto 1 *part* → ***revolver*** **2** *adj mar* rough; *gente* restless
rey *m* king
reyerta *f* fight
rezagarse ⟨1h⟩ *v/r* drop back, fall behind
rezar ⟨1f⟩ **1** *v/t oración* say **2** *v/i* pray; *de texto* say
rezo *m* prayer
rezongar ⟨1h⟩ *v/i* grumble
rezumar ⟨1a⟩ *v/t* & *v/i* ooze
ría 1 *vb* → ***reír*** **2** *f* estuary
riachuelo *m* stream
riada *f* flood
ribera *f* shore, bank
riberano *L.Am.* **1** *adj L.Am.* coastal; *de río* riverside *atr* **2** *m*, **-a** *f* person who lives by the sea / river
ribereño: ***ribereño de*** bordering (on)
rica *f* rich woman
rico 1 *adj* rich; *comida* delicious; F *niño* cute, sweet; ***rico en vitaminas*** rich in vitamins **2** *m* rich man; ***nuevo rico*** nouveau riche
ridiculizar ⟨1f⟩ *v/t* ridicule
ridículo 1 *adj* ridiculous **2** *m* ridicule; ***hacer el ridículo, quedar en ridículo*** make a fool of o.s.
ríe *vb* → ***reír***
riego 1 *vb* → ***regar*** **2** *m* AGR irrigation; ***riego sanguíneo*** blood flow
ríen *vb* → ***reír***
rienda *f* rein; ***dar rienda suelta a*** give free rein to
riesgo *m* risk; ***a riesgo de*** at the risk of; ***correr el riesgo*** run the risk (***de*** of)
riesgoso *adj L.Am.* risky
rifa *f* raffle
rifar ⟨1a⟩ **1** *v/t* raffle **2** *v/r* **rifarse** *fig* fight over
rifle *m* rifle
rige *vb* → ***regir***
rigidez *f* rigidity; *de carácter* inflexibility; *fig* strictness
rígido *adj* rigid; *carácter* inflexible; *fig* strict
rigor *m* rigo(u)r
riguroso *adj* rigorous, harsh
rima *f* rhyme
rimar ⟨1a⟩ *v/i* rhyme (***con*** with)
rimbombante *adj* ostentatious
rímel *m* mascara
rincón *m* corner
rinde *vb* → ***rendir***
rinoceronte *m* ZO rhino, rhinoceros
riña *f* quarrel, fight
riñe *vb* → ***reñir***
riñón *m* ANAT kidney; ***costar un riñón*** F cost an arm and a leg F
riñonera *f* fanny pack, *Br* bum bag
río 1 *m* river; ***río abajo / arriba*** up / down river; ***el Río de la Plata*** the River Plate **2** *vb* → ***reír***
rioplatense *adj* of / from the River Plate area, River Plate *atr*
riqueza *f* wealth
risa *f* laugh; ***risas*** *pl* laughter *sg*; ***dar risa*** be funny; ***morirse de risa*** kill o.s. laughing; ***tomar algo a risa*** treat sth as a joke
ristra *f* string
risueño *adj* cheerful
rítmico *adj* rhythmic(al)
ritmo *m* rhythm; *de desarrollo* rate, pace
rito *m* rite
ritual *m*/*adj* ritual
rival *m*/*f* rival
rivalidad *f* rivalry
rivalizar ⟨1f⟩ *v/i*: ***rivalizar con*** rival
rizado *adj* curly
rizar ⟨1f⟩ **1** *v/t* curl **2** **rizarse** *v/r* curl
rizo *m* curl
robar ⟨1a⟩ *v/t persona*, *banco* rob; *objeto* steal; *naipe* take, pick up
roble *m* BOT oak
robo *m* robbery; *en casa* burglary
robot *m* robot; ***robot de cocina*** food processor
robótica *f* robotics
robustecer ⟨2d⟩ **1** *v/t* strengthen **2** *v/r* **robustecerse** become stronger
robusto *adj* robust, sturdy
roca *f* rock
roce *m fig* friction; ***tener roces con*** come into conflict with
rociar ⟨1c⟩ *v/t* spray
rocín *m* F nag
rocío *m* dew
rock *m* MÚS rock
rococó *adj* rococo
rocódromo *m* climbing wall
rocoto *m S. Am.* hot red pepper
rodaballo *m* ZO turbot
rodaja *f* slice
rodaje *m de película* shooting, filming; AUTO breaking in, *Br* running in
rodapié *m* baseboard, *Br* skirting board
rodar ⟨1m⟩ **1** *v/i* roll; *de coche* go, travel (***a***

at); *sin rumbo fijo* wander **2** *v/t película* shoot; AUTO break in, *Br* run in

rodear ⟨1a⟩ **1** *v/t* surround **2** *v/r* **rodearse** surround o.s. (***de*** with)

rodeo *m* detour; *con caballos y vaqueros etc* rodeo; ***andarse con rodeos*** beat about the bush; ***hablar sin rodeos*** speak plainly, not beat about the bush

rodilla *f* knee; ***de rodillas*** kneeling, on one's knees; ***hincarse*** *or* ***ponerse de rodillas*** kneel (down)

rodillo *m* rolling pin; TÉC roller

rododendro *m* BOT rhododendron

roedor *m* rodent

roer ⟨2za⟩ *v/t* gnaw; *fig* eat into

rogar ⟨1h & 1m⟩ *v/t* ask for; (*implorar*) beg for, plead for; ***hacerse de rogar*** play hard to get

rojizo *adj* reddish

rojo **1** *adj* red; ***al rojo vivo*** red hot **2** *m color* red **3** *m*, **-a** *f* POL red, commie F

rol *m* role

rollizo *adj* F chubby

rollo *m* FOT roll; *fig* F drag F; ***buen / mal rollo*** F good / bad atmosphere; ***¡qué rollo!*** F what a drag! F

Roma Rome

romance *m* romance

románico *m/adj* Romanesque

romano **1** *adj* Roman **2** *m*, **-a** *f* Roman

romántico **1** *adj* romantic **2** *m*, **-a** *f* romantic

rombo *m* rhombus

romero *m* BOT rosemary

rompecabezas *m* puzzle

rompehielos *m inv* icebreaker

romper ⟨2a; *part* ***roto***⟩ **1** *v/t* break; (*hacer añicos*) smash; *tela, papel* tear **2** *v/i* break; ***romper a*** start to; ***romper con alguien*** break up with s.o. **3** *v/r* **romperse** break

rompopo *m C.Am., Méx bebida* eggnog

ron *m* rum

roncar ⟨1g⟩ *v/i* snore

roncha *f* MED bump, swelling

ronco *adj* hoarse; ***quedarse ronco*** go hoarse

ronda *f* round

rondar ⟨1a⟩ **1** *v/t* patrol; ***me ronda una idea*** I have an idea going around in my head **2** *v/i* F hang around

ronquido *m* snore; ***ronquidos*** *pl* snoring *sg*

ronronear ⟨1a⟩ *v/i de gato* purr

roña *f* grime

roñoso *adj* grimy, grubby

ropa *f* clothes *pl*; ***ropa de cama*** bedclothes *pl*; ***ropa interior*** underwear; ***ropa íntima*** *L.Am.* underwear

ropero *m* closet, *Br* wardrobe

rosa **1** *adj* pink **2** *f* BOT rose; ***fresco como una rosa*** fresh as a daisy; ***ver algo de color de rosa*** see sth through rose-colo(u)red glasses

rosado **1** *adj* pink; *vino* rosé **2** *m* rosé

rosal *m* rosebush

rosario *m* REL rosary; *fig* string

rosbif *m* GASTR roast beef

rosca *f* TÉC thread; GASTR F *pastry similar to a donut*

rosco *m* GASTR *pastry similar to a donut*; ***no comerse un rosco*** P not get anywhere

roscón *m* GASTR *large ring-shaped cake*

rosquilla *f pastry similar to a donut*

rosticería *f L.Am. type of deli that sells roast chicken*

rostro *m* face

rotación *f* rotation

rotisería *f L.Am.* deli, delicatessen

roto **1** *part* → ***romper*** **2** *adj pierna etc* broken; (*hecho añicos*) smashed; *tela, papel* torn **3** *m*, **-a** *f Chi* one of the urban poor

rotonda *f* traffic circle, *Br* roundabout

rotoso *adj Rpl* F scruffy

rotulador *m* fiber-tip, *Br* fibre-tip, felt-tip

rótulo *m* sign

rotundo *adj fig* categorical

rotura *f* breakage; ***una rotura de cadera*** MED a broken hip

rozadura *f* chafing, rubbing

rozagante *adj* healthy

rozar ⟨1f⟩ **1** *v/t* rub; (*tocar ligeramente*) brush; *fig* touch on **2** *v/i* rub **3** *v/r* **rozarse** rub; (*desgastarse*) wear

rte. *abr* (***= remitente***) sender

ruana *f Ecuad* poncho

rubeola, **rubéola** *f* MED German measles *sg*

rubí *m* ruby

rubicundo *adj* ruddy

rubio *adj* blond; ***tabaco rubio*** Virginia tobacco

ruborizarse ⟨1f⟩ *v/r* go red, blush

rúíbrica *f* heading; *de firma* flourish

rubro *m L.Am.* category, heading

rudeza *f* roughness

rudimentario *adj* rudimentary

rudo *adj* rough

rueda *f* wheel; ***rueda dentada*** cogwheel; ***rueda de prensa*** press conference; ***rueda de recambio*** spare wheel

ruedo *m* TAUR bullring

ruego **1** *vb* → ***rogar*** **2** *m* request

rufián *m* rogue

rugby *m* rugby

rugido *m* roar

rugir ⟨3c⟩ *v/i* roar

rugoso *adj superficie* rough
ruido *m* noise; ***hacer ruido*** make a noise; ***mucho ruido y pocas nueces*** all talk and no action
ruidoso *adj* noisy
ruin *adj* despicable, mean; (*tacaño*) mean, miserly
ruina *f* ruin; ***llevar a alguien a la ruina*** *fig* bankrupt s.o.
ruiseñor *m* zo nightingale
ruleta *f* roulette
ruletero *m Méx* cab *o* taxi driver
rulo *m* roller
rumbeador *m Rpl* tracker
rumbear ⟨1a⟩ *v/i L.Am.* head (***para*** for)
rumbo *m* course; ***tomar rumbo a*** head for; ***perder el rumbo*** *fig* lose one's way
rumboso *adj* lavish
rumiar ⟨1b⟩ *v/t fig* ponder
rumor *m* rumo(u)r
rumorearse ⟨1a⟩ *v/r* be rumo(u)red
rupestre *adj*: ***pintura rupestre*** cave painting
ruptura *f de relaciones* breaking off; *de pareja* break-up
rural 1 *adj* rural **2** *m Rpl* station wagon, *Br* estate car; ***rurales*** *Méx* (rural) police
Rusia Russia
ruso 1 *adj* Russian **2** *m*, **-a** *f* Russian
rúístico *adj* rustic
ruta *f* route
rutina *f* routine
rutinario *adj* routine *atr*

S

S *abr* (***= sur***) S (= South(ern))
S.A. *abr* (***= sociedad anónima***) inc (= incorporated), *Br* plc (= public limited company)
sábado *m* Saturday
sábana *f* sheet; ***sábana ajustable*** fitted sheet
sabana *f* savanna(h)
sabandija *f* bug, creepy-crawly
sabañón *m* chilblain
sabelotodo *m* F know-it-all F, *Br* know-all F
saber ⟨2n⟩ **1** *v/t* know (***de*** about); ***saber hacer algo*** know how to do sth, be able to do sth; ***no lo supe hasta más tarde*** I didn't find out till later; ***hacer saber algo a alguien*** let s.o. know sth; ***¡qué sé yo!*** who knows?; ***que yo sepa*** as far as I know; ***sabérselas todas*** F know every trick in the book **2** *v/i* taste (***a*** of); ***me sabe a quemado*** it tastes burnt to me; ***me sabe mal*** *fig* it upsets me **3** *m* knowledge, learning
sabiduría *f* wisdom; (*conocimientos*) knowledge
sabiendas *fpl*: ***a sabiendas*** knowingly; ***a sabiendas que*** knowing full well that
sabio 1 *adj* wise; (*sensato*) sensible **2** *m*, **-a** *f* wise person; (*experto*) expert
sabiondo *m*, **-a** *f* know- it-all F, *Br* know-all F
sablazo *m*: ***dar un sablazo a alguien*** F scrounge money off s.o.
sable *m* saber, *Br* sabre
sablear ⟨1a⟩ *v/t & v/i L.Am.* F scrounge (***a*** from)
sabor *m* flavo(u)r, taste; ***dejar mal sabor de boca*** *fig* leave a bad taste in the mouth
saborear ⟨1a⟩ *v/t* savo(u)r; *fig* relish
sabotaje *m* sabotage
saboteador *m*, **saboteadora** *f* saboteur
sabotear ⟨1a⟩ *v/t* sabotage
sabroso *adj* tasty; *fig* juicy; *L.Am.* (*agradable*) nice, pleasant
sabrosura *f L.Am.* tasty dish
sabueso *m fig* sleuth
sacacorchos *m inv* corkscrew
sacamuelas *m inv desp* F dentist
sacapuntas *m inv* pencil sharpener
sacar ⟨1g⟩ **1** *v/t* take out; *mancha* take out, remove; *información* get; *disco, libro* bring out; *fotocopias* make; ***sacar a alguien a bailar*** ask s.o. to dance; ***sacar algo en claro*** (*entender*) make sense of sth; ***sacar de paseo*** take for a walk **2** *v/r* **sacarse** *L.Am. ropa* take off
sacarina *f* saccharin(e)
sacerdote *m* priest
sacerdotisa *f* priestess
saciar ⟨1b⟩ *v/t fig* satisfy, fulfill
saciedad *f*: ***repetir algo hasta la saciedad*** *fig* repeat sth time and again, repeat sth ad nauseam

saco *m* sack; *L.Am.* jacket; ***saco de dormir*** sleeping bag; ***entrar a saco en*** F burst into, barge into F
sacramento *m* sacrament
sacrificar ⟨1g⟩ **1** *v/t* sacrifice; (*matar*) slaughter **2** *v/r* **sacrificarse** make sacrifices (***por*** for)
sacrificio *m* sacrifice
sacrilegio *m* sacrilege
sacristán *m* sexton
sacristía *f* vestry
sacudida *f* shake, jolt; EL shock
sacudir ⟨3a⟩ **1** *v/t tb fig* shake; F *niño* beat, wallop F **2** *v/r* **sacudirse** shake off, shrug off; ***sacudirse alguien*** (***de encima***) get rid of s.o.
sádico 1 *adj* sadistic **2** *m*, **-a** *f* sadist
sadismo *m* sadism
safari *m* safari; ***safari fotográfico*** photographic safari
sagaz *adj* shrewd, sharp
Sagitario *m/f inv* ASTR Sagittarius
sagrado *adj* sacred, holy
sagrario *m* tabernacle
Sahara Sahara
sainete *m* TEA short farce, one-act play
sal 1 *f* salt; ***sal comúín*** cooking salt; ***sal marina*** sea salt **2** *vb* → ***salir***
sala *f* room, hall; *de cine* screen; JUR court room; ***sala de embarque*** AVIA departure lounge; ***sala de espera*** waiting room; ***sala de estar*** living room; ***sala de fiestas*** night club; ***sala de sesiones*** *or* ***de juntas*** boardroom
saladero *m L.Am.* meat / fish salting factory
salado *adj* salted; (*con demasiada sal*) salty; (*no dulce*) savo(u)ry; *fig* funny, witty; *C.Am.*, *Chi*, *Rpl* F pric(e)y F
salamandra *f* ZO salamander
salamanquesa *f* ZO gecko
salami *m* salami
salar ⟨1a⟩ **1** *v/t* add salt to, salt; *para conservar* salt **2** *m Arg* salt mine
salarial *adj* salary *atr*
salario *m* salary; ***salario base*** basic wage; ***salario mínimo*** minimum wage
salazón *f* salted fish / meat; ***en salazón*** salt *atr*
salchicha *f* sausage
salchichón *m type of spiced sausage*
saldar ⟨1a⟩ *v/t disputa* settle; *deuda* settle, pay; *géneros* sell off
saldo *m* COM balance; (*resultado*) result; ***saldo acreedor*** credit balance; ***saldo deudor*** debit balance; ***de saldo*** reduced, on sale
saldré *vb* → ***salir***
salero *m* salt cellar; *fig* wit
saleroso *adj* funny, witty
salga *vb* → ***salir***
salgo *vb* → ***salir***
salida *f* exit, way out; TRANSP departure; *de carrera* start; ***salida de emergencia*** emergency exit; ***salida de tono*** ill--judged remark
saliente *adj* projecting, protruding; *presidente* retiring, outgoing
salir ⟨3r⟩ **1** *v/i* leave, go out; (*aparecer*) appear, come out; ***salir de*** (*ir fuera de*) leave, go out of; (*venir fuera de*) leave, come out of; ***salir a alguien*** take after s.o.; ***salir a 1000 pesetas*** cost 1000 pesetas; ***salir bien / mal*** turn out well / badly; ***el dibujo no me sale*** FI can't get this drawing right; ***no me salió el trabajo*** I didn't get the job; ***salir con alguien*** date s.o., go out with s.o.; ***salir perdiendo*** end up losing **2** *v/r* **salirse** *de líquido* overflow; (*dejar*) leave; ***salirse de la carretera*** leave the road, go off the road; ***salirse con la suya*** get what one wants
salitre *m* saltpeter, *Br* saltpetre
saliva *f* saliva; ***tragar saliva*** hold one's tongue
salmo *m* psalm
salmón *m* ZO salmon; ***color salmón*** salmon
salmonete *m* ZO red mullet
salmuera *f* pickle, brine
salobre *adj* salt; (*con demasiada sal*) salty
salomónico *adj* just, fair
salón *m* living room; ***salón de actos*** auditorium, hall; ***salón de baile*** dance hall; ***salón de belleza*** beauty parlo(u)r, beautician's
salpicadera *f Méx* AUTO fender, *Br* mudguard
salpicadero *m* AUTO dash(board)
salpicadura *f* stain
salpicar ⟨1g⟩ *v/t* splash, spatter (***con*** with); *fig* sprinkle, pepper
salpicón *m* GASTR *vegetable salad with chopped meat or fish*
salpimentar ⟨1k⟩ *v/t* season (with salt and pepper)
salsa *f* GASTR sauce; *baile* salsa; ***en su salsa*** *fig* in one's element
salsera *f* sauce boat
saltamontes *m inv* ZO grasshopper
saltar ⟨1a⟩ **1** *v/i* jump, leap; ***saltar a la vista*** *fig* be obvious, be clear; ***saltar sobre*** pounce on; ***saltar a la comba*** jump rope, *Br* skip **2** *v/t valla* jump **3** *v/r* **saltarse** (*omitir*) miss, skip
saltear ⟨1a⟩ *v/t* GASTR sauté
saltimbanqui *m* acrobat
salto *m* leap, jump; ***salto de agua*** water-

S

fall; ***salto de altura*** high jump; ***salto de longitud*** long jump; ***salto mortal*** somersault
saltón *adj*: ***ojos saltones*** bulging eyes
salubridad *f L.Am.* health; ***Salubridad*** *L.Am.* Department of Health
salud *f* health; ***¡(a tu) salud!*** cheers!
saludable *adj* healthy
saludar ⟨1a⟩ *v/t* say hello to, greet; MIL salute
saludo *m* greeting; MIL salute; ***saludos*** *en carta* best wishes
salva *f*: ***salva de aplausos*** round of applause
salvación *f* REL salvation
salvado *m* bran
salvador *m* REL savio(u)r
salvadoreño 1 *adj* Salvador(e)an **2** *m*, **-a** *f* Salvador(e)an
salvaguardar ⟨1a⟩ *v/t* safeguard, protect
salvajada *f* atrocity, act of savagery; ***decir una salvajada*** say something outrageous
salvaje 1 *adj* wild; (*bruto*) brutal **2** *m/f* savage
salvajismo *m* savagery
salvamanteles *m inv* table mat
salvamento *m* rescue; ***buque de salvamento*** life boat
salvapantallas *m inv* INFOR screensaver
salvar ⟨1a⟩ **1** *v/t* save; *obstáculo* get round, get over **2** *v/r* **salvarse** escape, get out
salvavidas *m inv* life belt
salvedad *f* (*excepción*) exception
salvo 1 *adj*: ***estar a salvo*** be safe (and sound); ***ponerse a salvo*** reach safety **2** *adv & prp* except, save; ***salvo error u omisión*** errors and omissions excepted
sambenito *m*: ***le han colgado el sambenito de vago*** F they've got him down as idle F
sambumbia *f L.Am. watery drink*
San *adj* Saint
sanar ⟨1a⟩ **1** *v/t* cure **2** *v/i de persona* get well, recover; *de herida* heal
sanatorio *m* sanitarium, clinic
sanción *f* JUR penalty, sanction
sancionar ⟨1a⟩ *v/t* penalize; (*multar*) fine
sancocho *m W.I. type of stew*
sandalia *f* sandal
sándalo *m* BOT sandalwood
sandez *f* nonsense; ***decir sandeces*** talk nonsense
sandía *f* watermelon
sandunga *f* F wit
sandunguero *adj L.Am.* F witty
sandwich *m tostado* toasted sandwich; *L.Am. sin tostar* sandwich
saneamiento *m* cleaning up; COM restructuring, rationalization
sanear ⟨1a⟩ *v/t* clean up; COM restructure, rationalize
sangrar ⟨1a⟩ **1** *v/t* ***sangrar a alguien*** *fig* F sponge off s.o. **2** *v/i* bleed
sangre *f* blood; ***sangre fría*** *fig* calmness, coolness; ***a sangre fría*** *fig* in cold blood; ***no llegará la sangre al río*** it won't come to that, it won't be that bad
sangría *f* GASTR sangria
sangriento *adj* bloody
sangrigordo *adj Méx* tedious, boring
sanguijuela *f* ZO, *fig* leech
sanguinario *adj* bloodthirsty
sanidad *f* health
sanitario *adj* (public) health *atr*
sanitarios *mpl* bathroom fittings
sano *adj* healthy; ***sano y salvo*** safe and well; ***cortar por lo sano*** take drastic measures
sanseacabó: ***y sanseacabó*** F and that's that F
santa *f* Saint
santiamén *m*: ***en un santiamén*** F in an instant
santidad *f*: ***Su Santidad*** His Holiness
santiguarse ⟨1i⟩ *v/r* cross o.s., make the sign of the cross
santo 1 *adj* holy **2** *m* saint; ***santo y seña*** F password; ***¿a santo de qué?*** F what on earth for? F; ***no es santo de mi devoción*** F I don't like him very much
santuario *m fig* sanctuary
santurrón *m*, **-ona** *f* sanctimonious person
saña *f* viciousness
sapo *m* ZO toad; ***echar sapos y culebras*** *fig* curse and swear
saque *m en tenis* serve; ***saque de banda*** *en fútbol* throw-in; ***saque de esquina*** corner (kick); ***tener buen saque*** F have a big appetite
saquear ⟨1a⟩ *v/t* sack, ransack
sarampión *m* MED measles
sarao *m* party
sarape *m Méx* poncho, blanket
sarcasmo *m* sarcasm
sarcástico *adj* sarcastic
sarcófago *m* sarcophagus
sardina *f* sardine; ***como sardinas en lata*** like sardines
sargento *m* sergeant
sarna *f* MED scabies
sarnoso *adj* scabby
sarpullido *m* MED rash
sarro *m* tartar
sarta *f* string, series

sartén *f* frying pan; ***tener la sartén por el mango*** *fig* be the boss, be in the driving seat
sastra *f* tailor(ess)
sastre *m* tailor
satán, **satanás** *m* Satan
satánico *adj* satanic
satélite *m* satellite; ***ciudad satélite*** satellite town
satén, **satín** *m* satin
sátira *f* satire
satírico *adj* satirical
satirizar ⟨1f⟩ *v/t* satirize
satisfacción *f* satisfaction
satisfacer ⟨2s; *part* ***satisfecho*** ⟩ *v/t* satisfy; *requisito*, *exigencia* meet, fulfil(l); *deuda* settle, pay off
satisfactorio *adj* satisfactory
satisfecho 1 *part* → ***satisfacer*** **2** *adj* satisfied; (*lleno*) full; ***darse por satisfecho*** be satisfied (***con*** with)
saturar ⟨1a⟩ *v/t* saturate
sauce *m* BOT willow; ***sauce llorón*** weeping willow
saúco *m* BOT elder
saudí *m/f* & *adj* Saudi
saudita *m/f* Saudi
sauna *f* sauna
savia *f* sap
saxofón, **saxófono** *m* saxophone, sax F
sazón *f*: ***a la sazón*** at that time
sazonar ⟨1a⟩ *v/t* GASTR season
scooter *m* motor scooter
se ◇ *pron complemento indirecto*: *a él* (to) him; *a ella* (to) her; *a usted*, *ustedes* (to) you; *a ellos* (to) them; ***se lo daré*** I will give it to him / her / you / them
◇ *reflexivo*: *con él* himself; *con ella* herself; *cosa* itself; *con usted* yourself; *con ustedes* yourselves; *con ellos* themselves; ***se vistió*** he got dressed, he dressed himself; ***se lavó las manos*** she washed her hands; ***se abrazaron*** they hugged each other
◇ *oración impersonal*: ***se cree*** it is thought; ***se habla español*** Spanish spoken
sé *vb* → ***saber***
sea *vb* → ***ser***
sebo *m* grease, fat
secador *m*: ***secador*** (***de pelo***) hair dryer
secadora *f* dryer
secar ⟨1g⟩ **1** *v/t* dry **2** *v/r* **secarse** dry
sección *f* section
secesión *f* POL secession
seco *adj* dry; *fig persona* curt, brusque; ***parar en seco*** stop dead
secreción *f* secretion
secretaria *f* secretary; ***secretaria de dirección*** executive secretary
secretaría *f* secretary's office; *de organización* secretariat
secretario *m tb* POL secretary
secreter *m mueble* writing desk
secretismo *m* secrecy
secreto 1 *adj* secret **2** *m* secret; ***un secreto a voces*** an open secret; ***en secreto*** in secret
secta *f* sect
sectario *adj* sectarian
sectarismo *m* sectarianism
sector *m* sector
secuaz *m/f* follower
secuela *f* MED after-effect
secuencia *f* sequence
secuencial *adj* INFOR sequential
secuestrador *m*, **secuestradora** *f* kidnapper
secuestrar ⟨1a⟩ *v/t barco*, *avión* hijack; *persona* abduct, kidnap
secuestro *m de barco*, *avión* hijacking; *de persona* abduction, kidnapping; ***secuestro aéreo*** hijacking
secundar ⟨1a⟩ *v/t* support, back
secundario *adj* secondary
sed *f tb fig* thirst; ***tener sed*** be thirsty
seda *f* silk; ***como una seda*** F as smooth as silk
sedal *m* fishing line
sedante *m* sedative
sede *f de organización* headquarters; *de acontecimiento* site; ***sede social*** head office
sedentario *adj* sedentary
sedición *f* sedition
sediento *adj* thirsty; ***estar sediento de*** *fig* thirst for
sedimentar ⟨1a⟩ *v/t* deposit
sedimento *m* sediment
sedoso *adj* silky
seducción *f* seduction; (*atracción*) attraction
seducir ⟨3o⟩ *v/t* seduce; (*atraer*) attract; (*cautivar*) captivate, charm
seductor 1 *adj* seductive; (*atractivo*) attractive; *oferta* tempting **2** *m* seducer
seductora *f* seductress
segadora *f* reaper, harvester
segar ⟨1h & 1k⟩ *v/t* reap, harvest
seglar *adj* secular, lay *atr*
segmento *m* segment
segregación *f* segregation; ***segregación racial*** racial segregation
segregar ⟨1h⟩ *v/t* segregate
seguida *f*: ***en seguida*** at once, immediately
seguido 1 *adj* consecutive, successive; ***ir todo seguido*** go straight on **2** *adv*

L.Am. often, frequently
seguidor *m*, **seguidora** *f* follower, supporter
seguimiento *m* monitoring
seguir ⟨3l & 3d⟩ **1** *v/t* follow; ***seguir a alguien*** follow s.o. **2** *v/i* continue, carry on; ***sigue enfadado conmigo*** he's still angry with me; ***seguir haciendo algo*** go on doing sth, continue to do sth
segúín 1 *prp* according to; ***segúín él*** according to him **2** *adv* it depends
segunda *f*: ***de segunda*** *fig* second-rate
segundero *m* second hand
segundo *m/adj* second
seguridad *f* safety; *contra crimen* security; (*certeza*) certainty; ***Seguridad Social*** *Esp* Social Security
seguro 1 *adj* safe; (*estable*) steady; (*cierto*) sure; ***es seguro*** (*cierto*) it's a certainty; ***seguro de sí mismo*** self-confident, sure of o.s. **2** *adv* for sure **3** *m* COM insurance; *de puerta, coche* lock; *L.Am.* (*imperdible*) safety pin; ***poner el seguro*** lock the door; ***ir sobre seguro*** be on the safe side
seis *adj* six
seiscientos *adj* six hundred
seísmo *m* earthquake
selección *f* selection; ***selección nacional*** DEP national team
seleccionador *m*, **seleccionadora** *f* DEP: ***seleccionador nacional*** national team manager
seleccionar ⟨1a⟩ *v/t* choose, select
selectividad *f en España* university entrance exam
selecto *adj* select, exclusive
sellar ⟨1a⟩ *v/t* seal
sello *m* stamp; *fig* hallmark; ***sello discográfico*** record label
selva *f* (*bosque*) forest; (*jungla*) jungle
semáforo *m* traffic light
semana *f* week; ***Semana Santa*** Holy Week, Easter
semanal *adj* weekly
semanario *m* weekly
semblante *m* face
sembrado *m* sown field
sembrar ⟨1k⟩ *v/t* sow; *fig*: *pánico, inquietud etc* spread
semejante 1 *adj* similar; ***jamás he oído semejante tontería*** I've never heard such nonsense **2** *m* fellow human being, fellow creature
semejanza *f* similarity
semejarse ⟨1a⟩ *v/r* look alike, resemble each other
semen *m* BIO semen
semental *m toro* stud bull; *caballo* stallion
semestre *m* six-month period; EDU semester
semicírculo *m* semicircle
semiconductor *m* EL semiconductor
semifinal *f* DEP semifinal
semilla *f* seed
seminario *m* seminary
seminarista *m* seminarian
semítico *adj* Semitic
sémola *f* semolina
senado *m* senate
senador *m*, **senadora** *f* senator
sencillez *f* simplicity
sencillo 1 *adj* simple **2** *m L.Am.* small change
senda *f* path, track
senderismo *m* trekking, hiking
senderista *m/f* walker, hiker
sendero *m* path, track
sendos, -as *adj pl*: ***les entregó sendos diplomas*** he presented each of them with a diploma
senil *adj* senile
seno *m tb fig* bosom; ***senos*** breasts
sensación *f* feeling, sensation; ***causar sensación*** *fig* cause a sensation
sensacional *adj* sensational
sensacionalista *adj* sensationalist
sensatez *f* good sense
sensato *adj* sensible
sensibilidad *f* feeling; (*emotividad*) sensitivity
sensibilizar ⟨1f⟩ *v/t* make aware (***sobre*** of)
sensible *adj* sensitive; (*apreciable*) appreciable, noticeable
sensiblero *adj* sentimental, schmaltzy F
sensor *m* sensor
sensorial *adj* sensory
sensual *adj* sensual
sensualidad *f* sensuality
sentada *f* sit-down
sentado *adj* sitting, seated; ***dar por sentado*** *fig* take for granted, assume
sentar ⟨1k⟩ **1** *v/t fig* establish, create; ***sentar las bases*** lay the foundations, pave the way **2** *v/i*: ***sentar bien a alguien*** *de comida* agree with s.o.; ***le sienta bien esa chaqueta*** that jacket suits her, she looks good in that jacket **3** *v/r* **sentarse** sit down
sentencia *f* JUR sentence
sentenciar ⟨1b⟩ *v/t* JUR sentence
sentido *m* sense; (*significado*) meaning; ***sentido comúín*** common sense; ***sentido del humor*** sense of humo(u)r; ***perder / recobrar el sentido*** lose / regain consciousness
sentimental *adj* emotional; ***ser senti-***

mental be sentimental

sentimentalismo *m* sentiment

sentimiento *m* feeling; ***lo acompaño en el sentimiento*** my condolences

sentir 1 *m* feeling, opinion **2** ⟨3i⟩ *v/t* feel; (*percibir*) sense; ***lo siento*** I'm sorry **3** *v/r* **sentirse** feel; *L.Am.* (*ofenderse*) take offense, *Br* take offence

seña *f* gesture, sign; ***me hizo una seña para que entrara*** he gestured to me to go in; ***señas*** *pl* address *sg*; ***hacer señas*** wave

señal *f* signal; *fig* sign, trace; COM deposit, down payment; ***en señal de*** as a token of, as a mark of

señalado *adj* special

señalar ⟨1a⟩ *v/t* indicate, point out

señalizar ⟨1f⟩ *v/t* signpost

Señor *m* Lord

señor 1 *m* gentleman, man; *trato* sir; *escrito* Mr; ***el señor López*** Mr López; ***los señores López*** Mr and Mrs López

señora *f* lady, woman; *trato* ma'am, *Br* madam; *escrito* Mrs, Ms; ***la señora López*** Mrs Lopez; ***mi señora*** my wife; ***señoras y señores*** ladies and gentlemen

señoría *f*: ***su señoría*** your Hono(u)r

señorial *adj* lordly, noble

señorita *f* young lady, young woman; *tratamiento* miss; *escrito* Miss; ***la señorita López*** Ms López, Miss López

señuelo *m* decoy

sepa *vb* → ***saber***

separación *f* separation; ***separación de bienes*** JUR division of property

separado *adj* separated; ***por separado*** separately

separar ⟨1a⟩ **1** *v/t* separate **2** *v/r* **separarse** separate, split up F

separatismo *m* separatism

separatista *m/f & adj* separatist

sepia *f* ZO cuttlefish

sept.[e] *abr* (***= septiembre***) Sept. (= September)

septentrional *adj* northern

septiembre *m* September

séptimo *adj* seventh

sepulcro *m* tomb

sepultar ⟨1a⟩ *v/t* bury

sepultura *f* burial; (*tumba*) tomb; ***dar sepultura a alguien*** bury s.o.

sequedad *f fig* curtness

sequía *f* drought

séquito *m* retinue, entourage

ser ⟨2w; *part* **sido** ⟩ **1** *v/i* be; ***ser de Sevilla*** be from Seville; ***ser de madera / plata*** be made of wood / silver; ***es de Juan*** it's Juan's, it belongs to Juan; ***ser para*** be for; ***a no ser que*** unless; ***¡eso es!*** exactly!, that's right!; ***es que ...*** the thing is ...; ***es de esperar*** it's to be hoped; ***¿cuánto es?*** how much is it?; ***¿qué es de ti?*** how's life?, how're things?; ***o sea*** in other words **2** *m* being

Serbia Serbia

serenarse ⟨1a⟩ *v/r* calm down; *del tiempo* clear up

serenata *f* MÚS serenade

serenidad *f* calmness, serenity

sereno 1 *m*: ***dormir al sereno*** sleep outdoors **2** *adj* calm, serene

serial *m* TV, RAD series

serie *f* series; ***fuera de serie*** out of this world, extraordinary

seriedad *f* seriousness

serio *adj* serious; (*responsable*) reliable; ***en serio*** seriously

sermón *m* sermon

sermonear ⟨1a⟩ *v/i* preach

seropositivo *adj* MED HIV positive

serpentina *f* streamer

serpiente *f* ZO snake; ***serpiente de cascabel*** rattlesnake

serranía *f* mountainous region

serrar ⟨1k⟩ *v/t* saw

serrín *m* sawdust

serrucho *m* handsaw

servicial *adj* obliging, helpful

servicio *m* service; ***servicios*** *pl* restroom *sg*, *Br* toilets; ***servicio doméstico*** domestic service; ***servicio militar*** military service; ***servicio pos(t)venta*** after-sales service; ***servicio de atención al cliente*** customer service; ***estar de servicio*** be on duty

servidor *m* INFOR server

servil *adj* servile

servilismo *m* servility

servilleta *f* napkin, serviette

servilletero *m* napkin ring

servir ⟨3l⟩ **1** *v/t* serve **2** *v/i* be of use; ***¿para qué sirve esto?*** what is this (used) for?; ***no servir de nada*** be no use at all **3** *v/r* **servirse** help o.s.; *comida* help oneself to

servodirección power steering

sésamo *m* sesame

sesenta *adj* sixty

sesgar ⟨1h⟩ *v/t* slant, skew

sesión *f* session; *en cine*, *teatro* show, performance

sesionar ⟨1a⟩ *v/i L.Am.* be in session

seso *m* ANAT brain; *fig* brains *pl*, sense; ***sesos*** GASTR brains

set *m tenis* set

seta *f* BOT mushroom; *venenosa* toadstool

setecientos *adj* seven hundred

setenta *adj* seventy

seto *m* hedge
s.e.u.o. *abr* (= ***salvo error u omisión***) E & OE (= errors and omissions excepted)
seudónimo *m* pseudonym
severo *adj* severe
sevillanas *fpl folk dance from Seville*
sexismo *m* sexism
sexista *m/f & adj* sexist
sexo *m* sex
sexto *adj* sixth
sexual *adj* sexual
sexualidad *f* sexuality
sexy *adj inv* sexy
shock *m* MED shock
si *conj* if; ***si no*** if not; ***como si*** as if; ***por si*** in case; ***me pregunto si vendrá*** I wonder whether he'll come
sí 1 *adv* yes **2** *pron tercera persona*: *singular masculino* himself; *femenino* herself; *cosa, animal* itself; *plural* themselves; *usted* yourself; *ustedes* yourselves; ***por sí solo*** by himself / itself, on his / its own
siamés *adj* Siamese
sibarita *m* bon vivant, epicure
Siberia Siberia
sicario *m* hired assassin
Sicilia Sicily
SIDA *abr* (= ***síndrome de inmunidad deficiente adquirida***) Aids (= acquired immune-deficiency syndrome)
sidecar *m* sidecar
sideral *adj viajes* space *atr*; ***espacio sideral*** outer space
siderurgia *f* iron and steel making
sido *part* → ***ser***
sidra *f* cider
siembra *f* sowing
siempre *adv* always; ***siempre que*** providing that, as long as; ***lo de siempre*** the same old story; ***para siempre*** for ever
sien *f* ANAT temple
siendo *vb* → ***ser***
siento *vb* → ***sentir***
sierra *f* saw; GEOG mountain range
siesta *f* siesta, nap; ***dormir la siesta*** have a siesta *o* nap
siete *adj* seven
sífilis *f* MED syphilis
siga *vb* → ***seguir***
sigilo *m* secrecy, stealth
sigiloso *adj* stealthy
sigla *f* abbreviation, acronym
siglo *m* century; ***hace siglos*** *or* ***un siglo que no le veo*** *fig* I haven't seen him in a long long time
signatario *m*, **-a** *f* signatory
significado *m* meaning
significar ⟨1g⟩ *v/t* mean, signify
significativo *adj* meaningful, significant
signo *m* sign; ***signo de admiración*** exclamation mark; ***signo de interrogación*** question mark; ***signo de puntuación*** punctuation mark
sigo *vb* → ***seguir***
siguiente 1 *adj* next, following **2** *pron* next (one)
sílaba *f* syllable
silbar ⟨1a⟩ *v/i & v/t* whistle
silbato *m* whistle
silbido *m* whistle
silenciador *m* AUTO muffler, *Br* silencer
silencio *m* silence; ***en silencio*** in silence, silently
silencioso *adj* silent
silicio *m* QUÍM silicon
silicona *f* silicone
silla *f* chair; ***silla de montar*** saddle; ***silla de ruedas*** wheelchair
sillín *m* saddle
sillón *m* armchair, easy chair
silueta *f* silhouette
silvestre *adj* wild
silvicultura *f* forestry
simbiosis *f* symbiosis
simbolismo *m* symbolism
simbolizar ⟨1f⟩ *v/t* symbolize
símbolo *m* symbol
simétrico *adj* symmetrical
similar *adj* similar
similitud *f* similarity
simio *m* ZO ape
simpatía *f* warmth, friendliness
simpático *adj* nice, lik(e)able
simpatizante *m/f* sympathizer, supporter
simpatizar ⟨1f⟩ *v/i* sympathize
simple 1 *adj* simple; (*mero*) ordinary **2** *m* simpleton
simplicidad *f* simplicity
simplificar ⟨1g⟩ *v/t* simplify
simplista *adj* simplistic
simposio *m* symposium
simulación *f* simulation
simulacro *m* (*cosa falsa*) pretense, *Br* pretence, sham; (*simulación*) simulation; ***simulacro de incendio*** fire drill
simulador *m* simulator
simular ⟨1a⟩ *v/t* simulate
simultanear ⟨1a⟩ *v/t*: ***simultanear dos cargos*** hold two positions at the same time
simultáneo *adj* simultaneous
sin *prp* without; ***sin que*** without; ***sin preguntar*** without asking
sinagoga *f* synagogue
sinceridad *f* sincerity
sincero *adj* sincere
síncope *m* MED blackout
sincronizar ⟨1f⟩ *v/t* synchronize

sindical *adj* (labor, *Br* trade) union *atr*
sindicalismo *m* (labor, *Br* trade) union movement
sindicalista *m/f* (labor, *Br* trade) union member
sindicato *m* (labor, *Br* trade) union
síndrome *m* syndrome
sinfín *m*: ***un sinfín de ...*** no end of ...
sinfonía *f* MÚS symphony
singular 1 *adj* singular; *fig* outstanding, extraordinary **2** *m* GRAM singular
siniestro 1 *adj* sinister **2** *m* accident; (*catástrofe*) disaster
sinnúímero *m*: ***un sinnúímero de*** no end of
sino 1 *m* fate **2** *conj* but; (*salvo*) except; ***no cena en casa, sino en el bar*** he doesn't have dinner at home, he has it in the bar
sinónimo 1 *adj* synonymous **2** *m* synonym
sinopsis *f inv* synopsis
sinsentido *m* nonsense
sintaxis *f* syntax
síntesis *f inv* synthesis; (*resumen*) summary
sintético *adj* synthetic
sintetizador *m* MÚS synthesizer
síntoma *m* symptom
sintonía *f melodía* theme tune, signature tune; RAD tuning, reception; ***estar en la sintonía de*** RAD be tuned to
sintonizar ⟨1f⟩ **1** *v/t radio* tune in **2** *v/i fig* be in tune (***con*** with)
sinuoso *adj* winding
sinusitis *f* MED sinusitis
sinvergüenza *m/f* swine; ***¡qué sinvergüenza!*** (*descarado*) what a nerve!
siquiera *adv*: ***ni siquiera*** not even; ***siquiera bebe algo*** *L.Am.* at least have a drink
sirena *f* siren; MYTH mermaid
Siria Syria
sirve *vb* → ***servir***
sirvienta *f* maid
sirviente *m* servant
sisar ⟨1a⟩ *v/t* F pilfer
sísmico *adj* seismic
sistema *m* system; ***sistema operativo*** operating system
sistemático *adj* systematic
sitiar ⟨1b⟩ *v/t* surround, lay siege to
sitio *m* place; (*espacio*) room; ***hacer sitio*** make room; ***en ningúín sitio*** nowhere; ***sitio web*** web site
situación *f* situation
situar ⟨1e⟩ **1** *v/t* place, put **2** *v/r* **situarse** be
S.L. *abr* (= ***sociedad limitada***) Ltd (= limited)
slip *m* underpants *pl*
s/n *abr* (= ***sin núímero***) not numbered
sobaco *m* armpit
sobar ⟨1a⟩ *v/t* handle, finger; F *sexualmente* grope F
soberanía *f* sovereignty
soberano *m*, **-a** *f* sovereign
soberbia *f* pride, arrogance
soberbio *adj* proud, arrogant; *fig* superb
sobornar ⟨1a⟩ *v/t* bribe
soborno *m* bribe
sobra *f* surplus, excess; ***hay de sobra*** there's more than enough; ***sobras*** leftovers
sobradamente *adv conocido* well
sobrar ⟨1a⟩ *v/t*: ***sobra comida*** there's food left over; ***me sobró pintura*** I had some paint left over; ***sobraba uno*** there was one left
sobre 1 *m* envelope **2** *prp* on; ***sobre esto*** about this; ***sobre las tres*** about three o'clock; ***sobre todo*** above all, especially
sobrecargar ⟨1h⟩ *v/t* overload
sobrecargo *m* AVIA chief flight attendant; MAR purser
sobrecoger ⟨2c⟩ *v/t* (*asustar*) strike fear into; (*impresionar*) have an effect on
sobredosis *f inv* overdose
sobrehumano *adj* superhuman
sobremesa *f*: ***de sobremesa*** afternoon *atr*
sobrenatural *adj* supernatural
sobrenombre *m* nickname
sobrentenderse ⟨2g⟩ *v/r*: ***se sobrentiende que ...*** needless to say, ...
sobrepasar ⟨1a⟩ **1** *v/t* exceed, surpass; ***me sobrepasa en altura*** he is taller than me **2** *v/r* **sobrepasarse** go too far
sobrepeso *m* excess weight
sobreponerse ⟨2r; *part* ***sobrepuesto***⟩ *v/r*: ***sobreponerse a*** overcome, get over
sobrepuesto *part* → ***sobreponerse***
sobresaliente *adj* outstanding, excellent
sobresalir ⟨3r⟩ *v/t* stick out, protrude; *fig* excel; ***sobresalir entre*** stand out among
sobresaltar ⟨1a⟩ **1** *v/t* startle **2** *v/r* **sobresaltarse** jump, start
sobresalto *m* jump, start
sobreseer ⟨2e⟩ *v/t* JUR dismiss
sobrestimar ⟨1a⟩ *v/t* overestimate
sobresueldo *m* bonus
sobrevalorar ⟨1a⟩ *v/t* overrate
sobrevenir ⟨3s⟩ *v/i* happen; *de guerra* break out
sobrevivir ⟨3a⟩ *v/i* survive
sobrevolar ⟨1m⟩ *v/t* fly over
sobriedad *f* soberness; *de comida*, *decoración* simplicity; (*moderación*) restraint
sobrina *f* niece

S

sobrino *m* nephew
sobrio *adj* sober; *comida, decoración* simple; (*moderado*) restrained
socarrón *adj* sarcastic, snide F
socavar ⟨1a⟩ *v/t tb fig* undermine
socavón *m* hollow
sociable *adj* sociable
social *adj* social
socialismo *m* socialism
socialista *m/f & adj* socialist
sociedad *f* society; ***sociedad anónima*** public corporation, *Br* public limited company; ***sociedad de consumo*** consumer society
socio *m*, **-a** *f de club, asociación etc* member; COM partner
sociología *f* sociology
socorrer ⟨2a⟩ *v/t* help, assist
socorrista *m/f* life guard
socorro *m* help, assistance; ***¡socorro!*** help!
soda *f* soda (water)
sodio *m* sodium
sofá *m* sofa
sofisticación *f* sophistication
sofisticado *adj* sophisticated
sofocante *adj* suffocating
sofocar ⟨1g⟩ **1** *v/t* suffocate; *incendio* put out **2** *v/r* **sofocarse** *fig* get embarrassed; (*irritarse*) get angry
sofoco *m fig* embarrassment
sofreír ⟨3m⟩ *v/t* sauté
sofrito *m* GASTR *mixture of fried onions, peppers etc*
software *m* INFOR software
soga *f* rope; ***estar con la soga al cuello*** F be in big trouble F
sois *vb* → ***ser***
soja *f* soy, *Br* soya
sol *m* sun; ***hace sol*** it's sunny; ***tomar el sol*** sunbathe
solamente *adv* only
solapa *f* lapel
solar *m* vacant lot
solariego *adj*: ***casa -a*** family seat
solario, solárium *m* solarium
soldado *m/f* soldier
soldador *m* welder
soldadura *f* welding, soldering
soldar ⟨1m⟩ *v/t* weld, solder
soleado *adj* sunny
soledad *f* solitude, loneliness
solemne *adj* solemn
soler ⟨2h⟩ *v/i*: ***soler hacer algo*** usually do sth; ***suele venir temprano*** he usually comes early; ***solía visitarme*** he used to visit me
solera *f* traditional character
solfeo *m* (tonic) sol-fa
solicitante *m/f* applicant
solicitar ⟨1a⟩ *v/t* request; *empleo, beca* apply for
solícito *adj* attentive
solicitud *f* application, request
solidaridad *f* solidarity
solidario *adj* supportive, understanding
solidarizarse ⟨1f⟩ *v/r*: ***solidarizarse con alguien*** support s.o., back s.o.
solidez *f* solidity; *fig* strength
sólido *adj* solid; *fig* sound
solista *m/f* soloist
solitaria *f* zo tapeworm
solitario 1 *adj* solitary; *lugar* lonely **2** *m* solitaire, *Br* patience; ***actuó en solitario*** he acted alone
soliviantar ⟨1a⟩ **1** *v/t* incite, stir up **2** *v/r* **soliviantarse** *v/r* rise up, rebel
sollozar ⟨1f⟩ *v/i* sob
sollozo *m* sob
solo *adj* single; ***estar solo*** be alone; ***sentirse solo*** feel lonely; ***un solo día*** a single day; ***a solas*** alone, by o.s.; ***por sí solo*** by o.s.
sólo *adv* only, just
solomillo *m* GASTR sirloin
solsticio *m* solstice
soltar ⟨1m⟩ **1** *v/t* let go of; (*librar*) release, let go; *olor* give off **2** *v/r* **soltarse** free o.s.; ***soltarse a andar / hablar*** begin *o* start to walk / talk
soltera *f* single *o* unmarried woman
soltero 1 *adj* single, not married **2** *m* bachelor, unmarried man
solterona *f desp* old maid
soltura *f* fluency, ease
soluble *adj* soluble
solución *f* solution
solucionar ⟨1a⟩ *v/t* solve
solventar ⟨1a⟩ *v/t* resolve, settle
solvente *adj* solvent
somanta *f* F beating
sombra *f* shadow; ***a la sombra de un árbol*** in the shade of a tree; ***a la sombra de*** *fig* under the protection of; ***sombra de ojos*** eye shadow
sombrero *m* hat; ***sombrero de copa*** top hat
sombrilla *f* sunshade, beach umbrella
sombrío *adj fig* somber, *Br* sombre
someter ⟨2a⟩ **1** *v/t* subject; ***someter algo a votación*** put sth to the vote **2** *v/r* **someterse** yield (***a*** to); *al ley* comply (***a*** with); (*rendirse*) give in (***a*** to); ***someterse a tratamiento*** undergo treatment
somier *m* bed base
somnífero *m* sleeping pill
somnolencia *f* sleepiness, drowsiness
somnoliento *adj* sleepy, drowsy

S

somos *vb* → ***ser***
son[1] *m* sound; ***al son de*** to the sound of; ***en son de paz*** in peace
son[2] *vb* → ***ser***
sonado *adj* F famous, well-known
sonajero *m* rattle
sonámbulo *m* sleep-walker
sonar ⟨1m⟩ **1** *v/i* ring out; ***sonar a*** sound like; ***me suena esa voz*** I know that voice, that voice sounds familiar **2** *v/r* **sonarse**: ***sonarse*** (***la nariz***) blow one's nose
sonata *f* MÚS sonata
sonda *f* MED catheter; ***sonda espacial*** space probe
sondaje *m L.Am.* poll, survey
sondear ⟨1a⟩ *v/t fig* survey, poll
sondeo *m*: ***sondeo*** (***de opinión***) survey, (opinion) poll
soneto *m* sonnet
sonido *m* sound
soniquete *m* droning
sonreír ⟨3m⟩ *v/i* smile
sonriente *adj* smiling
sonrisa *f* smile
sonrojar ⟨1a⟩ **1** *v/t*: ***sonrojar a alguien*** make s.o. blush **2** *v/r* **sonrojarse** blush
sonrojo *m* blush
sonsacar ⟨1g⟩ *v/t*: ***sonsacar algo*** worm sth out (***a*** of), wheedle sth out (***a*** of)
sonso *adj L.Am.* F silly
soñador **1** *adj* dreamy **2** *m* dreamer
soñar ⟨1m⟩ **1** *v/t* dream (***con*** about) **2** *v/i* dream; ***¡ni soñarlo!*** dream on! F
soñolencia *f* → ***somnolencia***
soñoliento *adj* → ***somnoliento***
sopa *f* soup; ***estar hecho una sopa*** F be sopping wet; ***hasta en la sopa*** F all over the place F
sopapo *m* F smack, slap
sopera *f* soup tureen
sopesar ⟨1a⟩ *v/t fig* weigh up
sopetón *m*: ***de sopetón*** unexpectedly
soplar ⟨1a⟩ **1** *v/i del viento* blow **2** *v/t vela* blow out; *polvo* blow away; ***soplar algo a la policía*** tip the police off about sth
soplete *m* welding torch
soplo *m*: ***en un soplo*** F in an instant
soplón *m* F informer, stool pigeon F
soponcio *m*: ***le dio un soponcio*** F he passed out
sopor *m* drowsiness, sleepiness
soporífero *adj* soporific
soportal *m* porch
soportar ⟨1a⟩ *v/t fig* put up with, bear; ***no puedo soportar a José*** I can't stand José
soporte *m* support, stand; ***soporte lógico*** INFOR software; ***soporte físico*** INFOR hardware
soprano MÚS **1** *m* soprano **2** *m/f* soprano
sorber ⟨2a⟩ *v/t* sip
sorbete *m* sorbet; *C.Am.* ice cream
sorbetería *f C.Am.* ice-cream parlo(u)r
sorbo *m* sip
sordera *f* deafness
sórdido *adj* sordid
sordo **1** *adj* deaf **2** *m*, **-a** *f* deaf person; ***hacerse el sordo*** turn a deaf ear
sordomudo **1** *adj* deaf and dumb **2** *m*, **-a** *f* deaf-mute
sorna *f* sarcasm; ***con sorna*** sarcastically, mockingly
sorocharse ⟨1a⟩ *v/r Pe, Bol* get altitude sickness
soroche *m Pe, Bol* altitude sickness
sorprendente *adj* surprising
sorprender ⟨2a⟩ *v/t* surprise
sorpresa *f* surprise; ***de*** *or* ***por sorpresa*** by surprise
sortear ⟨1a⟩ *v/t* draw lots for; *obstáculo* get round
sorteo *m* (*lotería*) lottery, (prize) draw
sortija *f* ring
sortilegio *m* spell, charm
SOS *m* SOS
sosa *f* QUÍM: ***sosa cáustica*** caustic soda
sosegado *adj* calm
sosegarse ⟨1h & 1k⟩ *v/r* calm down
sosería *f* insipidness, dullness
sosiego *m* calm, quiet
soslayo *adj*: ***de soslayo*** sideways
soso **1** *adj* tasteless, insipid; *fig* dull **2** *m*, **-a** *f* stick-in-the-mud F
sospecha *f* suspicion
sospechar ⟨1a⟩ **1** *v/t* suspect **2** *v/i* be suspicious; ***sospechar de alguien*** suspect someone
sospechoso **1** *adj* suspicious **2** *m*, **-a** *f* suspect
sostén *m* brassiere, bra; *fig* pillar, mainstay
sostener ⟨2l⟩ **1** *v/t familia* support; *opinión* hold **2** *v/r* **sostenerse** support o.s.; *de pie* stand up; *en el poder* stay, remain
sota *f naipes* jack
sotana *f* REL cassock
sótano *m* basement, *Br* cellar
soterrar ⟨1k⟩ *v/t* bury
soviético *adj* Soviet
soy *vb* → ***ser***
soya *f L.Am.* soy, *Br* soya
spot *m* TV commercial
spray *m* spray
sprint *m* sprint
squash *m* DEP squash
Sr. *abr* (***= señor***) Mr

S

Sra. *abr* (= ***señora***) Mrs
Sres. *abr* (= ***Señores***) Messrs (= Messieurs)
Srta. *abr* (= ***Señorita***) Miss
stand *m* COM stand
stock *m* stock; ***tener en stock*** have in stock
su, sus *adj pos*: *de él* his; *de ella* her; *de cosa* its; *de usted, ustedes* your; *de ellos* their; *de uno* one's
suave *adj* soft, smooth; *sabor, licor* mild
suavidad *f* softness, smoothness; *de sabor, licor* mildness
suavizante *m de pelo, ropa* conditioner
suavizar ⟨1f⟩ *v/t tb fig* soften
subacuático *adj* underwater
subalterno 1 *adj* subordinate **2** *m*, **-a** *f* subordinate
subasta *f* auction; ***sacar a subasta*** put up for auction
subastar ⟨1a⟩ *v/t* auction (off)
subcampeón *m* DEP runner-up
subconsciente *m/adj* subconscious
subcontrata(ción) *f* subcontracting
subdesarrollado *adj* underdeveloped
subdesarrollo *m* underdevelopment
subdirector *m*, **subdirectora** *f* deputy manager
súíbdito *m* subject
subestimar ⟨1a⟩ *v/t* underestimate
subida *f* rise, ascent; ***subida de los precios*** rise in prices
subido 1 *part* → ***subir*** **2** *adj*: ***subido de tono*** *fig* risqué, racy
subir ⟨3a⟩ **1** *v/t cuesta, escalera* go up, climb; *montaña* climb; *objeto* raise, lift; *intereses, precio* raise **2** *v/i para indicar acercamiento* come up; *para indicar alejamiento* go up; *de precio* rise, go up; *a un tren, autobúís* get on; *a un coche* get in **3** *v/r* **subirse** go up; *a un árbol* climb
súíbito *adj*: ***de súíbito*** suddenly, all of a sudden
subjetivo *adj* subjective
subjuntivo *m* GRAM subjunctive
sublevar ⟨1a⟩ **1** *v/t* incite to revolt; *fig* infuriate, get angry **2** *v/r* **sublevarse** rise up, revolt
sublimación *f fig* sublimation
sublime *adj* sublime, lofty
subliminal *adj* subliminal
submarinismo *m* scuba diving
submarinista *m/f* scuba diver
submarino 1 *adj* underwater **2** *m* submarine
subnormal *adj* subnormal
subordinado 1 *adj* subordinate **2** *m*, **-a** *f* subordinate
subproducto *m* by-product
subrayar ⟨1a⟩ *v/t* underline; *fig* underline, emphasize
subrepticio *adj* surreptitious
subsanar ⟨1a⟩ *v/t* put right, rectify
subsidiario *adj* subsidiary
subsidio *m* welfare, *Br* benefit; ***subsidio de paro*** *or* ***desempleo*** unemployment compensation (*Br* benefit)
subsistencia *f* subsistence, survival; *de pobreza, tradición* persistence
subsistir ⟨3a⟩ *v/i* live, survive; *de pobreza, tradición* live on, persist
subte *m Rpl* subway, *Br* underground
subterfugio *m* subterfuge
subterráneo 1 *adj* underground **2** *m L.Am.* subway, *Br* underground
subtítulo *m* subtitle
suburbio *m* slum area
subvención *f* subsidy
subvencionar ⟨1a⟩ *v/t* subsidize
subversivo *adj* subversive
subyacente *adj* underlying
subyugar ⟨1h⟩ *v/t* subjugate
succionar ⟨1a⟩ *v/t* suck
sucedáneo *m* substitute
suceder ⟨2a⟩ *v/i* happen, occur; ***suceder a*** follow; ***¿qué sucede?*** what's going on?
sucesión *f* succession; ***sucesión al trono*** succession to the throne
sucesivo *adj* successive; ***en lo sucesivo*** from now on
suceso *m* event
sucesor *m*, **sucesora** *f* successor
suciedad *f* dirt
sucio *adj tb fig* dirty
suculento *adj* succulent
sucumbir ⟨3a⟩ *v/i* succumb, give in
sucursal *f* COM branch
sudaca *m/f desp* South American
sudadera *f* sweatshirt
Sudáfrica South Africa
sudafricano 1 *adj* South African **2** *m*, **-a** *f* South African
Sudamérica South America
sudamericano 1 *adj* South American **2** *m*, **-a** *f* South American
sudar ⟨1a⟩ *v/i* sweat
sudario *m* REL shroud
sudeste *m* southeast
sudoeste *m* southwest
sudor *m* sweat
sudoración *f* perspiration
sudoroso *adj* sweaty
Suecia Sweden
sueco 1 *adj* Swedish **2** *m*, **-a** *f* Swede; ***hacerse el sueco*** F pretend not to hear, act dumb F
suegra *f* mother-in-law

suegro *m* father-in-law
suela *f de zapato* sole
sueldo *m* salary
suelo *m en casa* floor; *en el exterior* earth, ground; AGR soil; ***estar por los suelos*** F be at rock bottom F
suelto 1 *adj* loose, free; ***un pendiente suelto*** a single earring; ***andar suelto*** be at large **2** *m* loose change
sueño *m* (*estado de dormir*) sleep; (*fantasía, imagen mental*) dream; ***tener sueño*** be sleepy
suero *m* MED saline solution; *sanguíneo* blood serum
suerte *f* luck; ***por suerte*** luckily; ***echar a suertes*** toss for, draw lots for; ***probar suerte*** try one's luck
suertero *m*, **-a** *f L.Am.* F, **suertudo** *m*, **-a** *f L.Am.* F lucky devil F
suéter *m* sweater
suficiente 1 *adj* enough, sufficient **2** *m* EDU pass
sufragar ⟨1h⟩ *v/t* COM meet, pay
sufragio *m*: ***sufragio universal*** universal suffrage
sufrimiento *m* suffering
sufrir ⟨3a⟩ **1** *v/t fig* suffer, put up with **2** *v/i* suffer (***de*** from)
sugerencia *f* suggestion
sugerir ⟨3i⟩ *v/t* suggest
sugestionar ⟨1a⟩ *v/t* influence
sugestivo *adj* suggestive
suicida 1 *adj* suicidal **2** *m/f* suicide victim
suicidarse ⟨1a⟩ *v/r* commit suicide
suicidio *m* suicide
suite *f* suite
Suiza Switzerland
suizo 1 *adj* Swiss **2** *m*, **-a** *f* Swiss **3** *m* GASTR *sugar topped bun*
sujetador *m* brassiere, bra
sujetapapeles *m inv* paperclip
sujetar ⟨1a⟩ *v/t* hold (down), keep in place; (*sostener*) hold
sujeto 1 *adj* secure **2** *m* individual; GRAM subject
sulfurarse ⟨1a⟩ *v/r fig* F blow one's top F
suma *f* sum; ***en suma*** in short
sumamente *adv* extremely, highly
sumar ⟨1a⟩ **1** *v/t* add; ***5 y 6 suman 11*** 5 and 6 make 11 **2** *v/i* add up **3** *v/r* **sumarse**: ***sumarse a*** join
sumario *m* summary; JUR indictment
sumergir ⟨3c⟩ **1** *v/t* submerge, immerse **2** *v/r* **sumergirse** *fig* immerse o.s. (***en*** in), throw o.s. (***en*** into)
sumidero *m* drain
suministrar ⟨1a⟩ *v/t* supply, provide
suministro *m* supply
sumir ⟨3a⟩ **1** *v/t fig* plunge, throw (***en*** into) **2** *v/r* **sumirse** *fig* sink (***en*** into)
sumisión *f* submission
sumiso *adj* submissive
sumo *adj* supreme; ***con sumo cuidado*** with the utmost care; ***a lo sumo*** at the most
suntuoso *adj* sumptuous
supe *vb* → ***saber***
supeditar ⟨1a⟩ *v/t* make conditional (***a*** upon)
súper *adj* F super F, great F
superable *adj* surmountable
superación *f* overcoming, surmounting
superar ⟨1a⟩ **1** *v/t persona* beat; *límite* go beyond, exceed; *obstáculo* overcome, surmount **2** *v/r* **superarse** surpass o.s., excel o.s.
superávit *m* surplus
superchería *f* trick, swindle
superdotado *adj* gifted
superficial *adj* superficial, shallow
superficialidad *f* superficiality, shallowness
superficie *f* surface
superfluo *adj* superfluous
superior 1 *adj* upper; *en jerarquía* superior; ***ser superior a*** be superior to **2** *m* superior
superiora *f* REL Mother Superior
superioridad *f* superiority
superlativo *adj* superlative
supermercado *m* supermarket
superpoblación *f* overpopulation
superponer ⟨2r⟩ *v/t* superimpose
superpotencia *f* POL superpower
superpuesto *adj* superimposed
supersónico *adj* supersonic
superstición *f* superstition
supersticioso *adj* superstitious
supervisar ⟨1a⟩ *v/t* supervise
supervisor *m*, **supervisora** *f* supervisor
supervivencia *f* survival
superviviente 1 *adj* surviving **2** *m/f* survivor
suplantar ⟨1a⟩ *v/t* replace, take the place of
suplementario *adj* supplementary
suplemento *m* supplement
suplente *m/f* substitute, stand-in
súplica *f* plea
suplicar ⟨1g⟩ *v/t cosa* plead for, beg for; *persona* beg
suplicio *m fig* torment, ordeal
suplir ⟨3a⟩ *v/t carencia* make up for; (*sustituir*) substitute
supo *vb* → ***saber***
suponer ⟨2r; *part* **supuesto** ⟩ *v/t* suppose, assume
suposición *f* supposition

S

supositorio *m* MED suppository

supremacía *f* supremacy

supremo *adj* supreme

supresión *f* suppression; *de impuesto, ley* abolition; *de restricción* lifting; *de servicio* withdrawal

suprimir ⟨3a⟩ *v/t* suppress; *ley, impuesto* abolish; *restricción* lift; *servicio* withdraw; *puesto de trabajo* cut

supuesto 1 *part* → ***suponer* 2** *adj* supposed, alleged; ***por supuesto*** of course **3** *m* assumption

sur *m* south

surco *m* AGR furrow

sureño *adj* southern

surf(ing) *m* surfing

surfista *m/f* surfer

surgir ⟨3c⟩ *v/i fig* emerge; *de problema* come up; *de agua* spout

surrealismo *m* surrealism

surtido 1 *adj* assorted; ***bien surtido*** COM well stocked **2** *m* assortment, range

surtidor *m*: ***surtidor de gasolina*** *or* ***de nafta*** gas pump, *Br* petrol pump

surtir ⟨3a⟩ **1** *v/t* supply; ***surtir efecto*** have the desired effect **2** *v/i* spout **3** *v/r* **surtirse** stock up (***de*** with)

susceptible *adj* touchy; ***ser susceptible de mejora*** leave room for improvement

suscitar ⟨1a⟩ *v/t* arouse; *polémica* generate; *escándalo* provoke

suscribir ⟨3a; *part* ***suscrito*** ⟩ **1** *v/t* subscribe to **2** *v/r* **suscribirse** subscribe

suscripción *f* subscription

suscriptor *m*, **suscriptora** *f* subscriber

suscrito *part* → ***suscribir***

suspender ⟨2a⟩ **1** *v/t empleado, alumno* suspend; *objeto* hang; *reunión* adjourn; *examen* fail **2** *v/i* EDU fail

suspense *m fig* suspense

suspensión *f* suspension

suspenso 1 *adj* ***alumnos suspensos*** students who have failed; ***en suspenso*** suspended **2** *m* fail

suspensores *mpl L.Am.* suspenders, *Br* braces

suspicacia *f* suspicion

suspicaz *adj* suspicious

suspirar ⟨1a⟩ *v/i* sigh; ***suspirar por algo*** yearn for sth, long for sth

suspiro *m* sigh

sustancia *f* substance

sustancial *adj* substantial

sustantivo *m* GRAM noun

sustentar ⟨1a⟩ *v/t* sustain; *familia* support; *opinión* maintain

sustento *m* means of support

sustitución *f* substitution

sustituir ⟨3g⟩ *v/t*: ***sustituir X por Y*** replace X with Y, substitute Y for X

sustituto *m* substitute

susto *m* fright, scare; ***dar*** *or* ***pegar un susto a alguien*** give s.o. a fright

sustraer ⟨2p; *part* ***sustraido*** ⟩ *v/t* subtract, take away; (*robar*) steal

sustraido *part* → ***sustraer***

susurrar ⟨1a⟩ *v/t* whisper

susurro *m* whisper

sutil *adj fig* subtle

sutileza *f fig* subtlety

suyo, suya *pron pos*: *de él* his; *de ella* hers; *de usted, ustedes* yours; *de ellos* theirs; ***los suyos*** his / her etc folks, his / her etc family; ***hacer de las -as*** get up to one's old tricks; ***salirse con la -a*** get one's own way

T

tabaco *m* tobacco

tábano *m* ZO horsefly

tabarra *f*: ***dar la tabarra a alguien*** F bug s.o. F

taberna *f* bar

tabernero *m* bar owner, *Br* landlord; (*camarero*) bartender

tabique *m* partition, partition wall

tabla *f de madera* board, plank; PINT panel; (*cuadro*) table; ***tabla de multiplicar*** multiplication table; ***tabla de planchar*** ironing board; ***tabla de surf*** surf board; ***acabar*** *or* ***quedar en tablas*** end in a tie

tablero *m* board, plank; *de juego* board; ***tablero de mandos*** *or* ***de instrumentos*** AUTO dashboard

tableta *f*: ***tableta de chocolate*** chocolate bar

tablón *m* plank; ***tablón de anuncios*** bulletin board, *Br* notice board

tabúi *m* taboo

tabulador *m tb* INFOR tab key

taburete *m* stool
tacañería *f* F miserliness, stinginess F
tacaño 1 *adj* F miserly, stingy F **2** *m*, **-a** *f* F miser F, tightwad F
tacha *f* flaw, blemish; ***sin tacha*** beyond reproach
tachadura *f* crossing-out
tachar ⟨1a⟩ *v/t* cross out
tacho *m Rpl* (*papelera*) wastepaper basket; *en la calle* garbage can, *Br* litter basket
tachón *m* crossing-out
tachuela *f* thumbtack, *Br* drawing pin
tácito *adj* tacit
taciturno *adj* taciturn
taco *m* F (*palabrota*) swear word; *L.Am.* heel; GASTR taco (*filled tortilla*)
tacón *m de zapato* heel; ***zapatos de tacón*** high-heeled shoes
táctica *f* tactics *pl*
táctico *adj* tactical
tacto *m* (sense of) touch; *fig* tact, discretion
TAE *abr* (= ***tasa anual efectiva***) APR (= annual percentage rate)
tahona *f* bakery
tahúír *m* gambler, card-sharp F
taita *m S. Am.* F dad, pop F; *S. Am.* (*abuelo*) grandfather
tajada *f* GASTR slice; ***agarrar una tajada*** F get drunk; ***sacar tajada*** take a cut F
tajamar *m S. Am.* (*dique*) dike
tajante *adj* categorical
tajo *m* cut
tal 1 *adj* such; ***no dije tal cosa*** I said no such thing; ***el gerente era un tal Lucas*** the manager was someone called Lucas **2** *adv*: ***tal como*** such as; ***dejó la habitación tal cual la encontró*** she left the room just as she found it; ***tal para cual*** two of a kind; ***tal vez*** maybe, perhaps; ***¿qué tal?*** how's it going?; ***¿que tal la película?*** what was the movie like?; ***con tal de que*** + *subj* as long as, provided that
tala *f de árboles* felling
taladrar ⟨1a⟩ *v/t* drill
taladro *m* drill
talante *m* (*genio, humor*) mood; ***un talante bonachón*** a kindly nature; ***de mal talante*** in a bad mood
talar ⟨1a⟩ *v/t árbol* fell, cut down
talco *m* talc, talcum; ***polvos de talco*** talcum powder
talego *m* P 1000 pesetas
talento *m* talent
talismán *m* talisman
talla *f* size; (*estatura*) height; *C.Am.* F (*mentira*) lie; ***dar la talla*** *fig* make the grade
tallar ⟨1a⟩ *v/t* carve; *piedra preciosa* cut
tallarín *m* noodle
taller *m* workshop; ***taller mecánico*** AUTO repair shop; ***taller de reparaciones*** repair shop
tallo *m* BOT stalk, stem
talón *m* ANAT heel; COM stub; ***talón de Aquiles*** *fig* Achilles' heel; ***pisar los talones a alguien*** be hot on s.o.'s heels
talonario *m*: ***talonario de cheques*** check book, *Br* cheque book
tamal *m Méx, C.Am.* tamale (*meat wrapped in a leaf and steamed*)
tamaño 1 *adj*: ***tamaño fallo / problema*** such a great mistake / problem **2** *m* size
tambalearse ⟨1a⟩ *v/r* stagger, lurch; *de coche* sway
tambarria *f C.Am., Pe, Bol* F party
también *adv* also, too, as well; ***yo también*** me too; ***él también dice que …*** he also says that …
tambo *m Rpl* dairy farm; *Méx type of large container*
tambor *m* drum; *persona* drummer
tamborilear ⟨1a⟩ *v/i* drum with one's fingers
tamiz *m* sieve
tampoco *adv* neither; ***él tampoco va*** he's not going either
tampón *m* tampon; *de tinta* ink-pad
tan *adv* so; ***tan … como …*** as … as …; ***tan sólo*** merely
tanatorio *m* funeral parlo(u)r
tanda *f* series, batch; (*turno*) shift; *L.Am.* (commercial) break; ***tanda de penaltis*** DEP penalty shootout
tanga *m* tanga
tangente *f* MAT tangent; ***salir*** *or* ***irse por la tangente*** F sidestep the issue, duck the question F
tangible *adj fig* tangible
tango *m* tango
tanque *m tb* MIL tank
tantear ⟨1a⟩ *v/t* feel; (*calcular a ojo*) work out roughly; *situación* size up; *persona* sound out; (*probar*) try out; ***tantear el terreno*** *fig* see how the land lies
tantito *adv Méx* a little
tanto 1 *pron* so much; *igual cantidad* as much; ***un tanto*** a little; ***tantos*** *pl* so many *pl*; *igual núímero* as many; ***tienes tanto*** you have so much; ***no hay tantos como ayer*** there aren't as many as yesterday; ***a las -as de la noche*** in the small hours **2** *adv* so much; *igual cantidad* as much; *periodo* so long; ***tardó tanto como él*** she took as long as him; ***tanto mejor*** so much the better; ***no es para tanto***

it's not such a big deal; ***estar al tanto*** be informed (***de*** about); ***por lo tanto*** therefore, so **3** *m* point; ***tanto por ciento*** percentage
tapa *f* lid; ***tapa dura*** hardback
tapacubos *m inv* AUTO hub cap
tapadera *f* lid; *fig* front
tapadillo *m*: ***de tapadillo*** on the sly
tapado *m Arg*, *Chi* coat
tapar ⟨1a⟩ **1** *v/t* cover; *recipiente* put the lid on **2** *v/r* **taparse** wrap up; ***taparse los ojos*** cover one's eyes
taparrabo *m* loincloth
tapete *m* tablecloth; ***poner algo sobre el tapete*** bring sth up for discussion
tapia *f* wall; ***más sordo que una tapia*** as deaf as a post
tapicería *f* upholstery
tapicero *m*, **-a** *f* upholsterer
tapioca *f* tapioca
tapir *m* tapir
tapiz *m* tapestry
tapizar ⟨1f⟩ *v/t* upholster
tapón *m* top, cap; *de baño* plug; *de tráfico* traffic jam
taponar ⟨1a⟩ *v/t* block; *herida* swab
tapujo *m*: ***sin tapujos*** openly
taquicardia *f* MED tachycardia
taquigrafía *f* shorthand
taquilla *f* ticket office; TEA box-office; *C.Am.* (*bar*) small bar
taquillero 1 *adj cantante* popular; ***una película -a*** a hit movie, a box-office hit **2** *m*, **-a** *f* ticket clerk
tara *f* defect
tarado *adj* F stupid, dumb F
tarántula *f* ZO tarantula
tararear ⟨1a⟩ *v/t* hum
tardar ⟨1a⟩ *v/i* take a long time; ***tardamos dos horas*** we were two hours overdue *o* late; ***¡no tardes!*** don't be late; ***a más tardar*** at the latest; ***¿cuánto se tarda ...?*** how long does it take to ...?
tarde 1 *adv* late; ***tarde o temprano*** sooner or later **2** *f hasta las 5 ó 6* afternoon; *desde las 5 ó 6* evening; ***¡buenas tardes!*** good afternoon / evening; ***por la tarde*** in the afternoon / evening; ***de tarde en tarde*** from time to time
tardón *adj* F slow; (*impuntual*) late
tarea *f* task, job; ***tareas*** *pl* ***domésticas*** housework *sg*
tarifa *f* rate; *de tren* fare; ***tarifa plana*** flat rate
tarima *f* platform; ***suelo de tarima*** wooden floor
tarjeta *f* card; ***tarjeta amarilla*** DEP yellow card; ***tarjeta de crédito*** credit card; ***tarjeta de embarque*** AVIA boarding card; ***tarjeta de sonido*** INFOR sound card; ***tarjeta de visita*** (business) card; ***tarjeta gráfica*** INFOR graphics card; ***tarjeta inteligente*** smart card; ***tarjeta monedero*** electronic purse; ***tarjeta postal*** postcard; ***tarjeta roja*** DEP red card; ***tarjeta telefónica*** phone card
tarro *m* jar; P (*cabeza*) head
tarta *f* cake; *plana* tart; ***tarta helada*** ice-cream cake
tartamudear ⟨1a⟩ *v/i* stutter, stammer
tartamudez *f* stuttering, stammering
tartamudo 1 *adj* stuttering, stammering; ***ser tartamudo*** stutter, stammer **2** *m*, **-a** *f* stutterer, stammerer
tartera *f* lunch box
tarugo *m* F blockhead
tarumba F crazy F; ***volverse tarumba*** go crazy
tasa *f* rate; (*impuesto*) tax; ***tasa de desempleo*** *or* ***paro*** unemployment rate
tasar ⟨1a⟩ *v/t* fix a price for; (*valorar*) assess
tasca *f* F bar
tata *m L.Am.* F (*abuelo*) grandpa F
tatarabuela *f* great-great-grandmother
tatarabuelo *m* great-great-grandfather
tataranieta *f* great-great-granddaughter
tataranieto *m* great-great-grandson
tate *int* F (*ahora caigo*) oh I see; (*cuidado*) look out!
tatuaje *m* tattoo
taurino *adj* bullfighting *atr*
Tauro *m/f inv* ASTR Taurus
tauromaquia *f* bullfighting
taxi *m* cab, taxi
taxista *m/f* cab *o* taxi driver
taza *f* cup; *del wáter* bowl
tazón *m* bowl
te *pron directo* you; *indirecto* (to) you; *reflexivo* yourself
té *m* tea
teatral *adj fig* theatrical
teatro *m tb fig* theater, *Br* theatre
tebeo *m* children's comic
techar ⟨1a⟩ *v/t* roof
techo *m* ceiling; (*tejado*) roof; ***techo solar*** AUTO sun-roof; ***los sin techo*** the homeless; ***tocar techo*** *fig* peak
tecla *f* key
teclado *m* MÚS, INFOR keyboard
teclear ⟨1a⟩ *v/t* key
técnica *f* technique
técnico 1 *adj* technical **2** *m/f* technician; *de televisor, lavadora etc* repairman
tecnología *f* technology; ***alta tecnología*** hi-tech; ***tecnología punta*** state-of-the-art technology, leading-edge technology
tecolote *m Méx*, *C.Am.* (*búho*) owl

tedio *m* tedium
tedioso *adj* tedious
teja *f* roof tile; ***a toca teja*** in hard cash
tejado *m* roof
tejanos *mpl* jeans
tejemanejes *mpl* F scheming *sg*, plotting *sg*
tejer ⟨2a⟩ **1** *v/t* weave; (*hacer punto*) knit; F *intriga* devise **2** *v/i L.Am.* F plot, scheme
tejido *m* fabric; ANAT tissue
tejo *m* BOT yew; ***tirar a alguien los tejos*** F hit on s.o. F, come on to s.o. F
tejón *m* ZO badger
Tel. *abr* (= ***teléfono***) Tel. (= telephone)
tela *f* fabric, material; ***tela de araña*** spiderweb; ***poner en tela de juicio*** call into question; ***hay tela para rato*** F there's a lot to be done
telar *m* loom
telaraña *f* spiderweb
tele *f* F TV, *Br* telly F
telearrastre *m* drag lift
telebanca *f* telephone banking
telecabina *f* cable car
telecomedia *f* sitcom
telecompra *f* home shopping
telecomunicaciones *fpl* telecommunications
telediario *m* TV (television) news *sg*
teledirigido *adj* remote-controlled
teléf. *abr* (= ***teléfono***) tel. (= telephone)
teleférico *m* cable car
telefilm(e) *m* TV movie
telefonear ⟨1a⟩ *v/t & v/i* call, phone
telefonema *m L.Am.* (phone) message
telefónico *adj* (tele)phone *atr*
teléfono *m* (tele)phone; ***teléfono inalámbrico*** cordless (phone); ***teléfono móvil*** cellphone, *Br* mobile (phone)
telégrafo *m* telegraph
telegrama *m* telegram
telemando *m* remote control
telemática *f* data comms
telenovela *f* soap (opera)
teleobjetivo *m* FOT telephoto lens
telepatía *f* telepathy
telescópico *adj* telescopic
telescopio *m* telescope
teleserie *f* (television) series
telesilla *f* chair lift
telespectador *m*, **telespectadora** *f* (television) viewer
telesquí *m* drag lift
teletexto *m* teletext
teletienda *f* home shopping
teletrabajo *m* teleworking
teletrabajador *m*, **teletrabajadora** *f* teleworker
televidente *m/f* (television) viewer
televisar ⟨1a⟩ *v/t* televise
televisión *f* television; ***televisión por cable*** cable (television); ***televisión digital*** digital television; ***televisión de pago*** pay-per-view television; ***televisión vía satélite*** satellite television
televisivo *adj* television *atr*
televisor *m* TV, television (set); ***televisor en color*** color TV
télex *m* telex
telón *m* TEA curtain; ***el telón de acero*** POL the Iron Curtain; ***telón de fondo*** *fig* backdrop, background
telonero *m*, **-a** *f* supporting artist
tema *m* subject, topic; MÚS, *de novela* theme
temario *m* syllabus
temático *adj* thematic
temblar ⟨1k⟩ *v/i* tremble, shake; *de frío* shiver
temblor *m* trembling, shaking; *de frío* shivering; *L.Am.* (*terremoto*) earthquake; ***temblor de tierra*** earth tremor
tembloroso *adj* trembling, shaking; *de frío* shivering
temer ⟨2a⟩ **1** *v/t* be afraid of **2** *v/r* **temerse** be afraid; ***me temo que no podrá venir*** I'm afraid he won't be able to come; ***temerse lo peor*** fear the worst
temerario *adj* rash, reckless
temeridad *f* rashness, recklessness
temible *adj* terrifying
temor *m* fear
témpano *m* ice floe
temperamento *m* temperament
temperante *adj Méx* teetotal
temperatura *f* temperature
tempestad *f* storm
tempestuoso *adj tb fig* stormy
templado *adj* warm; *clima* temperate; *fig* moderate, restrained
templanza *f* restraint
templar ⟨1a⟩ *v/t ira, nervios etc* calm
templo *m* temple
temporada *f* season; ***una temporada*** a time, some time
temporal **1** *adj* temporary **2** *m* storm
temporizador *m* timer
tempranear ⟨1a⟩ *v/i L.Am.* get up early
temprano *adj & adv* early
ten *vb* → ***tener***
tenacidad *f* tenacity
tenaz *adj* determined, tenacious
tenaza *f* pincer, claw; ***tenazas*** pincers; *para las uñas* pliers
tendedero *m* clotheshorse, airer
tendencia *f* tendency; (*corriente*) trend
tendencioso *adj* tendentious

tender ⟨2g⟩ **1** *v/t ropa* hang out; *cable* lay; ***le tendió la mano*** he held out his hand to her **2** *v/i*: ***tender a*** tend to **3** *v/r* **tenderse** lie down
tenderete *m* stall
tendero *m*, **-a** *f* storekeeper, shopkeeper
tendido *m* EL: ***tendido eléctrico*** power lines *pl*
tendón *m* ANAT tendon; ***tendón de Aquiles*** Achilles' tendon
tenebroso *adj* dark, gloomy
tenedor *m* fork
tener ⟨2l⟩ **1** *v/t* have; ***tener 10 años*** be 10 (years old); ***tener un metro de ancho / largo*** be one metre (*Br* meter) wide / long; ***tener por*** consider to be; ***tengo que madrugar*** I must get up early, I have to *o* I've got to get up early; ***conque ¿esas tenemos?*** so that's how it is, eh? **2** *v/r* **tenerse** stand up; *fig* stand firm; ***se tiene por atractivo*** he thinks he's attractive
tenga *vb* → ***tener***
tengo *vb* → ***tener***
tenia *f* ZO tapeworm
teniente *m/f* MIL lieutenant
tenis *m* tennis; ***tenis de mesa*** table tennis
tenista *m/f* tennis player
tenor *m* MÚS tenor; ***a tenor de*** along the lines of
tenorio *m* lady-killer
tensar ⟨1a⟩ *v/t* tighten; *músculo* tense, tighten
tensión *f* tension; EL voltage; MED blood pressure
tenso *adj* tense; *cuerda*, *cable* taut
tentación *f* temptation
tentáculo *m* ZO, *fig* tentacle
tentador *adj* tempting
tentar ⟨1k⟩ *v/t* tempt, entice
tentativa *f* attempt
tentempié *m* F snack
tenue *adj* faint
teñir ⟨3h & 3l⟩ *v/t* dye; *fig* tinge
teología *f* theology
teorema *m* theorem
teoría *f* theory; ***en teoría*** in theory
tequila *m* tequila
terapeuta *m/f* therapist
terapéutico *adj* therapeutic
terapia *f* therapy
tercer *adj* third; ***Tercer Mundo*** Third World
tercermundista *adj* Third-World *atr*
tercero *m/adj* third
terciarse ⟨1b⟩ *v/r de oportunidad* come up
tercio *m* third
terciopelo *m* velvet
terco *adj* stubborn
tergiversar ⟨1a⟩ *v/t* distort, twist
termas *fpl* hot springs
térmico *adj* heat *atr*
terminación *f* GRAM ending
terminal **1** *m* INFOR terminal **2** *f* AVIA terminal; ***terminal de autobuses*** bus station
terminante *adj* categorical
terminar ⟨1a⟩ **1** *v/t* end, finish **2** *v/i* end, finish; (*parar*) stop **3** *v/r* **terminarse** run out; (*finalizar*) come to an end; ***se ha terminado la leche*** we've run out of milk, the milk's all gone
término *m* end, conclusion; (*palabra*) term; ***término municipal*** municipal area; ***por término medio*** on average; ***poner término a algo*** put an end to sth
terminología *f* terminology
termita *f* ZO termite
termo *m* thermos® (flask)
termómetro *m* thermometer
termostato *m* thermostat
ternera *f* calf; GASTR veal
ternero *m* calf
terno *m CSur* suit
ternura *f* tenderness
terracota *f* terracotta
terraplén *m* embankment
terrateniente *m/f* landowner
terraza *f* terrace; (*balcón*) balcony; (*café*) sidewalk café
terremoto *m* earthquake
terrenal *adj* earthly, worldly
terreno *m* land; *fig* field; ***un terreno*** a plot *o* piece of land; ***terreno de juego*** DEP field
terrestre *adj animal* land *atr*; *transporte* surface *atr*; ***la atmósfera terrestre*** the earth's atmosphere
terrible *adj* terrible, awful
territorial *adj* territorial
territorio *m* territory
terrón *m* lump, clod; ***terrón de azúícar*** sugar lump
terror *m* terror
terrorífico *adj* terrifying
terrorismo *m* terrorism
terrorista **1** *adj* terrorist *atr* **2** *m/f* terrorist
terso *adj* smooth
tertulia *f* TV debate, round table discussion
tertuliar ⟨1b⟩ *v/i L.Am.* get together for a discussion
tesina *f* dissertation
tesis *f inv* thesis
tesitura *f* situation
tesón *m* tenacity, determination
tesorero *m*, **-a** *f* treasurer

tesoro *m* treasure; ***tesoro púiblico*** treasury
test *m* test
testa *f* head
testaferro *m* front man
testamento *m* JUR will
testarudez *f* stubbornness
testarudo *adj* stubborn
testículo *m* ANAT testicle
testificar ⟨1g⟩ **1** *v/t* (*probar, mostrar*) be proof of; ***testificar que*** JUR testify that, give evidence that **2** *v/i* testify, give evidence
testigo 1 *m/f* JUR witness; ***testigo de cargo*** witness for the prosecution; ***testigo ocular*** *or* ***presencial*** eye witness **2** *m* DEP baton
testimonio *m* testimony, evidence
teta *f* F boob F; ZO teat, nipple
tétanos *m* MED tetanus
tetera *f* teapot
tetilla *f de hombre* nipple
tetina *f de biberón* teat
tetrabrik® *m* carton
tétrico *adj* gloomy
textil 1 *adj* textile *atr* **2** *mpl*: ***textiles*** textiles
texto *m* text
textual *adj* textual
textura *f* texture
tez *f* complexion
ti *pron* you; *reflexivo* yourself; ***¿y a ti qué te importa?*** so what?, what's it to you?
tía *f* aunt; F (*chica*) girl, chick F; ***¡tía buena!*** F hey gorgeous! F
tianguis *m Méx, C.Am.* market
tibio *adj tb fig* lukewarm
tiburón *m* ZO, *fig* F shark
tic *m* MED tic
ticket *m* (sales) receipt
tictac *m* tick-tock
tiempo *m* time; (*clima*) weather; GRAM tense; ***tiempo libre*** spare time, free time; ***tiempo real*** INFOR real time; ***a tiempo*** in time; ***a un tiempo, al mismo tiempo*** at the same time; ***antes de tiempo*** *llegar* ahead of time, early; *celebrar victoria* too soon; ***con tiempo*** in good time, early; ***desde hace mucho tiempo*** for a long time; ***hace buen / mal tiempo*** the weather's fine / bad; ***hace mucho tiempo*** a long time ago
tienda *f* store, shop; ***tienda de campaña*** tent; ***ir de tiendas*** go shopping
tiene *vb* → ***tener***
tientas *fpl*: ***andar a tientas*** *fig* feel one's way
tiento *m*: ***con tiento*** *fig* carefully
tierno *adj* soft; *carne* tender; *pan* fresh; *persona* tender-hearted
tierra *f* land; *materia* soil, earth; (*patria*) native land, homeland; ***la Tierra*** the earth; ***tierra firme*** dry land, terra firma; ***echar por tierra*** ruin, wreck
tieso *adj* stiff, rigid
tiesto *m* flower pot
tifón *m* typhoon
tifus *m* MED typhus
tigre *m* ZO tiger; *L.Am.* puma; *L.Am.* (*leopardo*) jaguar
tigresa *f* tigress
tijeras *fpl* scissors
tila *f* lime blossom tea
tildar ⟨1a⟩ *v/t*: ***tildar a alguien de*** *fig* brand s.o. as
tilde *f* accent; *en ñ* tilde
tilín *m*: ***me hizo tilín*** F I took an immediate liking to her
timador *m*, **timadora** *f* cheat
timar ⟨1a⟩ *v/t* cheat
timba *f* F gambling den
timbal *m* MÚS kettle drum
timbre *m de puerta* bell; *Méx* (postage) stamp
timidez *f* shyness, timidity
tímido *adj* shy, timid
timo *m* confidence trick, swindle
timón *m* MAR, AVIA rudder
tímpano *m* ANAT eardrum
tina *f* large jar; *L.Am.* (*bañera*) (bath)tub
tinglado *m fig* F mess
tinieblas *fpl* darkness *sg*
tino *m* aim, marksmanship; (*sensatez*) judg(e)ment; ***con mucho tino*** wisely, sensibly
tinta *f* ink; ***de buena tinta*** *fig* on good authority; ***medias tintas*** *fig* half measures
tinte *m* dye; *fig* veneer, gloss
tinterillo *m L.Am.* F shyster F
tintero *m* inkwell; ***dejarse algo en el tintero*** leave sth unsaid
tintin(e)ar ⟨1a⟩ *v/t* jingle
tinto *adj*: ***vino tinto*** red wine
tintorería *f* dry cleaner's
tío *m* uncle; F (*tipo*) guy F; F *apelativo* pal F
tiovivo *m* carousel, merry-go-round
típico *adj* typical (**de** of)
tipo *m* type, kind; F *persona* guy F; COM rate; ***tipo de cambio*** exchange rate; ***tipo de interés*** interest rate; ***tener buen tipo*** be well built; *de mujer* have a good figure
tipográfico *adj* typographic(al)
tíquet, **tiquete** *m L.Am.* receipt
tiquismiquis *m/f* F fuss-budget F, *Br* fusspot F
tira *f* strip; ***la tira de*** F loads of F, masses of F; ***tira y afloja*** *fig* give and take

T

tirabuzón *m* curl; (*sacacorchos*) corkscrew

tirachinas *m inv* slingshot, *Br* catapult

tirada *f* TIP print run; ***de una tirada*** in one go

tiradero *m Méx* dump

tirado *adj* P (*barato*) dirt-cheap F; ***estar tirado*** F (*fácil*) be a walkover F *o* a piece of cake F

tiradores *mpl Arg* suspenders, *Br* braces

tiranía *f* tyranny

tirano 1 *adj* tyrannical **2** *m*, **-a** *f* tyrant

tirante 1 *adj* taut; *fig* tense **2** *m* strap; ***tirantes*** suspenders, *Br* braces

tirantez *f fig* tension

tirar ⟨1a⟩ **1** *v/t* throw; *edificio*, *persona* knock down; (*volcar*) knock over; *basura* throw away; *dinero* waste, throw away F; TIP print; F *en examen* fail **2** *v/i* pull, attract; (*disparar*) shoot; ***tirar a*** tend toward; ***tirar a conservador*** have conservative tendencies; ***tirar de algo*** pull sth; ***ir tirando*** F get by, manage **3** *v/r* **tirarse** throw o.s.; F *tiempo* spend; ***tirarse a alguien*** P screw s.o. P

tirita *f* MED Bandaid®, *Br* plaster

tiritar ⟨1a⟩ *v/i* shiver

tiro *m* shot; ***tiro al blanco*** target practice; ***al tiro*** *CSur* F at once, right away; ***de tiros largos*** F dressed up; ***ni a tiros*** F for love nor money; ***le salió el tiro por la culata*** F it backfired on him; ***le sentó como un tiro*** F he needed it like a hole in the head F

tirón *m* tug, jerk; ***de un tirón*** at a stretch, without a break

tiroteo *m* shooting

tirria *f*: ***tener tirria a alguien*** F have it in for s.o. F

tisana *f* herbal tea

títere *m tb fig* puppet; ***no dejar títere con cabeza*** F spare no-one

titiritero *m*, **-a** *f* acrobat

titubear ⟨1a⟩ *v/i* waver, hesitate

titubeo *m* wavering, hesitation

titular *m de periódico* headline

titularse ⟨1a⟩ *v/r* be entitled

título *m* title; *universitario* degree; JUR title; COM bond; ***tener muchos títulos*** be highly qualified; ***a título de*** as; ***títulos de crédito*** credits

tiza *f* chalk

tiznar ⟨1a⟩ *v/t* blacken

tizón *m* ember

tlapalería *f Méx* hardware store

TLC *abr* (= ***Tratado de Libre Comercio***) NAFTA (= North American Free Trade Agreement)

toalla *f* towel; ***tirar*** *or* ***arrojar la toalla*** *fig* throw in the towel

toallero *m* towel rail

tobillo *m* ankle

tobogán *m* slide

tocadiscos *m inv* record player

tocado *adj*: ***estar tocado*** *fig* F be crazy F

tocador *m* dressing-table

tocante: ***en lo tocante a …*** with regard to …

tocar ⟨1g⟩ **1** *v/t* touch; MÚS play **2** *v/i L.Am. a la puerta* knock (on the door); *L.Am.* (*sonar la campanita*) ring the doorbell; ***te toca jugar*** it's your turn **3** *v/r* **tocarse** touch

tocateja: ***a tocateja*** in hard cash

tocayo *m*, **-a** *f* namesake

tocino *m* bacon

tocólogo *m*, **-a** *f* obstetrician

todavía *adv* still, yet; ***todavía no ha llegado*** he still hasn't come, he hasn't come yet; ***todavía no*** not yet

todo 1 *adj* all; ***todos los domingos*** every Sunday; ***-a la clase*** the whole *o* the entire class **2** *adv* all; ***estaba todo sucio*** it was all dirty; ***con todo*** all the same; ***del todo*** entirely, absolutely **3** *pron* all, everything; *pl* everybody, everyone; ***ir a por -as*** go all out

todoterreno *m* AUTO off-road *o* all-terrain vehicle

toldo *m* awning; *L.Am.* Indian hut

tolerancia *f* tolerance

tolerar ⟨1a⟩ *v/t* tolerate

toma *f* FOT shot, take; ***toma de conciencia*** realization; ***toma de corriente*** outlet, socket; ***toma de posesión*** POL taking office

tomado *adj Méx* F (*borracho*) drunk

tomadura *f*: ***tomadura de pelo*** F joke

tomar ⟨1a⟩ **1** *v/t* take; *decisión* make, take; *bebida*, *comida* have; ***tomarla con alguien*** F have it in for s.o. F; ***tomar el sol*** sunbathe; ***¡toma!*** here (you are); ***toma y daca*** give and take **2** *v/i L.Am.* drink; ***tomar por la derecha*** turn right **3** *v/r* **tomarse** take; *comida*, *bebida* have; ***se lo tomó a pecho*** he took it to heart

tomate *m* tomato

tomavistas *m inv* movie camera, cine camera

tomillo *m* BOT thyme

tomo *m* volume, tome; ***un timador de tomo y lomo*** F an out-and-out conman

ton *m*: ***sin ton ni son*** for no particular reason

tonada *f* song

tonalidad *f* tonality

tonel *m* barrel, cask

tonelada *f peso* ton

tónica *f* tonic
tónico *m* MED tonic
tonificar ⟨1g⟩ *v/t* tone up
tono *m* MÚS, MED, PINT tone
tontería *f fig* stupid *o* dumb F thing; ***tonterías*** *pl* nonsense *sg*
tonto 1 *adj* silly, foolish **2** *m*, **-a** *f* fool, idiot; ***hacer el tonto*** play the fool; ***hacerse el tonto*** act dumb F
top *m prenda* top
topacio *m* MIN topaz
toparse ⟨1a⟩ *v/r*: ***toparse con alguien*** bump into s.o., run into s.o.
tope *m* limit; *pieza* stop; *Méx en la calle* speed bump; ***pasarlo a tope*** F have a great time; ***estar hasta los topes*** F be bursting at the seams F
tópico *m* cliché, platitude
topo *m* ZO mole
toque *m*: ***toque de queda*** MIL, *fig* curfew; ***dar los úiltimos toques*** put the finishing touches (***a*** to)
toquilla *f* shawl
tórax *m* ANAT thorax
torbellino *m* whirlwind
torcer ⟨2b & 2h⟩ **1** *v/t* twist; (*doblar*) bend; (*girar*) turn **2** *v/i* turn; ***torcer a la derecha*** turn right **3** *v/r* **torcerse** twist, bend; *fig* go wrong; ***torcerse un pie*** sprain one's ankle
torcido *adj* twisted, bent
toreador *m esp L.Am.* bullfighter
torear ⟨1a⟩ **1** *v/i* fight bulls **2** *v/t* fight; *fig* dodge, sidestep
toreo *m* bullfighting
torera *f*: ***saltarse algo a la torera*** F flout sth, disregard sth
torero *m* bullfighter
tormenta *f* storm
tormento *m* torture
tornado *m* tornado, twister F
tornarse ⟨1a⟩ *v/r triste*, *difícil etc* become
torneo *m* competition, tournament
tornillo *m* screw; *con tuerca* bolt; ***le falta un tornillo*** F he's got a screw loose F
torniquete *m* turnstile; MED tourniquet
torno *m de alfarería* wheel; ***en torno a*** around, about
toro *m* bull; ***ir a los toros*** go to a bullfight; ***coger al toro por los cuernos*** take the bull by the horns
toronja *f L.Am.* grapefruit
torpe *adj* clumsy; (*tonto*) dense, dim
torpedo *m* MIL torpedo
torpeza *f* clumsiness; (*necedad*) stupidity
torre *f* tower; ***torre de control*** AVIA control tower
torrencial *adj* torrential
torrente *m fig* avalanche, flood
torrezno *m* GASTR fried rasher of bacon
tórrido *adj* torrid
torrija *f* GASTR French toast
torta *f* cake; *plana* tart; F slap
tortazo *m* F crash; (*bofetada*) punch
tortícolis *m* MED crick in the neck
tortilla *f* omelette; *L.Am.* tortilla
tortillera *f* V dyke F, lesbian
tortuga *f* ZO tortoise; *marina* turtle; ***a paso de tortuga*** *fig* at a snail's pace
tortuoso *adj fig* tortuous
tortura *f tb fig* torture
torturar ⟨1a⟩ *v/t* torture
tos *f* cough
tosco *adj fig* rough, coarse
toser ⟨2a⟩ *v/i* cough
tostada *f* piece of toast
tostado *adj* (*moreno*) brown, tanned
tostador *m* toaster
tostar ⟨1m⟩ **1** *v/t* toast; *café* roast; *al sol* tan **2** *v/r* **tostarse** tan, get brown
tostón *m* F bore
total 1 *adj* total, complete; ***en total*** altogether, in total **2** *m* whole; ***un total de 50 personas*** a total of 50 people
totalidad *f* totality
totalitario *adj* totalitarian
tóxico *adj* toxic
toxicómano *m*, **-a** *f* drug addict
toxina *f* toxin
tozudo *adj* obstinate
trabajador 1 *adj* hard-working **2** *m*, **trabajadora** *f* worker; ***trabajador eventual*** casual worker
trabajar ⟨1a⟩ **1** *v/i* work **2** *v/t* work; *tema*, *múísculos* work on
trabajo *m* work; ***trabajo en equipo*** team work; ***trabajo temporal*** temporary work; ***trabajo a tiempo parcial*** part--time work
trabajoso *adj* hard, laborious
trabalenguas *m inv* tongue twister
trabar ⟨1a⟩ **1** *v/t conversación*, *amistad* strike up **2** *v/r* **trabarse** get tangled up
trabucarse ⟨1g⟩ *v/r* get all mixed up
tracción *f* TÉC traction; ***tracción delantera/ trasera*** front / rear-wheel drive
tractor *m* tractor
tradición *f* tradition
tradicional *adj* traditional
traducción *f* translation
traducir ⟨3o⟩ *v/t* translate
traductor *m*, **traductora** *f* translator
traer ⟨2p; *part* **traido** ⟩ **1** *v/t* bring; ***traer consigo*** involve, entail; ***este periódico la trae en portada*** this newspaper carries it on the front page **2** *v/r* **traerse**: ***este asunto se las trae*** F it's a very tricky

matter
traficante *m* dealer
traficar ⟨1g⟩ *v/i* deal (***en*** in)
tráfico *m* traffic; ***tráfico de drogas*** drug trafficking, drug dealing
tragaperras *f inv* slot machine
tragar ⟨1h⟩ **1** *v/t* swallow; ***no lo trago*** I can't stand him *o* bear him **2** *v/r* **tragarse** *tb fig* F swallow
tragedia *f* tragedy
trágico *adj* tragic
tragicomedia *f* tragicomedy
trago *m* mouthful; F *bebida* drink; ***de un trago*** in one gulp; ***pasar un mal trago*** *fig* have a hard time
tragón *adj* greedy
traición *f* treachery, betrayal
traicionar ⟨1a⟩ *v/t* betray
traidor 1 *adj* treacherous **2** *m*, **traidora** *f* traitor
traido *part* → ***traer***
traigo *vb* → ***traer***
tráiler *m* trailer
traje 1 *m* suit; ***traje de baño*** swimsuit **2** *vb* → ***traer***
trajín *m* hustle and bustle
trajo *vb* → ***traer***
trama *f* (*tema*) plot
tramar ⟨1a⟩ *v/t complot* hatch
tramitar ⟨1a⟩ *v/t documento*: *de persona* apply for; *de banco etc* process
trámite *m* formality
tramo *m* section, stretch; *de escaleras* flight
trampa *f* trap; (*truco*) scam F, trick; ***hacer trampas*** cheat
trampilla *f* trapdoor
trampolín *m* diving board
tramposo *m*, **-a** *f* cheat, crook
tranca *f*: ***llevaba una tranca increíble*** F he was wasted F *o* smashed F; ***a trancas y barrancas*** with great difficulty
trancazo *m* F dose of flu
trance *m* (*momento difícil*) tough time; ***en trance*** in a trancc
tranquilidad *f* calm, quietness
tranquilizante *m* tranquilizer, *Br* tranquillizer
tranquilizar ⟨1f⟩ *v/t*: ***tranquilizar a alguien*** calm s.o. down
tranquillo *m*: ***coger el tranquillo de algo*** F get the hang of sth F
tranquilo *adj* calm, quiet; ***¡tranquilo!*** don't worry; ***déjame tranquilo*** leave me alone
transacción *f* COM deal, transaction;
transar ⟨1a⟩ *v/i L.Am.* (*ser vendido*) sell out
transatlántico 1 *adj* transatlantic **2** *m* liner
transbordador *m* ferry; ***transbordador espacial*** space shuttle
transbordo *m*: ***hacer transbordo*** TRANSP transfer, change
transcendental *adj fig* momentous
transcurrir ⟨3a⟩ *v/i de tiempo* pass, go by
transcurso *m* course; *de tiempo* passing
transeúinte *m/f* passer-by
transexual *m/f* transsexual
transferencia *f* COM transfer
transformación *f* transformation
transformador *m* EL transformer
transformar ⟨1a⟩ *v/t* transform
transfronterizo *adj* cross-border
tránsfuga *m/f* POL defector
transfusión *f*: ***transfusión de sangre*** blood transfusion
transgénico *adj* genetically modified
transgredir ⟨3a⟩ *v/t* infringe
transición *f* transition
transigir ⟨3c⟩ *v/i* compromise, make concessions
transistor *m* transistor
transitivo *adj* GRAM transitive
tránsito *m* COM transit; *L.Am.* (*circulación*) traffic
translúícido *adj* translucent
transmisión *f* transmission; ***transmisión de datos*** data transmission; ***enfermedad de transmisión sexual*** sexually transmitted disease
transmitir ⟨3a⟩ *v/t* spread; RAD, TV broadcast, transmit
transparencia *f para proyectar* transparency, slide
transparente *adj* transparent
transpiración *f* perspiration
transpirar ⟨1a⟩ *v/i* perspire
transplantar ⟨1a⟩ *v/t* transplant
transportar ⟨1a⟩ *v/t* transport
transporte *m* transport
tranvía *m* streetcar, *Br* tram
trapecio *m* trapeze
trapecista *m/f* trapeze artist(e)
trapiche *m CSur* sugar mill *o* press
trapicheo *m* F shady deal F
trapo *m viejo* rag; *para limpiar* cloth; ***trapos*** F clothes
trapujear ⟨1a⟩ *v/t & v/i C.Am.* smuggle
tráquea *f* ANAT windpipe, trachea
traqueteo *m* rattle, clatter
tras *prp en el espacio* behind; *en el tiempo* after
trasero 1 *adj* rear *atr*, back *atr* **2** *m* F butt F, *Br* rear end F
trasiego *m fig* bustle
trasladar ⟨1a⟩ **1** *v/t* move; *trabajador* transfer **2** *v/r* **trasladarse** move (***a*** to);

se traslada *Méx*: *en negocio* under new management
traslado *m* move; *de trabajador* transfer; ***traslado al aeropuerto*** airport transfer
trasluz *m*: ***al trasluz*** against the light
trasnochar ⟨1a⟩ *v/i* (*acostarse tarde*) go to bed late, stay up late; (*no dormir*) stay up all night; *L.Am.* stay overnight, spend the night
traspapelar ⟨1a⟩ *v/t* mislay
traspasar ⟨1a⟩ *v/t* (*atravesar*) go through; COM transfer
traspié *m* trip, stumble; ***dar un traspié*** *fig* slip up, blunder
trasplantar ⟨1a⟩ *v/t* AGR, MED transplant
trasplante *m* AGR, MED transplant
trastada *f* F prank, trick; ***hacer trastadas*** get up to mischief
traste *m*: ***irse al traste*** F fall through, go down the tubes F
trastero *m* lumber room
trasto *m desp* piece of junk; *persona* good-for-nothing
trastornar ⟨1a⟩ *v/t* upset; (*molestar*) inconvenience
trastorno *m* inconvenience; MED disorder
tratado *m esp* POL treaty; ***Tratado de Libre Comercio*** North American Free Trade Agreement
tratamiento *m* treatment; ***tratamiento de datos / textos*** INFOR data / word processing
tratar ⟨1a⟩ **1** *v/t* treat; (*manejar*) handle; (*dirigirse a*) address (***de*** as); *gente* come into contact with; *tema* deal with **2** *v/i*: ***tratar con alguien*** deal with s.o.; ***tratar de*** (*intentar*) try to **3** *v/r* **tratarse**: ***¿de qué se trata?*** what's it about?
trato *m de prisionero*, *animal* treatment; COM deal; ***malos tratos*** *pl* ill treatment *sg*, abuse *sg*,; ***tener trato con alguien*** have dealings with s.o.; ***¡trato hecho!*** it's a deal
trauma *m* trauma
traumatizar ⟨1f⟩ *v/t* traumatize
traumatólogo *m*, **-a** *f* trauma specialist, traumatologist
través *m*: ***a través de*** through
travesaño *m en fútbol* crossbar
travesía *f* crossing
travesti *m* transvestite, drag artist
travesura *f* bit of mischief, prank
travieso *adj niño* mischievous
trayecto *m* journey; ***10 dólares por trayecto*** 10 dollars each way
trayectoria *f fig* course, path
trazar ⟨1f⟩ *v/t* (*dibujar*) draw; *ruta* plot, trace; (*describir*) outline, describe
trazo *m* line
trébol *m* BOT clover
trece *adj* thirteen; ***mantenerse*** *or* ***seguir en sus trece*** stand firm, not budge
trecho *m* stretch, distance
tregua *f* truce, cease-fire; ***sin tregua*** relentlessly
treinta *adj* thirty
tremebundo *adj* horrendous, frightening
tremendo *adj* awful, dreadful; *éxito*, *alegría* tremendous
tren *m* FERR train; ***tren de alta velocidad*** high speed train; ***tren de lavado*** car wash; ***vivir a todo tren*** F live in style; ***estar como un tren*** F be absolutely gorgeous
trenca *f* duffel coat
trenza *f* plait
trepa *m* F *socialmente* social climber; *en el trabajo* careerist
trepar ⟨1a⟩ *v/i* climb (***a*** up), scale (***a*** sth)
trepidante *adj fig* frenetic
tres *adj* three
trescientos *adj* three hundred
tresillo *m* living-room suite, *Br* three--piece suite
treta *f* trick, ploy
triángulo *m* triangle
tribu *f* tribe
tribuna *f* grandstand
tribunal *m* court; ***Tribunal Supremo*** Supreme Court
tributo *m* tribute; (*impuesto*) tax
triciclo *m* tricycle
tricotar ⟨1a⟩ *v/i* knit
trifulca *f* F brawl, punch-up F
trigo *m* wheat
trillado *adj fig* hackneyed, clichéd
trillar ⟨1a⟩ *v/t* AGR thresh
trillizos *mpl* triplets
trillón *m* quintillion, *Br* trillion
trimestral *adj* quarterly
trimestre *m* quarter; *escolar* semester, *Br* term
trinar ⟨1a⟩ *v/i* trill, warble; ***está que trina*** *fig* F he's fuming F, he's hopping mad F
trincar ⟨1g⟩ *v/t* F *criminal* catch
trinchera *f* MIL trench
trineo *m* sled, sleigh
trino *m* trill, warble
trío *m* trio
tripa *f* F belly F, gut F; ***hacer de tripas corazón*** *fig* pluck up courage
triple *m*: ***el triple que el año pasado*** three times as much as last year
triplicar ⟨1g⟩ *v/t* triple, treble
trípode *m* tripod
tripulación *f* AVIA, MAR crew
tripular ⟨1a⟩ *v/t* man
triquiñuela *f* F dodge F, trick

tris *m*: ***estuvo en un tris de caerse*** F she came within an inch of falling
triste *adj* sad
tristeza *f* sadness
triturar ⟨1a⟩ *v/t* grind
triunfador 1 *adj* winning **2** *m*, **triunfadora** *f* winner, victor
triunfar ⟨1a⟩ *v/i* triumph, win
triunfo *m* triumph, victory; *en naipes* trump
trivial *adj* trivial
triza *f*: ***hacer trizas*** F *jarrón* smash to bits; *papel, vestido* tear to shreds
trocear ⟨1a⟩ *v/t* cut into pieces, cut up
troche: ***había errores a troche y moche*** F there were mistakes galore F
trofeo *m* trophy
troglodita *m/f* cave-dweller
troj(e) *f Arg* granary
trola *f* F fib
trolebús *m* trolley bus
tromba *f*: ***tromba de agua*** downpour
trombón *m* MÚS trombone
trombosis *f* MED thrombosis
trompa 1 *adj* F wasted F **2** *f* MÚS horn; ZO trunk
trompazo *m L.Am.* F whack F; ***darse un trompazo con algo*** F bang into sth
trompearse ⟨1a⟩ *L.Am.* F fight, lay into each other F
trompeta *f* MÚS trumpet
trompetista *m/f* MÚS trumpeter
trompicón *m*: ***a trompicones*** in fits and starts
trompo *m* spinning top
trona *f* high chair
tronar ⟨1m⟩ *v/i* thunder
troncha *f S. Am.* slice, piece
tronchante *adj* F sidesplitting
troncharse ⟨1a⟩ *v/r*: ***troncharse de risa*** F split one's sides laughing
tronco *m* trunk; *cortado* log; ***dormir como un tronco*** sleep like a log
trono *m* throne
tropa *f* MIL (*soldado raso*) ordinary soldier; ***tropas*** troops
tropel *m*: ***en tropel*** in a mad rush; ***salir en tropel*** pour out
tropezar ⟨1f & 1k⟩ *v/i* trip, stumble
tropical *adj* tropical
trópico *m* tropic
tropiezo *m fig* setback
tropilla *f L.Am.* herd
trotar ⟨1a⟩ *v/i fig* gad around
trote *m* trot; ***ya no estoy para esos trotes*** I'm not up to it any more
trozo *m* piece
trucha *f* ZO trout
truco *m* trick; ***coger el truco a algo*** F get the hang of sth F
truculento *adj* horrifying
trueno *m* thunder
trueque *m* barter
trufa *f* BOT truffle
truhán *m* rogue
Tte. *abr* (= ***Teniente***) Lieut. (= Lieutenant)
tú *pron sg* you; ***tratar de tú*** address as 'tu'
tu, **tus** *adj pos* your
tuberculosis *f* MED TB, tuberculosis
tubería *f* pipe
tubo *m* tube; ***tubo de escape*** AUTO exhaust (pipe); ***por un tubo*** F an enormous amount
tucán *m* ZO toucan
tuerca *f* TÉC nut
tulipán *m* BOT tulip
tullido *m* cripple
tumba *f* tomb, grave
tumbar ⟨1a⟩ **1** *v/t* knock down **2** *v/r* **tumbarse** lie down
tumbo *m* tumble; ***ir dando tumbos*** stagger along
tumbona *f* (sun) lounger
tumor *m* MED tumo(u)r
tumulto *m* uproar
tuna *f Méx fruta* prickly pear
tunda *f* F beating
tundra *f* GEOG tundra
túnel *m* tunnel; ***túnel de lavado*** car wash
Túnez Tunisia
túnica *f* tunic
tuntún: ***decir algo al buen tuntún*** say sth off the top of one's head
tupé *m* F quiff
tupido *adj pelo* thick; *vegetación* dense, thick
turbante *m* turban
turbar ⟨1a⟩ **1** *v/t* (*emocionar*) upset; *paz, tranquilidad* disturb; (*avergonzar*) embarrass **2** *v/r* **turbarse** (*emocionarse*) get upset; *de paz, tranquilidad* be disturbed; (*avergonzarse*) get embarrassed
turbina *f* turbine
turbio *adj* cloudy, murky; *fig* shady, murky
turbo *m* turbo
turbulencia *f* turbulence
turbulento *adj* turbulent
turco 1 *adj* Turkish **2** *m*, **-a** *f* Turk
turismo *m* tourism; *automóvil* sedan, *Br* saloon (car); ***turismo rural*** tourism in rural areas
turista *m/f* tourist
turístico *adj* tourist *atr*
turnarse ⟨1a⟩ *v/r* take it in turns

T

turno *m* turn; ***turno de noche*** night shift; ***por turnos*** in turns
turquesa *f piedra preciosa* turquoise; ***azul turquesa*** turquoise
Turquía Turkey
turrón *m* nougat
turulato *adj* F stunned, dazed
tute *m*: ***darse un tute*** F work like a dog F, slave F
tutear ⟨1a⟩ *v/t* address as 'tu'
tutiplén: ***había comida a tutiplén*** F there was loads *o* masses to eat F
tutor *m*, **tutora** *f* EDU tutor
tuve *vb* → ***tener***
tuvo *vb* → ***tener***
tuyo, **tuya** *pron pos* yours; ***los tuyos*** your folks, your family
TV *abr* (**= *televisión***) TV (= television)

U

u *conj* (*instead of* **o** *before words starting with o*) or
ubicación *f L.Am.* location; (*localización*) finding
ubicado *adj* located, situated
ubicar ⟨1g⟩ **1** *v/t L.Am.* place, put; (*localizar*) locate **2** *v/r* **ubicarse** be located, be situated; *en un empleo* get a job
ubicuo *adj* ubiquitous
ubre *f* udder
UCI *abr* (**= *Unidad de Cuidados Intensivos***) ICU (= Intensive Care Unit)
Ud. *pron* → ***usted***
Uds. *pron* → ***usted***
UE *abr* (**= *Unión Europea***) EU (= European Union)
ufano *adj* conceited; (*contento*) proud
ujier *m* usher
úlcera *f* MED ulcer
ulcerarse ⟨1a⟩ *v/r* MED become ulcerous, ulcerate
ulterior *adj* subsequent
últimamente *adv* lately
ultimar ⟨1a⟩ *v/t* finalize; *L.Am.* (*rematar*) finish off
ultimátum *m* ultimatum
último *adj* last; (*más reciente*) latest; *piso* top *atr*; ***-as noticias*** latest news *sg*; ***por último*** finally; ***está en las -as*** he doesn't have long (to live)
ultra *m* POL right-wing extremist
ultraderecha *f* POL extreme right
ultrajante *adj* outrageous; *palabras* insulting
ultrajar ⟨1a⟩ *v/t* outrage; (*insultar*) insult
ultraje *m* outrage; (*insulto*) insult
ultraligero *m* AVIA microlight
ultramarinos *mpl* groceries; ***tienda de ultramarinos*** grocery store, *Br* grocer's (shop)
ultramoderno *adj* ultramodern
ultranza: ***a ultranza*** for all one is worth; ***un defensor a ultranza de algo*** an ardent defender of sth
ultrasónico *adj* ultrasonic
ultrasonido *m* ultrasound
ultratumba *f*: ***la vida de ultratumba*** life beyond the grave
ultravioleta *adj* ultraviolet
ulular ⟨1a⟩ *v/i de viento* howl; *de búho* hoot
umbilical *adj* ANAT umbilical
umbral *m fig* threshold; ***en el umbral de*** *fig* on the threshold of
umbrío *adj* shady
un, **una** *art* a; *antes de vocal y h muda* an; ***unos coches / pájaros*** some cars / birds
unánime *adj* unanimous
unanimidad *f* unanimity; ***por unanimidad*** unanimously
unción *f fig* unction
undécimo *adj* eleventh
ungir ⟨3c⟩ *v/t* REL anoint
ungüento *m* ointment
únicamente *adv* only
único *adj* only; (*sin par*) unique; ***es único*** it's unique; ***hijo único*** only child; ***lo único que …*** the only thing that …
unicornio *m* MYTH unicorn
unidad *f* MIL, MAT unit; (*cohesión*) unity; ***unidad de cuidados intensivos, unidad de vigilancia intensiva*** MED intensive care unit; ***unidad de disco*** INFOR disk drive; ***unidad monetaria*** monetary unity
unido *adj* united; ***una familia -a*** a close-knit family
unificación *f* unification
unificar ⟨1g⟩ *v/t* unify
uniformar ⟨1a⟩ *v/t fig* standardize

uniforme 1 *adj* uniform; *superficie* even **2** *m* uniform
unilateral *adj* unilateral
unión *f* union; ***Unión Europea*** European Union
unir ⟨3a⟩ **1** *v/t* join; *personas* unite; *características* combine (***con*** with); *ciudades* link **2** *v/r* **unirse** join together; ***unirse a*** join
unisex *adj* unisex
unísono *adj*: ***al unísono*** in unison
unitario *adj* unitary; ***precio unitario*** unit price
universal *adj* universal
universidad *f* university; ***universidad a distancia*** *university correspondence school*, *Br* Open University
universitario 1 *adj* university *atr* **2** *m*, **-a** *f* (*estudiante*) university student
universo *m* universe
uno 1 *pron* one; ***es la -a*** it's one o'clock; ***me lo dijo uno*** someone *o* somebody told me; ***uno a uno, uno por uno, de uno en uno*** one by one; ***no dar ni -a*** F not get anything right; ***unos cuantos*** a few, some; ***unos niños*** some children; ***-as mil pesetas*** about a thousand pesetas **2** *m* one; ***el uno de enero*** January first, the first of January
untar ⟨1a⟩ *v/t* spread; ***untar a alguien*** F (*sobornar*) grease s.o.'s palm
untuoso *adj fig* oily
uña *f* ANAT nail; ZO claw; ***defenderse con uñas y dientes*** *fig* F fight tooth and nail; ***ser uña y carne*** *personas* be extremely close
uperisado *adj*: ***leche -a*** UHT milk
uranio *m* uranium
urbanidad *f* civility
urbanismo *m* city planning, *Br* town planning
urbanización *f* (urban) development; (*colonia*) housing development, *Br* housing estate
urbanizar ⟨1f⟩ *v/t terreno* develop
urbano *adj* urban; (*cortés*) courteous; ***guardia urbano*** local police officer
urbe *f* city
urdir ⟨3a⟩ *v/t complot* hatch
urea *f* urea
uretra *f* ANAT urethra
urgencia *f* urgency; (*prisa*) haste; MED emergency; ***urgencias*** *pl* emergency room *sg*, *Br* casualty *sg*
urgente *adj* urgent
urgir ⟨3c⟩ *v/i* be urgent
urinario *m* urinal
urna *f* urn; ***urna electoral*** ballot box
urólogo *m* MED urologist
urraca *f* ZO magpie
URSS *abr* (= ***Unión de las Repúíblicas Socialistas Soviéticas***) USSR (= Union of Soviet Socialist Republics)
urticaria *f* MED hives
Uruguay Uruguay
uruguayo 1 *adj* Uruguayan **2** *m*, **-a** *f* Uruguayan
usado *adj* (*gastado*) worn; (*de segunda mano*) second hand
usar ⟨1a⟩ **1** *v/t* use; *ropa*, *gafas* wear **2** *v/i*: ***listo para usar*** ready to use **3** *v/r* **usarse** be used
uso *m* use; (*costumbre*) custom; ***obligatorio el uso de casco*** helmets must be worn; ***en buen uso*** still in use
usted *pron* you; ***tratar de usted*** address as 'usted'; ***ustedes*** *pl* you; ***de usted / ustedes*** your; ***es de usted / ustedes*** it's yours
usual *adj* common, usual
usuario *m*, **-a** *f* INFOR user
usufructo *m* JUR usufruct
usura *f* usury
usurero *m*, **-a** *f* usurer
usurpar ⟨1a⟩ *v/t* usurp
utensilio *m* tool; *de cocina* utensil; ***utensilios*** *pl* equipment *sg*; ***utensilios*** *pl* ***de pesca*** fishing tackle *sg*
úítero *m* ANAT uterus
úítil 1 *adj* useful **2** *m* tool; ***úítiles*** *pl* ***de pesca*** fishing tackle *sg*
utilidad *f* usefulness
utilitario 1 *adj* functional, utilitarian **2** *m* AUTO compact
utilitarismo *m* utilitarianism
utilización *f* use
utilizar ⟨1f⟩ *v/t* use
utopía *f* utopia
utópico *adj* utopian
uva *f* BOT grape; ***estar de mala uva*** F be in a foul mood; ***tener mala uva*** F be a nasty piece of work F
UVI *abr* (= ***Unidad de Vigilancia Intensiva***) ICU (= Intensive Care Unit)
úívula *f* ANAT uvula

V

va *vb* → ***ir***
vaca *f* cow; GASTR beef; ***vaca lechera*** dairy cow; ***vaca marina*** manatee, sea cow; ***mal*** *or* ***enfermedad de las vacas locas*** F mad cow disease F
vacaciones *fpl* vacation *sg*, *Br* holiday *sg*; ***de vacaciones*** on vacation, *Br* on holiday
vacante 1 *adj* vacant, empty **2** *f* job opening, position, *Br* vacancy; ***cubrir una vacante*** fill a position
vaciar ⟨1b⟩ **1** *v/t* empty **2** *v/r* **vaciarse** empty
vacilación *f* hesitation
vacilante *adj* unsteady; (*dubitativo*) hesitant
vacilar ⟨1a⟩ **1** *v/i* hesitate; *de fe, resolución* waver; *de objeto* wobble, rock; *de persona* stagger; *Méx* F (*divertirse*) have fun **2** *v/t* F make fun of
vacío 1 *adj* empty **2** *m* FÍS vacuum; *fig espacio* void; ***vacío de poder*** power vacuum; ***vacío legal*** loophole; ***dejar un vacío*** *fig* leave a gap; ***envasado al vacío*** vacuum packed; ***hacer el vacío a alguien*** *fig* ostracize s.o.
vacuna *f* vaccine
vacunación *f* vaccination
vacunar ⟨1a⟩ *v/t* vaccinate
vacuno *adj* bovine; ***ganado vacuno*** cattle *pl*
vacuo *adj fig* vacuous
vadear ⟨1a⟩ *v/t río* ford; *dificultad* get around
vado *m* ford; *en la calle* entrance ramp; ***vado permanente*** *letrero* keep clear
vagabundear ⟨1a⟩ *v/i* drift around
vagabundo 1 *adj perro* stray **2** *m*, **-a** *f* hobo, *Br* tramp
vagancia *f* laziness, idleness
vagar ⟨1h⟩ *v/i* wander
vagido *m de bebe* cry
vagina *f* ANAT vagina
vago *adj* (*holgazán*) lazy; (*indefinido*) vague; ***hacer el vago*** laze around
vagón *m de carga* wagon; *de pasajeros* car, *Br* coach; ***vagón restaurante*** dining car, *Br tb* restaurant car
vaguear ⟨1a⟩ *v/i* laze around
vaguedad *f* vagueness
vahido *m* MED dizzy spell
vaho *m* (*aliento*) breath; (*vapor*) steam
vaina *f* BOT pod; *S. Am.* F drag F
vainilla *f* vanilla
vais *vb* → ***ir***
vaivén *m* to-and-fro, swinging; ***vaivenes*** *fig* ups and downs
vajilla *f* dishes *pl*; *juego* dinner service, set of dishes
vale *m* voucher, coupon
valedero *adj* valid
valentía *f* bravery
valer ⟨2q⟩ **1** *v/t* be worth; (*costar*) cost **2** *v/i de billete, carné* be valid; (*estar permitido*) be allowed; (*tener valor*) be worth; (*servir*) be of use; ***no valer para algo*** be no good at sth; ***vale más caro*** it's more expensive; ***sus consejos me valieron de mucho*** his advice was very useful to me; ***más vale ...*** it's better to ...; ***más te vale ...*** you'd better ...; ***¡vale!*** okay, sure **3** *v/r* **valerse** manage (by o.s.); ***valerse de*** make use of
valeriana *f* BOT valerian
valeroso *adj* valiant
valga *vb* → ***valer***
valgo *vb* → ***valer***
valía *f* worth
validar ⟨1a⟩ *v/t* validate
validez *f* validity
válido *adj* valid
valiente *adj* brave; *irón* fine
valija *f* (*maleta*) bag, suitcase, *Br tb* case; ***valija diplomática*** diplomatic bag
valioso *adj* valuable
valla *f* fence; DEP, *fig* hurdle; ***valla publicitaria*** billboard, *Br* hoarding; ***carrera de vallas*** DEP hurdles
vallado *m* fence
vallar ⟨1a⟩ *v/t* fence in
valle *m* valley
valor *m* value; (*valentía*) courage; ***valor añadido***, *L.Am.* ***valor agregado*** value added; ***valor nominal*** *de acción* nominal value; *de título* par value; ***objetos de valor*** valuables; ***valores*** COM securities
valoración *f* (*tasación*) valuation
valorar ⟨1a⟩ *v/t* value (***en*** at); (*estimar*) appreciate, value
vals *m* waltz
valuar ⟨1e⟩ *v/t* value
válvula *f* ANAT, EL valve; ***válvula de escape*** *fig* safety valve
vampiro *m fig* vampire
van *vb* → ***ir***
vanagloriarse ⟨1b⟩ *v/r* boast (***de*** about), brag (***de*** about)
vandálico *adj* destructive

vandalismo *m* vandalism
vándalo *m*, **-a** *f* vandal
vanguardia *f* MIL vanguard; ***de vanguardia*** *fig* avant-garde
vanidad *f* vanity
vanidoso *adj* conceited, vain
vano *adj* futile, vain; ***en vano*** in vain
vapor *m* vapo(u)r; *de agua* steam; ***cocinar al vapor*** steam
vaporizar ⟨1f⟩ **1** *v/t* vaporize **2** *v/r* **vaporizarse** vaporize
vaporoso *adj* vaporous; *fig*: *vestido* gauzy, filmy
vapulear ⟨1a⟩ *v/t* beat up
vapuleo *m* beating
vaquería *f* dairy
vaquero 1 *adj tela* denim; ***pantalones vaqueros*** jeans **2** *m* cowboy, cowhand
vaquilla *f* heifer
vara *f* stick; TÉC rod; (*bastón de mando*) staff
varapalo *m* F (*contratiempo*) hitch F, setback
variable *adj* variable; *tiempo* changeable
variación *f* variation
variado *adj* varied
variar ⟨1c⟩ **1** *v/t* vary; (*cambiar*) change **2** *v/i* vary; (*cambiar*) change; ***para variar*** for a change
varice *f* MED varicose vein
varicela *f* MED chickenpox
variedad *f* variety; ***variedades*** *pl* vaudeville *sg*, *Br* variety *sg*
variopinto *adj* varied, diverse
varios *adj* several
varita *f*: ***varita mágica*** magic wand
variz *f* varicose vein
varón *m* man, male
varonil *adj* manly, virile
vas *vb* → ***ir***
vasallo *m* vassal
vasco 1 *adj* Basque; ***País Vasco*** Basque country **2** *m idioma* Basque **3** *m*, **-a** *f* Basque
Vascongadas *fpl* Basque country *sg*
vascuence *m* Basque
vascular *adj* ANAT vascular
vasectomía *f* MED vasectomy
vaselina *f* Vaseline®
vasija *f* container, vessel
vaso *m* glass; ANAT vessel
vasto *adj* vast
Vaticano *m* Vatican
vaticinar ⟨1a⟩ *v/t* predict, forecast
vaticinio *m* prediction, forecast
vatio *m* EL watt
vaya 1 *vb* → ***ir* 2** *int* well!
V.º B.º *abr* (**= *visto bueno***) approved, OK
Vd. *pron* → ***usted***
Vds. *pron* → ***usted***
ve *vb* → ***ir***, ***ver***
vea *vb* → ***ver***
vecindad *f Méx* poor area
vecindario *m* neighbo(u)rhood
vecino 1 *adj* neighbo(u)ring **2** *m*, **-a** *f* neighbo(u)r
vedado *m*: ***vedado de caza*** game reserve
vedar ⟨1a⟩ *v/t* ban, prohibit
vedette *f* star
vegetación *f* vegetation
vegetal 1 *adj* vegetable, plant *atr* **2** *m* vegetable
vegetar ⟨1a⟩ *v/i fig* vegetate
vegetariano 1 *adj* vegetarian **2** *m*, **-a** *f* vegetarian
vehemente *adj* vehement
vehículo *m tb fig* vehicle; MED carrier
veinte *m/adj* twenty
veintena *f* twenty; *aproximadamente* about twenty
vejación *f* humiliation
vejar ⟨1a⟩ *v/t* humiliate
vejestorio *m* F old fossil F, old relic F
vejez *f* old age
vejiga *f* ANAT bladder
vela *f para alumbrar* candle; DEP sailing; *de barco* sail; ***a toda vela*** F flat out F, all out F; ***estar a dos velas*** F be broke F; ***pasar la noche en vela*** stay up all night
velada *f* evening
velador *m L.Am. lámpara* bedlamp, *Br* bedside light; *Chi mueble* nightstand, *Br* bedside table
velar ⟨1a⟩ *v/i*: ***velar por algo*** look after sth
velatorio *m* wake
velcro® *m* Velcro
veleidad *f* fickleness
velero *m* MAR sailing ship
veleta 1 *f* weathervane **2** *m/f fig* weathercock
vello *m* (body) hair
velo *m* veil
velocidad *f* speed; (*marcha*) gear
velódromo *m* velodrome
veloz *adj* fast, speedy
ven *vb* → ***venir***
vena *f* ANAT vein; ***le dio la vena y lo hizo*** F she just upped and did it F; ***estar en vena*** F be on form
venado *m* ZO deer
vencedor 1 *adj* winning **2** *m*, **vencedora** *f* winner
vencejo *m* ZO swift
vencer ⟨2b⟩ **1** *v/t* defeat; *fig* (*superar*) overcome **2** *v/i* win; COM *de plazo etc* expire

vencido *adj*: ***darse por vencido*** admit defeat, give in; ***a la tercera va la -a*** third time lucky
vencimiento *m* expiration, *Br* expiry; *de bono* maturity
venda *f* bandage
vendaje *m* MED dressing
vendar ⟨1a⟩ *v/t* MED bandage, dress; ***vendar los ojos a alguien*** blindfold s.o.
vendaval *m* gale
vendedor *m*, **vendedora** *f* seller
vender ⟨2a⟩ **1** *v/t* sell; *fig* (*traicionar*) betray **2** *v/r* **venderse** sell o.s.; ***venderse al enemigo*** sell out to the enemy
vendimia *f* grape harvest
vendimiar ⟨1b⟩ *v/t uvas* harvest, pick
vendré *vb* → ***venir***
veneno *m* poison
venenoso *adj* poisonous
venerable *adj* venerable
venerar ⟨1a⟩ *v/t* venerate, worship
venéreo *adj* MED venereal
venezolano 1 *adj* Venezuelan **2** *m*, **-** *f* Venezuelan
Venezuela Venezuela
venga *vb* → ***venir***
venganza *f* vengeance, revenge
vengar ⟨1h⟩ **1** *v/t* avenge **2** *v/r* **vengarse** take revenge (***de*** on; ***por*** for)
vengativo *adj* vengeful
vengo *vb* → ***venir***
venir ⟨3s⟩ **1** *v/i* come; ***venir de España*** come from Spain; ***venir bien*** be convenient; ***venir mal*** be inconvenient; ***le vino una idea*** an idea occurred to him; ***viene a ser lo mismo*** it comes down to the same thing; ***el año que viene*** next year; ***¡venga!*** come on; ***¿a qué viene eso?*** why do you say that? **2** *v/r* **venirse**: ***venirse abajo*** collapse; *fig*: *de persona* fall apart, go to pieces
venta *f* sale; ***venta por correo*** *or* ***por catálogo*** mail order; ***venta al detalle*** *or* ***al por menor*** retail; ***en venta*** for sale
ventaja *f* advantage; DEP *en carrera*, *partido* lead; ***ventaja fiscal*** tax advantage
ventajoso *adj* advantageous
ventana *f* window; ***ventana de la nariz*** nostril
ventanilla *f* AVIA, AUTO, FERR window; MAR porthole
ventilación *f* ventilation
ventilador *m* fan
ventilar ⟨1a⟩ *v/t* air; *fig*: *problema* talk over; *opiniones* air
ventisca *f* blizzard
ventosa *f* ZO sucker
ventosidad *f* wind, flatulence
ventrílocuo *m* ventriloquist
veo *vb* → ***ver***
ver ⟨2v; *part* **visto** ⟩ **1** *v/t* see; *televisión* watch; JUR *pleito* hear; *L.Am.* (*mirar*) look at; ***está por ver*** it remains to be seen; ***no puede verla*** *fig* he can't stand the sight of her; ***no tiene nada que ver con*** it doesn't have anything to do with; ***¡a v[illegible]*** let's see; ***¡hay que ver!*** would you bel[illegible]e it!; ***ya veremos*** we'll see **2** *v/i* *L.*[illegible]*.* (*mirar*) look; ***ve aquí dentro*** *L*[illegible]*n.* look in here **3** *v/r* **verse** see o[illegible], (*encontrarse*) see one another; [illegible]***ibráse visto!*** would you believe it!; [illegible]***e las verá conmigo!*** F he'll have me [illegible]o deal with!
[illegible]**eranear** ⟨1a⟩ *v/i* spend the summer vacation *o Br* holidays
veraniego *adj* summer *atr*
verano *m* summer
veras *f*: ***de veras*** really, truly
verbal *adj* GRAM verbal
verbena *f* (*fiesta*) party
verbo *m* GRAM verb
verborrea *f desp* verbosity
verdad *f* truth; ***a decir verdad*** to tell the truth; ***de verdad*** real, proper; ***no te gusta, ¿verdad?*** you don't like it, do you?; ***vas a venir, ¿verdad?*** you're coming, aren't you?; ***es verdad*** it's true, it's the truth
verdadero *adj* true; (*cierto*) real
verde 1 *adj* green; *fruta* unripe; F *chiste* blue, dirty; ***viejo verde*** dirty old man; ***poner verde a alguien*** F criticize s.o. **2** *m* green; ***los verdes*** POL the Greens
verdoso *adj* greenish
verdugo *m* executioner
verdulería *f* fruit and vegetable store, *Br* greengrocer's
verdura *f*: **verdura(s)** (*hortalizas*) greens *pl*, (green) vegetables *pl*
vereda *f S. Am.* sidewalk, *Br* pavement; ***meter alguien en vereda*** *fig* put s.o. back on the straight and narrow, bring s.o. into line
veredicto *m* JUR, *fig* verdict
verga *f* rod
vergel *m* orchard
vergonzoso *adj* disgraceful, shameful; (*tímido*) shy
vergüenza *f* shame; (*escándalo*) disgrace; ***me da vergüenza*** I'm embarrassed; ***es una vergüenza*** it's a disgrace; ***no sé cómo no se te cae la cara de vergüenza*** you should be ashamed (of yourself)
vericuetos *mpl fig* twists and turns
verídico *adj* true
verificar ⟨1g⟩ *v/t* verify
verja *f* railing; (*puerta*) iron gate

vermúí, **vermut** *m* vermouth
verosímil *adj* realistic; (*creíble*) plausible
verruga *f* wart
versado *adj* well-versed (***en*** in)
versar ⟨1a⟩ *v/i*: ***versar sobre*** deal with, be about
versátil *adj* fickle; *artista* versatile
versículo *m* verse
versión *f* version; ***en versión original*** *película* original language version
verso *m* verse
vértebra *f* ANAT vertebra
vertedero *m* dump, tip
verter ⟨2g⟩ *v/t* dump; (*derramar*) spill; *fig*: *opinión* voice
vertical *adj* vertical
vertido *m* dumping; ***vertidos*** *pl* waste *sg*
vertiente *f L.Am.* (*cuesta*) slope; (*lado*) side
vertiginoso *adj* dizzy; (*rápido*) frantic
vértigo *m* MED vertigo; ***darle a alguien vértigo*** make s.o. dizzy
vesícula *f* blister; ***vesícula biliar*** ANAT gall-bladder
vespa® *f* motorscooter
vestíbulo *m de casa* hall; *de edifico púíblico* lobby
vestido *m* dress; *L.Am. de hombre* suit
vestigio *m* vestige, trace
vestir ⟨3l⟩ **1** *v/t* dress; (*llevar puesto*) wear **2** *v/i* dress; ***vestir de negro*** wear black, dress in black; ***vestir de uniforme*** wear a uniform **3** *v/r* **vestirse** get dressed; (*disfrazarse*) dress up; ***vestirse de algo*** wear sth
vestuario *m* DEP locker room; TEA wardrobe
veta *f* MIN vein
vetar ⟨1a⟩ *v/t* POL veto
veterano 1 *adj* veteran; (*experimentado*) experienced **2** *m*, **-a** *f* veteran
veterinario 1 *adj* veterinary **2** *m*, **-a** *f* veterinarian, vet
veto *m* veto
vetusto *adj* ancient
vez *f* time; ***a la vez*** at the same time; ***a su vez*** for his / her part; ***cada vez que*** every time that; ***de vez en cuando*** from time to time; ***en vez de*** instead of; ***érase una vez*** once upon a time, there was; ***otra vez*** again; ***tal vez*** perhaps, maybe; ***una vez*** once; ***a veces*** sometimes; ***muchas veces*** (*con frecuencia*) often; ***hacer las veces de*** *de objeto* serve as; *de persona* act as
vi *vb* → ***ver***
vía 1 *f* FERR track; ***vía estrecha*** FERR narrow gauge; ***darle vía libre a alguien*** give s.o. a free hand; ***por vía aérea*** by air; ***en vías de*** *fig* in the process of **2** *prp* via
viable *adj plan, solución* viable, feasible
viaducto *m* viaduct
viajante *m/f* sales rep
viajar ⟨1a⟩ *v/i* travel
viaje *m* trip, journey; ***viaje organizado*** package tour; ***viaje de ida*** outward journey; ***viaje de ida y vuelta*** round trip; ***viaje de novios*** honeymoon; ***viaje de vuelta*** return journey
viajero *m*, **-a** *f* travel(l)er
viario *adj* road *atr*; ***educación -a*** instruction in road safety
víbora *f tb fig* viper
vibración *f* vibration
vibrante *adj fig* exciting
vibrar ⟨1a⟩ *v/t* vibrate
vicaría *f* pastor's house, vicarage; ***pasar por la vicaría*** F get married in church
vicecónsul *m* vice-consul
vicepresidente *m*, **-a** *f* POL vice-president; COM vice-president, *Br* deputy chairman
vicerrector *m* vice-rector
viceversa *adv*: ***y viceversa*** and vice versa
viciado *adj aire* stuffy
viciarse ⟨1b⟩ *v/r* fall into bad habits
vicio *m* vice; ***pasarlo de vicio*** F have a great time F
vicioso *adj* vicious; (*corrompido*) depraved
vicisitudes *fpl* ups and downs
víctima *f* victim
victimar ⟨1a⟩ *v/t L.Am.* kill
victoria *f* victory; ***cantar victoria*** claim victory
victorioso *adj* victorious
vicuña *f* ZO vicuna
vid *f* vine
vida *f* life; *esp* TÉC life span; ***de por vida*** for life; ***en mi vida*** never (in my life); ***ganarse la vida*** earn a living; ***hacer la vida imposible a alguien*** make s.o.'s life impossible; ***vida mía*** my love
vidente *m/f* seer, clairvoyant
vídeo *m* video
videocámara *f* video camera
videocas(s)et(t)e *m* video cassette
videoclip *m* pop video
videoconferencia *f* video conference
videojuego *m* video game
videotex(to) *m* videotext
vidriera *f L.Am.* shop window
vidrio *m L.Am.* glass; (*ventana*) window
vieira *f* ZO scallop
vieja *f* old woman
viejo 1 *adj* old **2** *m* old man; ***mis viejos*** F my folks F
viendo *vb* → ***ver***
viene *vb* → ***venir***

viento *m* wind; ***viento en popa*** *fig* F splendidly; ***contra viento y marea*** *fig* come what may; ***hacer viento*** be windy; ***proclamar a los cuatro vientos*** *fig* shout from the rooftops
vientre *m* belly
viernes *m inv* Friday; ***Viernes Santo*** Good Friday
Vietnam Vietnam
vietnamita *adj & m/f* Vietnamese
viga *f* beam, girder
vigente *adj legislación* in force
vigésimo *adj* twentieth
vigilante 1 *adj* watchful, vigilant **2** *m L.Am.* policeman; ***vigilante nocturno*** night watchman; ***vigilante jurado*** security guard
vigilar ⟨1a⟩ **1** *v/i* keep watch **2** *v/t* watch; *a un preso* guard
vigor *m* vigo(u)r; ***en vigor*** in force
vigoroso *adj* vigorous
vil *adj* vile, despicable
vilipendiar ⟨1b⟩ *v/t* insult, vilify *fml*; (*despreciar*) revile
villa *f* town
villancico *m* Christmas carol
villano 1 *adj* villainous **2** *m*, **-a** *f* villain
vilo: ***en vilo*** in the air; *fig* in suspense, on tenterhooks; ***levantar en vilo*** lift off the ground; ***tener a alguien en vilo*** *fig* keep s.o. in suspense *o* on tenterhooks
vinagre *m* vinegar
vinagrera *f* vinegar bottle; *S. Am.* (*indigestión*) indigestion; ***vinagreras*** *pl* cruet *sg*
vinagreta *f* vinaigrette
vincha *f S. Am.* hairband
vinculante *adj* binding
vincular ⟨1a⟩ *v/t* link (***a*** to); (*comprometer*) bind
vínculo *m* link; *fig* (*relación*) tie, bond
vindicar ⟨1g⟩ *v/t* vindicate
vine *vb* → ***venir***
vinícola *adj región, país* wine-growing *atr*; *industria* wine-making *atr*
viniendo *vb* → ***venir***
vinicultura *f* wine-growing
vino 1 *m* wine; ***vino blanco*** white wine; ***vino de mesa*** table wine; ***vino tinto*** red wine **2** *vb* → ***venir***
viña *f* vineyard
viñatero *m*, **-a** *f S. Am.* wine grower
viñedo *m* vineyard
viñeta *f* TIP vignette
vio *vb* → ***ver***
viola *f* MÚS viola
violación *f* rape; *de derechos* violation
violador *m*, **violadora** *f* rapist
violar ⟨1a⟩ *v/t* rape
violencia *f* violence
violentar ⟨1a⟩ *v/t puerta* force; (*incomodar*) embarrass
violento *adj* violent; (*embarazoso*) embarrassing; *persona* embarrassed
violeta 1 *f* BOT violet **2** *m/adj* violet
violín *m* violin
violinista *m/f* violinist
violonc(h)elo *m* cello
VIP *m* VIP
viperino *adj* malicious; ***lengua -a*** sharp tongue
viral *adj* viral
virar ⟨1a⟩ *v/t* MAR, AVIA turn
virgen 1 *adj* virgin; *cinta* blank; ***lana virgen*** pure new wool **2** *f* virgin
virginidad *f* virginity
Virgo *m/f inv* ASTR Virgo
virguería *f*: ***hace virguerías*** P he's a whizz F
vírico *adj* viral
viril *adj* virile, manly
virtual *adj* virtual
virtud *f* virtue; ***en virtud de*** by virtue of
virtuoso 1 *adj* virtuous **2** *m*, **-a** *f* virtuoso
viruela *f* MED smallpox
virulento *adj* MED, *fig* virulent
virus *m inv* MED virus; ***virus informático*** computer virus
viruta *f* shaving
visa *f L.Am.* visa
visado *m* visa
vísceras *fpl* guts, entrails
visceral *adj fig* gut *atr*, visceral
viscoso *adj* viscous
visera *f de gorra* peak; *de casco* visor
visibilidad *f* visibility
visible *adj* visible; *fig* evident, obvious
visillo *m* sheer, *Br* net curtain
visión *f* vision, sight; *fig* vision; (*opinión*) view; ***tener visión de futuro*** be forward looking
visita *f* visit; ***visita a domicilio*** house call; ***visita guiada*** guided tour; ***hacer una visita a alguien*** visit s.o.
visitante 1 *adj* visiting; DEP away **2** *m/f* visitor
visitar ⟨1a⟩ *v/t* visit
vislumbrar ⟨1a⟩ *v/t* glimpse
visos *mpl*: ***tener visos de*** show signs of
visón *m* ZO mink
víspera *f* eve; ***en vísperas de*** on the eve of
vista *f* (eye)sight; JUR hearing; ***vista cansada*** MED tired eyes; ***a la vista*** COM at sight, on demand; ***a primera vista*** at first sight; ***con vistas a*** with a view to; ***en vista de*** in view of; ***hasta la vista*** bye!, see you!; ***hacer la vista gorda*** *fig* F turn a

V

blind eye; ***tener vista para algo*** *fig* have a good eye for sth; ***volver la vista atrás*** *tb fig* look back
vistazo *m* look; ***echar un vistazo a*** take a (quick) look at
viste *vb* → ***ver, vestir***
visto 1 *part* → ***ver* 2** *adj*: ***está bien visto*** it's the done thing; ***está mal visto*** it's not done, it's not the done thing; ***está visto que*** it's obvious that; ***estar muy visto*** be old hat, not be original; ***por lo visto*** apparently **3** *m* check(mark), *Br* tick; ***dar el visto bueno*** give one's approval
vistoso *adj* eye-catching
visual *adj* visual
visualizar ⟨1f⟩ *v/t* visualize; *en pantalla* display
vital *adj* vital; *persona* lively
vitalicio *adj* life *atr*, for life; ***renta -a*** life annuity
vitalidad *f* vitality, liveliness
vitamina *f* vitamin
viticultor *m*, **viticultora** *f* wine grower
vitores *mpl* cheers, acclaim *sg*
vitorear ⟨1a⟩ *v/t* cheer
vítreo *adj* vitreous
vitrificar ⟨1g⟩ *v/t* vitrify
vitrina *f* display cabinet; *L.Am.* shop window
vitrocerámica *f* ceramic hob
vituperar ⟨1a⟩ *v/t* condemn
viuda *f* widow
viudedad *f* widowhood; ***pensión de viudedad*** widow's pension
viudo 1 *adj* widowed **2** *m* widower; ***quedarse viudo*** be widowed
viva *int* hurrah!; ***¡viva el rey!*** long live the king!
vivaz *adj* bright, sharp
vivencia *f* experience
víveres *mpl* provisions
vívido *adj* vivid
vivienda *f* housing; (*casa*) house
vivir ⟨3a⟩ **1** *v/t* live through, experience **2** *v/i* live; ***vivir de algo*** live on sth
vivo *adj* alive; *color* bright; *ritmo* lively; *fig* F sharp, smart
vocabulario *m* vocabulary
vocación *f* vocation
vocal 1 *m/f* member **2** *f* vowel
vocalista *m/f* vocalist
vocalizar ⟨1f⟩ *v/i* vocalize
voceador *m*, **voceadora** *f Méx* newspaper vendor
vocerío *m* uproar
vocero *m*, **-a** *f esp L.Am.* spokesperson
vociferar ⟨1a⟩ *v/i* shout
vodka *m* vodka
volador *adj* flying
volandas: ***en volandas*** *fig* in the air
volante 1 *adj* flying **2** *m* AUTO steering wheel; *de vestido* flounce; MED referral (slip)
volar ⟨1m⟩ **1** *v/i* fly; *fig* vanish **2** *v/t* fly; *edificio* blow up
volátil *adj tb fig* volatile
volatilizarse ⟨1f⟩ *v/r fig* vanish into thin air
volcán *m* volcano
volcánico *adj* volcanic
volcar ⟨1g & 1m⟩ **1** *v/t* knock over; (*vaciar*) empty; *barco, coche* overturn **2** *v/i de coche, barco* overturn **3** *v/r* **volcarse** tip over; ***volcarse por alguien*** F bend over backwards for s.o., go out of one's way for s.o.; ***volcarse en algo*** throw o.s. into sth
volea *f tenis* volley
voleibol *m* volleyball
voleo *m*: ***a voleo*** at random
voley-playa *m* beach volleyball
voltaje *m* EL voltage
voltear ⟨1a⟩ **1** *v/t L.Am.* (*invertir*) turn over; *Rpl* (*tumbar*) knock over; ***voltear el jersey*** turn the sweater inside out; ***voltear la cabeza*** turn one's head **2** *v/i* roll over; *de campanas* ring out
voltereta *f* somersault
voltio *m* EL volt
voluble *adj* erratic, unpredictable
volumen *m* TIP, MÚS, RAD volume; ***volumen de negocios*** COM turnover
voluntad *f* will; ***buena / mala voluntad*** good / ill will
voluntario 1 *adj* volunteer **2** *m*, **-a** *f* volunteer
voluntarioso *adj* willing, enthusiastic
voluptuoso *adj* voluptuous
volver ⟨2h; *part* **vuelto**⟩ **1** *v/t página, mirada etc* turn (***a*** to; ***hacia*** toward); ***volver loco*** drive crazy **2** *v/i* return; ***volver a hacer algo*** do sth again **3** *v/r* **volverse** turn round; ***volverse loco*** go crazy
vomitar ⟨1a⟩ **1** *v/t* throw up; *lava* hurl, throw out **2** *v/i* throw up, be sick; ***tengo ganas de vomitar*** I feel nauseous, *Br* I feel sick
vómito *m* MED vomit
vorágine *f* (*remolino*) whirlpool; *fig* whirl
voraz *adj* voracious; *incendio* fierce
vos *pron pers sg Rpl, C.Am., Ven* you
vosotros, **vosotras** *pron pers pl* you
votación *f* vote, ballot
votar ⟨1a⟩ **1** *v/t* (*aprobar*) vote **2** *v/i* vote
voto *m* POL vote; ***voto en blanco*** spoiled ballot paper
voy *vb* → ***ir***
voz *f* voice; *fig* rumo(u)r; ***voz activa / pa-***

siva GRAM active / passive voice; ***a media voz*** in a hushed voice, in a low voice; ***a voz en grito*** at the top of one's voice; ***en voz alta*** aloud; ***en voz baja*** in a low voice; ***correr la voz*** spread the word; ***llevar la voz cantante*** *fig* call the tune, call the shots; ***no tener voz ni voto*** *fig* not have a say; ***voz en off*** voice-over

vuelco 1 *vb* → ***volcar*** **2** *m*: ***dar un vuelco*** *fig* F take a dramatic turn; ***me dio un vuelco el corazón*** my heart missed a beat

vuelo 1 *vb* → ***volar*** **2** *m* flight; ***vuelo chárter*** charter flight; ***vuelo nacional*** domestic flight; ***al vuelo*** *coger, cazar* in mid-air; ***una falda con vuelo*** a full skirt

vuelta *f* return; *en carrera* lap; ***vuelta de carnero*** *L.Am.* half-somersault; ***vuelta al mundo*** round-the- world trip; ***a la vuelta*** on the way back; ***a la vuelta de la esquina*** *fig* just around the corner; ***dar la vuelta*** *llave etc* turn; ***dar media vuelta*** turn round; ***dar una vuelta*** go for a walk; ***dar cien vueltas a alguien*** F be a hundred times better than s.o. F

vuelto 1 *part* → ***volver*** **2** *m L.Am.* change

vuelvo *vb* → ***volver***

vuestro 1 *adj pos* your **2** *pron* yours

vulgar *adj* vulgar, common; *abundante* common

vulgaridad *f* vulgarity

vulgo *m* lower classes *pl*

vulnerable *adj* vulnerable

w. *abr* (**= *watio***) w (= watt)

walkman *m* personal stereo

wáter *m* bathroom, toilet

waterpolo *m* DEP water polo

WC *abr* WC

whisky *m* whiskey, *Br* whisky

windsurf(ing) *m* wind-surfing

windsurfista *m/f* windsurfer

X, Y

xenofobia *f* xenophobia

xilófono *m* MÚS xylophone

y *conj* and

ya *adv* already; (*ahora mismo*) now; ***¡ya!*** *incredulidad* oh, yeah!, sure!; *comprensión* I know, I understand; *asenso* OK, sure; *al terminar* finished!, done!; ***ya no vive aquí*** he doesn't live here any more, he no longer lives here; ***ya que*** since, as; ***ya lo sé*** I know; ***ya viene*** she's coming now; ***¿lo puede hacer? – ¡ya lo creo!*** can she do it? - you bet!; ***ya ... ya ...*** either … or …

yacaré *m L.Am.* ZO cayman

yacer ⟨2y⟩ *v/i* lie

yacimiento *m* MIN deposit

yanqui *m/f* Yankee

yapa *f L.Am.* bit extra (for free); *Pe, Bol* (*propina*) tip

yate *m* yacht

yaya *f* grandma

yayo *m* grandpa

yedra *f* BOT ivy

yegua *f* ZO mare

yema *f* yolk; ***yema del dedo*** fingertip

yendo *vb* → ***ir***

yerba *f L.Am.* grass; ***yerba mate*** maté

yerbatero *m*, **-a** *f Rpl* herbalist

yerno *m* son-in-law

yeso *m* plaster

yo *pron* I; ***soy yo*** it's me; ***yo que túí*** if I were you

yodo *m* iodine

yoga *m* yoga

yogur *m* yog(h)urt

yonqui *m/f* F junkie

yuca *f* BOT yucca
yugo *m* yoke
Yugoslavia Yugoslavia
yugoslavo 1 *adj* Yugoslav(ian) **2** *m*, **-a** *f* Yugoslav(ian)
yugular *adj* ANAT jugular
yute *m* jute
yuxtaposición *f* juxtaposition
yuyo *m L.Am.* weed

Z

zacatal *m C.Am.*, *Méx* pasture
zacate *m C.Am.*, *Méx* fodder
zafarse ⟨1a⟩ *v/r* get away (***de*** from); (*soltarse*) come undone; ***zafarse de algo*** (*evitar*) get out of sth
zafio *adj* coarse
zafiro *m* sapphire
zaga *f*: ***ir a la zaga*** bring up the rear
zalamero 1 *adj* flattering; *empalagoso* syrupy, sugary **2** *m*, **-a** *f* flatterer, sweet talker
zamba *f Arg* (*baile*) *Argentinian folk-dance*
zambomba *f* MÚS *type of drum*
zambullirse ⟨3h⟩ *v/r* dive (***en*** into); *fig* throw o.s. (***en*** into), immerse o.s. (***en*** in)
zamparse ⟨1a⟩ *v/r* F wolf down F
zanahoria *f* carrot
zancada *f* stride
zancadilla *f fig* obstacle; ***poner*** *or* ***echar la zancadilla a alguien*** trip s.o. up
zancudo *m L.Am.* mosquito
zángano *m* ZO drone; *fig* F lazybones *sg*
zanja *f* ditch
zanjar ⟨1a⟩ *v/t fig problemas* settle; *dificultades* overcome
zapatería *f* shoe store, shoe shop
zapatero *m*, **-a** *f* shoemaker; ***zapatero remendón*** shoe mender
zapatilla *f* slipper; *de deporte* sneaker, *Br* trainer
Zapatista *m/f Méx member or supporter of the Zapatista National Liberation Army*
zapato *m* shoe
zapear ⟨1a⟩ *v/i* TV F channel hop
zapeo, **zapping** *m* TV F channel hopping
zarandear ⟨1a⟩ *v/t* shake violently, buffet; ***zarandear a alguien*** *fig* give s.o. a hard time
zarpa *f* paw
zarpar ⟨1a⟩ *v/i* MAR set sail (***para*** for)
zarza *f* BOT bramble
zarzamora *f* BOT blackberry
zarzuela *f* MÚS *type of operetta*
zascandilear ⟨1a⟩ *v/i* mess around
zigzaguear ⟨1a⟩ *v/i* zigzag
zinc *m* zinc
zócalo *m* baseboard, *Br* skirting board
zodíaco, **zodiaco** *m* AST zodiac
zona *f* area, zone
zoncería *f L.Am.* F stupid thing
zonzo *adj L.Am.* F stupid
zoo *m* zoo
zoológico 1 *adj* zoological **2** *m* zoo
zoom *m* FOT zoom
zopilote *m L.Am.* ZO turkey buzzard
zorra *f* ZO vixen; P whore P
zorro 1 *adj* sly, crafty **2** *m* ZO fox; *fig* old fox
zozobrar ⟨1a⟩ *v/i* MAR overturn; *fig* go under
zueco *m* clog
zulo *m* hiding place
zumba *f L.Am.*, *Méx* (*paliza*) beating
zumbar ⟨1a⟩ **1** *v/i* buzz; ***me zumban los oídos*** my ears are ringing *o* buzzing **2** *v/t golpe*, *bofetada* give
zumbido *m* buzzing
zumo *m* juice
zurcir ⟨3b⟩ *v/t calcetines* darn; *chaqueta*, *pantalones* patch
zurdo 1 *adj* left-handed **2** *m*, *f* left-hander
zurrar ⟨1a⟩ *v/t* TÉC tan; ***zurrar a alguien*** F tan s.o.'s hide F

Activity & Reference Section

The following section contains three parts, each of which will help you in your learning:

Games and puzzles to help you learn to use this dictionary and practice your Spanish-language skills. You'll learn about the different features of this dictionary and how to look something up effectively.

Basic words and expressions to reinforce your learning and help you master the basics.

A short grammar reference to help you use the language correctly.

Using Your Dictionary

Using a bilingual dictionary is important if you want to speak, read or write in a foreign language. Unfortunately, if you don't understand the symbols in your dictionary or the format of the entries, you'll make mistakes.

What kind of mistakes? Think of some of the words you know in English that sound or look alike. For example, think about the word *ring*. How many meanings can you think of for this word, *ring*? Try to list at least three.

a. ______________________________

b. ______________________________

c. ______________________________

Now look up *ring* in the English side of the dictionary. There are nine Spanish words that correspond to the single English word *ring*. Some of these Spanish words are listed below in scrambled form.

Unscramble the jumbled Spanish words, then draw a line connecting each Spanish word with of the appropriate English meaning.

Spanish jumble	***English meanings***
1. ROSNA	**a.** a circle around something
2. LONAIL	**b.** the action of a bell or telephone (to ring)
3. ATSPI	**c.** jewelry worn on the finger
4. NOOT	**d.** the boxing venue
5. GNRI	**e.** one of the venues at a circus
6. LÍCCURO	**f.** the ring or tone of someone's voice

With so many Spanish words, each meaning something different, you must be careful to choose the right one. Using the wrong definition can obscure your meaning. Imagine the bizarre and misleading sentences you would make if you never looked beyond the first definition.

For example:

The boxer wearily entered the circle.

She always wore the circle left to her by her grandmother.

I was waiting for the phone circle when there was a knock at the door.

If you choose the wrong definition, you simply won't be understood. Mistakes like these are easy to avoid, once you know what to look for when using your dictionary. The following pages will review the structure of your bilingual dictionary and show you how to pick the right word when you use it. Read the tips and guidelines, then complete the puzzles and exercises to practice what you have learned.

Identifying Headwords

If you are looking for a single word in the dictionary, you simply look for that word's location in alphabetical order. However, if you are looking for a phrase, or an object that is described by several words, you will have to decide which word to look up.

Two-word terms are listed by their first word. If you are looking for the Spanish equivalent of *shooting star*, you will find it under *shooting*.

So-called phrasal verbs in English are found in a block under the main verb. The phrasal verbs *go ahead*, *go back*, *go off*, *go on*, *go out*, and *go up* are all found in a block after *go*.

Idiomatic expressions are found under the key word in the expression. The phrase *give someone a ring*, meaning to call someone, is found in the entry for *ring*.

Feminine headwords that are variants of a masculine headword and share a meaning with the masculine word will be found in alphabetical order with their masculine counterpart. In Spanish a male lawyer is called an **abogado** and a female lawyer is an **abogada**. Both of the words are found in alphabetical order under the masculine form, **abogado**.

Find the following words and phrases in your bilingual dictionary. Identify the headword under which you should look for each. Then, try to find all of the headwords in the word-search puzzle on the next page.

1. in the middle of

2. be in shock

3. break in

4. dog

5. bring up

6. string someone along

7. be in jeopardy

8. get away with it

9. that's a relief

10. take advantage of

11. bailarín

12. tan pronto como

13. sin duda

14. colgar de un hilo

15. menos mal

z	h	r	u	o	v	ó	l	x	q	r	e	r	p	o	u	j	k
u	g	e	d	u	a	v	c	l	x	f	í	u	e	t	e	c	i
í	a	e	z	ó	v	c	d	e	ñ	u	i	a	j	l	j	k	u
m	e	q	t	b	a	h	g	l	w	a	o	á	e	p	i	r	y
e	é	w	c	i	o	a	p	f	m	l	r	g	o	h	r	e	s
k	n	k	b	g	t	y	z	o	i	u	n	i	p	b	s	h	f
c	f	ñ	i	n	g	b	s	h	z	i	d	r	a	a	i	g	e
í	s	e	a	d	n	r	f	e	r	e	a	á	r	i	y	n	t
u	e	v	o	l	u	e	r	t	a	e	l	d	d	l	o	o	r
s	d	e	n	u	m	a	s	ó	m	s	e	z	y	a	e	t	y
a	h	d	s	o	i	k	b	r	i	n	g	w	o	r	l	m	s
ñ	e	o	d	q	m	i	d	d	l	e	j	d	l	í	r	a	q
b	d	g	c	o	r	g	l	e	y	d	n	i	o	n	u	l	l
e	z	g	n	k	z	w	a	c	s	u	n	s	e	i	e	a	f
l	w	y	u	f	v	e	ó	o	i	d	a	i	l	q	r	t	g
c	é	f	g	i	r	a	m	l	o	a	c	e	d	u	i	á	a
a	n	r	y	t	e	i	s	e	g	p	r	o	n	t	o	a	w
u	ñ	a	c	a	s	n	e	l	e	h	s	e	s	g	r	d	ó

Alphabetization

The entries in a bilingual dictionary are in alphabetical order. They are ordered from A to Z for each language. If words begin with the same letter or letters, they are alphabetized from A to Z using the first unique letter in each word.

Practice alphabetizing the following words. Rewrite the words in alphabetical order, using the space provided below. Next to each word also write the number that is associated with it. Then follow that order to connect the dots on the next page. Not all of the dots will be used, only those whose numbers appear in the word list.

universo	**1**	fecha	**48**
sueño	**2**	hasta	**57**
ciudad	**3**	calle	**59**
escuela	**4**	repente	**60**
nos	**7**	hoy	**62**
aquí	**8**	bastante	**65**
entender	**9**	mágico	**74**
disfraz	**10**	mañana	**75**
cuchillo	**15**	vida	**76**
jamás	**16**	algo	**77**
lente	**17**	zapato	**77**
tiempo	**20**	marrón	**79**
boleta	**21**	pie	**81**
nadie	**23**	otro	**82**
dulce	**27**	miel	**84**
más	**30**	lavaplatos	**86**
corazón	**41**	gritar	**87**
piel	**42**	miedo	**93**
así	**44**	flor	**95**
silla	**45**	despacio	**99**
llover	**46**		

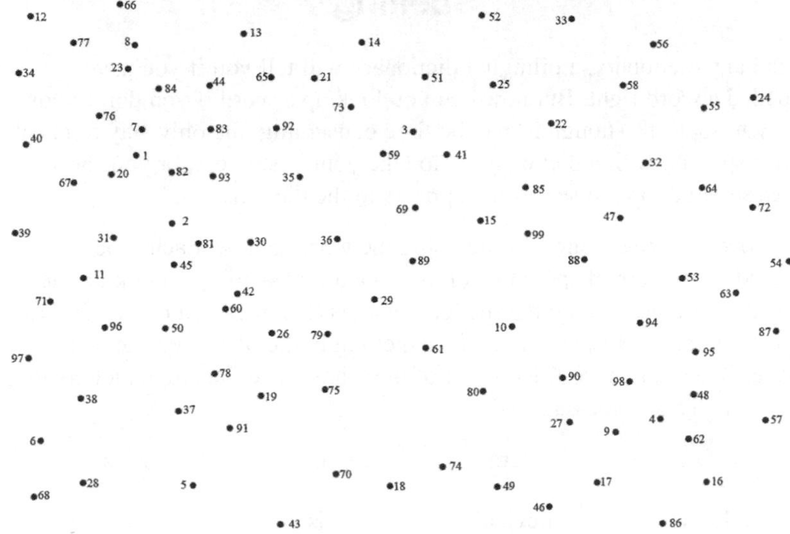

¿Qué país ve Ud.?

________ ________ ________ ________ ________ ________

Spelling

Like any dictionary, a bilingual dictionary will tell you if you have spelled a word right. But how can you look up a word if you don't know how to spell it? Though it may be time consuming, the only way to check your spelling with a dictionary is to take your best guess, or your best guesses, and look to see which appears in the dictionary.

Practice checking your spelling using the words below. Each group includes one correct spelling and three incorrect spellings. Look up the words and cross out the misspelled versions (the ones you do not find in the dictionary). Rewrite the correct spelling in the blanks on the next page. When you have filled in all of the blanks, use the circled letters to reveal a mystery message.

1. esfara	esfera	esfira	esfura
2. devisa	deviza	divisa	diviza
3. mendir	mentir	mindir	mintir
4. viata	viota	viuda	viuta
5. abagado	apagedo	apagado	apadato
6. paor	peor	pior	pour
7. mammeca	manmeca	mandeca	manteca
8. jarbín	jardén	jardín	jartiín
9. corana	corena	corona	coruna

1. ___ ___ ___ (___) ___ ___

2. ___ ___ ___ ___ (___) ___

3. ___ ___ ___ (___) ___ ___

4. ___ ___ (___) ___ ___

5. ___ (___) ___ ___ ___ ___ ___

6. ___ (___) ___ ___

7. ___ ___ (___) ___ ___ ___ ___

8. ___ ___ ___ (___) ___ ___

9. ___ ___ ___ (___) ___ ___

¡ ___ ___ ___ ___ ___ ___ ___ ___ ___!
1 2 3 4 5 6 7 8 9

Entries in Context

In addition to the literal translation of each headword in the dictionary, entries sometimes include phrases using that word.

Solve the crossword puzzle below using the correct word in context.

Hint: Each clue contains key words that will help you find the answer. Look up the key words in each clue. You'll find the answers in expressions within each entry.

ACROSS

4. The sticker in the no smoking section read "**prohibido** ____________."

5. The students read the story aloud. They read **en** _________ **alta**.

7. They wished us Merry Christmas, or _________ **Navidad**.

8. En primer ____________, he got off to a rough start. And in the second place, the competition was stiff.

9. The food was vacuum packed. **Fue envasado al** ________________.

11. I wondered what time it was; I asked a friend, "**¿Qué** ________ **es?**"

12. Hey! That's none of your business! **No es** ____________ **tuyo.**

16. ¿Gracias? Oh, don't mention it. **No** _________ **de qué.**

17. Oh, no! **Qué** ______________. What a shame!

DOWN

1. She had lost her lighter, so she asked her friend for a light, "**¿Tienes** _________**?**"

2. It's pouring rain! **Está lloviendo a** __________.

3. He plans to be in the lead soon. **Va a estar en** _____________.

5. Do you dine out once in a while? Sure, **de** ________ **en cuando.**

6. Tonight she will pick out her clothes and pack her bags (**hacer la** __________). Tomorrow she is leaving on vacation.

10. They have open-air seating on the patio, if you'd prefer to dine **al** ____________ **libre**.

11. __________ **en día** (nowadays), many women have careers. This may not have been the case for previous generations.

13. The weather is nice. It's sunny out. **Hace** ________.

14. Good night. **¡Buenas** ___________! See you again tomorrow.

15. You wonder if it is worth all the trouble? I think so. **En mi opinion, vale la** _____________.

1 2 3 4 5 6 7 8 9 10 11 12 13 14 15 16 17

Word Families

Some English words have several related meanings that are represented by different words in Spanish. These related meanings belong to the same word family and are grouped together under a single English headword. Other words, while they look the same, do not belong to the same word family. These words are written under a separate headword.

Think back to our first example, *ring*. The translations **círculo**, **anillo**, and **pista** all refer to related meanings of *ring* in English. They are all circular things, though in different contexts. **Timbrazo**, **dar un telefonazo a alguien**, and **sonar**, however, refer to a totally different meaning of *ring* in English: the sound a bell or phone makes.

The word family for circles, with all of its nuanced Spanish translations, is grouped together under *ring*[1]. The word family for sounds is grouped together under *ring*[2].

Study the lists of words below. Each group includes three Spanish translations belonging to one word family, and one Spanish translation of an identical-looking but unrelated English word. Eliminate the translation that is not in the same word family as the others. Then rewrite the misfit word in the corresponding blanks. When you have filled in all of the blanks, use the circled letters to reveal a bonus message.

Hint: Look up the Spanish words to find out what they mean. Then look up those words in the English-Spanish side of your dictionary to find the word family that contains the Spanish words.

1. encender	iluminar	ligero	luz
2. atasco	aprieto	embutir	mermelada
3. a juego	fósforo	igualar	partida
4. estampilla	patear	sello	timbre
5. anillo	cuadrilátero	pista	timbrazo

1. 

2. 

3. ___ ___ (___) ___ ___ ___ ___

4. ___ ___ (___) ___ ___ ___

5. ___ ___ ___ ___ ___ ___ ___ (___)

___ ___ ___ ___ ___

1 2 3 4 5

Regional variation

Spanish is a world language with several regional variants. Historical change and influence have produced diverse vocabularies across the Spanish-speaking world.

This dictionary leaves universal words unmarked. Words specific to a particular country or region are marked with abbreviations for that location. For example, words used only in Central America are marked in the dictionary with **C.Am**. Vocabulary used only in Mexico is marked with the abbreviation **Méx**, and so forth. A full list of these abbreviations is found on pages 10–11.

Look up the following words and indicate the regional or country affiliation in each box.

carro	majada	tuna	pelazón	abarrotes
afanar	papa	rebasar	terno	abalear
choclo	ñapa	corotos	chichera	chompa
chicha	frutilla	huachafo	egreso	okupa
plática	vecindad	hilachos	mañero	guanaco

If this puzzle were a BINGO card, which country or region would win?

____

Running Heads

Running heads are the words printed in blue at the top of each page. The running head on the left tells you the first headword on the left-hand page. The running head on the right tells you the last headword on the right-hand page. All the words that fall in alphabetical order between the two running heads appear on those two dictionary pages.

Look up the running head on the page where each headword appears, and write it in the space provided. Then unscramble the jumbled running heads and match them with what you wrote.

Headword	***Running head***	***Jumbled running head***
1. apenas	APAGAR	FOLOCNÓ
2. bombilla	__________	CILIMO
3. cómodo	__________	ÍTFICNOPE
4. famoso	__________	SUTOJ
5. joven	__________	MOOSS
6. magia	__________	RAAGAP
7. minuto	__________	OOPCA
8. oreja	__________	CEHILBO
9. polvo	__________	DARALSATR
10. sorna	__________	NEIVE
11. transición	__________	GIAAM
12. vetusto	__________	CAHFAAD

Parts of Speech

In Spanish and English, words are categorized into different ***parts of speech***. These labels tell us what function a word performs in a sentence. In this dictionary, the part of speech is given before a word's definition.

Nouns are things. ***Verbs*** describe actions. ***Adjectives*** describe nouns in sentences. For example, the adjective *pretty* tells you about the noun *girl* in the phrase *a pretty girl*. ***Adverbs*** also describe, but they modify verbs, adjectives, and other adverbs. The adverb *quickly* tells you more about how the action is carried out in the phrase *ran quickly*.

Prepositions specify relationships in time and space. They are words such as *in*, *on*, *before*, or *with*. ***Articles*** are words that accompany nouns. Words like *the* and *a* or *an* modify the noun, marking it as specific or general, and known or unknown.

Conjunctions are words like *and*, *but*, and *if* that join phrases and sentences together. ***Pronouns*** take the place of nouns in a sentence.

The following activity uses words from the dictionary in a Sudoku-style puzzle. In Sudoku puzzles, the numbers 1 to 9 are used to fill in grids. All digits 1 to 9 must appear, but cannot be repeated, in each square, row, and column.

In the following puzzles, you are given a set of words for each part of the grid. Look up each word to find out its part of speech. Then arrange the words within the square so that, in the whole puzzle, you do not repeat any part of speech within a column or row.

Hint: If one of the words given in the puzzle is a noun, then you know that no other nouns can be put in that row or column of the grid. Use the process of elimination to figure out where the other parts of speech can go.

Let's try a small puzzle first. You will use the categories noun *n*, verb *v*, adjective *adj*, and preposition *prp* to solve this puzzle. The sections are numbered from top left to bottom right.

Part 1

a, beber, cocina, **correcto**

Part 2

de, **donación**, escapar, espartano

Part 3

en, huelga, inferior, jugar

Part 4

lotería, **montar**, móvil, para

	correcto		
			donación
		montar	
en			

Now try a larger puzzle. For this puzzle, you will use the categories noun *n*, verb *v*, adjective *adj*, preposition *prp*, article *art*, and pronoun *pron*. The sections are numbered from top left to bottom right.

Part 1

antiguo, **ascensor**, **batir**, la, él, en

Part 2

charla, dócil, **educar**, ella, entre, los

Part 3

cierto, con, cola, **descansar**, **nosotros**, **una**

Part 4

cultura, **exclusivo**, ellos, leer, sin, un

Part 5

a, diferente, ejercer, ejemplo, **las**, **yo**

Part 6

de, el, familia, mantener, marinero, **Usted**

		batir	**charla**		
ascensor					**educar**
	descansar			**cultura**	
una	**nosotros**			**exclusivo**	
a		**las**			**Usted**
		yo	**de**		

Gender

Spanish nouns belong to one of two groups: feminine or masculine. A noun's gender is indicated in an entry after the headword or pronunciation with **m** for masculine, **f** for feminine, and **m/f** if the same form of the word can be used for a man or a woman.

In some cases, the masculine and feminine forms of one word mean two different things. For example, the masculine **un partido** means *a political party*. The feminine **una partida** means *a game or match*. The gender associated with each meaning follows the headword in the dictionary entry.

Look up the words in the grids below. Circle the feminine words. Put an **X** through the masculine words.

pie	persona	mano
distrito	huracán	computadora
lengua	jamón	disco

naranja	saco	manzana
estrella	mesa	objeto
miel	miedo	tren

gorro	océano	estación
escalera	onda	sirena
sabor	policía	lobo

Think of these as tic-tac-toe grids. Does masculine or feminine win more matches?

Adjectives

Adjectives in Spanish change form to agree in gender and number with the noun they modify. In many cases, the feminine form ends in –**a**, and the masculine form ends in –**o**. An –**s** is added to make the plural for either gender. Some adjectives have irregular forms, in this case, the irregular forms are written out after the headword.

Use the dictionary to determine whether the nouns in the following phrases are masculine or feminine, singular or plural. Then write in the correct inflected form of the adjective. Check your answers against the word search. The correct forms are found in the puzzle.

1. a difficult exam	un examen ____________
2. a tall woman	una mujer ____________
3. an important message	un mensaje _______________
4. secondary school	la escuela _________________
5. the red cars	los carros ______________
6. an unforgettable picnic	un picnic _______________
7. a beautiful girl	una chica _________
8. a romantic song	una canción ________________
9. the first time	la _____________ vez
10. two Peruvian monuments	dos monumentos _____________
11. a heavy backpack	una mochila ____________

t	r	v	g	m	l	u	o	b	p	o	á	o	a	e	l	é	ó
f	e	á	i	f	í	n	l	ú	b	i	s	ú	t	u	é	n	i
k	p	a	i	c	o	b	v	m	h	e	a	i	l	ú	q	a	r
p	r	c	b	ú	g	m	s	i	t	p	e	r	u	a	n	o	s
g	i	b	o	u	m	c	é	a	ñ	e	ú	w	e	k	s	g	u
q	m	i	n	r	d	e	c	y	o	d	i	g	í	f	k	e	é
á	e	s	i	d	o	i	e	á	c	z	i	b	e	m	f	o	b
n	r	á	t	á	t	s	i	e	u	e	ú	f	i	o	n	d	e
n	a	ó	a	n	u	é	i	a	ú	ú	p	l	í	u	t	i	ó
u	s	e	á	p	í	j	e	a	c	r	v	m	c	c	o	u	í
í	é	m	o	p	e	s	a	d	a	e	l	j	e	é	i	à	d
p	o	c	i	t	s	e	c	u	n	d	a	r	i	a	u	l	v
r	u	o	a	b	e	a	l	t	a	é	a	o	g	h	g	é	e
r	o	v	á	p	k	s	x	p	h	a	r	w	g	a	h	g	a
é	w	ó	ì	d	o	u	e	i	m	p	o	r	t	a	n	t	e
é	s	u	z	j	e	v	c	g	u	o	á	ú	o	i	é	v	u
v	o	n	o	i	e	n	i	z	é	e	i	v	u	h	o	k	í
p	z	r	i	n	o	l	v	i	d	a	b	l	e	b	p	l	t
i	s	c	f	a	i	p	e	t	k	ó	i	f	é	e	a	g	u
é	e	e	d	i	v	c	i	o	s	é	h	s	r	r	f	z	é

Verbs

Verbs are listed in the dictionary in their infinitive form. To use the verb in a sentence, you must conjugate it and use the form that agrees with the sentence's subject.

Most verbs fall into categories with other verbs that are conjugated in the same way. In the verb appendix of this dictionary, you will find an example of each category, along with conjugations of common irregular verbs.

For this puzzle, conjugate the given verbs in the present tense. Use the context and the subject pronoun to determine the person and number of the form you need. The correct answer fits in the crossword spaces provided.

Hint: The verb class code given in the verb's dictionary entry tells you which model conjugation to follow.

ACROSS

2. Los jugadores _______ Cubanos, de la Habana. **ser**

4. Yo _________ el periódico por la mañana. **leer**

5. Los sábados, yo ____________ con mi familia. **descansar**

8. Yo tengo un gato, y él __________ un perro. **tener**

9. Tú ___________ a la fiesta ¿verdad? **ir**

11. Nosotros ______________ al cine. **ir**

13. Mis hijos _____________ mucho la televisión. **mirar**

14. Yo __________ siempre las llaves. **perder**

15. Carlos __________ la maleta antes de ir de vacaciones. **hacer**

16. Tú __________ visitar Machu Picchu? **querer**

17. ¿Ustedes ___________ una palabra en el diccionario? **buscar**

18. Machu Picchu __________ en el Perú. **estar**

DOWN

1. Nosotros ____________ cuando habla el profesor. **comprender**

3. Los amigos ___________ algo en la cafetería antes de comer. **beber**

6. Los alumnos _____________ de la clase a las tres. **salir**

7. Yo _____________ por lo menos ocho horas por noche. **dormir**

9. Nosotros siempre ______________ a Sudamérica. **viajar**

10. El equipo argentino ______________ el partido. **ganar**

12. Ella ___________ la puerta cuando llega a casa. **cerrar**

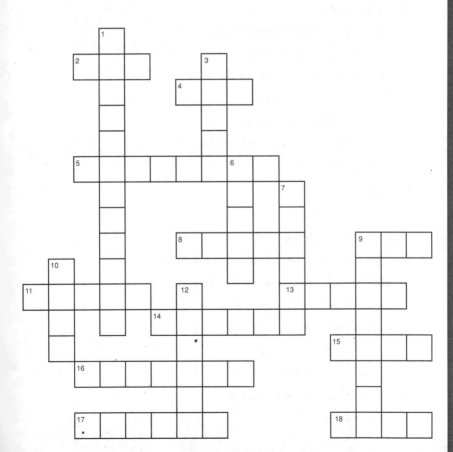

1 2 3 4 5 6 7 8 9 10 11 12 13 14 15 16 17 18

When you are reading Spanish, you face a different challenge. You see a conjugated verb in context and need to determine what its infinitive is in order to understand its meaning.

For the next puzzle, you will see conjugated verbs in the sentences. Figure out which verb the conjugated form represents, and write the infinitive (the headword form) in the puzzle.

ACROSS

3. Martín y Anita **llegaron** a las ocho.

5. ¿Por qué no **viene** a la fiesta tu novio?

7. ¡**Ganamos**!

10. Quiero que Ustedes **hagan** la tarea.

11. Las hojas **caen** en el otoño.

13. El chico **esconde** los caramelos.

15. No entiendo lo que **dices**.

16. Rita **cumple** diez años mañana.

18. Sofia **compartió** su bocadillo con sus amigos.

19. ¿Qué te **parece** el libro?

DOWN

1. No **volvimos** a casa.

2. Los alumnos **dieron** el examen.

4. A los niños les **gustan** mucho los videojuegos.

6. Ellos **hablaban** siempre con los amigos.

8. Las mujeres **prepararon** la cena.

9. Que yo **sepa**, está bien.

12. **Tomas** el sol en la playa.

14. El gato **se duerme** en el sillón.

16. Los abuelos **comieron** en casa.

17. El se **murió**.

1 2 3 4 5 6 7 8 9 10 11 12 13 14 15 16 17 18 19

Riddles

Solve the following riddles in English. Give the Spanish word for the riddle's solution.

1. This cold season is followed by spring.

___ ___ ___ ___ ___ ___ ___ ___
15 27 25 15 5 6 27 16

2. You don't want to forget this type of clothing when you go to the beach.

___ ___ ___ ___ ___   ___ ___   ___ ___ ___ ___
1 6 9 20 5   13 5   28 9 7 16

3. This thing protects you from the rain, but it's bad luck to open it indoors!

___ ___ ___ ___ ___ ___ ___ ___
17 9 6 9 11 14 9 10

4. This adjective is the opposite of "difficult."

___ ___ ___ ___ ___
12 29 24 15 18

5. This is the number that follows three and precedes five.

___ ___ ___ ___ ___ ___
24 14 9 1 6 16

6. If you are injured or very ill, you should go to this place.

___ ___ ___ ___ ___ ___ ___ ___
2 16 10 17 15 1 9 18

7. This mode of transportation has only two wheels. It is also good exercise!

___ ___ ___ ___ ___ ___ ___ ___ ___
28 15 24 15 24 18 5 1 5

8. This large mammal lives in the ocean.

___ ___ ___ ___ ___ ___ ___

28 9 18 18 5 27 9

9. This person is your mother's mother.

___ ___ ___ ___ ___ ___

9 28 14 9 18 9

10. There are twelve of these in a year.

___ ___ ___

26 5 10

11. Wearing this in the car is a safety precaution.

___ ___ ___ ___ ___ ___ ___ ___   ___ ___

24 15 27 1 14 6 30 27   13 5

___ ___ ___ ___ ___ ___ ___ ___ ___

10 5 11 14 6 15 13 9 13

12. Snow White bit into this red fruit and fell into a long slumber.

___ ___ ___ ___ ___ ___ ___

26 9 27 22 9 27 9

13. This professional brings letters and packages to your door.

___ ___ ___ ___ ___ ___ ___

24 9 6 1 5 6 16

14. This midday meal falls between breakfast and dinner.

___ ___ ___ ___ ___ ___ ___ ___

9 18 26 14 5 6 22 16

15. A very young dog is referred to as this.

___ ___ ___ ___ ___ ___ ___ ___

24 9 24 2 16 6 6 16

Cryptogram

Use the number-to-letter correspondence from the riddles to fill in the hidden message. When you are done, translate the Spanish message into English. What does it say?

14	27		26	16	13	15	10	26	16		5	27
5	10	17	9	7	16	18		13	15	24	5	
:		5	27		28	16	24	9				
	24	5	6	6	9	13	9	,		27	16	
5	27	1	6	9	27		26	16	10	24	9	10

Translation:

_____ _______________ _______ _______________ _________:

___________ _______________ _______________, _____

_________________ _______________.

Answer Key

Using Your Dictionary

a–c. Answers will vary

1. sonar, b
2. anillo, c
3. pista, e
4. tono, f
5. ring, d
6. círculo, a

Identifying Headwords

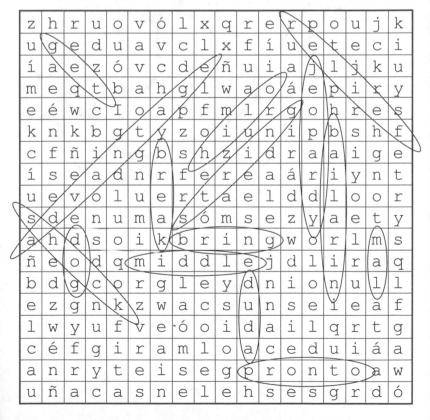

z	h	r	u	o	v	ó	l	x	q	r	e	r	p	o	u	j	k
u	g	e	d	u	a	v	c	l	x	f	í	u	e	t	e	c	i
í	a	e	z	ó	v	c	d	e	ñ	u	i	a	j	l	j	k	u
m	e	q	t	b	a	h	g	l	w	a	o	á	e	p	i	r	y
e	é	w	c	l	o	a	p	f	m	l	r	g	o	h	r	e	s
k	n	k	b	g	t	y	z	o	i	u	n	i	p	b	s	h	f
c	f	ñ	i	n	g	b	s	h	z	i	d	r	a	a	i	g	e
í	s	e	a	d	n	r	f	e	r	e	a	á	r	i	y	n	t
u	e	v	o	l	u	e	r	t	a	e	l	d	d	l	o	o	r
s	d	e	n	u	m	a	s	ó	m	s	e	z	y	a	e	t	y
a	h	d	s	o	i	k	b	r	i	n	g	w	o	r	l	m	s
ñ	e	o	d	q	m	i	d	d	l	e	j	d	l	i	r	a	q
b	d	g	c	o	r	g	l	e	y	d	n	i	o	n	u	l	l
e	z	g	n	k	z	w	a	c	s	u	n	s	e	i	e	a	f
l	w	y	u	f	v	e	ó	o	i	d	a	i	l	q	r	t	g
c	é	f	g	i	r	a	m	l	o	a	c	e	d	u	i	á	a
a	n	r	y	t	e	i	s	e	g	p	r	o	n	t	o	a	w
u	ñ	a	c	a	s	n	e	l	e	h	s	e	s	g	r	d	ó

Alphabetization

algo, aquí, así, bastante, boleta, calle, ciudad, corazón, cuchillo, despacio, disfraz, dulce, entender, escuela, fecha, flor, gritar, hasta, hoy, jamás, lavaplatos, lente, llover, mágico, mañana, marrón, más, miedo, miel, nadie, nos, otro, pie, piel, repente, silla, sueño, tiempo, universo, vida, zapato

M E X I K O

Spelling

1. **e**sfera
2. divi**s**a
3. men**t**ir
4. vi**u**da
5. a**p**agado
6. p**e**or
7. ma**n**teca
8. jar**d**ín
9. cor**o**na

¡E S T U P E N D O!

Entries in Context

							1 F			
							U			
							E			2 C
			3 C				G			Á
4 F	U	M	A	R		5 V	O	Z		N
			B			E				T
6 M		7 F	E	L	I	Z				A
A			Z							R
8 L	U	G	A	R		9 V	10 A	C	Í	O
E							I			S
T					11 H	O	R	A		
12 A	13 S	U	14 N	T	O		E			
	O		O		Y					
	L		C				15 P			
			16 H	A	Y		E			
			E				N			
	17 L	Á	S	T	I	M	A			

Word Families

1. ligero
2. mermelada
3. fósfero
4. patear
5. timbrazo

¡G E S T O!

Regional Variation

L. Am. carro	CSur majada	Mex tuna	C. Am. pelazón	L. Am. abarrotes
C. Am. afanar	L. Am. papa	Mex rebasar	CSur terno	S. Am. abalear
Rpl choclo	S. Am. ñapa	L. Am. corotos	C. Am. chichera	S. Am. chompa
L. Am. chicha	S. Am. frutilla	Pe huachafo	L. Am. egreso	Esp okupa
Mex plática	Mex vecindad	Mex hilachos	Rpl mañero	L. Am. guanaco

Latin America

Running Heads

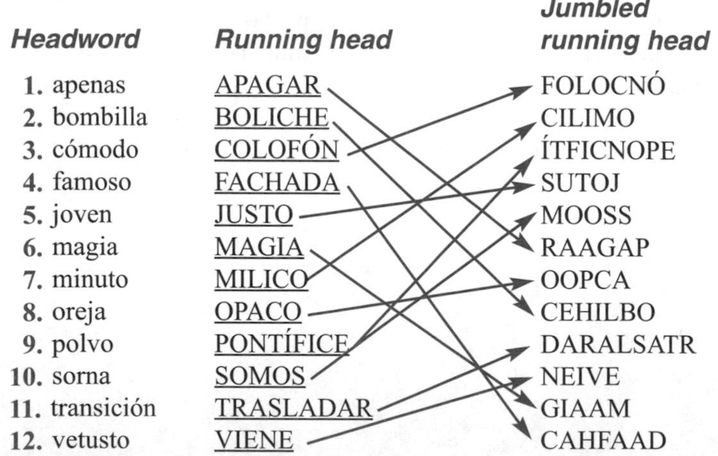

Headword
Running head
Jumbled running head
1. apenas
2. bombilla
3. cómodo
4. famoso
5. joven
6. magia
7. minuto
8. oreja
9. polvo
10. sorna
11. transición
12. vetusto
APAGAR
BOLICHE
COLOFÓN
FACHADA
JUSTO
MAGIA
MILICO
OPACO
PONTÍFICE
SOMOS
TRASLADAR
VIENE
FOLOCNÓ
CILIMO
ÍTFICNOPE
SUTOJ
MOOSS
RAAGAP
OOPCA
CEHILBO
DARALSATR
NEIVE
GIAAM
CAHFAAD

Parts of Speech

cocina	**correcto**	de	escapar
beber	a	espartano	**donación**
inferior	huelga	**montar**	para
en	jugar	lotería	móvil

él	la	**batir**	**charla**	entre	dócil
ascensor	en	antiguo	los	ella	**educar**
cierto	**descansar**	con	ellos	**cultura**	un
una	**nosotros**	cola	leer	**exclusivo**	sin
a	ejemplo	**las**	marinero	mantener	**Usted**
ejercer	diferente	**yo**	**de**	el	familia

Gender

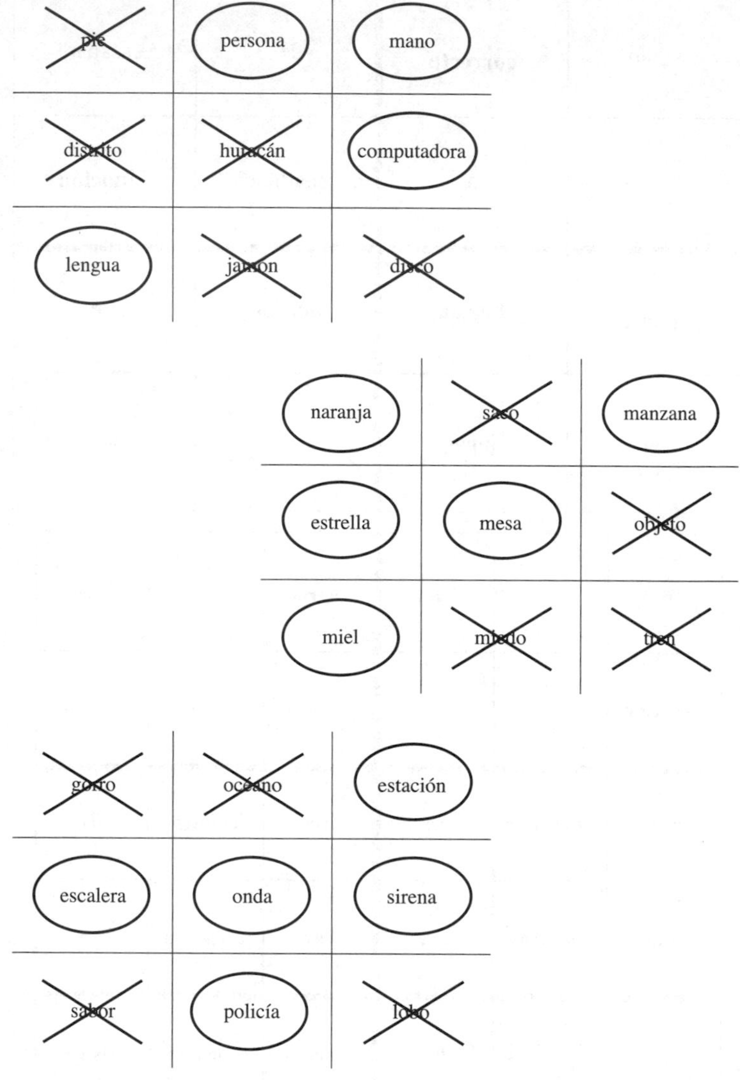

pie
persona
mano
distrito
huracán
computadora
lengua
jamón
disco
naranja
saco
manzana
estrella
mesa
objeto
miel
miedo
tren
gorro
océano
estación
escalera
onda
sirena
sabor
policía
lobo

Feminine wins the most matches.

Adjectives

1. un examen **difícil**
2. una mujer **alta**
3. un mensaje **importante**
4. la escuela **secundaria**
5. los carros **rojos**
6. un picnic **inolvidable**
7. una chica **bonita**
8. una canción **romántica**
9. la **primera** vez
10. dos monumentos **peruanos**
11. una mochila **pesada**

t	r	v	g	m	l	u	o	b	p	o	á	o	a	e	l	é	ó
f	e	á	i	f	í	n	l	ú	b	i	s	ú	t	u	é	n	i
k	p	a	i	c	o	b	v	m	h	e	a	i	l	ú	q	a	r
p	r	c	b	ú	g	m	s	i	t	p	e	r	u	a	n	o	s
g	i	b	o	u	m	c	é	a	ñ	e	ú	w	e	k	s	g	u
q	m	i	n	r	d	e	c	y	o	d	i	g	í	f	k	e	é
á	e	s	i	d	o	i	e	á	c	z	i	b	e	m	f	o	b
n	r	á	t	á	t	s	i	e	u	e	ú	f	i	o	n	d	e
n	a	ó	a	n	u	é	i	a	ú	ú	p	l	í	u	t	i	ó
u	s	e	á	p	í	j	e	a	c	r	v	m	c	c	o	u	í
í	é	m	o	p	e	s	a	d	a	e	l	j	e	é	i	á	d
p	o	c	i	t	s	e	c	u	n	d	a	r	i	a	u	l	v
r	u	o	a	b	e	a	l	t	a	é	a	o	g	h	g	é	e
r	o	v	á	p	k	s	x	p	h	a	r	w	g	a	h	g	a
é	w	ó	í	d	o	u	e	i	m	p	o	r	t	a	n	t	e
é	s	u	z	j	e	v	c	g	u	o	á	ú	o	i	é	v	u
v	o	n	o	i	e	n	i	z	é	e	i	v	u	h	o	k	í
p	z	r	i	n	o	l	v	i	d	a	b	l	e	b	p	l	t
i	s	c	f	a	i	p	e	t	k	ó	i	f	é	e	a	g	u
é	e	e	d	i	v	c	i	o	s	é	h	s	r	r	f	z	é

Verbs

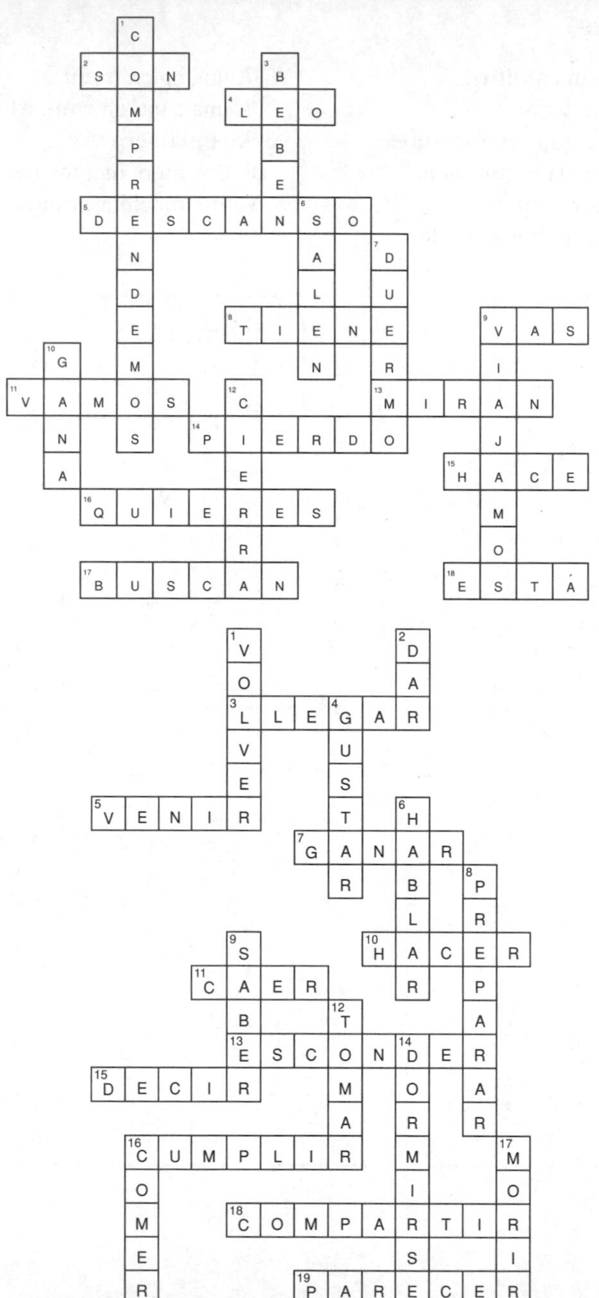
1 COMPRENDEMOS
2 SON
3 BEBE
4 LEO
5 DESCANSO
6 SALEN
7 DUERMO
8 TIENE
9 VAS
9 VIAJAMOS
10 GANA
11 VAMOS
12 CIERRA
13 MIRAN
14 PIERDO
15 HACE
16 QUIERES
17 BUSCAN
18 ESTÁ
1 VOLVER
2 DAR
3 LLEGAR
4 GUSTAR
5 VENIR
6 HABLAR
7 GANAR
8 PREPARAR
9 SABER
10 HACER
11 CAER
12 TOMAR
13 ESCONDER
14 DORMIR
15 DECIR
16 CUMPLIR
16 COMER
17 MORIR
18 COMPARTIR
19 PARECER

Riddles

1. invierno
2. traje de baño
3. paraguas
4. fácil
5. cuatro
6. hospital
7. bicicleta
8. ballena
9. abuela
10. mes
11. cinturón de seguridad
12. manzana
13. cartero
14. almuerzo
15. cachorro

Cryptogram

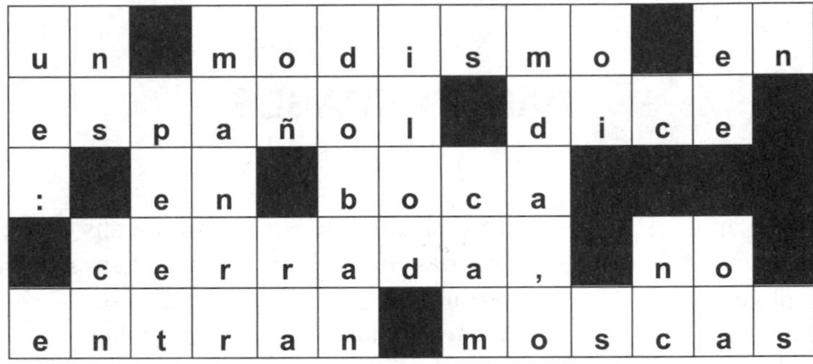

u	n		m	o	d	i	s	m	o		e	n
e	s	p	a	ñ	o	l		d	i	c	e	
:		e	n		b	o	c	a				
	c	e	r	r	a	d	a	,		n	o	
e	n	t	r	a	n		m	o	s	c	a	s

A Spanish proverb says: into a closed mouth, no flies enter.

BASIC SPANISH PHRASES & GRAMMAR

Pronunciation

In this section we have used a simplified phonetic system to represent the sounds of Spanish. Simply read the pronunciation as if it were English.

Stress

The acute accent (′) is used in Spanish to indicate a syllable is stressed, e.g. **río** (reeo). Since some words have more than one meaning, the accent mark is also used to distinguish between them, e.g.: **él** (*he*) and **el** (*the*); **sí** (*yes*) and **si** (*if*).

BASIC PHRASES

Essential

Good afternoon!	**¡Buenas tardes!**	bweh-nahs tahrdehs
Good evening!	**¡Buenas noches!**	bweh-nahs nochehs
Goodbye!	**¡Adiós!**	ah-deeyos
…, please!	**…, por favor.**	por fahbor
Thank you!	**¡Gracias!**	grah-seeyahs
Yes.	**Sí.**	see
No.	**No.**	no
Sorry!	**¡Lo siento!**	lo seeyehn-to
Where are the restrooms?	**¿Dónde están los baños?**	dondeh ehstahn los bahnyos
When?	**¿Cuándo?**	kwahn-doh
What?	**¿Qué?**	keh
Where?	**¿Dónde?**	dondeh
Here.	**Aquí.**	ahkee
There.	**Allí.**	ahyee
On the right.	**A la derecha.**	ah lah dehrehchah
On the left.	**A la izquierda.**	ah lah eeskeeyehr-dah
Do you have …?	**¿Tiene …?**	teeyeh-neh
I'd like …	**Quisiera …**	keeseeyeh-rah
How much is that?	**¿Cuánto cuesta?**	kwahn-to kwehs-tah

Where is …?	**¿Dónde está …?**	dondeh ehstah
Where can I get …?	**¿Dónde puedo encontrar …?**	dondeh pweh-doh ehnkontrahr

Communication Difficulties

Do you speak English?	**¿Habla inglés?**	ah-blah een-glehs
Does anyone here speak English?	**¿Hay alguien aquí que hable inglés?**	eye ahl-geeyehn ah-keeh keh ah-bleh een-glehs
Did you understand that?	**¿Ha entendido?**	ah ehntehn-dee-doh
I understand.	**Entiendo.**	ehntiehn-doh
I didn't understand that.	**No lo he entendido.**	no lo eh ehntehn-dee-doh
Could you speak a bit more slowly, please?	**¿Podría hablar un poco más despacio, por favor?**	podree-ah ah-blahr oon poko mahs despah-seeyo por fahbor
Could you please repeat that?	**¿Podría repetirlo, por favor?**	podree-ah rehpeh-teer-lo por fahbor
What does … mean?	**¿Qué significa …?**	keh seegnee-fee-kah
Could you write it down for me, please?	**¿Podría escribírmelo, por favor?**	podree-ah ehskree-beer-mehlo por fahbor

Greetings

Good morning!	**¡Buenos días!**	bwehnos dee-ahs
Good afternoon!	**¡Buenas tardes!**	bwehnahs tahrdehs
Good evening/night!	**¡Buenas noches!**	bwehnahs nocheh
Hello!	**¡Hola!**	Olah
How are you?	**¿Cómo está?**	komo ehstah
How are things?	**¿Qué tal?**	keh tahl
Fine, thanks. And you?	**Bien, gracias. ¿Y usted?**	beeyehn grah-seeyahs ee oostehd
I'm afraid I have to go now.	**Lo siento, pero me tengo que ir.**	lo seeyehn-toh pehro meh tehngo keh eer
Goodbye!	**¡Adiós!**	ah-deeyos
See you soon / tomorrow!	**¡Hasta pronto / mañana!**	ahstah pronto / mah-nyah-nah

It was nice meeting you.	**Me alegro de haberle conocido.**	meh ahleh-gro deh ah-behrleh kono-see-doh
Have a good trip!	**¡Buen viaje!**	bwehn beeyah-kheh

Meeting People

What's your name?	**¿Cómo se llama / te llamas?**	komo seh yahmah / teh yahmahs
My name is …	**Me llamo …**	meh yahmo
Where are you from?	**¿De dónde es / eres?**	deh dohndeh ehs /
ehrehs		
I'm from …	**Soy de …**	soy deh
– the US. –	**los Estados Unidos.**	los ehstah-dos oonee-dos
– Canada.	**Canadá.**	kah-nahdah
– the UK. –	**Gran Bretaña.**	grahn brehtah-nyah

Expressing Likes and Dislikes

Very good!	**¡Muy bien!**	mwee beeyehn
I'm very happy.	**Estoy muy contento** (m)/**contenta** (f).	ehs-toy mwee kon-tehnto/kon-tehn-tah
I like that.	**Me gusta.**	meh goos-tah
What a shame!	**¡Qué pena!**	keh pehnah
I'd rather …	**Preferiría …**	prehfehree-reeah
I don't like it.	**No me gusta.**	no meh goos-tah
I'd rather not.	**No me apetece.**	no meh ahpehteh-seh
Certainly not.	**¡De ninguna manera!**	deh neengoo-nah mahneh-rah

Expressing Requests and Thanks

Thank you very much.	**Muchas gracias.**	moochahs grah-seeyahs
Thanks, you too.	**Gracias, igualmente.**	grah-seeyahs eeg-wahl-mehnteh
May I?	**¿Puedo?**	pwehdoh

Please, …	**Por favor …**	por fahbor
No, thank you.	**No, gracias.**	no grah-seeyahs
Could you help me?	**¿Podría ayudarme?**	podree-ah ahy-oodahr-meh
That's very nice of you.	**Muy amable de su parte.**	mwee ahmah-bleh deh soo pahrteh
Thank you very much for all your trouble / help.	**Le agradezco las molestias / la ayuda.**	leh ahgrah-dehsko lahs molehs-teeyahs / lah ahyoodah
You're welcome.	**De nada.**	deh nahdah

Apologies

Sorry!	**¡Perdón!**	pehrdon
Excuse me!	**¡Perdone!**	pehr-doneh
I'm sorry about that.	**Lo siento.**	lo seeyehn-toh
Don't worry about it!	**¡No importa!**	no importah
How embarrassing!	**Esto me resulta muy desagradable.**	ehsto meh reh-sooltah mwee deh-sahgrah-dahbleh
It was a misunderstanding.	**Ha sido un malentendido.**	ah seedo oon mahlehn-tehndee-doh

GRAMMAR

Regular Verbs and Their Tenses

There are three verb types which follow a regular pattern, their infinitives ending in **-ar**, **-er**, and **-ir**, e.g. *to speak* **hablar**, *to eat* **comer**, *to live* **vivir**. Here are the most commonly used forms. The **vosotros** forms are only used in Spain. In Latin America **ustedes** is used to address more than one person formally or informally.

	Present	***Past***	***Future***
yo *I*	**hablo**	**hablé**	**hablaré**
tú *you (informal)*	**hablas**	**hablaste**	**hablarás**

él/ella/Ud. *he/she/ you (form.)*	**habla**	**habló**	**hablará**
nosotros *we*	**hablamos**	**hablamos**	**hablaremos**
vosotros *you (pl. inform.) [Spain]*	**habláis**	**hablasteis**	**hablaréis**
ellos/ellas/Uds. *they/you (form.)*	**hablan**	**hablaron**	**hablarán**
yo *I*	**como**	**comí**	**comeré**
tú *you (inform.)*	**comes**	**comiste**	**comerás**
él/ella/Ud. *he/she/ you (form.)*	**come**	**comió**	**comerá**
nosotros *we*	**comemos**	**comimos**	**comeremos**
vosotros *you (pl. inform.) [Spain]*	**coméis**	**comisteis**	**comeréis**
ellos/ellas/Uds. *they/you (form.)*	**comen**	**comieron**	**comerán**
yo *I*	**vivo**	**viví**	**viviré**
tú *you (inform.)*	**vives**	**viviste**	**vivirás**
él/ella/Ud. *he/she/ you (form.)*	**vive**	**vivió**	**vivirá**
nosotros *we*	**vivimos**	**vivimos**	**viviremos**
vosotros *you (pl. inform.) [Spain]*	**vivís**	**vivisteis**	**viviréis**
ellos/ellas/Uds. *they/you (form.)*	**viven**	**vivieron**	**vivirán**

Very often, people omit the pronoun, using only the verb form.

Examples: **Vivo en Madrid.** *I live in Madrid.*
¿Habla español? *Do you speak Spanish?*

There are many irregular verbs whose forms differ considerably.

To be – ser and estar

Spanish has two verbs for *to be*, **ser** and **estar**. Their usage is complex. Here are some general guidelines:

Ser is used to identify people or objects, to describe their basic and natural characteristics, also to tell time and dates.

Examples: **¡Es caro!** *That is expensive!*
Somos médicos. *We're doctors.*
Son las dos. *It's 2 o'clock.*

Estar is used when the state of a person or object is changeable and to indicate locations.

Examples: **Estoy cansado.** *I'm tired.*
¿Dónde estuvo? *Where was he?*
Estarán en Roma. *They'll be in Rome.*

	Present	***Past***	***Future***
yo	**soy/estoy**	**fui/estuve**	**seré/estaré**
tú	**eres/estás**	**fuiste/estuviste**	**serás/estarás**
él/ella/Ud.	**es/está**	**fue/estuvo**	**será/estará**
nosotros	**somos/ estamos**	**fuimos/estuvimos**	**seremos/ estaremos**
vosotros *[Spain]*	**sois/estáis**	**fuisteis/estuvisteis**	**seréis/estaréis**
ellos/ellas/Uds.	**son/están**	**fueron/estuvieron**	**serán/estarán**

Nouns and Articles

Generally nouns ending in **-o** are masculine, and those ending in **-a** are feminine. Their definite articles—meaning *the*—are **el** (m) and **la** (f). In the plural, the article is **los** (m) and **las** (f). Plural nouns end in **-s**, or **-es** when the singular form ends with a consonant.

Examples: Singular		Plural	
	el tren *the train*		**los trenes** *the trains*
	la mesa *the table*		**las mesas** *the tables*

The definite articles also change according to gender: **un** (m), **una** (f), **unos** (m/pl), **unas** (f/pl).

Examples: Singular		Plural	
	un libro *a book*		**unos libros** *books*
	una casa *a house*		**unas casas** *houses*

Possessive articles relate to the gender of the noun that follows:

Examples: **¿Dónde está su billete?** *Where is your ticket?*
Vuestro tren sale a las 8. *Your train leaves at 8.*
Busco mis maletas. *I'm looking for my suitcases.*

	Singular	***Plural***
my	**mi**	**mis**
your (inform.)	**tu**	**tus**
his/her/its/your (form.)	**su**	**sus**
our	**nuestro/a**	**nuestros/as**
your (pl. inform.)[Spain]	**vuestro/a**	**vuestros/as**
their/your (pl. form.)	**su**	**sus**

Word Order

The conjugated verb comes after the subject.

Examples: **Yo trabajo en Madrid.** *I work in Madrid.*

Questions are formed by reversing the order of subject and verb, changing the intonation of the affirmative sentence, or using key question words like *when?* **¿cuándo?**.

Examples: **¿Tiene Ud. mapas?** *Do you have maps?*
¿Cuándo cerrará el banco? *When will the bank close?*

Negations

Negative sentences are formed by adding **no** (*not*) to that part of the sentence which is to be negated.

Examples: **No fumamos.** *We don't smoke.*
No es nuevo. *It's not new.*
El autobús no llegó. *The bus didn't arrive.*
¿Por qué no escuchas? *Why don't you listen?*

Imperatives (Command Form)

Imperative sentences are formed by using the stem of the verb with the appropriate ending.

Examples:

tú *you (inform.)*	**¡Habla!** *Speak!*	**[no hables]**
Ud. *you (form.)*	**¡Hable!** *Speak!*	
nosotros *we*	**¡Hablemos!** *Let's speak!*	
vosotros *you (inform. pl.) [Spain]*	**¡Hablad!** *Speak!*	**[no habléis]**
Uds. *you (form. pl.)*	**¡Hablen!** *Speak!*	

Comparative and Superlative

Comparative and superlative are formed by adding **más** (*more*), **lo más** (*the most*), **menos** (*less*) or **lo menos** (*the least*) before the adjective or noun.

Adjective	***Comparative***	***Superlative***
grande	**más grande**	**lo más grande**
big, large	*bigger*	*the biggest*
costoso	**menos costoso**	**lo menos costoso**
expensive	*less expensive*	*the least expensive*

Examples: **Estas postales son las más baratas.** *These postcards are the cheapest.*
Pepe tiene menos dinero que Juan. *Pepe has less money than Juan.*

Possessive Pronouns

Pronouns serve as substitutes and relate to the gender.

	Singular	***Plural***
mine	**mío/a**	**míos/as**
yours (inform. sing.)	**tuyo/a**	**tuyos/as**
yours (form.)	**suyo/a**	**suyos/as**
his/her/its	**suyo/a**	**suyos/as**
ours	**nuestro/a**	**nuestros/as**
yours (pl. inform.) [Spain]	**vuestro/a**	**vuestros/as**
theirs	**suyo/a**	**suyos/as**

Examples: **Sus hijos y los míos.** *Your children and mine.*
¿Es tuyo este café? *Is this coffee yours?*

Adjectives

Adjectives describe nouns. They agree with the noun in gender and number. Masculine forms end in **-o**, feminine forms in **-a**. In general, adjectives come after the noun. The feminine form is generally the same if the masculine form ends in **-e** or with a consonant.

Examples: **Tenemos un coche viejo.** *We have an old car.*
Mi jefa es simpática. *My boss is nice.*
El mar/La flor es azul. *The ocean / flower is blue.*

Most adjectives form their plurals the same way as nouns:

Examples: **una casa roja** *a red house*
unas casas rojas *red houses*

Adverbs and Adverbial Expressions

Adverbs describe verbs. They are formed by adding **-mente** to the feminine form of the adjective if it differs from the masculine. Otherwise add **-mente** to the masculine form.

Examples: **María conduce lentamente.** *Maria drives very slowly.*
Roberto conduce rápidamente. *Robert drives fast.*
Ud. habla español bien. *You speak Spanish well.*

Some common adverbial time expressions:

actualmente *presently*
todavía *still*
todavía no *not yet*
ya no *not anymore*

Part 2

English-Spanish Dictionary

A

a [ə] *stressed* [eɪ] *art* un(a); ***$50 a ride*** 50 dólares por viaje

a·back [ə'bæk] *adv*: ***taken aback*** desconcertado (***by*** por)

a·ban·don [ə'bændən] *v/t* abandonar

a·bashed [ə'bæʃt] *adj* avergonzado

a·bate [ə'beɪt] *v/i of storm, flood* amainar

ab·at·toir ['æbətwɑːr] matadero *m*

ab·bey ['æbɪ] abadía *f*

ab·bre·vi·ate [ə'briːvɪeɪt] *v/t* abreviar

ab·bre·vi·a·tion [əbriːvɪ'eɪʃn] abreviatura *f*

ab·di·cate ['æbdɪkeɪt] *v/i* abdicar

ab·di·ca·tion [æbdɪ'keɪʃn] abdicación *f*

ab·do·men ['æbdəmən] abdomen *m*

ab·dom·i·nal [æb'dɑːmɪnl] *adj* abdominal

ab·duct [əb'dʌkt] *v/t* raptar, secuestrar

ab·duc·tion [əb'dʌkʃn] rapto *m*, secuestro *m*

◆ **a·bide by** [ə'baɪd] *v/t* atenerse a

a·bil·i·ty [ə'bɪlətɪ] capacidad *f*, habilidad *f*

a·blaze [ə'bleɪz] *adj* en llamas

a·ble ['eɪbl] *adj* (*skillful*) capaz, hábil; ***be able to*** poder; ***I wasn't able to see / hear*** no conseguí *or* pude ver / escuchar

a·ble-bod·ied [eɪbl'bɑːdiːd] *adj* sano

ab·nor·mal [æb'nɔːrml] *adj* anormal

ab·nor·mal·ly [æb'nɔːrməlɪ] *adv* anormalmente; *behave* de manera anormal

a·board [ə'bɔːrd] **1** *prep* a bordo de **2** *adv* a bordo; ***be aboard*** estar a bordo; ***go aboard*** subir a bordo

a·bol·ish [ə'bɑːlɪʃ] *v/t* abolir

ab·o·li·tion [æbə'lɪʃn] abolición *f*

a·bort [ə'bɔːrt] *v/t mission, launch* suspender, cancelar; COMPUT cancelar

a·bor·tion [ə'bɔːrʃn] aborto *m* (*provocado*); ***have an abortion*** abortar

a·bor·tive [ə'bɔːrtɪv] *adj* fallido

a·bout [ə'baʊt] **1** *prep* (*concerning*) acerca de, sobre; ***what's it about?*** *of book, movie* ¿de qué trata? **2** *adv* (*roughly*) más o menos; ***be about to ...*** (*be going to*) estar a punto de ...; ***be about*** (*somewhere near*) estar por ahí; ***there are a lot of people about*** hay un montón de gente por ahí

a·bove [ə'bʌv] **1** *prep* por encima de; ***500 m above sea level*** 500 m sobre el nivel del mar; ***above all*** por encima de todo, sobre todo **2** *adv*: ***on the floor above*** en el piso de arriba

a·bove-men·tioned [əbʌv'menʃnd] *adj* arriba mencionado

ab·ra·sion [ə'breɪʒn] abrasión *f*

ab·ra·sive [ə'breɪsɪv] *adj personality* abrasivo

a·breast [ə'brest] *adv* de frente, en fondo; ***keep abreast of*** mantenerse al tanto de

a·bridge [ə'brɪdʒ] *v/t* abreviar, condensar

a·broad [ə'brɒːd] *adv live* en el extranjero; *go* al extranjero

a·brupt [ə'brʌpt] *adj departure* brusco, repentino; *manner* brusco, rudo

a·brupt·ly [ə'brʌptlɪ] *adv* (*suddenly*) repentinamente; (*curtly*) bruscamente

ab·scess ['æbsɪs] absceso *m*

ab·sence ['æbsəns] *of person* ausencia *f*; (*lack*) falta *f*

ab·sent ['æbsənt] *adj* ausente

ab·sen·tee [æbsən'tiː] *n* ausente *m/f*

ab·sen·tee·ism [æbsən'tiːɪzm] absentismo *m*

ab·sent-mind·ed [æbsənt'maɪndɪd] *adj* despistado, distraído

ab·sent-mind·ed·ly [æbsənt'maɪndɪdlɪ] *adv* distraídamente

ab·so·lute ['æbsəluːt] *adj power* absoluto; *idiot* completo; *mess* total

ab·so·lute·ly ['æbsəluːtlɪ] *adv* (*completely*) absolutamente, completamente; ***absolutely not!*** ¡en absoluto!; ***do you agree? - absolutely!*** ¿estás de acuerdo? - ¡completamente!

ab·so·lu·tion [æbsə'luːʃn] REL absolución *f*

ab·solve [əb'zɑːlv] *v/t* absolver

ab·sorb [əb'sɔːrb] *v/t* absorber; ***absorbed in ...*** absorto en ...

ab·sorb·en·cy [əb'sɔːrbənsɪ] absorbencia *f*

ab·sorb·ent [əb'sɔːrbənt] *adj* absorbente

ab·sorb·ent 'cot·ton algodón *m* hidrófilo

ab·sorb·ing [əb'sɔːrbɪŋ] *adj* absorbente

ab·stain [əb'steɪn] *v/i from voting* abstenerse

ab·sten·tion [əb'stenʃn] *in voting* abstención *f*

ab·stract ['æbstrækt] *adj* abstracto

ab·struse [əb'struːs] *adj* abstruso

ab·surd [əb'sɜːrd] *adj* absurdo

ab·surd·i·ty [əb'sɜːrdətɪ] lo absurdo

a·bun·dance [ə'bʌndəns] abundancia *f*

a·bun·dant [ə'bʌndənt] *adj* abundante

a·buse¹ [ə'bjuːs] *n* (*insults*) insultos *mpl*; *of thing* maltrato *m*; ***he shouted abuse at me*** me insultó; (***child***) ***abuse*** *physical* malos tratos *mpl* a menores; *sexual* agre-

sión *f* sexual a menores
a·buse² [ə'bjuːz] *v/t* (*physically*) abusar de; (*verbally*) insultar
a·bu·sive [ə'bjuːsɪv] *adj language* insultante, injurioso; ***become abusive*** ponerse a insultar
a·bys·mal [ə'bɪʒml] *adj* F (*very bad*) desastroso F
a·byss [ə'bɪs] abismo *m*
AC ['eɪsiː] *abbr* (= ***alternating current***) CA (= corriente *f* alterna)
ac·a·dem·ic [ækə'demɪk] **1** *n* académico(-a) *m*(*f*), profesor(a) *m*(*f*) **2** *adj* académico
a·cad·e·my [ə'kædəmɪ] academia *f*
ac·cede [ək'siːd] *v/i* accede; ***accede to*** acceder a
ac·cel·e·rate [ək'seləreɪt] *v/t & v/i* acelerar
ac·cel·e·ra·tion [əkselə'reɪʃn] aceleración *f*
ac·cel·e·ra·tor [ək'seləreɪtər] *of car* acelerador *m*
ac·cent ['æksənt] *when speaking* acento *m*; (*emphasis*) énfasis *m*
ac·cen·tu·a·te [ək'sentʊeɪt] *v/t* acentuar
ac·cept [ək'sept] *v/t & v/i* aceptar
ac·cep·ta·ble [ək'septəbl] *adj* aceptable
ac·cept·ance [ək'septəns] aceptación *f*
ac·cess ['ækses] **1** *n* acceso *m*; ***have access to*** *computer* tener acceso a; *child* tener derecho a visitar **2** *v/t also* COMPUT acceder a
'ac·cess code COMPUT código *m* de acceso
ac·ces·si·ble [ək'sesəbl] *adj* accesible
ac·ces·sion [ək'seʃn] acceso *m*
ac·ces·so·ry [ək'sesərɪ] *for wearing* accesorio *m*, complemento *m*; LAW cómplice *m/f*
'ac·cess road carretera *f* de acceso
'ac·cess time COMPUT tiempo *m* de acceso
ac·ci·dent ['æksɪdənt] accidente *m*; ***by accident*** por casualidad
ac·ci·den·tal [æksɪ'dentl] *adj* accidental
ac·ci·den·tal·ly [æksɪ'dentlɪ] *adv* sin querer
ac·claim [ə'kleɪm] **1** *n* alabanza *f*, aclamación *f*; ***meet with acclaim*** ser alabado *or* aclamado **2** *v/t* alabar, aclamar
ac·cla·ma·tion [əklə'meɪʃn] aclamación *f*
ac·cli·mate, **ac·cli·ma·tize** [ə'klaɪmət, ə'klaɪmətaɪz] *v/t* aclimatarse
ac·com·mo·date [ə'kɑːmədeɪt] *v/t* alojar; *requirements* satisfacer, hacer frente a
ac·com·mo·da·tions [əkɑːmə'deɪʃnz] *npl* alojamiento *m*
ac·com·pa·ni·ment [ə'kʌmpənɪmənt] MUS acompañamiento *m*
ac·com·pa·nist [ə'kʌmpənɪst] MUS acompañante *m/f*
ac·com·pa·ny [ə'kʌmpənɪ] *v/t* (*pret & pp* ***accompanied***) *also* MUS acompañar
ac·com·plice [ə'kʌmplɪs] cómplice *m/f*
ac·com·plish [ə'kʌmplɪʃ] *v/t task* realizar; *goal* conseguir, lograr
ac·com·plished [ə'kʌmplɪʃt] *adj* consumado
ac·com·plish·ment [ə'kʌmplɪʃmənt] *of a task* realización *f*; (*talent*) habilidad *f*; (*achievement*) logro *m*
accord [ə'kɔːrd] acuerdo *m*; ***of one's own accord*** de motu propio
ac·cord·ance [ə'kɔːrdəns]: ***in accordance with*** de acuerdo con
ac·cord·ing [ə'kɔːrdɪŋ] *adv*: ***according to*** según
ac·cord·ing·ly [ə'kɔːrdɪŋlɪ] *adv* (*consequently*) por consiguiente; (*appropriately*) como corresponde
ac·cor·di·on [ə'kɔːrdɪən] acordeón *m*
ac·cor·di·on·ist [ə'kɔːrdɪənɪst] acordeonista *m/f*
ac·count [ə'kaʊnt] *financial* cuenta *f*; (*report, description*) relato *m*, descripción *f*; ***give an account of*** relatar, describir; ***on no account*** de ninguna manera, bajo ningún concepto; ***on account of*** a causa de; ***take sth into account, take account of sth*** tener algo en cuenta, tener en cuenta algo
◆ **account for** *v/t* (*explain*) explicar; (*make up, constitute*) suponer, constituir
ac·count·abil·i·ty [əkaʊntə'bɪlətɪ] responsabilidad *f*
ac·coun·ta·ble [ə'kaʊntəbl] *adj* responsable (***to*** ante); ***be held accountable*** ser considerado responsable
ac·coun·tant [ə'kaʊntənt] contable *m/f*, *L.Am.* contador(a) *m*(*f*)
ac'count hold·er titular *m/f* de una cuenta
ac'count num·ber número *m* de cuenta
ac·counts [ə'kaʊnts] *npl* contabilidad *f*
ac·cu·mu·late [ə'kjuːmjʊleɪt] **1** *v/t* acumular **2** *v/i* acumularse
ac·cu·mu·la·tion [əkjuːmjʊ'leɪʃn] acumulación *f*
ac·cu·ra·cy ['ækjʊrəsɪ] precisión *f*
ac·cu·rate ['ækjʊrət] *adj* preciso
ac·cu·rate·ly ['ækjʊrətlɪ] *adv* con precisión
ac·cu·sa·tion [ækjuː'zeɪʃn] acusación *f*
ac·cuse [ə'kjuːz] *v/t*: ***accuse s.o. of sth*** acusar a alguien de algo; ***be accused of*** LAW ser acusado de
ac·cused [ə'kjuːzd] *n* LAW acusado(-a) *m*(*f*)

ac·cus·ing [əˈkjuːzɪŋ] *adj* acusador
ac·cus·ing·ly [əˈkjuːzɪŋlɪ] *adv say* en tono acusador; ***he looked at me accusingly*** me lanzó una mirada acusadora
ac·cus·tom [əˈkʌstəm] *v/t* acostumbrar; ***get accustomed to*** acostumbrarse a; ***be accustomed to*** estar acostumbrado a
ace [eɪs] *in cards* as *m*; (*in tennis*: *shot*) ace *m*
ache [eɪk] **1** *n* dolor *m* **2** *v/i* doler
a·chieve [əˈʧiːv] *v/t* conseguir, lograr
a·chieve·ment [əˈʧiːvmənt] *of ambition* consecución *f*, logro *m*; (*thing achieved*) logro *m*
ac·id [ˈæsɪd] *n* ácido *m*
a·cid·i·ty [əˈsɪdətɪ] acidez *f*; *fig* sarcasmo *m*
ac·id ˈrain lluvia *f* ácida
ˈac·id test *fig* prueba *f* de fuego
ac·knowl·edge [əkˈnɑːlɪdʒ] *v/t* reconocer; ***acknowledge receipt of a letter*** acusar recibo de una carta
ac·knowl·edg(e)·ment [əkˈnɑːlɪdʒmənt] reconocimento *m*; *of a letter* acuse *m* de recibo
ac·ne [ˈæknɪ] MED acné *m*, acne *m*
a·corn [ˈeɪkɔːrn] BOT bellota *f*
a·cous·tics [əˈkuːstɪks] acústica *f*
ac·quaint [əˈkweɪnt] *v/t fml*: ***be acquainted with*** conocer
ac·quaint·ance [əˈkweɪntəns] *person* conocido(-a) *m(f)*
ac·qui·esce [ækwɪˈes] *v/i fml* acceder
ac·qui·es·cence [ækwɪˈesns] *fml* aquiescencia *f*
ac·quire [əˈkwaɪr] *v/t* adquirir
ac·qui·si·tion [ækwɪˈzɪʃn] adquisición *f*
ac·quis·i·tive [æˈkwɪzətɪv] *adj* consumista
ac·quit [əˈkwɪt] *v/t* LAW absolver
ac·quit·tal [əˈkwɪtl] LAW absolución *f*
a·cre [ˈeɪkər] acre *m* (*4.047m2*)
a·cre·age [ˈeɪkrɪdʒ] superficie *f* en acres
ac·ri·mo·ni·ous [ækrɪˈmoʊnɪəs] *adj* áspero, agrio
ac·ro·bat [ˈækrəbæt] acróbata *m/f*
ac·ro·bat·ic [ækrəˈbætɪk] *adj* acrobático
ac·ro·bat·ics [ækrəˈbætɪks] *npl* acrobacias *fpl*
ac·ro·nym [ˈækrənɪm] acrónimo *m*
a·cross [əˈkrɑːs] **1** *prep* al otro lado de; ***she lives across the street*** vive al otro lado de la calle; ***sail across the Atlantic*** cruzar el Atlántico navegando **2** *adv* de un lado a otro; ***it's too far to swim across*** está demasiado lejos como para cruzar a nado; ***once you're across*** cuando hayas llegado al otro lado; ***10 m across*** 10 m de ancho
a·cryl·ic [əˈkrɪlɪk] *adj* acrílico
act [ækt] **1** *v/i* THEA actuar; (*pretend*) hacer teatro; ***act as*** actuar *or* hacer de **2** *n* (*deed*), *of play* acto *m*; *in vaudeville* número *m*; (*law*) ley *f*; ***it's just an act*** (*pretense*) es puro teatro; ***act of God*** caso *m* fortuito
act·ing [ˈæktɪŋ] **1** *n in a play* interpretación *f*; *as profession* teatro *m* **2** *adj* (*temporary*) en funciones
ac·tion [ˈækʃn] acción *f*; ***out of action*** *machine* sin funcionar; *person* fuera de combate; ***take action*** actuar; ***bring an action against*** LAW demandar a
ac·tion ˈre·play TV repetición *f* (de la jugada)
ac·tive [ˈæktɪv] *adj also* GRAM activo; *party member* en activo
ac·tiv·ist [ˈæktɪvɪst] POL activista *m/f*
ac·tiv·i·ty [ækˈtɪvətɪ] actividad *f*
ac·tor [ˈæktər] actor *m*
ac·tress [ˈæktrɪs] actriz *f*
ac·tu·al [ˈækʧʊəl] *adj* verdadero, real
ac·tu·al·ly [ˈækʧʊəlɪ] *adv* (*in fact, to tell the truth*) en realidad; ***did you actually see her?*** ¿de verdad llegaste a verla?; ***he actually did it!*** ¡aunque parezca mentira lo hizo!; ***actually, I do know him*** (*stressing converse*) pues sí, de hecho lo conozco; ***actually, it's not finished yet*** el caso es que todavía no está terminado
ac·u·punc·ture [ˈækjəpʌŋkʧər] acupuntura *f*
a·cute [əˈkjuːt] *adj pain* agudo; *sense* muy fino
a·cute·ly [əˈkjuːtlɪ] *adv* (*extremely*) extremadamente; ***acutely aware*** plenamente consciente
ad [æd] → ***advertisement***
ad·a·mant [ˈædəmənt] *adj* firme
ad·a·mant·ly [ˈædəməntlɪ] *adv* firmemente
Ad·am's ap·ple [ædəmzˈæpəl] nuez *f*
a·dapt [əˈdæpt] **1** *v/t* adaptar **2** *v/i of person* adaptarse
a·dapt·a·bil·i·ty [ədæptəˈbɪlətɪ] adaptabilidad *f*
a·dap·ta·ble [əˈdæptəbl] *adj* adaptable
a·dap·ta·tion [ædæpˈteɪʃn] *of play etc* adaptación *f*
a·dapt·er [əˈdæptər] *electrical* adaptador *m*
add [æd] **1** *v/t* añadir; MATH sumar **2** *v/i of person* sumar
◆ **add on** *v/t 15% etc* sumar
◆ **add up** **1** *v/t* sumar **2** *v/i fig* cuadrar
ad·der [ˈædər] víbora *f*
ad·dict [ˈædɪkt] adicto(-a) *m(f)*; ***drug addict*** drogadicto(-a) *m(f)*

ad·dic·ted [ə'dɪktɪd] *adj* adicto; ***be addicted to*** ser adicto a
ad·dic·tion [ə'dɪkʃn] adicción *f*
ad·dic·tive [ə'dɪktɪv] *adj* adictivo
ad·di·tion [ə'dɪʃn] MATH suma *f*; *to list, company etc* incorporación *f*; *of new drive etc* instalación *f*; ***in addition*** además; ***in addition to*** además de
ad·di·tion·al [ə'dɪʃnl] *adj* adicional
ad·di·tive ['ædɪtɪv] aditivo *m*
add-on ['ædɑːn] extra *m*, accesorio *m*
ad·dress [ə'dres] **1** *n* dirección *f*; ***form of address*** tratamiento *m* **2** *v/t letter* dirigir; *audience* dirigirse a; ***how do you address the judge?*** ¿qué tratamiento se le da al juez?
ad'dress book agenda *f* de direcciones
ad·dress·ee [ædre'siː] destinatario(-a) *m(f)*
ad·ept ['ædept] *adj* experto; ***be adept at*** ser un experto en
ad·e·quate ['ædɪkwət] *adj* suficiente; (*satisfactory*) aceptable
ad·e·quate·ly ['ædɪkwətlɪ] *adv* suficientemente; (*satisfactorily*) aceptablemente
ad·here [əd'hɪr] *v/i* adherirse
◆ **adhere to** *v/t surface* adherirse a; *rules* cumplir
ad·he·sive [əd'hiːsɪv] *n* adhesivo *m*
ad·he·sive 'plas·ter esparadrapo *m*
ad·he·sive 'tape cinta *f* adhesiva
ad·ja·cent [ə'dʒeɪsnt] *adj* adyacente
ad·jec·tive ['ædʒɪktɪv] adjetivo *m*
ad·join [ə'dʒɔɪn] *v/t* lindar con
ad·join·ing [ə'dʒɔɪnɪŋ] *adj* contiguo
ad·journ [ə'dʒɜːrn] *v/i of court, meeting* aplazar
ad·journ·ment [ə'dʒɜːrnmənt] aplazamiento *m*
ad·just [ə'dʒʌst] *v/t* ajustar, regular
ad·just·a·ble [ə'dʒʌstəbl] *adj* ajustable, regulable
ad·just·ment [ə'dʒʌstmənt] ajuste *m*; *psychological* adaptación *f*
ad lib [æd'lɪb] **1** *adj* improvisado **2** *adv* improvisadamente **3** *v/i* (*pret & pp* ***adbed***) improvisar
ad·min·is·ter [əd'mɪnɪstər] *v/t* administrar
ad·min·is·tra·tion [ədmɪnɪ'streɪʃn] administración *f*
ad·min·is·tra·tive [ədmɪnɪ'strətɪv] *adj* administrativo
ad·min·is·tra·tor [əd'mɪnɪstreɪtər] administrador(a) *m(f)*
ad·mi·ra·ble ['ædmərəbl] *adj* admirable
ad·mi·ra·bly ['ædmərəblɪ] *adv* admirablemente
ad·mi·ral ['ædmərəl] almirante *m*
ad·mi·ra·tion [ædmə'reɪʃn] admiración *f*
ad·mire [əd'maɪr] *v/t* admirar
ad·mir·er [əd'maɪrər] admirador(a) *m(f)*
ad·mir·ing [əd'maɪrɪŋ] *adj* de admiración
ad·mir·ing·ly [əd'maɪrɪŋlɪ] *adv* con admiración
ad·mis·si·ble [əd'mɪsəbl] *adj* admisible
ad·mis·sion [əd'mɪʃn] (*confession*) confesión *f*; ***admission free*** entrada gratis
ad·mit [əd'mɪt] *v/t* (*pret & pp* ***admitted***) *to a place* dejar entrar; *to school, organization* admitir; *to hospital* ingresar; (*confess*) confesar; (*accept*) admitir
ad·mit·tance [əd'mɪtəns] admisión *f*; ***no admittance*** prohibido el paso
ad·mit·ted·ly [əd'mɪtedlɪ] *adv*: ***he didn't use those exact words, admittedly*** es verdad que no utilizó exactamente esas palabras
ad·mon·ish [əd'mɑːnɪʃ] *v/t fml* reprender
a·do [ə'duː]: ***without further ado*** sin más dilación
ad·o·les·cence [ædə'lesns] adolescencia *f*
ad·o·les·cent [ædə'lesnt] **1** *n* adolescente *m/f* **2** *adj* de adolescente
a·dopt [ə'dɑːpt] *v/t child, plan* adoptar
a·dop·tion [ə'dɑːpʃn] *of child* adopción *f*
adop·tive 'par·ents [ədɑːptɪv] *npl* padres *mpl* adoptivos
a·dor·a·ble [ə'dɔːrəbl] *adj* encantador
ad·o·ra·tion [ædə'reɪʃn] adoración *f*
a·dore [ə'dɔːr] *v/t* adorar; ***I adore chocolate*** me encanta el chocolate
a·dor·ing [ə'dɔːrɪŋ] *adj expression* lleno de adoración; ***his adoring fans*** sus entregados fans
ad·ren·al·in [ə'drenəlɪn] adrenalina *f*
a·drift [ə'drɪft] *adj* a la deriva; *fig* perdido
ad·u·la·tion [ædʊ'leɪʃn] adulación *f*
ad·ult ['ædʌlt] **1** *n* adulto(-a) *m(f)* **2** *adj* adulto
ad·ult ed·u'ca·tion educación *f* para adultos
a·dul·ter·ous [ə'dʌltərəs] *adj relationship* adúltero
a·dul·ter·y [ə'dʌltərɪ] adulterio *m*
'a·dult film *euph* película *f* para adultos
ad·vance [əd'væns] **1** *n money* adelanto *m*; *in science*, MIL avance *m*; ***in advance*** con antelación; *get money* por adelantado; ***48 hours in advance*** con 48 horas de antelación; ***make advances*** (*progress*) avanzar, progresar; *sexually* insinuarse **2** *v/i* MIL avanzar; (*make progress*) avanzar, progresar **3** *v/t theory* presentar; *sum of money* adelantar; *human knowledge, a cause* hacer avanzar
ad·vance 'book·ing reserva *f* (anticipa-

da)
ad·vanced [əd'vænst] *adj country, level, learner* avanzado
ad·vance 'no·tice aviso *m* previo
ad·vance 'pay·ment pago *m* por adelantado
ad·van·tage [əd'væntɪdʒ] ventaja *f*; ***there's no advantage to be gained*** no se gana nada; ***it's to your advantage*** te conviene; ***take advantage of*** aprovecharse de
ad·van·ta·geous [ædvən'teɪdʒəs] *adj* ventajoso
ad·vent ['ædvent] *fig* llegada *f*
'ad·vent cal·en·dar calendario *m* de Adviento
ad·ven·ture [əd'ventʃər] aventura *f*
ad·ven·tur·ous [əd'ventʃərəs] *adj person* aventurero; *investment* arriesgado
ad·verb ['ædvɜːrb] adverbio *m*
ad·ver·sa·ry ['ædvərserɪ] adversario(-a) *m(f)*
ad·verse ['ædvɜːrs] *adj* adverso
ad·vert ['ædvɜːrt] → ***advertisement***
ad·ver·tise ['ædvərtaɪz] **1** *v/t* anunciar **2** *v/i* anunciarse, poner un anuncio
ad·ver·tise·ment [ədvɜːr'taɪsmənt] anuncio *m*
ad·ver·tis·er ['ædvərtaɪzər] anunciante *m/f*
ad·ver·tis·ing ['ædvərtaɪzɪŋ] publicidad *f*
'ad·ver·tis·ing a·gen·cy agencia *f* de publicidad
'ad·ver·tis·ing budg·et presupuesto *m* para publicidad
'ad·ver·tis·ing cam·paign campaña *f* publicitaria
'ad·ver·tis·ing rev·e·nue ingresos *mpl* por publicidad
ad·vice [əd'vaɪs] consejo *m*; ***he gave me some advice*** me dio un consejo; ***take s.o.'s advice*** seguir el consejo de alguien
ad·vis·a·ble [əd'vaɪzəbl] *adj* aconsejable
ad·vise [əd'vaɪz] *v/t person, caution* aconsejar; *government* asesorar; ***I advise you to leave*** te aconsejo que te vayas
ad·vis·er [əd'vaɪzər] asesor(a) *m(f)*
ad·vo·cate ['ædvəkeɪt] *v/t* abogar por
aer·i·al ['erɪəl] *n* antena *f*
aer·i·al 'pho·to·graph fotografía *f* aérea
aer·o·bics [e'roʊbɪks] *nsg* aerobic *m*
aer·o·dy·nam·ic [eroʊdaɪ'næmɪk] *adj* aerodinámico
aer·o·nau·ti·cal [eroʊ'nɒːtɪkl] *adj* aeronáutico
aer·o·plane ['eroʊpleɪn] *Br* avión *m*
aer·o·sol ['erəsɑːl] aerosol *m*
aer·o·space in·dus·try ['erəspeɪs] industria *f* aeroespacial
aes·thet·ic *etc Br* → ***esthetic*** *etc*
af·fa·ble ['æfəbl] *adj* afable
af·fair [ə'fer] (*matter, business*) asunto *m*; (*love affair*) aventura *f*, lío *m*; ***foreign affairs*** asuntos *mpl* exteriores; ***have an affair with*** tener una aventura *or* lío con
affect [ə'fekt] *v/t also* MED afectar
af·fec·tion [ə'fekʃn] afecto *m*, cariño
af·fec·tion·ate [ə'fekʃnət] *adj* afectuoso, cariñoso
af·fec·tion·ate·ly [ə'fekʃnətlɪ] *adv* con afecto, cariñosamente
af·fin·i·ty [ə'fɪnətɪ] afinidad *f*
af·fir·ma·tive [ə'fɜːrmətɪv] *adj* afirmativo; ***answer in the affirmative*** responder afirmativamente
af·flu·ence ['æfluəns] prosperidad *f*, riqueza *f*
af·flu·ent ['æfluənt] *adj* próspero, acomodado; ***affluent society*** sociedad *f* opulenta
af·ford [ə'fɔːrd] *v/t* permitirse; ***be able to afford sth*** *financially* poder permitirse algo; ***I can't afford the time*** no tengo tiempo; ***it's a risk we can't afford to take*** es un riesgo que no podemos permitirnos tomar
af·ford·a·ble [ə'fɔːrdəbl] *adj* asequible
a·float [ə'floʊt] *adj boat* a flote; ***keep the company afloat*** mantener la compañía a flote
a·fraid [ə'freɪd] *adj*: ***be afraid*** tener miedo; ***be afraid of*** tener miedo de; ***I'm afraid of cats*** tengo miedo a los gatos; ***he's afraid of the dark*** le da miedo la oscuridad; ***I'm afraid of annoying him*** me da miedo enfadarle; ***I'm afraid*** *expressing regret* me temo; ***he's very ill, I'm afraid*** me temo que está muy enfermo; ***I'm afraid so*** (me) temo que sí; ***I'm afraid not*** (me) temo que no
a·fresh [ə'freʃ] *adv* de nuevo
Af·ri·ca ['æfrɪkə] África
Af·ri·can ['æfrɪkən] **1** *adj* africano **2** *n* africano(-a) *m(f)*
af·ter ['æftər] **1** *prep* después de; ***after all*** después de todo; ***after that*** después de eso; ***it's ten after two*** son las dos y diez **2** *adv* después; ***the day after*** el día siguiente
af·ter·math ['æftərmæθ] *time* periodo *m* posterior (***of*** a); *state of affairs* repercusiones *fpl*
afternoon [æftər'nuːn] tarde *f*; ***in the afternoon*** por la tarde; ***this afternoon*** esta tarde; ***good afternoon*** buenas tardes
'af·ter sales serv·ice servicio *m* posventa
'af·ter·shave loción *f* para después del afeitado, after shave *m*

'**af·ter·taste** regusto *m*
af·ter·ward ['æftərwərd] *adv* después
a·gain [ə'geɪn] *adv* otra vez; ***I never saw him again*** no lo volví a ver
a·gainst [ə'genst] *prep lean* contra; ***the USA against Brazil*** SP Estados Unidos contra *B*rasil; ***I'm against the idea*** estoy en contra de la idea; ***what do you have against her?*** ¿que tienes en contra de ella?; ***against the law*** ilegal
age [eɪdʒ] **1** *n of person, object* edad *f*; (*era*) era *f*; ***at the age of ten*** a los diez años; ***under age*** menor de edad; ***she's five years of age*** tiene cinco años; ***I've been waiting for ages*** llevo siglos esperando F; ***I haven't seen him for ages*** hace siglos que no lo veo F **2** *v/i* envejecer
aged[1] [eɪdʒd] *adj*: ***aged 16*** con 16 años de edad
a·ged[2] ['eɪdʒɪd] **1** *adj*: ***her aged parents*** sus ancianos padres **2** *n*: ***the aged*** los ancianos
'**age group** grupo *m* de edades
'**age lim·it** límite *m* de edad
a·gen·cy ['eɪdʒənsɪ] agencia *f*
a·gen·da [ə'dʒendə] orden *m* del día; ***on the agenda*** en el orden del día
a·gent ['eɪdʒənt] agente *m/f*, representante *m/f*
ag·gra·vate ['ægrəveɪt] *v/t* agravar; (*annoy*) molestar
ag·gre·gate ['ægrɪgət] *n* SP: ***win on aggregate*** ganar en el total de la eliminatoria
ag·gres·sion [ə'greʃn] agresividad *f*
ag·gres·sive [ə'gresɪv] *adj* agresivo; (*dynamic*) agresivo, enérgico
ag·gres·sive·ly [ə'gresɪvlɪ] *adv* agresivamente
a·ghast [ə'gæst] *adj* horrorizado
ag·ile ['ædʒəl] *adj* ágil
a·gil·i·ty [ə'dʒɪlətɪ] agilidad *f*
ag·i·tate ['ædʒɪteɪt] *v/i*: ***agitate for*** hacer campaña a favor de
ag·i·tat·ed ['ædʒɪteɪtɪd] *adj* agitado
ag·i·ta·tion [ædʒɪ'teɪʃn] agitación *f*
ag·i·ta·tor [ædʒɪ'teɪtər] agitador(a) *m(f)*
AGM [eɪdʒiː'em] *abbr* (= ***annual general meeting***) junta *f* general annual
ag·nos·tic [æg'nɑːstɪk] *n* agnóstico(-a) *m(f)*
a·go [ə'goʊ] *adv*: ***2 days ago*** hace dos días; ***long ago*** hace mucho tiempo; ***how long ago?*** ¿hace cuánto tiempo?; ***how long ago did he leave?*** ¿hace cuánto se marchó?
a·gog [ə'gɑːg] *adj*: ***be agog at sth*** estar emocionado con algo
ag·o·nize ['ægənaɪz] *v/i* atormentarse (***over*** por), angustiarse (***over*** por)
ag·o·niz·ing ['ægənaɪzɪŋ] *adj pain* atroz; *wait* angustioso
ag·o·ny ['ægənɪ] agonía *f*
a·gree [ə'griː] **1** *v/i* estar de acuerdo; *of figures* coincidir; (*reach agreement*) ponerse de acuerdo; ***I agree*** estoy de acuerdo; ***it doesn't agree with me*** *of food* no me sienta bien **2** *v/t price* acordar; ***agree that sth should be done*** acordar que hay que hacer algo
a·gree·a·ble [ə'griːəbl] *adj* (*pleasant*) agradable; ***be agreeable*** *fml* (*in agreement*) estar de acuerdo
a·gree·ment [ə'griːmənt] (*consent, contract*) acuerdo *m*; ***reach agreement on*** llegar a un acuerdo sobre
ag·ri·cul·tur·al [ægrɪ'kʌltʃərəl] *adj* agrícola
ag·ri·cul·ture ['ægrɪkʌltʃər] agricultura *f*
ahead [ə'hed] *adv position* delante; *movement* adelante; *in race* por delante, en cabeza; ***be ahead of*** estar por delante de; ***plan / think ahead*** planear con antelación / pensar con anticipación
aid [eɪd] **1** *n* ayuda *f*; ***come to s.o.'s aid*** acudir a ayudar a alguien **2** *v/t* ayudar
aide [eɪd] asistente *m/f*
Aids [eɪdz] sida *m*
ail·ing ['eɪlɪŋ] *adj economy* débil, frágil
ail·ment ['eɪlmənt] achaque *m*
aim [eɪm] **1** *n in shooting* puntería *f*; (*objective*) objetivo *m* **2** *v/i in shooting* apuntar; ***aim at doing sth, aim to do sth*** tener como intención hacer algo **3** *v/t remark* dirigir; ***he aimed the gun at me*** me apuntó con la pistola; ***be aimed at*** *of remark etc* estar dirigido a; *of gun* estar apuntando a
aim·less ['eɪmlɪs] *adj* sin objetivos
air [er] **1** *n* aire *m*; ***by air*** *travel* en avión; *send mail* por correo aéreo; ***in the open air*** al aire libre; ***on the air*** RAD, TV en el aire **2** *v/t room* airear; *fig*: *views* airear, ventilar
'**air·bag** airbag *m*, bolsa *f* de aire
'**air·base** base *f* aérea
'**air-con·di·tioned** *adj* con aire acondicionado, climatizado
'**air-con·di·tion·ing** aire *m* acondicionado
'**air·craft** avión *m*, aeronave *f*
'**air·craft car·ri·er** portaaviones *m inv*
'**air fare** (precio *m* del) *Span* billete *m or L.Am.* boleto *m* de avión
'**air·field** aeródromo *m*, campo *m* de aviación
'**air force** fuerza *f* aérea
'**air host·ess** azafata *f*, *L.Am.* aeromoza *f*
'**air let·ter** aerograma *m*

'air·lift 1 *n* puente m aéreo **2** *v/t* transportar mediante puente aéreo
'air·line línea *f* aérea
'air·lin·er avión *m* de pasajeros
'air·mail: ***by airmail*** por correo aéreo
'air·plane avión *m*
'air·pock·et bolsa *f* de aire
'air pol·lu·tion contaminación *f* del aire
'air·port aeropuerto *m*
'air·sick: ***get airsick*** marearse (*en avión*)
'air·space espacio *m* aéreo
'air ter·mi·nal terminal *f* aérea
'air·tight *adj container* hermético
'air traf·fic tráfico *m* aéreo
'air-traf·fic con·trol control *m* del tráfico aéreo
air-traf·fic con'trol·ler controlador(a) *m(f)* del tráfico aéreo
air·y ['erɪ] *adj room* aireado; *attitude* despreocupado, ligero
aisle [aɪl] pasillo *m*
'aisle seat asiento *m* de pasillo
a·jar [ə'dʒɑːr] *adj*: ***be ajar*** estar entreabierto
a·lac·ri·ty [ə'lækrətɪ] presteza *f*
a·larm [ə'lɑːrm] **1** *n* alarma *f*; ***raise the alarm*** dar la alarma **2** *v/t* alarmar
a'larm clock reloj *m* despertador
a·larm·ing [ə'lɑːrmɪŋ] *adj* alarmante
a·larm·ing·ly [ə'lɑːrmɪŋlɪ] *adv* de forma alarmante
al·bum ['ælbəm] *for photographs*, (*record*) álbum *m*
al·co·hol ['ælkəhɑːl] alcohol *m*
al·co·hol·ic [ælkə'hɑːlɪk] **1** *n* alcohólico(-a) *m(f)* **2** *adj* alcohólico
a·lert [ə'lɜːrt] **1** *n signal* alerta *f*; ***be on the alert*** estar alerta **2** *v/t* alertar **3** *adj* alerta
al·ge·bra ['ældʒɪbrə] álgebra *f*
al·i·bi ['ælɪbaɪ] coartada *f*
a·li·en ['eɪlɪən] **1** *n* (*foreigner*) extranjero(-a) *m(f)*; *from space* extraterrestre *m/f* **2** *adj* extraño; ***be alien to s.o.*** ser ajeno a alguien
a·li·en·ate ['eɪlɪəneɪt] *v/t* alienar, provocar el distanciamiento de
a·light [ə'laɪt] *adj* en llamas
a·lign [ə'laɪn] *v/t* alinear
a·like [ə'laɪk] **1** *adj*: ***be alike*** parecerse **2** *adv* igual; ***old and young alike*** viejos y jóvenes sin distinción
al·i·mo·ny ['ælɪmənɪ] pensión *f* alimenticia
a·live [ə'laɪv] *adj*: ***be alive*** estar vivo
all [ɒːl] **1** *adj* todo(s) **2** *pron* todo; ***all of us / them*** todos nosotros / ellos; ***he ate all of it*** se lo comió todo; ***that's all, thanks*** eso es todo, gracias; ***for all I care*** para lo que me importa; ***for all I know*** por lo que sé; ***all at once*** (*suddenly*) de repente; (*at the same time*) a la vez; ***all but*** (*except*) todos menos; (*nearly*) casi; ***all the better*** mucho mejor; ***all the time*** desde el principio; ***they're not at all alike*** no se parecen en nada; ***not at all!*** ¡en absoluto!; ***two all*** SP empate a dos; ***all right*** → ***alright***
al·lay [ə'leɪ] *v/t* apaciguar
al·le·ga·tion [ælɪ'geɪʃn] acusación *f*
al·lege [ə'ledʒ] *v/t* alegar
al·leged [ə'ledʒd] *adj* presunto
al·leg·ed·ly [ə'ledʒɪdlɪ] *adv* presuntamente, supuestamente
al·le·giance [ə'liːdʒəns] lealtad *f*
al·ler·gic [ə'lɜːrdʒɪk] *adj* alérgico; ***be allergic to*** ser alérgico a
al·ler·gy ['ælərdʒɪ] alergia *f*
al·le·vi·ate [ə'liːvɪeɪt] *v/t* aliviar
al·ley ['ælɪ] callejón *m*
al·li·ance [ə'laɪəns] alianza *f*
al·lo·cate ['æləkeɪt] *v/t* asignar
al·lo·ca·tion [ælə'keɪʃn] asignación *f*
al·lot [ə'lɑːt] *v/t* (*pret & pp* ***allotted***) asignar
al·low [ə'laʊ] *v/t* (*permit*) permitir; (*calculate for*) calcular; ***they don't allow smoking*** no está permitido fumar, está prohibido fumar; ***it's not allowed*** no está permitido; ***he allowed us to leave*** nos permitió salir
◆ **allow for** *v/t* tener en cuenta
al·low·ance [ə'laʊəns] (*money*) asignación *f*; (*pocket money*) paga *f*; ***make allowances*** *for weather etc* tener en cuenta; *for person* disculpar
al·loy ['ælɔɪ] aleación *f*
'all-pur·pose *adj* multiuso
'all-round *adj* completo
'all-time: ***be at an all-time low*** haber alcanzado un mínimo *histórico*
◆ **al·lude to** [ə'luːd] *v/t* aludir a
al·lur·ing [ə'luːrɪŋ] *adj* atractivo, seductor
all-wheel 'drive *adj* con tracción a las cuatro ruedas
al·ly ['ælaɪ] *n* aliado(-a) *m(f)*
Al·might·y [ɒːl'maɪtɪ]: ***the Almighty*** el Todopoderoso
al·mond ['ɑːmənd] almendra *f*
al·most ['ɒːlmoʊst] *adv* casi
a·lone [ə'loʊn] *adj* solo
a·long [ə'lɒːŋ] **1** *prep* (*situated beside*) a lo largo de; ***the shop is halfway along Baker Street*** la tienda está a mitad de Baker Street; ***walk along this path*** sigue por esta calle **2** *adv*: ***would you like to come along?*** ¿te gustaría venir con nosotros?; ***he always brings the dog along*** siempre trae al perro; ***along with*** junto con; ***all***

along (*all the time*) todo el tiempo, desde el principio
a·long·side [əlɒːŋ'saɪd] *prep* (*in co-operation with*) junto a; (*parallel to*) al lado de
a·loof [ə'luːf] *adj* distante, reservado
a·loud [ə'laʊd] *adv* en voz alta
al·pha·bet ['ælfəbet] alfabeto *m*
al·pha·bet·i·cal [ælfə'betɪkl] *adj* alfabético
al·read·y [ɒːl'redɪ] *adv* ya
al·right [ɒːlraɪt] *adj* (*not hurt, in working order*) bien; ***is it alright to leave now?*** (*permitted*) ¿puedo irme ahora?; ***is it alright to take these out of the country?*** ¿se pueden sacar éstos del país?; ***is it alright with you if I ...?*** ¿te importa si ...?; ***alright, you can have one!*** de acuerdo, ¡puedes tomar uno!; ***alright, I heard you!*** vale, ¡te he oído!; ***everything is alright now between them*** vuelven a estar bien; ***that's alright*** (*don't mention it*) de nada; (*I don't mind*) no importa
al·so ['ɒːlsoʊ] *adv* también
al·tar ['ɒːltər] altar *m*
al·ter ['ɒːltər] *v/t* alterar
al·ter·a·tion [ɒːltə'reɪʃn] alteración *f*
al·ter·nate 1 *v/i* ['ɒːltərneɪt] alternar **2** *adj* ['ɒːltərnət] alterno
al·ter·nat·ing cur·rent ['ɒːltərneɪtɪŋ] corriente *f* alterna
al·ter·na·tive [ɒːlt'ɜːrnətɪv] **1** *n* alternativa *f* **2** *adj* alternativo
al·ter·na·tive·ly [ɒːlt'ɜːrnətɪvlɪ] *adv* si no
al·though [ɒːl'ðoʊ] *conj* aunque, si bien
al·ti·tude ['æltɪtuːd] *of plane, city* altitud *f*; *of mountain* altura *f*
al·to·geth·er [ɒːltə'geðər] *adv* (*completely*) completamente; (*in all*) en total
al·tru·ism ['æltruːɪzm] altruismo *m*
al·tru·is·tic [æltruː'ɪstɪk] *adj* altruista
a·lu·min·i·um [ælјʊ'mɪnɪəm] *Br*, **a·lu·mi·num** [ə'luːmənəm] aluminio *m*
al·ways ['ɒːlweɪz] *adv* siempre
a. m. ['eɪem] *abbr* (= ***ante meridiem***) a. m.; ***at 11 a.m*** a las 11 de la mañana
a·mal·gam·ate [ə'mælgəmeɪt] *v/i of companies* fusionarse
a·mass [ə'mæs] *v/t* acumular
am·a·teur ['æmətʃʊr] *n unskilled* aficionado(-a) *m(f)*; SP amateur *m/f*
am·a·teur·ish ['æmətʃʊrɪʃ] *adj pej* chapucero
a·maze [ə'meɪz] *v/t* asombrar
a·mazed [ə'meɪzd] *adj* asombrado; ***we were amazed to hear ...*** nos asombró oír ...
a·maze·ment [ə'meɪzmənt] asombro *m*
a·maz·ing [ə'meɪzɪŋ] *adj* (*surprising*) asombroso; F (*very good*) alucinante F
a·maz·ing·ly [ə'meɪzɪŋlɪ] *adv* increíblemente
Am·a·zon ['æməzən] *n*: ***the Amazon*** el Amazonas
Am·a·zo·ni·an [æmə'zoʊnɪən] *adj* amazónico
am·bas·sa·dor [æm'bæsədər] embajador(a) *m(f)*
am·ber ['æmbər] *adj* ámbar; ***at amber*** en ámbar
am·bi·dex·trous [æmbɪ'dekstrəs] *adj* ambidiestro
am·bi·ence ['æmbɪəns] ambiente *m*
am·bi·gu·i·ty [æmbɪ'gjuːətɪ] ambigüedad *f*
am·big·u·ous [æm'bɪgjʊəs] *adj* ambiguo
am·bi·tion [æm'bɪʃn] *also pej* ambición *f*
am·bi·tious [æm'bɪʃəs] *adj* ambicioso
am·biv·a·lent [æm'bɪvələnt] *adj* ambivalente
am·ble ['æmbl] *v/i* deambular
am·bu·lance ['æmbjʊləns] ambulancia *f*
am·bush ['æmbʊʃ] **1** *n* emboscada *f* **2** *v/t* tender una emboscada a
a·mend [ə'mend] *v/t* enmendar
a·mend·ment [ə'mendmənt] enmienda *f*
a·mends [ə'mendz] *npl*: ***make amends for*** compensar
a·men·i·ties [ə'miːnətɪz] *npl* servicios *mpl*
A·mer·i·ca [ə'merɪkə] *continent* América; *USA* Estados *mpl* Unidos
A·mer·i·can [ə'merɪkən] **1** *n North American* estadounidense *m/f* **2** *adj North American* estadounidense
A'mer·i·can plan pensión *f* completa
a·mi·a·ble ['eɪmɪəbl] *adj* afable, amable
a·mi·ca·ble ['æmɪkəbl] *adj* amistoso
a·mi·ca·bly ['æmɪkəblɪ] *adv* amistosamente
am·mu·ni·tion [æmjʊ'nɪʃn] munición *f*; *fig* argumentos *mpl*
am·ne·sia [æm'niːzɪə] amnesia *f*
am·nes·ty ['æmnəstɪ] amnistía *f*
a·mong(st) [ə'mʌŋ(st)] *prep* entre
a·mor·al [eɪ'mɔːrəl] *adj* amoral
a·mount [ə'maʊnt] cantidad *f*; (*sum of money*) cantidad *f*, suma *f*
◆ **amount to** *v/t* ascender a; ***his contribution didn't amount to much*** su contribución no fue gran cosa
am·phib·i·an [æm'fɪbɪən] anfibio *m*
am·phib·i·ous [æm'fɪbɪəs] *adj animal, vehicle* anfibio
am·phi·the·a·ter, *Br* **am·phi·the·a·tre** ['æmfɪθɪətər] anfiteatro *m*
am·ple ['æmpl] *adj* abundante; ***$4 will be ample*** 4 dólares serán más que sufi-

cientes
am·pli·fi·er ['æmplɪfaɪr] amplificador *m*
am·pli·fy ['æmplɪfaɪ] *v/t* (*pret & pp* ***amplified***) *sound* amplificar
am·pu·tate ['æmpjʊteɪt] *v/t* amputar
am·pu·ta·tion [æmpjʊ'teɪʃn] amputación *f*
a·muse [ə'mjuːz] *v/t* (*make laugh etc*) divertir; (*entertain*) entretener
a·muse·ment [ə'mjuːzmənt] (*merriment*) diversión *f*; (*entertainment*) entretenimiento *m*; ***amusements*** (*games*) juegos *mpl*; ***what do you do for amusement?*** ¿qué haces para entretenerte?; ***to our great amusement*** para nuestro regocijo
a'muse·ment ar·cade [ɑːr'keɪd] salón *m* de juegos recreativos
a'muse·ment park parque *m* de atracciones
a·mus·ing [ə'mjuːzɪŋ] *adj* divertido
an·a·bol·ic ster·oid [ænə'bɑːlɪk] esteroide *m* anabolizante
a·nae·mi·a *etc Br* → ***anemia*** *etc*
an·aes·thet·ic *etc Br* → ***anesthetic*** *etc*
an·a·log ['ænəlɑːg] *adj* COMPUT analógico
a·nal·o·gy [ə'nælədʒɪ] analogía *f*
an·al·y·sis [ə'næləsɪs] (*pl* ***analyses*** [ə'næləsiːz]) análisis *m inv*; (*psychoanalysis*) psicoanálisis *m inv*
an·a·lyst ['ænəlɪst] analista *m/f*; PSYCH psicoanalista *m/f*
an·a·lyt·i·cal [ænə'lɪtɪkl] *adj* analítico
an·a·lyze ['ænəlaɪz] *v/t* analizar; (*psychoanalyse*) psicoanalizar
an·arch·y ['ænərkɪ] anarquía *f*
a·nat·o·my [ə'nætəmɪ] anatomía *f*
an·ces·tor ['ænsestər] antepasado(-a) *m(f)*
an·chor ['æŋkər] **1** *n* NAUT ancla *f* ; TV presentador(a) *m(f)* **2** *v/i* NAUT anclar
an·cient ['eɪnʃənt] *adj* antiguo
an·cil·lar·y [æn'sɪlərɪ] *adj staff* auxiliar
and [ənd] *stressed* [ænd] *conj* y
An·de·an ['ændɪən] *adj* andino
An·des ['ændiːz] *npl*: ***the Andes*** los Andes
an·ec·dote ['ænɪkdoʊt] anécdota *f*
a·ne·mia [ə'niːmɪə] anemia *f*
a·ne·mic [ə'niːmɪk] *adj* anémico
an·es·thet·ic [ænəs'θetɪk] *n* anestesia *f*
an·es·the·tist [ə'niːsθətɪst] anestesista *m/f*
an·gel ['eɪndʒl] REL ángel *m*; *fig* ángel *m*, cielo *m*
an·ger ['æŋgər] **1** *n* enfado *m*, enojo *m* **2** *v/t* enfadar, enojar
an·gi·na [æn'dʒaɪnə] angina *f* (de pecho)
an·gle ['æŋgl] *n* ángulo *m*
An·glo-Sax·on [æŋgloʊ'sæksn] **1** *adj* anglosajón **2** *n person* anglosajón(-ona) *m(f)*
an·gry ['æŋgrɪ] *adj* enfadado, enojado; ***be angry with s.o.*** estar enfadado *or* enojado con alguien
an·guish ['æŋgwɪʃ] angustia *f*
an·gu·lar ['æŋgjʊlər] *adj* anguloso
an·i·mal ['ænɪml] animal *m*
an·i·mated ['ænɪmeɪtɪd] *adj* animado
an·i·ma·ted car'toon dibujos *mpl* animados
an·i·ma·tion [ænɪ'meɪʃn] (*liveliness*), *of cartoon* animación *f*
an·i·mos·i·ty [ænɪ'mɑːsətɪ] animosidad *f*
an·kle ['æŋkl] tobillo *m*
an·nex ['æneks] **1** *n building* edificio *m* anexo **2** *v/t state* anexionar
an·nexe ['æneks] *n Br* edificio *m* anexo
an·ni·hi·late [ə'naɪəleɪt] *v/t* aniquilar
an·ni·hi·la·tion [ənaɪə'leɪʃn] aniquilación *f*
an·ni·ver·sa·ry [ænɪ'vɜːrsərɪ] (*wedding anniversary*) aniversario *m*
an·no·tate ['ænəteɪt] *v/t report* anotar
an·nounce [ə'naʊns] *v/t* anunciar
an·nounce·ment [ə'naʊnsmənt] anuncio *m*
an·nounc·er [ə'naʊnsər] TV, RAD presentador(a) *m(f)*
an·noy [ə'nɔɪ] *v/t* molestar, irritar; ***be annoyed*** estar molesto *or* irritado
an·noy·ance [ə'nɔɪəns] (*anger*) irritación *f*; (*nuisance*) molestia *f*
an·noy·ing [ə'nɔɪɪŋ] *adj* molesto, irritante
an·nu·al ['ænʊəl] *adj* anual
an·nu·al gen·er·al 'meet·ing junta *f* general anual
an·nu·i·ty [ə'nuːətɪ] anualidad *f*
an·nul [ə'nʌl] *v/t* (*pret & pp* ***annulled***) *marriage* anular
an·nul·ment [ə'nʌlmənt] anulación *f*
a·non·y·mous [ə'nɑːnɪməs] *adj* anónimo
an·o·rak ['ænəræk] *Br* anorak *m*
an·o·rex·i·a [ænə'reksɪə] anorexia *f*
an·o·rex·ic [ænə'reksɪk] *adj* anoréxico
an·oth·er [ə'nʌðər] **1** *adj* otro **2** *pron* otro(-a) *m(f)*; ***they helped one another*** se ayudaron (el uno al otro); ***do they know one another?*** ¿se conocen?
ans·wer ['ænsər] **1** *n to letter, person, question* respuesta *f*, contestación *f*; *to problem* solución *f* **2** *v/t letter, person, question* responder, contestar; ***answer the door*** abrir la puerta; ***answer the telephone*** responder *or Span* coger al teléfono
◆ **answer back** *v/t & v/i* contestar, replicar
◆ **answer for** *v/t* responder de

an·swer·ing ma·chine ['ænsərɪŋ] TELEC contestador *m* (automático)
ans·wer·phone ['ænsərfoʊn] TELEC contestador *m* (automático)
ant [ænt] hormiga *f*
an·tag·o·nism [æn'tægənɪzm] antagonismo *m*
an·tag·o·nis·tic [æntægə'nɪstɪk] *adj* hostil
an·tag·o·nize [æn'tægənaɪz] *v/t* antagonizar, enfadar
Ant·arc·tic [ænt'ɑːrktɪk] *n*: ***the Antarctic*** el Antártico
an·te·na·tal [æntɪ'neɪtl] *adj* prenatal
an·ten·na [æn'tenə] *of insect*, *for* TV antena *f*
an·thol·o·gy [æn'θɑːlədʒɪ] antología *f*
an·thro·pol·o·gy [ænθrə'pɑːlədʒɪ] antropología *f*
an·ti·bi·ot·ic [æntɪbaɪ'ɑːtɪk] *n* antibiótico *m*
an·ti·bod·y ['æntɪbɑːdɪ] anticuerpo *m*
an·tic·i·pate [æn'tɪsɪpeɪt] *v/t* esperar, prever
an·tic·i·pa·tion [æntɪsɪ'peɪʃn] expectativa *f*, previsión *f*
an·ti·clock·wise ['æntɪklɑːkwaɪz] *adv Br* en dirección contraria a las agujas del reloj
an·tics ['æntɪks] *npl* payasadas *fpl*
an·ti·dote ['æntɪdoʊt] antídoto *m*
an·ti·freeze ['æntɪfriːz] anticongelante *m*
an·tip·a·thy [æn'tɪpəθɪ] antipatía *f*
an·ti·quat·ed ['æntɪkweɪtɪd] *adj* anticuado
an·tique [æn'tiːk] *n* antigüedad *f*
an'tique dealer anticuario(-a) *m(f)*
an·tiq·ui·ty [æn'tɪkwətɪ] antigüedad *f*
an·ti·sep·tic [æntɪ'septɪk] **1** *adj* antiséptico **2** *n* antiséptico *m*
an·ti·so·cial [æntɪ'soʊʃl] *adj* antisocial, poco sociable
an·ti·vi·rus pro·gram [æntɪ'vaɪrəs] COMPUT (programa *m*) antivirus *m inv*
anx·i·e·ty [æŋ'zaɪətɪ] ansiedad *f*
anx·ious ['æŋkʃəs] *adj* preocupado; (*eager*) ansioso; ***be anxious for*** *for news etc* esperar ansiosamente
an·y ['enɪ] **1** *adj*: ***are there any diskettes / glasses?*** ¿hay disquetes / vasos?; ***is there any bread / improvement?*** ¿hay algo de pan / alguna mejora?; ***there aren't any diskettes / glasses*** no hay disquetes / vasos; ***there isn't any bread / improvement*** no hay pan / ninguna mejora; ***have you any idea at all?*** ¿tienes alguna idea?; ***any one of them could win*** cualquiera de ellos podría ganar **2** *pron* alguno(-a); ***do you have any?*** ¿tienes alguno(s)?; ***there aren't any left*** no queda ninguno; ***there isn't any left*** no queda; ***any of them could be guilty*** cualquiera de ellos podría ser culpable **3** *adv*: ***is that any better / easier?*** ¿es mejor / más fácil así?; ***I don't like it any more*** ya no me gusta
an·y·bod·y ['enɪbɒːdɪ] *pron* alguien; ***there wasn't anybody there*** no había nadie allí
an·y·how ['enɪhaʊ] *adv* en todo caso, de todos modos; ***if I can help you anyhow, please let me know*** si puedo ayudarte de alguna manera, por favor dímelo
an·y·one ['enɪwʌn] → ***anybody***
an·y·thing ['enɪθɪŋ] *pron* algo; *with negatives* nada; ***I didn't hear anything*** no oí nada; ***anything but*** todo menos; ***anything else?*** ¿algo más?
an·y·way ['enɪweɪ] → ***anyhow***
an·y·where ['enɪwer] *adv* en alguna parte; ***is Peter anywhere around?*** ¿está Peter por ahí?; ***he never goes anywhere*** nunca va a ninguna parte; ***I can't find it anywhere*** no lo encuentro por ninguna parte
a·part [ə'pɑːrt] *adv* aparte; ***the two cities are 250 miles apart*** las dos ciudades están a 250 millas la una de la otra; ***live apart*** *of people* vivir separado; ***apart from*** aparte de
a·part·ment [ə'pɑːrtmənt] apartamento *m*, *Span* piso *m*, *Am* departamento *m*
a'part·ment block bloque *m* de apartamentos *or Span* pisos
ap·a·thet·ic [æpə'θetɪk] *adj* apático
ap·a·thy ['æpəθɪ] apatía *f*
ape [eɪp] simio *m*
a·pe·ri·tif [ə'perɪtiːf] aperitivo *m*
ap·er·ture ['æpərtʃər] PHOT apertura *f*
a·piece [ə'piːs] *adv* cada uno
a·pol·o·get·ic [əpɑːlə'dʒetɪk] *adj letter* de disculpa; ***he was very apologetic about ...*** pedía constantes disculpas por ...
a·pol·o·gize [ə'pɑːlədʒaɪz] *v/i* disculparse, pedir perdón
a·pol·o·gy [ə'pɑːlədʒɪ] disculpa *f*
a·pos·tle [ə'pɑːsl] REL apóstol *m*
a·pos·tro·phe [ə'pɑːstrəfɪ] GRAM apóstrofo *m*
ap·pall [ə'pɒːl] *v/t* horrorizar, espantar
ap·pal·ling [ə'pɒːlɪŋ] *adj* horroroso
ap·pa·ra·tus [æpə'reɪtəs] aparatos *mpl*
ap·par·ent [ə'pærənt] *adj* aparente, evidente; ***become apparent that ...*** hacerse evidente que ...
ap·par·ent·ly [ə'pærəntlɪ] *adv* al parecer, por lo visto
ap·pa·ri·tion [æpə'rɪʃn] (*ghost*) aparición

f

ap·peal [ə'piːl] **1** *n* (*charm*) atractivo *m*; *for funds etc* llamamiento *m*; LAW apelación *f* **2** *v/i* LAW apelar

◆ **appeal to** *v/t* (*be attractive to*) atraer a

◆ **appeal for** *v/t* solicitar

ap·peal·ing [ə'piːlɪŋ] *adj idea, offer* atractivo; *glance* suplicante

ap·pear [ə'pɪr] *v/i* aparecer; *in court* comparecer; (*look, seem*) parecer; ***it appears that …*** parece que …

ap·pear·ance [ə'pɪrəns] aparición *f*; *in court* comparecencia *f*; (*look*) apariencia *f*, aspecto *m*; ***put in an appearance*** hacer acto de presencia

ap·pease [ə'piːz] *v/t* apaciguar

ap·pen·di·ci·tis [əpendɪ'saɪtɪs] apendicitis *m*

ap·pen·dix [ə'pendɪks] MED, *of book etc* apéndice *m*

ap·pe·tite ['æpɪtaɪt] *also fig* apetito *m*

ap·pe·tiz·er ['æpɪtaɪzər] aperitivo *m*

ap·pe·tiz·ing ['æpɪtaɪzɪŋ] *adj* apetitoso

ap·plaud [ə'plɒːd] **1** *v/i* aplaudir **2** *v/t also fig* aplaudir

ap·plause [ə'plɒːz] aplauso *m*

ap·ple ['æpl] manzana *f*

ap·ple 'pie tarta *f* de manzana

ap·ple 'sauce compota *f* de manzana

ap·pli·ance [ə'plaɪəns] aparato *m*; *household* electrodoméstico *m*

ap·plic·a·ble [ə'plɪkəbl] *adj* aplicable; ***it's not applicable to foreigners*** no se aplica a extranjeros

ap·pli·cant ['æplɪkənt] solicitante *m/f*

ap·pli·ca·tion [æplɪ'keɪʃn] *for job, passport etc* solicitud *f*; *for university* solicitud *f* (de admisión)

ap·pli'ca·tion form *for passport* impreso *m* de solicitud; *for university* impreso *m* de solicitud de admisión

ap·ply [ə'plaɪ] **1** *v/t* (*pret & pp* ***applied***) *rules, solution, ointment* aplicar **2** *v/i* (*pret & pp* ***applied***) *of rule, law* aplicarse

◆ **apply for** *v/t job, passport* solicitar; *university* solicitar el ingreso en

◆ **apply to** *v/t* (*contact*) dirigirse a; (*affect*) aplicarse a

ap·point [ə'pɔɪnt] *v/t to position* nombrar, designar

ap·point·ment [ə'pɔɪntmənt] *to position* nombramiento *m*, designación *f*; *meeting* cita *f*; ***make an appointment with the doctor*** pedir hora con el doctor

ap'point·ments di·a·ry agenda *f* de citas

ap·prais·al [ə'preɪz(ə)l] evaluación *f*

ap·pre·cia·ble [ə'priːʃəbl] *adj* apreciable

ap·pre·ci·ate [ə'priːʃɪeɪt] **1** *v/t* (*value*) apreciar; (*be grateful for*) agradecer; (*acknowledge*) ser consciente de; ***thanks, I appreciate it*** te lo agradezco **2** *v/i* FIN revalorizarse

ap·pre·ci·a·tion [əpriːʃɪ'eɪʃn] *of kindness etc* agradecimiento *m*; *of music etc* aprecio *m*

ap·pre·ci·a·tive [ə'priːʃətɪv] *adj* agradecido

ap·pre·hen·sive [æprɪ'hensɪv] *adj* aprensivo, temeroso

ap·pren·tice [ə'prentɪs] aprendiz(a) *m*(*f*)

ap·proach [ə'proʊʧ] **1** *n* aproximación *f*; (*proposal*) propuesta *f*; *to problem* enfoque *m* **2** *v/t* (*get near to*) aproximarse a; (*contact*) ponerse en contacto con; *problem* enfocar

ap·proach·a·ble [ə'proʊʧəbl] *adj person* accesible

ap·pro·pri·ate¹ [ə'proʊprɪət] *adj* apropiado, adecuado

ap·pro·pri·ate² [ə'proʊprɪeɪt] *v/t* apropiarse de; (*euph: steal*) apropiarse de

ap·prov·al [ə'pruːvl] aprobación *f*

ap·prove [ə'pruːv] **1** *v/i*: ***my parents don't approve*** a mis padres no les parece bien **2** *v/t* aprobar

◆ **approve of** *v/t* aprobar; ***her parents don't approve of me*** no les gusto a sus padres

ap·prox·i·mate [ə'prɑːksɪmət] *adj* aproximado

ap·prox·i·mate·ly [ə'prɑːksɪmətlɪ] *adv* aproximadamente

ap·prox·i·ma·tion [əprɑːksɪ'meɪʃn] aproximación *f*

APR [eɪpiː'ɑː] *abbr* (= ***annual percentage rate***) TAE *f* (= tasa *f* anual equivalente)

a·pri·cot ['æprɪkɑːt] albaricoque *m*, *L.Am.* damasco *m*

A·pril ['eɪprəl] abril *m*

apt [æpt] *adj remark* oportuno; ***be apt to …*** ser propenso a …

ap·ti·tude ['æptɪtuːd] aptitud *f*; ***he has a natural aptitude for …*** tiene aptitudes naturales para …

'ap·ti·tude test prueba *f* de aptitud

aq·ua·lung ['ækwəlʌŋ] escafandra *f* autónoma

a·quar·i·um [ə'kwerɪəm] acuario *m*

A·quar·i·us [ə'kwerɪəs] ASTR Acuario *m/f inv*

a·quat·ic [ə'kwætɪk] *adj* acuático

Ar·ab ['ærəb] **1** *adj* árabe **2** *n* árabe *m/f*

Ar·a·bic ['ærəbɪk] **1** *adj* árabe **2** *n* árabe *m*

ar·a·ble ['ærəbl] *adj* arable, cultivable

ar·bi·tra·ry ['ɑːrbɪtrerɪ] *adj* arbitrario

ar·bi·trate ['ɑːrbɪtreɪt] *v/i* arbitrar

ar·bi·tra·tion [ɑːrbɪ'treɪʃn] arbitraje *m*

ar·bi·tra·tor ['ɑːrbɪ'treɪtər] árbitro(-a) *m(f)*
arch [ɑːrtʃ] *n* arco *m*
ar·chae·ol·o·gy *etc Br* → ***archeology*** *etc*
ar·cha·ic [ɑːr'keɪɪk] *adj* arcaico
ar·che·o·log·i·cal [ɑːrkɪə'lɑːdʒɪkl] *adj* arqueológico
ar·che·ol·o·gist [ɑːrkɪ'ɑːlədʒɪst] arqueólogo(-a) *m(f)*
ar·che·ol·o·gy [ɑːrkɪ'ɑːlədʒɪ] arqueología *f*
ar·cher ['ɑːrtʃər] arquero(-a) *m(f)*
ar·chi·tec·t ['ɑːrkɪtekt] arquitecto(-a) *m(f)*
ar·chi·tec·tur·al [ɑːrkɪ'tektʃərəl] *adj* arquitectónico
ar·chi·tec·ture ['ɑːrkɪtektʃər] arquitectura *f*
ar·chives ['ɑːrkaɪvz] *npl* archivos *mpl*
arch·way ['ɑːrtʃweɪ] arco *m*
Arc·tic ['ɑːrktɪk] *n*: ***the Arctic*** el Ártico
ar·dent ['ɑːrdənt] *adj* ardiente, ferviente
ar·du·ous ['ɑːrdjʊəs] *adj* arduo
ar·e·a ['erɪə] área *f*, zona *f*; *of activity, study etc* área *f*, ámbito *m*
'ar·e·a code TELEC prefijo *m*
a·re·na [ə'riːnə] SP estadio *m*
Ar·gen·ti·na [ɑːrdʒən'tiːnə] Argentina
Ar·gen·tin·i·an [ɑːrdʒən'tɪnɪən] **1** *adj* argentino **2** *n* argentino(-a) *m(f)*
ar·gu·a·bly ['ɑːrgjʊəblɪ] *adv* posiblemente
ar·gue ['ɑːrgjuː] **1** *v/i* (*quarrel*) discutir; (*reason*) argumentar **2** *v/t*: ***argue that ...*** argumentar que ...
ar·gu·ment ['ɑːrgjʊmənt] (*quarrel*) discusión *m*; (*reasoning*) argumento *m*
ar·gu·ment·a·tive [ɑːrgjʊ'mentətɪv] *adj* discutidor
a·ri·a ['ɑːrɪə] MUS aria *f*
ar·id ['ærɪd] *adj land* árido
Ar·i·es ['eriːz] ASTR Aries *m/f inv*
a·rise [ə'raɪz] *v/i* (*pret* ***arose***, *pp* ***arisen***) *of situation, problem* surgir
a·ris·en [ə'rɪzn] *pp* → ***arise***
ar·is·toc·ra·cy [ærɪ'stɑːkrəsɪ] aristocracia *f*
ar·is·to·crat [ə'rɪstəkræt] aristócrata *m/f*
a·ris·to·crat·ic [ærɪstə'krætɪk] *adj* aristocrático
a·rith·me·tic [ə'rɪθmətɪk] aritmética *f*
arm[1] [ɑːrm] *n of person, chair* brazo *m*
arm[2] [ɑːrm] *v/t* armar
ar·ma·ments ['ɑːrməmənts] *npl* armamento *m*
arm·chair ['ɑːrmtʃer] sillón *m*
armed [ɑːrmd] *adj* armado
armed 'forc·es *npl* fuerzas *fpl* armadas
armed 'rob·ber·y atraco *m* a mano armada
ar·mor, *Br* **ar·mour** ['ɑːrmər] armadura *f*
ar·mored 've·hi·cle, *Br* **ar·moured 've·hi·cle** ['ɑːrmərd] vehículo *m* blindado
arm·pit ['ɑːrmpɪt] sobaco *m*
arms [ɑːrmz] *npl* (*weapons*) armas *fpl*
ar·my ['ɑːrmɪ] ejército *m*
a·ro·ma [ə'roʊmə] aroma *m*
a·rose [ə'roʊz] *pret* → ***arise***
a·round [ə'raʊnd] **1** *prep* (*enclosing*) alrededor de; ***it's around the corner*** está a la vuelta de la esquina **2** *adv* (*in the area*) por ahí; (*encircling*) alrededor; (*roughly*) alrededor de, aproximadamente; (*with expressions of time*) en torno a; ***he lives around here*** vive por aquí; ***walk around*** pasear; ***she has been around*** (*has traveled, is experienced*) tiene mucho mundo; ***he's still around*** F (*alive*) todavía está rondando por ahí F
a·rouse [ə'raʊz] *v/t* despertar; *sexually* excitar
ar·range [ə'reɪndʒ] *v/t* (*put in order*) ordenar; *furniture* ordenar, disponer; *flowers, music* arreglar; *meeting, party etc* organizar; *time and place* acordar; ***I've arranged to meet her*** he quedado con ella
◆ **arrange for** *v/t*: ***I arranged for Jack to collect it*** quedé para que Jack lo recogiera
ar·range·ment [ə'reɪndʒmənt] (*plan*) plan *m*, preparativo *m*; (*agreement*) acuerdo *m*; (*layout*: *of furniture etc*) orden *m*, disposición *f*; *of flowers, music* arreglo *m*; ***I've made arrangements for the neighbors to water my plants*** he quedado con los vecinos para que rieguen mis plantas
ar·rears [ə'rɪərz] *npl* atrasos *mpl*; ***be in arrears*** *of person* ir atrasado
ar·rest [ə'rest] **1** *n* detención *f*, arresto *m*; ***be under arrest*** estar detenido *or* arrestado **2** *v/t* detener, arrestar
ar·riv·al [ə'raɪvl] llegada *f*; ***on your arrival*** al llegar; ***arrivals*** *at airport* llegadas *fsg*
ar·rive [ə'raɪv] *v/i* llegar
◆ **arrive at** *v/t place, decision etc* llegar a
ar·ro·gance ['ærəgəns] arrogancia *f*
ar·ro·gant ['ærəgənt] *adj* arrogante
ar·ro·gant·ly ['ærəgəntlɪ] *adv* con arrogancia
ar·row ['æroʊ] flecha *f*
arse [ɑːrs] *Br* P culo *m* P
ar·se·nic ['ɑːrsənɪk] arsénico *m*
ar·son ['ɑːrsn] incendio *m* provocado
ar·son·ist ['ɑːrsənɪst] pirómano(-a) *m(f)*
art [ɑːrt] arte *m*; ***the arts*** las artes
ar·te·ry ['ɑːrtərɪ] MED arteria *f*

'art gal·ler·y *public* museo *m*; *private* galería *f* de arte
ar·thri·tis [ɑːr'θraɪtɪs] artritis *f*
ar·ti·choke ['ɑːrtɪʧoʊk] alcachofa *f*, *L.Am.* alcaucil *m*
ar·ti·cle ['ɑːrtɪkl] artículo *m*
ar·tic·u·late [ɑːr'tɪkjʊlət] *adj person* elocuente
ar·ti·fi·cial [ɑːrtɪ'fɪʃl] *adj* artificial
ar·ti·fi·cial in'tel·li·gence inteligencia *f* artificial
ar·til·le·ry [ɑːr'tɪlərɪ] artillería *f*
ar·ti·san ['ɑːrtɪzæn] artesano(-a) *m(f)*
ar·tist ['ɑːrtɪst] (*painter, artistic person*) artista *m/f*
ar·tis·tic [ɑːr'tɪstɪk] *adj* artístico
'arts de·gree licenciatura *f* en letras
as [æz] **1** *conj* (*while, when*) cuando; (*because, like*) como; ***as if*** como si; ***as usual*** como de costumbre; ***as necessary*** como sea necesario **2** *adv* como; ***as high / pretty as …*** tan alto / guapa como …; ***as much as that?*** ¿tanto? **3** *prep* como; ***work as a team*** trabajar en equipo; ***as a child / schoolgirl*** cuando era un niño / una colegiala; ***work as a teacher / translator*** trabajar como profesor / traductor; ***as for*** por lo que respecta a; ***as Hamlet*** en el papel del Hamlet
asap ['eɪzæp] *abbr* (= ***as soon as possible***) cuanto antes
as·bes·tos [æz'bestɑːs] amianto *m*, asbesto *m*
As·cen·sion [ə'senʃn] REL Ascensión *f*
ash [æʃ] ceniza *f*; ***ashes*** *of person* cenizas *fpl*
a·shamed [ə'ʃeɪmd] *adj* avergonzado, *L.Am.* apenado; ***be ashamed of*** estar avergonzado *or L.Am.* apenado de; ***you should be ashamed of yourself*** debería darte vergüenza *or L.Am.* pena; ***it's nothing to be ashamed of*** no tienes por qué avergonzarte *or L.Am.* apenarte
'ash bin, 'ash can cubo *m* de la basura
a·shore [ə'ʃɔːr] *adv* en tierra; ***go ashore*** desembarcar
ash·tray ['æʃtreɪ] cenicero *m*
A·sia ['eɪʃə] Asia
A·sian ['eɪʃən] **1** *adj* asiático **2** *n* asiático(-a) *m(f)*
a·side [ə'saɪd] *adv* a un lado; ***move aside please*** apártense, por favor; ***he took me aside*** me llevó aparte; ***aside from*** aparte de
ask [æsk] **1** *v/t person, question* preguntar; *question* hacer; (*invite*) invitar; *favor* pedir; ***can I ask you something?*** ¿puedo hacerte una pregunta?; ***ask s.o. for sth*** pedir algo a alguien; ***he asked me to leave*** me pidió que me fuera; ***ask s.o. about sth*** preguntar por algo a alguien **2** *v/i*: ***all you need to do is ask*** no tienes más que pedirlo
◆ **ask after** *v/t person* preguntar por
◆ **ask for** *v/t* pedir; *person* preguntar por
◆ **ask out** *v/t for a drink, night out* invitar a salir
ask·ing price ['æskɪŋ] precio *m* de salida
a·sleep [ə'sliːp] *adj* dormido; ***be (fast) asleep*** estar (profundamente) dormido; ***fall asleep*** dormirse, quedarse dormido
as·par·a·gus [ə'spærəgəs] espárragos *mpl*
as·pect ['æspekt] aspecto *m*
as·phalt ['æsfælt] *n* asfalto *m*
as·phyx·i·ate [æ'sfɪksɪeɪt] *v/t* asfixiar
as·phyx·i·a·tion [əsfɪksɪ'eɪʃn] asfixia *f*
as·pi·ra·tion [æspə'reɪʃn] aspiración *f*
as·pi·rin ['æsprɪn] aspirina *f*
ass[1] [æs] (*idiot*) burro(-a) *m(f)*
ass[2] [æs] P (*backside*) culo P; (*sex*) sexo *m*
as·sai·lant [ə'seɪlənt] asaltante *m/f*
as·sas·sin [ə'sæsɪn] asesino(-a) *m(f)*
as·sas·sin·ate [ə'sæsɪneɪt] *v/t* asesinar
as·sas·sin·a·tion [əsæsɪ'neɪʃn] asesinato *m*
as·sault [ə'sɒːlt] **1** *n* agresión *f*; (*attack*) ataque *m* **2** *v/t* atacar, agredir
as·sem·ble [ə'sembl] **1** *v/t parts* montar **2** *v/i of people* reunirse
as·sem·bly [ə'semblɪ] *of parts* montaje *m*; POL asamblea *f*
as'sem·bly line cadena *f* de montaje
as'sem·bly plant planta *f* de montaje
as·sent [ə'sent] *v/i* asentir, dar el consentimiento
as·sert [ə'sɜːrt] *v/t* afirmar, hacer valer; ***assert o.s.*** mostrarse firme
as·ser·tive [ə'sɜːrtɪv] *adj person* seguro y firme
as·sess [ə'ses] *v/t situation* evaluar; *value* valorar
as·sess·ment [ə'sesmənt] evaluación *f*
as·set ['æset] FIN activo *m*; *fig* ventaja *f*; ***she's an asset to the company*** es un gran valor para la compañía
ass·hole ['æshoʊl] V ojete *m* V; (*idiot*) *Span* gilipollas *m/f inv* V, *L.Am.* pendejo(-a) *m(f)* V
as·sign [ə'saɪn] *v/t person, thing* asignar
as·sign·ment [ə'saɪnmənt] (*task, study*) trabajo *m*
as·sim·i·late [ə'sɪmɪleɪt] *v/t information* asimilar; *person into group* integrar
as·sist [ə'sɪst] *v/t* ayudar
as·sist·ance [ə'sɪstəns] ayuda *f*, asistencia *f*
as·sis·tant [ə'sɪstənt] ayudante *m/f*; *Br in*

store dependiente(-a) *m(f)*

as·sis·tant di'rec·tor director(a) *m(f)* adjunto

as·sis·tant 'man·ag·er *of business* subdirector(a) *m(f)*; *of hotel, restaurant, store* subdirector(a) *m(f)*, subgerente *m/f*

as·so·ci·ate 1 *v/t* [ə'soʊʃɪeɪt] asociar; ***he has long been associated with the Royal Ballet*** ha estado vinculado al Royal Ballet durante mucho tiempo **2** *v/i* [ə'soʊʃɪeɪt]: ***associate with*** relacionarse con **3** *n* [ə'soʊʃɪət] colega *m/f*

as·so·ci·ate pro'fes·sor profesor(a) *m(f)* adjunto(a)

as·so·ci·a·tion [əsoʊsɪ'eɪʃn] asociación *f*; ***in association with*** conjuntamente con

as·sort·ed [ə'sɔːrtɪd] *adj* surtido, diverso

as·sort·ment [ə'sɔːrtmənt] *of food* surtido *m*; *of people* diversidad *f*

as·sume [ə'suːm] *v/t* (*suppose*) suponer

as·sump·tion [ə'sʌmpʃn] suposición *f*

as·sur·ance [ə'ʃʊrəns] garantía *f*; (*confidence*) seguridad *f*

as·sure [ə'ʃʊr] *v/t* (*reassure*) asegurar

as·sured [ə'ʃʊrd] *adj* (*confident*) seguro

as·ter·isk ['æstərɪsk] asterisco *m*

asth·ma ['æsmə] asma *f*

asth·mat·ic [æs'mætɪk] *adj* asmático

as·ton·ish [ə'stɑːnɪʃ] *v/t* asombrar, sorprender; ***be astonished*** estar asombrado *or* sorprendido

as·ton·ish·ing [ə'stɑːnɪʃɪŋ] *adj* asombroso, sorprendente

as·ton·ish·ing·ly [ə'stɑːnɪʃɪŋlɪ] *adv* asombrosamente

as·ton·ish·ment [ə'stɑːnɪʃmənt] asombro *m*, sorpresa *f*

as·tound [ə'staʊnd] *v/t* pasmar

as·tound·ing [ə'staʊndɪŋ] *adj* pasmoso

a·stray [ə'streɪ] *adv*: ***go astray*** extraviarse; *morally* descarriarse

a·stride [ə'straɪd] **1** *adv* a horcajadas **2** *prep* a horcajadas sobre

as·trol·o·ger [ə'strɑːlədʒər] astrólogo(-a) *m(f)*

as·trol·o·gy [ə'strɑːlədʒɪ] astrología *f*

as·tro·naut ['æstrənɒːt] astronauta *m/f*

as·tron·o·mer [ə'strɑːnəmər] astrónomo(-a) *m(f)*

as·tro·nom·i·cal [æstrə'nɑːmɪkl] *adj* *price etc* astronómico

as·tron·o·my [ə'strɑːnəmɪ] astronomía *f*

as·tute [ə'stuːt] *adj* astuto, sagaz

a·sy·lum [ə'saɪləm] (*mental asylum*) manicomio *m*; *political* asilo *m*

at [ət] *stressed* [æt] *prep with places* en; ***at Joe's*** *house* en casa de Joe; *bar* en el bar de Joe; ***at the door*** a la puerta; ***at 10 dollars*** a 10 dólares; ***at the age of 18*** a los 18 años; ***at 5 o'clock*** a las 5; ***at 150 km/h*** a 150 km./h.; ***be good / bad at sth*** ser bueno / malo haciendo algo

ate [eɪt] *pret* → ***eat***

a·the·ism ['eɪθɪɪzm] ateísmo *m*

a·the·ist ['eɪθɪɪst] ateo(-a) *m(f)*

ath·lete ['æθliːt] atleta *m/f*

ath·let·ic [æθ'letɪk] *adj* atlético

ath·let·ics [æθ'letɪks] atletismo *m*

At·lan·tic [ət'læntɪk] *n*: ***the Atlantic*** el Atlántico

at·las ['ætləs] atlas *m inv*

ATM [eɪtiː'em] *abbr* (= ***automatic teller machine***) cajero *m* automático

at·mos·phere ['ætməsfɪr] *of earth* atmósfera *f*; (*ambiance*) ambiente *m*

at·mos·pher·ic pol'lu·tion [ætməs'ferɪk] contaminación *f* atmosférica

at·om ['ætəm] átomo *m*

'at·om bomb bomba *f* atómica

a·tom·ic [ə'tɑːmɪk] *adj* atómico

a·tom·ic 'en·er·gy energía *f* atómica *or* nuclear

a·tom·ic 'waste desechos *mpl* radiactivos

a·tom·iz·er ['ætəmaɪzər] atomizador *m*

a·tone [ə'toʊn] *v/i*: ***atone for*** expiar

a·tro·cious [ə'troʊʃəs] *adj* atroz, terrible

a·troc·i·ty [ə'trɑːsətɪ] atrocidad *f*

at·tach [ə'tæʧ] *v/t* sujetar, fijar; *importance* atribuir; ***be attached to*** (*fond of*) tener cariño a

at·tach·ment [ə'tæʧmənt] (*fondness*) cariño *m* (***to*** por)

at·tack [ə'tæk] **1** *n* ataque *m* **2** *v/t* atacar

at·tempt [ə'tempt] **1** *n* intento *m*; ***an attempt on the world record*** un intento de batir el récord del mundo **2** *v/t* intentar

at·tend [ə'tend] *v/t* acudir a

◆ **attend to** *v/t* ocuparse de; *customer* atender

at·tend·ance [ə'tendəns] asistencia *f*

at·tend·ant [ə'tendənt] *in museum etc* vigilante *m/f*

at·ten·tion [ə'tenʃn] atención *f*; ***bring sth to s.o.'s attention*** informar a alguien de algo; ***your attention please*** atención, por favor; ***pay attention*** prestar atención

at·ten·tive [ə'tentɪv] *adj listener* atento

at·tic ['ætɪk] ático *m*

at·ti·tude ['ætɪtuːd] actitud *f*

attn *abbr* (= ***for the attention of***) atn (= a la atención de)

at·tor·ney [ə'tɜːrnɪ] abogado(-a) *m(f)*; ***power of attorney*** poder *m* (notarial)

at·tract [ə'trækt] *v/t* atraer; ***attract attention*** llamar la atención; ***attract s.o.'s attention*** atraer la atención de alguien; ***be***

attracted to s.o. sentirse atraído por alguien
at·trac·tion [ə'trækʃn] atracción *f*, atractivo *m*; *romantic* atracción *f*
at·trac·tive [ə'træktɪv] *adj* atractivo
at·trib·ute[1] [ə'trɪbjuːt] *v/t* atribuir; ***attribute sth to …*** atribuir algo a …
at·trib·ute[2] ['ætrɪbjuːt] *n* atributo *m*
au·ber·gine ['oʊbərʒiːn] *Br* berenjena *f*
auc·tion ['ɒːkʃn] **1** *n* subasta *f*, *L.Am.* remate *m* **2** *v/t* subastar, *L.Am.* rematar
◆ **auction off** *v/t* subastar, *L.Am.* rematar
auc·tio·neer [ɒːkʃə'nɪr] subastador(a) *m(f)*, *L.Am.* rematador(a) *m(f)*
au·da·cious [ɒː'deɪʃəs] *adj plan* audaz
au·dac·i·ty [ɒː'dæsətɪ] audacia *f*
au·di·ble ['ɒːdəbl] *adj* audible
au·di·ence ['ɒːdɪəns] *in theater, at show* público *m*, espectadores *mpl*; TV audiencia *f*
au·di·o ['ɒːdɪoʊ] *adj* de audio
au·di·o·vi·su·al [ɒːdɪoʊ'vɪʒʊəl] *adj* audiovisual
au·dit ['ɒːdɪt] **1** *n* auditoría *f* **2** *v/t* auditar; *course* asistir de oyente a
au·di·tion [ɒː'dɪʃn] **1** *n* audición *f* **2** *v/i* hacer una prueba
au·di·tor ['ɒːdɪtər] auditor(a) *m(f)*
au·di·to·ri·um [ɒːdɪ'tɔːrɪəm] *of theater etc* auditorio *m*
Au·gust ['ɒːgəst] agosto *m*
aunt [ænt] tía *f*
au pair [oʊ'per] au pair *m/f*
au·ra ['ɒːrə] aura *f*
aus·pic·es ['ɒːspɪsɪz] *npl* auspicios *mpl*; ***under the auspices of*** bajo los auspicios de
aus·pi·cious [ɒː'spɪʃəs] *adj* propicio
aus·tere [ɒː'stiːr] *adj interior* austero
aus·ter·i·ty [ɒːs'terətɪ] *economic* austeridad *f*
Aus·tra·li·a [ɒː'streɪlɪə] Australia
Aus·tra·li·an [ɒː'streɪlɪən] **1** *adj* australiano **2** *n* australiano(-a) *m(f)*
Aus·tri·a ['ɒːstrɪə] Austria
Aus·tri·an ['ɒːstrɪən] **1** *adj* austriaco **2** *n* austriaco(-a) *m(f)*
au·then·tic [ɒː'θentɪk] *adj* auténtico
au·then·tic·i·ty [ɒːθen'tɪsətɪ] autenticidad *f*
au·thor ['ɒːθər] *of story, novel* escritor(a) *m(f)*; *of text* autor(a) *m(f)*
au·thor·i·tar·i·an [əθɑːrɪ'terɪən] *adj* autoritario
au·thor·i·ta·tive [ə'θɑːrɪtətɪv] *adj* autorizado
au·thor·i·ty [ə'θɑːrətɪ] autoridad *f*; (*permission*) autorización *f*; ***be an authority on*** ser una autoridad en; ***the authorities*** las autoridades
au·thor·i·za·tion [ɒːθəraɪ'zeɪʃn] autorización *f*
au·thor·ize ['ɒːθəraɪz] *v/t* autorizar; ***be authorized to …*** estar autorizado para …
au·tis·tic [ɒː'tɪstɪk] *adj* autista
au·to·bi·og·ra·phy [ɒːtəbaɪ'ɑːgrəfɪ] autobiografía *f*
au·to·crat·ic [ɒːtə'krætɪk] *adj* autocrático
au·to·graph ['ɒːtəgræf] autógrafo *m*
au·to·mate ['ɒːtəmeɪt] *v/t* automatizar
au·to·mat·ic [ɒːtə'mætɪk] **1** *adj* automático **2** *n car* (coche *m*) automático *m*; *gun* pistola *f* automática; *washing machine* lavadora *f* automática
au·to·mat·i·cal·ly [ɒːtə'mætɪklɪ] *adv* automáticamente
au·to·ma·tion [ɒːtə'meɪʃn] automatización
au·to·mo·bile ['ɒːtəmoʊbiːl] automóvil *m*, coche *m*, *L.Am.* carro *m*, *Rpl* auto *m*
'au·to·mo·bile in·dus·try industria *f* automovilística
au·ton·o·mous [ɒː'tɑːnəməs] *adj* autónomo
au·ton·o·my [ɒː'tɑːnəmɪ] autonomía *f*
au·to·pi·lot ['ɒːtoʊpaɪlət] piloto *m* automático
au·top·sy ['ɒːtɑːpsɪ] autopsia *f*
au·tumn ['ɒːtəm] *Br* otoño *m*
aux·il·ia·ry [ɒːg'zɪljərɪ] *adj* auxiliar
a·vail [ə'veɪl] **1** *n*: ***to no avail*** en vano **2** *v/t*: ***avail o.s. of*** aprovechar
a·vai·la·ble [ə'veɪləbl] *adj* disponible
av·a·lanche ['ævəlænʃ] avalancha *f*, alud *m*
av·a·rice ['ævərɪs] avaricia *f*
av·e·nue ['ævənuː] avenida *f*; *fig* camino *m*
av·e·rage ['ævərɪdʒ] **1** *adj* medio; (*of mediocre quality*) regular **2** *n* promedio *m*, media *f*; ***above / below average*** por encima / por debajo del promedio; ***on average*** como promedio, de media **3** *v/t*: ***I average six hours of sleep a night*** duermo seis horas cada noche como promedio *or* de media
◆ **average out** *v/t* calcular el promedio *or* la media de
◆ **average out at** *v/t* salir a
a·verse [ə'vɜːrs] *adj*: ***not be averse to*** no ser reacio a
a·ver·sion [ə'vɜːrʃn] aversión *f*; ***have an aversion to*** tener aversión a
a·vert [ə'vɜːrt] *v/t one's eyes* apartar; *crisis* evitar
a·vi·a·tion [eɪvɪ'ɑɪʃn] aviación *f*
av·id ['ævɪd] *adj* ávido

av·o·ca·do [ɑːvə'kɑːdoʊ] aguacate *m*, *S. Am.* palta *f*
a·void [ə'vɔɪd] *v/t* evitar; ***you've been avoiding me*** has estado huyendo de mí
a·void·a·ble [ə'vɔɪdəbl] *adj* evitable
a·wait [ə'weɪt] *v/t* aguardar, esperar
a·wake [ə'weɪk] *adj* despierto; ***it kept me awake*** no me dejó dormir
a·ward [ə'wɔːrd] **1** *n* (*prize*) premio *m* **2** *v/t prize, damages* conceder
a·ware [ə'wer] *adj*: ***be aware of sth*** ser consciente de algo; ***become aware of sth*** darse cuenta de algo
a·ware·ness [ə'wernɪs] conciencia *f*
a·way [ə'weɪ] *adv*: ***look away*** mirar hacia otra parte; ***I'll be away until …*** *traveling* voy a estar fuera hasta …; *sick* no voy a ir hasta …; ***it's 2 miles away*** está a 2 millas; ***Christmas is still six weeks away*** todavía quedan seis semanas para Navidad; ***take sth away from s.o.*** quitar algo a alguien; ***put sth away*** guardar algo
a'way match SP partido *m* fuera de casa
awe·some ['ɒːsəm] *adj* F (*terrific*) alucinante F
aw·ful ['ɒːfəl] *adj* horrible, espantoso; ***I feel awful*** me siento fatal
aw·ful·ly ['ɒːfəlɪ] *adv* F (*very*) tremendamente; ***awfully bad*** malísimo
awk·ward ['ɒːkwərd] *adj* (*clumsy*) torpe; (*difficult*) difícil; (*embarrassing*) embarazoso; ***feel awkward*** sentirse incómodo
awn·ing ['ɒːnɪŋ] toldo *m*
ax, *Br* **axe** [æks] **1** *n* hacha *f* **2** *v/t project etc* suprimir; *budget, job* recortar
ax·le ['æksl] eje *m*

B

BA [biː'eɪ] *abbr* (= ***Bachelor of Arts***) Licenciatura *f* en Filosofía y Letras
ba·by ['beɪbɪ] *n* bebé *m*
'ba·by boom explosión *f* demográfica
'ba·by car·riage ['kærɪdʒ] cochecito *m* de bebé
ba·by·ish ['beɪbɪɪʃ] *adj* infantil
'ba·by-sit *v/i* (*pret & pp* ***baby-sat***) hacer de *Span* canguro *or L.Am.* babysitter
'ba·by-sit·ter ['sɪtər] *Span* canguro *m/f*, *L.Am.* babysitter *m/f*
bach·e·lor ['bætʃələr] soltero *m*
back [bæk] **1** *n of person, clothes* espalda *f*; *of car, bus, house* parte *f* trasera *or* de atrás; *of paper, book* dorso *m*; *of drawer* fondo *m*; *of chair* respaldo *m*; SP defensa *m/f*; ***in back*** *in store* en la trastienda; ***in the back*** (***of the car***) atrás (del coche); ***at the back of the bus*** en la parte trasera *or* de atrás del autobús; ***back to front*** del revés; ***at the back of beyond*** en el quinto pino **2** *adj* trasero; ***back road*** carretera *f* secundaria **3** *adv* atrás; ***please stand back*** pongase más para atrás **2** ***meters back from the edge*** a 2 metros del borde; ***back in 1935*** allá por el año 1935; ***give sth back to s.o.*** devolver algo a alguien; ***she'll be back tomorrow*** volverá mañana; ***when are you coming back?*** ¿cuándo volverás?; ***take sth back to the store*** *because unsatisfactory* devolver alguien a la tienda; ***they wrote / phoned back*** contestaron a la carta/a la llamada; ***he hit me back*** me devolvió el golpe **4** *v/t* (*support*) apoyar, respaldar; *horse* apostar por **5** *v/i* ***he backed into the garage*** entró en el garaje marcha atrás
◆ **back away** *v/i* alejarse (hacia atrás)
◆ **back down** *v/i* echarse atrás
◆ **back off** *v/i* echarse atrás
◆ **back onto** *v/t* dar por la parte de atrás a
◆ **back out** *v/i of commitment* echarse atrás
◆ **back up 1** *v/t* (*support*) respaldar; *file* hacer una copia de seguridad de; ***traffic was backed up all the way to …*** el atasco llegaba hasta … **2** *v/i in car* dar marcha atrás; *of drains* atascarse
'back·ache dolor *m* de espalda
'back·bit·ing cotilleo *m*, chismorreo *m*
'back·bone ANAT columna *f* vertebral, espina *f* dorsal; (*fig*: *courage*) agallas *fpl*; (*fig*: *mainstay*) columna *f* vertebral
'back-break·ing *adj* extenuante, deslomador
back 'burn·er: ***put sth on the back burner*** aparcar algo
'back·date *v/t*: ***a salary increase backdated to 1st January*** una subida salarial con efecto retroactivo a partir del 1 de enero

'**back·door** puerta *f* trasera
back·er ['bækər]: ***the backers of the movie*** *financially* las personas que financiaron la película
back'fire *v/i fig*: ***it backfired on us*** nos salió el tiro por la culata
'**back·ground** *n* fondo *m*; *of person* origen *m*, historia *f* personal; *of situation* contexto *m*; ***she prefers to stay in the background*** prefiere permanecer en un segundo plano
'**back·hand** *n in tennis* revés *m*
back·ing ['bækɪŋ] *n* (*support*) apoyo *m*, respaldo *m*; MUS acompañamiento *m*
'**back·ing group** MUS grupo *m* de acompañamiento
'**back·lash** reacción *f* violenta
'**back·log** acumulación *f*
'**back·pack 1** *n* mochila *f* **2** *v/i* viajar con la mochila a cuestas
'**back·pack·er** mochilero(-a) *m*(*f*)
'**back·pack·ing** viajes *mpl* con la mochila a cuestas
'**back·ped·al** *v/i fig* echarse atrás, dar marcha atrás
'**back seat** *of car* asiento *m* trasero *or* de atrás
back-seat 'driv·er: ***he's a terrible back-seat driver*** va siempre incordiando al conductor con sus comentarios
'**back·space (key)** (tecla *f* de) retroceso *m*
'**back·stairs** *npl* escalera *f* de servicio
'**back street** callejuela *f*
'**back streets** *npl* callejuelas *fpl*; *poorer, dirtier part of a city* zonas *fpl* deprimidas
'**back·stroke** SP espalda *f*
'**back·track** *v/i* volver atrás, retroceder
'**back·up** (*support*) apoyo *m*, respaldo *m*; *for police* refuerzos *mpl*; COMPUT copia *f* de seguridad; ***take a backup*** COMPUT haz una copia de seguridad
'**back·up disk** COMPUT disquete *m* con la copia de seguridad
back·ward ['bækwərd] **1** *adj child* retrasado; *society* atrasado; *glance* hacia atrás **2** *adv* hacia atrás
back'yard jardín *m* trasero; ***in s.o.'s backyard*** *fig* en la misma puerta de alguien
ba·con ['beɪkn] tocino *m*, *Span* bacon *m*
bac·te·ri·a [bæk'tɪrɪə] *npl* bacterias *fpl*
bad [bæd] *adj* malo; *before singular masculine noun* mal; *cold, headache etc* fuerte; *mistake, accident* grave; ***I've had a bad day*** he tenido un mal día; ***smoking is bad for you*** fumar es malo; ***it's not bad*** no está mal; ***that's really too bad*** (*shame*) es una verdadera pena; ***feel bad about*** (*guilty*) sentirse mal por; ***I'm bad at math*** se me dan mal las matemáticas; ***Friday's bad, how about Thursday?*** el viernes me viene mal, ¿qué tal el jueves?
bad 'debt deuda *f* incobrable
badge [bædʒ] insignia *f*, chapa *f*; *of policeman* placa *f*
bad·ger ['bædʒər] *v/t* acosar, importunar
bad 'lan·guage palabrotas *fpl*
bad·ly ['bædlɪ] *adv injured* gravemente; *damaged* seriamente; *work* mal; ***I did really badly in the exam*** el examen me salió fatal; ***he hasn't done badly*** *in life, business etc* no le ha ido mal; ***you're badly in need of a haircut*** necesitas urgentemente un corte de pelo; ***he is badly off*** *poor* anda mal de dinero
bad-man·nered [bæd'mænərd] *adj*: ***be bad-mannered*** tener malos modales
bad·min·ton ['bædmɪntən] bádminton *m*
bad-tem·pered [bæd'tempərd] *adj* malhumorado
baf·fle ['bæfl] *v/t* confundir, desconcertar; ***be baffled*** estar confundido *or* desconcertado; ***I'm baffled why she left*** no consigo entender por qué se fue
baf·fling ['bæflɪŋ] *adj mystery, software* desconcertante, incomprensible
bag [bæg] bolsa *f*; *for school* cartera *f*; (*purse*) bolso *m*, *S. Am.* cartera *f*, *Mex* bolsa *f*
bag·gage ['bægɪdʒ] equipaje *m*
'**bag·gage car** RAIL vagón *m* de equipajes
'**bag·gage check** consigna *f*
'**bag·gage re·claim** ['riːkleɪm] recogida *f* de equipajes
bag·gy ['bægɪ] *adj* ancho, holgado
'**bag·pipes** *npl* gaita *f*
bail [beɪl] *n* LAW libertad *f* bajo fianza; (*money*) fianza *f*; ***on bail*** bajo fianza
◆ **bail out 1** *v/t* LAW pagar la fianza de **2** *v/i of airplane* tirarse en paracaídas
bait [beɪt] *n* cebo *m*
bake [beɪk] *v/t* hornear, cocer al horno
baked 'beans [beɪkt] *npl alubias con salsa de tomate*
baked po'ta·to *Span* patata *f or L.Am.* papa *f* asada (*con piel*)
bak·er ['beɪkər] panadero(-a) *m*(*f*)
bak·er·y ['beɪkərɪ] panadería *f*
bak·ing pow·der ['beɪkɪŋ] levadura *f*
bal·ance ['bæləns] **1** *n* equilibrio *m*; (*remainder*) resto *m*; *of bank account* saldo *m* **2** *v/t* poner en equilibrio; ***balance the books*** cuadrar las cuentas **3** *v/i* mantenerse en equilibrio; *of accounts* cuadrar
bal·anced ['bælənst] *adj* (*fair*) objetivo; *diet, personality* equilibrado
bal·ance of 'pay·ments balanza *f* de pa-

gos
bal·ance of 'trade balanza *f* comercial
'bal·ance sheet balance *m*
bal·co·ny ['bælkənɪ] *of house* balcón *m*; *in theater* anfiteatro *m*
bald [bɒːld] *adj* calvo; ***he's going bald*** se está quedando calvo; ***bald spot*** calva *f*
bald·ing ['bɒːldɪŋ] *adj* medio calvo
Bal·kan ['bɒːlkən] *adj* balcánico
Bal·kans ['bɒːlkənz] *npl*: ***the Balkans*** los Balcanes
ball [bɒːl] *tennis-ball size* pelota *f*; *football size* balón *m*, pelota *f*; *billiard-ball size* bola *f*; ***on the ball*** despierto; ***play ball*** *fig* cooperar; ***the ball's in his court*** le toca actuar a él, la pelota está en su tejado
bal·lad ['bæləd] balada *f*
ball 'bear·ing rodamiento *m* de bolas
bal·le·ri·na [bælə'riːnə] bailarina *f*
bal·let [bæ'leɪ] ballet *m*
'bal·let danc·er bailarín (-ina) *m*(*f*)
'ball game (*baseball game*) partido *m* de béisbol; ***that's a different ball game*** F esa es otra cuestión F
bal·lis·tic mis·sile [bə'lɪstɪk] misil *m* balístico
bal·loon [bə'luːn] globo *m*
bal·loon·ist [bə'luːnɪst] piloto *m* de globo aerostático
bal·lot ['bælət] **1** *n* voto *m* **2** *v/t members* consultar por votación
'bal·lot box urna *f*
'bal·lot pa·per papeleta *f*
'ball·park (*baseball*) campo *m* de béisbol; ***you're in the right ballpark*** F no vas descaminado
'ball·park fig·ure F cifra *f* aproximada
'ball·point (pen) bolígrafo *m*, *Mex* pluma *f*, *Rpl* birome *m*
balls [bɒːlz] *npl* V huevos *mpl* V; (*courage*) huevos *mpl* V; (*nonsense*) tonterías *fpl*, paridas *fpl* F
bam·boo [bæm'buː] *n* bambú *m*
ban [bæn] **1** *n* prohibición *f* **2** *v/t* (*pret & pp* ***banned***) prohibir; ***ban s.o. from doing sth*** prohibir a alguien que haga algo
ba·nal [bə'næl] *adj* banal
ba·na·na [bə'nænə] plátano *m*, *Rpl* banana *f*
band [bænd] banda *f*; *pop* grupo *m*
ban·dage ['bændɪdʒ] **1** *n* vendaje *m* **2** *v/t* vendar
'Band-Aid® *Span* tirita *f*, *L.Am.* curita *f*
B&B [biːn'biː] *abbr* (= ***bed and breakfast***) hostal *m* familiar
ban·dit ['bændɪt] bandido *m*
'band·wagon: ***jump on the bandwagon*** subirse al carro
ban·dy ['bændɪ] *adj legs* arqueado
bang [bæŋ] **1** *n noise* estruendo *m*, estrépito *m*; (*blow*) golpe *m*; ***the door closed with a bang*** la puerta se cerró de un portazo **2** *v/t door* cerrar de un portazo; (*hit*) golpear; ***bang o.s. on the head*** golpearse la cabeza **3** *v/i* dar golpes; ***the door banged shut*** la puerta se cerró de un portazo
ban·gle ['bæŋgl] brazalete *m*, pulsera *f*
bangs [bæŋz] flequillo *m*
ban·is·ters ['bænɪstərz] *npl* barandilla *f*
ban·jo ['bændʒoʊ] banjo *m*
bank[1] [bæŋk] *of river* orilla *f*
bank[2] [bæŋk] **1** *n* FIN banco *m* **2** *v/i*: ***I bank with ...*** mi banco es el ... **3** *v/t money* ingresar, depositar
◆ **bank on** *v/t* contar con; ***don't bank on it*** no cuentes con ello
'bank ac·count cuenta *f* (bancaria)
'bank bal·ance saldo *m* bancario
'bank bill billete *m*
bank·er ['bæŋkər] banquero *m*
'bank·er's card tarjeta *f* bancaria
bank·ing ['bæŋkɪŋ] banca *f*
'bank loan préstamo *m* bancario
'bank man·ag·er director(a) *m*(*f*) de banco
'bank rate tipo *m* de interés bancario
'bank·roll *v/t* financiar
bank·rupt ['bæŋkrʌpt] **1** *adj* en bancarrota *or* quiebra; ***go bankrupt*** quebrar, ir a la quiebra; *of person* arruinarse **2** *v/t* llevar a la quiebra
bank·rupt·cy ['bæŋkrʌpsɪ] *of person, company* quiebra *f*, bancarrota *f*
'bank state·ment extracto *m* bancario
ban·ner ['bænər] pancarta *f*
banns [bænz] *npl* amonestaciones *fpl*
ban·quet ['bæŋkwɪt] *n* banquete *m*
ban·ter ['bæntər] *n* bromas *fpl*
bap·tism ['bæptɪzm] bautismo *m*
bap·tize [bæp'taɪz] *v/t* bautizar
bar[1] [bɑːr] *n of iron* barra *f*; *of chocolate* tableta *f*; *for drinks* bar *m*; (*counter*) barra *f*; ***a bar of soap*** una pastilla de jabón; ***be behind bars*** (*in prison*) estar entre barrotes
bar[2] [bɑːr] *v/t* (*pret & pp* ***barred***) *from premises* prohibir la entrada a; ***bar s.o. from doing sth*** prohibir a alguien que haga algo
bar[3] [bɑːr] *prep* (*except*) excepto
bar·bar·i·an [bɑːr'berɪən] bárbaro(-a) *m*(*f*)
bar·ba·ric [bɑːr'bærɪk] *adj* brutal, inhumano
bar·be·cue ['bɑːrbɪkjuː] **1** *n* barbacoa *f* **2**

v/t cocinar en la barbacoa
barbed 'wire [bɑːrbd] alambre *f* de espino
bar·ber ['bɑːrbər] barbero *m*
bar·bi·tu·rate [bɑːr'bɪtjərət] barbitúrico *m*
'bar code código *m* de barras
bare [ber] *adj* (*naked*) desnudo; (*empty*: *room*) vacío; *mountainside* pelado, raso; *floor* descubierto; ***in one's bare feet*** descalzo
'bare·foot *adj* descalzo
bare-head·ed [ber'hedɪd] *adj* sin sombrero
'bare·ly ['berlɪ] *adv* apenas; ***he's barely five*** acaba de cumplir cinco años
bar·gain ['bɑːrgɪn] **1** *n* (*deal*) trato *m*; (*good buy*) ganga *f*; ***into the bargain*** además **2** *v/i* regatear, negociar
◆ **bargain for** *v/t* (*expect*) imaginarse, esperar
barge [bɑːrdʒ] *n* NAUT barcaza *f*
◆ **barge into** *v/t person* tropezarse con; *room* irrumpir en
bar·i·tone ['bærɪtoʊn] *n* barítono *m*
bark[1] [bɑːrk] **1** *n of dog* ladrido *m* **2** *v/i* ladrar
bark[2] [bɑːrk] *of tree* corteza *f*
bar·ley ['bɑːrlɪ] cebada *f*
'bar·maid *Br* camarera *f*, *L.Am.* mesera *f*, *Rpl* moza *f*
'bar·man camarero *m*, *L.Am.* mesero *m*, *Rpl* mozo *m*
barn [bɑːrn] granero *m*
ba·rom·e·ter [bə'rɑːmɪtər] *also fig* barómetro *m*
Ba·roque [bə'rɑːk] *adj* barroco
bar·racks ['bærəks] *npl* MIL cuartel *m*
bar·rage [bə'rɑːʒ] MIL barrera *f* (de fuego); *fig* aluvión *m*
bar·rel ['bærəl] (*container*) tonel *m*, barril *m*
bar·ren ['bærən] *adj land* yermo, árido
bar·ri·cade [bærɪ'keɪd] *n* barricada *f*
bar·ri·er ['bærɪər] *also fig* barrera *f*; ***language barrier*** barrera *f* lingüística
bar·ring ['bɑːrɪŋ] *prep* salvo, excepto; ***barring accidents*** salvo imprevistos
bar·ris·ter ['bærɪstər] *Br* abogado(-a) *m*(*f*) (*que aparece en tribunales*)
bar·row ['bæroʊ] carretilla *f*
'bar ten·der camarero(-a) *m*(*f*), *L.Am.* mesero(-a) *m*(*f*), *Rpl* mozo(-a) *m*(*f*)
bar·ter ['bɑːrtər] **1** *n* trueque *m* **2** *v/t* cambiar, trocar (**for** por)
base [beɪs] **1** *n bottom, center* base *f*; ***base camp*** campamento *m* base **2** *v/t* basar (**on** en); ***be based in*** *of soldier* estar destinado en; *of company* tener su sede en
'base·ball *ball* pelota *f* de béisbol; *game* béisbol *m*
'base·ball bat bate *m* de béisbol
'base·ball cap gorra *f* de béisbol
'base·ball play·er jugador(a) *m*(*f*) de béisbol, *L.Am.* pelotero(-a) *m*(*f*)
'base·board rodapié *m*
base·less ['beɪslɪs] *adj* infundado
base·ment ['beɪsmənt] *of house, store* sótano *m*
'base rate FIN tipo *m* de interés básico
bash [bæʃ] **1** *n* F porrazo *m* F **2** *v/t* F dar un porrazo a F
ba·sic ['beɪsɪk] *adj* (*rudimentary*) básico; *room* modesto, sencillo; *language skills* elemental; (*fundamental*) fundamental; ***basic salary*** sueldo *m* base
ba·sic·al·ly ['beɪsɪklɪ] *adv* básicamente
ba·sics ['beɪsɪks] *npl*: ***the basics*** lo básico, los fundamentos; ***get down to basics*** centrarse en lo esencial
bas·il ['bæzɪl] albahaca *f*
ba·sil·i·ca [bə'zɪlɪkə] basílica *f*
ba·sin ['beɪsn] *for washing* barreño *m*; *in bathroom* lavabo *m*
ba·sis ['beɪsɪs] (*pl* ***bases*** ['beɪsiːz]) base *f*; ***on the basis of what you've told me*** de acuerdo con lo que me has dicho
bask [bæsk] *v/i* tomar el sol
bas·ket ['bæskɪt] cesta *f*; *in basketball* canasta *f*
'bas·ket·ball *game* baloncesto *m*, *L.Am.* básquetbol *m*; *ball* balón *m or* pelota *f* de baloncesto; ***basketball player*** baloncestista *m/f*, *L.Am.* basquebolista *m/f*
Basque [bæsk] **1** *adj* vasco **2** *n person* vasco(-a) *m*(*f*); *language* vasco *m*
bass [beɪs] **1** *n part, singer* bajo *m*; *instrument* contrabajo *m* **2** *adj* bajo
bas·tard ['bæstərd] ilegítimo(-a) *m*(*f*), bastardo(-a) *m*(*f*); P cabrón(-ona) *m*(*f*) P; ***poor bastard*** pobre desgraciado; ***stupid bastard*** desgraciado
bat[1] [bæt] **1** *n for baseball* bate *m*; *for table tennis* pala *f* **2** *v/i* (*pret & pp* ***batted***) *in baseball* batear
bat[2] [bæt] *v/t* (*pret & pp* ***batted***): ***he didn't bat an eyelid*** no se inmutó
bat[3] [bæt] (*animal*) murciélago *m*
batch [bætʃ] *n of students* tanda *f*; *of data* conjunto *m*; *of bread* hornada *f*; *of products* lote *m*
ba·ted ['beɪtɪd] *adj*: ***with bated breath*** con la respiración contenida
bath [bæθ] baño *m*; ***have a bath, take a bath*** darse *or* tomar un baño
bathe [beɪð] *v/i* (*swim, have a bath*) bañarse
bath·ing cost·ume, bathing suit ['beɪðɪŋ] bañador *m*, traje *m* de baño

'bath mat alfombra *f* de baño
'bath·robe albornoz *m*
'bath·room *for bath, washing hands*, cuarto *m* de baño; (*toilet*) servicio *m*, *L.Am.* baño *m*
'bath tow·el toalla *f* de baño
'bath·tub bañera *f*
bat·on [bə'tɑːn] *of conductor* batuta *f*
bat·tal·i·on [bə'tæliən] MIL batallón *m*
bat·ter ['bætər] *n* masa *f*; *in baseball* bateador(a) *m*(*f*)
bat·tered ['bætərd] *adj* maltratado
bat·ter·y ['bætəri] *in watch, flashlight* pila *f*; *in computer, car* batería *f*
'bat·ter·y charg·er ['tʃɑːrdʒər] cargador *m* de pilas / baterías
bat·ter·y-op·e·rat·ed [bætəri'ɑːpəreitid] *adj* que funciona con pilas
bat·tle ['bætl] **1** *n also fig* batalla *f* **2** *v/i against illness etc* luchar
'bat·tle·field, **'bat·tle·ground** campo *m* de batalla
'bat·tle·ship acorazado *m*
bawd·y ['bɒːdi] *adj* picante, subido de tono
bawl [bɒːl] *v/i* (*shout*) gritar, vociferar; (*weep*) berrear
◆ **bawl out** *v/t* F echar la bronca a F
bay [bei] (*inlet*) bahía *f*
bay·o·net ['beiənet] *n* bayoneta *f*
bay 'win·dow ventana *f* en saliente
BC [biː'siː] *abbr* (= ***before Christ***) a.C. (= antes de Cristo)
be [biː] ◇ *v/i* (*pret* ***was*** / ***were***, *pp* ***been***) *permanent characteristics, profession, nationality* ser; *position, temporary condition* estar; ***was she there?*** ¿estaba allí?; ***it's me*** soy yo; ***how much is / are ...?*** ¿cuánto es / son ...?; ***there is, there are*** hay; ***be careful*** ten cuidado; ***don't be sad*** no estés triste
◇ ***has the mailman been?*** ¿ha venido el cartero?; ***I've never been to Japan*** no he estado en Japón; ***I've been here for hours*** he estado aquí horas
◇ *tags*: ***that's right, isn't it?*** eso es, ¿no?; ***she's Chinese, isn't she?*** es china, ¿verdad?
◇ *v/aux*: ***I am thinking*** estoy pensando; ***he was running*** corría; ***you're being stupid*** estás siendo un estúpido
◇ *obligation*: ***you are to do what I tell you*** harás lo que yo te diga; ***I was to help him escape*** se suponía que le iba a ayudar a escaparse; ***you are not to tell anyone*** no debes decírselo a nadie
◇ *passive*: ***he was arrested*** fue detenido, lo detuvieron; ***they have been sold*** se han vendido

◆ **be in for** *v/t*: ***he's in for a big disappointment*** se va a llevar una gran desilusión
beach [biːtʃ] *n* playa *f*
'beach ball pelota *f* de playa
'beach·wear ropa *f* playera
beads [biːdz] *npl* cuentas *fpl*
beak [biːk] pico *m*
'be-all: ***the be-all and end-all*** lo más importante del mundo
beam [biːm] **1** *n in ceiling etc* viga *f* **2** *v/i* (*smile*) sonreír de oreja a oreja **3** *v/t* (*transmit*) emitir
bean [biːn] judía *f*, alubia *f*, *L.Am.* frijol *m*, *S. Am.* poroto *m*; ***green beans*** judías *fpl* verdes, *Mex* ejotes *mpl*, *S. Am.* porotos *mpl* verdes; ***coffee beans*** granos *mpl* de café; ***be full of beans*** F estar lleno de vitalidad
'bean·bag *cojín relleno de bolitas*
bear¹ [ber] *animal* oso(-a) *m*(*f*)
bear² [ber] **1** *v/t* (*pret* ***bore***, *pp* ***borne***) *weight* resistir; *costs* correr con; (*tolerate*) aguantar, soportar; *child* dar a luz; ***she bore him six children*** le dio seis hijos **2** *v/i* (*pret* ***bore***, *pp* ***borne***): ***bring pressure to bear on*** ejercer presión sobre
◆ **bear out** *v/t* (*confirm*) confirmar
bear·a·ble ['berəbl] *adj* soportable
beard [bird] barba *f*
beard·ed ['birdid] *adj* con barba
bear·ing ['beriŋ] *in machine* rodamiento *m*, cojinete *m*; ***that has no bearing on the case*** eso no tiene nada que ver con el caso
'bear mar·ket FIN mercado *m* a la baja
beast [biːst] *animal* bestia *f*; *person* bestia *m*/*f*
beat [biːt] **1** *n of heart* latido *m*; *of music* ritmo *m* **2** *v/i* (*pret* ***beat***, *pp* ***beaten***) *of heart* latir; *of rain* golpear; ***beat about the bush*** andarse por las ramas **3** *v/t* (*pret* ***beat***, *pp* ***beaten***) *in competition* derrotar, ganar a; (*hit*) pegar a; (*pound*) golpear; ***beat it!*** F ¡lárgate! F; ***it beats me*** no logro entender
◆ **beat up** *v/t* dar una paliza a
beat·en ['biːtən] **1** *adj*: ***off the beaten track*** retirado **2** *pp* → ***beat***
beat·ing ['biːtiŋ] (*physical*) paliza *f*
beat-up *adj* F destartalado F
beau·ti·cian [bjuː'tiʃn] esteticista *m*/*f*
beau·ti·ful ['bjuːtəfəl] *adj woman, house, day, story, movie* bonito, precioso, *L.Am.* lindo; *smell, taste, meal* delicioso, *L.Am.* rico; *vacation* estupendo; ***thanks, that's just beautiful!*** ¡muchísimas gracias, está maravilloso!
beau·ti·ful·ly ['bjuːtifəli] *adv cooked, do-*

ne perfectamente, maravillosamente
beaut·y ['bjuːtɪ] *of woman, sunset* belleza *f*
'**beaut·y par·lor** ['pɑːrlər] salón *m* de belleza
◆ **bea·ver away** *v/i* F trabajar como un burro F
be·came [bɪ'keɪm] *pret* → ***become***
be·cause [bɪ'kɑːz] *conj* porque; ***because it was too expensive*** porque era demasiado caro; ***because of*** debido a, a causa de; ***because of you, we can't go*** gracias a ti, no podemos ir
beck·on ['bekn] *v/i* hacer señas
be·come [bɪ'kʌm] *v/i* (*pret* ***became***, *pp* ***become***) hacerse, volverse; ***it became clear that ...*** quedó claro que ...; ***he became a priest*** se hizo sacerdote; ***she's becoming very forgetful*** cada vez es más olvidadiza; ***what's become of her?*** ¿qué fue de ella?
be·com·ing [bɪ'kʌmɪŋ] *adj* favorecedor, apropiado
bed [bed] *n* cama *f*; *of flowers* macizo; *of sea* fondo *m*; *of river* cauce *m*, lecho *m*; ***go to bed*** ir a la cama; ***he's still in bed*** aún está en la cama; ***go to bed with s.o.*** irse a la cama *or* acostarse con alguien
'**bed·clothes** *npl* ropa *f* de cama
bed·ding ['bedɪŋ] ropa *f* de cama
bed·lam ['bedləm] F locura *f*, jaleo *m*
bed·rid·den ['bedrɪdən] *adj*: ***be bedridden*** estar postrado en cama
'**bed·room** dormitorio *m*, *L.Am.* cuarto *m*
'**bed·side**: ***be at the bedside of*** estar junto a la cama de
'**bed·spread** colcha *f*
'**bed·time** hora *f* de irse a la cama
bee [biː] abeja *f*
beech [biːʧ] haya *f*
beef [biːf] **1** *n* carne *f* de vaca *or* vacuna; F (*complaint*) queja *f* **2** *v/i* F (*complain*) quejarse
◆ **beef up** *v/t* reforzar, fortalecer
'**beef·bur·ger** hamburguesa *f*
'**bee·hive** colmena *f*
'**bee·line**: ***make a beeline for*** ir directamente a
been [bɪn] *pp* → ***be***
beep [biːp] **1** *n* pitido *m* **2** *v/i* pitar **3** *v/t* (*call on pager*) llamar con el buscapersonas
beep·er ['biːpər] buscapersonas *m inv*, *Span* busca *m*
beer [bɪr] cerveza *f*
beet [biːt] remolacha *f*
bee·tle ['biːtl] escarabajo *m*
be·fore [bɪ'fɔːr] **1** *prep* (*time*) antes de; (*space, order*) antes de, delante de **2** *adv* antes; ***I've seen this movie before*** ya he visto esta película; ***have you been to Japan before?*** ¿habías estado antes *or* ya en Japón?; ***the week / day before*** la semana / el día anterior **3** *conj* antes de que
be'fore·hand *adv* de antemano
be·friend [bɪ'frend] *v/t* hacerse amigo de
beg [beg] **1** *v/i* (*pret & pp* ***begged***) mendigar, pedir **2** *v/t* (*pret & pp* ***begged***): ***beg s.o. to sth*** rogar *or* suplicar a alguien que haga algo
began [bɪ'gæn] *pret* → ***begin***
beg·gar ['begər] *n* mendigo(-a) *m*(*f*)
be·gin [bɪ'gɪn] **1** *v/i* (*pret* ***began***, *pp* ***begun***) empezar, comenzar; ***to begin with*** (*at first*) en un primer momento, al principio; (*in the first place*) para empezar **2** *v/t* (*pret* ***began***, *pp* ***begun***) empezar, comenzar; ***begin to do sth, begin doing sth*** empezar *or* comenzar a hacer algo
be·gin·ner [bɪ'gɪnər] principiante *m/f*
be·gin·ning [bɪ'gɪnɪŋ] principio *m*, comienzo *m*; (*origin*) origen *m*
be·grudge [bɪ'grʌdʒ] *v/t* (*envy*) envidiar; (*give reluctantly*) dar a regañadientes
be·gun [bɪ'gʌn] *pp* → ***begin***
be·half [bɪ'hɑːf]: ***on behalf of, in behalf of*** en nombre de; ***on my / his behalf*** en nombre mío / suyo
be·have [bɪ'heɪv] *v/i* comportarse, portarse; ***be·have (o.s.)*** comportarse *or* portarse bien; ***behave (yourself)!*** ¡pórtate bien!
be·hav·ior [bɪ'heɪvɪər] comportamiento *m*, conducta *f*
be·hind [bɪ'haɪnd] **1** *prep in position, order* detrás de; *in progress* por detrás de; ***be behind ...*** (*responsible for*) estar detrás de ...; (*support*) respaldar ... **2** *adv* (*at the back*) detrás; ***be behind*** *in match* ir perdiendo; ***be behind with sth*** estar atrasado con algo; ***leave sth behind*** dejarse algo
beige [beɪʒ] *adj* beige, *Span* beis
be·ing ['biːɪŋ] *existence, creature* ser *m*
be·lat·ed [bɪ'leɪtɪd] *adj* tardío
belch [belʧ] **1** *n* eructo *m* **2** *v/i* eructar
Bel·gian ['beldʒən] **1** *adj* belga **2** *n* belga *m/f*
Bel·gium ['beldʒəm] Bélgica
be·lief [bɪ'liːf] creencia *f*; ***it's my belief that*** creo que ...
be·lieve [bɪ'liːv] *v/t* creer
◆ **believe in** *v/t* creer en
be·liev·er [bɪ'liːvər] REL creyente *m/f*; *fig* partidario(a) *m*(*f*) (***in*** de)
be·lit·tle [bɪ'lɪtl] *v/t* menospreciar
Be·lize [be'liːz] *n* Belice

bell [bel] *of bike, door, school* timbre *m*; *of church* campana *f*
'bell·hop botones *m inv*
bel·lig·er·ent [bɪ'lɪdʒərənt] *adj* beligerante
bel·low ['beloʊ] **1** *n* bramido *m* **2** *v/i* bramar
bel·ly ['belɪ] *of person* estómago *m*, barriga *f*; (*fat stomach*) barriga *f*, tripa *f*; *of animal* panza *f*
'bel·ly·ache *v/i* F refunfuñar
be·long [bɪ'lɒːŋ] *v/i*: ***where does this belong?*** ¿dónde va esto?; ***I don't belong here*** no encajo aquí
◆ **belong to** *v/t of object, money* pertenecer a; *club* pertenecer a, ser socio de
be·long·ings [bɪ'lɒːŋɪŋz] *npl* pertenencias *fpl*
be·loved [bɪ'lʌvɪd] *adj* querido
be·low [bɪ'loʊ] **1** *prep* debajo de; *in amount, rate, level* por debajo de **2** *adv* abajo; *in text* más abajo; ***see below*** véase más abajo; ***10 degrees below*** 10 grados bajo cero
belt [belt] *n* cinturón *m*; ***tighten one's belt*** *fig* apretarse el cinturón
bench *seat* banco *m*; (*workbench*) mesa *f* de trabajo
'bench·mark punto *m* de referencia
bend [bend] **1** *n* curva *f* **2** *v/t* (*pret & pp* **bent**) doblar **3** *v/i* (*pret & pp* **bent**) torcer, girar; *of person* flexionarse
◆ **bend down** *v/i* agacharse
bend·er ['bendər] F parranda *f* F
be·neath [bɪ'niːθ] **1** *prep* debajo de; ***she thinks a job like that is beneath her*** cree que un trabajo como ése le supondría rebajarse **2** *adv* abajo
ben·e·fac·tor ['benɪfæktər] benefactor(a) *m(f)*
ben·e·fi·cial [benɪ'fɪʃl] *adj* beneficioso
ben·e·fi·ci·a·ry [benɪ'fɪʃərɪ] beneficiario(-a) *m(f)*
ben·e·fit ['benɪfɪt] **1** *n* beneficio *m*, ventaja *f* **2** *v/t* beneficiar **3** *v/i* beneficiarse
be·nev·o·lence [bɪ'nevələns] benevolencia *f*
be·nev·o·lent [bɪ'nevələnt] *adj* benevolente
be·nign [bɪ'naɪn] *adj* agradable; MED benigno
bent [bent] *pret & pp* → **bend**
be·queath [bɪ'kwiːð] *v/t also fig* legar
be·quest [bɪ'kwest] legado *m*
be·reaved [bɪ'riːvd] **1** *adj*: ***the bereaved parents*** los padres del difunto **2** *n*: ***the bereaved*** los familiares del difunto
be·ret ['bereɪ] boina *f*
ber·ry ['berɪ] baya *f*
ber·serk [bər'sɜːrk] *adv*: ***go berserk*** F volverse loco
berth [bɜːrθ] *on ship* litera *f*; *on train* camarote *m*; *for ship* amarradero *m*; ***give s.o. a wide berth*** evitar a alguien
be·seech [bɪ'siːtʃ] *v/t*: ***beseech s.o. to do sth*** suplicar a alguien que haga algo
be·side [bɪ'saɪd] *prep* al lado de, junto a; ***be beside o.s.*** estar fuera de sí; ***that's beside the point*** eso no tiene nada que ver
be·sides [bɪ'saɪdz] **1** *adv* además **2** *prep* (*apart from*) aparte de, además de
be·siege [bɪ'siːdʒ] *v/t fig* asediar, cercar
best [best] **1** *adj* mejor **2** *adv* mejor; ***which did you like best?*** ¿cuál te gustó más?; ***it would be best if ...*** sería mejor si ...; ***I like her best*** ella es la que más me gusta **3** *n*: ***do one's best*** hacer todo lo posible; ***I did my best to convince her*** hice todo lo posible por convencerla; ***the best*** *person, thing* el / la mejor; ***we insist on the best*** insistimos en lo mejor; ***we'll just have to make the best of it*** tendremos que arreglárnoslas; ***all the best!*** ¡buena suerte!, ¡que te vaya bien!
best be'fore date fecha *f* de caducidad
best 'man *at wedding* padrino *m*
'best-sell·er éxito *m* de ventas, best-seller *m*
bet [bet] **1** *n* apuesta *f*; ***place a bet*** hacer una apuesta **2** *v/i also fig* apostar; ***I bet he doesn't come*** apuesto a que no viene; ***you bet!*** ¡ya lo creo!
be·tray [bɪ'treɪ] *v/t* traicionar; *husband, wife* engañar
be·tray·al [bɪ'treɪəl] traición *f*; *of husband, wife* engaño *m*
bet·ter ['betər] **1** *adj* mejor; ***get better*** *in skills, health* mejorar; ***he's better*** *in health* está mejor **2** *adv* mejor; ***you'd better ask permission*** sería mejor que pidieras permiso; ***I'd really better not*** mejor no; ***all the better for us*** tanto mejor para nosotros; ***I like her better*** me gusta más ella
bet·ter 'off *adj* (*wealthier*) más rico
be·tween [bɪ'twiːn] *prep* entre; ***between you and me*** entre tú y yo
bev·er·age ['bevərɪdʒ] *fml* bebida *f*
be·ware [bɪ'wer] *v/t*: ***beware of*** tener cuidado con
be·wil·der [bɪ'wɪldər] *v/t* desconcertar
be·wil·der·ment [bɪ'wɪldərmənt] desconcierto *m*
be·yond [bɪ'jɑːnd] **1** *prep in space* más allá de; ***she has changed beyond recognition*** ha cambiado tanto que es di-

fícil reconocerla; ***it's beyond me*** (*don't understand*) no logro entender; (*can't do it*) me es imposible **2** *adv* más allá

bi·as ['baɪəs] *n against* prejuicio *m*; *in favor of* favoritismo *m*

bi·as(s)ed ['baɪəst] *adj* parcial

bib [bɪb] *for baby* babero *m*

Bi·ble ['baɪbl] Biblia *f*

bib·li·cal ['bɪblɪkl] *adj* bíblico

bib·li·og·ra·phy [bɪblɪ'ɑːgrəfɪ] bibliografía *f*

bi·car·bon·ate of so·da [baɪ'kɑːrbəneɪt] bicarbonato *m* sódico

bi·cen·ten·ni·al [baɪsen'tenɪəl] bicentenario *m*

bi·ceps ['baɪseps] *npl* bíceps *mpl*

bick·er ['bɪkər] *v/i* reñir, discutir

bi·cy·cle ['baɪsɪkl] bicicleta *f*

bid [bɪd] **1** *n at auction* puja *f*; (*attempt*) intento *m* **2** *v/i* (*pret & pp* **bid**) *at auction* pujar

bid·der ['bɪdər] postor(a) *m(f)*; ***the highest bidder*** el mejor postor

bi·en·ni·al [baɪ'enɪəl] *adj* bienal

bi·fo·cals [baɪ'foʊkəlz] *npl* gafas *fpl or L.Am.* lentes *mpl* bifocales

big [bɪg] **1** *adj* grande; *before singular nouns* gran; ***my big brother / sister*** mi hermano / hermana mayor; ***big name*** nombre *m* importante **2** *adv*: ***talk big*** alardear, fanfarronear

big·a·mist ['bɪgəmɪst] bígamo(-a) *m(f)*

big·a·mous ['bɪgəməs] *adj* bígamo

big·a·my ['bɪgəmɪ] bigamia *f*

'big·head F creído(-a) *m(f)* F

big-head·ed [bɪg'hedɪd] *adj* F creído F

big·ot ['bɪgət] fanático(-a) *m(f)*, intolerante *m/f*

bike [baɪk] **1** *n* F bici *f* F; *motorbike* moto *f* F **2** *v/i* ir en bici

bik·er ['baɪkər] motero(-a) *m(f)*

bi·ki·ni [bɪ'kiːnɪ] biquini *m*

bi·lat·er·al [baɪ'lætərəl] *adj* bilateral

bi·lin·gual [baɪ'lɪŋgwəl] *adj* bilingüe

bill [bɪl] **1** *n for gas, electricity* factura *f*, recibo *m*; *Br in hotel, restaurant* cuenta *f*; (*money*) billete *m*; POL proyecto *m* de ley; (*poster*) cartel *m* **2** *v/t* (*invoice*) enviar la factura a

'bill·board valla *f* publicitaria

'bill·fold cartera *f*, billetera *f*

bil·li·ards ['bɪljərdz] *nsg* billar *m*

bil·li·on ['bɪljən] mil millones *mpl*, millardo *m*

bill of ex'change FIN letra *f* de cambio

bill of 'sale escritura *f* de compraventa

bin [bɪn] *n* cubo *m*

bi·na·ry ['baɪnərɪ] *adj* binario

bind [baɪnd] *v/t* (*pret & pp* **bound**) (*connect*) unir; (*tie*) atar; (LAW: *oblige*) obligar

bind·ing ['baɪndɪŋ] **1** *adj agreement, promise* vinculante **2** *n of book* tapa *f*

bi·noc·u·lars [bɪ'nɑːkjʊlərz] *npl* prismáticos *mpl*

bi·o·chem·ist [baɪoʊ'kemɪst] bioquímico(-a) *m(f)*

bi·o·chem·is·try [baɪoʊ'kemɪstrɪ] bioquímica *f*

bi·o·de·gra·da·ble [baɪoʊdɪ'greɪdəbl] *adj* biodegradable

bi·og·ra·pher [baɪ'ɑːgrəfər] biógrafo(-a) *m(f)*

bi·og·ra·phy [baɪ'ɑːgrəfɪ] biografía *f*

bi·o·log·i·cal [baɪoʊ'lɑːdʒɪkl] *adj* biológico; ***biological parents*** padres *mpl* biológicos; ***biological detergent*** detergente *m* biológico

bi·ol·o·gist [baɪ'ɑːlədʒɪst] biólogo(-a) *m(f)*

bi·ol·o·gy [baɪ'ɑːlədʒɪ] biología *f*

bi·o·tech·nol·o·gy [baɪoʊtek'nɑːlədʒɪ] biotecnología *f*

bird [bɜːrd] ave *f*, pájaro *m*

'bird·cage jaula *f* para pájaros

bird of 'prey ave *f* rapaz

'bird sanc·tu·a·ry reserva *f* de aves

bird's eye 'view vista *f* panorámica; ***get a bird's eye view of sth*** ver algo a vista de pájaro

bi·ro® ['baɪroʊ] *Br* bolígrafo *m*, *Mex* pluma *f*, *Rpl* birome *m*

birth [bɜːrθ] *also fig* nacimiento *m*; (*labor*) parto *m*; ***give birth to*** *child* dar a luz; *of animal* parir; ***date of birth*** fecha *f* de nacimiento; ***the land of my birth*** mi tierra natal

'birth cer·tif·i·cate partida *f* de nacimiento

'birth con·trol control *m* de natalidad

'birth·day cumpleaños *m inv*; ***happy birthday!*** ¡feliz cumpleaños!

'birth·day cake tarta *f* de cumpleaños

'birth·mark marca *f* de nacimiento, antojo *m*

'birth·place lugar *m* de nacimiento

'birth·rate tasa *f* de natalidad

bis·cuit ['bɪskɪt] bollo *m*, panecillo *m*; *Br* galleta *f*

bi·sex·u·al ['baɪsekʃʊəl] **1** *adj* bisexual **2** *n* bisexual *m/f*

bish·op ['bɪʃəp] obispo *m*

bit [bɪt] *n* (*piece*) trozo *m*; (*part*) parte *f*; *of puzzle* pieza *f*; COMPUT bit *m*; ***a bit*** (*a little*) un poco; ***let's sit down for a bit*** sentémonos un rato; ***you haven't changed a bit*** no has cambiado nada; ***a bit of*** (*a little*) un poco de; ***a bit of news*** una noticia; ***a bit of advice*** un consejo; ***bit by***

bit poco a poco; ***I'll be there in a bit*** estaré allí dentro de un rato
bit² [bɪt] *pret* → ***bite***
bitch [bɪʧ] **1** *n dog* perra *f*; F *woman* zorra *f* F **2** *v/i* F (*complain*) quejarse
bitch·y ['bɪʧɪ] *adj* F *person* malicioso; *remark* a mala leche F
bite [baɪt] **1** *n of dog* mordisco *m*; *of spider, mosquito* picadura *f*; *of snake* mordedura *f*, picadura *f*; *of food* bocado *m*; ***let's have a bite*** (***to eat***) vamos a comer algo **2** *v/t* (*pret* ***bit***, *pp* ***bitten***) *of dog* morder; *of mosquito, flea* picar; *of snake* picar, morder; ***bite one's nails*** morderse las uñas **3** *v/i* (*pret* ***bit***, *pp* ***bitten***) *of dog* morder; *of mosquito, flea* picar; *of snake* morder, picar; *of fish* picar
bit·ten ['bɪtn] *pp* → ***bite***
bit·ter ['bɪtər] *adj taste* amargo; *person* resentido; *weather* helador; *argument* agrio
bit·ter·ly ['bɪtərlɪ] *adv resent* amargamente; ***it's bitterly cold*** hace un frío helador
bi·zarre [bɪ'zɑːr] *adj* extraño, peculiar
blab [blæb] *v/i* (*pret & pp* ***blabbed***) F irse de la lengua F
blab·ber·mouth ['blæbərmaʊθ] F bocazas *m/f inv* F
black [blæk] **1** *adj* negro; *coffee* solo; *tea* sin leche; *fig* negro, aciago **2** *n* (*color*) negro *m*; (*person*) negro(-a) *m*(*f*); ***be in the black*** FIN no estar en números rojos; ***in black and white*** en blanco y negro; *in writing* por escrito
◆ **black out** *v/i* perder el conocimiento
'**black·ber·ry** mora *f*
'**black·bird** mirlo *m*
'**black·board** pizarra *f*, encerado *m*
black 'box caja *f* negra
black 'cof·fee café *m* solo
black e'con·o·my economía *f* sumergida
black·en ['blækn] *v/t fig*: *person's name* manchar
black 'eye ojo *m* morado
'**black·head** espinilla *f*, punto *m* negro
black 'ice *Br* placas *fpl* de hielo
'**black·list 1** *n* lista *f* negra **2** *v/t* poner en la lista negra
'**black·mail 1** *n* chantaje *m*; ***emotional blackmail*** chantaje *m* emocional **2** *v/t* chantajear
'**black·mail·er** chantajista *m/f*
black 'mar·ket mercado *m* negro
black·ness ['blæknɪs] oscuridad *f*
'**black·out** ELEC apagón *m*; MED desmayo *m*; ***have a blackout*** desmayarse
'**black·smith** herrero *m*
blad·der ['blædər] vejiga *f*
blade [bleɪd] *of knife, sword* hoja *f*; *of propeller* pala *f*; *of grass* brizna *f*
blame [bleɪm] **1** *n* culpa *f*; ***I got the blame for it*** me echaron la culpa **2** *v/t* culpar; ***blame s.o. for sth*** culpar a alguien de algo
bland [blænd] *adj smile* insulso; *food* insípido, soso
blank [blæŋk] **1** *adj* (*not written on*) en blanco; *tape* virgen; *look* inexpresivo **2** *n* (*empty space*) espacio *m* en blanco; ***my mind's a blank*** tengo la mente en blanco
blank 'check, *Br* **blank 'cheque** cheque *m* en blanco
blan·ket ['blæŋkɪt] *n* manta *f*, *L.Am.* frazada *f*; ***a blanket of snow*** un manto de nieve
blare [bler] *v/i* retumbar
◆ **blare out 1** *v/i* retumbar **2** *v/t* emitir a todo volumen
blas·pheme [blæs'fiːm] *v/i* blasfemar
blas·phe·my ['blæsfəmɪ] blasfemia *f*
blast [blæst] **1** *n* (*explosion*) explosión *f*; (*gust*) ráfaga *f* **2** *v/t tunnel* abrir (con explosivos); *rock* volar; ***blast!*** F ¡mecachis! F
◆ **blast off** *v/i of rocket* despegar
'**blast fur·nace** alto horno *m*
'**blast-off** despegue *m*
bla·tant ['bleɪtənt] *adj* descarado
blaze [bleɪz] **1** *n* (*fire*) incendio *m*; ***a blaze of color*** una explosión de color **2** *v/i of fire* arder
◆ **blaze away** *v/i with gun* disparar sin parar
blaz·er ['bleɪzər] americana *f*
bleach [bliːʧ] **1** *n for clothes* lejía *f*; *for hair* decolorante *m* **2** *v/t hair* aclarar, desteñir
bleak [bliːk] *adj countryside* inhóspito; *weather* desapacible; *future* desolador
blear·y-eyed ['blɪrɪaɪd] *adj* con ojos de sueño
bleat [bliːt] *v/i of sheep* balar
bled [bled] *pret & pp* → ***bleed***
bleed [bliːd] **1** *v/i* (*pret & pp* ***bled***) sangrar; ***he's bleeding internally*** tiene una hemorragia interna; ***bleed to death*** desangrarse **2** *v/t* (*pret & pp* ***bled***) *fig* sangrar
bleed·ing ['bliːdɪŋ] *n* hemorragia *f*
bleep [bliːp] **1** *n* pitido *m* **2** *v/i* pitar **3** *v/t* (*call on pager*) llamar con el buscapersonas
bleep·er ['bliːpər] buscapersonas *m inv*, *Span* busca *m*
blem·ish ['blemɪʃ] **1** *n* imperfección *f* **2** *v/t*

reputation manchar
blend [blend] **1** *n of coffee etc* mezcla *f*; *fig* combinación *f* **2** *v/t* mezclar
◆ **blend in 1** *v/i of person in environment* pasar desapercibido; *of animal with surroundings etc* confundirse; *of furniture etc* combinar **2** *v/t in cooking* añadir
blend·er ['blendər] *machine* licuadora *f*
bless [bles] *v/t* bendecir; ***(God) bless you!*** ¡que Dios te bendiga!; *in response to sneeze* ¡Jesús!; ***be blessed with*** tener la suerte de
bless·ing ['blesɪŋ] *also fig* bendición *f*
blew [bluː] *pret* → **blow²**
blind [blaɪnd] **1** *adj* ciego; *corner* sin visibilidad; ***be blind to sth*** *fig* no ver algo **2** *npl*: ***the blind*** los ciegos, los invidentes **3** *v/t of sun* cegar; ***she was blinded in an accident*** se quedó ciega a raíz de un accidente; ***love blinded her to his faults*** el amor le impedía ver sus defectos
blind 'al·ley callejón *m* sin salida
blind 'date cita *f* a ciegas
'blind·fold 1 *n* venda *f* **2** *v/t* vendar los ojos a **3** *adv* con los ojos cerrados
blind·ing ['blaɪndɪŋ] *adj light* cegador; *headache* terrible
blind·ly ['blaɪndlɪ] *adv* a ciegas; *fig* ciegamente
'blind spot *in road* punto *m* sin visibilidad; *in driving mirror* ángulo *m* muerto; (*ability that is lacking*) punto *m* flaco
blink [blɪŋk] *v/i* parpadear
blink·ered ['blɪŋkərd] *adj fig* cerrado
blip [blɪp] *on radar screen* señal *f*, luz *f*; ***it's just a blip*** *fig* es algo momentáneo
bliss [blɪs] felicidad *f*; ***it was bliss*** fue fantástico
blis·ter ['blɪstər] **1** *n* ampolla *f* **2** *v/i* ampollarse; *of paint* hacer burbujas
bliz·zard ['blɪzərd] ventisca *f*
bloat·ed ['bloʊtɪd] *adj* hinchado
blob [blɑːb] *of liquid* goterón *m*
bloc [blɑːk] POL bloque *m*
block [blɑːk] **1** *n* bloque *m*; *buildings* manzana *f*, *L.Am.* cuadra *f*; *of shares* paquete *m*; (*blockage*) bloqueo *m* **2** *v/t* bloquear; *sink* atascar
◆ **block in** *v/t with vehicle* bloquear el paso a
◆ **block out** *v/t light* impedir el paso de
◆ **block up** *v/t sink etc* atascar
block·ade [blɑː'keɪd] **1** *n* bloqueo *m* **2** *v/t* bloquear
block·age ['blɑːkɪdʒ] obstrucción *f*
block·bust·er ['blɑːkbʌstər] gran éxito *m*
block 'let·ters *npl* letras *fpl* mayúsculas
blond [blɑːnd] *adj* rubio
blonde [blɑːnd] *n woman* rubia *f*
blood [blʌd] sangre *f*; ***in cold blood*** a sangre fría
'blood al·co·hol lev·el nivel *m* de alcohol en sangre
'blood bank banco *m* de sangre
'blood bath baño *m* de sangre
'blood do·nor donante *m*/*f* de sangre
'blood group grupo *m* sanguíneo
blood·less ['blʌdlɪs] *adj coup* incruento, pacífico
'blood poi·son·ing septicemia *f*
'blood pres·sure tensión *f* (arterial), presión *f* sanguínea
'blood re·la·tion: ***she's not a blood relation of mine*** no nos unen lazos de sangre
'blood sam·ple muestra *f* de sangre
'blood·shed derramamiento *m* de sangre
'blood·shot *adj* enrojecido
'blood·stain mancha *f* de sangre
'blood·stain·ed *adj* ensangrentado, manchado de sangre
'blood·stream flujo *m* sanguíneo
'blood test análisis *m inv* de sangre
'blood·thirst·y *adj* sanguinario; *movie* macabro
'blood trans·fu·sion transfusión *f* sanguínea
'blood ves·sel vaso *m* sanguíneo
blood·y ['blʌdɪ] *adj hands etc* ensangrentado; *battle* sangriento; *Br* F maldito F, *Span* puñetero F; ***bloody hell!*** ¡ostras! F
bloom [bluːm] **1** *n* flor *f*; ***in bloom*** en flor **2** *v/i also fig* florecer
blos·som ['blɑːsəm] **1** *n* flores *fpl* **2** *v/i also fig* florecer
blot [blɑːt] **1** *n* mancha *f*, borrón *m*; ***be a blot on the landscape*** estropear el paisaje **2** *v/t* (*pret & pp* **blotted**) (*dry*) secar
◆ **blot out** *v/t* borrar; *sun*, *view* ocultar
blotch [blɑːtʃ] *on skin* erupción *f*, mancha *f*
blotch·y ['blɑːtʃɪ] *adj*: ***blotchy skin*** piel con erupciones
blouse [blaʊz] blusa *f*
blow¹ [bloʊ] *n* golpe *m*
blow² [bloʊ] **1** *v/t* (*pret* **blew**, *pp* **blown**) *smoke* exhalar; *whistle* tocar; F (*spend*) fundir F; *opportunity* perder, desaprovechar; ***blow one's nose*** sonarse (la nariz) **2** *v/i* (*pret* **blew**, *pp* **blown**) *of wind*, *person* soplar; *of whistle* sonar; *of fuse* fundirse; *of tire* reventarse
◆ **blow off 1** *v/t* llevarse **2** *v/i* salir volando
◆ **blow out 1** *v/t candle* apagar **2** *v/i of candle* apagarse
◆ **blow over 1** *v/t* derribar, hacer caer **2** *v/i* caerse, derrumbarse; *of storm* amainar; *of argument* calmarse
◆ **blow up 1** *v/t with explosives* volar; *ba-*

lloon hinchar; *photograph* ampliar **2** *v/i* explotar; F (*become angry*) ponerse furioso
'**blow-dry** *v/t* (*pret & pp* **blow-dried**) secar (*con secador*)
'**blow·job** V mamada *f* V
'**blow·out** *of tire* reventón *m*; F (*big meal*) comilona *f* F
'**blow-up** *of photo* ampliación *f*
blown [bloʊn] *pp* → **blow²**
blue [blu:] **1** *adj* azul; F *movie* porno *inv* F **2** *n* azul *m*
'**blue·ber·ry** arándano *m*
blue 'chip *adj* puntero, de primera fila
blue-'col·lar work·er trabajador(a) *m*(*f*) manual
'**blue·print** plano *m*; (*fig*: *plan*) proyecto *m*, plan *m*
blues [blu:z] *npl* MUS blues *m inv*; ***have the blues*** estar deprimido
'**blues sing·er** cantante *m/f* de blues
bluff [blʌf] **1** *n* (*deception*) farol *m* **2** *v/i* ir de farol
blun·der ['blʌndər] **1** *n* error *m* de bulto, metedura *f* de pata **2** *v/i* cometer un error de bulto, meter la pata
blunt [blʌnt] *adj pencil* sin punta; *knife* desafilado; *person* franco
blunt·ly ['blʌntlɪ] *adv speak* francamente
blur [blɜ:r] **1** *n* imagen *f* desenfocada; ***everything is a blur*** todo está desenfocado **2** *v/t* (*pret & pp* **blurred**) desdibujar
blurb [blɜ:rb] *on book* nota *f* promocional
◆ **blurt out** [blɜ:rt] *v/t* soltar
blush [blʌʃ] **1** *n* rubor *m*, sonrojo *m* **2** *v/i* ruborizarse, sonrojarse
blush·er ['blʌʃər] *cosmetic* colorete *m*
blus·ter ['blʌstər] *v/i* protestar encolerizadamente
blus·ter·y ['blʌstərɪ] *adj* tempestuoso
BO [bi:'oʊ] *abbr* (= **body odor**) olor *m* corporal
board [bɔ:rd] **1** *n* tablón *m*, tabla *f*; *for game* tablero *m*; *for notices* tablón *m*; ***board*** (***of directors***) consejo *m* de administración; ***on board*** *on plane, boat, train* a bordo; ***take on board*** *comments etc* aceptar, tener en cuenta; (*fully realize truth of*) asumir; ***across the board*** de forma general **2** *v/t airplane etc* embarcar; *train* subir a **3** *v/i of passengers* embarcar; ***board with*** *as lodger* hospedarse con
◆ **board up** *v/t* cubrir con tablas
board·er ['bɔ:rdər] huésped *m/f*
'**board game** juego *m* de mesa
'**board·ing card** tarjeta *f* de embarque
'**board·ing house** hostal *m*, pensión *f*
'**board·ing pass** tarjeta *f* de embarque
'**board·ing school** internado *m*
'**board meet·ing** reunión *m* del consejo de administración
'**board room** sala *f* de reuniones *or* juntas
'**board·walk** paseo *m* marítimo con tablas
boast [boʊst] **1** *n* presunción *f*, jactancia *f* **2** *v/i* presumir, alardear (**about** de)
boat [boʊt] barco *m*; *small, for leisure* barca *f*; ***go by boat*** ir en barco
bob¹ [bɑ:b] *haircut* corte *m* a lo chico
bob² [bɑ:b] *v/i* (*pret & pp* **bobbed**) *of boat etc* mecerse
◆ **bob up** *v/i* aparecer
'**bob·sleigh**, '**bob·sled** bobsleigh *m*
bod·ice ['bɑ:dɪs] cuerpo *m*
bod·i·ly ['bɑ:dɪlɪ] **1** *adj* corporal; *needs* físico; *function* fisiológico **2** *adv eject* en volandas
bod·y ['bɑ:dɪ] cuerpo *m*; *dead* cadáver *m*; ***body of water*** masa *f* de agua
'**body·guard** guardaespaldas *m/f inv*
'**body lan·guage** lenguaje *m* corporal
'**bod·y o·dor** olor *m* corporal
'**bod·y pierc·ing** piercing *m*, perforaciones *fpl* corporales
'**body·shop** MOT taller *m* de carrocería
'**bod·y stock·ing** malla *f*
'**bod·y suit** body *m* '**body·work** MOT carrocería *f*
bog·gle ['bɑ:gl] *v/i*: ***the mind boggles!*** ¡no quiero ni pensarlo!
bo·gus ['boʊgəs] *adj* falso
boil¹ [bɔɪl] *n* (*swelling*) forúnculo
boil² [bɔɪl] **1** *v/t liquid* hervir; *egg, vegetables* cocer **2** *v/i* hervir
◆ **boil down to** *v/t* reducirse a
◆ **boil over** *v/i of milk etc* salirse
boil·er ['bɔɪlər] caldera *f*
boil·ing point ['bɔɪlɪŋ] *of liquid* punto *m* de ebullición; ***reach boiling point*** *fig* perder la paciencia
bois·ter·ous ['bɔɪstərəs] *adj* escandaloso
bold [boʊld] **1** *adj* valiente, audaz; *text* en negrita **2** *n* (*print*) negrita *f*; ***in bold*** en negrita
Bo·liv·i·a [bə'lɪvɪə] *n* Bolivia
Bo·liv·i·an [bə'lɪvɪən] **1** *adj* boliviano **2** *n* boliviano(-a) *m*(*f*)
bol·ster ['boʊlstər] *v/t confidence* reforzar
bolt [boʊlt] **1** *n on door* cerrojo *m*, pestillo *m*; *with nut* perno *m*; *of lightning* rayo *m*; ***like a bolt from the blue*** de forma inesperada **2** *adv*: ***bolt upright*** erguido **3** *v/t* (*fix with bolts*) atornillar; *close* cerrar con cerrojo *or* pestillo **4** *v/i* (*run off*) fugarse, escaparse
bomb [bɑ:m] **1** *n* bomba *f* **2** *v/t* MIL bombardear; *of terrorist* poner una bomba en

bom·bard [bɑːm'bɑːrd] *v/t* (*attack*) bombardear; ***bombard s.o. with questions*** bombardear alguien con preguntas
'**bomb attack** atentado *m* con bomba
bomb·er ['bɑːmər] *airplane* bombardero *m*; *terrorist* terrorista *m/f* (*que pone bombas*)
'**bomb·er jack·et** cazadora *f* de aviador
'**bomb·proof** *adj* a prueba de bombas
'**bomb scare** amenaza *f* de bomba
'**bomb·shell** (*fig*: *news*) bomba *f*
bond [bɑːnd] **1** *n* (*tie*) unión *f*; FIN bono *m* **2** *v/i of glue* adherirse
bone [boʊn] **1** *n* hueso *m*; *of fish* espina *f* **2** *v/t meat* deshuesar; *fish* quitar las espinas a
bon·fire ['bɑːnfaɪr] hoguera *f*
bon·net *Br of car* MOT capó *m*
bo·nus ['boʊnəs] *money* plus *m*, bonificación *f*; (*something extra*) ventaja *f* adicional; ***a Christmas bonus*** un plus por Navidad
boo [buː] **1** *n* abucheo *m* **2** *v/t & v/i* abuchear
boob [buːb] *n* P (*breast*) teta *f* P
boo·boo ['buːbuː] *n* F metedura *f* de pata
book [bʊk] **1** *n* libro *m*; *of matches* caja *f* (*de solapa*) **2** *v/t* (*reserve*) reservar; *of policeman* multar **3** *v/i* (*reserve*) reservar, hacer una reserva
'**book·case** estantería *f*, librería *f*
booked up [bʊkt'ʌp] *adj* lleno, completo; *person* ocupado
book·ie ['bʊkɪ] F corredor(a) *m*(*f*) de apuestas
book·ing ['bʊkɪŋ] (*reservation*) reserva *f*
'**book·ing clerk** taquillero(-a) *m*(*f*)
'**book·keep·er** tenedor(a) *m*(*f*) de libros
'**book·keep·ing** contabilidad *f*
book·let ['bʊklɪt] folleto *m*
'**book·mak·er** corredor(a) *m*(*f*) de apuestas
books [bʊks] *npl* (*accounts*) contabilidad *f*; ***do the books*** llevar la contabilidad; ***cook the books*** F falsificar las cuentas
'**book·sell·er** librero(-a) *m*(*f*)
'**book·shelf** estante *m*
'**book·store** librería *f*
'**book·stall** puesto *m* de venta de libros
'**book to·ken** vale *m* para comprar libros
boom¹ [buːm] **1** *n* boom *m* **2** *v/i of business* desarrollarse, experimentar un boom
boom² [buːm] *n noise* estruendo *m*
boon·ies ['buːnɪz] *npl* F: ***they live out in the boonies*** viven en el quinto pino F
boor [bʊr] basto *m*, grosero *m*
boor·ish ['bʊrɪʃ] *adj* basto, grosero
boost [buːst] **1** *n to sales*, *economy* impulso *m*; ***your confidence needs a boost*** necesitas algo que te dé más confianza **2** *v/t production*, *prices* estimular; *morale* levantar
boot [buːt] *n* bota *f*; *Br of car* maletero *m*, *C.Am.*, *Mex* cajuela *f*, *Rpl* baúl *m*
◆ **boot out** *v/t* F echar
◆ **boot up** *v/t & v/i* COMPUT arrancar
booth [buːð] *at market*, *fair* cabina *f*; (*in restaurant*) *mesa rodeada por bancos fijos*
booze [buːz] *n* F bebida *f*, *Span* priva *f* F
bor·der ['bɔːrdər] **1** *n between countries* frontera *f*; (*edge*) borde *m*; *on clothing* ribete *m* **2** *v/t country* limitar con; *river* bordear
◆ **border on** limitar con; (*be almost*) rayar en
'**bor·der·line** *adj*: ***a borderline case*** un caso dudoso
bore¹ [bɔːr] **1** *v/t hole* taladrar; ***bore a hole in sth*** taladrar algo
bore² [bɔːr] **1** *n* (*person*) pesado(-a) *m*(*f*), pelma *m/f inv* F; ***it's such a bore*** ¡qué pesadez *or Span* lata! **2** *v/t* aburrir
bore³ [bɔːr] *pret* → ***bear***²
bored [bɔːrd] *adj* aburrido; ***I'm bored*** me aburro, estoy aburrido
bore·dom ['bɔːrdəm] aburrimiento *m*
bor·ing ['bɔːrɪŋ] *adj* aburrido; ***be boring*** ser aburrido
born [bɔːrn] *adj*: ***be born*** nacer; ***where were you born?*** ¿dónde naciste?; ***be a born teacher*** haber nacido para ser profesor
borne [bɔːrn] *pp* → ***bear***²
bor·row ['bɑːroʊ] *v/t* tomar prestado
bos·om ['bʊzm] *of woman* pecho *m*
boss [bɑːs] jefe(-a) *m*(*f*)
◆ **boss about** *v/t* dar órdenes a
boss·y ['bɑːsɪ] *adj* mandón
bo·tan·i·cal [bə'tænɪkl] *adj* botánico
bo·tan·ic(·al) gar·dens *npl* jardín *m* botánico
bot·a·nist ['bɑːtənɪst] botánico(-a) *m*(*f*)
bot·a·ny ['bɑːtənɪ] botánica *f*
botch [bɑːtʃ] *v/t* arruinar, estropear
both [boʊθ] **1** *adj & pron* ambos, los dos; ***I know both (of the) brothers*** conozco a ambos hermanos, conozco a los dos hermanos; ***both of them*** ambos, los dos **2** *adv*: ***both my mother and I*** tanto mi madre como yo; ***he's both handsome and intelligent*** es guapo y además inteligente; ***is it business or pleasure? - both*** ¿es de negocios o de placer? - las dos cosas
both·er ['bɑːðər] **1** *n* molestias *fpl*; ***it's no bother*** no es ninguna molestia **2** *v/t* (*dis-*

turb) molestar; (*worry*) preocupar **3** *v/i* preocuparse; ***don't bother!*** (*you needn't do it*) ¡no te preocupes!; ***you needn't have bothered*** no deberías haberte molestado
bot·tle ['bɑːtl] **1** *n* botella *f*; *for baby* biberón *m* **2** *v/t* embotellar
◆ **bottle up** *v/t feelings* reprimir, contener
'**bot·tle bank** contenedor *m* de vidrio
bot·tled wa·ter ['bɑːtld] agua *f* embotellada
'**bot·tle·neck** *n in road* embotellamiento *m*, atasco *m*; *in production* cuello *m* de botella
'**bot·tle-o·pen·er** abrebotellas *m inv*
bot·tom ['bɑːtəm] **1** *adj* inferior, de abajo **2** *n of drawer, case, pan* fondo *m*; *of hill, page* pie *m*; *of pile* parte *f* inferior; (*underside*) parte *f* de abajo; *of street* final *m*; *of garden* fondo *m*; (*buttocks*) trasero *m*; ***at the bottom of the screen*** en la parte inferior de la pantalla
◆ **bottom out** *v/i* tocar fondo
bot·tom 'line (*fig: financial outcome*) saldo *m* final; (*real issue*) realidad *f*
bought [bɒːt] *pret & pp* → ***buy***
boul·der ['bouldər] roca *f* redondeada
bounce [bauns] **1** *v/t ball* botar **2** *v/i of ball* botar, rebotar; *on sofa etc* saltar; *of rain* rebotar; *of check* ser rechazado
bounc·er ['baunsər] portero *m*, gorila *m*
bounc·y ['baunsɪ] *adj ball* que bota bien; *cushion, chair* mullido
bound[1] [baund] *adj*: ***be bound to do sth*** (*obliged to*) estar obligado a hacer algo; ***she's bound to call an election soon*** (*sure to*) seguro que convoca elecciones pronto
bound[2] [baund] *adj*: ***be bound for*** *of ship* llevar destino a
bound[3] [baund] **1** *n* (*jump*) salto *m* **2** *v/i* saltar
bound[4] [baund] *pret & pp* → ***bind***
bound·a·ry ['baundərɪ] límite *m*; *between countries* frontera *f*
bound·less ['baundlɪs] *adj* ilimitado, infinito
bou·quet [bu'keɪ] (*flowers*) ramo *m*
bour·bon ['bɜːrbən] bourbon *m*
bout [baut] MED ataque *m*; *in boxing* combate *m*
bou·tique [buː'tiːk] boutique *f*
bow[1] [bau] **1** *n as greeting* reverencia *f* **2** *v/i* saludar con la cabeza **3** *v/t head* inclinar
bow[2] [bou] (*knot*) lazo *m*; MUS, *for archery* arco *m*
bow[3] [bau] *of ship* proa *f*
bow·els ['bauəlz] *npl* entrañas *fpl*
bowl[1] [boul] *for rice, cereals etc* cuenco *m*; *for soup* plato *m* sopero; *for salad* ensaladera *f*; *for washing* barreño *m*, palangana *f*
bowl[2] [boul] **1** *n* (*ball*) bola *f* **2** *v/i in bowling* lanzar la bola
◆ **bowl over** *v/t* (*fig: astonish*) impresionar, maravillar
bowl·ing ['boulɪŋ] bolos *mpl*
'**bowl·ing al·ley** bolera *f*
bow 'tie [bou] pajarita *f*
box[1] [bɑːks] *n container* caja *f*; *on form* casilla *f*
box[2] [bɑːks] *v/i* boxear
box·er ['bɑːksər] boxeador(a) *m(f)*
'**box·er shorts** *npl* calzoncillos *mpl*, boxers *mpl*
box·ing ['bɑːksɪŋ] boxeo *m*
'**box·ing glove** guante *m* de boxeo
'**box·ing match** combate *m* de boxeo
'**box·ing ring** cuadrilátero *m*, ring *m*
'**box num·ber** *at post office* apartado *m* de correos
'**box of·fice** taquilla *f*, *L.Am.* boletería *f*
boy [bɔɪ] niño *m*, chico *m*; (*son*) hijo *m*
boy·cott ['bɔɪkɑːt] **1** *n* boicot *m* **2** *v/t* boicotear
'**boy·friend** novio *m*
boy·ish ['bɔɪɪʃ] *adj* varonil
boy'scout boy scout *m*
bra [brɑː] *Br* sujetador *m*, sostén *m*
brace [breɪs] *on teeth* aparato *m*
brace·let ['breɪslɪt] pulsera *f*
brack·et ['brækɪt] *for shelf* escuadra *f*; (***square***) ***bracket*** *in text* corchete *m*
brag [bræg] *v/i* (*pret & pp* ***bragged***) presumir, fanfarronear
braid [breɪd] *n in hair* trenza *f*; *trimming* trenzado *m*
braille [breɪl] braille *m*
brain [breɪn] cerebro *m*; ***use your brain*** utiliza la cabeza
'**brain dead** *adj* MED clínicamente muerto
brain·less ['breɪnlɪs] *adj* F estúpido
brains [breɪnz] *npl* (*intelligence*) inteligencia *f*; ***the brains of the operation*** el cerebro de la operación
'**brain·storm** idea *f* genial
brain·storm·ing ['breɪnstɔːrmɪŋ] tormenta *f* de ideas
'**brain sur·geon** neurocirujano(-a) *m(f)*
'**brain sur·ger·y** neurocirugía *f*
'**brain tu·mor** tumor *m* cerebral
'**brain·wash** *v/t* lavar el cerebro a
'**brain·wave** (*brilliant idea*) idea *f* genial
brain·y ['breɪnɪ] *adj* F: ***be brainy*** tener mucho coco F, ser una lumbrera
brake [breɪk] **1** *n* freno *m*; ***act as a brake on*** frenar **2** *v/i* frenar

'brake flu·id MOT líquido *m* de frenos
'brake light MOT luz *f* de frenado
'brake ped·al MOT pedal *m* del freno
branch [bræntʃ] *n of tree* rama *f*; *of bank, company* sucursal *f*
◆ **branch off** *v/i of road* bifurcarse
◆ **branch out** *v/i* diversificarse; ***they've branched out into furniture*** han empezado a trabajar también con muebles
brand [brænd] **1** *n* marca *f* **2** *v/t*: ***be branded a liar*** ser tildado de mentiroso
brand 'im·age imagen *f* de marca
bran·dish ['brændɪʃ] *v/t* blandir
brand 'lead·er marca *f* líder del mercado
brand 'loy·al·ty lealtad *f* a una marca
'brand name nombre *m* comercial
brand-'new *adj* nuevo, flamante
bran·dy ['brændɪ] brandy *m*, coñac *m*
brass [bræs] *alloy* latón *m*; ***the brass*** MUS los metales
brass 'band banda *f* de música
bras·sière [brə'zɪr] sujetador *m*, sostén *m*
brat [bræt] *pej* niñato(-a) *m(f)*
bra·va·do [brə'vɑːdoʊ] bravuconería *f*
brave [breɪv] *adj* valiente, valeroso
brave·ly ['breɪvlɪ] *adv* valientemente, valerosamente
brav·er·y ['breɪvərɪ] valentía *f*, valor *m*
brawl [brɒːl] **1** *n* pelea *f* **2** *v/i* pelearse
brawn·y ['brɒːnɪ] *adj* fuerte, musculoso
Bra·zil [brə'zɪl] Brasil
Bra·zil·ian [brə'zɪlɪən] **1** *adj* brasileño **2** *n* brasileño(-a) *m(f)*
breach [briːtʃ] *n* (*violation*) infracción *f*, incumplimiento; *in party* ruptura *f*
breach of 'con·tract LAW incumplimiento *m* de contrato
bread [bred] *n* pan *m*
'bread·crumbs *npl for cooking* pan *m* rallado; *for birds* migas *fpl*
'bread knife cuchillo *m* del pan
breadth [bredθ] *of road* ancho *m*; *of knowledge* amplitud *f*
'bread·win·ner: ***be the breadwinner*** ser el que gana el pan
break [breɪk] **1** *n in bone etc* fractura *f*, rotura *f*; (*rest*) descanso *m*; *in relationship* separación *f* temporal; ***give s.o. a break*** F (*opportunity*) ofrecer una oportunidad a alguien; ***take a break*** descansar; ***without a break*** *work, travel* sin descanso **2** *v/t* (*pret* **broke**, *pp* **broken**) *machine, device* romper, estropear; *stick* romper, partir; *arm, leg* fracturar, romper; *glass, egg* romper; *rules, law* violar, incumplir; *promise* romper; *news* dar; *record* batir **3** *v/i* (*pret* **broke**, *pp* **broken**) *of machine, device* romperse, estropearse; *of glass, egg* romperse; *of stick* partirse, romperse; *of news* saltar; *of storm* estallar, comenzar; *of boy's voice* cambiar
◆ **break away** *v/i* (*escape*) escaparse; *from family* separarse; *from organization* escindirse; *from tradition* romper (**from** con)
◆ **break down 1** *v/i of vehicle* averiarse, estropearse; *of machine* estropearse; *of talks* romperse; *in tears* romper a llorar; *mentally* venirse abajo **2** *v/t door* derribar; *figures* detallar, desglosar
◆ **break even** *v/i* COM cubrir gastos
◆ **break in** *v/i* (*interrupt*) interrumpir; *of burglar* entrar
◆ **break off 1** *v/t* partir; *relationship* romper; ***they've broken it off*** han roto **2** *v/i* (*stop talking*) interrumpirse
◆ **break out** (*start up*) comenzar; *of fighting* estallar; *of disease* desatarse; *of prisoners* escaparse, darse a la fuga; ***he broke out in a rash*** le salió un sarpullido
◆ **break up 1** *v/t into component parts* descomponer; *fight* poner fin a **2** *v/i of ice* romperse; *of couple* terminar, separarse; *of band* separarse; *of meeting* terminar
break·a·ble ['breɪkəbl] *adj* rompible, frágil
break·age ['breɪkɪdʒ] rotura *f*
'break·down *of vehicle, machine* avería *f*; *of talks* ruptura *f*; (*nervous breakdown*) crisis *f inv* nerviosa; *of figures* desglose *m*
break-'e·ven point punto *m* de equilibrio
break·fast ['brekfəst] *n* desayuno *m*; ***have breakfast*** desayunar
'break·fast tel·e·vi·sion televisión *f* matinal
'break-in entrada *f* (*mediante la fuerza*); *robbery* robo *m*; ***we've had a break-in*** han entrado a robar
'break·through *in plan, negotiations* paso *m* adelante; *of science, technology* avance *m*
'break·up *of marriage, partnership* ruptura *f*, separación *f*
breast [brest] *of woman* pecho *m*
'breast·feed *v/t* (*pret & pp* **breastfed**) amamantar
'breast·stroke braza *f*
breath [breθ] respiración *f*; ***get your breath back*** recobrar el aliento; ***be out of breath*** estar sin respiración; ***take a deep breath*** respira hondo
Breath·a·lyz·er® ['breθəlaɪzər] alcoholímetro *m*
breathe [briːð] **1** *v/i* respirar **2** *v/t* (*inhale*) aspirar, respirar; (*exhale*) exhalar, espirar
◆ **breathe in** *v/t & v/i* aspirar, inspirar
◆ **breathe out** *v/i* espirar
breath·ing ['briːðɪŋ] *n* respiración *f*

breath·less ['breθlɪs] *adj*: ***arrive breathless*** llegar sin respiración, llegar jadeando
breath·less·ness ['breθlɪsnɪs] dificultad *f* para respirar
breath·tak·ing ['breθteɪkɪŋ] *adj* impresionante, sorprendente
bred [bred] *pret & pp* → ***breed***
breed [bri:d] **1** *n* raza *f* **2** *v/t* (*pret & pp **bred***) criar; *plants* cultivar; *fig* causar, generar **3** *v/i* (*pret & pp **bred***) *of animals* reproducirse
breed·er ['bri:dər] *of animals* criador(a) *m(f)*; *of plants* cultivador(a) *m(f)*
breed·ing ['bri:dɪŋ] *of animals* cría *f*; *of plants* cultivo *m*; *of person* educación *f*
breed·ing ground *fig* caldo *m* de cultivo
breeze [bri:z] brisa *f*
breez·i·ly ['bri:zɪlɪ] *adv fig* jovialmente, tranquilamente
breez·y ['bri:zɪ] *adj* ventoso; *fig* jovial, tranquilo
brew [bru:] **1** *v/t beer* elaborar; *tea* preparar, hacer **2** *v/i of storm* avecinarse; *of trouble* fraguarse
brew·er ['bru:ər] fabricante *m/f* de cerveza
brew·er·y ['bru:ərɪ] fábrica *f* de cerveza
bribe [braɪb] **1** *n* soborno *m*, *Mex* mordida *f*, *S. Am.* coima *f* **2** *v/t* sobornar
brib·er·y ['braɪbərɪ] soborno *m*, *Mex* mordida *f*, *S. Am.* coima *f*
brick [brɪk] ladrillo *m*
'**brick·lay·er** albañil *m/f*
brid·al suite ['braɪdl] suite *f* nupcial
bride [braɪd] novia *f* (*en boda*)
'**bride·groom** novio *m* (*en boda*)
'**brides·maid** dama *f* de honor
bridge[1] [brɪdʒ] **1** *n also* NAUT puente *m*; *of nose* caballete *m* **2** *v/t gap* superar, salvar
bridge[2] [brɪdʒ] *card game* bridge *m*
bri·dle [braɪdl] brida *f*
brief[1] ['bri:f] *adj* breve, corto
brief[2] [bri:f] **1** *n* (*mission*) misión *f* **2** *v/t*: ***brief s.o. on sth*** informar a alguien de algo
'**brief·case** maletín *m*
brief·ing ['bri:fɪŋ] reunión *f* informativa
brief·ly ['bri:flɪ] *adv* (*for a short period of time*) brevemente; (*in a few words*) en pocas palabras; (*to sum up*) en resumen
briefs [bri:fs] *npl for women* bragas *fpl*; *for men* calzoncillos *mpl*
bright [braɪt] *adj color* vivo; *smile* radiante; *future* brillante, prometedor; (*sunny*) soleado, luminoso; (*intelligent*) inteligente
◆ **bright·en up** ['braɪtn] **1** *v/t* alegrar **2** *v/i of weather* aclararse; *of face, person* alegrarse, animarse
bright·ly ['braɪtlɪ] *adv shine* intensamente, fuerte; *smile* alegremente
bright·ness ['braɪtnɪs] *of light* brillo *m*; *of weather* luminosidad *f*; *of smile* alegría *f*; (*intelligence*) inteligencia *f*
bril·liance ['brɪljəns] *of person* genialidad *f*; *of color* resplandor *m*
bril·liant ['brɪljənt] *adj sunshine etc* resplandeciente, radiante; (*very good*) genial; (*very intelligent*) brillante
brim [brɪm] *of container* borde *m*; *of hat* ala *f*
brim·ful ['brɪmfəl] *adj* rebosante
bring [brɪŋ] *v/t* (*pret & pp **brought***) traer; ***bring it here, will you*** tráelo aquí, por favor; ***can I bring a friend?*** ¿puedo traer a un amigo?, puedo venir con un amigo?
◆ **bring about** *v/t* ocasionar; ***bring about peace*** traer la paz
◆ **bring around** *v/t from a faint* hacer volver en sí; (*persuade*) convencer, persuadir
◆ **bring back** *v/t* (*return*) devolver; (*re-introduce*) reinstaurar; *memories* traer
◆ **bring down** *v/t fence, tree* tirar, echar abajo; *government* derrocar; *bird, airplane* derribar; *rates, inflation, price* reducir
◆ **bring in** *v/t interest, income* generar; *legislation* introducir; *verdict* pronunciar
◆ **bring on** *v/t illness* provocar
◆ **bring out** *v/t book, video, new product* sacar
◆ **bring to** *v/t from a faint* hacer volver en sí
◆ **bring up** *v/t child* criar, educar; *subject* mencionar, sacar a colación; (*vomit*) vomitar
brink [brɪŋk] borde *m*; ***be on the brink of sth*** *fig* estar a punto de hacer algo
brisk [brɪsk] *adj person, voice* enérgico; *walk* rápido; *trade* animado
bris·tle ['brɪsl] *v/i*: ***the streets are bristling with policemen*** las calles están atestadas de policías
brist·les ['brɪslz] *npl on chin* pelos *mpl*; *of brush* cerdas *fpl*
Brit [brɪt] F británico(-a) *m(f)*
Brit·ain ['brɪtn] Gran *Br*etaña
Brit·ish ['brɪtɪʃ] **1** *adj* británico **2** *n*: ***the British*** los británicos
Brit·on ['brɪtn] británico(-a) *m(f)*
brit·tle ['brɪtl] *adj* frágil, quebradizo
broach [broʊʧ] *v/t subject* sacar a colación
broad [brɒ:d] **1** *adj* ancho; *smile* amplio; (*general*) general; ***in broad daylight*** a plena luz del día; ***in broad terms*** en líneas generales **2** *n* F (*woman*) tía *f* F
'**broad·cast** **1** *n* emisión *f*; ***a live broad-***

cast una retransmisión en directo **2** *v/t* emitir, retransmitir
'broad·cast·er presentador(a) *m(f)*
'broad·cast·ing televisión *f*
broad·en ['brɒːdn] **1** *v/i* ensancharse, ampliarse **2** *v/t* ensanchar; ***broaden one's horizons*** ampliar los horizontes
'broad·jump salto *m* de longitud
broad·ly ['brɒːdlɪ] *adv* en general; ***broadly speaking*** en términos generales
broad·mind·ed [brɒːd'maɪndɪd] *adj* tolerante, abierto
broad·mind·ed·ness [brɒːd'maɪndɪdnɪs] mentalidad *f* abierta
broc·co·li ['brɑːkəlɪ] brécol *m*, brócoli *m*
bro·chure ['broʊʃər] folleto *m*
broil [brɔɪl] *v/t* asar a la parrilla
broil·er ['brɔɪlər] *on stove* parrilla *f*; *chicken* pollo *m* (para asar)
broke [broʊk] **1** *adj* F: ***be broke*** *temporarily* estar sin blanca F; *long term* estar arruinado; ***go broke*** (*go bankrupt*) arruinarse **2** *pret* → ***break***
bro·ken ['broʊkn] **1** *adj* roto; *home* deshecho; ***they talk in broken English*** chapurrean el inglés **2** *pp* → ***break***
bro·ken-heart·ed [broʊkn'hɑːrtɪd] *adj* desconsolado, destrozado
bro·ker ['broʊkər] corredor(a) *m(f)*, agente *m/f*
bron·chi·tis [brɑːŋ'kaɪtɪs] bronquitis *f*
bronze [brɑːnz] *n* bronce *m*
brooch [broʊʧ] broche *m*
brood [bruːd] *v/i of person* darle vueltas a las cosas; ***brood about sth*** darle vueltas a algo
broom [bruːm] escoba *f*
broth [brɑːθ] *soup* sopa *f*; *stock* caldo *m*
broth·el ['brɑːθl] burdel *m*
broth·er ['brʌðər] hermano *m*
'broth·er-in-law (*pl* ***brothers-in-law***) cuñado *m*
broth·er·ly ['brʌðərlɪ] *adj* fraternal
brought [brɒːt] *pret & pp* → ***bring***
brow [braʊ] (*forehead*) frente *f*; *of hill* cima *f*
brown [braʊn] **1** *n* marrón *m*, *L.Am.* color *m* café **2** *adj* marrón; *eyes, hair* castaño; (*tanned*) moreno **3** *v/t in cooking* dorar **4** *v/i in cooking* dorarse
'brown·bag *v/t* (*pret & pp* ***brownbagged***) F: ***brownbag it*** *llevar la comida al trabajo*
Brown·ie ['braʊnɪ] escultista *f*
'Brown·ie points *npl* tantos *mpl*; ***earn Brownie points*** anotarse tantos
brown·ie ['braʊnɪ] (*cake*) pastel *m* de chocolate y nueces
'brown-nose *v/t* P lamer el culo a P
brown 'pa·per papel *m* de estraza
brown pa·per 'bag bolsa *f* de cartón
brown 'sug·ar azúcar *m or f* moreno(-a)
browse [braʊz] *v/i in store* echar una ojeada; ***browse through a book*** hojear un libro
brows·er ['braʊzər] COMPUT navegador *m*
bruise [bruːz] **1** *n* magulladura *f*, cardenal *f*; *on fruit* maca *f* **2** *v/t arm, fruit* magullar; (*emotionally*) herir **3** *v/i of person* hacerse cardenales; *of fruit* macarse
bruis·ing ['bruːzɪŋ] *adj fig* doloroso
brunch [brʌnʧ] *combinación de desayuno y almuerzo*
bru·nette [bruː'net] *n* morena *f*
brunt [brʌnt]: ***this area bore the brunt of the flooding*** esta zona fue la más castigada por la inundación; ***we bore the brunt of the layoffs*** fuimos los más perjudicados por los despidos
brush [brʌʃ] **1** *n* cepillo *m*; *conflict* roce *m* **2** *v/t* cepillar; (*touch lightly*) rozar; (*move away*) quitar
◆ **brush against** *v/t* rozar
◆ **brush aside** *v/t* hacer caso omiso a, no hacer caso a
◆ **brush off** *v/t* sacudir; *criticism* no hacer caso a
◆ **brush up** *v/t* repasar
'brush·work PAINT pincelada *f*
brusque [brʊsk] *adj* brusco
Brus·sels ['brʌslz] Bruselas
Brus·sels sprouts *npl* coles *fpl* de *B*ruselas
bru·tal ['bruːtl] *adj* brutal
bru·tal·i·ty [bruː'tælətɪ] brutalidad *f*
bru·tal·ly ['bruːtəlɪ] *adv* brutalmente; ***be brutally frank*** ser de una sinceridad aplastante
brute [bruːt] bestia *m/f*
brute 'force fuerza *f* bruta
bub·ble ['bʌbl] *n* burbuja *f*
'bub·ble bath baño *m* de espuma
'bub·ble gum chicle *m*
'bub·ble wrap *n* plástico *m* para embalar (*con burbujas*)
bub·bly ['bʌblɪ] *n* F (*champagne*) champán *m*
buck[1] [bʌk] *n* F (*dollar*) dólar *m*
buck[2] [bʌk] *v/i of horse* corcovear
buck[3] [bʌk] *n*: ***pass the buck*** escurrir el bulto
buck·et ['bʌkɪt] *n* cubo *m*
buck·le[1] ['bʌkl] **1** *n* hebilla *f* **2** *v/t belt* abrochar
buck·le[2] ['bʌkl] *v/i of wood, metal* combarse
◆ **buckle down** *v/i* ponerse a trabajar

bud [bʌd] *n* BOT capullo *m*, brote *m*
bud·dy ['bʌdɪ] F amigo(-a) *m(f)*, *Span* colega *m/f* F; *form of address Span* colega *m/f* F, *L.Am.* compadre *m/f* F
budge [bʌdʒ] **1** *v/t* mover; (*make reconsider*) hacer cambiar de opinión **2** *v/i* moverse; (*change one's mind*) cambiar de opinión
bud·ger·i·gar ['bʌdʒərɪgɑːr] periquito *m*
bud·get ['bʌdʒɪt] **1** *n* presupuesto *m*; ***be on a budget*** tener un presupuesto limitado **2** *v/i* administrarse
◆ **budget for** *v/t* contemplar en el presupuesto
bud·gie ['bʌdʒɪ] F periquito *m*
buff[1] [bʌf] *adj color* marrón claro
buff[2] [bʌf] *n* aficionado(-a) *m(f)*; ***a movie buff*** un cinéfilo
buf·fa·lo ['bʌfəloʊ] búfalo *m*
buff·er ['bʌfər] RAIL tope *m*; COMPUT búfer *m*; *fig* barrera *f*
buf·fet[1] ['bʊfeɪ] *n* (*meal*) bufé *m*
buf·fet[2] ['bʌfɪt] *v/t of wind* sacudir
bug [bʌg] **1** *n insect* bicho *m*; *virus* virus *m inv*; (*spying device*) micrófono *m* oculto; COMPUT error *m* **2** *v/t* (*pret & pp* ***bugged***) *room* colocar un micrófono en; F (*annoy*) fastidiar F, jorobar F
bug·gy ['bʌgɪ] *for baby* silla *f* de paseo
bu·gle [bjuːgl] corneta *f*, clarín *m*
build [bɪld] **1** *n of person* constitución *f*, complexión *f* **2** *v/t* (*pret & pp* ***built***) construir, edificar
◆ **build up 1** *v/t strength* aumentar; *relationship* fortalecer; *collection* acumular **2** *v/i of dirt* acumularse; *of pressure, excitement* aumentar
'**build·er** ['bɪldər] albañil *m/f*; *company* constructora *f*
'**build·ing** ['bɪldɪŋ] edificio *m*; *activity* construcción *f*
'**build·ing blocks** *npl for child* piezas *fpl* de construcción
'**build·ing site** obra *f*
'**build·ing so·ci·e·ty** *Br* caja *f* de ahorros
'**build·ing trade** industria *f* de la construcción
'**build-up** (*accumulation*) accumulación *f*; ***after all the build-up*** *publicity* después de tantas expectativas
built [bɪlt] *pret & pp* → ***build***
built-in ['bɪltɪn] *adj cupboard* empotrado; *flash* incorporado
built-up 'ar·e·a zona *f* urbanizada
bulb [bʌlb] BOT bulbo *m*; (*light bulb*) bombilla *f*, *L.Am.* foco *m*
bulge [bʌldʒ] **1** *n* bulto *m*, abultamiento *m* **2** *v/i of eyes* salirse de las órbitas; *of wall* abombarse
bu·lim·i·a [bʊ'lɪmɪə] bulimia *f*
bulk [bʌlk]: ***the bulk of*** el grueso *or* la mayor parte de; ***in bulk*** a granel
'**bulk·y** ['bʌlkɪ] *adj* voluminoso
bull [bʊl] *animal* toro *m*
bull·doze ['bʊldoʊz] *v/t* (*demolish*) demoler, derribar; ***bulldoze s.o. into sth*** *fig* obligar a alguien a hacer algo
bull·doz·er ['bʊldoʊzər] bulldozer *m*
bul·let ['bʊlɪt] bala *f*
bul·le·tin ['bʊlɪtɪn] boletín *m*
'**bul·le·tin board** *on wall* tablón *m* de anuncios; COMPUT tablón *m* de anuncios, BBS *f*
'**bul·let-proof** *adj* antibalas *inv*
'**bull fight** corrida *f* de toros
'**bull fight·er** torero(-a) *m(f)*
'**bull fight·ing** tauromaquia *f*, los toros
'**bull mar·ket** FIN mercado *m* al alza
'**bull ring** plaza *f* de toros
'**bull's-eye** diana *f*, blanco *m*; ***hit the bull's-eye*** dar en el blanco
'**bull·shit 1** *n* V *Span* gilipollez *f* V, *L.Am.* pendejada *f* V **2** *v/i* (*pret & pp* ***bullshitted***) V decir *Span* gilipolleces V *or L.Am.* pendejadas V
bul·ly ['bʊlɪ] **1** *n* matón(-ona) *m(f)*; *child* abusón(-ona) *m(f)* **2** *v/t* (*pret & pp* ***bullied***) intimidar
bul·ly·ing ['bʊlɪɪŋ] *n* intimidación *f*
bum [bʌm] **1** *n* F (*tramp*) vagabundo(-a) *m(f)*; (*worthless person*) inútil *m/f* **2** *adj* F (*useless*) inútil **3** *v/t* (*pret & pp* ***bummed***) F *cigarette etc* gorronear
◆ **bum around**, **bum about** *v/i* F (*travel*) vagabundear (***in*** por); (*be lazy*) vaguear
bum·ble·bee ['bʌmblbiː] abejorro *m*
bump [bʌmp] **1** *n* (*swelling*) chichón *m*; *on road* bache *m*; ***get a bump on the head*** darse un golpe en la cabeza **2** *v/t* golpear
◆ **bump into** *v/t table* chocar con; (*meet*) encontrarse con
◆ **bump off** *v/t* F (*murder*) cargarse a F
◆ **bump up** *v/t* F (*prices*) aumentar
bump·er ['bʌmpər] **1** *n* MOT parachoques *m inv*; ***the traffic was bumper to bumper*** el tráfico estaba colapsado **2** *adj* (*extremely good*) excepcional, extraordinario
'**bump-start** *v/t car* arrancar un coche empujándolo; *fig*: *economy* reanimar
bump·y ['bʌmpɪ] *adj* con baches; *flight* movido
bun [bʌn] *hairstyle* moño *m*; *for eating* bollo *m*
bunch [bʌntʃ] *of people* grupo *m*; *of keys* manojo *m*; *of flowers* ramo *m*; *of grapes* racimo *m*; ***thanks a bunch*** *ironic* no sabes lo que te lo agradezco

bun·dle ['bʌndl] *of clothes* fardo *m*; *of wood* haz *m*

◆ **bundle up** *v/t* liar; (*dress warmly*) abrigar

bung [bʌŋ] *v/t Br* F echar

bun·gee jump·ing ['bʌndʒɪdʒʌmpɪŋ] puenting *m*

bun·gle ['bʌŋgl] *v/t* echar a perder

bunk [bʌŋk] litera *f*

bunk beds *npl* literas *fpl*

buoy [bɔɪ] *n* NAUT boya *f*

buoy·ant ['bɔɪənt] *adj* animado, optimista; *economy* boyante

bur·den ['bɜːrdn] **1** *n also fig* carga *f* **2** *v/t*: ***burden s.o. with sth*** *fig* cargar a alguien con algo

bu·reau ['bjʊroʊ] (*chest of drawers*) cómoda *f*; (*office*) departamento *m*, oficina *f*; ***a translation bureau*** una agencia de traducción

bu·reauc·ra·cy [bjʊ'rɑːkrəsɪ] burocracia *f*

bu·reau·crat ['bjʊrəkræt] burócrata *m/f*

bu·reau·crat·ic [bjʊrə'krætɪk] *adj* burocrático

burg·er ['bɜːrgər] hamburguesa *f*

bur·glar ['bɜːrglər] ladrón(-ona) *m(f)*

'**bur·glar a·larm** alarma *f* antirrobo

bur·glar·ize ['bɜːrgləraɪz] *v/t* robar

bur·glar·y ['bɜːrglərɪ] robo *m*

bur·gle ['bɜːgl] *v/t Br* robar

bur·i·al ['berɪəl] entierro *m*

bur·ly ['bɜːrlɪ] *adj* corpulento, fornido

burn [bɜːrn] **1** *n* quemadura *f* **2** *v/t* (*pret & pp* ***burnt***) quemar; ***be burned to death*** morir abrasado **3** *v/i* (*pret & pp* ***burnt***) *of wood, meat, in sun* quemarse

◆ **burn down 1** *v/t* incendiar **2** *v/i* incendiarse

◆ **burn out** *v/t*: ***burn o.s. out*** quemarse; ***a burned-out car*** un coche carbonizado

'**burn·out** F (*exhaustion*) agotamiento *m*

burnt [bɜːrnt] *pret & pp* → **burn**

burp [bɜːrp] **1** *n* eructo *m* **2** *v/i* eructar **3** *v/t baby* hacer eructar a

burst [bɜːrst] **1** *n in water pipe* rotura *f*; *of gunfire* ráfaga *f*; ***in a burst of energy*** en un arrebato de energía **2** *adj tire* reventado **3** *v/t* (*pret & pp* ***burst***) *balloon* reventar **4** *v/i* (*pret & pp* ***burst***) *of balloon, tire* reventar; ***burst into a room*** irrumpir en una habitación; ***burst into tears*** echarse a llorar; ***burst out laughing*** echarse a reír

bur·y ['berɪ] *v/t* (*pret & pp* ***buried***) enterrar; ***be buried under*** (*covered by*) estar sepultado por; ***bury o.s. in work*** meterse de lleno en el trabajo

bus [bʌs] **1** *n local* autobús *m*, *Mex* camión *m*, *Arg* colectivo *m*, *C.Am.* guagua *f*; *long distance* autobús *m*, *Span* autocar *m*; ***school bus*** autobús *m* escolar **2** *v/t* (*pret & pp* ***bussed***) llevar en autobús

'**bus·boy** ayudante *m* de camarero

'**bus driv·er** conductor(a) *m(f)* de autobús

bush [bʊʃ] *plant* arbusto *m*; *type of countryside* monte *m*

bushed [bʊʃt] *adj* F (*tired*) molido F

bush·y ['bʊʃɪ] *adj beard* espeso

busi·ness ['bɪznɪs] negocios *mpl*; (*company*) empresa *f*; (*sector*) sector *m*; (*affair, matter*) asunto *m*; *as subject of study* empresariales *fpl*; ***on business*** de negocios; ***that's none of your business!*** ¡no es asunto tuyo!; ***mind your own business!*** ¡no te metas en lo que no te importa!

'**busi·ness card** tarjeta *f* de visita

'**busi·ness class** clase *f* ejecutiva

'**busi·ness hours** *npl* horario *m* de oficina

busi·ness·like ['bɪznɪslaɪk] *adj* eficiente

'**busi·ness lunch** almuerzo *m* de negocios

'**busi·ness·man** hombre *m* de negocios, ejecutivo *m*

'**busi·ness meet·ing** reunión *f* de negocios

'**busi·ness school** escuela *f* de negocios

'**busi·ness stud·ies** *nsg course* empresariales *mpl*

'**busi·ness trip** viaje *m* de negocios

'**busi·ness·wom·an** mujer *f* de negocios, ejecutiva *f*

'**bus lane** carril *m* bus

'**bus shel·ter** marquesina *f*

'**bus sta·tion** estación *f* de autobuses

'**bus stop** parada *f* de autobús

'**bus tick·et** billete *m or L.Am.* boleto *m* de autobús

bust[1] [bʌst] *n of woman* busto *m*

bust[2] [bʌst] **1** *adj* F (*broken*) escacharrado F: ***go bust*** quebrar **2** *v/t* F escacharrar F

◆ **bus·tle about** ['bʌsl] *v/i* trajinar

'**bust-up** F corte *m* F

bust·y ['bʌstɪ] *adj* pechugona

bus·y ['bɪzɪ] **1** *adj also* TELEC ocupado; *full of people* abarrotado; *of restaurant etc: making money* ajetreado; ***the line was busy*** estaba ocupado, *Span* comunicaba; ***she leads a very busy life*** lleva una vida muy ajetreada; ***be busy doing sth*** estar ocupado *or* atareado haciendo algo **2** *v/t* (*pret & pp* ***busied***): ***busy o.s. with*** entretenerse con algo

'**bus·y·bod·y** metomentodo *m/f*, entro-

metido(-a) *m(f)*
'**bus·y sig·nal** señal *f* de ocupado *or Span* comunicando
but [bʌt] *unstressed* [bət] **1** *conj* pero; ***it's not me but my father you want*** no me quieres a mí sino a mi padre; ***but then*** (***again***) pero **2** *prep*: ***all but him*** todos excepto él; ***the last but one*** el penúltimo; ***the next but one*** el próximo no, el otro; ***the next page but one*** la página siguiente a la próxima; ***but for you*** si no hubiera sido por ti; ***nothing but the best*** sólo lo mejor
butch·er ['bʊtʃər] carnicero(-a) *m(f)*; *murderer* asesino(-a) *m(f)*
butt [bʌt] **1** *n of cigarette* colilla *f*; *of joke* blanco *m*; F (*buttocks*) trasero *m* F **2** *v/t* dar un cabezazo a; *of goat*, *bull* embestir
◆ **butt in** *v/i* inmiscuirse, entrometerse
but·ter ['bʌtər] **1** *n* mantequilla *f* **2** *v/t* untar de mantequilla
◆ **butter up** *v/t* F hacer la pelota a F
'**but·ter·fly** *insect* mariposa *f*
but·tocks ['bʌtəks] *npl* nalgas *fpl*
but·ton ['bʌtn] **1** *n on shirt*, *machine* botón *m*; (*badge*) chapa *f* **2** *v/t* abotonar
◆ **button up** *v/t* abotonar
'**but·ton·hole 1** *n in suit* ojal *m* **2** *v/t* acorralar
but·tress ['bʌtrəs] contrafuerte *m*
bux·om ['bʌksəm] *adj* de amplios senos
buy [baɪ] **1** *n* compra *f*, adquisición *f* **2** *v/t* (*pret & pp* **bought**) comprar; ***can I buy you a drink?*** ¿quieres tomar algo?; ***$5 doesn't buy much*** con 5 dólares no se puede hacer gran cosa
◆ **buy off** *v/t* (*bribe*) sobornar
◆ **buy out** *v/t* COM comprar la parte de
◆ **buy up** *v/t* acaparar
buy·er [baɪr] comprador(a) *m(f)*
buzz [bʌz] **1** *n* zumbido *m*; ***she gets a real buzz out of it*** F (*thrill*) le vuelve loca, le entusiasma **2** *v/i of insect* zumbar; *with buzzer* llamar por el interfono **3** *v/t with buzzer* llamar por el interfono a
◆ **buzz off** *v/i* F largarse F, *Span* pirarse F
buz·zard ['bʌzərd] ratonero *m*
buzz·er ['bʌzər] timbre *m*
'**buzz·word** palabra *f* de moda
by [baɪ] **1** *prep to show agent* por; (*near, next to*) al lado de, junto a; (*no later than*) no más tarde de; *mode of transport* en; ***she rushed by me*** pasó rápidamente por mi lado; ***as we drove by the church*** cuando pasábamos por la iglesia; ***side by side*** uno junto al otro; ***by day / night*** de día / noche; ***by bus / train*** en autobús / tren; ***by the dozen*** por docenas; ***by the hour / ton*** por hora / por tonelada; ***by my watch*** en mi reloj; ***by nature*** por naturaleza; ***a play by ...*** una obra de ...; ***by o.s.*** *without company* solo; ***I did it by myself*** lo hice yo solito; ***by a couple of minutes*** por un par de minutos; **2 *by* 4** *measurement* 2 por 4; ***by this time tomorrow*** mañana a esta hora; ***by this time next year*** el año que viene por estas fechas; ***go by, pass by*** pasar **2** *adv*: ***by and by*** (*soon*) dentro de poco
bye(**-bye**) [baɪ] adiós
by·gones ['baɪgɑːnz]: ***let bygones be bygones*** lo pasado, pasado está
'**by·pass 1** *n road* circunvalación *f*; MED bypass *m* **2** *v/t* sortear
'**by-prod·uct** subproducto *m*
by·stand·er ['baɪstændər] transeúnte *m/f*
byte [baɪt] byte *m*
'**by·word**: ***be a byword for*** ser sinónimo de

C

cab [kæb] (*taxi*) taxi *m*; *of truck* cabina *f*; ***cab driver*** taxista *m/f*
cab·a·ret ['kæbəreɪ] cabaret *m*
cab·bage ['kæbɪdʒ] col *f*, repollo *m*
cab·in ['kæbɪn] *of plane* cabina *f*; *of ship* camarote *m*
'**cab·in at·tend·ant** auxiliar *m/f* de vuelo
'**cab·in crew** personal *m* de a bordo
cab·i·net ['kæbɪnɪt] armario *m*; POL gabinete *m*; ***drinks cabinet*** mueble *m* bar; ***medicine cabinet*** botiquín *m*; ***display cabinet*** vitrina *f*
'**cab·i·net mak·er** ebanista *m/f*
ca·ble ['keɪbl] cable *m*; ***cable*** (***TV***) televisión *f* por cable
'**ca·ble car** teleférico *m*
'**ca·ble tel·e·vi·sion** televisión *f* por cable
'**cab rank**, '**cab stand** parada *f* de taxis

cac·tus ['kæktəs] cactus *m inv*
ca·dav·er [kə'dævər] cadáver *m*
CAD [kæd] *abbr* (= ***computer assisted design***) CAD *m* (= diseño asistido por *Span* ordenador *or L.Am.* computadora)
cad·die ['kædɪ] **1** *n in golf* caddie *m/f* **2** *v/i* hacer de caddie
ca·det [kə'det] cadete *m*
cadge [kædʒ] *v/t* F: ***cadge sth from s.o.*** gorronear algo a alguien
Cae·sar·e·an *Br* → ***Cesarean***
caf·é ['kæfeɪ] café *m*, cafetería *f*
caf·e·te·ri·a [kæfɪ'tɪrɪə] cafetería *f*, cantina *f*
caf·feine ['kæfiːn] cafeína *f*
cage [keɪdʒ] jaula *f*
ca·gey ['keɪdʒɪ] *adj* cauteloso, reservado; ***he's cagey about how old he is*** es muy reservado con respecto a su edad
ca·hoots [kə'huːts] *npl* F: ***be in cahoots with*** estar conchabado con
ca·jole [kə'dʒoʊl] *v/t* engatusar, persuadir
cake [keɪk] **1** *n big* tarta *f*; *small* pastel *m*; ***be a piece of cake*** F estar chupado F **2** *v/i* endurecerse
ca·lam·i·ty [kə'læmətɪ] calamidad *f*
cal·ci·um ['kælsɪəm] calcio *m*
cal·cu·late ['kælkjʊleɪt] *v/t* calcular
cal·cu·lat·ing ['kælkjʊleɪtɪŋ] *adj* calculador
cal·cu·la·tion [kælkjʊ'leɪʃn] cálculo *m*
cal·cu·la·tor ['kælkjʊleɪtər] calculadora *f*
cal·en·dar ['kælɪndər] calendario *m*
calf[1] [kæf] (*pl* ***calves*** [kævz]) (*young cow*) ternero(-a) *m(f)*, becerro(-a) *m(f)*
calf[2] [kæf] (*pl* ***calves*** [kævz]) *of leg* pantorrilla *f*
'**calf·skin** *n* piel *f* de becerro
cal·i·ber, *Br* **cal·i·bre** ['kælɪbər] *of gun* calibre *m*; ***a man of his calibre*** un hombre de su calibre
Cal·i·for·ni·an [kælɪ'fɔːnɪən] **1** *adj* californiano **2** *n* californiano(-a) *m(f)*
call [kɒːl] **1** *n* llamada *f*; (*demand*) llamamiento *m*; ***there's a call for you*** tienes una llamada, te llaman; ***I'll give you a call tomorrow*** te llamaré mañana; ***make a call*** hacer una llamada; ***a call for help*** una llamada de socorro; ***be on call*** estar de guardia **2** *v/t also* TELEC llamar; *meeting* convocar; ***he called him a liar*** le llamó mentiroso; ***what have they called the baby?*** ¿qué nombre le han puesto al bebé?; ***but we call him Tom*** pero le llamamos Tom; ***call s.o. names*** insultar a alguien; ***I called his name*** lo llamé **3** *v/i also* TELEC llamar; (*visit*) pasarse; ***can I tell him who's calling?*** ¿quién le llama?; ***call for help*** pedir ayuda a gritos
◆ **call at** *v/t* (*stop at*) pasarse por; *of train* hacer parada en
◆ **call back 1** *v/t* (*phone again*) volver a llamar; (*return call*) devolver la llamada; (*summon*) hacer volver **2** *v/i on phone* volver a llamar; (*make another visit*) volver a pasar
◆ **call for** *v/t* (*collect*) pasar a recoger; (*demand*) pedir, exigir; (*require*) requerir
◆ **call in 1** *v/t* (*summon*) llamar **2** *v/i* (*phone*) llamar; ***he called in sick*** llamó para decir que estaba enfermo
◆ **call off** *v/t* (*cancel*) cancelar; *strike* desconvocar
◆ **call on** *v/t* (*urge*) instar; (*visit*) visitar
◆ **call out** *v/t* (*shout*) gritar; (*summon*) llamar
◆ **call up** *v/t* (*on phone*) llamar; COMPUT abrir, visualizar
'**call cen·ter** centro *m* de atención telefónica
call·er ['kɒːlər] *on phone* persona *f* que llama; (*visitor*) visitante *m/f*
'**call girl** prostituta *f* (*que concierta sus citas por teléfono*)
cal·lous ['kæləs] *adj* cruel, desalmado
cal·lous·ly ['kæləslɪ] *adv* cruelmente
cal·lous·ness ['kæləsnɪs] crueldad *f*
calm [kɑːm] **1** *adj sea* tranquilo; *weather* apacible; *person* tranquilo, sosegado; ***please keep calm*** por favor mantengan la calma **2** *n* calma *f*; ***call for calm*** pedir calma
◆ **calm down 1** *v/t* calmar, tranquilizar **2** *v/i of sea, weather* calmarse; *of person* calmarse, tranquilizarse
calm·ly ['kɑːmlɪ] *adv* con calma, tranquilamente
cal·o·rie ['kælərɪ] caloría *f*
cam·cor·der ['kæmkɔːrdər] videocámara *f*
came [keɪm] *pret* → ***come***
cam·e·ra ['kæmərə] cámara *f*
'**cam·e·ra·man** cámara *m*, camarógrafo *m*
cam·i·sole ['kæmɪseʊl] camisola *f*
cam·ou·flage ['kæməflɑːʒ] **1** *n* camuflaje *m* **2** *v/t* camuflar
camp [kæmp] **1** *n* campamento *m*; ***make camp*** acampar; ***refugee camp*** campo *m* de refugiados **2** *v/i* acampar
cam·paign [kæm'peɪn] **1** *n* campaña *f* **2** *v/i* hacer campaña (***for*** a favor de)
cam·paign·er [kæm'peɪnər] defensor(a) *m(f)* (***for*** de); ***a campaigner against racism*** una persona que hace campaña contra el racismo
camp·er ['kæmpər] *person* campista *m/f*; *vehicle* autocaravana *f*

C

camp·ing ['kæmpɪŋ] acampada *f*; *on campsite* camping *m*; ***go camping*** ir de acampada *or* camping
'**camp·site** camping *m*
cam·pus ['kæmpəs] campus *m*
can[1] [kæn] *unstressed* [kən] *v/aux* (*pret* ***could***) ◇ (*ability*) poder; ***can you swim?*** ¿sabes nadar?; ***can you hear me?*** ¿me oyes?; ***I can't see*** no veo; ***can you speak French?*** ¿hablas francés?; ***can he call me back?*** ¿me podría devolver la llamada?; ***as fast / well as you can*** tan rápido / bien como puedas; ***I can't go any further - you can and you will!*** no puedo más - ¡ya lo creo que puedes!
◇ (*permission*) poder; ***can I help you?*** ¿te puedo ayudar?; ***can you help me?*** ¿me puedes ayudar?; ***can I have a beer / coffee?*** ¿me pones una cerveza / un café?; ***that can't be right*** debe haber un error
can[2] [kæn] **1** *n for drinks etc* lata *f* **2** *v/t* (*pret & pp* ***canned***) enlatar
Can·a·da ['kænədə] Canadá
Ca·na·di·an [kə'neɪdɪən] **1** *adj* canadiense **2** *n* canadiense *m/f*
ca·nal [kə'næl] *waterway* canal *m*
ca·nar·y [kə'nerɪ] canario *m*
can·cel ['kænsl] *v/t* cancelar
can·cel·la·tion [kænsə'leɪʃn] cancelación *f*
can·cel'la·tion fee tarifa *f* de cancelación de reserva
can·cer ['kænsər] cáncer *m*
Can·cer ['kænsər] ASTR Cáncer *m/f inv*
can·cer·ous ['kænsərəs] *adj* canceroso
c & f *abbr* (= ***cost and freight***) C&F (= costo y flete)
can·did ['kændɪd] *adj* sincero, franco
can·di·da·cy ['kændɪdəsɪ] candidatura *f*
can·di·date ['kændɪdət] *for position* candidato(-a) *m(f)*; *in exam* candidato(-a) *m(f)*, examinando(-a) *m(f)*
can·did·ly ['kændɪdlɪ] *adv* sinceramente, francamente
can·died ['kændiːd] *adj* confitado
can·dle ['kændl] vela *f*
'**can·dle·stick** candelero *m*; *short* palmatoria *f*
can·dor, *Br* **can·dour** ['kændər] sinceridad *f*, franqueza *f*
can·dy ['kændɪ] (*sweet*) caramelo *m*; (*sweets*) dulces *mpl*; ***a box of candy*** una caja de caramelos *or* dulces
cane [keɪn] caña *f*; *for walking* bastón *m*
can·is·ter ['kænɪstər] bote *m*
can·na·bis ['kænəbɪs] cannabis *m*, hachís *m*
canned [kænd] *adj fruit, tomatoes* enlatado, en lata; (*recorded*) grabado
can·ni·bal·ize ['kænɪbəlaɪz] *v/t* canibalizar
can·not ['kænɑːt] → ***can***[1]
can·ny ['kænɪ] *adj* (*astute*) astuto
ca·noe [kə'nuː] canoa *f*, piragua *f*
'**can o·pen·er** abrelatas *m inv*
can't [kænt] → ***can***[1]
can·tan·ker·ous [kæn'tæŋkərəs] *adj* arisco, cascarrabias
can·teen [kæn'tiːn] *in plant* cantina *f*, cafetería *f*
can·vas ['kænvəs] *for painting* lienzo *m*; *material* lona *f*
can·vass ['kænvəs] **1** *v/t* (*seek opinion of*) preguntar **2** *v/i* POL hacer campaña (***for*** en favor de)
can·yon ['kænjən] cañón *m*
cap [kæp] *n hat* gorro *m*; *with peak* gorra *f*; *of bottle*, *jar* tapón *m*; *of pen*, *of lens* tapa *f*
ca·pa·bil·i·ty [keɪpə'bɪlətɪ] capacidad *f*; ***it's beyond my capabilities*** no entra dentro de mis posibilidades
ca·pa·ble ['keɪpəbl] *adj* (*efficient*) capaz, competente; ***be capable of*** ser capaz de
ca·pac·i·ty [kə'pæsətɪ] capacidad *f*; *of car engine* cilindrada *f*; ***a capacity crowd*** un lleno absoluto; ***the job is well within your capacity*** el trabajo está dentro de tus posibilidades; ***in my capacity as ...*** en mi calidad de ...
cap·i·tal ['kæpɪtl] *n of country* capital *f*; (*capital letter*) mayúscula *f*; *money* capital *m*
cap·i·tal ex'pend·i·ture inversión *f* en activo fijo
cap·i·tal 'gains tax impuesto *m* sobre las plusvalías
cap·i·tal 'growth crecimiento *m* del capital
cap·i·tal·ism ['kæpɪtəlɪzm] capitalismo *m*
'**cap·i·tal·ist** ['kæpɪtəlɪst] **1** *adj* capitalista **2** *n* capitalista *m/f*
◆ **cap·i·tal·ize on** ['kæpɪtəlaɪz] *v/t* aprovecharse de
cap·i·tal 'let·ter letra *f* mayúscula
cap·i·tal 'pun·ish·ment pena *f* capital, pena *f* de muerte
ca·pit·u·late [kə'pɪtʊleɪt] *v/i* capitular
ca·pit·u·la·tion [kæpɪtʊ'leɪʃn] capitulación *f*
Cap·ri·corn ['kæprɪkɔːrn] ASTR Capricornio *m/f inv*
cap·size [kæp'saɪz] **1** *v/i* volcar **2** *v/t* hacer volcar
cap·sule ['kæpsʊl] *of medicine* cápsula *f*; (*space capsule*) cápsula *f* espacial

cap·tain ['kæptɪn] *n of ship, team*, MIL capitán(-ana) *m(f)*; *of aircraft* comandante *m/f*
cap·tion ['kæpʃn] *n* pie *m* de foto
cap·ti·vate ['kæptɪveɪt] *v/t* cautivar, fascinar
cap·tive ['kæptɪv] **1** *adj* prisionero **2** *n* prisionero(-a) *m(f)*
cap·tive 'mar·ket mercado *m* cautivo
cap·tiv·i·ty [kæp'tɪvətɪ] cautividad *f*
cap·ture ['kæptʃər] **1** *n of city* toma *f*; *of criminal, animal* captura *f* **2** *v/t person, animal* capturar; *city, building* tomar; *market share* ganar; (*portray*) captar
car [kɑːr] coche *m*, *L.Am.* carro *m*, *Rpl* auto *m*; *of train* vagón *m*; ***by car*** en coche
ca·rafe [kə'ræf] garrafa *f*, jarra *f*
car·at ['kærət] quilate *m*
car·bo·hy·drate [kɑːrboʊ'haɪdreɪt] carbohidrato *m*
'car bomb coche *m* bomba
car·bon mon·ox·ide [kɑːrbənmən'ɑːksaɪd] monóxido *m* de carbono
car·bu·ret·er, car·bu·ret·or [kɑːrbʊ'retər] carburador *m*
car·cass ['kɑːrkəs] cadáver *m*
car·cin·o·gen [kɑːr'sɪnədʒen] agente *m* cancerígeno *or* carcinogéno
car·cin·o·genic [kɑːrsɪnə'dʒenɪk] *adj* cancerígeno, carcinogéno
card [kɑːrd] *to mark occasion*, COMPUT, *business* tarjeta *f*; (*postcard*) (tarjeta *f*) postal *f*; (*playing card*) carta *f*, naipe *m*; ***game of cards*** partida *f* de cartas
'card·board cartón *m*
card·board 'box caja *f* de cartón
car·di·ac ['kɑːrdɪæk] *adj* cardíaco
car·di·ac ar'rest paro *m* cardíaco
car·di·gan ['kɑːrdɪgən] cárdigan *m*
car·di·nal ['kɑːrdɪnl] *n* REL cardenal *m*
'card in·dex fichero *m*
'card key llave *f* tarjeta
'card phone tarjeta *f* telefónica
care [ker] **1** *n* cuidado *m*; (*medical care*) asistencia *f* médica; (*worry*) preocupación *f*; ***care of*** → ***c/o***; ***take care*** (*be cautious*) tener cuidado; ***take care (of yourself)!*** (*goodbye*) ¡cuídate!; ***take care of*** *dog, tool, house, garden* cuidar; *baby* cuidar (de); (*deal with*) ocuparse de; ***I'll take care of the bill*** yo pago la cuenta; (***handle***) ***with care!*** *on label* frágil **2** *v/i* preocuparse; ***I don't care!*** ¡me da igual!; ***I couldn't care less*** ¡me importa un pimiento!; ***if you really cared …*** si de verdad te importara …
◆ **care about** *v/t* preocuparse por
◆ **care for** *v/t* (*look after: person*) cuidar (de); (*look after: plant*) cuidar; ***he doesn't care for me the way he used to*** ya no le gusto como antes; ***would you care for a drink?*** ¿le apetece tomar algo?
ca·reer [kə'rɪr] carrera *f*; ***career prospects*** perspectivas *fpl* profesionales
ca'reers of·fi·cer asesor(a) *m(f)* de orientación profesional
'care·free *adj* despreocupado
care·ful ['kerfəl] *adj* (*cautious, thorough*) cuidadoso; ***be careful*** tener cuidado; (***be***) ***careful!*** ¡(ten) cuidado!
care·ful·ly ['kerfəlɪ] *adv* (*with caution*) con cuidado; *worded etc* cuidadosamente
care·less ['kerlɪs] *adj* descuidado; ***you are so careless!*** ¡qué descuidado eres!
care·less·ly ['kerlɪslɪ] *adv* descuidadamente
car·er ['kerər] *persona que cuida de un familiar o enfermo*
ca·ress [kə'res] **1** *n* caricia *f* **2** *v/t* acariciar
care·tak·er ['kerteɪkər] conserje *m*
'care·worn *adj* agobiado
'car fer·ry ferry *m*, transbordador *m*
car·go ['kɑːrgoʊ] cargamento *m*
'car hire alquiler *m* de coches *or* automóviles
'car hire com·pa·ny empresa *f* de alquiler de coches *or* automóviles
car·i·ca·ture ['kærɪkətʃər] *n* caricatura *f*
car·ing ['kerɪŋ] *adj person* afectuoso, bondadoso; *society* solidario
'car me·chan·ic mecánico(-a) *m(f)* de coches *or* automóviles
car·nage ['kɑːrnɪdʒ] matanza *f*, carnicería *f*
car·na·tion [kɑːr'neɪʃn] clavel *m*
car·ni·val ['kɑːrnɪvl] feria *f*
car·ol ['kærəl] *n* villancico *m*
car·ou·sel [kærə'sel] *at airport* cinta *f* transportadora de equipajes; *for slide projector* carro *m*; (*merry-go-round*) tiovivo *m*
'car park *Br* estacionamiento *m*, *Span* aparcamiento *m*
car·pen·ter ['kɑːrpɪntər] carpintero(-a) *m(f)*
car·pet ['kɑːrpɪt] alfombra *f*
'car phone teléfono *m* de coche
'car·pool *n acuerdo para compartir el vehículo entre varias personas que trabajan en el mismo sitio*
'car port estacionamiento *m* con techo
'car ra·di·o autorradio *m*
car·ri·er ['kærɪər] *company* transportista *m*; *airline* línea *f* aérea; *of disease* portador(a) *m(f)*
car·rot ['kærət] zanahoria *f*
car·ry ['kærɪ] **1** *v/t* (*pret & pp* ***carried***) *of*

person llevar; *disease* ser portador de; *of ship, plane, bus etc* transportar; *proposal* aprobar; ***be carrying a child*** *of pregnant woman* estar embarazada; ***get carried away*** dejarse llevar por la emoción, emocionarse **2** *v/i* (*pret & pp* **carried**) *of sound* oírse

◆ **carry on 1** *v/i* (*continue*) seguir, continuar; (*make a fuss*) organizar un escándalo; (*have an affair*) tener un lío **2** *v/t* (*conduct*) mantener; *business* efectuar

◆ **carry out** *survey etc* llevar a cabo

'**car seat** *for child* asiento *m* para niño

cart [kɑːrt] carro *m*

car·tel [kɑːr'tel] cartel *m*

car·ton ['kɑːrtn] *for storage, transport* caja *f* de cartón; *for milk etc* cartón *m*, tetrabrik *m* ®; *for eggs, of cigarettes* cartón *m*

car·toon [kɑːr'tuːn] *in newspaper, magazine* tira *f* cómica; *on* TV, *movie* dibujos *mpl* animados

car·toon·ist [kɑːr'tuːnɪst] dibujante *m/f* de chistes

car·tridge ['kɑːrtrɪdʒ] *for gun* cartucho *m*

carve [kɑːrv] *v/t meat* trinchar; *wood* tallar

carv·ing ['kɑːrvɪŋ] *figure* talla *f*

'**car wash** lavado *m* de automóviles

case[1] [keɪs] *container* funda *f*; *of scotch, wine* caja *f*; (*suitcase*) maleta *f*

case[2] [keɪs] *n instance, criminal,* MED caso *m*; LAW causa *f*; ***I think there's a case for dismissing him*** creo que hay razones fundadas para despedirlo; ***the case for the prosecution*** (los argumentos jurídicos de) la acusación; ***make a case for sth*** defender algo; ***in case ...*** por si ...; ***in case of emergency*** en caso de emergencia; ***in any case*** en cualquier caso; ***in that case*** en ese caso

'**case his·to·ry** MED *historial m* médico

'**case·load** número *m* de casos

cash [kæʃ] **1** *n* (dinero *m* en) efectivo *m*; ***I'm a bit short of cash*** no tengo mucho dinero; ***cash down*** al contado; ***pay (in) cash*** pagar en efectivo; ***cash on delivery*** → ***COD*** **2** *v/t check* hacer efectivo

◆ **cash in on** *v/t* sacar provecho de

'**cash cow** fuente *f* de ingresos

'**cash desk** caja *f*

cash '**dis·count** descuento *m* por pago al contado

'**cash di·spens·er** *Br* cajero *m* automático

'**cash flow** flujo *m* de caja, cash-flow *m*; ***cash flow problems*** problemas *fpl* de liquidez

cash·ier [kæ'ʃɪr] *n in store etc* cajero(-a) *m(f)*

cash·mere ['kæʃmɪr] *adj* cachemir *m*

'**cash·point** cajero *m* automático

'**cash re·gis·ter** caja *f* registradora

ca·si·no [kə'siːnoʊ] casino *m*

cas·ket ['kæskɪt] (*coffin*) ataúd *m*

cas·se·role ['kæsəroʊl] *n meal* guiso *m*; *container* cacerola *f*, cazuela *f*

cas·sette [kə'set] cinta *f*, casete *f*

cas'sette play·er, cas'sette re·cord·er casete *m*

cast [kæst] **1** *n of play* reparto *m*; (*mold*) molde *m* **2** *v/t* (*pret & pp* **cast**) *doubt, suspicion* proyectar; *metal* fundir; *play* seleccionar el reparto de; ***they cast Alan as ...*** le dieron a Alan el papel de ...

◆ **cast off** *v/i of ship* soltar amarras

caste [kæst] casta *f*

cast·er ['kæstər] *on chair etc* ruedecita *f*

Cas·til·ian [kæs'tɪlɪən] **1** *adj* castellano **2** *n person* castellano(-a) *m(f)*; *language* castellano *m*

cast '**i·ron** *n* hierro *m* fundido

cast-'i·ron *adj* de hierro fundido

cas·tle ['kæsl] castillo *m*

'**cast·or** ['kæstər] → **caster**

cas·trate [kæ'streɪt] *v/t* castrar

cas·tra·tion [kæ'streɪʃn] castración *f*

cas·u·al ['kæʒʊəl] *adj* (*chance*) casual; (*offhand*) despreocupado; (*not formal*) informal; (*not permanent*) eventual; ***it was just a casual remark*** no era más que un comentario hecho de pasada; ***he was very casual about the whole thing*** parecía no darle mucha importancia al asunto; ***casual sex*** relaciones *fpl* sexuales (con parejas) ocasionales

cas·u·al·ly ['kæʒʊəlɪ] *adv dressed* de manera informal; *say* a la ligera

cas·u·al·ty ['kæʒʊəltɪ] víctima *f*

'**cas·u·al wear** ropa *f* informal

cat [kæt] gato *m*

Cat·a·lan ['kætəlæn] **1** *adj* catalán **2** *n person* catalán(-ana) *m(f)*; *language* catalán *m*

cat·a·log, *Br* **cat·a·logue** ['kætəlɑːg] *n* catálogo *m*

cat·a·lyst ['kætəlɪst] catalizador *m*

cat·a·lyt·ic con'vert·er [kætə'lɪtɪk] catalizador *m*

cat·a·pult ['kætəpʌlt] **1** *v/t fig to fame, stardom* catapultar, lanzar **2** *n* catapulta *f*; *toy* tirachinas *m inv*

cat·a·ract ['kætərækt] MED catarata *f*

ca·tas·tro·phe [kə'tæstrəfɪ] catástrofe *f*

cat·a·stroph·ic [kætə'strɑːfɪk] *adj* catastrófico

catch [kætʃ] **1** *n* parada *f* (*sin que la pelota toque el suelo*); *of fish* captura *f*, pesca *f*; (*locking device*) cierre *m*; (*problem*) pega *f*; ***there has to be a catch*** tiene que haber una trampa **2** *v/t* (*pret & pp* ***caught***) *ball* agarrar, *Span* coger; *animal* atrapar; *escaped prisoner* capturar; (*get on*: *bus, train*) tomar, *Span* coger; (*not miss*: *bus, train*) alcanzar, *Span* coger; *fish* pescar; *in order to speak to* alcanzar, pillar; (*hear*) oír; *illness* agarrar, *Span* coger; ***catch (a) cold*** agarrar *or Span* coger un resfriado, resfriarse; ***catch s.o.'s eye*** *of person, object* llamar la atención de alguien; ***catch sight of, catch a glimpse of*** ver; ***catch s.o. doing sth*** atrapar *or Span* coger a alguien haciendo algo

◆ **catch on** *v/i* (*become popular*) cuajar, ponerse de moda; (*understand*) darse cuenta

◆ **catch up** *v/i*: ***catch up with s.o.*** alcanzar a alguien; ***he's having to work hard to catch up*** tiene que trabajar muy duro para ponerse al día

◆ **catch up on** *v/t*: ***catch up on one's sleep*** recuperar sueño; ***there's a lot of work to catch up on*** hay mucho trabajo atrasado

catch-22 [kætʃtwentɪ'tu:]: ***it's a catch-22 situation*** es como la pescadilla que se muerde la cola

catch·er ['kætʃər] *in baseball* cácher *m*, cátcher *m*

catch·ing ['kætʃɪŋ] *adj also fig* contagioso

catch·y ['kætʃɪ] *adj tune* pegadizo

cat·e·go·ric [kætə'gɑ:rɪk] *adj* categórico

cat·e·gor·i·cal·ly [kætə'gɑ:rɪklɪ] *adv* categóricamente

cat·e·go·ry ['kætəgɔ:rɪ] categoría *f*

◆ **ca·ter for** ['keɪtər] *v/t* (*meet the needs of*) cubrir las necesidades de; (*provide food for*) organizar la comida para

ca·ter·er ['keɪtərər] hostelero(-a) *m(f)*

ca·ter·pil·lar ['kætərpɪlər] oruga *f*

ca·the·dral [kə'θi:drl] catedral *f*

Cath·o·lic ['kæθəlɪk] **1** *adj* católico **2** *n* católico(-a) *m(f)*

Ca·thol·i·cism [kə'θɑ:lɪsɪzm] catolicismo *m*

'**cat·nap 1** *n* cabezada *f* **2** *v/i* (*pret & pp* ***catnapped***) echarse una cabezada *f*

'**cat's eyes** *on road* captafaros *mpl* (*en el centro de la calzada*)

cat·sup ['kætsʌp] ketchup *m*, catchup *m*

cat·tle ['kætl] *npl* ganado *m*

cat·ty ['kætɪ] *adj* malintencionado

'**cat·walk** pasarela *f*

caught [kɒ:t] *pret & pp* → ***catch***

cau·li·flow·er ['kɒ:lɪflaʊər] coliflor *f*

cause [kɒ:z] **1** *n* causa *f*; (*grounds*) motivo *m*, razón *f* **2** *v/t* causar, provocar

caus·tic ['kɒ:stɪk] *adj fig* cáustico

cau·tion ['kɒ:ʃn] **1** *n* (*carefulness*) precaución *f*, prudencia *f*; ***caution is advised*** se recomienda prudencia **2** *v/t* (*warn*) prevenir (***against*** contra)

cau·tious ['kɒ:ʃəs] *adj* cauto, prudente

cau·tious·ly ['kɒ:ʃəslɪ] *adv* cautelosamente, con prudencia

cav·al·ry ['kævəlrɪ] caballería *f*

cave [keɪv] cueva *f*

◆ **cave in** *v/i of roof* hundirse

cav·i·ar ['kævɪɑ:r] caviar *m*

cav·i·ty ['kævətɪ] caries *f inv*

cc[1] [si:'si:] **1** *abbr* (= ***carbon copy***) copia *f* **2** *v/t memo* enviar una copia de; *person* enviar una copia a

cc[2] [si:'si:] *abbr* (= ***cubic centimeters***) cc (centimetros *mpl* cúbicos); MOT cilindrada *f*

CD [si:'di:] *abbr* (= ***compact disc***) CD *m* (= disco *m* compacto)

CD play·er (reproductor *m* de) CD *m*

CD-ROM [si:di:'rɑ:m] CD-ROM *m*

CD-ROM drive lector *m* de CD-ROM

cease [si:s] **1** *v/i* cesar **2** *v/t* suspender; ***cease doing sth*** dejar de hacer algo

'**cease-fire** alto *m* el fuego

cei·ling ['si:lɪŋ] *of room* techo *m*; (*limit*) tope *m*, límite *m*

cel·e·brate ['selɪbreɪt] **1** *v/i*: ***let's celebrate with a bottle of champagne*** celebrémoslo con una botella de champán **2** *v/t* celebrar, festejar; (*observe*) celebrar

cel·e·brat·ed ['selɪbreɪtɪd] *adj* célebre; ***be celebrated for*** ser célebre por

cel·e·bra·tion [selɪ'breɪʃn] celebración *f*

ce·leb·ri·ty [sɪ'lebrətɪ] celebridad *f*

cel·e·ry ['selərɪ] apio *m*

cel·i·ba·cy ['selɪbəsɪ] celibato *m*

cel·i·bate ['selɪbət] *adj* célibe

cell [sel] *for prisoner, in spreadsheet* celda *f*; BIO célula *f*

cel·lar ['selər] *of house* sótano *m*; *for wine* bodega *f*

cel·list ['tʃelɪst] violonchelista *m/f*

cel·lo ['tʃelou] violonchelo *m*

cel·lo·phane ['seləfeɪn] celofán *m*

'**cell phone, cel·lu·lar phone** ['seljələr] (teléfono *m*) móvil *m*, *L.Am.* (teléfono *m*) celular *m*

cel·lu·lite ['selju:laɪt] celulitis *f*

ce·ment [sɪ'ment] **1** *n* cemento *m* **2** *v/t* colocar con cemento; *friendship* consolidar

cem·e·tery ['seməterɪ] cementerio *m*

cen·sor ['sensər] *v/t* censor(a) *m(f)*

cen·sus ['sensəs] censo *m*

cent [sent] céntimo *m*

cen·te·na·ry [sen'ti:nərɪ] centenario *m*

cen·ter ['sentər] **1** *n* centro *m*; ***in the cen-***

C

ter of en el centro de **2** *v/t* centrar
◆ **center on** *v/t* centrarse en
cen·ter of 'grav·i·ty centro *m* de gravedad
cen·ti·grade ['sentɪgreɪd] *adj* centígrado; ***10 degrees centigrade*** 10 grados centígrados
cen·ti·me·ter, *Br* **cen·ti·me·tre** ['sentɪmiːter] centímetro *m*
cen·tral ['sentrəl] *adj* central; *location, apartment* céntrico; ***central Chicago*** el centro de Chicago; ***be central to sth*** ser el eje de algo
Cen·tral A'mer·i·ca *n* Centroamérica, América Central
Cen·tral A'mer·i·can 1 *adj* centroamericano, de (la) América *f* Central **2** *n* centroamericano(-a) *m(f)*
cen·tral 'heat·ing calefacción *f* central
cen·tral·ize ['sentrəlaɪz] *v/t* centralizar
cen·tral 'lock·ing MOT cierre *m* centralizado
cen·tral 'pro·ces·sing u·nit unidad *f* central de proceso
cen·tre *Br* → ***center***
cen·tu·ry ['senʧərɪ] siglo *m*
CEO [siːiː'oʊ] *abbr* (= ***Chief Executive Officer***) consejero(-a) *m(f)* delegado
ce·ram·ic [sɪ'ræmɪk] *adj* de cerámica
ce·ram·ics [sɪ'ræmɪks] (*pl*: *objects*) objetos *mpl* de cerámica; (*sing*: *art*) cerámica *f*
ce·re·al ['sɪrɪəl] (*grain*) cereal *m*; (*breakfast cereal*) cereales *mpl*
cer·e·mo·ni·al [serɪ'moʊnɪəl] **1** *adj* ceremonial **2** *n* ceremonial *m*
cer·e·mo·ny ['serɪmənɪ] (*event, ritual*) ceremonia *f*
cer·tain ['sɜːrtn] *adj* (*sure*) seguro; (*particular*) cierto; ***I'm certain*** estoy seguro; ***it's certain that …*** es seguro que …; ***a certain Mr S.*** un cierto Sr. S.; ***make certain*** asegurarse; ***know / say for certain*** saber / decir con certeza
cer·tain·ly ['sɜːrtnlɪ] *adv* (*definitely*) claramente; (*of course*) por supuesto; ***certainly not!*** ¡por supuesto que no!
cer·tain·ty ['sɜːrtntɪ] (*confidence*) certeza *f*, certidumbre *f*; (*inevitability*) seguridad *f*; ***it's a certainty*** es seguro; ***he's a certainty for the gold medal*** va a ganar seguro la medalla de oro
cer·tif·i·cate [sər'tɪfɪkət] (*qualification*) título *m*; (*official paper*) certificado *m*
cer·ti·fied pub·lic ac·count·ant ['sɜːrtɪfaɪd] censor(a) *m(f)* jurado de cuentas
cer·ti·fy ['sɜːrtɪfaɪ] *v/t* (*pret & pp **certified***) certificar
Ce·sar·e·an [sɪ'zerɪən] *n* cesárea *f*
ces·sa·tion [se'seɪʃn] cese *m*
c/f *abbr* (= ***cost and freight***) CF (= costo y flete)
CFC [siːef'siː] *abbr* (= ***chlorofluorocarbon***) CFC *m* (= clorofluorocarbono *m*)
chain [ʧeɪn] **1** *n also of hotels etc* cadena *f* **2** *v/t* encadenar: ***chain sth/s.o. to sth*** encadenar algo/a alguien a algo
chain re'ac·tion reacción *f* en cadena
'chain-smoke *v/i* fumar un cigarrillo tras otro, fumar como un carretero
'chain-smok·er *persona que fuma un cigarrillo tras otro*
'chain store *store* tienda *f* (de una cadena); *company* cadena *f* de tiendas
chair [ʧer] **1** *n* silla *f*; (*armchair*) sillón *m*; *at university* cátedra *f*; ***the chair*** (*electric chair*) la silla eléctrica; *at meeting* la presidencia; ***go to the chair*** ser ejecutado en la silla eléctrica; ***take the chair*** ocupar la presidencia **2** *v/t meeting* presidir
'chair lift telesilla *f*
'chair·man presidente *m*
chair·man·ship ['ʧermənʃɪp] presidencia *f*
'chair·per·son presidente(-a) *m(f)*
'chair·wom·an presidenta *f*
cha·let ['ʃæleɪ] chalet *m*, chalé *m*
chal·ice ['ʧælɪs] REL cáliz *m*
chalk [ʧɒːk] *for writing* tiza *f*; *in soil* creta *f*
chal·lenge ['ʧælɪndʒ] **1** *n* (*difficulty*) desafío *m*, reto *m*; *in race, competition* ataque *m* **2** *v/t* desafiar, retar; (*call into question*) cuestionar
chal·len·ger ['ʧælɪndʒər] aspirante *m/f*
chal·len·ging ['ʧælɪndʒɪŋ] *adj job, undertaking* estimulante
cham·ber·maid ['ʧeɪmbərmeɪd] camarera *f* (de hotel)
'cham·ber mu·sic música *f* de cámara
Cham·ber of 'Com·merce Cámara *f* de Comercio
cham·ois (leath·er) ['ʃæmɪ] ante *m*
cham·pagne [ʃæm'peɪn] champán *m*
cham·pi·on ['ʧæmpɪən] **1** *n* SP campeón(-ona) *m(f)*; *of cause* abanderado (-a) *m(f)* **2** *v/t* (*cause*) abanderar
cham·pi·on·ship ['ʧæmpɪənʃɪp] campeonato *m*
chance [ʧæns] (*possibility*) posibilidad *f*; (*opportunity*) oportunidad *f*; (*risk*) riesgo *m*; (*luck*) casualidad *f*, suerte *f*; ***there's not much chance of that happening*** no es probable que ocurra; ***leave nothing to chance*** no dejar nada a la improvisación; ***by chance*** por casualidad; ***take a chance*** correr el riesgo; ***I'm not taking any chances*** no voy a correr ningún riesgo
Chan·cel·lor ['ʧænsələr] *in Germany* can-

C

ciller *m*; ***Chancellor (of the Exchequer)*** *in Britain* Ministro(-a) *m(f)* de Hacienda

chan·de·lier [ʃændə'lɪr] araña *f* (de luces)

change [ʧeɪndʒ] **1** *n* cambio *m*; (*small coins*) suelto *m*; *from purchase* cambio *m*, *Span* vuelta *f*, *L.Am.* vuelto *m*; ***a change is as good as a rest*** a veces cambiar es lo mejor; ***that makes a nice change*** eso es una novedad bienvenida; ***for a change*** para variar; ***a change of clothes*** una muda **2** *v/t* cambiar; ***change trains*** hacer transbordo; ***change one's clothes*** cambiarse de ropa **3** *v/i* cambiar; (*put on different clothes*) cambiarse; (*take different train / bus*) hacer transbordo; ***the lights changed to green*** el semáforo se puso verde

change·a·ble ['ʧeɪndʒəbl] *adj* variable, cambiante

'**change·o·ver** transición *f* (***to*** a); *in relay race* relevo *m*

chang·ing room ['ʧeɪndʒɪŋ] SP vestuario *m*; *in shop* probador *m*

chan·nel ['ʧænl] *on* TV, *at sea* canal *m*

chant [ʧænt] **1** *n* REL canto *m*; *of fans* cántico *m*; *of demonstrators* consigna *f* **2** *v/i* gritar **3** *v/t* corear

cha·os ['keɪɑːs] caos *m*; ***it was chaos at the airport*** la situación en el aeropuerto era caótica

cha·ot·ic [keɪ'ɑːtɪk] *adj* caótico

chap [ʧæp] *n Br* F tipo *m* F, *Span* tío *m* F

chap·el ['ʧæpl] capilla *f*

chapped [ʧæpt] *adj lips* cortado; *hands* agrietado

chap·ter ['ʧæptər] *of book* capítulo *m*; *of organization* sección *f*

char·ac·ter ['kærɪktər] *nature, personality, in printing* carácter *m*; *person, in book, play* personaje *m*; ***he's a real character*** es todo un personaje

char·ac·ter·is·tic [kærɪktə'rɪstɪk] **1** *n* característica *f* **2** *adj* característico

char·ac·ter·is·ti·cal·ly [kærɪktə'rɪstɪklɪ] *adv* de modo característico; ***he was characteristically rude*** fue grosero como de costumbre

char·ac·ter·ize ['kærɪktəraɪz] *v/t* (*be typical of*) caracterizar; (*describe*) describir, clasificar

cha·rade [ʃə'rɑːd] *fig* farsa *f*

char·broil·ed ['ʧɑːrbrɔɪld] *adj* a la brasa

char·coal ['ʧɑːrkoʊl] *for barbecue* carbón *m* vegetal; *for drawing* carboncillo *m*

charge [ʧɑːrdʒ] **1** *n* (*fee*) tarifa *f*; LAW cargo *m*, acusación *f*; ***free of charge*** gratis; ***bank charges*** comisiones *fpl* bancarias; ***will that be cash or charge?*** ¿pagará en efectivo o con tarjeta?; ***be in charge*** estar a cargo; ***take charge*** hacerse cargo **2** *v/t sum of money* cobrar; (*put on account*) pagar con tarjeta; LAW acusar (***with*** de); *battery* cargar; ***please charge it to my account*** cárguelo a mi cuenta **3** *v/i* (*attack*) cargar

'**charge ac·count** cuenta *f* de crédito

'**charge card** tarjeta *f* de compra

cha·ris·ma [kə'rɪzmə] carisma *m*

char·is·ma·tic [kærɪz'mætɪk] *adj* carismático

char·i·ta·ble ['ʧærɪtəbl] *adj institution, donation* de caridad; *person* caritativo

char·i·ty ['ʧærətɪ] *assistance* caridad *f*; *organization* entidad *f* benéfica

char·la·tan ['ʃɑːrlətən] charlatán(-ana) *m(f)*

charm [ʧɑːrm] **1** *n* (*appealing quality*) encanto *m*; *on bracelet etc* colgante *m* **2** *v/t* (*delight*) encantar

charm·ing ['ʧɑːrmɪŋ] *adj* encantador

charred [ʧɑːrd] *adj* carbonizado

chart [ʧɑːrt] (*diagram*) gráfico *m*; (*map*) carta *f* de navegación; ***the charts*** MUS las listas de éxitos

'**char·ter flight** vuelo *m* chárter

chase [ʧeɪs] **1** *n* persecución *f* **2** *v/t* perseguir

◆ **chase away** *v/t* ahuyentar

chas·sis ['ʃæsɪ] *of car* chasis *m inv*

chat [ʧæt] **1** *n* charla *f*, *Mex* plática *f* **2** *v/i* (*pret & pp* ***chatted***) charlar, *Mex* platicar

'**chat show** tertulia *f* televisiva

'**chat show host** presentador(a) *m(f)* de tertulia televisiva

chat·ter ['ʧætər] **1** *n* cháchara *f* **2** *v/i talk* parlotear; *of teeth* castañetear

'**chat·ter·box** charlatán(-ana) *m(f)*

chat·ty ['ʧætɪ] *adj person* hablador

chauf·feur ['ʃoʊfər] *n* chófer *m*, *L.Am.* chofer *m*

'**chauf·feur-driv·en** *adj* con chófer *or L.Am.* chofer

chau·vin·ist ['ʃoʊvɪnɪst] *n* (*male chauvinist*) machista *m*

chau·vin·ist·ic [ʃoʊvɪ'nɪstɪk] *adj* chovinista; (*sexist*) machista

cheap [ʧiːp] *adj* (*inexpensive*) barato; (*nasty*) chabacano; (*mean*) tacaño

cheat [ʧiːt] **1** *n* (*person*) tramposo(-a) *m(f)* **2** *v/t* engañar; ***cheat s.o. out of sth*** estafar algo a alguien **3** *v/i in exam* copiar; *in cards etc* hacer trampa; ***cheat on one's wife*** engañar a la esposa

check¹ [ʧek] **1** *adj shirt* a cuadros **2** *n* cuadro *m*

check² [ʧek] FIN cheque *m*; *in restaurant etc* cuenta *f*; ***the check please*** la cuenta, por favor

C

check[3] [ʧek] **1** *n to verify sth* comprobación *f*; ***keep in check, hold in check*** mantener bajo control; ***keep a check on*** llevar el control de **2** *v/t* (*verify*) comprobar; *machinery* inspeccionar; (*restrain*, *stop*) contener, controlar; *with a checkmark* poner un tic en; *coat* dejar en el guardarropa; *package* dejar en consigna **3** *v/i* comprobar; ***check for*** comprobar

◆ **check in** *v/i at airport* facturar; *at hotel* registrarse

◆ **check off** *v/t* marcar (*como comprobada*)

◆ **check on** *v/t* vigilar

◆ **check out 1** *v/i of hotel* dejar el hotel **2** *v/t* (*look into*) investigar; *club*, *restaurant etc* probar

◆ **check up on** *v/t* hacer averiguaciones sobre, investigar

◆ **check with** *v/t of person* hablar con; (*tally*: *of information*) concordar con

'**check·book** talonario *m* de cheques, *L.Am.* chequera *f*

checked [ʧekt] *adj material* a cuadros

check·er·board ['ʧekərbɔːrd] tablero *m* de ajedrez

check·ered ['ʧekərd] *adj pattern* a cuadros; *career* accidentado

check·ers ['ʧekərz] *nsg* damas *fpl*

'**check-in** (**coun·ter**) mostrador *m* de facturación

check·ing ac·count ['ʧekɪŋ] cuenta *f* corriente

'**check-in time** hora *f* de facturación

'**check·list** lista *f* de verificación

'**check mark** tic *m*

'**check·mate** *n* jaque *m* mate

'**check-out** caja *f*

'**check-out time** *from hotel* hora *f* de salida

'**check·point** control *m*

'**check·room** *for coats* guardarropa *m*; *for baggage* consigna *f*

'**check·up** *medical* chequeo *m* (médico), revisión *f* (médica); *dental* revisión *f* (en el dentista)

cheek [ʧiːk] ANAT mejilla *f*

'**cheek·bone** pómulo *m*

cheer [ʧɪr] **1** *n* ovación *f*; ***cheers!*** *toast* ¡salud!; ***the cheers of the fans*** los vítores de los aficionados **2** *v/t* ovacionar, vitorear **3** *v/i* lanzar vítores

◆ **cheer on** *v/t* animar

◆ **cheer up 1** *v/i* animarse; ***cheer up!*** ¡anímate! **2** *v/t* animar

cheer·ful ['ʧɪrfəl] *adj* alegre, contento

cheer·ing ['ʧɪrɪŋ] *n* vítores *mpl*

cheer·i·o [ʧɪrɪ'oʊ] *Br* F ¡chao! F

'**cheer·lead·er** animadora *f*

cheese [ʧiːz] queso *m*

'**cheese·burg·er** hamburguesa *f* de queso

'**cheese·cake** tarta *f* de queso

chef [ʃef] chef *m*, jefe *m* de cocina

chem·i·cal ['kemɪkl] **1** *adj* químico **2** *n* producto *m* químico

chem·i·cal '**war·fare** guerra *f* química

chem·ist ['kemɪst] *in laboratory* químico(-a) *m*(*f*); *Br dispensing* farmacéutico(-a) *m*(*f*)

chem·is·try ['kemɪstrɪ] química *f*; *fig* sintonía *f*, química *f*

chem·o·ther·a·py [kiːmoʊ'θerəpɪ] quimioterapia *f*

cheque [ʧek] *Br* → ***check***[2]

cher·ish ['ʧerɪʃ] *v/t photo etc* apreciar mucho, tener mucho cariño a; *person* querer mucho; *hope* albergar

cher·ry ['ʧerɪ] *fruit* cereza *f*; *tree* cerezo *m*

cher·ub ['ʧerəb] *in painting*, *sculpture* querubín *m*

chess [ʧes] ajedrez *m*

'**chess·board** tablero *m* de ajedrez

'**chess·man**, '**chess·piece** pieza *f* de ajedrez

chest [ʧest] *of person* pecho *m*; *box* cofre *m*; ***get sth off one's chest*** desahogarse

chest·nut ['ʧesnʌt] castaña *f*; *tree* castaño *m*

chest of '**draw·ers** cómoda *f*

chew [ʧuː] *v/t* mascar, masticar; *of dog*, *rats* mordisquear

◆ **chew out** *v/t* F echar una bronca a F

chew·ing gum ['ʧuːɪŋ] chicle *m*

chic [ʃiːk] *adj* chic, elegante

chick [ʧɪk] *young chicken* pollito *m*; *young bird* polluelo *m*; F *girl* nena *f* F

chick·en ['ʧɪkɪn] **1** *n* gallina *f*; *food* pollo *m*; F (*coward*) gallina *f* F **2** *adj* F (*cowardly*) cobarde; ***be chicken*** ser un(a) gallina F

◆ **chicken out** *v/i* F acobardarse

'**chick·en·feed** F calderilla *f*

chief [ʧiːf] **1** *n* jefe(-a) *m*(*f*) **2** *adj* principal

chief ex·ec·u·tive '**of·fi·cer** consejero(-a) *m*(*f*) delegado

chief·ly ['ʧiːflɪ] *adv* principalmente

chil·blain ['ʧɪlbleɪn] sabañón *m*

child [ʧaɪld] (*pl* ***children*** ['ʧɪldrən]) niño(-a) *m*(*f*); *son* hijo *m*; *daughter* hija *f*; *pej* niño(-a) *m*(*f*), crío(-a) *m*(*f*)

'**child a·buse** malos tratos *mpl* a menores

'**child·birth** parto *m*

child·hood ['ʧaɪldhʊd] infancia *f*

child·ish ['ʧaɪldɪʃ] *adj pej* infantil

child·ish·ness ['ʧaɪldɪʃnɪs] *pej* infantilismo *m*

child·ish·ly [ˈʧaɪldɪʃlɪ] *adv pej* de manera infantil
child·less [ˈʧaɪldlɪs] *adj* sin hijos
child·like [ˈʧaɪldlaɪk] *adj* infantil
ˈ**child·mind·er** niñero(-a) *m(f)*
ˈ**child·ren** [ˈʧɪldrən] *pl* → ***child***
Chil·e [ˈʧɪlɪ] *n* Chile
Chil·e·an [ˈʧɪlɪən] **1** *adj* chileno **2** *n* chileno(-a) *m(f)*
chill [ʧɪl] **1** *n illness* resfriado *m*; ***there's a chill in the air*** hace bastante fresco **2** *v/t wine* poner a enfriar
◆ **chill out** *v/i* P tranquilizarse
chil·(l)i (pep·per) [ˈʧɪlɪ] chile *m*, *Span* guindilla *f*
chill·y [ˈʧɪlɪ] *adj weather, welcome* fresco; ***I'm feeling a bit chilly*** tengo fresco
chime [ʧaɪm] *v/i* campanada *f*
chim·ney [ˈʧɪmnɪ] chimenea *f*
chim·pan·zee [ʧɪmˈpænziː] chimpancé *m*
chin [ʧɪn] barbilla *f*
Chi·na [ˈʧaɪnə] China
chi·na [ˈʧaɪnə] porcelana *f*
Chi·nese [ʧaɪˈniːz] **1** *adj* chino **2** *n (language)* chino *m*; *(person)* chino(-a) *m(f)*
chink [ʧɪŋk] *gap* resquicio *m*; *sound* tintineo *m*
chip [ʧɪp] **1** *n of wood* viruta *f*; *of stone* lasca *f*; *damage* mella *f*; *in gambling* ficha *f*; ***chips*** patatas *fpl* fritas **2** *v/t (pret & pp* ***chipped****)* *(damage)* mellar
◆ **chip in** *v/i (interrupt)* interrumpir; *with money* poner dinero
chip·munk [ˈʧɪpmʌŋk] ardilla *f* listada
chi·ro·prac·tor [ˈkaɪroʊpræktər] quiropráctico(-a) *m(f)*
chirp [ʧɜːrp] *v/i* piar
chis·el [ˈʧɪzl] *n for stone* cincel *m*; *for wood* formón *m*
chit·chat [ˈʧɪtʧæt] charla *f*
chiv·al·rous [ˈʃɪvlrəs] *adj* caballeroso
chive [ʧaɪv] cebollino *m*
chlo·rine [ˈklɔːriːn] cloro *m*
chlor·o·form [ˈklɔːrəfɔːrm] *n* cloroformo *m*
choc·a·hol·ic [ʧɑːkəˈhɑːlɪk] *n* F adicto(-a) al chocolate
chock-a-block [ʧɑːkəˈblɑːk] *adj* F abarrotado F
chock-full [ʧɑːkˈfʊl] *adj* F de bote en bote F
choc·o·late [ˈʧɑːkələt] chocolate *m*; ***a box of chocolates*** una caja de bombones; ***hot chocolate*** chocolate *m* caliente
ˈ**choc·o·late cake** pastel *m* de chocolate
choice [ʧɔɪs] **1** *n* elección *f*; *(selection)* selección *f*; ***you have a choice of rice or potatoes*** puedes elegir entre arroz y patatas; ***the choice is yours*** tú eliges; ***I had no choice*** no tuve alternativa **2** *adj (top quality)* selecto
choir [kwaɪr] coro *m*
ˈ**choir·boy** niño *m* de coro
choke [ʧoʊk] **1** *n* MOT estárter *m* **2** *v/i* ahogarse; ***choke on sth*** atragantarse con algo **3** *v/t* estrangular; *screams* ahogar
cho·les·te·rol [kəˈlestəroʊl] colesterol *m*
choose [ʧuːz] *v/t & v/i (pret* ***chose****, pp* ***chosen****)* elegir, escoger
choos·ey [ˈʧuːzɪ] *adj* F exigente
chop [ʧɑːp] **1** *n meat* chuleta *f*; ***with one chop of the ax*** con un hachazo **2** *v/t (pret & pp* ***chopped****)* *wood* cortar; *meat* trocear; *vegetables* picar
◆ **chop down** *v/t tree* talar
chop·per [ˈʧɑːpər] F *(helicopter)* helicóptero *m*
ˈ**chop·sticks** *npl* palillos *mpl* (chinos)
cho·ral [ˈkɔːrəl] *adj* coral
chord [kɔːrd] MUS acorde *m*
chore [ʧɔːr] tarea *f*
chor·e·o·graph [ˈkɔːrɪəgræf] *v/t* coreografiar
chor·e·og·ra·pher [kɔːrɪˈɑːgrəfər] coreógrafo(-a) *m(f)*
chor·e·og·ra·phy [kɔːrɪˈɑːgrəfɪ] coreografía *f*
cho·rus [ˈkɔːrəs] *singers* coro *m*; *of song* estribillo *m*
chose [ʧoʊz] *pret* → ***choose***
cho·sen [ˈʧoʊzn] *pp* → ***choose***
Christ [kraɪst] Cristo; ***Christ!*** ¡Dios mío!
chris·ten [ˈkrɪsn] *v/t* bautizar
chris·ten·ing [ˈkrɪsnɪŋ] bautizo *m*
Chris·tian [ˈkrɪsʧən] **1** *n* cristiano(-a) *m(f)* **2** *adj* cristiano
Chris·ti·an·i·ty [krɪstɪˈænətɪ] cristianismo *m*
ˈ**Chris·tian name** nombre *m* de pila
Christ·mas [ˈkrɪsməs] Navidad(es) *f(pl)*; ***at Christmas*** en Navidad(es); ***Merry Christmas!*** ¡Feliz Navidad!
ˈ**Christ·mas card** crismas *m inv*, tarjeta *f* de Navidad
Christ·mas ˈ**Day** día *f* de Navidad
Christ·mas ˈ**Eve** Nochebuena *f*
ˈ**Christ·mas present** regalo *m* de Navidad
ˈ**Christ·mas tree** árbol *m* de Navidad
chrome, chro·mi·um [kroʊm, ˈkroʊmɪəm] cromo *m*
chro·mo·some [ˈkroʊməsoʊm] cromosoma *m*
chron·ic [ˈkrɑːnɪk] *adj* crónico
chron·o·log·i·cal [krɑːnəˈlɑːdʒɪkl] *adj* cronológico; ***in chronological order*** en orden cronológico
chrys·an·the·mum [krɪˈsænθəməm] cri-

santemo *m*
chub·by ['ʧʌbɪ] *adj* rechoncho
chuck [ʧʌk] *v/t* F tirar
◆ **chuck out** *v/t* F *object* tirar; *person* echar
chuck·le ['ʧʌkl] **1** *n* risita *f* **2** *v/i* reírse por lo bajo
chum [ʧʌm] amigo(-a) *m(f)*
chum·my ['ʧʌmɪ] *adj* F: ***be chummy with*** ser amiguete de F
chunk [ʧʌŋk] trozo *m*
chunk·y ['ʧʌŋkɪ] *adj sweater* grueso; *person, build* cuadrado, fornido
church [ʧɜːrʧ] iglesia *f*
church 'hall *sala parroquial empleada para diferentes actividades*
church 'serv·ice oficio *m* religioso
'church·yard cementerio *m* (al lado de iglesia)
churl·ish ['ʧɜːrlɪʃ] *adj* maleducado, grosero
chute [ʃuːt] rampa *f*; *for garbage* colector *m* de basura
CIA [siːaɪ'eɪ] *abbr* (= ***Central Intelligence Agency*** CIA *f* (= Agencia *f* Central de Inteligencia)
ci·der ['saɪdər] sidra *f*
CIF [siːaɪ'ef] *abbr* (= ***cost, insurance, freight***) CIF (= costo, seguro y flete)
ci·gar [sɪ'gɑːr] (cigarro *m*) puro *m*
cig·a·rette, **cig·a·ret** [sɪgə'ret] cigarrillo *m*
cig·a'rette end colilla *f*
cig·a'rette light·er encendedor *m*, mechero *m*
cig·a'rette pa·per papel *m* de fumar
cin·e·ma ['sɪnɪmə] cine *m*
cin·na·mon ['sɪnəmən] canela *f*
cir·cle ['sɜːrkl] **1** *n* círculo *m*; ***sit in a circle*** sentarse en círculo **2** *v/t* (*draw circle around*) poner un círculo alrededor de; ***his name was circled in red*** su nombre tenía un círculo rojo alrededor **3** *v/i of plane, bird* volar en círculo
cir·cuit ['sɜːrkɪt] circuito *m*; (*lap*) vuelta *f*
'cir·cuit board COMPUT placa *f or* tarjeta *f* de circuitos
'cir·cuit break·er ELEC cortacircuitos *m inv*
'cir·cuit train·ing SP: ***do circuit training*** hacer circuitos de entrenamiento
cir·cu·lar ['sɜːrkjʊlər] **1** *n giving information* circular *f* **2** *adj* circular
cir·cu·late ['sɜːrkjʊleɪt] **1** *v/i* circular **2** *v/t memo* hacer circular
cir·cu·la·tion [sərkjʊ'leɪʃn] circulación *f*; *of newspaper, magazine* tirada *f*
cir·cum·fer·ence [sər'kʌmfərəns] circunferencia *f*
cir·cum·stances ['sɜːrkəmstənsɪs] *npl* circunstancias *fpl*; *financial* situación *f* económica; ***under no circumstances*** en ningún caso, de ninguna manera; ***under the circumstances*** dadas las circunstancias
cir·cus ['sɜːrkəs] circo *m*
cir·rho·sis (of the liv·er) [sɪ'roʊsɪs] cirrosis *f* (hepática)
cis·tern ['sɪstɜːrn] cisterna *f*
cite [saɪt] *v/t* citar
cit·i·zen ['sɪtɪzn] ciudadano(-a) *m(f)*
cit·i·zen·ship ['sɪtɪznʃɪp] ciudadanía *f*
citr·us ['sɪtrəs] *adj* cítrico; ***citrus fruit*** cítrico *m*
cit·y ['sɪtɪ] ciudad *f*
city 'center centro *m* de la ciudad
city 'hall ayuntamiento *m*
civ·ic ['sɪvɪk] *adj* cívico
civ·il ['ʃɪvl] *adj* civil; (*polite*) cortés
civ·il en·gi'neer ingeniero(-a) *m(f)* civil
ci·vil·i·an [sɪ'vɪljən] **1** *n* civil *m/f* **2** *adj clothes* de civil
ci·vil·i·ty [sɪ'vɪlɪtɪ] cortesía *f*
civ·i·li·za·tion [sɪvəlaɪ'zeɪʃn] civilización *f*
civ·i·lize ['sɪvəlaɪz] *v/t person* civilizar
civ·il 'rights *npl* derechos *mpl* civiles
civ·il 'ser·vant funcionario(-a) *m(f)*
civ·il 'ser·vice administración *f* pública
civ·il 'war guerra *f* civil
claim [kleɪm] **1** *n* (*request*) reclamación *f* (***for*** de); (*right*) derecho *m*; (*assertion*) afirmación *f* **2** *v/t* (*ask for as a right*) reclamar; (*assert*) afirmar; *lost property* reclamar; ***they have claimed responsibility for the attack*** se han atribuido la responsabilidad del ataque
claim·ant ['kleɪmənt] reclamante *m/f*
clair·voy·ant [kler'vɔɪənt] *n* clarividente *m/f*, vidente *m/f*
clam [klæm] almeja *f*
◆ **clam up** *v/i* (*pret & pp* ***clammed***) F cerrarse, callarse
clam·ber ['klæmbər] *v/i* trepar (***over*** por)
clam·my ['klæmɪ] *adj* húmedo
clam·or, *Br* **clam·our** ['klæmər] *noise* griterío *m*; *outcry* clamor *m*
◆ **clamor for** *v/t justice* clamar por; *ice cream* pedir a gritos
clamp [klæmp] **1** *n fastener* abrazadera *f*, mordaza *f* **2** *v/t fasten* sujetar con abrazadera; *car* poner un cepo a
◆ **clamp down** *v/i* actuar contundentemente
◆ **clamp down on** *v/t* actuar contundentemente contra
clan [klæn] clan *m*
clan·des·tine [klæn'destɪn] *adj* clandesti-

no

clang [klæŋ] **1** *n* sonido *m* metálico **2** *v/i* resonar; ***the metal door clanged shut*** la puerta metálica se cerró con gran estrépito

clap [klæp] *v/t & v/i* (*pret & pp* ***clapped***) (*applaud*) aplaudir

clar·et ['klærɪt] *wine* burdeos *m inv*

clar·i·fi·ca·tion [klærɪfɪ'keɪʃn] aclaración *f*

clar·i·fy ['klærɪfaɪ] *v/t* (*pret & pp* ***clarified***) aclarar

clar·i·net [klærɪ'net] clarinete *m*

clar·i·ty ['klærətɪ] claridad *f*

clash [klæʃ] **1** *n* choque *m*, enfrentamiento *m*; *of personalities* choque *m* **2** *v/i* chocar, enfrentarse; *of colors* desentonar; *of events* coincidir

clasp [klæsp] **1** *n* broche *m*, cierre *m* **2** *v/t in hand* estrechar; ***he clasped the precious documents to him*** agarró firmemente los valiosos documentos

class [klæs] **1** *n lesson*, *students* clase *f*; ***social class*** clase *f* social **2** *v/t* clasificar (***as*** como)

clas·sic ['klæsɪk] **1** *adj* clásico **2** *n* clásico *m*

clas·si·cal ['klæsɪkl] *adj music* clásico

clas·si·fi·ca·tion [klæsɪfɪ'keɪʃn] clasificación *f*

clas·si·fied ['klæsɪfaɪd] *adj information* reservado

'clas·si·fied ad(ver·tise·ment) anuncio *m* por palabras

clas·si·fy ['klæsɪfaɪ] *v/t* (*pret & pp* ***classified***) clasificar

'class·mate compañero(-a) *m*(*f*) de clase

'class·room clase *f*, aula *f*

'class war·fare lucha *f* de clases

class·y ['klæsɪ] *adj* F con clase

clat·ter ['klætər] **1** *n* estrépito *m* **2** *v/i* hacer ruido

clause [klɒːz] *in agreement* cláusula *f*; GRAM cláusula *f*, oración *f*

claus·tro·pho·bi·a [klɒːstrə'foʊbɪə] claustrofobia *f*

claw [klɒː] **1** *n also fig* garra *f*; *of lobster* pinza *f* **2** *v/t* (*scratch*) arañar

clay [kleɪ] arcilla *f*

clean [kliːn] **1** *adj* limpio **2** *adv* F (*completely*) completamente **3** *v/t* limpiar; ***clean one's teeth*** limpiarse los dientes; ***I must have my coat cleaned*** tengo que llevar el abrigo a la tintorería

◆ **clean out** *v/t room*, *closet* limpiar por completo; *fig* desplumar

◆ **clean up 1** *v/t also fig* limpiar; *papers* recoger **2** *v/i* limpiar; (*wash*) lavarse; *on stock market etc* ganar mucho dinero

clean·er ['kliːnər] *person* limpiador(a) *m*(*f*); (***dry***) ***cleaner*** tintorería *f*

clean·ing wom·an ['kliːnɪŋ] señora *f* de la limpieza

cleanse [klenz] *v/t skin* limpiar

cleans·er ['klenzər] *for skin* loción *f* limpiadora

cleans·ing cream ['klenzɪŋ] crema *f* limpiadora

clear [klɪr] **1** *adj* claro; *weather*, *sky* despejado; *water* transparente; *conscience* limpio; ***I'm not clear about it*** no lo tengo claro; ***I didn't make myself clear*** no me expliqué claramente **2** *adv* ***stand clear of the doors*** apartarse de las puertas; ***steer clear of*** evitar **3** *v/t roads etc* despejar; (*acquit*) absolver; (*authorize*) autorizar; (*earn*) ganar, sacar; ***the guards cleared everybody out of the room*** los guardias sacaron a todo el mundo de la habitación; ***you're cleared for takeoff*** tiene autorización *or* permiso para despegar; ***clear one's throat*** carraspear **4** *v/i of sky*, *mist* despejarse; *of face* alegrarse

◆ **clear away** *v/t* quitar

◆ **clear off** *v/i* F largarse F

◆ **clear out 1** *v/t closet* ordenar, limpiar **2** *v/i* marcharse

◆ **clear up 1** *v/i* ordenar; *of weather* despejarse; *of illness*, *rash* desaparecer **2** *v/t* (*tidy*) ordenar; *mystery*, *problem* aclarar

clear·ance ['klɪrəns] *space* espacio *m*; (*authorization*) autorización *f*

clear·ance sale liquidación *f*

clear·ing ['klɪrɪŋ] claro *m*

clear·ly ['klɪrlɪ] *adv* claramente, ***she is clearly upset*** está claro que está disgustada

cleav·age ['kliːvɪdʒ] escote *m*

cleav·er ['kliːvər] cuchillo *m* de carnicero

clem·en·cy ['klemənsɪ] clemencia *f*

clench [klentʃ] *v/t teeth*, *fist* apretar

cler·gy ['klɜːrdʒɪ] clero *m*

cler·gy·man ['klɜːrdʒɪmæn] clérigo *m*

clerk [klɜːrk] *administrative* oficinista *m/f*; *in store* dependiente(-a) *m/f*

clev·er ['klevər] *adj person*, *animal* listo; *idea*, *gadget* ingenioso

clev·er·ly ['klevərlɪ] *adv designed* ingeniosamente

cli·ché ['kliːʃeɪ] tópico *m*, cliché *m*

cli·chéd ['kliːʃeɪd] *adj* estereotipado

click [klɪk] **1** *n* COMPUT clic *m* **2** *v/i* hacer clic

◆ **click on** *v/t* COMPUT hacer clic en

cli·ent ['klaɪənt] cliente *m/f*

cli·en·tele [kliːən'tel] clientela *f*

cli·mate ['klaɪmət] *also fig* clima *m*

C

'cli·mate change cambio *m* climático
cli·mat·ic [klaɪ'mætɪk] *adj* climático
cli·max ['klaɪmæks] *n* clímax *m*, punto *m* culminante
climb [klaɪm] **1** *n up mountain* ascensión *f*, escalada *f* **2** *v/t hill*, *ladder* subir; *mountain* subir, escalar; *tree* trepar a **3** *v/i* subir (***into*** a); *up mountain* subir, escalar; *of inflation etc* subir
◆ **climb down** *v/i from ladder etc* bajar
climb·er ['klaɪmər] *person* escalador(a) *m(f)*, alpinista *m/f*, *L.Am.* andinista *m/f*
climb·ing ['klaɪmɪŋ] escalada *f*, alpinismo *m*, *L.Am.* andinismo *m*
climb·ing wall rocódromo *m*
clinch [klɪntʃ] *v/t deal* cerrar; ***that clinches it*** ¡ahora sí que está claro!
cling [klɪŋ] *v/i* (*pret & pp* ***clung***) *of clothes* pegarse al cuerpo
◆ **cling to** *v/t person*, *idea* aferrarse a
'cling·film plástico *m* transparente (para alimentos)
cling·y ['klɪŋɪ] *adj child*, *boyfriend* pegajoso
clin·ic ['klɪnɪk] clínica *f*
clin·i·cal ['klɪnɪkl] *adj* clínico
clink [klɪŋk] **1** *n noise* tintineo *m* **2** *v/i* tintinear
clip[1] [klɪp] **1** *n fastener* clip *m* **2** *v/t* (*pret & pp* ***clipped***): ***clip sth to sth*** sujetar algo a algo
clip[2] [klɪp] **1** *n extract* fragmento *m* **2** *v/t* (*pret & pp* ***clipped***) *hair*, *grass* cortar; *hedge* podar
clip·pers ['klɪpərz] *npl for hair* maquinilla *f*; *for nails* cortaúñas *m inv*; *for gardening* tijeras *fpl* de podar
clip·ping ['klɪpɪŋ] *from newspaper* recorte *m*
clique [kliːk] camarilla *f*
cloak *n* capa *f*
'cloak·room *Br* guardarropa *m*
clock [klɑːk] reloj *m*
'clock ra·di·o radio *m* despertador
'clock·wise *adv* en el sentido de las agujas del reloj
'clock·work: ***it went like clockwork*** salió a la perfección
◆ **clog up** [klɑːg] **1** *v/i* (*pret & pp* ***clogged***) bloquearse **2** *v/t* (*pret & pp* ***clogged***) bloquear
clone [kloʊn] **1** *n* clon *m* **2** *v/t* clonar
close[1] [kloʊs] **1** *adj family* cercano; *friend* íntimo; ***bear a close resemblance to*** parecerse mucho a; ***the closest town*** la ciudad más cercana; ***be close to s.o.*** *emotionally* estar muy unido a alguien **2** *adv* cerca; ***close to the school*** cerca del colegio; ***close at hand*** a mano; ***close by*** cerca
close[2] [kloʊz] **1** *v/t* cerrar **2** *v/i of door*, *shop* cerrar; *of eyes* cerrarse
◆ **close down** *v/t & v/i* cerrar
◆ **close in** *v/i of fog* echarse encima; *of troops* aproximarse, acercarse
◆ **close up 1** *v/t building* cerrar **2** *v/i* (*move closer*) juntarse
closed [kloʊzd] *adj store*, *eyes* cerrado
closed-cir·cuit 'tel·e·vi·sion circuito *m* cerrado de televisión
'close-knit *adj* muy unido
close·ly ['kloʊslɪ] *adv listen*, *watch* atentamente; *cooperate* de cerca
clos·et ['klɑːzɪt] armario *m*
close-up ['kloʊsʌp] primer plano *m*
clos·ing date ['kloʊzɪŋ] fecha *f* límite
'clos·ing time hora *f* de cierre
clo·sure ['kloʊʒər] cierre *m*
clot [klɑːt] **1** *n of blood* coágulo *m* **2** *v/i* (*pret & pp* ***clotted***) *of blood* coagularse
cloth [klɑːθ] (*fabric*) tela *f*, tejido *m*; *for cleaning* trapo *m*
clothes [kloʊðz] *npl* ropa *f*
'clothes brush cepillo *m* para la ropa
'clothes hang·er percha *f*
'clothes·horse tendedero *m* plegable
'clothes·line cuerda *f* de tender la ropa
'clothes peg, **'clothes·pin** pinza *f* (de la ropa)
cloth·ing ['kloʊðɪŋ] ropa *f*
cloud [klaʊd] *n* nube *f*; ***a cloud of dust*** una nube de polvo
◆ **cloud over** *v/i of sky* nublarse
'cloud·burst chaparrón *m*
cloud·less ['klaʊdlɪs] *adj sky* despejado
cloud·y ['klaʊdɪ] *adj* nublado
clout [klaʊt] (*fig*: *influence*) influencia *f*
clove of 'gar·lic [kloʊv] diente *m* de ajo
clown [klaʊn] *also fig* payaso *m*
club [klʌb] *n weapon* palo *m*, garrote *m*; *in golf* palo *m*; *organization* club *m*; ***clubs*** *in cards* tréboles
clue [kluː] pista *f*; ***I haven't a clue*** F (*don't know*) no tengo idea F; ***he hasn't a clue*** F (*is useless*) no tiene ni idea F
clued-up [kluːd'ʌp] *adj* F puesto F; ***be clued-up on sth*** F estar puesto sobre algo F
clump [klʌmp] *n of earth* terrón *m*; *of flowers etc* grupo *m*
clum·si·ness ['klʌmzɪnɪs] torpeza *f*
clum·sy ['klʌmzɪ] *adj person* torpe
clung [klʌŋ] *pret & pp* → ***cling***
clus·ter ['klʌstər] **1** *n* grupo *m* **2** *v/i of people* apiñarse; *of houses* agruparse
clutch [klʌtʃ] **1** *n* MOT embrague *m* **2** *v/t* agarrar
◆ **clutch at** *v/t*: ***clutch at sth*** agarrarse a

algo
clut·ter ['klʌtər] **1** *n* desorden *m*; ***all the clutter on my desk*** la cantidad de cosas que hay encima de mi mesa **2** *v/t* (*also*: *clutter up*) abarrotar
Co. *abbr* (= ***Company***) Cía. (= Compañía *f*)
c/o *abbr* (= ***care of***) en el domicilio de
coach [koʊʧ] **1** *n* (*trainer*) entrenador(a) *m*(*f*); *of singer, actor* profesor(a) *m*(*f*); *on train* vagón *m*; *Br* (*bus*) autobús *m* **2** *v/t footballer* entrenar; *singer* preparar
coach·ing ['koʊʧɪŋ] entrenamiento *m*
co·ag·u·late [koʊ'ægjʊleɪt] *v/i of blood* coagularse
coal [koʊl] carbón *m*
co·a·li·tion [koʊə'lɪʃn] coalición *f*
'coal·mine mina *f* de carbón
coarse [kɔːrs] *adj* áspero; *hair* basto; (*vulgar*) basto, grosero
coarse·ly ['kɔːrslɪ] *adv* (*vulgarly*) de manera grosera; ***coarsely ground coffee*** café molido grueso
coast [koʊst] *n* costa *f*; ***at the coast*** en la costa
coast·al ['koʊstl] *adj* costero
coast·er ['koʊstər] posavasos *m inv*
'coast·guard *organization* servicio *m* de guardacostas; *person* guardacostas *m/f inv*
'coast·line litoral *m*, costa *f*
coat [koʊt] **1** *n* chaqueta *f*, *L.Am.* saco *m*; (*overcoat*) abrigo *m*; *of animal* pelaje *m*; *of paint etc* capa *f*, mano *f* **2** *v/t* (*cover*) cubrir (***with*** de)
'coat·hang·er percha *f*
coat·ing ['koʊtɪŋ] capa *f*
co-au·thor ['koʊɒːθər] **1** *n* coautor(a) *m*(*f*) **2** *v/t*: ***co-author a book*** escribir un libro conjuntamente
coax [koʊks] *v/t* persuadir; ***coax sth out of s.o.*** sonsacar algo a alguien
cob·bled ['kɑːbld] *adj* adoquinado
cob·ble·stone ['kɑːblstoʊn] adoquín *m*
cob·web ['kɑːbweb] telaraña *f*
co·caine [kə'keɪn] cocaína *f*
cock [kɑːk] *n* (*chicken*) gallo *m*; (*any male bird*) macho *m*
cock·eyed [kɑːk'aɪd] *adj* F *idea etc* ridículo
'cock·pit *of plane* cabina *f*
cock·roach ['kɑːkroʊʧ] cucaracha *f*
'cock·tail cóctel *m* (bebida)
'cock·tail par·ty cóctel *m* (fiesta)
'cock·tail shak·er coctelera *f*
cock·y ['kɑːkɪ] *adj* F creído, chulo
co·coa ['koʊkoʊ] *drink* cacao *m*
co·co·nut ['koʊkənʌt] coco *m*
'co·co·nut palm cocotero *m*
COD [siːoʊ'diː] *abbr* (= ***collect on delivery***) entrega *f* contra reembolso
cod·dle ['kɑːdl] *v/t sick person* cuidar; *pej*: *child* mimar
code [koʊd] *n* código *m*; ***in code*** cifrado
co·ed·u·ca·tion·al [koʊedʊ'keɪʃnl] *adj* mixto
co·erce [koʊ'ɜːrs] *v/t* coaccionar
co·ex·ist [koʊɪg'zɪst] *v/i* coexistir
co·ex·ist·ence [koʊɪg'zɪstəns] coexistencia *f*
cof·fee ['kɑːfɪ] café *m*; ***a cup of coffee*** un café
'cof·fee bean grano *m* de café
'cof·fee break pausa *f* para el café
'cof·fee cup taza *f* de café
'cof·fee grind·er ['graɪndər] molinillo *m* de café
'cof·fee mak·er cafetera *f* (para preparar)
'cof·fee pot cafetera *f* (para servir)
'cof·fee shop café *m*, cafetería *f*
'cof·fee ta·ble mesa *f* de centro
cof·fin ['kɑːfɪn] féretro *m*, ataúd *m*
cog [kɑːg] diente *m*
co·gnac ['kɑːnjæk] coñac *m*
'cog·wheel rueda *f* dentada
co·hab·it [koʊ'hæbɪt] *v/i* cohabitar
co·her·ent [koʊ'hɪrənt] *adj* coherente
coil [kɔɪl] **1** *n of rope* rollo *m*; *of smoke* espiral *f*; *of snake* anillo *m* **2** *v/t*: ***coil*** (***up***) enrollar
coin [kɔɪn] *n* moneda *f*
co·in·cide [koʊɪn'saɪd] *v/i* coincidir
co·in·ci·dence [koʊ'ɪnsɪdəns] coincidencia *f*
coke [koʊk] P (*cocaine*) coca *f*
Coke® [koʊk] Coca-Cola® *f*
cold [koʊld] **1** *adj also fig* frío; ***I'm*** (***feeling***) ***cold*** tengo frío; ***it's cold*** *of weather* hace frío; ***in cold blood*** a sangre fría; ***get cold feet*** F ponerse nervioso **2** *n* frío *m*; MED resfriado *m*; ***I have a cold*** estoy resfriado, tengo un resfriado
cold-blood·ed [koʊld'blʌdɪd] *adj* de sangre fría; *fig*: *murder* a sangre fría
cold call·ing ['kɒːlɪŋ] COM *visitas o llamadas comerciales hechas sin cita previa*
'cold cuts *npl* fiambres *mpl*
cold·ly ['koʊldlɪ] *adv* fríamente, con frialdad
cold·ness ['koʊldnɪs] frialdad *f*
'cold sore calentura *f*
cole·slaw ['koʊlslɒː] *ensalada de col, cebolla, zanahoria y mayonesa*
col·ic ['kɑːlɪk] cólico *m*
col·lab·o·rate [kə'læbəreɪt] *v/i* colaborar (***on*** en)
col·lab·o·ra·tion [kəlæbə'reɪʃn] colaboración *f*

col·lab·o·ra·tor [kə'læbəreɪtər] colaborador(a) *m(f)*; *with enemy* colaboracionista *m/f*
col·lapse [kə'læps] *v/i of roof, building* hundirse, desplomarse; *of person* desplomarse
col·lap·si·ble [kə'læpsəbl] *adj* plegable
col·lar ['kɑːlər] cuello *m*; *for dog* collar *m*
'col·lar-bone clavícula *f*
col·league ['kɑːliːg] colega *m/f*
col·lect [kə'lekt] **1** *v/t* recoger; *as hobby* coleccionar **2** *v/i* (*gather together*) reunirse **3** *adv*: ***call collect*** llamar a cobro revertido
col·lect call llamada *f* a cobro revertido
col·lect·ed [kə'lektɪd] *adj works, poems etc* completo; *person* sereno
col·lec·tion [kə'lekʃn] colección *f*; *in church* colecta *f*
col·lec·tive [kə'lektɪv] *adj* colectivo
col·lec·tive 'bar·gain·ing negociación *f* colectiva
col·lec·tor [kə'lektər] coleccionista *m/f*
col·lege ['kɑːlɪdʒ] universidad *f*
col·lide [kə'laɪd] *v/i* chocar, colisionar (***with*** con *or* contra)
col·li·sion [kə'lɪʒn] choque *m*, colisión *f*
col·lo·qui·al [kə'loʊkwɪəl] *adj* coloquial
Co·lom·bi·a [kə'lʌmbɪə] Colombia
Co·lom·bi·an [kə'lʌmbɪən] **1** *adj* colombiano **2** *n* colombiano(-a) *m(f)*
co·lon ['koʊlən] *punctuation*) dos puntos *mpl*; ANAT colon *m*
colo·nel ['kɜːrnl] coronel *m*
co·lo·ni·al [kə'loʊnɪəl] *adj* colonial
co·lo·nize ['kɑːlənaɪz] *v/t country* colonizar
co·lo·ny ['kɑːlənɪ] colonia *f*
col·or ['kʌlər] **1** *n* color *m*; ***in color*** *movie etc* en color; ***colors*** MIL bandera *f* **2** *v/t one's hair* teñir **3** *v/i* (*blush*) ruborizarse
'col·or-blind *adj* daltónico
col·ored ['kʌlərd] *adj person* de color
'col·or fast *adj* que no destiñe
col·or·ful ['kʌlərfəl] *adj* lleno de colores; *account* colorido
col·or·ing ['kʌlərɪŋ] color *m*
'col·or pho·to·graph fotografía *f* en color
'col·or scheme combinación *f* de colores
'col·or TV televisión *f* en color
co·los·sal [kə'lɑːsl] *adj* colosal
col·our *etc Br* → ***color*** *etc*
colt [koʊlt] potro *m*
Co·lum·bus [kə'lʌmbəs] Colón
col·umn ['kɑːləm] *architectural, of text* columna *f*
col·umn·ist ['kɑːləmɪst] columnista *m/f*
co·ma ['koʊmə] coma *m*; ***be in a coma*** estar en coma
comb [koʊm] **1** *n* peine *m* **2** *v/t hair, area* peinar; ***comb one's hair*** peinarse
com·bat ['kɑːmbæt] **1** *n* combate *m* **2** *v/t* combatir
com·bi·na·tion [kɑːmbɪ'neɪʃn] combinación *f*
com·bine [kəm'baɪn] **1** *v/t* combinar; *ingredients* mezclar **2** *v/i* combinarse
com·bine har·vest·er [kɑːmbaɪn'hɑːrvɪstər] cosechadora *f*
com·bus·ti·ble [kəm'bʌstɪbl] *adj* combustible
com·bus·tion [kəm'bʌstʃn] combustión *f*
come [kʌm] *v/i* (*pret* ***came***, *pp* ***come***) *toward speaker* venir; *toward listener* ir; *of train, bus* llegar, venir; ***don't come too close*** no te acerques demasiado; ***you'll come to like it*** llegará a gustarte; ***how come?*** F ¿y eso?; ***how come you've stopped going to the club?*** ¿cómo es que has dejado de ir al club?
◆ **come about** *v/i* (*happen*) pasar, suceder
◆ **come across 1** *v/t* (*find*) encontrar **2** *v/i*: ***his humor comes across as …*** su *humor* da la impresión de ser …; ***she comes across as …*** da la impresión de ser …
◆ **come along** *v/i* (*come too*) venir; (*turn up*) aparecer; (*progress*) marchar; ***why don't you come along?*** ¿por qué no te vienes con nosotros?
◆ **come apart** *v/i* desmontarse; (*break*) romperse
◆ **come around** *v/i to s.o.'s home* venir, pasarse; (*regain consciousness*) volver en sí
◆ **come away** *v/i* (*leave*) salir; *of button etc* caerse
◆ **come back** *v/i* volver; ***it came back to me*** lo recordé
◆ **come by 1** *v/i* pasarse **2** *v/t* (*acquire*) conseguir; ***how did you come by that bruise?*** ¿cómo te has dado ese golpe?
◆ **come down 1** *v/i* bajar; *of rain, snow* caer **2** *v/t*: ***he came down the stairs*** bajó las escaleras
◆ **come for** *v/t* (*attack*) atacar; (*collect thing*) venir a por; (*collect person*) venir a buscar a
◆ **come forward** *v/i* (*present o.s.*) presentarse
◆ **come from** *v/t* (*travel from*) venir de; (*originate from*) ser de
◆ **come in** *v/i* entrar; *of train* llegar; *of tide* subir; ***come in!*** ¡entre!, ¡adelante!
◆ **come in for** *v/t* recibir; ***come in for criticism*** recibir críticas
◆ **come in on** *v/t*: ***come in on a deal*** par-

ticipar en un negocio

◆ **come off** *v/i of handle etc* soltarse, caerse; *of paint etc* quitarse

◆ **come on** *v/i* (*progress*) marchar, progresar; ***come on!*** ¡vamos!; ***oh come on, you're exaggerating*** ¡vamos, hombre!, estás exagerando

◆ **come out** *v/i* salir; *of book* publicarse; *of stain* irse, quitarse; *of gay* declararse homosexual públicamente

◆ **come to 1** *v/t place* llegar a; *of hair, dress, water* llegar hasta; ***that comes to $70*** eso suma 70 dólares **2** *v/i* (*regain consciousness*) volver en sí

◆ **come up** *v/i* subir; *of sun* salir; ***something has come up*** ha surgido algo

◆ **come up with** *v/t solution* encontrar; ***John came up with a great idea*** a John se le ocurrió una idea estupenda

'come·back regreso *m*; ***make a comeback*** regresar

co·me·di·an [kə'miːdɪən] humorista *m/f*; *pej* payaso(-a) *m(f)*

'come·down gran decepción *f*

com·e·dy ['kɑːmədɪ] comedia *f*

com·et ['kɑːmɪt] cometa *m*

come·up·pance [kʌm'ʌpəns] *n* F: ***he'll get his comeuppance*** tendrá su merecido

com·fort ['kʌmfərt] **1** *n* comodidad *f*, confort *m*; (*consolation*) consuelo *m* **2** *v/t* consolar

com·for·ta·ble ['kʌmfərtəbl] *adj chair* cómodo; *house, room* cómodo, confortable; ***be comfortable*** *of person* estar cómodo; *financially* estar en una situación holgada

com·ic ['kɑːmɪk] **1** *n to read* cómic *m*; (*comedian*) cómico(-a) *m(f)* **2** *adj* cómico

com·i·cal ['kɑːmɪkl] *adj* cómico

'com·ic book cómic *m*

'com·ics ['kɑːmɪks] *npl* tiras *fpl* cómicas

'com·ic strip tira *f* cómica

com·ma ['kɑːmə] coma *f*

com·mand [kə'mænd] **1** *n* orden *f* **2** *v/t* ordenar, mandar

com·man·deer [kɑːmən'dɪr] *v/t* requisar

com·mand·er [kə'mændər] comandante *m/f*

com·mand·er-in-'chief comandante *m/f* en jefe

com·mand·ing of·fi·cer [kə'mændɪŋ] oficial *m/f* al mando

com·mand·ment [kə'mændmənt] mandamiento *m*: ***the Ten Commandments*** REL los Diez Mandamientos

com·mem·o·rate [kə'meməreɪt] *v/t* conmemorar

com·mem·o·ra·tion [kəmemə'reɪʃn]: ***in commemoration of*** en conmemoración de

com·mence [kə'mens] *v/t & v/i* comenzar

com·mend [kə'mend] *v/t* encomiar, elogiar

com·mend·able [kə'mendəbl] *adj* encomiable

com·men·da·tion [kəmen'deɪʃn] *for bravery* mención *f*

com·men·su·rate [kə'menʃərət] *adj*: ***commensurate with*** acorde con

com·ment ['kɑːment] **1** *n* comentario *m*; ***no comment!*** ¡sin comentarios! **2** *v/i* hacer comentarios (***on*** sobre)

com·men·ta·ry ['kɑːmənterɪ] comentarios *mpl*

com·men·tate ['kɑːmənteɪt] *v/i* hacer de comentarista

com·men·ta·tor ['kɑːmənteɪtər] comentarista *m/f*

com·merce ['kɑːmɜːrs] comercio *m*

com·mer·cial [kə'mɜːrʃl] **1** *adj* comercial **2** *n* (*advert*) anuncio *m* (publicitario)

com·mer·cial 'break pausa *f* publicitaria

com·mer·cial·ize [kə'mɜːrʃlaɪz] *v/t Christmas* comercializar

com·mer·cial 'trav·el·er viajante *m/f* de comercio

com·mis·e·rate [kə'mɪzəreɪt] *v/i*: ***she commiserated with me on my failure to get the job*** me dijo cuánto sentía que no hubiera conseguido el trabajo

com·mis·sion [kə'mɪʃn] **1** *n* (*payment, committee*) comisión *f*; (*job*) encargo *m* **2** *v/t*: ***she has been commissioned ...*** se le ha encargado ...

com·mit [kə'mɪt] *v/t* (*pret & pp* ***committed***) *crime* cometer; *money* comprometer; ***commit o.s.*** comprometerse

com·mit·ment [kə'mɪtmənt] compromiso *m* (***to*** con); ***he's afraid of commitment*** tiene miedo de comprometerse

com·mit·tee [kə'mɪtɪ] comité *m*

com·mod·i·ty [kə'mɑːdətɪ] *raw material* producto *m* básico; *product* bien *m* de consumo

com·mon ['kɑːmən] *adj* común; ***in common*** al igual (***with*** que); ***have sth in common with s.o.*** tener algo en común con alguien

com·mon·er ['kɑːmənər] plebeyo(-a) *m(f)*

com·mon 'law wife esposa *f* de hecho

com·mon·ly ['kɑːmənlɪ] *adv* comúnmente

Com·mon 'Mar·ket Mercado *m* Común

'com·mon·place *adj* común

Com·mons ['kɑːmənz] *npl*: ***the Commons*** *in Britain* la Cámara de los Co-

C

munes
com·mon 'sense sentido *m* común
com·mo·tion [kə'moʊʃn] alboroto *m*
com·mu·nal [kə'mju:nl] *adj* comunal
com·mu·nal·ly [kəm'ju:nəlɪ] *adv* en comunidad
com·mu·ni·cate [kə'mju:nɪkeɪt] **1** *v/i* comunicarse **2** *v/t* comunicar
com·mu·ni·ca·tion [kəmju:nɪ'keɪʃn] comunicación *f*
com·mu·ni'ca·tions *npl* comunicaciones *fpl*
com·mu·ni'ca·tions sat·el·lite satélite *m* de telecomunicaciones
com·mu·ni·ca·tive [kə'mju:nɪkətɪv] *adj person* comunicativo
Com·mu·nion [kə'mju:njən] REL comunión *f*
com·mu·ni·qué [kə'mju:nɪkeɪ] comunicado *m*
Com·mu·nism ['kɑ:mjʊnɪzəm] comunismo *m*
Com·mu·nist ['kɑ:mjʊnɪst] **1** *adj* comunista **2** *n* comunista *m/f*
com·mu·ni·ty [kə'mju:nətɪ] comunidad *f*
com'mu·ni·ty cen·ter centro *m* comunitario
com'mu·ni·ty serv·ice servicios *mpl* a la comunidad (como pena)
com·mute [kə'mju:t] **1** *v/i* viajar al trabajo; ***commute to work*** viajar al trabajo **2** *v/t* LAW conmutar
com·mut·er [kə'mju:tər] *persona que viaja al trabajo*
com'mut·er traf·fic *tráfico generado por los que se desplazan al trabajo*
com'mut·er train *tren de cercanías que utilizan los que se desplazan al trabajo*
com·pact **1** *adj* [kəm'pækt] compacto **2** *n* ['kɑ:mpækt] MOT utilitario *m*
com·pact 'disc (disco *m*) compacto *m*
com·pan·ion [kəm'pænjən] compañero(-a) *m(f)*
com·pan·ion·ship [kəm'pænjənʃɪp] compañía *f*
com·pa·ny ['kʌmpənɪ] COM empresa *f*, compañía *f*; (*companionship*, *guests*) compañía *f*; ***keep s.o. company*** hacer compañía a alguien
com·pa·ny 'car coche *m* de empresa
com·pa·ny 'law derecho *m* de sociedades
com·pa·ra·ble ['kɑ:mpərəbl] *adj* comparable
com·par·a·tive [kəm'pærətɪv] **1** *adj* (*relative*) relativo; *study* comparado; GRAM comparativo; ***comparative form*** GRAM comparativo *m* **2** *n* GRAM comparativo *m*
com·par·a·tive·ly [kəm'pærətɪvlɪ] *adv* relativamente
com·pare [kəm'per] **1** *v/t* comparar; ***compared with …*** comparado con …; ***you can't compare them*** no se pueden comparar **2** *v/i* compararse
com·pa·ri·son [kəm'pærɪsn] comparación *f*; ***there's no comparison*** no hay punto de comparación
com·part·ment [kəm'pɑ:rtmənt] compartimento *m*
com·pass ['kʌmpəs] brújula *f*; (***a pair of***) ***compasses*** GEOM un compás
com·pas·sion [kəm'pæʃn] compasión *f*
com·pas·sion·ate [kəm'pæʃənət] *adj* compasivo
com·pas·sion·ate 'leave *permiso laboral por muerte o enfermedad grave de un familiar*
com·pat·i·bil·i·ty [kəmpætə'bɪlɪtɪ] compatibilidad *f*
com·pat·i·ble [kəm'pætəbl] *adj* compatible; ***we're not compatible*** no somos compatibles
com·pel [kəm'pel] *v/t* (*pret & pp* ***compelled***) obligar
com·pel·ling [kəm'pelɪŋ] *adj argument* poderoso; *movie*, *book* fascinante
com·pen·sate ['kɑ:mpənseɪt] **1** *v/t with money* compensar **2** *v/i* ***compensate for*** compensar
com·pen·sa·tion [kɑ:mpən'seɪʃn] (*money*) indemnización *f*; (*reward*, *comfort*) compensación *f*
com·pete [kəm'pi:t] *v/i* competir (***for*** por)
com·pe·tence ['kɑ:mpɪtəns] competencia *f*
com·pe·tent ['kɑ:mpɪtənt] *adj* competente; ***I'm not competent to judge*** no estoy capacitado para juzgar
com·pe·tent·ly ['kɑ:mpɪtəntlɪ] *adv* competentemente
com·pe·ti·tion [kɑ:mpə'tɪʃn] (*contest*) concurso *f*; SP competición *f*; (*competitors*) competencia *f*; ***the government wants to encourage competition*** el gobierno quiere fomentar la competencia
com·pet·i·tive [kəm'petətɪv] *adj* competitivo
com·pet·i·tive·ly [kəm'petətɪvlɪ] *adv* competitivamente: ***competitively priced*** con un precio muy competitivo
com·pet·i·tive·ness [kəm'petɪtɪvnɪs] COM competitividad *f*; *of person* espíritu *m* competitivo
com·pet·i·tor [kəm'petɪtər] *in contest* concursante *m/f*; SP competidor(a) *m(f)*, contrincante *m/f*; COM competidor(a) *m(f)*
com·pile [kəm'paɪl] *v/t* compilar

com·pla·cen·cy [kəm'pleɪsənsɪ] complacencia *f*
com·pla·cent [kəm'pleɪsənt] *adj* complaciente
com·plain [kəm'pleɪn] *v/i* quejarse, protestar; *to shop, manager* quejarse; ***complain of*** MED estar aquejado de
com·plaint [kəm'pleɪnt] queja *f*, protesta *f*; MED dolencia *f*
com·ple·ment ['kɑːmplɪmənt] *v/t* complementar; ***they complement each other*** se complementan
com·ple·men·ta·ry [kɑːmplɪ'mentərɪ] *adj* complementario; ***the two are complementary*** los dos se complementan
com·plete [kəm'pliːt] **1** *adj* (*total*) absoluto, total; (*full*) completo; (*finished*) finalizado, terminado; ***I made a complete fool of myself*** quedé como un verdadero tonto **2** *v/t task, building etc* finalizar, terminar; *course* completar; *form* rellenar
com·plete·ly [kəm'pliːtlɪ] *adv* completamente
com·ple·tion [kəm'pliːʃn] finalización *f*, terminación *f*
com·plex ['kɑːmpleks] **1** *adj* complejo **2** *n also* PSYCH complejo *m*
com·plex·ion [kəm'plekʃn] *facial* tez *f*
com·plex·i·ty [kəm'pleksɪtɪ] complejidad *f*
com·pli·ance [kəm'plaɪəns] cumplimiento (***with*** de)
com·pli·cate ['kɑːmplɪkeɪt] *v/t* complicar
com·pli·cat·ed ['kɑːmplɪkeɪtɪd] *adj* complicado
com·pli·ca·tion [kɑːmplɪ'keɪʃn] complicación *f*; ***complications*** MED complicaciones *fpl*
com·pli·ment ['kɑːmplɪmənt] **1** *n* cumplido *m* **2** *v/t* hacer un cumplido a (***on*** por)
com·pli·men·ta·ry [kɑːmplɪ'mentərɪ] *adj* elogioso; (*free*) de regalo, gratis
'com·pli·ments slip nota *f* de cortesia
com·ply [kəm'plaɪ] *v/i* (*pret & pp* ***complied***) cumplir; ***comply with*** cumplir
com·po·nent [kəm'poʊnənt] pieza *f*, componente *m*
com·pose [kəm'poʊz] *v/t also* MUS componer; ***be composed of*** estar compuesto de; ***compose o.s.*** serenarse
com·posed [kəm'poʊzd] *adj* (*calm*) sereno
com·pos·er [kəm'poʊzər] MUS compositor(a) *m*(*f*)
com·po·si·tion [kɑːmpə'zɪʃn] *also* MUS composición *f*; (*essay*) redacción *f*
com·po·sure [kəm'poʊʒər] compostura *f*
com·pound ['kɑːmpaʊnd] *n* CHEM compuesto *m*
com·pound 'in·ter·est interés *m* compuesto *or* combinado
com·pre·hend [kɑːmprɪ'hend] *v/t* (*understand*) comprender
com·pre·hen·sion [kɑːmprɪ'henʃn] comprensión *f*
com·pre·hen·sive [kɑːmprɪ'hensɪv] *adj* detallado
com·pre·hen·sive in'sur·ance seguro *m* a todo riesgo
com·pre·hen·sive·ly [kɑːmprɪ'hensɪvlɪ] *adv* detalladamente
com·press **1** *n* ['kɑːmpres] MED compresa *f* **2** *v/t* [kəm'pres] *air, gas* comprimir; *information* condensar
com·prise [kəm'praɪz] *v/t* comprender; ***be comprised of*** constar de
com·pro·mise ['kɑːmprəmaɪz] **1** *n* solución *f* negociada; ***I've had to make compromises all my life*** toda mi vida he tenido que hacer concesiones **2** *v/i* transigir, efectuar concesiones **3** *v/t principles* traicionar; (*jeopardize*) poner en peligro; ***compromise o.s.*** ponerse en un compromiso
com·pul·sion [kəm'pʌlʃn] PSYCH compulsión *f*
com·pul·sive [kəm'pʌlsɪv] *adj behavior* compulsivo; *reading* absorbente
com·pul·so·ry [kəm'pʌlsərɪ] *adj* obligatorio
com·put·er [kəm'pjuːtər] *Span* ordenador *m*, *L.Am.* computadora *f*; ***have sth on computer*** tener algo en el *Span* ordenador *or L.Am.* computadora
com·put·er-aid·ed de'sign [kəmpjuːtər'eɪdɪd] diseño *m* asistido por *Span* ordenador *or L.Am.* computadora
com·put·er-aid·ed man·u'fac·ture fabricación *f* asistida por *Span* ordenador *or L.Am.* computadora
com·put·er-con'trolled *adj* controlado por *Span* ordenador *or L.Am.* computadora
com'puter game juego *m* de *Span* ordenador *or L.Am.* computadora
com·put·er·ize [kəm'pjuːtəraɪz] *v/t* informatizar, *L.Am.* computarizar
com·put·er 'lit·er·ate *adj* con conocimientos de informática *or L.Am.* computación
com·put·er 'sci·ence informática *f*, *L.Am.* computación *f*
com·put·er 'sci·en·tist informático(-a) *m*(*f*)
com·put·ing [kəm'pjuːtɪŋ] *n* informática *f*, *L.Am.* computación *f*
com·rade ['kɑːmreɪd] (*friend*) compañero(-a) *m*(*f*); POL camarada *m/f*

C

com·rade·ship ['kɑːmreɪdʃɪp] camaradería *f*
con [kɑːn] **1** *n* F timo *m* F **2** *v/t* (*pret & pp* ***conned***) F timar F
con·ceal [kən'siːl] *v/t* ocultar
con·ceal·ment [kən'siːlmənt] ocultación *f*
con·cede [kən'siːd] *v/t* (*admit*) admitir, reconocer; *goal* encajar
con·ceit [kən'siːt] engreimiento *m*, presunción *f*
con·ceit·ed [kən'siːtɪd] *adj* engreido, presuntuoso
con·cei·va·ble [kən'siːvəbl] *adj* concebible
con·ceive [kən'siːv] *v/i of woman* concebir; ***conceive of*** (*imagine*) imaginar; ***I can't conceive of that happening*** no puedo imaginar que eso vaya a pasar
con·cen·trate ['kɑːnsəntreɪt] **1** *v/i* concentrarse **2** *v/t one's attention, energies* concentrar
con·cen·trat·ed ['kɑːnsəntreɪtɪd] *adj juice etc* concentrado
con·cen·tra·tion [kɑːnsən'treɪʃn] concentración *f*
con·cept ['kɑːnsept] concepto *m*
con·cep·tion [kən'sepʃn] *of child* concepción *f*
con·cern [kən'sɜːrn] **1** *n* (*anxiety, care*) preocupación *f*; (*business*) asunto *m*; (*company*) empresa *f*; ***it's none of your concern*** no es asunto tuyo; ***cause concern*** preocupar, inquietar **2** *v/t* (*involve*) concernir, incumbir; (*worry*) preocupar, inquietar; ***concern o.s. with*** preocuparse de
con·cerned [kən'sɜːrnd] *adj* (*anxious*) preocupado, inquieto (***about*** por); (*caring*) preocupado (***about*** por); (*involved*) en cuestión; ***as far as I'm concerned*** por lo que a mí respecta
con·cern·ing [kən'sɜːrnɪŋ] *prep* en relación con, sobre
con·cert ['kɑːnsərt] concierto *m*
con·cert·ed [kən'sɜːrtɪd] *adj* (*joint*) concertado, conjunto
'con·cert·mas·ter primer violín *m/f*
con·cer·to [kən'ʧertoʊ] concierto *m*
con·ces·sion [kən'seʃn] (*compromise*) concesión *f*
con·cil·i·a·to·ry [kənsɪlɪ'eɪtərɪ] *adj* conciliador
con·cise [kən'saɪs] *adj* conciso
con·clude [kən'kluːd] *v/t & v/i* (*deduce, end*) concluir (***from*** de)
con·clu·sion [kən'kluːʒn] (*deduction*) conclusión *f*; (*end*) conclusión *f*; ***in conclusion*** en conclusión
con·clu·sive [kən'kluːsɪv] *adj* concluyente
con·coct [kən'kɑːkt] *v/t meal, drink* preparar; *excuse, story* urdir
con·coc·tion [kən'kɑːkʃn] *food* mejunje *m*; *drink* brebaje *m*, pócima *f*
con·crete ['kɑːŋkriːt] **1** *adj* concreto; ***concrete jungle*** jungla *f* de asfalto **2** *n* hormigón *m*, *L.Am.* concreto *m*
con·cur [kən'kɜːr] *v/i* (*pret & pp* ***concurred***) coincidir
con·cus·sion [kən'kʌʃn] conmoción *f* cerebral
con·demn [kən'dem] *v/t* condenar; *building* declarar en ruina; ***condemn s.o. to a life of poverty*** condenar a alguien a vivir en la miseria
con·dem·na·tion [kɑːndəm'neɪʃn] *of action* condena *f*
con·den·sa·tion [kɑːnden'seɪʃn] *on walls, windows* condensación *f*
con·dense [kən'dens] **1** *v/t* (*make shorter*) condensar **2** *v/i of steam* condensarse
con·densed 'milk [kən'densd] leche *f* condensada
con·de·scend [kɑːndɪ'send] *v/i*: ***he condescended to speak to me*** se dignó a hablarme
con·de·scend·ing [kɑːndɪ'sendɪŋ] *adj* (*patronizing*) condescendiente
con·di·tion [kən'dɪʃn] **1** *n* (*state*) condiciones *fpl*; *of health* estado *m*; *illness* enfermedad *f*; (*requirement, term*) condición *f*; ***conditions*** (*circumstances*) condiciones *fpl*; ***on condition that …*** a condición de que …; ***you're in no condition to drive*** no estás en condiciones de conducir **2** *v/t* PSYCH condicionar
con·di·tion·al [kən'dɪʃnl] **1** *adj acceptance* condicional **2** *n* GRAM condicional *m*
con·di·tion·er [kən'dɪʃnər] *for hair* suavizante *m*, acondicionador *m*; *for fabric* suavizante *m*
con·di·tion·ing [kən'dɪʃnɪŋ] PSYCH condicionamiento *m*
con·do ['kɑːndoʊ] F *apartment* apartamento *m*, *Span* piso *m*; *building* bloque de apartamentos
con·do·lences [kən'doʊlənsɪz] *npl* condolencias *fpl*
con·dom ['kɑːndəm] condón *m*, preservativo *m*
con·do·min·i·um [kɑːndə'mɪnɪəm] → ***condo***
con·done [kən'doʊn] *v/t actions* justificar
con·du·cive [kən'duːsɪv] *adj*: ***conducive to*** propicio para
con·duct **1** *n* ['kɑːndʌkt] (*behavior*) conducta *f* **2** *v/t* [kən'dʌkt] (*carry out*) real-

izar, hacer; ELEC conducir; MUS dirigir; ***conduct o.s.*** comportarse

con·duct·ed 'tour [kən'dʌktɪd] visita *f* guiada

con·duc·tor [kən'dʌktər] MUS director(a) *m(f)* de orquesta; *on train* revisor(-a) *m(f)*; PHYS conductor *m*

cone [koʊn] GEOM, *on highway* cono *m*; *for ice cream* cucurucho *m*; *of pine tree* piña *f*

con·fec·tion·er [kən'fekʃənər] pastelero(-a) *m(f)*

con·fec·tion·ers' sug·ar azúcar *m or f* glas

con·fec·tion·e·ry [kən'fekʃənərɪ] (*candy*) dulces *mpl*

con·fed·e·ra·tion [kənfedə'reɪʃn] confederación *f*

con·fer [kən'fɜːr] **1** *v/t* (*pret & pp* ***conferred***): ***confer sth on s.o.*** (*bestow*) conferir *or* otorgar algo a alguien **2** *v/i* (*pret & pp* ***conferred***) (*discuss*) deliberar

con·fe·rence ['kɑːnfərəns] congreso *m*; *discussion* conferencia *f*

'con·fe·rence room sala *f* de conferencias

con·fess [kən'fes] **1** *v/t* confesar; ***I confess I don't know*** confieso que no lo sé **2** *v/i* confesar; REL confesarse; ***confess to a weakness for sth*** confesar una debilidad por algo

con·fes·sion [kən'feʃn] confesión *f*; ***I've a confession to make*** tengo algo que confesar

con·fes·sion·al [kən'feʃnl] REL confesionario *m*

con·fes·sor [kən'fesər] REL confesor *m*

con·fide [kən'faɪd] **1** *v/t* confiar **2** *v/i*: ***confide in s.o.*** confiarse a alguien

con·fi·dence ['kɑːnfɪdəns] confianza *f*; (*secret*) confidencia *f*; ***in confidence*** en confianza, confidencialmente

con·fi·dent ['kɑːnfɪdənt] *adj* (*self-assured*) seguro de sí mismo; (*convinced*) seguro

con·fi·den·tial [kɑːnfɪ'denʃl] *adj* confidencial, secreto

con·fi·den·tial·ly [kɑːnfɪ'denʃlɪ] *adv* confidencialmente

con·fi·dent·ly ['kɑːnfɪdəntlɪ] *adv* con seguridad

con·fine [kən'faɪn] *v/t* (*imprison*) confinar, recluir; (*restrict*) limitar; ***be confined to one's bed*** tener que guardar cama

con·fined [kən'faɪnd] *adj space* limitado

con·fine·ment [kən'faɪnmənt] (*imprisonment*) reclusión *f*; MED parto *m*

con·firm [kən'fɜːrm] *v/t* confirmar

con·fir·ma·tion [kɑːnfər'meɪʃn] confirmación *f*

con·firmed [kɑːn'fɜːrmd] *adj* (*inveterate*) empedernido; ***I'm a confirmed believer in ...*** creo firmemente en ...

con·fis·cate ['kɑːnfɪskeɪt] *v/t* confiscar

con·flict 1 *n* ['kɑːnflɪkt] conflicto *m* **2** *v/i* [kən'flɪkt] (*clash*) chocar; ***conflicting loyalties*** lealtades *fpl* encontradas

con·form [kən'fɔːrm] *v/i* ser conformista; ***conform to*** *to standards etc* ajustarse a

con·form·ist [kən'fɔːrmɪst] *n* conformista *m/f*

con·front [kən'frʌnt] *v/t* (*face*) hacer frente a, enfrentarse; (*tackle*) hacer frente a

con·fron·ta·tion [kɑːnfrən'teɪʃn] confrontación *f*, enfrentamiento *m*

con·fuse [kən'fjuːz] *v/t* confundir; ***confuse s.o. with s.o.*** confundir a alguien con alguien

con·fused [kən'fjuːzd] *adj person* confundido; *situation, piece of writing* confuso

con·fus·ing [kən'fjuːzɪŋ] *adj* confuso

con·fu·sion [kən'fjuːʒn] (*muddle, chaos*) confusión *f*

con·geal [kən'dʒiːl] *v/i of blood* coagularse; *of fat* solidificarse

con·gen·ial [kən'dʒiːnɪəl] *adj person* simpático, agradable; *occasion, place* agradable

con·gen·i·tal [kən'dʒenɪtl] *adj* MED congénito

con·gest·ed [kən'dʒestɪd] *adj roads* congestionado

con·ges·tion [kən'dʒestʃn] *also* MED congestión *f*; ***traffic congestion*** congestión *f* circulatoria

con·grat·u·late [kən'grætʃʊleɪt] *v/t* felicitar

con·grat·u·la·tions [kəngrætʃʊ'leɪʃnz] *npl* felicitaciones *fpl*; ***congratulations on ...*** felicidades por ...; ***let me offer my congratulations*** permita que le dé la enhorabuena

con·grat·u·la·to·ry [kəngrætʃʊ'leɪtərɪ] *adj* de felicitación

con·gre·gate ['kɑːŋgrɪgeɪt] *v/i* (*gather*) congregarse

con·gre·ga·tion [kɑːŋgrɪ'geɪʃn] REL congregación *f*

con·gress ['kɑːŋgres] (*conference*) congreso *m*; ***Congress*** *in US* Congreso *m*

Con·gres·sion·al [kən'greʃnl] *adj* del Congreso

Con·gress·man ['kɑːŋgresmən] congresista *m*

Con·gress·wo·man ['kɑːŋgreswʊmən] congresista *f*

C

co·ni·fer ['kɑːnɪfər] conífera *f*
con·jec·ture [kən'dʒektʃər] *n* (*speculation*) conjetura *f*
con·ju·gate ['kɑːndʒʊgeɪt] *v/t* GRAM conjugar
con·junc·tion [kən'dʒʌŋkʃn] GRAM conjunción *f*; ***in conjunction with*** junto con
con·junc·ti·vi·tis [kəndʒʌŋktɪ'vaɪtɪs] conjuntivitis *f*
◆ **con·jure up** ['kʌndʒər] *v/t* (*produce*) hacer aparecer; (*evoke*) evocar
con·jur·er, **con·jur·or** ['kʌndʒərər] (*magician*) prestidigitador(a) *m*(*f*)
con·jur·ing tricks ['kʌndʒərɪŋ] *npl* juegos *mpl* de manos
con man ['kɑːnmæn] F timador *m* F
con·nect [kə'nekt] *v/t* conectar; (*link*) relacionar, vincular; *to power supply* enchufar
con·nect·ed [kə'nektɪd] *adj*: ***be well-connected*** estar bien relacionado; ***be connected with*** estar relacionado con
con·nect·ing flight [kə'nektɪŋ] vuelo *m* de conexión
con·nec·tion [kə'nekʃn] conexión *f*; *when traveling* conexión *f*, enlace; (*personal contact*) contacto *m*; ***in connection with*** en relación con
con·nois·seur [kɑːnə'sɜːr] entendido(-a) *m*(*f*)
con·quer ['kɑːŋkər] *v/t* conquistar; *fig*: *fear etc* vencer
con·quer·or ['kɑːŋkərər] conquistador(a) *m*(*f*)
con·quest ['kɑːŋkwest] *of territory* conquista *f*
con·science ['kɑːnʃəns] conciencia *f*; ***a guilty conscience*** un sentimiento de culpa; ***it was on my conscience*** me remordía la conciencia
con·sci·en·tious [kɑːnʃɪ'enʃəs] *adj* concienzudo
con·sci·en·tious·ness [kɑːnʃɪ'enʃəsnəs] aplicación *f*
con·sci·en·tious ob'ject·or objetor(a) *m*(*f*) de conciencia
con·scious ['kɑːnʃəs] *adj* consciente; ***be conscious of*** ser consciente de
con·scious·ly ['kɑːnʃəslɪ] *adv* conscientemente
con·scious·ness ['kɑːnʃəsnɪs] (*awareness*) conciencia *f*; MED con(s)ciencia *f*; ***lose / regain consciousness*** quedar inconsciente / volver en sí
con·sec·u·tive [kən'sekjʊtɪv] *adj* consecutivo
con·sen·sus [kən'sensəs] consenso *m*
con·sent [kən'sent] **1** *n* consentimiento *m* **2** *v/i* consentir (***to*** en)
con·se·quence ['kɑːnsɪkwəns] (*result*) consecuencia *f*; ***as a consequence of*** como consecuencia de
con·se·quent·ly ['kɑːnsɪkwəntlɪ] *adv* (*therefore*) por consiguiente
con·ser·va·tion [kɑːnsər'veɪʃn] (*preservation*) conservación *f*, protección *f*
con·ser·va·tion·ist [kɑːnsər'veɪʃnɪst] ecologista *m*/*f*
con·ser·va·tive [kən'sɜːrvətɪv] **1** *adj* (*conventional*) conservador; *estimate* prudente **2** *n Br* POL ***Conservative*** Conservador(a) *m*(*f*)
con·ser·va·to·ry [kən'sɜːrvətɔːrɪ] MUS conservatorio *m*
con·serve **1** *n* ['kɑːnsɜːrv] (*jam*) compota *f* **2** *v/t* [kən'sɜːrv] conservar
con·sid·er [kən'sɪdər] *v/t* (*regard*) considerar; (*show regard for*) mostrar consideración por; (*think about*) considerar; ***it is considered to be …*** se considera que es …
con·sid·e·ra·ble [kən'sɪdrəbl] *adj* considerable
con·sid·e·ra·bly [kən'sɪdrəblɪ] *adv* considerablemente
con·sid·er·ate [kən'sɪdərət] *adj* considerado
con·sid·er·ate·ly [kən'sɪdərətlɪ] *adv* con consideración
con·sid·e·ra·tion [kənsɪdə'reɪʃn] (*thoughtfulness, concern*) consideración *f*; (*factor*) factor *m*; ***take sth into consideration*** tomar algo en consideración; ***after much consideration*** tras muchas deliberaciones; ***your proposal is under consideration*** su propuesta está siendo estudiada
con·sign·ment [kən'saɪnmənt] COM envío *m*
◆ **con·sist of** [kən'sɪst] *v/t* consistir en
con·sis·ten·cy [kən'sɪstənsɪ] (*texture*) consistencia *f*; (*unchangingness*) coherencia *f*, consecuencia *f*; *of player* regularidad *f*, constancia *f*
con·sis·tent [kən'sɪstənt] *adj person* coherente, consecuente; *improvement, change* constante
con·sis·tent·ly [kən'sɪstəntlɪ] *adv perform* con regularidad *or* constancia; *improve* continuamente; ***he's consistently late*** llega tarde sistemáticamente
con·so·la·tion [kɑːnsə'leɪʃn] consuelo *m*; ***if it's any consolation*** si te sirve de consuelo
con·sole [kən'soʊl] *v/t* consolar
con·sol·i·date [kən'sɑːlɪdeɪt] *v/t* consolidar
con·so·nant ['kɑːnsənənt] *n* GRAM conso-

nante *f*

con·sor·ti·um [kən'sɔːrtɪəm] consorcio *m*

con·spic·u·ous [kən'spɪkjʊəs] *adj* llamativo; ***he felt very conspicuous*** sentía que estaba llamando la atención

con·spi·ra·cy [kən'spɪrəsɪ] conspiración *f*

con·spi·ra·tor [kən'spɪrətər] conspirador(a) *m(f)*

con·spire [kən'spaɪr] *v/i* conspirar

con·stant ['kɑːnstənt] *adj* (*continuous*) constante

con·stant·ly ['kɑːnstəntlɪ] *adv* constantemente

con·ster·na·tion [kɑːnstər'neɪʃn] consternación *f*

con·sti·pat·ed ['kɑːnstɪpeɪtɪd] *adj* estreñido

con·sti·pa·tion [kɑːnstɪ'peɪʃn] estreñimiento *m*

con·sti·tu·ent [kən'stɪtjʊənt] *n* (*component*) elemento *m* constitutivo, componente *m*

con·sti·tute ['kɑːnstɪtuːt] *v/t* constituir

con·sti·tu·tion [kɑːnstɪ'tuːʃn] constitución *f*

con·sti·tu·tion·al [kɑːnstɪ'tuːʃənl] *adj* POL constitucional

con·straint [kən'streɪnt] (*restriction*) restricción *f*, limite *m*

con·struct [kən'strʌkt] *v/t building etc* construir

con·struc·tion [kən'strʌkʃn] construcción *f*; ***under construction*** en construcción

con'struc·tion in·dus·try sector *m* de la construcción

con'struc·tion site obra *f*

con'struc·tion work·er obrero(-a) *m(f)* de la construcción

con·struc·tive [kən'strʌktɪv] *adj* constructivo

con·sul ['kɑːnsl] cónsul *m/f*

con·su·late ['kɑːnsʊlət] consulado *m*

con·sult [kən'sʌlt] *v/t* (*seek the advice of*) consultar

con·sul·tan·cy [kən'sʌltənsɪ] *company* consultoría *f*, asesoría *f*; (*advice*) asesoramiento *m*

con·sul·tant [kən'sʌltənt] *n* (*adviser*) asesor(a) *m(f)*, consultor(a) *m(f)*

con·sul·ta·tion [kɑːnsl'teɪʃn] consulta *f*; ***have a consultation with*** consultar con

con·sume [kən'suːm] *v/t* consumir

con·sum·er [kən'suːmər] (*purchaser*) consumidor(a) *m(f)*

con·sum·er 'con·fi·dence confianza *f* de los consumidores

con'sum·er goods *npl* bienes *mpl* de consumo

con'sum·er so·ci·e·ty sociedad *f* de consumo

con·sump·tion [kən'sʌmpʃn] consumo *m*

con·tact ['kɑːntækt] **1** *n* contacto; ***keep in contact with s.o.*** mantenerse en contacto con alguien; ***come into contact with s.o.*** entrar en contacto con alguien **2** *v/t* contactar con, ponerse en contacto con

'con·tact lens lentes *fpl* de contacto, *Span* lentillas *fpl*

'con·tact num·ber número *m* de contacto

con·ta·gious [kən'teɪdʒəs] *adj also fig* contagioso

con·tain [kən'teɪn] *v/t* (*hold, hold back*) contener; ***contain o.s.*** contenerse

con·tain·er [kən'teɪnər] (*recipient*) recipiente *m*; COM contenedor *m*

con'tain·er ship buque *m* de transporte de contenedores

con·tam·i·nate [kən'tæmɪneɪt] *v/t* contaminar

con·tam·i·na·tion [kəntæmɪ'neɪʃn] contaminación *f*

con·tem·plate ['kɑːntəmpleɪt] *v/t* contemplar

con·tem·po·ra·ry [kən'tempərerɪ] **1** *adj* contemporáneo **2** *n* contemporáneo(-a) *m(f)*

con·tempt [kən'tempt] desprecio *m*, desdén *m*; ***be beneath contempt*** ser despreciable

con·temp·ti·ble [kən'temptəbl] *adj* despreciable

con·temp·tu·ous [kən'temptʃʊəs] *adj* despectivo

con·tend [kən'tend] *v/i*: ***contend for ...*** competir por ...; ***contend with*** enfrentarse a

con·tend·er [kən'tendər] SP, POL contendiente *m/f*; *against champion* aspirante *m/f*

con·tent[1] ['kɑːntent] *n* contenido *m*

con·tent[2] [kən'tent] **1** *adj* satisfecho; ***I'm quite content to sit here*** me contento con sentarme aquí **2** *v/t*: ***content o.s. with*** contentarse con

con·tent·ed [kən'tentɪd] *adj* satisfecho

con·ten·tion [kən'tenʃn] (*assertion*) argumento *m*; ***be in contention for*** tener posibilidades de ganar

con·ten·tious [kən'tenʃəs] *adj* polémico

con·tent·ment [kən'tentmənt] satisfacción *f*

con·tents ['kɑːntents] *npl of house, letter, bag etc* contenido *m*; *list: in book* tabla *f* de contenidos

con·test[1] ['kɑːntest] *n* (*competition*) concurso *m*; (*struggle, for power*) lucha *f*

con·test² [kən'test] *v/t leadership etc* presentarse como candidato a; *decision, will* impugnar

con·tes·tant [kən'testənt] concursante *m/f*; *in competition* competidor(a) *m(f)*

con·text ['kɑːntekst] contexto *m*; ***look at sth in context / out of context*** examinar algo en contexto / fuera de contexto

con·ti·nent ['kɑːntɪnənt] *n* continente *m*

con·ti·nen·tal [kɑːntɪ'nentl] *adj* continental

con·tin·gen·cy [kən'tɪndʒənsɪ] contingencia *f*, eventualidad *f*

con·tin·u·al [kən'tɪnjʊəl] *adj* continuo

con·tin·u·al·ly [kən'tɪnjʊəlɪ] *adv* continuamente

con·tin·u·a·tion [kəntɪnjʊ'eɪʃn] continuación *f*

con·tin·ue [kən'tɪnjuː] **1** *v/t* continuar; ***to be continued*** continuará; ***he continued to drink*** continuó bebiendo **2** *v/i* continuar

con·ti·nu·i·ty [kɑːntɪ'njuːətɪ] continuidad *f*

con·tin·u·ous [kən'tɪnjʊəs] *adj* continuo

con·tin·u·ous·ly [kən'tɪnjʊəslɪ] *adv* continuamente, ininterrumpidamente

con·tort [kən'tɔːrt] *v/t face* contraer; *body* contorsionar

con·tour ['kɑːntʊr] contorno *m*

con·tra·cep·tion [kɑːntrə'sepʃn] anticoncepción *f*

con·tra·cep·tive [kɑːntrə'septɪv] *n (device, pill)* anticonceptivo *m*

con·tract¹ ['kɑːntrækt] *n* contrato *m*

con·tract² [kən'trækt] **1** *v/i (shrink)* contraerse **2** *v/t illness* contraer

con·trac·tor [kən'træktər] contratista *m/f*; ***building contractor*** constructora *f*

con·trac·tu·al [kən'træktʊəl] *adj* contractual

con·tra·dict [kɑːntrə'dɪkt] *v/t statement* desmentir; *person* contradecir

con·tra·dic·tion [kɑːntrə'dɪkʃn] contradicción *f*

con·tra·dic·to·ry [kɑːntrə'dɪktərɪ] *adj account* contradictorio

con·trap·tion [kən'træpʃn] F artilugio *m* F

con·trar·y¹ ['kɑːntrərɪ] **1** *adj* contrario; ***contrary to*** al contrario de **2** *n*: ***on the contrary*** al contrario

con·tra·ry² [kən'trerɪ] *adj (perverse)* difícil

con·trast 1 *n* ['kɑːntræst] contraste *m*; ***by contrast*** por contraste **2** *v/t & v/i* [kən'træst] contrastar

con·trast·ing [kən'træstɪŋ] *adj* opuesto

con·tra·vene [kɑːntrə'viːn] *v/t* contravenir

con·trib·ute [kən'trɪbjuːt] **1** *v/i* contribuir (***to*** a) **2** *v/t money, time, suggestion* contribuir con, aportar

con·tri·bu·tion [kɑːntrɪ'bjuːʃn] *money* contribución *f*; *to political party, church* donación *f*; *of time, effort, to debate* contribución *f*, aportación *f*; *to magazine* colaboración *f*

con·trib·u·tor [kən'trɪbjʊtər] *of money* donante *m/f*; *to magazine* colaborador(a) *m(f)*

con·trol [kən'troʊl] **1** *n* control *m*; ***take / lose control of*** tomar / perder el control de; ***lose control of o.s.*** perder el control; ***circumstances beyond our control*** circunstancias ajenas a nuestra voluntad; ***be in control of*** controlar; ***we're in control of the situation*** tenemos la situación controlada *or* bajo control; ***get out of control*** descontrolarse; ***under control*** bajo control; ***controls*** *of aircraft, vehicle* controles *mpl*; *(restrictions)* controles *mpl* **2** *v/t (pret & pp* ***controlled****) (govern)* controlar, dominar; *(restrict, regulate)* controlar; ***control o.s.*** controlarse

con'trol cen·ter, *Br* **con'trol centre** centro *m* de control

con'trol freak F *persona obsesionada con controlar todo*

con·trolled 'sub·stance [kən'troʊld] estupefaciente *m*

con·trol·ling 'in·ter·est [kən'troʊlɪŋ] FIN participación *f* mayoritaria, interés *m* mayoritario

con'trol pan·el panel *m* de control

con'trol tow·er torre *f* de control

con·tro·ver·sial [kɑːntrə'vɜːrʃl] *adj* polémico, controvertido

con·tro·ver·sy ['kɑːntrəvɜːrsɪ] polémica *f*, controversia *f*

con·va·lesce [kɑːnvə'les] *v/i* convalecer

con·va·les·cence [kɑːnvə'lesns] convalecencia *f*

con·vene [kən'viːn] *v/t* convocar

con·ve·ni·ence [kən'viːnɪəns] conveniencia *f*; ***at your / my convenience*** a su / mi conveniencia; ***all (modern) conveniences*** todas las comodidades

con've·ni·ence food comida *f* preparada

con've·ni·ence store tienda *f* de barrio

con·ve·ni·ent [kən'viːnɪənt] *adj location, device* conveniente; *time, arrangement* oportuno; ***it's very convenient living so near the office*** vivir cerca de la oficina es muy cómodo; ***the apartment is convenient for the station*** el apartamento está muy cerca de la estación; ***I'm afraid Monday isn't convenient***

me temo que el lunes no me va bien
con·ve·ni·ent·ly [kən'vi:nɪəntlɪ] *adv* convenientemente; ***conveniently located for theaters*** situado cerca de los teatros
con·vent ['kɑ:nvənt] convento *m*
con·ven·tion [kən'venʃn] (*tradition*) convención *f*; (*conference*) congreso *m*
con·ven·tion·al [kən'venʃnl] *adj* convencional
con'ven·tion cen·ter palacio *m* de congresos
con·ven·tion·eer [kən'venʃnɪr] congresista *m/f*
◆ **con·verge on** [kən'vɜ:rdʒ] *v/t* converger en
con·ver·sant [kən'vɜ:rsənt] *adj*: ***be conversant with*** estar familiarizado con
con·ver·sa·tion [kɑ:nvər'seɪʃn] conversación *f*; ***make conversation*** conversar; ***have a conversation*** mantener una conversación
con·ver·sa·tion·al [kɑ:nvər'seɪʃnl] *adj* coloquial
con·verse ['kɑ:nvɜ:rs] *n* (*opposite*): ***the converse*** lo opuesto
con·verse·ly [kən'vɜ:rslɪ] *adv* por el contrario
con·ver·sion [kən'vɜ:rʃn] conversión *f*
con'ver·sion ta·ble tabla *f* de conversión
con·vert 1 *n* ['kɑ:nvɜ:rt] converso(-a) *m*(*f*) (***to*** a) **2** *v/t* [kən'vɜ:rt] convertir
con·ver·ti·ble [kən'vɜ:rtəbl] *n car* descapotable *m*
con·vey [kən'veɪ] *v/t* (*transmit*) transmitir; (*carry*) transportar
con·vey·or belt [kən'veɪər] cinta *f* transportadora
con·vict 1 *n* ['kɑ:nvɪkt] convicto(-a) *m*(*f*) **2** *v/t* [kən'vɪkt] LAW: ***convict s.o. of sth*** declarar a alguien culpable de algo
con·vic·tion [kən'vɪkʃn] LAW condena *f*; (*belief*) convicción *f*
con·vince [kən'vɪns] *v/t* convencer: ***I'm convinced he's lying*** estoy convencido de que miente
con·vinc·ing [kən'vɪnsɪŋ] *adj* convincente
con·viv·i·al [kən'vɪvɪəl] *adj* (*friendly*) agradable
con·voy ['kɑ:nvɔɪ] *of ships, vehicles* convoy *m*
con·vul·sion [kən'vʌlʃn] MED convulsión *f*
cook [kʊk] **1** *n* cocinero(-a) *m*(*f*); ***I'm a good cook*** soy un buen cocinero, cocino bien **2** *v/t* cocinar; ***a cooked meal*** una comida caliente; ***cook the books*** F falsificar las cuentas **3** *v/i* cocinar
'cook·book libro *m* de cocina
cook·e·ry ['kʊkərɪ] cocina *f*
cook·ie ['kʊkɪ] galleta *f*
cook·ing ['kʊkɪŋ] *food* cocina *f*
cool [ku:l] **1** *n*: ***keep one's cool*** F mantener la calma; ***lose one's cool*** F perder la calma **2** *adj weather, breeze* fresco; *drink* frío; (*calm*) tranquilo, sereno; (*unfriendly*) frío **3** *v/i of food, interest* enfriarse; *of tempers* calmarse **4** *v/t*: ***cool it*** F cálmate
◆ **cool down 1** *v/i* enfriarse; *of weather* refrescar; *fig*: *of tempers* calmarse, tranquilizarse **2** *v/t food* enfriar; *fig* calmar, tranquilizar
cool·ing-'off pe·ri·od fase *f* de reflexión
co·op·e·rate [koʊ'ɑ:pəreɪt] *v/i* cooperar
co·op·e·ra·tion [koʊɑ:pə'reɪʃn] cooperación *f*
co·op·e·ra·tive [koʊ'ɑ:pərətɪv] **1** *n* COM cooperativa *f* **2** *adj* COM conjunto; (*helpful*) cooperativo
co·or·di·nate [koʊ'ɔ:rdɪneɪt] *v/t activities* coordinar
co·or·di·na·tion [koʊɔ:rdɪ'neɪʃn] coordinación *f*
cop [kɑ:p] *n* F poli *m/f* F
cope [koʊp] *v/i* arreglárselas; ***cope with*** poder con
cop·i·er ['kɑ:pɪər] *machine* fotocopiadora *f*
co·pi·lot ['koʊpaɪlət] copiloto *m/f*
co·pi·ous ['koʊpɪəs] *adj* copioso
cop·per ['kɑ:pər] *n metal* cobre *m*
cop·y ['kɑ:pɪ] **1** *n* copia *f*; *of book* ejemplar *m*; *of record, CD* copia *f*; (*written material*) texto *m*; ***make a copy of a file*** COMPUT hacer una copia de un archivo **2** *v/t* (*pret & pp* ***copied***) copiar
'cop·y cat F copión (-ona) *m*(*f*) F, copiota *m/f* F
'cop·y·cat crime *delito inspirado en otro*
'cop·y·right *n* copyright *m*, derechos *mpl* de reproducción
'cop·y-writ·er *in advertising* creativo(-a) *m*(*f*) (*de publicidad*)
cor·al ['kɑ:rəl] coral *m*
cord [kɔ:rd] (*string*) cuerda *f*, cordel *m*; (*cable*) cable *m*
cor·di·al ['kɔ:rdʒəl] *adj* cordial
cord·less 'phone ['kɔ:rdlɪs] teléfono *m* inalámbrico
cor·don ['kɔ:rdn] cordón *m*
◆ **cordon off** *v/t* acordonar
cords [kɔ:rdz] *npl pants* pantalones *mpl* de pana
cor·du·roy ['kɔ:rdərɔɪ] pana *f*
core [kɔ:r] **1** *n of fruit* corazón *m*; *of problem* meollo *m*; *of organization, party* núcleo *m* **2** *v/t fruit* sacar el corazón a

3 *adj issue*, *meaning* central
co·ri·an·der ['kɑːrɪændər] cilantro *m*
cork [kɔːrk] *in bottle* (tapón *m* de) corcho *m*; *material* corcho *m*
'cork·screw *n* sacacorchos *m inv*
corn [kɔːrn] *grain* maíz *m*
cor·ner ['kɔːrnər] **1** *n of page*, *street* esquina *f*; *of room* rincón *m*; (*bend*: *on road*) curva *f*; *in soccer* córner *m*, saque *m* de esquina; ***in the corner*** en el rincón; ***I'll meet you on the corner*** te veré en la esquina **2** *v/t person* arrinconar; ***corner a market*** monopolizar un mercado **3** *v/i of driver*, *car* girar
'cor·ner kick *in soccer* saque *m* de esquina, córner *m*
'corn·flakes *npl* copos *mpl* de maíz
'corn·starch harina *f* de maíz
corn·y ['kɔːrnɪ] *adj* F (*sentimental*) cursi F; *joke* manido
cor·o·na·ry ['kɑːrənerɪ] **1** *adj* coronario **2** *n* infarto *m* de miocardio
cor·o·ner ['kɑːrənər] *oficial encargado de investigar muertes sospechosas*
cor·po·ral ['kɔːrpərəl] *n* cabo *m/f*
cor·po·ral 'pun·ish·ment castigo *m* corporal
cor·po·rate ['kɔːrpərət] *adj* COM corporativo, de empresa; ***corporate image*** imagen *f* corporativa; ***corporate loyalty*** lealtad *f* a la empresa
cor·po·ra·tion [kɔːrpə'reɪʃn] (*business*) sociedad *f* anónima
corps [kɔːr] *nsg* cuerpo *m*
corpse [kɔːrps] cadáver *m*
cor·pu·lent ['kɔːrpjʊlənt] *adj* corpulento
cor·pus·cle ['kɔːrpʌsl] corpúsculo *m*
cor·ral [kə'ræl] *n* corral *m*
cor·rect [kə'rekt] **1** *adj* correcto; *time* exacto; ***you are correct*** tiene razón **2** *v/t* corregir
cor·rec·tion [kə'rekʃn] corrección *f*
cor·rect·ly [kə'rektlɪ] *adv* correctamente
cor·re·spond [kɑːrɪ'spɑːnd] *v/i* (*match*) corresponderse; ***correspond to*** corresponder a; ***correspond with*** corresponderse con; (*write letters*) mantener correspondencia con
cor·re·spon·dence [kɑːrɪ'spɑːndəns] (*matching*) correspondencia *f*, relación *f*; (*letters*) correspondencia *f*
cor·re·spon·dent [kɑːrɪ'spɑːndənt] (*letter writer*) correspondiente *m/f*; (*reporter*) corresponsal *m/f*
cor·re·spon·ding [kɑːrɪ'spɑːndɪŋ] *adj* (*equivalent*) correspondiente
cor·ri·dor ['kɔːrɪdər] *in building* pasillo *m*
cor·rob·o·rate [kə'rɑːbəreɪt] *v/t* corroborar
cor·rode [kə'roʊd] **1** *v/t* corroer **2** *v/i* corroerse
cor·ro·sion [kə'roʊʒn] corrosión *f*
cor·ru·gated 'card·board ['kɑːrəgeɪtɪd] cartón *m* ondulado
cor·ru·gated 'i·ron chapa *f* ondulada
cor·rupt [kə'rʌpt] **1** *adj* corrupto; COMPUT corrompido **2** *v/t* corromper; (*bribe*) sobornar
cor·rup·tion [kə'rʌpʃn] corrupción *f*
cos·met·ic [kɑːz'metɪk] *adj* cosmético; *fig* superficial
cos·met·ics [kɑːz'metɪks] *npl* cosméticos *mpl*
cos·met·ic 'sur·geon especialista *m/f* en cirugía estética
cos·met·ic 'sur·ger·y cirugía *f* estética
cos·mo·naut ['kɑːzmənɒːt] cosmonauta *m/f*
cos·mo·pol·i·tan [kɑːzmə'pɑːlɪtən] *adj city* cosmopolitano
cost¹ [kɑːst] **1** *n also fig* costo *m*, *Span* coste *m*; ***at all costs*** cueste lo que cueste; ***I've learnt to my cost*** por desgracia he aprendido **2** *v/t* (*pret & pp* ***cost***) *money*, *time* costar; ***how much does it cost?*** ¿cuánto cuesta?; ***it cost me my health*** me costó mi salud
cost² [kɑːst] *v/t* (*pret & pp* ***costed***) FIN *proposal*, *project* estimar el costo de
cost and 'freight COM costo *or Span* coste y flete
Cos·ta Ri·ca ['kɑːstə'riːkə] *n* Costa Rica
Cos·ta Ri·can ['kɑːstə'riːkən] **1** *adj* costarricense **2** *n* costarricense *m/f*
'cost-con·scious *adj* consciente del costo *or Span* coste
'cost-ef·fec·tive *adj* rentable
'cost, in·sur·ance, freight COM costo *or Span* coste, seguro y flete
cost·ly ['kɑːstlɪ] *adj mistake* caro
cost of 'liv·ing costo *m or Span* coste *m* de la vida
cost 'price precio *m* de costo *or Span* coste
cos·tume ['kɑːstuːm] *for actor* traje *m*
cos·tume 'jew·el·lery *Br*, **costume 'jew·el·ry** bisutería *f*
'cos·y *Br* → ***cozy***
cot [kɑːt] (*camp-bed*) catre *m*
cott·age ['kɑːtɪdʒ] casa *f* de campo, casita *f*
cot·tage 'cheese queso *m* fresco
cot·ton ['kɑːtn] **1** *n* algodón *m* **2** *adj* de algodón
◆ **cotton on** *v/i* F darse cuenta
◆ **cotton on to** *v/t* F darse cuenta de
◆ **cotton to** *v/t* F: ***I never cottoned to her*** nunca me cayó bien

cot·ton 'can·dy algodón *m* dulce
cot·ton 'wool *Br* algodón *m* (hidrófilo)
couch [kaʊʧ] *n* sofá *m*
'couch po·ta·to F teleadicto(-a) *m(f)* F
cou·chette [ku:'ʃet] litera *f*
cough [kɑ:f] **1** *n* tos *f*; *to get attention* carraspeo *m* **2** *v/i* toser; *to get attention* carraspear
◆ **cough up 1** *v/t blood etc* toser; F *money* soltar, *Span* apoquinar F **2** *v/i* F (*pay*) soltar dinero, *Span* apoquinar F
'cough med·i·cine, **'cough syr·up** jarabe *m* para la tos
could [kʊd] **1** *v/aux*: ***could I have my key?*** ¿me podría dar la llave?; ***could you help me?*** ¿me podrías ayudar?; ***this could be our bus*** puede que éste sea nuestro autobús; ***you could be right*** puede que tengas razón; ***I couldn't say for sure*** no sabría decirlo con seguridad; ***he could have got lost*** a lo mejor se ha perdido; ***you could have warned me!*** ¡me podías haber avisado! **2** *pret* → ***can***[1]
coun·cil ['kaʊnsl] *n* (*assembly*) consejo *m*
'coun·cil·man concejal *m*
coun·cil·or ['kaʊnsələr] concejal(a) *m(f)*
coun·sel ['kaʊnsl] **1** *n* (*advice*) consejo *m*; (*lawyer*) abogado(-a) *m(f)* **2** *v/t course of action* aconsejar; *person* ofrecer apoyo psicológico
coun·sel·ing, *Br* **coun·sel·ling** ['kaʊnslɪŋ] apoyo *m* psicológico
coun·sel·lor *Br*, **coun·sel·or** ['kaʊnslər] (*adviser*) consejero(-a) *m(f)*; *of student* orientador(a) *m(f)*; LAW abogado(-a) *m(f)*
count[1] [kaʊnt] **1** *n* (*number arrived at*) cuenta *f*; (*action of counting*) recuento *m*; *in baseball, boxing* cuenta *f*; ***what is your count?*** ¿cuántos has contado?; ***keep count of*** llevar la cuenta de; ***lose count of*** perder la cuenta de; ***at the last count*** en el último recuento **2** *v/i to ten etc* contar; (*be important*) contar; (*qualify*) contar, valer **3** *v/t* contar
◆ **count on** *v/t* contar con
count[2] [kaʊnt] *nobleman* conde *m*
'count·down cuenta *f* atrás
coun·te·nance ['kaʊntənəns] *v/t* tolerar
coun·ter[1] ['kaʊntər] *n in shop* mostrador *m*; *in café* barra *f*; *in game* ficha *f*
coun·ter[2] ['kaʊntər] **1** *v/t* contrarrestar **2** *v/i* (*retaliate*) responder
coun·ter[3] ['kaʊntər] *adv*: ***run counter to*** estar en contra de
'coun·ter·act *v/t* contrarrestar
coun·ter·at'tack 1 *n* contraataque *m* **2** *v/i* contraatacar
'coun·terbal·ance 1 *n* contrapeso *m* **2** *v/t* contrarrestar, contrapesar
coun·ter'clock·wise *adv* en sentido contrario al de las agujas del reloj
coun·ter'es·pi·o·nage contraespionaje *m*
coun·ter·feit ['kaʊntərfɪt] **1** *v/t* falsificar **2** *adj* falso
'coun·ter·part (*person*) homólogo(-a) *m(f)*
coun·ter·pro'duc·tive *adj* contraproducente
'coun·ter·sign *v/t* refrendar
coun·tess ['kaʊntes] condesa *f*
count·less ['kaʊntlɪs] *adj* incontables
coun·try ['kʌntrɪ] *n* (*nation*) país *m*; *as opposed to town* campo *m*; ***in the country*** en el campo
coun·try and 'west·ern MUS música *f* country
'coun·try·man (*fellow countryman*) compatriota *m*
'coun·try·side campo *m*
coun·ty ['kaʊntɪ] condado *m*
coup [ku:] POL golpe *m* (de Estado); *fig* golpe *m* de efecto
cou·ple ['kʌpl] *n* pareja *f*; ***just a couple*** un par; ***a couple of*** un par de
cou·pon ['ku:pɑ:n] cupón *m*
cour·age ['kʌrɪdʒ] valor *m*, coraje *m*
cou·ra·geous [kə'reɪdʒəs] *adj* valiente
cou·ra·geous·ly [kə'reɪdʒəslɪ] *adv* valientemente
cou·ri·er ['kʊrɪr] (*messenger*) mensajero(-a) *m(f)*; *with tourist party* guía *m/f*
course [kɔ:rs] *n* (*series of lessons*) curso *m*; (*part of meal*) plato *m*; *of ship, plane* rumbo *m*; *for horse race* circuito *m*; *for golf* campo *m*; *for skiing, marathon* recorrido *m*; ***change course*** *of ship, plane* cambiar de rumbo; ***of course*** (*certainly*) claro, por supuesto; (*naturally*) por supuesto; ***of course not*** claro que no; ***course of action*** táctica *f*; ***course of treatment*** tratamiento *m*; ***in the course of …*** durante …
court [kɔ:rt] *n* LAW tribunal *m*; (*courthouse*) palacio *m* de justicia; SP pista *f*, cancha *f*; ***take s.o. to court*** llevar a alguien a juicio
'court case proceso *m*, causa *f*
cour·te·ous ['kɜ:rtɪəs] *adj* cortés
cour·te·sy ['kɜ:rtəsɪ] cortesía *f*
'court·house palacio *m* de justicia
court 'mar·tial 1 *n* consejo *m* de guerra **2** *v/t* formar un consejo de guerra a
'court or·der orden *f* judicial
'court·room sala *f* de juicios
'court·yard patio *m*
cous·in ['kʌzn] primo(-a) *m(f)*

cove [kouv] (*small bay*) cala *f*

cov·er ['kʌvər] **1** *n protective* funda *f*; *of book, magazine* portada *f*; (*shelter*) protección *f*; (*insurance*) cobertura *f*; ***covers** for bed* manta y sábanas *fpl*; ***we took cover from the rain*** nos pusimos a cubierto de la lluvia **2** *v/t* cubrir

◆ **cover up 1** *v/t* cubrir; *scandal* encubrir **2** *v/i* disimular; ***cover up for s.o.*** encubrir a alguien

cov·er·age ['kʌvərɪdʒ] *by media* cobertura *f* informativa

cov·er·ing let·ter ['kʌvrɪŋ] carta *f*

cov·ert [kou'vɜːrt] *adj* encubierto

'**cov·er-up** encubrimiento *m*

cow [kau] vaca *f*

cow·ard ['kauərd] cobarde *m/f*

cow·ard·ice ['kauərdɪs] cobardía *f*

cow·ard·ly ['kauərdlɪ] *adj* cobarde

'**cow·boy** vaquero *m*

cow·er ['kauər] *v/i* agacharse, amilanarse

co-work·er ['kouwɜːrkər] compañero(a) *m(f)* de trabajo

coy [kɔɪ] *adj* (*evasive*) evasivo; (*flirtatious*) coqueto

co·zy ['kouzɪ] *adj room* acogedor; *job* cómodo

CPU [siːpiː'juː] *abbr* (= ***central processing unit***) CPU *f* (= unidad *f* central de proceso)

crab [kræb] *n* cangrejo *m*

crack [kræk] **1** *n* grieta *f*; *in cup, glass* raja *f*; (*joke*) chiste *m* (malo) **2** *v/t cup, glass* rajar; *nut* cascar; *code* descifrar; F (*solve*) resolver; ***crack a joke*** contar un chiste **3** *v/i* rajarse; ***get cracking*** F poner manos a la obra F

◆ **crack down on** *v/t* castigar severamente

◆ **crack up** *v/i* (*have breakdown*) sufrir una crisis nerviosa; F (*laugh*) desternillarse F

'**crack·brained** *adj* F chiflado F

'**crack·down** medidas *fpl* severas

cracked [krækt] *adj cup, glass* rajado; F (*crazy*) chiflado F

crack·er ['krækər] *to eat* galleta *f* salada

crack·le ['krækl] *v/i of fire* crepitar

cra·dle ['kreɪdl] *n for baby* cuna *f*

craft[1] [kræft] NAUT embarcación *f*

craft[2] [kræft] (*skill*) arte *m*; (*trade*) oficio *m*

crafts·man ['kræftsmən] artesano *m*

craft·y ['kræftɪ] *adj* astuto

crag [kræg] *rock* peñasco *m*, risco *m*

cram [kræm] *v/t* embutir

cramp [kræmp] *n* calambre *m*; ***stomach cramp*** retorcijón *m*

cramped [kræmpt] *adj room, apartment* pequeño

cramps [kræmps] *npl* calambre *m*; ***stomach cramps*** retorcijón *m*

cran·ber·ry ['krænberɪ] arándano *m* agrio

crane [kreɪn] **1** *n machine* grúa *f* **2** *v/t*: ***crane one's neck*** estirar el cuello

crank [krænk] *n person* maniático(-a) *m(f)*, persona *f* rara

'**crank·shaft** cigüeñal *m*

crank·y ['krænkɪ] *adj* (*bad-tempered*) gruñón

crash [kræʃ] **1** *n noise* estruendo *m*, estrépito *m*; *accident* accidente *m*; COM quiebra *f*, crac *m*; COMPUT bloqueo *m*; ***a crash of thunder*** un trueno **2** *v/i of car, airplane* estrellarse (***into*** con *or* contra); *of thunder* sonar; COM *of market* hundirse, desplomarse; COMPUT bloquearse, colgarse; F (*sleep*) dormir, *Span* sobar F; ***the waves crashed onto the shore*** las olas chocaban contra la orilla; ***the vase crashed to the ground*** el jarrón se cayó con estruendo **3** *v/t car* estrellar

◆ **crash out** *v/i* F (*fall asleep*) dormirse, *Span* quedarse sobado

'**crash bar·ri·er** quitamiedos *m inv*

'**crash course** curso *m* intensivo

'**crash di·et** dieta *f* drástica

'**crash hel·met** casco *m* protector

'**crash-land** *v/i* realizar un aterrizaje forzoso

'**crash 'land·ing** aterrizaje *m* forzoso

crate [kreɪt] (*packing case*) caja *f*

cra·ter ['kreɪtər] *of volcano* cráter *m*

crave [kreɪv] *v/t* ansiar

crav·ing ['kreɪvɪŋ] ansia *f*, deseo *m*; *of pregnant woman* antojo *m*; ***I have a craving for …*** me apetece muchísimo …

crawl [krɒːl] **1** *n in swimming* crol *m*; ***at a crawl*** (*very slowly*) muy lentamente **2** *v/i on floor* arrastrarse; *of baby* andar a gatas; (*move slowly*) avanzar lentamente

◆ **crawl with** *v/t* estar abarrotado de

cray·fish ['kreɪfɪʃ] *freshwater* cangrejo *m* de río; *saltwater* langosta *f*

cray·on ['kreɪɑːn] *n* lápiz *m* de color

craze [kreɪz] locura *f* (***for*** de); ***the latest craze*** la última locura *or* moda

cra·zy ['kreɪzɪ] *adj* loco; ***be crazy about*** estar loco por

creak [kriːk] **1** *n of hinge, door* chirrido *m*; *of floor* crujido *m* **2** *v/i of hinge, door* chirriar; *of floor, shoes* crujir

creak·y ['kriːkɪ] *adj hinge, door* que chirría; *floor, shoes* que cruje

cream [kriːm] **1** *n for skin* crema *f*; *for coffee, cake* nata *f*; (*color*) crema *m* **2** *adj* crema

cream 'cheese queso *m* blanco para un-

tar
cream·er ['kri:mər] (*pitcher*) jarra *f* para la nata; *for coffee* leche *f* en polvo
cream·y ['kri:mɪ] *adj with lots of cream* cremoso
crease [kri:s] **1** *n accidental* arruga *f*; *deliberate* raya *f* **2** *v/t accidentally* arrugar
cre·ate [kri:'eɪt] *v/t & v/i* crear
cre·a·tion [kri:'eɪʃn] creación *f*
cre·a·tive [kri:'eɪtɪv] *adj* creativo
cre·a·tor [kri:'eɪtər] creador(a) *m(f)*; (*founder*) fundador(a) *m(f)*; ***the Creator*** REL el Creador
crea·ture ['kri:ʧər] *animal, person* criatura *f*
crèche [kreʃ] *for children* guardería *f* (infantil); REL nacimiento *m*, belén *m*
cred·i·bil·i·ty [kredə'bɪlətɪ] credibilidad *f*
cred·i·ble ['kredəbl] *adj* creíble
cred·it ['kredɪt] **1** *n* FIN crédito *m*; (*honor*) crédito *m*, reconocimiento *m*; ***be in credit*** tener un saldo positivo; ***get the credit for sth*** recibir reconocimiento por algo **2** *v/t* (*believe*) creer; ***would you credit it!*** ¡te lo puedes creer!; ***credit an amount to an account*** abonar una cantidad en una cuenta
cred·i·ta·ble ['kredɪtəbl] *adj* estimable, honorable
'cred·it card tarjeta *f* de crédito
'cred·it lim·it límite *m* de crédito
cred·i·tor ['kredɪtər] acreedor(a) *m(f)*
'cred·it·wor·thy *adj* solvente
cred·u·lous ['kredʊləs] *adj* crédulo
creed [kri:d] (*beliefs*) credo *m*
creek [kri:k] (*stream*) arroyo *m*
creep [kri:p] **1** *n pej* asqueroso(-a) *m(f)* **2** *v/i* (*pret & pp* ***crept***) moverse sigilosamente
creep·er ['kri:pər] BOT enredadera *f*
creeps [kri:ps] *npl* F: ***the house / he gives me the creeps*** la casa / él me pone la piel de gallina F
creep·y ['kri:pɪ] *adj* F espeluznante F
cre·mate [krɪ'meɪt] *v/t* incinerar
cre·ma·tion [krɪ'meɪʃn] incineración *f*
cre·ma·to·ri·um [kremə'tɔ:rɪəm] crematorio *m*
crept [krept] *pret & pp* → ***creep***
cres·cent ['kresənt] *n shape* medialuna *f*; ***crescent moon*** cuarto *m* creciente
crest [krest] *of hill* cima *f*; *of bird* cresta *f*
crest·fal·len *adj* abatido
crev·ice ['krevɪs] grieta *f*
crew [kru:] *n of ship, airplane* tripulación *f*; *of repairmen etc* equipo *m*; (*crowd, group*) grupo *m*, pandilla *f*
'crew cut rapado *m*
'crew neck cuello *m* redondo
crib [krɪb] *n for baby* cuna *f*
crick [krɪk]: ***have a crick in the neck*** tener tortícolis
crick·et ['krɪkɪt] *insect* grillo *m*
crime [kraɪm] (*offense*) delito *m*; *serious, also fig* crimen *m*
crim·i·nal ['krɪmɪnl] **1** *n* delincuente *m/f*, criminal *m/f* **2** *adj* (*relating to crime*) criminal; (LAW: *not civil*) penal; (*shameful*) vergonzoso; *act* delictivo; ***it's criminal*** (*shameful*) es un crimen
crim·son ['krɪmzn] *adj* carmesí
cringe [krɪndʒ] *v/i with embarrassment* sentir vergüenza ajena
crip·ple ['krɪpl] **1** *n* (*disabled person*) inválido(-a) *m(f)* **2** *v/t person* dejar inválido; *fig*: *country, industry* paralizar
cri·sis ['kraɪsɪs] (*pl* ***crises*** ['kraɪsi:z]) crisis *f inv*
crisp [krɪsp] *adj weather, air* fresco; *lettuce, apple, bacon* crujiente; *new shirt, bills* flamante
cri·te·ri·on [kraɪ'tɪrɪən] (*standard*) criterio *m*
crit·ic ['krɪtɪk] crítico(-a) *m(f)*
crit·i·cal ['krɪtɪkl] *adj* (*making criticisms, serious*) crítico; *moment etc* decisivo
crit·i·cal·ly ['krɪtɪklɪ] *adv speak etc* en tono de crítica; ***critically ill*** en estado crítico
crit·i·cism ['krɪtɪsɪzm] crítica *f*
crit·i·cize ['krɪtɪsaɪz] *v/t* criticar
croak [kroʊk] **1** *n of frog* croar *m* **2** *v/i of frog* croar
cro·chet ['kroʊʃeɪ] **1** *n* ganchillo *m* **2** *v/t* hacer a ganchillo
crock·e·ry ['krɑ:kərɪ] vajilla *f*
croc·o·dile ['krɑ:kədaɪl] cocodrilo *m*
cro·cus ['kroʊkəs] azafrán *m*
cro·ny ['kroʊnɪ] F amiguete *m/f* F
crook [krʊk] *n* ladrón (-ona) *m(f)*; *dishonest trader* granuja *m/f*
crook·ed ['krʊkɪd] *adj* (*not straight*) torcido; (*dishonest*) deshonesto
crop [krɑ:p] **1** *n also fig* cosecha *f*; *plant grown* cultivo *m* **2** *v/t* (*pret & pp* ***cropped***) *hair* cortar; *photo* recortar
◆ **crop up** *v/i* salir
cross [krɑ:s] **1** *adj* (*angry*) enfadado, enojado **2** *n* cruz *f* **3** *v/t* (*go across*) cruzar; ***cross o.s.*** REL santiguarse; ***cross one's legs*** cruzar las piernas; ***keep one's fingers crossed*** cruzar los dedos; ***it never crossed my mind*** no se me ocurrió **4** *v/i* (*go across*) cruzar; *of lines* cruzarse, cortarse
◆ **cross off**, **cross out** *v/t* tachar
'cross·bar *of goal* larguero *m*; *of bicycle* barra *f*; *in high jump* listón *m*

C

ˈ**cross·check** **1** *n* comprobación *f* **2** *v/t* comprobar
cross-coun·try (ˈ**ski·ing**) esquí *m* de fondo
crossed ˈ**check**, *Br* **crossed** ˈ**cheque** [krɑːst] cheque *m* cruzado
cross-ex·am·iˈna·tion LAW interrogatorio *m*
cross-exˈam·ine *v/t* LAW interrogar
cross-ˈeyed *adj* bizco
cross·ing [ˈkrɑːsɪŋ] NAUT travesía *f*
ˈ**cross·roads** *nsg also fig* encrucijada *f*
ˈ**cross-sec·tion** *of people* muestra *f* representativa
ˈ**cross·walk** paso *m* de peatones
ˈ**cross·word** (**puz·zle**) crucigrama *m*
crotch [krɑːʧ] *of person, pants* entrepierna *f*
crouch [kraʊʧ] *v/i* agacharse
crow [kroʊ] *n bird* corneja *f*; ***as the crow flies*** en línea recta
ˈ**crow·bar** palanca *f*
crowd [kraʊd] *n* multitud *f*, muchedumbre *f*; *at sports event* público *m*
crowd·ed [ˈkraʊdɪd] *adj* abarrotado (***with*** de)
crown [kraʊn] **1** *n on head, tooth* corona *f* **2** *v/t tooth* poner una corona a
cru·cial [ˈkruːʃl] *adj* crucial
cru·ci·fix [ˈkruːsɪfɪks] crucifijo *m*
cru·ci·fix·ion [kruːsɪˈfɪkʃn] crucifixión *f*
cru·ci·fy [ˈkruːsɪfaɪ] *v/t* (*pret & pp* ***crucified***) *also fig* crucificar
crude [kruːd] **1** *adj* (*vulgar*) grosero; (*unsophisticated*) primitivo **2** *n*: ***crude*** (***oil***) crudo *m*
crude·ly [ˈkruːdlɪ] *adv speak* groseramente; *made* de manera primitiva
cru·el [ˈkruːəl] *adj* cruel (***to*** con)
cru·el·ty [ˈkruːəltɪ] crueldad *f* (***to*** con)
cruise [kruːz] **1** *n* crucero *m*; ***go on a cruise*** ir de crucero **2** *v/i of people* hacer un crucero; *of car* ir a velocidad de crucero; *of plane* volar
ˈ**cruise lin·er** transatlántico *m*
cruis·ing speed [ˈkruːzɪŋ] *of vehicle* velocidad *f* de crucero; *fig*: *of project etc* ritmo *m* normal
crumb [krʌm] miga *f*
crum·ble [ˈkrʌmbl] **1** *v/t* desmigajar **2** *v/i of bread* desmigajarse; *of stonework* desmenuzarse; *fig*: *of opposition etc* desmoronarse
crum·bly [ˈkrʌmblɪ] *adj cookie* que se desmigaja; *stonework* que se desmenuza
crum·ple [ˈkrʌmpl] **1** *v/t* (*crease*) arrugar **2** *v/i* (*collapse*) desplomarse
crunch [krʌnʧ] **1** *n*: ***when it comes to the crunch*** a la hora de la verdad **2** *v/i of snow, gravel* crujir
cru·sade [kruːˈseɪd] *n also fig* cruzada *f*
crush [krʌʃ] **1** *n* (*crowd*) muchedumbre *f*; ***have a crush on*** estar loco por **2** *v/t* aplastar; (*crease*) arrugar; ***they were crushed to death*** murieron aplastados **3** *v/i* (*crease*) arrugarse
crust [krʌst] *on bread* corteza *f*
crust·y [ˈkrʌstɪ] *adj bread* crujiente
crutch [krʌʧ] *for injured person* muleta *f*
cry [kraɪ] **1** *n* (*call*) grito *m*; ***have a cry*** llorar **2** *v/t* (*pret & pp* ***cried***) (*call*) gritar **3** *v/i* (*pret & pp* ***cried***) (*weep*) llorar
◆ **cry out** *v/t & v/i* gritar
◆ **cry out for** *v/t* (*need*) pedir a gritos
cryp·tic [ˈkrɪptɪk] *adj* críptico
crys·tal [ˈkrɪstl] cristal *m*
crys·tal·lize [ˈkrɪstəlaɪz] **1** *v/t* cristalizar **2** *v/i* cristalizarse
cub [kʌb] cachorro *m*; *of bear* osezno *m*
Cu·ba [ˈkjuːbə] Cuba
Cu·ban [ˈkjuːbən] **1** *adj* cubano **2** *n* cubano(-a) *m*(*f*)
cube [kjuːb] *shape* cubo *m*
cu·bic [ˈkjuːbɪk] *adj* cúbico
cu·bic caˈpac·i·ty TECH cilindrada *f*
cu·bi·cle [ˈkjuːbɪkl] (*changing room*) cubículo *m*
cu·cum·ber [ˈkjuːkʌmbər] pepino *m*
cud·dle [ˈkʌdl] **1** *n* abrazo **2** *v/t* abrazar
cud·dly [ˈkʌdlɪ] *adj kitten etc* tierno
cue [kjuː] *n for actor etc* pie *m*, entrada *f*; *for pool* taco *m*
cuff [kʌf] **1** *n of shirt* puño *m*; *of pants* vuelta *f*; (*blow*) cachete *m*; ***off the cuff*** improvisado **2** *v/t* (*hit*) dar un cachete a
ˈ**cuff link** gemelo *m*
cul-de-sac [ˈkʌldəsæk] callejón *m* sin salida
cu·li·nar·y [ˈkʌlɪnərɪ] *adj* culinario
cul·mi·nate [ˈkʌlmɪneɪt] *v/i* culminar (***in*** en)
cul·mi·na·tion [kʌlmɪˈneɪʃn] culminación *f*
cul·prit [ˈkʌlprɪt] culpable *m/f*
cult [kʌlt] (*sect*) secta *f*
cul·ti·vate [ˈkʌltɪveɪt] *v/t also fig* cultivar
cul·ti·vat·ed [ˈkʌltɪveɪtɪd] *adj person* culto
cul·ti·va·tion [kʌltɪˈveɪʃn] *of land* cultivo *m*
cul·tu·ral [ˈkʌlʧərəl] *adj* cultural
cul·ture [ˈkʌlʧər] *artistic* cultura *f*
cul·tured [ˈkʌlʧərd] *adj* (*cultivated*) culto
ˈ**cul·ture shock** choque *m* cultural
cum·ber·some [ˈkʌmbərsəm] *adj* engorroso
cu·mu·la·tive [ˈkjuːmjʊlətɪv] *adj* acumulativo

cun·ning ['kʌnɪŋ] **1** *n* astucia *f* **2** *adj* astuto
cup [kʌp] *n* taza *f*; *trophy* copa *f*
cup·board ['kʌbərd] armario *m*
'cup fi·nal final *f* de (la) copa
cu·po·la ['kjuːpələ] cúpula *f*
cu·ra·ble ['kjʊrəbl] *adj* curable
cu·ra·tor [kjʊ'reɪtər] conservador(a) *m(f)*
curb [kɜːrb] **1** *n of street* bordillo *m*; *on powers etc* freno *f* **2** *v/t* frenar
cur·dle ['kɜːrdl] *v/i of milk* cortarse
cure [kjʊr] **1** *n* MED cura *f* **2** *v/t* MED, *meat* curar
cur·few ['kɜːrfjuː] toque *m* de queda
cu·ri·os·i·ty [kjʊrɪ'ɑːsətɪ] (*inquisitiveness*) curiosidad *f*
cu·ri·ous ['kjʊrɪəs] *adj* (*inquisitive, strange*) curioso
cu·ri·ous·ly ['kjʊrɪəslɪ] *adv* (*inquisitively*) con curiosidad; (*strangely*) curiosamente; ***curiously enough*** curiosamente
curl [kɜːrl] **1** *n in hair* rizo *m*; *of smoke* voluta **2** *v/t hair* rizar; (*wind*) enroscar **3** *v/i of hair* rizarse; *of leaf, paper etc* ondularse
◆ **curl up** *v/i* acurrucarse
curl·y ['kɜːrlɪ] *adj hair* rizado; *tail* enroscado
cur·rant ['kʌrənt] (*dried fruit*) pasa *f* de Corinto
cur·ren·cy ['kʌrənsɪ] *money* moneda *f*; ***foreign currency*** divisas *fpl*
cur·rent ['kʌrənt] **1** *n in sea*, ELEC corriente *f* **2** *adj* (*present*) actual
cur·rent af'fairs, cur·rent e'vents *npl* la actualidad
cur·rent af'fairs pro·gram programa *m* de actualidad
'cur·rent ac·count *Br* cuenta *f* corriente
cur·rent·ly ['kʌrəntlɪ] *adv* actualmente
cur·ric·u·lum [kə'rɪkjʊləm] plan *m* de estudios
cur·ric·u·lum vi·tae ['viːtaɪ] *Br* currículum *m* vitae
cur·ry ['kʌrɪ] curry *m*
curse [kɜːrs] **1** *n* (*spell*) maldición *f*; (*swearword*) palabrota *f* **2** *v/t* maldecir; (*swear at*) insultar **3** *v/i* (*swear*) decir palabrotas
cur·sor ['kɜːrsər] COMPUT cursor *m*
cur·so·ry ['kɜːrsərɪ] *adj* rápido, superficial
curt [kɜːrt] *adj* brusco, seco
cur·tail [kɜːr'teɪl] *v/t* acortar
cur·tain ['kɜːrtn] cortina *f*; THEA telón *m*
curve [kɜːrv] **1** *n* curva *f* **2** *v/i* (*bend*) curvarse
cush·ion ['kʊʃn] **1** *n for couch etc* cojín *m* **2** *v/t blow, fall* amortiguar
cus·tard ['kʌstərd] natillas *fpl*
cus·to·dy ['kʌstədɪ] *of children* custodia *f*; ***in custody*** LAW detenido
cus·tom ['kʌstəm] (*tradition*) costumbre *f*; COM clientela *f*; ***it's the custom in France*** es costumbre en Francia; ***as was his custom*** como era costumbre en él; ***thank you for your custom*** *at shop* gracias por comprar aquí
cus·tom·a·ry ['kʌstəmərɪ] *adj* acostumbrado, de costumbre; ***it is customary to ...*** es costumbre ...
cus·tom-'built *adj* hecho de encargo
cus·tom-'made *adj* hecho de encargo
cus·tom·er ['kʌstəmər] cliente(-a) *m(f)*
cus·tom·er re'la·tions *npl* relaciones *fpl* con los clientes
cus·tom·er 'serv·ice atención *f* al cliente
cus·toms ['kʌstəmz] *npl* aduana *f*
'cus·toms clear·ance despacho *m* de aduanas
'cus·toms in·spec·tion inspección *f* aduanera
'cus·toms of·fi·cer funcionario(-a) *m(f)* de aduanas
cut [kʌt] **1** *n with knife etc, of garment* corte *m*; (*reduction*) recorte (***in*** de); ***my hair needs a cut*** necesito un corte de pelo **2** *v/t* (*pret & pp* **cut**) cortar; (*reduce*) recortar; *hours* acortar; ***get one's hair cut*** cortarse el pelo; ***I've cut my finger*** me he cortado el dedo
◆ **cut back 1** *v/i in costs* recortar gastos **2** *v/t staff numbers* recortar
◆ **cut down 1** *v/t tree* talar, cortar **2** *v/i in expenses* gastar menos; *in smoking / drinking* fumar / beber menos
◆ **cut down on** *v/t*: ***cut down on the cigarettes*** fumar menos; ***cut down on chocolate*** comer menos chocolate
◆ **cut off** *v/t with knife, scissors etc* cortar; (*isolate*) aislar; ***I was cut off*** se me ha cortado la comunicación
◆ **cut out** *v/t with scissors* recortar; (*eliminate*) eliminar; ***cut that out!*** F ¡ya está bien! F; ***be cut out for sth*** estar hecho para algo
◆ **cut up** *v/t meat etc* trocear
'cut·back recorte *m*
cute [kjuːt] *adj* (*pretty*) guapo, lindo; (*sexually attractive*) atractivo; (*smart, clever*) listo; ***it looks really cute on you*** eso te queda muy mono
cu·ti·cle ['kjuːtɪkl] cutícula *f*
'cut-off date fecha *f* límite
cut-'price *adj goods* rebajado; *store* de productos rebajados
'cut-throat *adj competition* despiadado
cut·ting ['kʌtɪŋ] **1** *n from newspaper etc*

recorte *m* **2** *adj remark* hiriente

cy·ber·space ['saɪbərspeɪs] ciberespacio *m*

cy·cle ['saɪkl] **1** *n* (*bicycle*) bicicleta *f*; (*series of events*) ciclo *m* **2** *v/i* ir en bicicleta

'cy·cle path vía *f* para bicicletas; *part of roadway* carril *m* bici

cy·cling ['saɪklɪŋ] ciclismo *m*

cy·clist ['saɪklɪst] ciclista *m/f*

cyl·in·der ['sɪlɪndər] cilindro *m*

cy·lin·dri·cal [sɪ'lɪndrɪkl] *adj* cilíndrico

cyn·ic ['sɪnɪk] escéptico(-a) *m*(*f*), suspicaz *m/f*

cyn·i·cal ['sɪnɪkl] *adj* escéptico, suspicaz

cyn·i·cal·ly ['sɪnɪklɪ] *adv smile, remark* con escepticismo *or* suspicacia

cyn·i·cism ['sɪnɪsɪzm] escepticismo *m*, suspicacia *f*

cy·press ['saɪprəs] ciprés *m*

cyst [sɪst] quiste *m*

Czech [tʃek] **1** *adj* checo; ***the Czech Republic*** la República Checa **2** *n person* checo(-a) *m*(*f*); *language* checo *m*

D

DA *abbr* (= ***district attorney***) fiscal *m/f* (del distrito)

dab [dæb] **1** *n small amount* pizca *f* **2** *v/t* (*pret & pp* ***dabbed***) (*remove*) quitar; (*apply*) poner

◆ **dab·ble in** *v/t* ser aficionado a

dad [dæd] *talking to him* papá *m*; *talking about him* padre *m*

dad·dy ['dædɪ] *talking to him* papi *m*; *talking about him* padre *m*

daf·fo·dil ['dæfədɪl] narciso *m*

dag·ger ['dægər] daga *f*

dai·ly ['deɪlɪ] **1** *n* (*paper*) diario *m* **2** *adj* diario

dain·ty ['deɪntɪ] *adj* grácil, delicado

dair·y ['derɪ] *on farm* vaquería *f*

'dair·y prod·ucts *npl* productos *mpl* lácteos

dais ['deɪɪs] tarima *f*

dai·sy ['deɪzɪ] margarita *f*

dam [dæm] **1** *n for water* presa *f* **2** *v/t* (*pret & pp* ***dammed***) *river* embalsar

dam·age ['dæmɪdʒ] **1** *n* daños *mpl*; *fig*: *to reputation etc* daño *m* **2** *v/t also fig* dañar; ***you're damaging your health*** estás perjudicando tu salud

dam·ages ['dæmɪdʒɪz] *npl* LAW daños *mpl* y perjuicios

dam·ag·ing ['dæmɪdʒɪŋ] *adj* perjudicial

dame [deɪm] F (*woman*) mujer *f*, *Span* tía *f* F

damn [dæm] **1** *interj* F ¡mecachis! F **2** *n* F: ***I don't give a damn!*** ¡me importa un pimiento! F **3** *adj* F maldito F **4** *adv* F muy; ***a damn stupid thing*** una tontería monumental **5** *v/t* (*condemn*) condenar; ***damn it!*** F ¡maldita sea! F; ***I'm damned if …*** F ya lo creo que … F

damned [dæmd] → ***damn*** *adj*, *adv*

damn·ing ['dæmɪŋ] *adj evidence* condenatorio; *report* crítico

damp [dæmp] *adj* húmedo

damp·en ['dæmpən] *v/t* humedecer

dance [dæns] **1** *n* baile *m* **2** *v/i* bailar; ***would you like to dance?*** ¿le gustaría bailar?

danc·er ['dænsər] bailarín (-ina) *m*(*f*)

danc·ing ['dænsɪŋ] baile *m*

dan·de·lion ['dændɪlaɪən] diente *m* de león

dan·druff ['dændrʌf] caspa *f*

dan·druff sham'poo champú *m* anticaspa

Dane [deɪn] danés(-esa) *m*(*f*)

dan·ger ['deɪndʒər] peligro *m*; ***be in danger*** estar en peligro; ***out of danger*** *of patient* estar fuera de peligro; ***be in no danger*** no estar en peligro

dan·ger·ous ['deɪndʒərəs] *adj* peligroso

dan·ger·ous 'driv·ing conducción *f* peligrosa

dan·ger·ous·ly ['deɪndʒərəslɪ] *adv drive* peligrosamente; ***dangerously ill*** gravemente enfermo

dan·gle ['dæŋgl] **1** *v/t* balancear **2** *v/i* colgar

Da·nish ['deɪnɪʃ] **1** *adj* danés **2** *n language* danés *m*

'Da·nish (pas·try) pastel *m* de hojaldre (*dulce*)

dare [der] **1** *v/i* atreverse; ***dare to do sth*** atreverse a hacer algo; ***how dare you!*** ¡cómo te atreves! **2** *v/t*: ***dare s.o. to do sth*** desafiar a alguien para que haga algo

dare·dev·il ['derdevɪl] temerario(-a) *m*(*f*)

dar·ing ['derɪŋ] *adj* atrevido

dark [dɑːrk] **1** *n* oscuridad *f*; ***in the dark*** en la oscuridad; ***after dark*** después de anochecer; ***keep s.o. in the dark about sth*** *fig* no revelar algo a alguien **2** *adj* oscuro; *hair* oscuro, moreno; ***dark green / blue*** verde / azul oscuro

dark·en ['dɑːrkn] *v/i of sky* oscurecerse

dark 'glass·es *npl* gafas *fpl* oscuras, *L.Am.* lentes *fpl* oscuras

dark·ness ['dɑːrknɪs] oscuridad *f*; ***in darkness*** a oscuras

'dark·room PHOT cuarto *m* oscuro

dar·ling ['dɑːrlɪŋ] **1** *n* cielo *m*; ***yes my darling*** sí cariño **2** *adj* encantador; ***darling Ann, how are you?*** querida Ann, ¿cómo estás?

darn[1] [dɑːrn] **1** *n* (*mend*) zurcido *m* **2** *v/t* (*mend*) zurcir

darn[2], **darned** [dɑːrn, dɑːrnd] → ***damn*** *adj*, *adv*

dart [dɑːrt] **1** *n for throwing* dardo *m* **2** *v/i* lanzarse, precipitarse

darts [dɑːrts] *nsg* dardos *mpl*

'dart(s)·board diana *f*

dash [dæʃ] **1** *n punctuation* raya *f*; (*small amount*) chorrito *m*; (MOT: *dashboard*) salpicadero *m*; ***make a dash for*** correr hacia **2** *v/i* correr; ***I must dash*** tengo que darme prisa; ***he dashed downstairs*** bajó las escaleras corriendo **3** *v/t hopes* frustrar, truncar

◆ **dash off 1** *v/i* irse **2** *v/t* (*write quickly*) escribir rápidamente

'dash·board salpicadero *m*

da·ta ['deɪtə] datos *mpl*

'da·ta·base base *f* de datos

da·ta 'cap·ture captura *f* de datos

da·ta 'pro·cess·ing proceso *m or* tratamiento *m* de datos

da·ta pro'tec·tion protección *f* de datos

da·ta 'stor·age almacenamiento *m* de datos

date[1] [deɪt] *fruit* dátil *m*

date[2] [deɪt] **1** *n* fecha *f*; (*meeting*) cita *f*; (*person*) pareja *f*; ***what's the date today?*** ¿qué fecha es hoy?, ¿a qué fecha estamos?; ***out of date*** *clothes* pasado de moda; *passport* caducado; ***up to date*** al día **2** *v/t letter, check* fechar; (*go out with*) salir con; ***that dates you*** (*shows your age*) eso demuestra lo viejo que eres

dat·ed ['deɪtɪd] *adj* anticuado

daub [dɒːb] *v/t* embadurnar

daugh·ter ['dɒːtər] hija *f*

'daugh·ter-in-law (*pl* **daughters-in-law**) nuera *f*

daunt [dɒːnt] *v/t* acobardar, desalentar

daw·dle ['dɒːdl] *v/i* perder el tiempo

dawn [dɒːn] **1** *n* amanecer *m*, alba *f*; *fig: of new age* albores *mpl* **2** *v/i* amanecer; ***it dawned on me that ...*** me di cuenta de que ...

day [deɪ] día *m*; ***what day is it today?*** ¿qué día es hoy?, ¿a qué día estamos?; ***day off*** día *m* de vacaciones; ***by day*** durante el día; ***day by day*** día tras día; ***the day after*** el día siguiente; ***the day after tomorrow*** pasado mañana; ***the day before*** el día anterior; ***the day before yesterday*** anteayer; ***day in day out*** un día sí y otro también; ***in those days*** en aquellos tiempos; ***one day*** un día; ***the other day*** (*recently*) el otro día; ***let's call it a day!*** ¡dejémoslo!

'day·break amanecer *m*, alba *f*

'day care servicio *m* de guardería

'day·dream 1 *n* fantasía *f* **2** *v/i* soñar despierto

'day dream·er soñador(a) *m*(*f*)

'day·light luz *f* del día

'day·light 'sav·ing time horario *m* de verano

'day·time: ***in the daytime*** durante el día

'day trip excursión *m* en el día

daze [deɪz] *n*: ***in a daze*** aturdido

dazed [deɪzd] *adj* aturdido

daz·zle ['dæzl] *v/t also fig* deslumbrar

DC [diː'siː] *abbr* (= ***direct current***) corriente *f* continua; (= ***District of Columbia***) Distrito *m* de Columbia

dead [ded] **1** *adj person, plant* muerto; *battery* agotado; *light bulb* fundido; F *place* muerto F; ***the phone is dead*** no hay línea **2** *adv* F (*very*) tela de F, la mar de F; ***dead beat, dead tired*** hecho polvo; ***that's dead right*** tienes toda la razón del mundo **3** *n*: ***the dead*** (*dead people*) los muertos; ***in the dead of night*** a altas horas de la madrugada

dead·en ['dedn] *v/t pain, sound* amortiguar

dead 'end (*street*) callejón *m* sin salida

dead-'end job trabajo *m* sin salidas

dead 'heat empate *m*

'dead·line fecha *f* tope; *for newspaper, magazine* hora *f* de cierre; ***meet a deadline*** cumplir un plazo

'dead·lock *n in talks* punto *m* muerto

dead·ly ['dedlɪ] *adj* (*fatal*) mortal; F (*boring*) mortal F

deaf [def] *adj* sordo

deaf-and-'dumb *adj* sordomudo

deaf·en ['defn] *v/t* ensordecer

deaf·en·ing ['defnɪŋ] *adj* ensordecedor

deaf·ness ['defnɪs] sordera *f*

deal [diːl] **1** *n* acuerdo *m*; ***I thought we had a deal?*** creía que habíamos hecho

D

un trato; ***it's a deal!*** ¡trato hecho!; ***a good deal*** (*bargain*) una ocasión; ***a good deal*** (*a lot*) mucho; ***a great deal of*** (*lots*) mucho(s) **2** *v/t* (*pret & pp* ***dealt***) *cards* repartir; ***deal a blow to*** asestar un golpe a

◆ **deal in** *v/t* (*trade in*) comerciar con; ***deal in drugs*** traficar con drogas

◆ **deal out** *v/t cards* repartir

◆ **deal with** *v/t* (*handle*) tratar; *situation* hacer frente a; *customer, applications* encargarse de; (*do business with*) hacer negocios con

deal·er ['diːlər] (*merchant*) comerciante *m/f*; (*drug dealer*) traficante *m/f*

deal·ing ['diːlɪŋ] (*drug dealing*) tráfico *m*

deal·ings ['diːlɪŋz] *npl* (*business*) tratos *mpl*

dealt [delt] *pret & pp* → ***deal***

dean [diːn] *of college* decano(-a) *m*(*f*)

dear [dɪr] *adj* querido; (*expensive*) caro; ***Dear Sir*** Muy Sr. Mío; ***Dear Richard / Margaret*** Querido Richard / Querida Margaret; (***oh***) ***dear!, dear me!*** ¡oh, cielos!

dear·ly ['dɪrlɪ] *adv love* muchísimo

death [deθ] muerte *f*

'**death cer·tif·i·cate** certificado *m* de defunción

'**death pen·al·ty** pena *f* de muerte

'**death toll** saldo *m* de víctimas mortales

de·ba·ta·ble [dɪ'beɪtəbl] *adj* discutible

de·bate [dɪ'beɪt] **1** *n also* POL debate *m* **2** *v/i* debatir; ***I debated with myself whether to go*** me debatía entre ir o no ir **3** *v/t* debatir

de·bauch·er·y [dɪ'bɒːʧərɪ] libertinaje *m*

deb·it ['debɪt] **1** *n* cargo *m* **2** *v/t account* cargar en; *amount* cargar

'**deb·it card** tarjeta *f* de débito

deb·ris ['debriː] *of building* escombros *mpl*; *of airplane, car* restos *mpl*

debt [det] deuda *f*; ***be in debt*** *financially* estar endeudado

debt·or ['detər] deudor(-a) *m*(*f*)

de·bug [diː'bʌg] *v/t* (*pret & pp* ***debugged***) *room* limpiar de micrófonos; COMPUT depurar

dé·but ['deɪbjuː] *n* debut *m*

dec·ade ['dekeɪd] década *f*

dec·a·dence ['dekədəns] decadencia *f*

dec·a·dent ['dekədənt] *adj* decadente

de·caf·fein·at·ed [dɪ'kæfɪneɪtɪd] *adj* descafeinado

de·cant·er [dɪ'kæntər] licorera *f*

de·cap·i·tate [dɪ'kæpɪteɪt] *v/t* decapitar

de·cay [dɪ'keɪ] **1** *n of wood, plant* putrefacción *f*; *of civilization* declive *m*; *in teeth* caries *f inv* **2** *v/i of wood, plant* pudrirse; *of civilization* decaer; *of teeth* cariarse

de·ceased [dɪ'siːst]: ***the deceased*** el difunto / la difunta

de·ceit [dɪ'siːt] engaño *m*, mentira *f*

de·ceit·ful [dɪ'siːtfəl] *adj* mentiroso

de·ceive [dɪ'siːv] *v/t* engañar

De·cem·ber [dɪ'sembər] diciembre *m*

de·cen·cy ['diːsənsɪ] decencia *f*; ***he had the decency to ...*** tuvo la delicadeza de ...

de·cent ['diːsənt] *adj* decente; (*adequately dressed*) presentable

de·cen·tral·ize [diː'sentrəlaɪz] *v/t* descentralizar

de·cep·tion [dɪ'sepʃn] engaño *m*

de·cep·tive [dɪ'septɪv] *adj* engañoso

de·cep·tive·ly [dɪ'septɪvlɪ] *adv*: ***it looks deceptively simple*** parece muy fácil

dec·i·bel ['desɪbel] decibelio *m*

de·cide [dɪ'saɪd] **1** *v/t* decidir **2** *v/i* decidir; ***you decide*** decide tú; ***it's so hard to decide*** es tan difícil decidirse

de·cid·ed [dɪ'saɪdɪd] *adj* (*definite*) tajante

de·cid·er [dɪ'saɪdər]: ***this match will be the decider*** este partido será el que decida

de·ci·du·ous [dɪ'sɪdʊəs] *adj* de hoja caduca

dec·i·mal ['desɪml] *n* decimal *m*

dec·i·mal 'point coma *f* (decimal)

dec·i·mate ['desɪmeɪt] *v/t* diezmar

de·ci·pher [dɪ'saɪfər] *v/t* descifrar

de·ci·sion [dɪ'sɪʒn] decisión *f*; ***come to a decision*** llegar a una decisión

de'ci·sion-mak·er: ***who's the decision-maker here?*** ¿quién toma aquí las decisiones?

de·ci·sive [dɪ'saɪsɪv] *adj* decidido; (*crucial*) decisivo

deck [dek] *of ship* cubierta *f*; *of cards* baraja *f*

'**deck·chair** tumbona *f*

dec·la·ra·tion [deklə'reɪʃn] (*statement*) declaración *f*

de·clare [dɪ'kler] *v/t* (*state*) declarar

de·cline [dɪ'klaɪn] **1** *n* (*fall*) descenso *m*; *in standards* caída *f*; *in health* empeoramiento *m* **2** *v/t invitation* declinar; ***decline to comment*** declinar hacer declaraciones **3** *v/i* (*refuse*) rehusar; (*decrease*) declinar; *of health* empeorar

de·clutch [diː'klʌʧ] *v/i* desembragar

de·code [diː'koʊd] *v/t* descodificar

de·com·pose [diːkəm'poʊz] *v/i* descomponerse

dé·cor ['deɪkɔːr] decoración *f*

dec·o·rate ['dekəreɪt] *v/t with paint* pintar; *with paper* empapelar; (*adorn*) decorar; *soldier* condecorar

dec·o·ra·tion [dekə'reɪʃn] *paint* pintado *m*; *paper* empapelado *m*; (*ornament*) decoración *f*

dec·o·ra·tive ['dekərətɪv] *adj* decorativo

dec·o·ra·tor ['dekəreɪtər] (*interior decorator*) decorador(a) *m(f)*; *with paint* pintor(a) *m(f)*; *with wallpaper* empapelador(a) *m(f)*

de·co·rum [dɪ'kɔːrəm] decoro *m*

de·coy ['diːkɔɪ] *n* señuelo *m*

de·crease 1 *n* ['diːkriːs] disminución *f*, reducción *f* (**in** de) **2** *v/t* [dɪ'kriːs] disminuir, reducir **3** *v/i* [dɪ'kriːs] disminuir, reducirse

de·crep·it [dɪ'krepɪt] *adj car, coat, shoes* destartalado; *person* decrépito

ded·i·cate ['dedɪkeɪt] *v/t book etc* dedicar; ***dedicate o.s. to*** dedicarse a

ded·i·ca·ted ['dedɪkeɪtɪd] *adj* dedicado

ded·i·ca·tion [dedɪ'keɪʃn] *in book* dedicatoria *f*; *to cause, work* dedicación *f*

de·duce [dɪ'duːs] *v/t* deducir

de·duct [dɪ'dʌkt] *v/t* descontar; ***deduct sth from sth*** descontar alguien de alguien

de·duc·tion [dɪ'dʌkʃn] *from salary*, (*conclusion*) deduccción *f*

dee·jay ['diːdʒeɪ] F disk jockey *m/f*, *Span* pincha *m/f* F

deed [diːd] *n* (*act*) acción *f*, obra *f*; LAW escritura *f*

deem [diːm] *v/t* estimar

deep [diːp] *adj* profundo; *color* intenso; ***be in deep trouble*** estar metido en serios apuros

deep·en ['diːpn] **1** *v/t* profundizar **2** *v/i* hacerse más profundo; *of crisis, mystery* agudizarse

'deep freeze *n* congelador *m*

'deep-froz·en food comida *f* congelada

'deep-fry *v/t* (*pret & pp* ***deep-fried***) freír (*en mucho aceite*)

deep 'fry·er freidora *f*

deer [dɪr] (*pl* ***deer***) ciervo *m*

de·face [dɪ'feɪs] *v/t* desfigurar, dañar

def·a·ma·tion [defə'meɪʃn] difamación *f*

de·fam·a·to·ry [dɪ'fæmətərɪ] *adj* difamatorio

de·fault ['diːfɒːlt] *adj* COMPUT por defecto

de·feat [dɪ'fiːt] **1** *n* derrota *f* **2** *v/t* derrotar; *of task, problem* derrotar, vencer

de·feat·ist [dɪ'fiːtɪst] *adj attitude* derrotista

de·fect ['diːfekt] *n* defecto *m*

de·fec·tive [dɪ'fektɪv] *adj* defectuoso

de'fence *etc Br* → ***defense*** *etc*

de·fend [dɪ'fend] *v/t* defender

de·fend·ant [dɪ'fendənt] acusado(-a) *m(f)*; *in civil case* demandado(-a) *m(f)*

de·fense [dɪ'fens] defensa *f*; ***come to s.o.'s defense*** salir en defensa de alguien

de'fense budg·et POL presupuesto *m* de defensa

de'fense law·yer abogado(-a) *m(f)* defensor(a)

de·fense·less [dɪ'fenslɪs] *adj* indefenso

de'fense play·er SP defensa *m/f*

De'fense Se·cre·ta·ry POL ministro(-a) *m(f)* de Defensa; *in USA* secretario *m* de Defensa

de'fense wit·ness LAW testigo *m/f* de la defensa

de·fen·sive [dɪ'fensɪv] **1** *n*: ***on the defensive*** a la defensiva; ***go on the defensive*** ponerse a la defensiva **2** *adj weaponry* defensivo; ***stop being so defensive!*** ¡no hace falta que te pongas tan a la defensiva!

de·fen·sive·ly [dɪ'fensɪvlɪ] *adv* a la defensiva

de·fer [dɪ'fɜːr] *v/t* (*pret & pp* ***deferred***) (*postpone*) aplazar, diferir

de·fer·ence ['defərəns] deferencia *f*

def·er·en·tial [defə'renʃl] *adj* deferente

de·fi·ance [dɪ'faɪəns] desafío *m*; ***in defiance of*** desafiando

de·fi·ant [dɪ'faɪənt] *adj* desafiante

de·fi·cien·cy [dɪ'fɪʃənsɪ] (*lack*) deficiencia *f*, carencia *f*

de·fi·cient [dɪ'fɪʃənt] *adj* deficiente, carente; ***be deficient in …*** carecer de …

def·i·cit ['defɪsɪt] déficit *m*

de·fine [dɪ'faɪn] *v/t word, objective* definir

def·i·nite ['defɪnɪt] *adj date, time, answer* definitivo; *improvement* claro; (*certain*) seguro; ***are you definite about that?*** ¿estás seguro de eso?; ***nothing definite has been arranged*** no se ha acordado nada de forma definitiva

def·i·nite 'ar·ti·cle GRAM artículo *m* determinado *or* definido

def·i·nite·ly ['defɪnɪtlɪ] *adv* con certeza, sin lugar a dudas

def·i·ni·tion [defɪ'nɪʃn] definición *f*

def·i·ni·tive [dɪ'fɪnətɪv] *adj* definitivo

de·flect [dɪ'flekt] *v/t* desviar; *criticism* distraer; ***be deflected from*** desviarse de

de·for·est·a·tion [dɪfɑːrɪs'teɪʃn] deforestación *f*

de·form [dɪ'fɔːrm] *v/t* deformar

de·for·mi·ty [dɪ'fɔːrmɪtɪ] deformidad *f*

de·fraud [dɪ'frɒːd] *v/t* defraudar

de·frost [diː'frɒːst] *v/t food, fridge* descongelar

deft [deft] *adj* hábil, diestro

de·fuse [diː'fjuːz] *v/t bomb* desactivar; *si-*

tuation calmar
de·fy [dɪ'faɪ] *v/t* (*pret & pp* ***defied***) desafiar
de·gen·e·rate [dɪ'dʒenəreɪt] *v/i* degenerar; ***degenerate into*** degenerar en
de·grade [dɪ'greɪd] *v/t* degradar
de·grad·ing [dɪ'greɪdɪŋ] *adj position, work* degradante
de·gree [dɪ'griː] *from university* título *m*; *of temperature, angle, latitude* grado *m*; ***there is a degree of truth in that*** hay algo de verdad en eso; ***a degree of compassion*** algo de compasión; ***by degrees*** gradualmente; ***get one's degree*** graduarse, *L.Am.* egresar
de·hy·drat·ed [diːhaɪ'dreɪtɪd] *adj* deshidratado
de-ice [diː'aɪs] *v/t* deshelar
de-ic·er [diː'aɪsər] *spray* descongelador *m*, descongelante *m*
deign [deɪn] *v/i*: ***deign to*** dignarse a
de·i·ty ['diːɪtɪ] deidad *f*
de·jec·ted [dɪ'dʒektɪd] *adj* abatido, desanimado
de·lay [dɪ'leɪ] **1** *n* retraso *m* **2** *v/t* retrasar; ***be delayed*** llevar retraso **3** *v/i* retrasarse
del·e·gate ['delɪgət] **1** *n* delegado(-a) *m*(*f*) **2** ['delɪgeɪt] *v/t task* delegar; *person* delegar en
del·e·ga·tion [delɪ'geɪʃn] delegación *f*
de·lete [dɪ'liːt] *v/t* borrar; (*cross out*) tachar; ***delete where not applicable*** táchese donde no corresponda
de·le·tion [dɪ'liːʃn] *act* borrado *m*; *that deleted* supresión *f*
del·i ['delɪ] → ***delicatessen***
de·lib·e·rate 1 *adj* [dɪ'lɪbərət] deliberado, intencionado **2** *v/i* [dɪ'lɪbəreɪt] deliberar
de·lib·e·rate·ly [dɪ'lɪbərətlɪ] *adv* deliberadamente, a propósito
del·i·ca·cy ['delɪkəsɪ] delicadeza *f*; *of health* fragilidad *f*; *food* exquisitez *f*, manjar *m*
del·i·cate ['delɪkət] *adj fabric, problem* delicado; *health* frágil
del·i·ca·tes·sen [delɪkə'tesn] *tienda de productos alimenticios de calidad*
del·i·cious [dɪ'lɪʃəs] *adj* delicioso
de·light [dɪ'laɪt] *n* placer *m*
de·light·ed [dɪ'laɪtɪd] *adj* encantado; ***I'd be delighted to come*** me encantaría venir
de·light·ful [dɪ'laɪtfəl] *adj* encantador
de·lim·it [diː'lɪmɪt] *v/t* delimitar
de·lin·quen·cy [dɪ'lɪŋkwənsɪ] delincuencia *f*
de·lin·quent [dɪ'lɪŋkwənt] *n* delincuente *m/f*
de·lir·i·ous [dɪ'lɪrɪəs] *adj* MED delirante; (*ecstatic*) entusiasmado; ***she's delirious about the new job*** está como loca con el nuevo trabajo
de·liv·er [dɪ'lɪvər] *v/t* entregar, repartir; *message* dar; *baby* dar a luz; *speech* pronunciar
de·liv·er·y [dɪ'lɪvərɪ] *of goods, mail* entrega *f*, reparto *m*; *of baby* parto *m*
de'liv·er·y charge gastos *mpl* de envío
de'liv·er·y date fecha *f* de entrega
de'liv·er·y man repartidor *m*
de'liv·er·y note nota *f* de entrega
de'liv·er·y serv·ice servicio *m* de reparto
de'liv·er·y van furgoneta *f* de reparto
de·lude [dɪ'luːd] *v/t* engañar; ***you're deluding yourself*** te estás engañando a ti mismo
de·luge ['deljuːdʒ] **1** *n* diluvio *m*; *fig* avalancha *f* **2** *v/t fig* inundar (***with*** de)
de·lu·sion [dɪ'luːʒn] engaño *m*; ***you're under a delusion if you think ...*** te engañas si piensas que ...
de luxe [də'luːks] *adj* de lujo
◆ **delve into** [delv] *v/t* rebuscar en
de·mand [dɪ'mænd] **1** *n* exigencia *f*; *by union* reivindicación *f*; COM demanda *f*; ***in demand*** solicitado **2** *v/t* exigir; (*require*) requirir
de·mand·ing [dɪ'mændɪŋ] *adj job* que exige mucho; *person* exigente
de·mean·ing [dɪ'miːnɪŋ] *adj* degradante
de·men·ted [dɪ'mentɪd] *adj* demente
de·mise [dɪ'maɪz] fallecimiento *m*; *fig* desaparición *f*
dem·i·tasse ['demɪtæs] taza *f* de café
dem·o ['demoʊ] *protest* manifestación *f*; *of video etc* maqueta *f*
de·moc·ra·cy [dɪ'mɑːkrəsɪ] democracia *f*
dem·o·crat ['deməkræt] demócrata *m/f*; ***Democrat*** POL Demócrata *m/f*
dem·o·crat·ic [demə'krætɪk] *adj* democrático
dem·o·crat·ic·ally [demə'krætɪklɪ] *adv* democráticamente
'dem·o disk disco *m* de demostración
de·mo·graph·ic [demoʊ'græfɪk] *adj* demográfico
de·mol·ish [dɪ'mɑːlɪʃ] *v/t building* demoler; *argument* destruir, echar por tierra
dem·o·li·tion [demə'lɪʃn] *of building* demolición *f*; *of argument* destrucción *f*
de·mon ['diːmən] demonio *m*
dem·on·strate ['demənstreɪt] **1** *v/t* demostrar **2** *v/i politically* manifestarse
dem·on·stra·tion [demən'streɪʃn] demostración *f*; *protest* manifestación *f*
de·mon·stra·tive [dɪ'mɑːnstrətɪv] *adj person* extrovertido, efusivo; GRAM demostrativo

de·mon·stra·tor ['demənstreɪtər] *protester* manifestante *m/f*

de·mor·al·ized [dɪ'mɔːrəlaɪzd] *adj* desmoralizado

de·mor·al·iz·ing [dɪ'mɔːrəlaɪzɪŋ] *adj* desmoralizador

de·mote [diː'mout] *v/t* degradar

de·mure [dɪ'mjuər] *adj* solemne, recatado

den [den] (*study*) estudio *m*

de·ni·al [dɪ'naɪəl] *of rumor, accusation* negación *f*; *of request* denegación *f*

den·im ['denɪm] tela *f* vaquera

den·ims ['denɪmz] *npl* (*jeans*) vaqueros *mpl*

Den·mark ['denmɑːrk] Dinamarca

de·nom·i·na·tion [dɪnɑːmɪ'neɪʃn] *of money* valor *m*; *religious* confesión *f*

de·nounce [dɪ'nauns] *v/t* denunciar

dense [dens] *adj smoke, fog* denso; *foliage* espeso; *crowd* compacto; F (*stupid*) corto

dense·ly ['denslɪ] *adv*: ***densely populated*** densamente poblado

den·si·ty ['densɪtɪ] *of population* densidad *f*

dent [dent] **1** *n* abolladura *f* **2** *v/t* abollar

den·tal ['dentl] *adj* dental; ***dental surgeon*** odontólogo(-a) *m(f)*

den·ted ['dentɪd] *adj* abollado

den·tist ['dentɪst] dentista *m/f*

den·tist·ry ['dentɪstrɪ] odontología *f*

den·tures ['dentʃərz] *npl* dentadura *f* postiza

de·ny [dɪ'naɪ] *v/t* (*pret & pp* ***denied***) *charge, rumor* negar; *right, request* denegar

de·o·do·rant [diː'oudərənt] desodorante *m*

de·part [dɪ'pɑːrt] *v/i* salir; ***depart from*** (*deviate from*) desviarse de

de·part·ment [dɪ'pɑːrtmənt] departamento *m*; *of government* ministerio *m*

De·part·ment of 'De·fense Ministerio *m* de Defensa

De·part·ment of the In'te·ri·or Ministerio *m* del Interior

De·part·ment of 'State Ministerio *m* de Asuntos Exteriores

de'part·ment store grandes almacenes *mpl*

de·par·ture [dɪ'pɑːrtʃər] salida *f*; *of person from job* marcha *f*; (*deviation*) desviación *f*; ***a new departure*** *for government, organization* una innovación; *for company* un cambio; *for actor, artist, writer* una nueva experiencia

de'par·ture lounge sala *f* de embarque

de'par·ture time hora *f* de salida

de·pend [dɪ'pend] *v/i* depender; ***that depends*** depende; ***it depends on the weather*** depende del tiempo; ***I depend on you*** dependo de ti

de·pen·da·ble [dɪ'pendəbl] *adj* fiable

de·pen·dant [dɪ'pendənt] → ***dependent***

de·pen·dence, de·pen·den·cy [dɪ'pendəns, dɪ'pendənsɪ] dependencia *f*

de·pen·dent [dɪ'pendənt] **1** *n persona a cargo de otra*; ***how many dependents do you have?*** ¿cuántas personas tiene a su cargo? **2** *adj* dependiente (***on*** de)

de·pict [dɪ'pɪkt] *v/t* describir

de·plete [dɪ'pliːt] *v/t* agotar, mermar

de·plor·a·ble [dɪ'plɔːrəbl] *adj* deplorable

de·plore [dɪ'plɔːr] *v/t* deplorar

de·ploy [dɪ'plɔɪ] *v/t* (*use*) utilizar; (*position*) desplegar

de·pop·u·la·tion [diːpɑːpjə'leɪʃn] despoblación *f*

de·port [dɪ'pɔːrt] *v/t* deportar

de·por·ta·tion [diːpɔːr'teɪʃn] deportación *f*

de·por'ta·tion or·der orden *f* de deportación

de·pose [dɪ'pouz] *v/t* deponer

de·pos·it [dɪ'pɑːzɪt] **1** *n in bank, of oil* depósito *m*; *of coal* yacimiento *m*; *on purchase* señal *f*, depósito *m* **2** *v/t money* depositar, *Span* ingresar; (*put down*) depositar

de'pos·it ac·count *Br* cuenta *f* de ahorro *or* de depósito

dep·o·si·tion [diːpou'zɪʃn] LAW declaración *f*

dep·ot ['diːpou] (*train station*) estación *f* de tren; (*bus station*) estación *f* de autobuses; *for storage* depósito *m*

de·praved [dɪ'preɪvd] *adj* depravado

de·pre·ci·ate [dɪ'priːʃɪeɪt] *v/i* FIN depreciarse

de·pre·ci·a·tion [dɪpriːʃɪ'eɪʃn] FIN depreciación *f*

de·press [dɪ'pres] *v/t person* deprimir

de·pressed [dɪ'prest] *adj person* deprimido

de·press·ing [dɪ'presɪŋ] *adj* deprimente

de·pres·sion [dɪ'preʃn] MED, *economic* depresión *f*; *meteorological* borrasca *f*

dep·ri·va·tion [deprɪ'veɪʃn] privación *f*

de·prive [dɪ'praɪv] *v/t* privar; ***deprive s.o. of sth*** privar a alguien de algo

de·prived [dɪ'praɪvd] *adj* desfavorecido

depth [depθ] profundidad *f*; *of color* intensidad *f*; ***in depth*** (*thoroughly*) en profundidad; ***in the depths of winter*** en pleno invierno; ***be out of one's depth*** *in water* no tocar el fondo; *fig*: *in discussion etc* saber muy poco

dep·u·ta·tion [depju'teɪʃn] delegación *f*

◆ **dep·u·tize for** ['depjutaɪz] *v/t* sustituir

dep·u·ty ['depjʊtɪ] segundo(-a) *m(f)*
'dep·u·ty lead·er vicelíder *m/f*
de·rail [dɪ'reɪl] *v/t* hacer descarrilar; ***be derailed*** *of train* descarrilar
de·ranged [dɪ'reɪndʒd] *adj* perturbado, trastornado
de·reg·u·late [dɪ'regjʊleɪt] *v/t* liberalizar, desregular
de·reg·u·la·tion [dɪregjʊ'leɪʃn] liberalización *f*, desregulación *f*
der·e·lict ['derəlɪkt] *adj* en ruinas
de·ride [dɪ'raɪd] *v/t* ridiculizar, mofarse de
de·ri·sion [dɪ'rɪʒn] burla *f*, mofa *f*
de·ri·sive [dɪ'raɪsɪv] *adj* burlón
de·ri·sive·ly [dɪ'raɪsɪvlɪ] *adv* burlonamente
de·ri·so·ry [dɪ'raɪsərɪ] *adj amount, salary* irrisorio
de·riv·a·tive [dɪ'rɪvətɪv] *adj* (*not original*) poco original
de·rive [dɪ'raɪv] *v/t* obtener, encontrar; ***be derived from*** *of word* derivar(se) de
der·ma·tol·o·gist [dɜːrmə'tɑːlədʒɪst] dermatólogo(-a) *m(f)*
de·rog·a·tory [dɪ'rɑːgətɔːrɪ] *adj* despectivo
de·scend [dɪ'send] **1** *v/t* descender por; ***be descended from*** descender de **2** *v/i* descender; *of mood, darkness* caer
de·scen·dant [dɪ'sendənt] descendiente *m/f*
de·scent [dɪ'sent] descenso *m*; (*ancestry*) ascendencia *f*; ***of Chinese descent*** de ascendencia china
de·scribe [dɪ'skraɪb] *v/t* describir; ***describe sth as sth*** definir a algo como algo
de·scrip·tion [dɪ'skrɪpʃn] descripción *f*
des·e·crate ['desɪkreɪt] *v/t* profanar
des·e·cra·tion [desɪ'kreɪʃn] profanación *f*
de·seg·re·gate [diː'segrəgeɪt] *v/t* acabar con la segregación racial en
des·ert[1] ['dezərt] *n also fig* desierto *m*
des·ert[2] [dɪ'zɜːrt] **1** *v/t* (*abandon*) abandonar **2** *v/i of soldier* desertar
des·ert·ed [dɪ'zɜːrtɪd] *adj* desierto
de·sert·er [dɪ'zɜːrtər] MIL desertor(a) *m(f)*
de·ser·ti·fi·ca·tion [dɪzɜːrtɪfɪ'keɪʃn] desertización *f*
de·ser·tion [dɪ'zɜːrʃn] (*abandonment*) abandono *m*; MIL deserción *f*
des·ert 'is·land isla *f* desierta
de·serve [dɪ'zɜːrv] *v/t* merecer
de·sign [dɪ'zaɪn] **1** *n* diseño *m*; (*pattern*) motivo *m* **2** *v/t* diseñar; ***not designed for heavy use*** no está diseñado para ser utilizado constantemente
des·ig·nate ['dezɪgneɪt] *v/t person* designar; *area* declarar
de·sign·er [dɪ'zaɪnər] diseñador(a) *m(f)*
de'sign·er clothes *npl* ropa *f* de diseño
de'sign fault defecto *m* de diseño
de'sign school escuela *f* de diseño
de·sir·a·ble [dɪ'zaɪrəbl] *adj* deseable; *house* apetecible, atractivo
de·sire [dɪ'zaɪr] *n* deseo *m*; ***I have no desire to see him*** no me apetece verle
desk [desk] *in classroom* pupitre *m*; *in home, office* mesa *f*; *in hotel* recepción *f*
'desk clerk recepcionista *m/f*
'desk di·a·ry agenda *f*
'desk·top *also on screen* escritorio *m*; *computer Span* ordenador *m* de escritorio, *L.Am.* computadora *f* de escritorio
desk·top 'pub·lish·ing autoedición *f*
des·o·late ['desələt] *adj place* desolado
de·spair [dɪ'sper] **1** *n* desesperación *f*; ***in despair*** desesperado **2** *v/i* desesperarse; ***I despair of finding something to wear*** he perdido la esperanza de encontrar algo para ponerme
des·per·ate ['despərət] *adj* desesperado; ***be desperate*** estar desesperado; ***be desperate for a drink / cigarette*** necesitar una bebida / un cigarrillo desesperadamente
des·per·a·tion [despə'reɪʃn] desesperación *f*; ***an act of desperation*** un acto desesperado
des·pic·a·ble [dɪs'pɪkəbl] *adj* despreciable
de·spise [dɪ'spaɪz] *v/t* despreciar
de·spite [dɪ'spaɪt] *prep* a pesar de
de·spon·dent [dɪ'spɑːndənt] *adj* abatido, desanimado
des·pot ['despɑːt] déspota *m/f*
des·sert [dɪ'zɜːrt] postre *m*
des·ti·na·tion [destɪ'neɪʃn] destino *m*
des·tined ['destɪnd] *adj*: ***be destined for*** *fig* estar destinado a
des·ti·ny ['destɪnɪ] destino *m*
des·ti·tute ['destɪtuːt] *adj* indigente; ***be destitute*** estar en la miseria
de·stroy [dɪ'strɔɪ] *v/t* destruir
de·stroy·er [dɪ'strɔɪr] NAUT destructor *m*
de·struc·tion [dɪ'strʌkʃn] destrucción *f*
de·struc·tive [dɪ'strʌktɪv] *adj* destructivo; *child* revoltoso
de·tach [dɪ'tætʃ] *v/t* separar, soltar
de·tach·a·ble [dɪ'tætʃəbl] *adj* desmontable, separable
de·tached [dɪ'tætʃt] *adj* (*objective*) distanciado
de·tach·ment [dɪ'tætʃmənt] (*objectivity*) distancia *f*
de·tail ['diːteɪl] *n* detalle *m*; ***in detail*** en detalle
de·tailed ['diːteɪld] *adj* detallado

de·tain [dɪ'teɪn] *v/t (hold back)* entretener; *as prisoner* detener
de·tain·ee [diːteɪn'iː] detenido(-a) *m(f)*
de·tect [dɪ'tekt] *v/t* percibir; *of device* detectar
de·tec·tion [dɪ'tekʃn] *of criminal, crime* descubrimiento *m*; *of smoke etc* detección *f*
de·tec·tive [dɪ'tektɪv] detective *m/f*
de'tec·tive nov·el novela *f* policiaca *or* de detectives
de·tec·tor [dɪ'tektər] detector *m*
dé·tente ['deɪtɑːnt] POL distensión *f*
de·ten·tion [dɪ'tenʃn] *(imprisonment)* detención *f*
de·ter [dɪ'tɜːr] *v/t (pret & pp* ***deterred****)* disuadir; ***deter s.o. from doing sth*** disuadir a alguien de hacer algo
de·ter·gent [dɪ'tɜːrdʒənt] detergente *m*
de·te·ri·o·rate [dɪ'tɪrɪəreɪt] *v/i* deteriorarse; *of weather* empeorar
de·te·ri·o·ra·tion [dɪtɪrɪə'reɪʃn] deterioro *m*; *of weather* empeoramiento *m*
de·ter·mi·na·tion [dɪtɜːrmɪ'neɪʃn] *(resolution)* determinación *f*
de·ter·mine [dɪ'tɜːrmɪn] *v/t (establish)* determinar
de·ter·mined [dɪ'tɜːrmɪnd] *adj* resuelto, decidido; ***I'm determined to succeed*** estoy decidido a triunfar
de·ter·rent [dɪ'terənt] *n* elemento *m* disuasorio; ***act as a deterrent*** actuar como elemento disuasorio; ***nuclear deterrent*** disuasión *f* nuclear
de·test [dɪ'test] *v/t* detestar
de·test·a·ble [dɪ'testəbl] *adj* detestable
de·to·nate ['detəneɪt] **1** *v/t* hacer detonar *or* explotar **2** *v/i* detonar, explotar
de·to·na·tion [detə'neɪʃn] detonación *f*, explosión *f*
de·tour ['diːtʊr] *n* rodeo *m*; *(diversion)* desvío *m*; ***make a detour*** dar un rodeo
◆ **de·tract from** [dɪ'trækt] *v/t achievement* quitar méritos a; *beauty* quitar atractivo a; ***the bad weather didn't detract from their enjoyment*** el mal tiempo no impidió que disfrutaran
de·tri·ment ['detrɪmənt]: ***to the detriment of*** en detrimento de
de·tri·men·tal [detrɪ'mentl] *adj* perjudicial (***to*** para)
deuce [duːs] *in tennis* deuce *m*
de·val·u·a·tion [diːvæljʊ'eɪʃn] *of currency* devaluación *f*
de·val·ue [diː'væljuː] *v/t currency* devaluar
dev·a·state ['devəsteɪt] *v/t crops, countryside, city* devastar; *fig: person* asolar
dev·a·stat·ing ['devəsteɪtɪŋ] *adj* devastador
de·vel·op [dɪ'veləp] **1** *v/t film* revelar; *land, site* urbanizar; *activity, business* desarrollar; *(originate)* desarrollar; *(improve on)* perfeccionar; *illness, cold* contraer **2** *v/i (grow)* desarrollarse; ***develop into*** convertirse en
de·vel·op·er [dɪ'veləpər] *of property* promotor(a) *m(f)* inmobiliario(-a)
de·vel·op·ing 'coun·try [dɪ'veləpɪŋ] país *m* en vías de desarrollo
de·vel·op·ment [dɪ'veləpmənt] *of film* revelado *m*; *of land, site* urbanización *f*; *of business, country* desarrollo *m*; *(event)* acontecimiento *m*; *(origination)* desarrollo *m*; *(improving)* perfeccionamiento *m*
de·vice [dɪ'vaɪs] *tool* aparato *m*, dispositivo *m*
dev·il ['devl] *also fig* diablo *m*, demonio *m*
de·vi·ous ['diːvɪəs] *adj (sly)* retorcido
de·vise [dɪ'vaɪz] *v/t* idear
de·void [dɪ'vɔɪd] *adj*: ***be devoid of*** estar desprovisto de
dev·o·lu·tion [diːvə'luːʃn] POL traspaso *m* de competencias
de·vote [dɪ'voʊt] *v/t* dedicar (***to*** a)
de·vot·ed [dɪ'voʊtɪd] *adj son etc* afectuoso; ***be devoted to s.o.*** tener mucho cariño a alguien
dev·o·tee [dɪvoʊ'tiː] entusiasta *m/f*
de·vo·tion [dɪ'voʊʃn] devoción *f*
de·vour [dɪ'vaʊər] *v/t food, book* devorar
de·vout [dɪ'vaʊt] *adj* devoto
dew [duː] rocío *m*
dex·ter·i·ty [dek'sterətɪ] destreza *f*
di·a·be·tes [daɪə'biːtiːz] *nsg* diabetes *f*
di·a·bet·ic [daɪə'betɪk] **1** *n* diabético(-a) *m(f)* **2** *adj* diabético; *foods* para diabéticos
di·ag·nose ['daɪəgnoʊz] *v/t* diagnosticar; ***she has been diagnosed as having cancer*** se le ha diagnosticado un cáncer
di·ag·no·sis [daɪəg'noʊsɪs] *(pl* ***diagnoses*** [daɪəg'noʊsiːz]) diagnóstico *m*
di·ag·o·nal [daɪ'ægənl] *adj* diagonal
di·ag·o·nal·ly [daɪ'ægənlɪ] *adv* diagonalmente, en diagonal
di·a·gram ['daɪəgræm] diagrama *m*
di·al ['daɪl] **1** *n of clock* esfera *f*; *of instrument* cuadrante *m*; TELEC disco *m* **2** *v/t & v/i (pret & pp* ***dialed****, Br* ***dialled****)* TELEC marcar
di·a·lect ['daɪəlekt] dialecto *m*
di·al·ling tone *Br* → ***dial tone***
di·a·log, *Br* **di·a·logue** ['daɪəlɑːg] diálogo *m*
di·a·log box COMPUT ventana *f* de diálogo

D

'di·al tone tono *m* de marcar

di·am·e·ter [daɪ'æmɪtər] diámetro *m*; ***a circle 6 cms in diameter*** un círculo de 6 cms. de diámetro

di·a·met·ri·cal·ly [daɪə'metrɪkəlɪ] *adv*: ***diametrically opposed*** diametralmente opuesto

di·a·mond ['daɪmənd] *also in cards* diamante *m*; *shape* rombo *m*

di·a·per ['daɪpər] pañal *m*

di·a·phragm ['daɪəfræm] ANAT, *contraceptive* diafragma *m*

di·ar·rhe·a, *Br* **di·ar·rhoe·a** [daɪə'riːə] diarrea *f*

di·a·ry ['daɪrɪ] *for thoughts* diario *m*; *for appointments* agenda *f*

dice [daɪs] **1** *n* dado *m*; *pl* dados *mpl* **2** *v/t food* cortar en dados

di·chot·o·my [daɪ'kɑːtəmɪ] dicotomía *f*

dic·ta·te [dɪk'teɪt] *v/t* dictar

dic·ta·tion [dɪk'teɪʃn] dictado *m*

dic·ta·tor [dɪk'teɪtər] POL dictador(a) *m(f)*

dic·ta·tori·al [dɪktə'tɔːrɪəl] *adj* dictatorial

dic·ta·tor·ship [dɪk'teɪtərʃɪp] dictadura *f*

dic·tion·a·ry ['dɪkʃənerɪ] diccionario *m*

did [dɪd] *pret* → ***do***

die [daɪ] *v/i* morir; ***die of cancer / Aids*** morir de cáncer / sida; ***I'm dying to know / leave*** me muero de ganas de saber / marchar

◆ **die away** *v/i of noise* desaparecer

◆ **die down** *v/i of noise* irse apagando; *of storm* amainar; *of fire* irse extinguiendo; *of excitement* calmarse

◆ **die out** *v/i of custom, species* desaparecer

die·sel ['diːzl] *fuel* gasoil *m*, gasóleo *m*

di·et ['daɪət] **1** *n* (*regular food*) dieta *f*; *for losing weight, for health reasons* dieta *f*, régimen *m* **2** *v/i to lose weight* hacer dieta *or* régimen

di·e·ti·tian [daɪə'tɪʃn] experto(-a) *m(f)* en dietética

dif·fer ['dɪfər] *v/i* (*be different*) ser distinto; (*disagree*) discrepar; ***the male differs from the female in ...*** el macho se diferencia de la hembra por ...

dif·fe·rence ['dɪfrəns] diferencia *f*; (*disagreement*) diferencia *f*, discrepancia *f*; ***it doesn't make any difference*** (*doesn't change anything*) no cambia nada; (*doesn't matter*) da lo mismo

dif·fe·rent ['dɪfrənt] *adj* diferente, distinto (***from, than*** de)

dif·fe·ren·ti·ate [dɪfə'renʃɪeɪt] *v/i* diferenciar, distinguir (***between*** entre); ***differentiate between*** *treat differently* establecer diferencias entre

dif·fe·rent·ly ['dɪfrəntlɪ] *adv* de manera diferente

dif·fi·cult ['dɪfɪkəlt] *adj* difícil

dif·fi·cul·ty ['dɪfɪkəltɪ] dificultad *f*; ***with difficulty*** con dificultades

dif·fi·dence ['dɪfɪdəns] retraimiento *m*

dif·fi·dent ['dɪfɪdənt] *adj* retraído

dig [dɪg] *v/t* & *v/i* (*pret* & *pp* ***dug***) cavar

◆ **dig out** *v/t* (*find*) encontrar

◆ **dig up** *v/t* levantar, cavar; *information* desenterrar

di·gest [daɪ'dʒest] *v/t also fig* digerir

di·gest·i·ble [daɪ'dʒestəbl] *adj food* digerible

di·ges·tion [daɪ'dʒestʃn] digestión *f*

di·ges·tive [daɪ'dʒestɪv] *adj* digestivo

dig·ger ['dɪgər] *machine* excavadora *f*

di·git ['dɪdʒɪt] (*number*) dígito *m*; ***a 4 digit number*** un número de 4 dígitos

di·gi·tal ['dɪdʒɪtl] *adj* digital

dig·ni·fied ['dɪgnɪfaɪd] *adj* digno

dig·ni·ta·ry ['dɪgnɪterɪ] dignatario(-a) *m(f)*

dig·ni·ty ['dɪgnɪtɪ] dignidad *f*

di·gress [daɪ'gres] *v/i* divagar, apartarse del tema

di·gres·sion [daɪ'greʃn] digresión *f*

dike [daɪk] *wall* dique *m*

di·lap·i·dat·ed [dɪ'læpɪdeɪtɪd] *adj* destartalado

di·late [daɪ'leɪt] *v/i of pupils* dilatarse

di·lem·ma [dɪ'lemə] dilema *m*; ***be in a dilemma*** estar en un dilema

dil·et·tante [dɪle'tæntɪ] diletante *m/f*

dil·i·gent ['dɪlɪdʒənt] *adj* diligente

di·lute [daɪ'luːt] *v/t* diluir

dim [dɪm] **1** *adj room* oscuro; *light* tenue; *outline* borroso, confuso; (*stupid*) tonto; *prospects* remoto **2** *v/t* (*pret* & *pp* ***dimmed***): atenuar; ***dim the headlights*** poner las luces cortas **3** *v/i* (*pret* & *pp* ***dimmed***) *of lights* atenuarse

dime [daɪm] *moneda de diez centavos*

di·men·sion [daɪ'menʃn] (*measurement*) dimensión *f*

di·min·ish [dɪ'mɪnɪʃ] *v/t* & *v/i* disminuir

di·min·u·tive [dɪ'mɪnʊtɪv] **1** *n* diminutivo *m* **2** *adj* diminuto

dim·ple ['dɪmpl] hoyuelo *m*

din [dɪn] *n* estruendo *m*

dine [daɪn] *v/i fml* cenar

din·er ['daɪnər] *person* comensal *m/f*; *restaurant* restaurante *m* barato

din·ghy ['dɪŋgɪ] (*small yacht*) bote *m* de vela; (*rubber boat*) lancha *f* neumática

din·gy ['dɪndʒɪ] *adj* sórdido; (*dirty*) sucio

din·ing car ['daɪnɪŋ] RAIL vagón *m* restaurante, coche *m* comedor

'din·ing room comedor *m*

'din·ing ta·ble mesa *f* de comedor
din·ner ['dɪnər] *in the evening* cena *f*; *at midday* comida *f*; (*formal gathering*) cena *f* de gala
'din·ner guest invitado(-a) *m*(*f*) a cenar
'din·ner jack·et esmoquin *m*
'din·ner par·ty cena *f*
'din·ner serv·ice vajilla *f*
di·no·saur ['daɪnəsɔːr] dinosaurio *m*
dip [dɪp] **1** *n* (*swim*) baño *m*, zambullida *f*; *for food* salsa *f*; (*slope*) inclinación *f*, pendiente *f*; (*depression*) hondonada *f* **2** *v/t* (*pret & pp* ***dipped***) meter; ***dip the headlights*** poner las luces cortas **3** *v/i* (*pret & pp* ***dipped***) *of road* bajar
di·plo·ma [dɪ'ploʊmə] diploma *m*
di·plo·ma·cy [dɪ'ploʊməsɪ] *also fig* diplomacia *f*
di·plo·mat ['dɪpləmæt] diplomático(-a) *m*(*f*)
di·plo·mat·ic [dɪplə'mætɪk] *adj also fig* diplomático
dip·lo·mat·i·cal·ly [dɪplə'mætɪklɪ] *adv* de forma diplomática
dip·lo·mat·ic im'mu·ni·ty inmunidad *f* diplomática
dire [daɪr] *adj* terrible; ***be in dire need of*** necesitar acuciantemente
di·rect [daɪ'rekt] **1** *adj* directo **2** *v/t play, movie, attention* dirigir; ***can you direct me to the museum?*** ¿me podría indicar cómo se va al museo?
di·rect 'cur·rent ELEC corriente *f* continua
di·rec·tion [dɪ'rekʃn] dirección *f*; ***directions*** *to a place* indicaciones *fpl*; (*instructions*) instrucciones *fpl*; *for medicine* posología *f*; ***let's ask for directions*** preguntemos cómo se va; ***directions for use*** modo *m* de empleo
di·rec·tion 'in·di·ca·tor MOT intermitente *m*
di·rec·tive [dɪ'rektɪv] directiva *f*
di·rect·ly [dɪ'rektlɪ] **1** *adv* (*straight*) directamente; (*soon*) pronto; (*immediately*) ahora mismo **2** *conj* en cuanto
di·rec·tor [dɪ'rektər] director(a) *m*(*f*)
di·rec·to·ry [dɪ'rektərɪ] directorio *m*; TELEC guía *f* telefónica
dirt [dɜːrt] suciedad *f*
'dirt cheap *adj* F tirado F
dirt·y ['dɜːrtɪ] **1** *adj* sucio; (*pornographic*) pornográfico, obsceno **2** *v/t* (*pret & pp* ***dirtied***) ensuciar
dirt·y 'trick jugarreta *f*; ***play a dirty trick on s.o.*** hacer una jugarreta a alguien
dis·a·bil·i·ty [dɪsə'bɪlətɪ] discapacidad *f*, minusvalía *f*
dis·a·bled [dɪs'eɪbld] **1** *n*: ***the disabled*** los discapacitados *mpl* **2** *adj* discapacitado
dis·ad·van·tage [dɪsəd'væntɪdʒ] (*drawback*) desventaja *f*; ***be at a disadvantage*** estar en desventaja
dis·ad·van·taged [dɪsəd'væntɪdʒd] *adj* desfavorecido
dis·ad·van·ta·geous [dɪsædvæn'teɪdʒəs] *adj* desventajoso, desfavorable
dis·a·gree [dɪsə'griː] *v/i of person* no estar de acuerdo, discrepar; ***let's agree to disagree*** aceptemos que no nos vamos a poner de acuerdo
◆ **disagree with** *v/t of person* no estar de acuerdo con, discrepar con; *of food* sentar mal; ***lobster disagrees with me*** la langosta me sienta mal
dis·a·gree·a·ble [dɪsə'griːəbl] *adj* desagradable
dis·a·gree·ment [dɪsə'griːmənt] desacuerdo *m*; (*argument*) discusión *f*
dis·ap·pear [dɪsə'pɪr] *v/i* desaparecer
dis·ap·pear·ance [dɪsə'pɪrəns] desaparición *f*
dis·ap·point [dɪsə'pɔɪnt] *v/t* desilusionar, decepcionar
dis·ap·point·ed [dɪsə'pɔɪntɪd] *adj* desilusionado, decepcionado
dis·ap·point·ing [dɪsə'pɔɪntɪŋ] *adj* decepcionante
dis·ap·point·ment [dɪsə'pɔɪntmənt] desilusión *f*, decepción *f*
dis·ap·prov·al [dɪsə'pruːvl] desaprobación *f*
dis·ap·prove [dɪsə'pruːv] *v/i* desaprobar, estar en contra; ***disapprove of*** desaprobar, estar en contra de
dis·ap·prov·ing [dɪsə'pruːvɪŋ] *adj* desaprobatorio, de desaprobación
dis·ap·prov·ing·ly [dɪsə'pruːvɪŋlɪ] *adv* con desaprobación
dis·arm [dɪs'ɑːrm] **1** *v/t* desarmar **2** *v/i* desarmarse
dis·ar·ma·ment [dɪs'ɑːrməmənt] desarme *m*
dis·arm·ing [dɪs'ɑːrmɪŋ] *adj* cautivador
dis·as·ter [dɪ'zæstər] desastre *m*
di'sas·ter ar·e·a zona *f* catastrófica; (*fig: person*) desastre *m*
di·sas·trous [dɪ'zæstrəs] *adj* desastroso
dis·band [dɪs'bænd] **1** *v/t* disolver **2** *v/i* disolverse
dis·be·lief [dɪsbə'liːf] incredulidad *f*; ***in disbelief*** con incredulidad
disc [dɪsk] (*CD*) compact *m* (disc)
dis·card [dɪ'skɑːrd] *v/t* desechar; *boyfriend* deshacerse de
di·scern [dɪ'sɜːrn] *v/t* distinguir, percibir
di·scern·i·ble [dɪ'sɜːrnəbl] *adj* perceptible

di·scern·ing [dɪ'sɜːrnɪŋ] *adj* entendido, exigente

dis·charge 1 *n* ['dɪstʃɑːrdʒ] *from hospital* alta *f*; *from army* licencia *f* **2** *v/t* [dɪs'tʃɑːrdʒ] *from hospital* dar el alta a; *from army* licenciar; *from job* despedir

di·sci·ple [dɪ'saɪpl] *religious* discípulo *m*

dis·ci·pli·nar·y [dɪsɪ'plɪnərɪ] *adj* disciplinario

dis·ci·pline ['dɪsɪplɪn] **1** *n* disciplina *f* **2** *v/t child, dog* castigar; *employee* sancionar

'disc jock·ey disc jockey *m/f*, *Span* pinchadiscos *m/f inv*

dis·claim [dɪs'kleɪm] *v/t* negar

dis·close [dɪs'kloʊs] *v/t* revelar

dis·clo·sure [dɪs'kloʊʒər] revelación *f*

dis·co ['dɪskoʊ] discoteca *f*

dis·col·or, *Br* **dis·col·our** [dɪs'kʌlər] *v/i* decolorar

dis·com·fort [dɪs'kʌmfərt] (*pain*) molestia *f*; (*embarrassment*) incomodidad *f*

dis·con·cert [dɪskən'sɜːrt] *v/t* desconcertar

dis·con·cert·ed [dɪskən'sɜːrtɪd] *adj* desconcertado

dis·con·nect [dɪskə'nekt] *v/t* desconectar

dis·con·so·late [dɪs'kɑːnsələt] *adj* desconsolado

dis·con·tent [dɪskən'tent] descontento *m*

dis·con·tent·ed [dɪskən'tentɪd] *adj* descontento

dis·con·tin·ue [dɪskən'tɪnjuː] *v/t product* dejar de producir; *bus, train service* suspender; *magazine* dejar de publicar

dis·cord ['dɪskɔːrd] MUS discordancia *f*; *in relations* discordia *f*

dis·co·theque ['dɪskətek] discoteca *f*

dis·count 1 *n* ['dɪskaʊnt] descuento *m* **2** *v/t* [dɪs'kaʊnt] *goods* descontar; *theory* descartar

dis·cour·age [dɪs'kʌrɪdʒ] *v/t* (*dissuade*) disuadir (***from*** de); (*dishearten*) desanimar, desalentar

dis·cour·age·ment [dɪs'kʌrɪdʒmənt] disuasión *f*; (*being disheartened*) desánimo *m*, desaliento *m*

dis·cov·er [dɪ'skʌvər] *v/t* descubrir

dis·cov·er·er [dɪ'skʌvərər] descubridor(a) *m(f)*

dis·cov·e·ry [dɪ'skʌvərɪ] descubrimiento *m*

dis·cred·it [dɪs'kredɪt] *v/t* desacreditar

di·screet [dɪ'skriːt] *adj* discreto

di·screet·ly [dɪ'skriːtlɪ] *adv* discretamente

di·screp·an·cy [dɪ'skrepənsɪ] discrepancia *f*

di·scre·tion [dɪ'skreʃn] discreción *f*; ***at your discretion*** a discreción; ***use your discretion*** usa tu criterio

di·scrim·i·nate [dɪ'skrɪmɪneɪt] *v/i* discriminar (***against*** contra); ***discriminate between*** (*distinguish*) distinguir entre

di·scrim·i·nat·ing [dɪ'skrɪmɪneɪtɪŋ] *adj* entendido, exigente

di·scrim·i·na·tion [dɪ'skrɪmɪneɪʃn] *sexual, racial etc* discriminación *f*

dis·cus ['dɪskəs] SP *object* disco *m*; *event* lanzamiento *m* de disco

di·scuss [dɪ'skʌs] *v/t* discutir; *of article* analizar

di·scus·sion [dɪ'skʌʃn] discusión *f*

'dis·cus throw·er lanzador(a) *m(f)* de disco

dis·dain [dɪs'deɪn] *n* desdén *m*

dis·ease [dɪ'ziːz] enfermedad *f*

dis·em·bark [dɪsəm'bɑːrk] *v/i* desembarcar

dis·en·chant·ed [dɪsən'tʃæntɪd] *adj*: ***disenchanted with*** desencantado con

dis·en·gage [dɪsən'geɪdʒ] *v/t* soltar

dis·en·tan·gle [dɪsən'tæŋgl] *v/t* desenredar

dis·fig·ure [dɪs'fɪgər] *v/t* desfigurar

dis·grace [dɪs'greɪs] **1** *n* vergüenza *f*; ***it's a disgrace!*** ¡qué vergüenza!; ***in disgrace*** desacreditado **2** *v/t* deshonrar

dis·grace·ful [dɪs'greɪsfəl] *adj behavior, situation* vergonzoso, lamentable

dis·grunt·led [dɪs'grʌntld] *adj* descontento

dis·guise [dɪs'gaɪz] **1** *n* disfraz *m*; ***in disguise*** disfrazado **2** *v/t voice, handwriting* cambiar; *fear, anxiety* disfrazar; ***disguise o.s. as*** disfrazarse de; ***he was disguised as*** iba disfrazado de

dis·gust [dɪs'gʌst] **1** *n* asco *m*, repugnancia *f*; ***in disgust*** asqueado **2** *v/t* dar asco, repugnar; ***I'm disgusted by ...*** me da asco *or* me repugna ...

dis·gust·ing [dɪs'gʌstɪŋ] *adj habit, smell, food* asqueroso, repugnante; ***it is disgusting that ...*** da asco que ..., es repugnante que ...

dish [dɪʃ] (*part of meal, container*) plato *m*

'dish·cloth paño *m* de cocina

dis·heart·en·ed [dɪs'hɑːrtnd] *adj* desalentado, descorazonado

dis·heart·en·ing [dɪs'hɑːrtnɪŋ] *adj* descorazonador

di·shev·eled [dɪ'ʃevld] *adj hair, clothes* desaliñado; *person* despeinado

dis·hon·est [dɪs'ɑːnɪst] *adj* deshonesto

dis·hon·est·y [dɪs'ɑːnɪstɪ] deshonestidad *f*

dis·hon·or [dɪs'ɑːnər] *n* deshonra *f*; ***bring dishonor on*** deshonrar a

dis·hon·o·ra·ble [dɪs'ɑːnərəbl] *adj* deshonroso
dis·hon·our *etc Br* → ***dishonor*** *etc*
'**dish·wash·er** *person* lavaplatos *m/f inv*; *machine* lavavajillas *m inv*, lavaplatos *m inv*
'**dish·wash·ing liq·uid** lavavajillas *m inv*
'**dish·wa·ter** agua *f* de lavar los platos
dis·il·lu·sion [dɪsɪ'luːʒn] *v/t* desilusionar
dis·il·lu·sion·ment [dɪsɪ'luːʒnmənt] desilusión *f*
dis·in·clined [dɪsɪn'klaɪnd] *adj*: ***she was disinclined to believe him*** no estaba inclinada a creerle
dis·in·fect [dɪsɪn'fekt] *v/t* desinfectar
dis·in·fec·tant [dɪsɪn'fektənt] desinfectante *m*
dis·in·her·it [dɪsɪn'herɪt] *v/t* desheredar
dis·in·te·grate [dɪs'ɪntəgreɪt] *v/i* desintegrarse; *of marriage* deshacerse
dis·in·terest·ed [dɪs'ɪntərestɪd] *adj* (*unbiased*) desinteresado
dis·joint·ed [dɪs'dʒɔɪntɪd] *adj* deshilvanado
disk [dɪsk] *also* COMPUT disco *m*; ***on disk*** en disco
'**disk drive** COMPUT unidad *f* de disco
disk·ette [dɪs'ket] disquete *m*
dis·like [dɪs'laɪk] **1** *n* antipatía *f* **2** *v/t*: ***she dislikes being kept waiting*** no le gusta que la hagan esperar; ***I dislike him*** no me gusta
dis·lo·cate ['dɪsləkeɪt] *v/t shoulder* dislocar
dis·lodge [dɪs'lɑːdʒ] *v/t* desplazar, mover de su sitio
dis·loy·al [dɪs'lɔɪəl] *adj* desleal
dis·loy·al·ty [dɪs'lɔɪəltɪ] deslealtad *f*
dis·mal ['dɪzməl] *adj weather* horroroso, espantoso; *news*, *prospect* negro; *person* (*sad*) triste; *person* (*negative*) negativo; *failure* estrepitoso
dis·man·tle [dɪs'mæntl] *v/t* desmantelar
dis·may [dɪs'meɪ] **1** *n* (*alarm*) consternación *f*; (*disappointment*) desánimo *m* **2** *v/t* consternar
dis·miss [dɪs'mɪs] *v/t employee* despedir; *suggestion* rechazar; *idea*, *possibility* descartar
dis·miss·al [dɪs'mɪsl] *of employee* despido *m*
dis·mount [dɪs'maʊnt] *v/i* desmontar
dis·o·be·di·ence [dɪsə'biːdɪəns] desobediencia *f*
dis·o·be·di·ent [dɪsə'biːdɪənt] *adj* desobediente
dis·o·bey [dɪsə'beɪ] *v/t* desobedecer
dis·or·der [dɪs'ɔːrdər] (*untidiness*) desorden *m*; (*unrest*) desórdenes *mpl*; MED dolencia *f*
dis·or·der·ly [dɪs'ɔːrdərlɪ] *adj room*, *desk* desordenado; *mob* alborotado
dis·or·gan·ized [dɪs'ɔːrgənaɪzd] *adj* desorganizado
dis·o·ri·ent·ed [dɪs'ɔːrɪəntɪd] *adj* desorientado
dis·own [dɪs'oʊn] *v/t* repudiar, renegar de
di·spar·ag·ing [dɪ'spærɪdʒɪŋ] *adj* despreciativo
di·spar·i·ty [dɪ'spærətɪ] disparidad *f*
dis·pas·sion·ate [dɪ'spæʃənət] *adj* (*objective*) desapasionado
di·spatch [dɪ'spætʃ] *v/t* (*send*) enviar
di·spen·sa·ry [dɪ'spensərɪ] *in pharmacy* dispensario *m*
◆ **di·spense with** [dɪ'spens] *v/t* prescindir de
di·sperse [dɪ'spɜːrs] **1** *v/t* dispersar **2** *v/i* *of crowd* dispersarse; *of mist* disiparse
di·spir·it·ed [dɪs'pɪrɪtɪd] *adj* desalentado, abatido
dis·place [dɪs'pleɪs] *v/t* (*supplant*) sustituir
di·splay [dɪ'spleɪ] **1** *n* muestra *f*; *in store window* objetos *mpl* expuestos; COMPUT pantalla *f*; ***be on display*** estar expuesto **2** *v/t emotion* mostrar; *at exhibition*, *for sale* exponer; COMPUT visualizar
di'splay cab·i·net *in museum*, *shop* vitrina *f*
dis·please [dɪs'pliːz] *v/t* desagradar, disgustar
dis·plea·sure [dɪs'pleʒər] desagrado *m*, disgusto *m*
dis·po·sa·ble [dɪ'spoʊzəbl] *adj* desechable; ***disposable income*** ingreso(s) *m*(*pl*) disponible(s)
dis·pos·al [dɪ'spoʊzl] eliminación *f*; ***I am at your disposal*** estoy a su disposición; ***put sth at s.o.'s disposal*** poner algo a disposición de alguien
◆ **dis·pose of** [dɪ'spoʊz] *v/t* (*get rid of*) deshacerse de
dis·posed [dɪ'spoʊzd] *adj*: ***be disposed to do sth*** (*willing*) estar dispuesto a hacer algo; ***be well disposed towards*** estar bien dispuesto hacia
dis·po·si·tion [dɪspə'zɪʃn] (*nature*) carácter *m*
dis·pro·por·tion·ate [dɪsprə'pɔːrʃənət] *adj* desproporcionado
dis·prove [dɪs'pruːv] *v/t* refutar
di·spute [dɪ'spjuːt] **1** *n* disputa *f*; *industrial* conflicto *m* laboral **2** *v/t* discutir; (*fight over*) disputarse; ***I don't dispute that*** eso no lo discuto
dis·qual·i·fi·ca·tion [dɪskwɑːlɪfɪ'keɪʃn] descalificación *f*

D

dis·qual·i·fy [dɪs'kwɑːlɪfaɪ] *v/t* (*pret & pp* ***disqualified***) descalificar
dis·re·gard [dɪsrə'gɑːrd] **1** *n* indiferencia *f* **2** *v/t* no tener en cuenta
dis·re·pair [dɪsrə'per]: ***in a state of disrepair*** deteriorado
dis·rep·u·ta·ble [dɪs'repjʊtəbl] *adj* poco respetable; *area* de mala reputación
dis·re·spect [dɪsrə'spekt] falta *f* de respeto
dis·re·spect·ful [dɪsrə'spektfəl] *adj* irrespetuoso
dis·rupt [dɪs'rʌpt] *v/t train service* trastornar, alterar; *meeting*, *class* interrumpir
dis·rup·tion [dɪs'rʌpʃn] *of train service* alteración *f*; *of meeting*, *class* interrupción *f*
dis·rup·tive [dɪs'rʌptɪv] *adj* perjudicial; ***he's very disruptive in class*** causa muchos problemas en clase
dis·sat·is·fac·tion [dɪssætɪs'fækʃn] insatisfacción *f*
dis·sat·is·fied [dɪs'sætɪsfaɪd] *adj* insatisfecho
dis·sen·sion [dɪ'senʃn] disensión *f*
dis·sent [dɪ'sent] **1** *n* discrepancia *f* **2** *v/i*: ***dissent from*** disentir de
dis·si·dent ['dɪsɪdənt] *n* disidente *m/f*
dis·sim·i·lar [dɪs'sɪmɪlər] *adj* distinto
dis·so·ci·ate [dɪ'soʊʃɪeɪt] *v/t* disociar; ***dissociate o.s. from*** disociarse de
dis·so·lute ['dɪsəluːt] *adj* disoluto
dis·so·lu·tion ['dɪsəluːʃn] POL disolución *f*
dis·solve [dɪ'zɑːlv] **1** *v/t substance* disolver **2** *v/i of substance* disolverse
dis·suade [dɪ'sweɪd] *v/t* disuadir; ***dissuade s.o. from doing sth*** disuadir a alguien de hacer algo
dis·tance ['dɪstəns] **1** *n* distancia *f*; ***in the distance*** en la lejanía **2** *v/t* distanciar; ***distance o.s. from*** distanciarse de
dis·tant ['dɪstənt] *adj place*, *time*, *relative* distante, lejano; (*fig*: *aloof*) distante
dis·taste [dɪs'teɪst] desagrado *m*
dis·taste·ful [dɪs'teɪstfəl] *adj* desagradable
dis·till·er·y [dɪs'tɪlərɪ] destilería *f*
dis·tinct [dɪ'stɪŋkt] *adj* (*clear*) claro; (*different*) distinto; ***as distinct from*** a diferencia de
dis·tinc·tion [dɪ'stɪŋkʃn] (*differentiation*) distinción *f*; ***hotel / product of distinction*** un hotel / producto destacado
dis·tinc·tive [dɪ'stɪŋktɪv] *adj* característico
dis·tinct·ly [dɪ'stɪŋktlɪ] *adv* claramente, con claridad; (*decidedly*) verdaderamente
dis·tin·guish [dɪ'stɪŋgwɪʃ] *v/t* distinguir; ***distinguish between X and Y*** distinguir entre X e Y
dis·tin·guished [dɪ'stɪŋgwɪʃt] *adj* distinguido
dis·tort [dɪ'stɔːrt] *v/t* distorsionar
dis·tract [dɪ'strækt] *v/t* distraer
dis·trac·tion [dɪ'strækʃn] distracción *f*; ***drive s.o. to distraction*** sacar a alguien de quicio
dis·traught [dɪ'strɒːt] *adj* angustiado, consternado
dis·tress [dɪ'stres] **1** *n* sufrimiento *m*; ***in distress*** *of ship*, *aircraft* en peligro **2** *v/t* (*upset*) angustiar
dis·tress·ing [dɪ'stresɪŋ] *adj* angustiante
dis'tress sig·nal señal *m* de socorro
dis·trib·ute [dɪ'strɪbjuːt] *v/t* distribuir, repartir; COM distribuir
dis·tri·bu·tion [dɪstrɪ'bjuːʃn] distribución *f*
dis·tri'bu·tion ar·range·ment COM acuerdo *m* de distribución
dis·trib·u·tor [dɪs'trɪbjuːtər] COM distribuidor(a) *m*(*f*)
dis·trict ['dɪstrɪkt] (*area*) zona *f*; (*neighborhood*) barrio *m*
dis·trict at'tor·ney fiscal *m/f* del distrito
dis·trust [dɪs'trʌst] **1** *n* desconfianza *f* **2** *v/t* desconfiar de
dis·turb [dɪ'stɜːrb] *v/t* (*interrupt*) molestar; (*upset*) preocupar; ***do not disturb*** no molestar
dis·turb·ance [dɪ'stɜːrbəns] (*interruption*) molestia *f*; ***disturbances*** (*civil unrest*) disturbios *mpl*
dis·turbed [dɪ'stɜːrbd] *adj* (*concerned*, *worried*) preocupado, inquieto; *mentally* perturbado
dis·turb·ing [dɪ'stɜːrbɪŋ] *adj* (*worrying*) inquietante; ***you may find some scenes disturbing*** algunas de las escenas pueden herir la sensibilidad del espectador
dis·used [dɪs'juːzd] *adj* abandonado
ditch [dɪʧ] **1** *n* zanja *f* **2** *v/t* F (*get rid of*) deshacerse de; *boyfriend* plantar F; *plan* abandonar
dith·er ['dɪðər] *v/i* vacilar
dive [daɪv] **1** *n* salto *m* de cabeza; *underwater* inmersión *f*; *of plane* descenso *m* en picado; F *bar etc* antro *m* F; ***take a dive*** F *of dollar etc* desplomarse **2** *v/i* (*pret also* ***dove***) tirarse de cabeza; *underwater* bucear; *of plane* descender en picado
div·er ['daɪvər] *off board* saltador(a) *m*(*f*) de trampolín; *underwater* buceador(a) *m*(*f*)
di·verge [daɪ'vɜːrdʒ] *v/i* bifurcarse
di·verse [daɪ'vɜːrs] *adj* diverso

di·ver·si·fi·ca·tion [daɪvɜːrsɪfɪ'keɪʃn] COM diversificación *f*
di·ver·si·fy [daɪ'vɜːrsɪfaɪ] *v/i* (*pret & pp* ***diversified***) COM diversificarse
di·ver·sion [daɪ'vɜːrʃn] *for traffic* desvío *f*; *to distract attention* distracción *f*
di·ver·si·ty [daɪ'vɜːrsətɪ] diversidad *f*
di·vert [daɪ'vɜːrt] *v/t traffic, attention* desviar
di·vest [daɪ'vest] *v/t*: ***divest s.o. of sth*** despojar a alguien de algo
di·vide [dɪ'vaɪd] *v/t also fig* dividir; ***divide 16 by 4*** dividir 16 entre 4
div·i·dend ['dɪvɪdend] FIN dividendo *m*; ***pay dividends*** *fig* resultar beneficioso
di·vine [dɪ'vaɪn] *adj also* F divino
div·ing ['daɪvɪŋ] *from board* salto *m* de trampolín; (*scuba diving*) buceo *m*, submarinismo *m*
'div·ing board trampolín *m*
di·vis·i·ble [dɪ'vɪzəbl] *adj* divisible
di·vi·sion [dɪ'vɪʒn] división *f*
di·vorce [dɪ'vɔːrs] **1** *n* divorcio *m*; ***get a divorce*** divorciarse **2** *v/t* divorciarse de; ***get divorced*** divorciarse **3** *v/i* divorciarse
di·vorced [dɪ'vɔːrst] *adj* divorciado
di·vor·cee [dɪvɔːr'siː] divorciado(-a) *m(f)*
di·vulge [daɪ'vʌldʒ] *v/t* divulgar, dar a conocer
DIY [diːaɪ'waɪ] *abbr* (= ***do it yourself***) bricolaje *m*
DI'Y store tienda *f* de bricolaje
diz·zi·ness ['dɪzɪnɪs] mareo *m*
diz·zy ['dɪzɪ] *adj* mareado; ***feel dizzy*** estar mareado
DJ ['diːdʒeɪ] *abbr* (= ***disc jockey***) disc jockey *m/f*, *Span* pinchadiscos *m/f inv*; (= ***dinner jacket***) esmoquin *m*
DNA [diːen'eɪ] *abbr* (= ***deoxyribonucleic acid***) AND *m* (= ácido *m* desoxirribonucleico)
do [duː] **1** *v/t* (*pret* ***did***, *pp* ***done***) hacer; *100 mph etc* ir a; ***do one's hair*** peinarse; ***what are you doing tonight?*** ¿qué vas a hacer esta noche?; ***I don't know what to do*** no sé qué hacer; ***do it right now!*** hazlo ahora mismo; ***have one's hair done*** arreglarse el pelo **2** *v/i* (*pret* ***did***, *pp* ***done***) (*be suitable, enough*): ***that'll do nicely*** eso bastará; ***that will do!*** ¡ya vale!; ***do well*** *of business* ir bien; ***he's doing well*** le van bien las cosas; ***well done!*** (*congratulations!*) ¡bien hecho!; ***how do you do?*** encantado de conocerle **3** *v/aux*: ***do you know him?*** ¿lo conoces?; ***I don't know*** no sé; ***do be quick*** date prisa, por favor; ***do you like Des Moines? - yes I do*** ¿te gusta Des Moines? - sí; ***he works hard, doesn't he?*** trabaja mucho, ¿verdad?; ***don't you believe me?*** ¿no me crees?; ***you do believe me, don't you?*** me crees, ¿verdad?; ***you don't know the answer, do you? - no I don't*** no sabes la respuesta, ¿no es así? - no, no la sé
◆ **do away with** *v/t* (*abolish*) abolir
◆ **do in** *v/t* F (*exhaust*) machacar F; ***I'm done in*** estoy hecho polvo F
◆ **do out of** *v/t*: ***do s.o. out of sth*** timar alguien a algo F
◆ **do up** *v/t* (*renovate*) renovar; *buttons, coat* abrocharse; *laces* atarse
◆ **do with** *v/t*: ***I could do with ...*** no me vendría mal ...; ***he won't have anything to do with it*** (*won't get involved*) no quiere saber nada de ello
◆ **do without 1** *v/i*: ***you'll have to do without*** te las tendrás que arreglar **2** *v/t* pasar sin
do·cile ['dousəl] *adj* dócil
dock[1] [dɑːk] **1** *n* NAUT muelle *m* **2** *v/i of ship* atracar; *of spaceship* acoplarse
dock[2] [dɑːk] *n* LAW banquillo *m* (de los acusados)
'dock·yard *Br* astillero *m*
doc·tor ['dɑːktər] *n* MED médico *m*; *form of address* doctor *m*
doc·tor·ate ['dɑːktərət] doctorado *m*
doc·trine ['dɑːktrɪn] doctrina *f*
doc·u·dra·ma ['dɑːkjʊdrɑːmə] docudrama *m*
doc·u·ment ['dɑːkjʊmənt] *n* documento *m*
doc·u·men·ta·ry [dɑːkjʊ'mentərɪ] *n program* documental *m*
doc·u·men·ta·tion [dɑːkjʊmen'teɪʃn] documentación *f*
dodge [dɑːdʒ] *v/t blow, person* esquivar; *issue, question* eludir
doe [doʊ] *deer* cierva *f*
dog [dɒːg] **1** *n* perro(-a) *m(f)* **2** *v/t* (*pret & pp* ***dogged***) *of bad luck* perseguir
'dog catch·er perrero(-a) *m(f)*
dog-eared ['dɒːgɪrd] *adj book* sobado, con las esquinas dobladas
dog·ged ['dɒːgɪd] *adj* tenaz
dog·gie ['dɒːgɪ] *in children's language* perrito *m*
dog·gy bag ['dɒːgɪbæg] *bolsa para las sobras de la comida*
'dog·house: ***be in the doghouse*** F haber caído en desgracia
dog·ma ['dɒːgmə] dogma *m*
dog·mat·ic [dɒːg'mætɪk] *adj* dogmático
do-good·er ['duːgʊdər] *pej* buen(a) samaritano(-a) *m(f)*

D

'**dog tag** MIL chapa *f* de identificación
'**dog-tired** *adj* F hecho polvo F
do-it-your·self [du:ɪtjər'self] bricolaje *m*
dol·drums ['doʊldrəmz]: ***be in the doldrums*** *of economy* estar en un bache; ***doldrums*** *of person* estar deprimido
◆ **dole out** *v/t* repartir
doll [dɑ:l] *toy* muñeca *f*; F *woman* muñeca *f* F
◆ **doll up** *v/t*: ***get dolled up*** emperifollarse
dol·lar ['dɑ:lər] dólar *m*
dol·lop ['dɑ:ləp] *n* F cucharada *f*
dol·phin ['dɑ:lfɪn] delfín *m*
dome [doʊm] *of building* cúpula *f*
do·mes·tic [də'mestɪk] **1** *adj chores* doméstico, del hogar; *news, policy* nacional **2** *n* empleado(-a) *m(f)* del hogar
do·mes·tic 'an·i·mal animal *m* doméstico
do·mes·ti·cate [də'mestɪkeɪt] *v/t animal* domesticar; ***be domesticated*** *of person* estar domesticado
do'mes·tic flight vuelo *m* nacional
dom·i·nant ['dɑ:mɪnənt] *adj* dominante
dom·i·nate ['dɑ:mɪneɪt] *v/t* dominar
dom·i·na·tion [dɑ:mɪ'neɪʃn] dominación *f*
dom·i·neer·ing [dɑ:mɪ'nɪrɪŋ] *adj* dominante
dom·i·no ['dɑ:mɪnoʊ] ficha *f* de dominó; ***play dominoes*** jugar al dominó
do·nate [doʊ'neɪt] *v/t* donar
do·na·tion [doʊ'neɪʃn] donación *f*, donativo *m*; MED donación *f*
done [dʌn] *pp* → ***do***
don·key ['dɑ:ŋkɪ] burro *m*
do·nor ['doʊnər] *of money*, MED donante *m/f*
do·nut ['doʊnʌt] dónut *m*
doo·dle ['du:dl] *v/i* garabatear
doom [du:m] *n* (*fate*) destino *m*; (*ruin*) fatalidad *f*
doomed [du:md] *adj project* condenado al fracaso; ***we are doomed*** (*bound to fail*) estamos condenados al fracaso; (*going to die*) vamos a morir
door [dɔ:r] puerta *f*; ***there's someone at the door*** hay alguien en la puerta
'**door·bell** timbre *m*
'**door·knob** pomo *m*
'**door·man** portero *m*
'**door·mat** felpudo *m*
'**door·step** umbral *m*
'**door·way** puerta *f*
dope [doʊp] **1** *n* (*drugs*) droga *f*; F (*idiot*) lelo(-a) *m(f)*; F (*information*) información *f* **2** *v/t* drogar
dor·mant ['dɔ:rmənt] *adj plant* aletargado; *volcano* inactivo
dor·mi·to·ry ['dɔ:rmɪtɔ:rɪ] dormitorio *m* (colectivo); (*hall of residence*) residencia *f* de estudiantes
dos·age ['doʊsɪdʒ] dosis *f inv*
dose [doʊs] *n* dosis *f inv*
dot [dɑ:t] *n* punto *m*; ***on the dot*** (*exactly*) en punto
◆ **dote on** [doʊt] *v/t* adorar a
dot.com (com·pany) [dɑ:t'kɑ:m] empresa *f* punto.com
dot·ing ['doʊtɪŋ] *adj*: ***my doting aunt*** mi tía, que tanto me adora
dot·ted line ['dɑ:tɪd] línea *f* de puntos
doub·le ['dʌbl] **1** *n person* doble *m/f*; *room* habitación *f* doble **2** *adj* doble; ***inflation is now in double figures*** la inflación ha superado ya el 10% **3** *adv*: ***they offered me double what the others did*** me ofrecieron el doble que la otra gente **4** *v/t* doblar, duplicar **5** *v/i* doblarse, duplicarse; ***it doubles as ...*** hace también de ...
◆ **double back** *v/i* (*go back*) volver sobre sus pasos
◆ **double up** *v/i in pain* doblarse; (*share*) compartir habitación
doub·le-'bass contrabajo *m*
doub·le 'bed cama *f* de matrimonio
doub·le-breast·ed [dʌbl'brestɪd] *adj* cruzado
doub·le'check *v/t & v/i* volver a comprobar
doub·le 'chin papada *f*
doub·le'cross *v/t* engañar, traicionar
doub·le 'glaz·ing doble acristalamiento *m*
doub·le'park *v/i* aparcar en doble fila
'**doub·le-quick** *adj*: ***in double-quick time*** muy rápidamente
'**doub·le room** habitación *f* doble
doub·les ['dʌblz] *in tennis* dobles *mpl*
doubt [daʊt] **1** *n* duda *f*; (*uncertainty*) dudas *fpl*; ***be in doubt*** ser incierto; ***not be in doubt*** estar claro; ***no doubt*** (*probably*) sin duda **2** *v/t* dudar; ***we never doubted you*** nunca dudamos de ti
doubt·ful ['daʊtfəl] *adj remark, look* dubitativo; ***be doubtful*** *of person* tener dudas; ***it is doubtful whether ...*** es dudoso que ...
doubt·ful·ly ['daʊtfəlɪ] *adv* lleno de dudas
doubt·less ['daʊtlɪs] *adj* sin duda, indudablemente
dough [doʊ] masa *f*; F (*money*) *Span* pasta *f* F, *L.Am.* plata *f* F
dough·nut ['doʊnʌt] dónut *m*
dove[1] [dʌv] *also fig* paloma *f*
dove[2] [doʊv] *pret* → ***dive***

dow·dy ['daʊdɪ] *adj* poco elegante
Dow Jones Av·er·age [daʊdʒoʊnz'ævərɪdʒ] índice *m* Dow Jones
down[1] [daʊn] *n* (*feathers*) plumón *m*
down[2] [daʊn] **1** *adv* (*downward*) (hacia) abajo; ***pull the blind down*** baja la persiana; ***put it down on the table*** ponlo en la mesa; ***when the leaves come down*** cuando se caen las hojas; ***cut down a tree*** cortar un árbol; ***she was down on her knees*** estaba arrodillada; ***the plane was shot down*** el avión fue abatido; ***down there*** allá abajo; ***fall down*** caerse; ***die down*** amainar; ***$200 down*** (*as deposit*) una entrada de 200 dólares; ***down south*** hacia el sur; ***be down*** *of price, rate* haber bajado; *of numbers, amount* haber descendido; (*not working*) no funcionar; F (*depressed*) estar deprimido *or* con la depre F **2** *prep*: ***run down the stairs*** bajar las escaleras corriendo; ***the lava rolled down the hill*** la lava descendía por la colina; ***walk down the street*** andar por la calle; ***down the corridor*** por el pasillo **3** *v/t* (*swallow*) tragar; (*destroy*) derribar
'**down-and-out** *n* vagabundo(-a) *m*(*f*)
'**down·cast** *adj* (*dejected*) deprimido
'**down·fall** caída *f*; *of person* perdición *f*
'**down·grade** *v/t* degradar; ***the hurricane has been downgraded to a storm*** el huracán ha sido reducido a la categoría de tormenta
down·heart·ed [daʊn'hɑːrtɪd] *adj* abatido
down'hill *adv* cuesta abajo; ***go downhill*** *fig* ir cuesta abajo
'**down·hill ski·ing** descenso *m*
'**down·load** *v/t* COMPUT descargar, bajar
'**down·mark·et** *adj* barato
'**down pay·ment** entrada *f*; ***make a down payment on sth*** pagar la entrada de algo
'**down·play** *v/t* quitar importancia a
'**down·pour** chaparrón *m*, aguacero *m*
'**down·right** **1** *adj lie* evidente; *idiot* completo **2** *adv dangerous* extremadamente; *stupid* completamente
'**down·side** (*disadvantage*) desventaja *f*, inconveniente *m*
'**down·size** **1** *v/t car* reducir el tamaño de; *company* reajustar la plantilla de **2** *v/i of company* reajustar la plantilla
'**down·stairs** **1** *adj* del piso de abajo; ***my downstairs neighbors*** los vecinos de abajo **2** *adv*: ***the kitchen is downstairs*** la cocina está en el piso de abajo; ***I ran downstairs*** bajé corriendo
down-to-'earth *adj approach, person* práctico, realista
'**down·town** **1** *n* centro *m* **2** *adj* del centro **2** *adv*: ***I'm going downtown*** voy al centro; ***he lives downtown*** vive en el centro
'**down·turn** *in economy* bajón *m*
'**down·ward** ['daʊnwərd] **1** *adj* descendente **2** *adv* a la baja
doze [doʊz] **1** *n* cabezada *f*, sueño *m* **2** *v/i* echar una cabezada
◆ **doze off** *v/i* quedarse dormido
doz·en ['dʌzn] docena *f*; ***dozens of*** F montonadas de F
drab [dræb] *adj* gris
draft [dræft] **1** *n of air* corriente *f*; *of document* borrador *m*; MIL reclutamiento *m*; ***draft*** (***beer***), ***beer on draft*** cerveza *f* de barril **2** *v/t document* redactar un borrador de; MIL reclutar
'**draft dodg·er** prófugo(-a) *m*(*f*)
draft·ee [dræft'iː] recluta *m/f*
drafts·man ['dræftsmən] delineante *m/f*
draft·y ['dræftɪ] *adj*: ***it's drafty here*** hace mucha corriente aquí
drag [dræg] **1** *n*: ***it's a drag having to …*** F es un latazo tener que … F; ***he's a drag*** F es un peñazo F; ***the main drag*** F la calle principal; ***in drag*** vestido de mujer **2** *v/t* (*pret & pp* ***dragged***) (*pull*) arrastrar; (*search*) dragar **3** *v/i* (*pret & pp* ***dragged***) *of time* pasar despacio; *of show, movie* ser pesado; ***drag s.o. into sth*** (*involve*) meter a alguien en algo; ***drag sth out of s.o.*** (*get information from*) arrancar algo de alguien
◆ **drag away** *v/t*: ***drag o.s. away from the TV*** despegarse de la TV
◆ **drag in** *v/t into conversation* introducir
◆ **drag on** *v/i* (*last long time*) alargarse
◆ **drag out** *v/t* (*prolong*) alargar
◆ **drag up** *v/t* F (*mention*) sacar a relucir
drag·on ['drægn] dragón *m*; *fig* ogro *m*
drain [dreɪn] **1** *n pipe* sumidero *m*, desagüe *m*; *under street* alcantarilla *f*; ***a drain on resources*** una sangría en los recursos **2** *v/t water, vegetables* escurrir; *land* drenar; *glass, tank, oil* vaciar; *person* agotar **3** *v/i of dishes* escurrir
◆ **drain away** *v/i of liquid* irse
◆ **drain off** *v/t water* escurrir
drain·age ['dreɪnɪdʒ] (*drains*) desagües *mpl*; *of water from soil* drenaje *m*
'**drain·pipe** tubo *m* de desagüe
dra·ma ['drɑːmə] (*art form*) drama *m*, teatro *m*; (*excitement*) dramatismo *m*; (*play*: *on* TV) drama *m*, obra *f* de teatro
dra·mat·ic [drə'mætɪk] *adj* dramático; *scenery* espectacular
dra·mat·i·cal·ly [drə'mætɪklɪ] *adv say* con dramatismo, de manera dramática; *decline, rise, change etc* espectacularmente

dram·a·tist ['dræmətɪst] dramaturgo(-a) *m(f)*
dram·a·ti·za·tion [dræmətaɪ'zeɪʃn] (*play*) dramatización *f*

D

dram·a·tize ['dræmətaɪz] *v/t also fig* dramatizar
drank [dræŋk] *pret* → ***drink***
drape [dreɪp] *v/t cloth* cubrir; ***draped in*** (*covered with*) cubierto con
drap·er·y ['dreɪpərɪ] ropajes *mpl*
drapes [dreɪps] *npl* cortinas *fpl*
dras·tic ['dræstɪk] *adj* drástico
draught *Br* → ***draft***
draw [drɒː] **1** *n in match, competition* empate *m*; *in lottery* sorteo *m*; (*attraction*) atracción *f* **2** *v/t* (*pret* ***drew***, *pp* ***drawn***) *picture, map* dibujar; *cart* tirar de; *curtain* correr; *in lottery* sortear; *gun, knife* sacar; (*attract*) atraer; (*lead*) llevar; *from bank account* sacar, retirar **3** *v/i* (*pret* ***drew***, *pp* ***drawn***) dibujar; *in match, competition* empatar; ***draw near*** acercarse
◆ **draw back 1** *v/i* (*recoil*) echarse atrás **2** *v/t* (*pull back*) retirar
◆ **draw on 1** *v/i* (*approach*) aproximarse **2** *v/t* (*make use of*) utilizar
◆ **draw out** *v/t wallet, money from bank* sacar
◆ **draw up 1** *v/t document* redactar; *chair* acercar **2** *v/i of vehicle* parar
'**draw·back** desventaja *f*, inconveniente *m*
draw·er[1] [drɔr] *of desk etc* cajón *m*
draw·er[2] [drɔr]: ***she's a good drawer*** dibuja muy bien
draw·ing ['drɒːɪŋ] dibujo *m*
'**draw·ing board** tablero *m* de dibujo; ***go back to the drawing board*** *fig* volver a empezar otra vez
'**draw·ing pin** *Br* chincheta *f*
drawl [drɒːl] *n* acento *m* arrastrado
drawn [drɒːn] *pp* → ***draw***
dread [dred] *v/t* tener pavor a; ***I dread him ever finding out*** me da pavor pensar que lo pueda llegar a descubrir; ***I dread going to the dentist*** me da pánico ir al dentista
dread·ful ['dredfəl] *adj* horrible, espantoso; ***it's a dreadful pity you won't be there*** es una auténtica pena que no vayas a estar ahí
dread·ful·ly ['dredfəlɪ] *adv* F (*extremely*) terriblemente, espantosamente F; *behave* fatal
dream [driːm] **1** *n* sueño *m* **2** *adj*: ***win your dream house!*** ¡gane la casa de sus sueños! **3** *v/t* soñar; (*daydream*) soñar (despierto) **4** *v/i* soñar; (*daydream*) soñar (despierto); ***I dreamt about you last night*** anoche soñé contigo
◆ **dream up** *v/t* inventar
dream·er ['driːmər] (*daydreamer*) soñador(a) *m(f)*
dream·y ['driːmɪ] *adj voice, look* soñador
drear·y ['drɪrɪ] *adj* triste, deprimente
dredge [dredʒ] *v/t harbor, canal* dragar
◆ **dredge up** *v/t fig* sacar a relucir
dregs [dregz] *npl of coffee* posos *mpl*; ***the dregs of society*** la escoria de la sociedad
drench [drentʃ] *v/t* empapar; ***get drenched*** empaparse
dress [dres] **1** *n for woman* vestido *m*; (*clothing*) traje *m*; ***he has no dress sense*** no sabe vestir(se); ***the company has a dress code*** la compañía tiene unas normas sobre la ropa que deben llevar los empleados **2** *v/t person* vestir; *wound* vendar; ***get dressed*** vestirse **3** *v/i* (*get dressed*) vestirse; *well, in black etc* vestir(se) (***in*** de)
◆ **dress up** *v/i* arreglarse, vestirse elegante; (*wear a disguise*) disfrazarse (***as*** de)
'**dress cir·cle** piso *m* principal
dress·er ['dresər] (*dressing table*) tocador *f*; *in kitchen* aparador *m*
dress·ing ['dresɪŋ] *for salad* aliño *m*, *Span* arreglo *m*; *for wound* vendaje *m*
dress·ing '**down** regaño *m*; ***give s.o. a dressing down*** regañar a alguien
'**dress·ing room** *in theater* camerino *m*
'**dress·ing ta·ble** tocador *f*
'**dress·mak·er** modisto(-a) *m(f)*
'**dress re·hears·al** ensayo *m* general
dress·y ['dresɪ] *adj* F elegante
drew [druː] *pret* → ***draw***
drib·ble ['drɪbl] *v/i of person, baby* babear; *of water* gotear; SP driblar
dried [draɪd] *adj fruit etc* seco
dri·er [draɪr] → ***dryer***
drift [drɪft] **1** *n of snow* ventisquero *m* **2** *v/i of snow* amontonarse; *of ship* ir a la deriva; (*go off course*) desviarse del rumbo; *of person* vagar
◆ **drift apart** *v/i of couple* distanciarse
drift·er ['drɪftər] vagabundo(-a) *m(f)*
drill [drɪl] **1** *n tool* taladro *m*; *exercise* simulacro *m*; MIL instrucción *f* **2** *v/t hole* taladrar, perforar **3** *v/i for oil* hacer perforaciones; MIL entrenarse
dril·ling rig ['drɪlɪŋrɪg] (*platform*) plataforma *f* petrolífera
dri·ly ['draɪlɪ] *adv remark* secamente, lacónicamente
drink [drɪŋk] **1** *n* bebida *f*; ***a drink of ...*** un vaso de ...; ***go for a drink*** ir a tomar algo **2** *v/t* (*pret* ***drank***, *pp* ***drunk***) beber **3** *v/i* (*pret* ***drank***, *pp* ***drunk***) beber, *L.Am.*

tomar; ***I don't drink*** no bebo

◆ **drink up 1** *v/i* (*finish drink*) acabarse la bebida **2** *v/t* (*drink completely*) beberse todo

drink·a·ble ['drɪŋkəbl] *adj* potable

drink 'driv·ing conducción *f* bajo los efectos del alcohol

drink·er ['drɪŋkər] bebedor(a) *m(f)*

drink·ing ['drɪŋkɪŋ]: ***I'm worried about his drinking*** me preocupa que beba tanto; ***a drinking problem*** un problema con la bebida

'drink·ing wa·ter agua *f* potable

'drinks ma·chine máquina *f* expendedora de bebidas

drip [drɪp] **1** *n* gota *f*; MED gotero *m*, suero *m* **2** *v/i* (*pret & pp* ***dripped***) gotear

'drip-dry *adj* que no necesita planchado

drip·ping ['drɪpɪŋ] *adv*: ***dripping wet*** empapado

drive [draɪv] **1** *n outing* vuelta *f*, paseo *m* (en coche); (*energy*) energía *f*; COMPUT unidad *f*; (*campaign*) campaña *f*; ***it's a short drive from the station*** está a poca distancia en coche de la estación; ***with left-/right-hand drive*** MOT con el volante a la izquierda/a la derecha **2** *v/t* (*pret* ***drove***, *pp* ***driven***) *vehicle* conducir, *L.Am.* manejar; (*own*) tener; (*take in car*) llevar (en coche); TECH impulsar; ***that noise / he is driving me mad*** ese ruido / él me está volviendo loco **3** *v/i* (*pret* ***drove***, *pp* ***driven***) conducir, *L.Am.* manejar; ***don't drink and drive*** si bebes, no conduzcas; ***I drive to work*** voy al trabajo en coche

◆ **drive at** *v/t*: ***what are you driving at?*** ¿qué insinuas?

◆ **drive away 1** *v/t* llevarse en un coche; (*chase off*) ahuyentar **2** *v/i* marcharse

◆ **drive in** *v/t nail* remachar

◆ **drive off** → ***drive away***

'drive-in *n* (*movie theater*) autocine *m*

driv·el ['drɪvl] *n* tonterías *fpl*

driv·en ['drɪvn] *pp* → ***drive***

driv·er ['draɪvər] conductor(a) *m(f)*; *Br of train* maquinista *m/f*; COMPUT controlador *m*

'driv·er's li·cense carné *m* de conducir

drive·thru ['draɪvθruː] *restaurante / banco etc en el que se atiende al cliente sin que salga del coche*

'drive·way camino *m* de entrada

driv·ing ['draɪvɪŋ] **1** *n* conducción *f*; ***his driving is appalling*** conduce *or L.Am.* maneja fatal **2** *adj rain* torrencial

driv·ing 'force fuerza *f* motriz

'driving in·struct·or profesor(a) *m(f)* de autoescuela

'driv·ing les·son clase *f* de conducir

'driv·ing li·cence *Br* carné *m* de conducir

'driv·ing school autoescuela *f*

'driv·ing test examen *m* de conducir *or L.Am.* manejar

driz·zle ['drɪzl] **1** *n* llovizna *f* **2** *v/i* lloviznar

drone [droʊn] *n noise* zumbido *m*

droop [druːp] *v/i of plant* marchistarse; ***her shoulders drooped*** se encorvó

drop [drɑːp] **1** *n* gota *f*; *in price, temperature* caída *f*; ***could I have a drop more milk, please?*** ¿me podría poner un poquitín más de leche, por favor? **2** *v/t* (*pret & pp* ***dropped***) *object* dejar caer; *person from car* dejar; *person from team* excluir; (*stop seeing*) abandonar; *charges, demand etc* retirar; (*give up*) dejar; ***drop a line to*** mandar unas líneas a **3** *v/i* (*pret & pp* ***dropped***) caer, caerse; (*decline*) caer; *of wind* amainar

◆ **drop in** *v/i* (*visit*) pasar a visitar

◆ **drop off 1** *v/t person* dejar; (*deliver*) llevar **2** *v/i* (*fall asleep*) dormirse; (*decline*) disminuir

◆ **drop out** *v/i* (*withdraw*) retirarse; ***drop out of school*** abandonar el colegio

'drop·out (*from school*) *alumno que ha abandonado los estudios*; *from society* marginado(-a) *m(f)*

drops [drɑːps] *npl for eyes* gotas *fpl*

drought [draʊt] sequía *f*

drove [droʊv] *pret* → ***drive***

drown [draʊn] **1** *v/i* ahogarse **2** *v/t person, sound* ahogar; ***be drowned*** ahogarse

drow·sy ['draʊzɪ] *adj* soñoliento(-a)

drudg·e·ry ['drʌdʒərɪ]: ***the job is sheer drudgery*** el trabajo es terriblemente pesado

drug [drʌg] **1** *n* MED, *illegal* droga *f*; ***be on drugs*** drogarse **2** *v/t* (*pret & pp* ***drugged***) drogar

'drug ad·dict drogadicto(-a) *m(f)*

'drug deal·er traficante *m/f* (de drogas)

drug·gist ['drʌgɪst] farmacéutico(-a) *m(f)*

'drug·store *tienda en la que se venden medicinas, cosméticos, periódicos y que a veces tiene un bar*

'drug traf·fick·ing tráfico *m* de drogas

drum [drʌm] *n* MUS tambor *m*; *container* barril *m*

◆ **drum into** *v/t* (*pret & pp* ***drummed***): ***drum sth into s.o.*** meter algo en la cabeza de alguien

◆ **drum up** *v/t*: ***drum up support*** buscar apoyos

drum·mer ['drʌmər] tambor *m*, tamborilero(-a) *m(f)*

'drum·stick MUS baqueta *f*; *of poultry*

muslo *m*
drunk [drʌŋk] **1** *n* borracho(-a) *m(f)* **2** *adj* borracho; ***get drunk*** emborracharse **3** *pp* → ***drink***
drunk·en [drʌŋkn] *voices, laughter* borracho; *party* con mucho alcohol
dry [draɪ] **1** *adj* seco; *where alcohol is banned* donde está prohibido el consumo de alcohol **2** *v/t & v/i* (*pret & pp* ***dried***) secar
◆ **dry out** *v/i* secarse; *of alcoholic* desintoxicarse
◆ **dry up** *v/i of river* secarse; F (*be quiet*) cerrar el pico F
'**dry·clean** *v/t* limpiar en seco
'**dry clean·er** tintorería *f*
'**dry·clean·ing** (*clothes*): ***would you pick up my drycleaning for me?*** ¿te importaría recogerme la ropa de la tintorería?
dry·er [draɪr] *machine* secadora *f*
DTP [di:ti:'pi:] *abbr* (= ***desk-top publishing***) autoedición *f*
du·al ['du:əl] *adj* doble
dub [dʌb] *v/t* (*pret & pp* ***dubbed***) *movie* doblar
du·bi·ous ['du:bɪəs] *adj* dudoso; (*having doubts*) inseguro; ***I'm still dubious about the idea*** todavía tengo mis dudas sobre la idea
duch·ess ['dʌtʃɪs] duquesa *f*
duck [dʌk] **1** *n* pato *m*, pata *f* **2** *v/i* agacharse **3** *v/t one's head* agachar; *question* eludir
dud [dʌd] *n* F (*false bill*) billete *m* falso
due [du:] *adj* (*proper*) debido; ***the money due me*** el dinero que se me debe; ***payment is now due*** el pago se debe hacer efectivo ahora; ***is there a train due soon?*** ¿va a pasar un tren pronto?; ***when is the baby due?*** ¿cuando está previsto que nazca el bebé?; ***he's due to meet him next month*** tiene previsto reunirse con él el próximo mes; ***due to*** (*because of*) debido a; ***be due to*** (*be caused by*) ser debido a; ***in due course*** en su debido momento
dues [du:z] *npl* cuota *f*
du·et [du:'et] MUS dúo *m*
dug [dʌg] *pret & pp* → ***dig***
duke [du:k] duque *m*
dull [dʌl] *adj weather* gris; *sound, pain* sordo; (*boring*) aburrido, soso
du·ly ['du:lɪ] *adv* (*as expected*) tal y como se esperaba; (*properly*) debidamente
dumb [dʌm] *adj* (*mute*) mudo; F (*stupid*); estúpido; ***a pretty dumb thing to do*** una tontería
dumb·found·ed [dʌm'faʊndɪd] *adj* boquiabierto
dum·my ['dʌmɪ] *for clothes* maniquí *m*
dump [dʌmp] **1** *n for garbage* vertedero *m*, basurero *m*; (*unpleasant place*) lugar *m* de mala muerte **2** *v/t* (*deposit*) dejar; (*dispose of*) deshacerse de; *toxic waste, nuclear waste* verter
dump·ling ['dʌmplɪŋ] *bola de masa dulce o salada*
dune [du:n] duna *f*
dung [dʌŋ] estiércol *m*
dun·ga·rees [dʌŋgə'ri:z] *npl* pantalones *mpl* de trabajo
dunk [dʌŋk] *v/t in coffee etc* mojar
du·o ['du:oʊ] MUS dúo *m*
du·plex (a·part·ment) ['du:pleks] dúplex *m*
du·pli·cate 1 *n* ['du:plɪkət] duplicado *m*; ***in duplicate*** por duplicado **2** *v/t* ['du:plɪkeɪt] (*copy*) duplicar, hacer un duplicado de; (*repeat*) repetir
du·pli·cate 'key llave *f* duplicada
du·ra·ble ['dʊrəbl] *adj material* duradero, durable; *relationship* duradero
du·ra·tion [dʊ'reɪʃn] duración *f*; ***for the duration of her visit*** mientras dure su visita
du·ress [dʊ'res]: ***under duress*** bajo coacción
dur·ing ['dʊrɪŋ] *prep* durante
dusk [dʌsk] crepúsculo *m*, anochecer *m*
dust [dʌst] **1** *n* polvo *m* **2** *v/t* quitar el polvo a; ***dust sth with sth*** (*sprinkle*) espolvorear algo con algo
'**dust cov·er** *for book* sobrecubierta *f*
dust·er ['dʌstər] (*cloth*) trapo *m* del polvo
'**dust jack·et** *of book* sobrecubierta *f*
'**dust·pan** recogedor *m*
dust·y ['dʌstɪ] *adj* polvoriento
Dutch [dʌtʃ] **1** *adj* holandés; ***go Dutch*** F pagar a escote F **2** *n* (*language*) neerlandés *m*; ***the Dutch*** los holandeses
du·ty ['du:tɪ] deber *m*; (*task*) obligación *f*, tarea *f*; *on goods* impuesto *m*; ***be on duty*** estar de servicio; ***be off duty*** estar fuera de servicio
du·ty-'free 1 *adj* libre de impuestos **2** *n* productos *mpl* libres de impuestos
du·ty-'free shop tienda *f* libre de impuestos
dwarf [dwɔ:rf] **1** *n* enano *m* **2** *v/t* empequeñecer
◆ **dwell on** [dwel] *v/t*: ***dwell on the past*** pensar en el pasado; ***don't dwell on what he said*** no des demasiada importancia a lo que ha dicho
dwin·dle ['dwɪndl] *v/i* disminuir, menguar
dye [daɪ] **1** *n* tinte *m* **2** *v/t* teñir
dy·ing ['daɪɪŋ] *adj person* moribundo; *industry, tradition* en vías de desaparición
dy·nam·ic [daɪ'næmɪk] *adj person* diná-

mico
dy·na·mism ['daɪnəmɪzm] dinamismo *m*
dy·na·mite ['daɪnəmaɪt] *n* dinamita *f*
dy·na·mo ['daɪnəmoʊ] TECH dinamo *f*, dínamo *f*
dy·nas·ty ['daɪnəstɪ] dinastía *f*
dys·lex·i·a [dɪs'leksɪə] dislexia *f*
dys·lex·ic [dɪs'leksɪk] **1** *adj* disléxico **2** *n* disléxico(-a) *m(f)*

E

each [iːʧ] **1** *adj* cada **2** *adv*: ***he gave us one each*** nos dio uno a cada uno; ***they're $1.50 each*** valen 1.50 dólares cada uno **3** *pron* cada uno; ***each other*** el uno al otro; ***we love each other*** nos queremos
ea·ger ['iːgər] *adj* ansioso; ***she's always eager to help*** siempre está deseando ayudar
ea·ger 'bea·ver F entusiasta *m/f*
ea·ger·ly ['iːgərlɪ] *adv* ansiosamente
ea·ger·ness ['iːgərnɪs] entusiasmo *m*
ea·gle ['iːgl] águila *f*
ea·gle-eyed [iːgl'aɪd] *adj* con vista de lince
ear[1] [ɪr] *of person, animal* oreja *f*; *sense* oído *m*
ear[2] [ɪr] *of corn* espiga *f*
'ear·ache dolor *m* de oídos
'ear·drum tímpano *m*
'ear·lobe lóbulo *m*
ear·ly ['ɜːrlɪ] **1** *adj* (*not late*) temprano; (*ahead of time*) anticipado; (*farther back in time*) primero; (*in the near future*) pronto; *music* antiguo; ***let's have an early supper*** cenemos temprano; ***in early October*** a principios de octubre; ***in the early hours of the morning*** a primeras horas de la madrugada; ***an early Picasso*** un Picasso de su primera época; ***I'm an early riser*** soy madrugador **2** *adv* (*not late*) pronto, temprano; (*ahead of time*) antes de tiempo; ***it's too early to say*** es demasiado pronto como para poder decir nada; ***earlier than*** antes que
'ear·ly bird madrugador(a) *m(f)*
ear·mark ['ɪrmɑːrk] *v/t* destinar; ***earmark sth for sth*** destinar algo a algo
earn [ɜːrn] *v/t salary* ganar; *interest* devengar; *holiday, drink etc* ganarse; ***earn one's living*** ganarse la vida
ear·nest ['ɜːrnɪst] *adj* serio; ***in earnest*** en serio
earn·ings ['ɜːrnɪŋz] *npl* ganancias *fpl*
'ear·phones *npl* auriculares *fpl*
'ear-pierc·ing *adj* estrepitoso
'ear·ring pendiente *m*
'ear·shot: ***within earshot*** al alcance del oído; ***out of earshot*** fuera del alcance del oído
earth [ɜːrθ] (*soil*) tierra *f*; (*world, planet*) Tierra *f*; ***where on earth …?*** F ¿dónde diablos …? F
earth·en·ware ['ɜːrθnwer] *n* loza *mpl*
earth·ly ['ɜːrθlɪ] *adj* terrenal; ***it's no earthly use*** F no sirve para nada
earth·quake ['ɜːrθkweɪk] terremoto *m*
earth-shat·ter·ing ['ɜːrθʃætərɪŋ] *adj* extraordinario
ease [iːz] **1** *n* facilidad *f*; ***be at (one's) ease, feel at ease*** sentirse cómodo; ***feel ill at ease*** sentirse incómodo **2** *v/t* (*relieve*) aliviar **3** *v/i of pain* disminuir
◆ **ease off 1** *v/t* (*remove*) quitar con cuidado **2** *v/i of pain* disminuir; *of rain* amainar
ea·sel ['iːzl] caballete *m*
eas·i·ly ['iːzəlɪ] *adv* (*with ease*) fácilmente; (*by far*) con diferencia
east [iːst] **1** *n* este *m* **2** *adj* oriental, este; *wind* del este **3** *adv travel* hacia el este
Eas·ter ['iːstər] Pascua *f*; *period* Semana *f* Santa
Eas·ter 'Day Domingo *m* de Resurrección
'Eas·ter egg huevo *m* de pascua
eas·ter·ly ['iːstərlɪ] *adj* del este
Eas·ter 'Mon·day Lunes *m* Santo
Eas·ter 'Sun·day Domingo *m* de Resurrección
east·ern ['iːstərn] *adj* del este; (*oriental*) oriental
east·er·ner ['iːstərnər] *habitante de la costa oeste estadounidense*
east·ward ['iːstwərd] *adv* hacia el este
eas·y ['iːzɪ] *adj* fácil; (*relaxed*) tranquilo; ***take things easy*** (*slow down*) tomarse las cosas con tranquilidad; ***take it easy!***

(*calm down*) ¡tranquilízate!
'eas·y chair sillón *m*
eas·y-go·ing ['iːzɪgoʊɪŋ] *adj* tratable
eat [iːt] *v/t & v/i* (*pret* ***ate***, *pp* ***eaten***) comer
◆ **eat out** *v/i* comer fuera
◆ **eat up** *v/t* comerse; *fig*: *use up* acabar con
eat·a·ble ['iːtəbl] *adj* comestible
eat·en ['iːtn] *pp* → ***eat***
eau de Co·logne [oʊdəkə'loʊn] agua *f* de colonia
eaves [iːvz] *npl* alero *m*
eaves·drop ['iːvzdrɑːp] *v/i* (*pret & pp* ***eavesdropped***) escuchar a escondidas (***on s.o.*** alguien)
ebb [eb] *v/i of tide* bajar
◆ **ebb away** *v/i fig of courage, strength* desvanecerse
ec·cen·tric [ɪk'sentrɪk] **1** *adj* excéntrico **2** *n* excéntrico(-a) *m*(*f*)
ec·cen·tric·i·ty [ɪksen'trɪsɪtɪ] excentricidad *f*
ech·o ['ekoʊ] **1** *n* eco *m* **2** *v/i* resonar **3** *v/t words* repetir; *views* mostrar acuerdo con
e·clipse [ɪ'klɪps] **1** *n* eclipse *m* **2** *v/t fig* eclipsar
e·co·lo·gi·cal [iːkə'lɑːdʒɪkl] *adj* ecológico
e·co·lo·gi·cal·ly [iːkə'lɑːdʒɪklɪ] *adv* ecológicamente
e·co·lo·gi·cal·ly 'friend·ly *adj* ecológico
e·col·o·gist [iː'kɑːlədʒɪst] ecologista *m/f*
e·col·o·gy [iː'kɑːlədʒɪ] ecología *f*
ec·o·nom·ic [iːkə'nɑːmɪk] *adj* económico
ec·o·nom·i·cal [iːkə'nɑːmɪkl] *adj* (*cheap*) económico; (*thrifty*) cuidadoso
ec·o·nom·i·cal·ly [iːkə'nɑːmɪklɪ] *adv* (*in terms of economics*) económicamente; (*thriftily*) de manera económica
ec·o·nom·ics [iːkə'nɑːmɪks] *nsg* (*science*) economía *f*; (*npl*: *financial aspects*) aspecto *m* económico
e·con·o·mist [ɪ'kɑːnəmɪst] economista *m/f*
e·con·o·mize [ɪ'kɑːnəmaɪz] *v/i* economizar, ahorrar
◆ **economize on** *v/t* economizar, ahorrar
e·con·o·my [ɪ'kɑːnəmɪ] *of a country* economía *f*; (*saving*) ahorro *m*
e'con·o·my class clase *f* turista
e'con·o·my drive intento *m* de ahorrar
e'con·o·my size tamaño *m* económico
e·co·sys·tem ['iːkoʊsɪstm] ecosistema *m*
e·co·tour·ism ['iːkoʊtʊrɪzm] ecoturismo *m*
ec·sta·sy ['ekstəsɪ] éxtasis *m*
ec·sta·t·ic [ɪk'stætɪk] *adj* muy emocionado, extasiado
Ec·ua·dor ['ekwədɔːr] *n* Ecuador
Ec·ua·dore·an [ekwə'dɔːrən] **1** *adj* ecuatoriano **2** *n* ecuatoriano(-a) *m*(*f*)
ec·ze·ma ['eksmə] eczema *f*
edge [edʒ] **1** *n of knife* filo *m*; *of table, seat, road, cliff* borde *m*; *in voice* irritación *f*; ***on edge*** tenso **2** *v/t* ribetear **3** *v/i* (*move slowly*) acercarse despacio
edge·wise ['edʒwaɪz] *adv* de lado; ***I couldn't get a word in edgewise*** no me dejó decir una palabra
edg·y ['edʒɪ] *adj* tenso
ed·i·ble ['edɪbl] *adj* comestible
ed·it ['edɪt] *v/t text* corregir; *book* editar; *newspaper* dirigir; TV *program, movie* montar
e·di·tion [ɪ'dɪʃn] edición *f*
ed·i·tor ['edɪtər] *of text, book* editor(a) *m*(*f*); *of newspaper* director(a) *m*(*f*); *of* TV *program, movie* montador(a) *m*(*f*); ***sports* / *political editor*** redactor(a) *m*(*f*) de deportes / política
ed·i·to·ri·al [edɪ'tɔːrɪəl] **1** *adj* editorial **2** *n in newspaper* editorial *m*
EDP [iːdiː'piː] *abbr* (= ***electronic data processing***) procesamiento *m* electrónico de datos
ed·u·cate ['edʒəkeɪt] *v/t child* educar; *consumers* concienciar
ed·u·cat·ed ['edʒəkeɪtɪd] *adj person* culto
ed·u·ca·tion [edʒə'keɪʃn] educación *f*; ***the education system*** el sistema educativo
ed·u·ca·tion·al [edʒə'keɪʃnl] *adj* educativo; (*informative*) instructivo
eel [iːl] anguila *f*
ee·rie ['ɪrɪ] *adj* escalofriante
ef·fect [ɪ'fekt] efecto *m*; ***take effect*** *of medicine, drug* hacer efecto; ***come into effect*** *of law* entrar en vigor
ef·fec·tive [ɪ'fektɪv] *adj* (*efficient*) efectivo; (*striking*) impresionante; ***effective May 1*** a partir del 1 de mayo
ef·fem·i·nate [ɪ'femɪnət] *adj* afeminado
ef·fer·ves·cent [efər'vesnt] *adj* efervescente; *personality* chispeante
ef·fi·cien·cy [ɪ'fɪʃənsɪ] *of person* eficiencia *f*; *of machine* rendimiento *f*; *of system* eficacia *f*
ef·fi·cient [ɪ'fɪʃənt] *adj person* eficiente; *machine* de buen rendimiento; *method* eficaz
ef·fi·cient·ly [ɪ'fɪʃəntlɪ] *adv* eficientemente
ef·flu·ent ['efluənt] aguas *fpl* residuales
ef·fort ['efərt] (*struggle, attempt*) esfuerzo *m*; ***make an effort to do sth*** hacer un esfuerzo por hacer algo
ef·fort·less ['efərtlɪs] *adj* fácil
ef·fron·te·ry [ɪ'frʌntərɪ] desvergüenza *f*

ef·fu·sive [ɪ'fjuːsɪv] *adj* efusivo
e.g. [iː'dʒiː] p. ej.
e·gal·i·tar·i·an [ɪgælɪ'terɪən] *adj* igualitario
egg [eg] huevo *m*; *of woman* óvulo *m*
◆ **egg on** *v/t* incitar
'egg·cup huevera *f*
'egg·head F cerebrito(-a) *m(f)* F
'egg·plant berenjena *f*
'egg·shell cáscara *f* de huevo
'egg tim·er reloj *m* de arena
e·go ['iːgoʊ] PSYCH ego *m*; (*self-esteem*) amor *m* propio
e·go·cen·tric [iːgoʊ'sentrɪk] *adj* egocéntrico
e·go·ism ['iːgoʊ'ɪzm] egoismo *m*
e·go·ist ['iːgoʊ'ɪst] egoísta *m/f*
E·gypt ['iːdʒɪpt] Egipto
E·gyp·tian [ɪ'dʒɪpʃn] **1** *adj* egipcio **2** *n* egipcio(-a) *m(f)*
ei·der·down ['aɪdərdaʊn] *quilt* edredón *m*
eight [eɪt] ocho
eigh·teen [eɪ'tiːn] dieciocho
eigh·teenth [eɪ'tiːnθ] *n & adj* decimoctavo
eighth [eɪtθ] *n & adj* octavo
eigh·ti·eth ['eɪtɪɪθ] *n & adj* octogésimo
eigh·ty ['eɪtɪ] ochenta
ei·ther ['aɪðər] **1** *adj* cualquiera de los dos; *with negative constructions* ninguno de los dos; (*both*) cada, ambos; ***he wouldn't accept either of the proposals*** no quería aceptar ninguna de las dos propuestas **2** *pron* cualquiera de los dos; *with negative constructions* ninguno de los dos **3** *adv* tampoco; ***I won't go either*** yo tampoco iré **4** *conj*: ***either ... or*** *choice* o ... o; *with negative constructions* ni ... ni
e·ject [ɪ'dʒekt] **1** *v/t* expulsar **2** *v/i from plane* eyectarse
◆ **eke out** [iːk] *v/t* (*make last*) hacer durar
el [el] → ***elevated railroad***
e·lab·o·rate 1 *adj* [ɪ'læbərət] elaborado **2** *v/t* [ɪ'læbəreɪt] elaborar **3** *v/i* [ɪ'læbəreɪt] dar detalles
e·lab·o·rate·ly [ɪ'læbəreɪtlɪ] *adv* elaboradamente
e·lapse [ɪ'læps] *v/i* pasar
e·las·tic [ɪ'læstɪk] **1** *adj* elástico **2** *n* elástico *m*
e·las·ti·ca·ted [ɪ'læstɪkeɪtɪd] *adj* elástico
e·las·ti·ci·ty [ɪlæs'tɪsətɪ] elasticidad *f*
e·las·ti·cized [ɪ'læstɪsaɪzd] *adj* elástico
e·lat·ed [ɪ'leɪtɪd] *adj* eufórico
el·at·ion [ɪ'leɪʃn] euforia *f*
el·bow ['elboʊ] **1** *n* codo *m* **2** *v/t* dar un codazo a; ***elbow out of the way*** apartar a codazos
el·der ['eldər] **1** *adj* mayor **2** *n* mayor *m/f*; ***she's two years my elder*** es dos años mayor que yo
el·der·ly ['eldərlɪ] **1** *adj* mayor **2** *n*: ***the elderly*** las personas mayores
el·dest ['eldəst] **1** *adj* mayor **2** *n* mayor *m/f*; ***the eldest*** el mayor
e·lect [ɪ'lekt] *v/t* elegir; ***elect to do sth*** decidir hacer algo
e·lect·ed [ɪ'lektɪd] *adj* elegido
e·lec·tion [ɪ'lekʃn] elección *f*; ***call an election*** convocar elecciones
e'lec·tion cam·paign campaña *f* electoral
e'lec·tion day día *m* de las elecciones
e·lec·tive [ɪ'lektɪv] *adj* opcional; *subject* optativo
e·lec·tor [ɪ'lektər] elector(a) *m(f)*, votante *m/f*
e·lec·to·ral sys·tem [ɪ'lektərəl] sistema *m* electoral
e·lec·to·rate [ɪ'lektərət] electorado *m*
e·lec·tric [ɪ'lektrɪk] *adj* eléctrico; *fig atmosphere* electrizado
e·lec·tri·cal [ɪ'lektrɪkl] *adj* eléctrico
e·lec·tri·cal en·gi'neer ingeniero(-a) *m(f)* electrónico
e·lec·tri·cal en·gi'neer·ing ingeniería *f* electrónica
e·lec·tric 'blan·ket manta *f or L.Am.* cobija *f* eléctrica
e·lec·tric 'chair silla *f* eléctrica
e·lec·tri·cian [ɪlek'trɪʃn] electricista *m/f*
e·lec·tri·ci·ty [ɪlek'trɪsətɪ] electricidad *f*
e·lec·tric 'ra·zor maquinilla *f* eléctrica
e·lec·tric 'shock descarga *f* eléctrica
e·lec·tri·fy [ɪ'lektrɪfaɪ] *v/t* (*pret & pp* ***electrified***) electrificar; *fig* electrizar
e·lec·tro·cute [ɪ'lektrəkjuːt] *v/t* electrocutar
e·lec·trode [ɪ'lektroʊd] electrodo *m*
e·lec·tron [ɪ'lektrɑːn] electrón *m*
e·lec·tron·ic [ɪlek'trɑːnɪk] *adj* electrónico
e·lec·tron·ic da·ta 'pro·ces·sing procesamiento *m* electrónico de datos
e·lec·tron·ic 'mail correo *m* electrónico
e·lec·tron·ics [ɪlek'trɑːnɪks] electrónica *f*
el·e·gance ['elɪgəns] elegancia *f*
el·e·gant ['elɪgənt] *adj* elegante
el·e·gant·ly ['elɪgəntlɪ] *adv* elegantemente
el·e·ment ['elɪmənt] *also* CHEM elemento *m*
el·e·men·ta·ry [elɪ'mentərɪ] *adj* (*rudimentary*) elemental
el·e'men·ta·ry school escuela *f* primaria
el·e'men·ta·ry teacher maestro(-a) *m(f)*
el·e·phant ['elɪfənt] elefante *m*
el·e·vate ['elɪveɪt] *v/t* elevar
el·e·vat·ed 'rail·road ['elɪveɪtɪd] ferrocarril *m* elevado

E

el·e·va·tion [elɪ'veɪʃn] (*altitude*) altura *f*
el·e·va·tor ['elɪveɪtər] ascensor *m*
el·e·ven [ɪ'levn] once
el·e·venth [ɪ'levnθ] *n* & *adj* undécimo; ***at the eleventh hour*** justo en el último minuto
el·i·gi·ble ['elɪdʒəbl] *adj* que reúne los requisitos; ***eligible to vote*** con derecho al voto; ***be eligible to do sth*** tener derecho a hacer algo
el·i·gi·ble 'bach·e·lor buen partido *m*
e·lim·i·nate [ɪ'lɪmɪneɪt] *v/t* eliminar; *poverty* acabar con; (*rule out*) descartar
e·lim·i·na·tion [ɪ'lɪmɪneɪʃn] eliminación *f*
e·lite [eɪ'li:t] **1** *n* élite *f* **2** *adj* de élite
elk [elk] ciervo *m* canadiense
el·lipse [ɪ'lɪps] elipse *f*
elm [elm] olmo *m*
e·lope [ɪ'loʊp] *v/i* fugarse con un amante
el·o·quence ['eləkwəns] elocuencia *f*
el·o·quent ['eləkwənt] *adj* elocuente
el·o·quent·ly ['eləkwəntlɪ] *adv* elocuentemente
El Sal·va·dor [el'sælvədɔːr] *n* El Salvador
else [els] *adv*: ***anything else?*** ¿algo más?; ***if you've got nothing else to do*** si no tienes nada más que hacer; ***no one else*** nadie más; ***everyone else is going*** todos (los demás) van, va todo el mundo; ***who else was there?*** ¿quién más estaba allí?; ***someone else*** otra persona; ***something else*** algo más; ***let's go somewhere else*** vamos a otro sitio; ***or else*** si no
else·where ['elswer] *adv* en otro sitio
e·lude [ɪ'lu:d] *v/t* (*escape from*) escapar de; (*avoid*) evitar; ***the name eludes me*** no recuerdo el nombre
e·lu·sive [ɪ'lu:sɪv] *adj* evasivo
e·ma·ci·ated [ɪ'meɪsɪeɪtɪd] *adj* demacrado
e-mail ['i:meɪl] **1** *n* correo *m* electrónico **2** *v/t person* mandar un correo electrónico a
'e-mail ad·dress dirección *f* de correo electrónico, dirección *f* electrónica
e·man·ci·pat·ed [ɪ'mænsɪpeɪtɪd] *adj* emancipado
e·man·ci·pa·tion [ɪmænsɪ'peɪʃn] emancipación *f*
em·balm [ɪm'bɑ:m] *v/t* embalsamar
em·bank·ment [ɪm'bæŋkmənt] *of river* dique *m*; RAIL terraplén *m*
em·bar·go [em'bɑ:rgoʊ] embargo *m*
em·bark [ɪm'bɑ:rk] *v/i* embarcar
◆ **embark on** *v/t* embarcarse en
em·bar·rass [ɪm'bærəs] *v/t* avergonzar; ***he embarrassed me in front of everyone*** me hizo pasar vergüenza delante de todos
em·bar·rassed [ɪm'bærəst] *adj* avergonzado; ***I was embarrassed to ask*** me daba vergüenza preguntar
em·bar·rass·ing [ɪm'bærəsɪŋ] *adj* embarazoso
em·bar·rass·ment [ɪm'bærəsmənt] embarazo *m*, apuro *m*
em·bas·sy ['embəsɪ] embajada *f*
em·bel·lish [ɪm'belɪʃ] *v/t* adornar; *story* exagerar
em·bers ['embərz] *npl* ascuas *fpl*
em·bez·zle [ɪm'bezl] *v/t* malversar
em·bez·zle·ment [ɪm'bezlmənt] malversación *f*
em·bez·zler [ɪm'bezlər] malversador(a) *m*(*f*)
em·bit·ter [ɪm'bɪtər] *v/t* amargar
em·blem ['embləm] emblema *m*
em·bod·i·ment [ɪm'bɑ:dɪmənt] personificación *f*
em·bod·y [ɪm'bɑ:dɪ] *v/t* (*pret & pp* ***embodied***) personificar
em·bo·lism ['embəlɪzm] embolia *f*
em·boss [ɪm'bɑ:s] *v/t metal* repujar; *paper* grabar en relieve
em·brace [ɪm'breɪs] **1** *n* abrazo *m* **2** *v/t* (*hug*) abrazar; (*take in*) abarcar **3** *v/i of two people* abrazarse
em·broi·der [ɪm'brɔɪdər] *v/t* bordar; *fig* adornar
em·broi·der·y [ɪm'brɔɪdərɪ] bordado *m*
em·bry·o ['embrɪoʊ] embrión *m*
em·bry·on·ic [embrɪ'ɑ:nɪk] *adj fig* embrionario
em·e·rald ['emərəld] esmeralda *f*
e·merge [ɪ'mɜ:rdʒ] *v/i* (*appear*) emerger, salir; *of truth* aflorar; ***it has emerged that*** se ha descubierto que
e·mer·gen·cy [ɪ'mɜ:rdʒənsɪ] emergencia *f*; ***in an emergency*** en caso de emergencia
emer·gen·cy 'ex·it salida *f* de emergencia
e'mer·gen·cy land·ing aterrizaje *m* forzoso
e'mer·gen·cy serv·ices *npl* servicios *mpl* de urgencia
em·er·y board ['emərɪ] lima *f* de uñas
em·i·grant ['emɪgrənt] emigrante *m/f*
em·i·grate ['emɪgreɪt] *v/i* emigrar
em·i·gra·tion [emɪ'greɪʃn] emigración *f*
Em·i·nence ['emɪnəns] REL: ***His Eminence*** Su Eminencia
em·i·nent ['emɪnənt] *adj* eminente
em·i·nent·ly ['emɪnəntlɪ] *adv* sumamente
e·mis·sion [ɪ'mɪʃn] *of gases* emisión *f*
e·mit [ɪ'mɪt] *v/t* (*pret & pp* ***emitted***) emitir; *heat, odor* desprender
e·mo·tion [ɪ'moʊʃn] emoción *f*

e·mo·tion·al [ɪ'moʊʃənl] *adj problems, development* sentimental; (*full of emotion*) emotivo
em·pa·thize ['empəθaɪz] *v/i*: ***empathize with*** identificarse con
em·pe·ror ['empərər] emperador *m*
em·pha·sis ['emfəsɪs] *in word* acento *m*; *fig* énfasis *m*
em·pha·size ['emfəsaɪz] *v/t syllable* acentuar; *fig* hacer hincapié en
em·phat·ic [ɪm'fætɪk] *adj* enfático
em·pire ['empaɪr] imperio *m*
em·ploy [ɪm'plɔɪ] *v/t* emplear; ***he's employed as a ...*** trabaja de ...
em·ploy·ee [emplɔɪ'iː] empleado(-a) *m(f)*
em·ploy·er [em'plɔɪər] empresario(-a) *m(f)*
em·ploy·ment [em'plɔɪmənt] empleo *m*; (*work*) trabajo *m*; ***be looking for employment*** buscar trabajo
em'ploy·ment a·gen·cy agencia *f* de colocaciones
em·press ['emprɪs] emperatriz *f*
emp·ti·ness ['emptɪnɪs] vacío *m*
emp·ty ['emptɪ] **1** *adj* vacío; *promise* vana **2** *v/t* (*pret & pp* ***emptied***) *drawer, pockets* vaciar; *glass, bottle* acabar **3** *v/i* (*pret & pp* ***emptied***) *of room, street* vaciarse
em·u·late ['emjʊleɪt] *v/t* emular
e·mul·sion [ɪ'mʌlʃn] *paint* emulsión *f*
en·a·ble [ɪ'neɪbl] *v/t* permitir; ***enable s.o. to do sth*** permitir a alguien hacer algo
en·act [ɪ'nækt] *v/t law* promulgar; THEA representar
e·nam·el [ɪ'næml] *n* esmalte *m*
enc *abbr* (= ***enclosure(s)***) documento(s) *m(pl)* adjunto(s)
en·chant [ɪn'ʧænt] *v/t* (*delight*) encantar
en·chant·ing [ɪn'ʧæntɪŋ] *adj* encantador
en·cir·cle [ɪn'sɜːrkl] *v/t* rodear
encl *abbr* (= ***en·clo·sure(s)***) documento(s) *m(pl)* adjunto(s)
en·close [ɪn'kloʊz] *v/t Br in letter* adjuntar; *area* rodear; ***please find enclosed ...*** remito adjunto ...
en·clo·sure [ɪn'kloʊʒər] *with letter* documento *m* adjunto
en·core ['ɑːŋkɔːr] bis *m*
en·coun·ter [ɪn'kaʊntər] **1** *n* encuentro *m* **2** *v/t person* encontrarse con; *problem, resistance* tropezar con
en·cour·age [ɪn'kʌrɪdʒ] *v/t* animar; *violence* fomentar
en·cour·age·ment [ɪn'kʌrɪdʒmənt] ánimo *m*
en·cour·ag·ing [ɪn'kʌrɪdʒɪŋ] *adj* alentador
◆ **en·croach on** [ɪn'kroʊʧ] *v/t land* invadir; *rights* usurpar; *time* quitar
en·cy·clo·pe·di·a [ɪnsaɪklə'piːdɪə] enciclopedia *f*
end [end] **1** *n of journey, month* final *m*; (*extremity*) extremo *m*; (*bottom*) fondo *m*; (*conclusion, purpose*) fin *m*; ***at the other end of town*** al otro lado de la ciudad; ***in the end*** al final; ***for hours on end*** durante horas y horas; ***stand sth on end*** poner de pie algo; ***at the end of July*** a finales de julio; ***in the end*** al final; ***put an end to*** poner fin a **2** *v/t* terminar, finalizar **3** *v/i* terminar
◆ **end up** *v/i* acabar
en·dan·ger [ɪn'deɪndʒər] *v/t* poner en peligro
en'dan·gered spe·cies especie *f* en peligro de extinción
en·dear·ing [ɪn'dɪrɪŋ] *adj* simpático
en·deav·or [ɪn'devər] **1** *n* esfuerzo *m* **2** *v/t* procurar
en·dem·ic [ɪn'demɪk] *adj* endémico
end·ing ['endɪŋ] final *m*; GRAM terminación *f*
end·less ['endlɪs] *adj* interminable
en·dorse [ɪn'dɔːrs] *v/t check* endosar; *candidacy* apoyar; *product* representar
en·dorse·ment [ɪn'dɔːrsmənt] *of check* endoso *m*; *of candidacy* apoyo *m*; *of product* representación *f*
end 'prod·uct producto *m* final
end re'sult resultado *m* final
en·dur·ance [ɪn'dʊrəns] resistencia *f*
en·dure [ɪn'dʊər] **1** *v/t* resistir **2** *v/i* (*last*) durar
en·dur·ing [ɪn'dʊrɪŋ] *adj* duradero
end-'us·er usuario(-a) *m(f)* final
en·e·my ['enəmɪ] enemigo(-a) *m(f)*
en·er·get·ic [enər'dʒetɪk] *adj* enérgico
en·er·get·ic·ally [enər'dʒetɪklɪ] *adv* enérgicamente
en·er·gy ['enərdʒɪ] energía *f*
'en·er·gy-sav·ing *adj device* que ahorra energía
'e·ner·gy sup·ply suministro *m* de energía
en·force [ɪn'fɔːrs] *v/t* hacer cumplir
en·gage [ɪn'geɪdʒ] **1** *v/t* (*hire*) contratar **2** *v/i* TECH engranar
◆ **engage in** *v/t* dedicarse a
en·gaged [ɪn'geɪdʒd] *adj to be married* prometido; ***get engaged*** prometerse
en'gaged tone *Br* TELEC señal *f* de ocupado *or Span* comunicando
en·gage·ment [ɪn'geɪdʒmənt] (*appointment, to be married*) compromiso *m*; MIL combate *m*
en'gage·ment ring anillo *m* de compromiso

en·gag·ing [ɪn'geɪdʒɪŋ] *adj smile, person* atractivo
en·gine ['endʒɪn] motor *m*
en·gi·neer [endʒɪ'nɪr] **1** *n* ingeniero(-a) *m(f)*; NAUT, RAIL maquinista *m/f* **2** *v/t fig: meeting etc* tramar
en·gi·neer·ing [endʒɪ'nɪrɪŋ] ingeniería *f*
En·gland ['ɪŋglənd] Inglaterra
En·glish ['ɪŋglɪʃ] **1** *adj* inglés(-esa) **2** *n language* inglés *m*; ***the English*** los ingleses
Eng·lish 'Chan·nel Canal *m* de la Mancha
'En·glish·man inglés *m*
'En·glish·wom·an inglesa *f*
en·grave [ɪn'greɪv] *v/t* grabar
en·grav·ing [ɪn'greɪvɪŋ] grabado *m*
en·grossed [ɪn'groʊst] *adj* absorto (***in*** en)
en·gulf [ɪn'gʌlf] *v/t* devorar
en·hance [ɪn'hæns] *v/t* realzar
e·nig·ma [ɪ'nɪgmə] enigma *m*
e·nig·mat·ic [enɪg'mætɪk] *adj* enigmático
en·joy [ɪn'dʒɔɪ] *v/t* disfrutar; ***enjoy o.s.*** divertirse; ***enjoy (your meal)!*** ¡que aproveche!
en·joy·a·ble [ɪn'dʒɔɪəbl] *adj* agradable
en·joy·ment [ɪn'dʒɔɪmənt] diversión *f*
en·large [ɪn'lɑːrdʒ] *v/t* ampliar
en·large·ment [ɪn'lɑːrdʒmənt] ampliación *f*
en·light·en [ɪn'laɪtn] *v/t* educar
en·list [ɪn'lɪst] **1** *v/i* MIL alistarse **2** *v/t*: ***I enlisted his help*** conseguí que me ayudara
en·liv·en [ɪn'laɪvn] *v/t* animar
en·mi·ty ['enmətɪ] enemistad *f*
e·nor·mi·ty [ɪ'nɔːrmətɪ] magnitud *f*
e·nor·mous [ɪ'nɔːrməs] *adj* enorme; *satisfaction, patience* inmenso
e·nor·mous·ly [ɪ'nɔːrməslɪ] *adv* enormemente
e·nough [ɪ'nʌf] **1** *adj pron* suficiente, bastante; ***will $50 be enough?*** ¿llegará con 50 dólares?; ***I've had enough!*** ¡estoy harto!; ***that's enough, calm down!*** ¡ya basta, tranquilízate! **2** *adv* suficientemente, bastante; ***the bag isn't big enough*** la bolsa no es lo suficientemente *or* bastante grande; ***strangely enough*** curiosamente
en·quire [ɪn'kwaɪr] → ***inquire***
en·raged [ɪn'reɪdʒd] *adj* enfurecido
en·rich [ɪn'rɪʧ] *v/t* enriquecer
en·roll [ɪn'roʊl] *v/i* matricularse
en·roll·ment [ɪn'roʊlmənt] matrícula *f*
en·sue [ɪn'suː] *v/i* sucederse
en suite ['ɑːnswiːt] *adj*: ***en suite bathroom*** baño *m* privado
en·sure [ɪn'ʃʊər] *v/t* asegurar
en·tail [ɪn'teɪl] *v/t* conllevar
en·tan·gle [ɪn'tæŋgl] *v/t in rope* enredar; ***become entangled in*** enredarse en; ***become entangled with*** *in love affair* liarse con
en·ter ['entər] **1** *v/t room, house* entrar en; *competition* participar en; *person, horse in race* inscribir; (*write down*) escribir; COMPUT introducir **2** *v/i* entrar; THEA entrar en escena; *in competition* inscribirse **3** *n* COMPUT intro *m*
en·ter·prise ['entərpraɪz] (*initiative*) iniciativa *f*; (*venture*) empresa *f*
en·ter·pris·ing ['entərpraɪzɪŋ] *adj* con iniciativa
en·ter·tain [entər'teɪn] **1** *v/t* (*amuse*) entretener; (*consider*: *idea*) considerar **2** *v/i* (*have guests*): ***we entertain a lot*** recibimos a mucha gente
en·ter·tain·er [entər'teɪnər] artista *m/f*
en·ter·tain·ing [entər'teɪnɪŋ] *adj* entretenido
en·ter·tain·ment [entər'teɪnmənt] entretenimiento *m*
en·thrall [ɪn'θrɒːl] *v/t* cautivar
en·thu·si·as·m [ɪn'θuːzɪæzm] entusiasmo *m*
en·thu·si·as·t [ɪn'θuːzɪ'æst] entusiasta *m/f*
en·thu·si·as·tic [ɪnθuːzɪ'æstɪk] *adj* entusiasta; ***be enthusiastic about sth*** estar entusiasmado con algo
en·thu·si·as·tic·al·ly [ɪnθuːzɪ'æstɪklɪ] *adv* con entusiasmo
en·tice [ɪn'taɪs] *v/t* atraer
en·tire [ɪn'taɪr] *adj* entero; ***the entire school is going*** va a ir todo el colegio
en·tire·ly [ɪn'taɪrlɪ] *adv* completamente
en·ti·tle [ɪn'taɪtld] *v/t*: ***entitle s.o. to sth*** dar derecho a alguien a algo; ***be entitled to*** tener derecho a
en·ti·tled [ɪn'taɪtld] *adj book* titulado
en·trance ['entrəns] entrada *f*; THEA entrada *f* en escena
en·tranced [ɪn'trænst] *adj* encantado
'en·trance ex·am(·i·na·tion) examen *m* de acceso
'en·trance fee (cuota *f* de) entrada *f*
en·trant ['entrənt] participante *m/f*
en·treat [ɪn'triːt] *v/t* suplicar; ***entreat s.o. to do sth*** suplicar a alguien que haga algo
en·trenched [ɪn'trenʧt] *adj attitudes* arraigado
en·tre·pre·neur [ɑːntrəprə'nɜːr] empresario(-a) *m(f)*
en·tre·pre·neur·i·al [ɑːntrəprə'nɜːrɪəl] *adj* empresarial
en·trust [ɪn'trʌst] *v/t* confiar; ***entrust s.o.***

with sth, entrust sth to s.o. confiar algo a alguien

en·try ['entrɪ] entrada *f*; *for competition* inscripción *f*; *in diary etc* entrada *f*; ***no entry*** prohibida la entrada; ***the winning entry was painted by …*** el cuadro ganador fue pintado por …

'en·try form impreso *m* de inscripción

'en·try·phone portero *m* automático

'en·try vi·sa visado *m*

e·nu·me·rate [ɪ'nuːməreɪt] *v/t* enumerar

en·vel·op [ɪn'veləp] *v/t* cubrir

en·ve·lope ['envəloʊp] sobre *m*

en·vi·a·ble ['envɪəbl] *adj* envidiable

en·vi·ous ['envɪəs] *adj* envidioso; ***be envious of s.o.*** tener envidia de alguien

en·vi·ron·ment [ɪn'vaɪrənmənt] (*nature*) medio *m* ambiente; (*surroundings*) entorno *m*, ambiente *m*

en·vi·ron·men·tal [ɪnvaɪrən'mentl] *adj* medioambiental

en·vi·ron·men·tal·ist [ɪnvaɪrən'm*m*əntəlɪst] ecologista *m/f*

en·vi·ron·men·tal·ly 'friend·ly [ɪnvaɪrən'mentəlɪ] *adj* ecológico, que no daña el medio ambiente

en·vi·ron·men·tal pol'lu·tion contaminación *f* medioambiental

en·vi·ron·men·tal pro'tec·tion protección *f* medioambiental

en·vi·rons [ɪn'vaɪrənz] *npl* alrededores *mpl*

en·vis·age [ɪn'vɪzɪdʒ] *v/t* imaginar

en·voy ['envɔɪ] enviado(-a) *m(f)*

en·vy ['envɪ] **1** *n* envidia *f*; ***be the envy of*** ser la envidia de **2** *v/t* (*pret & pp* ***envied***) envidiar; ***envy s.o. sth*** envidiar a alguien por algo

e·phem·er·al [ɪ'femərəl] *adj* efímero

ep·ic ['epɪk] **1** *n* epopeya *f* **2** *adj journey* épico; ***a task of epic proportions*** una tarea monumental

ep·i·cen·ter ['epɪsentr] epicentro *m*

ep·i·dem·ic [epɪ'demɪk] epidemia *f*

ep·i·lep·sy ['epɪlepsɪ] epilepsia *f*

ep·i·lep·tic [epɪ'leptɪk] epiléptico(-a) *m(f)*

ep·i·lep·tic 'fit ataque *m* epiléptico

ep·i·log, *Br* **ep·i·logue** ['epɪlɑːg] epílogo *m*

ep·i·sode ['epɪsoʊd] *of story, soap opera* episodio *m*, capítulo *m*; (*happening*) episodio *m*; ***let's forget the whole episode*** olvidemos lo sucedido

ep·i·taph ['epɪtæf] epitafio *m*

e·poch ['iːpɑːk] época *f*

e·poch-mak·ing ['iːpɑːkmeɪkɪŋ] *adj* que hace época

e·qual ['iːkwl] **1** *adj* igual; ***equal amounts of milk and water*** la misma cantidad de leche y de agua; ***equal opportunities*** igualdad *f* de oportunidades; ***be equal to*** *a task* estar capacitado para **2** *n* igual *m/f* **3** *v/t* (*pret & pp* ***equaled***, *Br* ***equalled***) (*with numbers*) equivaler; (*be as good as*) igualar; ***four times twelve equals 48*** cuatro por doce, (igual a) cuarenta y ocho

e·qual·i·ty [ɪ'kwɑːlətɪ] igualdad *f*

e·qual·ize ['iːkwəlaɪz] **1** *v/t* igualar **2** *v/i Br* SP empatar

e·qual·iz·er ['iːkwəlaɪzər] *Br* SP gol *m* del empate

e·qual·ly ['iːkwəlɪ] *adv* igualmente; *share, divide* en partes iguales; ***equally, …*** igualmente, …

e·qual 'rights *npl* igualdad *f* de derechos

e·quate [ɪ'kweɪt] *v/t* equiparar; ***equate sth with sth*** equiparar algo con algo

e·qua·tion [ɪ'kweɪʒn] MATH ecuación *f*

e·qua·tor [ɪ'kweɪtər] ecuador *m*

e·qui·lib·ri·um [iːkwɪ'lɪbrɪəm] equilibrio *m*

e·qui·nox ['iːkwɪnɑːks] equinoccio *m*

e·quip [ɪ'kwɪp] *v/t* (*pret & pp* ***equipped***) equipar; ***he's not equipped to handle it*** *fig* no está preparado para llevarlo

e·quip·ment [ɪ'kwɪpmənt] equipo *m*

eq·ui·ty ['ekwətɪ] FIN acciones *fpl* ordinarias

e·quiv·a·lent [ɪ'kwɪvələnt] **1** *adj* equivalente; ***be equivalent to*** equivaler a **2** *n* equivalente *m*

e·ra ['ɪrə] era *f*

e·rad·i·cate [ɪ'rædɪkeɪt] *v/t* erradicar

e·rase [ɪ'reɪz] *v/t* borrar

e·ras·er [ɪ'reɪzər] *for pencil* goma *f* (de borrar); *for chalk* borrador *m*

e·rect [ɪ'rekt] **1** *adj* erguido **2** *v/t* levantar, erigir

e·rec·tion [ɪ'rekʃn] *of building etc* construcción *f*; *of penis* erección *f*

er·go·nom·ic [ɜːrgoʊ'nɑːmɪk] *adj furniture* ergonómico

e·rode [ɪ'roʊd] *v/t also fig* erosionar

e·ro·sion [ɪ'roʊʒn] *also fig* erosión *f*

e·rot·ic [ɪ'rɑːtɪk] *adj* erótico

e·rot·i·cism [ɪ'rɑːtɪsɪzm] erotismo *m*

er·rand ['erənd] recado *m*; ***run errands*** hacer recados

er·rat·ic [ɪ'rætɪk] *adj* irregular; *course* errático

er·ror ['erər] error *m*

'er·ror mes·sage COMPUT mensaje *m* de error

e·rupt [ɪ'rʌpt] *v/i of volcano* entrar en erupción; *of violence* brotar; *of person* explotar

e·rup·tion [ɪ'rʌpʃn] *of volcano* erupción *f*; *of violence* brote *f*
es·ca·late ['eskəleɪt] *v/i* intensificarse
es·ca·la·tion [eskə'leɪʃn] intensificación *f*
es·ca·la·tor ['eskəleɪtər] escalera *f* mecánica
es·cape [ɪ'skeɪp] **1** *n of prisoner, animal* fuga *f*; *of gas* escape *m*, fuga *f*; ***have a narrow escape*** escaparse por los pelos **2** *v/i of prisoner, animal, gas* escaparse **3** *v/t*: ***the word escapes me*** no consigo recordar la palabra
es'cape chute AVIA tobogán *m* de emergencia
es·cort 1 *n* ['eskɔːrt] acompañante *m/f*; *guard* escolta *m/f*; ***under escort*** escoltado **2** *v/t* [ɪ'skɔːrt] escoltar; *socially* acompañar
es·pe·cial [ɪ'speʃl] → ***special***
es·pe·cial·ly [ɪ'speʃlɪ] *adv* especialmente
es·pi·o·nage ['espɪənɑːʒ] espionaje *m*
es·pres·so (cof·fee) [es'presoʊ] café *m* exprés
es·say ['eseɪ] *n creative* redacción *f*; *factual* trabajo *m*
es·sen·tial [ɪ'senʃl] *adj* esencial; ***the essential thing is ...*** lo esencial es ...
es·sen·tial·ly [ɪ'senʃlɪ] *adv* esencialmente; fundamentalmente
es·tab·lish [ɪ'stæblɪʃ] *v/t company* fundar; (*create, determine*) establecer; ***establish o.s. as*** establecerse como
es·tab·lish·ment [ɪ'stæblɪʃmənt] *firm, shop etc* establecimiento *m*; ***the Establishment*** el orden establecido
es·tate [ɪ'steɪt] (*area of land*) finca *f*; (*possessions of dead person*) patrimonio *m*
es'tate a·gen·cy *Br* agencia *f* inmobiliaria
es·thet·ic [ɪs'θetɪk] *adj* estético
es·ti·mate ['estɪmət] **1** *n* estimación *f*; *for job* presupuesto *m* **2** *v/t* estimar; ***estimated time of arrival*** hora *f* estimada de llegada
es·ti·ma·tion [estɪ'meɪʃn] estima *f*; ***he has gone up / down in my estimation*** le tengo en más / menos estima; ***in my estimation*** (*opinion*) a mi parecer
es·tranged [ɪs'treɪndʒd] *adj wife, husband* separado
es·tu·a·ry ['estʃəwerɪ] estuario *m*
ETA [iːtiː'eɪ] *abbr* (= ***estimated time of arrival***) hora *f* estimada de llegada
etc [et'setrə] *abbr* (= ***et cetera***) etc (= etcétera)
etch·ing ['etʃɪŋ] aguafuerte *m*
e·ter·nal [ɪ'tɜːrnl] *adj* eterno
e·ter·ni·ty [ɪ'tɜːrnətɪ] eternidad *f*
eth·i·cal ['eθɪkl] *adj* ético
eth·ics ['eθɪks] ética *f*; ***code of ethics*** código *m* ético
eth·nic ['eθnɪk] *adj* étnico
eth·nic 'group grupo *m* étnico
eth·nic mi'nor·i·ty minoría *f* étnica
EU [iː'juː] *abbr* (= ***European Union***) UE *f* (=Unión *f* Europea)
eu·phe·mism ['juːfəmɪzm] eufemismo *m*
eu·pho·ri·a [juː'fɔːrɪə] euforia *f*
eu·ro ['jʊroʊ] euro *m*
Eu·rope ['jʊrəp] Europa
Eu·ro·pe·an [jʊrə'pɪən] **1** *adj* europeo **2** *n* europeo(-a) *m(f)*
Eu·ro·pe·an Com'mis·sion Comisión *f* Europea
Eu·ro·pe·an 'Par·lia·ment Parlamento *m* Europeo
Eu·ro'pe·an plan media pensión *f*
Eu·ro·pe·an 'Un·ion Unión *f* Europea
eu·tha·na·si·a [jʊθə'neɪzɪə] eutanasia *f*
e·vac·u·ate [ɪ'vækjʊeɪt] *v/t* evacuar
e·vade [ɪ'veɪd] *v/t* evadir
e·val·u·ate [ɪ'væljʊeɪt] *v/t* evaluar
e·val·u·a·tion [ɪvæljʊ'eɪʃn] evaluación *f*
e·van·gel·ist [ɪ'vændʒəlɪst] evangelista *m/f*
e·vap·o·rate [ɪ'væpəreɪt] *v/i of water* evaporarse; *of confidence* desvanecerse
e·vap·o·ra·tion [ɪvæpə'reɪʃn] *of water* evaporación *f*
e·va·sion [ɪ'veɪʒn] evasión *f*
e·va·sive [ɪ'veɪsɪv] *adj* evasivo
eve [iːv] víspera *f*
e·ven ['iːvn] **1** *adj* (*regular*) regular; (*level*) llano; *number* par; *distribution* igualado; ***I'll get even with him*** me las pagará **2** *adv* incluso; ***even bigger / better*** incluso *or* aún mayor / mejor; ***not even*** ni siquiera; ***even so*** aun así; ***even if*** aunque; ***even if he begged me*** aunque me lo suplicara **3** *v/t*: ***even the score*** empatar, igualar el marcador
eve·ning ['iːvnɪŋ] tarde *f*; *after dark* noche *f*; ***in the evening*** por la tarde / noche; ***this evening*** esta tarde / noche; ***yesterday evening*** anoche *f*; ***good evening*** buenas *fpl* noches
'eve·ning class clase *f* nocturna
'eve·ning dress *for woman* traje *f* de noche; *for man* traje *f* de etiqueta
eve·ning 'pa·per periódico *m* de la tarde *or* vespertino
e·ven·ly ['iːvnlɪ] *adv* (*regularly*) regularmente
e·vent [ɪ'vent] acontecimiento *m*; SP prueba *f*; ***at all events*** en cualquier caso
e·vent·ful [ɪ'ventfəl] *adj* agitado, lleno de incidentes

e·ven·tu·al [ɪ'ventʃʊəl] *adj* final
e·ven·tu·al·ly [ɪ'ventʃʊəlɪ] *adv* finalmente
ev·er ['evər] *adv*: ***if I ever hear you ...*** como te oiga ...; ***have you ever been to Japan?*** ¿has estado alguna vez en Japón?; ***for ever*** siempre; ***ever since*** desde entonces; ***ever since she found out about it*** desde que se enteró de ello; ***ever since I've known him*** desde que lo conozco
ev·er·green ['evərgri:n] *n* árbol *m* de hoja perenne
ev·er·last·ing [evər'læstɪŋ] *adj love* eterno
ev·ery ['evrɪ] *adj* cada; ***I see him every day*** le veo todos los días; ***you have every reason to ...*** tienes toda la razón para ...; ***one in every ten*** uno de cada diez; ***every other day*** cada dos días; ***every now and then*** de vez en cuando
ev·ery·bod·y ['evrɪbɑ:dɪ] → ***everyone***
ev·ery·day ['evrɪdeɪ] *adj* cotidiano
ev·ery·one ['evrɪwʌn] *pron* todo el mundo
ev·ery·thing ['evrɪθɪŋ] *pron* todo
ev·ery·where ['evrɪwer] *adv* en *or* por todos sitios; (*wherever*) dondequiera que
e·vict [ɪ'vɪkt] *v/t* desahuciar
ev·i·dence ['evɪdəns] *also* LAW prueba(s) *f(pl)*; ***give evidence*** prestar declaración
ev·i·dent ['evɪdənt] *adj* evidente
ev·i·dent·ly ['evɪdəntlɪ] *adv* (*clearly*) evidentemente; (*apparently*) aparentemente, al parecer
e·vil ['i:vl] **1** *adj* malo **2** *n* mal *m*
e·voke [ɪ'voʊk] *v/t image* evocar
ev·o·lu·tion [i:və'lu:ʃn] evolución *f*
e·volve [ɪ'vɑ:lv] *v/i* evolucionar
ewe [ju:] oveja *f*
ex- [eks] *pref* ex-
ex [eks] F (*former wife, husband*) ex *m/f* F
ex·act [ɪg'zækt] *adj* exacto
ex·act·ing [ɪg'zæktɪŋ] *adj* exigente; *task* duro
ex·act·ly [ɪg'zæktlɪ] *adv* exactamente; ***exactly!*** ¡exactamente!
ex·ag·ge·rate [ɪg'zædʒəreɪt] *v/t & v/i* exagerar
ex·ag·ge·ra·tion [ɪgzædʒə'reɪʃn] exageración *f*
ex·am [ɪg'zæm] examen *m*; ***take an exam*** hacer un examen; ***pass / fail an exam*** aprobar/ suspender un examen
ex·am·i·na·tion [ɪgzæmɪ'neɪʃn] examen *m*; *of patient* reconocimiento *m*
ex·am·ine [ɪg'zæmɪn] *v/t* examinar; *patient* reconocer
ex·am·in·er [ɪg'zæmɪnər] EDU examinador(a) *m(f)*
ex·am·ple [ɪg'zæmpl] ejemplo *m*; ***for example*** por ejemplo; ***set a good / bad example*** dar buen / mal ejemplo
ex·as·pe·rat·ed [ɪg'zæspəreɪtɪd] *adj* exasperado
ex·as·pe·rat·ing [ɪg'zæspəreɪtɪŋ] *adj* exasperante
ex·ca·vate ['ekskəveɪt] *v/t* excavar
ex·ca·va·tion [ekskə'veɪʃn] excavación *f*
ex·ca·va·tor ['ekskəveɪtər] excavadora *f*
ex·ceed [ɪk'si:d] *v/t* (*be more than*) exceder; (*go beyond*) sobrepasar
ex·ceed·ing·ly [ɪk'si:dɪŋlɪ] *adj* sumamente
ex·cel [ɪk'sel] **1** *v/i* (*pret & pp* ***excelled***) sobresalir (***at*** en) **2** *v/t* (*pret & pp* ***excelled***): ***excel o.s.*** superarse a sí mismo
ex·cel·lence ['eksələns] excelencia *f*
ex·cel·lent ['eksələnt] *adj* excelente
ex·cept [ɪk'sept] *prep* excepto; ***except for*** a excepción de; ***except that*** sólo que
ex·cep·tion [ɪk'sepʃn] excepción *f*; ***with the exception of*** a excepción de; ***take exception to*** molestarse por
ex·cep·tion·al [ɪk'sepʃnl] *adj* excepcional
ex·cep·tion·al·ly [ɪk'sepʃnlɪ] *adv* (*extremely*) excepcionalmente
ex·cerpt ['eksɜ:rpt] extracto *m*
ex·cess [ɪk'ses] **1** *n* exceso *m*; ***eat / drink to excess*** comer / beber en exceso; ***in excess of*** superior a **2** *adj* excedente
ex·cess 'bag·gage exceso *m* de equipaje
ex·cess 'fare suplemento *m*
ex·ces·sive [ɪk'sesɪv] *adj* excesivo
ex·change [ɪks'tʃeɪndʒ] **1** *n* intercambio *m*; ***in exchange*** a cambio (***for*** de) **2** *v/t* cambiar
ex'change rate FIN tipo *m* de cambio
ex·ci·ta·ble [ɪk'saɪtəbl] *adj* excitable
ex·cite [ɪk'saɪt] *v/t* (*make enthusiastic*) entusiasmar
ex·cit·ed [ɪk'saɪtɪd] *adj* emocionado, excitado; *sexually* excitado; ***get excited*** emocionarse; ***get excited about*** emocionarse *or* excitarse con
ex·cite·ment [ɪk'saɪtmənt] emoción *f*, excitación *f*
ex·cit·ing [ɪk'saɪtɪŋ] *adj* emocionante, excitante
ex·claim [ɪk'skleɪm] *v/t* exclamar
ex·cla·ma·tion [eksklə'meɪʃn] exclamación *f*
ex·cla'ma·tion point signo *m* de admiración
ex·clude [ɪk'sklu:d] *v/t* excluir; *possibility* descartar
ex·clud·ing [ɪk'sklu:dɪŋ] *prep* excluyendo
ex·clu·sive [ɪk'sklu:sɪv] *adj* exclusivo
ex·com·mu·ni·cate [ekskə'mju:nɪkeɪt]

E

v/t REL excomulgar

ex·cru·ci·a·ting [ɪk'skruːʃɪeɪtɪŋ] *adj pain* terrible

ex·cur·sion [ɪk'skɜːrʃn] excursión *f*

ex·cuse **1** *n* [ɪk'skjuːs] excusa *f* **2** *v/t* [ɪk'skjuːz] (*forgive*) excusar, perdonar; (*allow to leave*) disculpar; ***excuse s.o. from sth*** dispensar a alguien de algo; ***excuse me*** *to get past, interrupting* perdone, disculpe; *to get attention* perdone, oiga

E

e·x·e·cute ['eksɪkjuːt] *v/t criminal, plan* ejecutar

ex·e·cu·tion [eksɪ'kjuːʃn] *of criminal, plan* ejecución *f*

ex·e·cu·tion·er [eksɪ'kjuːʃnər] verdugo *m*

ex·ec·u·tive [ɪg'zekjʊtɪv] ejecutivo(-a) *m(f)*

ex·ec·u·tive 'brief·case maletín *m* de ejecutivo

ex·ec·u·tive 'wash·room baño *m* para ejecutivos

ex·em·pla·ry [ɪg'zemplərɪ] *adj* ejemplar

ex·empt [ɪg'zempt] *adj* exento; ***be exempt from*** estar exento de

ex·er·cise ['eksərsaɪz] **1** *n* ejercicio *m*; ***take exercise*** hacer ejercicio **2** *v/t muscle* ejercitar; *dog* pasear; *caution* proceder con; ***exercise restraint*** controlarse **3** *v/i* hacer ejercicio

'ex·er·cise bike bicicleta *f* estática

'ex·er·cise book EDU cuaderno de ejercicios

ex·ert [ɪg'zɜːrt] *v/t authority* ejercer; ***exert o.s.*** esforzarse

ex·er·tion [ɪg'zɜːrʃn] esfuerzo *m*

ex·hale [eks'heɪl] *v/t* exhalar

ex·haust [ɪg'zɒːst] **1** *n fumes* gases *mpl* de la combustión; *pipe* tubo *m* de escape **2** *v/t* (*tire*) cansar; (*use up*) agotar

ex·haust·ed [ɪg'zɒːstɪd] *adj* (*tired*) agotado

ex'haust fumes *npl* gases *mpl* de la combustión

ex·haust·ing [ɪg'zɒːstɪŋ] *adj* agotador

ex·haus·tion [ɪg'zɒːstʃn] agotamiento *m*

ex·haus·tive [ɪg'zɒːstɪv] *adj* exhaustivo

ex'haust pipe tubo *m* de escape

ex·hib·it [ɪg'zɪbɪt] **1** *n in exhibition* objeto *m* expuesto **2** *v/t of gallery* exhibir; *of artist* exponer; (*give evidence of*) mostrar

ex·hi·bi·tion [eksɪ'bɪʃn] exposición *f*; *of bad behavior, skill* exhibición *f*

ex·hi·bi·tion·ist [eksɪ'bɪʃnɪst] exhibicionista *m/f*

ex·hil·a·rat·ing [ɪg'zɪləreɪtɪŋ] *adj* estimulante

ex·ile ['eksaɪl] **1** *n* exilio *m*; *person* exiliado(-a) *m(f)* **2** *v/t* exiliar

ex·ist [ɪg'zɪst] *v/i* existir; ***exist on*** subsistir a base de

ex·ist·ence [ɪg'zɪstəns] existencia *f*; ***be in existence*** existir; ***come into existence*** crearse, nacer

ex·ist·ing [ɪg'zɪstɪŋ] *adj* existente

ex·it ['eksɪt] **1** *n* salida *f*; THEA salida *f*, mutis *m* **2** *v/i* COMPUT salir

ex·on·e·rate [ɪg'zɑːnəreɪt] *v/t* exonerar de

ex·or·bi·tant [ɪg'zɔːrbɪtənt] *adj* exorbitante

ex·ot·ic [ɪg'zɑːtɪk] *adj* exótico

ex·pand [ɪk'spænd] **1** *v/t* expandir **2** *v/i* expandirse; *of metal* dilatarse

◆ **expand on** *v/t* desarrollar

ex·panse [ɪk'spæns] extensión *f*

ex·pan·sion [ɪk'spænʃn] expansión *f*; *of metal* dilatación *f*

ex·pat·ri·ate [eks'pætrɪət] **1** *adj* expatriado **2** *n* expatriado(-a) *m(f)*

ex·pect [ɪk'spekt] **1** *v/t* esperar; (*suppose*) suponer, imaginar(se); (*demand*) exigir **2** *v/i*: ***be expecting*** (*be pregnant*) estar en estado; ***I expect so*** eso espero, creo que sí

ex·pec·tant [ɪk'spektənt] *adj crowd* expectante

ex·pec·tant 'moth·er futura madre *f*

ex·pec·ta·tion [ekspek'teɪʃn] expectativa *f*; ***live up to people's expectations of you*** (*demands*) estar a la altura de lo que se espera de uno

ex·pe·dient [ɪk'spiːdɪənt] *adj* oportuno, conveniente

ex·pe·di·tion [ekspɪ'dɪʃn] expedición *f*

ex·pel [ɪk'spel] *v/t* (*pret & pp* ***expelled***) *person* expulsar

ex·pend [ɪk'spend] *v/t energy* gastar

ex·pend·a·ble [ɪk'spendəbl] *adj person* prescindible

ex·pen·di·ture [ɪk'spendɪtʃər] gasto *m*

ex·pense [ɪk'spens] gasto *m*; ***at great expense*** gastando mucho dinero; ***at the company's expense*** a cargo de la empresa; ***a joke at my expense*** una broma a costa mía; ***at the expense of his health*** a costa de su salud

ex'pense ac·count cuenta *f* de gastos

ex·pen·ses [ɪk'spensɪz] *npl* gastos *mpl*

ex·pen·sive [ɪk'spensɪv] *adj* caro

ex·pe·ri·ence [ɪk'spɪrɪəns] **1** *n* experiencia *f* **2** *v/t* experimentar

ex·pe·ri·enced [ɪk'spɪrɪənst] *adj* experimentado

ex·per·i·ment [ɪk'sperɪmənt] **1** *n* experimento *m* **2** *v/i* experimentar; ***experiment on*** *animals* experimentar con; ***experiment with*** (*try out*) probar

ex·per·i·men·tal [ɪksperɪ'mentl] *adj* experimental

ex·pert ['ekspɜːrt] **1** *adj* experto **2** *n* experto(-a) *m(f)*

ex·pert ad'vice la opinión de un experto

ex·pert·ise [ekspɜːr'tiːz] destreza *f*, pericia *f*

ex·pire [ɪk'spaɪr] *v/i* caducar

ex·pi·ry [ɪk'spaɪrɪ] *of lease, contract* vencimiento *m*; *of passport* caducidad *f*

ex'pi·ry date *of food, passport* fecha *f* de caducidad; ***be past its expiry date*** haber caducado

ex·plain [ɪk'spleɪn] **1** *v/t* explicar **2** *v/i* explicarse

ex·pla·na·tion [eksplə'neɪʃn] explicación *f*

ex·plan·a·tor·y [ɪk'splænətɔːrɪ] *adj* explicativo

ex·plic·it [ɪk'splɪsɪt] *adj instructions* explícito

ex·plic·it·ly [ɪk'splɪsɪtlɪ] *adv state* explícitamente; *forbid* terminantemente

ex·plode [ɪk'sploʊd] **1** *v/i of bomb* explotar **2** *v/t bomb* hacer explotar

ex·ploit¹ ['eksplɔɪt] *n* hazaña *f*

ex·ploit² [ɪk'splɔɪt] *v/t person, resources* explotar

ex·ploi·ta·tion [eksplɔɪ'teɪʃn] *of person* explotación *f*

ex·plo·ra·tion [eksplə'reɪʃn] exploración *f*

ex·plor·a·to·ry [ɪk'splɑːrətərɪ] *adj surgery* exploratorio

ex·plore [ɪk'splɔːr] *v/t country etc* explorar; *possibility* estudiar

ex·plo·rer [ɪk'splɔːrər] explorador(a) *m(f)*

ex·plo·sion [ɪk'sploʊʒn] *of bomb, in population* explosión *f*

ex·plo·sive [ɪk'sploʊsɪv] *n* explosivo *m*

ex·port ['ekspɔːrt] **1** *n action* exportación *f*; *item* producto *m* de exportación; ***exports*** *npl* exportaciones *fpl* **2** *v/t also* COMPUT exportar

'ex·port cam·paign campaña *f* de exportación

ex·port·er ['ekspɔːrtər] exportador(a) *m(f)*

ex·pose [ɪk'spoʊz] *v/t* (*uncover*) exponer; *scandal* sacar a la luz; ***he's been exposed as a liar*** ha quedado como un mentiroso; ***expose sth to sth*** exponer algo a algo

ex·po·sure [ɪk'spoʊʒər] exposición *f*; PHOT foto(grafía) *f*

ex·press [ɪk'spres] **1** *adj* (*fast*) rápido; (*explicit*) expreso **2** *n train* expreso *m*; *bus* autobús *m* directo **3** *v/t* expresar; ***express o.s. well / clearly*** expresarse bien / con claridad

ex'press el·e·va·tor *ascensor rápido que sólo para en algunos pisos*

ex·pres·sion [ɪk'spreʃn] *voiced* muestra *f*; *phrase, on face* expresión *f*; ***read with expression*** leer con sentimiento

ex·pres·sive [ɪk'spresɪv] *adj* expresivo

ex·press·ly [ɪk'spreslɪ] *adv state* expresamente; *forbid* terminantemente

ex·press·way [ɪk'spresweɪ] autopista *f*

ex·pul·sion [ɪk'spʌlʃn] *from school, of diplomat* expulsión *f*

ex·qui·site [ek'skwɪzɪt] *adj* (*beautiful*) exquisito

ex·tend [ɪk'stend] **1** *v/t house, investigation* ampliar; (*make wider*) ensanchar; (*make bigger*) agrandar; *runway, path* alargar; *contract, visa* prorrogar; *thanks, congratulations* extender **2** *v/i of garden etc* llegar

ex·ten·sion [ɪk'stenʃn] *to house* ampliación *f*; *of contract, visa* prórroga *f*; TELEC extensión *f*

ex'ten·sion ca·ble cable *m* de extensión

ex·ten·sive [ɪk'stensɪv] *adj damage* cuantioso; *knowledge* considerable; *search* extenso, amplio

ex·tent [ɪk'stent] alcance *m*; ***to such an extent that*** hasta el punto de que; ***to a certain extent*** hasta cierto punto

ex·ten·u·at·ing cir·cum·stances [ɪk'stenʊeɪtɪŋ] *npl* circunstancias *fpl* atenuantes

ex·te·ri·or [ɪk'stɪrɪər] **1** *adj* exterior **2** *n* exterior *m*

ex·ter·mi·nate [ɪk'stɜːrmɪneɪt] *v/t* exterminar

ex·ter·nal [ɪk'stɜːrnl] *adj* (*outside*) exterior, externo

ex·tinct [ɪk'stɪŋkt] *adj species* extinguido

ex·tinc·tion [ɪk'stɪŋkʃn] *of species* extinción *f*

ex·tin·guish [ɪk'stɪŋgwɪʃ] *v/t fire* extinguir, apagar; *cigarette* apagar

ex·tin·guish·er [ɪk'stɪŋgwɪʃər] extintor *m*

extort [ɪk'stɔːrt] *v/t* obtener mediante extorsión; ***extort money from*** extorsionar a

ex·tor·tion [ɪk'stɔːrʃn] extorsión *f*

ex·tor·tion·ate [ɪk'stɔːrʃənət] *adj prices* desorbitado

ex·tra ['ekstrə] **1** *n* extra *m*; *in movie* extra *m/f* **2** *adj* extra; ***meals are extra*** las comidas se pagan aparte; ***that's $1 extra*** cuesta 1 dólar más **3** *adv* super; ***extra strong*** extrafuerte; ***extra special*** muy especial

E

ex·tra 'charge recargo *m*
ex·tract[1] ['ekstrækt] *n* extracto *m*
ex·tract[2] [ɪk'strækt] *v/t* sacar; *coal, oil, tooth* extraer; *information* sonsacar
ex·trac·tion [ɪk'strækʃn] *of oil, coal, tooth* extracción *f*
ex·tra·dite ['ekstrədaɪt] *v/t* extraditar
ex·tra·di·tion [ekstrə'dɪʃn] extradición *f*
ex·tra'di·tion trea·ty tratado *m* de extradición
ex·tra·mar·i·tal [ekstrə'mærɪtl] *adj* extramarital
ex·tra·or·di·nar·i·ly [ekstrɔːrdɪn'erɪlɪ] *adv* extraordinariamente
ex·tra·or·di·na·ry [ɪk'strɔːrdɪnerɪ] *adj* extraordinario
ex·trav·a·gance [ɪk'strævəgəns] *with money* despilfarro *m*; *of claim etc* extravagancia *f*
ex·trav·a·gant [ɪk'strævəgənt] *adj with money* despilfarrador; *claim* extravagante
ex·treme [ɪk'striːm] **1** *n* extremo *m* **2** *adj* extremo; *views* extremista
ex·treme·ly [ɪk'striːmlɪ] *adv* extremadamente, sumamente
ex·trem·ist [ɪk'striːmɪst] extremista *m/f*
ex·tri·cate ['ekstrɪkeɪt] *v/t* liberar
ex·tro·vert ['ekstrəvɜːrt] **1** *adj* extrovertido **2** *n* extrovertido(-a) *m(f)*
ex·u·be·rant [ɪg'zuːbərənt] *adj* exuberante
ex·ult [ɪg'zʌlt] *v/i* exultar
eye [aɪ] **1** *n of person, needle* ojo *m*; ***keep an eye on*** (*look after*) estar pendiente de; (*monitor*) estar pendiente de, vigilar **2** *v/t* mirar
'eye·ball globo *m* ocular
'eye·brow ceja *f*
'eye-catch·ing *adj* llamativo
'eye·glass·es *npl* gafas *fpl*, *L.Am.* anteojos *mpl*, *L.Am.* lentes *mpl*
'eye·lash pestaña *f*
'eye·lid párpado *m*
'eye·lin·er lápiz *m* de ojos
'eye·sha·dow sombra *f* de ojos
'eye·sight vista *f*
'eye·sore engendro *m*, monstruosidad *f*
'eye strain vista *f* cansada
'eye·wit·ness testigo *m/f* ocular

F

F *abbr* (= ***Fahrenheit***) F
fab·ric ['fæbrɪk] (*material*) tejido *m*
fab·u·lous ['fæbjʊləs] *adj* fabuloso, estupendo
fab·u·lously ['fæbjʊləslɪ] *adv rich* tremendamente; *beautiful* increíblemente
fa·çade [fə'sɑːd] *of building, person* fachada *f*
face [feɪs] **1** *n* cara *f*; ***face to face*** cara a cara; ***lose face*** padecer una *hum*illación **2** *v/t* (*be opposite*) estar enfrente de; (*confront*) enfrentarse a
◆ **face up to** *v/t* hacer frente a
'face·cloth toallita *f*
'face·lift lifting *m*, estiramiento *m* de piel
'face pack mascarilla *f* (*facial*)
face 'val·ue: ***take sth at face value*** tomarse algo literalmente
fa·cial ['feɪʃl] *n* limpieza *f* de cutis
fa·cil·i·tate [fə'sɪlɪteɪt] *v/t* facilitar
fa·cil·i·ties [fə'sɪlətɪz] *npl* instalaciones *fpl*
fact [fækt] hecho *m*; ***in fact, as a matter of fact*** de hecho
faction ['fækʃn] facción *f*
fac·tor ['fæktər] factor *m*
fac·to·ry ['fæktərɪ] fábrica *f*
fac·ul·ty ['fækəltɪ] (*hearing etc*), *at university* facultad *f*
fad [fæd] moda *f*
fade [feɪd] *v/i of colors* desteñirse, perder color; *of memories* desvanecerse
fad·ed ['feɪdɪd] *adj color, jeans* desteñido, descolorido
fag[1] [fæg] F (*homosexual*) maricón *m* F
fag[2] [fæg] *Br* F (*cigarette*) pitillo *m* F
Fahr·en·heit ['færənhaɪt] *adj* Fahrenheit
fail [feɪl] **1** *v/i* fracasar; *of plan* fracasar, fallar **2** *n*: ***without fail*** sin falta
fail·ing ['feɪlɪŋ] *n* fallo *m*
fail·ure ['feɪljər] fracaso *m*; *in exam* suspenso *m*; ***I feel such a failure*** me siento un fracasado
faint [feɪnt] **1** *adj line, smile* tenue; *smell, noise* casi imperceptible **2** *v/i* desmayarse
faint·ly ['feɪntlɪ] *adv smile, smell* levemente
fair[1] [fer] *n* COM feria *f*

fair² [fer] *adj hair* rubio; *complexion* claro; (*just*) justo
fair·ly ['ferlɪ] *adv treat* justamente, con justicia; (*quite*) bastante
fair·ness ['fernɪs] *of treatment* imparcialidad *f*
fai·ry ['ferɪ] hada *f*
'fai·ry tale cuento *m* de hadas
faith [feɪθ] fe *f*, confianza *f*; REL fe *f*
faith·ful ['feɪθfəl] *adj* fiel; ***be faithful to one's partner*** ser fiel a la pareja
faith·ful·ly ['feɪθfəlɪ] *adv* religiosamente
Falk·land Is·lands ['fɒːlklənd] *npl*: ***the Falkland Islands*** las Islas Malvinas
fake [feɪk] **1** *n* falsificación *f* **2** *adj* falso **3** *v/t* (*forge*) falsificar; (*feign*) fingir
fall¹ [fɒːl] *n season* otoño *m*
fall² [fɒːl] **1** *v/i* (*pret* ***fell***, *pp* ***fallen***) *of person* caerse; *of government, prices, temperature, night* caer; ***it falls on a Tuesday*** cae en martes; ***fall ill*** enfermar, caer enfermo; ***I fell off the wall*** me caí del muro **2** *n* caída *f*
◆ **fall back on** *v/t* recurrir a
◆ **fall behind** *v/i with work, studies* retrasarse
◆ **fall down** *v/i* caerse
◆ **fall for** *v/t person* enamorarse de; (*be deceived by*) dejarse engañar por; ***I'm amazed you fell for it*** me sorprende mucho que picaras
◆ **fall out** *v/i of hair* caerse; (*argue*) pelearse
◆ **fall over** *v/i* caerse
◆ **fall through** *v/i of plans* venirse abajo
fal·len ['fɒːlən] *pp* → ***fall²***
fal·li·ble ['fæləbl] *adj* falible
'fall·out lluvia *f* radiactiva
false [fɑːls] *adj* falso
false a'larm falsa alarma *f*
false·ly ['fɑːlslɪ] *adv*: ***be falsely accused of sth*** ser acusado falsamente de algo
false 'start *in race* salida *f* nula
false 'teeth *npl* dentadura *f* postiza
fal·si·fy ['fɑːlsɪfaɪ] *v/t* (*pret & pp* ***falsified***) falsificar
fame [feɪm] fama *f*
fa·mil·i·ar [fə'mɪljər] *adj* familiar; ***get familiar*** (*intimate*) tomarse demasiadas confianzas; ***be familiar with sth*** estar familiarizado con algo; ***that looks familiar*** eso me resulta familiar; ***that sounds familiar*** me suena
fa·mil·i·ar·i·ty [fəmɪlɪ'ærɪtɪ] *with subject etc* familiaridad *f*
fa·mil·i·ar·ize [fə'mɪljəraɪz] *v/t*: ***familiarize o.s. with …*** familiarizarse con …
fam·i·ly ['fæməlɪ] familia *f*
fam·i·ly 'doc·tor médico *m/f* de familia
'fam·i·ly name apellido *m*
fam·i·ly 'plan·ning planificación *f* familiar
fam·i·ly 'plan·ning clin·ic clínica *f* de planificación familiar
fam·i·ly 'tree árbol *m* genealógico
fam·ine ['fæmɪn] hambruna *f*
fam·ished ['fæmɪʃt] *adj* F: ***I'm famished*** estoy muerto de hambre F
fa·mous ['feɪməs] *adj* famoso; ***be famous for …*** ser famoso por …
fan¹ [fæn] *n* (*supporter*) seguidor(a) *m*(*f*); *of singer, band* admirador(a) *m*(*f*), fan *m/f*
fan² [fæn] **1** *n electric* ventilador *m*; *handheld* abanico *m* **2** *v/t* (*pret & pp* ***fanned***) abanicar; ***fan o.s.*** abanicarse
fa·nat·ic [fə'nætɪk] *n* fanático(-a) *m*(*f*)
fa·nat·i·cal [fə'nætɪkl] *adj* fanático
fa·nat·i·cism [fə'nætɪsɪzm] fanatismo *m*
'fan belt MOT correa *f* del ventilador
'fan club club *m* de fans
fan·cy ['fænsɪ] **1** *adj* (*luxurious*) de lujo; (*complicated*) sofisticado **2** *n*: ***as the fancy takes you*** como te apetezca; ***take a fancy to s.o.*** encapricharse de alguien **3** *v/t* (*pret & pp* ***fancied***): ***do you fancy an ice cream?*** ¿te apetece un helado?
fan·cy 'dress disfraz *m*
fan·cy-'dress par·ty fiesta *f* de disfraces
fang [fæŋ] colmillo *m*
'fan mail cartas *fpl* de los fans
fan·ta·size ['fæntəsaɪz] *v/i* fantasear (***about*** sobre)
fan·tas·tic [fæn'tæstɪk] *adj* (*very good*) fantástico, excelente; (*very big*) inmenso
fan·tas·tic·al·ly [fæn'tæstɪklɪ] *adv* (*extremely*) sumamente, increíblemente
fan·ta·sy ['fæntəsɪ] fantasía *f*
far [fɑːr] *adv* lejos; (*much*) mucho; ***far bigger / faster*** mucho más grande / rápido; ***far away*** lejos; ***how far is it to …?*** ¿a cuánto está …?; ***as far as the corner / hotel*** hasta la esquina / el hotel; ***as far as I can see*** tal y como lo veo yo; ***as far as I know*** que yo sepa; ***you've gone too far*** *in behavior* te has pasado; ***so far so good*** por ahora muy bien
farce [fɑːrs] farsa *f*
fare [fer] *n price* tarifa *f*; *actual money* dinero *m*
Far 'East Lejano Oriente *m*
fare·well [fer'wel] *n* despedida *f*
fare'well par·ty fiesta *f* de despedida
far-fetched [fɑːr'fetʃt] *adj* inverosímil, exagerado
farm [fɑːrm] *n* granja *f*
farm·er ['fɑːrmər] granjero(-a) *m*(*f*)
'farm·house granja *f*, alquería *f*

farm·ing ['fɑːrmɪŋ] *n* agricultura *f*
'farm·work·er trabajador(a) *m(f)* del campo
'farm·yard corral *m*
far-'off *adj* lejano
far·sight·ed [fɑːr'saɪtɪd] *adj* previsor; *optically* hipermétrope
fart [fɑːrt] **1** *n* F pedo *m* F **2** *v/i* F tirarse un pedo F
far·ther ['fɑːðər] *adv* más lejos; ***farther away*** más allá, más lejos
far·thest ['fɑːrðəst] *adv travel etc* más lejos
fas·ci·nate ['fæsɪneɪt] *v/t* fascinar; ***be fascinated by ...*** estar fascinado por ...
fas·ci·nat·ing ['fæsɪneɪtɪŋ] *adj* fascinante
fas·ci·na·tion [fæsɪ'neɪʃn] fascinación *f*
fas·cism ['fæʃɪzm] fascismo *m*
fas·cist ['fæʃɪst] **1** *n* fascista *m/f* **2** *adj* fascista
fash·ion ['fæʃn] *n* moda *f*; (*manner*) modo *m*, manera *f*; ***in fashion*** de moda; ***out of fashion*** pasado de moda
fash·ion·a·ble ['fæʃnəbl] *adj* de moda
fash·ion·a·bly ['fæʃnəblɪ] *adv dressed* a la moda
'fash·ion-con·scious *adj* que sigue la moda
'fash·ion de·sign·er modisto(-a) *m(f)*
'fash·ion mag·a·zine revista *f* de modas
'fash·ion show desfile *f* de moda, pase *m* de modelos
fast[1] [fæst] **1** *adj* rápido; ***be fast*** *of clock* ir adelantado **2** *adv* rápido; ***stuck fast*** atascado; ***fast asleep*** profundamente dormido
fast[2] [fæst] *n not eating* ayuno *m*
fas·ten ['fæsn] **1** *v/t window, lid* cerrar (*poniendo el cierre*); *dress* abrochar; ***fasten sth onto sth*** asegurar algo a algo **2** *v/i of dress etc* abrocharse
fas·ten·er ['fæsnər] *for dress, lid* cierre *f*
fast 'food comida *f* rápida
fast-food 'res·tau·rant restaurante *f* de comida rápida
fast 'for·ward **1** *n on video etc* avance *m* rápido **2** *v/i* avanzar
'fast lane *on road* carril *f* rápido; ***in the fast lane*** *fig*: *of life* con un tren de vida acelerado
'fast train (tren *m*) rápido *m*
fat [fæt] **1** *adj* gordo **2** *n on meat, for baking* grasa *f*
fa·tal ['feɪtl] *adj illness* mortal; *error* fatal
fa·tal·i·ty [fə'tælətɪ] víctima *f* mortal
fa·tal·ly ['feɪtəlɪ] *adv* mortalmente; ***fatally injured*** herido mortalmente
fate [feɪt] destino *m*
fat·ed ['feɪtɪd] *adj*: ***be fated to do sth*** estar *pre*destinado a hacer algo
'fat-free *adj* sin grasas
fa·ther ['fɑːðər] *n* padre *m*; ***Father Martin*** REL el Padre Martin
Fa·ther 'Christ·mas *Br* Papá *m* Noel
fa·ther·hood ['fɑːðərhʊd] paternidad *f*
'fa·ther-in-law (*pl* ***fathers-in-law***) suegro *m*
fa·ther·ly ['fɑːðəlɪ] *adj* paternal
fath·om ['fæðəm] *n* NAUT braza *f*
◆ **fathom out** *v/t fig* entender
fa·tigue [fə'tiːg] *n* cansancio *m*, fatiga *f*
fat·so ['fætsoʊ] F gordinflón (-ona) *m(f)* F
fat·ten ['fætn] *v/t animal* engordar
fat·ty ['fætɪ] **1** *adj* graso **2** *n* F (*person*) gordinflón (-ona) *m(f)* F
fau·cet ['fɒːsɪt] *Span* grifo *m*, *L.Am.* llave *f*
fault [fɒːlt] *n* (*defect*) fallo *m*; ***it's your / my fault*** es culpa tuya / mía; ***find fault with ...*** encontrar defectos a ...
fault·less ['fɒːltlɪs] *adj* impecable
fault·y ['fɒːltɪ] *adj goods* defectuoso
fa·vor ['feɪvər] **1** *n* favor *m*; ***do s.o. a favor*** hacer un favor a alguien; ***do me a favor!*** (*don't be stupid*) ¡haz el favor!; ***in favor of ...*** a favor de ...; ***be in favor of ...*** estar a favor de ... **2** *v/t* (*prefer*) preferir
fa·vo·ra·ble ['feɪvərəbl] *adj reply etc* favorable
fa·vo·rite ['feɪvərɪt] **1** *n* favorito(-a) *m(f)*; *food* comida *f* favorita **2** *adj* favorito
fa·vor·it·ism ['feɪvrɪtɪzm] favoritismo *m*
fa·vour *etc Br* → ***favor*** *etc*
fax [fæks] **1** *n* fax *m*; ***send sth by fax*** enviar algo por fax **2** *v/t* enviar por fax: ***fax sth to s.o.*** enviar algo por fax a alguien
FBI [efbiː'aɪ] *abbr* (= ***Federal Bureau of Investigation***) FBI *m*
fear [fɪr] **1** *n* miedo *m*, temor *m* **2** *v/t* temer, tener miedo a
fear·less ['fɪrlɪs] *adj* valiente, audaz
fear·less·ly ['fɪrlɪslɪ] *adv* sin miedo
fea·si·bil·i·ty stud·y [fiːzə'bɪlətɪ] estudio *m* de viabilidad
fea·si·ble ['fiːzəbl] *adj* factible, viable
feast [fiːst] *n* banquete *m*, festín *m*
feat [fiːt] hazaña *f*, proeza *f*
fea·ther ['feðər] pluma *f*
fea·ture ['fiːʧər] **1** *n on face* rasgo *m*, facción *f*; *of city, building, plan, style* característica *f*; *article in paper* reportaje *m*; *movie* largometraje *f*; ***make a feature of ...*** destacar ... **2** *v/t* ***a movie featuring ...*** una película en la que aparece ...
'fea·ture film largometraje *m*
Feb·ru·a·ry ['februerɪ] febrero *m*
fed [fed] *pret & pp* → ***feed***

fed·e·ral ['fedərəl] *adj* federal
fed·e·ra·tion [fedə'reɪʃn] federación *f*
fed 'up *adj* F harto, hasta las narices F; ***be fed up with ...*** estar harto *or* hasta las narices de ...
fee [fiː] *of lawyer, doctor, consultant* honorarios *mpl*; *for entrance* entrada *f*; *for membership* cuota *f*
fee·ble ['fiːbl] *adj person, laugh* débil; *attempt* flojo; *excuse* pobre
feed [fiːd] *v/t* (*pret & pp* ***fed***) alimentar, dar de comer a
'feed·back *n* reacción *m*; ***we'll give you some feedback as soon as possible*** le daremos nuestra opinión *or* nuestras reacciones lo antes posible
feel [fiːl] **1** *v/t* (*pret & pp* ***felt***) (*touch*) tocar; (*sense*) sentir; (*think*) creer, pensar; ***you can feel the difference*** se nota la diferencia **2** *v/i* (*pret & pp* ***felt***): ***it feels like silk / cotton*** tiene la textura de la seda / algodón; ***your hand feels hot*** tienes la mano caliente; ***I feel hungry*** tengo hambre; ***I feel tired*** estoy cansado; ***how are you feeling today?*** ¿cómo te encuentras hoy?; ***how does it feel to be rich?*** ¿qué se siente siendo rico?; ***do you feel like a drink / meal?*** ¿te apetece una bebida / comida?; ***I feel like going / staying*** me apetece ir / quedarme; ***I don't feel like it*** no me apetece
◆ **feel up to** *v/t* sentirse con fuerzas para
feel·er ['fiːlər] *of insect* antena *f*
'feel·good fac·tor sensación *f* positiva
feel·ing ['fiːlɪŋ] sentimiento *m*; (*sensation*) sensación *f*; ***what are your feelings about it?*** ¿qué piensas sobre ello?; ***I have mixed feelings about him*** me inspira sentimientos contradictorios; ***I have this feeling that ...*** tengo el presentimiento de que ...
feet [fiːt] *pl* → ***foot***
fe·line ['fiːlaɪn] *adj* felino
fell [fel] *pret* → ***fall***[2]
fel·low ['feloʊ] *n* (*man*) tipo *m*
fel·low 'cit·i·zen conciudadano(-a) *m*(*f*)
fel·low 'coun·try·man compatriota *m*/*f*
fel·low 'man prójimo *m*
fel·o·ny ['felənɪ] delito *m* grave
felt [felt] **1** *n* fieltro *m* **2** *pret & pp* → ***feel***
felt 'tip, felt-tip 'pen rotulador *m*
fe·male ['fiːmeɪl] **1** *adj animal, plant* hembra; *relating to people* femenino **2** *n of animals, plants* hembra *f*; *person* mujer *f*
fem·i·nine ['femɪnɪn] **1** *adj also* GRAM femenino **2** *n* GRAM femenino *m*
fem·i·nism ['femɪnɪzm] feminismo *m*
fem·i·nist ['femɪnɪst] **1** *n* feminista *m*/*f* **2** *adj* feminista
fence [fens] *n around garden etc* cerca *f*, valla *f*; F *criminal* perista *m*/*f*; ***sit on the fence*** nadar entre dos aguas
◆ **fence in** *v/t land* cercar, vallar
fenc·ing ['fensɪŋ] SP esgrima *f*
fend [fend] *v/i*: ***fend for o.s.*** valerse por sí mismo
fend·er ['fendər] MOT aleta *f*
fer·ment[1] [fə'ment] *v/i of liquid* fermentar
fer·ment[2] ['fɜːrment] *n* (*unrest*) agitación *f*
fer·men·ta·tion [fɜːrmen'teɪʃn] fermentación *f*
fern [fɜːrn] helecho *m*
fe·ro·cious [fə'roʊʃəs] *adj* feroz
fer·ry ['ferɪ] *n* ferry *m*, transbordador *m*
fer·tile ['fɜːrtəl] *adj* fértil
fer·til·i·ty [fɜːr'tɪlətɪ] fertilidad *f*
fer'til·i·ty drug medicamento *m* para el tratamiento de la infertilidad
fer·ti·lize ['fɜːrtəlaɪz] *v/t* fertilizar
fer·ti·liz·er ['fɜːrtəlaɪzər] *for soil* fertilizante *m*
fer·vent ['fɜːrvənt] *adj admirer* ferviente
fer·vent·ly ['fɜːrvəntlɪ] *adv* fervientemente
fes·ter ['festər] *v/i of wound* enconarse
fes·ti·val ['festɪvl] festival *m*
fes·tive ['festɪv] *adj* festivo; ***the festive season*** la época navideña, las Navidades
fes·tiv·i·ties [fe'stɪvətɪz] *npl* celebraciones *fpl*
fe·tal ['fiːtl] *adj* fetal
fetch [fetʃ] *v/t person* recoger; *thing* traer, ir a buscar; *price* alcanzar
fe·tus ['fiːtəs] feto *m*
feud [fjuːd] **1** *n* enemistad *f* **2** *v/i* estar enemistado
fe·ver ['fiːvər] fiebre *f*
fe·ver·ish ['fiːvərɪʃ] *adj* con fiebre; *fig*: *excitement* febril
few [fjuː] **1** *adj* (*not many*) pocos; ***a few*** *things* unos pocos; ***quite a few, a good few*** (*a lot*) bastantes **2** *pron* (*not many*) pocos(-as); ***a few*** (*some*) unos pocos; ***quite a few, a good few*** (*a lot*) bastantes; ***few of them could speak English*** de ellos muy pocos hablaban inglés
fewer ['fjuːər] *adj* menos; ***fewer than ...*** menos que ...; *with numbers* menos de ...
fi·an·cé [fɪ'ɑːnseɪ] prometido *m*, novio *m*
fi·an·cée [fɪ'ɑːnseɪ] prometida *f*, novia *f*
fi·as·co [fɪ'æskoʊ] fiasco *m*
fib [fɪb] *n* F bola *f* F
fi·ber ['faɪbər] *n* fibra *f*
'fi·ber·glass *n* fibra *f* de vidrio
fi·ber 'op·tic *adj* de fibra óptica

fi·ber 'op·tics fibra *f* óptica
fi·bre *Br* → ***fiber***
fick·le ['fɪkl] *adj* inconstante, mudable
fic·tion ['fɪkʃn] *n* (*novels*) literatura *f* de ficción; (*made-up story*) ficción *f*
fic·tion·al ['fɪkʃnl] *adj* de ficción
fic·ti·tious [fɪk'tɪʃəs] *adj* ficticio
fid·dle ['fɪdl] **1** *n* (*violin*) violín *m*; ***it's a fiddle*** F (*cheat*) es un amaño **2** *v/i*: ***fiddle around with*** enredar con; ***fiddle around with*** enredar con **3** *v/t accounts, result* amañar
fi·del·i·ty [fɪ'delətɪ] fidelidad *f*
fid·get ['fɪdʒɪt] *v/i* moverse; ***stop fidgeting!*** ¡estáte quieto!
fid·get·y ['fɪdʒɪtɪ] *adj* inquieto
field [fiːld] *also of research etc* campo *m*; *for sport* campo *m*, *L.Am.* cancha *f*; (*competitors in race*) participantes *mpl*; ***that's not my field*** no es mi campo
field·er ['fiːldər] *in baseball* fildeador(-a) *m*(*f*)
'field e·vents *npl* pruebas *fpl* de salto y lanzamiento
fierce [fɪrs] *adj animal* feroz; *wind, storm* violento
fierce·ly ['fɪrslɪ] *adv* ferozmente
fi·er·y ['faɪrɪ] *adj* fogoso, ardiente
fif·teen [fɪf'tiːn] quince
fif·teenth [fɪf'tiːnθ] *n & adj* decimoquinto
fifth [fɪfθ] *n & adj* quinto
fif·ti·eth ['fɪftɪɪθ] *n & adj* quincuagésimo
fif·ty ['fɪftɪ] cincuenta
fif·ty-'fif·ty *adv* a medias
fig [fɪg] higo *m*
fight [faɪt] **1** *n* lucha *f*, pelea *f*; (*argument*) pelea *f*; *fig*: *for survival, championship etc* lucha *f*; *in boxing* combate *m*; ***have a fight*** (*argue*) pelearse **2** *v/t* (*pret & pp* ***fought***) *enemy, person* luchar contra, pelear contra; *in boxing* pelear contra; *disease, injustice* luchar contra, combatir **3** *v/i* (*pret & pp* ***fought***) luchar, pelear; (*argue*) pelearse
◆ **fight for** *v/t one's rights, a cause* luchar por
fight·er ['faɪtər] combatiente *m/f*; *airplane* caza *m*; (*boxer*) púgil *m*; ***she's a fighter*** tiene espíritu combativo
fight·ing ['faɪtɪŋ] *n physical, verbal* peleas *fpl*; MIL luchas *fpl*, combates *mpl*
fig·u·ra·tive ['fɪgjərətɪv] *adj* figurado
fig·ure ['fɪgər] **1** *n* figura *f*; (*digit*) cifra *f* **2** *v/t* F (*think*) imaginarse, pensar
◆ **figure on** *v/t* F (*plan*) pensar
◆ **figure out** *v/t* (*understand*) entender; *calculation* resolver
'fig·ure skat·er patinador(a) *m*(*f*) artístico(-a)
'fig·ure skat·ing patinaje *m* artístico
file[1] [faɪl] **1** *n of documents* expediente *m*; COMPUT archivo *m*, fichero *m* **2** *v/t documents* archivar
◆ **file away** *v/t documents* archivar
file[2] [faɪl] *n for wood, fingernails* lima *f*
'file cab·i·net archivador *m*
'file man·ag·er COMPUT administrador *m* de archivos
fi·li·al ['fɪlɪəl] *adj* filial
fill [fɪl] **1** *v/t* llenar; *tooth* empastar, *L.Am.* emplomar **2** *n*: ***eat one's fill*** hincharse
◆ **fill in** *v/t form, hole* rellenar; ***fill s.o. in*** poner a alguien al tanto
◆ **fill in for** *v/t* sustituir a
◆ **fill out 1** *v/t form* rellenar **2** *v/i* (*get fatter*) engordar
◆ **fill up 1** *v/t* llenar (hasta arriba) **2** *v/i of stadium, theater* llenarse
fil·let ['fɪlɪt] *n* filete *m*
fill·ing ['fɪlɪŋ] **1** *n in sandwich* relleno *m*; *in tooth* empaste *m*, *L.Am.* emplomadura *f* **2** *adj*: ***be filling*** *of food* llenar mucho
'fill·ing sta·tion estación *f* de servicio, gasolinera *f*
film [fɪlm] **1** *n for camera* carrete *m*; (*movie*) película *f* **2** *v/t person, event* filmar
'film-mak·er cineasta *m/f*
'film star estrella *f* de cine
fil·ter ['fɪltər] **1** *n* filtro *m* **2** *v/t coffee, liquid* filtrar
◆ **filter through** *v/i of news reports* filtrarse
'fil·ter pa·per papel *m* de filtro
'fil·ter tip (*cigarette*) cigarrillo *m* con filtro
filth [fɪlθ] suciedad *f*, mugre *f*
filth·y ['fɪlθɪ] *adj* sucio, mugriento; *language etc* obsceno
fin [fɪn] *of fish* aleta *f*
fi·nal ['faɪnl] **1** *adj* (*last*) último; *decision* final, definitivo **2** *n* SP final *f*
fi·na·le [fɪ'nælɪ] final *m*
fi·nal·ist ['faɪnəlɪst] finalista *m/f*
fi·nal·ize ['faɪnəlaɪz] *v/t plans, design* ultimar
fi·nal·ly ['faɪnəlɪ] *adv* finalmente, por último; (*at last*) finalmente, por fin
fi·nance ['faɪnæns] **1** *n* finanzas *fpl* **2** *v/t* financiar
fi·nan·ces ['faɪnænsɪz] *npl* finanzas *fpl*
fi·nan·cial [faɪ'nænʃl] *adj* financiero
fi·nan·cial·ly [faɪ'nænʃəlɪ] *adv* económicamente
fi·nan·cial 'year *Br* ejercicio *m* económico
fi·nan·cier [faɪ'nænsɪr] financiero(-a) *m*(*f*)
find [faɪnd] *v/t* (*pret & pp* ***found***) encon-

trar, hallar; ***if you find it too hot / cold*** si te parece demasiado frío / caliente; ***find s.o. innocent / guilty*** LAW declarar a alguien inocente / culpable; ***I find it strange that …*** me sorprende que …; ***how did you find the hotel?*** ¿qué te pareció el hotel?

◆ **find out 1** *v/t* descubrir, averiguar **2** *v/i* (*discover*) descubrir; ***can you try to find out?*** ¿podrías enterarte?

find·ings ['faɪndɪŋz] *npl of report* conclusiones *fpl*

fine[1] [faɪn] *adj day, weather* bueno; *wine, performance, city* excelente; *distinction, line* fino; ***how's that? - that's fine*** ¿qué tal está? - bien; ***that's fine by me*** por mí no hay ningún problema; ***how are you? - fine*** ¿cómo estás? - bien

fine[2] [faɪn] **1** *n* multa *f* **2** *v/t* multar, poner una multa a

fine-'tooth comb: ***go through sth with a fine-tooth comb*** revisar algo minuciosamente

fine-'tune *v/t engine, fig* afinar, hacer los últimos ajustes a

fin·ger ['fɪŋgər] **1** *n* dedo *m* **2** *v/t* tocar

'fin·ger·nail *n* uña *f*

'fin·ger·print 1 *n* huella *f* digital *or* dactilar **2** *v/t* tomar las huellas digitales *or* dactilares a

'fin·ger·tip *n* punta *f* del dedo; ***have sth at one's fingertips*** saberse algo al dedillo

fin·i·cky ['fɪnɪkɪ] *adj person* quisquilloso; *design* enrevesado

fin·ish ['fɪnɪʃ] **1** *v/t* acabar, terminar; ***finish doing sth*** acabar *or* terminar de hacer algo **2** *v/i* acabar, terminar **3** *n of product* acabado *m*; *of race* final *f*

◆ **finish off** *v/t* acabar, terminar

◆ **finish up** *v/t food* acabar, terminar; ***he finished up liking it*** acabó gustándole

◆ **finish with** *v/t boyfriend etc* cortar con

fin·ish·ing line ['fɪnɪʃɪŋ] línea *f* de meta

Fin·land ['fɪnlənd] Finlandia

Finn [fɪn] finlandés (-esa) *m(f)*

Finn·ish ['fɪnɪʃ] **1** *adj* finlandés **2** *n language* finés *m*

fir [fɜːr] abeto *m*

fire [faɪr] **1** *n* fuego *m*; *electric, gas* estufa *f*; (*blaze*) incendio *m*; (*bonfire, campfire etc*) hoguera *f*; ***be on fire*** estar ardiendo; ***catch fire*** prender; ***set sth on fire, set fire to sth*** prender fuego a algo **2** *v/i* (*shoot*) disparar (***on / at*** sobre/a) **3** *v/t* F (*dismiss*) despedir

'fire a·larm alarma *f* contra incendios

'fire·arm arma *f* de fuego

'fire·crack·er petardo *m*

'fire de·part·ment (cuerpo *m* de) bomberos *mpl*

'fire door puerta *f* contra incendios

'fire drill simulacro *m* de incendio; *Br* **'fire en·gine** coche *m* de bomberos

'fire es·cape salida *f* de incendios

'fire ex·tin·guish·er extintor *m*

'fire fight·er bombero (-a) *m(f)*

'fire·guard pantalla *f*, parachispas *m inv*; *Br* **'fire·man** bombero *m*

'fire·place chimenea *f*, hogar *m*

'fire sta·tion parque *m* de bomberos

'fire truck coche *m* de bomberos

'fire·wood leña *f*

'fire·works *npl* fuegos *mpl* artificiales

firm[1] [fɜːrm] *adj* firme; ***a firm deal*** un acuerdo en firme

firm[2] [fɜːrm] *n* COM empresa *f*

first [fɜːrst] **1** *adj* primero; ***who's first please?*** ¿quién es el primero, por favor? **2** *n* primero(-a) *m(f)* **3** *adv* primero; ***first of all*** (*for one reason*) en primer lugar; ***at first*** al principio

first 'aid primeros *mpl* auxilios

first-'aid box, first-'aid kit botiquín *m* de primeros auxilios

'first·born *adj* primogénito

'first class 1 *adj ticket, seat* de primera (clase); (*very good*) excelente **2** *adv travel* en primera (clase)

first 'floor planta *f* baja, *Br* primer piso *m*

first'hand *adj* de primera mano

First 'La·dy *of US* primera dama *f*

first·ly ['fɜːrstlɪ] *adv* en primer lugar

first 'name nombre *m* (de pila)

first 'night estreno *m*

first of'fend·er delincuente *m/f* sin antecedentes

first of'fense primer delito *m*

first-'rate *adj* excelente

fis·cal ['fɪskl] *adj* fiscal

fis·cal 'year año *m* fiscal

fish [fɪʃ] **1** *n* (*pl* **fish**) **1** *n* pez *m*; *to eat* pescado *m*; ***drink like a fish*** F beber como un cosaco F; ***feel like a fish out of water*** sentirse fuera de lugar **2** *v/i* pescar

'fish·bone espina *f* (de pescado)

fish·er·man ['fɪʃərmən] pescador *m*

fish·ing ['fɪʃɪŋ] pesca *f*

'fish·ing boat (barco *m*) pesquero *m*

'fish·ing line sedal *m*

'fish·ing rod caña *f* de pescar

'fish stick palito *m* de pescado

fish·y ['fɪʃɪ] *adj* F (*suspicious*) sospechoso

fist [fɪst] puño *m*

fit[1] [fɪt] *n* MED ataque *m*; ***a fit of rage / jealousy*** un arrebato de cólera / un ataque de celos

fit[2] [fɪt] *adj physically* en forma; *morally* adecuado; ***he's not fit to be President***

no está en condiciones ser Presidente; ***keep fit*** mantenerse en forma
fit³ [fɪt] **1** *v/t* (*attach*) colocar; ***these pants don't fit me any more*** estos pantalones ya no me entran; ***it fits you perfectly*** te queda perfectamente **2** *v/i* (*pret & pp* ***fitted***) *of clothes* quedar bien; *of piece of furniture etc* caber **3** *n*: ***it's a good fit*** *of jacket etc* queda bien; *of piece of furniture* cabe bien; ***it's a tight fit*** no hay mucho espacio
◆ **fit in 1** *v/i of person in group* encajar; ***it fits in with our plans*** encaja con nuestros planes **2** *v/t*: ***fit s.o. in*** *into schedule etc* hacer un hueco a alguien
fit·ful ['fɪtfəl] *adj sleep* intermitente
fit·ness ['fɪtnɪs] *physical* buena forma *f*
'fit·ness cen·ter, *Br* **'fit·ness cen·tre** gimnasio *m*
fit·ted 'kitch·en ['fɪtɪd] cocina *f* a medida
fit·ted 'sheet sábana *f* ajustable
fit·ter ['fɪtər] *n* técnico(-a) *m*(*f*)
fit·ting ['fɪtɪŋ] *adj* apropiado
fit·tings ['fɪtɪŋz] *npl* equipamiento *m*
five [faɪv] cinco
fix [fɪks] **1** *n* (*solution*) solución *f*; ***be in a fix*** F estar en un lío F **2** *v/t* (*attach*) fijar; (*repair*) arreglar, reparar; (*arrange: meeting etc*) organizar; *lunch* preparar; *dishonestly: match etc* amañar; ***fix sth onto sth*** fijar algo a algo; ***I'll fix you a drink*** te prepararé una bebida
◆ **fix up** *v/t meeting* organizar; ***it's all fixed up*** está todo organizado
fixed [fɪkst] *adj* fijo
fix·ings ['fɪkɪŋz] *npl* guarnición *f*
fix·ture ['fɪkstʃər] (*in room*) *parte fija del mobiliario o la decoración de una habitación*
◆ **fiz·zle out** ['fɪzl] *v/i* F quedarse en nada
fiz·zy ['fɪzɪ] *adj drink* con gas
flab [flæb] *on body* grasa *f*
flab·ber·gast ['flæbərgæst] *v/t* F: ***be flabbergasted*** quedarse estupefacto *or Span* alucinado F
flab·by ['flæbɪ] *adj muscles etc* fofo
flag¹ [flæg] *n* bandera *f*
flag² [flæg] *v/i* (*pret & pp* ***flagged***) (*tire*) desfallecer
'flag·pole asta *f* (de bandera)
fla·grant ['fleɪgrənt] *adj* flagrante
'flag·ship *fig* estandarte *m*
'flag·staff asta *f* (de bandera)
'flag·stone losa *f*
flair [fler] *n* (*talent*) don *m*; ***have a natural flair for*** tener dotes para
flake [fleɪk] *n of snow* copo *m*; *of skin* escama *f*; *of plaster* desconchón *m*
◆ **flake off** *v/i of skin* descamarse; *of plaster*, *paint* desconcharse
flak·y ['fleɪkɪ] *adj skin* con escamas; *paint* desconchado
flak·y 'pas·try hojaldre *m*
flam·boy·ant [flæm'bɔɪənt] *adj personality* extravagante
flam·boy·ant·ly [flæm'bɔɪəntlɪ] *adv dressed* extravagantemente
flame [fleɪm] *n* llama *f*; ***go up in flames*** ser pasto de las llamas
fla·men·co [flə'meŋkoʊ] flamenco *m*
fla'men·co danc·er bailaor(a) *m*(*f*)
flam·ma·ble ['flæməbl] *adj* inflamable
flan [flæn] tarta *f*
flank [flæŋk] **1** *n of horse etc* costado *m*; MIL flanco *m* **2** *v/t* flanquear; ***be flanked by*** estar flanqueado por
flap [flæp] **1** *n of envelope*, *pocket* solapa *f*; *of table* hoja *f*; ***be in a flap*** F estar histérico F **2** *v/t* (*pret & pp* ***flapped***) *wings* batir **3** *v/i* (*pret & pp* ***flapped***) *of flag etc* ondear
flare [fler] **1** *n* (*distress signal*) bengala *f*; *in dress* vuelo *m* **2** *v/t*: ***flare one's nostrils*** hinchar las narices resoplando
◆ **flare up** *v/i of violence* estallar; *of illness*, *rash* exacerbarse, empeorar; *of fire* llamear; (*get very angry*) estallar
flash [flæʃ] **1** *n of light* destello *m*; PHOT flash *m*; ***in a flash*** F en un abrir y cerrar de ojos; ***have a flash of inspiration*** tener una inspiración repentina; ***a flash of lightning*** un relámpago **2** *v/i of light* destellar **3** *v/t* ***flash one's headlights*** echar las luces
'flash·back *in movie* flash-back *m*, escena *f* retrospectiva
flash·er ['flæʃər] MOT intermitente *m*
'flash·light linterna *f*; PHOT flash *m*
flash·y ['flæʃɪ] *adj pej* ostentoso, chillón
flask [flæsk] (*hip flask*) petaca *f*
flat¹ [flæt] **1** *adj surface*, *land* llano, plano; *beer* sin gas; *battery* descargado; *tire* desinflado; *shoes* bajo; MUS bemol; ***and that's flat*** F y sanseacabó F **2** *adv* MUS demasiado bajo; ***flat out*** *work*, *run*, *drive* a tope; ***the factory is producing flat out*** la fábrica está al máximo de su capacidad productiva **3** *n Br* (*flat tire*) pinchazo *m*
flat² [flæt] *n Br* apartamento *m*, *Span* piso *m*
flat-chest·ed [flæt'tʃestɪd] *adj* plana de pecho
flat·ly ['flætlɪ] *adv refuse*, *deny* rotundamente
'flat rate tarifa *f* única
flat·ten ['flætn] *v/t land*, *road* allanar, aplanar; *by bombing*, *demolition* arrasar
flat·ter ['flætər] *v/t* halagar, adular

flat·ter·er ['flætərər] adulador(a) *m(f)*
flat·ter·ing ['flætərɪŋ] *adj comments* halagador; *color, clothes* favorecedor
flat·ter·y ['flætərɪ] halagos *mpl*, adulación *f*
flat·u·lence ['flætjʊləns] flatulencia *f*
'**flat·ware** (*cutlery*) cubertería *f*
flaunt [flɒːnt] *v/t* hacer ostentación de, alardear de
flau·tist ['flɒːtɪst] flautista *m/f*
fla·vor ['fleɪvər] **1** *n* sabor *m* **2** *v/t food* condimentar
fla·vor·ing ['fleɪvərɪŋ] *n* aromatizante *m*
fla·vour *etc Br* → ***flavor*** *etc*
flaw [flɒː] *n* defecto *m*, fallo *m*
flaw·less ['flɒːlɪs] *adj* impecable
flea [fliː] *n* pulga *f*
fleck [flek] mota *f*
fled [fled] *pret & pp* → ***flee***
flee [fliː] *v/i* (*pret & pp* ***fled***) escapar, huir
fleece [fliːs] *v/t* F desplumar F
fleet [fliːt] *n* NAUT, *of vehicles* flota *f*
fleet·ing ['fliːtɪŋ] *adj visit etc* fugaz; ***catch a fleeting glimpse of*** vislumbrar fugazmente a
flesh [fleʃ] *n* carne *f*; *of fruit* pulpa *f*; ***meet / see s.o. in the flesh*** conocer / ver a alguien en persona
flex [fleks] *v/t muscles* flexionar
flex·i·bil·i·ty [fleksə'bɪlətɪ] flexibilidad *f*
flex·i·ble ['fleksəbl] *adj* flexible; ***I'm quite flexible*** *about arrangements, timing* soy bastante flexible
'**flex·time** ['flekstaɪm] horario *m* flexible
flew [fluː] *pret* → ***fly***[3]
flick [flɪk] *v/t tail* sacudir; ***he flicked a fly off his hand*** espantó una mosca que tenía en la mano; ***she flicked her hair out of her eyes*** se apartó el pelo de los ojos
◆ **flick through** *v/t book, magazine* hojear
flick·er ['flɪkər] *v/i of light, screen* parpadear
fli·er [flaɪr] (*circular*) folleto *m*
flies [flaɪz] *npl Br on pants* bragueta *f*
flight [flaɪt] *n in airplane* vuelo *m*; (*fleeing*) huida *f*; ***not capable of flight*** incapaz de volar; ***flight (of stairs)*** tramo *m* (de escaleras)
'**flight at·tend·ant** auxiliar *m/f* de vuelo
'**flight crew** tripulación *f*
'**flight deck** AVIA cabina *f* del piloto
'**flight num·ber** número *m* de vuelo
'**flight path** ruta *f* de vuelo
'**flight re·cord·er** caja *f* negra
'**flight time** *departure* hora *f* del vuelo; *duration* duración *f* del vuelo
flight·y ['flaɪtɪ] *adj* inconstante
flim·sy ['flɪmzɪ] *adj structure, furniture* endeble; *dress, material* débil; *excuse* pobre
flinch [flɪntʃ] *v/i* encogerse
fling [flɪŋ] **1** *v/t* (*pret & pp* ***flung***) arrojar, lanzar; ***fling o.s. into a chair*** dejarse caer en una silla **2** *n* F (*affair*) aventura *f*
◆ **flip over** [flɪp] *v/i* volcar
◆ **flip through** *v/t* (*pret & pp* ***flipped***) *magazine* hojear
flip·per ['flɪpər] *for swimming* aleta *f*
flirt [flɜːrt] **1** *v/i* flirtear, coquetear **2** *n* ligón (-ona) *m(f)*
flir·ta·tious [flɜːr'teɪʃəs] *adj* coqueto
float [floʊt] *v/i also* FIN flotar
float·ing vot·er ['floʊtɪŋ] votante *m/f* indeciso(-a)
flock [flɑːk] **1** *n of sheep* rebaño *m* **2** *v/i* acudir en masa
flog [flɑːg] *v/t* (*pret & pp* ***flogged***) (*whip*) azotar
flood [flʌd] **1** *n* inundación *f* **2** *v/t of river* inundar
◆ **flood in** *v/i* llegar en grandes cantidades
flood·ing ['flʌdɪŋ] inundaciones *fpl*
'**flood·light** *n* foco *m*
flood·lit ['flʌdlɪt] *adj match* con luz artificial
'**flood wa·ters** *npl* crecida *f*
floor [flɔːr] *n* suelo *m*; (*story*) piso *m*
'**floor·board** *n* tabla *f* del suelo
'**floor cloth** trapo *m* del suelo
'**floor lamp** lámpara *f* de pie
flop [flɑːp] **1** *v/i* (*pret & pp* ***flopped***) dejarse caer; F (*fail*) pinchar F **2** *n* F (*failure*) pinchazo *m* F
flop·py ['flɑːpɪ] *adj ears* caído; *hat* blando; (*weak*) flojo
flop·py ('disk) disquete *m*
flor·ist ['flɔːrɪst] florista *m/f*
floss [flɑːs] **1** *n for teeth* hilo *m* dental **2** *v/t*: ***floss one's teeth*** limpiarse los dientes con hilo dental
flour [flaʊr] harina *f*
flour·ish ['flʌrɪʃ] *v/i of plant* crecer rápidamente; *of business, civilization* florecer, prosperar
flour·ish·ing ['flʌrɪʃɪŋ] *adj business, trade* floreciente, próspero
flow [floʊ] **1** *v/i* fluir **2** *n* flujo *m*
'**flow·chart** diagrama *m* de flujo
flow·er [flaʊr] **1** *n* flor *f* **2** *v/i* florecer
'**flow·er·bed** parterre *m*
'**flow·er·pot** tiesto *m*, maceta *f*
'**flow·er show** exposición *f* floral
flow·er·y ['flaʊrɪ] *adj pattern* floreado; *style of writing* florido
flown [floʊn] *pp* → ***fly***[3]
flu [fluː] gripe *f*

F

fluc·tu·ate ['flʌktjʊeɪt] *v/i* fluctuar
fluc·tu·a·tion [flʌktjʊ'eɪʃn] fluctuación *f*
flu·en·cy ['flu:ənsɪ] *in a language* fluidez *f*
flu·ent ['flu:ənt] *adj*: ***he speaks fluent Spanish*** habla español con soltura
flu·ent·ly ['flu:əntlɪ] *adv speak, write* con soltura
fluff [flʌf] *material* pelusa *f*
fluff·y ['flʌfɪ] *adj* esponjoso; ***fluffy toy*** juguete *m* de peluche
fluid ['flu:ɪd] *n* fluido *m*
flung [flʌŋ] *pret & pp* → ***fling***
flunk [flʌŋk] *v/t* F *subject* suspender, *Span* catear F
flu·o·res·cent [flʊ'resnt] *adj light* fluorescente
flur·ry ['flʌrɪ] *of snow* torbellino *m*
flush [flʌʃ] **1** *v/t*: ***flush the toilet*** tirar de la cadena; ***flush sth down the toilet*** tirar algo por el retrete **2** *v/i* (*go red in the face*) ruborizarse; ***the toilet won't flush*** la cisterna no funciona **3** *adj* (*level*): ***be flush with …*** estar a la misma altura que …
◆ **flush away** *v/t*: ***flush sth away*** *down toilet* tirar algo por el retrete
◆ **flush out** *v/t rebels etc* hacer salir
flus·ter ['flʌstər] *v/t*: ***get flustered*** ponerse nervioso
flute [flu:t] MUS flauta *f*; *glass* copa *f* de champán
flut·ist ['flu:tɪst] flautista *m/f*
flut·ter ['flʌtər] *v/i of bird, wings* aletear; *of flag* ondear; *of heart* latir con fuerza
fly[1] [flaɪ] *n insect* mosca *f*
fly[2] [flaɪ] *n on pants* bragueta *f*
fly[3] [flaɪ] **1** *v/i* (*pret* ***flew***, *pp* ***flown***) *of bird, airplane* volar; *in airplane* volar, ir en avión; *of flag* ondear; ***fly into a rage*** enfurecerse; ***she flew out of the room*** salió a toda prisa de la habitación **2** *v/t* (*pret* ***flew***, *pp* ***flown***) *airplane* pilotar; *airline* volar con; (*transport by air*) enviar por avión
◆ **fly away** *v/i of bird* salir volando; *of airplane* alejarse
◆ **fly back** *v/i* (*travel back*) volver en avión
◆ **fly in 1** *v/i of airplane, passengers* llegar en avión **2** *v/t supplies etc* transportar en avión
◆ **fly off** *v/i of hat etc* salir volando
◆ **fly out** *v/i* irse (*en avión*); ***when do you fly out?*** ¿cuándo os vais?
◆ **fly past** *v/i in formation* pasar volando en formación; *of time* volar
fly·ing ['flaɪɪŋ] *n* volar *m*
fly·ing 'sau·cer platillo *m* volante
foam [foʊm] *n on liquid* espuma *f*
foam 'rub·ber gomaespuma *f*
FOB [efoʊ'bi:] *abbr* (= ***free on board***) franco a bordo
fo·cus ['foʊkəs] **1** *n of attention*, PHOT foco *m*; ***be in focus / out of focus*** PHOT estar enfocado / desenfocado **2** *v/t*: ***focus one's attention on*** concentrar la atención en **3** *v/i* enfocar
◆ **focus on** *v/t problem, issue* concentrarse en; PHOT enfocar
fod·der ['fɑ:dər] forraje *m*
fog [fɑ:g] niebla *f*
◆ **fog up** *v/i* (*pret & pp* ***fogged***) empañarse
'fog·bound *adj* paralizado por la niebla
fog·gy ['fɑ:gɪ] *adj* neblinoso, con niebla; ***it's foggy*** hay niebla; ***I haven't the foggiest idea*** no tengo la más remota idea
foi·ble ['fɔɪbl] manía *f*
foil[1] [fɔɪl] *n* papel *m* de aluminio
foil[2] [fɔɪl] *v/t* (*thwart*) frustrar
fold[1] [foʊld] **1** *v/t paper etc* doblar; ***fold one's arms*** cruzarse de brazos **2** *v/i of business* quebrar **3** *n in cloth etc* pliegue *m*
◆ **fold up 1** *v/t* plegar **2** *v/i of chair, table* plegarse
fold[2] [foʊld] *n for sheep etc* redil *m*
fold·er ['foʊldər] *for documents*, COMPUT carpeta *f*
fold·ing ['foʊldɪŋ] *adj* plegable; ***folding chair*** silla *f* plegable
fo·li·age ['foʊlɪɪdʒ] follaje *m*
folk [foʊk] (*people*) gente *f*; ***my folks*** (*family*) mi familia; ***evening folks*** F buenas noches, gente F
'folk dance baile *m* popular
'folk mu·sic música *f* folk *or* popular
'folk sing·er cantante *m/f* de folk
'folk song canción *m/f* folk *or* popular
fol·low ['fɑ:loʊ] **1** *v/t* seguir; (*understand*) entender; ***follow me*** sígueme **2** *v/i logically* deducirse; ***it follows from this that …*** de esto se deduce que …; ***you go first and I'll follow*** tú ve primero que yo te sigo; ***the requirements are as follows*** los requisitos son los siguientes
◆ **follow up** *v/t letter, inquiry* hacer el seguimiento de
fol·low·er ['fɑ:loʊər] seguidor(a) *m(f)*
fol·low·ing ['fɑ:loʊɪŋ] **1** *adj* siguiente **2** *n people* seguidores(-as) *mpl* (*fpl*); ***the following*** lo siguiente
'fol·low-up meet·ing reunión *m* de seguimiento
'fol·low-up vis·it *to doctor etc* visita *f* de seguimiento
fol·ly ['fɑ:lɪ] (*madness*) locura *f*
fond [fɑ:nd] *adj* (*loving*) cariñoso; *memory* entrañable; ***he's fond of travel /***

music le gusta viajar / la música; ***I'm very fond of him*** le tengo mucho cariño
fon·dle ['fɑːndl] *v/t* acariciar
fond·ness ['fɑːndnɪs] *for s.o.* cariño *m* (***for*** por); *for wine, food* afición *f* (***for*** por)
font [fɑːnt] *for printing* tipo *m*; *in church* pila *f* bautismal
food [fuːd] comida *f*
'**food chain** cadena *f* alimentaria
food·ie ['fuːdɪ] F gourmet *m/f*
'**food mix·er** robot *m* de cocina
food poi·son·ing ['fuːdpɔɪznɪŋ] intoxicación *f* alimentaria
fool [fuːl] **1** *n* tonto(-a) *m(f)*, idiota *m/f*; ***you stupid fool!*** ¡estúpido!; ***make a fool of o.s.*** ponerse en ridículo **2** *v/t* engañar
◆ **fool about**, **fool around** *v/i* hacer el tonto; *sexually* tener un lío
◆ **fool around with** *v/t knife, drill etc* enredar con algo; *sexually* tener un lío con
'**fool·har·dy** *adj* temerario
fool·ish ['fuːlɪʃ] *adj* tonto
fool·ish·ly ['fuːlɪʃlɪ] *adv*: ***I foolishly ...*** cometí la tontería de ...
'**fool·proof** *adj* infalible
foot [fʊt] (*pl* ***feet*** [fiːt]) *also measurement* pie *m*; *of animal* pata *f*; ***on foot*** a pie, caminando, andando; ***I've been on my feet all day*** llevo todo el día de pie; ***be back on one's feet*** estar recuperado; ***at the foot of the page / hill*** al pie de la página / de la colina; ***put one's foot in it*** F meter la pata F
foot·age ['fʊtɪdʒ] secuencias *fpl*, imágenes *fpl*
'**foot·ball** *Br* (*soccer*) fútbol *m*; *American style* fútbol *m* americano; *ball* balón *m or* pelota *f* (de fútbol)
'**foot·ball play·er** *American style* jugador(a) *m(f)* de fútbol americano; *Br in soccer* jugador(a) *m(f)* de fútbol, futbolista *m/f*
'**foot·bridge** puente *m* peatonal
foot·er ['fʊtər] *in document* pie *m* de página
foot·hills ['fʊthɪlz] *npl* estribaciones *fpl*
'**foot·hold** *n in climbing* punto *m* de apoyo; ***gain a foothold*** *fig* introducirse
foot·ing ['fʊtɪŋ] (*basis*): ***put the business back on a secure footing***volver a afianzar la empresa; ***lose one's footing*** perder el equilibrio; ***be on the same/a different footing*** estar / no estar en igualdad de condiciones; ***be on a friendly footing with ...*** tener relaciones de amistad con ...
foot·lights ['fʊtlaɪts] *npl* candilejas *fpl*
'**foot·mark** pisada *f*
'**foot·note** nota *f* a pie de página
'**foot·path** sendero *m*
'**foot·print** pisada *f*
'**foot·step** paso *m*; ***follow in s.o.'s footsteps*** seguir los pasos de alguien
'**foot·stool** escabel *m*
'**foot·wear** calzado *m*
for [fər, fɔːr] *prep* ◇ *purpose, destination etc* para; ***a train for ...*** un tren para *or* hacia ...; ***clothes for children*** ropa para niños; ***it's too big / small for you*** te queda demasiado grande / pequeño; ***here's a letter for you*** hay una carta para ti; ***this is for you*** esto es para ti; ***what's for lunch?*** ¿qué hay para comer?; ***the steak is for me*** el filete es para mí; ***what is this for?*** ¿para qué sirve esto?; ***what for?*** ¿para qué?
◇ *time* durante; ***for three days / two hours*** durante tres días / dos horas; ***it lasts for two hours*** dura dos horas; ***please get it done for Monday*** por favor tenlo listo (para) el lunes
◇ *distance*: ***I walked for a mile*** caminé una milla; ***it stretches for 100 miles*** se extiende 100 millas
◇ (*in favor of*): ***I am for the idea*** estoy a favor de la idea
◇ (*instead of, in behalf of*): ***let me do that for you*** déjame que te lo haga; ***we are agents for ...*** somos representantes de ...
◇ (*in exchange for*) por; ***I bought it for $25*** lo compré por 25 dólares: ***how much did you sell it for?*** ¿por cuánto lo vendiste?
for·bade [fər'bæd] *pret* → ***forbid***
for·bid [fər'bɪd] *v/t* (*pret* ***forbade***, *pp* ***forbidden***) prohibir; ***forbid s.o. to do sth*** prohibir a alguien hacer algo
for·bid·den [fər'bɪdn] **1** *adj* prohibido; ***smoking / parking forbidden*** prohibido fumar / aparcar **2** *pp* → ***forbid***
for·bid·ding [fər'bɪdɪŋ] *adj person, tone, look* amenazador; *rockface* imponente; *prospect* intimidador
force [fɔːrs] **1** *n* fuerza *f*; ***come into force*** *of law etc* entrar en vigor; ***the forces*** MIL las fuerzas **2** *v/t door, lock* forzar; ***force s.o. to do sth*** forzar a alguien a hacer algo; ***force sth open*** forzar algo
◆ **force back** *v/t tears* contener
forced [fɔːrst] *adj* forzado
forced 'land·ing aterrizaje *m* forzoso
force·ful ['fɔːrsfəl] *adj argument* poderoso; *speaker* vigoroso; *character* enérgico
force·ful·ly ['fɔːrsfəlɪ] *adv* de manera convincente
for·ceps ['fɔːrseps] *npl* MED fórceps *m inv*

for·ci·ble ['fɔːrsəbl] *adj entry* por la fuerza
for·ci·bly ['fɔːrsəblɪ] *adv* por la fuerza
ford [fɔːrd] *n* vado *m*
fore [fɔːr] *n*: ***come to the fore*** salir a la palestra
'**fore·arm** antebrazo *m*
fore·bears ['fɔːrberz] *npl* antepasados *mpl*
fore·bod·ing [fər'boudɪŋ] premonición *f*
'**fore·cast 1** *n* pronóstico *m*; *of weather* pronóstico *m* (del tiempo) **2** *v/t* (*pret & pp* ***forecast***) pronosticar
'**fore·court** (*of garage*) *explanada en la parte de delante*
fore·fa·thers ['fɔːrfɑːðərz] *npl* ancestros *mpl*
'**fore·fin·ger** (dedo *m*) índice *m*
'**fore·front**: ***be in the forefront of*** estar a la vanguardia de
'**fore·gone** *adj*: ***that's a foregone conclusion*** eso ya se sabe de antemano
'**fore·ground** primer plano *m*
'**fore·hand** *in tennis* derecha *f*
'**fore·head** frente *f*
for·eign ['fɑːrən] *adj* extranjero; ***a foreign holiday*** unas vacaciones en el extranjero
for·eign af'fairs *npl* asuntos *mpl* exteriores
for·eign 'aid ayuda *f* al exterior
for·eign 'bod·y cuerpo *m* extraño
for·eign 'cur·ren·cy divisa *f* extranjera
for·eign·er ['fɑːrənər] extranjero(-a) *m(f)*
for·eign ex'change divisas *fpl*
for·eign 'lan·guage idioma *m* extranjero
'**For·eign Of·fice** *in UK* Ministerio *m* de Asuntos Exteriores
for·eign 'pol·i·cy política *f* exterior
For·eign 'Sec·re·ta·ry *in UK* Ministro(-a) *m(f)* de Asuntos Exteriores
'**fore·man** capataz *m*
'**fore·most** *adv* principal; ***what was foremost in my mind was the worry that …*** mi principal preocupación era que …
fo·ren·sic 'medi·cine [fə'rensɪk] medicina *f* forense
fo·ren·sic 'scien·tist forense *m/f*
'**fore·run·ner** predecesor(a) *m(f)*
fore'see *v/t* (*pret* ***foresaw***, *pp* ***foreseen***) prever
fore·see·a·ble [fər'siːəbl] *adj* previsible; ***in the foreseeable future*** en un futuro próximo
fore'seen *pp* → ***foresee***
'**fore·sight** previsión *f*
for·est ['fɑːrɪst] bosque *m*
for·est·ry ['fɑːrɪstrɪ] silvicultura
'**fore·taste** anticipo *m*
fore'tell *v/t* (*pret & pp* ***foretold***) predecir
for·ev·er [fə'revər] *adv* siempre; ***it is forever raining here*** aquí llueve constantemente; ***I will remember this day forever*** no me olvidaré nunca de ese día
fore·word ['fɔːrwɜːrd] prólogo *m*
for·feit ['fɔːrfət] *v/t* (*lose*) perder; (*give up*) renunciar a
for·gave [fər'geɪv] *pret* → ***forgive***
forge [fɔːrdʒ] *v/t* falsificar
◆ **forge ahead** *v/i* progresar rápidamente
forg·er ['fɔːrdʒər] falsificador(a) *m(f)*
forg·er·y ['fɔːrdʒərɪ] falsificación *f*
for·get [fər'get] *v/t* (*pret* ***forgot***, *pp* ***forgotten***) olvidar; ***I forgot his name*** se me olvidó su nombre; ***forget to do sth*** olvidarse de hacer algo
for·get·ful [fər'getfəl] *adj* olvidadizo
for'get-me-not *flower* nomeolvides *m inv*
for·give [fər'gɪv] *v/t & v/i* (*pret* ***forgave***, *pp* ***forgiven***) perdonar
for·gi·ven [fər'gɪvn] *pp* → ***forgive***
for·give·ness [fər'gɪvnɪs] perdón *m*
for·got [fər'gɑːt] *pret* → ***forget***
for·got·ten [fər'gɑːtn] *pp* → ***forget***
fork [fɔːrk] *n for eating* tenedor *m*; *for garden* horca *f*; *in road* bifurcación *f*
◆ **fork out** *v/t & v/i* F (*pay*) apoquinar F
forked *adj tongue* bífido; *stick* bifurcado
fork·lift 'truck carretilla *f* elevadora
form [fɔːrm] **1** *n shape* forma *f*; (*document*) formulario *m*, impreso *m*; ***be on / off form*** estar / no estar en forma **2** *v/t in clay etc* moldear; *friendship* establecer; *opinion* formarse; *past tense etc* formar; (*constitute*) formar, constituir **3** *v/i* (*take shape, develop*) formarse
form·al ['fɔːrml] *adj* formal; *recognition etc* oficial; *dress* de etiqueta
for·mal·i·ty [fər'mælətɪ] formalidad *f*; ***it's just a formality*** sólo es una formalidad; ***the formalities*** las formalidades
for·mal·ly ['fɔːrməlɪ] *adv speak, behave* formalmente; *accepted, recognized* oficialmente
for·mat ['fɔːrmæt] **1** *v/t* (*pret & pp* ***formatted***) *diskette, document* formatear **2** *n of paper, program etc* formato *m*
for·ma·tion [fɔːr'meɪʃn] formación *f*; ***formation flying*** vuelo *m* en formación
for·ma·tive ['fɔːrmətɪv] *adj* formativo; ***in his formative years*** en sus años de formación
for·mer ['fɔːrmər] *adj* antiguo; ***the former*** el primero; ***the former arrangement*** la situación de antes
for·mer·ly ['fɔːrmərlɪ] *adv* antiguamente
for·mi·da·ble ['fɔːrmɪdəbl] *adj persona-*

lity formidable; *opponent*, *task* terrible
for·mu·la ['fɔːrmjʊlə] MATH, CHEM, *fig* fórmula *f*
for·mu·late ['fɔːrmjʊleɪt] *v/t* (*express*) formular
for·ni·cate ['fɔːrnɪkeɪt] *v/i fml* fornicar
for·ni·ca·tion [fɔːrnɪ'keɪʃn] *fml* fornicación *f*
fort [fɔːrt] MIL fuerte *m*
forth [fɔːrθ] *adv*: ***back and forth*** de un lado para otro; ***and so forth*** y así sucesivamente; ***from that day forth*** desde ese día en adelante
forth·com·ing ['fɔːrθkʌmɪŋ] *adj* (*future*) próximo; *personality* comunicativo
'forth·right *adj* directo
for·ti·eth ['fɔːrtɪɪθ] *n & adj* cuadragésimo
fort·night ['fɔːrtnaɪt] *Br* quincena *f*
for·tress ['fɔːrtrɪs] MIL fortaleza *f*
for·tu·nate ['fɔːrʧnət] *adj* afortunado
for·tu·nate·ly ['fɔːrʧnətlɪ] *adv* afortunadamente
for·tune ['fɔːrʧən] (*fate*, *money*) fortuna *f*; (*luck*) fortuna *f*, suerte *f*; ***tell s.o.'s fortune*** decir a alguien la buenaventura
'for·tune-tell·er adivino(-a) *m*(*f*)
for·ty ['fɔːrtɪ] cuarenta; ***have forty winks*** F echarse una siestecilla F
fo·rum ['fɔːrəm] *fig* foro *m*
for·ward ['fɔːrwərd] **1** *adv* hacia delante **2** *adj pej*: *person* atrevido **3** *n* SP delantero(-a) *m*(*f*) **4** *v/t letter* reexpedir
'for·ward·ing ad·dress ['fɔːrwərdɪŋ] *dirección a la que reexpedir correspondencia*
'for·ward·ing a·gent COM transitario(-a) *m*(*f*)
'for·ward-look·ing *adj* con visión de futuro, moderno
fos·sil ['fɑːsəl] fósil *m*
fos·sil·ized ['fɑːsəlaɪzd] *adj* fosilizado
fos·ter ['fɑːstər] *v/t child* acoger, adoptar (temporalmente); *attitude*, *belief* fomentar
'fos·ter child niño(-a) *m*(*f*) en régimen de acogida
'fos·ter home hogar *m* de acogida
'fos·ter par·ents *npl* familia *f* de acogida
fought [fɒːt] *pret & pp* → ***fight***
foul [faʊl] **1** *n* SP falta *f* **2** *adj smell*, *taste* asqueroso; *weather* terrible **3** *v/t* SP hacer (una) falta a
found[1] [faʊnd] *v/t school etc* fundar
found[2] [faʊnd] *pret & pp* → ***find***
foun·da·tion [faʊn'deɪʃn] *of theory etc* fundamento *m*; (*organization*) fundación *f*
foun·da·tions [faʊn'deɪʃnz] *npl of building* cimientos *mpl*
found·er ['faʊndər] *n* fundador(a) *m*(*f*)
found·ing ['faʊndɪŋ] *n* fundación *f*
foun·dry ['faʊndrɪ] fundición *f*
foun·tain ['faʊntɪn] fuente *f*
'foun·tain pen pluma *f* (estilográfica)
four [fɔːr] cuatro; ***on all fours*** a gatas, a cuatro patas
four-let·ter 'word palabrota *f*
four-post·er ('bed) cama *f* de dosel
'four-star *adj hotel etc* de cuatro estrellas
four·teen [fɔːr'tiːn] catorce
four·teenth [fɔːr'tiːnθ] *n & adj* decimocuarto
fourth [fɔːrθ] *n & adj* cuarto
four-wheel 'drive MOT vehículo *m* con tracción a las cuatro ruedas; *type of drive* tracción *f* a las cuatro ruedas
fowl [faʊl] ave *f* de corral
fox [fɑːks] **1** *n* zorro *m* **2** *v/t* (*puzzle*) dejar perplejo
foy·er ['fɔɪər] vestíbulo *m*
frac·tion ['frækʃn] fracción *f*; MATH fracción *f*, quebrado *m*
frac·tion·al·ly ['frækʃnəlɪ] *adv* ligeramente
frac·ture ['frækʧər] **1** *n* fractura *f* **2** *v/t* fracturar; ***he fractured his arm*** se fracturó el brazo
fra·gile ['frædʒəl] *adj* frágil
frag·ment ['frægmənt] *n* fragmento *m*
frag·men·tar·y [fræg'məntərɪ] *adj* fragmentario
fra·grance ['freɪgrəns] fragancia *f*
fra·grant ['freɪgrənt] *adj* fragante
frail [freɪl] *adj* frágil, delicado
frame [freɪm] **1** *n of picture*, *window* marco *m*; *of eyeglasses* montura *f*; *of bicycle* cuadro *m*; ***frame of mind*** estado *m* de ánimo **2** *v/t picture* enmarcar; F *person* tender una trampa a
'frame-up F trampa *f*
'frame·work estructura *f*; *for agreement* marco *m*
France [fræns] Francia
fran·chise ['frænʧaɪz] *n for business* franquicia *f*
frank [fræŋk] *adj* franco
frank·furt·er ['fræŋkfɜːrtər] salchicha *f* de Fráncfort
frank·ly ['fræŋklɪ] *adv* francamente; ***frankly, it's not worth it*** francamente *or* la verdad, no vale la pena
frank·ness ['fræŋknɪs] franqueza *f*
fran·tic ['fræntɪk] *adj* frenético
fran·ti·cal·ly ['fræntɪklɪ] *adv* frenéticamente
fra·ter·nal [frə'tɜːrnl] *adj* fraternal
fraud [frɒːd] fraude *m*; *person* impostor(a) *m*(*f*)

fraud·u·lent ['frɒːdjʊlənt] *adj* fraudulento
fraud·u·lent·ly ['frɒːdjʊləntlɪ] *adv* fraudulentamente
frayed [freɪd] *adj cuffs* deshilachado
freak [friːk] **1** *n unusual event* fenómeno *m* anormal; *two-headed person, animal etc* monstruo *m*, monstruosidad *f*; F *strange person* bicho *m* raro F; ***movie / jazz freak*** F un fanático del cine / jazz F **2** *adj wind, storm etc* anormal

F

freck·le ['frekl] peca *f*
free [friː] **1** *adj* libre; *no cost* gratis, gratuito; ***are you free this afternoon?*** ¿estás libre esta tarde?; ***free and easy*** relajado; ***for free*** *travel, get sth* gratis **2** *v/t prisoners* liberar
free·bie ['friːbɪ] F regalo *m*; ***as a freebie*** de regalo
free·dom ['friːdəm] libertad *f*
free·dom of 'speech libertad *f* de expresión
free·dom of the 'press libertad *f* de prensa
free 'en·ter·prise empresa *f* libre
free 'kick *in soccer* falta *f*, golpe *m* franco
free·lance ['friːlæns] **1** *adj* autónomo, free-lance **2** *adv*: ***work freelance*** trabajar como autónomo *or* free-lance
free·lanc·er ['friːlænsər] autónomo(-a) *m(f)*, free-lance *m/f*
free·load·er ['friːloʊdər] F gorrón (-ona) *m(f)*
free·ly ['friːlɪ] *adv admit* libremente
free mar·ket e'con·o·my economía *f* de libre mercado
free-range 'chick·en pollo *m* de corral
free-range 'eggs *npl* huevos *mpl* de corral
free 'sam·ple muestra *f* gratuita
free 'speech libertad *f* de expresión
'free·way autopista *f*
free'wheel *v/i on bicycle* ir sin pedalear
free 'will libre albedrío *m*; ***he did it of his own free will*** lo hizo por propia iniciativa
freeze [friːz] **1** *v/t* (*pret* ***froze***, *pp* ***frozen***) *food, wages, video* congelar; *river* congelar, helar **2** *v/i* (*pret* ***froze***, *pp* ***frozen***) *of water* congelarse, helarse
◆ **freeze over** *v/i of river* helarse
'freeze-dried *adj* liofilizado
freez·er ['friːzər] congelador *m*
freez·ing ['friːzɪŋ] **1** *adj* muy frío; ***it's freezing (cold)*** *of weather* hace mucho frío; *of water* está muy frío; ***I'm freezing (cold)*** tengo mucho frío **2** *n*: ***10 below freezing*** diez grados bajo cero
'freez·ing com·part·ment congelador *m*
'freez·ing point punto *m* de congelación
freight [freɪt] *n* transporte; *costs* flete *m*
'freight car *on train* vagón *m* de mercancías
freight·er ['freɪtər] *ship* carguero *m*; *airplane* avión *m* de carga
'freight train tren *m* de mercancías
French [frentʃ] **1** *adj* francés **2** *n language* francés *m*; ***the French*** los franceses
French 'bread pan *m* de barra
French 'doors *npl* puerta *f* cristalera
'French fries *npl Span* patatas *fpl or L.Am.* papas *fpl* fritas
'French·man francés *m*
'French·wom·an francesa *f*
fren·zied ['frenzɪd] *adj attack, activity* frenético; *mob* desenfrenado
fren·zy ['frenzɪ] frenesí *m*; ***whip s.o. into a frenzy*** poner a alguien frenético
fre·quen·cy ['friːkwənsɪ] *also* RAD frecuencia *f*
fre·quent[1] ['friːkwənt] *adj* frecuente; ***how frequent are the trains?*** ¿con qué frecuencia pasan trenes?
fre·quent[2] [frɪ'kwent] *v/t bar* frecuentar
fre·quent·ly ['frɪkwentlɪ] *adv* con frecuencia
fres·co ['freskoʊ] fresco *m*
fresh [freʃ] *adj* fresco; *start* nuevo; ***don't you get fresh with your mother!*** ¡no seas descarado con tu madre!
fresh 'air aire *m* fresco
fresh·en ['freʃn] *v/i of wind* refrescar
◆ **freshen up 1** *v/i* refrescarse **2** *v/t room, paintwork* renovar, revivir
fresh·ly ['freʃlɪ] *adv* recién
'fresh·man estudiante *m/f* de primer año
fresh·ness ['freʃnɪs] frescura *f*
'fresh·wa·ter *adj* de agua dulce
fret [fret] *v/i* (*pret & pp* ***fretted***) ponerse nervioso, inquietarse
Freud·i·an ['frɔɪdɪən] *adj* freudiano
fric·tion ['frɪkʃn] PHYS rozamiento *m*; *between people* fricción *f*
'fric·tion tape cinta *f* aislante
Fri·day ['fraɪdeɪ] viernes *m inv*
fridge [frɪdʒ] nevera *f*, frigorífico *m*
fried 'egg [fraɪd] huevo *m* frito
fried po'ta·toes *npl Span* patatas *fpl or L.Am.* papas *fpl* fritas
friend [frend] amigo(-a) *m(f)*; ***make friends*** *of one person* hacer amigos; *of two people* hacerse amigos; ***make friends with s.o.*** hacerse amigo de alguien
friend·li·ness ['frendlɪnɪs] simpatía *f*
friend·ly ['frendlɪ] *adj atmosphere* agradable; *person* agradable, simpático; (*easy to use*) fácil de usar; *argument, match, re-*

lations amistoso; ***be friendly with s.o.*** (*be friends*) ser amigo de alguien
'friend·ship ['frendʃɪp] amistad *f*
fries [fraɪz] *npl Span* patatas *fpl or L.Am.* papas *fpl* fritas
fright [fraɪt] susto *m*; ***give s.o. a fright*** dar un susto a alguien, asustar a alguien; ***scream with fright*** gritar asustado
fright·en ['fraɪtn] *v/t* asustar; ***be frightened*** estar asustado, tener miedo; ***don't be frightened*** no te asustes, no tengas miedo; ***be frightened of*** tener miedo de
◆ **frighten away** *v/t* ahuyentar, espantar
fright·en·ing ['fraɪtnɪŋ] *adj noise, person, prospect* aterrador, espantoso
fri·gid ['frɪdʒɪd] *adj sexually* frígido
frill [frɪl] *on dress etc* volante *m*; (*fancy extra*) extra *m*
frill·y ['frɪlɪ] *adj* de volantes
fringe [frɪndʒ] *on dress, curtains etc* flecos *mpl*; *Br in hair* flequillo *m*; (*edge*) margen *m*
fringe ben·e·fits *npl* ventajas *fpl* adicionales
frisk [frɪsk] *v/t* cachear
frisk·y ['frɪskɪ] *adj puppy etc* juguetón
◆ **frit·ter away** ['frɪtər] *v/t time* desperdiciar; *fortune* despilfarrar
fri·vol·i·ty [frɪ'vɑːlətɪ] frivolidad *f*
friv·o·lous ['frɪvələs] *adj* frívolo
frizz·y ['frɪzɪ] *adj hair* crespo
frog [frɑːg] rana *f*
'frog·man hombre *m* rana
from [frɑːm] *prep* ◇ *in time* desde; ***from 9 to 5 (o'clock)*** de 9 a 5; ***from the 18th century*** desde el siglo XVIII; ***from today on*** a partir de hoy; ***from next Tuesday*** a partir del próximo martes
◇ *in space* de, desde; ***from here to there*** de *or* desde aquí hasta allí; ***we drove here from Paris*** vinimos en coche desde París
◇ *origin* de; ***a letter from Jo*** una carta de Jo; ***a gift from the management*** un regalo de la dirección; ***it doesn't say who it's from*** no dice de quién es; ***I am from New Jersey*** soy de Nueva Jersey; ***made from bananas*** hecho con plátanos
◇ (*because of*): ***tired from the journey*** cansado del viaje; ***it's from overeating*** es por comer demasiado
front [frʌnt] **1** *n of building, book* portada *f*; (*cover organization*) tapadera *f*; MIL, *of weather* frente *m*; ***in front*** delante; *in a race* en cabeza; ***the car in front*** el coche de delante; ***in front of*** delante de; ***at the front of*** en la parte de delante de **2** *adj wheel, seat* delantero **3** *v/t* TV *program* presentar
front 'cov·er portada *f*
front 'door puerta *f* principal
front 'en·trance entrada *f* principal
fron·tier ['frʌntɪr] frontera *f*; *fig*: *of knowledge, science* límite *m*
front 'line MIL línea *f* del frente
front 'page *of newspaper* portada *f*, primera *f* plana
front page 'news *nsg* noticia *f* de portada *or* de primera plana
front 'row primera fila *f*
front seat 'pas·sen·ger *in car* pasajero(-a) *m*(*f*) de delante
front-wheel 'drive tracción *f* delantera
frost [frɑːst] *n* escarcha *f*; ***there was a frost last night*** anoche cayó una helada
'frost·bite congelación *f*
'frost·bit·ten *adj* congelado
frost·ed glass ['frɑːstɪd] vidrio *m* esmerilado
frost·ing ['frɑːstɪŋ] *on cake* glaseado *m*
frost·y ['frɑːstɪ] *adj weather* gélido; *fig*: *welcome* glacial
froth [frɑːθ] *n* espuma *f*
froth·y ['frɑːθɪ] *adj cream etc* espumoso
frown [fraʊn] **1** *n*: ***what's that frown for?*** ¿por qué frunces el ceño? **2** *v/i* fruncir el ceño
froze [froʊz] *pret* → ***freeze***
fro·zen ['froʊzn] **1** *adj ground, food* congelado; *wastes* helado; ***I'm frozen*** F estoy helado *or* congelado F **2** *pp* → ***freeze***
fro·zen 'food comida *f* congelada
fruit [fruːt] fruta *f*
'fruit cake bizcocho *m* de frutas
fruit·ful ['fruːtfəl] *adj discussions etc* fructífero
'fruit juice *Span* zumo *m or L.Am.* jugo *m* de fruta
fruit 'sal·ad macedonia *f*
frus·trate [frʌ'streɪt] *v/t person, plans* frustrar
frus·trat·ed [frʌ'streɪtɪd] *adj* frustrado
frus·trat·ing [frʌ'streɪtɪŋ] *adj* frustrante
frus·tra·tion [frʌ'streɪʃn] frustración *f*; ***sexual frustration*** frustración *f* sexual; ***the frustrations of modern life*** las frustraciones de la vida moderna
fry [fraɪ] *v/t* (*pret & pp* ***fried***) freír
'fry·pan sartén *f*
fuck [fʌk] *v/t* V *Span* follar con V, *L.Am.* coger V; ***fuck!*** ¡joder! V; ***fuck him!*** ¡que se joda! V
◆ **fuck off** *v/i* V: ***fuck off!*** ¡vete a la mierda! V
fuck·ing ['fʌkɪŋ] **1** *adj* V puto V **2** *adv* V: ***it's fucking crazy*** es un estupidez ¡coño!; ***it was fucking brilliant!*** ¡estuvo

de puta madre! V

fu·el ['fjʊəl] **1** *n* combustible *m* **2** *v/t fig* avivar

fu·gi·tive ['fjuːdʒətɪv] *n* fugitivo(-a) *m(f)*

ful·fil *Br*, **ful·fill** [fʊl'fɪl] *v/t dream* cumplir, realizar; *task* realizar; *contract* cumplir; ***feel fulfilled*** *in job, life* sentirse realizado

ful·fill·ing [fʊl'fɪlɪŋ] *adj*: ***I have a fulfilling job*** mi trabajo me llena

F

ful·fil·ment *Br*, **ful·fill·ment** [fʊl'fɪlmənt] *of contract etc* cumplimiento *m*; *moral, spiritual* satisfacción *f*

full [fʊl] *adj* lleno; *account, schedule* completo; *life* pleno; ***full of*** *of water etc* lleno de; ***full up*** *hotel etc, with food* lleno; ***pay in full*** pagar al contado

full 'board *Br* pensión *f* completa

'full-grown *adj* completamente desarrollado

'full-length *adj dress* de cuerpo entero; ***full-length movie*** largometraje *m*

full 'moon luna *f* llena

full 'stop *Br* punto *m*

full 'time 1 *adj worker, job* a tiempo completo **2** *adv work* a tiempo completo

ful·ly ['fʊlɪ] *adv* completamente; *describe* en detalle

fum·ble ['fʌmbl] *v/t ball* dejar caer

◆ **fumble about** *v/i* rebuscar

fume [fjuːm] *v/i*: ***be fuming*** F *with anger* echar *humo* F

fumes [fjuːmz] *npl* humos *mpl*

fun [fʌn] diversión *f*; ***it was great fun*** fue muy divertido; ***bye, have fun!*** ¡adiós, que lo paséis bien!; ***for fun*** para divertirse; ***make fun of*** burlarse de

func·tion ['fʌŋkʃn] **1** *n* (*purpose*) función *f*; (*reception etc*) acto *m* **2** *v/i* funcionar; ***function as*** hacer de

func·tion·al ['fʌŋkʃnl] *adj* funcional

fund [fʌŋd] **1** *n* fondo *m* **2** *v/t project etc* financiar

fun·da·men·tal [fʌndə'mentl] *adj* fundamental; (*crucial*) esencial

fun·da·men·tal·ist [fʌndə'mentlɪst] *n* fundamentalista *m/f*

fun·da·men·tal·ly [fʌndə'mentlɪ] *adv* fundamentalmente

fund·ing ['fʌndɪŋ] (*money*) fondos *mpl*, financiación *f*

fu·ne·ral ['fjuːnərəl] funeral *m*

'fu·ne·ral di·rec·tor encargado(-a) *m(f)* de una funeraria

'fu·ne·ral home funeraria *f*

fun·gus ['fʌŋgəs] hongos *mpl*

fu·nic·u·lar (**'rail·way**) [fjuː'nɪkjʊlər] funicular *m*

fun·nel ['fʌnl] *n of ship* chimenea *f*

fun·nies ['fʌnɪz] *npl* F *sección de humor*

fun·ni·ly ['fʌnɪlɪ] *adv* (*oddly*) de modo extraño; (*comically*) de forma divertida; ***funnily enough*** curiosamente

fun·ny ['fʌnɪ] *adj* (*comical*) divertido, gracioso; (*odd*) curioso, raro; ***that's not funny*** eso no tiene gracia

'fun·ny bone hueso *m* de la risa

fur [fɜːr] piel *f*

fu·ri·ous ['fjʊrɪəs] *adj* (*angry*) furioso; (*intense*) furioso, feroz; *effort* febril; ***at a furious pace*** a un ritmo vertiginoso

fur·nace ['fɜːrnɪs] horno *m*

fur·nish ['fɜːrnɪʃ] *v/t room* amueblar; (*supply*) suministrar

fur·ni·ture ['fɜːrnɪtʃər] mobiliario *m*, muebles *mpl*; ***a piece of furniture*** un mueble

fur·ry ['fɜːrɪ] *adj animal* peludo

fur·ther ['fɜːrðər] **1** *adj* (*additional*) adicional; (*more distant*) más lejano; ***there's been a further development*** ha pasado algo nuevo; ***until further notice*** hasta nuevo aviso; ***have you anything further to say?*** ¿tiene algo más que añadir? **2** *adv walk, drive* más lejos; ***further, I want to say ...*** además, quiero decir ...; ***two miles further*** (***on***) dos millas más adelante **3** *v/t cause etc* promover

fur·ther'more *adv* es más

fur·thest ['fɜːrðɪst] **1** *adj*: ***the furthest point north*** el punto más al norte; ***the furthest stars*** las estrellas más lejanas **2** *adv* más lejos; ***this is the furthest north I've ever been*** nunca había estado tan al norte

fur·tive ['fɜːrtɪv] *adj glance* furtivo

fur·tive·ly ['fɜːrtɪvlɪ] *adv* furtivamente

fu·ry ['fjʊrɪ] (*anger*) furia *f*, ira *f*

fuse [fjuːz] **1** *n* ELEC fusible *m* **2** *v/i* ELEC fundirse; ***the lights have fused*** se han fundido los plomos **3** *v/t* ELEC fundir

'fuse·box caja *f* de fusibles

fu·se·lage ['fjuːzəlɑːʒ] fuselaje *m*

'fuse wire fusible *m* (*hilo*)

fu·sion ['fjuːʒn] fusión *f*

fuss [fʌs] *n* escándalo *m*; ***make a fuss*** (*complain*) armar un escándalo; (*behave in exaggerated way*) armar un escándalo; ***make a fuss of*** (*be very attentive to*) deshacerse en atenciones con

fuss·y ['fʌsɪ] *adj person* quisquilloso; *design etc* recargado; ***be a fussy eater*** ser un quisquilloso a la hora de comer

fu·tile ['fjuːtl] *adj* inútil, vano

fu·til·i·ty [fjuː'tɪlətɪ] inutilidad *f*

fu·ture ['fjuːtʃər] **1** *n also* GRAM futuro *m*; ***in future*** en el futuro **2** *adj* futuro

fu·tures ['fjuːtʃərz] *npl* FIN futuros *mpl*

'fu·tures mar·ket FIN mercado *m* de futuros
fu·tur·is·tic [fju:ʧə'rɪstɪk] *adj design* futurista
fuze [fju:z] → ***fuse***
fuzz·y ['fʌzɪ] *adj hair* crespo; (*out of focus*) borroso

G

gab [gæb] *n*: ***have the gift of the gab*** F tener labia F
gab·ble ['gæbl] *v/i* farfullar
◆ **gad about** [gæd] *v/i* (*pret & pp* ***gadded***) pendonear
gad·get ['gædʒɪt] artilugio *m*, chisme *m*
gaffe [gæf] metedura *f* de pata
gag [gæg] **1** *n over mouth* mordaza *f*; (*joke*) chiste *m* **2** *v/t* (*pret & pp* ***gagged***) *also fig* amordazar
gain [geɪn] *v/t* (*acquire*) ganar; *victory* obtener; ***gain speed*** cobrar velocidad; ***gain 10 pounds*** engordar 10 libras
ga·la ['gælə] gala *f*
gal·ax·y ['gæləksɪ] AST galaxia *f*
gale [geɪl] vendaval *m*
gal·lant ['gælənt] *adj* galante
gall blad·der ['gɒ:lblædər] vesícula *f* biliar
gal·le·ry ['gælərɪ] *for art* museo *m*; *in theater* galería *f*
gal·ley ['gælɪ] *on ship* cocina *f*
◆ **gal·li·vant around** ['gælɪvænt] *v/i* pendonear
gal·lon ['gælən] galón *m* (*en EE.UU. 3,785 litros, en GB 4,546*); ***gallons of tea*** F toneladas de té F
gal·lop ['gæləp] *v/i* galopar
gal·lows ['gæloʊz] *npl* horca *f*
gall·stone ['gɒ:lstoʊn] cálculo *m* biliar
ga·lore [gə'lɔ:r] *adj*: ***apples / novels galore*** manzanas / novelas a montones
gal·va·nize ['gælvənaɪz] *v/t* TECH galvanizar; ***galvanize s.o. into activity*** hacer que alguien se vuelva más activo
gam·ble ['gæmbl] *v/i* jugar
gam·bler ['gæmblər] jugador(a) *m*(*f*)
gam·bling ['gæmblɪŋ] *n* juego *m*
game [geɪm] *n* (*sport*) partido *m*; *children's* juego *m*; *in tennis* juego *m*
'game re·serve coto *m* de caza
gang [gæŋ] *of friends* cuadrilla *f*, pandilla *f*; *of criminals* banda *f*
◆ **gang up on** *v/t* compincharse contra
'gang rape 1 *n* violación *f* colectiva **2** *v/t* violar colectivamente
gan·grene ['gæŋgri:n] MED gangrena *f*
gang·ster ['gæŋstər] gángster *m*
'gang war·fare lucha *f* entre bandas
'gang·way pasarela *f*
gaol [dʒeɪl] → ***jail***
gap [gæp] *in wall* hueco *m*; *for parking*, *in figures* espacio *m*; *in time* intervalo *m*; *in conversation* interrupción *f*; *between two people's characters* diferencia *f*
gape [geɪp] *v/i of person* mirar boquiabierto
◆ **gape at** *v/t* mirar boquiabierto a
gap·ing ['geɪpɪŋ] *adj hole* enorme
gar·age [gə'rɑ:ʒ] *n for parking* garaje *m*; *for gas* gasolinera *f*; *for repairs* taller *m*
gar·bage ['gɑ:rbɪdʒ] basura *f*; (*fig: nonsense*) tonterías *fpl*
'gar·bage bag bolsa *f* de la basura
'gar·bage can cubo *m* de la basura
'gar·bage truck camión *m* de la basura
gar·bled ['gɑ:rbld] *adj message* confuso
gar·den ['gɑ:rdn] jardín *m*
'gar·den cen·ter, *Br* **'gar·den cen·tre** vivero *m*, centro *m* de jardinería
gar·den·er ['gɑ:rdnər] aficionado(-a) *m*(*f*) a la jardinería; *professional* jardinero(-a) *m*(*f*)
gar·den·ing ['gɑ:rdnɪŋ] jardinería *f*
gar·gle ['gɑ:rgl] *v/i* hacer gárgaras
gar·goyle ['gɑ:rgɔɪl] ARCHI gárgola *f*
gar·ish ['gerɪʃ] *adj color* chillón; *design* estridente
gar·land ['gɑ:rlənd] *n* guirnalda *f*
gar·lic ['gɑ:rlɪk] ajo *m*
gar·lic 'bread pan *m* con ajo
gar·ment ['gɑ:rmənt] prenda *f* (de vestir)
gar·nish ['gɑ:rnɪʃ] *v/t* guarnecer (***with*** con)
gar·ret ['gærɪt] buhardilla *f*
gar·ri·son ['gærɪsn] *n place* plaza *f*; *troops* guarnición *f*
gar·ter ['gɑ:rtər] liga *f*
gas [gæs] *n* gas *m*; (*gasoline*) gasolina *f*, *Rpl* nafta *f*

G

gash [gæʃ] *n* corte *m* profundo
gas·ket ['gæskɪt] junta *f*
gas·o·line ['gæsəliːn] gasolina *f*, *Rpl* nafta *f*
gasp [gæsp] **1** *n* grito *m* apagado **2** *v/i* lanzar un grito apagado; ***gasp for breath*** luchar por respirar
'gas ped·al acelerador *m*
'gas pipe·line gasoducto *m*
'gas pump surtidor *m* (de gasolina)
'gas stove cocina *f* de gas **'gas sta·tion** gasolinera *f*, *S. Am.* bomba *f*
gas·tric ['gæstrɪk] *adj* MED gástrico
gas·tric 'flu MED gripe *f* gastrointestinal
gas·tric 'juices *npl* jugos *mpl* gástricos
gas·tric 'ul·cer MED úlcera *f* gástrica
gate [geɪt] *of house*, *at airport* puerta *f*; *made of iron* verja *f*
'gate·crash *v/t*: ***gatecrash a party*** colarse en una fiesta
'gate·way *also fig* entrada *f*
gath·er ['gæðər] **1** *v/t facts*, *information* reunir; ***am I to gather that ...?*** ¿debo entender que ...?; ***gather speed*** ganar velocidad **2** *v/i of crowd* reunirse
◆ **gather up** *v/t possessions* recoger
gather·ing ['gæðərɪŋ] *n* (*group of people*) grupo *m* de personas
gau·dy ['gɒːdɪ] *adj* chillón, llamativo
gauge [geɪdʒ] **1** *n* indicador *m* **2** *v/t pressure* medir, calcular; *opinion* estimar, evaluar
gaunt [gɒːnt] *adj* demacrado
gauze [gɒːz] gasa *f*
gave [geɪv] *pret* → ***give***
gaw·ky ['gɒːkɪ] *adj* desgarbado
gawp [gɒːp] *v/i* F mirar boquiabierto; ***don't just stand there gawping!*** ¡no te quedes ahí boquiabierto!
gay [geɪ] **1** *n* (*homosexual*) homosexual *m*, gay *m* **2** *adj* homosexual, gay
gaze [geɪz] **1** *n* mirada *f* **2** *v/i* mirar fijamente
◆ **gaze at** *v/t* mirar fijamente
GB [dʒiː'biː] *abbr* (= ***Great Britain***) GB (= Gran *Br*etaña)
GDP [dʒiːdiː'piː] *abbr* (= ***gross domestic product***) PIB *m* (= producto *m* interior bruto)
gear [gɪr] *n equipment* equipo *m*; *in vehicles* marcha *f*
'gear·box MOT caja *f* de cambios
'gear le·ver, **'gear shift** MOT palanca *f* de cambios
geese [giːs] *pl* → ***goose***
gel [dʒel] *for hair* gomina *f*; *for shower* gel *m*
gel·a·tine ['dʒelətiːn] gelatina *f*
gel·ig·nite ['dʒelɪgnaɪt] gelignita *f*
gem [dʒem] gema *f*; (*fig: book etc*) joya *f*; (*person*) cielo *m*
Gem·i·ni ['dʒemɪnaɪ] ASTR Géminis *m/f inv*
gen·der ['dʒendər] género *m*
gene [dʒiːn] gen *m*; ***it's in his genes*** lo lleva en los genes
gen·e·ral ['dʒenrəl] **1** *n* MIL general *m*; ***in general*** en general, por lo general **2** *adj* general
gen·e·ral e'lec·tion elecciones *fpl* generales
gen·er·al·i·za·tion [dʒenrəlaɪ'zeɪʃn] generalización *f*; ***that's a generalization*** eso es generalizar
gen·e·ral·ize ['dʒenrəlaɪz] *v/i* generalizar
gen·er·al·ly ['dʒenrəlɪ] *adv* generalmente, por lo general; ***generally speaking*** en términos generales
gen·e·ral prac'ti·tion·er médico(-a) *m*(*f*) de cabecera *or* de familia
gen·e·rate ['dʒenəreɪt] *v/t* generar; *a feeling* provocar
gen·e·ra·tion [dʒenə'reɪʃn] generación *f*
gen·e'ra·tion gap conflicto *m* generacional
gen·e·ra·tor ['dʒenəreɪtər] generador *m*
ge·ner·ic drug [dʒə'nerɪk] MED medicamento *m* genérico
gen·e·ros·i·ty [dʒenə'rɑːsətɪ] generosidad *f*
gen·e·rous ['dʒenərəs] *adj* generoso
ge·net·ic [dʒɪ'netɪk] *adj* genético
ge·net·i·cal·ly [dʒɪ'netɪklɪ] *adv* genéticamente; ***genetically modified*** *crops* transgénico; ***be genetically modified*** estar modificado genéticamente
ge·net·ic 'code código *m* genético
ge·net·ic en·gi'neer·ing ingeniería *f* genética
ge·net·ic 'fin·ger·print identificación *f* genética
ge·net·i·cist [dʒɪ'netɪsɪst] genetista *m/f*, especialista *m/f* en genética
ge·net·ics [dʒɪ'netɪks] genética *f*
ge·ni·al ['dʒiːnjəl] *adj* afable, cordial
gen·i·tals ['dʒenɪtlz] *npl* genitales *mpl*
ge·ni·us ['dʒiːnjəs] genio *m*
gen·o·cide ['dʒenəsaɪd] genocidio *m*
gen·tle ['dʒentl] *adj person* tierno, delicado; *touch*, *detergent* suave; *breeze* suave, ligero; *slope* poco inclinado; ***be gentle with it, it's fragile*** ten mucho cuidado con él, es frágil
gen·tle·man ['dʒentlmən] caballero *m*; ***he's a real gentleman*** es todo un caballero
gen·tle·ness ['dʒentlnɪs] *of person* ternura *f*, delicadeza; *of touch*, *detergent*,

breeze suavidad *f*; *of slope* poca inclinación *f*

gen·tly ['dʒentlɪ] *adv* con delicadeza, poco a poco; ***a breeze blew gently*** sopla una ligera *or* suave brisa

gents [dʒents] *nsg Br toilet* servicio *m* de caballeros

gen·u·ine ['dʒenʊɪn] *adj antique* genuino, auténtico; (*sincere*) sincero

gen·u·ine·ly ['dʒenʊɪnlɪ] *adv* realmente, de verdad

ge·o·graph·i·cal [dʒɪə'græfɪkl] *adj features* geográfico

ge·og·ra·phy [dʒɪ'ɑːgrəfɪ] geografía *f*

ge·o·log·i·cal [dʒɪə'lɑːdʒɪkl] *adj* geológico

ge·ol·o·gist [dʒɪ'ɑːlədʒɪst] geólogo(-a) *m(f)*

ge·ol·o·gy [dʒɪ'ɑːlədʒɪ] geología *f*

ge·o·met·ric, ge·o·met·ri·cal [dʒɪə'metrɪk(l)] *adj* geométrico

ge·om·e·try [dʒɪ'ɑːmətrɪ] geometría *f*

ge·ra·ni·um [dʒə'reɪnɪəm] geranio *m*

ger·i·at·ric [dʒerɪ'ætrɪk] **1** *adj* geriátrico **2** *n* anciano(-a) *m(f)*

germ [dʒɜːrm] *also fig* germen *m*

Ger·man ['dʒɜːrmən] **1** *adj* alemán **2** *n person* alemán (-ana) *m(f)*; *language* alemán *m*

Ger·man 'mea·sles *nsg* rubeola *f*

Ger·man 'shep·herd pastor *m* alemán

Germany ['dʒɜːrmənɪ] Alemania

ger·mi·nate ['dʒɜːrmɪneɪt] *v/i of seed* germinar

germ 'war·fare guerra *f* bacteriológica

ges·tic·u·late [dʒe'stɪkjʊleɪt] *v/i* gesticular

ges·ture ['dʒestʃər] *n also fig* gesto *m*

get [get] *v/t* (*pret* **got**, *pp* **got, gotten**) (*obtain*) conseguir; (*fetch*) traer; (*receive*: *letter, knowledge, respect*) recibir; (*catch*: *bus, train etc*) tomar, *Span* coger; (*arrive*) llegar; (*understand*) entender; ***you can get them at the corner shop*** los puedes comprar en la tienda de la esquina; ***can I get you something to drink?*** ¿quieres tomar algo?; ***get tired*** cansarse; ***get drunk*** emborracharse; ***I'm getting old*** me estoy haciendo mayor; ***get the TV fixed*** hacer que arreglen la televisión; ***get s.o. to do sth*** hacer que alguien haga algo; ***get to do sth*** (*have opportunity*) llegar a hacer algo; ***get one's hair cut*** cortarse el pelo; ***get sth ready*** preparar algo; ***get going*** (*leave*) marcharse, irse; ***have got*** tener; ***he's got a lot of money*** tiene mucho dinero; ***I have got to study / see him*** tengo que estudiar / verlo; ***I don't want to, but I've got to*** no quiero, pero tengo que hacerlo; ***get to know*** llegar a conocer

◆ **get about** *v/i* (*travel*) viajar; (*be mobile*) desplazarse

◆ **get along** *v/i* (*come to party etc*) ir; *with s.o.* llevarse bien; ***how are you getting along at school?*** ¿cómo te van las cosas en el colegio?; ***the patient is getting along nicely*** el paciente está progresando satisfactoriamente

◆ **get at** *v/t* (*criticize*) meterse con; (*imply, mean*) querer decir

◆ **get away 1** *v/i* (*leave*) marcharse, irse **2** *v/t*: ***get sth away from s.o.*** quitar algo a alguien

◆ **get away with** *v/t* salir impune de; ***get away with it*** salirse con la suya; ***she lets him get away with anything*** le permite todo; ***I'll let you get away with it this time*** por esta vez te perdonaré

◆ **get back 1** *v/i* (*return*) volver; ***I'll get back to you on that tomorrow*** le responderé a eso mañana **2** *v/t* (*obtain again*) recuperar

◆ **get by** *v/i* (*pass*) pasar; *financially* arreglárselas

◆ **get down 1** *v/i from ladder etc* bajarse (**from** de); (*duck etc*) agacharse **2** *v/t* (*depress*) desanimar, deprimir

◆ **get down to** *v/t* (*start*: *work*) ponerse a; ***get down to the facts*** ir a los hechos

◆ **get in 1** *v/i* (*arrive*) llegar; *to car* subir(se), meterse; ***how did they get in?*** *of thieves, mice etc* ¿cómo entraron? **2** *v/t to suitcase etc* meter

◆ **get into** *v/t house* entrar en, meterse en; *car* subir(se) a, meterse en; *computer system* introducirse en

◆ **get off 1** *v/i from bus etc* bajarse; (*finish work*) salir; (*not be punished*) librarse **2** *v/t* (*remove*) quitar; *clothes, hat, footgear* quitarse; ***get off my bike!*** ¡bájate de mi bici!; ***get off the grass!*** ¡no pises la hierba!

◆ **get off with** *v/t*: ***get off with a small fine*** tener que pagar sólo una pequeña multa

◆ **get on 1** *v/i to bike, bus, train* montarse, subirse; (*be friendly*) llevarse bien; (*advance*: *of time*) hacerse tarde; (*become old*) hacerse mayor; (*make progress*) progresar; ***how are you getting on with the new subjects?*** ¿cómo te va con las nuevas asignaturas?; ***it's getting on*** *getting late* se está haciendo tarde; ***he's getting on*** se está haciendo mayor; ***he's getting on for 50*** está a punto de cumplir 50 **2** *v/t*: ***get on the bus / one's bike*** montarse en el autobús/ la bici; ***get one's shoes on***

G

ponerse los zapatos; ***I can't get these pants on*** estos pantalones no me entran
◆ **get out 1** *v/i of car, prison etc* salir; ***get out!*** ¡vete!, ¡fuera de aquí!; ***let's get out of here*** ¡salgamos de aquí!; ***I don't get out much these days*** últimamente no salgo mucho **2** *v/t nail, something jammed* sacar, extraer; *stain* quitar; *gun, pen* sacar
◆ **get over** *v/t fence etc* franquear; *disappointment* superar; *lover etc* olvidar
◆ **get over with** *v/t* terminar con; ***let's get it over with*** quitémonoslo de encima
◆ **get through** *v/i on telephone* conectarse; ***obviously I'm just not getting through*** está claro que no me estoy haciendo entender; ***get through to s.o.*** (*make self understood*) comunicarse con alguien
◆ **get up 1** *v/i* levantarse **2** *v/t* (*climb*) subir
'get·a·way *from robbery* fuga *f*, huida *f*
'get·a·way car coche *m* utilizado en la fuga
'get-to·geth·er reunión *f*
ghast·ly ['gæstlɪ] *adj* terrible
gher·kin ['gɜːrkɪn] pepinillo *m*
ghet·to ['getoʊ] gueto *m*
ghost [goʊst] fantasma *m*
ghost·ly ['goʊstlɪ] *adj* fantasmal
'ghost town ciudad *f* fantasma
ghoul [guːl] macabro(-a) *m*(*f*), morboso(-a) *m*(*f*)
ghoul·ish ['guːlɪʃ] *adj* macabro, morboso
gi·ant ['dʒaɪənt] **1** *n* gigante *m* **2** *adj* gigantesco, gigante
gib·ber·ish ['dʒɪbərɪʃ] F memeces *fpl* F, majaderías *fpl* F
gibe [dʒaɪb] *n* pulla *f*
gib·lets ['dʒɪblɪts] *npl* menudillos *mpl*
gid·di·ness ['gɪdɪnɪs] mareo *m*
gid·dy ['gɪdɪ] *adj* mareado; ***feel giddy*** estar mareado
gift [gɪft] regalo *m*
gift cer·ti·fi·cate vale *m* de regalo
gift·ed ['gɪftɪd] *adj* con talento
'gift·wrap 1 *n* papel *m* de regalo **2** *v/t* (*pret & pp* ***giftwrapped***) envolver para regalo
gig [gɪg] F concierto *m*, actuación *f*
gi·ga·byte ['gɪgəbaɪt] COMPUT gigabyte *m*
gi·gan·tic [dʒaɪ'gæntɪk] *adj* gigantesco
gig·gle ['gɪgl] **1** *v/i* soltar risitas **2** *n* risita *f*
gig·gly ['gɪglɪ] *adj* que suelta risitas
gill [gɪl] *of fish* branquia *f*
gilt [gɪlt] *n* dorado *m*; ***gilts*** FIN valores *mpl* del Estado
gim·mick ['gɪmɪk] truco *m*, reclamo *m*
gim·mick·y ['gɪmɪkɪ] *adj* superficial, artificioso
gin [dʒɪn] ginebra *f*; ***gin and tonic*** gin-tonic *m*
gin·ger ['dʒɪndʒər] **1** *n spice* jengibre *m* **2** *adj cat* color fuego; ***he has ginger hair*** es pelirrojo
gin·ger 'beer *refresco con sabor a jengibre*
'gin·ger·bread pan *m* de jengibre
gin·ger·ly ['dʒɪndʒərlɪ] *adv* cuidadosamente, delicadamente
gip·sy ['dʒɪpsɪ] gitano(-a) *m*(*f*)
gi·raffe [dʒɪ'ræf] jirafa *f*
gir·der ['gɜːrdər] *n* viga *f*
girl [gɜːrl] chica *f*; ***young girl*** niña *f*, chica *f*
'girl·friend *of boy* novia *f*; *of girl* amiga *f*
girl·ie mag·a·zine ['gɜːrlɪ] revista *f* porno
girl·ish ['gɜːrlɪʃ] *adj* de niñas
girl 'scout escultista *f*, scout *f*
gist [dʒɪst] esencia *f*
give [gɪv] *v/t* (*pret* ***gave***, *pp* ***given***) dar; *as present* regalar; (*supply: electricity etc*) proporcionar; *talk, lecture* dar, pronunciar; *cry, groan* soltar; ***give her my love*** dale recuerdos (de mi parte); ***give s.o. a present*** hacer un regalo a alguien
◆ **give away** *v/t as present* regalar; (*betray*) traicionar; ***give o.s. away*** descubrirse, traicionarse
◆ **give back** *v/t* devolver
◆ **give in 1** *v/i* (*surrender*) rendirse **2** *v/t* (*hand in*) entregar
◆ **give off** *v/t smell, fumes* emitir, despedir
◆ **give onto** *v/t* (*open onto*) dar a
◆ **give out 1** *v/t leaflets etc* repartir **2** *v/i of supplies, strength* agotarse
◆ **give up 1** *v/t smoking etc* dejar de; ***give o.s. up to the police*** entregarse a la policía **2** *v/i* (*stop making effort*) rendirse; ***I find it hard to give up*** me cuesta mucho dejarlo
◆ **give way** *v/i of bridge etc* hundirse
give-and-'take toma *m* y daca
giv·en ['gɪvn] *pp* → ***give***
'giv·en name nombre *m* de pila
gla·ci·er ['gleɪʃər] glaciar *m*
glad [glæd] *adj* contento, alegre; ***I was glad to see you*** me alegré de verte
glad·ly ['glædlɪ] *adv* con mucho gusto
glam·or ['glæmər] atractivo *m*, glamour *m*
glam·or·ize ['glæməraɪz] *v/t* hacer atractivo, ensalzar
glam·or·ous ['glæmərəs] *adj* atractivo, glamoroso
glam·our *Br* → ***glamor***
glance [glæns] **1** *n* ojeada *f*, vistazo **2** *v/i* echar una ojeada *or* vistazo
◆ **glance at** *v/t* echar una ojeada *or* vista-

zo a
gland [glænd] glándula *f*
glan·du·lar 'fe·ver ['glændʒələr] mononucleosis *f inv* infecciosa
glare [gler] **1** *n of sun, headlights* resplandor *m* **2** *v/i of headlights* resplandecer
◆ **glare at** *v/t* mirar con furia a
glar·ing ['glerɪŋ] *adj mistake* garrafal
glar·ing·ly ['glerɪŋlɪ] *adv*: ***it's glaringly obvious*** está clarísimo
glass [glæs] *material* vidrio *m*; *for drink* vaso *m*
glass 'case vitrina *f*
glass·es *npl* gafas *fpl*, *L.Am.* lentes *mpl*, *L.Am.* anteojos *mpl*
'glass·house invernadero *m*
glaze [gleɪz] *n* vidriado *m*
◆ **glaze over** *v/i of eyes* vidriarse
glazed [gleɪzd] *adj expression* vidrioso
gla·zi·er ['gleɪzɪr] cristalero(-a) *m(f)*, vidriero(-a) *m(f)*
glaz·ing ['gleɪzɪŋ] cristales *mpl*, vidrios *mpl*
gleam [gli:m] **1** *n* resplandor *m*, brillo *m* **2** *v/i* resplandecer, brillar
glee [gli:] júbilo *m*, regocijo *m*
glee·ful ['gli:fəl] *adj* jubiloso
glib [glɪb] *adj* fácil
glib·ly ['glɪblɪ] *adv* con labia
glide [glaɪd] *v/i of bird, plane* planear; *of piece of furniture* deslizarse
glid·er ['glaɪdər] planeador *m*
glid·ing ['glaɪdɪŋ] *n sport* vuelo *m* sin motor
glim·mer ['glɪmər] **1** *n of light* brillo *m* tenue; ***glimmer of hope*** rayo *m* de esperanza **2** *v/i* brillar tenuamente
glimpse [glɪmps] **1** *n* vistazo *m*; ***catch a glimpse of*** vislumbrar **2** *v/t* vislumbrar
glint [glɪnt] **1** *n* destello *m*; *in eyes* centelleo *m* **2** *v/i of light* destellar; *of eyes* centellear
glis·ten ['glɪsn] *v/i* relucir, centellear
glit·ter ['glɪtər] *v/i* resplandecer, destellar
glit·ter·ati *npl* famosos *mpl*
gloat [gloʊt] *v/i* regodearse
◆ **gloat over** *v/t* regodearse de
glo·bal ['gloʊbl] *adj* global
glo·bal e'con·o·my economía *f* global
glo·bal 'mar·ket mercado *m* global
glo·bal 'war·ming calentamiento *m* global
globe [gloʊb] (*the earth*) globo *m*; (*model of earth*) globo *m* terráqueo
gloom [glu:m] (*darkness*) tinieblas *fpl*, oscuridad *f*; *mood* abatimiento *m*, melancolía *f*
gloom·i·ly ['glu:mɪlɪ] *adv* con abatimiento, melancólicamente
gloom·y ['glu:mɪ] *adj room* tenebroso, oscuro; *mood, person* abatido, melancólico
glo·ri·ous ['glɔ:rɪəs] *adj weather, day* espléndido, maravilloso; *victory* glorioso
glo·ry ['glɔ:rɪ] *n* gloria *f*
gloss [glɑ:s] *n* (*shine*) lustre *m*, brillo *m*; (*general explanation*) glosa *f*
◆ **gloss over** *v/t* pasar por alto
glos·sa·ry ['glɑ:sərɪ] glosario *m*
'gloss paint pintura *f* brillante
gloss·y ['glɑ:sɪ] **1** *adj paper* cuché, satinado **2** *n magazine* revista *f* en color (en papel cuché *or* satinado)
glove [glʌv] guante *m*
'glove com·part·ment *in car* guantera *f*
'glove pup·pet marioneta *f* de guiñol (de guante)
glow [gloʊ] **1** *n of light, fire* resplandor *m*, brillo *m*; *in cheeks* rubor *m* **2** *v/i of light, fire* resplandecer, brillar; *of cheeks* ruborizarse
glow·er [glaʊr] *v/i* fruncir el ceño
glow·ing ['gloʊɪŋ] *adj description* entusiasta
glu·cose ['glu:koʊs] glucosa *f*
glue [glu:] **1** *n* pegamento *m*, cola *f* **2** *v/t* pegar, encolar; ***glue sth to sth*** pegar *or* encolar algo a algo; ***be glued to the radio / TV*** F estar pegado a la radio / televisión F
glum [glʌm] *adj* sombrío, triste
glum·ly ['glʌmlɪ] *adv* con tristeza
glut [glʌt] *n* exceso *m*, superabundancia *f*
glut·ton ['glʌtən] glotón(-ona) *m(f)*
glut·ton·y ['glʌtənɪ] gula *f*, glotonería *f*
GMT [dʒi:em'ti:] *abbr* (= ***Greenwich Mean Time***) hora *f* del meridiano de Greenwich
gnarled [nɑ:rld] *adj* nudoso
gnat [næt] *tipo de mosquito*
gnaw [nɒ:] *v/t bone* roer
GNP [dʒi:en'pi:] *abbr* (= ***gross national product***) PNB *m* (= producto *m* nacional bruto)
go [goʊ] **1** *n* (*try*) intento *m*; ***it's my go*** me toca a mí; ***have a go at sth*** (*try*) intentar algo; (*complain about*) protestar contra algo; ***on the go*** en marcha; ***in one go*** *drink, write etc* de un tirón **2** *v/i* (*pret* ***went***, *pp* ***gone***) ir (***to*** a); (*leave*) irse, marcharse; (*work, function*) funcionar; (*come out*: *of stain etc*) irse; (*cease*: *of pain etc*) pasarse; (*match*: *of colors etc*) ir bien, pegar; ***go shopping / jogging*** ir de compras/a hacer footing; ***I must be going*** me tengo que ir; ***let's go!*** ¡vamos!; ***go for a walk*** ir a pasear *or* a dar un paseo; ***go to bed*** ir(se) a la cama; ***go to school*** ir al colegio; ***how's the work***

going? ¿cómo va el trabajo?; ***they're going for $50*** (*being sold at*) se venden por 50 dólares; ***hamburger to go*** hamburguesa para llevar; ***be all gone*** (*finished*) haberse acabado; ***go green*** ponerse verde; ***be going to do sth*** ir a hacer algo

◆ **go ahead** *v/i and do sth* seguir adelante; ***can I? - sure, go ahead*** ¿puedo? - por supuesto, adelante

◆ **go ahead with** *v/t plans etc* seguir adelante con

◆ **go along with** *v/t suggestion* aceptar

◆ **go at** *v/t* (*attack*) atacar

◆ **go away** *v/i of person* irse, marcharse; *of rain, pain, clouds* desaparecer

◆ **go back** *v/i* (*return*) volver; (*date back*) remontarse; ***we go back a long way*** nos conocemos desde hace tiempo; ***go back to sleep*** volver a dormirse

◆ **go by** *v/i of car, time* pasar

◆ **go down** *v/i* bajar; *of sun* ponerse; *of ship* hundirse; ***go down well / badly*** *of suggestion etc* sentar bien / mal

◆ **go for** *v/t* (*attack*) atacar; ***I don't much go for gin*** no me va mucho la ginebra

◆ **go in** *v/i to room, house* entrar; *of sun* ocultarse; (*fit: of part etc*) ir, encajar

◆ **go in for** *v/t competition, race* tomar parte en; ***I used to go in for badminton quite a lot*** antes jugaba mucho al bádminton

◆ **go off 1** *v/i* (*leave*) marcharse; *of bomb* explotar, estallar; *of gun* dispararse; *of alarm* saltar; *of milk etc* echarse a perder **2** *v/t*: ***I've gone off whisky*** ya no me gusta el whisky

◆ **go on** *v/i* (*continue*) continuar; (*happen*) ocurrir, pasar; ***go on, do it!*** (*encouraging*) ¡venga, hazlo!; ***what's going on?*** ¿qué pasa?

◆ **go on at** *v/t* (*nag*) meterse con

◆ **go out** *v/i of person* salir; *of light, fire* apagarse

◆ **go out with** *v/t romantically* salir con

◆ **go over** *v/t* (*check*) examinar; (*do again*) repasar

◆ **go through** *v/t illness, hard times* atravesar; (*check*) revisar, examinar; (*read through*) estudiar

◆ **go under** *v/i* (*sink*) hundirse; *of company* ir a la quiebra

◆ **go up** *v/i* subir

◆ **go without 1** *v/t food etc* pasar sin **2** *v/i* pasar privaciones

goad [goʊd] *v/t* pinchar; ***goad s.o. into doing sth*** pinchar a alguien para que haga algo

'go-a·head 1 *n* luz *f* verde; ***when we get the go-ahead*** cuando nos den la luz verde **2** *adj* (*enterprising, dynamic*) dinámico

goal [goʊl] SP *target* portería *f*, *L.Am.* arco *m*; SP *point* gol *m*; (*objective*) objetivo *m*, meta *f*

goal·ie ['goʊlɪ] F portero(-a) *m*(*f*), *L.Am.* arquero(-a) *m*(*f*)

'goal·keep·er portero(-a) *m*(*f*), guardameta *m/f*, *Am* arquero(-a) *m*(*f*)

'goal kick saque *m* de puerta

'goal·mouth portería *f*

'goal·post poste *m*

goat [goʊt] cabra *f*

gob·ble ['gɑːbl] *v/t* engullir

◆ **gobble up** *v/t* engullir

gob·ble·dy·gook ['gɑːbldɪguːk] F jerigonza *f* F

'go-be·tween intermediario(-a) *m*(*f*)

god [gɑːd] dios *m*; ***thank God!*** ¡gracias a Dios!; ***oh God!*** ¡Dios mío!

'god·child ahijado(-a) *m*(*f*)

'god·daugh·ter ahijada *f*

god·dess ['gɑːdɪs] diosa *f*

'god·fa·ther *also in mafia* padrino *m*

god·for·sak·en ['gɑːdfərseɪkən] *adj place* dejado de la mano de Dios

'god·moth·er madrina *f*

'god·pa·rent *man* padrino *m*; *woman* madrina *f*

'god·send regalo *m* del cielo

'god·son ahijado *m*

go·fer ['goʊfər] F recadero(-a) *m*(*f*)

gog·gles ['gɑːglz] *npl* gafas *fpl*

go·ing ['goʊɪŋ] *adj price etc* vigente; ***going concern*** empresa *f* en marcha

go·ings-on [goʊɪŋz'ɑːn] *npl* actividades *fpl*

gold [goʊld] **1** *n* oro *m* **2** *adj* de oro

gold·en ['goʊldn] *adj sky, hair* dorado

gold·en 'hand·shake *gratificación entregada tras la marcha de un directivo*

gold·en 'wed·ding (an·ni·ver·sa·ry) bodas *fpl* de oro

'gold·fish pez *m* de colores

'gold mine *fig* mina *f*

'gold·smith orfebre *m/f*

golf [gɑːlf] golf *m*

'golf ball pelota *f* de golf

'golf club *organization* club *m* de golf; *stick* palo *m* de golf

'golf course campo *m* de golf

golf·er ['gɑːlfər] golfista *m/f*

gone [gɑːn] *pp* → ***go***

gong [gɑːŋ] gong *m*

good [gʊd] *adj* bueno; *food* bueno, rico; ***a good many*** muchos; ***he's good at chess*** se le da muy bien el ajedrez; ***be good for s.o.*** ser bueno para alguien

good·bye [gʊd'baɪ] adiós *m*, despedida *f*;

say goodbye to s.o., wish s.o. goodbye decir adiós a alguien, despedirse de alguien
'good-for-no·thing *n* inútil *m/f*
Good 'Fri·day Viernes *m inv* Santo
good-hu·mored, *Br* **good-hu·moured** [gʊd'hjuːmərd] *adj* jovial, afable
good-'look·ing [gʊd'lʊkɪŋ] *adj woman, man* guapo
good-na·tured [gʊd'neɪʧərd] bondadoso
good·ness ['gʊdnɪs] *adj moral* bondad *f*; *of fruit etc* propiedades *fpl*, valor *m* nutritivo; ***thank goodness!*** ¡gracias a Dios!
goods [gʊdz] *npl* COM mercancías *fpl*, productos *mpl*
good'will buena voluntad *f*
good·y-good·y ['gʊdɪgʊdɪ] *n* F: ***she's a real goody-goody*** es demasiado buenaza F
goo·ey ['guːɪ] *adj* pegajoso
goof [guːf] *v/i* F meter la pata F
goose [guːs] (*pl* ***geese*** [giːs]) ganso *m*, oca *f*
goose·ber·ry ['gʊzberɪ] grosella *f*
'goose bumps *npl* carne *f* de gallina
'goose pim·ples *npl* carne *f* de gallina
gorge [gɔːrdʒ] **1** *n* garganta *f*, desfiladero *m* **2** *v/t*: ***gorge o.s. on sth*** comer algo hasta hartarse
gor·geous ['gɔːrdʒəs] *adj weather* maravilloso; *dress, hair* precioso; *woman, man* buenísimo; *smell* estupendo
go·ril·la [gə'rɪlə] gorila *m*
gosh [gɑːʃ] *int* ¡caramba!, ¡vaya!
go-'slow huelga *f* de celo
gos·pel ['gɑːspl] *in Bible* evangelio *m*; ***it's the gospel truth*** es la pura verdad
gos·sip ['gɑːsɪp] **1** *n* cotilleo *m*; *person* cotilla *m/f* **2** *v/i* cotillear
'gos·sip col·umn ecos *mpl* de sociedad
'gos·sip col·um·nist escritor(a) *m(f)* de los ecos de sociedad
gos·sip·y ['gɑːsɪpɪ] *adj letter* lleno de cotilleos
got [gɑːt] *pret & pp* → ***get***
got·ten ['gɑːtn] *pp* → ***get***
gour·met ['gʊrmeɪ] *n* gastrónomo(-a) *m(f)*, gourmet *m/f*
gov·ern ['gʌvərn] *v/t country* gobernar
gov·ern·ment ['gʌvərnmənt] gobierno *m*
gov·er·nor ['gʌvərnər] gobernador(a) *m(f)*
gown [gaʊn] *long dress* vestido *m*; *wedding dress* traje *m*; *of academic, judge* toga *f*; *of surgeon* bata *f*
grab [græb] *v/t* (*pret & pp* ***grabbed***) agarrar; *food* tomar; ***grab some sleep*** dormir
grace [greɪs] *of dancer etc* gracia *f*, elegancia *f*; ***say grace*** bendecir la mesa
grace·ful ['greɪsfəl] *adj* elegante
grace·ful·ly ['greɪsfəlɪ] *adv move* con gracia *or* elegancia
gra·cious ['greɪʃəs] *adj person* amable; *style, living* elegante; ***good gracious!*** ¡Dios mío!
grade [greɪd] **1** *n quality* grado *m*; EDU curso *m*; (*mark*) nota *f* **2** *v/t* clasificar
'grade cross·ing paso *m* a nivel
'grade school escuela *f* primaria
gra·di·ent ['greɪdɪənt] pendiente *f*
grad·u·al ['grædʒʊəl] *adj* gradual
grad·u·al·ly ['grædʒʊəlɪ] *adv* gradualmente, poco a poco
grad·u·ate ['grædʒʊət] **1** *n* licenciado (-a) *m(f)*; *from high school* bachiller *m/f* **2** *v/i from university* licenciarse, *L.Am.* egresarse; *from high school* sacar el bachillerato
grad·u·a·tion [grædʒʊ'eɪʃn] graduación *f*
graf·fi·ti [grə'fiːtiː] graffiti *m*
graft [græft] **1** *n* BOT, MED injerto *m*; *corruption* corrupción *f* **2** *v/t* BOT, MED injertar
grain [greɪn] grano *m*; *in wood* veta *f*; ***go against the grain*** ir contra la naturaleza de alguien
gram [græm] gramo *m*
gram·mar ['græmər] gramática *f*
gram·mat·i·cal [grə'mætɪkl] *adj* gramatical
gram·mat·i·cal·ly *adv* gramaticalmente
grand [grænd] **1** *adj* grandioso; F (*very good*) estupendo, genial **2** *n* F (*$1000*) mil dólares
gran·dad ['grændæd] abuelito *m*
'grand·child nieto(-a) *m(f)*
'grand·daugh·ter nieta *f*
gran·deur ['grændʒər] grandiosidad *f*
'grand·fa·ther abuelo *m*
'grand·fa·ther clock reloj *m* de pie
gran·di·ose ['grændɪoʊs] *adj* grandioso
grand 'jur·y jurado *m* de acusación, gran jurado
'grand·ma F abuelita *f*, yaya *f* F
'grand·moth·er abuela *f* ABWAYLA
'grand·pa F abuelito *m*, yayo *m* F
'grand·par·ents *npl* abuelos *mpl*
grand pi'an·o piano *m* de cola
grand 'slam gran slam *m*
'grand·son nieto *m*
'grand·stand tribuna *f*
gran·ite ['grænɪt] granito *m*
gran·ny ['grænɪ] F abuelita *f*, yaya *f* F
grant [grænt] **1** *n money* subvención *f* **2** *v/t* conceder; ***take sth for granted*** dar algo por sentado; ***take s.o. for granted*** no

apreciar a alguien lo suficiente
gran·u·lat·ed sug·ar ['grænuleɪtɪd] azúcar *m or f* granulado(-a)
gran·ule ['grænjuːl] gránulo *m*
grape [greɪp] uva *f*
'grape·fruit pomelo *m*, *L.Am.* toronja *f*
'grape·fruit juice *Span* zumo *m* de pomelo, *L.Am.* jugo *m* de toronja
'grape·vine: ***I've heard on the grapevine that …*** me ha contado un pajarito que …
graph [græf] gráfico *m*, gráfica *f*
graph·ic ['græfɪk] **1** *adj* (*vivid*) gráfico **2** *n* COMPUT gráfico *m*
graph·ic·ally ['græfɪklɪ] *adv describe* gráficamente
graph·ic de'sign·er diseñador(a) *m(f)* gráfico(-a)
◆ **grap·ple with** ['græpl] *v/t attacker* forcejear con; *problem etc* enfrentarse a
grasp [græsp] **1** *n physical* asimiento *m*; *mental* comprensión *m* **2** *v/t physically* agarrar; (*understand*) comprender
grass [græs] *n* hierba *f*
'grass·hop·per saltamontes *m inv*
grass 'roots *npl people* bases *fpl*
grass 'wid·ow *mujer cuyo marido está a menudo ausente durante largos periodos de tiempo*
grass 'wid·ow·er *hombre cuya mujer está a menudo ausente durante largos periodos de tiempo*
gras·sy ['græsɪ] *adj* lleno de hierba
grate[1] [greɪt] *n metal* parrilla *f*, reja *f*
grate[2] [greɪt] **1** *v/t in cooking* rallar **2** *v/i of sound* rechinar
grate·ful ['greɪtfəl] *adj* agradecido; ***we are grateful for your help*** (le) agradecemos su ayuda; ***I'm grateful to him*** le estoy agradecido
grate·ful·ly ['greɪtfəlɪ] *adv* con agradecimiento
grat·er ['greɪtər] rallador *m*
grat·i·fy ['grætɪfaɪ] *v/t* (*pret & pp* ***gratified***) satisfacer, complacer
grat·ing ['greɪtɪŋ] **1** *n* reja *f* **2** *adj sound, voice* chirriante
grat·i·tude ['grætɪtuːd] gratitud *f*
gra·tu·i·tous [grə'tuːɪtəs] *adj* gratuito
gra·tu·i·ty [grə'tuːətɪ] propina *f*, gratificación *f*
grave[1] [greɪv] *n* tumba *f*, sepultura *f*
grave[2] [greɪv] *adj* grave
grav·el ['grævl] *n* gravilla *f*
'grave·stone lápida *f*
'grave·yard cementerio *m*
◆ **grav·i·tate toward** ['grævɪteɪt] *v/t* verse atraído por
grav·i·ty ['grævətɪ] PHYS gravedad *f*
gra·vy ['greɪvɪ] jugo *m* (de la carne)
gray [greɪ] *adj* gris; ***be going gray*** encanecer
gray-haired [greɪ'herd] *adj* canoso
'gray·hound galgo *m*
graze[1] [greɪz] *v/i of cow etc* pastar, pacer
graze[2] [greɪz] **1** *v/t arm etc* rozar, arañar **2** *n* rozadura *f*, arañazo *m*
grease [griːs] *n* grasa *f*
grease·proof 'pa·per papel *m* de cera *or* parafinado
greas·y ['griːsɪ] *adj food, hands, plate* grasiento; *hair, skin* graso
great [greɪt] *adj* grande, *before singular noun* gran; F (*very good*) estupendo, genial; ***how was it? - great!*** ¿cómo fue? - ¡estupendo *or* genial!; ***great to see you again!*** ¡me alegro de volver a verte!
Great 'Brit·ain Gran Bretaña
great-'grand·child bisnieto(-a) *m(f)*
great-'grand·daugh·ter bisnieta *f*
great-'grand·fa·ther bisabuelo *m*
great-'grand·moth·er bisabuela *f*
great-'grand·par·ents *npl* bisabuelos *mpl*
great-'grand·son bisnieto *m*
great·ly ['greɪtlɪ] *adv* muy
great·ness ['greɪtnɪs] grandeza *f*
Greece [griːs] Grecia
greed [griːd] *for money* codicia *f*; *for food* gula *f*, glotonería *f*
greed·i·ly ['griːdɪlɪ] *adv* con codicia; *eat* con gula *or* glotonería
greed·y ['griːdɪ] *adj for food* glotón; *for money* codicioso
Greek [griːk] **1** *adj* griego **2** *n person* griego(-a) *m(f)*; *language* griego *m*
green [griːn] *adj* verde; *environmentally* ecologista, verde
green 'beans *npl* judías *fpl* verdes, *L.Am.* porotos *mpl* verdes, *Mex* ejotes *mpl*
'green belt cinturón *m* verde
'green card (*work permit*) permiso *m* de trabajo
'green·field site terreno *m* edificable en el campo
'green·horn F novato(-a) *m(f)* F
'green·house invernadero *m*
'green·house ef·fect efecto *m* invernadero
'green·house gas gas *m* invernadero
greens [griːnz] *npl* verduras *f*
green 'thumb: ***have a green thumb*** tener buena mano con la jardinería
greet [griːt] *v/t* saludar
greet·ing ['griːtɪŋ] saludo *m*
'greet·ing card tarjeta *f* de felicitación
gre·gar·i·ous [grɪ'gerɪəs] *adj person* sociable
gre·nade [grɪ'neɪd] granada *f*

grew [gruː] *pret* → ***grow***
grey *Br* → ***gray***
grid [grɪd] reja *f*, rejilla *f*
'**grid·iron** SP *campo de fútbol americano*
'**grid·lock** *in traffic* paralización *m* del tráfico
grief [griːf] dolor *m*, aflicción *f*
grief-strick·en ['griːfstrɪkn] *adj* afligido
griev·ance ['griːvəns] queja *f*
grieve [griːv] *v/i* sufrir; ***grieve for s.o.*** llorar por alguien
grill [grɪl] **1** *n on window* reja *f* **2** *v/t* (*interrogate*) interrogar
grille [grɪl] reja *f*
grim [grɪm] *adj face* severo; *prospects* desolador; *surroundings* lúgubre
gri·mace ['grɪməs] *n* gesto *m*, mueca *f*
grime [graɪm] mugre *f*
grim·ly ['grɪmlɪ] *adv speak* en tono grave
grim·y ['graɪmɪ] *adj* mugriento
grin [grɪn] **1** *n* sonrisa *f* (amplia) **2** *v/i* (*pret & pp* ***grinned***) sonreír abiertamente
grind [graɪnd] *v/t* (*pret & pp* ***ground***) *coffee* moler; *meat* picar; ***grind one's teeth*** hacer rechinar los dientes
grip [grɪp] **1** *n*: ***he lost his grip on the rope*** se le escapó la cuerda; ***be losing one's grip*** (*losing one's skills*) estar perdiendo el control **2** *v/t* (*pret & pp* ***gripped***) agarrar
gripe [graɪp] **1** *n* F queja *f* **2** *v/i* F quejarse
grip·ping ['grɪpɪŋ] *adj* apasionante
gris·tle ['grɪsl] cartílago *m*
grit [grɪt] **1** *n* (*dirt*) arenilla *f*; *for roads* gravilla *f* **2** *v/t* (*pret & pp* ***gritted***): ***grit one's teeth*** apretar los dientes
grit·ty ['grɪtɪ] *adj* F *book, movie etc* duro F, descarnado
groan [groʊn] **1** *n* gemido *m* **2** *v/i* gemir
gro·cer ['groʊsər] tendero(-a) *m*(*f*)
gro·cer·ies ['groʊsərɪz] *npl* comestibles *mpl*
gro·cer·y store ['groʊsərɪ] tienda *f* de comestibles *or Mex* abarrotes
grog·gy ['grɑːgɪ] *adj* F grogui F
groin [grɔɪn] ANAT ingle *f*
groom [gruːm] **1** *n for bride* novio *m*; *for horse* mozo *m* de cuadra **2** *v/t horse* almohazar; (*train, prepare*) preparar; ***well groomed*** *in appearance* bien arreglado
groove [gruːv] ranura *f*
grope [groʊp] **1** *v/i in the dark* caminar a tientas **2** *v/t sexually* manosear
◆ **grope for** *v/t door handle, the right word* intentar encontrar
gross [groʊs] *adj* (*coarse, vulgar*) grosero; *exaggeration* tremendo; *error* craso; FIN bruto
gross do·mes·tic 'prod·uct producto *m* interior bruto
gross na·tion·al 'prod·uct producto *m* nacional bruto
ground[1] [graʊnd] **1** *n* suelo *m*, tierra *f*; (*reason*) motivo *m*; ELEC tierra *f*; ***on the ground*** en el suelo **2** *v/t* ELEC conectar a tierra
ground[2] [graʊnd] *pret & pp* → ***grind***
'**ground con·trol** control *m* de tierra
'**ground crew** personal *m* de tierra
ground·ing ['graʊndɪŋ] *in subject* fundamento *m*; ***he's had a good grounding in electronics*** tiene buenos fundamentos de electrónica
ground·less ['graʊndlɪs] *adj* infundado
ground 'meat carne *f* picada
'**ground·nut** cacahuete *m*, *L.Am.* maní *m*, *Mex* cacahuate *m*
'**ground plan** plano *m*
'**ground staff** SP personal *m* de mantenimiento; *at airport* personal *m* de tierra
'**ground·work** trabajos *mpl* preliminares
group [gruːp] **1** *n* grupo *m* **2** *v/t* agrupar
group·ie ['gruːpɪ] F grupi *f* F
group 'ther·a·py terapia *f* de grupo
grouse [graʊs] **1** *n* F queja *f* **2** *v/i* F quejarse, refunfuñar
grov·el ['grɑːvl] *v/i fig* arrastrarse
grow [groʊ] **1** *v/i* (*pret* ***grew***, *pp* ***grown***) crecer; *of number, amount* crecer, incrementarse; ***grow old / tired*** envejecer / cansarse **2** *v/t* (*pret* ***grew***, *pp* ***grown***) *flowers* cultivar
◆ **grow up** *v/i of person, city* crecer; ***grow up!*** ¡no seas crío!
growl [graʊl] **1** *n* gruñido *m* **2** *v/i* gruñir
grown [groʊn] *pp* → ***grow***
grown-up ['groʊnʌp] **1** *n* adulto(-a) *m*(*f*) **2** *adj* maduro
growth [groʊθ] *of person, economy* crecimiento *m*; (*increase*) incremento *m*; MED bulto *m*
grub [grʌb] *of insect* larva *f*, gusano
grub·by ['grʌbɪ] *adj* mugriento *m*
grudge [grʌdʒ] **1** *n* rencor *m*; ***bear s.o. a grudge*** guardar rencor a alguien **2** *v/t*: ***grudge s.o. sth*** *feel envy* envidiar algo a alguien
grudg·ing ['grʌdʒɪŋ] *adj* rencoroso
grudg·ing·ly ['grʌdʒɪŋlɪ] *adv* de mala gana
gru·el·ing, *Br* **gru·el·ling** ['gruːəlɪŋ] *adj* agotador
gruff [grʌf] *adj* seco, brusco
grum·ble ['grʌmbl] *v/i* murmurar, refunfuñar
grum·bler ['grʌmblər] quejica *m/f*
grump·y ['grʌmpɪ] *adj* cascarrabias
grunt [grʌnt] **1** *n* gruñido *m* **2** *v/i* gruñir

guar·an·tee [gærən'tiː] **1** *n* garantía *f*; ***guarantee period*** periodo *m* de garantía **2** *v/t* garantizar
guar·an·tor [gærən'tɔːr] garante *m/f*
guard [gɑːrd] **1** *n* (*security guard*) guardia *m/f*, guarda *m/f*; MIL guardia *f*; *in prison* guardián (-ana) *m(f)*; ***be on one's guard against*** estar en guardia contra **2** *v/t* guardar, proteger
◆ **guard against** *v/t* evitar
'**guard dog** perro *m* guardián
guard·ed ['gɑːrdɪd] *adj reply* cauteloso
guard·i·an ['gɑːrdɪən] LAW tutor(a) *m(f)*
guard·i·an 'an·gel ángel *m* de la guardia
Gua·te·ma·la [gwætə'mɑːlə] *n* Guatemala
Gua·te·ma·lan [gwætə'mɑːlən] **1** *adj* guatemalteco **2** *n* guatemalteco(-a) *m(f)*
guer·ril·la [gə'rɪlə] guerrillero(-a) *m(f)*
guer·ril·la 'war·fare guerra *f* de guerrillas
guess [ges] **1** *n* conjetura *f*, suposición *f* **2** *v/t the answer* adivinar; ***I guess so*** me imagino *or* supongo que sí; ***I guess not*** me imagino *or* supongo que no **3** *v/i* adivinar
'**guess·work** conjeturas *fpl*
guest [gest] invitado(-a) *m(f)*
'**guest·house** casa *f* de huéspedes
'**guest·room** habitación *f* para invitados
guf·faw [gʌ'fɒː] **1** *n* carcajada *f*, risotada *f* **2** *v/i* carcajearse
guid·ance ['gaɪdəns] orientación *f*, consejo *m*
guide [gaɪd] **1** *n person* guía *m/f*; *book* guía *f* **2** *v/t* guiar
'**guide·book** guía *f*
guid·ed mis·sile ['gaɪdɪd] misil *m* teledirigido
'**guide dog** *Br* perro *m* lazarillo
guid·ed 'tour visita *f* guiada
guide·lines ['gaɪdlaɪnz] *npl* directrices *fpl*, normas *fpl* generales
guilt [gɪlt] culpa *f*, culpabilidad *f*; LAW culpabilidad *f*
guilt·y ['gɪltɪ] *adj also* LAW culpable; ***be guilty of sth*** ser culpable de algo; ***have a guilty conscience*** tener remordimientos de conciencia
guin·ea pig ['gɪnɪpɪg] conejillo *m* de Indias, cobaya *f*; *fig* conejillo *m* de Indias
guise [gaɪz] apariencia *f*; ***under the guise of*** bajo la apariencia de
gui·tar [gɪ'tɑːr] guitarra *f*
gui'tar case estuche *m* de guitarra
gui·tar·ist [gɪ'tɑːrɪst] guitarrista *m/f*
gui'tar play·er guitarrista *m/f*
gulf [gʌlf] golfo *m*; *fig* abismo *m*; ***the Gulf*** el Golfo
Gulf of 'Mex·i·co Golfo *m* de México
gull [gʌl] *bird* gaviota *f*
gul·let ['gʌlɪt] ANAT esófago *m*
gul·li·ble ['gʌlɪbl] *adj* crédulo, ingenuo
gulp [gʌlp] **1** *n of water etc* trago *m* **2** *v/i in surprise* tragar saliva
◆ **gulp down** *v/t drink* tragar; *food* engullir
gum[1] [gʌm] *in mouth* encía *f*
gum[2] [gʌm] *n* (*glue*) pegamento *m*, cola *f*; (*chewing gum*) chicle *m*
gump·tion ['gʌmpʃn] sentido *m* común
gun [gʌn] *pistol, revolver* pistola *f*; *rifle* rifle *m*; *cannon* cañón *m*
◆ **gun down** *v/t* (*pret & pp* ***gunned***) matar a tiros
'**gun·fire** disparos *mpl*
'**gun·man** hombre *m* armado
'**gun·point**: ***at gunpoint*** a punta de pistola
'**gun·shot** disparo *m*, tiro *m*
'**gun·shot wound** herida *f* de bala
gur·gle ['gɜːrgl] *v/i of baby* gorjear; *of drain* gorgotear
gu·ru ['guru] *fig* gurú *m*
gush [gʌʃ] *v/i of liquid* manar, salir a chorros
gush·y ['gʌʃɪ] *adj* F (*enthusiastic*) efusivo, exagerado
gust [gʌst] ráfaga *f*
gus·to ['gʌstoʊ] entusiasmo *m*; ***with gusto*** con entusiasmo
gust·y ['gʌstɪ] *adj weather* ventoso, con viento racheado; ***gusty wind*** viento *m* racheado
gut [gʌt] **1** *n* intestino *m*; F (*stomach*) tripa *f* F **2** *v/t* (*pret & pp* ***gutted***) (*destroy*) destruir
guts [gʌts] *npl* F (*courage*) agallas *fpl* F
guts·y ['gʌtsɪ] *adj* F (*brave*) valiente, con muchas agallas F
gut·ter ['gʌtər] *on sidewalk* cuneta *f*; *on roof* canal *m*, canalón *m*
guy [gɑɪ] F tipo *m* F, *Span* tío *m* F; ***hey, you guys*** eh, gente
guz·zle ['gʌzl] *v/t* tragar, engullir
gym [dʒɪm] gimnasio *m*
gym·na·si·um [dʒɪm'neɪzɪəm] gimnasio *m*
gym·nast ['dʒɪmnæst] gimnasta *m/f*
gym·nas·tics [dʒɪm'næstɪks] gimnasia *f*
'**gym shoes** *npl* zapatillas *fpl* de gimnasia
gy·nae·col·o·gy *etc Br* → ***gynecology*** *etc*
gy·ne·col·o·gy [gaɪnɪ'kɑːlədʒɪ] ginecología *f*
gy·ne·col·ogist [gaɪnɪ'kɑːlədʒɪst] ginecólogo(-a) *m(f)*
gyp·sy ['dʒɪpsɪ] gitano(-a) *m(f)*

H

hab·it ['hæbɪt] hábito *m*, costumbre *m*; ***get into the habit of doing sth*** adquirir el hábito de hacer algo
hab·it·a·ble ['hæbɪtəbl] *adj* habitable
hab·i·tat ['hæbɪtæt] hábitat *m*
ha·bit·u·al [hə'bɪtʊəl] *adj* habitual
hack [hæk] *n poor writer* gacetillero(-a) *m(f)*
hack·er ['hækər] COMPUT pirata *m/f* informático(-a)
hack·neyed ['hæknɪd] *adj* manido
had [hæd] *pret & pp* → ***have***
had·dock ['hædək] eglefino *m*
hag·gard ['hægərd] *adj* demacrado
hag·gle ['hægl] *v/i* regatear; ***haggle over sth*** regatear algo
hail [heɪl] *n* granizo *m*
'**hail·stone** piedra *f* de granizo
'**hail·storm** granizada *f*
hair [her] pelo *m*, cabello *m*; *single* pelo *m*; (*body hair*) vello *m*; ***have short / long hair*** tener el pelo corto / largo
'**hair·brush** cepillo *m*
'**hair·cut** corte *m* de pelo; ***have a haircut*** cortarse el pelo
'**hair·do** F peinado *m*
'**hair·dress·er** peluquero(-a) *m(f)*; ***at the hairdresser*** en la peluquería
'**hair·dri·er**, '**hair·dry·er** secador *m* (de pelo)
hair·less ['herlɪs] *adj* sin pelo
'**hair·pin** horquilla *f*
hair·pin 'bend curva *f* muy cerrada
hair-rais·ing ['hereɪzɪŋ] *adj* espeluznante
hair re·mov·er [herɪ'muːvər] depilatorio *m*
'**hair's breadth** *fig*: ***by a hair's breadth*** por un pelo
hair-split·ting ['hersplɪtɪŋ] *n* sutilezas *fpl*
'**hair spray** laca *f*
'**hair·style** peinado *m*
'**hair·styl·ist** estilista *m/f*, peluquero(-a) *m(f)*
hair·y ['herɪ] *adj arm*, *animal* peludo; F (*frightening*) espeluznante
half [hæf] **1** *n* (*pl* ***halves*** [hævz]) mitad *f*; ***half past ten*** las diez y media; ***half after ten*** las diez y media; ***half an hour*** media hora; ***half a pound*** media libra; ***go halves with s.o. on sth*** ir a medias con alguien en algo **2** *adj* medio; ***at half price*** a mitad de precio **3** *adv* a medias; ***half finished*** a medio acabar
half 'board *Br* media pensión *f*
half-heart·ed [hæf'hɑːrtɪd] *adj* desganado
half 'time 1 *n* SP descanso *m* **2** *adj*: ***half time job*** trabajo *m* a tiempo parcial; ***half time score*** marcador *m* en el descanso
half'way 1 *adj stage*, *point* intermedio **2** *adv* a mitad de camino
hall [hɒːl] *large room* sala *f*; (*hallway in house*) vestíbulo *m*
Hal·low·e'en [hæloʊ'wiːn] *víspera de Todos los Santos*
halo ['heɪloʊ] halo *m*
halt [hɒːlt] **1** *v/i* detenerse **2** *v/t* detener **3** *n* alto *m*; ***come to a halt*** detenerse
halve [hæv] *v/t input*, *costs*, *effort* reducir a la mitad; *apple* partir por la mitad
ham [hæm] jamón *m*
ham·burg·er ['hæmbɜːrgər] hamburguesa *f*
ham·mer ['hæmər] **1** *n* martillo *m* **2** *v/i*: ***hammer at the door*** golpear la puerta
ham·mock ['hæmək] hamaca *f*
ham·per[1] ['hæmpər] *n for food* cesta *f*
ham·per[2] *v/t* (*obstruct*) estorbar, obstaculizar
ham·ster ['hæmstər] hámster *m*
hand [hænd] *n* mano *m*; *of clock* manecilla *f*; (*worker*) brazo *m*; ***at hand, to hand*** a mano; ***at first hand*** de primera mano, directamente; ***by hand*** a mano; ***on the one hand ..., on the other hand*** por una parte ..., por otra parte; ***the work is in hand*** el trabajo se está llevando a cabo; ***on your right hand*** a mano derecha; ***hands off!*** ¡fuera las manos!; ***hands up!*** ¡arriba las manos!; ***change hands*** cambiar de manos; ***give s.o. a hand*** echar un a mano a alguien
◆ **hand down** *v/t* transmitir
◆ **hand in** *v/t* entregar
◆ **hand on** *v/t* pasar
◆ **hand out** *v/t* repartir
◆ **hand over** *v/t* entregar
'**hand·bag** *Br* bolso *m*, *L.Am.* cartera *f*
'**hand·book** manual *m*
'**hand·cuff** *v/t* esposar
hand·cuffs ['hæn(d)kʌfs] *npl* esposas *fpl*
hand·i·cap ['hændɪkæp] *n* desventaja *f*
hand·i·capped ['hændɪkæpt] *adj physically* minusválido, disminuido; ***handicapped by lack of funds*** en desventaja por carecer de fondos
hand·i·craft ['hændɪkræft] artesanía *f*
hand·i·work ['hændɪwɜːrk] manuali-

dades *fpl*
hand·ker·chief ['hæŋkərʧɪf] pañuelo *m*
han·dle ['hændl] **1** *n of door* manilla *f*; *of suitcase* asa *f*; *of pan, knife* mango *m* **2** *v/t goods, difficult person* manejar; *case, deal* llevar, encargarse de; ***let me handle this*** deja que me ocupe yo de esto
han·dle·bars ['hændlbɑːrz] *npl* manillar *m*, *L.Am.* manubrio *m*
'**hand lug·gage** equipaje *m* de mano
hand·made [hæn(d)'meɪd] *adj* hecho a mano
'**hand·rail** barandilla *f*
'**hand·shake** apretón *m* de manos
hands-off [hændz'ɑːf] *adj* no intervencionista
hand·some ['hænsəm] *adj* guapo, atractivo
hands-on [hændz'ɑːn] *adj* práctico; ***he has a hands-on style of management*** le gusta implicarse en todos los aspectos de la gestión
'**hand·writ·ing** caligrafía *f*
hand·writ·ten ['hændrɪtn] *adj* escrito a mano
hand·y ['hændɪ] *adj tool, device* práctico; ***it's handy for the shops*** está muy cerca de las tiendas; ***it might come in handy*** nos puede venir muy bien
hang [hæŋ] **1** *v/t* (*pret & pp* **hung**) *picture* colgar; *person* colgar, ahorcar (*pret & pp* **hanged**) **2** *v/i* (*pret & pp* **hung**) colgar; *of dress, hair* caer, colgar **3** *n*: ***get the hang of sth*** F agarrarle el tranquillo a algo F
◆ **hang about** *v/i*: ***he's always hanging about on the street corner*** siempre está rondando por la esquina; ***hang about a minute!*** F ¡un momento!
◆ **hang on** *v/i* (*wait*) esperar
◆ **hang on to** *v/t* (*keep*) conservar; ***do you mind if I hang on to it for a while?*** ¿te importa si me lo quedo durante un tiempo?
◆ **hang up** *v/i* TELEC colgar
han·gar ['hæŋər] hangar *m*
hang·er ['hæŋər] *for clothes* percha *f*
hang glid·er ['hæŋglaɪdər] *person* piloto *m* de ala delta; *device* ala *f* delta
hang glid·ing ['hæŋglaɪdɪŋ] ala *f* delta
'**hang·o·ver** resaca *f*
◆ **han·ker after** ['hæŋkər] *v/t* anhelar
han·kie, **han·ky** ['hæŋkɪ] F pañuelo *m*
hap·haz·ard [hæp'hæzərd] *adj* descuidado
hap·pen ['hæpn] *v/i* ocurrir, pasar, suceder; ***if you happen to see him*** si por casualidad lo vieras; ***what has happened to you?*** ¿qué te ha pasado?
◆ **happen across** *v/t* encontrar por casualidad
hap·pen·ing ['hæpnɪŋ] suceso *m*
hap·pi·ly ['hæpɪlɪ] *adv* alegremente; (*luckily*) afortunadamente
hap·pi·ness ['hæpɪnɪs] felicidad *f*
hap·py ['hæpɪ] *adj* feliz, contento; *coincidence* afortunado
hap·py-go-'luck·y *adj* despreocupado
'**hap·py hour** *franja horaria en la que las bebidas son más baratas en los bares*
har·ass [hə'ræs] *v/t* acosar; *enemy* asediar, hostigar
har·assed [hər'æst] *adj* agobiado
har·ass·ment [hə'ræsmənt] acoso *m*; ***sexual harassment*** acoso *m* sexual
har·bor, *Br* **har·bour** ['hɑːrbər] **1** *n* puerto *m* **2** *v/t criminal* proteger; *grudge* albergar
hard [hɑːrd] *adj* duro; (*difficult*) difícil; *facts, evidence* real; ***hard of hearing*** duro de oído
'**hard·back** *n* libro *m* de tapas duras
hard-boiled [hɑːrd'bɔɪld] *adj egg* duro
'**hard cop·y** copia *f* impresa
'**hard core** *n* (*pornography*) porno *m* duro
hard 'cur·ren·cy divisa *f* fuerte
hard 'disk disco *m* duro
hard·en ['hɑːrdn] **1** *v/t* endurecer **2** *v/i of glue, attitude* endurecerse
'**hard hat** casco *m*; (*construction worker*) obrero(-a) *m*(*f*) (de la construcción)
hard·head·ed [hɑːrd'hedɪd] *adj* pragmático
hard·heart·ed [hɑːrd'hɑːrtɪd] *adj* insensible
hard 'line línea *f* dura; ***take a hard line on*** adoptar una línea dura en cuanto a
hard'lin·er partidario(-a) *m*(*f*) de la línea dura
hard·ly ['hɑːrdlɪ] *adv* apenas; ***did you agree? - hardly!*** ¿estuviste de acuerdo? - ¡en absoluto!
hard·ness ['hɑːrdnɪs] dureza *f*; (*difficulty*) dificultad *f*
hard'sell venta *f* agresiva
hard·ship ['hɑːrdʃɪp] penuria *f*, privación *f*
hard 'up *adj*: ***be hard up*** andar mal de dinero
'**hard·ware** ferretería *f*; COMPUT hardware *m*
'**hard·ware store** ferretería *f*
hard-work·ing [hɑːrd'wɜːrkɪŋ] *adj* trabajador
har·dy ['hɑːrdɪ] *adj* resistente
hare [her] liebre *f*
hare·brained ['herbreɪnd] *adj* alocado
harm [hɑːrm] **1** *n* daño *m*; ***it wouldn't do***

any harm to buy two por comprar dos no pasa nada **2** *v/t* hacer daño a, dañar
harm·ful ['hɑːrmfəl] *adj* dañino, perjudicial
harm·less ['hɑːrmlɪs] *adj* inofensivo; *fun* inocente
har·mo·ni·ous [hɑːr'moʊnɪəs] *adj* armonioso
har·mo·nize ['hɑːrmənaɪz] *v/i* armonizar
har·mo·ny ['hɑːrmənɪ] MUS, *fig* armonía *f*
harp [hɑːrp] *n* arpa *f*
◆ **harp on about** *v/t* F dar la lata con F
har·poon [hɑːr'puːn] *n* arpón *m*
harsh [hɑːʃ] *adj criticism, words* duro, severo; *color* chillón; *light* potente
harsh·ly ['hɑːrʃlɪ] *adv* con dureza *or* severidad
har·vest ['hɑːrvɪst] *n* cosecha *f*
hash [hæʃ] F: ***make a hash of*** fastidiar
hash browns *npl Span* patatas *fpl or L.Am.* papas *fpl* fritas
hash·ish ['hæʃiːʃ] hachís *m*
'**hash mark** almohadilla *f*, *el signo* '#'
haste [heɪst] *n* prisa *f*
has·ten ['heɪsn] *v/i*: ***hasten to do sth*** apresurarse en hacer algo
hast·i·ly ['heɪstɪlɪ] *adv* precipitadamente
hast·y ['heɪstɪ] *adj* precipitado
hat [hæt] sombrero *m*
hatch [hætʃ] *n for serving food* trampilla *f*; *on ship* escotilla *f*
◆ **hatch out** *v/i of eggs* romperse; *of chicks* salir del cascarón
hatch·et ['hætʃɪt] hacha *f*; ***bury the hatchet*** enterrar el hacha de guerra
hate [heɪt] **1** *n* odio *m* **2** *v/t* odiar
ha·tred ['heɪtrɪd] odio *m*
haugh·ty ['hɒːtɪ] *adj* altanero
haul [hɒːl] **1** *n of fish* captura *f*; *of robbery* botín *m* **2** *v/t* (*pull*) arrastrar
haul·age ['hɒːlɪdʒ] transporte *m*
'**haul·age com·pa·ny** empresa *f* de transportes
haul·i·er ['hɒːlɪr] transportista *m*
haunch [hɒːntʃ] *of person* trasero *m*; *of animal* pierna *f*
haunt [hɒːnt] **1** *v/t*: ***this place is haunted*** en este lugar hay fantasmas **2** *n* lugar *m* favorito
haunt·ing ['hɒːntɪŋ] *adj tune* fascinante
Ha·van·a [hə'vænə] *n* La Habana
have [hæv] **1** *v/t* (*pret & pp* ***had***) (*own*) tener ◇ *breakfast, lunch* tomar
◇ ***I don't have a TV*** no tengo televisión; ***can I have a coffee?*** ¿me da un café?; ***can I have more time?*** ¿me puede dar más tiempo?; ***do you have …?*** ¿tiene …?
◇ *must*: ***have*** (***got***) ***to*** tener que
◇ *causative*: ***I'll have it faxed to you*** te lo mandaré por fax; ***I'll have have it repaired*** haré que lo arreglen; ***I had my hair cut*** me corté el pelo
◇ *v/aux*: ***I have eaten*** he comido; ***have you seen her?*** ¿la has visto?
◆ **have back** *v/t*: ***when can I have it back?*** ¿cuándo me lo devolverá?
◆ **have on** *v/t* (*wear*) llevar puesto; ***do you have anything on tonight?*** (*have planned*) ¿tenéis algo planeado para esta noche?
ha·ven ['heɪvn] *fig* refugio *m*
hav·oc ['hævək] estragos *mpl*; ***play havoc with*** hacer estragos en
hawk [hɒːk] *also fig* halcón *m*
hay [heɪ] heno *m*
'**hay fe·ver** fiebre *f* del heno
haz·ard ['hæzərd] *n* riesgo *m*, peligro *m*
'**haz·ard lights** *npl* MOT luces *fpl* de emergencia
haz·ard·ous ['hæzərdəs] *adj* peligroso, arriesgado; ***hazardous waste*** residuos *mpl* peligrosos
haze [heɪz] neblina *f*
ha·zel ['heɪzl] *n tree* avellano *m*
'**ha·zel·nut** avellana *f*
haz·y ['heɪzɪ] *adj image, memories* confuso, vago; ***I'm a bit hazy about it*** no lo tengo muy claro
he [hiː] *pron* él; ***he is French/a doctor*** es francés / médico; ***you're funny, he's not*** tú tienes gracia, él no
head [hed] **1** *n* cabeza *f*; (*boss, leader*) jefe(-a) *m*(*f*); *of school* director(a) *m*(*f*); *on beer* espuma *f*; *of nail, line* cabeza *f*; ***$15 a head*** 15 dólares por cabeza; ***heads or tails?*** ¿cara o cruz?; ***at the head of the list*** encabezando la lista; ***head over heels*** *fall* rodando; *fall in love* locamente; ***lose one's head*** (*go crazy*) perder la cabeza **2** *v/t* (*lead*) estar a la cabeza de; *ball* cabecear
◆ **head for** *v/t* dirigirse a *or* hacia
'**head·ache** dolor *m* de cabeza
'**head·band** cinta *f* para la cabeza
head·er ['hedər] *in soccer* cabezazo *m*; *in document* encabezamiento *m*
'**head·hunt** *v/t* COM buscar, captar
'**head·hunt·er** COM cazatalentos *m/f inv*
head·ing ['hedɪŋ] *in list* encabezamiento *m*
'**head·lamp** faro *m*
'**head·light** faro *m*
'**head·line** *n in newspaper* titular *m*; ***make the headlines*** saltar a los titulares
'**head·long** *adv fall* de cabeza
'**head·mas·ter** director *m*
'**head·mis·tress** directora *f*

H

head 'of·fice *of company* central *f*
head-'on 1 *adv crash* de frente **2** *adj crash* frontal
'head·phones *npl* auriculares *mpl*
'head·quar·ters *npl of party, organization* sede *f*; *of army* cuartel *m* general
'head·rest reposacabezas *f inv*
'head·room *under bridge* gálibo *m*; *in car* espacio *m* vertical
'head·scarf pañuelo *m* (para la cabeza)
'head·strong *adj* cabezudo, testarudo
head 'teach·er director(a) *m(f)*
head 'wait·er maître *m*
'head·wind viento *m* contrario
head·y ['hedɪ] *adj drink, wine etc* que se sube a la cabeza
heal [hiːl] *v/t* curar
◆ **heal up** *v/i* curarse
health [helθ] salud *f*; ***your health!*** ¡a tu salud!
'health club gimnasio *m* (*con piscina, pista de tenis, sauna etc*)
'health food comida *f* integral
'health food store tienda *f* de comida integral
'health in·su·rance seguro *m* de enfermedad
'health re·sort centro *m* de reposo
health·y ['helθɪ] *adj person* sano; *food, lifestyle* saludable; *economy* saneado
heap [hiːp] *n* montón *m*
◆ **heap up** *v/t* amontonar
hear [hɪr] *v/t & v/i* (*pret & pp* ***heard***) oír
◆ **hear about** *v/t*: ***have you heard about Mike?*** ¿te has enterado de lo de Mike?; ***they're bound to hear about it sooner or later*** se van a enterar tarde o temprano
◆ **hear from** *v/t* (*have news from*) tener noticias de
hear·ing ['hɪrɪŋ] oído *m*; LAW vista *f*; ***his hearing is not so good now*** ahora ya no oye tan bien; ***she was within hearing / out of hearing*** estaba / no estaba lo suficientemente cerca como para oírlo
'hear·ing aid audífono *m*
'hear·say rumores *mpl*; ***by hearsay*** de oídas
hearse [hɜːrs] coche *m* fúnebre
heart [hɑːrt] *also fig* corazón *m*; *of problem* meollo *m*; ***know sth by heart*** saber algo de memoria; ***hearts*** *in cards* corazones *mpl*
'heart at·tack infarto *m*
'heart·beat latido *m*
heart·break·ing ['hɑːrtbreɪkɪŋ] *adj* desgarrador
'heart·brok·en *adj* descorazonado
'heart·burn acidez *f* (de estómago)
'heart fail·ure paro *m* cardíaco
heart·felt ['hɑːrtfelt] *adj sympathy* sincero
hearth [hɑːrθ] chimenea *f*
heart·less ['hɑːrtlɪs] *adj* despiadado
heart·rend·ing ['hɑːrtrendɪŋ] *adj plea, sight* desgarrador
'heart throb F ídolo *m*
'heart trans·plant transplante *m* de corazón
heart·y ['hɑːrtɪ] *adj appetite* voraz; *meal* copioso; *person* cordial, campechano
heat [hiːt] *n* calor *m*
◆ **heat up** *v/t* calentar
heat·ed ['hiːtɪd] *adj swimming pool* climatizado; *discussion* acalorado
heat·er ['hiːtər] *in room* estufa *f*; ***turn on the heater*** *in car* enciende la calefacción
hea·then ['hiːðn] *n* pagano(-a) *m(f)*
heath·er ['heðər] brezo *m*
heat·ing ['hiːtɪŋ] calefacción *f*
'heat·proof, **'heat-re·sis·tant** *adj* resistente al calor
'heat·stroke insolación *f*
'heat·wave ola *f* de calor
heave [hiːv] *v/t* (*lift*) subir
heav·en ['hevn] cielo *m*; ***good heavens!*** ¡Dios mío!
heav·en·ly ['hevənlɪ] *adj* F divino F
heav·y ['hevɪ] *adj* pesado; *cold, rain, accent, loss* fuerte; *smoker, drinker* empedernido; *loss of life* grande; *bleeding* abundante; ***there's heavy traffic*** hay mucho tráfico
heav·y-'du·ty *adj* resistente
'heav·y·weight *adj* SP de los pesos pesados
heck·le ['hekl] *v/t* interrumpir (*molestando*)
hec·tic ['hektɪk] *adj* vertiginoso, frenético
hedge [hedʒ] *n* seto *m*
hedge·hog ['hedʒhɑːg] erizo *m*
hedge·row ['hedʒroʊ] seto *m*
heed [hiːd] *v/t*: ***pay heed to ...*** hacer caso de ...
heel [hiːl] *of foot* talón *m*; *of shoe* tacón *m*
'heel bar zapatería *f*
hef·ty ['heftɪ] *adj weight, suitcase* pesado; *person* robusto
height [haɪt] altura *f*; ***at the height of the season*** en plena temporada
height·en ['haɪtn] *v/t effect, tension* intensificar
heir [er] heredero *m*
heir·ess ['erɪs] heredera *f*
held [held] *pret & pp* → ***hold***
hel·i·cop·ter ['helɪkɑːptər] helicóptero *m*
hell [hel] infierno *m*; ***what the hell are you doing / do you want?*** F ¿qué de-

H

monios estás haciendo / quieres? F: ***go to hell!*** F ¡vete a paseo! F; ***a hell of a lot*** F un montonazo F; ***one hell of a nice guy*** F un tipo muy simpático *or Span* legal F
hel·lo [hə'loʊ] hola; TELEC ¿sí?, *Span* ¿diga?, *Am* ¿alo?, *Rpl* ¿oigo?, *Mex* ¿bueno?; ***say hello to s.o.*** saludar a alguien
helm [helm] NAUT timón *m*
hel·met ['helmɪt] casco *m*
help [help] **1** *n* ayuda *f*; ***help!*** ¡socorro! **2** *v/t* ayudar; ***just help yourself** to food* toma lo que quieras; ***I can't help it*** no puedo evitarlo; ***I couldn't help laughing*** no pude evitar reírme
help·er ['helpər] ayudante *m/f*
help·ful ['helpfəl] *adj advice* útil; *person* servicial
help·ing ['helpɪŋ] *of food* ración *f*
help·less ['helplɪs] *adj* (*unable to cope*) indefenso; (*powerless*) impotente
help·less·ly ['helplɪslɪ] *adv* impotentemente
help·less·ness ['helplɪsnɪs] impotencia *f*
'help screen COMPUT pantalla *f* de ayuda
hem [hem] *n of dress etc* dobladillo *m*
hem·i·sphere ['hemɪsfɪr] hemisferio *m*
'hem·line bajo *m*
hem·or·rhage ['hemərɪdʒ] **1** *n* hemorragia *f* **2** *v/i* sangrar
hen [hen] gallina *f*
hench·man ['hentʃmən] *pej* sicario *m*
'hen par·ty despedida *f* de soltera
hen·pecked ['henpekt] *adj*: ***henpecked husband*** calzonazos *mpl*
hep·a·ti·tis [hepə'taɪtɪs] hepatitis *f*
her [hɜːr] **1** *adj* su; ***her ticket*** su entrada; ***her books*** sus libros **2** *pron direct object* la; *indirect object* le; *after prep* ella; ***I know her*** la conozco; ***I gave her the keys*** le di las llaves; ***I sold it to her*** se lo vendí; ***this is for her*** esto es para ella; ***who do you mean? - her*** ¿a quién te refieres? - a ella
herb [ɜːrb] hierba *f*
herb(al) 'tea ['ɜːrb(əl)] infusión *f*
herd [hɜːrd] *n* rebaño *m*; *of elephants* manada *f*
here [hɪr] *adv* aquí; ***over here*** aquí; ***here's to you!*** *as toast* ¡a tu salud!; ***here you are*** *giving sth* ¡aquí tienes!; ***here we are!*** *finding sth* ¡aquí está!
he·red·i·ta·ry [hə'redɪterɪ] *adj disease* hereditario
he·red·i·ty [hə'redɪtɪ] herencia *f*
her·i·tage ['herɪtɪdʒ] patrimonio *m*
her·mit ['hɜːrmɪt] ermitaño(-a) *m(f)*
her·ni·a ['hɜːrnɪə] MED hernia *f*
he·ro ['hɪroʊ] héroe *m*
he·ro·ic [hɪ'roʊɪk] *adj* heroico
he·ro·i·cal·ly [hɪ'roʊɪklɪ] *adv* heroicamente
her·o·in ['heroʊɪn] heroína *f*
'her·o·in ad·dict heroinómano(-a) *m(f)*
her·o·ine ['heroʊɪn] heroína *f*
her·o·ism ['heroʊɪzm] heroísmo *m*
her·on ['herən] garza *f*
her·pes ['hɜːrpiːz] MED herpes *m*
her·ring ['herɪŋ] arenque *m*
hers [hɜːrz] *pron* el suyo, la suya; ***hers are red*** los suyos son rojos; ***that book is hers*** ese libro es suyo; ***a cousin of hers*** un primo suyo
her·self [hɜːr'self] *pron reflexive* se; *emphatic* ella misma; ***she hurt herself*** se hizo daño; ***when she saw herself in the mirror*** cuando se vio en el espejo; ***he saw it herself*** lo vio ella misma; ***by herself*** (*alone*) sola; (*without help*) ella sola, ella misma
hes·i·tant ['hezɪtənt] *adj* indeciso
hes·i·tant·ly ['hezɪtəntlɪ] *adv* con indecisión
hes·i·tate ['hezɪteɪt] *v/i* dudar, vacilar
hes·i·ta·tion [hezɪ'teɪʃn] vacilación *f*
het·er·o·sex·u·al [hetəroʊ'sekʃʊəl] *adj* heterosexual
hey·day ['heɪdeɪ] apogeo *m*
hi [haɪ] *int* ¡hola!
hi·ber·nate ['haɪbərneɪt] *v/i* hibernar
hic·cup ['hɪkʌp] *n* hipo *m*; (*minor problem*) tropiezo *m*, traspié *m*; ***have the hiccups*** tener hipo
hick [hɪk] *pej* F palurdo(-a) *m(f)* F, pueblerino(-a) *m(f)* F
'hick town *pej* F ciudad *f* provinciana
hid [hɪd] *pret* → ***hide***[1]
hid·den ['hɪdn] **1** *adj meaning, treasure* oculto **2** *pp* → ***hide***[1]
hid·den a'gen·da *fig* objetivo *m* secreto
hide[1] [haɪd] **1** *v/t* (*pret* ***hid***, *pp* ***hidden***) esconder **2** *v/i* (*pret* ***hid***, *pp* ***hidden***) esconderse
hide[2] *n of animal* escondrijo *m*
hide-and-'seek escondite *m*
'hide·a·way escondite *m*
hid·e·ous ['hɪdɪəs] *adj* espantoso, horrendo; *person* repugnante
hid·ing[1] ['haɪdɪŋ] (*beating*) paliza *f*
hid·ing[2] ['haɪdɪŋ]: ***be in hiding*** estar escondido; ***go into hiding*** esconderse
'hid·ing place escondite *m*
hi·er·ar·chy ['haɪrɑːrkɪ] jerarquía *f*
hi-fi ['haɪfaɪ] equipo *m* de alta fidelidad
high [haɪ] **1** *adj* alto; *wind* fuerte; (*on drugs*) colocado P; ***have a very high opinion of*** tener muy buena opinión de; ***high in the sky*** en lo alto; ***it is high time you understood*** ya va siendo hora de

H

que entiendas **2** *n* MOT directa *f*; *in statistics* máximo *m*; EDU escuela *f* secundaria, *Span* instituto *m* **3** *adv*: ***that's as high as we can go*** eso es lo máximo que podemos ofrecer
'high·brow *adj* intelectual
'high·chair trona *f*
high·'class *adj* de categoría
High 'Court Tribunal *m* Supremo
high 'div·ing salto *m* de trampolín
high-'fre·quen·cy *adj* de alta frecuencia
high-'grade *adj* de calidad superior
high-hand·ed [haɪ'hændɪd] *adj* despótico
high-heeled [haɪ'hiːld] *adj* de tacón alto
'high jump salto *m* de altura
high-'lev·el *adj* de alto nivel
'high life buena vida *f*
'high·light 1 *n* (*main event*) momento *m* cumbre; *in hair* reflejo *m* **2** *v/t with pen* resaltar; COMPUT seleccionar, resaltar
'high·light·er *pen* fluorescente *m*
high·ly ['haɪlɪ] *adv desirable*, *likely* muy; ***be highly paid*** estar muy bien pagado; ***think highly of s.o.*** tener una buena opinión de alguien
high·ly 'strung *adj* muy nervioso
high per'form·ance *adj drill*, *battery* de alto rendimiento
high-pitched [haɪ'pɪʧt] *adj* agudo
'high point *of life*, *career* punto *m* culminante
high-pow·ered [haɪ'paʊərd] *adj engine* potente; *intellectual* de alto(s) vuelo(s); *salesman* enérgico
high 'pres·sure 1 *n weather* altas presiones *fpl* **2** *adj* TECH a gran presión; *salesman* agresivo; *job*, *lifestyle* muy estresante
high 'priest sumo sacerdote *m*
'high school escuela *f* secundaria, *Span* instituto *m*
high so'ci·e·ty alta sociedad *f*
high-speed 'train tren *m* de alta velocidad
high 'tech 1 *n* alta *f* tecnología **2** *adj* de alta tecnología
high 'tide marea *f* alta
high 'wa·ter: ***at high water*** con la marea alta
'high·way autopista *f*
'high wire *in circus* cuerda *f* floja
hi·jack ['haɪdʒæk] **1** *v/t plane*, *bus* secuestrar **2** *n of plane*, *bus* secuestro *m*
hi·jack·er ['haɪdʒækər] *of plane*, *bus* secuestrador(a) *m*(*f*)
hike[1] [haɪk] **1** *n* caminata *f* **2** *v/i* caminar
hike[2] [haɪk] *n in prices* subida *f*
hik·er ['haɪkər] senderista *m/f*
hik·ing ['haɪkɪŋ] senderismo *m*
'hik·ing boots *npl* botas *fpl* de senderismo
hi·lar·i·ous [hɪ'lerɪəs] *adj* divertidísimo, graciosísimo
hill [hɪl] colina *f*; (*slope*) cuesta *f*
hill-bil·ly ['hɪlbɪlɪ] F *rústico montañés*
hill·side ['hɪlsaɪd] ladera *f*
hill·top ['hɪltɑːp] cumbre *f*
hill·y ['hɪlɪ] *adj* con colinas
hilt [hɪlt] puño *m*
him [hɪm] *pron direct object* lo; *indirect object* le; *after prep* él; ***I know him*** lo conozco; ***I gave him the keys*** le di las llaves; ***I sold it to him*** se lo vendí; ***this is for him*** esto es para él; ***who do you mean? - him*** ¿a quién te refieres? - a él
him·self [hɪm'self] *pron reflexive* se; *emphatic* él mismo; ***he hurt himself*** se hizo daño; ***when he saw himself in the mirror*** cuando se vio en el espejo; ***he saw it himself*** lo vio él mismo; ***by himself*** (*alone*) solo; (*without help*) él solo, él mismo
hind [haɪnd] *adj* trasero
hin·der ['hɪndər] *v/t* obstaculizar, entorpecer
hin·drance ['hɪndrəns] estorbo *m*, obstáculo *m*
hind·sight ['haɪndsaɪt]: ***with hindsight*** a posteriori
hinge [hɪndʒ] *n* bisagra *f*
◆ **hinge on** *v/t* depender de
hint [hɪnt] *n* (*clue*) pista *f*; (*piece of advice*) consejo *m*; (*implied suggestion*) indirecta *f*; *of red*, *sadness etc* rastro *m*
hip [hɪp] *n* cadera *f*
hip 'pock·et bolsillo *m* trasero
hip·po·pot·a·mus [hɪpə'pɑːtəməs] hipopótamo *m*
hire [haɪr] *v/t* alquilar
his [hɪz] **1** *adj* su; ***his ticket*** su entrada; ***his books*** sus libros **2** *pron* el suyo, la suya; ***his are red*** los suyos son rojos; ***that ticket is his*** esa entrada es suya; ***a cousin of his*** un primo suyo
His·pan·ic [hɪ'spænɪk] **1** *n* hispano(-a) *m*(*f*) **2** *adj* hispano, hispánico
hiss [hɪs] *v/i of snake*, *audience* silbar
his·to·ri·an [hɪ'stɔːrɪən] historiador(a) *m*(*f*)
his·tor·ic [hɪ'stɑːrɪk] *adj* histórico
his·tor·i·cal [hɪ'stɑːrɪkl] *adj* histórico
his·to·ry ['hɪstərɪ] historia *f*
hit [hɪt] **1** *v/t* (*pret & pp* ***hit***) golpear; (*collide with*) chocar contra; ***he was hit by a bullet*** le alcanzó una bala; ***it suddenly hit me*** (*I realized*) de repente me di cuenta; ***hit town*** (*arrive*) llegar a la ciudad **2** *n* (*blow*) golpe *m*; MUS, (*success*)

éxito *m*
◆ **hit back** *v/i physically* devolver el golpe; *verbally, with actions* responder
◆ **hit on** *v/t idea* dar con
◆ **hit out at** *v/t* (*criticize*) atacar
hit-and-run *adj*: ***hit-and-run accident*** *accidente en el que el vehículo causante se da a la fuga*
hitch [hɪʧ] **1** *n* (*problem*) contratiempo *m*; ***without a hitch*** sin ningún contratiempo **2** *v/t* enganchar; ***hitch sth to sth*** enganchar algo a algo; ***hitch a ride*** hacer autoestop **3** *v/i* (*hitchhike*) hacer autoestop
◆ **hitch up** *v/t wagon, trailer* enganchar
'**hitch·hike** *v/i* hacer autoestop
'**hitch·hik·er** autoestopista *m/f*
'**hitch·hik·ing** autoestop *m*
hi-'tech 1 *n* alta tecnología *f* **2** *adj* de alta tecnología
'**hit·list** lista *f* de blancos
'**hit·man** asesino *m* a sueldo
hit-or-'miss *adj* a la buena ventura
'**hit squad** grupo *m* de intervención especial
HIV [eɪʧaɪ'viː] *abbr* (= ***human immunodeficiency virus***) VIH *m* (= virus *m inv* de la inmunodeficiencia *hum*ana)
hive [haɪv] *for bees* colmena *f*
◆ **hive off** *v/t* (COM: *separate off*) desprenderse de
HIV-'pos·i·tive *adj* seropositivo
hoard [hɔːrd] **1** *n* reserva *f* **2** *v/t* hacer acopio de; *money* acumular
hoard·er ['hɔːrdər] acaparador(a) *m*(*f*)
hoarse [hɔːrs] *adj* ronco
hoax [hoʊks] *n* bulo *m*, engaño *m*; ***bomb hoax*** amenaza *f* falsa de bomba
hob [hɑːb] *on cooker* placa *f*
hob·ble ['hɑːbl] *v/i* cojear
hob·by ['hɑːbɪ] hobby *m*, afición *f*
ho·bo ['hoʊboʊ] F vagabundo(-a) *m*(*f*)
hock·ey ['hɑːkɪ] (*ice hockey*) hockey *m* sobre hielo
hog [hɑːg] *n* (*pig*) cerdo *m*, *L.Am.* chancho *m*
hoist [hɔɪst] **1** *n* montacargas *m inv*; *manual* elevador *m* **2** *v/t* (*lift*) levantar, subir; *flag* izar; ***they hoisted the winner up onto their shoulders*** subieron al ganador a hombros
ho·kum ['hoʊkəm] F (*nonsense*) tonterías *fpl*; (*sentimental stuff*) cursilería *f*
hold [hoʊld] **1** *v/t* (*pret & pp* ***held***) *in hand* llevar; (*support, keep in place*) sostener; *passport, license* tener; *prisoner, suspect* retener; (*contain*) contener; *job, post* ocupar; *course* mantener; ***hold my hand*** dame la mano; ***hold one's breath*** aguantar la respiración; ***he can hold his drink*** sabe beber; ***hold s.o. responsible*** hacer a alguien responsable; ***hold that …*** (*believe, maintain*) mantener que …; ***hold the line, please*** TELEC espere, por favor **2** *n in ship, plane* bodega *f*; ***take hold of sth*** agarrar algo; ***lose one's hold on sth*** *on rope* soltar algo; *on reality* perder el contacto con algo
◆ **hold against** *v/t*: ***hold sth against s.o.*** tener algo contra alguien
◆ **hold back 1** *v/t crowds* contener; *facts, information* guardar **2** *v/i* (*not tell all*): ***I'm sure he's holding back*** estoy seguro de que no dice todo lo que sabe
◆ **hold on** *v/i* (*wait*) esperar; ***now hold on a minute!*** ¡un momento!
◆ **hold on to** *v/t* (*keep*) guardar; *belief* aferrarse a
◆ **hold out 1** *v/t hand* tender; *prospect* ofrecer **2** *v/i of supplies* durar; (*survive*) resistir, aguantar
◆ **hold up 1** *v/t hand* levantar; *bank etc* atracar; (*make late*) retrasar; ***I was held up by the traffic*** he llegado tarde por culpa del tráfico; ***hold sth up as an example*** poner a alguien como ejemplo
◆ **hold with** *v/t* (*approve of*): ***I don't hold with that sort of behavior*** no me parece bien ese tipo de comportamiento
'**hold·all** *Br* bolsa *f*
hold·er ['hoʊldər] (*container*) receptáculo *m*; *of passport, ticket etc* titular *m/f*; *of record* poseedor(a) *m*(*f*)
'**hold·ing com·pa·ny** holding *m*
'**hold·up** (*robbery*) atraco *m*; (*delay*) retraso *m*
hole [hoʊl] *in sleeve, wood, bag* agujero *m*; *in ground* hoyo *m*
hol·i·day ['hɑːlədeɪ] *single day* día *f* de fiesta; *period* vacaciones *fpl*; ***take a holiday*** tomarse vacaciones
Hol·land ['hɑːlənd] Holanda
hol·low ['hɑːloʊ] *adj object* hueco; *cheeks* hundido; *promise* vacío
hol·ly ['hɑːlɪ] acebo *m*
hol·o·caust ['hɑːləkɒːst] holocausto *m*
hol·o·gram ['hɑːləgræm] holograma *m*
hol·ster ['hoʊlstər] pistolera *f*
ho·ly ['hoʊlɪ] *adj* santo
Ho·ly 'Spir·it Espíritu *m* Santo
'**Ho·ly Week** Semana *f* Santa
home [hoʊm] **1** *n* casa *f*; (*native country*) tierra *f*; *for old people* residencia *f*; ***New York is my home*** Nueva York es mi hogar; ***at home*** (*in house*) en casa; (*in country*) en mi / su / nuestra tierra; ***make yourself at home*** ponte cómodo; ***at home and abroad*** en el país y en el extranjero; ***at home*** SP en casa; ***work from ho-***

H

me trabajar desde casa **2** *adv* a casa; ***go home*** ir a casa; *to country* ir a mi / tu / su tierra; *to town, part of country* ir a mi / tu / su ciudad
ˈhome ad·dress domicilio *m*
home ˈbank·ing telebanca *f*, banca *f* electrónica
ˈhome·com·ing vuelta *f* a casa
home comˈput·er *Span* ordenador *m*, *L.Am.* computadora *f* doméstica
home·less [ˈhoʊmlɪs] *adj* sin casa; ***the homeless*** los sin casa
ˈhome·lov·ing *adj* hogareño
home·ly [ˈhoʊmlɪ] *adj* (*homeloving*) hogareño; (*not good-looking*) feúcho
H
homeˈmade *adj* casero
ˈhome match partido *m* en casa
home ˈmov·ie película *f* casera
ho·me·op·a·thy [hoʊmɪˈɑːpəθɪ] homeopatía *f*
ˈhome page *web site* página *f* personal; *on web site* página *f* inicial
ˈhome·sick *adj* nostálgico; ***be homesick*** tener morriña
ˈhome town ciudad *f* natal
home·ward [ˈhoʊmwərd] *adv to own house* a casa; *to own country* a mi país
ˈhome·work EDU deberes *mpl*
ˈhome·work·ing COM teletrabajo *m*
hom·i·cide [ˈhɑːmɪsaɪd] *crime* homicidio *m*; *police department* brigada *f* de homicidios
hom·o·graph [ˈhɑːməgræf] homógrafo *m*
ho·mo·pho·bi·a [hɑːməˈfoʊbɪə] homofobia *f*
ho·mo·sex·u·al [hɑːməˈsekʃʊəl] **1** *adj* homosexual **2** *n* homosexual *m/f*
Hon·du·ras [hɑːnˈdʊrəs] *n* Honduras
Hon·du·ran [hɑːnˈdʊrən] **1** *adj* hondureño **2** *n* hondureño(-a) *m(f)*
hon·est [ˈɑːnɪst] *adj* honrado
hon·est·ly [ˈɑːnɪstlɪ] *adv* honradamente; ***honestly!*** ¡desde luego!
hon·es·ty [ˈɑːnɪstɪ] honradez *f*
hon·ey [ˈhʌnɪ] miel *f*; F (*darling*) cariño *m*, vida *f* mía
ˈhon·ey·comb panal *m*
ˈhon·ey·moon *n* luna *f* de miel
honk [hɑːŋk] *v/t horn* tocar
hon·or [ˈɑːnər] **1** *n* honor *m* **2** *v/t* honrar
hon·or·a·ble [ˈɑːnrəbl] *adj* honorable
hon·our *etc Br* → ***honor*** *etc*
hood [hʊd] *over head* capucha *f*; *over cooker* campana *f* extractora; MOT capó *m*; F (*gangster*) matón(-ona) *m(f)*
hood·lum [ˈhuːdləm] matón(-ona) *m(f)*
hoof [huːf] casco *m*
hook [hʊk] gancho *m*; *to hang clothes on* colgador *m*; *for fishing* anzuelo *m*; ***off the hook*** TELEC descolgado
hooked [hʊkt] *adj* enganchado; ***be hooked on sth*** *on drugs, fig* estar enganchado a algo
hook·er [ˈhʊkər] F fulana *f* F
hook·ey [ˈhʊkɪ] F: ***play hookey*** hacer novillos, *Mex* irse de pinta, *S. Am.* hacerse la rabona
hoo·li·gan [ˈhuːlɪgən] gamberro(-a) *m(f)*
hoo·li·gan·ism [ˈhuːlɪgənɪzm] gamberrismo *m*
hoop [huːp] aro *m*
hoot [huːt] **1** *v/t horn* tocar **2** *v/i of car* dar bocinazos; *of owl* ulular
hoo·ver® [ˈhuːvər] **1** *n* aspirador *m*, aspiradora *f* **2** *v/t carpets, room* pasar el aspirador por, aspirar
hop¹ [hɑːp] *n plant* lúpulo *m*
hop² [hɑːp] *v/i* (*pret & pp* ***hopped***) saltar
hope [hoʊp] **1** *n* esperanza *f*; ***there's no hope of that*** no hay esperanza de eso **2** *v/i* esperar; ***hope for sth*** esperar algo; ***we all hope for peace*** todos ansiamos la paz **3** *v/t*: ***I hope you like it*** espero que te guste; ***I hope so*** eso espero; ***I hope not*** espero que no
hopeful [ˈhoʊpfəl] *adj* prometedor; ***I'm hopeful that …*** espero que …
hope·ful·ly [ˈhoʊpfəlɪ] *adv say, wait* esperanzadamente; ***hopefully he hasn't forgotten*** esperemos que no se haya olvidado
hope·less [ˈhoʊplɪs] *adj position, prospect* desesperado; (*useless: person*) inútil
ho·ri·zon [həˈraɪzn] horizonte *m*
hor·i·zon·tal [hɑːrɪˈzɑːntl] *adj* horizontal
hor·mone [ˈhɔːrmoʊn] hormona *f*
horn [hɔːrn] *of animal* cuerno *m*; MOT bocina *f*, claxon *m*
hor·net [ˈhɔːrnɪt] avispón *m*
horn-rimmed ˈspec·ta·cles [ˈhɔːrnrɪmd] *npl* gafas *fpl* de concha
horn·y [ˈhɔːrnɪ] *adj* F *sexually* cachondo F
hor·o·scope [ˈhɑːrəskoʊp] horóscopo *m*
hor·ri·ble [ˈhɑːrɪbl] *adj* horrible; *person* muy antipático
hor·ri·fy [ˈhɑːrɪfaɪ] *v/t* (*pret & pp* ***horrified***) horrorizar; ***I was horrified*** me quedé horrorizado
hor·ri·fy·ing [ˈhɑːrɪfaɪɪŋ] *adj* horroroso
hor·ror [ˈhɑːrər] horror *m*
ˈhor·ror mov·ie película *f* de terror
hors d'oeu·vre [ɔːrˈdɜːrv] entremés *m*
horse [hɔːrs] caballo *m*
ˈhorse·back: ***on horseback*** a caballo
horse ˈchest·nut castaño *m* de Indias
ˈhorse·pow·er caballo *m* (de vapor)
ˈhorse race carrera *f* de caballos
ˈhorse·shoe herradura *f*

hor·ti·cul·ture ['hɔːrtɪkʌltʃər] horticultura *f*
hose [hoʊz] *n* manguera *f*
hos·pice ['hɑːspɪs] hospital *m* para enfermos terminales
hos·pi·ta·ble [hɑː'spɪtəbl] *adj* hospitalario
hos·pi·tal ['hɑːspɪtl] hospital *m*; ***go into the hospital*** ir al hospital
hos·pi·tal·i·ty [hɑːspɪ'tælətɪ] hospitalidad *f*
host [hoʊst] *n at party, reception* anfitrión *m*; *of* TV *program* presentador(a) *m(f)*
hos·tage ['hɑːstɪdʒ] rehén *m*; ***take s.o. hostage*** tomar a alguien como rehén
'hos·tage tak·er *persona que toma rehenes*
hos·tel ['hɑːstl] *for students* residencia *f*; (*youth hostel*) albergue *m*
hos·tess ['hoʊstɪs] *at party, reception* anfitriona *f*; *on airplane* azafata *f*; *in bar* cabaretera *f*
hos·tile ['hɑːstl] *adj* hostil
hos·til·i·ty [hɑː'stɪlətɪ] *of attitude* hostilidad *f*; ***hostilities*** hostilidades *fpl*
hot [hɑːt] *adj weather* caluroso; *object, water, food* caliente; (*spicy*) picante; ***it's hot*** *of weather* hace calor; ***I'm hot*** tengo calor; ***she's pretty hot at math*** F (*good*) es una fenómena con las matemáticas F
'hot dog perrito *m* caliente
ho·tel [hoʊ'tel] hotel *m*
'hot·plate placa *f*
'hot spot *military, political* punto *m* caliente
hour [aʊr] hora *f*
hour·ly ['aʊrlɪ] *adj*: ***at hourly intervals*** a intervalos de una hora; ***an hourly bus*** un autobús que pasa cada hora
house [haʊs] *n* casa *f*; ***at your house*** en tu casa
'house·boat barco-vivienda *f*
'house·break·ing allanamiento *m* de morada
'house·hold hogar *m*
house·hold 'name nombre *m* conocido
'house hus·band amo *m* de casa
'house·keep·er ama *f* de llaves
'house·keep·ing *activity* tareas *fpl* domésticas; *money* dinero *m* para gastos domésticos
House of Rep·re'sent·a·tives *npl* Cámara *f* de Representantes
house·warm·ing (party) ['haʊswɔːrmɪŋ] fiesta *f* de estreno de una casa
'house·wife ama *f* de casa
'house·work tareas *fpl* domésticas
hous·ing ['haʊzɪŋ] vivienda *f*; TECH cubierta *f*
'hous·ing con·di·tions *npl* condiciones *fpl* de la vivienda
hov·el ['hɑːvl] chabola *f*
hov·er ['hɑːvər] *v/i of bird* cernerse; *of helicopter* permanecer inmóvil en el aire
'hov·er·craft aerodeslizador *m*, hovercraft *m*
how [haʊ] *adv* cómo; ***how are you?*** ¿cómo estás?; ***how about …?*** ¿qué te parece …?; ***how about a drink?*** ¿te apetece tomar algo?; ***how much?*** ¿cuánto?; ***how much is it?*** *of cost* ¿cuánto vale *or* cuesta?; ***how many?*** ¿cuántos?; ***how often?*** ¿con qué frecuencia?; ***how funny / sad!*** ¡qué divertido / triste!
how'ev·er *adv* sin embargo; ***however big / rich / small they are*** independientemente de lo grandes / ricos / pequeños que sean
howl [haʊl] *v/i of dog* aullido *m*; *of person in pain* alarido *m*; *with laughter* risotada *f*
howl·er ['haʊlər] (*mistake*) error *m* garrafal
hub [hʌb] *of wheel* cubo *m*
'hub·cap tapacubos *m inv*
◆ **hud·dle together** ['hʌdl] *v/i* apiñarse, acurrucarse
hue [hjuː] tonalidad *f*
huff [hʌf]: ***be in a huff*** estar enfurruñado
hug [hʌg] *v/t* (*pret & pp* ***hugged***) abrazar
huge [hjuːdʒ] *adj* enorme
hull [hʌl] casco *m*
hul·la·ba·loo [hʌləbə'luː] alboroto *m*
hum [hʌm] **1** *v/t* (*pret & pp* ***hummed***) *song, tune* tararear **2** *v/i* (*pret & pp* ***hummed***) *of person* tararear; *of machine* zumbar
hu·man ['hjuːmən] **1** *n* humano *m* **2** *adj* humano; ***human error*** error *m or* fallo *m* humano
hu·man 'be·ing ser *m* humano
hu·mane [hjuː'meɪn] *adj* humano
hu·man·i·tar·i·an [hjuːmænɪ'terɪən] *adj* humanitario
hu·man·i·ty [hjuː'mænətɪ] humanidad *f*
hu·man 'race raza *f* humana
hu·man re'sources *npl* recursos *mpl* humanos
hum·ble ['hʌmbl] *adj* humilde
hum·drum ['hʌmdrʌm] *adj* monótono, anodino
hu·mid ['hjuːmɪd] *adj* húmedo
hu·mid·i·fi·er [hjuː'mɪdɪfaɪr] humidificador *m*
hu·mid·i·ty [hjuː'mɪdətɪ] humedad *f*
hu·mil·i·ate [hjuː'mɪlɪeɪt] *v/t* humillar
hu·mil·i·at·ing [hjuː'mɪlɪeɪtɪŋ] *adj* humillante

hu·mil·i·a·tion [hjuːmɪlɪ'eɪʃn] humillación *f*
hu·mil·i·ty [hjuː'mɪlətɪ] humildad *f*
hu·mor ['hjuːmər] humor *m*; ***sense of humor*** sentido *m* del *hum*or
hu·mor·ous ['hjuːmərəs] *adj* gracioso
hu·mour *Br* → **humor**
hump [hʌmp] **1** *n of camel, person* joroba *f*; *on road* bache *m* **2** *v/t* F (*carry*) acarrear
hunch [hʌntʃ] *n* (*idea*) presentimiento *m*, corazonada *f*
hun·dred ['hʌndrəd] cien *m*; ***a hundred dollars*** cien dólares; ***hundreds of birds*** cientos *or* centenares de aves; ***a hundred and one*** ciento uno; ***two hundred*** doscientos
hun·dredth ['hʌndrədθ] *n & adj* centésimo
'hun·dred·weight *43 kilogramos*
hung [hʌŋ] *pret & pp* → **hang**
Hun·gar·i·an [hʌŋ'gerɪən] **1** *adj* húngaro **2** *n person* húngaro(-a) *m*(*f*); *language* húngaro *m*
Hun·ga·ry ['hʌŋgərɪ] Hungría
hun·ger ['hʌŋgər] *n* hambre *f*
hung-'o·ver *adj*: ***be hung-over*** tener resaca
hun·gry ['hʌŋgrɪ] *adj* hambriento; ***I'm hungry*** tengo hambre
hunk [hʌŋk] *n* cacho *m*, pedazo *m*; F *man* cachas *m inv* F
hun·ky-dor·y [hʌŋkɪ'dɔːrɪ] *adj* F: ***everything's hunky-dory*** todo va de perlas
hunt [hʌnt] **1** *n* caza *f*, búsqueda *f* **2** *v/t animal* cazar
◆ **hunt for** *v/t* buscar
hunt·er ['hʌntər] cazador(a) *m*(*f*)
hunt·ing ['hʌntɪŋ] caza *f*
hur·dle ['hɜːrdl] SP valla *f*; (*fig*: *obstacle*) obstáculo *m*
hur·dler ['hɜːrdlər] SP vallista *m/f*
hur·dles *npl* SP vallas *fpl*
hurl [hɜːrl] *v/t* lanzar
hur·ray [hʊ'reɪ] *int* ¡hurra!
hur·ri·cane ['hʌrɪkən] huracán *m*
hur·ried ['hʌrɪd] *adj* apresurado
hur·ry ['hʌrɪ] **1** *n* prisa *f*; ***be in a hurry*** tener prisa **2** *v/i* (*pret & pp* ***hurried***) darse prisa
◆ **hurry up 1** *v/i* darse prisa; ***hurry up!*** ¡date prisa! **2** *v/t* meter prisa a
hurt [hɜːrt] **1** *v/i* (*pret & pp* ***hurt***) doler; ***does it hurt?*** ¿te duele? **2** *v/t* (*pret & pp* ***hurt***) *physically* hacer daño a; *emotionally* herir; ***I've hurt my hand*** me he hecho daño en la mano; ***did he hurt you?*** ¿te hizo daño?
hus·band ['hʌzbənd] marido *m*
hush [hʌʃ] *n* silencio *m*; ***hush!*** ¡silencio!
◆ **hush up** *v/t scandal etc* acallar
husk [hʌsk] *of peanuts etc* cáscara *f*
hus·ky ['hʌskɪ] *adj voice* áspero
hus·tle ['hʌsl] **1** *n* agitación *f*; ***hustle and bustle*** ajetreo *m* **2** *v/t person* empujar
hut [hʌt] cabaña *f*, refugio *m*; *workman's* cobertizo *m*
hy·a·cinth ['haɪəsɪnθ] jacinto *m*
hy·brid ['haɪbrɪd] *n* híbrido *m*
hy·drant ['haɪdrənt] boca *f* de riego *or* de incendios
hy·draul·ic [haɪ'drɒːlɪk] *adj* hidráulico
hy·dro·e'lec·tric [haɪdroʊɪ'lektrɪk] *adj* hidroeléctrico
'hy·dro·foil ['haɪdrəfɔɪl] *boat* hidroplaneador *m*
hy·dro·gen ['haɪdrədʒən] hidrógeno *m*
'hy·dro·gen bomb bomba *f* de hidrógeno
hy·giene ['haɪdʒiːn] higiene *f*
hy·gien·ic [haɪ'dʒiːnɪk] *adj* higiénico
hymn [hɪm] himno *m*
hype [haɪp] *n* bombo *m*
hy·per·ac·tive [haɪpər'æktɪv] *adj* hiperactivo
hy·per·sen·si·tive [haɪpər'sensɪtɪv] *adj* hipersensible
hy·per·ten·sion [haɪpər'tenʃn] hipertensión *f*
hy·per·text ['haɪpərtekst] COMPUT hipertexto *m*
hy·phen ['haɪfn] guión *m*
hyp·no·sis [hɪp'noʊsɪs] hipnosis *f*
hyp·no·ther·a·py [hɪpnoʊ'θerəpɪ] hipnoterapia *f*
hyp·no·tize ['hɪpnətaɪz] *v/t* hipnotizar
hy·po·chon·dri·ac [haɪpə'kɑːndrɪæk] *n* hipocondríaco(-a) *m*(*f*)
hy·poc·ri·sy [hɪ'pɑːkrəsɪ] hipocresía *f*
hyp·o·crite ['hɪpəkrɪt] hipócrita *m/f*
hyp·o·crit·i·cal [hɪpə'krɪtɪkl] *adj* hipócrita
hy·po·ther·mi·a [haɪpoʊ'θɜːrmɪə] hipotermia *f*
hy·poth·e·sis [haɪ'pɑːθəsɪs] (*pl* ***hypotheses*** [haɪ'pɑːθəsiːz]) hipótesis *f inv*
hy·po·thet·i·cal [haɪpə'θetɪkl] *adj* hipotético
hys·ter·ec·to·my [hɪstə'rektəmɪ] histerectomía *f*
hys·te·ri·a [hɪ'stɪrɪə] histeria *f*
hys·ter·i·cal [hɪ'sterɪkl] *adj person, laugh* histérico; F (*very funny*) tronchante F; ***become hysterical*** ponerse *hist*érico
hys·ter·ics [hɪ'sterɪks] *npl* ataque *f* de *hist*eria; (*laughter*) ataque *f* de risa

H

I

I [aɪ] *pron* yo; ***I am English/a student*** soy inglés / estudiante; ***you're crazy, I'm not*** tú estás loco, yo no
ice [aɪs] *in drink, on road* hielo *m*; ***break the ice*** *fig* romper el hielo
◆ **ice up** *v/i of engine, wings* helarse
ice·berg ['aɪsbɜːrg] iceberg *m*
'ice·box nevera *f*, *Rpl* heladera *f*
'ice·break·er *ship* rompehielos *m inv*
'ice cream helado *m*
'ice cream par·lor heladería *f*
'ice cube cubito *m* de hielo
iced [aɪst] *adj drink* helado
iced 'cof·fee café *m* helado
'ice hock·ey hockey *m* sobre hielo
'ice rink pista *f* de hielo
'ice skate patín *m* de cuchilla
'ice skat·ing patinaje *m* sobre hielo
i·ci·cle ['aɪsɪkl] carámbano *m*
i·con ['aɪkɑːn] *also* COMPUT icono *m*
icy ['aɪsɪ] *adj road* con hielo; *surface* helado; *welcome* frío
ID [aɪ'diː] *abbr* (= ***identity***) documentación *f*; ***have you got any ID on you?*** ¿lleva algún tipo de documentación?
idea [aɪ'diːə] idea *f*; ***good idea!*** ¡buena idea!; ***I have no idea*** no tengo ni idea; ***it's not a good idea to …*** no es buena idea …
i·deal [aɪ'diːəl] *adj* (*perfect*) ideal
i·deal·is·tic [aɪdiːə'lɪstɪk] *adj* idealista
i·deal·ly [aɪ'diːəlɪ] *adv*: ***ideally situated*** en una posición ideal; ***ideally, we would do it like this*** lo ideal sería que lo hiciéramos así
i·den·ti·cal [aɪ'dentɪkl] *adj* idéntico; ***identical twins*** gemelos(-as) *mpl* (*fpl*) idénticos(-as)
i·den·ti·fi·ca·tion [aɪdentɪfɪ'keɪʃn] identificación *f*; *papers etc* documentación *f*
i·den·ti·fy [aɪ'dentɪfaɪ] *v/t* (*pret & pp* ***identified***) identificar
i·den·ti·ty [aɪ'dentətɪ] identidad *f*; ***identity card*** carné *m* de identidad
i·de·o·log·i·cal [aɪdɪə'lɑːdʒɪkl] *adj* ideológico
i·de·ol·o·gy [aɪdɪ'ɑːlədʒɪ] ideología *f*
id·i·om ['ɪdɪəm] (*saying*) modismo *m*
id·i·o·mat·ic [ɪdɪə'mætɪk] *adj natural* natural
id·i·o·syn·cra·sy [ɪdɪə'sɪŋkrəsɪ] peculiaridad *f*, rareza *f*
id·i·ot ['ɪdɪət] idiota *m/f*, estúpido(-a) *m/f*
id·i·ot·ic [ɪdɪ'ɑːtɪk] *adj* idiota, estúpido
i·dle ['aɪdl] **1** *adj not working* desocupado; (*lazy*) vago; *threat* vano; *machinery* inactivo; ***in an idle moment*** en un momento libre **2** *v/i of engine* funcionar al ralentí
◆ **idle away** *v/t the time etc* pasar ociosamente
i·dol ['aɪdl] ídolo *m*
i·dol·ize ['aɪdəlaɪz] *v/t* idolatrar
i·dyl·lic [ɪ'dɪlɪk] *adj* idílico
if [ɪf] *conj* si; ***if only I hadn't shouted at her*** ojalá no le hubiera gritado
ig·nite [ɪg'naɪt] *v/t* inflamar
ig·ni·tion [ɪg'nɪʃn] *in car* encendido *m*; ***ignition key*** llave *m* de contacto
ig·no·rance ['ɪgnərəns] ignorancia *f*
ig·no·rant ['ɪgnərənt] *adj* ignorante; (*rude*) maleducado; ***be ignorant of sth*** desconocer *or* ignorar algo
ig·nore [ɪg'nɔːr] *v/t* ignorar; COMPUT omitir
ill [ɪl] *adj* enfermo; ***fall ill, be taken ill*** caer enfermo; ***feel ill at ease*** no sentirse a gusto, sentirse incómodo
il·le·gal [ɪ'liːgl] *adj* ilegal
il·le·gi·ble [ɪ'ledʒəbl] *adj* ilegible
il·le·git·i·mate [ɪlɪ'dʒɪtɪmət] *adj child* ilegítimo
ill-fat·ed [ɪl'feɪtɪd] *adj* infortunado
il·li·cit [ɪ'lɪsɪt] *adj* ilícito
il·lit·e·rate [ɪ'lɪtərət] *adj* analfabeto
ill-man·nered [ɪl'mænərd] *adj* maleducado
ill-na·tured [ɪl'neɪʧərd] *adj* malhumorado
ill·ness ['ɪlnɪs] enfermedad *f*
il·log·i·cal [ɪ'lɑːdʒɪkl] *adj* ilógico
ill-tem·pered [ɪl'tempərd] *adj* malhumorado
ill'treat *v/t* maltratar
il·lu·mi·nate [ɪ'luːmɪneɪt] *v/t building etc* iluminar
il·lu·mi·nat·ing [ɪ'luːmɪneɪtɪŋ] *adj remarks etc* iluminador, esclarecedor
il·lu·sion [ɪ'luːʒn] ilusión *f*
il·lus·trate ['ɪləstreɪt] *v/t* ilustrar
il·lus·tra·tion [ɪlə'streɪʃn] ilustración *f*
il·lus·tra·tor [ɪlə'streɪtər] ilustrador(a) *m(f)*
ill 'will rencor *m*
im·age ['ɪmɪdʒ] imagen *f*; ***he's the image of his father*** es la viva imagen de su padre
'im·age-con·scious *adj* preocupado por la imagen
i·ma·gi·na·ble [ɪ'mædʒɪnəbl] *adj* imagi-

nable; ***the biggest / smallest size imaginable*** la talla más grande / más pequeña que se pueda imaginar

i·ma·gi·na·ry [ɪ'mædʒɪnərɪ] *adj* imaginario

i·ma·gi·na·tion [ɪmædʒɪ'neɪʃn] imaginación *f*; ***it's all in your imagination*** son imaginaciones tuyas

i·ma·gi·na·tive [ɪ'mædʒɪnətɪv] *adj* imaginativo

i·ma·gine [ɪ'mædʒɪn] *v/t* imaginar, imaginarse; ***I can just imagine it*** me lo imagino; ***you're imagining things*** son imaginaciones tuyas

im·be·cile ['ɪmbəsiːl] imbécil *m/f*

IMF [aɪem'ef] *abbr* (= ***International Monetary Fund***) FMI *m* (= Fondo *m* Monetario Internacional)

im·i·tate ['ɪmɪteɪt] *v/t* imitar

im·i·ta·tion [ɪmɪ'teɪʃn] imitación *f*; ***learn by imitation*** aprender imitando

im·mac·u·late [ɪ'mækjʊlət] *adj* inmaculado

im·ma·te·ri·al [ɪmə'tɪrɪəl] *adj* (*not relevant*) irrelevante

im·ma·ture [ɪmə'ʧʊər] *adj* inmaduro

im·me·di·ate [ɪ'miːdɪət] *adj* inmediato; ***the immediate family*** los familiares más cercanos; ***in the immediate neighborhood*** en las inmediaciones

im·me·di·ate·ly [ɪ'miːdɪətlɪ] *adv* inmediatamente; ***immediately after the bank / church*** justo después del banco / la iglesia

im·mense [ɪ'mens] *adj* inmenso

im·merse [ɪ'mɜːrs] *v/t* sumergir; ***immerse o.s. in*** sumergirse en

im·mer·sion heat·er [ɪ'mɜːrʃn] calentador *m* de agua eléctrico

im·mi·grant ['ɪmɪgrənt] *n* inmigrante *m/f*

im·mi·grate ['ɪmɪgreɪt] *v/i* inmigrar

im·mi·gra·tion [ɪmɪ'greɪʃn] inmigración *f*; ***Immigration*** *government department* (Departamento *m* de) Inmigración *f*

im·mi·nent ['ɪmɪnənt] *adj* inminente

im·mo·bi·lize [ɪ'moʊbɪlaɪz] *v/t factory* paralizar; *person*, *car* inmovilizar

im·mo·bi·liz·er [ɪ'moʊbɪlaɪzər] *on car* inmovilizador *m*

im·mod·e·rate [ɪ'mɑːdərət] *adj* desmedido, exagerado

im·mor·al [ɪ'mɔːrəl] *adj* inmoral

im·mor·al·i·ty [ɪmɔː'rælɪtɪ] inmoralidad *f*

im·mor·tal [ɪ'mɔːrtl] *adj* inmortal

im·mor·tal·i·ty [ɪmɔːr'tælɪtɪ] inmortalidad *f*

im·mune [ɪ'mjuːn] *adj to illness*, *infection* inmune; *from ruling*, *requirement* con inmunidad

im'mune sys·tem MED sistema *m* inmunológico

im·mu·ni·ty [ɪ'mjuːnətɪ] inmunidad *f*; ***diplomatic immunity*** inmunidad *f* diplomática

im·pact ['ɪmpækt] *n* impacto *m*; ***the warning had no impact on him*** el aviso no le hizo cambiar lo más mínimo

im·pair [ɪm'per] *v/t* dañar

im·paired [ɪm'perd] *adj*: ***with impaired hearing / sight*** con problemas auditivos / visuales

im·par·tial [ɪm'pɑːrʃl] *adj* imparcial

im·pass·a·ble [ɪm'pæsəbl] *adj road* intransitable

im·passe ['ɪmpæs] *in negotations etc* punto *m* muerto

im·pas·sioned [ɪm'pæʃnd] *adj speech*, *plea* apasionado

im·pas·sive [ɪm'pæsɪv] *adj* impasible

im·pa·tience [ɪm'peɪʃəns] impaciencia *f*

im·pa·tient [ɪm'peɪʃənt] *adj* impaciente

im·pa·tient·ly [ɪm'peɪʃəntlɪ] *adv* impacientemente

im·peach [ɪm'piːʧ] *v/t President* iniciar un proceso de destitución contra

im·pec·ca·ble [ɪm'pekəbl] *adj* impecable

im·pec·ca·bly [ɪm'pekəblɪ] *adv* impecablemente

im·pede [ɪm'piːd] *v/t* dificultar

im·ped·i·ment [ɪm'pedɪmənt] *in speech* defecto *m* del habla

im·pend·ing [ɪm'pendɪŋ] *adj* inminente

im·pen·e·tra·ble [ɪm'penɪtrəbl] *adj* impenetrable

im·per·a·tive [ɪm'perətɪv] **1** *adj* imprescindible **2** *n* GRAM imperativo *m*

im·per·cep·ti·ble [ɪmpɜːr'septɪbl] *adj* imperceptible

im·per·fect [ɪm'pɜːrfekt] **1** *adj* imperfecto **2** *n* GRAM imperfecto *m*

im·pe·ri·al [ɪm'pɪrɪəl] *adj* imperial

im·per·son·al [ɪm'pɜːrsənl] *adj* impersonal

im·per·so·nate [ɪm'pɜːrsəneɪt] *v/t as a joke* imitar; *illegally* hacerse pasar por

im·per·ti·nence [ɪm'pɜːrtɪnəns] impertinencia *f*

im·per·ti·nent [ɪm'pɜːrtɪnənt] *adj* impertinente

im·per·tur·ba·ble [ɪmpər'tɜːrbəbl] *adj* imperturbable

im·per·vi·ous [ɪm'pɜːrvɪəs] *adj*: ***impervious to*** inmune a

im·pe·tu·ous [ɪm'peʧʊəs] *adj* impetuoso

im·pe·tus ['ɪmpɪtəs] *of campaign etc* ímpetu *m*

im·ple·ment **1** *n* ['ɪmplɪmənt] utensilio *m* **2** *v/t* ['ɪmplɪment] *measures etc* poner en práctica

im·pli·cate ['ɪmplɪkeɪt] *v/t* implicar; ***implicate s.o. in sth*** implicar a alguien en algo

im·pli·ca·tion [ɪmplɪ'keɪʃn] consecuencia *f*; ***the implication is that …*** implica que …

im·pli·cit [ɪm'plɪsɪt] *adj* implícito; *trust* inquebrantable

im·plore [ɪm'plɔːr] *v/t* implorar

im·ply [ɪm'plaɪ] *v/i* (*pret & pp* ***implied***) implicar; ***are you implying I lied?*** ¿insinúas que mentí?

im·po·lite [ɪmpə'laɪt] *adj* maleducado

im·port ['ɪmpɔːrt] **1** *n* importación *f* **2** *v/t* importar

im·por·tance [ɪm'pɔːrtəns] importancia *f*

im·por·tant [ɪm'pɔːrtənt] *adj* importante

im·por·ter [ɪm'pɔːrtər] importador(a) *m(f)*

im·pose [ɪm'pouz] *v/t tax* imponer; ***impose o.s. on s.o.*** molestar a alguien

im·pos·ing [ɪm'pouzɪŋ] *adj* imponente

im·pos·si·bil·i·ty [ɪmpɑːsɪ'bɪlɪtɪ] imposibilidad *f*

im·pos·si·ble [ɪm'pɑːsɪbəl] *adj* imposible

im·pos·tor [ɪm'pɑːstər] impostor(a) *m(f)*

im·po·tence ['ɪmpətəns] impotencia *f*

im·po·tent ['ɪmpətənt] *adj* impotente

im·pov·e·rished [ɪm'pɑːvərɪʃt] *adj* empobrecido

im·prac·ti·cal [ɪm'præktɪkəl] *adj* poco práctico

im·press [ɪm'pres] *v/t* impresionar; ***be impressed by s.o./sth*** quedar impresionado por alguien / algo; ***I'm not impressed*** no me parece nada extraordinario

im·pres·sion [ɪm'preʃn] impresión *f*; (*impersonation*) imitación *f*; ***make a good / bad impression on s.o.*** causar a alguien buena / mala impresión; ***I get the impression that …*** me da la impresión de que …

im·pres·sion·a·ble [ɪm'preʃənəbl] *adj* influenciable

im·pres·sive [ɪm'presɪv] *adj* impresionante

im·print ['ɪmprɪnt] *n of credit card* impresión *f*

im·pris·on [ɪm'prɪzn] *v/t* encarcelar

im·pris·on·ment [ɪm'prɪznmənt] encarcelamiento *m*

im·prob·a·ble [ɪm'prɑːbəbəl] *adj* improbable

im·prop·er [ɪm'prɑːpər] *adj behavior* incorrecto

im·prove [ɪm'pruːv] *v/t & v/i* mejorar

im·prove·ment [ɪm'pruːvmənt] mejora *f*, mejoría *f*

im·pro·vise ['ɪmprəvaɪz] *v/i* improvisar

im·pu·dent ['ɪmpjʊdənt] *adj* insolente, desvergonzado

im·pulse ['ɪmpʌls] impulso *m*; ***do sth on an impulse*** hacer algo impulsivamente

'impulse buy compra *f* impulsiva

im·pul·sive [ɪm'pʌlsɪv] *adj* impulsivo

im·pu·ni·ty [ɪm'pjuːnətɪ] impunidad *f*; ***with impunity*** impunemente

im·pure [ɪm'pjʊr] *adj* impuro

in [ɪn] **1** *prep* ◇ en; ***in Washington / Milan*** en Washington / Milán; ***in the street*** en la calle; ***in the box*** en la caja; ***put it in your pocket*** méteteloen el bolsillo; ***wounded in the leg / arm*** herido en la pierna / el brazo
◇ ***in 1999*** en 1999; ***in two hours*** *from now* dentro de dos horas
◇ (*over period of*) en; ***in the morning*** por la mañana; ***in the summer*** en verano; ***in August*** en agosto
◇ ***in English / Spanish*** en inglés / español; ***in a loud voice*** en voz alta; ***in his style*** en su estilo; ***in yellow*** de amarillo
◇ ***in crossing the road*** (*while*) al cruzar la calle; ***in agreeing to this*** (*by virtue of*) al expresar acuerdo con esto
◇ ***in his novel*** en su novela; ***in Faulkner*** en Faulkner
◇ ***three in all*** tres en total; ***one in ten*** uno de cada diez **2** *adv*: ***is he in?*** *at home* ¿está en casa?; ***is the express in yet?*** ¿ha llegado ya el expreso?; ***when the diskette is in*** cuando el disquete está dentro; ***in here*** aquí dentro **3** *adj* (*fashionable, popular*) de moda; ***be in*** estar de moda

in·a·bil·i·ty [ɪnə'bɪlɪtɪ] incapacidad *f*

in·ac·ces·si·ble [ɪnək'sesɪbl] *adj* inaccesible

in·ac·cu·rate [ɪn'ækjʊrət] *adj* inexacto

in·ac·tive [ɪn'æktɪv] *adj* inactivo

in·ad·e·quate [ɪn'ædɪkwət] *adj* insuficiente

in·ad·vis·a·ble [ɪnəd'vaɪzəbl] *adj* poco aconsejable

in·an·i·mate [ɪn'ænɪmət] *adj* inanimado

in·ap·pro·pri·ate [ɪnə'proupriət] *adj remark, thing to do* inadecuado, improcedente; *choice* inapropiado

in·ar·tic·u·late [ɪnɑːr'tɪkjʊlət] *adj*: ***be inarticulate*** expresarse mal

in·au·di·ble [ɪn'ɒːdəbl] *adj* inaudible

in·au·gu·ral [ɪ'nɒːgjʊrəl] *adj speech* inaugural

in·au·gu·rate [ɪ'nɒːgjʊreɪt] *v/t* inaugurar

in·born ['ɪnbɔːrn] *adj* innato

in·breed·ing ['ɪnbriːdɪŋ] endogamia *f*

inc. *abbr* (= ***incorporated***) S.A. (= sociedad *f* anónima)

incalculable [ɪn'kælkjʊləbl] *adj damage* incalculable

in·ca·pa·ble [ɪn'keɪpəbl]] *adj* incapaz; ***be incapable of doing sth*** ser incapaz de hacer algo

in·cen·di·a·ry de'vice [ɪn'sendɪrɪ] artefacto *m* incendiario

in·cense[1] ['ɪnsens] *n* incienso *m*

in·cense[2] [ɪn'sens] *v/t* encolerizar

in·cen·tive [ɪn'sentɪv] incentivo *m*

in·ces·sant [ɪn'sesnt] *adj* incesante

in·ces·sant·ly [ɪn'sesntlɪ] *adv* incesantemente

in·cest ['ɪnsest] incesto *m*

inch [ɪntʃ] *n* pulgada *f*

in·ci·dent ['ɪnsɪdənt] incidente *m*

in·ci·den·tal [ɪnsɪ'dentl] *adj* sin importancia; ***incidental expenses*** gastos *mpl* varios

in·ci·den·tal·ly [ɪnsɪ'dentlɪ] *adv* a propósito

in·cin·e·ra·tor [ɪn'sɪnəreɪtər] incinerador *m*

in·ci·sion [ɪn'sɪʒn] incisión *f*

in·ci·sive [ɪn'saɪsɪv] *adj* incisivo

in·cite [ɪn'saɪt] *v/t* incitar; ***incite s.o. to do sth*** incitar a alguien a que haga algo

in·clem·ent [ɪn'klemənt] *adj* inclemente

in·cli·na·tion [ɪnklɪ'neɪʃn] (*tendency, liking*) inclinación *f*

in·cline [ɪn'klaɪn] *v/t*: ***be inclined to do sth*** tender a hacer algo

in·close, in·clos·ure → ***enclose, enclosure***

in·clude [ɪn'klu:d] *v/t* incluir

in·clud·ing [ɪn'klu:dɪŋ] *prep* incluyendo

in·clu·sive [ɪn'klu:sɪv] **1** *adj price* total, global **2** *prep*: ***inclusive of*** incluyendo, incluido **3** *adv*: ***from Monday to Thursday inclusive*** de lunes al jueves, ambos inclusive; ***it costs $ 1000 inclusive*** cuesta 1.000 dólares todo incluido

in·co·her·ent *adj* incoherente

in·come ['ɪnkəm] ingresos *mpl*

'in·come tax impuesto *m* sobre la renta

in·com·ing ['ɪnkʌmɪŋ] *adj tide* que sube; ***incoming flight*** vuelo *f* que llega; ***incoming mail*** correo *m* recibido; ***incoming calls*** llamadas *fpl* recibidas

in·com·pa·ra·ble [ɪn'kɑ:mpərəbl] *adj* incomparable

in·com·pat·i·bil·i·ty [ɪnkəmpætɪ'bɪlɪtɪ] incompatibilidad *f*

in·com·pat·i·ble [ɪnkəm'pætɪbl] *adj* incompatible

in·com·pe·tence [ɪn'kɑ:mpɪtəns] incompetencia *f*

in·com·pe·tent [ɪn'kɑ:mpɪtənt] *adj* incompetente

in·com·plete [ɪnkəm'pli:t] *adj* incompleto

in·com·pre·hen·si·ble [ɪnkɑ:mprɪ'hensɪbl] *adj* incomprensible

in·con·cei·va·ble [ɪnkən'si:vəbl] *adj* inconcebible

in·con·clu·sive [ɪnkən'klu:sɪv] *adj* no concluyente

in·con·gru·ous [ɪn'kɑ:ŋgrʊəs] *adj* incongruente

in·con·sid·er·ate [ɪnkən'sɪdərət] *adj* desconsiderado

in·con·sis·tent [ɪnkən'sɪstənt] *adj argument, behavior* incoherente, inconsecuente; *player* irregular; ***be inconsistent with sth*** no ser consecuente con algo

in·con·so·la·ble [ɪnkən'soʊləbl] *adj* inconsolable, desconsolado

in·con·spic·u·ous [ɪnkən'spɪkjʊəs] *adj* discreto

in·con·ve·ni·ence [ɪnkən'vi:nɪəns] *n* inconveniencia *f*

in·con·ve·ni·ent [ɪnkən'vi:nɪənt] *adj* inconveniente, inoportuno

in·cor·po·rate [ɪn'kɔ:rpəreɪt] *v/t* incorporar

in·cor·po·rat·ed [ɪn'kɔ:rpəreɪtɪd] *adj* COM: ***ABC Incorporated*** ABC, sociedad *f* anónima

in·cor·rect [ɪnkə'rekt] *adj* incorrecto

in·cor·rect·ly [ɪnkə'rektlɪ] *adv* incorrectamente

in·cor·ri·gi·ble [ɪn'kɑ:rɪdʒəbl] *adj* incorregible

in·crease 1 *v/t & v/i* [ɪn'kri:s] aumentar **2** *n* ['ɪnkri:s] aumento *m*

in·creas·ing [ɪn'kri:sɪŋ] *adj* creciente

in·creas·ing·ly [ɪn'kri:sɪŋlɪ] *adv* cada vez más; ***we're getting increasingly concerned*** cada vez estamos más preocupados

in·cred·i·ble [ɪn'kredɪbl] *adj* (*amazing, very good*) increíble

in·crim·i·nate [ɪn'krɪmɪneɪt] *v/t* incriminar; ***incriminate o.s.*** incriminarse

in·cu·ba·tor ['ɪŋkjʊbeɪtər] incubadora *f*

in·cur [ɪn'kɜ:r] *v/t* (*pret & pp* ***incurred***) *costs* incurrir en; *debts* contraer; *s.o.'s anger* provocar

in·cu·ra·ble [ɪn'kjʊrəbl] *adj* incurable

in·debt·ed [ɪn'detɪd] *adj*: ***be indebted to s.o.*** estar en deuda con alguien

in·de·cent [ɪn'di:snt] *adj* indecente

in·de·ci·sive [ɪndɪ'saɪsɪv] *adj* indeciso

in·de·ci·sive·ness [ɪndɪ'saɪsɪvnɪs] indecisión *f*

in·deed [ɪn'di:d] *adv* (*in fact*) ciertamente,

efectivamente; *yes, agreeing* ciertamente, en efecto; ***very much indeed*** muchísimo; ***thank you very much indeed*** muchísimas gracias

in·de·fi·na·ble [ɪndɪ'faɪnəbl] *adj* indefinible

in·def·i·nite [ɪn'defɪnɪt] *adj* indefinido; ***indefinite article*** GRAM artículo *m* indefinido

in·def·i·nite·ly [ɪn'defɪnɪtlɪ] *adv* indefinidamente

in·del·i·cate [ɪn'delɪkət] *adj* poco delicado

in·dent 1 *n* ['ɪndent] *in text* sangrado *m* **2** *v/t* [ɪn'dent] *line* sangrar

in·de·pen·dence [ɪndɪ'pendəns] independencia *f*

In·de'pen·dence Day Día *m* de la Independencia

in·de·pen·dent [ɪndɪ'pendənt] *adj* independiente

in·de·pen·dent·ly [ɪndɪ'pendəntlɪ] *adv deal with* por separado; ***independently of*** al margen de

in·de·scri·ba·ble [ɪndɪ'skraɪbəbl] *adj* indescriptible

in·de·scrib·a·bly [ɪndɪ'skraɪbəblɪ] *adv* indescriptiblemente

in·de·struc·ti·ble [ɪndɪ'strʌktəbl] *adj* indestructible

in·de·ter·mi·nate [ɪndɪ'tɜːrmɪnət] *adj* indeterminado

in·dex ['ɪndeks] *n for book* índice *m*

'in·dex card ficha *f*

'in·dex fin·ger (dedo *m*) índice *m*

in·dex-'linked *adj* indexado

In·di·a ['ɪndɪə] (la) India

In·di·an ['ɪndɪən] **1** *adj* indio **2** *n from India* indio(-a) *m(f)*, hindú *m/f*; *American* indio(-a) *m(f)*

In·di·an 'sum·mer *in northern hemisphere* veranillo *m* de San Martín; *in southern hemisphere* veranillo *m* de San Juan

in·di·cate ['ɪndɪkeɪt] **1** *v/t* indicar **2** *v/i when driving* poner el intermitente

in·di·ca·tion [ɪndɪ'keɪʃn] indicio *m*

in·di·ca·tor ['ɪndɪkeɪtər] *on car* intermitente *m*

in·dict [ɪn'daɪt] *v/t* acusar

in·dif·fer·ence [ɪn'dɪfrəns] indiferencia *f*

in·dif·fer·ent [ɪn'dɪfrənt] *adj* indiferente; (*mediocre*) mediocre; ***are you totally indifferent to the way I feel?*** ¿no te importa lo más mínimo lo que sienta yo?

in·di·ges·ti·ble [ɪndɪ'dʒestɪbl] *adj* indigesto

in·di·ges·tion [ɪndɪ'dʒestʃn] indigestión *f*

in·dig·nant [ɪn'dɪgnənt] *adj* indignado

in·dig·na·tion [ɪndɪg'neɪʃn] indignación *f*

in·di·rect [ɪndɪ'rekt] *adj* indirecto

in·di·rect·ly [ɪndɪ'rektlɪ] *adv* indirectamente

in·dis·creet [ɪndɪ'skriːt] *adj* indiscreto

in·dis·cre·tion [ɪndɪ'skreʃn] indiscreción *f*

in·dis·crim·i·nate [ɪndɪ'skrɪmɪnət] *adj* indiscriminado

in·dis·pen·sa·ble [ɪndɪ'spensəbl] *adj* indispensable, imprescindible

in·dis·posed [ɪndɪ'spoʊzd] *adj* (*not well*) indispuesto; ***be indisposed*** hallarse indispuesto

in·dis·pu·ta·ble [ɪndɪ'spjuːtəbl] *adj* indiscutible

in·dis·pu·ta·bly [ɪndɪ'spjuːtəblɪ] *adv* indiscutiblemente

in·dis·tinct [ɪndɪ'stɪŋkt] *adj* indistinto, impreciso

in·dis·tin·guish·a·ble [ɪndɪ'stɪŋgwɪʃəbl] *adj* indistinguible

in·di·vid·u·al [ɪndɪ'vɪdʒʊəl] **1** *n* individuo *m* **2** *adj* individual

in·di·vid·u·a·list [ɪndɪ'vɪdʒʊəlɪst] *adj* individualista

in·di·vid·u·al·ly [ɪndɪ'vɪdʒʊəlɪ] *adv* individualmente

in·di·vis·i·ble [ɪndɪ'vɪzɪbl] *adj* indivisible

in·doc·tri·nate [ɪn'dɑːktrɪneɪt] *v/t* adoctrinar

in·do·lence ['ɪndələns] indolencia *f*

in·do·lent ['ɪndələnt] *adj* indolente

In·do·ne·sia [ɪndə'niːʒə] Indonesia

In·do·ne·sian [ɪndə'niːʒən] **1** *adj* indonesio **2** *n person* indonesio(-a) *m(f)*

in·door ['ɪndɔːr] *adj activities* de interior; *sport* de pista cubierta; *arena* cubierto; *athletics* en pista cubierta

in·doors [ɪn'dɔːrz] *adv* dentro

in·dorse → ***endorse***

in·dulge [ɪn'dʌldʒ] **1** *v/t o.s., one's tastes* satisfacer **2** *v/i*: ***indulge in a pleasure*** entregarse a un placer; ***if I might indulge in a little joke*** si se me permite contar un chiste

in·dul·gent [ɪn'dʌldʒənt] *adj* indulgente

in·dus·tri·al [ɪn'dʌstrɪəl] *adj* industrial; ***industrial action*** acciones *fpl* reivindicativas

in·dus·tri·al dis'pute conflicto *m* laboral

in·dus·tri·al·ist [ɪn'dʌstrɪəlɪst] industrial *m/f*

in·dus·tri·al·ize [ɪn'dʌstrɪəlaɪz] **1** *v/t* industrializar **2** *v/i* industrializarse

in·dus·tri·al 'waste residuos *mpl* industriales

in·dus·tri·ous [ɪn'dʌstrɪəs] *adj* trabajador, aplicado

in·dus·try ['ɪndəstrɪ] industria *f*

I

in·ef·fec·tive [ɪnɪ'fektɪv] *adj* ineficaz
in·ef·fec·tu·al [ɪnɪ'fektʃʊəl] *adj person* inepto, incapaz
in·ef·fi·cient [ɪnɪ'fɪʃənt] *adj* ineficiente
in·eli·gi·ble [ɪn'elɪdʒɪbl] *adj*: ***be ineligible*** no reunir las condiciones
in·ept [ɪ'nept] *adj* inepto
in·e·qual·i·ty [ɪnɪ'kwɑːlɪtɪ] desigualdad *f*
in·es·ca·pa·ble [ɪnɪ'skeɪpəbl] *adj* inevitable
in·es·ti·ma·ble [ɪn'estɪməbl] *adj* inestimable
in·ev·i·ta·ble [ɪn'evɪtəbl] *adj* inevitable
in·ev·i·ta·bly [ɪn'evɪtəblɪ] *adv* inevitablemente
in·ex·cu·sa·ble [ɪnɪk'skjuːzəbl] *adj* inexcusable, injustificable
in·ex·haus·ti·ble [ɪnɪg'zɒːstəbl] *adj supply* inagotable
in·ex·pen·sive [ɪnɪk'spensɪv] *adj* barato, económico
in·ex·pe·ri·enced [ɪnɪk'spɪrɪənst] *adj* inexperto
in·ex·plic·a·ble [ɪnɪk'splɪkəbl] *adj* inexplicable
in·ex·pres·si·ble [ɪnɪk'spresɪbl] *adj joy* indescriptible
in·fal·li·ble [ɪn'fælɪbl] *adj* infalible
in·fa·mous ['ɪnfəməs] *adj* infame
in·fan·cy ['ɪnfənsɪ] infancia *f*
in·fant ['ɪnfənt] bebé *m*
in·fan·tile ['ɪnfəntaɪl] *adj pej* infantil, pueril
in·fan·try ['ɪnfəntrɪ] infantería *f*
in·fan·try 'sol·dier soldado *m/f* de infantería, infante *m/f*
'in·fant school colegio *m* de párvulos
in·fat·u·at·ed [ɪn'fætʃʊeɪtɪd] *adj*: ***be infatuated with s.o.*** estar encaprichado de alguien
in·fect [ɪn'fekt] *v/t* infectar; ***he infected everyone with his cold*** contagió el resfriado a todo el mundo; ***become infected*** *of wound* infectarse; *of person* contagiarse
in·fec·tion [ɪn'fekʃn] infección *f*
in·fec·tious [ɪn'fekʃəs] *adj disease* infeccioso; *laughter* contagioso
in·fer [ɪn'fɜːr] *v/t* (*pret & pp* ***inferred***) inferir, deducir (***from*** de)
in·fe·ri·or [ɪn'fɪrɪər] *adj* inferior (***to*** a)
in·fe·ri·or·i·ty [ɪnfɪrɪ'ɑːrətɪ] *in quality* inferioridad *f*
in·fe·ri'or·i·ty com·plex complejo *m* de inferioridad
in·fer·tile [ɪn'fɜːrtl] *adj woman, plant* estéril; *soil* estéril, yermo
in·fer·til·i·ty [ɪnfər'tɪlɪtɪ] esterilidad *f*
in·fi·del·i·ty [ɪnfɪ'delɪtɪ] infidelidad *f*
in·fil·trate ['ɪnfɪltreɪt] *v/t* infiltrarse en
in·fi·nite ['ɪnfɪnət] *adj* infinito
in·fin·i·tive [ɪn'fɪnətɪv] infinitivo *m*
in·fin·i·ty [ɪn'fɪnətɪ] infinidad *f*
in·firm [ɪn'fɜːrm] *adj* enfermo, achacoso
in·fir·ma·ry [ɪn'fɜːrmərɪ] enfermería *f*
in·fir·mi·ty [ɪn'fɜːrmətɪ] debilidad *f*
in·flame [ɪn'fleɪm] *v/t* despertar
in·flam·ma·ble [ɪn'flæməbl] *adj* inflamable
in·flam·ma·tion [ɪnflə'meɪʃn] MED inflamación *f*
in·flat·a·ble [ɪn'fleɪtəbl] *adj dinghy* hinchable, inflable
inflate [ɪn'fleɪt] *v/t tire, dinghy* hinchar, inflar; *economy* inflar
in·fla·tion [ɪn'fleɪʃən] inflación *f*
in·fla·tion·a·ry [ɪn'fleɪʃənərɪ] *adj* inflacionario, inflacionista
in·flec·tion [ɪn'flekʃn] inflexión *f*
in·flex·i·ble [ɪn'fleksɪbl] *adj* inflexible
in·flict [ɪn'flɪkt] *v/t* infligir; ***inflict sth on s.o.*** infligir algo a alguien
'in-flight *adj*: ***in-flight entertainment*** entretenimiento *m* durante el vuelo
in·flu·ence ['ɪnflʊəns] **1** *n* influencia *f*; ***be a good / bad influence on s.o.*** tener una buena / mala influencia en alguien **2** *v/t* influir en, influenciar
in·flu·en·tial [ɪnflʊ'enʃl] *adj* influyente
in·flu·en·za [ɪnflʊ'enzə] gripe *f*
in·form [ɪn'fɔːrm] **1** *v/t* informar; ***inform s.o. about sth*** informar a alguien de algo; ***please keep me informed*** por favor manténme informado **2** *v/i*: ***inform on s.o.*** delatar a alguien
in·for·mal [ɪn'fɔːrməl] *adj* informal
in·for·mal·i·ty [ɪnfɔːr'mælɪtɪ] informalidad *f*
in·form·ant [ɪn'fɔːrmənt] confidente *m/f*
in·for·ma·tion [ɪnfər'meɪʃn] información *f*; ***a piece of information*** una información
in·for·ma·tion 'sci·ence informática *f*
in·for·ma·tion 'sci·en·tist informático(-a) *m(f)*
in·for·ma·tion tech'nol·o·gy tecnologías *fpl* de la información
in·for·ma·tive [ɪn'fɔːrmətɪv] *adj* informativo; ***you're not being very informative*** no estás dando mucha información
in·form·er [ɪn'fɔːrmər] confidente *m/f*
infra-red [ɪnfrə'red] *adj* infrarrojo
in·fra·struc·ture ['ɪnfrəstrʌktʃər] infraestructura *f*
in·fre·quent [ɪn'friːkwənt] *adj* poco frecuente
in·fu·ri·ate [ɪn'fjʊrɪeɪt] *v/t* enfurecer, exasperar

in·fu·ri·at·ing [ɪn'fjʊrɪeɪtɪŋ] *adj* exasperante
in·fuse [ɪn'fju:z] *v/i of tea* infundir
in·fu·sion [ɪn'fju:ʒn] (*herb tea*) infusión *f*
in·ge·ni·ous [ɪn'dʒi:nɪəs] *adj* ingenioso
in·ge·nu·i·ty [ɪndʒɪ'nu:ətɪ] lo ingenioso
in·got ['ɪŋgət] lingote *m*
in·gra·ti·ate [ɪn'greɪʃɪeɪt] *v/t*: ***ingratiate o.s. with s.o.*** congraciarse con alguien
in·grat·i·tude [ɪn'grætɪtu:d] ingratitud *f*
in·gre·di·ent [ɪn'gri:dɪənt] *also fig* ingrediente *m*
in·hab·it [ɪn'hæbɪt] *v/t* habitar
in·hab·it·a·ble [ɪn'hæbɪtəbl] *adj* habitable
in·hab·i·tant [ɪn'hæbɪtənt] habitante *m/f*
in·hale [ɪn'heɪl] **1** *v/t* inhalar **2** *v/i when smoking* tragarse el *humo*
in·ha·ler [ɪn'heɪlər] inhalador *m*
in·her·it [ɪn'herɪt] *v/t* heredar
in·her·i·tance [ɪn'herɪtəns] herencia *f*
in·hib·it [ɪn'hɪbɪt] *v/t growth* impedir; *conversation* inhibir, cohibir
in·hib·it·ed [ɪn'hɪbɪtɪd] *adj* inhibido, cohibido
in·hi·bi·tion [ɪnhɪ'bɪʃn] inhibición *f*
in·hos·pi·ta·ble [ɪnhɑ:'spɪtəbl] *adj person* inhospitalario; *city, climate* inhóspito
'in-house **1** *adj facilities* en el lugar de trabajo; ***in-house team*** equipo *m* en plantilla **2** *adv work* en la empresa
in·hu·man [ɪn'hju:mən] *adj* inhumano
i·ni·tial [ɪ'nɪʃl] **1** *adj* inicial **2** *n* inicial *f* **3** *v/t* (*write initials on*) poner las iniciales en
i·ni·tial·ly [ɪ'nɪʃlɪ] *adv* inicialmente, al principio
i·ni·ti·ate [ɪ'nɪʃɪeɪt] *v/t* iniciar
i·ni·ti·a·tion [ɪnɪʃɪ'eɪʃn] iniciación *f*, inicio *m*
i·ni·tia·tive [ɪ'nɪʃətɪv] iniciativa *f*; ***do sth on one's own initiative*** hacer algo por iniciativa propia
in·ject [ɪn'dʒekt] *v/t drug, fuel, capital* inyectar
in·jec·tion [ɪn'dʒekʃn] *of drug, fuel, capital* inyección *f*
'in-joke: ***it's an in-joke*** es un chiste que entendemos nosotros
in·jure ['ɪndʒər] *v/t* lesionar; ***he injured his leg*** se lesionó la pierna
in·jured ['ɪndʒərd] **1** *adj leg* lesionado; *feelings* herido **2** *npl*: ***the injured*** los heridos
in·ju·ry ['ɪndʒərɪ] lesión *f*; *wound* herida *f*
'in·jury time SP tiempo *m* de descuento
in·jus·tice [ɪn'dʒʌstɪs] injusticia *f*
ink [ɪŋk] tinta *f*
ink·jet ('prin·ter) impresora *f* de chorro de tinta
in·land ['ɪnlənd] *adj* interior; *mail* nacional
in-laws ['ɪnlɒ:z] *npl* familia *f* política
in·lay ['ɪnleɪ] *n* incrustación *f*
in·let ['ɪnlet] *of sea* ensenada *f*; *in machine* entrada *f*
in·mate ['ɪnmeɪt] *of prison* recluso(-a) *m(f)*; *of mental hospital* paciente *m/f*
inn [ɪn] posada *f*, mesón *m*
in·nate [ɪ'neɪt] *adj* innato
in·ner ['ɪnər] *adj* interior; ***the inner ear*** el oído interno
in·ner 'cit·y *barrios degradados del centro de la ciudad*; ***inner city decay*** degradación *m* del centro de la ciudad
'in·ner·most *adj feelings* más íntimo; *recess* más recóndito
in·ner 'tube cámara *f* (de aire)
in·no·cence ['ɪnəsəns] inocencia *f*
in·no·cent ['ɪnəsənt] *adj* inocente
in·no·cu·ous [ɪ'nɑ:kjʊəs] *adj* inocuo
in·no·va·tion [ɪnə'veɪʃn] innovación *f*
in·no·va·tive [ɪnə'veɪtɪv] *adj* innovador
in·no·va·tor ['ɪnəveɪtər] innovador(a) *m(f)*
in·nu·me·ra·ble [ɪ'nu:mərəbl] *adj* innumerable
i·noc·u·late [ɪ'nɑ:kjʊleɪt] *v/t* inocular
i·noc·u·la·tion [ɪ'nɑ:kjʊ'leɪʃn] inoculación *f*
in·of·fen·sive [ɪnə'fensɪv] *adj* inofensivo
in·or·gan·ic [ɪnɔ:r'gænɪk] *adj* inorgánico
'in·pa·tient paciente *m/f* interno(-a)
in·put ['ɪnpʊt] **1** *n into project etc* contribución *f*, aportación *f*; COMPUT entrada *f* **2** *v/t* (*pret & pp* ***inputted*** *or* ***input***) *into project* contribuir, aportar; COMPUT introducir
in·quest ['ɪnkwest] investigación *f* (***into*** sobre)
in·quire [ɪn'kwaɪr] *v/i* preguntar; ***inquire into sth*** investigar algo
in·quir·y [ɪn'kwaɪrɪ] consulta *f*, pregunta *f*; *into rail crash etc* investigación *f*
in·quis·i·tive [ɪn'kwɪzətɪv] *adj* curioso, inquisitivo
in·sane [ɪn'seɪn] *adj person* loco, demente; *idea* descabellado
in·san·i·ta·ry [ɪn'sænɪterɪ] *adj* antihigiénico
in·san·i·ty [ɪn'sænɪtɪ] locura *f*, demencia *f*
in·sa·tia·ble [ɪn'seɪʃəbl] *adj* insaciable
in·scrip·tion [ɪn'skrɪpʃn] inscripción *f*
in·scru·ta·ble [ɪn'skru:təbl] *adj* inescrutable
in·sect ['ɪnsekt] insecto *m*
in·sec·ti·cide [ɪn'sektɪsaɪd] insecticida *f*
'in·sect re·pel·lent repelente *m* contra insectos

in·se·cure [ɪnsɪ'kjʊr] *adj* inseguro
in·se·cu·ri·ty [ɪnsɪ'kjʊrɪtɪ] inseguridad *f*
in·sen·si·tive [ɪn'sensɪtɪv] *adj* insensible
in·sen·si·tiv·i·ty [ɪnsensɪ'tɪvɪtɪ] insensibilidad *f*
in·sep·a·ra·ble [ɪn'seprəbl] *adj* inseparable
in·sert 1 *n* ['ɪnsɜːrt] *in magazine etc* encarte *m* **2** *v/t* [ɪn'sɜːrt] *coin, finger, diskette* introducir, meter; *extra text* insertar; ***insert sth into sth*** introducir *or* meter algo en algo
in·ser·tion [ɪn'sɜːrʃn] *act* introducción *f*, inserción *f*; *of text* inserción *f*
in·side [ɪn'saɪd] **1** *n of house, box* interior *m*; ***somebody on the inside*** alguien de dentro; ***inside out*** del revés; ***turn sth inside out*** dar la vuelta a algo (*de dentro a fuera*); ***know sth inside out*** saberse algo al dedillo **2** *prep* dentro de; ***inside the house*** dentro de la casa; ***inside of 2 hours*** dentro de 2 horas **3** *adv stay, remain* dentro; *go, carry* adentro; ***we went inside*** entramos **4** *adj*: ***inside information*** información *f* confidencial; ***inside lane*** SP calle *f* de dentro; *on road* carril *m* de la derecha; ***inside pocket*** bolsillo *m* interior
in·sid·er [ɪn'saɪdər] *persona con acceso a información confidencial*
in·sid·er 'deal·ing FIN uso *m* de información privilegiada
in·sides [ɪn'saɪdz] *npl* tripas *mpl*
in·sid·i·ous [ɪn'sɪdɪəs] *adj* insidioso
in·sight ['ɪnsaɪt]: ***this film offers an insight into local customs*** esta película permite hacerse una idea de las costumbres locales; ***full of insight*** muy perspicaz
in·sig·nif·i·cant [ɪnsɪg'nɪfɪkənt] *adj* insignificante
in·sin·cere [ɪnsɪn'sɪr] *adj* poco sincero, falso
in·sin·cer·i·ty [ɪnsɪn'serɪtɪ] falta *f* de sinceridad
in·sin·u·ate [ɪn'sɪnʊeɪt] *v/t* (*imply*) insinuar
in·sist [ɪn'sɪst] *v/i* insistir; ***please keep it, I insist*** por favor, insisto en que te lo quedes
◆ **insist on** *v/t* insistir en
in·sis·tent [ɪn'sɪstənt] *adj* insistente
in·so·lent ['ɪnsələnt] *adj* insolente
in·sol·u·ble [ɪn'sɑːljʊbl] *adj problem* irresoluble; *substance* insoluble
in·sol·vent [ɪn'sɑːlvənt] *adj* insolvente
in·som·ni·a [ɪn'sɑːmnɪə] insomnio *m*
in·spect [ɪn'spekt] *v/t* inspeccionar
in·spec·tion [ɪn'spekʃn] inspección *f*
in·spec·tor [ɪn'spektər] *in factory, of police* inspector(a) *m*(*f*); *on buses* revisor(a) *m*(*f*)
in·spi·ra·tion [ɪnspə'reɪʃn] inspiración *f*
in·spire [ɪn'spaɪr] *v/t respect etc* inspirar; ***be inspired by s.o./sth*** estar inspirado por alguien / algo
in·sta·bil·i·ty [ɪnstə'bɪlɪtɪ] *of character, economy* inestabilidad *f*
in·stall [ɪn'stɒːl] *v/t* instalar
in·stal·la·tion [ɪnstə'leɪʃn] instalación *f*; ***military installation*** instalación *f* militar
in·stal·ment *Br*, **in·stall·ment** [ɪn'stɒːlmənt] *of story*, TV *drama etc* episodio *m*; *payment* plazo *m*
in'stall·ment plan compra *f* a plazos
in·stance ['ɪnstəns] (*example*) ejemplo *m*; ***for instance*** por ejemplo
in·stant ['ɪnstənt] **1** *adj* instantáneo **2** *n* instante *m*; ***in an instant*** en un instante
in·stan·ta·ne·ous [ɪnstən'teɪnɪəs] *adj* instantáneo
in·stant 'cof·fee café *m* instantáneo
in·stant·ly ['ɪnstəntlɪ] *adv* al instante
in·stead [ɪn'sted] *adv*: ***I'll take that one instead*** me llevaré mejor ese otro; ***would you like coffee instead?*** ¿preferiría mejor café?; ***I'll have coffee instead of tea*** tomaré té en vez de café; ***he went instead of me*** fue en mi lugar
in·step ['ɪnstep] empeine *m*
in·stinct ['ɪnstɪŋkt] instinto *m*
in·stinc·tive [ɪn'stɪŋktɪv] *adj* instintivo
in·sti·tute ['ɪnstɪtuːt] **1** *n* instituto *m*; *for elderly* residencia *f* de ancianos; *for mentally ill* psiquiátrico *m* **2** *v/t new law* establecer; *inquiry* iniciar
in·sti·tu·tion [ɪnstɪ'tuːʃn] institución *f*; (*setting up*) iniciación *f*
in·struct [ɪn'strʌkt] *v/t* (*order*) dar instrucciones a; (*teach*) instruir; ***instruct s.o. to do sth*** (*order*) ordenar a alguien que haga algo
in·struc·tion [ɪn'strʌkʃn] instrucción *f*; ***instructions for use*** instrucciones *fpl* de uso
in'struc·tion man·u·al manual *m* de instrucciones
in·struc·tive [ɪn'strʌktɪv] *adj* instructivo
in·struc·tor [ɪn'strʌktər] instructor(a) *m*(*f*)
in·stru·ment ['ɪnstrʊmənt] MUS, *tool* instrumento *m*
in·sub·or·di·nate [ɪnsə'bɔːrdɪnət] *adj* insubordinado
in·suf·fi·cient [ɪnsə'fɪʃnt] *adj* insuficiente
in·su·late ['ɪnsəleɪt] *v/t also* ELEC aislar
in·su·la·tion [ɪnsə'leɪʃn] ELEC aislamiento *m*; *against cold* aislamiento *m* (térmico)

in·su·lin ['ɪnsəlɪn] insulina *f*
in·sult 1 *n* ['ɪnsʌlt] insulto *m* **2** *v/t* [ɪn'sʌlt] insultar
in·sur·ance [ɪn'ʃʊrəns] seguro *m*
in'sur·ance com·pa·ny compañía *f* de seguros, aseguradora *f*
in'sur·ance pol·i·cy póliza *f* de seguros
in'sur·ance pre·mi·um prima *f* (del seguro)
in·sure [ɪn'ʃʊr] *v/t* asegurar
in·sured [ɪn'ʃʊrd] **1** *adj* asegurado; ***be insured*** estar asegurado **2** *n*: ***the insured*** el asegurado, la asegurada
in·sur·moun·ta·ble [ɪnsər'maʊntəbl] *adj* insuperable
in·tact [ɪn'tækt] *adj* (*not damaged*) intacto
in·take ['ɪnteɪk] *of college etc* remesa *f*; ***we have an annual intake of 300 students*** cada año admitimos a 300 alumnos
in·te·grate ['ɪntɪgreɪt] *v/t* integrar (***into*** en)
in·te·grat·ed 'cir·cuit ['ɪntɪgreɪtɪd] circuito *m* integrado
in·teg·ri·ty [ɪn'tegrətɪ] (*honesty*) integridad *f*; ***a man of integrity*** un hombre íntegro
in·tel·lect ['ɪntəlekt] intelecto *m*
in·tel·lec·tual [ɪntə'lektʃʊəl] **1** *adj* intelectual **2** *n* intelectual *m/f*
in·tel·li·gence [ɪn'telɪdʒəns] inteligencia *f*; (*information*) información *f* secreta
in'tel·li·gence of·fi·cer agente *m/f* del servicio de inteligencia
in'tel·li·gence ser·vice servicio *m* de inteligencia
in·tel·li·gent [ɪn'telɪdʒənt] *adj* inteligente
in·tel·li·gi·ble [ɪn'telɪdʒəbl] *adj* inteligible
in·tend [ɪn'tend] *v/i*: ***intend to do sth*** tener la intención de hacer algo; ***that's not what I intended*** esa no era mi intención
in·tense [ɪn'tens] *adj sensation*, *pleasure*, *heat*, *pressure* intenso; *personality* serio
in·ten·si·fy [ɪn'tensɪfaɪ] **1** *v/t* (*pret & pp* ***intensified***) *effect*, *pressure* intensificar **2** *v/i* (*pret & pp* ***intensified***) intensificarse
in·ten·si·ty [ɪn'tensətɪ] intensidad *f*
in·ten·sive [ɪn'tensɪv] *adj study*, *training*, *treatment* intensivo
in·ten·sive 'care (u·nit) MED (unidad *f* de) cuidados *mpl* intensivos
in·ten·sive 'course *of language study* curso *m* intensivo
in·tent [ɪn'tent] *adj*: ***be intent on doing sth*** (*determined to do*) estar decidido a hacer algo; (*concentrating on*) estar concentrado haciendo algo
in·ten·tion [ɪn'tenʃn] intención *f*; ***I have no intention of …*** (*refuse to*) no tengo intención de …
in·ten·tion·al [ɪn'tenʃənl] *adj* intencionado
in·ten·tion·al·ly [ɪn'tenʃnlɪ] *adv* a propósito, adrede
in·ter·ac·tion [ɪntər'ækʃn] interacción *f*
in·ter·ac·tive [ɪntər'æktɪv] *adj* interactivo
in·ter·cede [ɪntər'siːd] *v/i* interceder
in·ter·cept [ɪntər'sept] *v/t* interceptar
in·ter·change ['ɪntərtʃeɪndʒ] *n of highways* nudo *m* vial
in·ter·change·a·ble [ɪntər'tʃeɪndʒəbl] *adj* intercambiable
in·ter·com ['ɪntərkɑːm] *in office*, *ship* interfono *m*; *for front door* portero *m* automático
in·ter·course ['ɪntərkɔːrs] *sexual* coito *m*
in·ter·de·pend·ent [ɪntərdɪ'pendənt] *adj* interdependiente
in·ter·est ['ɪntrəst] **1** *n also* FIN interés *m*; ***take an interest in sth*** interesarse por algo **2** *v/t* interesar; ***does that offer interest you?*** ¿te interesa esa oferta?
in·terest·ed ['ɪntrəstɪd] *adj* interesado; ***be interested in sth*** estar interesado en algo; ***thanks, but I'm not interested*** gracias, pero no me interesa
in·terest-free 'loan préstamo *m* sin intereses
in·terest·ing ['ɪntrəstɪŋ] *adj* interesante
'in·terest rate tipo *m* de interés
interface ['ɪntərfeɪs] **1** *n* interface *m*, interfaz *f* **2** *v/i* relacionarse
in·ter·fere [ɪntər'fɪr] *v/i* interferir, entrometerse
◆ **interfere with** *v/t* afectar a; ***the lock had been interfered with*** alguien había manipulado la cerradura
in·ter·fer·ence [ɪntər'fɪrəns] intromisión *f*; *on radio* interferencia *f*
in·te·ri·or [ɪn'tɪrɪər] **1** *adj* interior **2** *n* interior *m*; ***Department of the Interior*** Ministerio *m* del Interior
in·te·ri·or 'dec·o·ra·tor interiorista *m/f*, decorador(a) *m*(*f*) de interiores
in·te·ri·or de'sign interiorismo *m*
in·te·ri·or de'sign·er interiorista *m/f*
in·ter·lude ['ɪntərluːd] *at theater* entreacto *m*, intermedio *m*; *at concert* intermedio *m*; (*period*) intervalo
in·ter·mar·ry [ɪntər'mærɪ] *v/i* (*pret & pp* ***intermarried***) casarse (*con miembros de otra raza*, *religión o grupo*); ***the two tribes intermarried*** los dos tribus se casaron entre sí
in·ter·me·di·ar·y [ɪntər'miːdɪərɪ] *n* intermediario

in·ter·me·di·ate [ɪntər'miːdɪət] *adj* intermedio *m*
in·ter·mis·sion [ɪntər'mɪʃn] *in theater* entreacto *m*, intermedio *m*; *in movie theater* intermedio *m*, descanso *m*
in·tern [ɪn'tɜːrn] *v/t* recluir
in·ter·nal [ɪn'tɜːrnl] *adj* interno
in·ter·nal com'bus·tion en·gine motor *m* de combustión interna
in·ter·nal·ly [ɪn'tɜːrnəlɪ] *adv* internamente
In·ter·nal 'Rev·e·nue (Ser·vice) Hacienda *f*, *Span* Agencia *f* Tributaria
in·ter·na·tion·al [ɪntər'næʃnl] **1** *adj* internacional **2** *n match* partido *m* internacional; *player* internacional *m/f*
In·ter·na·tion·al Court of 'Jus·tice Tribunal *m* Internacional de Justicia
in·ter·na·tion·al·ly [ɪntər'næʃnəlɪ] *adv* internacionalmente
In·ter·na·tion·al 'Mon·e·tar·y Fund Fondo *m* Monetario Internacional
In·ter·net ['ɪntərnet] Internet *f*; ***on the Internet*** en Internet
in·ter·nist [ɪn'tɜːrnɪst] internista *m/f*
in·ter·pret [ɪn'tɜːrprɪt] *v/t & v/i* interpretar
in·ter·pre·ta·tion [ɪntɜːrprɪ'teɪʃn] interpretación *f*
in·ter·pret·er [ɪn'tɜːrprɪtər] intérprete *m/f*
in·ter·re·lat·ed [ɪntərrɪ'leɪtɪd] *adj facts* interrelacionado
in·ter·ro·gate [ɪn'terəgeɪt] *v/t* interrogar
in·ter·ro·ga·tion [ɪnterə'geɪʃn] interrogatorio *m*
in·ter·rog·a·tive [ɪntər'rɑːgətɪv] *n* GRAM (forma *f*) interrogativa *f*
in·ter·ro·ga·tor [ɪnterə'geɪtər] interrogador(a) *m(f)*
in·ter·rupt [ɪntər'rʌpt] **1** *v/t speaker* interrumpir **2** *v/i* interrumpir
in·ter·rup·tion [ɪntər'rʌpʃn] interrupción *f*
in·ter·sect [ɪntər'sekt] **1** *v/t* cruzar **2** *v/i* cruzarse
in·ter·sec·tion ['ɪntərsekʃn] (*crossroads*) intersección *f*
in·ter·state ['ɪntərsteɪt] *n* autopista *f* interestatal
in·ter·val ['ɪntərvl] intervalo *m*; *in theater* entreacto *m*, intermedio *m*; *at concert* intermedio *m*
in·ter·vene [ɪntər'viːn] *v/i of person, police etc* intervenir
in·ter·ven·tion [ɪntər'venʃn] intervención *f*
in·ter·view ['ɪntərvjuː] **1** *n* entrevista *f* **2** *v/t* entrevistar
in·ter·view·ee [ɪntərvjuː'iː] *on* TV entrevistado(-a) *m(f)*; *for job* candidato(-a) *m(f)*
in·ter·view·er ['ɪntərvjuːər] entrevistador(a) *m(f)*
in·testine [ɪn'testɪn] intestino *m*
in·ti·ma·cy ['ɪntɪməsɪ] *of friendship* intimidad *f*; *sexual* relaciones *fpl* íntimas
in·ti·mate ['ɪntɪmət] *adj* íntimo
in·tim·i·date [ɪn'tɪmɪdeɪt] *v/t* intimidar
in·tim·i·da·tion [ɪntɪmɪ'deɪʃn] intimidación *f*
in·to ['ɪntʊ] *prep* en; ***he put it into his suitcase*** lo puso en su maleta; ***translate into English*** traducir al inglés; ***he's into classical music*** F (*likes*) le gusta *or Span* le va mucho la música clásica; ***he's into local politics*** F (*is involved with*) está muy metido en el mundillo de la política local; ***when you're into the job*** cuando te hayas metido en el trabajo
in·tol·e·ra·ble [ɪn'tɑːlərəbl] *adj* intolerable
in·tol·e·rant [ɪn'tɑːlərənt] *adj* intolerante
in·tox·i·cat·ed [ɪn'tɑːksɪkeɪtɪd] *adj* ebrio, embriagado
in·tran·si·tive [ɪn'trænsɪtɪv] *adj* intransitivo
in·tra·ve·nous [ɪntrə'viːnəs] *adj* intravenoso
in·trep·id [ɪn'trepɪd] *adj* intrépido
in·tri·cate ['ɪntrɪkət] *adj* intrincado, complicado
in·trigue **1** *n* ['ɪntriːg] intriga *f* **2** *v/t* [ɪn'triːg] intrigar; ***I would be intrigued to know …*** tendría curiosidad por saber …
in·trigu·ing [ɪn'triːgɪŋ] *adj* intrigante
in·tro·duce [ɪntrə'duːs] *v/t* presentar; *new technique etc* introducir; ***may I introduce …?*** permítame presentarle a …; ***he introduced me to his wife*** me presentó a su esposa; ***introduce s.o. to a new sport*** iniciar a alguien en un deporte nuevo
in·tro·duc·tion [ɪntrə'dʌkʃn] *to person* presentación *f*; *to a new food, sport etc* iniciación *f*; *in book, of new techniques et* introducción *f*
in·tro·vert ['ɪntrəvɜːrt] *n* introvertido(-a) *m(f)*
in·trude [ɪn'truːd] *v/i* molestar
in·trud·er [ɪn'truːdər] intruso(-a) *m(f)*
in·tru·sion [ɪn'truːʒn] intromisión *f*
in·tu·i·tion [ɪntuː'ɪʃn] intuición *f*
in·vade [ɪn'veɪd] *v/t* invadir
in·val·id[1] [ɪn'vælɪd] *adj* nulo
in·va·lid[2] ['ɪnvəlɪd] *n* MED minusválido(-a) *m(f)*

in·val·i·date [ɪn'vælɪdeɪt] *v/t claim, theory* invalidar
in·val·u·a·ble [ɪn'væljʊbl] *adj help, contributor* inestimable
in·var·i·a·bly [ɪn'veɪrɪəblɪ] *adv (always)* invariablemente, siempre
in·va·sion [ɪn'veɪʒn] invasión *f*
in·vent [ɪn'vent] *v/t* inventar
in·ven·tion [ɪn'venʃn] *action* invención *f*; *thing invented* invento *m*
in·ven·tive [ɪn'ventɪv] *adj* inventivo, imaginativo
in·ventor [ɪn'ventər] inventor(-a) *m(f)*
in·ven·tory ['ɪnvəntɔːrɪ] inventorio *m*
in·verse [ɪn'vɜːrs] *adj order* inverso
in·vert [ɪn'vɜːrt] *v/t* invertir
in·vert·ed 'com·mas [ɪn'vɜːrtɪd] *npl* comillas *fpl*
in·ver·te·brate [ɪn'vɜːrtɪbrət] *n* invertebrado *m*
invest [ɪn'vest] **1** *v/t* invertir **2** *v/i* invertir (***in*** en)
in·ves·ti·gate [ɪn'vestɪgeɪt] *v/t* investigar
in·ves·ti·ga·tion [ɪnvestɪ'geɪʃn] investigación *f*
in·ves·ti·ga·tive 'jour·nal·ism [ɪn'vestɪgətɪv] periodismo *m* de investigación
in·vest·ment [ɪn'vestmənt] inversión *f*
in'vest·ment bank banco *m* de inversiones
in·ves·tor [ɪn'vestər] inversor(a) *m(f)*
in·vig·or·at·ing [ɪn'vɪgəreɪtɪŋ] *adj climate* vigorizante
in·vin·ci·ble [ɪn'vɪnsəbl] *adj* invencible
in·vis·i·ble [ɪn'vɪzɪbl] *adj* invisible
in·vi·ta·tion [ɪnvɪ'teɪʃn] invitación *f*
in·vite [ɪn'vaɪt] *v/t* invitar; ***he invited me out for a meal*** me invitó a comer
◆ **invite in** *v/t*: ***invite s.o. in*** invitar a alguien a que entre
in·voice ['ɪnvɔɪs] **1** *n* factura *f* **2** *v/t customer* enviar la factura a
in·vol·un·ta·ry [ɪn'vɑːlənterɪ] *adj* involuntario
in·volve [ɪn'vɑːlv] *v/t hard work, expense* involucrar, entrañar; ***it would involve emigrating*** supondría emigrar; ***this doesn't involve you*** esto no tiene nada que ver contigo; ***what does it involve?*** ¿en qué consiste?; ***get involved with sth*** involucrarse *or* meterse en algo; ***the police didn't want to get involved*** la policía no quería intervenir; ***get involved with s.o.*** *emotionally, romantically* tener una relación sentimental con alguien
in·volved [ɪn'vɑːlvd] *adj (complex)* complicado
in·volve·ment [ɪn'vɑːlvmənt] *in a project, crime etc* participación *f*, intervención *f*
in·vul·ne·ra·ble [ɪn'vʌlnərəbl] *adj* invulnerable
in·ward ['ɪnwərd] **1** *adj feeling, smile* interior **2** *adv* hacia dentro
in·ward·ly ['ɪnwərdlɪ] *adv* por dentro
i·o·dine ['aɪoʊdiːn] yodo *m*
IOU [aɪoʊ'juː] *abbr* (= ***I owe you***) pagaré *m*
IQ [aɪ'kjuː] *abbr* (= ***intelligence quotient***) cociente *m* intelectual
I·ran [ɪ'rɑːn] Irán
I·ra·ni·an [ɪ'reɪnɪən] **1** *adj* iraní **2** *n* iraní *m/f*
I·raq [ɪ'ræːk] Iraq, Irak
I·ra·qi [ɪ'rækɪ] **1** *adj* iraquí **2** *n* iraquí *m/f*
Ire·land ['aɪrlənd] Irlanda
i·ris ['aɪrɪs] *of eye* iris *m inv*; *flower* lirio *m*
I·rish ['aɪrɪʃ] *adj* irlandés
'I·rish·man irlandés *m*
'I·rish·wom·an irlandesa *f*
i·ron ['aɪərn] **1** *n substance* hierro *m*; *for clothes* plancha *f* **2** *v/t shirts etc* planchar
i·ron·ic(al) [aɪ'rɑːnɪk(l)] *adj* irónico
i·ron·ing ['aɪərnɪŋ] planchado *m*; ***do the ironing*** planchar
'i·ron·ing board tabla *f* de planchar
'i·ron·works fundición *f*
i·ron·y ['aɪrənɪ] *ironía f*; ***the irony of it all is that …*** lo irónico del tema es que …
ir·ra·tion·al [ɪ'ræʃənl] *adj* irracional
ir·rec·on·ci·la·ble [ɪrekən'saɪləbl] *adj* irreconciliable
ir·re·cov·e·ra·ble [ɪrɪ'kʌvərəbl] *adj* irrecuperable
ir·re·gu·lar [ɪ'regjʊlər] *adj* irregular
ir·rel·e·vant [ɪ'reləvənt] *adj* irrelevante
ir·rep·a·ra·ble [ɪ'repərəbl] *adj* irreparable
ir·re·place·a·ble [ɪrɪ'pleɪsəbl] *adj object, person* irreemplazable
ir·re·pres·si·ble [ɪrɪ'presəbl] *adj sense of humor* incontenible; *person* irreprimible
ir·re·proa·cha·ble [ɪrɪ'proʊtʃəbl] *adj* irreprochable
ir·re·sis·ti·ble [ɪrɪ'zɪstəbl] *adj* irresistible
ir·re·spec·tive [ɪrɪ'spektɪv] *adv*: ***irrespective of*** independientemente de
ir·re·spon·si·ble [ɪrɪ'spɑːnsəbl] *adj* irresponsable
ir·re·trie·va·ble [ɪrɪ'triːvəbl] *adj* irrecuperable
ir·rev·e·rent [ɪ'revərənt] *adj* irreverente
ir·rev·o·ca·ble [ɪ'revəkəbl] *adj* irrevocable
ir·ri·gate ['ɪrɪgeɪt] *v/t* regar
ir·ri·ga·tion [ɪrɪ'geɪʃn] riego *m*
ir·ri·ga·tion ca'nal acequia *f*
ir·ri·ta·ble ['ɪrɪtəbl] *adj* irritable
ir·ri·tate ['ɪrɪteɪt] *v/t* irritar

ir·ri·tat·ing ['ɪrɪteɪtɪŋ] *adj* irritante
ir·ri·ta·tion [ɪrɪ'teɪʃn] irritación *f*
Is·lam ['ɪzlɑːm] (el) Islam
Is·lam·ic [ɪz'læmɪk] *adj* islámico
is·land ['aɪlənd] isla *f*; **(*traffic*) *island*** isleta *f*
is·land·er ['aɪləndər] isleño(-a) *m*(*f*)
i·so·late ['aɪsəleɪt] *v/t* aislar
i·so·lat·ed ['aɪsəleɪtɪd] *adj* aislado
i·so·la·tion [aɪsə'leɪʃn] *of a region* aislamiento *m*; ***in isolation*** aisladamente
i·so'la·tion ward pabellón *m* de enfermedades infecciosas
ISP [aɪes'piː] *abbr* (= ***Internet service provider***) proveedor *m* de (acceso a) Internet
Is·rael ['ɪzreɪl] Israel
Is·rae·li [ɪz'reɪlɪ] **1** *adj* israelí **2** *n person* israelí *m/f*
is·sue ['ɪʃuː] **1** *n* (*matter*) tema *m*, asunto *m*; *of magazine* número *m*; ***the point at issue*** el tema que se debate; ***take issue with s.o./sth*** discrepar de algo / alguien **2** *v/t coins* emitir; *passports, visa* expedir; *warning* dar; ***issue s.o. with sth*** entregar algo a alguien
IT [aɪ'tiː] *abbr* (= ***information technology***) tecnologías *fpl* de la información; ***IT department*** departamento de informática
it [ɪt] *pron as object* lo *m*, la *f*; ***what color is it? - it is red*** ¿de qué color es? - es rojo; ***it's raining*** llueve; ***it's me / him*** soy yo / es él; ***it's Charlie here*** TELEC soy Charlie; ***it's your turn*** te toca; ***that's it!*** (*that's right*) ¡eso es!; (*finished*) ¡ya está!
I·tal·i·an [ɪ'tæljən] **1** *adj* italiano **2** *n person* italiano(-a) *m*(*f*); *language* italiano *m*
I·ta·ly ['ɪtəlɪ] Italia
itch [ɪʧ] **1** *n* picor *m* **2** *v/i* picar
i·tem ['aɪtəm] *in list, accounts*, (*article*) artículo *m*; *on agenda* punto *m*; *of news* noticia *f*
i·tem·ize ['aɪtəmaɪz] *v/t invoice* detallar
i·tin·e·ra·ry [aɪ'tɪnərerɪ] itinerario *m*
its [ɪts] *poss adj* su; ***where is its box?*** ¿dónde está su caja?; ***the dog has hurt its leg*** el perro se ha hecho daño en la pata
it's [ɪts] → ***it is***, ***it has***
it·self [ɪt'self] *pron reflexive* se; ***the dog hurt itself*** el perro se hizo daño; ***the hotel itself is fine*** el hotel en sí (mismo) está bien; ***by itself*** (*alone*) aislado, solo; (*automatically*) solo
i·vo·ry ['aɪvərɪ] marfil *m*
i·vy ['aɪvɪ] hiedra *f*

J

jab [dʒæb] *v/t* (*pret & pp* ***jabbed***) clavar; ***he jabbed his elbow into my ribs*** me clavó el codo en las costillas
jab·ber ['dʒæbər] *v/i* parlotear
jack [dʒæk] MOT gato *m*; *in cards* jota *f*
◆ **jack up** *v/t* MOT levantar con el gato
jack·et ['dʒækɪt] (*coat*) chaqueta *f*; *of book* sobrecubierta *f*
jack·et po'ta·to *Span* patata *f or L.Am.* papa *f* asada (*con piel*)
'jack-knife 1 *n* navaja *f* **2** *v/i* derrapar (*por la parte del remolque*)
'jack·pot gordo *m*; ***he hit the jackpot*** le tocó el gordo
ja·cuz·zi [dʒə'kuːzɪ] jacuzzi *m*
jade [dʒeɪd] *n* jade *m*
jad·ed ['dʒeɪdɪd] *adj* harto; *appetite* hastiado
jag·ged ['dʒægɪd] *adj* accidentado
jag·u·ar ['dʒægʊər] jaguar *m*
jail [dʒeɪl] *n* cárcel *f*; ***he's in jail*** está en la cárcel
jam[1] [dʒæm] *n for bread* mermelada *f*
jam[2] [dʒæm] **1** *n* MOT atasco *m*; F (*difficulty*) aprieto *m*; ***be in a jam*** estar en un aprieto **2** *v/t* (*pret & pp* ***jammed***) (*ram*) meter, embutir; (*cause to stick*) atascar; *broadcast* provocar interferencias en; ***be jammed*** *of roads* estar colapsado; *of door, window* estar atascado; ***jam on the brakes*** dar un frenazo **3** *v/i* (*pret & pp* ***jammed***) (*stick*) atascarse; ***all ten of us managed to jam into the car*** nos las arreglamos para meternos los diez en el coche
jam-'packed *adj* F abarrotado (***with*** de)
jan·i·tor ['dʒænɪtər] portero(-a) *m*(*f*)
Jan·u·a·ry ['dʒænʊerɪ] enero *m*

Ja·pan [dʒə'pæn] Japón
Jap·a·nese [dʒæpə'niːz] **1** *adj* japonés **2** *n person* japonés(-esa) *m(f)*; *language* japonés *m*; ***the Japanese*** los japoneses
jar[1] [dʒɑːr] *n container* tarro *m*
jar[2] [dʒɑːr] *v/i* (*pret & pp* ***jarred***) *of noise* rechinar; ***jar on*** rechinar en
jar·gon ['dʒɑːrgən] jerga *f*
jaun·dice ['dʒɒːndɪs] *n* ictericia *f*
jaun·diced ['dʒɒːndɪst] *adj fig* resentido
jaunt [dʒɒːnt] *n* excursión *f*; ***go on a jaunt*** ir de excursión
jaunt·y ['dʒɒːntɪ] *adj* desenfadado
jav·e·lin ['dʒævlɪn] (*spear*) jabalina *f*; *event* (lanzamiento *m* de) jabalina *f*
jaw [dʒɒː] *n* mandíbula *f*
jay·walk·er ['dʒeɪwɒːkər] peatón(-ona) *m(f)* imprudente
'jay·walk·ing *cruzar la calle de manera imprudente*
jazz [dʒæz] *n* jazz *m*
◆ **jazz up** *v/t* F animar
jeal·ous ['dʒeləs] *adj* celoso; ***be jealous of*** *in love* tener celos de; *of riches etc* tener envidia de
jeal·ous·ly ['dʒeləslɪ] *adv* celosamente; *relating to possessions* con envidia
jeal·ous·y ['dʒeləsɪ] celos *mpl*; *of possessions* envidia *f*
jeans [dʒiːnz] *npl* vaqueros *mpl*, jeans *mpl*
jeep [dʒiːp] jeep *m*
jeer [dʒɪr] **1** *n* abucheo *m* **2** *v/i* abuchear; ***jeer at*** burlarse de
Jel·lo® ['dʒeloʊ] gelatina *f*
jel·ly ['dʒelɪ] mermelada *f*
'jel·ly bean gominola *f*
'jel·ly·fish medusa *f*
jeop·ar·dize ['dʒepərdaɪz] *v/t* poner en peligro
jeop·ar·dy ['dʒepərdɪ]: ***be in jeopardy*** estar en peligro
jerk[1] [dʒɜːrk] **1** *n* sacudida *f* **2** *v/t* dar un tirón a
jerk[2] [dʒɜːrk] *n* F imbécil *m/f*, *Span* gilipollas *m/f inv* F
jerk·y ['dʒɜːrkɪ] *adj movement* brusco
jer·sey ['dʒɜːrzɪ] (*sweater*) suéter *m*, *Span* jersey *m*
jest [dʒest] **1** *n* broma *f*; ***in jest*** en broma **2** *v/i* bromear
Je·sus ['dʒiːzəs] Jesús
jet [dʒet] **1** *n of water* chorro *m*; (*nozzle*) boquilla *f*; (*airplane*) reactor *m*, avión *m* a reacción **2** *v/i* (*pret & pp* ***jetted***) *travel* viajar en avión
jet-'black *adj* azabache
'jet en·gine reactor *m*
'jet·lag desfase *m* horario, jet lag *m*
jet·ti·son ['dʒetɪsn] *v/t also fig* tirar por la borda
jet·ty ['dʒetɪ] malecón *m*
Jew [dʒuː] judío(-a) *m(f)*
jew·el ['dʒuːəl] joya *f*, alhaja *f*; *fig*: *person* joya *f*
jew·el·er, *Br* **jew·el·ler** ['dʒuːlər] joyero(-a) *m(f)*
jew·el·lery *Br*, **jew·el·ry** ['dʒuːlrɪ] joyas *fpl*, alhajas *fpl*
Jew·ish ['dʒuːɪʃ] *adj* judío
jif·fy [dʒɪfɪ] F: ***in a jiffy*** en un periquete F
jig·saw (puzzle) ['dʒɪgsɒː] rompecabezas *m inv*, puzzle *m*
jilt [dʒɪlt] *v/t* dejar plantado
jin·gle ['dʒɪŋgl] **1** *n* (*song*) melodía *f* publicitaria **2** *v/i of keys, coins* tintinear
jinx [dʒɪŋks] *n* gafe *m*; ***there's a jinx on this project*** este proyecto está gafado
jit·ters ['dʒɪtərz] *npl* F: ***I got the jitters*** me entró el pánico *or Span* canguelo F
jit·ter·y ['dʒɪtərɪ] *adj* F nervioso
job [dʒɑːb] (*employment*) trabajo *m*, empleo *m*; (*task*) tarea *f*, trabajo *m*; ***it's not my job to answer the phone*** no me corresponde a mí contestar el teléfono; ***I've got a few jobs to do around the house*** tengo que hacer unas cuantas cosas en la casa; ***out of a job*** sin trabajo *or* empleo; ***it's a good job you warned me*** menos mal que me aviaste; ***you'll have a job*** (*it'll be difficult*) te va a costar Dios y ayuda
'job de·scrip·tion (descripción *f* de las) responsabilidades *fpl* del puesto
'job hunt *v/i*: ***be job hunting*** buscar trabajo
job·less ['dʒɑːblɪs] *adj* desempleado, *Span* parado
job sat·is'fac·tion satisfacción *f* con el trabajo
jock·ey ['dʒɑːkɪ] *n* jockey *m/f*
jog ['dʒɑːg] **1** *n*: ***go for a jog*** ir a hacer jogging *or* footing **2** *v/i* (*pret & pp* ***jogged***) *as exercise* hacer jogging *or* footing **3** *v/t* (*pret & pp* ***jogged***) ***jog s.o.'s memory*** refrescar la memoria de alguien; ***somebody jogged my elbow*** alguien me dio en el codo
◆ **jog along** *v/i* F ir tirando P
jog·ger ['dʒɑːgər] *person* persona *f* que hace jogging *or* footing; *shoe* zapatilla *f* de jogging *or* footing
jog·ging ['dʒɑːgɪŋ] jogging *m*, footing *m*; ***go jogging*** ir a hacer jogging *or* footing
'jog·ging suit chándal *m*
john [dʒɑːn] P (*toilet*) baño *m*, váter *m*
join [dʒɔɪn] **1** *n* juntura *f* **2** *v/i of roads, rivers* juntarse; (*become a member*) ha-

cerse socio **3** *v/t* (*connect*) unir; *person* unirse a; *club* hacerse socio de; (*go to work for*) entrar en; *of road* desembocar en; ***I'll join you at the theater*** me runiré contigo en el teatro

◆ **join in** *v/i* participar

◆ **join up** *v/i* MIL alistarse

join·er ['dʒɔɪnər] carpintero(-a) *m(f)*

joint [dʒɔɪnt] **1** *n* ANAT articulación *f*; *in woodwork* junta *f*; *of meat* pieza *f*; F (*place*) garito *m* F; *of cannabis* porro *m* F, canuto *m* F **2** *adj* (*shared*) conjunto

joint ac'count cuenta *f* conjunta

joint 'ven·ture empresa *f* conjunta

joke [dʒoʊk] **1** *n story* chiste *m*; (*practical joke*) broma *f*; ***play a joke on*** gastar una broma a; ***it's no joke*** no tiene ninguna gracia **2** *v/i* bromear

jok·er ['dʒoʊkər] *person* bromista *m/f*; F *pej* payaso(-a) *m(f)*; *in cards* comodín *m*

jok·ing ['dʒoʊkɪŋ]: ***joking apart*** bromas aparte

jok·ing·ly ['dʒoʊkɪŋlɪ] *adv* en broma

jol·ly ['dʒɑːlɪ] *adj* alegre

jolt [dʒoʊlt] **1** *n* (*jerk*) sacudida *f* **2** *v/t* (*push*) ***somebody jolted my elbow*** alguien me dio en el codo

jos·tle ['dʒɑːsl] *v/t* empujar

◆ **jot down** [dʒɑːt] *v/t* (*pret & pp* ***jotted***) apuntar, anotar

jour·nal ['dʒɜːrnl] (*magazine*) revista *f*; (*diary*) diario *m*

jour·nal·ism ['dʒɜːrnəlɪzm] periodismo *m*

jour·nal·ist ['dʒɜːrnəlɪst] periodista *m/f*

jour·ney ['dʒɜːrnɪ] *n* viaje *m*

jo·vi·al ['dʒoʊvɪəl] *adj* jovial

joy [dʒɔɪ] alegría *f*, gozo *m*

'joy·stick COMPUT joystick *m*

ju·bi·lant ['dʒuːbɪlənt] *adj* jubiloso

ju·bi·la·tion [dʒuːbɪ'leɪʃn] júbilo *m*

judge [dʒʌdʒ] **1** *n* LAW juez *m/f*, jueza *f*; *in competition* juez *m/f*, miembro *m* del jurado **2** *v/t* juzgar; (*estimate*) calcular **3** *v/i* juzgar; ***judge for yourself*** júzgalo por ti mismo

judg·ment ['dʒʌdʒmənt] LAW fallo *m*; (*opinion*) juicio *m*; ***an error of judgment*** una equivocación; ***he showed good judgment*** mostró tener criterio; ***against my better judgment*** a pesar de no estar convencido; ***the Last Judgment*** REL el Juicio Final

'Judg(e)·ment Day Día *m* del Juicio Final

ju·di·cial [dʒuː'dɪʃl] *adj* judicial

ju·di·cious [dʒuː'dɪʃəs] *adj* juicioso

ju·do ['dʒuːdoʊ] judo *m*

jug·gle [dʒʌgl] *v/t also fig* hacer malabarismos con

jug·gler ['dʒʌglər] malabarista *m/f*

juice [dʒuːs] *n Span* zumo *m*, *L.Am.* jugo *m*

juic·y ['dʒuːsɪ] *adj* jugoso; *news, gossip* jugoso, sabroso

juke·box ['dʒuːkbɑːks] máquina *f* de discos

Ju·ly [dʒʊ'laɪ] julio *m*

jum·ble ['dʒʌmbl] *n* revoltijo *m*

◆ **jumble up** *v/t* revolver

jum·bo (jet) ['dʒʌmboʊ] jumbo *m*

'jum·bo(-sized) *adj* gigante

jump [dʒʌmp] **1** *n* salto *m*; (*increase*) incremento *m*, subida *f*; ***give a jump*** *of surprise* dar un salto **2** *v/i* saltar; (*increase*) dispararse; ***you made me jump!*** ¡me diste un susto!; ***jump to one's feet*** ponerse de pie de un salto; ***jump to conclusions*** sacar conclusiones precipitadas **3** *v/t fence etc* saltar; F (*attack*) asaltar; ***jump the lights*** saltarse el semáforo, pasarse un semáforo en rojo

◆ **jump at** *v/t opportunity* no dejar escapar

jump·er[1] ['dʒʌmpər] *dress* pichi *m*

jump·er[2] ['dʒʌmpər] SP saltador(a) *m(f)*; *horse* caballo *m* de saltos

jump·y ['dʒʌmpɪ] *adj* nervioso; ***get jumpy*** ponerse nervioso

junc·tion ['dʒʌŋkʃn] *of roads* cruce *m*

junc·ture ['dʒʌŋktʃər] *fml*: ***at this juncture*** en esta coyuntura

June [dʒuːn] junio *m*

jun·gle ['dʒʌŋgl] selva *f*, jungla *f*

ju·ni·or ['dʒuːnjər] **1** *adj subordinate* de rango inferior; *younger* más joven **2** *n in rank* subalterno(-a) *m(f)*; ***she is ten years my junior*** es diez años más joven que yo

ju·ni·or 'high escuela *f* secundaria (*para alumnos de entre 12 y 14 años*)

junk [dʒʌŋk] *n* trastos *mpl*

'junk food comida *f* basura

junk·ie ['dʒʌŋkɪ] F drogota *m/f* F

'junk mail propaganda *f* postal

'junk shop cacharrería *f*

'junk·yard depósito *m* de chatarra

jur·is·dic·tion [dʒʊrɪs'dɪkʃn] LAW jurisdicción *f*

ju·ror ['dʒʊrər] miembro *m* del jurado

ju·ry ['dʒʊrɪ] jurado *m*

just [dʒʌst] **1** *adj law, cause* justo **2** *adv* (*barely*) justo; (*exactly*) justo, justamente; (*only*) sólo, solamente; ***have just done sth*** acabar de hacer algo; ***I've just seen her*** la acabo de ver; ***just about*** (*almost*) casi; ***I was just about to leave when …*** estaba a punto de salir cuando …; ***just like that*** (*abruptly*) de repente;

just now (*at the moment*) ahora mismo; ***I saw her just now*** (*a few moments ago*) la acabo de ver; ***just you wait!*** ¡ya verás!; ***just be quiet!*** ¡cállate de una vez!

jus·tice ['dʒʌstɪs] justicia *f*

jus·ti·fi·a·ble [dʒʌstɪ'faɪəbl] *adj* justificable

jus·ti·fia·bly [dʒʌstɪ'faɪəblɪ] *adv* justificadamente

jus·ti·fi·ca·tion [dʒʌstɪfɪ'keɪʃn] justificación *f*; ***there's no justification for behavior like that*** ese comportamiento es injustificable *or* no tiene justificación

jus·ti·fy ['dʒʌstɪfaɪ] *v/t* (*pret & pp* ***justified***) *also text* justificar

just·ly ['dʒʌstlɪ] *adv* (*fairly*) con justicia; (*rightly*) con razón

◆ **jut out** [dʒʌt] *v/i* (*pret & pp* ***jutted***) sobresalir

ju·ve·nile ['dʒuːvənl] **1** *adj crime* juvenil; *court* de menores; *pej* infantil **2** *n fml* menor *m/f*

ju·ve·nile de'lin·quen·cy delincuencia *f* juvenil

ju·ve·nile de'lin·quent delincuente *m/f* juvenil

K

k [keɪ] *abbr* (= ***kilobyte***) k (= kilobyte *m*); (= ***thousand***) mil

kan·ga·roo [kæŋgə'ruː] canguro *m*

ka·ra·te [kə'rɑːtɪ] kárate *m*

ka'ra·te chop golpe *m* de kárate

ke·bab [kɪ'bæb] pincho *m*, brocheta *f*

keel [kiːl] NAUT quilla *f*

◆ **keel over** *v/i of structure* desplomarse; *of person* desmayarse

keen [kiːn] *adj* entusiasta, interesado; *interest* gran; *competition* reñido; ***she's keen to learn*** tiene mucho interés en aprender; ***he's keen on football / her*** le gusta el fútbol / ella; ***I'm not keen on the idea*** no me entusiasma la idea; ***be keen to do sth*** estar muy interesado en hacer algo

keep [kiːp] **1** *n* (*maintenance*) manutención *f*; ***for keeps*** F para siempre **2** *v/t* (*pret & pp* ***kept***) guardar; (*not lose*) conservar; (*detain*) entretener; *family* mantener; *animals* tener, criar; ***you can keep it*** (*it's for you*) te lo puedes quedar; ***keep trying!*** ¡sigue intentándolo!; ***don't keep interrupting!*** ¡deja de interrumpirme!; ***keep a promise*** cumplir una promesa; ***keep s.o. company*** hacer compañía a alguien; ***keep s.o. waiting*** hacer esperar a alguien; ***he can't keep anything to himself*** no sabe guardar un secreto; ***I kept the news of the accident to myself*** no dije nada sobre el accidente; ***keep sth from s.o.*** ocultar algo a alguien; ***we kept the news from him*** no le contamos la noticia **3** *v/i* (*pret & pp* ***kept***) *of food*, *milk* aguantar, conservarse; ***keep calm!*** ¡tranquilízate!; ***keep quiet!*** ¡cállate!

◆ **keep away 1** *v/i*: ***keep away from that building*** no te acerques a ese edificio **2** *v/t*: ***keep the children away from the stove*** no dejes que los niños se acerquen a la cocina

◆ **keep back** *v/t* (*hold in check*) contener; *information* ocultar

◆ **keep down** *v/t voice* bajar; *costs*, *inflation etc* reducir; *food* retener; ***keep your voices down in the library*** hablen en voz baja en la biblioteca; ***tell the kids to keep the noise down*** diles a los niños que no hagan tanto ruido; ***I can't keep anything down*** devuelvo todo lo que como

◆ **keep in** *v/t in school* castigar (*a quedarse en clase*); ***the hospital's keeping her in*** la tienen en observación

◆ **keep off 1** *v/t* (*avoid*) evitar; ***keep off the grass!*** ¡prohibido pisar el césped! **2** *v/i*: ***if the rain keeps off*** si no llueve

◆ **keep on 1** *v/i* continuar; ***if you keep on interrupting me*** si no dejas de interrumpirme; ***keep on trying*** sigue intentándolo **2** *v/t*: ***the company kept them on*** la empresa los mantuvo en el puesto; ***keep your coat on!*** *item of clothing* ¡no te quites el abrigo!

◆ **keep on at** *v/t* (*nag*): ***my parents keep on at me to get a job*** mis padres no dejan de decirme que busque un trabajo

◆ **keep out 1** *v/t*: ***it keeps the cold out*** protege del frío; ***they must be kept out*** no pueden entrar **2** *v/i*: ***I told you***

to keep out! *of a place* ¡te dije que no entraras!; ***I would keep out of it if I were you*** *of discussion etc* yo en tu lugar no me metería; ***keep out*** *as sign* prohibida la entrada, prohibido el paso

◆ **keep to** *v/t path* seguir; *rules* cumplir, respetar

◆ **keep up 1** *v/i when walking, running etc* seguir *or* mantener el ritmo (***with*** de); ***keep up with s.o.*** (*stay in touch with*) mantener contacto con alguien **2** *v/t pace* seguir, mantener; *payments* estar al corriente de; *bridge, pants* sujetar

keep·ing ['ki:pɪŋ] *n*: ***be in keeping with*** *decor* combinar con; ***in keeping with*** *promises* de acuerdo con

'**keep·sake** recuerdo *m*

keg [keg] barril *m*

ken·nel ['kenl] *n* caseta *f* del perro

ken·nels ['kenlz] *npl* residencia *f* canina

kept [kept] *pret & pp* → ***keep***

ker·nel ['kɜ:rnl] almendra *f*

ker·o·sene ['kerəsi:n] queroseno *m*

K

ketch·up ['ketʃʌp] ketchup *m*

ket·tle ['ketl] hervidor *m*

key [ki:] **1** *n to door, drawer* llave *f*; *on keyboard, piano* tecla *f*; *of piece of music* clave *f*; *on map* leyenda *f* **2** *adj* (*vital*) clave, crucial **3** *v/t & v/i* COMPUT teclear

◆ **key in** *v/t data* introducir, teclear

'**key·board** COMPUT, MUS teclado *m*

key·board·er COMPUT operador(a) *m(f)*, *persona que introduce datos en el ordenador*

'**key·card** tarjeta *f* (de hotel)

keyed-up [ki:d'ʌp] *adj* nervioso

'**key·hole** ojo *m* de la cerradura

key·note '**speech** discurso *m* central

'**key·ring** llavero *m*

kha·ki ['kækɪ] *adj* caqui

kick [kɪk] **1** *n* patada *f*; ***he got a kick out of watching them suffer*** disfrutó viéndoles sufrir; (***just***) ***for kicks*** F por diversión **2** *v/t* dar una patada a; F *habit* dejar; ***I kicked him in the shins*** le di una patada en la espinilla **3** *v/i of person* patalear; *of horse, mule* cocear

◆ **kick around** *v/t ball* dar patadas a; F (*discuss*) comentar

◆ **kick in** *v/t* P *money* apoquinar F

◆ **kick off** *v/i* comenzar, sacar de centro; F (*start*) empezar

◆ **kick out** *v/t of bar, company* echar; *of country, organization* expulsar

◆ **kick up** *v/t*: ***kick up a fuss*** montar un numerito

'**kick·back** F (*bribe*) soborno *m*

'**kick·off** SP saque *m*

kid [kɪd] **1** *n* F (*child*) crío *m* F, niño *m*; ***when I was a kid*** cuando era pequeño; ***kid brother*** hermano *m* pequeño; ***kid sister*** hermana *f* pequeña **2** *v/t* (*pret & pp* ***kidded***) F tomar el pelo a F **3** *v/i* (*pret & pp* ***kidded***) F bromear; ***I was only kidding*** estaba bromeando

kid·der ['kɪdər] F vacilón *m* F

kid '**gloves**: ***handle s.o. with kid gloves*** tratar a alguien con guante de seda

kid·nap ['kɪdnæp] *v/t* (*pret & pp* ***kidnapped***) secuestrar

kid·nap·(p)er ['kɪdnæpər] secuestrador *m*

'**kid·nap·(p)ing** ['kɪdnæpɪŋ] secuestro *m*

kid·ney ['kɪdnɪ] ANAT riñón *m*; *in cooking* riñones *mpl*

'**kid·ney bean** alubia *f* roja de riñón

'**kid·ney ma·chine** MED riñón *m* artificial, máquina *f* de diálisis

kill [kɪl] *v/t* matar; ***the drought killed all the plants*** las plantas murieron como resultado de la sequía; ***I had six hours to kill*** tenía seis horas sin nada que hacer; ***be killed in an accident*** matarse en un accidente, morirse en un accidente; ***kill o.s.*** suicidarse; ***kill o.s. laughing*** F morirse de risa F

kil·ler ['kɪlər] (*murderer*) asesino *m*; ***be a killer*** *of disease* ser mortal

kil·ling ['kɪlɪŋ] *n* asesinato *m*; ***make a killing*** F (*lots of money*) forrarse F

kil·ling·ly ['kɪlɪŋlɪ] *adv* F: ***killingly funny*** para morirse de risa

kiln [kɪln] horno *m*

ki·lo ['ki:loʊ] kilo *m*

ki·lo·byte ['kɪloʊbaɪt] COMPUT kilobyte *m*

ki·lo·gram ['kɪloʊgræm] kilogramo *m*

ki·lo·me·ter, *Br* **ki·lo·me·tre** [kɪ'lɑ:mɪtər] kilómetro *m*

kind¹ [kaɪnd] *adj* agradable, amable

kind² [kaɪnd] *n* (*sort*) tipo *m*; (*make, brand*) marca *f*; ***all kinds of people*** toda clase de personas; ***I did nothing of the kind!*** ¡no hice nada parecido!; ***kind of ...*** *sad, lonely, etc* un poco ...; ***that's very kind of you*** gracias por tu amabilidad

kin·der·gar·ten ['kɪndərgɑ:rtn] guardería *f*, jardín *m* de infancia

kind-heart·ed [kaɪnd'hɑ:rtɪd] *adj* agradable, amable

kind·ly ['kaɪndlɪ] **1** *adj* amable, agradable **2** *adv* con amabilidad; ***kindly don't interrupt*** por favor, no me interrumpa; ***kindly lower your voice*** ¿le importaría hablar más bajo?

kind·ness ['kaɪndnɪs] amabilidad *f*

king [kɪŋ] rey *m*

king·dom ['kɪŋdəm] reino *m*

'**king-size(d)** *adj* F *cigarettes* extralargo; ***king-size(d) bed*** cama *f* de matrimonio

grande
kink [kɪŋk] *n in hose etc* doblez *f*
kink·y ['kɪŋkɪ] *adj* F vicioso
kiosk ['kiːɑːsk] quiosco *m*
kiss [kɪs] **1** *n* beso *m* **2** *v/t* besar **3** *v/i* besarse
kiss of 'life boca *m* a boca, respiración *f* artificial; ***give s.o. the kiss of life*** hacer a alguien el boca a boca
kit [kɪt] (*equipment*) equipo *m*; ***first aid kit*** botiquín *m*; ***tool kit*** caja *f* de herramientas
kitch·en ['kɪʧɪn] cocina *f*
kitch·en·ette [kɪʧɪ'net] *cocina pequeña*
kitch·en 'sink: ***you've got everything but the kitchen sink*** F llevas la casa a cuestas F
kite [kaɪt] cometa *f*
kit·ten ['kɪtn] gatito *m*
kit·ty ['kɪtɪ] *money* fondo *m*
klutz [klʌts] F (*clumsy person*) manazas *m* F
knack [næk] habilidad *f*; ***he has a knack of upsetting people*** tiene la habilidad de disgustar a la gente; ***I soon got the knack of the new machine*** le pillé el truco a la nueva máquina rápidamente
knead [niːd] *v/t dough* amasar
knee [niː] *n* rodilla *f*
'knee·cap *n* rótula *f*
kneel [niːl] *v/i* (*pret & pp* ***knelt***) arrodillarse
'knee-length *adj* hasta la rodilla
knelt [nelt] *pret & pp* → ***kneel***
knew [nuː] *pret* → ***know***
knick-knacks ['nɪknæks] *npl* F baratijas *fpl*
knife [naɪf] **1** *n* (*pl* ***knives*** [naɪvz]) *for food* cuchillo *m*; *carried outside* navaja *f* **2** *v/t* acuchillar, apuñalar
knight [naɪt] *n* caballero *m*
knit [nɪt] **1** *v/t* (*pret & pp* ***knitted***) tejer **2** *v/i* (*pret & pp* ***knitted***) tricotar
◆ **knit together** *v/i of broken bone* soldarse
knit·ting ['nɪtɪŋ] punto *m*
'knit·ting nee·dle aguja *f* para hacer punto
'knit·wear prendas *fpl* de punto
knob [nɑːb] *on door* pomo *m*; *on drawer* tirador *m*; *of butter* nuez *f*, trocito *m*
knock [nɑːk] **1** *n on door* golpe *m*; (*blow*) golpe *m*; ***there was a knock on the door*** llamaron a la puerta **2** *v/t* (*hit*) golpear; F (*criticize*) criticar, meterse con F; ***he was knocked to the ground*** le tiraron al suelo **3** *v/i on the door* llamar
◆ **knock around 1** *v/t* F (*beat*) pegar a **2** *v/i* F (*travel*) viajar
◆ **knock down** *v/t of car* atropellar; *building* tirar; *object* tirar al suelo; F (*reduce the price of*) rebajar
◆ **knock off 1** *v/t* P (*steal*) mangar P **2** *v/i* F (*stop work for the day*) acabar, *Span* plegar F
◆ **knock out** *v/t* (*make unconscious*) dejar K.O.; *of medicine* dejar para el arrastre F; *power lines etc* destruir; (*eliminate*) eliminar
◆ **knock over** *v/t* tirar; *of car* atropellar
'knock·down *adj*: ***at a knockdown price*** tirado
knock-kneed [nɑːk'niːd] *adj* patizambo
'knock·out *n in boxing* K.O. *m*
knot [nɑːt] **1** *n* nudo *m* **2** *v/t* (*pret & pp* ***knotted***) anudar
'knot·ty ['nɑːtɪ] *adj problem* complicado
know [noʊ] **1** *v/t* (*pret* ***knew***, *pp* ***known***) *fact, language, how to do sth* saber; *person, place* conocer; (*recognize*) reconocer; ***will you let him know that …?*** ¿puedes decirle que …? **2** *v/i* (*pret* ***knew***, *pp* ***known***) saber; ***I don't know*** no (lo) sé; ***yes, I know*** sí, lo sé **3** *n*: ***people in the know*** los enterados
'know·how pericia *f*
know·ing ['noʊɪŋ] *adj* cómplice
know·ing·ly ['noʊɪŋlɪ] *adv* (*wittingly*) deliberadamente; *smile etc* con complicidad
'know-it-all F sabiondo F
knowl·edge ['nɑːlɪdʒ] conocimiento *m*; ***to the best of my knowledge*** por lo que sé; ***have a good knowledge of …*** tener buenos conocimientos de …
knowl·edge·a·ble ['nɑːlɪdʒəbl] *adj*: ***she's very knowledgeable about music*** sabe mucho de música
known [noʊn] *pp* → ***know***
knuck·le ['nʌkl] nudillo *m*
◆ **knuckle down** *v/i* F aplicarse F
◆ **knuckle under** *v/i* F pasar por el aro F
KO [keɪ'oʊ] (*knockout*) K.O.
Ko·ran [kə'ræn] Corán *m*
Ko·re·a [kə'riːə] Corea
Ko·re·an [kə'riːən] **1** *adj* coreano **2** *n* coreano(a) *m*(*f*); *language* coreano *m*
ko·sher ['koʊʃər] *adj* REL kosher; F legal F
kow·tow ['kaʊtaʊ] *v/i* F reverenciar
ku·dos ['kjuːdɑːs] reconocimiento *m*, prestigio *m*

L

lab [læb] laboratorio *m*
la·bel ['leɪbl] **1** *n* etiqueta *f* **2** *v/t baggage* etiquetar
la·bor ['leɪbər] *n* (*work*) trabajo *m*; *in pregnancy* parto *m*; ***be in labor*** estar de parto
la·bor·a·to·ry ['læbrətoʊrɪ] laboratorio *m*
la·bor·a·to·ry tech'ni·cian técnico(-a) *m*(*f*) de laboratorio
la·bo·ri·ous [lə'bɔːrɪəs] *adj* laborioso
la·bored ['leɪbərd] *adj style*, *speech* elaborado
la·bor·er ['leɪbərər] obrero(-a) *m*(*f*)
'la·bor u·ni·on sindicato *m*
'la·bor ward MED sala *f* de partos
la·bour *etc Br* → ***labor*** *etc*
lace [leɪs] *n material* encaje *m*; *for shoe* cordón *m*
◆**lace up** *v/t shoes* atar
lack [læk] **1** *n* falta *f*, carencia *f* **2** *v/t* carecer de; ***he lacks confidence*** le falta confianza **3** *v/i*: ***be lacking*** faltar
lac·quer ['lækər] *n for hair* laca *f*
lad [læd] muchacho *m*, chico *m*
lad·der ['lædər] *n* escalera *f* (de mano)
la·den ['leɪdn] *adj* cargado (***with*** de)
la·dies room ['leɪdiːz] servicio *m* de señoras
la·dle ['leɪdl] *n* cucharón *m*, cazo *m*
la·dy ['leɪdɪ] señora *f*
'la·dy·bug mariquita *f*
'la·dy·like *adj* femenino
lag [læg] *v/t* (*pret & pp* ***lagged***) *pipes* revestir con aislante
◆**lag behind** *v/i* quedarse atrás
la·ger ['lɑːgər] cerveza *f* rubia
la·goon [lə'guːn] laguna *f*
laid [leɪd] *pret & pp* → ***lay***[1]
laid·back [leɪd'bæk] *adj* tranquilo, despreocupado
lain [leɪn] *pp* → ***lie***[2]
lake [leɪk] lago *m*
lamb [læm] *animal*, *meat* cordero *m*
lame [leɪm] *adj person* cojo; *excuse* pobre
la·ment [lə'ment] **1** *n* lamento *m* **2** *v/t* lamentar
lam·en·ta·ble ['læməntəbl] *adj* lamentable
lam·i·nat·ed ['læmɪneɪtɪd] *adj surface* laminado; *paper* plastificado
lam·i·nat·ed 'glass cristal *m* laminado
lamp [læmp] lámpara *f*
'lamp·post farola *f*
'lamp·shade pantalla *f* (*de lámpara*)
land [lænd] **1** *n* tierra *f*; ***by land*** por tierra; ***on land*** en tierra; ***work on the land*** *as farmer* trabajar la tierra **2** *v/t airplane* aterrizar; *job* conseguir **3** *v/i of airplane* aterrizar; *of capsule on the moon* alunizar; *of ball*, *sth thrown* caer; ***it landed right on top of his head*** le cayó justo en la cabeza
land·ing ['lændɪŋ] *n of airplane* aterrizaje *m*; *on moon* alunizaje *m*; *of staircase* rellano *m*
'land·ing field pista *f* de aterrizaje
'land·ing gear tren *m* de aterrizaje
'land·ing strip pista *f* de aterrizaje
'land·la·dy *of bar* patrona *f*; *of hostel etc* dueña *f*; *of rented room* casera *f*
'land·lord *of bar* patrón *m*; *of hostel etc* dueño *m*; *of rented room* casero *m*
'land·mark punto *m* de referencia; *fig* hito *m*
'land own·er terrateniente *m/f*
land·scape ['lændskeɪp] **1** *n* (*also painting*) paisaje *m* **2** *adv print* en formato apaisado
'land·slide corrimiento *m* de tierras
land·slide 'vic·to·ry victoria *f* arrolladora
lane [leɪn] *in country* camino *m*, vereda *f*; (*alley*) callejón *m*; MOT carril *m*
lan·guage ['læŋgwɪdʒ] lenguaje *m*; *of nation* idioma *f*, lengua *f*
'lan·guage lab laboratorio *m* de idiomas
lank [læŋk] *adj hair* lacio
lank·y ['læŋkɪ] *adj person* larguirucho
lan·tern ['læntərn] farol *f*
lap[1] [læp] *n of track* vuelta *f*
lap[2] [læp] *n of water* chapoteo *m*
◆**lap up** *v/t* (*pret & pp* ***lapped***) *drink*, *milk* beber a lengüetadas; *flattery* deleitarse con
lap[3] [læp] *n of person* regazo *m*
la·pel [lə'pel] solapa *f*
lapse [læps] **1** *n* (*mistake*, *slip*) desliz *m*; *of time* lapso *m*; ***a lapse of attention*** un momento de distracción; ***a lapse of memory*** un olvido **2** *v/i of membership* vencer; ***lapse into silence / despair*** sumirse en el silencio / la desesperación; ***she lapsed into English*** empezó a hablar en inglés
lap·top ['læptɑːp] COMPUT ordenador *m* portátil, *L.Am.* computadora *f* portátil
lar·ce·ny ['lɑːrsənɪ] latrocinio *m*
lard [lɑːrd] manteca *f* de cerdo
lar·der ['lɑːrdər] despensa *f*

large [lɑːrdʒ] *adj* grande; ***be at large*** *of criminal, wild animal* andar suelto
large·ly ['lɑːrdʒlɪ] *adv* (*mainly*) en gran parte, principalmente
lark [lɑːrk] *bird* alondra *f*
lar·va ['lɑːrvə] larva *f*
lar·yn·gi·tis [lærɪn'dʒaɪtɪs] laringitis *f*
lar·ynx ['lærɪŋks] laringe *f*
la·ser ['leɪzər] láser *m*
'la·ser beam rayo *m* láser
'la·ser print·er impresora *f* láser
lash¹ [læʃ] *v/t with whip* azotar
◆ **lash down** *v/t with rope* amarrar
◆ **lash out** *v/i with fists, words* atacar (***at*** a), arremeter (***at*** contra)
lash² [læʃ] *n* (*eyelash*) pestaña *f*
lass [læs] muchacha *f*, chica *f*
last¹ [læst] **1** *adj in series* último; (*preceding*) anterior; ***last Friday*** el viernes pasado; ***last but one*** penúltimo; ***last night*** anoche; ***last but not least*** por último, pero no por ello menos importante **2** *adv* ***at last*** por fin, al fin
last² [læst] *v/i* durar
last·ing ['læstɪŋ] *adj* duradero
last·ly ['læstlɪ] *adv* por último, finalmente
latch [lætʃ] *n* pestillo *m*
late [leɪt] **1** *adj*: ***the bus is late again*** el autobús vuelve a llegar tarde; ***it's late*** es tarde; ***it's getting late*** se está haciendo tarde; ***of late*** últimamente, recientemente; ***the late 19th/20th century*** la última parte del siglo XIX / XX; ***in the late 19th/20th century*** a finales del siglo XIX / XX **2** *adv arrive, leave* tarde
late·ly ['leɪtlɪ] *adv* últimamente, recientemente
lat·er ['leɪtər] *adv* más tarde; ***see you later!*** ¡hasta luego!; ***later on*** más tarde
lat·est ['leɪtɪst] *adj news, girlfriend* último
lathe [leɪð] *n* torno *m*
la·ther ['lɑːðər] *n from soap* espuma *f*; ***in a lather*** (*sweaty*) empapado de sudor
Lat·in ['lætɪn] **1** *adj* latino **2** *n* latín *m*
Lat·in A'mer·i·ca Latinoamérica, *América* Latina
La·tin A'mer·i·can 1 *n* latinoamericano(-a) *m*(*f*) **2** *adj* latinoamericano
La·ti·no [læ'tiːnoʊ] **1** *adj* latino **2** *n* latino(-a)
lat·i·tude ['lætɪtuːd] *geographical* latitud *f*; (*freedom to act*) libertad *f*
lat·ter ['lætər] **1** *adj* último **2** *n*: ***Mr Brown and Mr White, of whom the latter was ...*** el Señor *B*rown y el Señor White, de quien el segundo *or* este último era ...
laugh [læf] **1** *n* risa *f*; ***it was a laugh*** F fue genial **2** *v/i* reírse
◆ **laugh at** *v/t* reírse de
'laugh·ing stock: ***make o.s. a laughing stock*** ponerse en ridículo; ***become a laughing stock*** ser el hazmerreír
laugh·ter ['læftər] risas *fpl*
launch [lɒːntʃ] **1** *n small boat* lancha *f*; *of ship* botadura *f*; *of rocket, new product* lanzamiento *m* **2** *v/t rocket, new product* lanzar; *ship* botar
'launch cer·e·mo·ny ceremonia *f* de lanzamiento
launch·(ing) pad plataforma *f* de lanzamiento
laun·der ['lɒːndər] *v/t clothes* lavar (y planchar); *money* blanquear
laun·dro·mat ['lɒːndrəmæt] lavandería *f*
laun·dry ['lɒːndrɪ] *place* lavadero *m*; *dirty clothes* ropa *f* sucia; *clean clothes* ropa *f* lavada; ***do the laundry*** lavar la ropa, *Span* hacer la colada
lau·rel ['lɑːrəl] laurel *m*
lav·a·to·ry ['lævətɔːrɪ] *place* cuarto *m* de baño, lavabo *m*; *equipment* retrete *m*
lav·en·der ['lævəndər] espliego *m*, lavanda *f*
lav·ish ['lævɪʃ] *adj* espléndido
law [lɒː] ley *f*; *subject* derecho *m*; ***be against the law*** estar prohibido, ser ilegal
law-a·bid·ing ['lɒːəbaɪdɪŋ] *adj* respetuoso con la ley
'law court juzgado *m*
law·ful ['lɒːfəl] *adj* legal; *wife* legítimo
law·less ['lɒːlɪs] *adj* sin ley
lawn [lɒːn] césped *m*
'lawn mow·er cortacésped *m*
'law·suit pleito *m*
law·yer ['lɒːjər] abogado(-a) *m*(*f*)
lax [læks] *adj* poco estricto
lax·a·tive ['læksətɪv] *n* laxante *m*
lay¹ [leɪ] *v/t* (*pret & pp* ***laid***) (*put down*) dejar, poner; *eggs* poner; V *sexually* tirarse a V
lay² [leɪ] *pret* → ***lie²***
◆ **lay into** *v/t* (*attack*) arremeter contra
◆ **lay off** *v/t workers* despedir
◆ **lay on** *v/t* (*provide*) organizar
◆ **lay out** *v/t objects* colocar, disponer; *page* diseñar, maquetar
'lay·a·bout F gandul(a) *m*(*f*) F
'lay-by *on road* área *f* de descanso
lay·er ['leɪər] estrato *m*; *of soil, paint* capa *f*
'lay·man laico *m*
'lay-off despido *m*
◆ **laze around** [leɪz] *v/i* holgazanear
la·zy ['leɪzɪ] *adj person* holgazán, perezoso; *day* ocioso
lb *abbr* (= ***pound***) libra *f* (*de peso*)
LCD [elsiː'diː] *abbr* (= ***liquid crystal dis-***

play) LCD, pantalla *f* de cristal líquido
lead¹ [liːd] **1** *v/t* (*pret & pp* ***led***) *procession, race* ir al frente de; *company, team* dirigir; (*guide, take*) conducir **2** *v/i* (*pret & pp* ***led***) *in race, competition* ir en cabeza; (*provide leadership*) tener el mando; ***a street leading off the square*** una calle que sale de la plaza; ***where is this leading?*** ¿adónde nos lleva esto? **3** *n in race* ventaja *f*; ***be in the lead*** estar en cabeza; ***take the lead*** ponerse en cabeza; ***lose the lead*** perder la cabeza
◆ **lead on** *v/i* (*go in front*) ir delante
◆ **lead up to** *v/t* preceder a; ***I wonder what she's leading up to*** me pregunto a dónde quiere ir a parar
lead² [liːd] *for dog* correa *f*
lead³ [led] *substance* plomo *m*
lead·ed ['ledɪd] *adj gas* con plomo
lead·er ['liːdər] líder *m*
lead·er·ship ['liːdərʃɪp] *of party etc* liderazgo *m*; ***under his leadership*** bajo su liderazgo
'lead·er·ship con·test pugna *f* por el liderazgo
lead-free ['ledfriː] *adj gas* sin plomo
lead·ing ['liːdɪŋ] *adj runner* en cabeza; *company, product* puntero
'lead·ing-edge *adj company* en la vanguardia; *technology* de vanguardia
leaf [liːf] (*pl* ***leaves*** [liːvz]) hoja *f*
◆ **leaf through** *v/t* hojear
leaf·let ['liːflət] folleto *m*
league [liːg] liga *f*
leak [liːk] **1** *n in roof* gotera *f*; *in pipe* agujero *m*; *of air, gas* fuga *f*, escape *m*; *of information* filtración *f* **2** *v/i of boat* hacer agua; *of pipe* tener un agujero; *of liquid, gas* fugarse, escaparse
◆ **leak out** *v/i of air, gas* fugarse, escaparse; *of news* filtrarse
leak·y ['liːkɪ] *adj pipe* con agujeros; *boat* que hace agua
lean¹ [liːn] **1** *v/i* (*be at an angle*) estar inclinado; ***lean against sth*** apoyarse en algo **2** *v/t* apoyar; ***lean sth against sth*** apoyar algo contra algo
lean² [liːn] *adj meat* magro; *style, prose* pobre, escueto
leap [liːp] **1** *n* salto *m*; ***a great leap forward*** un gran salto adelante **2** *v/i* (*pret & pp* ***leaped*** *or* ***leapt***) saltar; ***he leapt over the fence*** saltó la valla; ***they leapt into the river*** se tiraron al río
leapt [lept] *pret & pp* → ***leap***
'leap year año *m* bisiesto
learn [lɜːrn] **1** *v/t* aprender; (*hear*) enterarse de; ***learn how to do sth*** aprender a hacer algo **2** *v/i* aprender
learn·er ['lɜːrnər] estudiante *m/f*
'learn·er driv·er conductor(a) *m*(*f*) en prácticas
learn·ing ['lɜːrnɪŋ] *n* (*knowledge*) conocimientos *mpl*; *act* aprendizaje *m*
'learn·ing curve curva *f* de aprendizaje; ***be on the learning curve*** tener que aprender cosas nuevas
lease [liːs] **1** *n* (contrato *m* de) arrendamiento *m* **2** *v/t apartment, equipment* arrendar
◆ **lease out** *v/t apartment, equipment* arrendar
lease 'pur·chase arrendamiento *m* con opción de compra
leash [liːʃ] *for dog* correa *f*
least [liːst] **1** *adj* (*slightest*) menor; ***the least*** *amount, money, baggage* menos; ***there's not the least reason to ...*** no hay la más mínima razón para que ... **2** *adv* menos **3** *n* lo menos; ***he drank the least*** fue el que menos bebió; ***not in the least surprised*** en absoluto sorprendido; ***at least*** por lo menos
leath·er ['leðər] **1** *n* piel *f*, cuero **2** *adj* de piel, de cuero
leave [liːv] **1** *n* (*vacation*) permiso *m*; ***on leave*** de permiso **2** *v/t* (*pret & pp* ***left***) *city, place* marcharse de, irse de; *person, food, memory*, (*forget*) dejar; ***let's leave things as they are*** dejemos las cosas tal y como están; ***how did you leave things with him?*** ¿cómo quedaron las cosas con él?; ***leave s.o./sth alone*** (*not touch, not interfere with*) dejar a alguien / algo en paz; ***be left*** quedar; ***there is nothing left*** no queda nada; ***I only have one left*** sólo me queda uno **3** *v/i* (*pret & pp* ***left***) *of person* marcharse, irse; *of plane, train, bus* salir
◆ **leave behind** *v/t intentionally* dejar; (*forget*) olvidarse
◆ **leave on** *v/t hat, coat* dejar puesto; TV, *computer* dejar encendido
◆ **leave out** *v/t word, figure* omitir; (*not put away*) no guardar; ***leave me out of this*** a mí no me metas en esto
'leav·ing par·ty fiesta *f* de despedida
lec·ture ['lekʧər] **1** *n* clase *f*; *to general public* conferencia *f* **2** *v/i at university* dar clases (***in*** de); *to general public* dar una conferencia
'lec·ture hall sala *f* de conferencias
'lec·tur·er ['lekʧərər] profesor(a) *m*(*f*)
LED [eliː'diː] *abbr* (= ***light-emitting diode***) LED *m* (= diodo *m* emisor de luz)
led [led] *pret & pp* → ***lead¹***
ledge [ledʒ] *of window* alféizar *f*; *on rock face* saliente *m*

ledg·er ['ledʒər] COM libro *m* mayor
leek [liːk] puerro *m*
leer [lɪr] *n sexual* mirada *f* impúdica; *evil* mirada *f* maligna
left [left] **1** *adj* izquierdo **2** *n also* POL izquierda *f*; ***on the left*** a la izquierda; ***on the left of sth*** a la izquierda de algo; ***to the left*** *turn, look* a la izquierda **3** *adv turn, look* a la izquierda
left² [left] *pret & pp* → ***leave***
'left-hand *adj* de la izquierda; ***on your left-hand side*** a tu izquierda; *bend* a la izquierda
left-hand 'drive: ***this car is left-hand drive*** este coche tiene el volante a la izquierda
left-'handed *adj* zurdo
left 'lug·gage (of·fice) *Br* consigna *f*
'left-overs *npl food* sobras *fpl*
'left-wing *adj* POL izquierdista, de izquierdas
leg [leg] *of person* pierna *f*; *of animal* pata *f*; ***pull s.o.'s leg*** tomar el pelo a alguien
leg·a·cy ['legəsɪ] legado *m*
le·gal ['liːgl] *adj* legal
le·gal ad'vis·er asesor(a) *m(f)* jurídico(-a)
le·gal·i·ty [lɪ'gælətɪ] legalidad *f*
le·gal·ize ['liːgəlaɪz] *v/t* legalizar
le·gend ['ledʒənd] leyenda *f*
le·gen·da·ry ['ledʒəndrɪ] *adj* legendario
le·gi·ble ['ledʒəbl] *adj* legible
le·gis·late ['ledʒɪsleɪt] *v/i* legislar
le·gis·la·tion [ledʒɪs'leɪʃn] legislación *f*
le·gis·la·tive ['ledʒɪslətɪv] *adj* legislativo
le·gis·la·ture ['ledʒɪslətʃər] POL legislativo *m*
le·git·i·mate [lɪ'dʒɪtɪmət] *adj* legítimo
'leg room espacio *m* para las piernas
lei·sure ['liːʒər] ocio *m*; ***I look forward to having more leisure*** estoy deseando tener más tiempo libre; ***do it at your leisure*** tómate tu tiempo para hacerlo
'lei·sure cen·ter, *Br* **'lei·sure cen·tre** centro *m* recreativo
lei·sure·ly ['liːʒəlɪ] *adj pace, lifestyle* tranquilo, relajado
'lei·sure time tiempo *m* libre
le·mon ['lemən] limón *m*
le·mon·ade [lemə'neɪd] limonada *f*
'le·mon juice zumo *m* de limón, *L.Am.* jugo de limón
le·mon 'tea té *m* con limón
lend [lend] *v/t* (*pret & pp* ***lent***) prestar
length [leŋθ] longitud *f*; (*piece*: *of material etc*) pedazo *m*; ***at length*** *describe, explain* detalladamente; (*finally*) finalmente
length·en ['leŋθən] *v/t* alargar
length·y ['leŋθɪ] *adj speech, stay* largo
le·ni·ent ['liːnɪənt] *adj* indulgente, poco severo
lens [lenz] *of camera* objetivo *m*, lente *f*; *of eyeglasses* cristal *m*; *of eye* cristalino *m*; (*contact lens*) lente *m* de contacto, *Span* lentilla *f*
'lens cov·er *of camera* tapa *f* del objetivo
Lent [lent] REL Cuaresma *f*
lent [lent] *pret & pp* → ***lend***
len·til ['lentl] lenteja *f*
len·til 'soup sopa *f* de lentejas
Leo ['liːoʊ] Leo ASTR *m/f inv*
leop·ard ['lepərd] leopardo *m*
le·o·tard ['liːoʊtɑːrd] malla *f*
les·bi·an ['lezbɪən] **1** *n* lesbiana *f* **2** *adj* lésbico, lesbiano
less [les] *adv* menos; ***eat / talk less*** comer / hablar menos; ***less interesting / serious*** menos interesante / serio; ***it costs less*** cuesta menos; ***less than $200*** menos de 200 dólares
les·sen ['lesn] **1** *v/t* disminuir **2** *v/i* reducirse, disminuir
les·son ['lesn] lección *f*
let [let] *v/t* (*pret & pp* ***let***) (*allow*) dejar, permitir; ***let s.o. do sth*** dejar a alguien hacer algo; ***let me go!*** ¡déjame!; ***let him come in!*** ¡déjale entrar!; ***let's go / stay*** vamos / quedémonos; ***let's not argue*** no discutamos; ***let alone*** mucho menos; ***let go of sth*** *of rope, handle* soltar algo; ***let go of me!*** ¡suéltame!
◆ **let down** *v/t hair* soltarse; *blinds* bajar; (*disappoint*) decepcionar, defraudar; *dress, pants* alargar
◆ **let in** *v/t to house* dejar pasar
◆ **let off** *v/t* (*not punish*) perdonar; *from car* dejar; ***the court let him off with a small fine*** el tribunal sólo le impuso una pequeña multa
◆ **let out** *v/t of room, building* alquilar, *Mex* rentar; *jacket etc* agrandar; *groan, yell* soltar
◆ **let up** *v/i* (*stop*) amainar
le·thal ['liːθl] *adj* letal
leth·ar·gic [lɪ'θɑːrdʒɪk] *adj* aletargado, apático
leth·ar·gy ['leθərdʒɪ] sopor *m*, apatía *f*
let·ter ['letər] *of alphabet* letra *f*; *in mail* carta *f*
'let·ter·box buzón *m*
'let·ter·head (*heading*) membrete *m*; (*headed paper*) papel *m* con membrete
let·ter of 'cred·it COM carta *f* de crédito
let·tuce ['letɪs] lechuga *f*
'let·up: ***without a letup*** sin interrupción
leu·ke·mia [luː'kiːmɪə] leucemia *f*
lev·el ['levl] **1** *adj field, surface* nivelado,

L

llano; *in competition*, *scores* igualado; ***draw level with s.o.*** *in race* ponerse a la altura de alguien **2** *n on scale*, *in hierarchy*, (*amount*) nivel *m*; ***on the level*** F (*honest*) honrado

lev·el-head·ed [levl'hedɪd] *adj* ecuánime, sensato

le·ver ['liːvər] **1** *n* palanca *f* **2** *v/t*: ***lever sth open*** abrir algo haciendo palanca

lev·er·age ['liːvrɪdʒ] apalancamiento *m*; (*influence*) influencia *f*

lev·y ['levɪ] *v/t* (*pret & pp* ***levied***) *taxes* imponer

lewd [luːd] *adj* obsceno

li·a·bil·i·ty [laɪə'bɪlətɪ] (*responsibility*) responsabilidad *f*; (*likeliness*) propensión *f* (***to*** a)

li·a·ble ['laɪəbl] *adj* (*responsible*) responsable (***for*** de); ***be liable to*** (*likely*) ser propenso a

◆ **li·ai·se with** [lɪ'eɪz] *v/t* actuar de enlace con

li·ai·son [lɪ'eɪzɑːn] (*contacts*) contacto *m*, enlace *m*

li·ar [laɪr] mentiroso(-a) *m*(*f*)

li·bel ['laɪbl] **1** *n* calumnia *f*, difamación *f* **2** *v/t* calumniar, difamar

lib·e·ral ['lɪbərəl] *adj* (*broad-minded*), POL liberal; (*generous*: *portion etc*) abundante

lib·e·rate ['lɪbəreɪt] *v/t* liberar

lib·e·rat·ed ['lɪbəreɪtɪd] *adj* liberado

lib·e·ra·tion [lɪbə'reɪʃn] liberación *f*

lib·er·ty ['lɪbərtɪ] libertad *f*; ***at liberty*** *of prisoner etc* en libertad; ***be at liberty to do sth*** tener libertad para hacer algo

Libra ['liːbrə] ASTR Libra *m/f inv*

li·brar·i·an [laɪ'brerɪən] bibliotecario(-a) *m*(*f*)

li·bra·ry ['laɪbrerɪ] biblioteca *f*

Lib·y·a ['lɪbɪə] Libia

Lib·y·an ['lɪbɪən] **1** *adj* libio **2** *n* libio(-a) *m*(*f*)

lice [laɪs] *pl* → ***louse***

li·cence *Br* → ***license 1*** *n*

li·cense ['laɪsns] **1** *n* permiso *m*, licencia *f* **2** *v/t* autorizar; ***be licensed*** tener permiso *or* licencia

'**li·cense num·ber** (número *m* de) matrícula *f*

'**li·cense plate** *of car* (placa *f* de) matrícula *f*

lick [lɪk] **1** *n* lamedura *f* **2** *v/t* lamer; ***lick one's lips*** relamerse

lick·ing ['lɪkɪŋ] F (*defeat*): ***we got a licking*** nos dieron una paliza F

li·co·rice ['lɪkərɪs] regaliz *m*

lid [lɪd] (*top*) tapa *f*

lie¹ [laɪ] **1** *n* mentira *f* **2** *v/i* mentir

lie² [laɪ] *v/i* (*pret* ***lay***, *pp* ***lain***) *of person* estar tumbado; *of object* estar; (*be situated*) estar, encontrarse; ***lie on your stomach*** túmbate boca abajo

◆ **lie down** *v/i* tumbarse

'**lie-in**: ***have a lie-in*** quedarse un rato más en la cama

lieu [luː]: ***in lieu of*** en lugar de

lieu·ten·ant [lʊ'tenənt] teniente *m/f*

life [laɪf] (*pl* ***lives*** [laɪvz]) vida *f*; *of machine* vida *f*, duración *f*; ***all her life*** toda su vida; ***that's life!*** ¡así es la vida!

'**life belt** salvavidas *m inv*

'**life·boat** *from ship* bote *m* salvavidas; *from land* lancha *f* de salvamento

'**life ex·pect·an·cy** esperanza *f* de vida

'**life·guard** socorrista *m/f*

'**life his·to·ry** historia *f* de la vida

life im'pris·on·ment cadena *f* perpetua

'**life jack·et** chaleco *m* salvavidas

life·less ['laɪflɪs] *adj* sin vida

life·like ['laɪflaɪk] *adj* realista

'**life·long** de toda la vida

'**life pre·serv·er** salvavidas *m inv*

'**life-sav·ing** *adj medical equipment*, *drug* que salva vidas

'**life·sized** *adj* de tamaño natural

'**life-threat·en·ing** *adj* que puede ser mortal

'**life·time** vida *f*; ***in my lifetime*** durante mi vida

lift [lɪft] **1** *v/t* levantar **2** *v/i of fog* disiparse **3** *n* (*Br*: *elevator*) ascensor *m*; ***give s.o. a lift*** llevar a alguien (en coche)

◆ **lift off** *v/i of rocket* despegar

'**lift-off** *of rocket* despegue *m*

lig·a·ment ['lɪgəmənt] ligamento *m*

light¹ [laɪt] **1** *n* luz *f*; ***in the light of*** a la luz de; ***have you got a light?*** ¿tienes fuego? **2** *v/t* (*pret & pp* ***lighted*** *or* ***lit***) *fire*, *cigarette* encender; (*illuminate*) iluminar **3** *adj color*, *sky* claro; *room* luminoso

light² [laɪt] **1** *adj* (*not heavy*) ligero **2** *adv*: ***travel light*** viajar ligero de equipaje

◆ **light up 1** *v/t* (*illuminate*) iluminar **2** *v/i* (*start to smoke*) encender un cigarrillo

'**light bulb** bombilla *f*

light·en¹ ['laɪtn] *v/t color* aclarar

light·en² ['laɪtn] *v/t load* aligerar

◆ **lighten up** *v/i of person* alegrarse; ***come on, lighten up*** venga, no te tomes las cosas tan en serio

light·er ['laɪtər] *for cigarettes* encendedor *m*, *Span* mechero *m*

light-head·ed [laɪt'hedɪd] (*dizzy*) mareado

light-'heart·ed [laɪt'hɑːrtɪd] *adj* alegre

'**light·house** faro *m*

light·ing ['laɪtɪŋ] iluminación *f*

light·ly ['laɪtlɪ] *adv touch* ligeramente; ***get off lightly*** salir bien parado
light·ness[1] ['laɪtnɪs] *of room, color* claridad *f*
light·ness[2] ['laɪtnɪs] *in weight* ligereza *f*
light·ning ['laɪtnɪŋ]: ***a flash of lightning*** un relámpago; ***they were struck by lightning*** les cayó un rayo
'light·ning con·duc·tor pararrayos *m inv*
'light pen lápiz *m* óptico
'light·weight *n in boxing* peso *m* ligero
'light year año *m* luz
like[1] [laɪk] **1** *prep* como; ***be like s.o.*** ser como alguien; ***what is she like?*** ¿cómo es?; ***it's not like him*** (*not his character*) no es su estilo **2** *conj* F (*as*) como; ***like I said*** como dije
like[2] [laɪk] *v/t*: ***I like it / her*** me gusta; ***I would like ...*** querría ...; ***I would like to ...*** me gustaría ...; ***would you like ...?*** ¿querrías ...?; ***would you like to ...?*** ¿querrías ...?; ***she likes to swim*** le gusta nadar; ***if you like*** si quieres
like·a·ble ['laɪkəbl] *adj* simpático
like·li·hood ['laɪklɪhʊd] probabilidad *f*; ***in all likelihood*** con toda probabilidad
like·ly ['laɪklɪ] *adj* (*probable*) probable; ***not likely!*** ¡ni hablar!
like·ness ['laɪknɪs] (*resemblance*) parecido *m*
'like·wise ['laɪkwaɪz] *adv* igualmente; ***pleased to meet you - likewise!*** encantado de conocerle - ¡lo mismo digo!
lik·ing ['laɪkɪŋ] afición *f* (***for*** a); ***to your liking*** a su gusto; ***take a liking to s.o.*** tomar cariño a alguien
li·lac ['laɪlək] *flower* lila *f*; *color* lila *m*
li·ly ['lɪlɪ] lirio *m*
li·ly of the 'val·ley lirio *m* de los valles
limb [lɪm] miembro *m*
lime[1] [laɪm] *fruit, tree* lima *f*
lime[2] [laɪm] *substance* cal *f*
lime'green *adj* verde lima
'lime·light: ***be in the limelight*** estar en el candelero
lim·it ['lɪmɪt] **1** *n* límite *m*; ***within limits*** dentro de un limite; ***be off limits*** *of place* ser zona prohibida; ***that's the limit!*** F ¡es el colmo! F **2** *v/t* limitar
lim·i·ta·tion [lɪmɪ'teɪʃn] limitación *f*
lim·it·ed 'com·pa·ny sociedad *f* limitada
li·mo ['lɪmoʊ] F limusina *f*
lim·ou·sine ['lɪməziːn] limusina *f*
limp[1] [lɪmp] *adj* flojo
limp[2] [lɪmp] *n*: ***he has a limp*** cojea
line[1] [laɪn] *n of text, on road*, TELEC línea *f*; *of trees* fila *f*, hilera *f*; *of people* fila *f*, cola *f*; *of business* especialidad *f*; ***what line are you in?*** ¿a qué te dedicas?; ***the line is busy*** está ocupado, *Span* está comunicando; ***hold the line*** no cuelgue; ***draw the line at sth*** no estar dispuesto a hacer algo; ***line of inquiry*** línea *f* de investigación; ***line of reasoning*** argumentación *f*; ***stand in line*** hacer cola; ***in line with ...*** (*conforming with*) en las mismas líneas que
line[2] [laɪn] *v/t* forrar
◆ **line up** *v/i* hacer cola
lin·e·ar ['lɪnɪər] *adj* lineal
lin·en ['lɪnɪn] *material* lino *m*; (*sheets etc*) ropa *f* blanca
lin·er ['laɪnər] *ship* transatlántico *m*
lines·man ['laɪnzmən] SP juez *m* de línea, linier *m*
lin·ger ['lɪŋgər] *v/i of person* entretenerse; *of pain* persistir
lin·ge·rie ['lænʒəriː] lencería *f*
lin·guist ['lɪŋgwɪst] lingüista *m/f*; ***she's a good linguist*** se le dan bien los idiomas
lin·guis·tic [lɪŋ'gwɪstɪk] *adj* lingüístico
lin·ing ['laɪnɪŋ] *of clothes* forro *m*; *of brakes, pipe* revestimiento *m*
link [lɪŋk] **1** *n* (*connection*) conexión *f*; *between countries* vínculo *m*; *in chain* eslabón *m* **2** *v/t* conectar
◆ **link up** *v/i* encontrarse; TV conectar
li·on ['laɪən] león *m*
lip [lɪp] labio *m*
'lip·read *v/i* (*pret & pp* **lipread** [red]) leer los labios
'lip·stick barra *f* de labios
li·queur [lɪ'kjʊr] licor *m*
liq·uid ['lɪkwɪd] **1** *n* líquido *m* **2** *adj* líquido
liq·ui·date ['lɪkwɪdeɪt] *v/t assets* liquidar; F (*kill*) cepillarse a F
liq·ui·da·tion [lɪkwɪ'deɪʃn] liquidación *f*; ***go into liquidation*** ir a la quiebra
liq·ui·di·ty [lɪ'kwɪdɪtɪ] FIN liquidez *f*
liq·uid·ize ['lɪkwɪdaɪz] *v/t* licuar
liq·uid·iz·er ['lɪkwɪdaɪzər] licuadora *f*
liq·uor ['lɪkər] bebida *f* alcohólica
'liq·uor store tienda *f* de bebidas alcohólicas
lisp [lɪsp] **1** *n* ceceo *m* **2** *v/i* cecear
list [lɪst] **1** *n* lista *f* **2** *v/t* enumerar; COMPUT listar
lis·ten ['lɪsn] *v/i* escuchar; ***I tried to persuade him, but he wouldn't listen*** intenté convencerle, pero no me hizo ningún caso
◆ **listen in** *v/i* escuchar
◆ **listen to** *v/t radio, person* escuchar
lis·ten·er ['lɪsnər] *to radio* oyente *m/f*; ***he's a good listener*** sabe escuchar
list·ings mag·a·zine ['lɪstɪŋz] guía *f* de espectáculos

L

list·less ['lɪstlɪs] *adj* apático, lánguido
lit [lɪt] *pret & pp* → ***light***[1]
li·ter ['liːtər] litro *m*
lit·e·ral ['lɪtərəl] *adj* literal
lit·e·ral·ly ['lɪtərəlɪ] *adv* literalmente
lit·e·ra·ry ['lɪtərerɪ] *adj* literario
lit·e·rate ['lɪtərət] *adj* culto; ***be literate*** saber leer y escribir
lit·e·ra·ture ['lɪtrəʧər] literatura *f*; *about a product* folletos *mpl*, prospectos *mpl*
li·tre *Br* → ***liter***
lit·ter ['lɪtər] basura *f*; *of animal* camada *f*
'lit·ter bas·ket papelera *f*
'lit·ter bin cubo *m* de la basura
lit·tle ['lɪtl] **1** *adj* pequeño; ***the little ones*** los pequeños **2** *n* poco *m*; ***the little I know*** lo poco que sé; ***a little*** un poco; ***a little bread / wine*** un poco de pan / vino; ***a little is better than nothing*** más vale poco que nada **3** *adv*: poco; ***little by little*** poco a poco; ***a little better / bigger*** un poco mejor / más grande; ***a little before 6*** un poco antes de las 6
live[1] [lɪv] *v/i* vivir
◆ **live on 1** *v/t rice, bread* sobrevivir a base de **2** *v/i* (*continue living*) sobrevivir, vivir
◆ **live up**: ***live it up*** pasarlo bien
◆ **live up to** *v/t* responder a
◆ **live with** *v/t* vivir con
live[2] [laɪv] *adj broadcast* en directo; *ammunition* real; *wire* con corriente
live·li·hood ['laɪvlɪhʊd] vida *f*, sustento *m*; ***earn one's livelihood*** ganarse la vida
live·li·ness ['laɪvlɪnɪs] *of person, music* vivacidad *f*; *of debate* lo animado
live·ly ['laɪvlɪ] *adj* animado
liv·er ['lɪvər] MED, *food* hígado *m*
live·stock ['laɪvstɑːk] ganado *m*
liv·id ['lɪvɪd] *adj* (*angry*) enfurecido, furioso
liv·ing ['lɪvɪŋ] **1** *adj* vivo **2** *n* vida *f*; ***what do you do for a living?*** ¿en qué trabajas?; ***earn one's living*** ganarse la vida; ***standard of living*** estándar *m* de vida
'liv·ing room sala *f* de estar, salón *m*
liz·ard ['lɪzərd] lagarto *m*
load [loʊd] **1** *n also* ELEC carga *f*; ***loads of*** F montones de F **2** *v/t car, truck, gun* cargar; *camera* poner el carrete a; COMPUT: *software* cargar (en memoria); ***load sth onto sth*** cargar algo en algo
load·ed ['loʊdɪd] *adj* F (*very rich*) forrado F; (*drunk*) como una cuba
loaf [loʊf] *n* (*pl* ***loaves*** [loʊvz]) pan *m*; ***a loaf of bread*** una barra de pan, un pan
◆ **loaf about** *v/i* F gandulear F
loaf·er ['loʊfər] *shoe* mocasín *m*
loan [loʊn] **1** *n* préstamo *m*; ***on loan*** prestado **2** *v/t* prestar; ***loan s.o. sth*** prestar algo a alguien
loathe [loʊð] *v/t* detestar, aborrecer
loath·ing ['loʊðɪŋ] odio *m*, aborrecimiento *m*
lob·by ['lɑːbɪ] *n in hotel, theater* vestíbulo *m*; POL lobby *m*, grupo *m* de presión
lobe [loʊb] *of ear* lóbulo *m*
lob·ster ['lɑːbstər] langosta *f*
lo·cal ['loʊkl] **1** *adj* local; ***the local people*** la gente del lugar; ***I'm not local*** no soy de aquí **2** *n*: ***the locals*** los del lugar; ***are you a local?*** ¿eres de aquí?
'lo·cal call TELEC llamada *f* local
lo·cal e'lec·tions *npl* elecciones *fpl* municipales
lo·cal 'gov·ern·ment administración *f* municipal
lo·cal·i·ty [loʊ'kælətɪ] localidad *f*
lo·cal·ly ['loʊkəlɪ] *adv live, work* cerca, en la zona; ***it's well known locally*** es muy conocido en la zona; ***they are grown locally*** son cultivados en la región
lo·cal 'pro·duce productos *mpl* del lugar
'lo·cal time hora *f* local
lo·cate [loʊ'keɪt] *v/t new factory etc* emplazar, ubicar; (*identify position of*) situar; ***be located*** encontrarse
lo·ca·tion [loʊ'keɪʃn] (*siting*) emplazamiento *m*; (*identifying position of*) localización *f*; ***on location*** *movie* en exteriores
lock[1] [lɑːk] *of hair* mechón *m*
lock[2] [lɑːk] **1** *n on door* cerradura *f* **2** *v/t door* cerrar (con llave)
◆ **lock away** *v/t* guardar bajo llave
◆ **lock in** *v/t person* encerrar; ***I locked myself in*** me quedé encerrado
◆ **lock out** *v/t of house* dejar fuera
◆ **lock up** *v/t in prison* encerrar
lock·er ['lɑːkər] taquilla *f*
'lock·er room vestuario *m*
lock·et ['lɑːkɪt] guardapelo *m*
lock·smith ['lɑːksmɪθ] cerrajero(-a) *m*(*f*)
lo·cust ['loʊkəst] langosta *f*
lodge [lɑːdʒ] **1** *v/t complaint* presentar **2** *v/i of bullet* alojarse
lodg·er ['lɑːdʒər] húesped *m/f*
loft [lɑːft] buhardilla *f*, desván *m*
loft·y ['lɑːftɪ] *adj heights, ideals* elevado
log [lɑːg] *n wood* tronco *m*; *written record* registro *m*
◆ **log off** *v/i* (*pret & pp* ***logged***) salir
◆ **log on** *v/i* entrar
◆ **log on to** *v/t* entrar a
'log·book *captain's* cuaderno *m* de bitácora; *driver's* documentación *f* del vehículo
log 'cab·in cabaña *f*
log·ger·heads ['lɑːgərhedz]: ***be at log-***

gerheads estar enfrentado
lo·gic ['lɑːdʒɪk] lógica *f*
lo·gic·al ['lɑːdʒɪkl] *adj* lógico
lo·gic·al·ly ['lɑːdʒɪklɪ] *adv* lógicamente
lo·gis·tics [lə'dʒɪstɪks] logística *f*
lo·go ['loʊgoʊ] logotipo *m*
loi·ter ['lɔɪtər] *v/i* holgazanear
lol·li·pop ['lɑːlɪpɑːp] piruleta *f*
Lon·don ['lʌndən] Londres
lone·li·ness ['loʊnlɪnɪs] *of person, place* soledad *f*
lone·ly ['loʊnlɪ] *adj person* solo; *place* solitario
lon·er ['loʊnər] solitario(-a) *m*(*f*)
long[1] [lɒːŋ] **1** *adj* largo; ***it's a long way*** hay un largo camino; ***it's two feet long*** mide dos pies de largo; ***the movie is three hours long*** la película dura tres horas **2** *adv* mucho tiempo; ***don't be long*** no tardes mucho; ***5 weeks is too long*** 5 semanas son mucho tiempo; ***will it take long?*** ¿llevará mucho tiempo?; ***that was long ago*** eso fue hace mucho tiempo; ***long before then*** mucho antes; ***before long*** al poco tiempo; ***we can't wait any longer*** no podemos esperar más tiempo; ***she no longer works here*** ya no trabaja aquí; ***so long as*** (*provided*) siempre que; ***so long!*** ¡hasta la vista!
long[2] [lɒːŋ] *v/i*: ***long for sth*** *home* echar en falta algo; *change* anhelar *or* desear algo; ***be longing to do sth*** anhelar *or* desear hacer algo
long-'dis·tance *adj race* de fondo; *flight* de larga distancia; ***a long-distance phonecall*** una llamada de larga distancia, una conferencia interurbana
lon·gev·i·ty [lɑːn'dʒevɪtɪ] longevidad *f*
long·ing ['lɒːŋɪŋ] *n* anhelo *m*, deseo *m*
lon·gi·tude ['lɑːŋgɪtuːd] longitud *f*
'long jump *Br* salto *m* de longitud
'long-range *missile* de largo alcance; *forecast* a largo plazo
long-sight·ed [lɒːŋ'saɪtɪd] *adj* hipermétrope
long-sleeved [lɒːŋ'sliːvd] *adj* de manga larga
long-'stand·ing *adj* antiguo
'long-term *adj* a largo plazo
'long wave RAD onda *f* larga
'long·wind·ed [lɒːŋ'wɪndɪd] *adj* prolijo
look [lʊk] **1** *n* (*appearance*) aspecto *m*; (*glance*) mirada *f*; ***give s.o./sth a look*** mirar a alguien / mirar algo; ***have a look at sth*** (*examine*) echar un vistazo a algo; ***can I have a look?*** ¿puedo echarle un vistazo?; ***can I have a look around?*** *in shop etc* ¿puedo echar un vistazo?; ***looks*** (*beauty*) atractivo *m*, guapura *f* **2** *v/i* mirar; (*search*) buscar; (*seem*) parecer; ***you look tired / different*** pareces cansado / diferente; ***he looks about 25*** aparenta 25 años; ***how do things look to you?*** ¿qué te parece cómo están las cosas?; ***that looks good*** tiene buena pinta
◆ **look after** *v/t children* cuidar (de); *property, interests* proteger
◆ **look ahead** *v/i fig* mirar hacia el futuro
◆ **look around 1** *v/i* mirar **2** *v/t museum, city* dar una vuelta por
◆ **look at** *v/t* mirar; (*examine*) estudiar; (*consider*) considerar; ***it depends how you look at it*** depende de cómo lo mires
◆ **look back** *v/i* mirar atrás
◆ **look down on** *v/t* mirar por encima del hombro a
◆ **look for** *v/t* buscar
◆ **look forward to** *v/t* estar deseando; ***I'm looking forward to the vacation*** tengo muchas ganas de empezar las vacaciones
◆ **look in on** *v/t* (*visit*) hacer una visita a
◆ **look into** *v/t* (*investigate*) investigar
◆ **look on 1** *v/i* (*watch*) quedarse mirando **2** *v/t*: ***look on s.o./sth as*** (*consider*) considerar a alguien / algo como
◆ **look onto** *v/t garden, street* dar a
◆ **look out** *v/i through, from window etc* mirar; (*pay attention*) tener cuidado; ***look out!*** ¡cuidado!
◆ **look out for** *v/t* buscar; (*be on guard against*) tener cuidado con
◆ **look out of** *v/t window* mirar por
◆ **look over** *v/t translation* revisar, repasar; *house* inspeccionar
◆ **look round** *v/t museum, city* dar una vuelta por
◆ **look through** *v/t magazine, notes* echar un vistazo a, hojear
◆ **look to** *v/t* (*rely on*): ***we look to you for help*** acudimos a usted en busca de ayuda
◆ **look up 1** *v/i from paper etc* levantar la mirada; (*improve*) mejorar; ***things are looking up*** las cosas están mejorando **2** *v/t word, phone number* buscar; (*visit*) visitar
◆ **look up to** *v/t* (*respect*) admirar
'look·out *person* centinela *m*, vigía *m*; ***be on the lookout for*** estar buscando
◆ **loom up** [luːm] *v/i* aparecer (***out of*** de entre)
loon·y ['luːnɪ] **1** *n* F chalado(-a) *m*(*f*) F **2** *adj* F chalado F
loop [luːp] *n* bucle *m*
'loop·hole *in law etc* resquicio *m or* vacío *m* legal
loose [luːs] *adj connection, button* suelto; *clothes* suelto, holgado; *morals* disoluto,

relajado; *wording* impreciso; ***loose change*** suelto *m*, *L.Am.* sencillo *m*; ***loose ends*** *of problem, discussion* cabos *mpl* sueltos
loose·ly ['luːslɪ] *adv worded* vagamente
loos·en ['luːsn] *v/t collar, knot* aflojar
loot [luːt] **1** *n* botín *m* **2** *v/i* saquear
loot·er ['luːtər] saqueador(a) *m(f)*
◆**lop off** [lɑːp] *v/t* (*pret & pp* ***lopped***) *branch* cortar; podar
lop·sid·ed [lɑːp'saɪdɪd] *adj* torcido; *balance of committee* desigual
Lord [lɔːrd] (*God*) Señor *m*
Lord's 'Prayer padrenuestro *m*
lor·ry ['lɑːrɪ] *Br* camión *m*
lose [luːz] **1** *v/t* (*pret & pp* ***lost***) *object, match* perder **2** *v/i* (*pret & pp* ***lost***) SP perder; *of clock* retrasarse; ***I'm lost*** me he perdido; ***get lost!*** F ¡vete a paseo!
◆**lose out** *v/i* salir perdiendo
los·er ['luːzər] perdedor(-a) *m(f)*; F *in life* fracasado(-a) *m(f)*
loss [lɑːs] pérdida *f*; ***make a loss*** tener pérdidas; ***I'm at a loss what to say*** no sé qué decir
L
lost [lɑːst] **1** *adj* perdido **2** *pret & pp* → ***lose***
lost-and-'found, *Br* **lost 'prop·er·ty (office)** oficina *f* de objetos perdidos
lot [lɑːt]: ***the lot*** todo; ***a lot (of), lots (of)*** mucho, muchos; ***a lot of books, lots of books*** muchos libros; ***a lot of butter, lots of butter*** mucha mantequilla; ***a lot better / easier*** mucho mejor / más fácil
lo·tion ['loʊʃn] loción *f*
lot·te·ry ['lɑːtərɪ] lotería *f*
loud [laʊd] *adj voice, noise* fuerte; *music* fuerte, alto; *color* chillón
loud'speak·er altavoz *m*, *L.Am.* altoparlante *m*
lounge [laʊndʒ] *in house* salón *m*
◆**lounge about** *v/i* holgazanear
'lounge suit traje *m* de calle
louse [laʊs] (*pl* ***lice*** [laɪs]) piojo *m*
lous·y ['laʊzɪ] *adj* F asqueroso F; ***I feel lousy*** me siento de pena F
lout [laʊt] gamberro *m*
lov·a·ble ['lʌvəbl] *adj* adorable, encantador
love [lʌv] **1** *n* amor *m*; *in tennis* nada *f*; ***be in love*** estar enamorado (***with*** de); ***I'm in love with you*** estoy enamorado de ti; ***fall in love*** enamorarse (***with*** de); ***make love*** hacer el amor; ***make love to ...*** hacer el amor con; ***yes, my love*** sí, amor **2** *v/t person, country, wine* amar; ***she loves to watch tennis*** le encanta ver tenis
'love af·fair aventura *f* amorosa
'love·life vida *f* amorosa
'love let·ter carta *f* de amor
love·ly ['lʌvlɪ] *adj face, hair, color, tune* precioso, lindo; *person, character* encantador; *holiday, weather, meal* estupendo; ***we had a lovely time*** nos lo pasamos de maravilla
lov·er ['lʌvər] amante *m/f*
lov·ing ['lʌvɪŋ] *adj* cariñoso
lov·ing·ly ['lʌvɪŋlɪ] *adv* con cariño
low [loʊ] **1** *adj bridge, salary, price, voice, quality* bajo; ***be feeling low*** estar deprimido; ***we're low on gas / tea*** nos queda poca gasolina / té **2** *n in weather* zona *f* de bajas presiones, borrasca *f*; *in sales, statistics* mínimo *m*
low·brow ['loʊbraʊ] *adj* poco intelectual, popular
low-'cal·o·rie *adj* bajo en calorías
'low-cut *adj dress* escotado
low·er ['loʊər] *v/t to the ground, hemline, price* bajar; *flag* arriar; *pressure* reducir
'low-fat *adj* de bajo contenido graso
'low·key *adj* discreto, mesurado
'low·lands *npl* tierras *fpl* bajas
low-'pres·sure ar·e·a zona *f* de bajas presiones, borrasca *f*
'low sea·son temporada *f* baja
'low tide marea *f* baja
loy·al ['lɔɪəl] *adj* leal, fiel (***to*** a)
loy·al·ly ['lɔɪəlɪ] *adv* lealmente, fielmente
loy·al·ty ['lɔɪəltɪ] lealtad *f* (***to*** a)
loz·enge ['lɑːzɪndʒ] *shape* rombo *m*; *tablet* pastilla *f*
Ltd *abbr* (= ***limited***) S.L. (= sociedad *f* limitada)
lu·bri·cant ['luːbrɪkənt] lubricante *m*
lu·bri·cate ['luːbrɪkeɪt] *v/t* lubricar
lu·bri·ca·tion [luːbrɪ'keɪʃn] lubricación *f*
lu·cid ['luːsɪd] *adj* (*clear, sane*) lúcido
luck [lʌk] suerte *f*; ***bad luck*** mala suerte; ***hard luck!*** ¡mala suerte!; ***good luck!*** ¡buena suerte!
◆**luck out** *v/i* F tener mucha suerte
luck·i·ly ['lʌkɪlɪ] *adv* afortunadamente, por suerte
luck·y ['lʌkɪ] *adj person, coincidence* afortunado; *day, number* de la suerte; ***you were lucky*** tuviste suerte; ***she's lucky to be alive*** tiene suerte de estar con vida; ***that's lucky!*** ¡qué suerte!
lu·cra·tive ['luːkrətɪv] *adj* lucrativo
lu·di·crous ['luːdɪkrəs] *adj* ridículo
lug [lʌg] *v/t* (*pret & pp* ***lugged***) arrastrar
lug·gage ['lʌgɪdʒ] equipaje *m*
luke·warm ['luːkwɔːrm] *adj water* tibio, templado; *reception* indiferente
lull [lʌl] **1** *n in storm, fighting* tregua *f*; *in conversation* pausa *f* **2** *v/t*: ***lull s.o. into a***

false sense of security dar a alguien una falsa sensación de seguridad
lul·la·by ['lʌləbaɪ] canción *f* de cuna, nana *f*
lum·ba·go [lʌmbeɪgoʊ] lumbago *m*
lum·ber ['lʌmbər] *n* (*timber*) madera *f*
lu·mi·nous ['luːmɪnəs] *adj* luminoso
lump [lʌmp] *n of sugar, earth* terrón *m*; (*swelling*) bulto *m*
◆ **lump together** *v/t* agrupar
lump 'sum pago *m* único
lump·y ['lʌmpɪ] *adj liquid, sauce* grumoso; *mattress* lleno de bultos
lu·na·cy ['luːnəsɪ] locura *f*
lu·nar ['luːnər] *adj* lunar
lu·na·tic ['luːnətɪk] *n* lunático(-a) *m*(*f*), loco(-a) *m*(*f*)
lunch [lʌntʃ] *n* almuerzo *m*, comida *f*; ***have lunch*** almorzar, comer
'lunch box fiambrera *f*
'lunch break pausa *f* para el almuerzo
'lunch hour hora *f* del almuerzo
'lunch·time hora *f* del almuerzo
lung [lʌŋ] pulmón *m*
'lung can·cer cáncer *m* de pulmón
◆ **lunge at** [lʌndʒ] *v/t* arremeter contra
lurch [lɜːrtʃ] *v/i of drunk* tambalearse; *of ship* dar sacudidas
lure [lʊr] **1** *n* atractivo *m* **2** *v/t* atraer
lu·rid ['lʊrɪd] *adj color* chillón; *details* espeluznante
lurk [lɜːrk] *v/i of person* estar oculto, estar al acecho
lus·cious ['lʌʃəs] *adj fruit, dessert* jugoso, exquisito; F *woman, man* cautivador
lush [lʌʃ] *adj vegetation* exuberante
lust [lʌst] *n* lujuria *f*
lux·u·ri·ous [lʌg'ʒʊrɪəs] *adj* lujoso
lux·u·ri·ous·ly [lʌg'ʒʊrɪəslɪ] *adv* lujosamente
lux·u·ry ['lʌkʃərɪ] **1** *n* lujo *m* **2** *adj* de lujo
lymph gland ['lɪmfglænd] ganglio *m* linfático
lynch [lɪntʃ] *v/t* linchar
lyr·i·cist ['lɪrɪsɪst] letrista *m/f*
lyr·ics ['lɪrɪks] *npl* letra *f*

M

M [em] *abbr* (= ***medium***) M (= talla *f* media)
MA [em'eɪ] *abbr* (= ***Master of Arts***) Máster *m* en Humanidades
ma'am [mæm] señora *f*
mac [mæk] F (*mackintosh*) impermeable *m*
ma·chine [mə'ʃiːn] **1** *n* máquina *f* **2** *v/t with sewing machine* coser a máquina; TECH trabajar a máquina
ma'chine gun *n* ametralladora *f*
ma·chine-'read·a·ble *adj* legible por *Span* el ordenador *or L.Am.* la computadora
ma·chin·e·ry [mə'ʃiːnərɪ] (*machines*) maquinaria *f*
ma·chine trans'la·tion traducción *f* automática
ma·chis·mo [mə'kɪzmoʊ] machismo *m*
mach·o ['mætʃoʊ] *adj* macho
mack·in·tosh ['mækɪntɑːʃ] impermeable *m*
mac·ro ['mækroʊ] COMPUT macro *m*
mad [mæd] *adj* (*insane*) loco; F (*angry*) enfadado; ***a mad idea*** una idea disparatada; ***be mad about*** F estar loco por; ***drive s.o. mad*** volver loco a alguien; ***go mad*** (*become insane*) volverse loco; F (*with enthusiasm*) volverse loco F; ***like mad*** F *run, work* como un loco F; ***Pa got real mad when I told him*** papá se puso hecho una furia cuando se lo conté
mad·den ['mædən] *v/t* (*infuriate*) sacar de quicio
mad·den·ing ['mædnɪŋ] *adj* exasperante
made [meɪd] *pret & pp* → ***make***
'mad·house *fig* casa *f* de locos
mad·ly ['mædlɪ] *adv* como loco; ***madly in love*** locamente enamorado
'mad·man loco *m*
mad·ness ['mædnɪs] locura *f*
Ma·don·na [mə'dɑːnə] madona *f*
Ma·fi·a ['mɑːfɪə]: ***the Mafia*** la mafia
mag·a·zine [mægə'ziːn] (*printed*) revista *f*
mag·got ['mægət] gusano *m*
Ma·gi ['meɪdʒaɪ] REL: ***the Magi*** los Reyes Magos
ma·gic ['mædʒɪk] **1** *n* magia *f*; ***as if by magic, like magic*** como por arte de magia **2** *adj* mágico; ***there's nothing magic about it*** no tiene nada de mágico

mag·i·cal ['mædʒɪkl] *adj* mágico
ma·gi·cian [mə'dʒɪʃn] *performer* mago(-a) *m(f)*
ma·gic 'spell hechizo *m*
ma·gic 'trick truco *m* de magia
mag·ic 'wand varita *f* mágica
mag·nan·i·mous [mæg'nænɪməs] *adj* magnánimo
mag·net ['mægnɪt] imán *m*
mag·net·ic [mæg'netɪk] *adj* magnético; *fig: personality* cautivador
mag·net·ic 'stripe banda *f* magnética
mag·net·ism [mæg'netɪzm] *of person* magnetismo *m*
mag·nif·i·cence [mæg'nɪfɪsəns] magnificencia *f*
mag·nif·i·cent [mæg'nɪfɪsənt] *adj* magnífico
mag·ni·fy ['mægnɪfaɪ] *v/t* (*pret & pp* ***magnified***) aumentar; *difficulties* magnificar
'mag·ni·fy·ing glass lupa *f*
mag·ni·tude ['mægnɪtuːd] magnitud *f*
ma·hog·a·ny [mə'hɑːgənɪ] caoba *f*
maid [meɪd] (*servant*) criada *f*; *in hotel* camarera *f*
'maid·en name ['meɪdn] apellido *m* de soltera
maid·en 'voy·age viaje *m* inaugural
mail [meɪl] **1** *n* correo *m*; ***put sth in the mail*** echar algo al correo **2** *v/t letter* enviar (por correo)
'mail·box *also* COMPUT buzón *m*
'mail·ing list lista *f* de direcciones
'mail·man cartero *m*
mail-'or·der cat·a·log, *Br* **mail-'or·der cat·a·logue** catálogo *m* de venta por correo
mail-'or·der firm empresa *f* de venta por correo
'mail·shot mailing *m*
maim [meɪm] *v/t* mutilar
main [meɪn] *adj* principal; ***she's alive, that's the main thing*** está viva, que es lo principal
'main course plato *m* principal
main 'en·trance entrada *f* principal
'main·frame *Span* ordenador *m* central, *L.Am.* computadora *f* central
'main·land tierra *f* firme; ***on the mainland*** en el continente
main·ly ['meɪnlɪ] *adv* principalmente
main 'road carretera *f* general
'main street calle *f* principal
main·tain [meɪn'teɪn] *v/t* mantener
main·te·nance ['meɪntənəns] mantenimiento *m*; ***pay maintenance*** pagar una pensión alimenticia
'main·te·nance costs *npl* gastos *mpl* de mantenimiento
'main·te·nance staff personal *m* de mantenimiento
ma·jes·tic [mə'dʒestɪk] *adj* majestuoso
ma·jes·ty ['mædʒestɪ] majestuosidad *f*; ***Her Majesty*** Su Majestad
ma·jor ['meɪdʒər] **1** *adj* (*significant*) importante, principal; ***in C major*** MUS en C mayor **2** *n* MIL comandante *m*
◆ **major in** *v/t* especializarse en
ma·jor·i·ty [mə'dʒɑːrətɪ] *also* POL mayoría *f*; ***be in the majority*** ser mayoría
make [meɪk] **1** *n* (*brand*) marca *f* **2** *v/t* (*pret & pp* ***made***) hacer; *cars* fabricar, producir; *movie* rodar; *speech* pronunciar; (*earn*) ganar; MATH hacer; ***two and two make four*** dos y dos son cuatro; ***make s.o. do sth*** (*force to*) obligar a alguien a hacer algo; (*cause to*) hacer que alguien haga algo; ***you can't make me do it!*** ¡no puedes obligarme a hacerlo!; ***make s.o. happy / angry*** hacer feliz/ enfadar a alguien; ***make a decision*** tomar una decisión; ***make a telephone call*** hacer una llamada telefónica; ***made in Japan*** hecho en Japón; ***make it*** (*catch bus, train*) llegar a tiempo; (*come*) ir; (*succeed*) tener éxito; (*survive*) sobrevivir; ***what time do you make it?*** ¿qué hora llevas?; ***make believe*** imaginarse; ***make do with*** conformarse con; ***what do you make of it?*** ¿qué piensas?
◆ **make for** *v/t* (*go toward*) dirigirse hacia
◆ **make off** *v/i* escaparse
◆ **make off with** *v/t* (*steal*) llevarse
◆ **make out** *v/t list* hacer, elaborar; *check* extender; (*see*) distinguir; (*imply*) pretender
◆ **make over** ceder
◆ **make up 1** *v/i of woman, actor* maquillarse; *after quarrel* reconciliarse **2** *v/t story, excuse* inventar; *face* maquillar; (*constitute*) suponer, formar; ***be made up of*** estar compuesto de; ***make up one's mind*** decidirse; ***make it up*** *after quarrel* reconciliarse
◆ **make up for** *v/t* compensar por
'make-be·lieve *n* ficción *f*, fantasía *f*
mak·er ['meɪkər] (*manufacturer*) fabricante *m*
make·shift ['meɪkʃɪft] *adj* improvisado
make-up ['meɪkʌp] (*cosmetics*) maquillaje *m*
'make-up bag bolsa *f* del maquillaje
mal·ad·just·ed [mælə'dʒʌstɪd] *adj* inadaptado
male [meɪl] **1** *adj* (*masculine*) masculino; *animal, bird, fish* macho; ***male bosses*** los jefes varones; ***a male teacher*** un profesor **2** *n man* hombre *m*, varón *m*; *ani-*

mal, bird, fish macho *m*
male 'chau·vin·ism machismo *m*
male chau·vin·ist 'pig machista *m*
male 'nurse enfermero *m*
ma·lev·o·lent [mə'levələnt] *adj* malévolo
mal·func·tion [mæl'fʌŋkʃn] **1** *n* fallo *m* (***in*** de) **2** *v/i* fallar
mal·ice ['mælɪs] malicia *f*
ma·li·cious [mə'lɪʃəs] *adj* malicioso
ma·lig·nant [mə'lɪgnənt] *adj tumor* maligno
mall [mɒːl] (*shopping mall*) centro *m* comercial
mal·nu·tri·tion [mælnuː'trɪʃn] desnutrición *f*
mal·treat [mæl'triːt] *v/t* maltratar
mal·treat·ment [mæl'triːtmənt] maltrato *m*
mam·mal ['mæml] mamífero *m*
mam·moth ['mæməθ] *adj* (*enormous*) gigantesco
man [mæn] **1** *n* (*pl* ***men*** [men]) hombre *m*; (*humanity*) el hombre; *in checkers* ficha *f* **2** *v/t* (*pret & pp* ***manned***) *telephones, front desk* atender; *spacecraft* tripular
man·age ['mænɪdʒ] **1** *v/t business* dirigir; *money* gestionar; *suitcase* poder con; ***manage to ...*** conseguir ... **2** *v/i* (*cope*) arreglárselas
man·age·a·ble ['mænɪdʒəbl] *adj* (*easy to handle*) manejable; (*feasible*) factible
man·age·ment ['mænɪdʒmənt] (*managing*) gestión *f*, administración *f*; (*managers*) dirección *f*; ***under his management*** bajo su gestión
man·age·ment 'buy·out *compra de una empresa por sus directivos*
man·age·ment con'sult·ant consultor(a) *m*(*f*) en administración de empresas
'man·age·ment stud·ies estudios *mpl* de administración de empresas
'man·age·ment team equipo *m* directivo
man·ag·er ['mænɪdʒər] *of hotel, company* director(a) *m*(*f*); *of shop, restaurant* encargado(a) *m*(*f*)
man·a·ge·ri·al [mænɪ'dʒɪrɪəl] *adj* de gestión; ***a managerial post*** un puesto directivo
man·ag·ing di'rec·tor director(a) *m*(*f*) gerente
man·da·rin (or·ange) [mændərɪn'(ɔːrɪndʒ)] mandarina *f*
man·date ['mændeɪt] (*authority*) mandato *m*; (*task*) tarea *f*
man·da·to·ry ['mændətɔːrɪ] *adj* obligatorio
mane [meɪn] *of horse* crines *fpl*
ma·neu·ver [mə'nuːvər] **1** *n* maniobra *f* **2** *v/t* maniobrar; ***she maneuvered him into giving her the assignment*** consiguió convencerle para que le diera el trabajo
man·gle ['mæŋgl] *v/t* (*crush*) destrozar
man·han·dle ['mænhændl] *v/t* mover a la fuerza
man·hood ['mænhʊd] (*maturity*) madurez *f*; (*virility*) virilidad *f*
'man-hour hora-hombre *f*
'man·hunt persecución *f*
ma·ni·a ['meɪnɪə] (*craze*) pasión *f*
ma·ni·ac ['meɪnɪæk] F chiflado(-a) *m*(*f*) F
man·i·cure ['mænɪkjʊr] manicura *f*
man·i·fest ['mænɪfest] **1** *adj* manifiesto **2** *v/t* manifestar; ***manifest itself*** manifestarse
ma·nip·u·late [mə'nɪpjəleɪt] *v/t person, bones* manipular
ma·nip·u·la·tion [mənɪpjə'leɪʃn] *of person, bones* manipulación *f*
ma·nip·u·la·tive [mə'nɪpjələtɪv] *adj* manipulador
man'kind la *hum*anidad
man·ly ['mænlɪ] *adj* (*brave*) de hombres; (*strong*) varonil
'man-made *adj fibers, materials* sintético; *crater, structure* artificial
man·ner ['mænər] *of doing sth* manera *f*, modo *m*; (*attitude*) actitud *f*
man·ners ['mænərz] *npl* modales *mpl*; ***good / bad manners*** buena / mala educación; ***have no manners*** ser un maleducado
ma·noeu·vre *Br* → ***maneuver***
'man·pow·er (*workers*) mano *f* de obra; *for other tasks* recursos *mpl* humanos
man·sion ['mænʃn] mansión *f*
'man·slaugh·ter *Br* homicidio *m* sin premeditación
man·tel·piece ['mæntlpiːs] repisa *f* de chimenea
man·u·al ['mænjʊəl] **1** *adj* manual **2** *n* manual *m*
man·u·al·ly ['mænjʊəlɪ] *adv* a mano
man·u·fac·ture [mænjʊ'fækʧər] **1** *n* fabricación *f* **2** *v/t equipment* fabricar
man·u·fac·tur·er [mænjʊ'fækʧərər] fabricante *m*
man·u·fac·tur·ing [mænjʊ'fækʧərɪŋ] *adj industry* manufacturero
ma·nure [mə'nʊr] estiércol *m*
man·u·script ['mænjʊskrɪpt] manuscrito *m*
man·y ['menɪ] **1** *adj* muchos; ***take as many apples as you like*** toma todas las manzanas que quieras; ***many times*** muchas veces; ***not many people / taxis*** no mucha gente / muchos taxis; ***too many problems / beers*** demasiados problemas / demasiadas cervezas **2** *pron*

muchos; ***a great many, a good many*** muchos; ***how many do you need?*** ¿cuántos necesitas?; ***as many as 200 are still missing*** hay hasta 200 desaparecidos

'man-year año-hombre *m*

map [mæp] mapa *m*

◆ **map out** *v/t* (*pret & pp* ***mapped***) proyectar

ma·ple ['meɪpl] arce *m*

mar [mɑːr] *v/t* (*pret & pp* ***marred***) empañar

mar·a·thon ['mærəθɑːn] *race* maratón *m or f*

mar·ble ['mɑːrbl] *material* mármol *m*

March [mɑːrʧ] marzo *m*

march [mɑːrʧ] **1** *n* marcha *f* **2** *v/i* marchar

march·er ['mɑːrʧər] manifestante mf

mare [mer] yegua *f*

mar·ga·rine [mɑːrdʒə'riːn] margarina *f*

mar·gin ['mɑːrdʒɪn] *also* COM margen *m*; ***by a narrow margin*** por un estrecho margen

mar·gin·al ['mɑːrdʒɪnl] *adj* (*slight*) marginal

mar·gin·al·ly ['mɑːrdʒɪnlɪ] *adv* (*slightly*) ligeramente

mar·i·hua·na, **mar·i·jua·na** [mærɪ'hwɑːnə] marihuana *f*

ma·ri·na [mə'riːnə] puerto *m* deportivo

mar·i·nade [mærɪ'neɪd] *n* adobo *m*

mar·i·nate ['mærɪneɪt] *v/t* adobar, marinar

ma·rine [mə'riːn] **1** *adj* marino **2** *n* MIL marine *m/f*, infante *m/f* de marina

mar·i·tal ['mærɪtl] *adj* marital

mar·i·tal 'sta·tus estado *m* civil

mar·i·time ['mærɪtaɪm] *adj* marítimo

mar·jo·ram ['mɑːrdʒərəm] mejorana *f*

mark¹ [mɑːrk] FIN marco *m*

mark² [mɑːrk] **1** *n* señal *f*, marca *f*; (*stain*) marca *f*, mancha *f*; (*sign, token*) signo *m*, señal *f*; (*trace*) señal *f*; EDU nota *f*; ***leave one's mark*** dejar huella **2** *v/t* (*stain*) manchar; EDU calificar; (*indicate, commemorate*) marcar **3** *v/i of fabric* mancharse

◆ **mark down** *v/t goods* rebajar

◆ **mark out** *v/t with a line etc* marcar; (*fig: set apart*) distinguir

◆ **mark up** *v/t price* subir; *goods* subir de precio

marked [mɑːrkt] *adj* (*definite*) marcado, notable

mark·er ['mɑːrkər] (*highlighter*) rotulador *m*

mar·ket ['mɑːrkɪt] **1** *n* mercado *m*; (*stock market*) bolsa *f*; ***on the market*** en el mercado **2** *v/t* comercializar

mar·ket·a·ble ['mɑːrkɪtəbl] *adj* comercializable

mar·ket e'con·o·my economía *f* de mercado

'mar·ket for·ces *npl* fuerzas *fpl* del mercado

mar·ket·ing ['mɑːrkɪtɪŋ] marketing *m*

'mar·ket·ing cam·paign campaña *f* de marketing

'mar·ket·ing de·part·ment departamento *m* de marketing

'mar·ket·ing mix marketing mix *m*, *el producto, el precio, la distribución y la promoción*

'mar·ket·ing strat·e·gy estrategia *f* de marketing

mar·ket 'lead·er líder *m* del mercado

'mar·ket-place *in town* plaza *f* del mercado; *for commodities* mercado *m*

mar·ket re'search investigación *m* de mercado

mar·ket 'share cuota *f* de mercado

mark-up ['mɑːrkʌp] margen *m*

mar·ma·lade ['mɑːrməleɪd] mermelada *f* de naranja

mar·quee [mɑːr'kiː] carpa *f*

mar·riage ['mærɪdʒ] matrimonio *m*; *event* boda *f*

'mar·riage cer·tif·i·cate certificado *m* de matrimonio

mar·riage 'guid·ance coun·se·lor consejero(-a) *m*(*f*) matrimonial

mar·ried ['mærɪd] *adj* casado; ***be married to …*** estar casado con …

mar·ried 'life vida *f* matrimonial

mar·ry ['mærɪ] *v/t* (*pret & pp* ***married***) casarse con; *of priest* casar; ***get married*** casarse

marsh [mɑːrʃ] pantano *m*, ciénaga *f*

mar·shal ['mɑːrʃl] *n in police* jefe(-a) *m*(*f*) de policía; *in security service* miembro *m* del servicio de seguridad

marsh·mal·low [mɑːrʃ'mæloʊ] *dulce de consistencia blanda*

marsh·y ['mɑːrʃɪ] *adj* pantanoso

mar·tial arts [mɑːrʃl'ɑːrts] *npl* artes *fpl* marciales

mar·tial 'law ley *f* marcial

mar·tyr ['mɑːrtər] mártir *m/f*

mar·tyred ['mɑːrtərd] *adj fig* de mártir

mar·vel ['mɑːrvl] maravilla *f*

◆ **marvel at** *v/t* maravillarse de

mar·ve·lous, *Br* **mar·vel·lous** ['mɑːrvələs] *adj* maravilloso

Marx·ism ['mɑːrksɪzm] marxismo *m*

Marx·ist ['mɑːrksɪst] **1** *adj* marxista **2** *n* marxista *m/f*

mar·zi·pan ['mɑːrzɪpæn] mazapán *m*

mas·ca·ra [mæ'skærə] rímel *m*

mas·cot ['mæskət] mascota *f*

mas·cu·line ['mæskjʊlɪn] *adj* masculino
mas·cu·lin·i·ty [mæskjʊ'lɪnətɪ] (*virility*) masculinidad *f*
mash [mæʃ] *v/t* hacer puré de, majar
mashed po·ta·toes [mæʃt] *npl* puré *m* de patatas *or L.Am.* papas
mask [mæsk] **1** *n* máscara *f*; *to cover mouth, nose* mascarilla *f* **2** *v/t feelings* enmascarar
'mask·ing tape cinta *f* adhesiva de pintor
mas·och·ism ['mæsəkɪzm] masoquismo *m*
mas·och·ist ['mæsəkɪst] masoquista *m/f*
ma·son ['meɪsn] cantero *m*
ma·son·ry ['meɪsnrɪ] albañilería *f*
mas·que·rade [mæskə'reɪd] **1** *n fig* mascarada *f* **2** *v/i*: ***masquerade as*** hacerse pasar por
mass[1] [mæs] **1** *n* (*great amount*) gran cantidad *f*; (*body*) masa *f*; ***the masses*** las masas; ***masses of*** F un montón de F **2** *v/i* concentrarse
mass[2] [mæs] REL misa *f*
mas·sa·cre ['mæsəkər] **1** *n* masacre *f*, matanza *f*; F *in sport* paliza *f* **2** *v/t* masacrar; F *in sport* dar una paliza a
mas·sage ['mæsɑːʒ] **1** *n* masaje *m* **2** *v/t* dar un masaje en; *figures* maquillar
'mas·sage par·lor, *Br* **'mas·sage parlour** salón *m* de masajes
mas·seur [mæ'sɜːr] masajista *m*
mas·seuse [mæ'sɜːrz] masajista *f*
mas·sive ['mæsɪv] *adj* enorme; *heart attack* muy grave
mass 'me·di·a *npl* medios *mpl* de comunicación
mass-pro'duce *v/t* fabricar en serie
mass pro'duc·tion fabricación *f* en serie
mast [mæst] *of ship* mástil *m*; *for radio signal* torre *f*
mas·ter ['mæstər] **1** *n of dog* dueño *m*, amo *m*; *of ship* patrón *m*; ***be a master of*** ser un maestro de **2** *v/t skill, language, situation* dominar
'mas·ter bed·room dormitorio *m* principal
'mas·ter key llave *f* maestra
mas·ter·ly ['mæstəlɪ] *adj* magistral
'mas·ter·mind 1 *n* cerebro *m* **2** *v/t* dirigir, organizar
Mas·ter of 'Arts Máster *m* en Humanidades
mas·ter of 'cer·e·mo·nies maestro *m* de ceremonias
'mas·ter·piece obra *f* maestra
'mas·ter's (de·gree) máster *m*
mas·ter·y ['mæstərɪ] dominio *m*
mas·tur·bate ['mæstərbeɪt] *v/i* masturbarse
mat [mæt] *for floor* estera *f*; *for table* salvamanteles *m inv*
match[1] [mætʃ] *for cigarette* cerilla *f*, fósforo *m*
match[2] [mætʃ] **1** *n* SP partido *m*; *in chess* partida *f*; ***be no match for s.o.*** no estar a la altura de alguien; ***meet one's match*** encontrar la horma de su zapato **2** *v/t* (*be the same as*) coincidir con; (*be in harmony with*) hacer juego con; (*equal*) igualar **3** *v/i of colors, patterns* hacer juego
'match·box caja *f* de cerillas
match·ing ['mætʃɪŋ] *adj* a juego
'match stick cerilla *f*, fósforo *m*
mate [meɪt] **1** *n of animal* pareja *f*; NAUT oficial *m/f* **2** *v/i* aparearse; ***these birds mate for life*** estas aves viven con la misma pareja toda la vida
ma·te·ri·al [mə'tɪrɪəl] **1** *n* (*fabric*) tejido *m*; (*substance*) material *m*; ***materials*** materiales *mpl* **2** *adj* material
ma·te·ri·al·ism [mə'tɪrɪəlɪzm] materialismo *m*
ma·te·ri·al·ist [mətɪrɪə'lɪst] materialista *m/f*
ma·te·ri·al·is·tic [mətɪrɪə'lɪstɪk] *adj* materialista
ma·te·ri·al·ize [mə'tɪrɪəlaɪz] *v/i* (*appear*) aparecer; (*come into existence*) hacerse realidad
ma·ter·nal [mə'tɜːrnl] *adj* maternal; ***my maternal grandfather*** mi abuelo materno
ma·ter·ni·ty [mə'tɜːrnətɪ] maternidad *f*
ma'ter·ni·ty dress vestido *m* premamá
ma'ter·ni·ty leave baja *m* por maternidad
ma'ter·ni·ty ward pabellón *m* de maternidad
math [mæθ] matemáticas *fpl*
math·e·mat·i·cal [mæθə'mætɪkl] *adj* matemático
math·e·ma·ti·cian [mæθmə'tɪʃn] matemático(-a) *m*(*f*)
math·e·mat·ics [mæθ'mætɪks] matemáticas *fpl*
maths *Br* → ***math***
mat·i·née ['mætɪneɪ] sesión *f* de tarde
ma·tri·arch ['meɪtrɪɑːrk] matriarca *f*
mat·ri·mo·ny ['mætrəmoʊnɪ] matrimonio *m*
matt [mæt] *adj* mate
mat·ter ['mætər] **1** *n* (*affair*) asunto *m*; PHYS materia *f*; ***you're only making matters worse*** sólo estás empeorando las cosas; ***as a matter of course*** automáticamente; ***as a matter of fact*** de hecho; ***what's the matter?*** ¿qué pasa?; ***no matter what she says*** diga lo que diga **2** *v/i*

M

importar; ***it doesn't matter*** no importa
mat·ter-of-'fact *adj* tranquilo
mat·tress ['mætrɪs] colchón *m*
ma·ture [mə'ʧʊr] **1** *adj* maduro **2** *v/i of person* madurar; *of insurance policy etc* vencer
ma·tu·ri·ty [mə'ʧʊrətɪ] madurez *f*
maul [mɒːl] *v/t of lion, tiger* atacar; *of critics* destrozar
max·i·mize ['mæksɪmaɪz] *v/t* maximizar
max·i·mum ['mæksɪməm] **1** *adj* máximo; ***it will cost $500 maximum*** costará 500 dólares como máximo **2** *n* máximo *m*
May [meɪ] mayo *m*
may [meɪ] *v/aux* ◇ *possibility*: ***it may rain*** puede que llueva; ***you may be right*** puede que tengas razón; ***it may not happen*** puede que no ocurra
◆
◆ *permission* poder; ***may I help / smoke?*** ¿puedo ayudar / fumar?
may·be ['meɪbiː] *adv* quizás, tal vez
'May Day el Primero de Mayo
may·o, **may·on·naise** ['meɪoʊ, meɪə'neɪz] mayonesa *f*
may·or [mer] alcalde *m*
maze [meɪz] laberinto *m*
MB *abbr* (= ***megabyte***) MB (= megabyte *m*)
MBA [embiː'eɪ] *abbr* (= ***Master of Business Administration***) MBA *m* (= Máster *m* en Administración de Empresas)
MBO [embiː'oʊ] *abbr* (= ***management buyout***) *compra de una empresa por sus directivos*
MC [em'siː] *abbr* (= ***master of ceremonies***) maestro *m* de ceremonias
MD [em'diː] *abbr* (= ***Doctor of Medicine***) Doctor(a) *m(f)* en Medicina; (= ***managing director***) director(a) *m(f)* gerente
me [miː] *pron direct & indirect object* me; *after prep* mí; ***he knows me*** me conoce; ***he gave me the keys*** me dio las llaves; ***he sold it to me*** me lo vendió; ***this is for me*** esto es para mí; ***who do you mean? - me?*** ¿a quién te refieres? - ¿a mí?; ***with me*** conmigo; ***it's me*** soy yo; ***taller than me*** más alto que yo
mead·ow ['medoʊ] prado *m*
mea·ger, *Br* **mea·gre** ['miːgər] *adj* escaso, exiguo
meal [miːl] comida *f*; ***enjoy your meal*** ¡que aproveche!
'meal·time hora *f* de comer
mean[1] [miːn] *adj with money* tacaño; (*nasty*) malo, cruel; ***that was a mean thing to say*** ha estado fatal que dijeras eso
mean[2] [miːn] **1** *v/t* (*pret & pp* ***meant***) (*intend to say*) querer decir; (*signify*) querer decir, significar; ***you weren't meant to hear that*** no era mi intención que oyeras eso; ***mean to do sth*** tener la intención de hacer algo; ***be meant for*** ser para; *of remark* ir dirigido a; ***doesn't it mean anything to you?*** (*doesn't it matter?*) ¿no te importa para nada? **2** *v/i* (*pret & pp* ***meant***): ***mean well*** tener buena intención
mean·ing ['miːnɪŋ] *of word* significado *m*
mean·ing·ful ['miːnɪŋfəl] *adj* (*comprehensible*) con sentido; (*constructive*), *glance* significativo
mean·ing·less ['miːnɪŋlɪs] *adj* sin sentido
means [miːnz] *npl financial* medios *mpl*; (*nsg*: *way*) medio *m*; ***a means of transport*** un medio de transporte; ***by all means*** (*certainly*) por supuesto; ***by all means check my figures*** comprueba mis cifras, faltaría más; ***by no means rich / poor*** ni mucho menos rico / pobre; ***by means of*** mediante
meant [ment] *pret & pp* → ***mean***[2]
mean·time ['miːntaɪm] **1** *adv* mientras tanto **2** *n*: ***in the meantime*** mientras tanto
mean·while ['miːnwaɪl] **1** *adv* mientras tanto **2** *n*: ***in the meanwhile*** mientras tanto
mea·sles ['miːzlz] *nsg* sarampión *m*
mea·sure ['meʒər] **1** *n* (*step*) medida *f*; ***we've had a measure of success*** (*certain amount*) hemos tenido cierto éxito **2** *v/t* medir **3** *v/i* medir
◆ **measure out** *v/t area, drink, medicine* medir; *sugar, flour, ingredients* pesar
◆ **measure up** *v/i* estar a la altura (***to*** de)
mea·sure·ment ['meʒərmənt] medida *f*; ***system of measurement*** sistema *m* de medidas
meas·ur·ing jug ['meʒərɪŋ] jarra *m* graduada
'mea·sur·ing tape cinta *f* métrica
meat [miːt] carne *f*
'meat·ball albóndiga *f*
'meat·loaf *masa de carne cocinada en forma de barra de pan que se come fría*
me·chan·ic [mɪ'kænɪk] mecánico(-a) *m(f)*
me·chan·i·cal [mɪ'kænɪkl] *adj also fig* mecánico
me·chan·i·cal en·gi'neer ingeniero(-a) *m(f)* industrial
me·chan·i·cal en·gi'neer·ing ingeniería *f* industrial
me·chan·i·cal·ly [mɪ'kænɪklɪ] *adv also fig* mecánicamente

mech·a·nism ['mekənɪzm] mecanismo *m*
mech·a·nize ['mekənaɪz] *v/t* mecanizar
med·al ['medl] medalla *f*
med·a·list, *Br* **med·al·list** ['medəlɪst] medallista *m/f*
med·dle ['medl] *v/i* entrometerse; ***don't meddle with the TV*** no enredes con la televisión
me·di·a ['miːdɪə] *npl*: ***the media*** los medios de comunicación
'**me·di·a cov·er·age** cobertura *f* informativa
'**me·di·a e·vent** acontecimiento *m* informativo
me·di·a '**hype** revuelo *m* informativo
'**me·d·ia stud·ies** ciencias *fpl* de la información
me·di·an strip [miːdɪən'strɪp] mediana *f*
me·di·ate ['miːdɪeɪt] *v/i* mediar
me·di·a·tion [miːdɪ'eɪʃn] mediación *f*
me·di·a·tor ['miːdɪeɪtər] mediador(a) *m(f)*
med·i·cal ['medɪkl] **1** *adj* médico **2** *n* reconocimiento *m* médico
'**med·i·cal cer·tif·i·cate** certificado *m* médico
'**med·i·cal ex·am·i·na·tion** reconocimiento *m* médico
'**med·i·cal his·to·ry** historial *m* médico
'**med·i·cal pro·fes·sion** profesión *f* médica; (*doctors*) médicos *mpl*
'**med·i·cal re·cord** ficha *m* médica
Med·i·care ['medɪker] *seguro de enfermedad para los ancianos en Estados Unidos*
med·i·cat·ed ['medɪkeɪtɪd] *adj* medicinal
med·i·ca·tion [medɪ'keɪʃn] medicamento *m*, medicina *f*; ***are you on any medication?*** ¿está tomando algún medicamento?
me·di·ci·nal [mɪ'dɪsɪnl] *adj* medicinal
medi·cine ['medsən] *science* medicina *f*; (*medication*) medicina *f*, medicamento *m*
'**med·i·cine cab·i·net** botiquín *m*
med·i·e·val [medɪ'iːvl] *adj* medieval
me·di·o·cre [miːdɪ'oʊkər] *adj* mediocre
me·di·oc·ri·ty [miːdɪ'ɑːkrətɪ] *of work etc*, *person* mediocridad *f*
med·i·tate ['medɪteɪt] *v/i* meditar
med·i·ta·tion [medɪ'teɪʃn] meditación *f*
Med·i·ter·ra·ne·an [medɪtə'reɪnɪən] **1** *adj* mediterráneo **2** *n*: ***the Mediterranean*** el Mediterráneo
me·di·um ['miːdɪəm] **1** *adj* (*average*) medio; *steak* a punto **2** *n size* talla *f* media; (*means*) medio *m*; (*spiritualist*) médium *m/f*
me·di·um-sized ['miːdɪəmsaɪzd] *adj* de tamaño medio
me·di·um '**term**: ***in the medium term*** a medio plazo
'**me·di·um wave** RAD onda *f* media
med·ley ['medlɪ] (*assortment*) mezcla *f*
meek [miːk] *adj* manso, dócil
meet [miːt] **1** *v/t* (*pret & pp* ***met***) *by appointment* encontrarse con, reunirse con; *by chance*, *of eyes* encontrarse con; (*get to know*) conocer; (*collect*) ir a buscar; *in competition* enfrentarse con; (*satisfy*) satisfacer; ***meet a deadline*** cumplir un plazo **2** *v/i* (*pret & pp* ***met***) encontrarse; *in competition* enfrentarse; *of committee etc* reunirse; ***have you two met?*** ¿os conocíais? **3** *n* SP reunión *f*
◆ **meet with** *v/t person*, *opposition*, *approval* encontrarse con; ***my attempts met with failure*** mis intentos fracasaron
meet·ing ['miːtɪŋ] *by chance* encuentro *m*; *of committee*, *in business* reunión *f*; ***he's in a meeting*** está reunido
'**meet·ing place** lugar *m* de encuentro
meg·a·byte ['megəbaɪt] COMPUT megabyte *m*
mel·an·chol·y ['melənkəlɪ] *adj* melancólico
mel·low ['meloʊ] **1** *adj* suave **2** *v/i of person* suavizarse, sosegarse
me·lo·di·ous [mɪ'loʊdɪəs] *adj* melodioso
mel·o·dra·mat·ic [melədrə'mætɪk] *adj* melodramático
mel·o·dy ['melədɪ] melodía *f*
mel·on ['melən] melón *m*
melt [melt] **1** *v/i* fundirse, derretirse **2** *v/t* fundir, derretir
◆ **melt away** *v/i fig* desvanecerse
◆ **melt down** *v/t metal* fundir
melt·ing pot ['meltɪŋpɑːt] *fig* crisol *m*
mem·ber ['membər] miembro *m*
Mem·ber of '**Con·gress** diputado(-a) *m(f)*
Mem·ber of '**Par·lia·ment** *Br* diputado(-a) *m(f)*
mem·ber·ship ['membərʃɪp] afiliación *f*; (*number of members*) número *m* de miembros; ***he applied for membership of the club*** solicitó ser admitido en el club
'**mem·ber·ship card** tarjeta *f* de socio
mem·brane ['membreɪn] membrana *f*
me·men·to [me'mentoʊ] recuerdo *m*
mem·o ['memoʊ] nota *f*
mem·oirs ['memwɑːrz] *npl* memorias *fpl*
'**mem·o pad** bloc *m* de notas
mem·o·ra·ble ['memərəbl] *adj* memorable
me·mo·ri·al [mɪ'mɔːrɪəl] **1** *adj* conmemorativo **2** *n* monumento *m* conmemorativo

Me'mo·ri·al Day Día *f* de los Caídos
mem·o·rize ['meməraɪz] *v/t* memorizar
mem·o·ry ['memərɪ] (*recollection*) recuerdo *m*; (*power of recollection*), COMPUT memoria *f*; ***I have no memory of the accident*** no recuerdo el accidente; ***have a good / bad memory*** tener buena / mala memoria; ***in memory of*** en memoria de
men [men] *pl* → ***man***
men·ace ['menɪs] **1** *n* (*threat*) amenaza *f*; *person* peligro *m* **2** *v/t* amenazar
men·ac·ing ['menɪsɪŋ] amenazador
mend [mend] **1** *v/t* reparar; *clothes* coser, remendar; *shoes* remendar **2** *n*: ***be on the mend*** *after illness* estar recuperándose
me·ni·al ['miːnɪəl] *adj* ingrato, penoso
men·in·gi·tis [menɪn'dʒaɪtɪs] meningitis *f*
men·o·pause ['menəpɒːz] menopausia *f*
'men's room servicio *m* de caballeros
men·stru·ate ['menstrʊeɪt] *v/i* menstruar
men·stru·a·tion [menstrʊ'eɪʃn] menstruación *f*
men·tal ['mentl] *adj* mental; F (*crazy*) chiflado F, pirado F
men·tal a'rith·me·tic cálculo *m* mental
men·tal 'cru·el·ty crueldad *f* mental
'men·tal hos·pi·tal hospital *m* psiquiátrico
men·tal 'ill·ness enfermedad *f* mental
men·tal·i·ty [men'tælətɪ] mentalidad *f*
men·tal·ly ['mentəlɪ] *adv* (*inwardly*) mentalmente
men·tal·ly 'hand·i·capped *adj* con minusvalía psíquica
men·tal·ly 'ill *adj*: ***be mentally ill*** sufrir una enfermedad mental
men·tion ['menʃn] **1** *n* mención *f*; ***she made no mention of it*** no lo mencionó **2** *v/t* mencionar; ***don't mention it*** (*you're welcome*) no hay de qué
men·tor ['mentɔːr] mentor(a) *m(f)*
men·u ['menuː] *for food*, COMPUT menú *m*
mer·ce·na·ry ['mɜːrsɪnərɪ] **1** *adj* mercenario **2** *n* MIL mercenario(-a) *m(f)*
mer·chan·dise ['mɜːrʧəndaɪz] mercancías *fpl*, *L.Am.* mercadería *f*
mer·chant ['mɜːrʧənt] comerciante *m/f*
mer·chant 'bank *Br* banco *m* mercantil
mer·ci·ful ['mɜːrsɪfəl] *adj* compasivo, piadoso
mer·ci·ful·ly ['mɜːrsɪfəlɪ] *adv* (*thankfully*) afortunadamente
mer·ci·less ['mɜːrsɪlɪs] *adj* despiadado
mer·cu·ry ['mɜːrkjʊrɪ] mercurio *m*
mer·cy ['mɜːrsɪ] clemencia *f*, compasión *f*; ***be at s.o.'s mercy*** estar a merced de alguien
mere [mɪr] *adj* mero, simple
mere·ly ['mɪrlɪ] *adv* meramente, simplemente
merge [mɜːrdʒ] *v/i of two lines etc* juntarse, unirse; *of companies* fusionarse
merg·er ['mɜːrdʒər] COM fusión *f*
mer·it ['merɪt] **1** *n* (*worth*) mérito *m*; (*advantage*) ventaja *f*; ***she got the job on merit*** consiguió el trabajo por méritos propios **2** *v/t* merecer
mer·ry ['merɪ] *adj* alegre; ***Merry Christmas!*** ¡Feliz Navidad!
'mer·ry-go-round tiovivo *m*
mesh [meʃ] malla *f*
mess [mes] (*untidiness*) desorden *m*; (*trouble*) lío *m*; ***I'm in a bit of a mess*** estoy metido en un lío; ***be a mess*** *of room, desk* estar desordenado; *of hair* estar revuelto; *of situation, s.o.'s life* ser un desastre
◆ **mess about, mess around 1** *v/i* enredar **2** *v/t person* jugar con
◆ **mess around with** *v/t* enredar con; *s.o.'s wife* tener un lío con
◆ **mess up** *v/t room, papers* desordenar; *task* convertir en una chapuza; *plans, marriage* estropear, arruinar
mes·sage ['mesɪdʒ] *also of movie etc* mensaje *m*
mes·sen·ger ['mesɪndʒər] (*courier*) mensajero(-a) *m(f)*
mess·y ['mesɪ] *adj room, person* desordenado; *job* sucio; *divorce, situation* desagradable
met [met] *pret & pp* → ***meet***
me·tab·o·lism [mətæ'bəlɪzm] metabolismo *m*
met·al ['metl] **1** *adj* metálico **2** *n* metal *m*
me·tal·lic [mɪ'tælɪk] *adj* metálico
met·a·phor ['metəfər] metáfora *f*
me·te·or ['miːtɪər] meteoro *m*
me·te·or·ic [miːtɪ'ɑːrɪk] *adj fig* meteórico
me·te·or·ite ['miːtɪəraɪt] meteorito *m*
me·te·or·o·log·i·cal [miːtɪrə'lɑːdʒɪkl] *adj* meteorológico
me·te·or·ol·o·gist [miːtɪə'rɑːlədʒɪst] meteorólogo(-a) *m(f)*
me·te·o·rol·o·gy [miːtɪə'rɑːlədʒɪ] meteorología *f*
me·ter[1] ['miːtər] *for gas, electricity* contador *m*; (*parking meter*) parquímetro *m*
me·ter[2] ['miːtər] *unit of length* metro *m*
'me·ter read·ing lectura *f* del contador
meth·od ['meθəd] método *m*
me·thod·i·cal [mɪ'θɑːdɪkl] *adj* metódico
me·thod·i·cal·ly [mɪ'θɑːdɪklɪ] *adv* metódicamente
me·tic·u·lous [mə'tɪkjʊləs] *adj* meticuloso, minucioso
me·tre *Br* → ***meter***[2]

met·ric ['metrɪk] *adj* métrico
me·trop·o lis [mɪ'trɑːpəlɪs] metrópolis *f inv*
met·ro·pol·i·tan [metrə'pɑːlɪtən] *adj* metropolitano
mew [mjuː] → ***miaow***
Mex·i·can ['meksɪkən] **1** *adj* mexicano, mejicano **2** *n* mexicano(-a) *m(f)*, mejicano(-a) *m(f)*
Mex·i·co ['meksɪkoʊ] México, Méjico
Mex·i·co 'Cit·y *n* Ciudad *f* de México, *Mex* México, *Mex* el Distrito Federal, *Mex* el D.F.
mez·za·nine (floor) ['mezəniːn] entresuelo *m*
mi·aow [mɪaʊ] **1** *n* maullido *m* **2** *v/i* maullar
mice [maɪs] *pl* → ***mouse***
mick·ey mouse [mɪkɪ'maʊs] *adj* P *course, qualification* de tres al cuarto P
mi·cro·bi·ol·o·gy [maɪkroʊbaɪ'ɑːlədʒɪ] microbiología *f*
'mi·cro·chip microchip *m*
'mi·cro·cli·mate microclima *m*
mi·cro·cosm ['maɪkroʊkɑːzm] microcosmos *m inv*
'mi·cro·e·lec·tron·ics microelectrónica *f*
'mi·cro·film microfilm *m*
'mi·cro·or·gan·ism microorganismo *m*
'mi·cro·phone micrófono *m*
mi·cro'pro·ces·sor microprocesador *m*
'mi·cro·scope microscopio *m*
mi·cro·scop·ic [maɪkrə'skɑːpɪk] *adj* microscópico
'mi·cro·wave *oven* microondas *m inv*
mid·air [mɪd'er]: ***in midair*** en pleno vuelo
mid·day [mɪd'deɪ] mediodía *m*
mid·dle ['mɪdl] **1** *adj* del medio; ***the middle child of five*** el tercero de cinco hermanos **2** *n* medio *m*; ***it's the middle of the night!*** ¡estamos en plena noche!; ***in the middle of*** *of floor, room* en medio de; *of period of time* a mitad *or* mediados de; ***in the middle of winter*** en pleno invierno; ***be in the middle of doing sth*** estar ocupado haciendo algo
'mid·dle-aged *adj* de mediana edad
'Mid·dle Ages *npl* Edad *f* Media
mid·dle 'class *adj* de clase media; ***the middle class(es)*** las clases medias
Mid·dle 'East Oriente *m* Medio
'mid·dle·man intermediario *m*
mid·dle 'man·age·ment mandos *mpl* intermedios
mid·dle 'name segundo nombre *m*
'mid·dle·weight *boxer* peso *m* medio
mid·dling ['mɪdlɪŋ] *adj* regular
mid·field·er [mɪd'fiːldər] centrocampista *m/f*
midge [mɪdʒ] mosquito *m* (pequeño)
midg·et ['mɪdʒɪt] *adj* en miniatura
'mid·night ['mɪdnaɪt] medianoche *f*; ***at midnight*** a medianoche
'mid·sum·mer pleno verano *m*
'mid·way *adv*: ***we'll stop for lunch midway*** pararemos para comer a mitad de camino; ***midway through the meeting*** a mitad de la reunión
'mid·week *adv* a mitad de semana
'Mid·west Medio Oeste *m* (de Estados Unidos)
'mid·wife comadrona *f*
'mid·win·ter pleno invierno *m*
might¹ [maɪt] *v/aux* poder, ser posible que; ***I might be late*** puede *or* es posible que llegue tarde; ***it might rain*** puede *or* es posible que llueva; ***it might never happen*** puede *or* es posible que no ocurra nunca; ***he might have left*** a lo mejor se ha ido; ***you might have told me!*** ¡me lo podías haber dicho!
might² [maɪt] (*power*) poder *m*, fuerza *f*
might·y ['maɪtɪ] **1** *adj* poderoso **2** *adv* F (*extremely*) muy, cantidad de F
mi·graine ['miːgreɪn] migraña *f*
mi·grant work·er ['maɪgrənt] trabajador(a) *m(f)* itinerante
mi·grate [maɪ'greɪt] *v/i* emigrar
mi·gra·tion [maɪ'greɪʃn] emigración *f*
mike [maɪk] F micro *m* F
mild [maɪld] *adj weather, climate* apacible; *cheese, voice* suave; *curry* no muy picante; *person* afable, apacible
mil·dew ['mɪlduː] moho *m*
mild·ly ['maɪldlɪ] *adv say sth* con suavidad; *spicy* ligeramente; ***to put it mildly*** por no decir algo peor
mild·ness ['maɪldnɪs] *of weather, voice* suavidad *f*; *of person* afabilidad *f*
mile [maɪl] milla *f*; ***be miles better / easier*** F ser mil veces mejor / más fácil F
mile·age ['maɪlɪdʒ] millas *fpl* recorridas; ***unlimited mileage*** kilometraje *m* ilimitado
'mile·stone *fig* hito *m*
mil·i·tant ['mɪlɪtənt] **1** *adj* militante **2** *n* militante *m/f*
mil·i·ta·ry ['mɪlɪterɪ] **1** *adj* militar **2** *n*: ***the military*** el ejército, las fuerzas armadas
mil·i·ta·ry a'cad·e·my academia *f* militar
mil·i·ta·ry po'lice policía *f* militar
mil·i·tar·y 'serv·ice servicio *m* militar
mi·li·tia [mɪ'lɪʃə] milicia *f*
milk [mɪlk] **1** *n* leche *f* **2** *v/t* ordeñar
milk 'choc·o·late chocolate *m* con leche
'milk jug jarra *f* de leche
milk of mag'ne·sia leche *f* de magnesia
'milk·shake batido *m*

ˈ**milk·y** [ˈmɪlkɪ] *adj with lots of milk* con mucha leche; *made with milk* con leche
Milk·y ˈWay Vía *f* Láctea
mill [mɪl] *for grain* molino *m*; *for textiles* fábrica *f* de tejidos
◆ **mill about**, **mill around** *v/i* pulular
mil·len·ni·um [mɪˈlenɪəm] milenio *m*
mil·li·gram, *Br* **mil·li·gramme** [ˈmɪlɪgræm] miligramo *m*
mil·li·me·ter, *Br* **mil·li·me·tre** [ˈmɪlɪmiːtər] milímetro *m*
mil·lion [ˈmɪljən] millón *m*
mil·lion·aire [mɪljəˈner] millonario(-a) *m(f)*
mime [maɪm] *v/t* representar con gestos
mim·ic [ˈmɪmɪk] **1** *n* imitador(a) *m(f)* **2** *v/t* (*pret & pp* ***mimicked***) imitar
mince [mɪns] *v/t* picar
ˈ**mince·meat** carne *f* picada
mince ˈpie *empanada de carne picada*
mind [maɪnd] **1** *n* mente *f*; ***it's uppermost in my mind*** es lo que más me preocupa; ***it's all in your mind*** son imaginaciones tuyas; ***be out of one's mind*** haber perdido el juicio; ***bear, keep sth in mind*** recordar; ***I've a good mind to …*** estoy considerando seriamente …; ***change one's mind*** cambiar de opinión; ***it didn't enter my mind*** no se me ocurrió; ***give s.o. a piece of one's mind*** cantarle a alguien las cuarenta; ***make up one's mind*** decidirse; ***have something on one's mind*** tener algo en la cabeza; ***keep one's mind on sth*** concentrarse en algo **2** *v/t* (*look after*) cuidar (de); (*heed*) prestar atención a; ***I don't mind what we do*** no me importa lo que hagamos; ***do you mind if I smoke?, do you mind my smoking?*** ¿le importa que fume?; ***would you mind opening the window?*** ¿le importaría abrir la ventana?; ***mind the step!*** ¡cuidado con el escalón!; ***mind your own business!*** ¡métete en tus asuntos! **3** *v/i*: ***mind!*** ¡ten cuidado!; ***never mind!*** ¡no importa!; ***I don't mind*** no me importa, me da igual
mind-bog·gling [ˈmaɪndbɑːglɪŋ] *adj* increíble
mind·less [ˈmaɪndlɪs] *adj violence* gratuito
mine[1] [maɪn] *pron* el mío, la mía; ***mine are red*** los míos son rojos; ***that book is mine*** eso libro es mío; ***a cousin of mine*** un primo mío
mine[2] [maɪn] **1** *n for coal etc* mina *f* **2** *v/i*: ***mine for*** extraer
mine[3] [maɪn] **1** *n* (*explosive*) mina *f* **2** *v/t* minar
ˈ**mine·field** MIL campo *m* de minas; *fig* campo *m* minado
min·er [ˈmaɪnər] minero(-a) *m(f)*
min·e·ral [ˈmɪnərəl] *n* mineral *m*
ˈ**min·e·ral wa·ter** agua *f* mineral
ˈ**mine·sweep·er** NAUT dragaminas *m inv*
min·gle [ˈmɪŋgl] *v/i of sounds, smells* mezclarse; *at party* alternar
min·i [ˈmɪnɪ] *skirt* minifalda *f*
min·i·a·ture [ˈmɪnɪʧər] *adj* en miniatura
ˈ**min·i·bus** microbús *m*
min·i·mal [ˈmɪnɪməl] *adj* mínimo
min·i·mal·ism [ˈmɪnɪməlɪzm] minimalismo *m*
min·i·mize [ˈmɪnɪmaɪz] *v/t risk, delay* minimizar, reducir al mínimo; (*downplay*) minimizar, quitar importancia a
min·i·mum [ˈmɪnɪməm] **1** *adj* mínimo **2** *n* mínimo *m*
min·i·mum ˈwage salario *m* mínimo
min·ing [ˈmaɪnɪŋ] minería *f*
ˈ**min·i·se·ries** TV miniserie *f*
ˈ**min·i·skirt** minifalda *f*
min·is·ter [ˈmɪnɪstər] POL ministro(-a) *m(f)*; REL ministro(-a) *m(f)*, pastor(a) *m(f)*
min·is·te·ri·al [mɪnɪˈstɪrɪəl] *adj* ministerial
min·is·try [ˈmɪnɪstrɪ] POL ministerio *m*
mink [mɪŋk] *animal, fur* visón *m*; *coat* abrigo *m* de visón
mi·nor [ˈmaɪnər] **1** *adj problem, setback* menor, pequeño; *operation, argument* de poca importancia; *aches and pains* leve; ***in D minor*** MUS en D menor **2** *n* LAW menor *m/f* de edad
mi·nor·i·ty [maɪˈnɑːrətɪ] minoría *f*; ***be in the minority*** ser minoría
mint [mɪnt] *n herb* menta *f*; *chocolate* pastilla *f* de chocolate con sabor a menta; *hard candy* caramelo *m* de menta
mi·nus [ˈmaɪnəs] **1** *n* (*minus sign*) (signo *m* de) menos *m* **2** *prep* menos; ***temperatures of minus 18*** temperaturas de 18 grados bajo cero
mi·nus·cule [ˈmɪnəskjuːl] *adj* minúsculo
min·ute[1] [ˈmɪnɪt] *of time* minuto *m*; ***in a minute*** (*soon*) en un momento; ***just a minute*** un momento
mi·nute[2] [maɪˈnuːt] *adj* (*tiny*) diminuto, minúsculo; (*detailed*) minucioso; ***in minute detail*** minuciosamente
ˈ**mi·nute hand** [ˈmɪnɪt] minutero *m*
mi·nute·ly [maɪˈnuːtlɪ] *adv in detail* minuciosamente; (*very slightly*) mínimamente
min·utes [ˈmɪnɪts] *npl of meeting* acta(s) *f(pl)*
mir·a·cle [ˈmɪrəkl] milagro *m*
mi·rac·u·lous [mɪˈrækjʊləs] *adj* milagro-

M

so

mi·rac·u·lous·ly [mɪ'rækjʊləslɪ] *adv* milagrosamente

mi·rage ['mɪrɑːʒ] espejismo *m*

mir·ror ['mɪrər] **1** *n* espejo *m*; MOT (espejo *m*) retrovisor *m* **2** *v/t* reflejar

mis·an·thro·pist [mɪ'zænθrəpɪst] misántropo(-a) *m(f)*

mis·ap·pre·hen·sion [mɪsæprɪ'henʃn]: ***be under a misapprehension*** estar equivocado

mis·be·have [mɪsbə'heɪv] *v/i* portarse mal

mis·be·hav·ior, *Br* **mis·be·hav·iour** [mɪsbə'heɪvɪər] mal comportamiento *m*

mis·cal·cu·late [mɪs'kælkjʊleɪt] *v/t & v/i* calcular mal

mis·cal·cu·la·tion [mɪs'kælkjʊleɪʃn] error *m* de cálculo

mis·car·riage ['mɪskærɪdʒ] MED aborto *m* (espontáneo); ***miscarriage of justice*** error *m* judicial

mis·car·ry ['mɪskærɪ] *v/i* (*pret & pp* ***miscarried***) *of plan* fracasar

mis·cel·la·ne·ous [mɪsə'leɪnɪəs] *adj* diverso; ***put it in the file marked "miscellaneous"*** ponlo en la carpeta de "varios"

mis·chief ['mɪstʃɪf] (*naughtiness*) travesura *f*, trastada *f*

mis·chie·vous ['mɪstʃɪvəs] *adj* (*naughty*) travieso; (*malicious*) malicioso

mis·con·cep·tion [mɪskən'sepʃn] idea *f* equivocada

mis·con·duct [mɪs'kɑːndʌkt] mala conducta *f*

mis·con·strue [mɪskən'struː] *v/t* malinterpretar

mis·de·mea·nor, *Br* **mis·de·mea·nour** [mɪsdə'miːnər] falta *f*, delito *m* menor

mi·ser ['maɪzər] avaro(-a) *m(f)*

mis·e·ra·ble ['mɪzrəbl] *adj* (*unhappy*) triste, infeliz; *weather, performance* horroroso

mi·ser·ly ['maɪzərlɪ] *adj person* avaro; ***a miserly $150*** 150 míseros dólares

mis·e·ry ['mɪzərɪ] (*unhappiness*) tristeza *f*, infelicidad *f*; (*wretchedness*) miseria *f*

mis·fire [mɪs'faɪr] *v/i of joke, scheme* salir mal

mis·fit ['mɪsfɪt] *in society* inadaptado(-a) *m(f)*

mis·for·tune [mɪs'fɔːrtʃən] desgracia *f*

mis·giv·ings [mɪs'gɪvɪŋz] *npl* recelo *m*, duda *f*

mis·guid·ed [mɪs'gaɪdɪd] *adj person* equivocado; *attempt, plan* desacertado

mis·han·dle [mɪs'hændl] *v/t situation* llevar mal

mis·hap ['mɪshæp] contratiempo *m*

mis·in·form [mɪsɪn'fɔːrm] *v/t* informar mal

mis·in·ter·pret [mɪsɪn'tɜːrprɪt] *v/t* malinterpretar

mis·in·ter·pre·ta·tion [mɪsɪntɜːrprɪ'teɪʃn] mala interpretación *f*

mis·judge [mɪs'dʒʌdʒ] *v/t person, situation* juzgar mal

mis·lay [mɪs'leɪ] *v/t* (*pret & pp* ***mislaid***) perder

mis·lead [mɪs'liːd] *v/t* (*pret & pp* ***misled***) engañar

mis·lead·ing [mɪs'liːdɪŋ] *adj* engañoso

mis·man·age [mɪs'mænɪdʒ] *v/t* gestionar mal

mis·man·age·ment [mɪs'mænɪdʒmənt] mala gestión *f*

mis·match ['mɪsmætʃ]: ***there's a mismatch between the two sets of figures*** los dos grupos de cifras no se corresponden

mis·placed ['mɪspleɪst] *adj loyalty* inmerecido; *enthusiasm* inoportuno

mis·print ['mɪsprɪnt] errata *f*

mis·pro·nounce [mɪsprə'naʊns] *v/t* pronunciar mal

mis·pro·nun·ci·a·tion [mɪsprənʌnsɪ'eɪʃn] pronunciación *f* incorrecta

mis·read [mɪs'riːd] *v/t* (*pret & pp* ***misread*** [red]) *word, figures* leer mal; *situation* malinterpretar

mis·rep·re·sent [mɪsreprɪ'zent] *v/t* deformar, tergiversar

miss[1] [mɪs]: ***Miss Smith*** la señorita Smith; ***miss!*** ¡señorita!

miss[2] [mɪs] **1** *n* SP fallo *m*; ***give sth a miss*** *meeting, party etc* no ir a algo **2** *v/t target* no dar en; *emotionally* echar de menos; *bus, train, airplane* perder; (*not notice*) pasar por alto; (*not be present at*) perderse; ***I ducked and he missed me*** me agaché y no me dio; ***you just missed her*** (*she's just left*) se acaba de marchar; ***we must have missed the turnoff*** nos hemos debido pasar el desvío; ***you don't miss much!*** ¡no se te escapa una!; ***miss a class*** faltar a una clase **3** *v/i* fallar

mis·shap·en [mɪs'ʃeɪpən] *adj* deforme

mis·sile ['mɪsəl] arma *f* arrojadiza; *weapon* misil *m*

miss·ing ['mɪsɪŋ] *adj* desaparecido; ***be missing*** *of person, plane* haber desaparecido; ***the missing money*** el dinero que falta

mis·sion ['mɪʃn] *task* misión *f*; *people* delegación *f*

mis·sion·a·ry ['mɪʃənrɪ] REL misionero(-a) *m(f)*

mis·spell [mɪs'spel] *v/t* escribir incorrectamente
mist [mɪst] neblina *f*
◆ **mist over** *v/i of eyes* empañarse
◆ **mist up** *v/i of mirror, window* empañarse
mis·take [mɪ'steɪk] **1** *n* error *m*, equivocación *f*; ***make a mistake*** cometer un error *or* una equivocación, equivocarse; ***by mistake*** por error *or* equivocación **2** *v/t* (*pret* ***mistook***, *pp* ***mistaken***) confundir; ***mistake X for Y*** confundir X con Y
mis·tak·en [mɪ'steɪkən] **1** *adj* erróneo, equivocado; ***be mistaken*** estar equivocado **2** *pp* → ***mistake***
mis·ter ['mɪstər] → ***Mr***
mis·took [mɪ'stʊk] *pret* → ***mistake***
mis·tress ['mɪstrɪs] *lover* amante *f*, querida *f*; *of servant* ama *f*; *of dog* dueña *f*, ama *f*
mis·trust [mɪs'trʌst] **1** *n* desconfianza *f* (***of*** en) **2** *v/t* desconfiar de
mist·y ['mɪstɪ] *adj weather* neblinoso; *eyes* empañado; *color* borroso
mis·un·der·stand [mɪsʌndər'stænd] *v/t* (*pret & pp* ***misunderstood***) entender mal
mis·un·der·stand·ing [mɪsʌndər'stændɪŋ] (*mistake*) malentendido *m*; (*argument*) desacuerdo *m*
mis·use **1** *n* [mɪs'juːs] uso *m* indebido **2** *v/t* [mɪs'juːz] usar indebidamente
miti·ga·ting cir·cum·stances ['mɪtɪgeɪtɪŋ] *npl* circunstancias *fpl* atenuantes
mitt [mɪt] *in baseball* guante *m* de béisbol
mit·ten ['mɪtən] mitón *m*
mix [mɪks] **1** *n* (*mixture*) mezcla *f*; *cooking*: *ready to use* preparado *m* **2** *v/t* mezclar; ***mix the flour in well*** mezclar la harina bien; *cement* preparar **3** *v/i socially* relacionarse
◆ **mix up** *v/t* (*confuse*) confundir (***with*** con); (*put in wrong order*) revolver, desordenar; ***be mixed up*** *emotionally* tener problemas emocionales; *of figures* estar confundido; *of papers* estar revuelto *or* desordenado; ***be mixed up in*** estar metido en; ***get mixed up with*** verse liado con
◆ **mix with** *v/t* (*associate with*) relacionarse con
mixed [mɪkst] *adj feelings* contradictorio; *reactions*, *reviews* variado
mixed 'mar·riage matrimonio *m* mixto
mix·er ['mɪksər] *for food* batidora *f*; *drink* refresco *m* (*para mezclar con bebida alcohólica*); ***she's a good mixer*** es muy sociable
mix·ture ['mɪkstʃər] mezcla *f*; *medicine* preparado *m*
mix-up ['mɪksʌp] confusión *f*
moan [moʊn] **1** *n of pain* gemido *m* **2** *v/i in pain* gemir
mob [mɑːb] **1** *n* muchedumbre *f* **2** *v/t* (*pret & pp* ***mobbed***) asediar, acosar
mo·bile ['moʊbəl] **1** *adj person* con movilidad; (*that can be moved*) móvil; ***she's a lot less mobile now*** ahora tiene mucha menos movilidad **2** *n* móvil *m*
mo·bile 'home casa *f* caravana
mo·bile 'phone *Br* teléfono *m* móvil
mo·bil·i·ty [mə'bɪlətɪ] movilidad *f*
mob·ster ['mɑːbstər] gángster *m*
mock [mɑːk] **1** *adj* fingido, simulado; ***mock-Tudor houses*** casas de estilo Tudor simulado; ***mock exams / elections*** exámenes *mpl*/elecciones *fpl* de prueba **2** *v/t* burlarse de
mock·er·y ['mɑːkərɪ] (*derision*) burlas *fpl*; (*travesty*) farsa *f*
mock-up ['mɑːkʌp] (*model*) maqueta *f*, modelo *m*
mode [moʊd] (*form*), COMPUT modo *m*; ***mode of transportation*** medio *m* de transporte
mod·el ['mɑːdl] **1** *adj employee, husband* modélico, modelo; ***model boat / plane*** maqueta *f* de un barco / avión **2** *n miniature* maqueta *f*, modelo *m*; (*pattern*) modelo *m*; (*fashion model*) modelo *m/f*; ***male model*** modelo *m* **3** *v/t*: ***model clothes*** trabajar de modelo; ***she models swimsuits*** trabaja de modelo de bañadores **4** *v/i for designer* trabajar de modelo; *for artist, photographer* posar
mo·dem ['moʊdem] módem *m*
mod·e·rate **1** *adj* ['mɑːdərət] moderado **2** *n* ['mɑːdərət] POL moderado(-a) *m(f)* **3** *v/t* ['mɑːdəreɪt] moderar
mod·e·rate·ly ['mɑːdərətlɪ] *adv* medianamente, razonablemente
mod·e·ra·tion [mɑːdə'reɪʃn] (*restraint*) moderación *f*; ***in moderation*** con moderación
mod·ern ['mɑːdn] *adj* moderno; ***in the modern world*** en el mundo contemporáneo
mod·ern·i·za·tion [mɑːdənaɪ'zeɪʃn] modernización *f*
mod·ern·ize ['mɑːdənaɪz] **1** *v/t* modernizar **2** *v/i of business, country* modernizarse
mod·ern 'lan·guages *npl* lenguas *fpl* modernas
mod·est ['mɑːdɪst] *adj* modesto
mod·es·ty ['mɑːdɪstɪ] modestia *f*
mod·i·fi·ca·tion [mɑːdɪfɪ'keɪʃn] modificación *f*

M

mod·i·fy ['mɑːdɪfaɪ] *v/t* (*pret & pp* ***modified***) modificar
mod·u·lar ['mɑːdʊlər] *adj furniture* por módulos
mod·ule ['mɑːduːl] módulo *m*
moist [mɔɪst] *adj* húmedo
moist·en ['mɔɪsn] *v/t* humedecer
mois·ture ['mɔɪstʃər] humedad *f*
mois·tur·iz·er ['mɔɪstʃəraɪzər] *for skin* crema *f* hidratante
mo·lar ['moʊlər] muela *f*, molar *m*
mo·las·ses [mə'læsɪz] *npl* melaza *f*
mold[1] [moʊld] *on food* moho *m*
mold[2] [moʊld] **1** *n* molde *m* **2** *v/t clay, character* moldear
mold·y ['moʊldɪ] *adj food* mohoso
mole [moʊl] *on skin* lunar *m*
mo·lec·u·lar [mə'lekjʊlər] *adj* molecular
mol·e·cule ['mɑːlɪkjuːl] molécula *f*
mo·lest [mə'lest] *v/t child, woman* abusar sexualmente de
mol·ly·cod·dle ['mɑːlɪkɑːdl] *v/t* F mimar, consentir
mol·ten ['moʊltən] *adj* fundido
mom [mɑːm] F mamá *f*
mo·ment ['moʊmənt] momento *m*; ***at the moment*** en estos momentos, ahora mismo; ***for the moment*** por el momento, por ahora
mo·men·tar·i·ly [moʊmən'terɪlɪ] *adv* (*for a moment*) momentáneamente; (*in a moment*) de un momento a otro
mo·men·ta·ry ['moʊmənterɪ] *adj* momentáneo
mo·men·tous [mə'mentəs] *adj* trascendental, muy importante
mo·men·tum [mə'mentəm] cobrar / perder impulso
mon·arch ['mɑːnərk] monarca *m/f*
mon·ar·chy ['mɑːnərkɪ] monarquía *f*
mon·as·tery ['mɑːnəsterɪ] monasterio *m*
mo·nas·tic [mə'næstɪk] *adj* monástico
Mon·day ['mʌndeɪ] lunes *m inv*
mon·e·ta·ry ['mɑːnɪterɪ] *adj* monetario
mon·ey ['mʌnɪ] dinero *m*; ***he's making a lot of money*** está ganando mucho dinero
'**mon·ey belt** faltriquera *f*
'**mon·ey-lend·er** prestamista *m/f*
'**mon·ey mar·ket** mercado *m* monetario
'**mon·ey or·der** giro *m* postal
mon·grel ['mʌngrəl] perro *m* cruzado
mon·i·tor ['mɑːnɪtər] **1** *n* COMPUT monitor *m* **2** *v/t* controlar
monk [mʌŋk] monje *m*
mon·key ['mʌŋkɪ] mono *m*; F *child* diablillo *m* F
◆ **monkey about with** *v/t* F enredar con
'**mon·key wrench** llave *f* inglesa
mon·o·gram ['mɑːnəgræm] monograma *m*
mon·o·grammed ['mɑːnəgræmd] con monograma
mon·o·log, *Br* **mon·o·logue** ['mɑːnəlɑːg] monólogo *m*
mo·nop·o·lize [mə'nɑːpəlaɪz] *v/t* monopolizar
mo·nop·o·ly [mə'nɑːpəlɪ] monopolio *m*
mo·not·o·nous [mə'nɑːtənəs] *adj* monótono
mo·not·o·ny [mə'nɑːtənɪ] monotonía *f*
mon·soon [mɑːn'suːn] monzón *m*
mon·ster ['mɑːnstər] *n* monstruo *m*
mon·stros·i·ty [mɑːn'strɑːsətɪ] monstruosidad *f*
mon·strous ['mɑːnstrəs] *adj* (*frightening, huge*) monstruoso; (*shocking*) escandaloso
month [mʌnθ] mes *m*; ***how much do you pay a month?*** ¿cuánto pagas al mes?
month·ly ['mʌnθlɪ] **1** *adj* mensual **2** *adv* mensualmente **3** *n magazine* revista *f* mensual
mon·u·ment ['mɑːnʊmənt] monumento *m*
mon·u·ment·al [mɑːnʊ'mentl] *adj fig* monumental
mood [muːd] (*frame of mind*) humor *m*; (*bad mood*) mal *humor m*; *of meeting, country* atmósfera *f*; ***be in a good / bad mood*** estar de buen / mal *humor*; ***I'm in the mood for a pizza*** me apetece una pizza
mood·y ['muːdɪ] *adj* temperamental; (*bad-tempered*) malhumorado
moon [muːn] *n* luna *f*
'**moon·light** **1** *n* luz *f* de luna **2** *v/i* F estar pluriempleado irregularmente; ***he's moonlighting as a barman*** tiene un segundo empleo de camarero
'**moon·lit** *adj* iluminado por la luna
moor [mʊr] *v/t boat* atracar
moor·ing ['mʊrɪŋ] atracadero *m*
moose [muːs] alce *m* americano
mop [mɑːp] **1** *n for floor* fregona *f*; *for dishes* estropajo *m* (*con mango*) **2** *v/t* (*pret & pp* ***mopped***) *floor* fregar; *eyes, face* limpiar
◆ **mop up** *v/t* limpiar; MIL acabar con
mope [moʊp] *v/i* estar abatido
mor·al ['mɔːrəl] **1** *adj* moral; *person, behavior* moralista **2** *n of story* moraleja *f*; ***morals*** moral *f*, moralidad *f*
mo·rale [mə'ræl] moral *f*
mo·ral·i·ty [mə'rælətɪ] moralidad *f*
mor·bid ['mɔːrbɪd] *adj* morboso
more [mɔːr] **1** *adj* más; ***there are no more eggs*** no quedan huevos; ***some more***

M

tea? ¿más té?; ***more and more students / time*** cada vez más estudiantes / tiempo **2** *adv* más; ***more important*** más importante; ***more often*** más a menudo; ***more and more*** cada vez más; ***more or less*** más o menos; ***once more*** una vez más; ***he paid more than $100 for it*** pagó más de 100 dólares por él; ***he earns more than I do*** gana más que yo; ***I don't live there any more*** ya no vivo allí **3** *pron* más; ***do you want some more?*** ¿quieres más?; ***a little more*** un poco más

more·o·ver [mɔːˈrouvər] *adv* además, lo que es más

morgue [mɔːrg] depósito *m* de cadáveres

morn·ing [ˈmɔːrnɪŋ] mañana *f*; ***in the morning*** por la mañana; ***this morning*** esta mañana; ***tomorrow morning*** mañana por la mañana; ***good morning*** buenos días

morn·ing ˈsick·ness náuseas *fpl* matutinas (*típicas del embarazo*)

mo·ron [ˈmɔːrɑːn] F imbécil *m/f* F, subnormal *m/f* F

mo·rose [məˈrous] *adj* hosco, malhumorado

mor·phine [ˈmɔːrfiːn] morfina *f*

mor·sel [ˈmɔːrsl] pedacito *m*

mor·tal [ˈmɔːrtl] **1** *adj* mortal **2** *n* mortal *m/f*

mor·tal·i·ty [mɔːrˈtæləti] mortalidad *f*

mor·tar[1] [ˈmɔːrtər] MIL mortero *m*

mor·tar[2] [ˈmɔːrtər] (*cement*) mortero *m*, argamasa *f*

mort·gage [ˈmɔːrgɪdʒ] **1** *n* hipoteca *f*, préstamo *m* hipotecario **2** *v/t* hipotecar

mor·ti·cian [mɔːrˈtɪʃn] encargado(-a) *m(f)* de una funeraria

mor·tu·a·ry [ˈmɔːrtʊerɪ] depósito *m* de cadáveres

mo·sa·ic [moʊˈzeɪɪk] mosaico *m*

Mos·cow [ˈmɑːskaʊ] Moscú

Mos·lem [ˈmʊzlɪm] **1** *adj* musulmán **2** *n* musulmán(-ana) *m(f)*

mosque [mɑːsk] mezquita *f*

mos·qui·to [mɑːsˈkiːtoʊ] mosquito *m*

moss [mɑːs] musgo *m*

moss·y [ˈmɑːsɪ] *adj* cubierto de musgo

most [moʊst] **1** *adj* la mayoría de **2** *adv* (*very*) muy, sumamente; ***the most beautiful / interesting*** el más hermoso / interesante; ***that's the one I like most*** ése es el que más me gusta; ***most of all*** sobre todo **3** *pron* la mayoría de; ***I've read most of her novels*** he leído la mayoría de sus novelas; ***at (the) most*** como mucho; ***make the most of*** aprovechar al máximo

most·ly [ˈmoʊstlɪ] *adv* principalmente, sobre todo

mo·tel [moʊˈtel] motel *m*

moth [mɑːθ] mariposa *f* nocturna; (*clothes moth*) polilla *f*

ˈmoth·ball bola *f* de naftalina

moth·er [ˈmʌðər] **1** *n* madre *f* **2** *v/t* mimar

ˈmoth·er·board COMPUT placa *f* madre

ˈmoth·er·hood maternidad *f*

Moth·er·ing ˈSun·day → ***Mother's Day***

ˈmoth·er-in-law (*pl* ***mothers-in-law***) suegra *f*

moth·er·ly [ˈmʌðərlɪ] *adj* maternal

moth·er-of-ˈpearl nácar *m*

ˈMoth·er's Day Día *f* de la Madre

ˈmoth·er tongue lengua *f* materna

mo·tif [moʊˈtiːf] motivo *m*

mo·tion [ˈmoʊʃn] **1** *n* (*movement*) movimiento *m*; (*proposal*) moción *f*; ***put, set things in motion*** poner las cosas en marcha **2** *v/t*: ***he motioned me forward*** me indicó con un gesto que avanzara

mo·tion·less [ˈmoʊʃnlɪs] *adj* inmóvil

mo·ti·vate [ˈmoʊtɪveɪt] *v/t person* motivar

mo·ti·va·tion [moʊtɪˈveɪʃn] motivación *f*

mo·tive [ˈmoʊtɪv] motivo *m*

mo·tor [ˈmoʊtər] motor *m*

ˈmo·tor·bike moto *f*

ˈmo·tor·boat lancha *f* motora

mo·tor·cade [ˈmoʊtəkeɪd] caravana *f*, desfile *m* de coches

ˈmo·tor·cy·cle motocicleta *f*

ˈmo·tor·cy·clist motociclista *m/f*

ˈmo·tor home autocaravana *f*

mo·tor·ist [ˈmoʊtərɪst] conductor(a) *m(f)*, automovilista *m/f*

ˈmo·tor me·chan·ic mecánico(-a) *m(f)* (de automóviles)

ˈmo·tor rac·ing carreras *fpl* de coches

ˈmo·tor·scoot·er vespa® *f*

ˈmo·tor ve·hi·cle vehículo *m* de motor

ˈmo·tor·way *Br* autopista *f*

mot·to [ˈmɑːtoʊ] lema *f*

mould *etc Br* → ***mold***[2] *etc*

mound [maʊnd] montículo *m*

mount [maʊnt] **1** *n* (*mountain*) monte *m*; (*horse*) montura *f*; ***Mount McKinley*** el Monte McKinley **2** *v/t steps* subir; *horse, bicycle* montar en; *campaign, photo* montar **3** *v/i* aumentar, crecer

◆ **mount up** *v/i* acumularse

moun·tain [ˈmaʊntɪn] montaña *f*

ˈmoun·tain bike bicicleta *f* de montaña

moun·tain·eer [maʊntɪˈnɪr] montañero(-a) *m(f)*, alpinista *m/f*, *L.Am.* andinista *m/f*

moun·tain·eer·ing [maʊntɪˈnɪrɪŋ] montañismo *m*, alpinismo *m*, *L.Am.* andinismo *m*

M

moun·tain·ous ['maʊntɪnəs] *adj* montañoso
mount·ed po'lice ['maʊntɪd] policía *f* montada
mourn [mɔːrn] **1** *v/t* llorar **2** *v/i*: ***mourn for s.o.*** llorar la muerte de alguien
mourn·er ['mɔːrnər] doliente *m/f*
mourn·ful ['mɔːrnfəl] *adj voice*, *face* triste
mourn·ing ['mɔːrnɪŋ] luto *m*, duelo *m*; ***be in mourning*** estar de luto; ***wear mourning*** vestir de luto
mouse [maʊs] (*pl* ***mice*** [maɪs]) *also* COMPUT ratón *m*
'**mouse mat** COMPUT alfombrilla *f*
mous·tache → ***mustache***
mouth [maʊθ] *of person* boca *f*; *of river* desembocadura *f*
mouth·ful ['maʊθfəl] *of food* bocado *m*; *of drink* trago *m*
'**mouth·or·gan** armónica *f*
'**mouth·piece** *of instrument* boquilla *f*; (*spokesperson*) portavoz *m/f*
'**mouth·wash** enjuague *m* bucal, elixir *m* bucal
'**mouth·wa·ter·ing** *adj* apetitoso
move [muːv] **1** *n in chess*, *checkers* movimiento *m*; (*step*, *action*) paso *m*; (*change of house*) mudanza *f*; ***make the first move*** dar el primer paso; ***get a move on!*** F ¡espabílate! F; ***don't make a move!*** ¡ni te muevas! **2** *v/t object* mover; (*transfer*) trasladar; *emotionally* conmover; ***move those papers out of your way*** aparta esos papeles; ***move house*** mudarse de casa **3** *v/i* moverse; (*transfer*) trasladarse
◆ **move around** *v/i in room* andar; *from place to place* trasladarse, mudarse
◆ **move away** *v/i* alejarse, apartarse; (*move house*) mudarse
◆ **move in** *v/i to house*, *neighborhood* mudarse; *to office* trasladarse
◆ **move on** *v/i to another town* mudarse; *to another job* cambiarse; *to another subject* pasar a hablar de
◆ **move out** *v/i of house* mudarse; *of area* marcharse
◆ **move up** *v/i in league* ascender, subir; (*make room*) correrse
move·ment ['muːvmənt] *also organization*, MUS movimiento *m*
mov·ers ['muːvərz] *npl firm* empresa *f* de mudanzas; (*men*) empleados *mpl* de una empresa de mudanzas
mov·ie ['muːvɪ] película *f*; ***go to a movie, the movies*** ir al cine
mov·ie·go·er ['muːvɪgoʊər] aficionado(a) *m/f* al cine
'**mov·ie thea·ter** cine *m*, sala *f* de cine
mov·ing ['muːvɪŋ] *adj which can move* movible; *emotionally* conmovedor
mow [moʊ] *v/t grass* cortar
◆ **mow down** *v/t* segar la vida de
mow·er ['moʊər] cortacésped *m*
MP [em'piː] *abbr* (= ***Member of Parliament***) *Br* diputado(-a) *m*(*f*); *abbr* (= ***Military Policeman***) policía *m* militar
mph [empiː'eɪtʃ] *abbr* (= ***miles per hour***) millas *fpl* por hora
Mr ['mɪstər] Sr.
Mrs ['mɪsɪz] Sra.
Ms [mɪz] Sra. (*casda o no casada*)
Mt *abbr* (= ***Mount***) Monte *m*
much [mʌtʃ] **1** *adj* mucho; ***so much money*** tanto dinero; ***as much ... as ...*** tanto ... como **2** *adv* mucho; ***I don't like him much*** no me gusta mucho; ***he's much more intelligent than ...*** es mucho más inteligente que ...; ***the house is much too large for one person*** la casa es demasiado grande para una sola persona; ***very much*** mucho; ***thank you very much*** muchas gracias; ***I love you very much*** te quiero muchísimo; ***too much*** demasiado; ***as much as ...*** tanto ... como; ***it may cost as much as half a million dollars*** puede que haya malversado hasta medio millón de dólares; ***I thought as much*** eso es lo que pensaba **3** *pron* mucho; ***what did she say? - nothing much*** ¿qué dijo? - no demasiado
muck [mʌk] (*dirt*) suciedad *f*
mu·cus ['mjuːkəs] mocos *mpl*, mucosidad *f*
mud [mʌd] barro *m*
mud·dle ['mʌdl] **1** *n* lío *m* **2** *v/t person* liar; ***you've got the story all muddled*** te has hecho un lío con la *historia*
◆ **muddle up** *v/t* desordenar; (*confuse*) liar
mud·dy ['mʌdɪ] *adj* embarrado
mues·li ['mjuːzlɪ] muesli *m*
muf·fin ['mʌfɪn] magdalena *f*
muf·fle ['mʌfl] *v/t* ahogar, amortiguar
◆ **muffle up** *v/i* abrigarse
muf·fler ['mʌflər] MOT silenciador *m*
mug[1] [mʌg] *for tea*, *coffee* taza *f*; F (*face*) jeta *f* F, *Span* careto *m* F
mug[2] [mʌg] *v/t* (*pret & pp* ***mugged***) (*attack*) atracar
mug·ger ['mʌgər] atracador(a) *m*(*f*)
mug·ging ['mʌgɪŋ] atraco *m*
mug·gy ['mʌgɪ] *adj* bochornoso
mule [mjuːl] *animal* mulo(-a) *m*(*f*); (*slipper*) pantufla *f*
◆ **mull over** [mʌl] *v/t* reflexionar sobre
mul·ti·lat·e·ral [mʌltɪ'lætərəl] *adj* POL multilateral

M

mul·ti·lin·gual [mʌltɪ'lɪŋgwəl] *adj* multilingüe
mul·ti·me·di·a [mʌltɪ'mi:dɪə] **1** *n* multimedia *f* **2** *adj* multimedia
mul·ti·na·tion·al [mʌltɪ'næʃnl] **1** *adj* multinacional **2** *n* COM multinacional *f*
mul·ti·ple ['mʌltɪpl] *adj* múltiple
mul·ti·ple 'choice ques·tion pregunta *f* tipo test
mul·ti·ple scle·ro·sis [skle'roʊsɪs] esclerosis *f* múltiple
mul·ti·pli·ca·tion [mʌltɪplɪ'keɪʃn] multiplicación *f*
mul·ti·ply ['mʌltɪplaɪ] **1** *v/t* (*pret & pp* ***multiplied***) multiplicar **2** *v/i* (*pret & pp* ***multiplied***) multiplicarse
mum·my ['mʌmɪ] *Br* mamá *f*
mum·ble ['mʌmbl] **1** *n* murmullo *m* **2** *v/t* farfullar **3** *v/i* hablar entre dientes
mumps [mʌmps] *nsg* paperas *fpl*
munch [mʌntʃ] **1** *v/t* mascar **2** *v/i* mascar
mu·ni·ci·pal [mju:'nɪsɪpl] *adj* municipal
mu·ral ['mjʊrəl] mural *m*
mur·der ['mɜ:rdər] **1** *n* asesinato *m* **2** *v/t* *person* asesinar, matar; *song* destrozar
mur·der·er ['mɜ:rdərər] asesino(-a) *m(f)*
mur·der·ous ['mɜ:rdrəs] *adj rage, look* asesino
murk·y ['mɜ:rkɪ] *adj water* turbio, oscuro; *fig* turbio
mur·mur ['mɜ:rmər] **1** *n* murmullo *m* **2** *v/t* murmurar
mus·cle ['mʌsl] músculo *m*
mus·cu·lar ['mʌskjʊlər] *adj pain, strain* muscular; *person* musculoso
muse [mju:z] *v/i* meditar, reflexionar
mu·se·um [mju:'zɪəm] museo *m*
mush·room ['mʌʃrʊm] **1** *n* seta *f*, hongo *m*; (*button mushroom*) champiñón *m* **2** *v/i* crecer rápidamente
mu·sic ['mju:zɪk] música *f*; *in written form* partitura *f*
mu·sic·al ['mju:zɪkl] **1** *adj* musical; *person* con talento para la música **2** *n* musical *m*
'mu·sic(·al) box caja *f* de música
mu·sic·al 'in·stru·ment instrumento *m* musical
mu·si·cian [mju:'zɪʃn] músico(-a) *m(f)*
mus·sel ['mʌsl] mejillón *m*
must [mʌst] *v/aux* ◇ *necessity* tener que, deber; ***I must be on time*** tengo que *or* debo llegar a la hora; ***do you have to leave now? yes, I must*** ¿tienes que marcharte ahora? - sí, debo marcharme; ***I mustn't be late*** no tengo que llegar tarde, no debo llegar tarde
◇ *probability* deber de; ***it must be about 6 o'clock*** deben de ser las seis; ***they must have arrived by now*** ya deben de haber llegado
mus·tache [mə'stæʃ] bigote *m*
mus·tard ['mʌstərd] mostaza *f*
must·y ['mʌstɪ] *adj room* que huele a humedad; *smell* a humedad
mute [mju:t] *adj animal* mudo
mut·ed ['mju:tɪd] *adj color* apagado; *criticism* débil
mu·ti·late ['mju:tɪleɪt] *v/t* mutilar
mu·ti·ny ['mju:tɪnɪ] **1** *n* motín *m* **2** *v/i* (*pret & pp* ***mutinied***) amotinarse
mut·ter ['mʌtər] *v/t & v/i* murmurar
mut·ton ['mʌtn] carnero *m*
mu·tu·al ['mju:tʃʊəl] *adj* mutuo
muz·zle ['mʌzl] **1** *n of animal* hocico *m*; *for dog* bozal *m* **2** *v/t* poner un bozal a; ***muzzle the press*** amordazar a la prensa
my [maɪ] *adj* mi; ***my house*** mi casa; ***my parents*** mis padres
my·op·ic [maɪ'ɑ:pɪk] *adj* miope
my·self [maɪ'self] *pron reflexive* me; *emphatic* yo mismo(-a); ***when I saw myself in the mirror*** cuando me vi en el espejo; ***I saw it myself*** lo vi yo mismo; ***by myself*** (*alone*) solo; (*without help*) yo solo, yo mismo
mys·te·ri·ous [mɪ'stɪrɪəs] *adj* misterioso
mys·te·ri·ous·ly [mɪ'stɪrɪəslɪ] *adv* misteriosamente
mys·te·ry ['mɪstərɪ] misterio *m*; ***mystery*** (***story***) relato *m* de misterio
mys·ti·fy ['mɪstɪfaɪ] *v/t* (*pret & pp* ***mystified***) dejar perplejo
myth [mɪθ] *also fig* mito *m*
myth·i·cal ['mɪθɪkl] *adj* mítico
my·thol·o·gy [mɪ'θɑ:lədʒɪ] mitología *f*

N

nab [næb] *v/t* (*pret & pp* ***nabbed***) F (*take for o.s.*) pescar F, agarrar
nag [næg] **1** *v/i* (*pret & pp* ***nagged***) *of person* dar la lata **2** *v/t* (*pret & pp* ***nagged***): ***nag s.o. to do sth*** dar la lata a alguien para que haga algo
nag·ging ['nægɪŋ] *adj person* quejica; *doubt* persistente; *pain* continuo
nail [neɪl] *for wood* clavo *m*; *on finger, toe* uña *f*
'nail clip·pers *npl* cortaúñas *m inv*
'nail file lima *f* de uñas
'nail pol·ish esmalte *m* de uñas
'nail pol·ish re·mov·er quitaesmaltes *m inv*
'nail scis·sors *npl* tijeras *fpl* de manicura
'nail var·nish esmalte *m* de uñas
na·ive [naɪ'iːv] *adj* ingenuo
naked ['neɪkɪd] *adj* desnudo; ***to the naked eye*** a simple vista
name [neɪm] **1** *n* nombre *m*; ***what's your name?*** ¿cómo te llamas?; ***call s.o. names*** insultar a alguien; ***make a name for o.s.*** hacerse un nombre **2** *v/t*: ***they named him Ben*** le llamaron Ben
◆ **name for** *v/t*: ***name s.o. for s.o.*** poner a alguien el nombre de alguien
name·ly ['neɪmlɪ] *adv* a saber
'name·sake tocayo(-a) *m(f)*; homónimo(-a) *m(f)*
'name·tag *on clothing etc* etiqueta *f*
nan·ny ['nænɪ] niñera *f*
nap [næp] *n* cabezada *f*; ***have a nap*** echar una cabezada
nape [neɪp]: ***nape of the neck*** nuca *f*
nap·kin ['næpkɪn] (*table napkin*) servilleta *f*; (*sanitary napkin*) compresa *f*
nar·cot·ic [nɑːr'kɑːtɪk] *n* narcótico *m*, estupefaciente *m*
nar'cot·ics a·gent agente *m/f* de la brigada de estupefacientes
nar·rate [nə'reɪt] *v/t* narrar
nar·ra·tion [nə'reɪʃn] (*telling*) narración *f*
nar·ra·tive ['nærətɪv] **1** *n* (*story*) narración *f* **2** *adj poem*, *style* narrativo
nar·ra·tor [nə'reɪtər] narrador(a) *m(f)*
nar·row ['nærou] *adj street*, *bed*, *victory* estrecho; *views*, *mind* cerrado
nar·row·ly ['nærouli] *adv win* por poco; ***narrowly escape sth*** escapar por poco de algo
nar·row-mind·ed [nærou'maɪndɪd] *adj* cerrado
na·sal ['neɪzl] *adj voice* nasal
nas·ty ['næstɪ] *adj person*, *smell* desagradable, asqueroso; *thing to say* malintencionado; *weather* horrible; *cut*, *wound* feo; *disease* serio
na·tion ['neɪʃn] nación *f*
na·tion·al ['næʃənl] **1** *adj* nacional **2** *n* ciudadano(-a) *m(f)*
na·tion·al 'an·them himno *m* nacional
na·tion·al 'debt deuda *f* pública
na·tion·al·ism ['næʃənəlɪzm] nacionalismo *m*
na·tion·al·i·ty [næʃə'nælətɪ] nacionalidad *f*
na·tion·al·ize ['næʃənəlaɪz] *v/t industry etc* nacionalizar
na·tion·al 'park parque *m* nacional
na·tive ['neɪtɪv] **1** *adj* nativo; ***native language*** lengua *f* materna **2** *n* nativo(-a) *m(f)*, natural *m/f*; *tribesman* nativo(-a) *m(f)*, indígena *m/f*; ***he's a native of New York*** es natural de Nueva York
na·tive 'coun·try país *m* natal
na·tive 'speak·er hablante *m/f* nativo(-a)
NATO ['neɪtou] *abbr* (= ***North Atlantic Treaty Organization***) OTAN *f* (= Organización *f* del Tratado del Atlántico Norte)
nat·u·ral ['nætʃrəl] *adj* natural; ***a natural blonde*** una rubia natural
nat·u·ral 'gas gas *m* natural
nat·u·ral·ist ['nætʃrəlɪst] naturalista *m/f*
nat·u·ral·ize ['nætʃrəlaɪz] *v/t*: ***become naturalized*** naturalizarse, nacionalizarse
nat·u·ral·ly ['nætʃərəlɪ] *adv* (*of course*) naturalmente; *behave*, *speak* con naturalidad; (*by nature*) por naturaleza
nat·u·ral 'sci·ence ciencias *fpl* naturales
nat·u·ral 'sci·en·tist experto(-a) *m(f)* en ciencias naturales
na·ture ['neɪtʃər] naturaleza *f*
na·ture re'serve reserva *f* natural
naugh·ty ['nɒːtɪ] *adj* travieso, malo; *photograph*, *word etc* picante
nau·se·a ['nɒːzɪə] náusea *f*
nau·se·ate ['nɒːzɪeɪt] *v/t* (*fig*: *disgust*) dar náuseas a
nau·se·at·ing ['nɒːzɪeɪtɪŋ] *adj smell*, *taste* nauseabundo; *person* repugnante
nau·seous ['nɒːʃəs] *adj* nauseabundo; ***feel nauseous*** tener náuseas
nau·ti·cal ['nɒːtɪkl] *adj* náutico
'nau·ti·cal mile milla *f* náutica
na·val ['neɪvl] *adj* naval
'na·val base base *f* naval

na·vel ['neɪvl] ombligo *m*
nav·i·ga·ble ['nævɪgəbl] *adj river* navegable
nav·i·gate ['nævɪgeɪt] *v/i in ship, airplane,* COMPUT navegar; *in car* hacer de copiloto
nav·i·ga·tion [nævɪ'geɪʃn] navegación *f*; *in car* direcciónes *fpl*
nav·i·ga·tor ['nævɪgeɪtər] *on ship* oficial *m* de derrota; *in airplane* navegante *m/f*; *in car* copiloto *m/f*
na·vy ['neɪvɪ] armada *f*, marina *f* (de guerra)
na·vy 'blue 1 *n* azul *m* marino **2** *adj* azul marino
near [nɪr] **1** *adv* cerca; ***come a bit nearer*** acércate un poco más **2** *prep* cerca de; ***near the bank*** cerca del banco; ***do you go near the bank?*** ¿pasa cerca del banco? **3** *adj* cercano, próximo; ***the nearest bus stop*** la parada de autobús más cercana *or* próxima; ***in the near future*** en un futuro próximo
near·by [nɪr'baɪ] *adv live* cerca
near·ly ['nɪrlɪ] *adv* casi
near-sight·ed [nɪr'saɪtɪd] *adj* miope
neat [ni:t] *adj* ordenado; *whisky* solo, seco; *solution* ingenioso; F (*terrific*) genial F, estupendo F
ne·ces·sar·i·ly ['nesəserəlɪ] *adv* necesariamente
ne·ces·sa·ry ['nesəserɪ] *adj* necesario, preciso; ***it is necessary to …*** es necesario …, hay que …
ne·ces·si·tate [nɪ'sesɪteɪt] *v/t* exigir, hacer necesario
ne·ces·si·ty [nɪ'sesɪtɪ] (*being necessary*) necesidad *f*; (*something necessary*) necesidad *f*, requisito *m* imprescindible
neck [nek] cuello *m*
neck·lace ['neklɪs] collar *m*
'neck·line *of dress* escote *m*
'neck·tie corbata *f*
née [neɪ] *adj* de soltera
need [ni:d] **1** *n* necesidad *f*; ***if need be*** si fuera necesario; ***in need*** necesitado; ***be in need of sth*** necesitar algo; ***there's no need to be rude / upset*** no hace falta ser grosero /que te enfades **2** *v/t* necesitar; ***you'll need to buy one*** tendrás que comprar uno; ***you don't need to wait*** no hace falta que esperes; ***I need to talk to you*** tengo que *or* necesito hablar contigo; ***need I say more?*** ¿hace falta que añada algo?
nee·dle ['ni:dl] *for sewing, injection, on dial* aguja *f*
'nee·dle·work costura *f*
need·y ['ni:dɪ] *adj* necesitado
neg·a·tive ['negətɪv] *adj* negativo; ***answer in the negative*** dar una respuesta negativa
ne·glect [nɪ'glekt] **1** *n* abandono *m*, descuido *m* **2** *v/t garden, one's health* descuidar, desatender; ***neglect to do sth*** no hacer algo
ne·glect·ed [nɪ'glektɪd] *adj gardens* abandonado, descuidado; *author* olvidado; ***feel neglected*** sentirse abandonado
neg·li·gence ['neglɪdʒəns] negligencia *f*
neg·li·gent ['neglɪdʒənt] *adj* negligente
neg·li·gi·ble ['neglɪdʒəbl] *adj quantity, amount* insignificante
ne·go·ti·a·ble [nɪ'goʊʃəbl] *adj salary, contract* negociable
ne·go·ti·ate [nɪ'goʊʃɪeɪt] **1** *v/i* negociar **2** *v/t deal, settlement* negociar; *obstacles* franquear, salvar; *bend in road* tomar
ne·go·ti·a·tion [nɪgoʊʃɪ'eɪʃn] negociación *f*; ***be under negotiation*** estar siendo negociado
ne·go·ti·a·tor [nɪ'goʊʃɪeɪtər] negociador(a) *m*(*f*)
Ne·gro ['ni:groʊ] negro(-a) *m*(*f*)
neigh [neɪ] *v/i* relinchar
neigh·bor ['neɪbər] vecino(-a) *m*(*f*)
neigh·bor·hood ['neɪbərhʊd] *in town* vecindario *m*, barrio *m*; ***in the neighborhood of …*** *fig* alrededor de …
neigh·bor·ing ['neɪbərɪŋ] *adj house, state* vecino, colindante
neigh·bor·ly ['neɪbərlɪ] *adj* amable
neigh·bour *etc Br* → ***neighbor*** *etc*
nei·ther ['ni:ðər] **1** *adj* ninguno; ***neither applicant was any good*** ninguno de los candidatos era bueno **2** *pron* ninguno(-a) *m*(*f*) **3** *adv*: ***neither … nor …*** ni … ni **4** *conj*: ***neither do I*** yo tampoco; ***neither can I*** yo tampoco
ne·on light ['ni:ɑ:n] luz *f* de neón
neph·ew ['nefju:] sobrino *m*
nerd [nɜ:rd] F petardo(-a) *m*(*f*)
nerve [nɜ:rv] nervio *m*; (*courage*) valor *m*; (*impudence*) descaro *m*; ***it's bad for my nerves*** me pone de los nervios; ***get on s.o.'s nerves*** sacar de quicio a alguien
nerve-rack·ing ['nɜ:rvrækɪŋ] *adj* angustioso, exasperante
ner·vous ['nɜ:rvəs] *adj person* nervioso, inquieto; *twitch* nervioso; ***I'm nervous about meeting them*** la reunión con ellos me pone muy nervioso
ner·vous 'break·down crisis *f inv* nerviosa
ner·vous 'en·er·gy energía *f*
ner·vous·ness ['nɜ:rvəsnɪs] nerviosismo *m*
ner·vous 'wreck manojo *m* de nervios

nerv·y ['nɜːrvɪ] *adj* (*fresh*) descarado
nest [nest] *n* nido *m*
nes·tle ['nesl] *v/i* acomodarse
net¹ [net] *for fishing*, *tennis* red *f*
net² [net] *adj price*, *weight* neto
net 'cur·tain visillo *m*
net 'pro·fit beneficio *m* neto
net·tle ['netl] ortiga *f*
'net·work *of contacts*, *cells*, COMPUT red *f*
neu·rol·o·gist [nʊə'rɑːlədʒɪst] neurólogo(-a) *m*(*f*)
neu·ro·sis [nʊ'roʊsɪs] neurosis *f inv*
neu·rot·ic [nʊ'rɑːtɪk] *adj* neurótico
neu·ter ['nuːtər] *v/t animal* castrar
neu·tral ['nuːtrl] **1** *adj country* neutral; *color* neutro **2** *n gear* punto *m* muerto; ***in neutral*** en punto muerto
neu·tral·i·ty [nʊ'trælətɪ] neutralidad *f*
neu·tral·ize ['nʊtrəlaɪz] *v/t* neutralizar
nev·er ['nevər] *adv* nunca; ***you're never going to believe this*** no te vas a creer esto; ***you never promised, did you?*** no lo llegaste a prometer, ¿verdad?
nev·er-'end·ing *adj* interminable
nev·er·the·less [nevərðə'les] *adv* sin embargo, no obstante
new [nuː] *adj* nuevo; ***this system is still new to me*** todavía no me he hecho con este sistema; ***I'm new to the job*** soy nuevo en el trabajo; ***that's nothing new*** no es nada nuevo
'new·born *adj* recién nacido
new·com·er ['nuːkʌmər] recién llegado(-a) *m*(*f*)
new·ly ['nuːlɪ] *adv* (*recently*) recientemente, recién
new·ly weds [wedz] *npl* recién casados *mpl*
new 'moon luna *f* nueva
news [nuːz] *nsg* noticias *fpl*; *on* TV noticias *fpl*, telediario *m*; *on radio* noticias *fpl*; ***that's news to me*** no sabía eso
'news a·gen·cy agencia *f* de noticias
'news·a·gent quiosquero(-a) *m*(*f*)
'news·cast TV noticias *fpl*, telediario *m*; *on radio* noticias *fpl*
'news·cast·er TV presentador(a) *m*(*f*) de informativos
'news flash flash *m* informativo, noticia *f* de última hora
'newspaper periódico *m*
'news·read·er TV *etc* presentador(a) *m*(*f*) de informativos
'news re·port reportaje *m*
'news·stand quiosco *m*
'news·ven·dor vendedor(a) *m*(*f*) de periódicos
'New Year año *m* nuevo; ***Happy New Year!*** ¡Feliz Año Nuevo!
New Year's 'Day Día *m* de Año Nuevo
New Year's 'Eve Nochevieja *f*
New York [jɔːrk] **1** *adj* neoyorquino **2** *n*: ***New York*** (***City***) Nueva York
New York·er ['jɔːrkər] *n* neoyorquino(-a) *m*(*f*)
New Zea·land ['ziːlənd] Nueva Zelanda
New Zea·land·er ['ziːləndər] neozelandés(-esa) *m*(*f*), neocelandés(-esa) *m*(*f*)
next [nekst] **1** *adj in time* próximo, siguiente; *in space* siguiente, de al lado; ***next week*** la próxima semana, la semana que viene; ***the next week he came back again*** volvió a la semana siguiente; ***who's next?*** ¿quién es el siguiente? **2** *adv* luego, después; ***next, we're going to study …*** a continuación, vamos a estudiar …; ***next to*** (*beside*) al lado de; (*in comparison with*) en comparación con
next 'door 1 *adj neighbor* de al lado **2** *adv live* al lado
next of 'kin pariente *m* más cercano
nib·ble ['nɪbl] *v/t* mordisquear
Nic·a·ra·gua [nɪkə'rɑːgwə] Nicaragua
Nic·a·ra·guan [nɪkə'rɑːgwən] **1** *adj* nicaragüense **2** *n* nicaragüense *m/f*
nice [naɪs] *adj trip*, *house*, *hair* bonito, *L.Am.* lindo; *person* agradable, simpático; *weather* bueno, agradable; *meal*, *food* bueno, rico; ***be nice to your sister!*** ¡trata bien a tu hermana!; ***that's very nice of you*** es muy amable de tu parte
nice·ly ['naɪslɪ] *adv written*, *presented* bien; (*pleasantly*) amablemente
nice·ties ['naɪsətɪz] *npl* sutilezas *fpl*; refinamientos *mpl*; ***social niceties*** cumplidos *mpl*
niche [niːʃ] *in market* hueco *m*, nicho *m*; (*special position*) hueco *m*
nick [nɪk] *n* (*cut*) muesca *f*, mella *f*; ***in the nick of time*** justo a tiempo
nick·el ['nɪkl] níquel *m*; (*coin*) *moneda de cinco centavos*
'nick·name *n* apodo *m*, mote *m*
niece [niːs] sobrina *f*
nig·gard·ly ['nɪgərdlɪ] *adj amount*, *person* mísero
night [naɪt] noche *f*; ***tomorrow night*** mañana por la noche; ***11 o'clock at night*** las 11 de la noche; ***travel by night*** viajar de noche; ***during the night*** por la noche; ***stay the night*** quedarse a dormir; ***a room for 2 nights*** una habitación para 2 noches; ***work nights*** trabajar de noche; ***good night*** buenas noches; ***in the middle of the night*** en mitad de la noche
'night·cap *drink* copa *f* (*tomada antes de ir a dormir*)
'night·club club *m* nocturno, discoteca *f*

'night·dress camisón *m*
'night·fall: ***at nightfall*** al anochecer
'night flight vuelo *m* nocturno
'night·gown camisón *m*
night·ie ['naɪtɪ] camisón *m*
nigh·tin·gale ['naɪtɪŋgeɪl] ruiseñor *m*
'night·life vida *f* nocturna
night·ly ['naɪtlɪ] **1** *adj*: ***a nightly event*** algo que sucede todas las noches **2** *adv* todas las noches
'night·mare *also fig* pesadilla *f*
'night por·ter portero *m* de noche
'night school escuela *f* nocturna
'night shift turno *m* de noche
'night·shirt camisa *f* de dormir
'night·spot local *m* nocturno
'night·time: ***at nighttime, in the nighttime*** por la noche
nil [nɪl] *Br* cero
nim·ble ['nɪmbl] *adj* ágil
nine [naɪn] nueve
nine·teen [naɪn'tiːn] diecinueve
nine·teenth [naɪn'tiːnθ] *n & adj* decimonoveno
nine·ti·eth ['naɪntɪɪθ] *n & adj* nonagésimo
nine·ty ['naɪntɪ] noventa
ninth [naɪnθ] *n & adj* noveno
nip [nɪp] *n* (*pinch*) pellizco *m*; (*bite*) mordisco *m*
nip·ple ['nɪpl] pezón *m*
ni·tro·gen ['naɪtrədʒn] nitrógeno *m*
no [noʊ] **1** *adv* no **2** *adj*: ***there's no coffee / tea left*** no queda café / té; ***I have no family / money*** no tengo familia / dinero; ***I'm no linguist / expert*** no soy un lingüista / experto; ***no smoking / parking*** prohibido fumar / aparcar
no·bil·i·ty [noʊ'bɪlətɪ] nobleza *f*
no·ble ['noʊbl] *adj* noble
no·bod·y ['noʊbədɪ] *pron* nadie; ***nobody knows*** nadie lo sabe; ***there was nobody at home*** no había nadie en casa
nod [nɑːd] **1** *n* movimiento *m* de la cabeza **2** *v/i* (*pret & pp* ***nodded***) asentir con la cabeza
◆ **nod off** *v/i* (*fall asleep*) quedarse dormido
no-hop·er [noʊ'hoʊpər] F inútil *m/f* F
noise [nɔɪz] ruido *m*
nois·y ['nɔɪzɪ] *adj* ruidoso
nom·i·nal ['nɑːmɪnl] *adj amount* simbólico
nom·i·nate ['nɑːmɪneɪt] *v/t* (*appoint*) nombrar; ***nominate s.o. for a post*** (*propose*) proponer a alguien para un puesto
nom·i·na·tion [nɑːmɪ'neɪʃn] (*appointment*) nombramiento *m*; (*proposal*) nominación *f*; ***who was your nomination?*** ¿a quién propusiste?
nom·i·nee [nɑːmɪ'niː] candidato(-a) *m(f)*
non ... [nɑːn] no ...
non·al·co'hol·ic *adj* sin alcohol
non·a'ligned *adj* no alineado
non·cha·lant ['nɑːnʃəlɑːnt] *adj* despreocupado
non·com·mis·sioned 'of·fi·cer suboficial *m/f*
non·com'mit·tal *adj person, response* evasivo
non·de·script ['nɑːndɪskrɪpt] *adj* anodino
none [nʌn] *pron*: ***none of the students*** ninguno de los estudiantes; ***none of the water*** nada del agua; ***there are none left*** no queda ninguno; ***there is none left*** no queda nada
non'en·ti·ty nulidad *f*
none·the·less [nʌnðə'les] *adv* sin embargo, no obstante
non·ex'ist·ent *adj* inexistente
non'fic·tion no ficción *f*
non·(in)'flam·ma·ble *adj* incombustible, no inflamable
non·in·ter'fer·ence, **non·in·ter'ven·tion** no intervención *f*
non-'i·ron *adj shirt* que no necesita plancha
'no-no: ***that's a no-no*** F de eso nada
no-'non·sense *adj approach* directo
non'payment impago *m*
non·pol'lut·ing *adj* que no contamina
non'res·i·dent *n* no residente *m/f*
non·re·turn·a·ble [nɑːnrɪ'tɜːrnəbl] *adj* no retornable
non·sense ['nɑːnsəns] disparate *m*, tontería *f*; ***don't talk nonsense*** no digas disparates *or* tonterías; ***nonsense, it's easy!*** tonterías, ¡es fácil!
non'skid *adj tires* antideslizante
non'slip *adj surface* antideslizante
non'smok·er *person* no fumador(a) *m(f)*
non'stand·ard *adj* no estándar
non'stick *adj pans* antiadherente
non'stop 1 *adj flight, train* directo, sin escalas; *chatter* ininterrumpido **2** *adv fly, travel* directamente; *chatter, argue* sin parar
non'swim·mer: ***be a nonswimmer*** no saber nadar
non'u·nion *adj* no sindicado
non'vi·o·lence no violencia *f*
non'vi·o·lent *adj* no violento
noo·dles ['nuːdlz] *npl* tallarines *mpl* (chinos)
nook [nʊk] rincón *m*
noon [nuːn] mediodía *m*; ***at noon*** al mediodía
noose [nuːs] lazo *m* corredizo

N

nor [nɔːr] *conj* ni; ***nor do I*** yo tampoco, ni yo
norm [nɔːrm] norma *f*
nor·mal ['nɔːrml] *adj* normal
nor·mal·i·ty [nɔːr'mælətɪ] normalidad *f*
nor·mal·ize ['nɔːrməlaɪz] *v/t relationships* normalizar
nor·mal·ly ['nɔːrməlɪ] *adv* (*usually*) normalmente; (*in a normal way*) normalmente, con normalidad
north [nɔːrθ] **1** *n* norte *m*; ***to the north of*** al norte de **2** *adj* norte **3** *adv travel* al norte; ***north of*** al norte de
North Am'er·i·ca *Am*érica del Norte, Norteamérica
North Am'er·i·can **1** *n* norteamericano(-a) *m*(*f*) **2** *adj* norteamericano
north'east *n* nordeste *m*, noreste *m*
nor·ther·ly ['nɔːrðəlɪ] *adj* norte, del norte
nor·thern ['nɔːrðən] norteño, del norte
nor·thern·er ['nɔːrðənər] norteño(-a) *m*(*f*)
North Ko're·a Corea del Norte
North Ko're·an **1** *adj* norcoreano **2** *n* norcoreano(-a) *m*(*f*)
North 'Pole Polo *m* Norte
north·ward ['nɔːrðwərd] *adv travel* hacia el norte
north·west [nɔːrð'west] *n* noroeste *m*
Nor·way ['nɔːrweɪ] Noruega
Nor·we·gian [nɔːr'wiːdʒn] **1** *adj* noruego **2** *n person* noruego(-a) *m*(*f*); *language* noruego *m*
nose [noʊz] nariz *m*; *of animal* hocico *m*; ***it was right under my nose!*** ¡lo tenía delante de mis narices!
◆ **nose about** *v/i* F husmear
'nose·bleed: ***have a nosebleed*** sangrar por la nariz
nos·tal·gia [nɑː'stældʒɪə] nostalgia *f*
nos·tal·gic [nɑː'stældʒɪk] *adj* nostálgico
nos·tril ['nɑːstrəl] ventana *f* de la nariz
nos·y ['noʊzɪ] *adj* F entrometido
not [nɑːt] *adv* no; ***not this one, that one*** éste no, ése; ***not now*** ahora no; ***not there*** no allí; ***not like that*** así no; ***not before Tuesday / next week*** no antes del martes / de la próxima semana; ***not for me, thanks*** para mí no, gracias; ***not a lot*** no mucho; ***it's not ready / allowed*** no está listo / permitido; ***I don't know*** no lo sé; ***I am not American*** no soy americano; ***he didn't help*** no ayudó
no·ta·ble ['noʊtəbl] *adj* notable
no·ta·ry ['noʊtərɪ] notario(-a) *m*(*f*)
notch [nɑːtʃ] muesca *f*, mella *f*
note [noʊt] *n written*, MUS nota *f*; ***take notes*** tomar notas; ***take note of sth*** prestar atención a algo
◆ **note down** *v/t* anotar
'note·book cuaderno *m*, libreta *f*; COMPUT *Span* ordenador *m* portátil, *L.Am.* computadora *f* portátil
not·ed ['noʊtɪd] *adj* destacado
'note·pad bloc *m* de notas
'note·pa·per papel *m* de carta
noth·ing ['nʌθɪŋ] *pron* nada; ***nothing but*** sólo; ***nothing much*** no mucho; ***for nothing*** (*for free*) gratis; (*for no reason*) por nada; ***I'd like nothing better*** me encantaría
no·tice ['noʊtɪs] **1** *n on bulletin board*, *in street* cartel *m*, letrero *m*; (*advance warning*) aviso *m*; *in newspaper* anuncio *m*; ***at short notice*** con poca antelación; ***until further notice*** hasta nuevo aviso; ***give s.o. his / her notice*** *to quit job* despedir a alguien; *to leave house* comunicar a alguien que tiene que abandonar la casa; ***hand in one's notice*** *to employer* presentar la dimisión; ***four weeks' notice*** cuatro semanas de preaviso; ***take notice of sth*** observar algo, prestar atención a algo; ***take no notice of s.o./sth*** no hacer caso de alguien / algo **2** *v/t* notar, fijarse en
no·tice·a·ble ['noʊtɪsəbl] *adj* apreciable, evidente
no·ti·fy ['noʊtɪfaɪ] *v/t* (*pret & pp* **notified**) notificar, informar
no·tion ['noʊʃn] noción *f*, idea *f*
no·tions ['noʊsnz] *npl* artículos *mpl* de costura
no·to·ri·ous [noʊ'tɔːrɪəs] *adj* de mala fama
nou·gat ['nuːgət] *especie de turrón*
nought [nɒːt] cero *m*
noun [naʊn] nombre *m*, sustantivo *m*
nou·rish·ing ['nʌrɪʃɪŋ] *adj* nutritivo
nou·rish·ment ['nʌrɪʃmənt] alimento *m*, alimentación *f*
nov·el ['nɑːvl] *n* novela *f*
nov·el·ist ['nɑːvlɪst] novelista *m*/*f*
no·vel·ty ['nɑːvəltɪ] (*being new*) lo novedoso; (*something new*) novedad *f*
No·vem·ber [noʊ'vembər] noviembre *m*
nov·ice ['nɑːvɪs] principiante *m*/*f*
now [naʊ] *adv* ahora; ***now and again, now and then*** de vez en cuando; ***by now*** ya; ***from now on*** de ahora en adelante; ***right now*** ahora mismo; ***just now*** (*at this moment*) en este momento; (*a little while ago*) hace un momento; ***now, now!*** ¡vamos!, ¡venga!; ***now, where did I put it?*** ¿y ahora dónde lo he puesto?
now·a·days ['naʊədeɪz] *adv* hoy en día
no·where ['noʊwer] *adv* en ningún lugar;

it's nowhere near finished no está acabado ni mucho menos; ***he was nowhere to be seen*** no se le veía en ninguna parte
noz·zle ['nɑːzl] boquilla *f*
nu·cle·ar ['nuːklɪər] *adj* nuclear
nu·cle·ar 'en·er·gy energía *f* nuclear
nu·cle·ar 'fis·sion fisión *f* nuclear
'nu·cle·ar-free *adj* desnuclearizado
nu·cle·ar 'phys·ics física *f* nuclear
nu·cle·ar 'pow·er energía *f* nuclear; POL potencia *f* nuclear
nu·cle·ar 'pow·er sta·tion central *f* nuclear
nu·cle·ar re'ac·tor reactor *m* nuclear
nu·cle·ar 'waste residuos *mpl* nucleares
nu·cle·ar 'weap·on arma *f* nuclear
nude [nuːd] **1** *adj* desnudo **2** *n painting* desnudo *m*; ***in the nude*** desnudo
nudge [nʌdʒ] *v/t* dar un toque con el codo a
nud·ist ['nuːdɪst] *n* nudista *m/f*
nui·sance ['nuːsns] incordio *m*, molestia *f*; ***make a nuisance of o.s.*** dar la lata; ***what a nuisance!*** ¡qué incordio!
nuke [nuːk] *v/t* F atacar con armas nucleares
null and 'void [nʌl] *adj* nulo y sin efecto
numb [nʌm] *adj* entumecido; *emotionally* insensible
num·ber ['nʌmbər] **1** *n* número *m*; ***a number of people*** un cierto número de personas **2** *v/t* (*put a number on*) numerar
numeral ['nuːmərəl] número *m*
nu·me·rate ['nuːmərət] *adj* que sabe sumar y restar
nu·me·rous ['nuːmərəs] *adj* numeroso
nun [nʌn] monja *f*
nurse [nɜːrs] enfermero(-a) *m*(*f*)
nur·se·ry ['nɜːrsərɪ] guardería *f*; *for plants* vivero *m*
'nur·se·ry rhyme canción *f* infantil
'nur·se·ry school parvulario *m*, jardín *m* de infancia
'nur·se·ry school teach·er profesor(a) *m*(*f*) de parvulario
nurs·ing ['nɜːrsɪŋ] enfermería *f*
'nurs·ing home *for old people* residencia *f*
nut [nʌt] nuez *f*; *for bolt* tuerca *f*; ***nuts*** F (*testicles*) pelotas *fpl* F
'nut·crack·ers *npl* cascanueces *m inv*
nu·tri·ent ['nuːtrɪənt] *n* nutriente *m*
nu·tri·tion [nuː'trɪʃn] nutrición *f*
nu·tri·tious [nuː'trɪʃəs] *adj* nutritivo
nuts [nʌts] *adj* F (*crazy*) chalado F, pirado F; ***be nuts about s.o.*** estar coladito por alguien F
'nut·shell: ***in a nutshell*** en una palabra
nut·ty ['nʌtɪ] *adj taste* a nuez; F (*crazy*) chalado F, pirado F
ny·lon ['naɪlɑːn] **1** *n* nylon *m* **2** *adj* de nylon

O

oak [oʊk] *tree, wood* roble *m*
oar [ɔːr] remo *m*
o·a·sis [oʊ'eɪsɪs] (*pl* ***oases*** [oʊ'eɪsiːz]) *also fig* oasis *m inv*
oath [oʊθ] LAW, (*swearword*) juramento *m*; ***on oath*** bajo juramento
'oat·meal harina *f* de avena
oats [oʊts] *npl* copos *mpl* de avena
o·be·di·ence [oʊ'biːdɪəns] obediencia *f*
o·be·di·ent [oʊ'biːdɪənt] *adj* obediente
o·be·di·ent·ly [oʊ'biːdɪəntlɪ] *adv* obedientemente
o·bese [oʊ'biːs] *adj* obeso
o·bes·i·ty [oʊ'biːsɪtɪ] obesidad *f*
o·bey [oʊ'beɪ] *v/t* obedecer
o·bit·u·a·ry [ə'bɪtʊerɪ] *n* necrología *f*, obituario *m*
ob·ject[1] ['ɑːbdʒɪkt] *n* (*thing*) objeto *m*; (*aim*) objetivo *m*; GRAM objeto *m*
ob·ject[2] [əb'dʒekt] *v/i* oponerse
◆ **object to** *v/t* oponerse a
ob·jec·tion [əb'dʒekʃn] objeción *f*
ob·jec·tio·na·ble [əb'dʒekʃnəbl] *adj* (*unpleasant*) desagradable
ob·jec·tive [əb'dʒektɪv] **1** *adj* objetivo **2** *n* objetivo *m*
ob·jec·tive·ly [əb'dʒektɪvlɪ] *adv* objetivamente
ob·jec·tiv·i·ty [əb'dʒektɪvətɪ] objetividad *f*
ob·li·ga·tion [ɑːblɪ'geɪʃn] obligación *f*; ***be under an obligation to s.o.*** tener una obligación para con alguien
ob·lig·a·to·ry [ə'blɪgətɔːrɪ] *adj* obligatorio
o·blige [ə'blaɪdʒ] *v/t* obligar; ***much o-***

O

bliged! muy agradecido
o·blig·ing [əˈblaɪdʒɪŋ] *adj* atento, servicial
o·blique [əˈbliːk] **1** *adj reference* indirecto **2** *n in punctuation* barra *f* inclinada
o·blit·er·ate [əˈblɪtəreɪt] *v/t city* destruir, arrasar; *memory* borrar
o·bliv·i·on [əˈblɪvɪən] olvido *m*; ***fall into oblivion*** caer en el olvido
o·bliv·i·ous [əˈblɪvɪəs] *adj*: ***be oblivious of sth*** no ser consciente de algo
ob·long [ˈɑːblɒːŋ] *adj* rectangular
ob·nox·ious [əbˈnɑːkʃəs] *adj person* detestable, odioso; *smell* repugnante
ob·scene [ɑːbˈsiːn] *adj* obsceno; *salary, poverty* escandaloso
ob·scen·i·ty [əbˈsenətɪ] obscenidad *f*
ob·scure [əbˈskjʊr] *adj* oscuro
ob·scu·ri·ty [əbˈskjʊrətɪ] oscuridad *f*
ob·ser·vance [əbˈzɜːrvns] *of festival* práctica *f*
ob·ser·vant [əbˈzɜːrvnt] *adj* observador
ob·ser·va·tion [ɑːbzəˈveɪʃn] *of nature, stars* observación *f*; (*comment*) observación *f*, comentario *m*
ob·ser·va·to·ry [əbˈzɜːrvətɔːrɪ] observatorio *m*
ob·serve [əbˈzɜːrv] *v/t* observar
ob·serv·er [əbˈzɜːrvər] observador(a) *m*(*f*)
ob·sess [ɑːbˈses] *v/t* obsesionar; ***be obsessed by / with*** estar obsesionado con / por
ob·ses·sion [ɑːbˈseʃn] obsesión *f*
ob·ses·sive [ɑːbˈsesɪv] *adj* obsesivo
ob·so·lete [ˈɑːbsəliːt] *adj* obsoleto
ob·sta·cle [ˈɑːbstəkl] obstáculo *m*
ob·ste·tri·cian [ɑːbstəˈtrɪʃn] obstetra *m/f*, tocólogo(-a) *m*(*f*)
ob·stet·rics [ɑːbˈstetrɪks] obstetricia *f*, tocología *f*
ob·sti·na·cy [ˈɑːbstɪnəsɪ] obstinación *f*
ob·sti·nate [ˈɑːbstɪnət] *adj* obstinado
ob·sti·nate·ly [ˈɑːbstɪnətlɪ] *adv* obstinadamente
ob·struct [ɑːbˈstrʌkt] *v/t road* obstruir; *investigation, police* obstaculizar
ob·struc·tion [əbˈstrʌkʧn] *on road etc* obstrucción *f*
ob·struc·tive [əbˈstrʌktɪv] *adj behavior, tactics* obstruccionista
ob·tain [əbˈteɪn] *v/t* obtener, lograr
ob·tain·a·ble [əbˈteɪnəbl] *adj products* disponible
ob·tru·sive [əbˈtruːsɪv] *adj* molesto; ***the plastic chairs are rather obtrusive*** las sillas de plástico desentonan por completo
ob·tuse [əbˈtuːs] *adj fig* duro de mollera
ob·vi·ous [ˈɑːbvɪəs] *adj* obvio, evidente
ob·vi·ous·ly [ˈɑːbvɪəslɪ] *adv* obviamente; ***obviously!*** ¡por supuesto!
oc·ca·sion [əˈkeɪʒn] ocasión *f*
oc·ca·sion·al [əˈkeɪʒənl] *adj* ocasional, esporádico; ***I like the occasional whisky*** me gusta tomarme un whisky de vez en cuando
oc·ca·sion·al·ly [əˈkeɪʒnlɪ] *adv* ocasionalmente, de vez en cuando
oc·cult [əˈkʌlt] **1** *adj* oculto **2** *n*: ***the occult*** lo oculto
oc·cu·pant [ˈɑːkjʊpənt] ocupante *m/f*
oc·cu·pa·tion [ɑːkjʊˈpeɪʃn] ocupación *f*
oc·cu·pa·tion·al ˈther·a·pist [ɑːkjʊˈpeɪʃnl] terapeuta *m/f* ocupacional
oc·cu·pa·tion·al ˈther·a·py terapia *f* ocupacional
oc·cu·py [ˈɑːkjʊpaɪ] *v/t* (*pret & pp* ***occupied***) ocupar
oc·cur [əˈkɜːr] *v/i* (*pret & pp* ***occurred***) ocurrir, suceder; ***it occurred to me that ...*** se me ocurrió que ...
oc·cur·rence [əˈkʌrəns] acontecimiento *m*
o·cean [ˈoʊʃn] océano *m*
o·ce·a·nog·ra·phy [oʊʃnˈɑːgrəfɪ] oceanografía *f*
o'clock [əˈklɑːk]: ***at five / six o'clock*** a las cinco / seis
Oc·to·ber [ɑːkˈtoʊbər] octubre *m*
oc·to·pus [ˈɑːktəpəs] pulpo *m*
OD [oʊˈdiː] *v/i* F ***OD on*** *drug* tomar una sobredosis de
odd [ɑːd] *adj* (*strange*) raro, extraño; (*not even*) impar; ***the odd one out*** el bicho raro; ***50 odd*** cerca de 50
ˈodd·ball F bicho *m* raro F
odds [ɑːdz] *npl*: ***be at odds with sth/s.o.*** no concordar con algo / estar peleado con alguien; ***the odds are 10 to one*** las apuestas están en 10 a 1; ***the odds are that ...*** lo más probable es que ...; ***against all the odds*** contra lo que se esperaba
odds and ˈends *npl objects* cacharros *mpl*; *things to do* cosillas *fpl*
ˈodds-on *adj favorite* indiscutible
o·di·ous [ˈoʊdɪəs] *adj* odioso
o·dom·e·ter [oʊˈdɑːmətər] cuentakilómetros *m inv*
o·dor, *Br* **o·dour** [ˈoʊdər] olor *m*
of [ɑːv], [əv] *prep possession* de; ***the name of the street / hotel*** el nombre de la calle / del hotel; ***the color of the car*** el color del coche; ***the works of Dickens*** las obras de Dickens; ***five / ten minutes of twelve*** las doce menos cinco / diez; ***die of cancer*** morir de cáncer; ***love of***

money* / *adventure amor por el dinero / la aventura; ***of the three this is …*** de los tres éste es …

off [ɑːf] **1** *prep*: ***off the main road*** (*away from*) apartado de la carretera principal; (*leading off*) saliendo de la carretera principal; ***$20 off the price*** una rebaja en el precio de 20 dólares; ***he's off his food*** no come nada, está desganado **2** *adv*: ***be off*** *of light*, TV, *machine* estar apagado; *of brake*, *lid*, *top* no estar puesto; *not at work* faltar; *on vacation* estar de vacaciones; (*canceled*) estar cancelado; ***we're off tomorrow*** (*leaving*) nos vamos mañana; ***I'm off to New York*** me voy a Nueva York; ***with his pants* / *hat off*** sin los pantalones / el sombrero; ***take a day off*** tomarse un día de fiesta *or* un día libre; ***it's 3 miles off*** está a tres millas de distancia; ***it's a long way off*** *in distance* está muy lejos; *in future* todavía queda mucho tiempo; ***he got into his car and drove off*** se subió al coche y se marchó; ***off and on*** de vez en cuando **3** *adj*: ***the off switch*** el interruptor de apagado

of·fence *Br* → ***offense***

of·fend [ə'fend] *v/t* (*insult*) ofender

of·fend·er [ə'fendər] LAW delincuente *m/f*; ***offenders will be prosecuted*** se procesará a los infractores

of·fense [ə'fens] LAW delito *m*; ***take offense at sth*** ofenderse por algo

of·fen·sive [ə'fensɪv] **1** *adj behavior*, *remark* ofensivo; *smell* repugnante **2** *n* (MIL: *attack*) ofensiva *f*; ***go on*(*to*) *the offensive*** pasar a la ofensiva

of·fer ['ɑːfər] **1** *n* oferta *f* **2** *v/t* ofrecer; ***offer s.o. sth*** ofrecer algo a alguien

off'hand *adj attitude* brusco

of·fice ['ɑːfɪs] *building* oficina *f*; *room* oficina *f*, despacho *m*; *position* cargo *m*

'of·fice block bloque *m* de oficinas

'of·fice hours *npl* horas *fpl* de oficina

of·fi·cer ['ɑːfɪsər] MIL oficial *m/f*; *in police* agente *m/f*

of·fi·cial [ə'fɪʃl] **1** *adj* oficial **2** *n* funcionario(-a) *m*(*f*)

of·fi·cial·ly [ə'fɪʃlɪ] *adv* oficialmente

of·fi·ci·ate [ə'fɪʃɪeɪt] *v/i*: ***with X officiating*** con X celebrando la ceremonia

of·fi·cious [ə'fɪʃəs] *adj* entrometido

'off-line *adv work* fuera de línea; ***be off-line*** *of printer etc* estar desconectado; ***go off-line*** desconectarse

'off·peak *adj rates* en horas valle, fuera de las horas punta; ***offpeak electricity*** electricidad *f* en horas valle *or* fuera de las horas punta

'off-sea·son 1 *adj rates*, *vacation* de temporada baja **2** *n* temporada *f* baja

'off·set *v/t* (*pret & pp* ***offset***) *losses*, *disadvantage* compensar

'off·shore *adj drilling rig* cercano a la costa; *investment* en el exterior

'off·side 1 *adj wheel etc* del lado del conductor **2** *adv* SP fuera de juego

'off·spring *of person* vástagos *mpl*, hijos *mpl*; *of animal* crías *fpl*

off-the-'rec·ord *adj* confidencial

'off-white *adj* blancuzco

of·ten ['ɑːfn] *adv* a menudo, frecuentemente *m*

oil [ɔɪl] **1** *n for machine*, *food*, *skin* aceite *m*; *petroleum* petróleo *m* **2** *v/t hinges*, *bearings* engrasar

'oil change cambio *m* del aceite

'oil com·pa·ny compañía *f* petrolera

'oil·field yacimiento *m* petrolífero

'oil-fired *adj central heating* de gasóleo *or* fuel

'oil paint·ing óleo *m*

'oil-pro·duc·ing coun·try país *m* productor de petróleo

'oil re·fin·e·ry refinería *f* de petróleo

'oil rig plataforma *f* petrolífera

'oil·skins *npl* ropa *f* impermeable

'oil slick marea *f* negra

'oil tank·er petrolero *m*

'oil well pozo *m* petrolífero

oil·y ['ɔɪlɪ] *adj* grasiento

oint·ment ['ɔɪntmənt] ungüento *m*, pomada *f*

ok [oʊ'keɪ] *adj*, *adv* F ***can I? - ok*** ¿puedo? - de acuerdo *or Span* vale; ***is it ok with you if …?*** ¿te parecería bien si …?; ***does that look ok?*** ¿queda bien?; ***that's ok by me*** por mí, ningún problema; ***are you ok?*** (*well*, *not hurt*) ¿estás bien?; ***are you ok for Friday?*** ¿te va bien el viernes?; ***he's ok*** (*is a good guy*) es buena persona; ***is this bus ok for …?*** ¿este autobús va a …?

old [oʊld] *adj* viejo; (*previous*) anterior, antiguo; ***an old man* / *woman*** un anciano / una anciana, un viejo / una vieja; ***how old are you* / *is he?*** ¿cuántos años tienes / tiene?; ***he's getting old*** está haciéndose mayor

old 'age vejez *f*

old-'fash·ioned *adj clothes*, *style*, *ideas* anticuado, pasado de moda, *word* anticuado

ol·ive ['ɑːlɪv] aceituna *f*, oliva *f*

'ol·ive oil aceite *m* de oliva

O·lym·pic 'Games [ə'lɪmpɪk] *npl* Juegos *mpl* Olímpicos

om·e·let, *Br* **om·e·lette** ['ɑːmlɪt] tortilla *f* (francesa)

om·i·nous ['ɑːmɪnəs] *adj* siniestro
o·mis·sion [oʊ'mɪʃn] omisión *f*
o·mit [ə'mɪt] *v/t* (*pret & pp* ***omitted***) omitir; ***omit to do sth*** no hacer algo
om·nip·o·tent [ɑːm'nɪpətənt] *adj* omnipotente
om·nis·ci·ent [ɑːm'nɪsɪənt] *adj* omnisciente
on [ɑːn] **1** *prep* en; ***on the table / wall*** en la mesa / la pared; ***on the bus / train*** en el autobús / el tren; ***on TV / the radio*** en la televisión / la radio; ***on Sunday*** el domingo; ***on the 1st of …*** el uno de …; ***this is on me*** (*I'm paying*) invito yo; ***have you any money on you?*** ¿llevas dinero encima?; ***on his arrival / departure*** cuando llegue / se marche; ***on hearing this*** al escuchar esto **2** *adv*: ***be on*** *of light*, TV, *computer etc* estar encendido *or L.Am.* prendido; *of brake*, *lid*, *top* estar puesto; *of meeting etc*: *be scheduled to happen* haber sido acordado; ***it's on at 5 am*** *of* TV *program* lo dan *or Span* ponen a las cinco; ***what's on tonight?*** *on* TV *etc* ¿qué dan *or Span* ponen esta noche?; (*what's planned?*) ¿qué planes hay para esta noche?; ***with his hat on*** con el sombrero puesto; ***you're on*** (*I accept your offer etc*) trato hecho; ***that's not on*** (*not allowed*, *not fair*) eso no se hace; ***on you go*** (*go ahead*) adelante; ***walk / talk on*** seguir caminando / hablando; ***and so on*** etcétera; ***on and on*** *talk etc* sin parar **3** *adj*: ***the on switch*** el interruptor de encendido
once [wʌns] **1** *adv* (*one time*, *formerly*) una vez; ***once again, once more*** una vez más; ***at once*** (*immediately*) de inmediato, inmediamente; ***all at once*** (*suddenly*) de repente; (***all***) ***at once*** (*together*) al mismo tiempo; ***once upon a time there was …*** érase una vez …; ***once in a while*** de vez en cuando; ***once and for all*** de una vez por todas; ***for once*** por una vez **2** *conj* una vez que; ***once you have finished*** una vez que hayas acabado
one [wʌn] **1** *number* uno *m* **2** *adj* un(a); ***one day*** un día **3** *pron* uno(-a); ***which one?*** ¿cuál?; ***one by one*** *enter*, *deal with* uno por uno; ***we help one another*** nos ayudamos mutuamente; ***what can one say / do?*** ¿qué puede uno decir / hacer?; ***the little ones*** los pequeños; ***I for one*** yo personalmente
one-'off *n* (*unique event*, *person*) hecho *m* aislado; (*exception*) excepción *f*
one-par·ent 'fam·i·ly familia *f* monoparental
one'self *pron* uno(-a) mismo(-a) *m*(*f*); ***do sth by oneself*** hacer algo sin ayuda; ***look after oneself*** cuidarse; ***be by oneself*** estar solo
one-sid·ed [wʌn'saɪdɪd] *adj discussion*, *fight* desigual
one-track 'mind *hum*: ***have a one-track mind*** ser un obseso
'one-way street calle *f* de sentido único
'one-way tick·et billete *m* de ida
on·ion ['ʌnjən] cebolla *f*
'on-line *adv* en línea; ***go on-line to*** conectarse a
'on-line serv·ice COMPUT servicio *m* en línea
on·look·er ['ɑːnlʊkər] espectador(a) *m*(*f*), curioso(-a) *m*(*f*)
on·ly ['oʊnlɪ] **1** *adv* sólo, solamente; ***he was here only yesterday*** estuvo aquí ayer mismo; ***not only … but also …*** no sólo *or* solamente … sino también …; ***only just*** por poco **2** *adj* único; ***only son*** hijo único
'on·set comienzo *m*
'on·side *adv* SP en posición reglamentaria
on-the-job 'train·ing formación *f* continua
on·to ['ɑːntuː] *prep*: ***put sth onto sth*** poner algo encima de algo
on·ward ['ɑːnwərd] *adv* hacia adelante; ***from … onward*** de … en adelante
ooze [uːz] **1** *v/i of liquid*, *mud* rezumar **2** *v/t* rezumar; ***he oozes charm*** rezuma *or* rebosa encanto
o·paque [oʊ'peɪk] *adj glass* opaco
OPEC ['oʊpek] *abbr* (= ***Organization of Petroleum Exporting Countries***) OPEP *f* (= Organización *f* de Países Exportadores de Petróleo)
o·pen ['oʊpən] **1** *adj* (*also honest*) abierto; ***in the open air*** al aire libre **2** *v/t* abrir **3** *v/i of door*, *shop* abrir; *of flower* abrirse
◆ **open up** *v/i of person* abrirse
o·pen-'air *adj meeting*, *concert* al aire libre; *pool* descubierto
'o·pen day jornada *f* de puertas abiertas
o·pen-'end·ed *adj contract etc* abierto
o·pen·ing ['oʊpənɪŋ] *in wall etc* abertura *f*; (*beginning*: *of film*, *novel etc*) comienzo *m*; (*job*) puesto *m* vacante
'o·pen·ing hours *npl* horario *m* de apertura
o·pen·ly ['oʊpənlɪ] *adv* (*honestly*, *frankly*) abiertamente
o·pen-mind·ed [oʊpən'maɪndɪd] *adj* de mentalidad abierta
o·pen 'plan of·fice oficina *f* de planta abierta
'o·pen tick·et billete *m* abierto
op·e·ra ['ɑːpərə] ópera *f*

'op·e·ra glass·es *npl* gemelos *mpl*, prismáticos *mpl*
'op·e·ra house (teatro *m* de la) ópera *f*
'op·e·ra sing·er cantante *m/f* de ópera
op·e·rate ['ɑːpəreɪt] **1** *v/i of company* operar, actuar; *of airline, bus service,* MED operar; *of machine* funcionar (**on** con) **2** *v/t machine* manejar
◆ **operate on** *v/t* MED operar; ***they operated on his leg*** le operaron de la pierna
'op·e·rat·ing in·struc·tions *npl* instrucciones *fpl* de funcionamiento
'op·e·rating room MED quirófano *m*
'op·e·rat·ing sys·tem COMPUT sistema *m* operativo
op·e·ra·tion [ɑːpə'reɪʃn] MED operación *f*; *of machine* manejo *m*; ***operations*** *of company* operaciones *fpl*, actividades *fpl*; ***have an operation*** MED ser operado
op·e·ra·tor ['ɑːpəreɪtər] TELEC operador(a) *m(f)*; *of machine* operario(-a) *m(f)*; (*tour operator*) operador *m* turístico
oph·thal·mol·o·gist [ɑːfθæl'mɑːlədʒɪst] oftalmólogo(-a) *m(f)*
o·pin·ion [ə'pɪnjən] opinión *f*; ***in my opinion*** en mi opinión
o'pin·ion poll encuesta *f* de opinión
op·po·nent [ə'pounənt] oponente *m/f*, adversario(-a) *m(f)*
op·por·tune ['ɑːpərtuːn] *adj fml* oportuno
op·por·tun·ist [ɑːpər'tuːnɪst] oportunista *m/f*
op·por·tu·ni·ty [ɑːpər'tuːnətɪ] oportunidad *f*
op·pose [ə'pouz] *v/t* oponerse a; ***be opposed to …*** estar en contra de …; ***John, as opposed to George …*** John, al contrario que George …
op·po·site ['ɑːpəzɪt] **1** *adj* contrario; *views, characters, meaning* opuesto; ***the opposite side of town / end of the road*** el otro lado de la ciudad / el otro extremo de la calle; ***the opposite sex*** el sexo opuesto **2** *n*: ***the opposite of*** lo contrario de
op·po·site 'num·ber homólogo(-a) *m(f)*
op·po·si·tion [ɑːpə'zɪʃn] *to plan,* POL oposición *f*; ***meet with opposition*** encontrar oposición
op·press [ə'pres] *v/t the people* oprimir
op·pres·sive [ə'presɪv] *adj rule, dictator* opresor; *weather* agobiante
opt [ɑːpt] *v/t*: ***opt to do sth*** optar por hacer algo
op·ti·cal il·lu·sion ['ɑːptɪkl] ilusión *f* óptica
op·ti·cian [ɑːp'tɪʃn] óptico(-a) *m(f)*
op·ti·mism ['ɑːptɪmɪzm] optimismo *m*
op·ti·mist ['ɑːptɪmɪst] optimista *m/f*
op·ti·mist·ic [ɑːptɪ'mɪstɪk] *adj* optimista
op·timist·ic·ally [ɑːptɪ'mɪstɪklɪ] *adv* con optimismo
optimum ['ɑːptɪməm] **1** *adj* óptimo **2** *n*: ***the optimum*** lo ideal
op·tion ['ɑːpʃn] opción *f*
op·tion·al ['ɑːpʃnl] *adj* optativo
op·tion·al 'ex·tras *npl* accesorios *mpl* opcionales
or [ɔːr] *conj* o; *before a word beginning with the letter o* u ; ***or else!*** ¡más vale que no llegues tarde, ¡de lo contrario!
o·ral ['ɔːrəl] *adj exam, sex* oral; *hygiene* bucal
or·ange ['ɔːrɪndʒ] **1** *adj color* naranja **2** *n fruit* naranja *f*; *color* naranja *m*
'or·ange juice *Span* zumo *m or L.Am.* jugo de naranja
or·ange 'squash naranjada *f*
or·a·tor ['ɔːrətər] orador(a) *m(f)*
or·bit ['ɔːrbɪt] **1** *n of earth* órbita *f*; ***send sth into orbit*** poner algo en órbita **2** *v/t the earth* girar alrededor de
or·chard ['ɔːrtʃərd] huerta *f* (de frutales)
or·ches·tra ['ɔːrkɪstrə] orquesta *f*
or·chid ['ɔːrkɪd] orquídea *f*
or·dain [ɔːr'deɪn] *v/t* ordenar
or·deal [ɔːr'diːl] calvario *m*, experiencia *f* penosa
or·der ['ɔːrdər] **1** *n* (*command*) orden *f*; (*sequence, being well arranged*) orden *m*; *for goods* pedido *m*; ***take s.o.'s order*** *in restaurant* preguntar a alguien lo que va a tomar; ***in order to*** para; ***out of order*** (*not functioning*) estropeado; (*not in sequence*) desordenado **2** *v/t* (*put in sequence, proper layout*) ordenar; *goods* pedir, encargar; *meal* pedir; ***order s.o. to do sth*** ordenar a alguien hacer algo *or* que haga algo **3** *v/i in restaurant* pedir
or·der·ly ['ɔːrdəlɪ] **1** *adj lifestyle* ordenado, metódico **2** *n in hospital* celador(a) *m(f)*
or·di·nal num·ber ['ɔːrdɪnl] (número *m*) ordinal *m*
or·di·nar·i·ly [ɔːrdɪ'nerɪlɪ] *adv* (*as a rule*) normalmente
or·di·nary ['ɔːrdɪnerɪ] *adj* común, normal
ore [ɔːr] mineral, mena *f*
or·gan ['ɔːrgən] ANAT, MUS órgano *m*
or·gan·ic [ɔːr'gænɪk] *adj food* ecológico, biológico; *fertilizer* orgánico
or·gan·i·cal·ly [ɔːr'gænɪklɪ] *adv grown* ecológicamente, biológicamente
or·gan·ism ['ɔːrgənɪzm] organismo *m*
or·gan·i·za·tion [ɔːrgənaɪ'zeɪʃn] organización *f*

or·gan·ize ['ɔːrgənaɪz] *v/t* organizar
or·gan·ized 'crime crimen *m* organizado
or·gan·iz·er ['ɔːrgənaɪzər] *person* organizador(a) *m(f)*
or·gas·m ['ɔːrgæzm] orgasmo *m*
O·ri·ent ['ɔːrɪənt] Oriente
O·ri·en·tal [ɔːrɪ'entl] **1** *adj* oriental **2** *n* oriental *m/f*
o·ri·en·tate ['ɔːrɪənteɪt] *v/t* (*direct*) orientar; ***orientate o.s.*** (*get bearings*) orientarse
or·i·gin ['ɑːrɪdʒɪn] origen *m*; ***idea / person of Chinese origin*** una idea / una persona de origen chino
o·rig·i·nal [ə'rɪdʒənl] **1** *adj* (*not copied, first*) original **2** *n painting etc* original *m*
o·rig·i·nal·i·ty [ərɪdʒən'ælətɪ] originalidad *f*
o·rig·i·nal·ly [ə'rɪdʒənəlɪ] *adv* originalmente; (*at first*) originalmente, en un principio
o·rig·i·nate [ə'rɪdʒɪneɪt] **1** *v/t scheme, idea* crear **2** *v/i of idea, belief* originarse; *of family* proceder
o·rig·i·na·tor [ə'rɪdʒɪneɪtər] *of scheme etc* creador(a) *m(f)*; ***he's not an originator*** no es un creador nato
or·na·ment ['ɔːrnəmənt] adorno *m*
or·na·men·tal [ɔːrnə'mentl] *adj* ornamental
or·nate [ɔːr'neɪt] *adj style, architecture* recargado
or·phan ['ɔːrfn] *n* huérfano(-a) *m(f)*
or·phan·age ['ɔːrfənɪdʒ] orfanato *m*
or·tho·dox ['ɔːrθədɑːks] *adj* REL, *fig* ortodoxo
or·tho·pe·dic [ɔːrθə'piːdɪk] *adj* ortopédico
os·ten·si·bly [ɑː'stensəblɪ] *adv* aparentemente
os·ten·ta·tion [ɑːsten'teɪʃn] ostentación *f*
os·ten·ta·tious [ɑːsten'teɪʃəs] *adj* ostentoso
os·ten·ta·tious·ly [ɑːsten'teɪʃəslɪ] *adv* de forma ostentosa
os·tra·cize ['ɑːstrəsaɪz] *v/t* condenar al ostracismo
oth·er ['ʌðər] **1** *adj* otro; ***other people might not agree*** puede que otros no estén de acuerdo; ***the other day*** (*recently*) el otro día; ***every other day / person*** cada dos días / personas **2** *n*: ***the other*** el otro; ***the others*** los otros
oth·er·wise ['ʌðərwaɪz] *adv* de lo contrario, si no; (*differently*) de manera diferente
ot·ter ['ɑːtər] nutria *f*
ought [ɒːt] *v/aux*: ***I/you ought to know*** debo / debes saberlo; ***he / they ought to know*** debe / deben saberlo; ***you ought to have done it*** deberías haberlo hecho
ounce [aʊns] onza *f*
our [aʊr] *adj* nuestro *m*, nuestra *f*; ***our brother*** nuestro hermano; ***our books*** nuestros libros
ours [aʊrz] *pron* el nuestro, la nuestra; ***ours are red*** los nuestros son rojos; ***that book is ours*** ese libro es nuestro; ***a friend of ours*** un amigo nuestro
our·selves [aʊr'selvz] *pron reflexive* nos; *emphatic* nosotros mismos *mpl*, nosotras mismas *fpl*; ***we hurt ourselves*** nos hicimos daño; ***when we saw ourselves in the mirror*** cuando nos vimos en el espejo; ***we saw it ourselves*** lo vimos nosotros mismos; ***by ourselves*** (*alone*) solos; (*without help*) nosotros solos, nosotros mismos
oust [aʊst] *v/t from office* derrocar
out [aʊt] *adv*: ***be out*** *of light, fire* estar apagado; *of flower* estar en flor; (*not at home, not in building*), *of sun* haber salido; *of calculations* estar equivocado; (*be published*) haber sido publicado; (*no longer in competition*) estar eliminado; (*no longer in fashion*) estar pasado de moda; ***the secret is out*** el secreto ha sido revelado; ***out here in Dallas*** aquí en Dallas; ***he's out in the garden*** está en el jardín; (***get***) ***out!*** ¡vete!; (***get***) ***out of my room!*** ¡fuera de mi habitación!; ***that's out!*** (*out of the question*) ¡eso es imposible!; ***he's out to win*** (*fully intends to*) va a por la victoria
out·board 'mo·tor motor *m* de fueraborda
'out·break *of violence, war* estallido *m*
'out·build·ing edificio *m* anexo
'out·burst *emotional* arrebato *m*, arranque *m*
'out·cast *n* paria *m/f*
'out·come resultado *m*
'out·cry protesta *f*
out'dat·ed *adj* anticuado
out'do *v/t* (*pret* ***outdid***, *pp* ***outdone***) superar
out'door *adj toilet, activities, life* al aire libre
out'doors *adv* fuera
out·er ['aʊtər] *adj wall etc* exterior
out·er 'space espacio *m* exterior
'out·fit *clothes* traje *m*, conjunto *m*; (*company, organization*) grupo *m*
'out·go·ing *adj flight* saliente; *personality* extrovertido
out'grow *v/t* (*pret* ***outgrew***, *pp* ***outgrown***) *old ideas* dejar atrás

O

out·ing ['aʊtɪŋ] (*trip*) excursión *f*
out'last *v/t* durar más que
'out·let *of pipe* desagüe *m*; *for sales* punto *m* de venta
'out·line 1 *n of person, building etc* perfil *m*, contorno *m*; *of plan, novel* resumen *m* **2** *v/t plans etc* resumir
out'live *v/t* sobrevivir a
'out·look (*prospects*) perspectivas *fpl*
'out·ly·ing *adj areas* periférico
out'num·ber *v/t* superar en número
out of *prep* ◇ *motion* fuera de; ***run out of the house*** salir corriendo de la casa; ***it fell out of the window*** se cayó por la ventana
◇ *position*: ***20 miles out of of Detroit*** a 20 millas de Detroit
◇ *cause* por; ***out of jealousy / curiosity*** por celos / curiosidad
◇ *without*: ***we're out of gas / beer*** no nos queda gasolina / cerveza
◇ *from a group* de cada; ***5 out of 10*** 5 de cada 10
out-of-'date *adj* anticuado, desfasado
out-of-the-'way *adj* apartado
'out·pa·tient paciente *m/f* externo(-a)
'out·pa·tients' (clin·ic) clínica *f* ambulatoria
'out·per·form *v/t* superar a
'out·put 1 *n of factory* producción *f*; COMPUT salida *f* **2** *v/t* (*pret & pp* ***outputted*** *or* ***output***) (*produce*) producir
'out·rage 1 *n feeling* indignación *f*; *act* ultraje *m*, atrocidad *f* **2** *v/t* indignar, ultrajar; ***I was outraged to hear ...*** me indignó escuchar que ...
out·ra·geous [aʊt'reɪdʒəs] *adj acts* atroz; *prices* escandaloso
'out·right 1 *adj winner* absoluto **2** *adv win* completamente; *kill* en el acto
out'run *v/t* (*pret* ***outran***, *pp* ***outrun***) correr más que
'out·set principio *m*, comienzo *m*; ***from the outset*** desde el principio *or* comienzo
out'shine *v/t* (*pret & pp* ***outshone***) eclipsar
'out·side 1 *adj surface, wall* exterior; *lane* de fuera **2** *adv sit, go* fuera **3** *prep* fuera de; (*apart from*) aparte de **4** *n of building, case etc* exterior *m*; ***at the outside*** a lo sumo
out·side 'broad·cast emisión *f* desde exteriores
out·sid·er [aʊt'saɪdər] *in life* forastero(-a) *m*(*f*); ***be an outsider*** *in election, race* no ser uno de los favoritos
'out·size *adj clothing* de talla especial
'out·skirts *npl* afueras *fpl*
out'smart → ***outwit***
out'stand·ing *adj success, quality* destacado, sobresaliente; *writer, athlete* excepcional; FIN: *invoice, sums* pendiente
out·stretched ['aʊtstretʃt] *adj hands* extendido
out'vote *v/t*: ***be outvoted*** perder la votación
out·ward ['aʊtwərd] *adj appearance* externo; ***outward journey*** viaje *m* de ida
out·ward·ly ['aʊtwərdlɪ] *adv* aparentemente
out'weigh *v/t* pesar más que
out'wit *v/t* (*pret & pp* ***outwitted***) mostrarse más listo que
o·val ['oʊvl] *adj* oval, ovalado
o·va·ry ['oʊvərɪ] ovario *m*
o·va·tion [oʊ'veɪʃn] ovación *f*; ***give s.o. a standing ovation*** aplaudir a alguien de pie
ov·en ['ʌvn] horno *m*
'ov·en glove, **'ov·en mitt** manopla *f* para el horno
'ov·en·proof *adj* refractario
'ov·en-read·y *adj* listo para el horno
o·ver ['oʊvər] **1** *prep* (*above*) sobre, encima de; (*across*) al otro lado de; (*more than*) más de; (*during*) durante; ***she walked over the street*** cruzó la calle; ***travel all over Brazil*** viajar por todo Brasil; ***let's talk over a drink / meal*** hablemos mientras tomamos una bebida / comemos; ***we're over the worst*** lo peor ya ha pasado; ***over and above*** además de **2** *adv*: ***be over*** (*finished*) haber acabado; ***there were just 6 over*** sólo quedaban seis; ***over to you*** (*your turn*) te toca a ti; ***over in Japan*** allá en Japón; ***over here / there*** por aquí / allá; ***it hurts all over*** me duele por todas partes; ***painted white all over*** pintado todo de blanco; ***it's all over*** se ha acabado; ***over and over again*** una y otra vez; ***do sth over (again)*** volver a hacer algo
o·ver·all ['oʊvərɒːl] **1** *adj length* total **2** *adv* (*in general*) en general; ***it measures six feet overall*** mide en total seis pies
o·ver·alls ['oʊvərɒːlz] *npl Span* mono *m*, *L.Am.* overol *m*
o·ver'awe *v/t* intimidar; ***be overawed by s.o./sth*** sentirse intimidado por alguien / algo
o·ver'bal·ance *v/i* perder el equilibrio
o·ver'bear·ing *adj* dominante, despótico
'o·ver·board *adv* por la borda; ***man overboard!*** ¡hombre al agua!; ***go overboard for s.o./sth*** entusiasmarse muchísimo con alguien / algo
'o·ver·cast *adj day* nublado; *sky* cubierto

o·ver'charge *v/t customer* cobrar de más a
'o·ver·coat abrigo *m*
o·ver'come *v/t* (*pret* ***overcame***, *pp* ***overcome***) *difficulties*, *shyness* superar, vencer; ***be overcome by emotion*** estar embargado por la emoción
o·ver'crowd·ed *adj train* atestado; *city* superpoblado
o·ver'do *v/t* (*pret* ***overdid***, *pp* ***overdone***) (*exaggerate*) exagerar; *in cooking* recocer, cocinar demasiado; ***you're overdoing things*** te estás excediendo
o·ver'done *adj meat* demasiado hecho
'o·ver·dose *n* sobredosis *f inv*
'o·ver·draft descubierto *m*; ***have an overdraft*** tener un descubierto
o·ver'draw *v/t* (*pret* ***overdrew***, *pp* ***overdrawn***) *account* dejar al descubierto; ***be $800 overdrawn*** tener un descubierto de 800 dólares
o·ver'dressed *adj* demasiado trajeado
'o·ver·drive MOT superdirecta *f*
o·ver'due *adj*: ***his apology was long overdue*** se debía haber disculpado hace tiempo; ***an overdue alteration*** un cambio que había que haber efectuado hace tiempo
o·ver'es·ti·mate *v/t abilities*, *value* sobreestimar
o·ver'ex·pose *v/t photograph* sobreexponer
'o·ver·flow[1] *n pipe* desagüe *m*, rebosadero *m*
o·ver'flow[2] *v/i of water* desbordarse
o·ver'grown *adj garden* abandonado, cubierto de vegetación; ***he's an overgrown baby*** es como un niño
o·ver'haul *v/t engine*, *plans* revisar
'o·ver·head 1 *adj lights*, *railway* elevado **2** *n* FIN gastos *mpl* generales
o·ver'hear *v/t* (*pret & pp* ***overheard***) oír por casualidad
o·ver'heat·ed *adj* recalentado
o·ver·joyed [oʊvər'dʒɔɪd] *adj* contentísimo, encantado
'o·ver·kill: ***that's overkill*** eso es exagerar
'o·ver·land 1 *adj route* terrestre **2** *adv travel* por tierra
o·ver'lap *v/i* (*pret & pp* ***overlapped***) *of tiles etc* solaparse; *of periods of time* coincidir; *of theories* tener puntos en común
o·ver'leaf *adv*: ***see overleaf*** véase al dorso
o·ver'load *v/t vehicle*, ELEC sobrecargar
o·ver'look *v/t of tall building etc* dominar; (*not see*) pasar por alto
o·ver·ly ['oʊvərlɪ] *adv* excesivamente, demasiado
'o·ver·night *adv travel* por la noche; ***stay overnight*** quedarse a pasar la noche
o·ver·night 'bag bolso *m* de viaje
o·ver'paid *adj*: ***be overpaid*** cobrar demasiado
'o·ver·pass paso *m* elevado
o·verpop·u·lat·ed [oʊvə'pɑːpjʊleɪtɪd] *adj* superpoblado
o·ver'pow·er *v/t physically* dominar
o·ver·pow·ering [oʊvər'paʊrɪŋ] *adj smell* fortísimo; *sense of guilt* insoportable
o·ver·priced [oʊvər'praɪst] *adj* demasiado caro
o·ver·rat·ed [oʊvə'reɪtɪd] *adj* sobrevalorado
o·ver·re'act *v/i* reaccionar exageradamente
o·ver'ride *v/t* (*pret* ***overrode***, *pp* ***overridden***) anular
o·ver'rid·ing *adj concern* primordial
o·ver'rule *v/t decision* anular
o·ver'run *v/t* (*pret* ***overran***, *pp* ***overrun***) *country* invadir; *time* superar; ***be overrun with*** estar plagado de
o·ver'seas 1 *adv live*, *work* en el extranjero; *go* al extranjero **2** *adj* extranjero
o·ver'see *v/t* (*pret* ***oversaw***, *pp* ***overseen***) supervisar
o·ver'shad·ow *v/t fig* eclipsar
'o·ver·sight descuido *m*
o·ver·sim·pli·fi'ca·tion simplificación *f* excesiva
o·ver'sim·pli·fy *v/t* (*pret & pp* ***oversimplified***) simplificar en exceso
o·ver'sleep *v/i* (*pret & pp* ***overslept***) quedarse dormido
o·ver'state *v/t* exagerar
o·ver'state·ment exageración *f*
o·ver'step *v/t* (*pret & pp* ***overstepped***) *fig* traspasar; ***overstep the mark*** propasarse, pasarse de la raya
o·ver'take *v/t* (*pret* ***overtook***, *pp* ***overtaken***) *in work*, *development* adelantarse a; *Br* MOT adelantar
o·ver'throw[1] *v/t* (*pret* ***overthrew***, *pp* ***overthrown***) derrocar
'o·verthrow[2] *n* derrocamiento *m*
'o·ver·time 1 *n* SP: ***in overtime*** en la prórroga **2** *adv*: ***work in overtime*** hacer horas extras
'o·ver·ture ['oʊvərtʃʊr] MUS obertura *f*; ***make overtures to*** establecer contactos con
o·ver'turn 1 *v/t vehicle* volcar; *object* dar la vuelta a; *government* derribar **2** *v/i of vehicle* volcar
'o·ver·view visión *f* general
o·ver'weight *adj* con sobrepeso; ***be overweight*** estar demasiado gordo

o·ver'whelm [oʊvər'welm] *v/t with work* abrumar, inundar; *with emotion* abrumar; ***be overwhelmed by*** *by response* estar abrumado por
o·verwhelm·ing [oʊvər'welmɪŋ] *adj feeling* abrumador; *majority* aplastante
o·ver'work **1** *n* exceso *m* de trabajo **2** *v/i* trabajar en exceso **3** *v/t* hacer trabajar en exceso
owe [oʊ] *v/t* deber; ***owe s.o. $500*** deber a alguien 500 dólares; ***owe s.o. an apology*** deber disculpas a alguien; ***how much do I owe you?*** ¿cuánto te debo?
ow·ing to ['oʊɪŋ] *prep* debido a
owl [aʊl] búho *m*
own[1] [oʊn] *v/t* poseer; ***who owns the restaurant?*** ¿de quién es el restaurante?, ¿quién es el propietario del restaurante?
own[2] [oʊn] **1** *adj* propio **2** *pron*: ***a car / an apartment of my own*** mi propio coche/ apartamento; ***on my / his own*** yo / él solo
◆ **own up** *v/i* confesar
own·er ['oʊnər] dueño(-a) *m(f)*, propietario(-a) *m(f)*
own·er·ship ['oʊnərʃɪp] propiedad *f*
ox [ɑːks] buey *m*
ox·ide ['ɑːksaɪd] óxido *m*
ox·y·gen ['ɑːksɪdʒən] oxígeno *m*
oy·ster ['ɔɪstər] ostra *f*
oz *abbr* (= ***ounce*(*s*)**) onza(s) *f(pl)*
o·zone ['oʊzoʊn] ozono *m*
'o·zone lay·er capa *f* de ozono

P

PA [piː'eɪ] *abbr* (= ***personal assistant***) secretario(-a) *m(f)* personal
pace [peɪs] **1** *n* (*step*) paso *m*; (*speed*) ritmo *m* **2** *v/i*: ***pace up and down*** pasear de un lado a otro
'pace·mak·er MED marcapasos *m inv*; SP liebre *f*
Pa·cif·ic [pə'sɪfɪk]: ***the Pacific*** (***Ocean***) el (Océano) Pacífico
pac·ifi·er ['pæsɪfaɪər] chupete *m*
pac·i·fism ['pæsɪfɪzm] pacifismo *m*
pac·i·fist ['pæsɪfɪst] *n* pacifista *m/f*
pac·i·fy ['pæsɪfaɪ] *v/t* (*pret & pp* ***pacified***) tranquilizar; *country* pacificar
pack [pæk] **1** *n* (*backpack*) mochila *f*; *of cereal, food, cigarettes* paquete *m*; *of cards* baraja *f* **2** *v/t item of clothing etc* meter en la maleta; *goods* empaquetar; *groceries* meter en una bolsa; ***pack one's bag / suitcase*** hacer la bolsa / la maleta **3** *v/i* hacer la maleta
pack·age ['pækɪdʒ] **1** *n* paquete *m*; ***employment package*** *of offers etc* condiciones *fpl* de empleo **2** *v/t in packs* embalar; *idea, project* presentar
'pack·age deal *for holiday* paquete *m*
'pack·age tour viaje *m* organizado
pack·ag·ing ['pækɪdʒɪŋ] *of product* embalaje *m*; *of idea, project* presentación *f*; ***it's all packaging*** *fig* es sólo imagen
pack·ed [pækt] *adj* (*crowded*) abarrotado
pack·et ['pækɪt] paquete *m*
pact [pækt] pacto *m*
pad[1] [pæd] **1** *n for protection* almohadilla *f*; *for absorbing liquid* compresa *f*; *for writing* bloc *m* **2** *v/t* (*pret & pp* ***padded***) *with material* acolchar; *speech, report* meter paja en
pad[2] *v/i* (*move quietly*) caminar silenciosamente
pad·ded shoulders ['pædɪd] hombreras *fpl*
pad·ding ['pædɪŋ] *material* relleno *m*; *in speech etc* paja *f*
pad·dle ['pædəl] **1** *n for canoe* canalete *m*, remo *m* **2** *v/i in canoe* remar; *in water* chapotear
pad·dling pool ['pædlɪŋ] piscina *f* para niños
pad·dock ['pædək] potrero *m*
pad·lock ['pædlɑːk] **1** *n* candado *m* **2** *v/t gate* cerrar con candado; ***I padlocked my bike to the railings*** até mi bicicleta a la verja con candado
page[1] [peɪdʒ] *n of book etc* página *f*; ***page number*** número *m* de página
page[2] [peɪdʒ] *v/t* (*call*) llamar; *by PA* llamar por megafonía; *by beeper* llamar por el buscapersonas *or Span* busca
pag·er ['peɪdʒər] buscapersonas *m inv*, *Span* busca *m*
paid [peɪd] *pret & pp* → ***pay***
paid em'ploy·ment empleo *m* remunerado

pail [peɪl] cubo *m*
pain [peɪn] dolor *m*; ***be in pain*** sentir dolor; ***take pains to ...*** tomarse muchas molestias por ...; ***a pain in the neck*** F una lata F, un tostón F
pain·ful ['peɪnfəl] *adj* dolorido; *blow, condition, subject* doloroso; (*laborious*) difícil; ***my arm is still very painful*** me sigue doliendo mucho el brazo
pain·ful·ly ['peɪnfəlɪ] *adv* (*extremely, acutely*) extremadamente
pain·kill·er ['peɪnkɪlər] analgésico *m*
pain·less ['peɪnlɪs] *adj* indoloro; ***be completely painless*** doler nada
pains·tak·ing ['peɪnzteɪkɪŋ] *adj* meticuloso
paint [peɪnt] **1** *n* pintura *f* **2** *v/t* pintar
paint·brush ['peɪntbrʌʃ] *large* brocha *f*; *small* pincel *m*
paint·er ['peɪntər] *decorator* pintor(a) *m(f)* (de brocha gorda); *artist* pintor(a) *m(f)*
paint·ing ['peɪntɪŋ] *activity* pintura *f*; *picture* cuadro *m*
paint·work ['peɪntwɜːrk] pintura *f*
pair [per] *of shoes, gloves, objects* par *m*; *of people, animals* pareja *f*
pa·ja·ma 'jack·et camisa *f* de pijama
pa·ja·ma 'pants pantalón *m* de pijama
pa·ja·mas [pə'dʒɑːməz] *npl* pijama *m*
Pa·ki·stan [pɑːkɪ'stɑːn] Paquistán, Pakistán
Pa·ki·sta·ni [pɑːkɪ'stɑːnɪ] **1** *n* paquistaní *m/f*, pakistaní *m/f* **2** *adj* paquistaní, pakistaní
pal [pæl] F (*friend*) amigo(-a) *m(f)*; *Span* colega *m/f* F; ***hey pal, got a light?*** oye amigo *or Span* tío, ¿tienes fuego?
pal·ace ['pælɪs] palacio *m*
pal·ate ['pælət] paladar *m*
pa·la·tial [pə'leɪʃl] *adj* palaciego
pale [peɪl] *adj person* pálido; ***she went pale*** palideció; ***pale pink / blue*** rosa / azul claro
Pal·e·stine ['pæləstaɪn] Palestina
Pal·e·stin·i·an [pælə'stɪnɪən] **1** *n* palestino(-a) *m(f)* **2** *adj* palestino
pal·let ['pælɪt] palé *m*
pal·lor ['pælər] palidez *f*
palm [pɑːm] *of hand* palma *f*; *tree* palmera *f*
pal·pi·ta·tions [pælpɪ'teɪʃnz] *npl* MED palpitaciones *fpl*
pal·try ['pɒːltrɪ] *adj* miserable
pam·per ['pæmpər] *v/t* mimar
pam·phlet ['pæmflɪt] *for information* folleto *m*; *political* panfleto *m*
pan [pæn] **1** *n for cooking* cacerola *f*; *for frying* sartén *f* **2** *v/t* (*pret & pp **panned***) F (*criticize*) poner por los suelos F
◆ **pan out** *v/i* (*develop*) salir
Pan·a·ma ['pænəmɑː] *n* Panamá
Pan·a·ma Ca'nal *n*: ***the Panama Canal*** el Canal de Panamá
Pan·a·ma 'Cit·y *n* Ciudad *f* de Panamá
Pan·a·ma·ni·an [pænə'meɪnɪən] **1** *adj* panameño **2** *n* panameño(-a) *m(f)*
pan·cake ['pænkeɪk] crepe *m*, *L.Am.* panqueque *m*
pan·da ['pændə] (oso *m*) panda *m*
pan·de·mo·ni·um [pændɪ'moʊnɪəm] pandemónium *m*, pandemonio *m*
◆ **pan·der to** ['pændər] *v/t* complacer
pane [peɪn] *of glass* hoja *f*
pan·el ['pænl] panel *m*; *people* grupo *m*, panel *m*
pan·el·ing ['pænəlɪŋ] paneles *mpl*; *of ceiling* artesonado *m*
pang [pæŋ]: ***pangs of hunger*** retortijones *mpl*; ***pangs of remorse*** remordimientos *mpl*
'pan·han·dle *v/i* F mendigar
pan·ic ['pænɪk] **1** *n* pánico *m* **2** *v/i* (*pret & pp **panicked***) ser presa del pánico; ***don't panic*** ¡que no cunda el pánico!
'pan·ic buy·ing FIN compra *f* provocada por el pánico
'pan·ic sel·ling FIN venta *f* provocada por el pánico
'pan·ic-strick·en presa del pánico
pan·o·ra·ma [pænə'rɑːmə] panorama *m*
pa·no·ra·mic [pænə'ræmɪk] *adj view* panorámico
pan·sy ['pænzɪ] *flower* pensamiento *m*
pant [pænt] *v/i* jadear
pan·ties ['pæntɪz] *npl Span* bragas *fpl*, *L.Am.* calzones *mpl*
pantihose → ***pantyhose***
pants [pænts] *npl* pantalones *mpl*
pan·ty·hose ['pæntɪhoʊz] medias *fpl*, pantis *mpl*
pa·pal ['peɪpəl] *adj* papal
pa·per ['peɪpər] **1** *n* papel *m*; (*newspaper*) periódico *m*; *academic* estudio *m*; *at conference* ponencia *f*; (*examination paper*) examen *m*; ***papers*** (*documents*) documentos *mpl*; *of vehicle* (*identity papers*) papeles *mpl*, documentación *f*; ***a piece of paper*** un trozo de papel **2** *adj* de papel **3** *v/t room, walls* empapelar
'paperback libro *m* en rústica
paper 'bag bolsa *f* de papel
'paper boy repartidor *m* de periódicos
'paper clip clip *m*
'paper cup vaso *m* de papel
'paperwork papeleo *m*
par [pɑːr] *in golf* par *m*; ***be on a par with*** ser comparable a; ***feel below par*** sen-

P

tirse en baja forma

par·a·chute ['pærəʃuːt] **1** *n* paracaídas *m inv* **2** *v/i* saltar en paracaídas **3** *v/t troops, supplies* lanzar en paracaídas

par·a·chut·ist ['pærəʃuːtɪst] paracaidista *m/f*

pa·rade [pə'reɪd] **1** *n procession* desfile *m* **2** *v/i* desfilar; (*walk about*) pasearse **3** *v/t knowledge, new car* hacer ostentación de

par·a·dise ['pærədaɪs] paraíso *m*

par·a·dox ['pærədɑːks] paradoja *f*

par·a·dox·i·cal [pærə'dɑːksɪkl] *adj* paradójico

par·a·dox·i·cal·ly [pærə'dɑːksɪklɪ] *adv* paradójicamente

par·a·graph ['pærəgræf] párrafo *m*

Par·a·guay ['pærəgwaɪ] *n* Paraguay

Par·a·guay·an [pærə'gwaɪən] **1** *adj* paraguayo **2** *n* paraguayo(-a) *m*(*f*)

par·al·lel ['pærəlel] **1** *n in geometry* paralela *f*; GEOG paralelo *m*; *fig* paralelismo *m*; ***draw a parallel*** establecer un paralelismo; ***do two things in parallel*** hacer dos cosas al mismo tiempo **2** *adj also fig* paralelo **3** *v/t* (*match*) equipararse a

pa·ral·y·sis [pə'ræləsɪs] parálisis *f*

par·a·lyze ['pærəlaɪz] *v/t also fig* paralizar

par·a·med·ic [pærə'medɪk] *n* auxiliar *m/f* sanitario(a)

pa·ram·e·ter [pə'ræmɪtər] parámetro *m*

par·a·mil·i·tar·y [pærə'mɪlɪterɪ] **1** *adj* paramilitar **2** *n* paramilitar *m/f*

par·a·mount ['pærəmaʊnt] *adj* supremo, extremo; ***be paramount*** ser de importancia capital

par·a·noi·a [pærə'nɔɪə] paranoia *f*

par·a·noid ['pærənɔɪd] *adj* paranoico

par·a·pher·na·li·a [pærəfər'neɪlɪə] parafernalia *f*

par·a·phrase ['pærəfreɪz] *v/t* parafrasear

par·a·pleg·ic [pærə'pliːdʒɪk] *n* parapléjico(-a) *m*(*f*)

par·a·site ['pærəsaɪt] *also fig* parásito *m*

par·a·sol ['pærəsɑːl] sombrilla *f*

par·a·troop·er ['pærətruːpər] paracaidista *m/f* (*militar*)

par·cel ['pɑːrsl] *n* paquete *m*

◆ **parcel up** *v/t* empaquetar

parch [pɑːrʧ] *v/t* secar; ***be parched*** F *of person* estar muerto de sed F

par·don ['pɑːrdn] **1** *n* LAW indulto *m*; ***I beg your pardon?*** (*what did you say?*) ¿cómo ha dicho?; ***I beg your pardon*** (*I'm sorry*) discúlpeme **2** *v/t* perdonar; LAW indultar; ***pardon me?*** ¿perdón?; ***pardon me?*** ¿qué?

pare [per] *v/t* (*peel*) pelar

par·ent ['perənt] *father* padre *m*; *mother* madre *f*; ***my parents*** mis padres

pa·ren·tal [pə'rentl] *adj* de los padres

'**par·ent company** empresa *f* matriz

par·ent-'teacher association asociación *f* de padres y profesores

pa·ren·the·sis [pə'renθəsɪs] (*pl* ***parentheses*** [pə'renθəsiːz]) paréntesis *m inv*

par·ish ['pærɪʃ] parroquia *f*

park[1] [pɑːrk] *n* parque *m*

park[2] *v/t & v/i* MOT estacionar, *Span* aparcar

par·ka ['pɑːrkə] parka *f*

par·king ['pɑːrkɪŋ] MOT estacionamiento *m*, *Span* aparcamiento *m*; ***no parking*** prohibido aparcar

'**par·king disc** disco *m* (de aparcamiento)

'**par·king ga·rage** párking *m*, *Span* aparcamiento *m*

'**par·king lot** estacionamiento *m*, *Span* aparcamiento *m* (*al aire libre*)

'**par·king me·ter** parquímetro *m*

'**par·king place** (plaza *f* de) estacionamiento *or Span* aparcamiento, sitio *m* para estacionar *or Span* aparcar

'**par·king tick·et** multa *f* de estacionamiento

par·lia·ment ['pɑːrləmənt] parlamento *m*

par·lia·men·ta·ry [pɑːrlə'mentərɪ] *adj* parlamentario

pa·role [pə'roʊl] **1** *n* libertad *f* condicional; ***be on parole*** estar en libertad condicional **2** *v/t* poner en libertad condicional; ***be paroled*** salir en libertad condicional

par·rot ['pærət] loro *m*

pars·ley ['pɑːrslɪ] perejil *m*

part [pɑːrt] **1** *n* (*portion, area*) parte *f*; (*episode*) parte *f*, episodio *m*; *of machine* pieza *f* (de repuesto); *in play, film* papel *m*; *in hair* raya *f*; ***take part in*** tomar parte en **2** *adv* (*partly*) en parte; ***part American part Spanish*** medio americano medio español; ***part fact, part fiction*** con una parte de realidad y una parte de ficción **3** *v/i* separarse **4** *v/t*: ***part one's hair*** hacerse la raya

◆ **part with** *v/t* desprenderse de

'**part ex·change**: ***take sth in part exchange*** llevarse algo como parte del pago

par·tial ['pɑːrʃl] *adj* (*incomplete*) parcial; ***be partial to*** tener debilidad por

par·tial·ly ['pɑːrʃəlɪ] *adv* parcialmente

par·ti·ci·pant [pɑːr'tɪsɪpənt] participante *m/f*

par·ti·ci·pate [pɑːr'tɪsɪpeɪt] *v/i* participar

par·ti·ci·pa·tion [pɑːrtɪsɪ'peɪʃn] participación *f*

par·ti·cle ['pɑːrtɪkl] PHYS partícula *f*; (*small amount*) pizca *f*

par·tic·u·lar [pər'tɪkjələr] *adj* (*specific*) particular, concreto; (*demanding*) exigente; *about friends, employees* selectivo; *pej* especial, quisiquilloso; ***you know how particular she is*** ya sabes lo especial que es; ***this particular morning*** precisamente esta mañana; ***in particular*** en particular; ***it's a particular favorite of mine*** es uno de mis preferidos

par·tic·u·lar·ly [pər'tɪkjələrlɪ] *adv* particularmente, especialmente

par·ti·tion [pɑːr'tɪʃn] **1** *n* (*screen*) tabique *m*; *of country* partición *f*, división *f* **2** *v/t country* dividir

◆ **partition off** *v/t* dividir con tabiques

part·ly ['pɑːrtlɪ] *adv* en parte

part·ner ['pɑːrtnər] COM socio(-a) *m*(*f*); *in relationship* compañero(-a) *m*(*f*); *in tennis, dancing* pareja *f*

part·ner·ship ['pɑːrtnərʃɪp] COM sociedad *f*; *in particular activity* colaboración *f*

part of 'speech parte *f* de la oración

'part own·er copropietario(-a) *m*(*f*)

'part-time **1** *adj* a tiempo parcial **2** *adv work* a tiempo parcial

part-'tim·er: ***be a part-timer*** trabajar a tiempo parcial

par·ty ['pɑːrtɪ] **1** *n* (*celebration*) fiesta *f*; POL partido *m*; (*group of people*) grupo *m*; ***be a party to*** tomar parte en **2** *v/i* (*pret & pp* ***partied***) F salir de marcha F

pass [pæs] **1** *n for entry*, SP pase *m*; *in mountains* desfiladero *m*; ***make a pass at*** tirarle los tejos a **2** *v/t* (*hand*) pasar; (*go past*) pasar por delante de; (*overtake*) adelantar; (*go beyond*) sobrepasar; (*approve*) aprobar; ***pass an exam*** aprobar un examen; ***pass sentence*** LAW dictar sentencia; ***pass the time*** pasar el tiempo **3** *v/i of time* pasar; *in exam* aprobar; (*go away*) pasarse

◆ **pass around** *v/t* repartir

◆ **pass away** *v/i euph* fallcccr, pasar a mejor vida

◆ **pass by** **1** *v/t* (*go past*) pasar por **2** *v/i* (*go past*) pasarse

pass on **1** *v/t information, book* pasar; ***pass on the savings to ...*** *of supermarket etc* revertir el ahorro en ... **2** *v/i* (*euph: die*) fallecer, pasar a mejor vida

◆ **pass out** *v/i* (*faint*) desmayarse

◆ **pass through** *v/t town* pasar por

◆ **pass up** *v/t opportunity* dejar pasar

pass·a·ble ['pæsəbl] *adj road* transitable; (*acceptable*) aceptable

pas·sage ['pæsɪdʒ] (*corridor*) pasillo *m*; *from poem, book* pasaje *m*; *of time* paso *m*

pas·sage·way ['pæsɪdʒweɪ] pasillo *m*

pas·sen·ger ['pæsɪndʒər] pasajero(-a) *m*(*f*)

'pas·sen·ger seat asiento *m* de pasajero

pas·ser-by [pæsər'baɪ] (*pl* ***passers-by***) transeúnte *m*/*f*

pas·sion ['pæʃn] pasión *f*; ***a crime of passion*** un crimen pasional

pas·sion·ate ['pæʃnət] *adj lover* apasionado; (*fervent*) fervoroso

pas·sive ['pæsɪv] **1** *adj* pasivo **2** *n* GRAM (voz *f*) pasiva *f*; ***in the passive*** en pasiva

'pass mark EDU nota *f* mínima para aprobar

Pass·o·ver ['pæsouvər] REL Pascua *f* de los hebreos

pass·port ['pæspɔːrt] pasaporte *m*

'pass·port control control *m* de pasaportes

pass·word ['pæswɜːrd] contraseña *f*

past [pæst] **1** *adj* (*former*) pasado; ***his past life*** su pasado; ***the past few days*** los últimos días; ***that's all past now*** todo eso es agua pasada **2** *n* pasado; ***in the past*** antiguamente **3** *prep in position* después de; ***it's half past two*** son las dos y media; ***it's past seven o'clock*** pasan de las siete; ***it's past your bedtime*** hace rato que tenías que haberte ido a la cama **4** *adv*: ***run / walk past*** pasar

pas·ta ['pæstə] pasta *f*

paste [peɪst] **1** *n* (*adhesive*) cola *f* **2** *v/t* (*stick*) pegar

pas·tel ['pæstl] **1** *n color* pastel *m* **2** *adj* pastel

pas·time ['pæstaɪm] pasatiempo *m*

past par'ti·ci·ple GRAM participio *m* pasado

pas·tra·mi [pæ'strɑːmɪ] pastrami *m*, *carne de vaca ahumada con especias*

pas·try ['peɪstrɪ] *for pie* masa *f*; *small cake* pastel *m*

'past tense GRAM (tiempo *m*) pasado *m*

pas·ty ['peɪstɪ] *adj complexion* pálido

pat [pæt] **1** *n* palmadita *f*; ***give s.o. a pat on the back*** *fig* dar una palmadita a alguien en la espalda **2** *v/t* (*pret & pp* ***patted***) dar palmaditas a

patch [pætʃ] **1** *n on clothing* parche *m*; (*area*) mancha *f*; ***a bad patch*** (*period of time*) un mal momento, una mala racha; ***patches of fog*** zonas de niebla; ***not be a patch on*** *fig* no tener ni punto de comparación con **2** *v/t clothing* remendar

◆ **patch up** *v/t* (*repair temporarily*) hacer un remiendo a, arreglar a medias; *quarrel* solucionar

patch·work ['pætʃwɜːrk] **1** *n needlework* labor *f* de retazo **2** *adj hecho de remiendos*

P

patch·y ['pætʃɪ] *quality* desigual; *work, performance* irregular
pâ·té [pɑː'teɪ] paté *m*
pa·tent ['peɪtnt] **1** *adj* patente, evidente **2** *n for invention* patente *f* **3** *v/t invention* patentar
pa·tent 'leath·er charol *m*
pa·tent·ly ['peɪtntlɪ] (*clearly*) evidentemente, claramente
pa·ter·nal [pə'tɜːrnl] *relative* paterno; *pride, love* paternal
pa·ter·nal·ism [pə'tɜːrnlɪzm] paternalismo *m*
pa·ter·nal·is·tic [pətɜːrnl'ɪstɪk] *adj* paternalista
pa·ter·ni·ty [pə'tɜːrnɪtɪ] paternidad *f*
path [pæθ] *also fig* camino *m*
pa·thet·ic [pə'θetɪk] *adj invoking pity* patético; F (*very bad*) lamentable F
path·o·log·i·cal [pæθə'lɑːdʒɪkl] *adj* patológico
pa·thol·o·gy [pə'θɑːlədʒɪ] patología *f*
pa·thol·o·gist [pə'θɑːlədʒɪst] patólogo(-a) *m(f)*
pa·tience ['peɪʃns] paciencia *f*
pa·tient ['peɪʃnt] **1** *n* paciente *m/f* **2** *adj* paciente; ***just be patient!*** ¡ten paciencia!
pa·tient·ly ['peɪʃntlɪ] *adv* pacientemente
pat·i·o ['pætɪoʊ] patio *m*
pat·ri·ot ['peɪtrɪət] patriota *m/f*
pat·ri·ot·ic [peɪtrɪ'ɑːtɪk] *adj* patriótico
pa·tri·ot·ism ['peɪtrɪətɪzm] patriotismo *m*
pa·trol [pə'troʊl] **1** *n* patrulla *f*; ***be on patrol*** estar de patrulla **2** *v/t* (*pret & pp* ***patrolled***) *streets, border* patrullar
pa'trol car coche *m* patrulla
pa'trol·man policía *m*, patrullero *m*
pa'trol wag·on furgón *m* policial
pa·tron ['peɪtrən] *of store, movie theater* cliente *m/f*; *of artist, charity etc* patrocinador(a) *m(f)*
pa·tron·ize ['pætrənaɪz] *v/t store* ser cliente de; *person* tratar con condescendencia *or* como a un niño
pa·tron·iz·ing ['pætrənaɪzɪŋ] condescendiente
pa·tron 'saint santo(-a) *m(f)* patrón(-ona), patrón(-ona) *m(f)*
pat·ter ['pætər] **1** *n of rain etc* repiqueteo *m*; F (*of salesman*) parloteo *m* F **2** *v/i* repiquetear
pat·tern ['pætərn] *n on wallpaper, fabric* estampado *m*; *for knitting, sewing* diseño *m*; (*model*) modelo *m*; *in behavior, events* pauta *f*
pat·terned ['pætərnd] *adj* estampado
paunch [pɒːntʃ] barriga *f*
pause [pɒːz] **1** *n* pausa *f* **2** *v/i* parar; *when speaking* hacer una pausa **3** *v/t tape* poner en pausa
pave [peɪv] *with concrete* pavimentar; *with slabs* adoquinar; ***pave the way for*** *fig* preparar el terreno para
pave·ment ['peɪvmənt] (*Am*: *roadway*) calzada *f*; (*Br*: *sidewalk*) acera *f*
pav·ing stone ['peɪvɪŋ] losa *f*
paw [pɒː] **1** *n of animal* pata *f*; F (*hand*) pezuña *f* F **2** *v/t* F sobar F
pawn[1] [pɒːn] *n in chess* peón *m*; *fig* títere *m*
pawn[2] [pɒːn] *v/t* empeñar
'pawn·bro·ker prestamista *m/f*
'pawn·shop casa *f* de empeños
pay [peɪ] **1** *n* paga *f*, sueldo *m*; ***in the pay of*** a sueldo de **2** *v/t* (*pret & pp* ***paid***) *employee, sum, bill* pagar; ***pay attention*** prestar atención; ***pay s.o. a compliment*** hacer un cumplido a alguien **3** *v/i* (*pret & pp* ***paid***) pagar; (*be profitable*) ser rentable; ***it doesn't pay to …*** no conviene …; ***pay for*** *purchase* pagar; ***you'll pay for this!*** *fig* ¡me las pagarás!
◆ **pay back** *v/t person* devolver el dinero a *loan* devolver
◆ **pay in** *v/t to bank* ingresar
◆ **pay off 1** *v/t debt* liquidar; (*bribe*) sobornar **2** *v/i* (*be profitable*) valer la pena
◆ **pay up** *v/i* pagar
pay·a·ble ['peɪəbl] *adj* pagadero
'pay check cheque *m* del sueldo
'pay·day día *m* de paga
pay·ee [peɪ'iː] beneficiario(-a) *m(f)*
'pay en·ve·lope sobre *m* con la paga
pay·er ['peɪər] pagador(a) *m(f)* ***they are good payers*** pagan puntualmente
pay·ment ['peɪmənt] pago *m*
'pay phone teléfono *m* público
pay·roll ['peɪroʊl] *money* salarios *mpl*; *employees* nómina *f*; ***be on the payroll*** estar en nómina
pay·slip ['peɪslɪp] nómina *f* (*papel*)
PC [piː'siː] *abbr* (= ***personal computer***) PC *m*, *Span* ordenador *m or L.Am.* computadora personal; (= ***politically correct***) políticamente correcto
pea [piː] *Span* guisante *m*, *L.Am.* arveja *f*, *Mex* chícharo *m*
peace [piːs] paz *f*; (*quietness*) tranquilidad
peace·a·ble ['piːsəbl] *adj person* pacífico
'Peace Corps *organización gubernamental estadounidense de ayuda al desarrollo*
peace·ful ['piːsfəl] *adj* tranquilo; *demonstration* pacífico
peace·ful·ly ['piːsfəlɪ] *adv* pacíficamente
peach [piːtʃ] *fruit* melocotón *m*, *L.Am.* durazno *m*; *tree* melocotonero *m*, *L.Am.* duraznero *m*

P

pea·cock ['piːkɑːk] pavo *m* real
peak [piːk] **1** *n of mountain* cima *f*; *mountain* pico *m*; *fig* clímax *m* **2** *v/i* alcanzar el máximo
'**peak hours** *npl* horas *fpl* punta
pea·nut ['piːnʌt] cacahuete *m*, *L.Am.* maní *m*, *Mex* cacahuate *m*; ***get paid peanuts*** F cobrar una miseria F; ***that's peanuts to him*** F eso es calderilla para él F
pea·nut 'but·ter crema *f* de cacahuete
pear [per] pera *f*
pearl [pɜːrl] perla *f*
peas·ant ['peznt] campesino(-a) *m*(*f*)
peb·ble ['pebl] guijarro *m*
pe·can ['piːkən] pacana *f*
peck [pek] **1** *n bite* picotazo *m*; *kiss* besito *m* **2** *v/t bite* picotear; *kiss* dar un besito a
pe·cu·li·ar [pɪ'kjuːljər] *adj* (*strange*) raro; ***peculiar to*** (*special*) característico de
pe·cu·li·ar·i·ty [pɪkjuːlɪ'ærətɪ] (*strangeness*) rareza *f*; (*special feature*) peculiaridad *f*, característica *f*
ped·al ['pedl] **1** *n of bike* pedal *m* **2** *v/i* (*turn pedals*) pedalear; (*cycle*) recorrer en bicicleta
pe·dan·tic [pɪ'dæntɪk] *adj* puntilloso
ped·dle ['pedl] *v/t drugs* traficar *or* trapichear con
ped·es·tal ['pedəstl] *for statue* pedestal *m*
pe·des·tri·an [pɪ'destrɪən] *n* peatón(-ona) *m*(*f*)
pe·des·tri·an 'cros·sing paso *m* de peatones
pe·di·at·ric [piːdɪ'ætrɪk] *adj* pediátrico
pe·di·a·tri·cian [piːdɪə'trɪʃn] pediatra *m*/*f*
pe·di·at·rics [piːdɪ'ætrɪks] pediatría *f*
ped·i·cure ['pedɪkjʊr] pedicura *f*
ped·i·gree ['pedɪgriː] **1** *n of animal* pedigrí; *of person* linaje *m* **2** *adj* con pedigrí
pee [piː] *v/i* F hacer pis F, mear F
peek [piːk] **1** *n* ojeada *f*, vistazo *m* **2** *v/i* echar una ojeada *or* vistazo
peel [piːl] **1** *n* piel *f* **2** *v/t fruit, vegetables* pelar **3** *v/i of nose, shoulders* pelarse; *of paint* levantarse
◆ **peel off 1** *v/t wrapper etc* quitar; *jacket etc* quitarse **2** *v/i of wrapper* quitarse
peep [piːp] → ***peek***
peep·hole ['piːphoʊl] mirilla *f*
peer[1] [pɪr] *n* (*equal*) igual *m*
peer[2] [pɪr] *v/i* mirar; ***peer through the mist*** buscar con la mirada entre la niebla; ***peer at*** forzar la mirada para ver
peeved [piːvd] F mosqueado F
peg [peg] *n for hat, coat* percha *f*; *for tent* clavija *f*; ***off the peg*** de confección
pe·jo·ra·tive [pɪ'dʒɑːrətɪv] *adj* peyorativo
pel·let ['pelɪt] pelotita *f*; (*bullet*) perdigón *m*
pelt [pelt] **1** *v/t*: ***pelt s.o. with sth*** tirar algo a alguien **2** *v/i*: ***they pelted along the road*** F fueron a toda mecha por la carretera F; ***it's pelting down*** F está diluviando F
pel·vis ['pelvɪs] pelvis *f*
pen[1] [pen] *n* (*ballpoint pen*) bolígrafo *m*; (*fountain pen*) pluma *f* (estilográfica)
pen[2] [pen] (*enclosure*) corral *m*
pen[3] [pen] → ***penitentiary***
pe·nal·ize ['piːnəlaɪz] *v/t* penalizar
pen·al·ty ['penəltɪ] sanción *f*; SP penalti *m*; ***take the penalty*** *in soccer* lanzar el penalti
'**pen·al·ty ar·e·a** SP área *f* de castigo
'**pen·al·ty clause** LAW cláusula *f* de penalización
'**pen·al·ty kick** (lanzamiento *m* de) penalti *m*
pen·al·ty 'shoot-out tanda *f* de penalties
'**pen·al·ty spot** punto *m* de penalti
pen·cil ['pensɪl] lápiz *m*
pen·cil sharp·en·er sacapuntas *m inv*
pen·dant ['pendənt] (*necklace*) colgante *m*
pend·ing ['pendɪŋ] **1** *prep* en espera de **2** *adj* pendiente; ***be pending*** *awaiting a decision* estar pendiente; *about to happen* ser inminente
pen·e·trate ['penɪtreɪt] *v/t* (*pierce*) penetrar; *market* penetrar en
pen·e·trat·ing ['penɪtreɪtɪŋ] *adj stare, scream* penetrante; *analysis* exhaustivo
pen·e·tra·tion [penɪ'treɪʃn] penetración *f*; *of defences* incursión *f*; *of market* entrada *f*
'**pen friend** amigo(-a) *m*(*f*) por correspondencia
pen·guin ['peŋgwɪn] pingüino *m*
pen·i·cil·lin [penɪ'sɪlɪn] penicilina *f*
pe·nin·su·la [pə'nɪnsʊlə] península *f*
pe·nis ['piːnɪs] pene *m*
pen·i·tence ['penɪtəns] (*remorse*) arrepentimiento *m*
pen·i·tent ['penɪtənt] *adj* arrepentido
pen·i·tent·ia·ry [penɪ'tenʃərɪ] prisión *f*, cárcel *f*
pen·knife ['pennaɪf] navaja *f*
'**pen name** seudónimo *m*
pen·nant ['penənt] banderín *f*
pen·ni·less ['penɪlɪs] *adj* sin un centavo
pen·ny ['penɪ] penique *m*
'**pen pal** amigo(-a) *m*(*f*) por correspondencia
pen·sion ['penʃn] pensión *f*
◆ **pension off** *v/t* jubilar
'**pen·sion fund** fondo *m* de pensiones
'**pen·sion scheme** plan *m* de jubilación
pen·sive ['pensɪv] *adj* pensativo

Pen·ta·gon ['pentəgɑːn]: ***the Pentagon*** el Pentágono
pen·tath·lon [pen'tæθlən] pentatlón *m*
Pen·te·cost ['pentɪkɑːst] Pentecostés *m*
pent·house ['penthaʊs] ático *m* (*de lujo*)
pent-up ['pentʌp] *adj* reprimido
pe·nul·ti·mate [pe'nʌltɪmət] *adj* penúltimo
peo·ple ['piːpl] *npl* gente *f*; (*individuals*) personas *fpl*; (*nsg*: *race*, *tribe*) pueblo *m*; ***the people*** (*citizens*) el pueblo, los ciudadanos; ***the Spanish people*** los españoles; ***a lot of people think …*** muchos piensan que …; ***people say …*** se dice que …, dicen que …
pep·per ['pepər] *spice* pimienta *f*; *vegetable* pimiento *m*
pep·per·mint *sweet* caramelo *m* de menta
pep talk ['peptɒːk]: ***give a pep talk*** decir unas palabras de aliento
per [pɜːr] *prep* por; ***per annum*** al año, por año
per·ceive [pər'siːv] *v/t with senses* percibir; (*view*, *interpret*) interpretar
per·cent [pər'sent] *adv* por ciento
per·cen·tage [pər'sentɪdʒ] porcentaje *m*, tanto *m* por ciento
per·cep·ti·ble [pər'septəbl] *adj* perceptible
per·cep·ti·bly [pər'septəblɪ] *adv* visiblemente
per·cep·tion [pər'sepʃn] *through senses* percepción *f*; *of situation* apreciación *f*; (*insight*) perspicacia *f*
per·cep·tive [pər'septɪv] *adj* perceptivo
perch [pɜːrtʃ] **1** *n for bird* percha *f* **2** *v/i of bird* posarse; *of person* sentarse
per·co·late ['pɜːrkəleɪt] *v/i of coffee* filtrarse
per·co·la·tor ['pɜːrkəleɪtər] cafetera *f* de filtro
per·cus·sion [pər'kʌʃn] percusión *f*
per'cus·sion in·stru·ment instrumento *m* de percusión
pe·ren·ni·al [pə'renɪəl] *n* BOT árbol *m* de hoja perenne
per·fect **1** *n* ['pɜːrfɪkt] GRAM pretérito *m* perfecto **2** *adj* perfecto **3** *v/t* [pər'fekt] perfeccionar
per·fec·tion [pər'fekʃn] perfección *f*; ***do sth to perfection*** hacer algo a la perfección
per·fec·tion·ist [pər'fekʃnɪst] perfeccionista *m/f*
per·fect·ly ['pɜːrfɪktlɪ] perfectamente; (*totally*) completamente
per·fo·rat·ed ['pɜːrfəreɪtɪd] *adj line* perforado
per·fo·ra·tions [pɜːrfə'reɪʃnz] *npl* perforaciones *fpl*
per·form [pə'fɔːrm] **1** *v/t* (*carry out*) realizar, llevar a cabo; *of actors*, *musician etc* interpretar, representar **2** *v/i of actor*, *musician*, *dancer* actuar; *of machine* funcionar
per·form·ance [pə'fɔːrməns] *by actor*, *musician etc* actuación *f*, interpretación *f*; *of play* representación *f*; *of employee* rendimiento *m*; *of official*, *company*, *in sport* actuación *f*; *of machine* rendimiento *m*
per'form·ance car coche *m* de gran rendimiento
per·form·er [pə'fɔːrmər] intérprete *m/f*
per·fume ['pɜːrfjuːm] perfume *m*
per·func·to·ry [pər'fʌŋktərɪ] *adj* superficial
per·haps [pər'hæps] *adv* quizá(s), tal vez; ***perhaps it's not too late*** puede que no sea demasiado tarde
per·il ['perəl] peligro *m*
per·il·ous ['perələs] *adj* peligroso
pe·rim·e·ter [pə'rɪmɪtər] perímetro *m*
pe'rim·e·ter fence cerca *f*
pe·ri·od ['pɪrɪəd] periodo *m*, período *m*; (*menstruation*) periodo, regla *f*; *punctuation mark* punto *m*; ***I don't want to, period!*** F ¡no me da la gana y punto! F
pe·ri·od·ic [pɪrɪ'ɑːdɪk] *adj* periódico
pe·ri·od·i·cal [pɪrɪ'ɑːdɪkl] *n* publicación *f* periódica
pe·ri·od·i·cal·ly [pɪrɪ'ɑːdɪklɪ] *adv* periódicamente, con periodicidad
pe·riph·e·ral [pə'rɪfərəl] **1** *adj* (*not crucial*) secundario **2** *n* COMPUT periférico *m*
pe·riph·e·ry [pə'rɪfərɪ] periferia *f*
per·ish ['perɪʃ] *v/i of rubber* estropearse, picarse; *of person* perecer
per·ish·a·ble ['perɪʃəbl] *adj food* perecedero
per·jure ['pɜːrdʒər] *v/t*: ***perjure o.s.*** perjurar
per·ju·ry ['pɜːrdʒərɪ] perjurio *m*
perk [pɜːrk] *n of job* ventaja *f*
◆**perk up** **1** *v/t* animar **2** *v/i* animarse
perk·y ['pɜːrkɪ] (*cheerful*) animado
perm [pɜːrm] **1** *n* permanente *f* **2** *v/t* hacer la permanente; ***she had her hair permed*** se hizo la permanente
per·ma·nent ['pɜːrmənənt] *adj* permanente
per·ma·nent·ly ['pɜːrmənəntlɪ] *adv* permanentemente
per·me·a·ble ['pɜːrmɪəbl] *adj* permeable
per·me·ate ['pɜːrmɪeɪt] *v/t* impregnar
per·mis·si·ble [pər'mɪsəbl] *adj* permisible
per·mis·sion [pər'mɪʃn] permiso *m*; ***ask***

s.o.'s permission to ... pedir permiso a alguien para ...

per·mis·sive [pər'mɪsɪv] *adj* permisivo

per·mit ['pɜːrmɪt] **1** *n* licencia *f* **2** *v/t* (*pret & pp* ***permitted***) [pər'mɪt] permitir; ***permit s.o. to do sth*** permitir a alguien que haga algo

per·pen·dic·u·lar [pɜːrpən'dɪkjʊlər] *adj* perpendicular

per·pet·u·al *adj* perpetuo; *interruptions* continuo

per·pet·u·al·ly [pər'petʃʊəlɪ] *adv* constantemente

per·pet·u·ate [pər'petʃʊeɪt] *v/t* perpetuar

per·plex [pər'pleks] *v/t* dejar perplejo

per·plexed [pər'plekst] *adj* perplejo

per·plex·i·ty [pər'pleksɪtɪ] perplejidad *f*

per·se·cute ['pɜːrsɪkjuːt] *v/t* perseguir; (*hound*) acosar

per·se·cu·tion [pɜːrsɪ'kjuːʃn] persecución *f*; (*harassment*) acoso *m*

per·se·cu·tor [pɜːrsɪ'kjuːtər] perseguidor(a) *m*(*f*)

per·se·ver·ance [pɜːrsɪ'vɪrəns] perseverancia *f*

per·se·vere [pɜːrsɪ'vɪr] *v/i* perseverar

per·sist [pər'sɪst] *v/i* persistir; ***persist in*** persistir en

per·sis·tence [pər'sɪstəns] (*perseverance*) perseverancia *f*; (*continuation*) persistencia *f*

per·sis·tent [pər'sɪstənt] *adj person, questions* perseverante; *rain, unemployment etc* persistente

per·sis·tent·ly [pər'sɪstəntlɪ] *adv* (*continually*) constantemente

per·son ['pɜːrsn] persona *f*; ***in person*** en persona

per·son·al ['pɜːrsənl] *adj* (*private*) personal; *life* privado; ***don't make personal remarks*** no hagas comentarios personales

per·son·al as'sist·ant secretario(-a) *m*(*f*) personal

'per·son·al col·umn sección *f* de anuncios personales

per·son·al com'put·er *Span* ordenador *m* personal, *L.Am.* computadora *f* personal

per·son·al 'hy·giene higiene *f* personal

per·son·al·i·ty [pɜːrsə'nælətɪ] personalidad *f*; (*celebrity*) personalidad *f*, personaje *m*

per·son·al·ly ['pɜːrsənəlɪ] *adv* (*for my part*) personalmente; (*in person*) en persona; ***don't take it personally*** no te lo tomes como algo personal

per·son·al 'or·gan·iz·er organizador *m* personal

per·son·al 'pro·noun pronombre *m* personal

per·son·al 'ster·e·o walkman *m* ®

per·son·i·fy [pɜːr'sɑːnɪfaɪ] *v/t* (*pret & pp* ***personified***) *of person* personificar

per·son·nel [pɜːrsə'nel] *employees, department* personal *m*

per·son'nel man·a·ger director(a) *m*(*f*) de personal

per·spec·tive [pər'spektɪv] PAINT perspectiva *f*; ***get sth into perspective*** poner algo en perspectiva

per·spi·ra·tion [pɜːrspɪ'reɪʃn] sudor *m*, transpiración *f*

per·spire [pɜːr'spaɪr] *v/i* sudar, transpirar

per·suade [pər'sweɪd] *v/t person* persuadir; ***persuade s.o. to do sth*** persuadir a alguien para que haga algo

per·sua·sion [pər'sweɪʒn] persuasión *f*

per·sua·sive [pər'sweɪsɪv] persuasivo

per·ti·nent ['pɜːrtɪnənt] *adj fml* pertinente

per·turb [pər'tɜːrb] *v/t* perturbar

per·turb·ing [pər'tɜːrbɪŋ] *adj* perturbador

Pe·ru [pə'ruː] *n* Perú

pe·ruse [pə'ruːz] *v/t fml* leer atentamente

Pe·ru·vi·an [pə'ruːvɪən] **1** *adj* peruano **2** *n* peruano(-a) *m*(*f*)

per·va·sive [pər'veɪsɪv] *adj influence, ideas* dominante

per·verse [pər'vɜːrs] *adj* (*awkward*) terco; ***just to be perverse*** sólo para llevar la contraria

per·ver·sion [pər'vɜːrʃn] *sexual* perversión *f*

per·vert ['pɜːrvɜːrt] *n sexual* pervertido(-a) *m*(*f*)

pes·si·mism ['pesɪmɪzm] pesimismo *m*

pes·si·mist ['pesɪmɪst] pesimista *m/f*

pes·si·mist·ic [pesɪ'mɪstɪk] *adj* pesimista

pest [pest] plaga *f*; F *person* tostón *m* F

pes·ter ['pestər] *v/t* acosar; ***pester s.o. to do sth*** molestar *or* dar la lata a alguien para que haga algo

pes·ti·cide ['pestɪsaɪd] pesticida *f*

pet [pet] **1** *n animal* animal *m* doméstico *or* de compañía; (*favorite*) preferido(-a) *m*(*f*) **2** *adj* preferido, favorito **3** *v/t* (*pret & pp* ***petted***) *animal* acariciar **4** *v/i* (*pret & pp* ***petted***) *of couple* magrearse F

pet·al ['petl] pétalo *m*

◆**pe·ter out** ['piːtər] *v/i of rain* amainar; *of rebellion* irse extinguiendo; *of path* ir desapareciendo

pe·tite [pə'tiːt] *adj* chiquito(-a); *size* menudo

pe·ti·tion [pə'tɪʃn] *n* petición *f*

'pet name nombre *m* cariñoso

pet·ri·fied ['petrɪfaɪd] *adj person* petrifi-

P

cado; *scream*, *voice* aterrorizado

pet·ri·fy ['petrɪfaɪ] *v/t* (*pret & pp* ***petrified***) dejar petrificado

pet·ro·chem·i·cal [petroʊ'kemɪkl] *adj* petroquímico

pet·rol ['petrl] *Br* gasolina *f*, *Arg* nafta *f*

pe·tro·le·um [pɪ'troʊlɪəm] petróleo *m*

pet·ting ['petɪŋ] magreo *m* F

pet·ty ['petɪ] *adj person*, *behavior* mezquino; *details*, *problem* sin importancia

pet·ty 'cash dinero *m* para gastos menores

pet·u·lant ['petʃələnt] *adj* caprichoso

pew [pjuː] banco *m* (*de iglesia*)

pew·ter ['pjuːtər] peltre *m*

phar·ma·ceu·ti·cal [fɑːrmə'suːtɪkl] *adj* farmaceútico

phar·ma·ceu·ti·cals [fɑːmə'suːtɪklz] *npl* fármacos *mpl*

phar·ma·cist ['fɑːrməsɪst] *in store* farmaceútico(-a) *m(f)*

phar·ma·cy ['fɑːrməsɪ] *store* farmacia *f*

phase [feɪz] fase *f*; ***go through a difficult phase*** atravesar una mala etapa

◆ **phase in** *v/t* introducir gradualmente

◆ **phase out** *v/t* eliminar gradualmente

PhD [piːeɪtʃ'diː] *abbr* (= ***Doctor of Philosophy***) Doctorado *m*

phe·nom·e·nal [fɪ'nɑːmɪnl] *adj* fenomenal

phe·nom·e·nal·ly [fɪ'nɑːmɪnlɪ] *adv* extraordinariamente; *stupid* increíblemente

phe·nom·e·non [fɪ'nɑːmɪnɑːn] fenómeno *m*

phil·an·throp·ic [fɪlən'θrɑːpɪk] *adj* filantrópico

phi·lan·thro·pist [fɪ'lænθrəpɪst] filántropo(-a) *m(f)*

phi·lan·thro·py [fɪ'lænθrəpɪ] filantropía *f*

Phil·ip·pines ['fɪlɪpiːnz] *npl*: ***the Philippines*** las Filipinas

phil·is·tine ['fɪlɪstaɪn] *n* filisteo(-a) *m(f)*

phi·los·o·pher [fɪ'lɑːsəfər] filósofo(-a) *m(f)*

phil·o·soph·i·cal [fɪlə'sɑːfɪkl] *adj* filosófico

phi·los·o·phy [fɪ'lɑːsəfɪ] filosofía *f*

pho·bi·a ['foʊbɪə] fobia *f*

phone [foʊn] **1** *n* teléfono *m*; ***be on the phone*** *have a phone* tener teléfono; *be talking* estar hablando por teléfono **2** *v/t* llamar (por teléfono) a **3** *v/i* llamar (por teléfono)

'phone book guía *f* (de teléfonos)

'phone booth cabina *f* (de teléfonos)

'phone call llamada *f* (telefónica)

'phone card *Br* tarjeta *f* telefónica

'phone num·ber número *m* de teléfono

pho·net·ics [fə'netɪks] fonética *f*

pho·n(e)y ['foʊnɪ] *adj* F falso

pho·to ['foʊtoʊ] *n* foto *f*

'pho·to al·bum álbum *m* de fotos

'pho·to·cop·i·er fotocopiadora *f*

'pho·to·cop·y 1 *n* fotocopia *f* **2** *v/t* (*pret & pp* ***photocopied***) fotocopiar

pho·to·gen·ic [foʊtoʊ'dʒenɪk] *adj* fotogénico

pho·to·graph ['foʊtəgræf] **1** *n* fotografía *f* **2** *v/t* fotografiar

pho·tog·ra·pher [fə'tɑːgrəfər] fotógrafo(-a) *m(f)*

pho·tog·ra·phy [fə'tɑːgrəfɪ] fotografía *f*

phrase [freɪz] **1** *n* frase *f* **2** *v/t* expresar

'phrase·book guía *f* de conversación

phys·i·cal ['fɪzɪkl] **1** *adj* físico **2** *n* MED reconocimiento *m* médico

phys·i·cal 'hand·i·cap minusvalía *f* física

phys·i·cal·ly ['fɪzɪklɪ] *adv* físicamente

phys·i·cal·ly 'hand·i·cap·ped disminuído(-a) *m(f)* físico

phy·si·cian [fɪ'zɪʃn] médico(-a) *m(f)*

phys·i·cist ['fɪzɪsɪst] físico(-a) *m(f)*

phys·ics ['fɪzɪks] física *f*

phys·i·o·ther·a·pist [fɪzɪoʊ'θerəpɪst] fisioterapeuta *m/f*

phys·i·o·ther·a·py [fɪzɪoʊ'θerəpɪ] fisioterapia *f*

phy·sique [fɪ'ziːk] físico *m*

pi·a·nist ['pɪənɪst] pianista *m/f*

pi·an·o [pɪ'ænoʊ] piano *m*

pick [pɪk] **1** *n*: ***take your pick*** elige el que prefieras **2** *v/t* (*choose*) escoger, elegir; *flowers*, *fruit* recoger; ***pick one's nose*** meterse el dedo en la nariz **3** *v/i*: ***pick and choose*** ser muy exigente

◆ **pick at** *v/t*: ***pick at one's food*** comer como un pajarito

◆ **pick on** *v/t* (*treat unfairly*) meterse con; (*select*) elegir

◆ **pick out** *v/t* (*identify*) identificar

◆ **pick up 1** *v/t object* recoger, *Span* coger; *habit* adquirir, *Span* coger; *illness* contraer, *Span* coger; *in car*, *from ground*, *from airport etc* recoger; *telephone* descolgar; *language*, *skill* aprender; (*buy*) comprar; *criminal* detener; ***pick s.o. up*** *sexually* ligar con alguien; ***pick up the tab*** F pagar **2** *v/i* (*improve*) mejorar

pick·et ['pɪkɪt] **1** *n of strikers* piquete *m* **2** *v/t* hacer piquete delante de

'pick·et fence valla *f* de estacas

'pick·et line piquete *m*

pick·le ['pɪkl] *v/t* encurtir; *fish* poner en escabeche; *meat* poner en adobo

pick·les ['pɪklz] *npl* (*dill pickles*) encurtidos *mpl*

'pick·pocket carterista *m/f*

pick-up (truck) ['pɪkʌp] camioneta *f*
pick·y ['pɪkɪ] *adj* F tiquismiquis F
pic·nic ['pɪknɪk] **1** *n* picnic *m* **2** *v/i* (*pret & pp* ***picnicked***) ir de picnic
pic·ture ['pɪktʃər] **1** *n* (*photo*) fotografía *f*; (*painting*) cuadro *m*; (*illustration*) dibujo *m*; (*movie*) película *f*; *on* TV imagen *f*; ***keep s.o. in the picture*** mantener a alguien al día **2** *v/t* imaginar
'pic·ture book libro *m* ilustrado
pic·ture 'post·card postal *f*
pic·tur·esque [pɪktʃə'resk] *adj* pintoresco
pie [paɪ] pastel *m*
piece [pi:s] (*fragment*) fragmento *m*; *component, in board game* pieza *f*; ***a piece of pie / bread*** un trozo de pastel / una rebanada de pan; ***a piece of advice*** un consejo; ***go to pieces*** derrumbarse; ***take to pieces*** desmontar
◆ **piece together** *v/t broken plate* recomponer; *facts, evidence* reconstruir
piece·meal ['pi:smi:l] *adv* poco a poco
piece·work ['pi:swɜ:rk] *n* trabajo *m* a destajo
pier [pɪr] *at seaside* malecón *m*
pierce [pɪrs] *v/t* (*penetrate*) perforar; *ears* agujerear
pierc·ing ['pɪrsɪŋ] *adj scream* desgarrador; *gaze* penetrante; *wind* cortante
pig [pɪg] *also fig* cerdo *m*; *greedy* glotón(-a) *m*(*f*)
pi·geon ['pɪdʒɪn] paloma *f*
'pi·geon·hole 1 *n* casillero *m* **2** *v/t person* encasillar; *proposal* archivar
pig·gy·bank ['pɪgɪbæŋk] hucha *f*
pig·head·ed [pɪg'hedɪd] *adj* F cabezota F
'pig·pen *also fig* pocilga *f*
'pig·skin piel *f* de cerdo
'pig·tail coleta *f*
pile [paɪl] montón *m*, pila *f*; ***a pile of work*** F un montón de trabajo F
◆ **pile up 1** *v/i of work, bills* acumularse **2** *v/t* amontonar
piles [paɪlz] *nsg* MED hemorroides *fpl*
pile-up ['paɪlʌp] MOT choque *m* múltiple
pil·fer·ing ['pɪlfərɪŋ] hurtos *mpl*
pil·grim ['pɪlgrɪm] peregrino(-a) *m*(*f*)
pil·grim·age ['pɪlgrɪmɪdʒ] peregrinación *f*
pill [pɪl] pastilla *f*; ***be on the pill*** tomar la píldora
pil·lar ['pɪlər] pilar *m*
pil·lion ['pɪljən] *of motor bike* asiento *m* trasero
pil·low ['pɪloʊ] *n* almohada *f*
'pill·ow·case, 'pil·low·slip funda *f* de almohada
pi·lot ['paɪlət] **1** *n of airplane* piloto *m/f*; *for ship* práctico *m* **2** *v/t airplane* pilotar
'pi·lot scheme plan *m* piloto
pimp [pɪmp] *n* proxeneta *m*, *Span* chulo *m* F
pim·ple ['pɪmpl] grano *m*
pin [pɪn] **1** *n for sewing* alfiler *m*; *in bowling* bolo *m*; (*badge*) pin *m*; ELEC clavija *f*; ***safety pin*** imperdible *m* **2** *v/t* (*pret & pp* ***pinned***) (*hold down*) mantener; (*attach*) sujetar
◆ **pin down** *v/t*: ***pin s.o. down to a date*** forzar a alguien a concretar una fecha
◆ **pin up** *v/t notice* sujetar con chinchetas
PIN [pɪn] PIN *m* ***personal identification number*** número *m* de identificación personal
pin·cers ['pɪnsərz] *npl of crab* pinzas *fpl*; *tool* tenazas *fpl*; ***a pair of pincers*** unas tenazas *fpl*
pinch [pɪntʃ] **1** *n* pellizco *m*; *of salt, sugar etc* pizca *f*; ***at a pinch*** si no queda otro remedio; ***at a pinch*** *with numbers* como máximo **2** *v/t* pellizcar **3** *v/i of shoes* apretar
pine[1] [paɪn] *n tree* pino *m*; *wood* (madera *f* de) pino *m*
pine[2] [paɪn] *v/i*: ***pine for*** echar de menos
pine·ap·ple ['paɪnæpl] piña *f*, *L.Am.* ananá(s) *f*
ping [pɪŋ] **1** *n* sonido *m* metálico **2** *v/i* hacer un sonido metálico
ping-pong ['pɪŋgpɑ:ng] pimpón *m*, ping-pong *m*
pink [pɪŋk] *adj* rosa
pin·na·cle ['pɪnəkl] *fig* cima *f*
'pin·point determinar
pins and 'nee·dles hormigueo *m*
'pin·stripe *adj* a rayas
pint [paɪnt] pinta *f*, *medida equivalente a 0,473 litros en Estados Unidos o a 0,568 litros en Gran Bretaña*
'pin-up modelo *m/f* de revista
pi·o·neer [paɪə'nɪr] **1** *n fig* pionero(-a) *m*(*f*) **2** *v/t* ser pionero en
pi·o·neer·ing [paɪə'nɪrɪŋ] *adj work* pionero
pi·ous ['paɪəs] piadoso
pip [pɪp] *n of fruit* pepita *f*
pipe [paɪp] **1** *n for smoking* pipa *f*; *for water, gas, sewage* tubería *f* **2** *v/t* conducir por tuberías
◆ **pipe down** *v/i* F cerrar el pico F
piped mu·sic [paɪpt'mju:zɪk] hilo *m* musical
pipe·line *for oil* oleoducto *m*; *for gas* gasoducto *m*; ***in the pipeline*** *fig* en trámite
pip·ing hot [paɪpɪŋ'hɑ:t] *adj* muy caliente
pi·rate ['paɪrət] **1** *n* pirata *m/f* **2** *v/t software* piratear
Pis·ces ['paɪsi:z] ASTR Piscis *m/f inv*
piss [pɪs] **1** *v/i* P (*urinate*) mear P; ***take the***

P

piss out of s.o. P cachondearse de alguien P **2** *n* P (*urine*) meada *f* P
◆ **piss off** *v/i* P largarse F; ***piss off!*** P ¡vete al cuerno! P
pissed [pɪst] *adj* P (*annoyed*) cabreado P; *Br* P (*drunk*) borracho, pedo F
pis·tol ['pɪstl] pistola *f*
pis·ton ['pɪstən] pistón *m*
pit [pɪt] *n* (*hole*) hoyo *m*; (*coal mine*) mina *f*
pitch[1] [pɪʧ] *n* MUS tono *m*
pitch[2] [pɪʧ] **1** *v/i in baseball* lanzar la pelota **2** *v/t tent* montar; *ball* lanzar
'**pitch black** *adj* negro como el carbón
pitch·er[1] ['pɪʧər] *baseball player* lanzador(a) *m*(*f*), pítcher *m/f*
pitch·er[2] ['pɪʧər] *container* jarra *f*
pit·e·ous ['pɪtɪəs] *adj* patético
pit·fall ['pɪtfɒːl] dificultad *f*
pith [pɪθ] *of citrus fruit* piel *f* blanca
pit·i·ful ['pɪtɪfəl] *adj sight* lastimoso; *excuse, attempt* lamentable
pit·i·less ['pɪtɪləs] *adj* despiadado
pits [pɪts] *npl in motor racing* boxes *mpl*
'**pit stop** *in motor racing* parada *f* en boxes
pit·tance ['pɪtns] miseria *f*
pit·y ['pɪtɪ] **1** *n* pena *f*, lástima *f*; ***it's a pity that*** es una pena *or* lástima que; ***what a pity!*** ¡qué pena!; ***take pity on*** compadecerse de **2** *v/t* (*pret & pp* ***pitied***) *person* compadecerse de
piv·ot ['pɪvət] *v/i* pivotar
piz·za ['piːtsə] pizza *f*
plac·ard ['plækɑːrd] pancarta *f*
place [pleɪs] **1** *n* sitio *m*; *in race, competition* puesto *m*; (*seat*) sitio *m*, asiento; ***I've lost my place*** *in book* no sé por dónde iba; ***at my / his place*** en mi / su casa; ***in place of*** en lugar de; ***feel out of place*** sentirse fuera de lugar; ***take place*** tener lugar, llevarse a cabo; ***in the first place*** (*firstly*) en primer lugar; (*in the beginning*) en principio **2** *v/t* (*put*) poner, colocar; ***I know you but I can't quite place you*** te conozco pero no recuerdo de qué; ***place an order*** hacer un pedido
'**place mat** mantel *m* individual
plac·id ['plæsɪd] *adj* apacible
pla·gia·rism ['pleɪdʒərɪzm] plagio *m*
pla·gia·rize ['pleɪdʒəraɪz] *v/t* plagiar
plague [pleɪg] **1** *n* plaga *f* **2** *v/t* (*bother*) molestar
plain[1] [pleɪn] *n* llanura *f*
plain[2] [pleɪn] **1** *adj* (*clear, obvious*) claro; (*not fancy*) simple; (*not pretty*) feíllo; (*not patterned*) liso; (*blunt*) directo; ***plain chocolate*** chocolate amargo **2** *adv* verdaderamente; ***it's plain crazy*** es una verdadera locura
'**plain-clothes**: ***in plain-clothes*** de paisano
plain·ly ['pleɪnlɪ] *adv* (*clearly*) evidentemente; (*bluntly*) directamente; (*simply*) con sencillez; ***he's plainly upset*** está claro que está enfadado
plain 'spo·ken *adj* directo
plain·tiff ['pleɪntɪf] demandante *m/f*
plain·tive ['pleɪntɪv] *adj* quejumbroso
plan [plæn] **1** *n* (*project, intention*) plan *m*; (*drawing*) plano *m*; ***wedding plans*** preparaciones *fpl* para la boda **2** *v/t* (*pret & pp* ***planned***) (*prepare*) planear; (*design*) hacer los planos de; ***plan to do sth, plan on doing sth*** planear hacer algo **3** *v/i* (*pret & pp* ***planned***) hacer planes
plane[1] [pleɪn] *n* (*airplane*) avión *m*
plane[2] [pleɪn] *tool* cepillo *m*
plan·et ['plænɪt] planeta *f*
plank [plæŋk] *of wood* tablón *m*; *fig*: *of policy* punto *m*
plan·ning ['plænɪŋ] planificación *f*; ***at the planning stage*** en fase de estudio
plant[1] [plænt] **1** *n* planta *f* **2** *v/t* plantar
plant[2] [plænt] *n* (*factory*) fábrica *f*, planta *f*; (*equipment*) maquinaria *f*
plan·ta·tion [plæn'teɪʃn] plantación *f*
plaque [plæk] *on wall, teeth* placa *f*
plas·ter ['plæstər] **1** *n on wall, ceiling* yeso *m* **2** *v/t wall, ceiling* enyesar; ***be plastered with*** estar recubierto de
plas·ter cast escayola *f*
plas·tic ['plæstɪk] **1** *n* plástico *m* **2** *adj* (*made of plastic*) de plástico
plas·tic 'bag bolsa *f* de plástico
'**plas·tic (mon·ey)** plástico *m*, tarjetas *fpl* de pago
plas·tic 'sur·geon cirujano(-a) *m*(*f*) plástico(-a)
plas·tic 'sur·ge·ry cirugía *f* estética
plate [pleɪt] *n for food* plato *m*; (*sheet of metal*) chapa *f*; F PHOT placa *f*
pla·teau ['plætoʊ] meseta *f*
plat·form ['plætfɔːrm] (*stage*) plataforma *f*; *of railroad station* andén *m*; *fig*: *political* programa *f*
plat·i·num ['plætɪnəm] **1** *n* platino *m* **2** *adj* de platino
plat·i·tude ['plætɪtuːd] tópico *m*
pla·ton·ic [plə'tɑːnɪk] *adj relationship* platónico
pla·toon [plə'tuːn] *of soldiers* sección *f*
plat·ter ['plætər] *for meat, fish* fuente *f*
plau·si·ble ['plɒːzəbl] *adj* plausible
play [pleɪ] **1** *n in theater, on* TV obra *f* (de teatro); *of children, in match,* TECH juego *m* **2** *v/i* jugar; *of musician* tocar **3** *v/t musical instrument* tocar; *piece of music* in-

terpretar, tocar; *game* jugar; *tennis*, *football* jugar a; *opponent* jugar contra; (*perform*: *Macbeth etc*) representar; *particular role* interpretar, hacer el papel de; ***play a joke on*** gastar una broma a

◆ **play around** *v/i* F (*be unfaithful*) acostarse con otras personas

◆ **play down** *v/t* quitar importancia a

◆ **play up** *v/i of machine* dar problemas; *of child* dar guerra

play·act ['pleɪækt] *v/i* (*pretend*) fingir

play·boy ['pleɪbɔɪ] playboy *m*

play·er ['pleɪr] SP jugador(a) *m*(*f*); (*musician*) intérprete *m*/*f*; (*actor*) actor *m*, actriz *f*

play·ful ['pleɪfəl] *adj punch etc* de broma

play·ground ['pleɪgraʊnd] zona *f* de juegos

'**play·group** guardería *f*

play·ing card ['pleɪɪŋkɑːrd] carta *f*

play·ing field ['pleɪɪŋfiːld] campo *m* de deportes

play·mate ['pleɪmeɪt] compañero(-a) *m*(*f*) de juego

play·wright ['pleɪraɪt] autor(a) *m*(*f*)

pla·za ['plɑːzə] *for shopping* centro *m* comercial

plc [piːel'siː] *abbr* (= *Br* ***public limited company***) S.A. *f* (= sociedad *f* anónima)

plea [pliː] *n* súplica *f*

plead [pliːd] *v/i*: ***plead for mercy*** pedir clemencia; ***plead guilty / not guilty*** declararse culpable / inocente; ***she pleaded with me not to go*** me suplicó que no fuera

pleas·ant ['pleznt] *adj* agradable

please [pliːz] **1** *adv* por favor; ***more tea? - yes, please*** ¿más té? - sí, por favor; ***please do*** claro que sí, por supuesto **2** *v/t* complacer; ***please yourself!*** ¡haz lo que quieras!

pleased [pliːzd] *adj* contento; (*satisfied*) satisfecho; ***pleased to meet you*** encantado de conocerle; ***I'm very pleased to be here*** estoy muy contento de estar aquí

pleas·ing ['pliːzɪŋ] *adj* agradable

pleas·ure ['pleʒər] (*happiness, satisfaction, delight*) satisfacción *f*; *as opposed to work* placer *m*; ***it's a pleasure*** (*you're welcome*) no hay de qué; ***with pleasure*** faltaría más

pleat [pliːt] *n in skirt* tabla *f*

pleat·ed skirt ['pliːtɪd] falda *f* de tablas

pledge [pledʒ] **1** *n* (*promise*) promesa *f*; (*guarantee*) compromiso *m*; (*money*) donación *f*; ***Pledge of Allegiance*** *juramento de lealtad a la bandera estadounidense* **2** *v/t* (*promise*) prometer; (*guarantee*) comprometerse; *money* donar

plen·ti·ful ['plentɪfəl] *adj* abundante

plen·ty ['plentɪ] (*abundance*) abundancia *f*; ***plenty of books / food*** muchos libros / mucha comida; ***we've got plenty of room*** tenemos espacio más que suficiente; ***that's plenty*** es suficiente; ***there's plenty for everyone*** hay (suficiente) para todos

pli·a·ble ['plaɪəbl] *adj* flexible

pli·ers ['plaɪərz] *npl* alicates *mpl*; ***a pair of pliers*** unos alicates

plight [plaɪt] situación *f* difícil

plod [plɑːd] *v/i* (*pret & pp* ***plodded***) (*walk*) arrastrarse

◆ **plod on** *v/i with a job* avanzar laboriosamente

plod·der ['plɑːdər] (*at work, school*) *persona no especialmente lista pero muy trabajadora*

plot¹ [plɑːt] *n* (*land*) terreno *m*

plot² [plɑːt] **1** *n* (*conspiracy*) complot *m*; *of novel* argumento *m* **2** *v/t* (*pret & pp* ***plotted***) tramar **3** *v/i* (*pret & pp* ***plotted***) conspirar

plot·ter ['plɑːtər] conspirador(a) *m*(*f*); COMPUT plóter *m*

plough *Br*, **plow** [plaʊ] **1** *n* arado *m* **2** *v/t & v/i* arar

◆ **plow back** *v/t profits* reinvertir

pluck [plʌk] *v/t eyebrows* depilar; *chicken* desplumar

◆ **pluck up** *v/t*: ***pluck up courage to ...*** reunir el valor para ...

plug [plʌg] **1** *n for sink, bath* tapón *m*; *electrical* enchufe *m*; (*spark plug*) bujía *f*; ***give a book a plug*** dar publicidad a un libro **2** *v/t* (*pret & pp* ***plugged***) *hole* tapar; *new book etc* hacer publicidad de

◆ **plug away at** *v/t* F trabajar con esfuerzo en

◆ **plug in** *v/t* enchufar

plum [plʌm] **1** *n fruit* ciruela *f*; *tree* ciruelo *m* **2** *adj* F: ***plum job*** un chollo de trabajo

plum·age ['pluːmɪdʒ] plumaje *m*

plumb [plʌm] *adj* vertical

◆ **plumb in** *v/t washing machine* conectar a la red del agua

plumb·er ['plʌmər] *Span* fontanero(-a) *m*(*f*), *L.Am.* plomero(-a) *m*(*f*)

plumb·ing ['plʌmɪŋ] (*pipes*) tuberías *fpl*

plume [pluːm] *n* (*feather*) pluma *f*; *of smoke* nube *f*

plum·met ['plʌmɪt] *v/i of airplane, prices* caer en picado

plump [plʌmp] *adj* rellenito

◆ **plump for** *v/t* decidirse por

plunge [plʌndʒ] **1** *n* salto *m*; *in prices* caída *f*; ***take the plunge*** dar el paso **2** *v/i* precipitarse; *of prices* caer en picado **3**

v/t hundir; (*into water*) sumergir; ***the city was plunged into darkness*** la ciudad quedó inmersa en la oscuridad; ***the news plunged him into despair*** la noticia lo hundió en la desesperación
plung·ing ['plʌndʒɪŋ] *adj neckline* escotado
plu·per·fect ['pluːpɜːrfɪkt] *n* GRAM pluscuamperfecto *m*
plu·ral ['plʊərəl] **1** *n* plural *m* **2** *adj* plural
plus [plʌs] **1** *prep* más; ***I want John plus two other volunteers ...*** quiero a John y a otros dos voluntarios **2** *adj* más de; ***$500 plus*** más de 500 dólares **3** *n symbol* signo *m* más; (*advantage*) ventaja *f* **4** *conj* (*moreover, in addition*) además
plush [plʌʃ] *adj* lujoso
'**plus sign** signo *m* más
ply·wood ['plaɪwʊd] madera *f* contrachapada
PM [piː'em] *Br abbr* (= ***Prime Minister***) Primer(a) *m*(*f*) Ministro(-a)
p.m. [piː'em] *abbr* (= ***post meridiem***) p.m.; ***at 3 p.m*** a las 3 de la tarde; ***at 11 p.m*** a las 11 de la noche
pneu·mat·ic [nuː'mætɪk] *adj* neumático
pneu·mat·ic 'drill martillo *m* neumático
pneu·mo·ni·a [nuː'moʊnɪə] pulmonía *f*, neumonía *f*
poach¹ [poʊʧ] *v/t* (*cook*) hervir
poach² [poʊʧ] *v/t* & *v/i* (*hunt*) cazar furtivamente; *fish* pescar furtivamente
poached egg [poʊʧt'eg] huevo *m* escalfado
poach·er ['poʊʧər] *of game* cazador(a) *m*(*f*) furtivo(a); *of fish* pescador(a) *m*(*f*) furtivo(a)
P.O. Box [piː'oʊbɑːks] apartado *m* de correos
pock·et ['pɑːkɪt] **1** *n* bolsillo *m*; ***line one's pockets*** llenarse los bolsillos; ***be $10 out of pocket*** salir perdiendo 10 dólares **2** *adj radio, dictionary* de bolsillo **3** *v/t* meter en el bolsillo
'**pock·et·book** (*handbag*) bolso *m*; (*wallet*) cartera *f*; (*book*) libro *m* de bolsillo
pock·et 'cal·cu·la·tor calculadora *f* de bolsillo
'**pock·et·knife** navaja *f*
po·di·um ['poʊdɪəm] podio *m*
po·em ['poʊɪm] poema *m*
po·et ['poʊɪt] poeta *m*; poeta *f*, poetisa *f*
po·et·ic [poʊ'etɪk] *adj* poético
po·et·ic 'jus·tice justicia *f* divina
po·et·ry ['poʊɪtrɪ] poesía *f*
poign·ant ['pɔɪnjənt] *adj* conmovedor
point [pɔɪnt] **1** *n of pencil, knife* punta *f*; *in competition, argument* punto *m*; (*purpose*) objetivo *m*; (*moment*) momento *m*; *in decimals* coma *f*; ***what's the point of telling him?*** ¿qué se consigue diciéndoselo?; ***the point I'm trying to make ...*** lo que estoy intentando decir ...; ***at one point*** en un momento dado; ***that's beside the point*** eso no viene a cuento; ***be on the point of*** estar a punto de; ***get to the point*** ir al grano; ***the point is ...*** la cuestión es que ...; ***there's no point in waiting / trying*** no vale la pena esperar / intentarlo **2** *v/i* señalar con el dedo **3** *v/t*: ***he pointed the gun at me*** me apuntó con la pistola
◆ **point out** *v/t sights* indicar; *advantages etc* destacar
◆ **point to** *v/t with finger* señalar con el dedo; (*fig: indicate*) indicar
'**point-blank** **1** *adj refusal, denial* categórico; ***at point-blank range*** a quemarropa **2** *adv refuse, deny* categóricamente
point·ed ['pɔɪntɪd] *adj remark* mordaz
point·er ['pɔɪntər] *for teacher* puntero *m*; (*hint*) consejo *m*; (*sign, indication*) indicador *m*
point·less ['pɔɪntləs] *adj* inútil; ***it's pointless trying*** no sirve de nada intentarlo
'**point of sale** *place* punto *m* de venta; *promotional material* material *m* promocional
'**point of view** punto *m* de vista
poise [pɔɪz] confianza *f*
poised [pɔɪzd] *adj person* con aplomo
poi·son ['pɔɪzn] **1** *n* veneno *m* **2** *v/t* envenenar
poi·son·ous ['pɔɪznəs] *adj* venenoso
poke [poʊk] **1** *n* empujón *m* **2** *v/t* (*prod*) empujar; (*stick*) clavar; ***he poked his head out of the window*** asomó la cabeza por la ventana; ***poke fun at*** reírse de; ***poke one's nose into*** F meter las narices en F
◆ **poke around** *v/i* F husmear
pok·er ['poʊkər] *card game* póquer *m*
pok·y ['poʊkɪ] *adj* F (*cramped*) enano, minúsculo
Po·land ['poʊlənd] Polonia
po·lar ['poʊlər] *adj* polar
po·lar bear oso *m* polar *or* blanco
po·lar·ize ['poʊləraɪz] *v/t* polarizar
Pole [poʊl] polaco(-a) *m*(*f*)
pole¹ [poʊl] *for support* poste *m*; *for tent, pushing things* palo *m*
pole² [poʊl] *of earth* polo *m*
'**pole star** estrella *f* polar
'**pole·vault** salto *m* con pértiga
'**pole-vault·er** saltador(a) *m*(*f*) de pértiga
po·lice [pə'liːs] *n* policía *f*
po'lice car coche *m* de policía
po'lice·man policía *m*

po'lice state estado *m* policial
po'lice sta·tion comisaría *f* (de policía)
po'lice·wo·man (mujer *f*) policía *f*
pol·i·cy¹ ['pɑːlɪsɪ] política *f*
pol·i·cy² ['pɑːlɪsɪ] (*insurance policy*) póliza *f*
po·li·o ['poʊlɪoʊ] polio *f*
Pol·ish ['poʊlɪʃ] **1** *adj* polaco **2** *n* polaco *m*
pol·ish ['pɑːlɪʃ] **1** *n* abrillantador *m*; (*nail polish*) esmalte *m* de uñas **2** *v/t* dar brillo a; *speech* pulir
◆ **polish off** *v/t food* acabar, comerse
◆ **polish up** *v/t skill* perfeccionar
pol·ished ['pɑːlɪʃt] *adj performance* brillante
po·lite [pə'laɪt] *adj* educado
po·lite·ly [pə'laɪtlɪ] *adv* educadamente
po·lite·ness [pə'laɪtnɪs] educación *f*
po·lit·i·cal [pə'lɪtɪkl] *adj* político
po·lit·i·cal·ly cor·rect [pə'lɪtɪklɪ kə'rekt] políticamente correcto
pol·i·ti·cian [pɑːlɪ'tɪʃn] político(-a) *m*(*f*)
pol·i·tics ['pɑːlətɪks] política *f*; ***I'm not interested in politics*** no me interesa la política; ***what are his politics?*** ¿cuáles son sus ideas políticas?
poll [poʊl] **1** *n* (*survey*) encuesta *f*, sondeo *m*; ***the polls*** (*election*) las elecciones; ***go to the polls*** (*vote*) acudir a las urnas **2** *v/t people* sondear; *votes* obtener
pol·len ['pɑːlən] polen *m*
'pol·len count concentración *f* de polen en el aire
'poll·ing booth ['poʊlɪŋ] cabina *f* electoral
'poll·ing day día *m* de las elecciones
poll·ster ['pɑːlstər] encuestador(a) *m*(*f*)
pol·lu·tant [pə'luːtənt] contaminante *m*
pol·lute [pə'luːt] *v/t* contaminar
pol·lu·tion [pə'luːʃn] contaminación *f*
po·lo ['poʊloʊ] SP polo *m*
'po·lo neck *sweater* suéter *m* de cuello alto
'po·lo shirt polo *m*
pol·y·eth·yl·ene [pɑːlɪ'eθɪliːn] polietileno *m*
pol·y·es·ter [pɑːlɪ'estər] poliéster *m*
pol·y·sty·rene [pɑːlɪ'staɪriːn] poliestireno *m*
pol·y·un·sat·u·rat·ed [pɑːlɪʌn'sætjəreɪtɪd] *adj* poliinsaturado
pom·pous ['pɑːmpəs] *adj* pomposo
pond [pɑːnd] estanque *m*
pon·der ['pɑːndər] *v/i* reflexionar
pon·tiff ['pɑːntɪf] pontífice *m*
pon·y ['poʊnɪ] poni *m*
'pon·y·tail coleta *f*
poo·dle ['puːdl] caniche *m*
pool¹ [puːl] (*swimming pool*) piscina *f*, *L.Am.* pileta *f*, *Mex* alberca *f*; *of water, blood* charco *m*
pool² [puːl] *game* billar *m* americano
pool³ [puːl] **1** *n* (*common fund*) bote *m*, fondo *m* común **2** *v/t resources* juntar
'pool hall sala *f* de billares
'pool table mesa *f* de billar americano
poop·ed [puːpt] *adj* F hecho polvo F
poor [pʊr] **1** *adj* pobre; (*not good*) mediocre, malo; ***be in poor health*** estar enfermo; ***poor old Tony!*** ¡pobre(cito) Tony! **2** *n*: ***the poor*** los pobres
poor·ly ['pʊlɪ] **1** *adv* mal **2** *adj* (*unwell*): ***feel poorly*** encontrarse mal
pop¹ [pɑːp] **1** *n noise* pequeño *m* ruido **2** *v/i* (*pret & pp* ***popped***) *of balloon etc* estallar **3** *v/t* (*pret & pp* ***popped***) *cork* hacer saltar; *balloon* pinchar
pop² [pɑːp] **1** *n* MUS pop *m* **2** *adj* pop
pop³ [pɑːp] F (*father*) papá *m* F
pop⁴ [pɑːp] F (*put*) meter
◆ **pop in** *v/i* F (*make a brief visit*) pasar un momento
◆ **pop out** *v/i* F (*go out for a short time*) salir un momento
◆ **pop up** *v/i* F (*appear suddenly*) aparecer
'pop con·cert concierto *m* (de música) pop
pop·corn ['pɑːpkɔːrn] palomitas *fpl* de maíz
pope [poʊp] papa *m*
'pop group grupo *m* (de música) pop
pop·py ['pɑːpɪ] amapola *f*
Pop·sicle® ['pɑːpsɪkl] polo *m* (*helado*)
'pop song canción *f* pop
pop·u·lar ['pɑːpjʊlər] *adj* popular; ***contrary to popular belief*** contrariamente a lo que se piensa
pop·u·lar·i·ty [pɑːpjʊ'lærətɪ] popularidad *f*
pop·u·late ['pɑːpjʊleɪt] *v/t* poblar
pop·u·la·tion [pɑːpjʊ'leɪʃn] población *f*
porce·lain ['pɔːrsəlɪn] **1** *n* porcelana *f* **2** *adj* de porcelana
porch [pɔːrʧ] porche *m*
por·cu·pine ['pɔːrkjʊpaɪn] puercoespín *m*
pore [pɔːr] *of skin* poro *m*
◆ **pore over** *v/t* estudiar detenidamente
pork [pɔːrk] cerdo *m*
porn [pɔːrn] *n* F porno *m*
porn(o) [pɔːrn, 'pɔːrnoʊ] *adj* F porno F
por·no·graph·ic [pɔːrnə'græfɪk] *adj* pornográfico
porn·og·ra·phy [pɔːr'nɑːgrəfɪ] pornografía *f*
po·rous ['pɔːrəs] *adj* poroso
port¹ [pɔːrt] *n town, area* puerto *m*
port² [pɔːrt] *adj* (*left-hand*) a babor

P

por·ta·ble ['pɔːrtəbl] **1** *adj* portátil **2** *n* COMPUT portátil *m*; TV televisión *f* portátil
por·ter ['pɔːrtər] mozo(-a) *m(f)*
port·hole ['pɔːrthoʊl] NAUT portilla *f*
por·tion ['pɔːrʃn] *n* parte *f*; *of food* ración *f*
por·trait ['pɔːrtreɪt] **1** *n* retrato *m* **2** *adv print* en formato vertical
por·tray [pɔːr'treɪ] *of artist, photographer* retratar; *of actor* interpretar; *of author* describir
por·tray·al [pɔːr'treɪəl] *by actor* interpretación *f*, representación *f*; *by author* descripción *f*
Por·tu·gal ['pɔːrʧʊgl] Portugal
Por·tu·guese [pɔːrʧʊ'giːz] **1** *adj* portugués **2** *n person* portugués(-esa) *m(f)*; *language* portugués *m*
pose [poʊz] **1** *n* (*pretense*) pose *f*; ***it's all a pose*** no es más que una pose **2** *v/i for artist, photographer* posar; ***pose as*** hacerse pasar por **3** *v/t*: ***pose a problem/a threat*** representar un problema / una amenaza
posh [pɑːʃ] *adj Br* F elegante, *pej* pijo
po·si·tion [pə'zɪʃn] **1** *n* posición *f*; (*stance, point of view*) postura *f*; (*job*) puesto *m*, empleo *m*; (*status*) posición *f* (social) **2** *v/t* situar, colocar
pos·i·tive ['pɑːzətɪv] *adj* positivo; ***be positive*** (*sure*) estar seguro
pos·i·tive·ly ['pɑːzətɪvlɪ] *adv* (*decidedly*) verdaderamente, sin lugar a dudas; (*definitely*) claramente
pos·sess [pə'zes] *v/t* poseer
pos·ses·sion [pə'zeʃn] posesión *f*; ***possessions*** posesiones *fpl*
pos·ses·sive [pə'zesɪv] *adj person*, GRAM posesivo
pos·si·bil·i·ty [pɑːsə'bɪlətɪ] posibilidad *f*; ***there is a possibility that …*** cabe la posibilidad de que …
pos·si·ble ['pɑːsəbl] *adj* posible; ***the shortest / quickest route possible*** la ruta más corto / rápido posible; ***the best possible …*** el mejor …
possibly ['pɑːsəblɪ] *adv* (*perhaps*) puede ser, quizás; ***that can't possibly be right*** no puede ser cierto; ***they're doing everything they possibly can*** están haciendo todo lo que pueden; ***could you possibly tell me …?*** ¿tendría la amabilidad de decirme …?
post[1] [poʊst] **1** *n of wood, metal* poste *m* **2** *v/t notice* pegar; *on notice board* poner; *profits* presentar; ***keep s.o. posted*** mantener a alguien al corriente
post[2] [poʊst] **1** *n* (*place of duty*) puesto *m* **2** *v/t soldier, employee* destinar; *guards* apostar
post[3] [poʊst] **1** *n Br* (*mail*) correo *m* **2** *v/t Br letter* echar al correo
post·age ['poʊstɪdʒ] franqueo *m*
'**post·age stamp** *fml* sello *m*, *L.Am.* estampilla *f*, *Mex* timbre *m*
post·al ['poʊstl] *adj* postal
'**post·card** (tarjeta *f*) postal *f*
'**post·code** *Br* código *m* postal
'**post·date** *v/t* posfechar
post·er ['poʊstər] póster *m*, *L.Am.* afiche *m*
pos·te·ri·or [pɑː'stɪrɪər] *n* (*hum*: *buttocks*) trasero *m*
pos·ter·i·ty [pɑː'sterətɪ] posteridad *f*; ***for posterity*** para la posteridad
post·grad·u·ate ['poʊstgrædʒʊət] **1** *n* posgraduado(-a) *m(f)* **2** *adj* de posgrado
post·hu·mous ['pɑːstʊməs] *adj* póstumo
post·hu·mous·ly ['pɑːstʊməslɪ] *adv* póstumamente
post·ing ['poʊstɪŋ] (*assignment*) destino *m*
post·mark ['poʊstmɑːrk] matasellos *m inv*
post-mor·tem [poʊst'mɔːrtəm] autopsia *f*
'**post of·fice** oficina *f* de correos
post·pone [poʊst'poʊn] *v/t* posponer, aplazar
post·pone·ment [poʊst'poʊnmənt] aplazamiento *m*
pos·ture ['pɑːsʧər] postura *f*
'**post-war** *adj* de posguerra
pot[1] [pɑːt] *for cooking* olla *f*; *for coffee* cafetera *f*; *for tea* tetera *f*; *for plant* maceta *f*
pot[2] [pɑːt] F (*marijuana*) maría *f* F
po·ta·to [pə'teɪtoʊ] *Span* patata *f*, *L.Am.* papa *f*
po·ta·to chips, *Br* **po·ta·to crisps** *npl Span* patatas *fpl* fritas, *L.Am.* papas *fpl* fritas
'**pot·bel·ly** ['pɑːtbelɪ] barriga *f*
po·tent ['poʊtənt] *adj* potente
po·ten·tial [pə'tenʃl] **1** *adj* potencial **2** *n* potencial *m*
po·ten·tial·ly [pə'tenʃəlɪ] *adv* potencialmente
pot·hole ['pɑːthoʊl] *in road* bache *m*
pot·ter ['pɑːtər] *n* alfarero(-a) *m(f)*
pot·ter·y ['pɑːtərɪ] *n* alfarería *f*
pot·ty ['pɑːtɪ] *n for baby* orinal *m*
pouch [paʊʧ] (*bag*) bolsa *f*; *for tobacco* petaca *f*; *for amunition* cartuchera *f*; *for mail* saca *m*
poul·try ['poʊltrɪ] *birds* aves *fpl* de corral; *meat* carne *f* de ave
pounce [paʊns] *v/i of animal* saltar; *fig* echarse encima

pound¹ [paʊnd] *n weight* libra *f* *(453,6 gr)*
pound² [paʊnd] *n for strays* perrera *f*; *for cars* depósito *m*
pound³ [paʊnd] *v/i of heart* palpitar con fuerza; ***pound on*** *(hammer on)* golpear en
pound 'ster·ling libra *f* esterlina
pour [pɔːr] **1** *v/t into a container* verter; *spill* derramar; ***pour s.o. some coffee*** servir café a alguien **2** *v/i*: ***it's pouring (with rain)*** está lloviendo a cántaros
◆ **pour out** *v/t liquid* servir; *troubles* contar
pout [paʊt] *v/i* hacer un mohín
pov·er·ty ['pɑːvərtɪ] pobreza *f*
pov·er·ty-strick·en ['pɑːvərtɪstrɪkn] depauperado
pow·der ['paʊdər] **1** *n* polvo *m*; *for face* polvos *m*, colorete *m* **2** *v/t face* empolvarse
pow·er ['paʊər] **1** *n (strength)* fuerza *f*; *of engine* potencia; *(authority)* poder *m*; *(energy)* energía *f*; *(electricity)* electricidad *f*; ***in power*** POL en el poder; ***fall from power*** POL perder el poder **2** *v/t*: ***be powered by*** estar impulsado por
'pow·er-as·sist·ed steering dirección *f* asistida
'pow·er cut apagón *m*
'pow·er fail·ure apagón *m*
pow·er·ful ['paʊərfəl] *adj* poderoso; *car* potente; *drug* fuerte
pow·er·less ['paʊərlɪs] *adj* impotente; ***be powerless to ...*** ser incapaz de ...
'pow·er line línea *f* de conducción eléctrica
'pow·er out·age apagón *m*
'pow·er sta·tion central *f* eléctrica
'pow·er steer·ing dirección *f* asistida
'pow·er u·nit fuente *f* de alimentación
PR [piː'ɑːr] *abbr* (= ***public relations***) relaciones *fpl* públicas
prac·ti·cal ['præktɪkl] *adj* práctico; *layout* funcional
prac·ti·cal 'joke broma *f* *(que se gasta)*
prac·tic·al·ly ['præktɪklɪ] *adv behave, think* de manera práctica; *(almost)* prácticamente, casi
prac·tice ['præktɪs] **1** *n* práctica *f*; *(rehearsal)* ensayo *m*; *(custom)* costumbre *f*; ***in practice*** *(in reality)* en la práctica; ***be out of practice*** estar desentrenado; ***practice makes perfect*** a base de práctica se aprende **2** *v/i* practicar; *of musician* ensayar; *of footballer* entrenarse **3** *v/t* practicar; *law, medicine* ejercer
prac·tise *Br* → ***practice*** *v/i & v/t*
prag·mat·ic [præg'mætɪk] *adj* pragmático
prag·ma·tism ['prægmətɪzm] pragmatismo *m*
prai·rie ['prerɪ] pradera *f*
praise [preɪz] **1** *n* elogio *m*, alabanza *f* **2** *v/t* elogiar
'praise·wor·thy *adj* elogiable
prank [præŋk] *n* travesura *f*
prat·tle ['prætl] *v/i* F parlotear F
prawn [prɒːn] gamba *f*
pray [preɪ] *v/i* rezar
prayer [prer] oración *f*
preach [priːʧ] **1** *v/i in church* predicar; *(moralize)* sermonear **2** *v/t sermon* predicar
preach·er ['priːʧər] predicador(a) *m(f)*
pre·am·ble [priː'æmbl] preámbulo *m*
pre·car·i·ous [prɪ'kerɪəs] *adj* precario
pre·car·i·ous·ly [prɪ'kerɪəslɪ] *adv* precariamente
pre·cau·tion [prɪ'kɒːʃn] precaución *f*; ***as a precaution*** como precaución
pre·cau·tion·a·ry [prɪ'kɒːʃnrɪ] *adj measure* preventivo
pre·cede [prɪ'siːd] *v/t in time* preceder; *(walk in front of)* ir delante de
pre·ce·dent ['presɪdənt] precedente *m*
pre·ce·ding [prɪ'siːdɪŋ] *adj week, chapter* anterior
pre·cinct ['priːsɪŋkt] *(district)* distrito *m*
pre·cious ['preʃəs] *adj* preciado; *gem* precioso
pre·cip·i·tate [prɪ'sɪpɪteɪt] *v/t crisis* precipitar
pré·cis ['preɪsiː] *n* resumen *m*
pre·cise [prɪ'saɪs] *adj* preciso
pre·cise·ly [prɪ'saɪslɪ] *adv* exactamente
pre·ci·sion [prɪ'sɪʒn] precisión *f*
pre·co·cious [prɪ'koʊʃəs] *adj child* precoz
pre·con·ceived ['priːkənsiːvd] *adj idea* preconcebido
pre·con·di·tion [priːkən'dɪʃn] condición *f* previa
pred·a·tor ['predətər] *animal* depredador(a) *m(f)*
pred·a·to·ry ['predətɔːrɪ] *adj* depredador
pre·de·ces·sor ['priːdɪsesər] *in job* predecesor(a) *m(f)*; *machine* modelo *m* anterior
pre·des·ti·na·tion [priːdestɪ'neɪʃn] predestinación *f*
pre·des·tined [priː'destɪnd] *adj*: ***be predestined to*** estar *pred*estinado a
pre·dic·a·ment [prɪ'dɪkəmənt] apuro *m*
pre·dict [prɪ'dɪkt] *v/t* predecir, pronosticar
pre·dict·a·ble [prɪ'dɪktəbl] *adj* predecible
pre·dic·tion [prɪ'dɪkʃn] predicción *f*, pronóstico *m*
pre·dom·i·nant [prɪ'dɑːmɪnənt] *adj* pre-

dominante

pre·dom·i·nant·ly [prɪ'dɑːmɪnəntlɪ] *adv* predominantemente

pre·dom·i·nate [prɪ'dɑːmɪneɪt] *v/i* predominar

pre·fab·ri·cat·ed [priː'fæbrɪkeɪtɪd] *adj* prefabricado

pref·ace ['prefɪs] *n* prólogo *m*, prefacio *m*

pre·fer [prɪ'fɜːr] *v/t* (*pret & pp* ***preferred***) preferir; ***prefer X to Y*** preferir X a Y; ***prefer to do*** preferir hacer

pref·e·ra·ble ['prefərəbl] *adj* preferible; ***anywhere is preferable to this*** cualquier sitio es mejor que éste

pref·e·ra·bly ['prefərəblɪ] *adv* preferentemente

pref·e·rence ['prefərəns] preferencia *f*

pref·er·en·tial [prefə'renʃl] *adj* preferente

pre·fix ['priːfɪks] prefijo *m*

preg·nan·cy ['pregnənsɪ] embarazo *m*

preg·nant ['pregnənt] *adj woman* embarazada; *animal* preñada

pre·heat ['priːhiːt] *v/t oven* precalentar

pre·his·tor·ic [priːhɪs'tɑːrɪk] *adj* prehistórico

pre·judge [priː'dʒʌdʒ] *v/t* prejuzgar, juzgar de antemano

prej·u·dice ['predʒʊdɪs] **1** *n* prejuicio *m* **2** *v/t person* predisponer, influir; *chances* perjudicar

prej·u·diced ['predʒʊdɪst] *adj* parcial, *pre*dispuesto

pre·lim·i·na·ry [prɪ'lɪmɪnerɪ] *adj* preliminar

pre·mar·i·tal [priː'mærɪtl] *adj* prematrimonial

pre·ma·ture ['priːmətʊr] *adj* prematuro

pre·med·i·tat·ed [priː'medɪteɪtɪd] *adj* premeditado

prem·i·er ['premɪr] *n* (*Prime Minister*) primer(a) ministro(-a) *m(f)*

prem·i·ère ['premɪer] *n* estreno *m*

prem·is·es ['premɪsɪz] *npl* local *m*

pre·mi·um ['priːmɪəm] *n in insurance* prima *f*

pre·mo·ni·tion [premə'nɪʃn] premonición *f*, presentimiento *m*

pre·na·tal [priː'neɪtl] *adj* prenatal

pre·oc·cu·pied [prɪ'ɑːkjʊpaɪd] *adj* preocupado

prep·a·ra·tion [prepə'reɪʃn] preparación *f*; ***in preparation for*** como preparación a; ***preparations*** preparativos *mpl*

pre·pare [prɪ'per] **1** *v/t* preparar; ***be prepared to do sth*** (*willing*) estar dispuesto a hacer algo; ***be prepared for sth*** (*be expecting*, *ready*) estar preparado para algo **2** *v/i* prepararse

prep·o·si·tion [prepə'zɪʃn] preposición *f*

pre·pos·ter·ous [prɪ'pɑːstərəs] *adj* ridículo, absurdo

prep school ['prepskuːl] escuela *f* primaria privada

pre·req·ui·site [priː'rekwɪzɪt] requisito *m* previo

pre·scribe [prɪ'skraɪb] *v/t of doctor* recetar

pre·scrip·tion [prɪ'skrɪpʃn] MED receta *f*

pres·ence ['prezns] presencia *f*; ***in the presence of*** en presencia de, delante de

pres·ence of 'mind presencia *f* de ánimo

pres·ent[1] ['preznt] **1** *adj* (*current*) actual; ***be present*** estar presente **2** *n*: ***the present*** *also* GRAM el presente; ***at present*** en este momento

pres·ent[2] ['preznt] *n* (*gift*) regalo *m*

pre·sent[3] [prɪ'zent] *v/t* presentar; *award* entregar; *program* presentar; ***present s.o. with sth, present sth to s.o.*** entregar algo a alguien

pre·sen·ta·tion [prezn'teɪʃn] *to audience* presentación *f*

pres·ent-day [preznt'deɪ] *adj* actual

pre·sent·er [prɪ'zentər] presentador(a) *m(f)*

pres·ent·ly ['prezntlɪ] *adv* (*at the moment*) actualmente; (*soon*) pronto

'pres·ent tense tiempo *m* presente

pres·er·va·tion [prezər'veɪʃn] conservación *f*; *of standards*, *peace* mantenimiento *m*

pre·ser·va·tive [prɪ'zɜːrvətɪv] *n* conservante *m*

pre·serve [prɪ'zɜːrv] **1** *n* (*domain*) dominio *m* **2** *v/t standards*, *peace etc* mantener; *food*, *wood* conservar

pre·side [prɪ'zaɪd] *v/i at meeting* presidir; ***preside over*** *meeting* presidir

pres·i·den·cy ['prezɪdənsɪ] presidencia *f*

pres·i·dent ['prezɪdnt] POL, *of company* presidente(-a) *m(f)*

pres·i·den·tial [prezɪ'denʃl] *adj* presidencial

press [pres] **1** *n*: ***the press*** la prensa **2** *v/t button* pulsar, presionar; (*urge*) presionar; (*squeeze*) apretar; *clothes* planchar **3** *v/i*: ***press for*** presionar para obtener

'press a·gen·cy agencia *f* de prensa

'press con·fer·ence rueda *f or* conferencia *f* de prensa

press·ing ['presɪŋ] *adj* urgente

pres·sure ['preʃər] **1** *n* presión *f*; ***be under pressure*** estar sometido a presión; ***he is under pressure to resign*** lo están presionando para que dimita **2** *v/t* presionar

pres·tige [pre'stiːʒ] prestigio *m*

pres·ti·gious [pre'stɪdʒəs] *adj* prestigioso

pre·su·ma·bly [prɪ'zuːməblɪ] *adv* presumiblemente, probablemente
pre·sume [prɪ'zuːm] suponer; ***they were presumed dead*** los dieron por muertos; ***presume to do sth*** *fml* tomarse la libertad de hacer algo
pre·sump·tion [prɪ'zʌmpʃn] *of innocence, guilt* presunción *f*
pre·sump·tu·ous [prɪ'zʌmptʊəs] *adj* presuntuoso
pre·sup·pose [priːsə'poʊs] *v/t* presuponer
pre-tax ['priːtæks] *adj* antes de impuestos
pre·tence *Br* → ***pretense***
pre·tend [prɪ'tend] **1** *v/t* fingir, hacer como si; *claim* pretender; ***pretend to be s.o.*** hacerse pasar por alguien; ***the children are pretending to be spacemen*** los niños están jugando a que son astronautas **2** *v/i* fingir
pre·tense [prɪ'tens] farsa *f*
pre·ten·tious [prɪ'tenʃəs] *adj* pretencioso
pre·text ['priːtekst] pretexto *m*
pret·ty ['prɪtɪ] **1** *adj village, house, fabric etc* bonito, lindo; *child, woman* guapo, lindo **2** *adv* (*quite*) bastante
pre·vail [prɪ'veɪl] *v/i* (*triumph*) prevalecer
pre·vail·ing [prɪ'veɪlɪŋ] *adj* predominante
pre·vent [prɪ'vent] *v/t* impedir, evitar; ***prevent s.o.*** (***from***) ***doing sth*** impedir que alguien haga algo
pre·ven·tion [prɪ'venʃn] prevención *f*
pre·ven·tive [prɪ'ventɪv] *adj* preventivo
pre·view ['priːvjuː] **1** *n of movie, exhibition* preestreno *m* **2** *v/t* hacer la presentación previa de
pre·vi·ous ['priːvɪəs] *adj* anterior, previo
pre·vi·ously ['priːvɪəslɪ] *adv* anteriormente, antes
pre-war ['priːwɔːr] *adj* de preguerra, de antes de la guerra
prey [preɪ] *n* presa *f*; ***prey to*** presa de
◆ **prey on** *v/t* atacar; *fig*: *of con man etc* aprovecharse de
price [praɪs] **1** *n* precio *m* **2** *v/t* COM poner precio a
price·less ['praɪslɪs] *adj* que no tiene precio
'**price tag** etiqueta *f* del precio
'**price war** guerra *f* de precios
price·y ['praɪsɪ] *adj* F carillo F
prick[1] [prɪk] **1** *n pain* punzada *f* **2** *v/t* (*jab*) pinchar
prick[2] [prɪk] *n* V (*penis*) polla *f* V, carajo *m* V; V *person Span* gilipollas *m inv* V, *L.Am.* pendejo *m* V
◆ **prick up** *v/t*: ***prick up one's ears*** *of dog* aguzar las orejas; *of person* prestar atención
prick·le ['prɪkl] *on plant* espina *f*
prick·ly ['prɪklɪ] *adj beard, plant* que pincha; (*irritable*) irritable
pride [praɪd] **1** *n in person, achievement* orgullo *m*; (*self-respect*) amor *m* propio **2** *v/t*: ***pride o.s. on*** enorgullecerse de
priest [priːst] sacerdote *m*; (*parish priest*) cura *m*
pri·ma·ri·ly [praɪ'merɪlɪ] *adv* principalmente
pri·ma·ry ['praɪmərɪ] **1** *adj* principal **2** *n* POL elecciones *fpl* primarias
prime [praɪm] **1** *n*: ***be in one's prime*** estar en la flor de la vida **2** *adj example, reason* primordial; ***of prime importance*** de suprema importancia
prime '**min·is·ter** primer(a) ministro(-a) *m*(*f*)
'**prime time** *n* TV horario *m* de mayor audiencia
prim·i·tive ['prɪmɪtɪv] *adj* primitivo
prince [prɪns] príncipe *m*
prin·cess [prɪn'ses] princesa *f*
prin·ci·pal ['prɪnsəpl] **1** *adj* principal **2** *n of school* director(a) *m*(*f*); *of university* rector(a) *m*(*f*)
prin·ci·pal·ly ['prɪnsəplɪ] *adv* principalmente
prin·ci·ple ['prɪnsəpl] principio *m*; ***on principle*** por principios; ***in principle*** en principio
print [prɪnt] **1** *n in book, newspaper etc* letra *f*; (*photograph*) grabado *m*; ***out of print*** agotado **2** *v/t* imprimir; *use block capitals* escribir en mayúsculas
◆ **print out** *v/t* imprimir
print·ed mat·ter ['prɪntɪd] impresos *mpl*
print·er ['prɪntər] *person* impresor(a) *m*(*f*); *machine* impresora *f*; *company* imprenta *f*
print·ing press ['prɪntɪŋpres] imprenta *f*
'**print·out** copia *f* impresa
pri·or [praɪr] **1** *adj* previo **2** *prep*: ***prior to*** antes de
pri·or·i·tize [praɪ'ɔːrətaɪz] *v/t* (*put in order of priority*) ordenar atendiendo a las prioridades; (*give priority to*) dar prioridad a
pri·or·i·ty [praɪ'ɑːrətɪ] prioridad *f*; ***have priority*** tener prioridad
pris·on ['prɪzn] prisión *f*, cárcel *f*
pris·on·er ['prɪznər] prisionero(-a) *m*(*f*); ***take s.o. prisoner*** hacer prisionero a alguien
pris·on·er of '**war** prisionero(-a) *m*(*f*) de guerra
priv·a·cy ['prɪvəsɪ] intimidad *f*
pri·vate ['praɪvət] **1** *adj* privado **2** *n* MIL soldado *m/f* raso; ***in private*** en privado

pri·vate·ly ['praɪvətlɪ] *adv* (*in private*) en privado; *with one other* a solas; (*inwardly*) para sí; ***privately owned*** en manos privadas
'pri·vate sec·tor sector *m* privado
pri·va·tize ['praɪvətaɪz] *v/t Br* privatizar
priv·i·lege ['prɪvəlɪdʒ] (*special treatment*) privilegio *m*; (*honor*) honor *m*
priv·i·leged ['prɪvəlɪdʒd] *adj* privilegiado
prize [praɪz] **1** *n* premio *m* **2** *v/t* apreciar, valorar
prize·win·ner ['praɪzwɪnər] premiado(-a) *m*(*f*)
prize·win·ning ['praɪzwɪnɪŋ] *adj* premiado
pro[1] [proʊ] *n*: ***the pros and cons*** los pros y los contras
pro[2] [proʊ] → ***professional***
pro[3] [proʊ]: ***be pro …*** (*in favor of*) estar a favor de; ***the pro Clinton Democrats*** los demócratas partidarios de Clinton
prob·a·bil·i·ty [prɑːbə'bɪlətɪ] probabilidad *f*
prob·a·ble ['prɑːbəbl] *adj* probable
prob·a·bly ['prɑːbəblɪ] *adv* probablemente
pro·ba·tion [prə'beɪʃn] *in job* período *m* de prueba; LAW libertad *f* condicional; ***be given probation*** ser puesto en libertad condicional
pro·'ba·tion of·fi·cer *oficial encargado de la vigilancia de los que están en libertad condicional*
pro·'ba·tion pe·ri·od *in job* período *m* de prueba
probe [proʊb] **1** *n* (*investigation*) investigación *f*; *scientific* sonda *f* **2** *v/t* examinar; (*investigate*) investigar
prob·lem ['prɑːbləm] problema *f*; ***no problem!*** ¡claro!
pro·ce·dure [prə'siːdʒər] procedimiento *m*
pro·ceed [prə'siːd] *v/i* (*go*: *of people*) dirigirse; *of work etc* proseguir, avanzar; ***proceed to do sth*** pasar a hacer algo
pro·ceed·ings [prə'siːdɪŋz] *npl* (*events*) actos *mpl*
pro·ceeds ['proʊsiːdz] *npl* recaudación *f*
pro·cess ['prɑːses] **1** *n* proceso *m*; ***in the process*** (*while doing it*) al hacerlo **2** *v/t food* tratar; *raw materials*, *data* procesar; *application* tramitar
pro·ces·sion [prə'seʃn] desfile *m*; *religious* procesión *f*
pro·claim [prə'kleɪm] *v/t* declarar, proclamar
prod [prɑːd] **1** *n* empujoncito *m* **2** *v/t* (*pret & pp* ***prodded***) dar un empujoncito a; *with elbow* dar un codazo a
prod·i·gy ['prɑːdɪdʒɪ]: (***infant***) ***prodigy*** niño(-a) *m*(*f*) prodigio
prod·uce[1] ['prɑːduːs] *n* productos *mpl* del campo
pro·duce[2] [prə'duːs] *v/t* producir; (*manufacture*) fabricar; (*bring out*) sacar
pro·duc·er [prə'duːsər] productor(a) *m*(*f*); (*manufacturer*) fabricante *m/f*
prod·uct ['prɑːdʌkt] producto *m*
pro·duc·tion [prə'dʌkʃn] producción *f*
pro'duc·tion ca·pac·i·ty capacidad *f* de producción
pro'duc·tion costs *npl* costos *mpl* de producción
pro·duc·tive [prə'dʌktɪv] *adj* productivo
pro·duc·tiv·i·ty [prɑːdʌk'tɪvətɪ] productividad *f*
pro·fane [prə'feɪn] *adj language* profano
pro·fess [prə'fes] *v/t* manifestar
pro·fes·sion [prə'feʃn] profesión *f*; ***what's your profession?*** ¿a qué se dedica?
pro·fes·sion·al [prə'feʃnl] **1** *adj* profesional; ***turn professional*** hacerse profesional **2** *n* profesional *m/f*
pro·fes·sion·al·ly [prə'feʃnlɪ] *adv play sport* profesionalmente; (*well*, *skillfully*) con profesionalidad
pro·fes·sor [prə'fesər] catedrático(-a) *m*(*f*)
pro·fi·cien·cy [prə'fɪʃnsɪ] competencia *f*
pro·fi·cient [prə'fɪʃnt] competente; (*skillful*) hábil
pro·file ['proʊfaɪl] *of face* perfil *m*
prof·it ['prɑːfɪt] **1** *n* beneficio *m* **2** *v/i*: ***profit by, profit from*** beneficiarse de
prof·it·a·bil·i·ty [prɑːfɪtə'bɪlətɪ] rentabilidad *f*
prof·i·ta·ble ['prɑːfɪtəbl] *adj* rentable
'prof·it mar·gin margen *m* de beneficios
pro·found [prə'faʊnd] *adj* profundo
pro·found·ly [prə'faʊndlɪ] *adv* profundamente, enormemente; *thank*, *apologize* efusivamente
prog·no·sis [prɑːg'noʊsɪs] pronóstico *m*
pro·gram, *Br* **pro·gramme** ['proʊgræm] **1** *n* programa *m* **2** *v/t* (*pret & pp* ***programmed***) COMPUT programar
pro·gram·mer ['proʊgræmər] COMPUT programador(a) *m*(*f*)
pro·gress **1** *n* ['prɑːgres] progreso *m*; ***make progress*** hacer progresos; ***in progress*** en curso **2** *v/i* [prə'gres] (*advance in time*) avanzar; (*move on*) pasar; (*make progress*) progresar; ***how is the work progressing?*** ¿cómo avanza el trabajo?
pro·gres·sive [prə'gresɪv] *adj* (*enlightened*) progresista; (*which progresses*) progresivo

pro·gres·sive·ly [prə'gresɪvlɪ] *adv* progresivamente
pro·hib·it [prə'hɪbɪt] *v/t* prohibir
pro·hi·bi·tion [proʊhɪ'bɪʃn] prohibición *f*; ***during Prohibition*** durante la ley seca
pro·hib·i·tive [prə'hɪbɪtɪv] *adj prices* prohibitivo
proj·ect¹ ['prɑːdʒekt] *n* (*plan, undertaking*) proyecto *m*; EDU trabajo *m*; *housing area* barriada *f* de viviendas sociales
pro·ject² [prə'dʒekt] **1** *v/t movie* proyectar; *figures, sales* calcular **2** *v/i* (*stick out*) sobresalir
pro·jec·tion [prə'dʒekʃn] (*forecast*) previsión *f*
pro·jec·tor [prə'dʒektər] *for slides* proyector *m*
pro·lif·ic [prə'lɪfɪk] *adj writer, artist* prolífico
pro·log, *Br* **pro·logue** ['proʊlɑːg] prólogo *m*
pro·long [prə'lɒːŋ] *v/t* prolongar
prom [prɑːm] (*school dance*) *baile de fin de curso*
prom·i·nent ['prɑːmɪnənt] *adj nose, chin* prominente; (*significant*) destacado
prom·is·cu·i·ty [prɑːmɪ'skjuːətɪ] promiscuidad *f*
pro·mis·cu·ous [prə'mɪskjʊəs] *adj* promiscuo
prom·ise ['prɑːmɪs] **1** *n* promesa *f* **2** *v/t* prometer; ***she promised to help*** prometió ayudar; ***promise sth to s.o.*** prometer algo a alguien **3** *v/i*: ***do you promise?*** ¿lo prometes?
prom·ising ['prɑːmɪsɪŋ] *adj* prometedor
pro·mote [prə'moʊt] *v/t employee* ascender; (*encourage, foster*) promover; COM promocionar
pro·mot·er [prə'moʊtər] *of sports event* promotor(a) *m*(*f*)
pro·mo·tion [prə'moʊʃn] *of employee* ascenso *m*; *of scheme, idea*, COM promoción *f*
prompt [prɑːmpt] **1** *adj* (*on time*) puntual; (*speedy*) rápido **2** *adv*: ***at two o'clock prompt*** a las dos en punto **3** *v/t* (*cause*) provocar; *actor* apuntar **4** *n* COMPUT mensaje *m*; ***go to the c prompt*** ir a c:\
prompt·ly ['prɑːmptlɪ] *adv* (*on time*) puntualmente; (*immediately*) inmediatamente
prone [proʊn] *adj*: ***be prone to*** ser propenso a
pro·noun ['proʊnaʊn] pronombre *m*
pro·nounce [prə'naʊns] *v/t word* pronunciar; (*declare*) declarar
pro·nounced [prə'naʊnst] *adj accent* marcado; *views* fuerte

pron·to ['prɑːntoʊ] *adv* F ya, en seguida
pro·nun·ci·a·tion [prənʌnsɪ'eɪʃn] pronunciación *f*
proof [pruːf] *n* prueba(s) *f*(*pl*); *of book* prueba *f*
prop [prɑːp] **1** *v/t* (*pret & pp* ***propped***) apoyar **2** *n* THEA accesorio *m*
◆ **prop up** *v/t* apoyar
prop·a·gan·da [prɑːpə'gændə] propaganda *f*
pro·pel [prə'pel] *v/t* (*pret & pp* ***propelled***) propulsar
pro·pel·lant [prə'pelənt] *in aerosol* propelente *m*
pro·pel·ler [prə'pelər] *of boat* hélice *f*
prop·er ['prɑːpər] *adj* (*real*) de verdad; (*fitting*) adecuado; ***it's not proper*** no está bien; ***put it back in its proper place*** vuelve a ponerlo en su sitio
prop·er·ly ['prɑːpərlɪ] *adv* (*correctly*) bien; (*fittingly*) adecuadamente
prop·er·ty ['prɑːpərtɪ] propiedad *f*; (*land*) propiedad(es) *f*(*pl*)
prop·er·ty de'vel·op·er promotor(a) *m*(*f*) inmobiliario(a)
proph·e·cy ['prɑːfəsɪ] profecía *f*
proph·e·sy ['prɑːfəsaɪ] *v/t* (*pret & pp* ***prophesied***) profetizar
pro·por·tion [prə'pɔːrʃn] proporción *f*; ***a large proportion of North Americans*** gran parte de los norteamericanos; ***proportions*** (*dimensions*) proporciones *fpl*
pro·por·tion·al [prə'pɔːrʃnl] *adj* proporcional
pro·por·tion·al rep·re·sen'ta·tion POL representación *f* proporcional
pro·pos·al [prə'poʊzl] (*suggestion*) propuesta *f*; *of marriage* proposición *f*
pro·pose [prə'poʊz] **1** *v/t* (*suggest*) sugerir, proponer; (*plan*) proponerse **2** *v/i* (*make offer of marriage*) pedir la mano
prop·o·si·tion [prɑːpə'zɪʃn] **1** *n* propuesta *f* **2** *v/t woman* hacer proposiciones a
pro·pri·e·tor [prə'praɪətər] propietario(-a) *m*(*f*)
pro·pri·e·tress [prə'praɪətrɪs] propietaria *f*
prose [proʊz] prosa *f*
pros·e·cute ['prɑːsɪkjuːt] *v/t* LAW procesar
pros·e·cu·tion [prɑːsɪ'kjuːʃn] LAW procesamiento *m*; *lawyers* acusación *f*; ***he's facing prosecution*** lo van a procesar
pros·e·cu·tor → ***public prosecutor*** fiscal *m/f*
pros·pect ['prɑːspekt] **1** *n* (*chance, likelihood*) probabilidad *f*; (*thought of something in the future*) perspectiva *f*; ***prospects*** perspectivas *fpl* (de futuro)

P

2 *v/i*: ***prospect for** gold* buscar
pro·spec·tive [prə'spektɪv] *adj* potencial
pros·per ['prɑːspər] *v/i* prosperar
pros·per·i·ty [prɑː'sperətɪ] prosperidad *f*
pros·per·ous ['prɑːspərəs] *adj* próspero
pros·ti·tute ['prɑːstɪtuːt] *n* prostituta *f*; ***male prostitute*** prostituto *m*
pros·ti·tu·tion [prɑːstɪ'tuːʃn] prostitución *f*
pros·trate ['prɑːstreɪt] *adj* postrado; ***be prostrate with grief*** postrado por el dolor
pro·tect [prə'tekt] *v/t* proteger
pro·tec·tion [prə'tekʃn] protección *f*
pro'tec·tion mon·ey *dinero pagado a delincuentes a cambio de obtener protección; paid to terrorists* impuesto *m* revolucionario
pro·tec·tive [prə'tektɪv] *adj* protector
pro·tec·tive 'cloth·ing ropa *f* protectora
pro·tec·tor [prə'tektər] protector(a) *m(f)*
pro·tein ['proʊtiːn] proteína *f*
pro·test 1 *n* ['proʊtest] protesta *f* **2** *v/t* [prə'test] protestar, quejarse de; (*object to*) protestar contra **3** *v/i* [prə'test] protestar
Prot·es·tant ['prɑːtɪstənt] **1** *n* protestante *m/f* **2** *adj* protestante
pro·test·er [prə'testər] manifestante *m/f*
pro·to·col ['proʊtəkɑːl] protocolo *m*
pro·to·type ['proʊtətaɪp] prototipo *m*
pro·tracted [prə'træktɪd] *adj* prolongado, largo
pro·trude [prə'truːd] *v/i* sobresalir
pro·trud·ing [prə'truːdɪŋ] *adj* saliente; *ears, teeth* prominente
proud [praʊd] *adj* orgulloso; ***be proud of*** estar orgulloso de
proud·ly ['praʊdlɪ] *adv* con orgullo, orgullosamente
prove [pruːv] *v/t* demostrar, probar
prov·erb ['prɑːvɜːrb] proverbio *m*, refrán *m*
pro·vide [prə'vaɪd] *v/t* proporcionar; ***provide sth to s.o., provide s.o. with sth*** proporcionar algo a alguien; ***provided*** (***that***) (*on condition that*) con la condición de que, siempre que
◆ **provide for** *v/t family* mantener; *of law etc* prever
prov·ince ['prɑːvɪns] provincia *f*
pro·vin·cial [prə'vɪnʃl] *adj city* provincial; *pej*: *attitude* de pueblo, provinciano
pro·vi·sion [prə'vɪʒn] (*supply*) suministro *m*; *of law, contract* disposición *f*
pro·vi·sion·al [prə'vɪʒnl] *adj* provisional
pro·vi·so [prə'vaɪzoʊ] condición *f*
prov·o·ca·tion [prɑːvə'keɪʃn] provocación *f*
pro·voc·a·tive [prə'vɑːkətɪv] *adj* provocador; *sexually* provocativo
pro·voke [prə'voʊk] *v/t* (*cause, annoy*) provocar
prow [praʊ] NAUT proa *f*
prow·ess ['praʊɪs] proezas *fpl*
prowl [praʊl] *v/i of tiger, burglar* merodear
prowl·er ['praʊlər] merodeador(a) *m(f)*
prox·im·i·ty [prɑːk'sɪmətɪ] proximidad *f*
prox·y ['prɑːksɪ] (*authority*) poder *m*; *person* apoderado(-a) *m(f)*
prude [pruːd] mojigato(-a) *m(f)*
pru·dence ['pruːdns] prudencia *f*
pru·dent ['pruːdnt] *adj* prudente
prud·ish ['pruːdɪʃ] *adj* mojigato
prune[1] [pruːn] *n* ciruela *f* pasa
prune[2] [pruːn] *v/t plant* podar; *fig* reducir
pry [praɪ] *v/i* (*pret & pp* ***pried***) entrometerse
◆ **pry into** *v/t* entrometerse en
PS ['piːes] *abbr* (= ***postscript***) PD (= posdata *f*)
pseu·do·nym ['suːdənɪm] pseudónimo *m*
psy·chi·at·ric [saɪkɪ'ætrɪk] *adj* psiquiátrico
psy·chi·a·trist [saɪ'kaɪətrɪst] psiquiatra *m/f*
psy·chi·a·try [saɪ'kaɪətrɪ] psiquiatría *f*
psy·chic ['saɪkɪk] *adj research* paranormal; ***I'm not psychic*** no soy vidente
psy·cho·a·nal·y·sis [saɪkoʊən'æləsɪs] psicoanálisis *m*
psy·cho·an·a·lyst [saɪkoʊ'ænəlɪst] psicoanalista *m/f*
psy·cho·an·a·lyze [saɪkoʊ'ænəlaɪz] *v/t* psicoanalizar
psy·cho·log·i·cal [saɪkə'lɑːdʒɪkl] *adj* psicológico
psy·cho·log·i·cal·ly [saɪkə'lɑːdʒɪklɪ] *adv* psicológicamente
psy·chol·o·gist [saɪ'kɑːlədʒɪst] psicólogo(-a) *m(f)*
psy·chol·o·gy [saɪ'kɑːlədʒɪ] psicología *f*
psy·chop·ath ['saɪkoʊpæθ] psicópata *m/f*
psy·cho·so·mat·ic [saɪkoʊsə'mætɪk] *adj* psicosomático
PTO [piːtiː'oʊ] *abbr* (= ***please turn over***) véase al dorso
pub [pʌb] *Br* bar *m*
pu·ber·ty ['pjuːbərtɪ] pubertad *f*
pu·bic hair ['pjuːbɪk] vello *m* púbico
pub·lic ['pʌblɪk] **1** *adj* público **2** *n*: ***the public*** el público; ***in public*** en público
pub·li·ca·tion [pʌblɪ'keɪʃn] publicación *f*
pub·lic 'hol·i·day día *m* festivo
pub·lic·i·ty [pʌb'lɪsətɪ] publicidad *f*
pub·li·cize ['pʌblɪsaɪz] *v/t* (*make known*) publicar, hacer público; COM dar publici-

dad a
pub·lic 'li·bra·ry biblioteca *f* pública
pub·lic·ly ['pʌblɪklɪ] *adv* públicamente
pub·lic 'pros·e·cu·tor fiscal *m/f*
pub·lic re'la·tions *npl* relaciones públicas *fpl*
'pub·lic school *Br* colegio *m* privado, *Am* colegio *m* público
'pub·lic sec·tor sector *m* público
pub·lish ['pʌblɪʃ] *v/t* publicar
pub·lish·er ['pʌblɪʃər] *person* editor(a) *m(f)*; *company* editorial *f*
pub·lish·ing ['pʌblɪʃɪŋ] industria *f* editorial
'pub·lish·ing com·pa·ny editorial *f*
pud·ding ['pʊdɪŋ] *Br dish* pudín *m*; *part of meal* postre *m*
pud·dle ['pʌdl] charco *m*
Puer·to Ri·can [pwertoʊ'ri:kən] **1** *adj* portorriqueño, puertorriqueño **2** *n* portorriqueño(-a) *m(f)*, puertorriqueño(-a) *m(f)*
Puer·to Ri·co [pwertoʊ'ri:koʊ] *n* Puerto Rico
puff [pʌf] **1** *n of wind* racha *f*; *from cigarette* calada *f*; *of smoke* bocanada *f* **2** *v/i* (*pant*) resoplar; ***puff on a cigarette*** dar una calada a un cigarrillo
puff·y ['pʌfɪ] *adj eyes, face* hinchado
puke [pju:k] **1** *n* P *substance* vomitona *f* P **2** *v/i* P echar la pota P
pull [pʊl] **1** *n on rope* tirón *m*; F (*appeal*) gancho *m* F; F (*influence*) enchufe *m* F **2** *v/t* (*drag*) arrastrar; (*tug*) tirar de; *tooth* sacar; ***pull a muscle*** sufrir un tirón en un músculo **3** *v/i* tirar
◆ **pull ahead** *v/i in race, competition* adelantarse
◆ **pull apart** *v/t* (*separate*) separar
◆ **pull away** *v/t* apartar
◆ **pull down** *v/t* (*lower*) bajar; (*demolish*) derribar
◆ **pull in** *v/i of bus, train* llegar
◆ **pull off** *v/t* quitar; *item of clothing* quitarse; F conseguir
◆ **pull out 1** *v/t* sacar; *troops* retirar; **2** *v/i of an agreement, of troops* retirarse; *of ship* salir
◆ **pull over** *v/i* parar en el arcén
◆ **pull through** *v/i from an illness* recuperarse
◆ **pull together 1** *v/i* (*cooperate*) cooperar **2** *v/t*: ***pull o.s. together*** tranquilizarse
◆ **pull up 1** *v/t* (*raise*) subir; *item of clothing* subirse; *plant, weeds* arrancar **2** *v/i of car etc* parar
pul·ley ['pʊlɪ] polea *f*
pull·o·ver ['pʊloʊvər] suéter *m*, *Span* jersey *m*
pulp [pʌlp] *of fruit* pulpa *f*; *for paper-making* pasta *f*
pul·pit ['pʊlpɪt] púlpito *m*
pul·sate [pʌl'seɪt] *v/i of heart, blood* palpitar; *of music* vibrar
pulse [pʌls] pulso *m*
pul·ver·ize ['pʌlvəraɪz] *v/t* pulverizar
pump [pʌmp] **1** *n* bomba *f*; (*gas pump*) surtidor *m* **2** *v/t* bombear
◆ **pump up** *v/t* inflar
pump·kin ['pʌmpkɪn] calabaza *f*
pun [pʌn] juego *m* de palabras
punch [pʌntʃ] **1** *n* (*blow*) puñetazo *m*; *implement* perforadora *f* **2** *v/t with fist* dar un puñetazo a; *hole, ticket* agujerear
'punch line *última frase de un chiste*
punc·tu·al ['pʌŋktʃʊəl] *adj* puntual
punc·tu·al·i·ty [pʌŋktʃʊ'ælətɪ] puntualidad *f*
punc·tu·al·ly ['pʌŋktʃʊəlɪ] *adv* puntualmente
punc·tu·ate ['pʌŋktʃʊəɪt] *v/t* puntuar
punc·tu·a·tion ['pʌŋktʃʊ'eɪʃn] puntuación *f*
punc·tu'a·tion mark signo *m* de puntuación
punc·ture ['pʌŋktʃər] **1** *n* perforación *f* **2** *v/t* perforar
pun·gent ['pʌndʒənt] *adj* fuerte
pun·ish ['pʌnɪʃ] *v/t person* castigar
pun·ish·ing ['pʌnɪʃɪŋ] *adj schedule* exigente; *pace* fuerte
pun·ish·ment ['pʌnɪʃmənt] castigo *m*
punk (rock) ['pʌŋk(rɑ:k)] MUS (música *f*) punk *m*
pu·ny ['pju:nɪ] *adj person* enclenque
pup [pʌp] cachorro *m*
pu·pil[1] ['pju:pl] *of eye* pupila *f*
pu·pil[2] ['pju:pl] (*student*) alumno(-a) *m(f)*
pup·pet ['pʌpɪt] *also fig* marioneta *f*
'pup·pet gov·ern·ment gobierno *m* títere
pup·py ['pʌpɪ] cachorro *m*
pur·chase[1] ['pɜ:rtʃəs] **1** *n* adquisición *f*, compra *f* **2** *v/t* adquirir, comprar
pur·chase[2] ['pɜ:rtʃəs] (*grip*) agarre *m*
pur·chas·er ['pɜ:rtʃəsər] comprador(a) *m(f)*
pure [pjʊr] *adj* puro; ***pure new wool*** pura lana *f* virgen
pure·ly ['pjʊrlɪ] *adv* puramente
pur·ga·to·ry ['pɜ:rgətɔ:rɪ] purgatorio *m*
purge [pɜ:rdʒ] **1** *n of political party* purga *f* **2** *v/t* purgar *f*
pu·ri·fy ['pjʊrɪfaɪ] *v/t* (*pret & pp* ***purified***) *water* depurar
pu·ri·tan ['pjʊrɪtən] puritano(-a) *m(f)*
pu·ri·tan·i·cal [pjʊrɪ'tænɪkl] *adj* puritano
pu·ri·ty ['pjʊrɪtɪ] pureza *f*

P

pur·ple ['pɜːrpl] *adj* morado
Pur·ple 'Heart MIL *medalla concedida a los soldados heridos en combate*
pur·pose ['pɜːrpəs] (*aim, object*) propósito *m*, objeto *m*; ***on purpose*** a propósito; ***what is the purpose of your visit?*** ¿cuál es el objeto de su visita?
pur·pose·ful ['pɜːrpəsfəl] *adj* decidido
pur·pose·ly ['pɜːrpəslɪ] *adv* decididamente
purr [pɜːr] *v/i of cat* ronronear
purse [pɜːrs] *n* (*pocket book*) bolso *m*; *Br*: *for money* monedero *m*
pur·sue [pər'suː] *v/t person* perseguir; *career* ejercer; *course of action* proseguir
pur·su·er [pər'suːər] perseguidor(a) *m*(*f*)
pur·suit [pər'suːt] (*chase*) persecución *f*; *of happiness etc* búsqueda *f*; (*activity*) actividad *f*; ***those in pursuit*** los perseguidores
pus [pʌs] pus *m*
push [pʊʃ] **1** *n* (*shove*) empujón *m*; ***at the push of a button*** apretando un botón **2** *v/t* (*shove*) empujar; *button* apretar, pulsar; (*pressurize*) presionar; F *drugs* pasar F, mercadear con; ***be pushed for cash*** F estar pelado F, estar sin un centavo; ***be pushed for time*** F ir mal de tiempo F; ***be pushing 40*** F rondar los 40 **3** *v/i* empujar
◆ **push ahead** *v/i* seguir adelante
◆ **push along** *v/t cart etc* empujar
◆ **push away** *v/t* apartar
◆ **push off 1** *v/t lid* destapar; **2** *v/i Br* F (*leave*) largarse F
◆ **push on** *v/i* (*continue*) continuar
◆ **push up** *v/t prices* hacer subir
push·er ['pʊʃər] F *of drugs* camello *m* F
push-up ['pʊʃʌp] flexión *f* (de brazos)
push·y ['pʊʃɪ] *adj* F avasallador, agresivo
puss, pus·sy (cat) [pʊs, 'pʊsɪ (kæt)] F minino *m* F
◆ **pussy foot about** ['pʊsɪfʊt] *v/i* F andarse con rodeos
put [pʊt] *v/t* (*pret & pp* ***put***) poner; *question* hacer; ***put the cost at …*** estimar el costo en …
◆ **put across** *v/t idea etc* hacer llegar
◆ **put aside** *v/t money* apartar, ahorrar; *work* dejar a un lado
◆ **put away** *v/t in closet etc* guardar; *in institution* encerrar; F (*consume*) consumir, cepillarse F; *money* apartar, ahorrar; *animal* sacrificar
◆ **put back** *v/t* (*replace*) volver a poner
◆ **put by** *v/t money* apartar, ahorrar
◆ **put down** *v/t* dejar; *deposit* entregar; *rebellion* reprimir; (*belittle*) dejar en mal lugar; ***put down in writing*** poner por escrito; ***put one's foot down*** *in car* apretar el acelerador; (*be firm*) plantarse; ***put sth down to sth*** (*attribute*) atribuir algo a algo
◆ **put forward** *v/t idea etc* proponer, presentar
◆ **put in** *v/t* meter; *time* dedicar; *request, claim* presentar
◆ **put in for** *v/t* (*apply for*) solicitar
◆ **put off** *v/t light, radio*, TV apagar; (*postpone*) posponer, aplazar; (*deter*) desalentar; (*repel*) desagradar; ***I was put off by the smell*** el olor me quitó las ganas; ***that put me off shellfish for life*** me quitó las ganas de volver a comer marisco
◆ **put on** *v/t light, radio*, TV encender, *L.Am.* prender; *tape, music* poner; *jacket, shoes, eye glasses* ponerse; (*perform*) representar; (*assume*) fingir; ***put on make-up*** maquillarse; ***put on the brake*** frenar; ***put on weight*** engordar; ***she's just putting it on*** está fingiendo
◆ **put out** *v/t hand* extender; *fire, light* apagar
◆ **put through** *v/t*: ***put s.o. through to s.o.*** *on phone* poner a alguien con alguien
◆ **put together** *v/t* (*assemble, organize*) montar
◆ **put up** *v/t hand* levantar; *person* alojar; (*erect*) levantar; *prices* subir; *poster, notice* colocar; *money* aportar; ***put your hands up!*** ¡arriba las manos!; ***put up for sale*** poner en venta
◆ **put up with** *v/t* (*tolerate*) aguantar
putt [pʌt] *v/i* SP golpear con el putter
put·ty ['pʌtɪ] masilla *f*
puz·zle ['pʌzl] **1** *n* (*mystery*) enigma *m*; *game* pasatiempos *mpl*; (*jigsaw puzzle*) puzzle *m*; (*crossword puzzle*) crucigrama *m* **2** *v/t* desconcertar; ***one thing puzzles me*** hay algo que no acabo de entender
puz·zling ['pʌzlɪŋ] *adj* desconcertante
PVC [piːviː'siː] *abbr* (= ***polyvinyl chloride***) PVC *m* (= cloruro *m* de polivinilo)
py·ja·mas *Br* → ***pajamas***
py·lon ['paɪlən] torre *f* de alta tensión

P

Q

quack[1] [kwæk] **1** *n of duck* graznido *m* **2** *v/i* graznar
quack[2] [kwæk] *n* F (*bad doctor*) matasanos *m/f inv* F
quad·ran·gle ['kwɑːdræŋgl] *figure* cuadrángulo *m*; *courtyard* patio *m*
quad·ru·ped ['kwɑːdrʊped] cuadrúpedo *m*
quad·ru·ple ['kwɑːdrʊpl] *v/i* cuadruplicarse
quad·ru·plets ['kwɑːdrʊplɪts] *npl* cuatrillizos(-as) *mpl* (*fpl*)
quads [kwɑːdz] *npl* F cuatrillizos(-as) *mpl f*(*fpl*)
quag·mire ['kwɑːgmaɪr] *fig* atolladero *m*
quail [kweɪl] *v/i* temblar (***at*** ante)
quaint [kweɪnt] *adj cottage* pintoresco; (*slightly eccentric*: *ideas etc*) extraño
quake [kweɪk] **1** *n* (*earthquake*) terremoto *m* **2** *v/i of earth*, *with fear* temblar
qual·i·fi·ca·tion [kwɑːlɪfɪ'keɪʃn] *from university etc* título *m*; ***have the right qualifications for a job*** estar bien cualificado para un trabajo
qual·i·fied ['kwɑːlɪfaɪd] *adj doctor*, *engineer*, *plumber etc* titulado; (*restricted*) limitado; ***I am not qualified to judge*** no estoy en condiciones de poder juzgar
qual·i·fy ['kwɑːlɪfaɪ] **1** *v/t* (*pret & pp* ***qualified***) *of degree*, *course etc* habilitar; *remark etc* matizar **2** *v/i* (*pret & pp* ***qualified***) (*get degree etc*) titularse, *L.Am.* egresar; *in competition* calificarse; ***they qualified for the final*** se clasificaron para la final; ***that doesn't qualify as …*** eso no cuenta como …
qual·i·ty ['kwɑːlətɪ] calidad *f*; (*characteristic*) cualidad *f*
qual·i·ty con'trol control *m* de calidad
qualm [kwɑːm]: ***have no qualms about …*** no tener reparos en …
quan·da·ry ['kwɑːndərɪ] dilema *m*
quan·ti·fy ['kwɑːntɪfaɪ] *v/t* (*pret & pp* ***quantified***) cuantificar
quan·ti·ty ['kwɑːntətɪ] cantidad *f*
quan·tum 'phys·ics ['kwɑːntəm] física *f* cuántica
quar·an·tine ['kwɑːrəntiːn] cuarentena *f*
quar·rel ['kwɑːrəl] **1** *n* pelea *f* **2** *v/i* (*pret & pp* ***quarreled***, *Br* ***quarrelled***) pelearse
quar·rel·some ['kwɑːrəlsʌm] *adj* peleón
quar·ry[1] ['kwɑːrɪ] *in hunt* presa *f*
quar·ry[2] ['kwɑːrɪ] *for mining* cantera *f*
quart [kwɔːrt] cuarto *m* de galón
quar·ter ['kwɔːrtər] cuarto *m*; *25 cents* cuarto *m* de dólar; *part of town* barrio *m*; ***a quarter of an hour*** un cuarto de hora; ***a quarter of 5*** las cinco menos cuarto; ***a quarter after 5*** las cinco y cuarto
'quar·ter·back SP quarterback *m*, *en fútbol americano*, *jugador que dirige el juego de ataque*
quar·ter-'fi·nal cuarto *m* de final
quar·ter-'fi·nal·ist cuartofinalista *m/f*
quar·ter·ly ['kwɔːrtəlɪ] **1** *adj* trimestral **2** *adv* trimestralmente
'quar·ter·note MUS negra *f*
quar·ters ['kwɔːrtəz] *npl* MIL alojamiento *m*
quar·tet [kwɔːr'tet] MUS cuarteto *m*
quartz [kwɔːrts] cuarzo *m*
quash [kwɑːʃ] *v/t rebellion* aplastar, sofocar; *court decision* revocar
qua·ver ['kweɪvər] **1** *n in voice* temblor *m* **2** *v/i of voice* temblar
quay [kiː] muelle *m*
'quay·side muelle *m*
quea·sy ['kwiːzɪ] *adj* mareado; ***get queasy*** marearse
queen [kwiːn] reina *f*
queen 'bee abeja *f* reina
queer [kwɪr] *adj* (*peculiar*) raro, extraño
queer·ly ['kwɪrlɪ] *adv* de manera extraña
quell [kwel] *v/t protest*, *crowd* acallar; *riot* aplastar, sofocar
quench [kwentʃ] *v/t thirst* apagar, saciar; *flames* apagar
que·ry ['kwɪrɪ] **1** *n* duda *f*, pregunta *f* **2** *v/t* (*pret & pp* ***queried***) (*express doubt about*) cuestionar; (*check*) comprobar; ***query sth with s.o.*** preguntar algo a alguien
quest [kwest] busca *f*
ques·tion ['kwestʃn] **1** *n* pregunta *f*; (*matter*) cuestión *f*, asunto *m*; ***in question*** (*being talked about*) en cuestión; (*in doubt*) en duda; ***it's a question of money / time*** es una cuestión de dinero / tiempo; ***that's out of the question*** eso es imposible **2** *v/t person* preguntar a; LAW interrogar; (*doubt*) cuestionar, poner en duda
ques·tion·a·ble ['kwestʃnəbl] *adj* cuestionable, dudoso
ques·tion·ing ['kwestʃnɪŋ] **1** *adj look*, *tone* inquisitivo **2** *n* interrogatorio *m*
'ques·tion mark signo *m* de interrogación

ques·tion·naire [kwestʃə'ner] cuestionario *m*
queue [kjuː] *n Br* cola *f*
quib·ble ['kwɪbl] *v/i* discutir (*por algo insignificante*)
quick [kwɪk] *adj* rápido; ***be quick!*** ¡date prisa!; ***let's have a quick drink*** vamos a tomarnos algo rápidamente; ***can I have a quick look?*** ¿me dejas echarle un vistazo?; ***that was quick!*** ¡qué rápido!
quick·ie ['kwɪkɪ]: ***have a quickie*** F (*quick drink*) tomarse una copa rápida
quick·ly ['kwɪklɪ] *adv* rápidamente, rápido, deprisa
'**quick·sand** arenas *fpl* movedizas
'**quick·sil·ver** azogue *m*
quick·wit·ted [kwɪk'wɪtɪd] *adj* agudo
qui·et ['kwaɪət] *adj* tranquilo; *engine* silencioso; ***keep quiet about sth*** guardar silencio sobre algo; ***quiet!*** ¡silencio!
◆ **qui·et·en down** ['kwaɪətn] **1** *v/t children, class* tranquilizar, hacer callar **2** *v/i of children* tranquilizarse, callarse; *of political situation* calmarse
quiet·ly ['kwaɪətlɪ] *adv* (*not loudly*) silenciosamente; (*without fuss*) discretamente; (*peacefully*) tranquilamente; ***speak quietly*** hablar en voz baja
quiet·ness ['kwaɪətnɪs] *n of voice* suavidad *f*; *of night*, *street* silencio *m*, calma *f*
quilt [kwɪlt] *on bed* edredón *m*
quilt·ed ['kwɪltɪd] *adj* acolchado
quin·ine ['kwɪniːn] quinina *f*
quin·tet [kwɪn'tet] MUS quinteto *m*
quip [kwɪp] **1** *n joke* broma *f*; *remark* salida *f* **2** *v/i* (*pret & pp* ***quipped***) bromear
quirk [kwɜːrk] peculiaridad *f*, rareza *f*
quirk·y ['kwɜːrkɪ] *adj* peculiar, raro
quit [kwɪt] **1** *v/t* (*pret & pp* ***quit***) *job* dejar, abandonar; ***quit doing sth*** dejar de hacer algo **2** *v/i* (*pret & pp* ***quit***) (*leave job*) dimitir; COMPUT salir; ***get one's notice to quit*** *from landlord* recibir la notificación de desalojo
quite [kwaɪt] *adv* (*fairly*) bastante; (*completely*) completamente; ***not quite ready*** no listo del todo; ***I didn't quite understand*** no entendí bien; ***is that right? - not quite*** ¿es verdad? - no exactamente; ***quite!*** ¡exactamente!; ***quite a lot*** bastante; ***quite a few*** bastantes; ***it was quite a surprise / change*** fue toda una sorpresa / un cambio
quits [kwɪts] *adj*: ***be quits with s.o.*** estar en paz con alguien
quit·ter ['kwɪtər] F *persona que abandona fácilmente*
quiv·er ['kwɪvər] *v/i* estremecerse
quiz [kwɪz] **1** *n* concurso *m* (*de preguntas y respuestas*) **2** *v/t* (*pret & pp* ***quizzed***) interrogar (***about*** sobre)
'**quiz mas·ter** *presentador de un concurso de preguntas y respuestas*
'**quiz pro·gram**, *Br* '**quiz pro·gramme** programa *m* concurso (*de preguntas y respuestas*)
quo·ta ['kwoʊtə] cuota *f*
quo·ta·tion [kwoʊ'teɪʃn] *from author* cita *f*; (*price*) presupuesto *m*
quo'ta·tion marks *npl* comillas *fpl*
quote [kwoʊt] **1** *n from author* cita *f*; (*price*) presupuesto *m*; (*quotation mark*) comilla *f*; ***in quotes*** entre comillas **2** *v/t text* citar; *price* dar **3** *v/i*: ***quote from an author*** citar de un autor

R

rab·bi ['ræbaɪ] rabino *m*
rab·bit ['ræbɪt] conejo *m*
rab·ble ['ræbl] chusma *f*, multitud *f*
rab·ble-rous·er ['ræblraʊzər] agitador(a) *m*(*f*)
ra·bies ['reɪbiːz] *nsg* rabia *f*
rac·coon [rə'kuːn] mapache *m*
race[1] [reɪs] *n of people* raza *f*
race[2] [reɪs] **1** *n* SP carrera *f*; ***the races*** *horse races* las carreras **2** *v/i* (*run fast*) correr; ***he raced through his meal / work*** acabó su comida / trabajo a toda velocidad **3** *v/t* correr contra; ***I'll race you*** te echo una carrera
'**race·course** hipódromo *m*
'**race·horse** caballo *m* de carreras
'**race riot** disturbios *mpl* raciales
'**race·track** circuito *m*; *for horses* hipódromo *m*
ra·cial ['reɪʃl] *adj* racial; ***racial equality*** igualdad *f* racial
rac·ing ['reɪsɪŋ] carreras *fpl*

rac·ism ['reɪsɪzm] racismo *m*
ra·cist ['reɪsɪst] **1** *n* racista *m/f* **2** *adj* racista
rack [ræk] **1** *n* (*for bikes*) *barras para aparcar bicicletas*; *for bags on train* portaequipajes *m inv*; *for CDs* mueble *m* **2** *v/t*: ***rack one's brains*** devanarse los sesos
rack·et¹ ['rækɪt] SP raqueta *f*
rack·et² ['rækɪt] (*noise*) jaleo *m*; (*criminal activity*) negocio *m* sucio
ra·dar ['reɪdɑːr] radar *m*
'ra·dar screen pantalla *f* de radar
'ra·dar trap control *m* de velocidad por radar
ra·di·al 'tire, *Br* **ra·di·al 'tyre** ['reɪdɪəl] neumático *m* radial
ra·di·ance ['reɪdɪəns] esplendor *m*, brillantez *f*
ra·di·ant ['reɪdɪənt] *adj smile*, *appearance* resplandeciente, brillante
ra·di·ate ['reɪdɪeɪt] *v/i of heat*, *light* irradiar
ra·di·a·tion [reɪdɪ'eɪʃn] PHYS radiación *f*
ra·di·a·tor ['reɪdɪeɪtər] *in room*, *car* radiador *m*
rad·i·cal ['rædɪkl] **1** *adj* radical **2** *n* POL radical *m/f*
rad·i·cal·ism ['rædɪkəlɪzm] POL radicalismo *m*
rad·i·cal·ly ['rædɪklɪ] *adv* radicalmente
ra·di·o ['reɪdɪoʊ] radio *f*; ***on the radio*** en la radio; ***by radio*** por radio
ra·di·o·ac·tive [reɪdɪoʊ'æktɪv] *adj* radiactivo
ra·di·o·ac·tive 'waste residuos *mpl* radiactivos
ra·di·o·ac·tiv·i·ty [reɪdɪoʊæk'tɪvətɪ] radiactividad *f*
ra·di·o a'larm radio *f* despertador
ra·di·og·ra·pher [reɪdɪ'ɑːgrəfər] técnico(-a) *m*(*f*) de rayos X
ra·di·og·ra·phy [reɪdɪ'ɑːgrəfɪ] radiografía *f*
'ra·di·o sta·tion emisora *f* de radio
'ra·di·o tax·i radiotaxi *m*
ra·di·o'ther·a·py radioterapia *f*
rad·ish ['rædɪʃ] rábano *m*
ra·di·us ['reɪdɪəs] radio *m*
raf·fle ['ræfl] *n* rifa *f*
raft [ræft] balsa *f*
raf·ter ['ræftər] viga *f*
rag [ræg] *n for cleaning etc* trapo *m*; ***in rags*** con harapos
rage [reɪdʒ] **1** *n* ira *f*, cólera *f*; ***be in a rage*** estar encolerizado; ***be all the rage*** F estar arrasando F **2** *v/i of storm* bramar
rag·ged ['rægɪd] *adj* andrajoso
raid [reɪd] **1** *n by troops* incursión *f*; *by police* redada *f*; *by robbers* atraco *m*; FIN ataque *m*, incursión *f* **2** *v/t of troops* realizar una incursión en; *of police* realizar una redada en; *of robbers* atracar; *fridge*, *orchard* saquear
raid·er ['reɪdər] *on bank etc* atracador(a) *m*(*f*)
rail [reɪl] *n on track* riel *m*, carril *m*; (*handrail*) pasamanos *m inv*, baranda *f*; *for towel* barra *f*; ***by rail*** en tren
rail·ings ['reɪlɪŋz] *npl around park etc* verja *f*
rail·road ['reɪlroʊd] ferrocarril *m*
'rail·road sta·tion estación *f* de ferrocarril *or* de tren
rail·way ['reɪlweɪ] *Br* ferrocarril *m*
rain [reɪn] **1** *n* lluvia *f*; ***in the rain*** bajo la lluvia **2** *v/i* llover; ***it's raining*** llueve
'rain·bow arco *m* iris
'rain·check: ***can I take a raincheck on that?*** F ¿lo podríamos aplazar para algún otro momento?
'rain·coat impermeable *m*
'rain·drop gota *f* de lluvia
'rain·fall pluviosidad *f*, precipitaciones *fpl*
'rain for·est selva *f*
'rain·proof *adj fabric* impermeable
'rain·storm tormenta *f*, aguacero *m*
rain·y ['reɪnɪ] *adj* lluvioso; ***it's rainy*** llueve mucho
'rain·y sea·son estación *f* de las lluvias
raise [reɪz] **1** *n in salary* aumento *m* de sueldo **2** *v/t shelf etc* levantar; *offer* incrementar; *children* criar; *question* plantear; *money* reunir
rai·sin ['reɪzn] pasa *f*
rake [reɪk] *n for garden* rastrillo *m*
◆ **rake up** *v/t leaves* rastrillar; *fig* sacar a la luz
ral·ly ['rælɪ] *n* (*meeting*, *reunion*) concentración *f*; *political* mitin *m*; MOT rally *m*; *in tennis* peloteo *m*
◆ **rally round** **1** *v/i* (*pret & pp* ***rallied***) acudir a ayudar **2** *v/t* (*pret & pp* ***rallied***): ***rally round s.o.*** acudir a ayudar a alguien
ram [ræm] **1** *n* carnero *m* **2** *v/t* (*pret & pp* ***rammed***) *ship*, *car* embestir
RAM [ræm] COMPUT *abbr* (= ***random access memory***) RAM *f* (= memoria *f* de acceso aleatorio)
ram·ble ['ræmbl] **1** *n walk* caminata *f*, excursión *f* **2** *v/i walk* caminar; *in speaking* divagar; (*talk incoherently*) hablar sin decir nada coherente
ram·bler ['ræmblər] *walker* senderista *m/f*, excursionista *m/f*
ram·bling ['ræmblɪŋ] **1** *n walking* senderismo *m*; *in speech* divagaciones *fpl* **2** *adj speech* inconexo

ramp [ræmp] rampa *f*; *for raising vehicle* elevador *m*
ram·page ['ræmpeɪdʒ] **1** *v/i* pasar arrasando con todo **2** *n*: ***go on the rampage*** pasar arrasando con todo
ram·pant ['ræmpənt] *adj inflation* galopante
ram·part ['ræmpɑːrt] muralla *f*
ram·shack·le ['ræmʃækl] *adj* destartalado, desvencijado
ran [ræn] *pret* → ***run***
ranch [ræntʃ] rancho *m*
ranch·er ['ræntʃər] ranchero(-a) *m(f)*
ran·cid ['rænsɪd] *adj* rancio
ran·cor ['ræŋkər] rencor
R & D [ɑːrən'diː] *abbr* (= ***research and development***) I+D *f* (= investigación *f* y desarrollo)
ran·dom ['rændəm] **1** *adj* al azar; ***random sample*** muestra *f* aleatoria **2** *n*: ***at random*** al azar
ran·dy ['rændɪ] *adj Br* F cachondo F; ***it makes me randy*** me pone cachondo
rang [ræŋ] *pret* → ***ring***[2]
range [reɪndʒ] **1** *n of products* gama *f*; *of gun, airplane* alcance *m*; *of voice* registro *m*; *of mountains* cordillera *f*; ***at close range*** de cerca **2** *v/i*: ***range from X to Y*** ir desde X a Y
rang·er ['reɪndʒər] guardabosques *m/f inv*
rank [ræŋk] **1** *n* MIL, *in society* rango *m*; ***the ranks*** MIL la tropa **2** *v/t* clasificar
◆ **rank among** *v/t* figurar entre
ran·kle ['ræŋkl] *v/i* doler; ***it still rankles*** (***with him***) todavía le duele
ran·sack ['rænsæk] *v/t* saquear
ran·som ['rænsəm] *n* rescate *m*; ***hold s.o. to ransom*** pedir un rescate por alguien
'**ran·som mon·ey** (dinero *m* del) rescate *m*
rant [rænt] *v/i*: ***rant and rave*** despotricar
rap [ræp] **1** *n at door etc* golpe *m*; MUS rap *m* **2** *v/t* (*pret & pp* ***rapped***) *table etc* golpear
◆ **rap at** *v/t window etc* golpear
rape[1] [reɪp] **1** *n* violación *f* **2** *v/t* violar
rape[2] [reɪp] *n* BOT colza *f*
'**rape vic·tim** víctima *m/f* de una violación
rap·id ['ræpɪd] *adj* rápido
ra·pid·i·ty [rə'pɪdətɪ] rapidez *f*
rap·id·ly ['ræpɪdlɪ] *adv* rápidamente
rap·ids ['ræpɪdz] *npl* rápidos *mpl*
rap·ist ['reɪpɪst] violador(a) *m(f)*
rap·port [ræ'pɔːr] relación *f*; ***we've got a good rapport*** nos entendemos muy bien
rap·ture ['ræptʃər]: ***go into raptures over*** extasiarse con
rap·tur·ous ['ræptʃərəs] *adj* clamoroso
rare [rer] *adj* raro; *steak* poco hecho
rare·ly ['rerlɪ] *adv* raramente, raras veces
rar·i·ty ['rerətɪ] rareza *f*
ras·cal ['ræskl] pícaro(-a) *m(f)*
rash[1] [ræʃ] *n* MED sarpullido *m*, erupción *f* cutánea
rash[2] [ræʃ] *adj action, behavior* precipitado
rash·ly ['ræʃlɪ] *adv* precipitadamente
rasp·ber·ry ['ræzberɪ] frambuesa *f*
rat [ræt] *n* rata *f*
rate [reɪt] **1** *n of exchange* tipo *m*; *of pay* tarifa *f*; (*price*) tarifa *f*, precio *m*; (*speed*) ritmo *m*; ***rate of interest*** FIN tipo *m* de interés; ***at this rate*** (*at this speed*) a este ritmo; (*if we carry on like this*) si seguimos así; ***at any rate*** (*anyway*) en todo caso; (*at least*) por lo menos **2** *v/t*: ***rate s.o. as …*** considerar a alguien (como) …; ***rate s.o. highly*** tener buena opinión de alguien
rather ['ræðər] *adv* bastante; ***I would rather stay here*** preferiría quedarme aquí; ***or would you rather …?*** ¿o preferiría …?
rat·i·fi·ca·tion [rætɪfɪ'keɪʃn] ratificación *f*
rat·i·fy ['rætɪfaɪ] *v/t* (*pret & pp* ***ratified***) ratificar
rat·ings ['reɪtɪŋz] *npl* índice *m* de audiencia
ra·ti·o ['reɪʃɪoʊ] proporción *f*
ra·tion ['ræʃn] **1** *n* ración *f* **2** *v/t supplies* racionar
ra·tion·al ['ræʃənl] *adj* racional
ra·tion·al·i·ty [ræʃə'nælɪtɪ] racionalidad *f*
ra·tion·al·i·za·tion [ræʃənəlaɪ'zeɪʃn] racionalización *f*
ra·tion·al·ize ['ræʃənəlaɪz] **1** *v/t* racionalizar **2** *v/i* buscar una explicación racional
ra·tion·al·ly ['ræʃənlɪ] *adv* racionalmente
'**rat race** *la vida frenética y competitiva*
rat·tle ['rætl] **1** *n noise* traqueteo *m*, golpeteo *m*; *toy* sonajero *m* **2** *v/t chains etc* entrechocar **3** *v/i of chains etc* entrechocarse; *of crates* traquetear
◆ **rattle off** *v/t poem, list of names* decir rápidamente
◆ **rattle through** *v/t* hacer rápidamente
'**rat·tle·snake** serpiente *f* de cascabel
rau·cous ['rɒːkəs] *adj laughter, party* estridente
rav·age ['rævɪdʒ] **1** *n*: ***the ravages of time*** los estragos del tiempo **2** *v/t* arrasar; ***ravaged by war*** arrasado por la guerra
rave [reɪv] **1** *v/i* (*talk deliriously*) delirar; (*talk wildly*) desvariar; ***rave about sth*** (*be very enthusiastic*) estar muy entusiasmado con algo **2** *n party* fiesta *f* tecno
rave re'view crítica *f* muy entusiasta
ra·ven ['reɪvn] cuervo *m*

R

rav·e·nous ['rævənəs] *adj appetite* voraz; ***have a ravenous appetite*** tener un hambre canina
rav·e·nous·ly ['rævənəslɪ] *adv* con voracidad
ra·vine [rə'viːn] barranco *m*
rav·ing ['reɪvɪŋ] *adv*: ***raving mad*** chalado
rav·ish·ing ['rævɪʃɪŋ] *adj* encantador, cautivador
raw [rɒː] *adj meat, vegetable* crudo; *sugar* sin refinar; *iron* sin tratar
raw ma'te·ri·als *npl* materias *fpl* primas
ray [reɪ] rayo *m*; ***a ray of hope*** un rayo de esperanza
raze [reɪz] *v/t*: ***raze to the ground*** arrasar *or* asolar por completo
ra·zor ['reɪzər] maquinilla *f* de afeitar
'ra·zor blade cuchilla *f* de afeitar
re [riː] *prep* COM con referencia a
reach [riːʧ] **1** *n*: ***within reach*** al alcance; ***out of reach*** fuera del alcance **2** *v/t* llegar a; *decision, agreement, conclusion* alcanzar, llegar a; ***can you reach it?*** ¿alcanzas?, ¿llegas?
◆ **reach out** *v/i* extender el brazo
re·act [rɪ'ækt] *v/i* reaccionar
re·ac·tion [rɪ'ækʃn] reacción *f*
re·ac·tion·ar·y [rɪ'ækʃnrɪ] **1** *n* POL reaccionario(-a) *m(f)* **2** *adj* POL reaccionario
re·ac·tor [rɪ'æktər] *nuclear* reactor *m*
read [riːd] **1** *v/t* (*pret & pp* ***read*** [red]) *also* COMPUT leer **2** *v/i* (*pret & pp* ***read*** [red]) leer; ***read to s.o.*** leer a alguien
◆ **read out** *v/t aloud* leer en voz alta
◆ **read up on** *v/t* leer mucho sobre, estudiar
rea·da·ble ['riːdəbl] *adj handwriting* legible; *book* ameno
read·er ['riːdər] *person* lector(a) *m(f)*
read·i·ly ['redɪlɪ] *adv admit, agree* de buena gana
read·i·ness ['redɪnɪs]: ***in a state of readiness*** preparado par actuar; ***their readiness to help*** la facilidad con la que ayudaron
read·ing ['riːdɪŋ] *activity* lectura *f*; ***take a reading from the meter*** leer el contador
'read·ing mat·ter lectura *f*
re·ad·just [riːə'dʒʌst] **1** *v/t equipment, controls* reajustar **2** *v/i to conditions* volver a adaptarse
read-'on·ly file COMPUT archivo *m* sólo de lectura
read-'on·ly mem·o·ry COMPUT memoria *f* sólo de lectura
read·y ['redɪ] *adj* (*prepared*) listo, preparado; (*willing*) dispuesto; ***get*** (***o.s.***) ***ready*** prepararse; ***get sth ready*** preparar algo
read·y 'cash dinero *m* contante y sonante
read·y-made *adj stew etc* precocinado; *solution* ya hecho
read·y-to-wear *adj* de confección
real [riːl] *adj* real; *surprise, genius* auténtico; ***he's a real idiot*** es un auténtico idiota
'real es·tate bienes *mpl* inmuebles
'real es·tate a·gent agente *m/f* inmobiliario(-a)
re·al·ism ['rɪəlɪzəm] realismo *m*
re·a·list ['rɪəlɪst] realista *m/f*
re·a·lis·tic [rɪə'lɪstɪk] *adj* realista
re·a·lis·tic·al·ly [rɪə'lɪstɪklɪ] *adv* realísticamente
re·al·i·ty [rɪ'ælətɪ] realidad *f*
re·a·li·za·tion [rɪəlaɪ'zeɪʃn]: ***the realization dawned on me that ...*** me di cuenta de que ...
re·a·lize ['rɪəlaɪz] *v/t* darse cuenta de; FIN (*yield*) producir; (*sell*) realizar, liquidar; ***I realize now that ...*** ahora me doy cuenta de que ...
real·ly ['rɪəlɪ] *adv in truth* de verdad; *big, small* muy; ***I am really really sorry*** lo siento en el alma; ***really?*** ¿de verdad?; ***not really*** *as reply* la verdad es que no
real 'time *n* COMPUT tiempo *m* real
real-time *adj* COMPUT en tiempo real
re·al·tor ['riːltər] agente *m/f* inmobiliario(-a)
re·alty ['riːltɪ] bienes *mpl* inmuebles
reap [riːp] *v/t* cosechar
re·ap·pear [riːə'pɪr] *v/i* reaparecer
reappearance [riːə'pɪrəns] reaparición *f*
rear [rɪr] **1** *n* parte *f* de atrás **2** *adj legs* de atrás; *seats, wheels, lights* trasero
rear 'end 1 *n* F *of person* trasero *m* **2** *v/t* MOT F dar un golpe por atrás a
rear 'light *of car* luz *f* trasera
re·arm [riː'ɑːrm] **1** *v/t* rearmar **2** *v/i* rearmarse
'rear·most *adj* último
re·ar·range [riːə'reɪnʒ] *v/t flowers* volver a colocar; *furniture* reordenar; *schedule, meetings* cambiar
rear-view 'mir·ror espejo *m* retrovisor
rea·son ['riːzn] **1** *n faculty* razón *f*; (*cause*) razón *f*, motivo *m*; ***see / listen to reason*** atender a razones **2** *v/i*: ***reason with s.o.*** razonar con alguien
rea·so·na·ble ['riːznəbl] *adj person* razonable; ***a reasonable number of people*** un buen número de personas
rea·son·a·bly ['riːznəblɪ] *adv act, behave* razonablemente; (*quite*) bastante
rea·son·ing ['riːznɪŋ] razonamiento *m*
re·as·sure [riːə'ʃʊr] *v/t* tranquilizar; ***she reassured us of her continued support*** nos aseguró que continuábamos contan-

R

do con su apoyo
re·as·sur·ing [riːə'ʃʊrɪŋ] *adj* tranquilizador
re·bate ['riːbeɪt] *money back* reembolso *m*
reb·el[1] ['rebl] *n* rebelde *m/f*; ***rebel troops*** tropas *fpl* rebeldes
re·bel[2] [rɪ'bel] *v/i* (*pret & pp* ***rebelled***) rebelarse
reb·el·lion [rɪ'belɪən] rebelión *f*
reb·el·lious [rɪ'belɪəs] *adj* rebelde
reb·el·lious·ly [rɪ'belɪəslɪ] *adv* con rebeldía
reb·el·lious·ness [rɪ'belɪəsnɪs] rebeldía *f*
re·bound [rɪ'baʊnd] *v/i of ball etc* rebotar
re·buff [rɪ'bʌf] *n* desaire *m*, rechazo *m*
re·build ['riːbɪld] *v/t* (*pret & pp* ***rebuilt***) reconstruir
re·buke [rɪ'bjuːk] *v/t* reprender
re·call [rɪ'kɒːl] *v/t goods* retirar del mercado; (*remember*) recordar
re·cap ['riːkæp] *v/i* (*pret & pp* ***recapped***) recapitular
re·cap·ture [riː'kæptʃər] *v/t* MIL reconquistar; *criminal* volver a detener
re·cede [rɪ'siːd] *v/i of flood waters* retroceder
re·ced·ing [rɪ'siːdɪŋ] *adj forehead, chin* hundido; ***have a receding hairline*** tener entradas
re·ceipt [rɪ'siːt] *for purchase* recibo *m*; ***acknowledge receipt of sth*** acusar recibo de algo; ***receipts*** FIN ingresos *mpl*
re·ceive [rɪ'siːv] *v/t* recibir
re·ceiv·er [rɪ'siːvər] *of letter* destinatario(-a) *m(f)*; TELEC auricular *m*; *for radio* receptor *m*; *in tennis* jugador(a) *m(f)* al resto
re·ceiv·er·ship [rɪ'siːvərʃɪp]: ***be in receivership*** estar en suspensión de pagos
re·cent ['riːsnt] *adj* reciente
re·cent·ly ['riːsntlɪ] *adv* recientemente
re·cep·tion [rɪ'sepʃn] recepción *f*; (*welcome*) recibimiento *m*
re'cep·tion desk recepción *f*
re·cep·tion·ist [rɪ'sepʃnɪst] recepcionista *m/f*
re·cep·tive [rɪ'septɪv] *adj*: ***be receptive to sth*** ser receptivo a algo
re·cess ['riːses] *n in wall etc* hueco *m*; EDU recreo *m*; *of parliament* periodo *m* vacacional
re·ces·sion [rɪ'seʃn] *economic* recesión *f*
re·charge [riː'tʃɑːrdʒ] *v/t battery* recargar
re·ci·pe ['resəpɪ] receta *f*
're·ci·pe book libro *m* de cocina, recetario *m*
re·cip·i·ent [rɪ'sɪpɪənt] *of parcel etc* destinatario(-a) *m(f)*; *of payment* receptor(a) *m(f)*
re·cip·ro·cal [rɪ'sɪprəkl] *adj* recíproco
re·cit·al [rɪ'saɪtl] MUS recital *m*
re·cite [rɪ'saɪt] *v/t poem* recitar; *details, facts* enumerar
reck·less ['reklɪs] *adj* imprudente; *driving* temerario
reck·less·ly ['reklɪslɪ] *adv* con imprudencia; *drive* con temeridad
reck·on ['rekən] *v/i* (*think, consider*) estimar, considerar; ***I reckon it won't happen*** creo que no va a pasar
◆ **reckon on** *v/t* contar con
◆ **reckon with** *v/t*: ***have s.o./sth to reckon with*** tener que vérselas con alguien / algo
reck·on·ing ['rekənɪŋ] estimaciones *fpl*, cálculos *mpl*; ***by my reckoning*** según mis cálculos
re·claim [rɪ'kleɪm] *v/t land from sea* ganar, recuperar; *lost property, rights* reclamar
re·cline [rɪ'klaɪn] *v/i* reclinarse
re·clin·er [rɪ'klaɪnər] *chair* sillón *m* reclinable
re·cluse [rɪ'kluːs] solitario(-a) *m(f)*
rec·og·ni·tion [rekəg'nɪʃn] *of state, s.o.'s achievements* reconocimiento *m*; ***in recognition of*** en reconocimiento a; ***be changed beyond recognition*** estar irreconocible
rec·og·niz·a·ble [rekəg'naɪzəbl] *adj* reconocible
rec·og·nize ['rekəgnaɪz] *v/t* reconocer
re·coil [rɪ'kɔɪl] *v/i* echarse atrás, retroceder
rec·ol·lect [rekə'lekt] *v/t* recordar
rec·ol·lec·tion [rekə'lekʃn] recuerdo *m*; ***I have no recollection of the accident*** no me acuerdo del accidente
rec·om·mend [rekə'mend] *v/t* recomendar
rec·om·men·da·tion [rekəmen'deɪʃn] recomendación *f*
rec·om·pense ['rekəmpens] *n* recompensa *f*
rec·on·cile ['rekənsaɪl] *v/t people* reconciliar; *differences, facts* conciliar; ***reconcile o.s. to …*** hacerse a la idea de …; ***be reconciled*** *of two people* haberse reconciliado
rec·on·cil·i·a·tion [rekənsɪlɪ'eɪʃn] *of people* reconciliación *f*; *of differences, facts* conciliación *f*
re·con·di·tion [riːkən'dɪʃn] *v/t* reacondicionar
re·con·nais·sance [rɪ'kɑːnɪsns] MIL reconocimiento *m*
re·con·sid·er [riːkən'sɪdər] **1** *v/t offer, one's position* reconsiderar **2** *v/i*: ***won't***

you please reconsider? ¿por qué no lo reconsideras, por favor?

re·con·struct [riːkən'strʌkt] *v/t* reconstruir

rec·ord[1] ['rekɔːrd] *n* MUS disco *m*; SP *etc* récord *m*; *written document etc* registro *m*, documento *m*; *in database* registro *m*; ***records*** archivos *mpl*; ***say sth off the record*** decir algo oficiosamente; ***have a criminal record*** tener antecedentes penales; ***have a good record for sth*** tener un buen *historial* en materia de algo

re·cord[2] [rɪ'kɔːrd] *v/t electronically* grabar; *in writing* anotar

'rec·ord-break·ing *adj* récord

re·cor·der [rɪ'kɔːrdər] MUS flauta *f* dulce

'rec·ord hold·er plusmarquista *m/f*

re·cord·ing [rɪ'kɔːrdɪŋ] grabación *f*

re'cord·ing stu·di·o estudio *m* de grabación

'rec·ord play·er tocadiscos *m inv*

re·count [rɪ'kaʊnt] *v/t* (*tell*) relatar

re-count ['riːkaʊnt] **1** *n of votes* segundo recuento *m* **2** *v/t* (*count again*) volver a contar

re·coup [rɪ'kuːp] *v/t financial losses* resarcirse de

re·cov·er [rɪ'kʌvər] **1** *v/t sth lost, stolen goods* recuperar; *composure* recobrar **2** *v/i from illness* recuperarse

re·cov·er·y [rɪ'kʌvərɪ] recuperación *f*; ***he has made a good recovery*** se ha recuperado muy bien

rec·re·a·tion [rekrɪ'eɪʃn] ocio *m*

rec·re·a·tion·al [rekrɪ'eɪʃnl] *adj done for pleasure* recreativo

re·cruit [rɪ'kruːt] **1** *n* MIL recluta *m/f*; *to company* nuevo(-a) trabajador(a) **2** *v/t new staff* contratar

re·cruit·ment [rɪ'kruːtmənt] MIL reclutamiento *m*; *to company* contratación *f*

re'cruit·ment drive MIL campaña *f* de reclutamiento; *to company* campaña *f* de contratación

rec·tan·gle ['rektæŋgl] rectángulo *m*

rec·tan·gu·lar [rek'tæŋgjʊlər] *adj* rectangular

rec·ti·fy ['rektɪfaɪ] *v/t* (*pret & pp* ***rectified***) rectificar

re·cu·pe·rate [rɪ'kuːpəreɪt] *v/i* recuperarse

re·cur [rɪ'kɜːr] *v/i* (*pret & pp* ***recurred***) *of error, event* repetirse; *of symptoms* reaparecer

re·cur·rent [rɪ'kʌrənt] *adj* recurrente

re·cy·cla·ble [riː'saɪkləbl] *adj* reciclable

re·cy·cle [riː'saɪkl] *v/t* reciclar

re·cy·cling [riː'saɪklɪŋ] reciclado *m*

red [red] *adj* rojo; ***in the red*** FIN en números rojos

Red 'Cross Cruz *f* Roja

red·den ['redn] *v/i* (*blush*) ponerse colorado

re·dec·o·rate [riː'dekəreɪt] *v/t with paint* volver a pintar; *with paper* volver a empapelar

re·deem [rɪ'diːm] *v/t debt* amortizar; REL redimir

re·deem·ing feat·ure [rɪ'diːmɪŋ]: ***his one redeeming feature is that …*** lo único que lo salva es que …

re·demp·tion [rɪ'dempʃn] REL redención *f*

re·de·vel·op [riːdɪ'veləp] *v/t part of town* reedificar

red-hand·ed [red'hændɪd] *adj*: ***catch s.o. red-handed*** coger a alguien con las manos en la masa

'red·head pelirrojo(-a) *m*(*f*)

red-'hot *adj* al rojo vivo

red-'let·ter day día *m* señalado

red 'light *at traffic light* semáforo *m* (en) rojo

red 'light dis·trict zona *f* de prostitución

red 'meat carne *f* roja

'red·neck F *individuo racista y reaccionario, normalmente de clase trabajadora*

re·dou·ble [riː'dʌbl] *v/t*: ***redouble one's efforts*** redoblar los esfuerzos

red 'pep·per *vegetable* pimiento *m* rojo

red 'tape F burocracia *f*, papeleo *m*

re·duce [rɪ'duːs] *v/t* reducir; *price* rebajar

re·duc·tion [rɪ'dʌkʃn] reducción *f*; *in price* rebaja *f*

re·dun·dant [rɪ'dʌndənt] *adj* (*unnecessary*) innecesario; ***be made redundant*** *Br at work* ser despedido

reed [riːd] BOT junco *m*

reef [riːf] *in sea* arrecife *m*

'reef knot nudo *m* de rizos

reek [riːk] *v/i* apestar (***of*** a)

reel [riːl] *n of film* rollo *m*; *of thread* carrete *m*

◆ **reel off** *v/t* soltar

re-e'lect *v/t* reelegir

re-e'lec·tion reelección *f*

re-'entry *of spacecraft* reentrada *f*

ref [ref] F árbitro(-a) *m*(*f*)

re·fer [rɪ'fɜːr] *v/t* (*pret & pp* ***referred***): ***refer a decision / problem to s.o.*** remitir una decisión / un problema a alguien

◆ **refer to** *v/t* (*allude to*) referirse a; *dictionary etc* consultar

ref·er·ee [refə'riː] SP árbitro(-a) *m*(*f*); (*for job*) *persona que pueda dar referencias*

ref·er·ence ['refərəns] referencia *f*; ***with reference to*** con referencia a

'ref·er·ence book libro *m* de consulta

R

'**reference li·bra·ry** biblioteca *f* de consulta

'**ref·er·ence num·ber** número *m* de referencia

ref·e·ren·dum [refə'rendəm] referéndum *m*

re·fill ['riːfɪl] *v/t tank*, *glass* volver a llenar

re·fine [rɪ'faɪn] *v/t oil*, *sugar* refinar; *technique* perfeccionar

re·fined [rɪ'faɪnd] *adj manners*, *language* refinado

re·fine·ment [rɪ'faɪnmənt] *to process*, *machine* mejora *f*

re·fin·e·ry [rɪ'faɪnərɪ] refinería *f*

re·fla·tion ['riːfleɪʃn] reflación *f*

reflect [rɪ'flekt] **1** *v/t light* reflejar; ***be reflected in*** reflejarse en **2** *v/i* (*think*) reflexionar

re·flec·tion [rɪ'flekʃn] *in water*, *glass etc* reflejo *f*; (*consideration*) reflexión *f*

re·flex ['riːfleks] *in body* reflejo *m*

re·flex re'ac·tion acto *m* reflejo

re·form [rɪ'fɔːrm] **1** *n* reforma *f* **2** *v/t* reformar

re·form·er [rɪ'fɔːrmər] reformador(a) *m*(*f*)

re·frain[1] [rɪ'freɪn] *v/i fml* abstenerse; ***please refrain from smoking*** se ruega no fumar

re·frain[2] [rɪ'freɪn] *n in song*, *poem* estribillo *m*

re·fresh [rɪ'freʃ] *v/t person* refrescar; ***feel refreshed*** sentirse fresco

refresh·er course [rɪ'freʃər] curso *m* de actualización *or* reciclaje

re·fresh·ing [rɪ'freʃɪŋ] *adj drink* refrescante; *experience* reconfortante

re·fresh·ments [rɪ'freʃmənts] *npl* refrigerio *m*

re·fri·ge·rate [rɪ'frɪdʒəreɪt] *v/t* refrigerar; ***keep refrigerated*** conservar refrigerado

re·fri·ge·ra·tor [rɪ'frɪdʒəreɪtər] frigorífico *m*, refrigerador *m*

re·fu·el [riːf'jʊəl] **1** *v/t airplane* reabastecer de combustible a **2** *v/i of airplane* repostar

ref·uge ['refjuːdʒ] refugio *m*; ***take refuge*** *from storm etc* refugiarse

ref·u·gee [refjʊ'dʒiː] refugiado(-a) *m*(*f*)

ref·u'gee camp campo *m* de refugiados

re·fund ['riːfʌnd] **1** *n* ['riːfʌnd] reembolso *m*; ***give s.o. a refund*** devolver el dinero a alguien **2** *v/t* [rɪ'fʌnd] reembolsar

re·fus·al [rɪ'fjuːzl] negativa *f*

re·fuse[1] [rɪ'fjuːz] **1** *v/i* negarse **2** *v/t help*, *food* rechazar; ***refuse s.o. sth*** negar algo a alguien; ***refuse to do sth*** negarse a hacer algo

ref·use[2] ['refjuːs] (*garbage*) basura *f*

'**ref·use col·lec·tion** recogida *f* de basuras

'**ref·use dump** vertedero *m*

re·gain [rɪ'geɪn] *v/t* recuperar

re·gal ['riːgl] *adj* regio

re·gard [rɪ'gɑːrd] **1** *n*: ***have great regard for s.o.*** sentir gran estima por alguien; ***in this regard*** en este sentido; ***with regard to*** con respecto a; (***kind***) ***regards*** saludos; ***give my regards to Paula*** dale saludos *or* recuerdos a Paula de mi parte; ***with no regard for*** sin tener en cuenta **2** *v/t*: ***regard s.o./sth as sth*** considerar a alguien / algo como algo; ***I regard it as an honor*** para mí es un honor; ***as regards*** con respecto a

re·gard·ing [rɪ'gɑːrdɪŋ] *prep* con respecto a

re·gard·less [rɪ'gɑːrdlɪs] *adv* a pesar de todo; ***regardless of*** sin tener en cuenta

re·gime [reɪ'ʒiːm] (*government*) régimen *m*

re·gi·ment ['redʒɪmənt] *n* regimiento *m*

re·gion ['riːdʒən] región *f*; ***in the region of*** del orden de

re·gion·al ['riːdʒənl] *adj* regional

re·gis·ter ['redʒɪstər] **1** *n* registro *m*; *at school* lista *f* **2** *v/t birth*, *death* registrar; *vehicle* matricular; *letter* certificar; *emotion* mostrar; ***send a letter registered*** enviar una carta por correo certificado **3** *v/i at university*, *for a course* matricularse; *with police* registrarse

re·gis·tered let·ter ['redʒɪstərd] carta *f* certificada

re·gis·tra·tion [redʒɪ'streɪʃn] registro *m*; *at university*, *for course* matriculación *f*

re·gis'tra·tion num·ber *Br* MOT (número *m* de) matrícula *f*

re·gret [rɪ'gret] **1** *v/t* (*pret & pp* ***regretted***) lamentar, sentir **2** *n* arrepentimiento *m*, pesar *m*

re·gret·ful [rɪ'gretfəl] *adj* arrepentido

re·gret·ful·ly [rɪ'gretfəlɪ] *adv* lamentablemente

re·gret·ta·ble [rɪ'gretəbl] *adj* lamentable

re·gret·ta·bly [rɪ'gretəblɪ] *adv* lamentablemente

reg·u·lar ['regjʊlər] **1** *adj* regular; (*normal*, *ordinary*) normal **2** *n at bar etc* habitual *m/f*

reg·u·lar·i·ty [regjʊ'lærətɪ] regularidad *f*

reg·u·lar·ly ['regjʊlərlɪ] *adv* regularmente

reg·u·late ['regʊleɪt] *v/t* regular

reg·u·la·tion [regʊ'leɪʃn] (*rule*) regla *f*, norma *f*

re·hab ['riːhæb] F rehabilitación *f*

re·ha·bil·i·tate [riːhə'bɪlɪteɪt] *v/t ex-criminal* rehabilitar

R

re·hears·al [rɪ'hɜːrsl] ensayo *m*
re·hearse [rɪ'hɜːrs] *v/t & v/i* ensayar
reign [reɪn] **1** *n* reinado *m* **2** *v/i* reinar
re·im·burse [riːɪm'bɜːrs] *v/t* reembolsar
rein [reɪn] rienda *f*
re·in·car·na·tion [riːɪnkɑːr'neɪʃn] reencarnación *f*
re·in·force [riːɪn'fɔːrs] *v/t structure* reforzar; *beliefs* reafirmar
re·in·forced con·crete [riːɪn'fɔːrst] hormigón *m* armado
re·in·force·ments [riːɪn'fɔːrsmənts] *npl* MIL refuerzos *mpl*
re·in·state [riːɪn'steɪt] *v/t person in office* reincorporar; *paragraph in text* volver a colocar
re·it·e·rate [riː'ɪtəreɪt] *v/t fml* reiterar
re·ject [rɪ'dʒekt] *v/t* rechazar
re·jec·tion [rɪ'dʒekʃn] rechazo *m*; ***he felt a sense of rejection*** se sintió rechazado
re·lapse ['riːlæps] *n* MED recaída *f*; ***have a relapse*** sufrir una recaída
re·late [rɪ'leɪt] **1** *v/t story* relatar, narrar; ***relate sth to sth*** *connect* relacionar algo con algo **2** *v/i*: ***relate to*** *be connected with* estar relacionado con; ***he doesn't relate to people*** no se relaciona fácilmente con la gente
re·lat·ed [rɪ'leɪtɪd] *adj by family* emparentado; *events*, *ideas etc* relacionado; ***are you two related?*** ¿sois parientes?
re·la·tion [rɪ'leɪʃn] *in family* pariente *m/f*; (*connection*) relación *f*; ***business / diplomatic relations*** relaciones *fpl* comerciales / diplomáticas
re·la·tion·ship [rɪ'leɪʃnʃɪp] relación *f*
rel·a·tive ['relətɪv] **1** *n* pariente *m/f* **2** *adj* relativo; ***X is relative to Y*** X está relacionado con Y
rel·a·tive·ly ['relətɪvlɪ] *adv* relativamente
re·lax [rɪ'læks] **1** *v/i* relajarse; ***relax!, don't get angry*** ¡tranquilízate!, no te enfades **2** *v/t muscle*, *pace* relajar
re·lax·a·tion [riːlæk'seɪʃn] relajación *f*; ***what do you do for relaxation?*** ¿qué haces para relajarte?
re·laxed [rɪ'lækst] *adj* relajado
re·lax·ing [rɪ'læksɪŋ] *adj* relajante
re·lay [riː'leɪ] **1** *v/t message* pasar; *radio*, TV *signals* retransmitir **2** *n*: ***relay*** (***race***) carrera *f* de relevos
re·lease [rɪ'liːs] **1** *n from prison* liberación *f*, puesta *f* en libertad; *of CD etc* lanzamiento *m*; *CD*, *record* trabajo *m* **2** *v/t prisoner* liberar, poner en libertad; *parking brake* soltar; *information* hacer público
rel·e·gate ['relɪgeɪt] *v/t* relegar
re·lent [rɪ'lent] *v/i* ablandarse, ceder
re·lent·less [rɪ'lentlɪs] *adj* (*determined*) implacable; *rain etc* que no cesa
re·lent·less·ly [rɪ'lentlɪslɪ] *adv* implacablemente; *rain* sin cesar
rel·e·vance ['reləvəns] pertinencia *f*
rel·e·vant ['reləvənt] *adj* pertinente
re·li·a·bil·i·ty [rɪlaɪə'bɪlətɪ] fiabilidad *f*
re·li·a·ble [rɪ'laɪəbl] *adj* fiable; *information* fiable, fidedigna
re·li·a·bly [rɪ'laɪəblɪ] *adv*: ***I am reliably informed that*** sé de buena fuente que
re·li·ance [rɪ'laɪəns] confianza *f*, dependencia *f*; ***reliance on s.o./sth*** confianza en alguien / algo, dependencia de alguien / algo
re·li·ant [rɪ'laɪənt] *adj*: ***be reliant on*** depender de
rel·ic ['relɪk] reliquia *f*
re·lief [rɪ'liːf] alivio *m*; ***that's a relief*** qué alivio; ***in relief*** *in art* en relieve
re·lieve [rɪ'liːv] *v/t pressure*, *pain* aliviar; (*take over from*) relevar; ***be relieved*** *at news etc* sentirse aliviado
re·li·gion [rɪ'lɪdʒən] religión *f*
re·li·gious [rɪ'lɪdʒəs] *adj* religioso
re·li·gious·ly [rɪ'lɪdʒəslɪ] *adv* (*conscientiously*) religiosamente
re·lin·quish [rɪ'lɪŋkwɪʃ] *v/t* renunciar a
rel·ish ['relɪʃ] **1** *n sauce* salsa *f*; (*enjoyment*) goce *m* **2** *v/t idea*, *prospect* gozar con; ***I don't relish the idea*** la idea no me entusiasma
re·live [riː'lɪv] *v/t the past*, *an event* revivir
re·lo·cate [riːlə'keɪt] *v/i of business*, *employee* trasladarse
re·lo·ca·tion [riːlə'keɪʃn] *of business*, *employee* traslado *m*
re·luc·tance [rɪ'lʌktəns] reticencia *f*
re·luc·tant [rɪ'lʌktənt] *adj* reticente, reacio; ***be reluctant to do sth*** ser reacio a hacer algo
re·luc·tant·ly [rɪ'lʌktəntlɪ] *adv* con reticencia
◆ **re·ly on** [rɪ'laɪ] *v/t* (*pret & pp* ***relied***) depender de; ***rely on s.o. to do sth*** contar con alguien para hacer algo
re·main [rɪ'meɪn] *v/i* (*be left*) quedar; MATH restar; (*stay*) permanecer
re·main·der [rɪ'meɪndər] **1** *n also* MATH resto *m* **2** *v/t* vender como saldo
re·main·ing [rɪ'meɪnɪŋ] *adj* restante
re·mains [rɪ'meɪnz] *npl of body* restos *mpl* (mortales)
re·make ['riːmeɪk] *n of movie* nueva versión *f*
re·mand [rɪ'mænd] **1** *v/t*: ***remand s.o. in custody*** poner a alguien en prisión preventiva **2** *n*: ***be on remand*** *in prison* estar en prisión preventiva; *on bail* estar en libertad bajo fianza

re·mark [rɪ'mɑːrk] **1** *n* comentario *m*, observación *f* **2** *v/t* comentar, observar

re·mar·ka·ble [rɪ'mɑːrkəbl] *adj* notable, extraordinario

re·mark·a·bly [rɪ'mɑːrkəblɪ] *adv* extraordinariamente

re·mar·ry [riː'mærɪ] *v/i* (*pret & pp* ***remarried***) volver a casarse

rem·e·dy ['remədɪ] *n* MED, *fig* remedio *m*

re·mem·ber [rɪ'membər] **1** *v/t s.o., sth* recordar, acordarse de; ***remember to lock the door*** acuérdate de cerrar la puerta; ***remember me to her*** dale recuerdos de mi parte **2** *v/i* recordar, acordarse; ***I don't remember*** no recuerdo, no me acuerdo

re·mind [rɪ'maɪnd] *v/t*: ***remind s.o. of sth*** recordar algo a alguien; ***remind s.o. of s.o.*** recordar alguien a alguien; ***you remind me of your father*** me recuerdas a tu padre

re·mind·er [rɪ'maɪndər] recordatorio *m*; *for payment* recordatorio *m* de pago

rem·i·nisce [remɪ'nɪs] *v/i* contar recuerdos

rem·i·nis·cent [remɪ'nɪsənt] *adj*: ***be reminiscent of sth*** recordar a algo, tener reminiscencias de algo

re·miss [rɪ'mɪs] *adj fml* negligente, descuidado

re·mis·sion [rɪ'mɪʃn] remisión *f*; ***go into remission*** MED remitir

rem·nant ['remnənt] resto *m*

re·morse [rɪ'mɔːrs] remordimientos *mpl*

re·morse·less [rɪ'mɔːrslɪs] *adj person* despiadado; *pace, demands* implacable

re·mote [rɪ'moʊt] *adj village, possibility* remoto; (*aloof*) distante; *ancestor* lejano

re·mote 'ac·cess COMPUT acceso *m* remoto

re·mote con'trol control *m* remoto; *for* TV mando *m* a distancia

re·mote·ly [rɪ'moʊtlɪ] *adv related, connected* remotamente; ***it's just remotely possible*** es una posibilidad muy remota

re·mote·ness [rɪ'moʊtnəs]: ***the remoteness of the house*** la lejanía *or* lo aislado de la casa

re·mov·a·ble [rɪ'muːvəbl] *adj* de quita y pon

re·mov·al [rɪ'muːvl] eliminación *f*

re·move [rɪ'muːv] *v/t* eliminar; *top, lid* quitar; *coat etc* quitarse; *doubt, suspicion* despejar; *growth, organ* extirpar

re·mu·ner·a·tion [rɪmjuːnə'reɪʃn] remuneración *f*

re·mu·ner·a·tive [rɪ'mjuːnərətɪv] *adj* bien remunerado

re·name [riː'neɪm] *v/t* cambiar el nombre a

ren·der ['rendər] *v/t service* prestar; ***render s.o. helpless / unconscious*** dejar a alguien indefenso / inconsciente

ren·der·ing ['rendərɪŋ] *of piece of music* interpretación *f*

ren·dez-vous ['rɑːndeɪvuː] *romantic* cita *f*; MIL encuentro *m*

re·new [rɪ'nuː] *v/t contract, license* renovar; *discussions* reanudar; ***feel renewed*** sentirse como nuevo

re·new·al [rɪ'nuːəl] *of contract etc* renovación *f*; *of discussions* reanudación *f*

re·nounce [rɪ'naʊns] *v/t title, rights* renunciar a

ren·o·vate ['renəveɪt] *v/t* renovar

ren·o·va·tion [renə'veɪʃn] renovación *f*

re·nown [rɪ'naʊn] renombre *m*

re·nowned [rɪ'naʊnd] *adj* renombrado; ***be renowned for sth*** ser célebre por algo

rent [rent] **1** *n* alquiler *m*; ***for rent*** se alquila **2** *v/t apartment, car, equipment* alquilar, *Mex* rentar

rent·al ['rentl] *for apartment, for* TV alquiler *m*, *Mex* renta *f*

'rent·al a·gree·ment acuerdo *m* de alquiler

'rent·al car coche *m* de alquiler

rent-'free *adv* sin pagar alquiler

re·o·pen [riː'oʊpn] **1** *v/t* reabrir; *negotiations* reanudar **2** *v/i of theater etc* volver a abrir

re·or·gan·i·za·tion [riːɔːrgənaɪz'eɪʃn] reorganización *f*

re·or·gan·ize [riː'ɔːrgənaɪz] *v/t* reorganizar

rep [rep] COM representante *m/f*, comercial *m/f*

re·paint [riː'peɪnt] *v/t* repintar

re·pair [rɪ'per] **1** *v/t fence*, TV reparar; *shoes* arreglar **2** *n to fence*, TV reparación *f*; *of shoes* arreglo *m*; ***in a good / bad state of repair*** en buen / mal estado

re'pair·man técnico *m*

re·pa·tri·ate [riː'pætrɪeɪt] *v/t* repatriar

re·pa·tri·a·tion [riː'pætrɪ'eɪʃn] repatriación *f*

re·pay [riː'peɪ] *v/t* (*pret & pp* ***repaid***) *money* devolver; *person* pagar

re·pay·ment [riː'peɪmənt] devolución *f*; *installment* plazo *m*

re·peal [rɪ'piːl] *v/t law* revocar

re·peat [rɪ'piːt] **1** *v/t* repetir; ***am I repeating myself?*** ¿me estoy repitiendo? **2** *n* TV *program etc* repetición *f*

re·peat 'busi·ness COM negocio *m* que se repite

re·peat·ed [rɪ'piːtɪd] *adj* repetido

re·peat·ed·ly [rɪ'pi:tɪdlɪ] *adv* repetidamente, repetidas veces
re·peat 'or·der COM pedido *m* repetido
re·pel [rɪ'pel] *v/t* (*pret & pp* ***repelled***) *invaders, attack* rechazar; *insects* repeler, ahuyentar; (*disgust*) repeler, repugnar
re·pel·lent [rɪ'pelənt] **1** *n* (*insect repellent*) repelente *m* **2** *adj* repelente, repugnante
re·pent [rɪ'pent] *v/i* arrepentirse
re·per·cus·sions [ri:pər'kʌʃnz] *npl* repercusiones *fpl*
rep·er·toire ['repərtwɑ:r] repertorio *m*
rep·e·ti·tion [repɪ'tɪʃn] repetición *f*
re·pet·i·tive [rɪ'petɪtɪv] *adj* repetitivo
re·place [rɪ'pleɪs] *v/t* (*put back*) volver a poner; (*take the place of*) reemplazar, sustituir
re·place·ment [rɪ'pleɪsmənt] *n person* sustituto(-a) *m*(*f*); *thing* recambio *m*, reemplazo *m*
re·place·ment 'part (pieza *f* de) recambio *m*
re·play ['ri:pleɪ] **1** *n recording* repetición *f* (de la jugada); *match* repetición *f* (del partido) **2** *v/t match* repetir
re·plen·ish [rɪ'plenɪʃ] *v/t container* rellenar; *supplies* reaprovisionar
rep·li·ca ['replɪkə] réplica *f*
re·ply [rɪ'plaɪ] **1** *n* respuesta *f*, contestación *f* **2** *v/t & v/i* (*pret & pp* ***replied***) responder, contestar
re·port [rɪ'pɔ:rt] **1** *n* (*account*) informe *m*; *by journalist* reportaje *m* **2** *v/t facts* informar; *to authorities* informar de, dar parte de; ***report a person to the police*** denunciar a alguien a la policía; ***he is reported to be in Washington*** se dice que está en Washington **3** *v/i of journalist* informar; (*present o.s.*) presentarse (***to*** ante)
◆ **report to** *v/t in business* trabajar a las órdenes de
re'port card boletín *m* de evaluación
re·port·er [rɪ'pɔ:rtər] reportero(-a) *m*(*f*)
re·pos·sess [ri:pə'zes] *v/t* COM embargar
rep·re·hen·si·ble [reprɪ'hensəbl] *adj* recriminable
rep·re·sent [reprɪ'zent] *v/t* representar
rep·re·sen·ta·tive [reprɪ'zentətɪv] **1** *n* representante *m/f*; POL representante *m/f*, diputado(-a) *m*(*f*)/ **2** *adj* (*typical*) representativo
re·press [rɪ'pres] *v/t revolt* reprimir; *feelings, laughter* reprimir, controlar
re·pres·sion [rɪ'preʃn] POL represión *f*
re·pres·sive [rɪ'presɪv] *adj* POL represivo
re·prieve [rɪ'pri:v] **1** *n* LAW indulto *m*; *fig* aplazamiento *m* **2** *v/t prisoner* indultar
rep·ri·mand ['reprɪmænd] *v/t* reprender
re·print ['ri:prɪnt] **1** *n* reimpresión *f* **2** *v/t* reimprimir
re·pri·sal [rɪ'praɪzl] represalia *f*; ***take reprisals*** tomar represalias; ***in reprisal for*** en represalia por
re·proach [rɪ'proʊʧ] **1** *n* reproche *m*; ***be beyond reproach*** ser irreprochable **2** *v/t*: ***reproach s.o. for sth*** reprochar algo a alguien
re·proach·ful [rɪ'proʊʧfəl] *adj* de reproche
re·proach·ful·ly [rɪ'proʊʧfəlɪ] *adv look* con una mirada de reproche; *say* con tono de reproche
re·pro·duce [ri:prə'du:s] **1** *v/t atmosphere, mood* reproducir **2** *v/i* BIO reproducirse
re·pro·duc·tion [ri:prə'dʌkʃn] reproducción *f*
re·pro·duc·tive [rɪprə'dʌktɪv] *adj* reproductivo
rep·tile ['reptaɪl] reptil *m*
re·pub·lic [rɪ'pʌblɪk] república *f*
re·pub·li·can [rɪ'pʌblɪkn] **1** *n* republicano(-a) *m*(*f*) **2** *adj* republicano
re·pu·di·ate [rɪ'pju:dɪeɪt] *v/t* (*deny*) rechazar
re·pul·sive [rɪ'pʌlsɪv] *adj* repulsivo
rep·u·ta·ble ['repjʊtəbl] *adj* reputado, acreditado
rep·u·ta·tion [repjʊ'teɪʃn] reputación *f*; ***have a good / bad reputation*** tener una buena / mala reputación
re·put·ed [rep'jʊtəd] *adj*: ***be reputed to be*** tener fama de ser
re·put·ed·ly [rep'jʊtədlɪ] *adv* según se dice
re·quest [rɪ'kwest] **1** *n* petición *f*, solicitud *f*; ***on request*** por encargo **2** *v/t* pedir, solicitar
re·quiem ['rekwɪəm] MUS réquiem *m*
re·quire [rɪ'kwaɪr] *v/t* (*need*) requerir, necesitar; ***it requires great care*** se requiere mucho cuidado; ***as required by law*** como estipula la ley; ***guests are required to ...*** se ruega a los los invitados que ...
re·quired [rɪ'kwaɪrd] *adj* (*necessary*) necesario
re·quire·ment [rɪ'kwaɪrmənt] (*need*) necesidad *f*; (*condition*) requisito *m*
req·ui·si·tion [rekwɪ'zɪʃn] *v/t* requisar
re-route [ri:'ru:t] *v/t airplane etc* desviar
re·run ['ri:rʌn] **1** *n of* TV *program* reposición *f* **2** *v/t* (*pret* ***reran***, *pp* ***rerun***) *tape* volver a poner
re·sched·ule [ri:'ʃedu:l] *v/t* volver a programar
res·cue ['reskju:] **1** *n* rescate *m*; ***come to***

s.o.'s rescue acudir al rescate de alguien **2** *v/t* rescatar
'res·cue par·ty equipo *m* de rescate
re·search [rɪ'sɜːrʧ] *n* investigación *f*
◆ **research into** *v/t* investigar
re·search and de'vel·op·ment investigación *f* y desarrollo
re'search as·sist·ant ayudante *m/f* de investigación
re·search·er [rɪ'sɜːrʧər] investigador(a) *m(f)*
re'search proj·ect proyecto *m* de investigación
re·sem·blance [rɪ'zembləns] parecido *m*, semejanza *f*
re·sem·ble [rɪ'zembl] *v/t* parecerse a
re·sent [rɪ'zent] *v/t* estar molesto por
re·sent·ful [rɪ'zentfəl] *adj* resentido
re·sent·ful·ly [rɪ'zentfəlɪ] *adv* con resentimiento
re·sent·ment [rɪ'zentmənt] resentimiento *m*
res·er·va·tion [rezər'veɪʃn] reserva *f*; ***I have a reservation*** *in hotel, restaurant* tengo una reserva
re·serve [rɪ'zɜːrv] **1** *n* reserva *f*; SP reserva *m/f*; ***reserves*** FIN reservas *fpl*; ***keep sth in reserve*** tener algo en la reserva **2** *v/t seat, table* reservar; *judgment* reservarse
re·served [rɪ'zɜːrvd] *adj table, manner* reservado
res·er·voir ['rezərvwɑːr] *for water* embalse *m*, pantano *m*
re·shuf·fle ['riːʃʌfl] **1** *n* POL remodelación *f* **2** *v/t* POL remodelar
re·side [rɪ'zaɪd] *v/i fml* residir
res·i·dence ['rezɪdəns] (*fml*: *house etc*) residencia *f*; (*stay*) estancia *f*
'res·i·dence per·mit permiso *m* de residencia
'res·i·dent ['rezɪdənt] **1** *n* residente *m/f* **2** *adj* (*living in a building*) residente
res·i·den·tial [rezɪ'denʃl] *adj district* residencial
res·i·due ['rezɪduː] residuo *m*
re·sign [rɪ'zaɪn] **1** *v/t position* dimitir de; ***resign o.s. to*** resignarse a **2** *v/i from job* dimitir
res·ig·na·tion [rezɪg'neɪʃn] *from job* dimisión *f*; *mental* resignación *f*
re·signed [re'zaɪnd] *adj* resignado; ***we have become resigned to the fact that ...*** nos hemos resignado a aceptar que ...
re·sil·i·ent [rɪ'zɪlɪənt] *adj personality* fuerte; *material* resistente
res·in ['rezɪn] resina *f*
re·sist [rɪ'zɪst] **1** *v/t* resistir; *new measures* oponer resistencia a **2** *v/i* resistir
re·sist·ance [rɪ'zɪstəns] resistencia *f*
re·sis·tant [rɪ'zɪstənt] *adj material* resistente; ***resistant to heat / rust*** resistente al calor/a la oxidación
res·o·lute ['rezəluːt] *adj* resuelto
res·o·lu·tion [rezə'luːʃn] resolución *f*; *made at New Year etc* propósito *m*
re·solve [rɪ'zɑːlv] *v/t problem, mystery* resolver; ***resolve to do sth*** resolver hacer algo
re·sort [rɪ'zɔːrt] *n place* centro *m* turístico; ***as a last resort*** como último recurso
◆ **resort to** *v/t violence, threats* recurrir a
◆ **re·sound with** [rɪ'zaʊnd] *v/t* resonar con
re·sound·ing [rɪ'zaʊndɪŋ] *adj success, victory* clamoroso
re·source [rɪ'sɔːrs] recurso *m*; ***leave s.o. to his own resources*** dejar que alguien se las arregle solo
re·source·ful [rɪ'sɔːrsfəl] *adj person* lleno de recursos; *attitude, approach* ingenioso
re·spect [rɪ'spekt] **1** *n* respeto *m*; ***show respect to*** mostrar respeto hacia; ***with respect to*** con respecto a; ***in this / that respect*** en cuanto a esto / eso; ***in many respects*** en muchos aspectos; ***pay one's last respects to s.o.*** decir el último adiós a alguien **2** *v/t* respetar
re·spect·a·bil·i·ty [rɪspektə'bɪlətɪ] respetabilidad *f*
re·spec·ta·ble [rɪ'spektəbl] *adj* respetable
re·spec·ta·bly [rɪ'spektəblɪ] *adv* respetablemente
re·spect·ful [rɪ'spektfəl] *adj* respetuoso
re·spect·ful·ly [rɪ'spektfəlɪ] *adv* respetuosamente, con respeto
re·spec·tive [rɪ'spektɪv] *adj* respectivo
re·spec·tive·ly [rɪ'spektɪvlɪ] *adv* respectivamente
res·pi·ra·tion [respɪ'reɪʃn] respiración *f*
res·pi·ra·tor [respɪ'reɪtər] MED respirador *m*
re·spite ['respaɪt] respiro *m*; ***without respite*** sin respiro
re·spond [rɪ'spɑːnd] *v/i* responder
re·sponse [rɪ'spɑːns] respuesta *f*
re·spon·si·bil·i·ty [rɪspɑːnsɪ'bɪlətɪ] responsabilidad *f*; ***accept responsibility for*** aceptar responsabilidad de; ***a job with more responsibility*** un trabajo con más responsabilidad
re·spon·si·ble [rɪ'spɑːnsəbl] *adj* reponsable (***for*** de); *job* de responsabilidad
re·spon·sive [rɪ'spɑːnsɪv] *adj brakes* que responde bien; ***a responsive audience*** una audiencia que muestra interés
rest[1] [rest] **1** *n* descanso *m*; ***he needs a rest*** necesita descansar; ***set s.o.'s mind***

at rest tranquilizar a alguien **2** *v/i* descansar; ***rest on*** *of theory, box* apoyarse en; ***it all rests with him*** todo depende de él **3** *v/t* (*lean, balance*) apoyar

rest[2] [rest]: ***the rest*** el resto

res·tau·rant ['restrɑːnt] restaurante *m*

'res·tau·rant car vagón *m or* coche *m* restaurante

'rest cure cura *f* de reposo *or* descanso

rest·ful ['restfəl] *adj* tranquilo, relajante

'rest home residencia *f* de ancianos

rest·less ['restlɪs] *adj* inquieto; ***have a restless night*** pasar una mala noche

rest·less·ly ['restlɪslɪ] *adv* sin descanso

res·to·ra·tion [restə'reɪʃn] restauración *f*

re·store [rɪ'stɔːr] *v/t building etc* restaurar; (*bring back*) devolver

re·strain [rɪ'streɪn] *v/t* contener; ***restrain o.s.*** contenerse

re·straint [rɪ'streɪnt] (*moderation*) moderación *f*, comedimiento *m*

re·strict [rɪ'strɪkt] *v/t* restringir, limitar; ***I'll restrict myself to …*** me limitaré a …

re·strict·ed [rɪ'strɪktɪd] *adj view* limitado

re·strict·ed 'ar·e·a MIL zona *f* de acceso restringido

re·stric·tion [rɪ'strɪkʃn] restricción *f*, limitación *f*; ***place restrictions upon s.o.*** imponer restricciones *or* limitaciones a alguien

'rest room *Am* aseo *m*, servicios *mpl*

re·sult [rɪ'zʌlt] *n* resultado *m*; ***as a result of this*** como resultado de esto

◆ **result from** *v/t* resultar de

◆ **result in** *v/t* tener como resultado

re·sume [rɪ'zjuːm] **1** *v/t* reanudar **2** *v/i* continuar

ré·su·mé ['rezʊmeɪ] currículum *m* (vitae)

re·sump·tion [rɪ'zʌmpʃn] reanudación *f*

re·sur·face [riː'sɜːfɪs] **1** *v/t roads* volver a asfaltar **2** *v/i* (*reappear*) reaparecer

res·ur·rec·tion [rezə'rekʃn] REL resurrección *f*

re·sus·ci·tate [rɪ'sʌsɪteɪt] *v/t* resucitar, revivir

re·sus·ci·ta·tion [rɪsʌsɪ'teɪʃn] resucitación *f*

re·tail ['riːteɪl] **1** *adv*: ***sell sth retail*** vender algo al por menor **2** *v/i*: ***retail at …*** su precio de venta al público es de …

re·tail·er ['riːteɪlər] minorista *m/f*

're·tail out·let punto *m* de venta

're·tail price precio *m* de venta al público

re·tain [rɪ'teɪn] *v/t* conservar; *heat* retener

re·tain·er [rɪ'teɪnər] FIN anticipo *m*

re·tal·i·ate [rɪ'tælɪeɪt] *v/i* tomar represalias

re·tal·i·a·tion [rɪtælɪ'eɪʃn] represalias *fpl*; ***in retaliation for*** como represalia por

re·tard·ed [rɪ'tɑːrdɪd] *adj mentally* retrasado mental

re·think [riː'θɪŋk] *v/t* (*pret & pp* ***rethought***) replantear

re·ti·cence ['retɪsns] reserva *f*

re·ti·cent ['retɪsnt] *adj* reservado

re·tire [rɪ'taɪr] *v/i from work* jubilarse

re·tired [rɪ'taɪrd] *adj* jubilado

re·tire·ment [rɪ'taɪrmənt] jubilación *f*

re'tire·ment age edad *f* de jubilación

re·tir·ing [rɪ'taɪrɪŋ] *adj* retraído, reservado

re·tort [rɪ'tɔːrt] **1** *n* réplica *f* **2** *v/t* replicar

re·trace [rɪ'treɪs] *v/t*: ***they retraced their footsteps*** volvieron sobre sus pasos

re·tract [rɪ'trækt] *v/t claws* retraer; *undercarriage* replegar; *statement* retirar

re·train [riː'treɪn] *v/i* reciclarse

re·treat [rɪ'triːt] **1** *v/i* retirarse **2** *n* MIL retirada *f*; *place* retiro *m*

re·trieve [rɪ'triːv] *v/t* recuperar

re·triev·er [rɪ'triːvər] *dog* perro *m* cobrador

ret·ro·ac·tive [retroʊ'æktɪv] *adj law etc* retroactivo

ret·ro·ac·tive·ly [retroʊ'æktɪvlɪ] *adv* con retroactividad

ret·ro·grade ['retrəgreɪd] *adj move, decision* retrógrado

ret·ro·spect ['retrəspekt]: ***in retrospect*** en retrospectiva

ret·ro·spec·tive [retrə'spektɪv] *n* retrospectiva *f*

re·turn [rɪ'tɜːrn] **1** *n to a place* vuelta *f*, regreso *m*; (*giving back*) devolución *f*; COMPUT retorno *m*; *in tennis* resto *m*; (*profit*) rendimiento *m*; *Br ticket* billete *m or L.Am.* boleto *m* de ida y vuelta; ***by return (of post)*** a vuelta de correo; ***many happy returns (of the day)*** feliz cumpleaños; ***in return for*** a cambio de **2** *v/t* devolver; (*put back*) volver a colocar **3** *v/i* (*go back, come back*) volver, regresar; *of good times, doubts etc* volver

re·turn 'flight vuelo *m* de vuelta

re·turn 'jour·ney viaje *m* de vuelta

re·u·ni·fi·ca·tion [riːjuːnɪfɪ'keɪʃn] reunificación *f*

re·u·nion [riː'juːnjən] reunión *f*

re·u·nite [riːjuː'naɪt] *v/t* reunir

re·us·a·ble [riː'juːzəbl] *adj* reutilizable

re·use [riː'juːz] *v/t* reutilizar

rev [rev] *n* revolución *f*; ***revs per minute*** revoluciones por minuto

◆ **rev up** *v/t* (*pret & pp* ***revved***) *engine* revolucionar

re·val·u·a·tion [riːvæljʊ'eɪʃn] revaluación *f*

re·veal [rɪ'viːl] *v/t* (*make visible*) revelar;

(*make known*) revelar, desvelar
re·veal·ing [rɪ'viːlɪŋ] *adj remark* revelador; *dress* insinuante, atrevido
◆ **rev·el in** ['revl] *v/t* (*pret & pp* ***reveled***, *Br* ***revelled***) deleitarse con
rev·e·la·tion [revə'leɪʃn] revelación *f*
re·venge [rɪ'vendʒ] *n* venganza *f*; ***take one's revenge*** vengarse; ***in revenge for*** como venganza por
rev·e·nue ['revənuː] ingresos *mpl*
re·ver·be·rate [rɪ'vɜːrbəreɪt] *v/i of sound* reverberar
re·vere [rɪ'vɪr] *v/t* reverenciar
rev·e·rence ['revərəns] reverencia *f*
Rev·e·rend ['revərənd] REL Reverendo *m*
rev·e·rent ['revərənt] *adj* reverente
re·verse [rɪ'vɜːrs] **1** *adj sequence* inverso; ***in reverse order*** en orden inverso **2** *n* (*back*) dorso *m*; MOT marcha *f* atrás; ***the reverse*** (*the opposite*) lo contrario **3** *v/t sequence* invertir; ***reverse a vehicle*** hacer marcha atrás con un vehículo **4** *v/i* MOT hacer marcha atrás
revert [rɪ'vɜːrt] *v/i*: ***revert to*** volver a
re·view [rɪ'vjuː] **1** *n of book, movie* reseña *f*, crítica *f*; *of troops* revista *f*; *of situation etc* revisión *f* **2** *v/t book, movie* reseñar, hacer una crítica de; *troops* pasar revista a; *situation etc* revisar; EDU repasar
re·view·er [rɪ'vjuːər] *of book, movie* crítico(-a) *m(f)*
re·vise [rɪ'vaɪz] *v/t opinion, text* revisar
re·vi·sion [rɪ'vɪʒn] *of opinion, text* revisión *f*
re·viv·al [rɪ'vaɪvl] *of custom, old style etc* resurgimiento *m*; *of patient* reanimación *f*
re·vive [rɪ'vaɪv] **1** *v/t custom, old style etc* hacer resurgir; *patient* reanimar **2** *v/i of business, exchange rate etc* reactivarse
re·voke [rɪ'voʊk] *v/t law* derogar; *license* revocar
re·volt [rɪ'voʊlt] **1** *n* rebelión *f* **2** *v/i* rebelarse
re·volt·ing [rɪ'voʊltɪŋ] *adj* (*disgusting*) repugnante
rev·o·lu·tion [revə'luːʃn] POL revolución *f*; (*turn*) vuelta *f*, revolución *f*
rev·o·lu·tion·ar·y [revə'luːʃn ərɪ] **1** *n* POL revolucionario(-a) *m(f)* **2** *adj* revolucionario
rev·o·lu·tion·ize [revə'luːʃnaɪz] *v/t* revolucionar
re·volve [rɪ'vɑːlv] *v/i* girar (***around*** en torno a)
re·volv·er [rɪ'vɑːlvər] revólver *m*
re·volv·ing 'door [rɪ'vɑːlvɪŋ] puerta *f* giratoria

R

re·vue [rɪ'vjuː] THEA revista *f*
re·vul·sion [rɪ'vʌlʃn] repugnancia *f*
re·ward [rɪ'wɔːrd] **1** *n* recompensa *f* **2** *v/t financially* recompensar
re·ward·ing [rɪ'wɔːrdɪŋ] *adj experience* gratificante
re·wind [riː'waɪnd] *v/t* (*pret & pp* ***rewound***) *film, tape* rebobinar
re·write [riː'raɪt] *v/t* (*pret* ***rewrote***, *pp* ***rewritten***) reescribir
rhe·to·ric ['retərɪk] retórica *f*
rhe·to·ric·al 'ques·tion [rɪ'tɑːrɪkl] pregunta *f* retórica
rheu·ma·tism ['ruːmətɪzm] reumatismo *m*
rhi·no·ce·ros [raɪ'nɑːsərəs] rinoceronte *m*
rhu·barb ['ruːbɑːrb] ruibarbo *m*
rhyme [raɪm] **1** *n* rima *f* **2** *v/i* rimar
rhythm ['rɪðm] ritmo *m*
rib [rɪb] ANAT costilla *f*
rib·bon ['rɪbən] cinta *f*
rice [raɪs] arroz *m*
rich [rɪʧ] **1** *adj* (*wealthy*) rico; *food* sabroso; ***it's too rich*** es muy pesado **2** *n*: ***the rich*** los ricos
rich·ly ['rɪʧlɪ] *adv*: ***be richly deserved*** ser muy merecido
rick·et·y ['rɪkətɪ] *adj* desvencijado
ric·o·chet ['rɪkəʃeɪ] *v/i* rebotar
rid [rɪd]: ***get rid of*** deshacerse de
rid·dance ['rɪdns] F: ***good riddance to her!*** ¡espero no volver a verla nunca!
rid·den ['rɪdn] *pp* → ***ride***
rid·dle ['rɪdl] **1** *n* acertijo *m* **2** *v/t*: ***be riddled with*** estar lleno de
ride [raɪd] **1** *n on horse, in vehicle* paseo *m*, vuelta *f*; (*journey*) viaje *m*; ***do you want a ride into town?*** ¿quieres que te lleve al centro? **2** *v/t* (*pret* ***rode***, *pp* ***ridden***) *horse* montar a; *bike* montar en **3** *v/i* (*pret* ***rode***, *pp* ***ridden***) *on horse* montar; ***can you ride?*** ¿sabes montar?; ***those who were riding at the back of the bus*** los que iban en la parte de atrás del autobús
rid·er ['raɪdər] *on horse* jinete *m*, amazona *f*; *on bicycle* ciclista *m/f*; *on motorbike* motorista *m/f*
ridge [rɪdʒ] *raised strip* borde *m*; *of mountain* cresta *f*; *of roof* caballete *m*
rid·i·cule ['rɪdɪkjuːl] **1** *n* burlas *fpl* **2** *v/t* ridiculizar, poner en ridículo
ri·dic·u·lous [rɪ'dɪkjʊləs] *adj* ridículo
ri·dic·u·lous·ly [rɪ'dɪkjʊləslɪ] *adv expensive, difficult* terriblemente; ***it's ridiculously easy*** es facilísimo
rid·ing ['raɪdɪŋ] *on horseback* equitación *f*
ri·fle ['raɪfl] *n* rifle *m*

rift [rɪft] *in earth* grieta *f*; *in party etc* escisión *f*

rig [rɪg] **1** *n* (*oil rig*) plataforma *f* petrolífera; (*truck*) camión *m* **2** *v/t* (*pret & pp* ***rigged***) *elections* amañar

right [raɪt] **1** *adj* (*correct*) correcto; (*suitable*) adecuado, apropiado; (*not left*) derecho; ***it's not right to treat people like that*** no está bien tratar así a la gente; ***it's the right thing to do*** es lo que hay que hacer; ***be right*** *of answer* estar correcto; *of person* tener razón; *of clock* ir bien; ***put things right*** arreglar las cosas; ***that's right!*** ¡eso es!; ***that's all right*** *doesn't matter* no te preocupes; *when s.o. says thank you* de nada; *is quite good* está bastante bien; ***I'm all right*** *not hurt* estoy bien; *have got enough* no, gracias; ***all right, that's enough!*** ¡ahora sí que ya está bien! **2** *adv* (*directly*) justo; (*correctly*) correctamente; (*not left*) a la derecha; ***he broke it right off*** lo rompió por completo; ***right back in 1982*** allá en 1982; ***right now*** ahora mismo **3** *n civil, legal etc* derecho *m*; *not left*, POL derecha *f*; ***on the right*** *also* POL a la derecha; ***turn to the right, take a right*** gira a la derecha; ***be in the right*** tener razón; ***know right from wrong*** distinguir lo que está bien de lo que está mal

right-'an·gle ángulo *m* recto; ***at right-angles to*** en *or* formando ángulo recto con

right·ful ['raɪtfəl] *adj heir, owner etc* legítimo

'right-hand *adj*: ***on the right-hand side*** a mano derecha

right-hand 'drive *n* MOT vehículo *m* con el volante a la derecha

right-hand·ed [raɪt'hændɪd] *adj person* diestro

right-hand 'man mano *f* derecha

right of 'way *in traffic* preferencia *f*; *across land* derecho *m* de paso

right 'wing *n* POL la derecha *f*; SP la banda derecha

right-'wing *adj* POL de derechas

right-wing ex'trem·ism POL extremismo *m* de derechas

right-'wing·er POL derechista *m/f*

rig·id ['rɪdʒɪd] *adj* rígido

rig·or ['rɪgər] *of discipline* rigor *m*; ***the rigors of the winter*** los rigores del invierno

rig·or·ous ['rɪgərəs] *adj* riguroso

rig·or·ous·ly ['rɪgərəslɪ] *adv check, examine* rigurosamente

rig·our *Br* → ***rigor***

rile [raɪl] *v/t* F fastidiar, *Span* mosquear F

rim [rɪm] *of wheel* llanta *f*; *of cup* borde *m*; *of eye glasses* montura *f*

ring[1] [rɪŋ] *n* (*circle*) círculo *m*; *on finger* anillo *m*; *in boxing* cuadrilátero *m*, ring *m*; *at circus* pista *f*

ring[2] [rɪŋ] **1** *n of bell* timbrazo; *of voice* tono *m*; ***give s.o. a ring*** *Br* TELEC dar un telefonazo a alguien **2** *v/t* (*pret* ***rang***, *pp* ***rung***) *bell* hacer sonar **3** *v/i* (*pret* ***rang***, *pp* ***rung***) *of bell* sonar; ***please ring for attention*** toque el timbre para que lo atiendan

'ring·lead·er cabecilla *m/f*

'ring-pull anilla *f*

rink [rɪŋk] pista *f* de patinaje

rinse [rɪns] **1** *n for hair color* reflejo *m* **2** *v/t* aclarar

ri·ot ['raɪət] **1** *n* disturbio *m* **2** *v/i* causar disturbios

ri·ot·er ['raɪətər] alborotador(a) *m*(*f*)

'riot police policía *f* antidisturbios

rip [rɪp] **1** *n in cloth etc* rasgadura *f* **2** *v/t* (*pret & pp* ***ripped***) *cloth etc* rasgar; ***rip sth open*** romper algo rasgándolo

◆ **rip off** *v/t* F *customers* robar F, clavar F; (*cheat*) timar

◆ **rip up** *v/t letter, sheet* hacer pedazos

ripe [raɪp] *adj fruit* maduro

rip·en ['raɪpn] *v/i of fruit* madurar

ripe·ness ['raɪpnɪs] *of fruit* madurez *f*

'rip-off *n* F robo *m* F

rip·ple ['rɪpl] *on water* onda *f*

rise [raɪz] **1** *v/i* (*pret* ***rose***, *pp* ***risen***) *from chair etc* levantarse; *of sun* salir; *of rocket* ascender, subir; *of price, temperature, water* subir **2** *n in price, temperature* subida *f*, aumento *m*; *in water level* subida *f*; *in salary* aumento *m*; ***give rise to*** dar pie a

ris·en ['rɪzn] *pp* → ***rise***

ris·er ['raɪzər]: ***be an early riser*** ser un madrugador; ***be a late riser*** levantarse tarde

risk [rɪsk] **1** *n* riesgo *m*, peligro *m*; ***take a risk*** arriesgarse **2** *v/t* arriesgar; ***let's risk it*** arriesguémonos

risk·y ['rɪskɪ] *adj* arriesgado

ris·qué [rɪ'skeɪ] *adj* subido de tono

rit·u·al ['rɪtʊəl] **1** *n* ritual *m* **2** *adj* ritual

ri·val ['raɪvl] **1** *n* rival *m/f* **2** *v/t* rivalizar con; ***I can't rival that*** no puedo rivalizar con eso

ri·val·ry ['raɪvlrɪ] rivalidad *f*

riv·er ['rɪvər] río *m*

'riv·er·bank ribera *f*

'riv·er·bed lecho *m*

Riv·er 'Plate *n*: ***the River Plate*** el Río de la Plata

'riv·er·side **1** *adj* a la orilla del río **2** *n* ribera *f*, orilla *f* del río

riv·et ['rɪvɪt] **1** *n* remache *m* **2** *v/t* remachar; ***rivet sth to sth*** unir algo a algo con remaches
riv·et·ing ['rɪvɪtɪŋ] *adj* fascinante
road [roʊd] *in country* carretera *f*; *in city* calle *f*; ***it's just down the road*** está muy cerca
'**road·block** control *m* de carretera
'**road hog** *conductor(a) temerario(-a)*
'**road-hold·ing** *of vehicle* adherencia *f*, agarre *m*
'**road map** mapa *m* de carreteras
road 'safe·ty seguridad *f* vial
'**road·side**: ***at the roadside*** al borde de la carretera
'**road·sign** señal *f* de tráfico
'**road·way** calzada *f*
'**road·wor·thy** *adj* en condiciones de circular
roam [roʊm] *v/i* vagar
roar [rɔːr] **1** *n of traffic, engine* estruendo *m*; *of lion* rugido *m*; *of person* grito *m*, bramido *m* **2** *v/i of engine, lion* rugir; *of person* gritar, bramar; ***roar with laughter*** reírse a carcajadas
roast [roʊst] **1** *n of beef etc* asado *m* **2** *v/t* asar **3** *v/i of food* asarse; ***we're roasting*** nos estamos asando
roast 'beef rosbif *m*
'**roast·ing tin** [roʊstɪŋ] fuente *f* para asar
roast 'pork cerdo *m* asado
rob [rɑːb] *v/t* (*pret & pp* ***robbed***) *person* robar a; *bank* atracar, robar; ***I've been robbed*** me han robado
rob·ber ['rɑːbər] atracador(a) *m(f)*
rob·ber·y ['rɑːbərɪ] atraco *m*, robo *m*
robe [roʊb] *of judge* toga *f*; *of priest* sotana *f*; (*bathrobe*) bata *f*
rob·in ['rɑːbɪn] petirrojo *m*
ro·bot ['roʊbɑːt] robot *m*
ro·bust [roʊ'bʌst] *adj person, structure* robusto; *material* resistente; ***be in robust health*** tener una salud de hierro
rock [rɑːk] **1** *n* roca *f*; MUS rock *m*; ***on the rocks*** *of drink* con hielo; ***their marriage is on the rocks*** su matrimonio está en crisis **2** *v/t baby* acunar; *cradle* mecer; (*surprise*) sorprender, impactar **3** *v/i on chair* mecerse; *of boat* balancearse
'**rock band** grupo *m* de rock
rock 'bot·tom: ***reach rock bottom*** tocar fondo
'**rock-bot·tom** *adj prices* mínimo
'**rock climb·er** escalador(a) *m(f)*
'**rock climb·ing** escalada *f* (en roca)
rock·et ['rɑːkɪt] **1** *n* cohete *m* **2** *v/i of prices etc* dispararse
rock·ing chair ['rɑːkɪŋ] mecedora *f*
'**rock·ing horse** caballito *m* de juguete
rock 'n roll [rɑːkn'roʊl] rock and roll *m*
'**rock star** estrella *f* del rock
rock·y ['rɑːkɪ] *adj beach, path* pedregoso
rod [rɑːd] vara *f*; *for fishing* caña *f*
rode [roʊd] *pret* → ***ride***
ro·dent ['roʊdnt] roedor *m*
rogue [roʊg] granuja *m/f*, bribón(-ona) *m(f)*
role [roʊl] papel *m*
'**role mod·el** ejemplo *m*
roll [roʊl] **1** *n* (*bread roll*) panecillo *m*; *of film* rollo *m*; *of thunder* retumbo *m*; (*list, register*) lista *f* **2** *v/i of ball etc* rodar; *of boat* balancearse **3** *v/t*: ***roll sth into a ball*** hacer una bola con algo; ***roll sth along the ground*** hacer rodar algo por el suelo
◆ **roll over 1** *v/i* darse la vuelta **2** *v/t person, object* dar la vuelta a; (*renew*) renovar; (*extend*) refinanciar
◆ **roll up 1** *v/t sleeves* remangar **2** *v/i* F (*arrive*) llegar
'**roll-call** lista *f*
roll·er ['roʊlər] *for hair* rulo *m*
'**roll·er blade**® *n* patín *m* en línea
'**roll·er blind** persiana *f*
roll·er coast·er ['roʊlerkoʊstər] montaña *f* rusa
'**roll·er skate** *n* patín *m* (de ruedas)
roll·ing pin ['roʊlɪŋ] rodillo *m* de cocina
ROM [rɑːm] COMPUT *abbr* (= ***read only memory***) ROM *f* (= memoria *f* de sólo lectura)
Ro·man ['roʊmən] **1** *adj* romano **2** *n* romano(-a) *m(f)*
Ro·man 'Cath·o·lic 1 *n* REL católico(-a) *m(f)* romano(-a) **2** *adj* católico romano
ro·mance [rə'mæns] (*affair*) aventura *f* (amorosa); *novel* novela *f* rosa; *movie* película *f* romántica
ro·man·tic [roʊ'mæntɪk] *adj* romántico
ro·man·tic·al·ly [roʊ'mæntɪklɪ] *adv*: ***be romantically involved with s.o.*** tener un romance con alguien
roof [ruːf] techo *m*, tejado *m*; ***have a roof over one's head*** tener un techo donde dormir
'**roof-rack** MOT baca *f*
rook·ie ['rʊkɪ] F novato(-a) *m(f)*
room [ruːm] habitación *f*; (*space*) espacio *m*, sitio *m*; ***there's no room for …*** no hay sitio para …, no cabe …
'**room clerk** recepcionista *m/f*
'**room·mate** *sharing room* compañero(-a) *m(f)* de habitación; *sharing apartment* compañero(-a) *m(f)* de apartamento
'**room ser·vice** servicio *m* de habitaciones
room 'tem·per·a·ture temperatura *f* ambiente
room·y ['ruːmɪ] *adj house, car etc* espacio-

R

so; *clothes* holgado

root [ruːt] *n* raíz *f*; ***roots*** *of person* raíces *fpl*

◆ **root for** *v/t* F apoyar

◆ **root out** *v/t* (*get rid of*) cortar de raíz; (*find*) encontrar

rope [roʊp] cuerda *f*; *thick* soga *f*; ***show s.o. the ropes*** F poner a alguien al tanto

◆ **rope off** *v/t* acordonar

ro·sa·ry ['roʊzərɪ] REL rosario *m*

rose[1] [roʊz] BOT rosa *f*

rose[2] [roʊz] *pret* → ***rise***

rose·ma·ry ['roʊzmerɪ] romero *m*

ros·trum ['rɑːstrəm] estrado *m*

ros·y ['roʊzɪ] *adj cheeks* sonrosado; *future* de color de rosa

rot [rɑːt] **1** *n in wood* putrefacción *f* **2** *v/i* (*pret & pp* ***rotted***) *of food, wood* pudrirse; *of teeth* cariarse

ro·ta ['roʊtə] turnos *mpl*; *actual document* calendario *m* con los turnos

ro·tate [roʊ'teɪt] **1** *v/i of blades, earth* girar **2** *v/t* hacer girar; *crops* rotar

ro·ta·tion [roʊ'teɪʃn] *around the sun etc* rotación *f*; ***do sth in rotation*** hacer algo por turnos rotatorios

rot·ten ['rɑːtn] *adj food, wood etc* podrido; *weather, luck* horrible; ***that was a rotten trick*** ¡qué mala idea!

rough [rʌf] **1** *adj surface, ground* accidentado; *hands, skin* áspero; *voice* ronco; (*violent*) bruto; *crossing* movido; *seas* bravo; (*approximate*) aproximado; ***rough draft*** borrador *m* **2** *adv*: ***sleep rough*** dormir a la intemperie **3** *n in golf* rough *m* **4** *v/t*: ***rough it*** apañárselas

◆ **rough up** *v/t* F dar una paliza a

rough·age ['rʌfɪdʒ] *in food* fibra *f*

rough·ly ['rʌflɪ] *adv* (*approximately*) aproximadamente; (*harshly*) brutalmente; ***roughly speaking*** aproximadamente

rou·lette [ruː'let] ruleta *f*

round [raʊnd] **1** *adj* redondo; ***in round figures*** en números redondos **2** *n of mailman, doctor, drinks, competition* ronda *f*; *of toast* rebanada *f*; *in boxing match* round *m*, asalto *m* **3** *v/t corner* doblar **4** *adv, prep* → ***around***

◆ **round off** *v/t edges* redondear; *meeting, night out* concluir

◆ **round up** *v/t figure* redondear (hacia la cifra más alta); *suspects, criminals* detener

round·a·bout ['raʊndəbaʊt] **1** *adj route, way of saying sth* indirecto **2** *n Br on road* rotonda *f*, *Span* glorieta *f*

'**round-the-world** *adj* alrededor del mundo

round 'trip viaje *m* de ida y vuelta

round trip 'tick·et billete *m or L.Am.* boleto *m* de ida y vuelta

'**round-up** *of cattle* rodeo *m*; *of suspects, criminals* redada *f*; *of news* resumen *m*

rouse [raʊz] *v/t from sleep* despertar; *interest, emotions* excitar, provocar

rous·ing ['raʊzɪŋ] *adj speech, finale* emocionante

route [raʊt] *n* ruta *f*, recorrido *m*

rou·tine [ruː'tiːn] **1** *adj* habitual **2** *n* rutina *f*; ***as a matter of routine*** como rutina

row[1] [roʊ] *n* (*line*) hilera *f*; ***5 days in a row*** 5 días seguidos

row[2] [roʊ] **1** *v/t boat* llevar remando **2** *v/i* remar

row[3] [raʊ] *n* (*quarrel*) pelea *f*, discusión *f*; (*noise*) alboroto *m*

row·boat ['roʊboʊt] bote *m* de remos

row·dy ['raʊdɪ] *adj* alborotador, *Span* follonero

roy·al [rɔɪəl] *adj* real

roy·al·ty ['rɔɪəltɪ] *royal persons* realeza *f*; *on book, recording* derechos *mpl* de autor

rub [rʌb] *v/t* (*pret & pp* ***rubbed***) frotar

◆ **rub down** *v/t to clean* lijar

◆ **rub in** *v/t cream, ointment* extender, frotar; ***don't rub it in!*** *fig* ¡no me lo restriegues por las narices!

◆ **rub off 1** *v/t dirt* limpiar frotando; *paint etc* borrar **2** *v/i*: ***it rubs off on you*** se te contagia

rub·ber ['rʌbər] **1** *n material* goma *f*, caucho *m*; P (*condom*) goma *f* P **2** *adj* de goma *or* caucho

rub·ber 'band goma *f* elástica

rub·ber 'gloves *npl* guantes *mpl* de goma

rub·bish ['rʌbɪʃ] basura *f*; *poor quality* basura *f*, porquería *f*; (*nonsense*) tonterías *fpl*; ***this radio is rubbish*** esta radio es una basura *or* porquería; ***don't talk rubbish!*** ¡no digas tonterías!

rub·ble ['rʌbl] escombros *mpl*

ru·by ['ruːbɪ] *jewel* rubí *m*

ruck·sack ['rʌksæk] mochila *f*

rud·der ['rʌdər] timón *m*

rud·dy ['rʌdɪ] *adj complexion* rubicundo

rude [ruːd] *adj person, behavior* maleducado, grosero; *language* grosero; ***it is rude to ...*** es de mala educación ...; ***I didn't mean to be rude*** no pretendía faltar al respeto

rude·ly ['ruːdlɪ] *adv* (*impolitely*) groseramente

rude·ness ['ruːdnɪs] mala *f* educación, grosería *f*

ru·di·men·ta·ry [ruːdɪ'mentərɪ] *adj* rudimentario

ru·di·ments ['ruːdɪmənts] *npl* rudimentos *mpl*
rue·ful ['ruːfəl] *adj* arrepentido, compungido
rue·ful·ly ['ruːfəlɪ] *adv* con arrepentimiento
ruf·fi·an ['rʌfɪən] rufián *m*
ruf·fle ['rʌfl] **1** *n on dress* volante *m* **2** *v/t hair* despeinar; *clothes* arrugar; *person* alterar, enfadar; ***get ruffled*** alterarse
rug [rʌg] alfombra *f*; (*blanket*) manta *f* (de viaje)
rug·by ['rʌgbɪ] rugby *m*
'rug·by match partido *m* de rugby
'rug·by play·er jugador(a) *m(f)* de rugby
rug·ged ['rʌgɪd] *adj scenery, cliffs* escabroso, accidentado; *face* de rasgos duros; *resistance* decidido
ru·in ['ruːɪn] **1** *n* ruina *f*; ***ruins*** ruinas *fpl*; ***in ruins*** *city, building* en ruinas; *of plans, marriage* arruinado **2** *v/t* arruinar; ***be ruined*** *financially* estar arruinado *or* en la ruina
rule [ruːl] **1** *n of club, game* regla *f*, norma *f*; *of monarch* reinado *m*; *for measuring* regla *f*; ***as a rule*** por regla general **2** *v/t country* gobernar; ***the judge ruled that …*** el juez dictaminó que … **3** *v/i of monarch* reinar
◆ **rule out** *v/t* descartar
rul·er ['ruːlər] *for measuring* regla *f*; *of state* gobernante *m/f*
rul·ing ['ruːlɪŋ] **1** *n* fallo *m*, decisión *f* **2** *adj party* gobernante, en el poder
rum [rʌm] *n drink* ron *m*
rum·ble ['rʌmbl] *v/i of stomach* gruñir; *of train in tunnel* retumbar
◆ **rum·mage around** ['rʌmɪdʒ] *v/i* buscar revolviendo
'rum·mage sale rastrillo *m* benéfico
ru·mor ['ruːmər] **1** *n* rumor *m* **2** *v/t*: ***it is rumored that …*** se rumorea que …
rump [rʌmp] *of animal* cuartos *mpl* traseros
rum·ple ['rʌmpl] *v/t clothes, paper* arrugar
rump·'steak filete *m* de lomo
run [rʌn] **1** *n on foot* carrera *f*; *in car* viaje *m*; *in tights* carrera *f*; THEA: *of play* temporada *f*; ***it has had a three year run*** *of play* lleva tres años en cartel; ***go for a run*** ir a correr; ***go for a run in the car*** ir a dar una vuelta en el coche; ***make a run for it*** salir corriendo; ***a criminal on the run*** un criminal fugado; ***in the short / long run*** a corto / largo plazo; ***a run on the dollar*** un movimiento especulativo contra el dólar **2** *v/i* (*pret* ***ran***, *pp* ***run***) *of person, animal* correr; *of river* correr, discurrir; *of paint, make-up* correrse; *of play* estar en cartel; *of engine, machine, software* funcionar; *in election* presentarse; ***run for President*** presentarse a las elecciones presidenciales; ***the trains run every ten minutes*** pasan trenes cada diez minutos; ***it doesn't run on Saturdays*** *of bus, train* no funciona los sábados; ***don't leave the tap running*** no dejes el grifo abierto; ***his nose is running*** le moquea la nariz; ***her eyes are running*** le lloran los ojos **3** *v/t* (*pret* ***ran***, *pp* ***run***) *race* correr; *business, hotel, project etc* dirigir; *software* usar; (*start*) ejecutar; *car* tener; (*use*) usar; ***can I run you to the station?*** ¿te puedo llevar hasta la estación?; ***he ran his eye down the page*** echó una ojeada a la página
◆ **run across** *v/t* (*meet*) encontrarse con; (*find*) encontrar
◆ **run away** *v/i* salir corriendo, huir; *from home* escaparse
◆ **run down 1** *v/t* (*knock down*) atropellar; (*criticize*) criticar; *stocks* reducir **2** *v/i of battery* agotarse
◆ **run into** *v/t* (*meet*) encontrarse con; *difficulties* tropezar con
◆ **run off 1** *v/i* salir corriendo **2** *v/t* (*print off*) tirar
◆ **run out** *v/i of contract* vencer; *of supplies* agotarse; ***time has run out*** se ha acabado el tiempo
◆ **run out of** *v/t time, supplies* quedarse sin; ***I ran out of gas*** me quedé sin gasolina; ***I'm running out of patience*** se me está acabando la paciencia
◆ **run over 1** *v/t* (*knock down*) atropellar; ***can we run over the details again?*** ¿podríamos repasar los detalles otra vez? **2** *v/i of water etc* desbordarse
◆ **run through** *v/t* (*rehearse, go over*) repasar
◆ **run up** *v/t debts, large bill* acumular; *clothes* coser
run·a·way ['rʌnəweɪ] *n persona que se ha fugado de casa*
run-'down *adj person* débil, apagado; *part of town, building* ruinoso
rung[1] [rʌŋ] *of ladder* peldaño *m*
rung[2] [rʌŋ] *pp* → ***ring***[2]
run·ner ['rʌnər] *athlete* corredor(a) *m(f)*
run·ner 'beans *npl* judías *fpl* verdes, *L.Am.* porotos *mpl* verdes, *Mex* ejotes *mpl*
run·ner-'up subcampeón(-ona) *m(f)*
run·ning ['rʌnɪŋ] **1** *n* SP el correr; (*jogging*) footing *m*; *of business* gestión *f* **2** *adj*: ***for two days running*** durante dos días seguidos
run·ning 'wa·ter agua *f* corriente

run·ny ['rʌnɪ] *adj mixture* fluido, líquido; *nose* que moquea
'run-up SP carrerilla *f*; ***in the run-up to*** en el periodo previo a
'run·way pista *f* de aterrizaje / despegue
rup·ture ['rʌptʃər] **1** *n* ruptura *f* **2** *v/i of pipe etc* romperse
ru·ral ['rʊrəl] *adj* rural
ruse [ruːz] artimaña *f*
rush [rʌʃ] **1** *n* prisa *f*; ***do sth in a rush*** hacer algo con prisas; ***be in a rush*** tener prisa; ***what's the big rush?*** ¿qué prisa tenemos? **2** *v/t person* meter prisa a; *meal* comer a toda prisa; ***rush s.o. to hospital*** llevar a alguien al hospital a toda prisa **3** *v/i* darse prisa
'rush hour hora *f* punta
Rus·sia ['rʌʃə] Rusia
Rus·sian ['rʌʃən] **1** *adj* ruso **2** *n* ruso(-a) *m(f)*; *language* ruso *m*
rust [rʌst] **1** *n* óxido *m* **2** *v/i* oxidarse
rus·tle ['rʌsl] **1** *n of silk, leaves* susurro *m* **2** *v/i of silk, leaves* susurrar
'rust-proof *adj* inoxidable
rust re·mov·er ['rʌstrɪmuːvər] desoxidante *m*
rust·y ['rʌstɪ] *adj* oxidado; ***my French is pretty rusty*** tengo el francés muy abandonado; ***I'm a little rusty*** estoy un poco falto de forma
rut [rʌt] *in road* rodada *f*; ***be in a rut*** *fig* estar estancado
ruth·less ['ruːθlɪs] *adj* implacable, despiadado
ruth·less·ly ['ruːθlɪslɪ] *adv* sin compasión, despiadadamente
ruth·less·ness ['ruːθlɪsnɪs] falta *f* de compasión
rye [raɪ] centeno *m*
'rye bread pan *m* de centeno

S

sab·bat·i·cal [sə'bætɪkl] *n year* año *m* sabático; ***a 6 month sabbatical*** 6 meses de excedencia
sab·o·tage ['sæbətɑːʒ] **1** *n* sabotaje *m* **2** *v/t* sabotear
sab·o·teur [sæbə'tɜːr] saboteador(a) *m(f)*
sac·cha·rin ['sækərɪn] *n* sacarina *f*
sa·chet ['sæʃeɪ] *of shampoo, cream etc* sobrecito *m*
sack [sæk] **1** *n bag* saco *m*; *for groceries* bolsa *f*; ***he got the sack*** F lo echaron **2** *v/t* F echar
sa·cred ['seɪkrɪd] *adj* sagrado
sac·ri·fice ['sækrɪfaɪs] **1** *n* sacrificio *m*; ***make sacrifices*** *fig* hacer sacrificios **2** *v/t* sacrificar
sac·ri·lege ['sækrɪlɪdʒ] sacrilegio *m*
sad [sæd] *adj person, face, song* triste; *state of affairs* lamentable, desgraciado
sad·dle ['sædl] **1** *n* silla *f* de montar **2** *v/t horse* ensillar; ***saddle s.o. with sth*** *fig* endilgar algo a alguien
sa·dism ['seɪdɪzm] sadismo *m*
sa·dist ['seɪdɪst] sádico(-a) *m(f)*
sa·dis·tic [sə'dɪstɪk] *adj* sádico
sad·ly ['sædlɪ] *adv look, say etc* con tristeza; (*regrettably*) lamentablemente
sad·ness ['sædnɪs] tristeza *f*
safe [seɪf] **1** *adj* seguro; *driver* prudente; (*not in danger*) a salvo; ***is it safe to walk here?*** ¿se puede andar por aquí sin peligro? **2** *n* caja *f* fuerte
'safe·guard **1** *n* garantía *f*; ***as a safeguard against*** como garantía contra **2** *v/t* salvaguardar
safe·ly ['seɪflɪ] *adv arrive* sin percances; (*successfully*) sin problemas; *drive* prudentemente; *assume* con certeza
'safe keep·ing: ***give sth to s.o. for safe keeping*** dar algo a alguien para que lo custodie
safe·ty ['seɪftɪ] seguridad *f*
'safety belt cinturón *m* de seguridad
'safe·ty-con·scious *adj*: ***be safety-conscious*** tener en cuenta la seguridad
safe·ty 'first prevención *f* de accidentes
'safe·ty pin imperdible *m*
sag [sæg] **1** *n in ceiling etc* combadura *f* **2** *v/i* (*pret & pp* ***sagged***) *of ceiling* combarse; *of rope* destensarse; *of tempo* disminuir
sa·ga ['sægə] saga *f*
sage [seɪdʒ] *n herb* salvia *f*
Sa·git·tar·i·us [sædʒɪ'terɪəs] ASTR Sagitario *m/f inv*
said [sed] *pret & pp* → ***say***
sail [seɪl] **1** *n of boat* vela *f*; *trip* viaje *m* (en

S

barco); ***go for a sail*** salir a navegar **2** *v/t yacht* manejar **3** *v/i* navegar; (*depart*) zarpar, hacerse a la mar
'sail·board 1 *n* tabla *f* de windsurf **2** *v/i* hacer windsurf
'sail·board·ing windsurf *m*
'sail·boat barco *m* de vela, velero *m*
sail·ing ['seɪlɪŋ] SP vela *f*
'sail·ing ship barco de vela, velero *m*
sail·or ['seɪlər] *in the navy* marino *m/f*; *in the merchant navy*, SP marinero(-a) *m(f)*; ***I'm a good / bad sailor*** no me mareo / me mareo con facilidad
saint [seɪnt] santo *m*
sake [seɪk]: ***for my sake*** por mí; ***for the sake of peace*** por la paz
sal·ad ['sæləd] ensalada *f*
sal·ad 'dress·ing aliño *m* *or* aderezo *m* para ensalada
sal·a·ry ['sælərɪ] sueldo *m*, salario *f*
'sal·a·ry scale escala *f* salarial
sale [seɪl] venta *f*; *reduced prices* rebajas *fpl*; ***for sale*** *sign* se vende; ***is this for sale?*** ¿está a la venta?; ***be on sale*** estar a la venta; *at reduced prices* estar de rebajas
sales [seɪlz] *npl department* ventas *fpl*
'sales clerk *in store* vendedor(a) *m(f)*, dependiente(-a) *m(f)*
'sales fig·ures *npl* cifras *fpl* de ventas
'sales·man vendedor *m*
sales 'man·ag·er jefe(-a) *m(f)* de ventas
'sales meet·ing reunión *f* del departamento de ventas
'sales·wo·man vendedora *f*
sa·lient ['seɪlɪənt] *adj* sobresaliente, destacado
sa·li·va [sə'laɪvə] saliva *f*
salm·on ['sæmən] (*pl* ***salmon***) salmón *m*
sa·loon [sə'luːn] MOT turismo *m*; (*bar*) bar *m*
salt [sɒːlt] **1** *n* sal *f* **2** *v/t food* salar
'salt·cel·lar salero *m*
salt 'wa·ter agua *f* salada
'salt-wa·ter fish pez *m* de agua salada
salt·y ['sɒːltɪ] *adj* salado
sal·u·tar·y ['sæljʊterɪ] *adj experience* beneficioso
sa·lute [sə'luːt] **1** *n* MIL saludo; ***take the salute*** presidir un desfile **2** *v/t* saludar; *fig* (*hail*) elogiar **3** *v/i* MIL saludar
Sal·va·dor(e)·an [sælvə'dɔːrən] **1** *adj* salvadoreño **2** *n* salvadoreño(-a) *m(f)*
sal·vage ['sælvɪdʒ] *v/t from wreck* rescatar
sal·va·tion [sæl'veɪʃn] *also fig* salvación *f*
Sal·va·tion 'Ar·my Ejército *m* de Salvación
same [seɪm] **1** *adj* mismo **2** *pron*: ***the same*** lo mismo; ***Happy New Year - the same to you*** Feliz Año Nuevo - igualmente; ***he's not the same any more*** ya no es el mismo; ***life isn't the same without you*** la vida es distinta sin ti; ***all the same*** (*even so*) aun así; ***men are all the same*** todos los hombres son iguales; ***it's all the same to me*** me da lo mismo, me da igual **3** *adv*: ***the same*** igual
sam·ple ['sæmpl] *n* muestra *f*
sanc·ti·mo·ni·ous [sæŋktɪ'moʊnɪəs] *adj* mojigato
sanc·tion ['sæŋkʃn] **1** *n* (*approval*) consentimiento *m*, aprobación *f*; (*penalty*) sanción *f* **2** *v/t* (*approve*) sancionar
sanc·ti·ty ['sæŋktətɪ] carácter *m* sagrado
sanc·tu·a·ry ['sæŋktʃʊerɪ] santuario *m*
sand [sænd] **1** *n* arena *f* **2** *v/t with sandpaper* lijar
san·dal ['sændl] sandalia *f*
'sand·bag saco *m* de arena
'sand·blast *v/t* arenar
'sand dune duna *f*
sand·er ['sændər] *tool* lijadora *f*
'sand·pa·per 1 *n* lija *f* **2** *v/t* lijar
'sand·stone arenisca *f*
sand·wich ['sænwɪtʃ] **1** *n Span* bocadillo *m*, *L.Am.* sandwich *m* **2** *v/t*: ***be sandwiched between two …*** estar encajonado entre dos …
sand·y ['sændɪ] *adj soil* arenoso; *feet, towel etc* lleno de arena; *hair* rubio oscuro; ***sandy beach*** playa *f* de arena
sane [seɪn] *adj* cuerdo
sang [sæŋ] *pret* → ***sing***
san·i·tar·i·um [sænɪ'terɪəm] sanatorio *m*
san·i·ta·ry ['sænɪterɪ] *adj conditions* salubre, higiénico; ***sanitary installations*** instalaciones *fpl* sanitarias
'san·i·ta·ry nap·kin compresa *f*
san·i·ta·tion [sænɪ'teɪʃn] (*sanitary installations*) instalaciones *fpl* sanitarias; (*removal of waste*) saneamiento *f*
san·i'ta·tion de·part·ment servicio *m* de limpieza
san·i·ty ['sænətɪ] razón *f*, juicio *m*
sank [sæŋk] *pret* → ***sink***
San·ta Claus ['sæntəklɒːz] Papá Noel *m*, Santa Claus *m*
sap [sæp] **1** *n in tree* savia *f* **2** *v/t* (*pret & pp* ***sapped***) *s.o.'s energy* consumir
sap·phire ['sæfaɪr] *n jewel* zafiro *m*
sar·cas·m ['sɑːrkæzm] sarcasmo *m*
sar·cas·tic [sɑːr'kæstɪk] *adj* sarcástico
sar·cas·tic·al·ly [sɑːr'kæstɪklɪ] *adv* sarcásticamente
sar·dine [sɑːr'diːn] sardina *f*
sar·don·ic [sɑːr'dɑːnɪk] *adj* sardónico
sar·don·ic·al·ly [sɑːr'dɑːnɪklɪ] *adv* sardó-

S

nicamente
sash [sæʃ] *on dress* faja *f*; *on uniform* fajín *m*
sat [sæt] *pret & pp* → ***sit***
Sa·tan ['seɪtn] Satán, Satanás
satch·el ['sætʃl] *for schoolchild* cartera *f*
sat·el·lite ['sætəlaɪt] satélite *m*
'sat·el·lite dish antena *f* parabólica
sat·el·lite T'V televisión *f* por satélite
sat·in ['sætɪn] **1** *adj* satinado **2** *n* satín *m*
sat·ire ['sætaɪr] sátira *f*
sa·tir·i·cal [sə'tɪrɪkl] *adj* satírico
sat·i·rist ['sætərɪst] escritor(a) *m(f)* de sátiras
sat·ir·ize ['sætəraɪz] *v/t* satirizar
sat·is·fac·tion [sætɪs'fækʃn] satisfacción *f*; ***I get satisfaction out of my job*** mi trabajo me produce satisfacción; ***is that to your satisfaction madam?*** *fml* ¿está al gusto de la señora?
sat·is·fac·to·ry [sætɪs'fæktərɪ] *adj* satisfactorio; (*just good enough*) suficiente
sat·is·fy ['sætɪsfaɪ] *v/t* (*pret & pp* ***satisfied***) satisfacer; *conditions* cumplir; ***I am satisfied*** (*had enough to eat*) estoy lleno; ***I am satisfied that ...*** (*convinced*) estoy convencido *or* satisfecho de que ...; ***I hope you're satisfied!*** ¡estarás contento!
Sat·ur·day ['sætərdeɪ] sábado *m*
sauce [sɒːs] salsa *f*
'sauce·pan cacerola *f*
sau·cer ['sɒːsər] plato *m* (*de taza*)
sauc·y ['sɒːsɪ] *adj person, dress* descarado
Sa·u·di A·ra·bi·a [saʊdɪə'reɪbɪə] Arabia Saudí *or* Saudita
Sa·u·di A·ra·bi·an [saʊdɪə'reɪbɪən] **1** *adj* saudita, saudí **2** *n* saudita *m/f*, saudí *m/f*
sau·na ['sɒːnə] sauna *f*
saun·ter ['sɒːntər] *v/i* andar sin prisas
saus·age ['sɒːsɪdʒ] salchicha *f*
sav·age ['sævɪdʒ] **1** *adj animal*, *attack* salvaje; *criticism* feroz **2** *n* salvaje *m/f*
sav·age·ry ['sævɪdʒrɪ] crueldad *f*
save [seɪv] **1** *v/t* (*rescue*) rescatar, salvar; *money, time, effort* ahorrar; (*collect*) guardar; COMPUT guardar; *goal* parar; REL salvar **2** *v/i* (*put money aside*) ahorrar; SP hacer una parada **3** *n* SP parada *f*
◆ **save up for** *v/t* ahorrar para
sav·er ['seɪvər] *person* ahorrador(a) *m(f)*
savi·ng ['seɪvɪŋ] *amount saved, activity* ahorro *m*
sav·ings ['seɪvɪŋz] *npl* ahorros *mpl*
'sav·ings ac·count cuenta *f* de ahorros
sav·ings and 'loan caja *f* de ahorros
'sav·ings bank caja *f* de ahorros
sa·vior, *Br* **sa·viour** ['seɪvjər] REL salvador *m*
sa·vor ['seɪvər] *v/t* saborear
sa·vor·y ['seɪvərɪ] *adj not sweet* salado
sa·vour *etc Br* → ***savor*** *etc*
saw¹ [sɒː] **1** *n tool* serrucho *m*, sierra *f* **2** *v/t* aserrar
saw² [sɒː] *pret* → ***see***
◆ **saw off** *v/t* cortar (con un serrucho)
'saw·dust serrín *m*, aserrín *m*
sax·o·phone ['sæksəfoʊn] saxofón *m*
say [seɪ] **1** *v/t* (*pret & pp* ***said***) decir; *poem* recitar; ***that is to say*** es decir; ***what do you say to that?*** ¿qué opinas de eso?; ***what does the note say?*** ¿qué dice la nota?, ¿qué pone en la nota? **2** *n*: ***have one's say*** expresar una opinión
say·ing ['seɪɪŋ] dicho *m*
scab [skæb] *on skin* costra *f*
scaf·fold·ing ['skæfəldɪŋ] *on building* andamiaje *m*
scald [skɒːld] *v/t* escaldar
scale¹ [skeɪl] *on fish, reptile* escama *f*
scale² [skeɪl] **1** *n* (*size*) escala *f*, tamaño *m*; *on thermometer, map*, MUS escala *f*; ***on a larger scale*** a gran escala; ***on a smaller scale*** a pequeña escala **2** *v/t cliffs etc* escalar
◆ **scale down** *v/t* disminuir, reducir
scale 'draw·ing dibujo *m* a escala
scales [skeɪlz] *npl for weighing* báscula *f*, peso *m*
scal·lop ['skæləp] *n shellfish* vieira *f*
scalp [skælp] *n* cuero *m* cabelludo
scal·pel ['skælpl] bisturí *m*
scam [skæm] F chanchullo *m* F
scam·pi ['skæmpɪ] gambas *fpl* rebozadas
scan [skæn] **1** *v/t* (*pret & pp* ***scanned***) *horizon* otear; *page* ojear; COMPUT escanear **2** *n of brain* escáner *m*; *of fetus* ecografía *f*
◆ **scan in** *v/t* COMPUT escanear
scan·dal ['skændl] escándalo *m*
scan·dal·ize ['skændəlaɪz] *v/t* escandalizar
scan·dal·ous ['skændələs] *adj affair, prices* escandaloso
Scan·di·na·vi·a [skændɪ'neɪvɪə] Escandinavia
scan·ner ['skænər] MED, COMPUT escáner *m*; *for foetus* ecógrafo *m*
scant [skænt] *adj* escaso
scant·i·ly ['skæntɪlɪ] *adv*: ***be scantily clad*** andar ligero de ropa
scant·y ['skæntɪ] *adj skirt* cortísimo; *bikini* mínimo
scape·goat ['skeɪpgoʊt] cabeza *f* de turco, chivo *m* expiatorio
scar [skɑːr] **1** *n* cicatriz *f* **2** *v/t* (*pret & pp*

scarred) cicatrizar

scarce [skers] *adj in short supply* escaso; ***make o.s. scarce*** desaparecer

scarce·ly ['skerslı] *adv*: ***he had scarcely said it when ...*** apenas lo había dicho cuando ...; ***there was scarcely anything left*** no quedaba casi nada; ***I scarcely know her*** apenas la conozco

scar·ci·ty ['skersıtı] escasez *f*

scare [sker] **1** *v/t* asustar, atemorizar; ***be scared of*** tener miedo de **2** *n* (*panic, alarm*) miedo *m*, temor *m*; ***give s.o. a scare*** dar a alguien un susto

◆ **scare away** *v/t* ahuyentar

'**scare·crow** espantapájaros *m inv*

scare·mon·ger ['skermʌŋgər] alarmista *m/f*

scarf [skɑːrf] *around neck, over head* pañuelo *m*; *woollen* bufanda *f*

scar·let ['skɑːrlət] *adj* escarlata

scar·let 'fe·ver escarlatina *f*

scar·y ['skerı] *adj sight* espeluznante; ***scary music*** música de miedo

scath·ing ['skeıðıŋ] *adj* feroz

scat·ter ['skætər] **1** *v/t leaflets* esparcir; *seeds* diseminar; ***be scattered all over the room*** estar esparcido por toda la habitación **2** *v/i of people* dispersarse

scat·ter·brained ['skætərbreınd] *adj* despistado

scat·tered ['skætərd] *adj showers, family, villages* disperso

scav·enge ['skævındʒ] *v/i* rebuscar; ***scavenge for sth*** rebuscar en busca de algo

scav·eng·er ['skævındʒər] *animal, bird* carroñero *m*; (*person*) *persona que busca comida entre la basura*

sce·na·ri·o [sı'nɑːrıoʊ] situación *f*

scene [siːn] escena *f*; *of accident, crime etc* lugar *m*; (*argument*) escena *f*, número *m*; ***make a scene*** hacer una escena, montar un número; ***scenes*** THEA decorados *mpl*; ***jazz / rock scene*** mundo del jazz / rock; ***behind the scenes*** entre bastidores

sce·ne·ry ['siːnərı] THEA escenario *m*

scent [sent] *n* olor *m*; (*perfume*) perfume *m*, fragancia *m*

scep·tic *etc Br* → ***skeptic*** *etc*

sched·ule ['ʃeduːl] **1** *n of events, work* programa *m*; *of exams* calendario *m*; *for train, work, of lessons* horario *m*; ***be on schedule*** *of work* ir según lo previsto; *of train* ir a la hora prevista; ***be behind schedule*** *of work, train etc* ir con retraso **2** *v/t* (*put on schedule*) programar; ***it's scheduled for completion next month*** está previsto que se complete el próximo mes

sched·uled 'flight ['ʃeduːld] vuelo *m* regular

scheme [skiːm] **1** *n* (*plan*) plan *m*, proyecto *m*; (*plot*) confabulación *f* **2** *v/i* (*plot*) confabularse

schem·ing ['skiːmıŋ] *adj* maquinador

schiz·o·phre·ni·a [skıtsə'friːnıə] esquizofrenia *f*

schiz·o·phren·ic [skıtsə'frenık] **1** *n* esquizofrénico(-a) *m*(*f*) **2** *adj* esquizofrénico

schol·ar ['skɑːlər] erudito(-a) *m*(*f*)

schol·ar·ly ['skɑːlərlı] *adj* erudito

schol·ar·ship ['skɑːlərʃıp] *scholarly work* estudios *mpl*; *financial award* beca *f*

school [skuːl] escuela *f*, colegio *m*; (*university*) universidad *f*

'**school bag** (*satchel*) cartera *f*

'**school·boy** escolar *m*

'**school·children** *npl* escolares *mpl*

'**school days** *npl*; ***do you remember your school days?*** ¿te acuerdas de cuándo ibas al colegio?

'**school·girl** escolar *f*

'**school·mate** compañero *m* de colegio

'**school·teach·er** maestro(-a) *m*(*f*), profesor(a) *m*(*f*)

sci·at·i·ca [saı'ætıkə] ciática *f*

sci·ence ['saıəns] ciencia *f*

sci·ence 'fic·tion ciencia *f* ficción

sci·en·tif·ic [saıən'tıfık] *adj* científico

sci·en·tist ['saıəntıst] científico(-a) *m*(*f*)

scis·sors ['sızərz] *npl* tijeras *fpl*

scoff[1] [skɑːf] *v/t* F (*eat fast*) zamparse F

scoff[2] [skɑːf] *v/i* (*mock*) burlarse, mofarse

◆ **scoff at** *v/t* burlarse de, mofarse de

scold [skoʊld] *v/t child, husband* regañar

scoop [skuːp] **1** *n implement* cuchara *f*; *for mud* pala *f*; (*story*) exclusiva *f* **2** *v/t*: ***scoop sth into sth*** recoger algo para meterlo en algo

◆ **scoop up** *v/t* recoger

scoot·er ['skuːtər] *with motor* escúter *m*; *child's* patinete *m*

scope [skoʊp] alcance *m*; (*freedom, opportunity*) oportunidad *f*; ***he wants more scope to do his own thing*** quiere más libertad para hacer lo que quiere

scorch [skɔːrʧ] *v/t* quemar

scorch·ing ['skɔːrʧıŋ] *adj* abrasador

score [skɔːr] **1** *n* SP resultado *m*; *in competition* puntuación *f*; (*written music*) partitura *f*; *of movie etc* banda *f* sonora, música *f*; ***what's the score?*** SP ¿cómo van?; ***have a score to settle with s.o.*** tener una cuenta pendiente con alguien; ***keep (the) score*** llevar el tanteo **2** *v/t goal* marcar; *point* anotar; (*cut: line*)

S

marcar **3** *v/i* marcar; (*keep the score*) llevar el tanteo; ***that's where he scores*** ése es su punto fuerte

'score·board marcador *m*

scor·er ['skɔːrər] *of goal* goleador(a) *m(f)*; *of point* anotador(a) *m(f)*; (*official score-keeper*) *encargado del marcador*

scorn [skɔːrn] **1** *n* desprecio *m*; ***pour scorn on sth*** despreciar algo, menospreciar algo **2** *v/t idea*, *suggestion* despreciar

scorn·ful ['skɔːrnfəl] *adj* despreciativo

scorn·ful·ly ['skɔːrnfəlɪ] *adv* con desprecio

Scor·pi·o ['skɔːrpɪoʊ] ASTR Escorpio *m/f inv*

Scot [skɑːt] escocés(-esa) *m(f)*

Scotch [skɑːʧ] (*whisky*) whisky *m* escocés

Scotch 'tape® celo *m*, *L.Am.* Durex® *m*

scot-'free *adv*: ***get off scot-free*** salir impune

Scot·land ['skɑːtlənd] Escocia

Scots·man ['skɑːtsmən] escocés *m*

Scots·wom·an ['skɑːtswʊmən] escocesa *f*

Scot·tish ['skɑːtɪʃ] *adj* escocés

scoun·drel ['skaʊndrəl] canalla *m/f*

scour¹ ['skaʊər] *v/t* (*search*) rastrear, peinar

scour² ['skaʊər] *v/t pans* fregar

scout [skaʊt] *n* (*boy scout*) boy-scout *m*

scowl [skaʊl] **1** *n* ceño *m* **2** *v/i* fruncir el ceño

scram [skræm] *v/i* (*pret & pp* ***scrammed***) F largarse F; ***scram!*** ¡largo!

scram·ble ['skræmbl] **1** *n* (*rush*) prisa *f* **2** *v/t message* cifrar, codificar **3** *v/i* (*climb*) trepar; ***he scrambled to his feet*** se levantó de un salto

scram·bled 'eggs ['skræmbld] *npl* huevos *mpl* revueltos

scrap [skræp] **1** *n metal* chatarra *f*; (*fight*) pelea *f*; *of food* trocito *m*; *of evidence* indicio *m*; *of common sense* pizca *f* **2** *v/t* (*pret & pp* ***scrapped***) *plan*, *project* abandonar; *paragraph* borrar

'scrap·book álbum *m* de recortes

scrape [skreɪp] **1** *n on paintwork etc* arañazo *m* **2** *v/t paintwork* rayar; ***scrape a living*** apañarse

◆ **scrape through** *v/i in exam* aprobar por los pelos

'scrap heap: ***be good for the scrap heap*** *of person* estar para el arrastre; *of object* estar para tirar

scrap 'met·al chatarra *f*

scrap 'pa·per papel *m* usado

scrap·py ['skræpɪ] *adj work*, *writing* desorganizado

scratch [skræʧ] **1** *n mark* marca *f*; ***have a scratch*** *to stop itching* rascarse; ***start from scratch*** empezar desde cero; ***your work isn't up to scratch*** tu trabajo es insuficiente **2** *v/t* (*mark: skin*) arañar; (*mark: paint*) rayar; *because of itch* rascarse **3** *v/i of cat etc* arañar; *because of itch* rascarse

scrawl [skrɒːl] **1** *n* garabato *m* **2** *v/t* garabatear

scraw·ny ['skrɒːnɪ] *adj* escuálido

scream [skriːm] **1** *n* grito *m*; ***screams of laughter*** carcajadas *fpl* **2** *v/i* gritar

screech [skriːʧ] **1** *n of tires* chirrido *m*; (*scream*) chillido *m* **2** *v/i of tires* chirriar; (*scream*) chillar

screen [skriːn] **1** *n in room*, *hospital* mampara *f*; *protective* cortina *f*; *in movie theater* pantalla *f*; COMPUT monitor *m*, pantalla *f* **2** *v/t* (*protect*, *hide*) ocultar; *movie* proyectar; *for security reasons* investigar

'screen·play guión *m*

'screen sav·er COMPUT salvapantallas *m inv*

'screen test *for movie* prueba *f*

screw [skruː] **1** *n* tornillo *m*; V (*sex*) polvo *m* V **2** *v/t*: ***screw sth to sth*** atornillar algo a algo; V (*have sex with*) echar un polvo con V; F (*cheat*) timar F

◆ **screw up 1** *v/t eyes* cerrar; *piece of paper* arrugar; F (*make a mess of*) fastidiar F **2** *v/i* F (*make a bad mistake*) meter la pata F

'screw·driv·er destornillador *m*

screwed 'up [skruːd'ʌp] *adj* F *psychologically* acomplejado

'screw top *on bottle* tapón *m* de rosca

screw·y ['skruːɪ] *adj* F chiflado F; *idea*, *film* descabellado F

scrib·ble ['skrɪbl] **1** *n* garabato *m* **2** *v/t & v/i* garabatear

scrimp [skrɪmp] *v/i*: ***scrimp and scrape*** pasar apuros, pasar estrecheces

script [skrɪpt] *for movie*, *play* guión *m*; *form of writing* caligrafía *f*

scrip·ture ['skrɪpʧər] escritura *f*; ***the (Holy) Scriptures*** las Sagradas Escrituras

'script·writ·er guionista *m/f*

scroll [skroʊl] *n* (*manuscript*) manuscrito *m*

◆ **scroll down** *v/i* COMPUT avanzar

◆ **scroll up** *v/i* COMPUT retroceder

scrounge [skraʊndʒ] *v/t* gorronear

scroung·er ['skraʊndʒər] gorrón(-ona) *m(f)*

scrub [skrʌb] *v/t* (*pret & pp* ***scrubbed***) *floors* fregar; *hands* frotar

scrub·bing brush ['skrʌbɪŋ] *for floor* ce-

pillo *m* para fregar
scruff·y ['skrʌfɪ] *adj* andrajoso, desaliñado
scrum [skrʌm] *in rugby* melé *f*
◆ **scrunch up** [skrʌntʃ] *v/t plastic cup etc* estrujar
scru·ples ['skru:plz] *npl* escrúpulos *mpl*
scru·pu·lous ['skru:pjələs] *adj with moral principles* escrupuloso; (*thorough*) meticuloso; *attention to detail* minucioso
scru·pu·lous·ly ['skru:pjələslɪ] *adv* (*meticulously*) minuciosamente
scru·ti·nize ['skru:tɪnaɪz] *v/t* (*examine closely*) estudiar, examinar
scru·ti·ny ['skru:tɪnɪ] escrutinio *m*; ***come under scrutiny*** ser objeto de investigación
scu·ba div·ing ['sku:bə] submarinismo *m*
scuf·fle ['skʌfl] *n* riña *f*
sculp·tor ['skʌlptər] escultor(a) *m*(*f*)
sculp·ture ['skʌlptʃər] escultura *f*
scum [skʌm] *on liquid* película *f* de suciedad; (*pej*: *people*) escoria *f*
sea [si:] mar *m*; ***by the sea*** junto al mar
'**sea·bed** fondo *m* marino
'**sea·bird** ave *f* marina
sea·far·ing ['si:ferɪŋ] *adj nation* marinero
'**sea·food** marisco *m*
'**sea·front** paseo *m* marítimo
'**sea·go·ing** *adj vessel* de altura
'**sea·gull** gaviota *f*
seal[1] [si:l] *n animal* foca *f*
seal[2] [si:l] **1** *n on document* sello *m*; TECH junta *f*, sello *m* **2** *v/t container* sellar
◆ **seal off** *v/t area* aislar
'**sea lev·el**: ***above sea level*** sobre el nivel del mar; ***below sea level*** bajo el nivel del mar
seam [si:m] *n on garment* costura *f*; *of ore* filón *m*
'**sea·man** marinero *m*
seam·stress ['si:mstrɪs] modista *f*
'**sea·port** puerto *m* marítimo
'**sea pow·er** *nation* potencia *f* marítima
search [sɜ:rtʃ] **1** *n* búsqueda *f*; ***be in search of*** estar en busca de **2** *v/t baggage, person* registrar; ***search a place for s.o.*** buscar a alguien en un lugar
◆ **search for** *v/t* buscar
search·ing ['sɜ:rtʃɪŋ] *adj look* escrutador; *question* difícil
'**search·light** reflector *m*
'**search par·ty** grupo *m* de rescate
'**search war·rant** orden *f* de registro
'**sea·shore** orilla *f*
'**sea·sick** *adj* mareado; ***get seasick*** marearse
'**sea·side** costa *f*, playa *f*; ***seaside resort*** centro *m* de veraneo costero
sea·son ['si:zn] *n* (*winter, spring etc*) estación *f*; *for tourism etc* temporada *f*; ***plums aren't in season at the moment*** ahora no es temporada de ciruelas
sea·son·al ['si:znl] *adj fruit, vegetables* del tiempo; *employment* temporal
sea·soned ['si:znd] *adj wood* seco; *traveler, campaigner* experimentado
sea·son·ing ['si:znɪŋ] condimento *m*
'**sea·son tick·et** abono *m*
seat [si:t] **1** *n in room, bus, plane* asiento; *in theater* butaca *f*; *of pants* culera *f*; ***please take a seat*** por favor, siéntese **2** *v/t* (*have seating for*): ***the hall can seat 200 people*** la sala tiene capacidad para 200 personas; ***please remain seated*** por favor, permanezcan sentados
'**seat belt** cinturón *m* de seguridad
'**sea ur·chin** erizo *m* de mar
'**sea·weed** alga(s) *f*(pl)
se·clud·ed [sɪ'klu:dɪd] *adj* apartado
se·clu·sion [sɪ'klu:ʒn] aislamiento *m*
sec·ond[1] ['sekənd] **1** *n of time* segundo *m* **2** *adj* segundo **3** *adv come in* en segundo lugar **4** *v/t motion* apoyar
se·cond[2] [sɪ'kɑ:nd] *v/t*: ***be seconded to*** ser asignado a
sec·ond·a·ry ['sekənderɪ] *adj* secundario; ***of secondary importance*** de menor importancia
sec·ond·a·ry ed·u'ca·tion educación *f* secundaria
se·cond 'best *adj*: ***be second best*** ser el segundo mejor; *inferior* ser un segundón; ***the second best runner in the school*** el segundo mejor corredor del colegio
sec·ond 'big·gest *adj*: ***it is the second biggest company in the area*** es la segunda empresa más grande de la zona
sec·ond 'class *adj ticket* de segunda clase
sec·ond 'floor tercer piso *m*, *Br* segundo piso *m*
'**sec·ond hand** *n on clock* segundero *m*
sec·ond-'hand **1** *adj* de segunda mano **2** *adv buy* de segunda mano
sec·ond·ly ['sekəndlɪ] *adv* en segundo lugar
sec·ond-'rate *adj* inferior
sec·ond 'thoughts: ***I've had second thoughts*** he cambiado de idea
se·cre·cy ['si:krəsɪ] secretismo *m*
se·cret ['si:krət] **1** *n* secreto *m*; ***in secret*** en secreto **2** *adj* secreto
se·cret 'a·gent agente *m/f* secreto
sec·re·tar·i·al [sekrə'terɪəl] *adj tasks, job* de secretario
sec·re·tar·y ['sekrəterɪ] secretario(-a) *m*(*f*); POL ministro(-a) *m*(*f*)

Sec·re·tar·y of 'State *in USA* Secretario(-a) *m(f)* de Estado
se·crete [sɪ'kriːt] *v/t* (*give off*) segregar; (*hide away*) esconder
se·cre·tion [sɪ'kriːʃn] secreción *f*
se·cre·tive ['siːkrətɪv] *adj* reservado
se·cret·ly ['siːkrətlɪ] *adv* en secreto
se·cret po'lice policía *f* secreta
se·cret 'ser·vice servicio *m* secreto
sect [sekt] secta *f*
sec·tion ['sekʃn] *of book, company, text* sección *f*; *of building* zona *f*; *of apple* parte *f*
sec·tor ['sektər] sector *m*
sec·u·lar ['sekjələr] *adj* laico
se·cure [sɪ'kjʊr] **1** *adj shelf etc* seguro; *job, contract* fijo **2** *v/t shelf etc* asegurar; *s.o.'s help* conseguir
se·cu·ri·ty [sɪ'kjʊrətɪ] seguridad *f*; *for investment* garantía *f*
se'cu·ri·ties mar·ket FIN mercado *m* de valores
se'cu·ri·ty a·lert alerta *f*
se'cu·ri·ty check control *m* de seguridad
se'cu·ri·ty-con·scious *adj* consciente de la seguridad
se'cu·ri·ty forces *npl* fuerzas *fpl* de seguridad
se'cu·ri·ty guard guardia *m/f* de seguridad
se'cu·ri·ty risk *person* peligro *m* (para la seguridad)
se·dan [sɪ'dæn] turismo *m*
se·date [sɪ'deɪt] *v/t* sedar
se·da·tion [sɪ'deɪʃn]: ***be under sedation*** estar sedado
sed·a·tive ['sedətɪv] *n* sedante *m*
sed·en·ta·ry ['sedənterɪ] *adj job* sedentario
sed·i·ment ['sedɪmənt] sedimento *m*
se·duce [sɪ'duːs] *v/t* seducir
se·duc·tion [sɪ'dʌkʃn] seducción *f*
se·duc·tive [sɪ'dʌktɪv] *adj dress* seductor; *offer* tentador
see [siː] *v/t* (*pret* ***saw***, *pp* ***seen***) ver; (*understand*) entender, ver; *romantically* ver, salir con; ***I see*** ya veo; ***can I see the manager?*** ¿puedo ver al encargado?; ***you should see a doctor*** deberías ir a que te viera un médico; ***see s.o. home*** acompañar a alguien a casa; ***see you!*** F ¡hasta la vista!, ¡chao! F
◆ **see about** *v/t* (*look into*): ***I'll see about getting it repaired*** me encargaré de que lo arreglen
◆ **see off** *v/t at airport etc* despedir; (*chase away*) espantar
◆ **see out** *v/t*: ***see s.o. out*** acompañar a alguien a la puerta
◆ **see to** *v/t*: ***see to sth*** ocuparse de algo; ***see to it that sth gets done*** asegurarse de que algo se haga
seed [siːd] semilla *f*; *in tennis* cabeza *f* de serie; ***go to seed*** *of person* descuidarse; *of district* empeorarse
seed·ling ['siːdlɪŋ] planta *f* de semillero
seed·y ['siːdɪ] *adj bar, district* de mala calaña
see·ing 'eye dog ['siːɪŋ] perro *m* lazarillo
see·ing (that) ['siːɪŋ] *conj* dado que, ya que
seek [siːk] *v/t* (*pret & pp* ***sought***) buscar
seem [siːm] *v/i* parecer; ***it seems that ...*** parece que ...
seem·ing·ly ['siːmɪŋlɪ] *adv* aparentemente
seen [siːn] *pp* → ***see***
seep [siːp] *v/i of liquid* filtrarse
◆ **seep out** *v/i of liquid* filtrarse
see·saw ['siːsɒː] *n* sube y baja *m*
seethe [siːð] *v/i*: ***be seething with anger*** estar a punto de estallar (de cólera)
'see-through *adj dress, material* transparente
seg·ment ['segmənt] segmento *m*
seg·ment·ed [seg'məntɪd] *adj* segmentado, dividido
seg·re·gate ['segrɪgeɪt] *v/t* segregar
seg·re·ga·tion [segrɪ'geɪʃn] segregación *f*
seis·mol·o·gy [saɪz'mɑːlədʒɪ] sismología *f*
seize [siːz] *v/t s.o., s.o.'s arm* agarrar; *opportunity* aprovechar; *of Customs, police etc* incautarse de
◆ **seize up** *v/i of engine* atascarse
sei·zure ['siːʒər] MED ataque *m*; *of drugs etc* incautación *f*; *amount seized* alijo *m*
sel·dom ['seldəm] *adv* raramente, casi nunca
se·lect [sɪ'lekt] **1** *v/t* seleccionar **2** *adj* (*exclusive*) selecto
se·lec·tion [sɪ'lekʃn] selección *f*; (*choosing*) elección *f*
se'lec·tion pro·cess proceso *m* de selección
se·lec·tive [sɪ'lektɪv] *adj* selectivo
self [self] (*pl* ***selves*** [selvz]) ego *m*; ***my other self*** mi otro yo
self-ad·dressed 'en·ve·lope [selfə'drest]: ***send us a self-addressed envelope*** envíenos un sobre con sus datos
self-as'sur·ance confianza *f* en sí mismo
self-assured [selfə'ʃʊrd] *adj* seguro de sí mismo
self-ca·ter·ing a'part·ment [self'keɪtərɪŋ] *Br* apartamento *m or Span* piso *m* sin servicio de comidas
self-'cen·tered, *Br* **self-'cen·tred** [self-

S

'sentərd] *adj* egoísta
self-'clean·ing *adj oven* con autolimpieza
self-con'fessed [selfkən'fest] *adj*: ***he's a self-confessed megalomaniac*** se confiesa megalómano
self-'con·fi·dence confianza *f* en sí mismo
self-'con·fi·dent *adj* seguro de sí mismo
self-'con·scious *adj* tímido
self-'con·scious·ness timidez *f*
self-con·tained [selfkən'teɪnd] *adj apartment* independiente
self con'trol autocontrol *m*
self-de'fence *Br*, **self-de'fense** autodefensa *f*; ***in self-defence*** en defensa propia
self-'dis·ci·pline autodisciplina *f*
self-'doubt inseguridad *f*
self-em·ployed [selfɪm'plɔɪd] *adj* autónomo
self-e'steem autoestima *f*
self-ex'pres·sion autoexpresión *f*
self-'ev·i·dent *adj* obvio
self-'gov·ern·ment autogobierno *m*
self-'in·terest interés *m* propio
self·ish ['selfɪʃ] *adj* egoísta
self·less ['selflɪs] *adj* desinteresado
self-made 'man [self'meɪd] hombre *m* hecho a sí mismo
self-'pit·y autocompasión *f*
self-'por·trait autorretrato *m*
self-pos·sessed [selfpə'zest] *adj* sereno
self-re'li·ant *adj* autosuficiente
self-re'spect amor *m* propio
self-right·eous [self'raɪʧəs] *adj pej* santurrón, intolerante
self-sat·is·fied [self'sætɪzfaɪd] *adj pej* pagado de sí mismo
self-'ser·vice *adj* de autoservicio
self-ser·vice 'res·tau·rant (restaurante *m*) autoservicio *m*
self-taught [self'tɒːt] *adj* autodidacta
sell [sel] *v/t & v/i* (*pret & pp* ***sold***) vender
◆ **sell out** *v/i of product* agotarse; ***we've sold out*** se nos ha(n) agotado
◆ **sell out of** *v/t* agotar las existencias de
◆ **sell up** *v/i* vender todo
'sell-by date fecha *f* límite de venta; ***be past its sell-by date*** haber pasado la fecha límite de venta
sell·er ['selər] vendedor(a) *m*(*f*)
sell·ing ['selɪŋ] *n* COM ventas *fpl*
'sell·ing point COM ventaja *f*
Sel·lo·tape® ['seləteɪp] *Br* celo *m*, *L.Am.* Durex® *m*
se·men ['siːmən] semen *m*
se·mes·ter [sɪ'mestər] semestre *m*
sem·i ['semɪ] *n truck* camión *m* semirremolque
'sem·i·cir·cle semicírculo *m*
sem·i'cir·cu·lar *adj* semicircular
semi-'co·lon punto *m* y coma
sem·i·con'duc·tor ELEC semiconductor *m*
semi'fi·nal semifinal *f*
semi'fi·nal·ist semifinalista *m/f*
sem·i·nar ['semɪnɑːr] seminario *m*
sem·i'skilled *adj* semicualificado
sen·ate ['senət] senado *m*
sen·a·tor ['senətər] senador(a) *m*(*f*); ***Senator George Schwarz*** el Senador George Schwarz
send [send] *v/t* (*pret & pp* ***sent***) enviar, mandar; ***the doctor sent him to a specialist*** el médico lo envió *or* mandó a un especialista; ***send her my best wishes*** dale recuerdos de mi parte
◆ **send back** *v/t* devolver
◆ **send for** *v/t* mandar buscar
◆ **send in** *v/t troops, application* enviar, mandar; *next interviewee* hacer pasar
◆ **send off** *v/t letter, fax etc* enviar, mandar
send·er ['sendər] *of letter* remitente *m/f*
se·nile ['siːnaɪl] *adj* senil
se·nil·i·ty [sɪ'nɪlətɪ] senilidad *f*
se·ni·or ['siːnjər] *adj* (*older*) mayor; *in rank* superior
se·ni·or 'cit·i·zen persona *f* de la tercera edad
se·ni·or·i·ty [siːnj'ɑːrətɪ] *in job* antigüedad *f*
sen·sa·tion [sen'seɪʃn] sensación *f*
sen·sa·tion·al [sen'seɪʃnl] *adj news, discovery* sensacional
sense [sens] **1** *n* (*meaning, point, hearing etc*) sentido *m*; (*feeling*) sentimiento *m*; (*common sense*) sentido *m* común, sensatez *f*; ***in a sense*** en cierto sentido; ***talk sense, man!*** ¡no digas tonterías!; ***come to one's senses*** entrar en razón; ***it doesn't make sense*** no tiene sentido; ***there's no sense in waiting*** no tiene sentido que esperemos **2** *v/t s.o.'s presence* sentir, notar; ***I could sense that something was wrong*** tenía la sensación de que algo no iba bien
sense·less ['senslɪs] *adj* (*pointless*) absurdo
sen·si·ble ['sensəbl] *adj* sensato; *clothes, shoes* práctico, apropiado
sen·si·bly ['sensəblɪ] *adv* con sensatez; ***she wasn't sensibly dressed*** no llevaba ropa apropiada
sen·si·tive ['sensətɪv] *adj skin, person* sensible
sen·si·tiv·i·ty [sensə'tɪvətɪ] *of skin, person* sensibilidad *f*
sen·sor ['sensər] sensor *m*

sen·su·al ['senʃʊəl] *adj* sensual
sen·su·al·i·ty [senʃʊ'ælətɪ] sensualidad *f*
sen·su·ous ['senʃʊəs] *adj* sensual
sent [sent] *pret & pp* → ***send***
sen·tence ['sentəns] **1** *n* GRAM oración *f*; LAW sentencia *f* **2** *v/t* LAW sentenciar, condenar
sen·ti·ment ['sentɪmənt] (*sentimentality*) sentimentalismo *m*; (*opinion*) opinión *f*
sen·ti·ment·al [sentɪ'mentl] *adj* sentimental
sen·ti·men·tali·ty [sentɪmen'tælətɪ] sentimentalismo *m*
sen·try ['sentrɪ] centinela *m*
sep·a·rate¹ ['sepərət] *adj* separado; ***keep sth separate from sth*** guardar algo separado de algo
separate² ['sepəreɪt] **1** *v/t* separar; ***separate sth from sth*** separar algo de algo **2** *v/i of couple* separarse
sep·a·rat·ed ['sepəreɪtɪd] *adj couple* separado
sep·a·rate·ly ['sepərətlɪ] *adv pay, treat* por separado
sep·a·ra·tion [sepə'reɪʃn] separación *f*
Sep·tem·ber [sep'tembər] septiembre *m*
sep·tic ['septɪk] *adj* séptico; ***go septic*** *of wound* infectarse
se·quel ['siːkwəl] continuación *f*
se·quence ['siːkwəns] *n* secuencia *f*; ***in sequence*** en orden; ***out of sequence*** en desorden; ***the sequence of events*** la secuencia de hechos
se·rene [sɪ'riːn] *adj* sereno
ser·geant ['sɑːrdʒənt] sargento *m/f*
se·ri·al ['sɪrɪəl] *n on* TV, *radio* serie *f*, serial *m*; *in magazine* novela *f* por entregas
se·ri·al·ize ['sɪrɪəlaɪz] *v/t novel on* TV emitir en forma de serie; *in newspaper* publicar por entregas
'se·ri·al kill·er asesino(-a) *m(f)* en serie
'se·ri·al num·ber *of product* número *m* de serie
'se·ri·al port COMPUT puerto *m* (en) serie
se·ries ['sɪriːz] *nsg* serie *f*
se·ri·ous ['sɪrɪəs] *adj situation, damage, illness* grave; (*person: earnest*) serio; *company* serio; ***I'm serious*** lo digo en serio; ***we'd better take a serious look at it*** deberíamos examinarlo seriamente
se·ri·ous·ly ['sɪrɪəslɪ] *adv injured* gravemente; ***seriously intend to …*** tener intenciones firmes de …; ***seriously?*** ¿en serio?; ***take s.o. seriously*** tomar a alguien en serio
se·ri·ous·ness ['sɪrɪəsnɪs] *of person* seriedad *f*; *of situation* seriedad *f*, gravedad *f*; *of illness* gravedad *f*
ser·mon ['sɜːrmən] sermón *m*
ser·vant ['sɜːrvənt] sirviente(-a) *m(f)*
serve [sɜːrv] **1** *n in tennis* servicio *m*, saque *m* **2** *v/t food, meal* servir; *customer in shop* atender; *one's country, the people* servir a; ***it serves you right*** ¡te lo mereces! **3** *v/i* servir; *in tennis* servir, sacar
◆ **serve up** *v/t meal* servir
serv·er ['sɜːrvər] *in tennis* jugador(a) *m(f)* al servicio; COMPUT servidor *m*
ser·vice ['sɜːrvɪs] **1** *n to customers, community* servicio *m*; *for vehicle, machine* revisión *f*; *in tennis* servicio *m*, saque *m*; ***services*** (*service sector*) el sector servicios; ***the services*** MIL las fuerzas armadas **2** *v/t vehicle, machine* revisar
'ser·vice ar·e·a área *f* de servicio
'ser·vice charge *in restaurant* servicio *m* (*tarifa*)
'ser·vice in·dus·try industria *f* de servicios
'ser·vice·man MIL militar *m*
'ser·vice pro·vid·er COMPUT proveedor *m* de servicios
'ser·vice sec·tor sector *m* servicios
'ser·vice sta·tion estación *f* de servicio
ser·vi·ette [sɜːrvɪ'et] servilleta *f*
ser·vile ['sɜːrvəl] *adj pej* servil
serv·ing ['sɜːrvɪŋ] *n of food* ración *f*
ses·sion ['seʃn] sesión *f*; *with boss* reunión *f*
set [set] **1** *n of tools* juego *m*; *of books* colección *f*; (*group of people*) grupo *m*; MATH conjunto *m*; (THEA: *scenery*) decorado *m*; *where a movie is made* plató *m*; *in tennis* set *m*; ***television set*** televisor *m*; ***a set of dishes*** una vajilla; ***a set of glasses*** una cristalería **2** *v/t* (*pret & pp* ***set***) (*place*) colocar; *movie, novel etc* ambientar; *date, time, limit* fijar; *mechanism, alarm* poner; *clock* poner en hora; *broken limb* recomponer; *jewel* engastar; (*typeset*) componer; ***set the table*** poner la mesa **3** *v/i* (*pret & pp* ***set***) *of sun* ponerse; *of glue* solidificarse **4** *adj views, ideas* fijo; (*ready*) preparado; ***be dead set on sth*** estar empeñado en hacer algo; ***be very set in one's ways*** ser de ideas fijas; ***set meal*** menú *m* (del día)
◆ **set apart** *v/t* distinguir
◆ **set aside** *v/t material, food* apartar; *money* ahorrar
◆ **set back** *v/t in plans etc* retrasar; ***it set me back $400*** me salió por 400 dólares
◆ **set off** **1** *v/i on journey* salir **2** *v/t explosion* provocar; *bomb* hacer explotar; *chain reaction* desencadenar; *alarm* activar
◆ **set out** **1** *v/i on journey* salir (***for*** hacia) **2** *v/t ideas, goods* exponer; ***set out to do***

S

sth (*intend*) tener la intención de hacer algo

◆ **set to** *v/i* (*start on a task*) empezar a trabajar

◆ **set up 1** *v/t new company* establecer; *equipment*, *machine* instalar; *market stall* montar; *meeting* organizar; F (*frame*) tender una trampa a **2** *v/i in business* emprender un negocio

'set·back contratiempo *m*

set·tee [se'tiː] (*couch*, *sofa*) sofá *m*

set·ting ['setɪŋ] *n of novel etc* escenario *m*; *of house* ubicación *f*

set·tle ['setl] **1** *v/i of bird*, *dust* posarse; *of building* hundirse; *to live* establecerse **2** *v/t dispute*, *uncertainty* resolver, solucionar; *debts* saldar; *nerves*, *stomach* calmar; ***that settles it!*** ¡está decidido!

◆ **settle down** *v/i* (*stop being noisy*) tranquilizarse; (*stop wild living*) sentar la cabeza; *in an area* establecerse

◆ **settle for** *v/t* (*take*, *accept*) conformarse con

◆ **settle up** *v/i* (*pay*) ajustar cuentas con

set·tled ['setld] *adj weather* estable

set·tle·ment ['setlmənt] *of claim* resolución *f*; *of debt* liquidación *f*; *of dispute* acuerdo *m*; (*payment*) suma *f*; *of building* hundimiento *m*

set·tler ['setlər] *in new country* colono *m*

'set-up (*structure*) estructura *f*; (*relationship*) relación *f*; F (*frameup*) trampa *f*

sev·en ['sevn] siete

sev·en·teen [sevn'tiːn] diecisiete

sev·en·teenth [sevn'tiːnθ] *n & adj* decimoséptimo

sev·enth ['sevnθ] *n & adj* séptimo

sev·en·ti·eth ['sevntɪɪθ] *n & adj* septuagésimo

sev·en·ty ['sevntɪ] setenta

sev·er ['sevər] *v/t* cortar; *relations* romper

sev·e·ral ['sevrl] **1** *adj* varios **2** *pron* varios(-as) *mpl* (*fpl*)

se·vere [sɪ'vɪr] *adj illness* grave; *penalty*, *winter*, *weather* severo; *teacher* estricto

se·vere·ly [sɪ'vɪrlɪ] *adv punish*, *speak* con severidad; *injured*, *disrupted* gravemente

se·ver·i·ty [sɪ'verətɪ] severidad *f*; *of illness* gravedad *f*

Se·ville [sə'vɪl] *n* Sevilla

sew [soʊ] *v/t & v/i* (*pret* ***sewed***, *pp* ***sewn***) coser

◆ **sew on** *v/t button* coser

sew·age ['suːɪdʒ] aguas *fpl* residuales

'sew·age plant planta *f* de tratamiento de aguas residuales, depuradora *f*

sew·er ['suːər] alcantarilla *f*, cloaca *f*

sew·ing ['soʊɪŋ] *skill* costura *f*; *that being sewn* labor *f*

'sew·ing ma·chine máquina *f* de coser

sewn [soʊn] *pp* → ***sew***

sex [seks] (*act*, *gender*) sexo *m*; ***have sex with*** tener relaciones sexuales con, acostarse con

sex·ist ['seksɪst] **1** *adj* sexista **2** *n* sexista *m/f*

sex·u·al ['sekʃʊəl] *adj* sexual

sex·u·al as'sault agresión *f* sexual

sex·u·al ha'rass·ment acoso *m* sexual

sex·u·al 'in·ter·course relaciones *fpl* sexuales

sex·u·al·i·ty [sekʃʊ'ælətɪ] sexualidad *f*

sex·u·al·ly ['sekʃʊlɪ] *adv* sexualmente; ***sexually transmitted disease*** enfermedad *f* de transmisión sexual

sex·y ['seksɪ] *adj* sexy *inv*

shab·bi·ly ['ʃæbɪlɪ] *adv dressed* con desaliño; *treat* muy mal, de manera muy injusta

shab·by ['ʃæbɪ] *adj coat etc* desgastado, raído; *treatment* malo, muy injusto

shack [ʃæk] choza *f*

shade [ʃeɪd] **1** *n for lamp* pantalla *f*; *of color* tonalidad *f*; *on window* persiana *f*; ***in the shade*** a la sombra **2** *v/t from sun*, *light* proteger de la luz

shad·ow ['ʃædoʊ] *n* sombra *f*

shad·y ['ʃeɪdɪ] *adj spot* umbrío; *character*, *dealings* sospechoso

shaft [ʃæft] TECH eje *m*, árbol *m*; *of mine* pozo *m*

shag·gy ['ʃægɪ] *adj hair*, *dog* greñudo

shake [ʃeɪk] **1** *n* sacudida *f*; ***give sth a good shake*** agitar algo bien **2** *v/t* (*pret* ***shook***, *pp* ***shaken***) agitar; *emotionally* conmocionar; ***he shook his head*** negó con la cabeza; ***shake hands*** estrechar *or* darse la mano; ***shake hands with s.o.*** estrechar *or* dar la mano a alguien **3** *v/i* (*pret* ***shook***, *pp* ***shaken***) *of voice*, *building*, *person* temblar

shak·en ['ʃeɪkən] **1** *adj emotionally* conmocionado **2** *pp* → ***shake***

'shake-up reestructuración *f*

'shak·y ['ʃeɪkɪ] *adj table etc* inestable; *after illness* débil; *after shock* conmocionado; *grasp of sth*, *grammar etc* flojo; *voice*, *hand* tembloroso

shall [ʃæl] *v/aux* ◇ *future*: ***I shall do my best*** haré todo lo que pueda; ***I shan't see them*** no los veré

◇ *suggesting*: ***shall we go?*** ¿nos vamos?

shal·low ['ʃæloʊ] *adj water* poco profundo; *person* superficial

sham·bles ['ʃæmblz] *nsg* caos *m*

shame [ʃeɪm] **1** *n* vergüenza *f*, *Col*, *Mex*, *Ven* pena *f*; ***bring shame on*** avergonzar

or Col, Mex, Ven apenar a; ***shame on you!*** ¡deberías darte vergüenza!; ***what a shame!*** ¡qué pena *or* lástima! **2** *v/t* avergonzar, *Col, Mex, Ven* apenar; ***shame s.o. into doing sth*** avergonzar a alguien para que haga algo
shame·ful [ˈʃeɪmfəl] *adj* vergonzoso
shame·ful·ly [ˈʃeɪmfəlɪ] *adv* vergonzosamente
shame·less [ˈʃeɪmlɪs] *adj* desvergonzado
sham·poo [ʃæmˈpuː] **1** *n* champú *m* **2** *v/t customer* lavar la cabeza a; *hair* lavar
shan·ty town [ˈʃæntɪ] *Span* barrio *m* de chabolas, *Am* barriada *f*
shape [ʃeɪp] **1** *n* forma *f* **2** *v/t clay* modelar; *person's life, character* determinar; *the future* dar forma a
shape·less [ˈʃeɪplɪs] *adj dress etc* amorfo
shape·ly [ˈʃeɪplɪ] *adv figure* esbelto
share [ʃer] **1** *n* parte *f*; FIN acción *f*; ***I did my share of the work*** hice la parte del trabajo que me correspondía **2** *v/t feelings, opinions* compartir **3** *v/i* compartir
◆ **share out** *v/t* repartir
ˈ**share·hold·er** accionista *m/f*
shark [ʃɑːrk] *fish* tiburón *m*
sharp [ʃɑːrp] **1** *adj knife* afilado; *mind* vivo; *pain* agudo; *taste* ácido **2** *adv* MUS demasiado alto; ***at 3 o'clock sharp*** a las tres en punto
sharp·en [ˈʃɑːrpn] *v/t knife* afilar; *pencil* sacar punta a; *skills* perfeccionar
sharp ˈ**prac·tice** triquiñuelas *fpl*, tejemanejes *mpl*
shat [ʃæt] *pret & pp* → ***shit***
shat·ter [ˈʃætər] **1** *v/t glass* hacer añicos; *illusions* destrozar **2** *v/i of glass* hacerse añicos
shat·tered [ˈʃætərd] *adj* F *(exhausted)* destrozado F, hecho polvo F; *(very upset)* destrozado F
shat·ter·ing [ˈʃætərɪŋ] *adj news, experience* demoledor, sorprendente
shave [ʃeɪv] **1** *v/t* afeitar **2** *v/i* afeitarse **3** *n* afeitado *m*; ***have a shave*** afeitarse; ***that was a close shave*** ¡le faltó un pelo!
◆ **shave off** *v/t beard* afeitar; *from piece of wood* rebajar
shav·en [ˈʃeɪvn] *adj head* afeitado
shav·er [ˈʃeɪvər] *electric* máquinilla *f* de afeitar (eléctrica)
shav·ing brush [ˈʃeɪvɪŋ] brocha *f* de afeitar
ˈ**shav·ing soap** jabón *m* de afeitar
shawl [ʃɒːl] chal *m*
she [ʃiː] *pron* ella; ***she is German/a student*** es alemana / estudiante; ***you're funny, she's not*** tú tienes gracia, ella no
shears [ʃɪrz] *npl for gardening* tijeras *fpl* (de podar); *for sewing* tijeras *fpl* (*grandes*)
sheath [ʃiːθ] *n for knife* funda *f*; *contraceptive* condón *m*
shed[1] [ʃed] *v/t* (*pret & pp* ***shed***) *blood, tears* derramar; *leaves* perder; ***shed light on*** *fig* arrojar luz sobre
shed[2] [ʃed] *n* cobertizo *m*
sheep [ʃiːp] (*pl* ***sheep***) oveja *f*
ˈ**sheep·dog** perro *m* pastor
sheep-herd·er [ˈʃiːphɜːrdər] pastor *m*
sheep·ish [ˈʃiːpɪʃ] *adj* avergonzado
ˈ**sheep·skin** *adj lining* (de piel) de borrego
sheer [ʃɪr] *adj madness, luxury* puro, verdadero; *hell* verdadero; *drop, cliffs* escarpado
sheet [ʃiːt] *for bed* sábana *f*; *of paper* hoja *f*; *of metal* chapa *f*, plancha *f*; *of glass* hoja *f*, lámina *f*
shelf [ʃelf] (*pl* ***shelves*** [ʃelvz]) estante *m*; ***shelves*** estanterías *fpl*
shell [ʃel] **1** *n of mussel etc* concha *f*; *of egg* cáscara *f*; *of tortoise* caparazón *m*; MIL proyectil *m*; ***come out of one's shell*** *fig* salir del caparazón **2** *v/t peas* pelar; MIL bombardear (*con artillería*)
ˈ**shell·fire** fuego *m* de artillería
ˈ**shell·fish** marisco *m*
shel·ter [ˈʃeltər] **1** *n* refugio *m*; (*bus shelter*) marquesina *f* **2** *v/i from rain, bombing etc* refugiarse **3** *v/t* (*protect*) proteger
shel·tered [ˈʃeltərd] *adj place* resguardado; ***lead a sheltered life*** llevar una vida protegida
shelve [ʃelv] *v/t fig* posponer
shep·herd [ˈʃepərd] *n* pastor *m*
sher·iff [ˈʃerɪf] sheriff *m/f*
sher·ry [ˈʃerɪ] jerez *m*
shield [ʃiːld] **1** *n* escudo *m*; *sports trophy* trofeo *m* (*en forma de escudo*); TECH placa *f* protectora; *of policeman* placa *f* **2** *v/t* (*protect*) proteger
shift [ʃɪft] **1** *n* cambio *m*; (*period of work*) turno *m* **2** *v/t* (*move*) mover; *stains etc* eliminar **3** *v/i* (*move*) moverse; (*change*) trasladarse, desplazarse; *of wind* cambiar; ***he was shifting!*** F iba a toda mecha F
ˈ**shift key** COMPUT tecla *f* de mayúsculas
ˈ**shift work** trabajo *m* por turnos
ˈ**shift work·er** trabajador(a) *m(f)* por turnos
shift·y [ˈʃɪftɪ] *adj pej* sospechoso
shilly-shally [ˈʃɪlɪʃælɪ] *v/i* (*pret & pp* ***shilly-shallied***) F titubear
shim·mer [ˈʃɪmər] *v/i* brillar; *of roads in heat* reverberar

shin [ʃɪn] *n* espinilla *f*
shine [ʃaɪn] **1** *v/i* (*pret & pp* ***shone***) brillar; *fig*: *of student etc* destacar (***at*** en) **2** *v/t* (*pret & pp* ***shone***): ***could you shine a light in here?*** ¿podrías alumbrar aquí? **3** *n on shoes etc* brillo *m*
shin·gle ['ʃɪŋgl] *on beach* guijarros *mpl*
shin·gles ['ʃɪŋglz] *nsg* MED herpes *m*
shin·y ['ʃaɪnɪ] *adj surface* brillante
ship [ʃɪp] **1** *n* barco *m*, buque *m* **2** *v/t* (*pret & pp* ***shipped***) (*send*) enviar; *by sea* enviar por barco
ship·ment ['ʃɪpmənt] (*consignment*) envío *m*
'ship·own·er naviero(-a) *m(f)*, armador(a) *m(f)*
ship·ping ['ʃɪpɪŋ] *n* (*sea traffic*) navíos *mpl*, buques *mpl*; (*sending*) envío *m*; (*sending by sea*) envío *m* por barco
'ship·ping com·pa·ny (compañía *f*) naviera *f*
ship·ping costs *npl* gastos *mpl* de envío
ship'shape *adj* ordenado, organizado
'ship·wreck **1** *n* naufragio *m* **2** *v/t*: ***be shipwrecked*** naufragar
'ship·yard astillero *m*
shirk [ʃɜːrk] *v/t* eludir
shirk·er ['ʃɜːrkər] vago(-a) *m(f)*
shirt [ʃɜːrt] camisa *f*; ***in his shirt sleeves*** en mangas de camisa
shit [ʃɪt] **1** *n* P mierda *f* P; ***I need a shit*** tengo que cagar P **2** *v/i* (*pret & pp* ***shat***) P cagar P **3** *interj* P mierda P
shit·ty ['ʃɪtɪ] *adj* F asqueroso F; ***I feel shitty*** me encuentro de pena F
shiv·er ['ʃɪvər] *v/i* tiritar
shock [ʃɑːk] **1** *n* shock *m*, impresión *f*; ELEC descarga *f*; ***be in shock*** MED estar en estado de shock **2** *v/t* impresionar, dejar boquiabierto; ***I was shocked by the news*** la noticia me impresionó *or* dejó boquiabierto; ***an artist who tries to shock his public*** un artista que intenta escandalizar a su público
'shock ab·sorb·er [əb'sɔːrbər] MOT amortiguador *m*
shock·ing ['ʃɑːkɪŋ] *adj behavior, poverty* impresionante, escandaloso; F *prices* escandaloso; F *weather, spelling* terrible
shock·ing·ly ['ʃɑːkɪŋlɪ] *adv behave* escandalosamente
shod·dy ['ʃɑːdɪ] *adj goods* de mala calidad; *behavior* vergonzoso
shoe [ʃuː] zapato *m*
'shoe·horn *n* calzador *m*
'shoe-lace cordón *m*
'shoe·mak·er zapatero(-a) *m(f)*
'shoe mender zapatero(-a) *m(f)* remendón(-ona)
'shoe·store zapatería *f*
'shoe·string: ***do sth on a shoestring*** hacer algo con cuatro duros
shone [ʃɑːn] *pret & pp* → ***shine***
◆ **shoo away** [ʃuː] *v/t children, chicken* espantar
shook [ʃuːk] *pret* → ***shake***
shoot [ʃuːt] **1** *n* BOT brote *m* **2** *v/t* (*pret & pp* ***shot***) disparar; *and kill* matar de un tiro; *movie* rodar; ***shoot s.o. in the leg*** disparar a alguien en la pierna
◆ **shoot down** *v/t airplane* derribar; *fig*: *suggestion* echar por tierra
◆ **shoot off** *v/i* (*rush off*) irse deprisa
◆ **shoot up** *v/i of prices* dispararse; *of children* crecer mucho; *of new suburbs, buildings etc* aparecer de repente; F *of drug addict* chutarse F
shoot·ing 'star ['ʃuːtɪŋ] estrella *f* fugaz
shop [ʃɑːp] **1** *n* tienda *f*; ***talk shop*** hablar del trabajo **2** *v/i* (*pret & pp* ***shopped***) comprar; ***go shopping*** ir de compras
shop·keep·er ['ʃɑːkiːpər] tendero(-a) *m(f)*
shop·lift·er ['ʃɑːplɪftər] ladrón(-ona) *m(f)* (*en tienda*)
shop·lift·ing ['ʃɑːplɪftɪŋ] *n* hurtos *mpl* (*en tiendas*)
shop·per ['ʃɑːpər] *person* comprador(a) *m(f)*
shop·ping ['ʃɑːpɪŋ] *items* compra *f*; ***I hate shopping*** odio hacer la compra; ***do one's shopping*** hacer la compra
'shop·ping bag bolsa *f* de la compra
'shop·ping cen·ter, *Br* **'shop·ping cen·tre** centro *m* comercial
'shop·ping list lista *f* de la compra
'shop·ping mall centro *m* comercial
shop 'stew·ard representante *m/f* sindical
shop 'win·dow escaparate *m*, *L.Am.* vidriera *f*, *Mex* aparador *m*
shore [ʃɔːr] orilla *f*; ***on shore*** (*not at sea*) en tierra
short [ʃɔːrt] **1** *adj* corto; *in height* bajo; ***it's just a short walk*** está a poca distancia a pie; ***we're short of fuel*** nos queda poco combustible; ***he's not short of ideas*** no le faltan ideas; ***time is short*** hay poco tiempo **2** *adv*: ***cut short*** *vacation, meeting* interrumpir; ***stop a person short*** hacer pararse a una persona; ***go short of*** pasar sin; ***in short*** en resumen
short·age ['ʃɔːrtɪdʒ] escasez *f*, falta *f*
short 'cir·cuit *n* cortocircuito *m*
short·com·ing ['ʃɔːrtkʌmɪŋ] defecto *m*
'short cut atajo *m*
short·en ['ʃɔːrtn] *v/t dress, hair, vacation* acortar; *chapter, article* abreviar; *work*

day reducir

short·en·ing ['ʃɔːrtnɪŋ] *n grasa utilizada para hacer masa de pastelería*

'**short·fall** déficit *m*

'**short·hand** *n* taquigrafía *f*

short-hand·ed [ʃɔːrt'hændɪd] *adj* falto de personal

short-lived ['ʃɔːrtlɪvd] *adj* efímero

short·ly ['ʃɔːrtlɪ] *adv* (*soon*) pronto; ***shortly before / after*** justo antes / después

short·ness ['ʃɔːrtnɪs] *of visit* brevedad *f*; *in height* baja *f* estatura

shorts [ʃɔːrts] *npl* pantalones *mpl* cortos, shorts *mpl*; *underwear* calzoncillos *mpl*

short·sight·ed [ʃɔːrt'saɪtɪd] *adj* miope; *fig* corto de miras

short-sleeved ['ʃɔːrtsliːvd] *adj* de manga corta

short-staffed [ʃɔːrt'stæft] *adj* falto de personal

short 'sto·ry relato *m or* cuento corto

short-tem·pered [ʃɔːrt'tempərd] *adj* irascible

'**short-term** *adj* a corto plazo

'**short time**: ***be on short time*** *of workers* trabajar a jornada reducida

'**short wave** onda *f* corta

shot[1] [ʃɑːt] *from gun* disparo *m*; (*photograph*) fotografía *f*; (*injection*) inyección *f*; ***be a good / poor shot*** tirar bien / mal; ***he accepted like a shot*** aceptó al instante; ***he ran off like a shot*** se fue como una bala

shot[2] [ʃɑːt] *pret & pp* → ***shoot***

'**shot·gun** escopeta *f*

should [ʃʊd] *v/aux*: ***what should I do?*** ¿qué debería hacer?; ***you shouldn't do that*** no deberías hacer eso; ***that should be long enough*** debería ser lo suficientemente largo; ***you should have heard him!*** ¡tendrías que haberle oído!

shoul·der ['ʃoʊldər] *n* ANAT hombro *m*

'**shoul·der bag** bolso *m* (de bandolera)

'**shoul·der blade** omóplato *m*, omoplato

'**shoul·der strap** *of brassiere, dress* tirante *m*; *of bag* correa *f*

shout [ʃaʊt] **1** *n* grito *m* **2** *v/t & v/i* gritar

◆ **shout at** *v/t* gritar a

shout·ing ['ʃaʊtɪŋ] *n* griterío *m*

shove [ʃʌv] **1** *n* empujón *m* **2** *v/t & v/i* empujar

◆ **shove in** *v/i in line* meterse empujando

◆ **shove off** *v/i* F (*go away*) largarse F

shov·el ['ʃʌvl] **1** *n* pala *f* **2** *v/t*: ***shovel snow off the path*** retirar a paladas la nieve del camino

show [ʃoʊ] **1** *n* THEA espectáculo *m*; TV programa *m*; *of emotion* muestra *f*; ***on show*** *at exhibition* expuesto, en exposición **2** *v/t* (*pret* ***showed***, *pp* ***shown***) *passport, ticket* enseñar, mostrar; *interest, emotion* mostrar; *at exhibition* exponer; *movie* proyectar; ***show s.o. sth, show sth to s.o.*** enseñar *or* mostrar algo a alguien **3** *v/i* (*pret* ***showed***, *pp* ***shown***) (*be visible*) verse; ***what's showing at ...?*** *of movie* qué ponen en el ...?

◆ **show around** *v/t* enseñar; ***he showed us around*** nos enseñó la casa / el edificio *etc*

◆ **show in** *v/t* hacer pasar a

◆ **show off** **1** *v/t skills* mostrar **2** *v/i pej* presumir, alardear

◆ **show up** **1** *v/t shortcomings etc* poner de manifiesto; ***don't show me up in public*** (*embarrass*) no me avergüences en público **2** *v/i* (*be visible*) verse; F (*arrive, turn up*) aparecer

'**show busi·ness** el mundo del espectáculo

'**show·case** *n* vitrina *f*; *fig* escaparate *m*

'**show·down** enfrentamiento *m*

show·er ['ʃaʊər] **1** *n of rain* chaparrón *m*, chubasco *m*; *to wash* ducha *f*, *Mex* regadera *f*; (*party*) *fiesta con motivo de un bautizo, una boda etc., en la que los invitados llevan obsequios*; ***take a shower*** ducharse **2** *v/i* ducharse **3** *v/t*: ***shower s.o. with compliments / praise*** colmar a alguien de cumplidos / alabanzas

'**show·er cap** gorro *m* de baño

'**show·er cur·tain** cortina *f* de ducha

'**shower·proof** *adj* impermeable

'**show·jump·ing** concurso *m* de saltos

shown [ʃoʊn] *pp* → ***show***

'**show-off** *n pej* fanfarrón(-ona) *m(f)*

'**show·room** sala *f* de exposición *f*; ***in showroom condition*** como nuevo

show·y ['ʃoʊɪ] *adj jacket, behavior* llamativo

shrank [ʃræŋk] *pret* → ***shrink***[1]

shred [ʃred] **1** *n of paper etc* trozo *m*; *of fabric* jirón *m*; ***there isn't a shred of evidence*** no hay prueba alguna **2** *v/t* (*pret & pp* ***shredded***) *paper* hacer trizas; *in cooking* cortar en tiras

shred·der ['ʃredər] *for documents* trituradora *f* (de documentos)

shrewd [ʃruːd] *adj person* astuto; *judgment, investment* inteligente

shrewd·ness ['ʃruːdnɪs] *of person* astucia *f*; *of decision* inteligencia *f*

shriek [ʃriːk] **1** *n* alarido *m*, chillido *m* **2** *v/i* chillar

shrill [ʃrɪl] *adj* estridente, agudo

shrimp [ʃrɪmp] gamba *f*; *larger Span* langostino *m*, *L.Am.* camarón *m*

shrine [ʃraɪn] santuario *m*
shrink¹ [ʃrɪŋk] *v/i* (*pret* ***shrank***, *pp* ***shrunk***) *of material* encoger(se); *level of support etc* reducirse
shrink² [ʃrɪŋk] *n* F (*psychiatrist*) psiquiatra *m/f*
'shrink-wrap *v/t* (*pret & pp* ***shrink-wrapped***) envolver en plástico adherente
'shrink-wrap·ping *material plástico adherente para envolver*
shriv·el ['ʃrɪvl] *v/i of skin* arrugarse; *of leaves* marchitarse
Shrove 'Tues·day [ʃroʊv] martes *m inv* de Carnaval
shrub [ʃrʌb] arbusto *m*
shrub·be·ry ['ʃrʌbərɪ] arbustos *mpl*
shrug [ʃrʌg] **1** *n*: ***... he said with a shrug*** ... dijo encogiendo los hombros **2** *v/i* (*pret & pp* ***shrugged***) encoger los hombros **3** *v/t* (*pret & pp* ***shrugged***): ***shrug one's shoulders*** encoger los hombros
shrunk [ʃrʌŋk] *pp* → ***shrink¹***
shud·der ['ʃʌdər] **1** *n of fear, disgust* escalofrío *m*; *of earth, building* temblor *m* **2** *v/i with fear, disgust* estremecerse; *of earth, building* temblar; ***I shudder to think*** me estremezco de pensar
shuf·fle ['ʃʌfl] **1** *v/t cards* barajar **2** *v/i in walking* arrastrar los pies
shun [ʃʌn] *v/t* (*pret & pp* ***shunned***) rechazar
shut [ʃʌt] *v/t & v/i* (*pret & pp* ***shut***) cerrar
◆ **shut down** **1** *v/t business* cerrar; *computer* apagar **2** *v/i of business* cerrarse; *of computer* apagarse
◆ **shut off** *v/t* cortar
◆ **shut up** *v/i* F (*be quiet*) callarse; ***shut up!*** ¡cállate!
shut·ter ['ʃʌtər] *on window* contraventana *f*; PHOT obturador *m*
'shut·ter speed PHOT tiempo *m* de exposición
shut·tle ['ʃʌtl] *v/i*: ***shuttle between*** *of bus* conectar; *of airplane* hacer el puente aéreo entre
'shut·tle·bus *at airport* autobús *m* de conexión
'shut·tle·cock SP volante *m*
'shut·tle ser·vice servicio *m* de conexión
shy [ʃaɪ] *adj* tímido
shy·ness ['ʃaɪnɪs] timidez *f*
Si·a·mese 'twins [saɪə'miːz] *npl* siameses *mpl* (*fpl*)
sick [sɪk] *adj* enfermo; *sense of humor* morboso, macabro; *society* enfermo; ***be sick of*** (*fed up with*) estar harto de
sick·en ['sɪkn] **1** *v/t* (*disgust*) poner enfermo **2** *v/i*: ***be sickening for sth*** estar incubando algo
sick·en·ing ['sɪknɪŋ] *adj stench* nauseabundo; *behavior, crime* repugnante
'sick leave baja *f* (por enfermedad); ***be on sick leave*** estar de baja
sick·ly ['sɪklɪ] *adj person* enfermizo; *color* pálido
sick·ness ['sɪknɪs] enfermedad *f*; (*vomiting*) vómitos *mpl*
side [saɪd] *n of box, house, field* lado *m*; *of mountain* ladera *f*, vertiente *f*; *of person* costado *m*; SP equipo *m*; ***take sides*** (*favor one side*) tomar partido (***with*** por); ***I'm on your side*** estoy de parte tuya; ***side by side*** uno al lado del otro; ***at the side of the road*** al lado de la carretera; ***on the big / small side*** un poco grande / pequeño
◆ **side with** *v/t* tomar partido por
'side·board aparador *m*
'sideburns *npl* patillas *fpl*
'side dish plato *m* de acompañamiento
'side ef·fect efecto *m* secundario
'side·light MOT luz *f* de posición
'side·line **1** *n* actividad *f* complementaria **2** *v/t*: ***feel sidelined*** sentirse marginado
'side·step *v/t* (*pret & pp* ***sidestepped***) *fig* evadir
'side street bocacalle *f*
'side·track *v/t* distraer; ***get sidetracked*** distraerse
'side·walk acera *f*, *Rpl* vereda *f*, *Mex* banqueta *f*
side·walk 'caf·é terraza *f*
side·ways ['saɪdweɪz] *adv* de lado
siege [siːdʒ] sitio *m*; ***lay siege to*** sitiar
sieve [sɪv] *n* tamiz *m*
sift [sɪft] *v/t flour* tamizar; *data* examinar a fondo
◆ **sift through** *v/t details, data* pasar por el tamiz
sigh [saɪ] **1** *n* suspiro *m*; ***heave a sigh of relief*** suspirar de alivio **2** *v/i* suspirar
sight [saɪt] *n* vista *f*; (*power of seeing*) vista *f*, visión *f*; ***sights*** *of city* lugares *mpl* de interés; ***he can't stand the sight of blood*** no aguanta ver sangre; ***I caught sight of him just as ...*** lo vi justo cuando ...; ***know by sight*** conocer de vista; ***within sight of*** a la vista de; ***as soon as the car was out of sight*** en cuanto se dejó de ver el coche; ***what a sight you look!*** ¡qué pintas llevas!; ***lose sight of*** *objective etc* olvidarse de
sight·see·ing ['saɪtsiːɪŋ] *n*: ***we like sightseeing*** nos gusta hacer turismo; ***go sightseeing*** hacer turismo
'sight·see·ing tour visita *f* turística
sight·seer ['saɪtsiːər] turista *m/f*
sign [saɪn] **1** *n* señal *f*; *outside shop*, *on*

building cartel *m*, letrero *m*; ***it's a sign of the times*** es un signo de los tiempos que corren **2** *v/t & v/i* firmar

◆ **sign in** *v/i* registrarse

◆ **sign up** *v/i* (*join the army*) alistarse

sig·nal ['sɪgnl] **1** *n* señal *f*; ***send out all the wrong signals*** dar a una impresión equivocada **2** *v/i of driver* poner el intermitente

sig·na·to·ry ['sɪgnətɔːrɪ] *n* signatario(-a) *m*(*f*), firmante *m/f*

sig·na·ture ['sɪgnətʃər] *n* firma *f*

sig·na·ture 'tune sintonía *f*

sig·net ring ['sɪgnɪt] sello *m* (*anillo*)

sig·nif·i·cance [sɪg'nɪfɪkəns] importancia *f*, relevancia *f*

sig·nif·i·cant [sɪg'nɪfɪkənt] *adj event etc* importante, relevante; (*quite large*) considerable

sig·nif·i·cant·ly [sɪg'nɪfɪkəntlɪ] *adv larger, more expensive* considerablemente

sig·ni·fy ['sɪgnɪfaɪ] *v/t* (*pret & pp* ***signified***) significar, suponer

'sign lan·guage lenguaje *m* por señas

'sign·post señal *f*

si·lence ['saɪləns] **1** *n* silencio *m*; ***in silence*** *work, march* en silencio; ***silence!*** ¡silencio! **2** *v/t* hacer callar

si·lenc·er ['saɪlənsər] *on gun* silenciador *m*

si·lent ['saɪlənt] *adj* silencioso; *movie* mudo; ***stay silent*** (*not comment*) permanecer callado

sil·hou·ette [sɪluː'et] *n* silueta *f*

sil·i·con ['sɪlɪkən] silicio *m*

sil·i·con 'chip chip *m* de silicio

sil·i·cone ['sɪlɪkoʊn] silicona *f*

silk [sɪlk] **1** *n* seda *f* **2** *adj shirt etc* de seda

silk·y ['sɪlkɪ] *adj hair, texture* sedoso

sil·li·ness ['sɪlɪnɪs] tontería *f*, estupidez

sil·ly ['sɪlɪ] *adj* tonto, estúpido

si·lo ['saɪloʊ] silo *m*

sil·ver ['sɪlvər] **1** *n metal, medal* plata *f*; (*silver objects*) (objetos *mpl* de) plata *f* **2** *adj ring* de plata; *hair* canoso

sil·ver-plat·ed [sɪlvər'pleɪtɪd] *adj* plateado

sil·ver·ware ['sɪlvərwer] plata *f*

sil·ver 'wed·ding bodas *fpl* de plata

sim·i·lar ['sɪmɪlər] *adj* parecido, similar; ***be similar to*** ser parecido a, parecerse a

sim·i·lar·i·ty [sɪmɪ'lærətɪ] parecido *m*, similitud *f*

sim·i·lar·ly ['sɪmɪlərlɪ] *adv* de la misma manera

sim·mer ['sɪmər] *v/i in cooking* cocer a fuego lento; ***be simmering (with rage)*** estar a punto de explotar

◆ **simmer down** *v/i* tranquilizarse

sim·ple ['sɪmpl] *adj* (*easy, not fancy*) sencillo; *person* simple

sim·ple-mind·ed [sɪmpl'maɪndɪd] *adj pej* simplón

sim·pli·ci·ty [sɪm'plɪsətɪ] *of task, design* sencillez *f*, simplicidad *f*

sim·pli·fy ['sɪmplɪfaɪ] *v/t* (*pret & pp* ***simplified***) simplificar

sim·plis·tic [sɪm'plɪstɪk] *adj* simplista

sim·ply ['sɪmplɪ] *adv* sencillamente; ***it is simply the best*** es sin lugar a dudas el mejor

sim·u·late ['sɪmjʊleɪt] *v/t* simular

sim·ul·ta·ne·ous [saɪml'teɪnɪəs] *adj* simultáneo

sim·ul·ta·ne·ous·ly [saɪml'teɪnɪəslɪ] *adv* simultáneamente

sin [sɪn] **1** *n* pecado *m* **2** *v/i* (*pret & pp* ***sinned***) pecar

since [sɪns] **1** *prep* desde; ***since last week*** desde la semana pasada **2** *adv* desde entonces; ***I haven't seen him since*** no lo he visto desde entonces **3** *conj in expressions of time* desde que; (*seeing that*) ya que, dado que; ***since you left*** desde que te marchaste; ***since I have been living here*** desde que vivo acquí; ***since you don't like it*** ya que *or* dado que no te gusta

sin·cere [sɪn'sɪr] *adj* sincero

sin·cere·ly [sɪn'sɪrlɪ] *adv* sinceramente; ***I sincerely hope he appreciates it*** espero de verdad que lo aprecie; ***Yours sincerely*** atentamente

sin·cer·i·ty [sɪn'serətɪ] sinceridad *f*

sin·ful ['sɪnfəl] *adj person* pecador; *things* pecaminoso; ***it is sinful to …*** es pecado …

sing [sɪŋ] *v/t & v/i* (*pret* ***sang***, *pp* ***sung***) cantar

singe [sɪndʒ] *v/t* chamuscar

sing·er ['sɪŋər] cantante *m/f*

sin·gle ['sɪŋgl] **1** *adj* (*sole*) único, solo; (*not double*) único; (*not married*) soltero *m*; ***there wasn't a single mistake*** no había ni un solo error; ***in single file*** en fila india; ***single currency*** moneda única **2** *n* MUS sencillo *m*; (*single room*) habitación *f* individual; *person* soltero(-a) *m*(*f*); *Br ticket* billete *m or L.Am.* boleto *m* de ida; ***holidays for singles*** vacaciones para gente sin pareja; ***singles*** *in tennis* individuales *mpl*

◆ **single out** *v/t* (*choose*) seleccionar; (*distinguish*) distinguir

sin·gle-breast·ed [sɪŋgl'brestɪd] *adj* recto, con una fila de botones

sin·gle-'hand·ed [sɪŋgl'hændɪd] **1** *adj* en solitario **2** *adv* en solitario

S

sin·gle-mind·ed [sɪŋgl'maɪndɪd] *adj* determinado, resuelto
Sin·gle 'Mar·ket Mercado *m* Único
sin·gle 'moth·er madre *f* soltera
sin·gle 'pa·rent padre *m*/madre *f* soltero(-a)
sin·gle pa·rent 'fam·i·ly familia *f* monoparental
sin·gle 'room habitación *f* individual
sin·gu·lar ['sɪŋgjʊlər] **1** *adj* GRAM singular **2** *n* GRAM singular *m*; ***in the singular*** en singular
sin·is·ter ['sɪnɪstər] *adj* siniestro; *sky* amenazador
sink [sɪŋk] **1** *n in kitchen* fregadero *m*; *in bathroom* lavabo *m* **2** *v/i* (*pret* ***sank***, *pp* ***sunk***) *of ship*, *object* hundirse; *of sun* ponerse; *of interest rates*, *pressure etc* descender, bajar; ***he sank onto the bed*** se tiró a la cama **3** *v/t* (*pret* ***sank***, *pp* ***sunk***) *ship* hundir; *funds* investir
◆ **sink in** *v/i of liquid* penetrar; ***it still hasn't really sunk in*** *of realization* todavía no lo he asumido
sin·ner ['sɪnər] pecador(a) *m*(*f*)
si·nus ['saɪnəs] seno *m* (*nasal*)
si·nus·i·tis [saɪnə'saɪtɪs] MED sinusitis *f*
sip [sɪp] **1** *n* sorbo *m* **2** *v/t* (*pret & pp* ***sipped***) sorber
sir [sɜːr] señor *m*; ***excuse me, sir*** perdone, caballero
si·ren ['saɪrən] sirena *f*
sir·loin ['sɜːrlɔɪn] solomillo *m*
sis·ter ['sɪstər] hermana *f*
'sis·ter-in-law (*pl* ***sisters-in-law***) cuñada *f*
sit [sɪt] **1** *v/i* (*pret & pp* ***sat***) estar sentado; (*sit down*) sentarse **2** *v/t* (*pret & pp* ***sat***) *exam* presentarse a
◆ **sit down** *v/i* sentarse
◆ **sit up** *v/i in bed* incorporarse; (*straighten back*) sentarse derecho; (*wait up at night*) esperar levantado
sit·com ['sɪtkɑːm] telecomedia *f*, comedia *f* de situación
site [saɪt] **1** *n* emplazamiento *m*; *of battle* lugar *m* **2** *v/t new offices etc* situar
sit·ting ['sɪtɪŋ] *n of committee*, *court*, *for artist* sesión *f*; *for meals* turno *m*
'sit·ting room sala *f* de estar, salón *m*
sit·u·at·ed ['sɪtʊeɪtɪd] *adj* situado
sit·u·a·tion [sɪtʊ'eɪʃn] situación *f*
six [sɪks] seis
six·teen [sɪks'tiːn] dieciséis
six·teenth [sɪks'tiːnθ] *n & adj* decimosexto
sixth [sɪksθ] *n & adj* sexto
six·ti·eth ['sɪkstɪɪθ] *n & adj* sexagésimo
six·ty ['sɪkstɪ] sesenta
size [saɪz] tamaño *m*; *of loan* importe *m*; *of jacket* talla *f*; *of shoes* número *m*
◆ **size up** *v/t* evaluar, examinar
size·a·ble ['saɪzəbl] *adj house*, *order* considerable; *meal* copioso
siz·zle ['sɪzl] *v/i* chisporrotear
skate [skeɪt] **1** *n* patín *m* **2** *v/i* patinar
skate·board ['skeɪtbɔːrd] *n* monopatín *m*
skate·board·er ['skeɪtbɔːrdər] *persona que patina en monopatín*
skate·board·ing ['skeɪtbɔːrdɪŋ] patinaje *m* en monopatín
skat·er ['skeɪtər] patinador(a) *m*(*f*)
skat·ing ['skeɪtɪŋ] *n* patinaje *m*
'skat·ing rink pista *f* de patinaje
skel·e·ton ['skelɪtn] esqueleto *m*
'skel·e·ton key llave *f* maestra
skep·tic ['skeptɪk] escéptico(-a) *m*(*f*)
skep·ti·cal ['skeptɪkl] *adj* escéptico
skep·ti·cism ['skeptɪsɪzm] escepticismo *m*
sketch [sketʃ] **1** *n* boceto *m*, esbozo *m*; THEA sketch *m* **2** *v/t* bosquejar
'sketch·book cuaderno *m* de dibujo
sketch·y ['sketʃɪ] *adj knowledge etc* básico, superficial
skew·er ['skjʊər] *n* brocheta *f*
ski [skiː] **1** *n* esquí *m* **2** *v/i* esquiar
'ski boots *npl* botas *fpl* de esquí
skid [skɪd] **1** *n of car* patinazo *m*; *of person* resbalón *m* **2** *v/i* (*pret & pp* ***skidded***) *of car* patinar; *of person* resbalar
ski·er ['skiːər] esquiador(a) *m*(*f*)
ski·ing ['skiːɪŋ] esquí *m*
'ski in·struc·tor monitor(a) *m*(*f*) de esquí
skil·ful *etc Br* → ***skillful*** *etc*
'ski lift remonte *m*
skill [skɪl] destreza *f*, habilidad *f*
skilled [skɪld] *adj* capacitado, preparado
skilled 'work·er trabajador(a) *m*(*f*) cualificado
'skill·ful ['skɪlfəl] *adj* hábil, habilidoso
skill·ful·ly ['skɪlfəlɪ] *adv* con habilidad *or* destreza
skim [skɪm] *v/t* (*pret & pp* ***skimmed***) *surface* rozar; *milk* desnatar, descremar
◆ **skim off** *v/t the best* escoger
◆ **skim through** *v/t text* leer por encima
skimmed 'milk [skɪmd] leche *f* desnatada *or* descremada
skimp·y ['skɪmpɪ] *adj account etc* superficial; *dress* cortísimo; *bikini* mínimo
skin [skɪn] **1** *n* piel *f* **2** *v/t* (*pret & pp* ***skinned***) despellejar, desollar
'skin div·ing buceo *m* (en bañador)
skin·flint ['skɪnflɪnt] F agarrado(a) *m*(*f*) F, roñoso(-a) *m*(*f*)
'skin graft injerto *m* de piel
skin·ny ['skɪnɪ] *adj* escuálido

'**skin-tight** *adj* ajustado
skip [skɪp] **1** *n* (*little jump*) brinco *m*, saltito *m* **2** *v/i* (*pret & pp* ***skipped***) brincar **3** *v/t* (*pret & pp* ***skipped***) (*omit*) pasar por alto
'**ski pole** bastón *m* de esquí
skip·per ['skɪpər] NAUT patrón(-ona) *m*(*f*), capitán (-ana) *m*(*f*); *of team* capitán(-ana) *m*(*f*)
'**ski re·sort** estación *f* de esquí
skirt [skɜːrt] *n* falda *f*
'**ski run** pista *f* de esquí
'**ski tow** telesquí *m*
skull [skʌl] cráneo *m*
skunk [skʌŋk] mofeta *f*
sky [skaɪ] cielo *m*
'**sky·light** claraboya *f*
'**sky·line** horizonte *m*
'**sky·scrap·er** ['skaɪskreɪpər] rascacielos *m inv*
slab [slæb] *of stone* losa *f*; *of cake etc* trozo *m* grande
slack [slæk] *adj rope* flojo; *work* descuidado; *period* tranquilo; ***discipline is very slack*** no hay disciplina
slack·en ['slækn] *v/t rope*, *pace* aflojar; *pace*
◆ **slacken off** *v/i of trading*, *pace* disminuir
slacks [slæks] *npl* pantalones *mpl*
slain [sleɪn] *pp* → ***slay***
slam [slæm] **1** *v/t* (*pret & pp* ***slammed***) *door* cerrar de un golpe **2** *v/i* (*pret & pp* ***slammed***) *of door* cerrarse de golpe
◆ **slam down** *v/t* estampar
slan·der ['slændər] **1** *n* difamación *f* **2** *v/t* difamar
slan·der·ous ['slændərəs] *adj* difamatorio
slang [slæŋ] argot *m*, jerga *f*; *of a specific group* jerga *f*
slant [slænt] **1** *v/i* inclinarse **2** *n* inclinación *f*; *given to a story* enfoque *m*
slant·ing ['slæntɪŋ] *adj roof* inclinado; *eyes* rasgado
slap [slæp] **1** *n* (*blow*) bofetada *f*, cachete *m* **2** *v/t* (*pret & pp* ***slapped***) dar una bofetada *or* un cachete a; ***slap s.o. in the face*** dar una bofetada a alguien
'**slap·dash** *adj* chapucero
slash [slæʃ] **1** *n* (*cut*) corte *m*, raja *f*; *in punctuation* barra *f* **2** *v/t skin etc* cortar; *prices*, *costs* recortar drásticamente; ***slash one's wrists*** cortarse las venas
slate [sleɪt] *n* pizarra *f*
slaugh·ter ['slɒːtər] **1** *n of animals* sacrificio *m*; *of people*, *troops* matanza *f* **2** *v/t animals* sacrificar; *people*, *troops* masacrar
'**slaugh·ter·house** *for animals* matadero *m*
Slav [slɑːv] *adj* eslavo
slave [sleɪv] *n* esclavo(-a) *m*(*f*)
'**slave-driv·er** F negrero(-a) *m*(*f*) F
slay [sleɪ] *v/t* (*pret* ***slew***, *pp* ***slain***) asesinar
slay·ing ['sleɪɪŋ] (*murder*) asesinato *m*
sleaze [sliːz] POL corrupción *f*
slea·zy ['sliːzɪ] *adj bar* sórdido; *person* de mala calaña
sled, **sledge** [sled, sledʒ] *n* trineo *m*
'**sledge ham·mer** mazo *m*
sleep [sliːp] **1** *n* sueño *m*; ***go to sleep*** dormirse; ***I need a good sleep*** necesito dormir bien; ***I couldn't get to sleep*** no pude dormirme **2** *v/i* (*pret & pp* ***slept***) dormir
◆ **sleep in** *v/i* (*have a long lie*) dormir hasta tarde
◆ **sleep on** *v/t*: ***sleep on sth*** *decision* consultar algo con la almohada
◆ **sleep with** *v/t* (*have sex with*) acostarse con
sleep·i·ly ['sliːpɪlɪ] *adv*: ***say sth sleepily*** decir algo medio dormido
'**sleep·ing bag** ['sliːpɪŋ] saco *m* de dormir
'**sleep·ing car** RAIL coche *m* cama
'**sleep·ing pill** somnífero *m*, pastilla *f* para dormir
sleep·less ['sliːplɪs] *adj*: ***have a sleepless night*** pasar la noche en blanco
'**sleep walk·er** sonámbulo(-a) *m*(*f*)
'**sleep walk·ing** sonambulismo *m*
sleep·y ['sliːpɪ] *adj* adormilado, somnoliento; *town* tranquilo; ***I'm sleepy*** tengo sueño
sleet [sliːt] *n* aguanieve *f*
sleeve [sliːv] *of jacket etc* manga *f*
sleeve·less ['sliːvlɪs] *adj* sin mangas
sleigh [sleɪ] *n* trineo *m*
sleight of '**hand** [slaɪt] juegos *mpl* de manos
slen·der ['slendər] *adj figure*, *arms* esbelto; *income*, *margin* escaso; *chance* remoto
slept [slept] *pret & pp* → ***sleep***
slew [sluː] *pret* → ***slay***
slice [slaɪs] **1** *n of bread* rebanada *f*; *of cake* trozo *m*; *of salami*, *cheese* loncha *f*; *fig*: *of profits etc* parte *f* **2** *v/t loaf etc* cortar (en rebanadas)
sliced '**bread** [slaɪst] pan *m* de molde en rebanadas; ***the greatest thing since sliced bread*** F lo mejor desde que se inventó la rueda F
slick [slɪk] **1** *adj performance* muy logrado; (*pej*: *cunning*) con mucha labia **2** *n of oil* marea *f* negra
slid [slɪd] *pret & pp* → ***slide***
slide [slaɪd] **1** *n for kids* tobogán *m*; PHOT

diapositiva *f* **2** *v/i* (*pret & pp* ***slid***) deslizarse; *of exchange rate etc* descender **3** *v/t* (*pret & pp* ***slid***) deslizar

slid·ing 'door ['slaɪdɪŋ] puerta *f* corredera

slight [slaɪt] **1** *adj person, figure* menudo; (*small*) pequeño; *accent* ligero; ***I have a slight headache*** me duele un poco la cabeza; ***no, not in the slightest*** no, en absoluto

slight·ly ['slaɪtlɪ] *adv* un poco

slim [slɪm] **1** *adj* delgado; *chance* remoto **2** *v/i* (*pret & pp* ***slimmed***): ***I'm slimming*** estoy a dieta

slime [slaɪm] (*mud*) lodo *m*; *of slug etc* baba *f*

slim·y ['slaɪmɪ] *adj liquid* viscoso; *river bed* lleno de lodo

sling [slɪŋ] **1** *n for arm* cabestrillo *m* **2** *v/t* (*pret & pp* ***slung***) F (*throw*) tirar

slip [slɪp] **1** *n on ice etc* resbalón *m*; (*mistake*) desliz *m*; ***a slip of paper*** un trozo de papel; ***a slip of the tongue*** un lapsus; ***give s.o. the slip*** dar esquinazo a alguien **2** *v/i* (*pret & pp* ***slipped***) *on ice etc* resbalar; *of quality etc* empeorar; ***he slipped out of the room*** se fue de la habitación sigilosamente **3** *v/t* (*pret & pp* ***slipped***) (*put*): ***he slipped it into his briefcase*** lo metió en su maletín sigilosamente; ***it slipped my mind*** se me olvidó

◆ **slip away** *v/i of time* pasar; *of opportunity* esfumarse; (*die quietly*) morir tranquilamente

◆ **slip off** *v/t jacket etc* quitarse

◆ **slip on** *v/t jacket etc* ponerse

◆ **slip out** *v/i* (*go out*) salir (sigilosamente)

◆ **slip up** *v/i* equivocarse

slipped 'disc [slɪpt] hernia *f* discal

slip·per ['slɪpər] zapatilla *f* (*de estar por casa*)

slip·pery ['slɪpərɪ] *adj surface, road* resbaladizo; *fish* escurridizo

slip·shod ['slɪpʃɑːd] *adj* chapucero

'slip-up (*mistake*) error *m*

slit [slɪt] **1** *n* (*tear*) raja *f*; (*hole*) rendija *f*; *in skirt* corte *m* **2** *v/t* (*pret & pp* ***slit***) abrir; ***slit s.o.'s throat*** degollar a alguien

slith·er ['slɪðər] *v/i* deslizarse

sliv·er ['slɪvər] trocito *m*; *of wood, glass* astilla *f*

slob [slɑːb] *pej* dejado(-a) *m/f*, guarro(-a) *m/f*

slob·ber ['slɑːbər] *v/i* babear

slog [slɑːg] *n* paliza *f*

slo·gan ['sloʊgən] eslogan *m*

slop [slɑːp] *v/t* (*pret & pp* ***slopped***) derramar

slope [sloʊp] **1** *n of roof, handwriting* inclinación *f*; *of mountain* ladera *f*; ***built on a slope*** construido en una pendiente **2** *v/i* inclinarse; ***the road slopes down to the sea*** la carretera baja hasta el mar

slop·py ['slɑːpɪ] *adj* descuidado; *too sentimental* sensiblero

slot [slɑːt] **1** *n* ranura *f*; *in schedule* hueco *m*

◆ **slot in 1** *v/t* (*pret & pp* ***slotted***) introducir **2** *v/i* (*pret & pp* ***slotted***) encajar

'slot ma·chine *for cigarettes, food* máquina *f* expendedora; *for gambling* máquina *f* tragaperras

slouch [slaʊʧ] *v/i*: ***don't slouch*** ponte derecho

slov·en·ly ['slʌvnlɪ] *adj* descuidado

slow [sloʊ] *adj* lento; ***be slow*** *of clock* ir retrasado

◆ **slow down 1** *v/t work, progress* restrasar; *traffic, production* ralentizar **2** *v/i in walking, driving* reducir la velocidad; *of production etc* relantizarse; ***you need to slow down*** *in lifestyle* tienes que tomarte las cosas con calma

'slow·down *in production* ralentización *f*

slow·ly ['sloʊlɪ] *adv* despacio, lentamente

slow 'mo·tion: ***in slow motion*** a cámara lenta

slow·ness ['sloʊnɪs] lentitud *f*

'slow·poke F tortuga *f* F

slug [slʌg] *n animal* babosa *f*

slug·gish ['slʌgɪʃ] *adj* lento

slum [slʌm] *n* suburbio *m*, arrabal

slump [slʌmp] **1** *n in trade* desplome *m* **2** *v/i economically* desplomarse, hundirse; (*collapse: of person*) desplomarse

slung [slʌŋ] *pret & pp* → ***sling***

slur [slɜːr] **1** *n on s.o.'s character* difamación *f* **2** *v/t* (*pret & pp* ***slurred***) *words* arrastrar

slurp [slɜːrp] *v/t* sorber

slurred [slɜːrd] *adj*: ***his speech was slurred*** habló arrastrando las palabras

slush [slʌʃ] nieve *f* derretida; (*pej: sentimental stuff*) sensiblería *f*

'slush fund fondo *m* para corruptelas

slush·y ['slʌʃɪ] *adj snow* derretido; *movie, novel* sensiblero

slut [slʌt] *pej* fulana *f*

sly [slaɪ] *adj* ladino; ***on the sly*** a escondidas

smack [smæk] **1** *n*: ***a smack on the bottom*** un azote; ***a smack in the face*** una bofetada **2** *v/t child* pegar; *bottom* dar un azote en

small [smɒːl] *adj* pequeño, *L.Am.* chico

small 'change cambio *m*, suelto *m*,

L.Am. sencillo *m*
small 'hours *npl* madrugada *f*
small·pox ['smɒːlpɑːks] viruela *f*
'small print letra *f* pequeña
'small talk: ***make small talk*** hablar de banalidades *or* trivialidades
smart [smɑːrt] **1** *adj* (*elegant*) elegante; (*intelligent*) inteligente; *pace* rápido; ***get smart with*** hacerse el listillo con **2** *v/i* (*hurt*) escocer
'smart ass F sabelotodo *m/f* F
'smart card tarjeta *f* inteligente
◆ **smart·en up** ['smɑːrtn] *v/t appearance* mejorar; *room* arreglar
smart·ly ['smɑːrtlɪ] *adv dressed* con elegancia
smash [smæʃ] **1** *n noise* estruendo *m*; (*car crash*) choque *m*; *in tennis* smash *m*, mate *m* **2** *v/t break* hacer pedazos *or* añicos; ***he smashed the toys against the wall*** estrelló los juguetes contra la pared; ***he smashed his fist on the table*** dio un puñetazo en la mesa; ***smash sth to pieces*** hacer algo añicos **3** *v/i break* romperse; ***the driver smashed into …*** el conductor se estrelló contra …
◆ **smash up** *v/t place* destrozar
smash 'hit F exitazo *m* F
smat·ter·ing ['smætərɪŋ] *of a language* nociones *fpl*
smear [smɪr] **1** *n of ink* borrón *m*; *of paint* mancha *f*; MED citología *f*; *on character* difamación *f* **2** *v/t character* difamar; ***smear X over Y*** untar *or* embadurnar Y de X
'smear cam·paign campaña *f* de difamación
smell [smel] **1** *n* olor *m*; ***it has no smell*** no huele a nada; ***sense of smell*** sentido *m* del olfato **2** *v/t* oler **3** *v/i unpleasantly* oler (mal); (*sniff*) olfatear; ***you smell of beer*** hueles a cerveza; ***it smells good*** huele bien
smell·y ['smelɪ] *adj* apestoso; ***she had smelly feet*** le olían los pies; ***it's so smelly in here!*** ¡qué mal huele aquí!
smile [smaɪl] **1** *n* sonrisa *f* **2** *v/i* sonreír
◆ **smile at** *v/t* sonreir a
smirk [smɜːrk] **1** *n* sonrisa *f* maligna **2** *v/i* sonreír malignamente
smog [smɑːg] niebla *f* tóxica
smoke [smoʊk] **1** *n* humo *m*; ***have a smoke*** fumarse un cigarrillo **2** *v/t cigarettes* fumar; *bacon* ahumar **3** *v/i of person* fumar
smok·er ['smoʊkər] *person* fumador(a) *m*(a)
smok·ing ['smoʊkɪŋ]: ***smoking is bad for you*** fumar es malo; ***no smoking*** *sign* prohibido fumar
'smok·ing com·part·ment RAIL compartimento *m* de fumadores
smok·y ['smoʊkɪ] *adj room, air* lleno de *humo*
smooth [smuːð] **1** *adj surface, skin* liso, suave; *sea* en calma; (*peaceful*) tranquilo; *ride, drive* sin vibraciones; *transition* sin problemas; *pej*: *person* meloso **2** *v/t hair* alisar
◆ **smooth down** *v/t with sandpaper etc* alisar
◆ **smooth out** *v/t paper, cloth* alisar
◆ **smooth over** *v/t*: ***smooth things over*** suavizar las cosas
smooth·ly ['smuːðlɪ] *adv without any problems* sin incidentes
smoth·er ['smʌðər] *v/t flames* apagar, sofocar; *person* asfixiar; ***smother s.o. with kisses*** comerse a alguien a besos; ***he smothered the bread with jam*** cubrío *or* embardurnó el pan de mermelada
smol·der, *Br* **smoul·der** ['smoʊldər] *v/i of fire* arder (*los rescoldos*); *fig*: *with anger* arder de rabia; *fig*: *with desire* arder en deseos
smudge [smʌdʒ] **1** *n of paint* mancha *f*; *of ink* borrón *m* **2** *v/t ink* emborronar; *paint* difuminar
smug [smʌg] *adj* engreído
smug·gle ['smʌgl] *v/t* pasar de contrabando
smug·gler ['smʌglər] contrabandista *m/f*
smug·gling ['smʌglɪŋ] contrabando *m*
smug·ly ['smʌglɪ] *adv* con engreimiento *or* suficiencia
smut·ty ['smʌtɪ] *adj joke, sense of humor* obsceno
snack [snæk] *n* tentempié *m*, aperitivo *m*
'snack bar cafetería *f*
snag [snæg] *n* (*problem*) inconveniente *m*, pega *f*
snail [sneɪl] caracol *m*
snake [sneɪk] *n* serpiente *f*
snap [snæp] **1** *n* chasquido *m*; PHOT foto *f* **2** *v/t* (*pret & pp* ***snapped***) *break* romper **3** *v/i* (*pret & pp* ***snapped***) *break* romperse; ***none of your business, she snapped*** no es asunto tuyo, saltó **4** *adj decision, judgment* rápido, súbito
◆ **snap up** *v/t bargains* llevarse
snap fast·en·er ['snæpfæsnər] automático *m*, corchete *m*
snap·py ['snæpɪ] *adj person, mood* irascible; *decision, response* rápido; (*elegant*) elegante
'snap·shot foto *f*
snarl [snɑːrl] **1** *n of dog* gruñido *m* **2** *v/i* gruñir

S

snatch [snætʃ] **1** *v/t* arrebatar; (*steal*) robar; (*kidnap*) secuestrar; ***snatch sth from s.o.*** arrebatar algo a alguien **2** *v/i*: ***don't snatch*** no lo agarres
◆ **snatch at** *v/t* intentar agarrar
snaz·zy ['snæzɪ] *adj* F vistoso, *Span* chulo F
sneak [sniːk] **1** *n* (*telltale*) chivato(-a) *m*(*f*) **2** *v/t* (*remove, steal*) llevarse; ***sneak a glance at*** mirar con disimulo a **3** *v/i* (*tell tales*) chivarse; ***sneak into the room*** entrar a la habitación a hurtadillas
sneak·ers ['sniːkərz] *npl* zapatillas *fpl* de deporte
sneak·ing ['sniːkɪŋ] *adj*: ***have a sneaking suspicion that …*** sospechar que …
sneak·y ['sniːkɪ] *adj* F (*crafty*) ladino, cuco F
sneer [sniːr] **1** *n* mueca *f* desdeñosa **2** *v/i* burlarse (***at*** de)
sneeze [sniːz] **1** *n* estornudo *m* **2** *v/i* estornudar
snick·er ['snɪkər] **1** *n* risita *f* **2** *v/i* reírse (*en voz baja*)
sniff [snɪf] **1** *v/i to clear nose* sorberse los mocos; *of dog* olfatear **2** *v/t* (*smell*) oler; *of dog* olfatear
snip [snɪp] *n* F (*bargain*) ganga *f*
snip·er ['snaɪpər] francotirador(a) *m*(*f*)
sniv·el ['snɪvl] *v/i* gimotear
snob [snɑːb] presuntuoso(-a) *m*(*f*)
snob·ber·y ['snɑːbərɪ] presuntuosidad *f*
snob·bish ['snɑːbɪʃ] *adj* presuntuoso
snoop [snuːp] *n* fisgón(-ona) *m*(*f*)
◆ **snoop around** *v/i* fisgonear
snoot·y ['snuːtɪ] *adj* presuntuoso
snooze [snuːz] **1** *n* cabezada *f*; ***have a snooze*** echar una cabezada **2** *v/i* echar una cabezada
snore [snɔːr] *v/i* roncar
snor·ing ['snɔːrɪŋ] *n* ronquidos *mpl*
snor·kel ['snɔːrkl] *n* snorkel *m*, tubo *m* para buceo
snort [snɔːrt] *v/i of bull, person* bufar, resoplar
snout [snaʊt] *of pig, dog* hocico *m*
snow [snoʊ] **1** *n* nieve *f* **2** *v/i* nevar
◆ **snow under** *v/i*: ***be snowed under*** estar desbordado
'**snow·ball** bola *f* de nieve
'**snow·bound** *adj* aislado por la nieve
'**snow chains** *npl* MOT cadenas *fpl* para la nieve
'**snow·drift** nevero *m*
'**snow·drop** campanilla *f* de invierno
'**snow·flake** copo *m* de nieve
'**snow·man** muñeco *m* de nieve
'**snow·plow** quitanieves *f inv*
'**snow·storm** tormenta *f* de nieve
snow·y ['snoʊɪ] *adj weather* de nieve; *roads, hills* nevado
snub [snʌb] **1** *n* desaire **2** *v/t* (*pret & pp* ***snubbed***) desairar
snub-nosed ['snʌbnoʊzd] *adj* con la nariz respingona
snug [snʌg] *adj* (*tight-fitting*) ajustado; ***we are nice and snug in here*** aquí se está muy a gusto
◆ **snug·gle down** ['snʌgl] *v/i* acurrucarse
◆ **snug·gle up to** *v/t* acurrucarse contra
so [soʊ] **1** *adv* tan; ***it was so easy*** fue tan fácil; ***I'm so cold*** tengo tanto frío; ***that was so kind of you*** fue muy amable de tu parte; ***not so much*** no tanto; ***so much easier*** mucho más fácil; ***you shouldn't eat / drink so much*** no deberías comer / beber tanto; ***I miss you so*** te echo tanto de menos; ***so am / do I*** yo también; ***so is she / does she*** ella también; ***and so on*** etcétera **2** *pron*: ***I hope / think so*** eso espero / creo; ***you didn't tell me - I did so*** no me lo dijiste - sí que lo hice; ***50 or so*** unos 50 **3** *conj for that reason* así que; *in order that* para que; ***I got up late and so I missed the train*** me levanté tarde y por eso perdí el tren; ***so (that) I could come too*** para que yo también pudiera venir; ***so what?*** F ¿y qué? F
soak [soʊk] *v/t* (*steep*) poner en remojo; *of water, rain* empapar
◆ **soak up** *v/t liquid* absorber; ***soak up the sun*** tostarse al sol
soaked [soʊkt] *adj* empapado; ***be soaked to the skin*** estar calado hasta los huesos
soak·ing (wet) ['soʊkɪŋ] *adj* empapado
so-and-so ['soʊənsoʊ] F (*unknown person*) fulanito *m*; (*euph*: *annoying person*) canalla *m/f*
soap [soʊp] *for washing* jabón *m*
'**soap (op·e·ra)** telenovela *f*
soap·y ['soʊpɪ] *adj water* jabonoso
soar [sɔːr] *v/i of rocket etc* elevarse; *of prices* dispararse
sob [sɑːb] **1** *n* sollozo *m* **2** *v/i* (*pret & pp* ***sobbed***) sollozar
so·ber ['soʊbər] *adj* (*not drunk*) sobrio; (*serious*) serio
◆ **sober up** *v/i*: ***he sobered up*** se le pasó la borrachera
so-'called *adj* (*referred to as*) así llamado; (*incorrectly referred to as*) mal llamado
soc·cer ['sɑːkər] fútbol *m*
'**soc·cer hoo·li·gan** hincha *m* violento
so·cia·ble ['soʊʃəbl] *adj* sociable
so·cial ['soʊʃl] *adj* social
so·cial 'dem·o·crat socialdemócrata *m/f*

so·cial·ism ['soʊʃəlɪzm] socialismo *m*
so·cial·ist ['soʊʃəlɪst] **1** *adj* socialista **2** *n* socialista *m/f*
so·cial·ize ['soʊʃəlaɪz] *v/i* socializar (***with*** con)
'**soc·ial life** vida *f* social
so·cial 'sci·ence ciencia *f* social
'**so·cial work** trabajo *m* social
'**so·cial work·er** asistente(-a) *m(f)* social
so·ci·e·ty [sə'saɪətɪ] sociedad *f*
so·ci·ol·o·gist [soʊsɪ'ɑːlədʒɪst] sociólogo(-a) *m(f)*
so·ci·ol·o·gy [soʊsɪ'ɑːlədʒɪ] sociología *f*
sock[1] [sɑːk] *for wearing* calcetín *m*
sock[2] [sɑːk] **1** *n* (*punch*) puñetazo *m* **2** *v/t* (*punch*) dar un puñetazo a
sock·et ['sɑːkɪt] *for light bulb* casquillo *m*; *of arm* cavidad *f*; *of eye* cuenca *f*; *Br electrical* enchufe *m*
so·da ['soʊdə] (*soda water*) soda *f*; (*ice--cream soda*) *refresco de soda con helado*
sod·den ['sɑːdn] *adj* empapado
so·fa ['soʊfə] sofá *m*
'**so·fa-bed** sofá cama *m*
soft [sɑːft] *adj voice, light, color, skin* suave; *pillow, attitude* blando; ***have a soft spot for*** tener una debilidad por
'**soft drink** refresco *m*
'**soft drug** droga *f* blanda
soft·en ['sɑːfn] **1** *v/t position* ablandar; *impact, blow* amortiguar **2** *v/i of butter, ice cream* ablandarse, reblandecerse
soft·ly ['sɑːftlɪ] *adv* suavemente
soft 'toy peluche *m*
soft·ware ['sɑːftwer] software *m*
sog·gy ['sɑːgɪ] *adj* empapado
soil [sɔɪl] **1** *n* (*earth*) tierra *f* **2** *v/t* ensuciar
so·lar 'en·er·gy ['soʊlər] energía *f* solar
'**so·lar pan·el** panel *m* solar
'**solar system** sistema *m* solar
sold [soʊld] *pret & pp* → ***sell***
sol·dier ['soʊldʒər] soldado *m*
◆ **soldier on** *v/i* seguir adelante; ***we'll have to soldier on without her*** nos las tendremos que arreglar sin ella
sole[1] [soʊl] *n of foot* planta *f*; *of shoe* suela *f*
sole[2] [soʊl] *adj* único
sole·ly ['soʊlɪ] *adv* únicamente
sol·emn ['sɑːləm] *adj* solemne
so·lem·ni·ty [sə'lemnətɪ] solemnidad *f*
sol·emn·ly ['sɑːləmlɪ] *adv* solemnemente
so·lic·it [sə'lɪsɪt] *v/i of prostitute* abordar clientes
so·lic·i·tor [sə'lɪsɪtər] *Br* abogado(-a) *m(f)* (*que no aparece en tribunales*)
sol·id ['sɑːlɪd] *adj* sólido; (*without holes*) compacto; *gold, silver* macizo; ***a solid hour*** una hora seguida
sol·i·dar·i·ty [sɑːlɪ'dærətɪ] solidaridad *f*
so·lid·i·fy [sə'lɪdɪfaɪ] *v/i* (*pret & pp* ***solidified***) solidificarse
sol·id·ly ['sɑːlɪdlɪ] *adv built* sólidamente; *in favor of sth* unánimente
so·lil·o·quy [sə'lɪləkwɪ] soliloquio *f*
sol·i·taire [sɑːlɪ'ter] *card game* solitario *m*
sol·i·ta·ry ['sɑːlɪterɪ] *adj life, activity* solitario; (*single*) único
sol·i·ta·ry con'fine·ment prisión *f* incomunicada
sol·i·tude ['sɑːlɪtuːd] soledad *f*
so·lo ['soʊloʊ] **1** *n* MUS solo *m* **2** *adj* en solitario
so·lo·ist ['soʊloʊɪst] solista *m/f*
sol·u·ble ['sɑːljʊbl] *adj substance, problem* soluble
so·lu·tion [sə'luːʃn] solución *f* (***to*** a); (*mixture*) solución *f*
solve [sɑːlv] *v/t problem* solucionar, resolver; *mystery* resolver; *crossword* resolver, sacar
sol·vent ['sɑːlvənt] *adj financially* solvente
som·ber, *Br* **som·bre** ['sɑːmbər] *adj* (*dark*) oscuro; (*serious*) sombrío
some [sʌm] **1** *adj*: ***would you like some water / cookies?*** ¿quieres agua / galletas?; ***some countries*** algunos países; ***I gave him some money*** le di (algo de) dinero; ***some people say that …*** hay quien dice … **2** *pron*: ***some of the group*** parte del grupo; ***would you like some?*** ¿quieres?; ***milk? - no thanks, I've got some*** ¿leche? - gracias, ya tengo **3** *adv* (*a bit*): ***we'll have to wait some*** tendremos que esperar algo *or* un poco
some·bod·y ['sʌmbədɪ] *pron* alguien
'**some·day** *adv* algún día
'**some·how** *adv* (*by one means or another*) de alguna manera; (*for some unknown reason*) por alguna razón; ***I've never liked him somehow*** por alguna razón u otra nunca me cayó bien
'**some·one** *pron* → ***somebody***
'**some·place** *adv* → ***somewhere***
som·er·sault ['sʌmərsɒːlt] **1** *n* salto mortal **2** *v/i* dar un salto mortal
'**some·thing** *pron* algo; ***would you like something to drink / eat?*** ¿te gustaría beber / comer algo?; ***is something wrong?*** ¿pasa algo?
'**some·time** *adv*: ***let's have lunch sometime*** quedemos para comer un día de éstos; ***sometime last year*** en algún momento del año pasado
'**some·times** ['sʌmtaɪmz] *adv* a veces
'**some·what** *adv* un tanto
'**some·where** **1** *adv* en alguna parte *or* al-

S

gún lugar **2** *pron*: ***let's go to somewhere quiet*** vamos a algún sitio tranquilo; ***I was looking for somewhere to park*** buscaba un sitio donde aparcar
son [sʌn] hijo *m*
so·na·ta [sə'nɑːtə] MUS sonata *f*
song [sɒːŋ] canción *f*
'song·bird pájaro *m* cantor
'song·writ·er cantautor(a) *m(f)*
'son-in-law (*pl* **sons-in-law**) yerno *m*
'son·net ['sɑːnɪt] soneto *m*
soon [suːn] *adv* pronto; ***how soon can you be ready to leave?*** ¿cuándo estarás listo para salir?; ***he left soon after I arrived*** se marchó al poco de llegar yo; ***can't you get here any sooner?*** ¿no podrías llegar antes?; ***as soon as*** tan pronto como; ***as soon as possible*** lo antes posible; ***sooner or later*** tarde o temprano; ***the sooner the better*** cuanto antes mejor
soot [sʊt] hollín *m*
soothe [suːð] *v/t* calmar
so·phis·ti·cat·ed [sə'fɪstɪkeɪtɪd] *adj* sofisticado
so·phis·ti·ca·tion [sə'fɪstɪkeɪʃn] sofisticación *f*
soph·o·more ['sɑːfəmɔːr] estudiante *m/f* de segundo año
sop·py ['sɑːpɪ] *adj* F sensiblero
so·pra·no [sə'prænoʊ] *n singer* soprano *m/f*; *voice* voz *f* de soprano
sor·did ['sɔːrdɪd] *adj affair, business* sórdido
sore [sɔːr] **1** *adj* (*painful*) dolorido; F (*angry*) enojado, *Span* mosqueado F; ***is it sore?*** ¿duele?; ***I'm sore all over*** me duele todo el cuerpo **2** *n* llaga *f*
sor·row ['sɑːroʊ] *n* pena *f*
sor·ry ['sɑːrɪ] *adj* (*sad*: *day, sight*) triste; (***I'm***) ***sorry!*** *apologizing* ¡lo siento!; ***I'm sorry that I didn't tell you sooner*** lamento no habértelo dicho antes; ***I was so sorry to hear of her death*** me dio mucha pena oír lo de su muerte; (***I'm***) ***sorry but I can't help*** lo siento pero no puedo ayudar; ***I won't be sorry to leave here*** no me arrepentiré de irme de aquí; ***I feel sorry for her*** siento pena *or* lástima por ella; ***be a sorry sight*** ofrecer un espectáculo lamentable
sort [sɔːrt] **1** *n* clase *f*, tipo *m*; ***sort of*** F un poco, algo; ***is it finished? - sort of*** F ¿está acabado? - más o menos **2** *v/t* ordenar, clasificar; COMPUT ordenar
◆ **sort out** *v/t papers* ordenar, clasificar; *problem* resolver, arreglar
SOS [esoʊ'es] SOS *m*; *fig* llamada *f* de auxilio
so-'so *adv* F así así F
sought [sɒːt] *pret & pp* → ***seek***
soul [soʊl] REL, *fig*: *of a nation etc* alma *f*; *character* personalidad *f*; ***the poor soul*** el pobrecillo
sound[1] [saʊnd] **1** *adj* (*sensible*) sensato; (*healthy*) sano; *sleep* profundo **2** *adv*: ***be sound asleep*** estar profundamente dormido
sound[2] [saʊnd] **1** *n* sonido *m*; (*noise*) ruido *m* **2** *v/t* (*pronounce*) pronunciar; MED auscultar; ***sound one's horn*** tocar la bocina **3** *v/i*: ***that sounds interesting*** parece interesante; ***she sounded unhappy*** parecía triste
◆ **sound out** *v/t* sondear; ***I sounded her out about the idea*** sondeé a ver qué le parecía la idea
'sound card COMPUT tarjeta *f* de sonido
'sound ef·fects *npl* efectos *mpl* sonoros
sound·ly ['saʊndlɪ] *adv sleep* profundamente; *beaten* rotundamente
'sound·proof *adj* insonorizado
'sound·track banda *f* sonora
soup [suːp] sopa *f*
'soup bowl cuenco *m*
souped-up [suːpt'ʌp] *adj* F trucado
'soup plate plato *m* sopero
'soup spoon cuchara *f* sopera
sour [saʊr] *adj apple, orange* ácido, agrio; *milk* cortado; *comment* agrio
source [sɔːrs] *n* fuente *f*; *of river* nacimiento *m*; (*person*) fuente *f*
'sour cream nata *f* agria
south [saʊθ] **1** *adj* sur, del sur **2** *n* sur *m*; ***to the south of*** al sur de **3** *adv* al sur; ***south of*** al sur de
South 'Af·ric·a Sudáfrica
South 'Af·ri·can 1 *adj* sudafricano **2** *n* sudafricano(-a) *m(f)*
South A'mer·i·ca Sudamérica, *América* del Sur
South A'mer·i·can 1 *adj* sudamericano **2** *n* sudamericano(-a) *m(f)*
south'east 1 *n* sudeste *m*, sureste *m* **2** *adj* sudeste, sureste **3** *adv* al sudeste *or* sureste; ***southeast of*** al sudeste de
south'·east·ern *adj* del sudeste
south·er·ly ['sʌðərlɪ] *adj wind* sur, del sur; *direction* sur
south·ern ['sʌðərn] *adj* sureño
south·ern·er ['sʌðərnər] sureño(-a) *m(f)*
south·ern·most ['sʌðərnmoʊst] *adj* más al sur
South 'Pole Polo *m* Sur
south·ward ['saʊθwərd] *adv* hacia el sur
south·'west 1 *n* sudoeste *m*, suroeste *m* **2** *adj* sudoeste, suroeste **3** *adv* al sudeste *or* suroeste; ***southwest of*** al sudoeste *or*

S

suroeste de
south'west·ern *adj* del sudoeste *or* suroeste
sou·ve·nir [suːvə'nɪr] recuerdo *m*
sove·reign ['sɑːvrɪn] *adj state* soberano
sove·reign·ty ['sɑːvrɪntɪ] *of state* soberanía *f*
So·vi·et ['soʊvɪət] *adj* soviético
So·vi·et 'U·nion Unión *f* Soviética
sow[1] [saʊ] *n* (*female pig*) cerda *f*, puerca *f*
sow[2] [soʊ] *v/t* (*pret* ***sowed***, *pp* ***sown***) *seeds* sembrar
sown [soʊn] *pp* → ***sow***[2]
'soy bean [sɔɪ] semilla *f* de soja
soy 'sauce salsa *f* de soja
space [speɪs] *n* espacio *m*
◆ **space out** *v/t* espaciar
'space-bar COMPUT barra *f* espaciadora
'space·craft nave *f* espacial
'space·ship nave *f* espacial
'space shut·tle transbordador *m* espacial
'space sta·tion estación *f* espacial
'space·suit traje *m* espacial
spa·cious ['speɪʃəs] *adj* espacioso
spade [speɪd] *for digging* pala *f*; ***spades*** *in card game* picas *fpl*
'spade·work *fig* trabajo *m* preliminar
spa·ghet·ti [spə'getɪ] *nsg* espaguetis *mpl*
Spain [speɪn] España
span [spæn] *v/t* (*pret & pp* ***spanned***) abarcar; *of bridge* cruzar
Span·iard ['spænjərd] español(a) *m*(*f*)
Span·ish ['spænɪʃ] **1** *adj* español **2** *n language* español *m*; ***the Spanish*** los españoles
spank [spæŋk] *v/t* azotar
spank·ing ['spæŋkɪŋ] azotaina *f*
span·ner ['spænər] *Br* llave *f*
spare [sper] **1** *v/t*: ***can you spare me $50?*** ¿me podrías dejar 50 dólares?; ***we can't spare a single employee*** no podemos prescindir ni de un solo trabajador; ***can you spare the time?*** ¿tienes tiempo?; ***I have time to spare*** me sobra el tiempo; ***there were 5 to spare*** sobraban cinco **2** *adj pair of glasses, set of keys* de repuesto; ***do you have any spare cash?*** ¿no te sobrará algo de dinero? **3** *n* recambio *m*, repuesto *m*
spare 'part pieza *f* de recambio *or* repuesto
spare 'ribs *npl* costillas *fpl* de cerdo
spare 'room habitación *f* de invitados
spare 'time tiempo *m* libre
spare 'tire, *Br* **spare 'tyre** MOT rueda *f* de recambio *or* repuesto
spar·ing ['sperɪŋ] *adj* moderado; ***be sparing with*** no derrochar
spa·ring·ly ['sperɪŋlɪ] *adv* con moderación
spark [spɑːrk] *n* chispa *f*
spar·kle ['spɑːrkl] *v/i* destellar
spar·kling 'wine ['spɑːrklɪŋ] vino *m* espumoso
'spark plug bujía *f*
spar·row ['spæroʊ] gorrión *m*
sparse [spɑːrs] *adj vegetation* escaso
sparse·ly ['spɑːrslɪ] *adv*: ***sparsely populated*** poco poblado
spar·tan ['spɑːrtn] *adj room* espartano
spas·mod·ic [spæz'mɑːdɪk] *adj* intermitente
spat [spæt] *pret & pp* → ***spit***
spate [speɪt] *fig* oleada *f*
spa·tial ['speɪʃl] *adj* espacial
spat·ter ['spætər] *v/t*: ***the car spattered mud all over me*** el coche me salpicó de barro
speak [spiːk] **1** *v/i* (*pret* ***spoke***, *pp* ***spoken***) hablar (***to*** con); (*make a speech*) dar una charla; ***we're not speaking*** (***to each other***) (*we've quarreled*) no nos hablamos; ***speaking*** TELEC al habla **2** *v/t* (*pret* ***spoke***, *pp* ***spoken***) *foreign language* hablar; ***she spoke her mind*** dijo lo que pensaba
◆ **speak for** *v/t* hablar en nombre de
◆ **speak out** *v/i*: ***speak out against injustice*** denunciar la injusticia
◆ **speak up** *v/i* (*speak louder*) hablar más alto
speak·er ['spiːkər] *at conference* conferenciante *m/f*; (*orator*) orador(a) *m*(*f*); *of sound system* altavoz *m*, *L.Am.* altoparlante *m*; *of language* hablante *m/f*
spear [spɪr] lanza *f*
spear·mint ['spɪrmɪnt] hierbabuena *f*
spe·cial ['speʃl] *adj* especial; ***be on special*** estar de oferta
spe·cial ef·fects *npl* efectos *mpl* especiales
spe·cial·ist ['speʃlɪst] especialista *m/f*
spe·cial·ize ['speʃəlaɪz] *v/i* especializarse (***in*** en)
spe·cial·ly ['speʃlɪ] *adv* → ***especially***
spe·cial·i·ty [speʃɪ'ælətɪ] *Br*, **spe·cial·ty** ['speʃəltɪ] especialidad *f*
spe·cies ['spiːʃiːz] *nsg* especie *f*
spe·cif·ic [spə'sɪfɪk] *adj* específico
spe·cif·i·cal·ly [spə'sɪfɪklɪ] *adv* específicamente
spec·i·fi·ca·tions [spesɪfɪ'keɪʃnz] *npl of machine etc* especificaciones *fpl*
spe·ci·fy ['spesɪfaɪ] *v/t* (*pret & pp* ***specified***) especificar
spe·ci·men ['spesɪmən] muestra *f*
speck [spek] *of dust, soot* mota *f*
specs [speks] *npl* F (*spectacles*) gafas *fpl*,

L.Am. lentes *mpl*

spec·ta·cle ['spektəkl] (*impressive sight*) espectáculo *m*; **(*a pair of*) *spectacles*** unas gafas, *L.Am.* unos lentes

spec·tac·u·lar [spek'tækjʊlər] *adj* espectacular

spec·ta·tor [spek'teɪtər] espectador(a) *m(f)*

spec'ta·tor sport deporte *m* espectáculo

spec·trum ['spektrəm] *fig* espectro *m*

spec·u·late ['spekjʊleɪt] *v/i also* FIN especular

spec·u·la·tion [spekjʊ'leɪʃn] *also* FIN especulación *f*

spec·u·la·tor ['spekjʊleɪtər] FIN especulador(a) *m(f)*

sped [sped] *pret & pp* → ***speed***

speech [spiːʧ] (*address*) discurso *m*; *in play* parlamento *m*; (*ability to speak*) habla *f*, dicción *f*; (*way of speaking*) forma *f* de hablar

'**speech de·fect** defecto *m* del habla

speech·less ['spiːʧlɪs] *adj with shock, surprise* sin habla; ***I was left speechless*** me quedé sin habla

'**speech ther·a·pist** logopeda *m/f*

'**speech ther·a·py** logopedia *f*

'**speech writ·er** redactor(a) *m(f)* de discursos

speed [spiːd] **1** *n* velocidad *f*; (*promptness*) rapidez *f*; ***at a speed of 150 mph*** a una velocidad de 150 millas por hora **2** *v/i* (*pret & pp* ***sped***) *run* correr; *drive too quickly* sobrepasar el límite de velocidad; ***we were speeding along*** íbamos a toda velocidad

◆ **speed by** *v/i* pasar a toda velocidad

◆ **speed up 1** *v/i of car, driver* acelerar; *when working* apresurarse **2** *v/t process* acelerar

'**speed·boat** motora *f*, planeadora *f*

'**speed bump** resalto *m* (*para reducir la velocidad del tráfico*), *Arg* despertador *m*, *Mex* tope *m*

speed·i·ly ['spiːdɪlɪ] *adv* con rapidez

speed·ing ['spiːdɪŋ] *n*: ***fined for speeding*** multado por exceso de velocidad

'**speed·ing fine** multa *f* por exceso de velocidad

'**speed lim·it** *on roads* límite *m* de velocidad

speed·om·e·ter [spiː'dɑːmɪtər] velocímetro *m*

'**speed trap** control *m* de velocidad por radar

speed·y ['spiːdɪ] *adj* rápido

spell[1] [spel] **1** *v/t word* deletrear ***how do you spell …?*** ¿cómo se escribe … ? **2** *v/i* deletrear

spell[2] [spel] *n* (*period of time*) periodo *m*, temporada; ***I'll take a spell at the wheel*** te relevaré un rato al volante

'**spell·bound** *adj* hechizado

'**spell·check** COMPUT: ***do a spellcheck on*** pasar el corrector ortográfico a

'**spell·check·er** COMPUT corrector *m* ortográfico

spell·ing ['spelɪŋ] ortografía *f*

spend [spend] *v/t* (*pret & pp* ***spent***) *money* gastar; *time* pasar

'**spend·thrift** *n pej* derrochador(a) *m(f)*

spent [spent] *pret & pp* → ***spend***

sperm [spɜːrm] espermatozoide *m*; (*semen*) esperma *f*

'**sperm bank** banco *m* de esperma

'**sperm count** recuento *m* espermático

sphere [sfɪr] *also fig* esfera *f*; ***sphere of influence*** ámbito *m* de influencia

spice [spaɪs] *n* (*seasoning*) especia *f*

spic·y ['spaɪsɪ] *adj food* con especias; (*hot*) picante

spi·der ['spaɪdər] araña *f*

'**spi·der·web** telaraña *f*, tela *f* de araña

spike [spaɪk] *n* pincho *m*; *on running shoe* clavo *m*

spill [spɪl] **1** *v/t* derramar **2** *v/i* derramarse **3** *n* derrame *m*

spin[1] [spɪn] **1** *n* (*turn*) giro *m* **2** *v/t* (*pret & pp* ***spun***) hacer girar **3** *v/i* (*pret & pp* ***spun***) *of wheel* girar, dar vueltas; ***my head is spinning*** me da vueltas la cabeza

spin[2] [spɪn] *v/t wool, cotton* hilar; *web* tejer

◆ **spin around** *v/i of person, car* darse la vuelta

◆ **spin out** *v/t* alargar

spin·ach ['spɪnɪdʒ] espinacas *fpl*

spin·al ['spaɪnl] *adj* de la columna vertebral

spin·al 'col·umn columna *f* vertebral

spin·al 'cord médula *f* espinal

'**spin doc·tor** F *asesor encargado de dar la mejor prensa posible a un político o asunto*

'**spin-dry** *v/t* centrifugar

spin-'dry·er centrifugadora *f*

spine [spaɪn] *of person, animal* columna *f* vertebral; *of book* lomo *m*; *on plant, hedgehog* espina *f*

spine·less ['spaɪnlɪs] *adj* (*cowardly*) débil

'**spin-off** producto *m* derivade

spin·ster ['spɪnstər] solterona *f*

spin·y ['spaɪnɪ] *adj* espinoso

spi·ral ['spaɪrəl] **1** *n* espiral **2** *v/i* (*rise quickly*) subir vertiginosamente

spi·ral 'stair·case escalera *f* de caracol

spire [spaɪr] aguja *f*

spir·it ['spɪrɪt] *n* espíritu *m*; (*courage*) valor *m*; ***in a spirit of cooperation*** con espíritu de cooperación

spir·it·ed ['spɪrɪtɪd] *adj* (*energetic*) enérgico

'**spir·it lev·el** nivel *m* de burbuja

spir·its[1] ['spɪrɪts] *npl* (*alcohol*) licores *mpl*

spirits[2] ['spɪrɪts] *npl* (*morale*) la moral; ***be in good / poor spirits*** tener la moral alta / baja

spir·i·tu·al ['spɪrɪʧʊəl] *adj* espiritual

spir·it·u·al·ism ['spɪrɪʧəlɪzm] espiritismo *m*

spir·it·u·al·ist ['spɪrɪʧəlɪst] *n* espiritista *m/f*

spit [spɪt] *v/i* (*pret & pp* ***spat***) *of person* escupir; ***it's spitting with rain*** está chispeando

◆ **spit out** *v/t food, liquid* escupir

spite [spaɪt] *n* rencor *m*; ***in spite of*** a pesar de

spite·ful ['spaɪtfəl] *adj* malo, malicioso

spite·ful·ly ['spaɪtfəlɪ] *adv* con maldad *or* malicia

spit·ting '**im·age** ['spɪtɪŋ]: ***be the spitting image of s.o.*** ser el vivo retrato de alguien

splash [splæʃ] **1** *n small amount of liquid* chorrito *m*; *of color* mancha *f* **2** *v/t person* salpicar; ***the car splashed mud all over me*** el coche me salpicó de barro **3** *v/i* chapotear; *of water* salpicar

◆ **splash down** *v/i of spacecraft* amerizar

◆ **splash out** *v/i in spending* gastarse una fortuna

'**splash·down** amerizaje *m*

splen·did ['splendɪd] *adj* espléndido

splen·dor, *Br* **splen·dour** ['splendər] esplendor *m*

splint [splɪnt] *n* MED tablilla *f*

splin·ter ['splɪntər] **1** *n* astilla *f* **2** *v/i* astillarse

'**splin·ter group** grupo *m* escindido

split [splɪt] **1** *n damage* raja *f*; (*disagreement*) escisión *f*; (*division, share*) reparto *m* **2** *v/t* (*pret & pp* ***split***) *damage* rajar; *logs* partir en dos; (*cause disagreement in*) escindir; (*share*) repartir **3** *v/i* (*pret & pp* ***split***) (*tear*) rajarse; (*disagree*) escindirse

◆ **split up** *v/i of couple* separarse

split per·son'al·i·ty PSYCH doble personalidad *f*

split·ting ['splɪtɪŋ] *adj*: ***splitting headache*** dolor *m* de cabeza atroz

splut·ter ['splʌtər] *v/i* farfullar

spoil [spɔɪl] *v/t* estropear, arruinar

'**spoil·sport** F aguafiestas *m/f inv* F

spoilt [spɔɪlt] *adj child* consentido, mimado; ***be spoilt for choice*** tener mucho donde elegir

spoke[1] [spoʊk] *of wheel* radio *m*

spoke[2] [spoʊk] *pret* → ***speak***

spo·ken ['spoʊkən] *pp* → ***speak***

spokes·man ['spoʊksmən] portavoz *m*

spokes·per·son ['spoʊkspɜːrsən] portavoz *m/f*

spokes·wom·an ['spoʊkswʊmən] portavoz *f*

sponge [spʌndʒ] *n* esponja *f*

◆ **sponge off**, **sponge on** *v/t* F vivir a costa de

'**sponge cake** bizcocho *m*

spong·er ['spʌndʒər] F gorrón(-ona) *m(f)* F

spon·sor ['spɑːnsər] **1** *n* patrocinador *m* **2** *v/t* patrocinar

spon·sor·ship ['spɑːnsərʃɪp] patrocinio *m*

spon·ta·ne·ous [spɑːn'teɪnɪəs] *adj* espontáneo

spon·ta·ne·ous·ly [spɑːn'teɪnɪəslɪ] *adv* espontáneamente

spook·y ['spuːkɪ] *adj* F espeluznante, terrorífico

spool [spuːl] *n* carrete *m*

spoon [spuːn] *n* cuchara *f*

'**spoon·feed** *v/t* (*pret & pp* ***spoonfed***) *fig* dar todo mascado a

spoon·ful ['spuːnfʊl] cucharada *f*

spo·rad·ic [spə'rædɪk] *adj* esporádico

sport [spɔːrt] *n* deporte *m*

sport·ing ['spɔːrtɪŋ] *adj* deportivo; ***a sporting gesture*** un gesto deportivo

'**sports car** [spɔːrts] (coche *m*) deportivo *m*

'**sports·coat** chaqueta *f* de sport

sports '**jour·nal·ist** periodista *m/f* deportivo(-a)

'**sports·man** deportista *m*

'**sports med·i·cine** medicina *f* deportiva

'**sports news** *nsg* noticias *fpl* deportivas

'**sports page** página *f* de deportes

'**sports·wear** ropa *f* de deporte

'**sports·wom·an** deportista *f*

sport·y ['spɔːrtɪ] *adj person* deportista; *clothes* deportivo

spot[1] [spɑːt] (*pimple etc*) grano *m*; (*part of pattern*) lunar *m*; ***a spot of …*** (*a little*) algo de …, un poco de …

spot[2] [spɑːt] (*place*) lugar *m*, sitio *m*; ***on the spot*** (*in the place in question*) en el lugar; (*immediately*) en ese momento; ***put s.o. on the spot*** poner a alguien en un aprieto

spot[3] [spɑːt] *v/t* (*pret & pp* ***spotted***) (*notice*) ver; (*identify*) ver, darse cuenta de

spot '**check** *n* control *m* al azar; ***carry out***

spot check checks llevar a cabo controles al azar
spot·less ['spɑːtlɪs] *adj* inmaculado, impecable
'spot·light *n* foco *m*
spot·ted ['spɑːtɪd] *adj fabric* de lunares
spot·ty ['spɑːtɪ] *adj with pimples* con granos
spouse [spaʊs] *fml* cónyuge *m/f*
spout [spaʊt] **1** *n* pitorro *m* **2** *v/i of liquid* chorrear **3** *v/t* F soltar F
sprain [spreɪn] **1** *n* esguince *m* **2** *v/t* hacerse un esguince en
sprang [spræŋ] *pret* → ***spring³***
sprawl [sprɒːl] *v/i* despatarrarse; *of city* expandirse; ***send s.o. sprawling*** *of punch* derribar de un golpe
sprawl·ing ['sprɒːlɪŋ] *adj city, suburbs* en expansión
spray [spreɪ] **1** *n of sea water, from fountain* rociada *f*; *for hair* spray *m*; *container* aerosol *m*, spray *m* **2** *v/t* rociar; ***spray sth with sth*** rociar algo de algo
'spray·gun pistola *f* pulverizadora
spread [spred] **1** *n of disease, religion etc* propagación *f*; F (*big meal*) comilona *f* F **2** *v/t* (*pret & pp* ***spread***) (*lay*) extender; *butter, jelly* untar; *news, rumor* difundir; *disease* propagar; *arms, legs* extender **3** *v/i* (*pret & pp* ***spread***) *of disease, fire* propagarse; *of rumor, news* difundirse; *of butter* extenderse, untarse
'spread·sheet COMPUT hoja *f* de cálculo
spree [spriː] F: ***go (out) on a spree*** ir de juerga; ***go on a shopping spree*** salir a comprar a lo loco
sprig [sprɪg] ramita *f*
spright·ly ['spraɪtlɪ] *adj* lleno de energía
spring¹ [sprɪŋ] *n* (*season*) primavera *f*
spring² [sprɪŋ] *n* (*device*) muelle *m*
spring³ [sprɪŋ] **1** *n* (*jump*) brinco *m*, salto *m*; (*stream*) manantial *m* **2** *v/i* (*pret* ***sprang***, *pp* ***sprung***) brincar, saltar; ***spring from*** proceder de; ***he sprang to his feet*** se levantó de un salto
'spring·board trampolín *m*
spring 'chick·en *hum*: ***she's no spring chicken*** no es ninguna niña
spring-'clean·ing limpieza *f* a fondo
'spring·time primavera *f*
spring·y ['sprɪŋɪ] *adj mattress, ground* mullido; *walk* ligero; *piece of elastic* elástico
sprin·kle ['sprɪŋkl] *v/t* espolvorear; ***sprinkle sth with sth*** espolvorear algo con algo
sprin·kler ['sprɪŋklər] *for garden* aspersor *m*; *in ceiling* rociador *m* contra incendios
sprint [sprɪnt] **1** *n* esprint *m*; SP carrera *f* de velocidad **2** *v/i* (*run fast*) correr a toda velocidad; *of runner* esprintar
sprint·er ['sprɪntər] SP esprínter *m/f*, velocista *m/f*
sprout [spraʊt] **1** *v/i of seed* brotar **2** *n*: (***Brussels***) ***sprouts*** coles *fpl* de Bruselas
spruce [spruːs] *adj* pulcro
sprung [sprʌŋ] *pp* → ***spring³***
spry [spraɪ] *adj* lleno *m* de energía
spun [spʌn] *pret & pp* → ***spin¹***
spur [spɜːr] *n* espuela *f*; *fig* incentivo; ***on the spur of the moment*** sin pararse a pensar
◆ **spur on** *v/t* (*pret & pp* ***spurred***) (*encourage*) espolear
spurt [spɜːrt] **1** *n in race* arrancada *f*; ***put on a spurt*** acelerar **2** *v/i of liquid* chorrear
sput·ter ['spʌtər] *v/i of engine* chisporrotear
spy [spaɪ] **1** *n* espía *m/f* **2** *v/i* (*pret & pp* ***spied***) espiar **3** *v/t* (*pret & pp* ***spied***) (*see*) ver
◆ **spy on** *v/t* espiar
squab·ble ['skwɑːbl] **1** *n* riña *f* **2** *v/i* reñir
squal·id ['skwɒːlɪd] *adj* inmundo, miserable
squal·or ['skwɒːlər] inmunidcia *f*
squan·der ['skwɒːndər] *v/t money* despilfarrar
square [skwer] **1** *adj in shape* cuadrado; ***square miles*** millas cuadradas **2** *n also* MATH cuadrado *m*; *in town* plaza *f*; *in board game* casilla *f*; ***we're back to square one*** volvemos al punto de partida
◆ **square up** *v/i* hacer cuentas
square 'root raíz *f* cuadrada
squash¹ [skwɑːʃ] *n vegetable* calabacera *f*
squash² [skwɑːʃ] *n game* squash *m*
squash³ [skwɑːʃ] *v/t* (*crush*) aplastar
squat [skwɑːt] **1** *adj person, build* chaparro; *figure, buildings* bajo **2** *v/i* (*pret & pp* ***squatted***) *sit* agacharse; ***squat in a building*** ocupar ilegalmente un edificio
squat·ter ['skwɑːtər] ocupante *m/f* ilegal, *Span* okupa *m/f* F
squeak [skwiːk] **1** *n of mouse* chillido *m*; *of hinge* chirrido *m* **2** *v/i of mouse* chillar; *of hinge* chirriar; *of shoes* crujir
squeak·y ['skwiːkɪ] *adj hinge* chirriante; *shoes* que crujen; *voice* chillón
'squeak·y clean *adj* F bien limpio
squeal [skwiːl] **1** *n* chillido; ***there was a squeal of brakes*** se oyó una frenada estruendosa **2** *v/i* chillar; *of brakes* armar un estruendo
squeam·ish ['skwiːmɪʃ] *adj* aprensivo
squeeze [skwiːz] **1** *n of hand, shoulder*

apretón *m* **2** *v/t* (*press*) apretar; (*remove juice from*) exprimir

◆ **squeeze in 1** *v/i to a car etc* meterse a duras penas **2** *v/t* hacer hueco para

◆ **squeeze up** *v/i to make space* apretarse

squid [skwɪd] calamar *m*

squint [skwɪnt] *n*: ***she has a squint*** es estrábica, tiene estrabismo

squirm [skwɜːrm] *v/t* retorcerse

squir·rel ['skwɪrl] *n* ardilla *f*

squirt [skwɜːrt] **1** *v/t* lanzar un chorro de **2** *n* F *pej* canijo(-a) *m*(*f*) F, mequetrefe *m/f* F

St *abbr* (= ***saint***) Sto; Sta (= santo *m*; santa *f*); (= ***street***) c/ (= calle *f*)

stab [stæb] **1** *n* F intento *m*; ***have a stab at sth*** intentar algo **2** *v/t* (*pret & pp* ***stabbed***) *person* apuñalar

sta·bil·i·ty [stə'bɪlətɪ] estabilidad *f*

sta·bil·ize ['steɪbɪlaɪz] **1** *v/t prices, boat* estabilizar **2** *v/i of prices etc* estabilizarse

sta·ble[1] ['steɪbl] *n for horses* establo *m*

sta·ble[2] ['steɪbl] *adj* estable; *patient's condition* estacionario

stack [stæk] **1** *n* (*pile*) pila *f*; (*smokestack*) chimenea *f*; ***stacks of*** F montones de F **2** *v/t* apilar

sta·di·um ['steɪdɪəm] estadio *m*

staff [stæf] *npl* (*employees*) personal *m*; (*teachers*) profesorado *m*; ***staff are not allowed to ...*** los empleados no tienen permitido ...

staf·fer ['stæfər] empleado(-a) *m*(*f*)

'**staff·room** *in school* sala *f* de profesores

stag [stæg] ciervo *m*

stage[1] [steɪdʒ] *in life, project etc* etapa *f*

stage[2] [steɪdʒ] **1** *n* THEA escenario *m*; ***go on the stage*** hacerse actor / actriz **2** *v/t play* escenificar, llevar a escena; *demonstration* llevar a cabo

stage 'door entrada *f* de artistas

'**stage fright** miedo *m* escénico

'**stage hand** tramoyista *m/f*

stag·ger ['stægər] **1** *v/i* tambalearse **2** *v/t* (*amaze*) dejar anonadado; *coffee breaks etc* escalonar

stag·ger·ing ['stægərɪŋ] *adj* asombroso

stag·nant ['stægnənt] *adj also fig* estancado

stag·nate [stæg'neɪt] *v/i fig* estancarse

stag·na·tion [stæg'neɪʃn] estancamiento *m*

'**stag par·ty** despedida *f* de soltero

stain [steɪn] **1** *n* (*dirty mark*) mancha *f*; *for wood* tinte *m* **2** *v/t* (*dirty*) manchar; *wood* teñir **3** *v/i of wine etc* manchar, dejar mancha; *of fabric* mancharse

stained-glass 'win·dow [steɪnd] vidriera *f*

stain·less 'steel ['steɪnlɪs] *n* acero *m* inoxidable

'**stain re·mov·er** [rɪ'muːvər] quitamanchas *m inv*

stair [ster] escalón *m*; ***the stairs*** la(s) escalera(s)

'**stair·case** escalera(s) *f*(/pl)

stake [steɪk] **1** *n of wood* estaca *f*; *when gambling* apuesta *f*; (*investment*) participación *f*; ***be at stake*** estar en juego **2** *v/t tree* arrodrigar; *money* apostar; *reputation* jugarse; *person* ayudar (*económicamente*)

stale [steɪl] *adj bread* rancio; *air* viciado; *fig*: *news* viejo

'**stale·mate** *in chess* tablas *fpl* (*por rey ahogado*); *fig* punto *m* muerto

stalk[1] [stɒːk] *n of fruit, plant* tallo *m*

stalk[2] [stɒːk] *v/t* (*follow*) acechar; *person* seguir

stalk·er ['stɒːkər] *persona que sigue a otra obsesivamente*

stall[1] [stɒːl] *n at market* puesto *m*; *for cow, horse* casilla *f*

stall[2] [stɒːl] **1** *v/i of vehicle, engine* calarse; *of plane* entrar en pérdida; (*play for time*) intentar ganar tiempo **2** *v/t engine* calar; *person* retener

stal·li·on ['stæljən] semental *m*

stalls [stɒːlz] *npl* patio *m* de butacas

stal·wart ['stɒːlwərt] *adj support, supporter* incondicional

stam·i·na ['stæmɪnə] resistencia *f*

stam·mer ['stæmər] **1** *n* tartamudeo *m* **2** *v/i* tartamudear

stamp[1] [stæmp] **1** *n for letter* sello *m*, *L.Am.* estampilla *f*, *Mex* timbre *m*; *device* tampón *m*; *mark made with device* sello *m* **2** *v/t* sellar; ***stamped addressed envelope*** sobre *m* franqueado con la dirección

stamp[2] [stæmp] *v/t*: ***stamp one's feet*** patear

◆ **stamp out** *v/t* (*eradicate*) terminar con

'**stamp collec·ting** filatelia *f*

'**stamp col·lec·tion** collección *f* de sellos *or L.Am.* estampillas *or Mex* timbres

'**stamp col·lec·tor** coleccionista *m/f* de sellos *or L.Am.* estampillas *or Mex* timbres

stam·pede [stæm'piːd] **1** *n of cattle etc* estampida *f*; *of people* desbandada *f* **2** *v/i of cattle etc* salir de estampida; *of people* salir en desbandada

stance [stæns] (*position*) postura *f*

stand [stænd] **1** *n at exhibition* puesto *m*, stand *m*; (*witness stand*) estrado *m*; (*support, base*) soporte *m*; ***take the stand*** LAW subir al estrado **2** *v/i* (*pret & pp* ***stood***) *of*

S

building encontrarse, hallarse; *as opposed to sit* estar de pie; (*rise*) ponerse de pie; ***did you notice two men standing near the window?*** ¿viste a dos hombres al lado de la ventana?; ***there was a large box standing in the middle of the floor*** había una caja muy grande en mitad del suelo; ***the house stands at the corner of ...*** la casa se encuentra en la esquina de ...; ***stand still*** quedarse quieto; ***where do you stand with Liz?*** ¿cual es tu situación con Liz? **3** *v/t* (*pret & pp* ***stood***) (*tolerate*) aguantar, soportar; (*put*) colocar; ***you don't stand a chance*** no tienes ninguna posibilidad; ***stand s.o. a drink*** invitar a alguien a una copa; ***stand one's ground*** mantenerse firme

◆ **stand back** *v/i* echarse atrás

◆ **stand by 1** *v/i* (*not take action*) quedarse sin hacer nada; (*be ready*) estar preparado **2** *v/t person* apoyar; *decision* atenerse a

◆ **stand down** *v/i* (*withdraw*) retirarse

◆ **stand for** *v/t* (*tolerate*) aguantar; (*represent*) significar

◆ **stand in for** *v/t* sustituir

◆ **stand out** *v/i* destacar

◆ **stand up 1** *v/i* levantarse **2** *v/t* F plantar F

◆ **stand up for** *v/t* defender; ***stand up for yourself!*** ¡defiéndete!

◆ **stand up to** *v/t* hacer frente a

stan·dard ['stændərd] **1** *adj* (*usual*) habitual **2** *n* (*level of excellence*) nivel *m*; TECH estándar *m*; ***be up to standard*** cumplir el nivel exigido; ***not be up to standard*** estar por debajo del nivel exigido; ***my parents set very high standards*** mis padres exigen mucho

stan·dard·ize ['stændərdaɪz] *v/t* normalizar

stan·dard of 'li·ving nivel *m* de vida

'stand·by 1 *n ticket* billete *m* stand-by; ***be on standby*** estar en stand-by *or* en lista de espera **2** *adv fly* con un billete stand--by

'stand·by pas·sen·ger pasajero(-a) *m*(*f*) en stand-by *or* en lista de espera

stand·ing ['stændɪŋ] *n in society etc* posición *f*; (*repute*) reputación *f*; ***a musician / politician of some standing*** un reputado músico / político; ***a relationship of long standing*** una relación establecida hace mucho tiempo

'stand·ing room: ***standing room only*** no quedan asientos

stand·off·ish [stænd'ɑːfɪʃ] *adj* distante

'stand·point punto *m* de vista

'stand·still: ***be at a standstill*** estar paralizado; ***bring to a standstill*** paralizar

stank [stæŋk] *pret* → ***stink***

stan·za ['stænzə] estrofa *f*

sta·ple[1] ['steɪpl] *n foodstuff* alimento *m* básico

sta·ple[2] ['steɪpl] **1** *n* (*fastener*) grapa *f* **2** *v/t* grapar

sta·ple 'di·et dieta *f* básica

'sta·ple gun grapadora *f* industrial

sta·pler ['steɪplər] grapadora *f*

star [stɑːr] **1** *n also person* estrella *f* **2** *v/t* (*pret & pp* ***starred***) *of movie* estar protagonizado por **3** *v/i* (*pret & pp* ***starred***) *in movie*: ***Depardieu starred in ...*** Depardieu protagonizó ...

'star·board *adj* de estribor

starch [stɑːrtʃ] *in foodstuff* fécula *f*

stare [ster] **1** *n* mirada *f* fija **2** *v/i* mirar fijamente; ***stare at*** mirar fijamente

'star·fish estrella *f* de mar

stark [stɑːrk] **1** *adj landscape* desolado; *reminder, picture etc* desolador; ***in stark contrast to*** en marcado contraste con **2** *adv*: ***stark naked*** completamente desnudo

star·ling ['stɑːrlɪŋ] estornino *m*

star·ry ['stɑːrɪ] *adj night* estrellado

star·ry-eyed [stɑːrɪ'aɪd]] *adj person* cándido, ingenuo

Stars and 'Stripes *la bandera estadounidense*

start [stɑːrt] **1** *n* (*beginning*) comienzo *m*, principio *m*; *of race* salida *f*; ***get off to a good / bad start*** empezar bien / mal; ***from the start*** desde el principio; ***well, it's a start!*** bueno, ¡algo es algo! **2** *v/i* empezar, comenzar; *of engine, car* arrancar; ***starting from tomorrow*** a partir de mañana **3** *v/t* empezar, comenzar; *engine, car* arrancar; *business* montar; ***start to do sth, start doing sth*** empezar *or* comenzar a hacer algo; ***he started to cry*** se puso a llorar

start·er ['stɑːrtər] (*part of meal*) entrada *m*, entrante *m*; *of car* motor *m* de arranque

'start·ing point punto *m* de partida

'start·ing sal·a·ry sueldo *m* inicial

start·le ['stɑːrtl] *v/t* sobresaltar

start·ling ['stɑːrtlɪŋ] *adj* sorprendente, asombroso

starv·a·tion [stɑːr'veɪʃn] inanición *f*, hambre *f*

starve [stɑːrv] *v/i* pasar hambre; ***starve to death*** morir de inanición *or* hambre; ***I'm starving*** F me muero de hambre F

state[1] [steɪt] **1** *n* (*condition, country*) estado *m*; ***the States*** (los) Estados Unidos **2** *adj capital etc* estatal, del estado; *ban-*

S

quet etc de estado
state² [steɪt] *v/t* declarar
ˈ**State De·part·ment** Departamento *m* de Estado, *Ministerio de Asuntos Exteriores*
state·ment [ˈsteɪtmənt] declaración *f*; (*bank statement*) extracto *m*
state of eˈmer·gen·cy estado *m* de emergencia
state-of-the-ˈart *adj* modernísimo
states·man [ˈsteɪtsmən] hombre *m* de estado
state ˈtroop·er policía *m/f* estatal
state ˈvis·it visita *f* de estado
stat·ic (e·lecˈtric·i·ty) [ˈstætɪk] electricidad *f* estática
sta·tion [ˈsteɪʃn] **1** *n* RAIL estación *f*; RAD emisora *f*; TV canal *m* **2** *v/t guard etc* apostar; ***be stationed in*** *of soldier* estar destinado en
sta·tion·a·ry [ˈsteɪʃnərɪ] *adj* parado
sta·tion·er [ˈsteɪʃənər] papelería *f*
sta·tion·er·y [ˈsteɪʃənərɪ] artículos *mpl* de papelería
sta·tion ˈman·ag·er RAIL jefe *m* de estación
ˈ**sta·tion wag·on** ranchera *f*
sta·tis·ti·cal [stəˈtɪstɪkl] *adj* estadístico
sta·tis·ti·cal·ly [stəˈtɪstɪklɪ] *adv* estadísticamente
sta·tis·ti·cian [stætɪsˈtɪʃn] estadístico(-a) *m(f)*
sta·tis·tics [stəˈtɪstɪks] (*nsg*: *science*) estadística *f*; (*npl*: *figures*) estadísticas *fpl*
stat·ue [ˈstætʃuː] estatua *f*
Stat·ue of ˈLib·er·ty Estatua *f* de la Libertad
sta·tus [ˈsteɪtəs] categoría *f*, posición *f*; ***women want equal status with men*** las mujeres quieren igualdad con los hombres
ˈ**sta·tus bar** COMPUT barra *f* de estado
ˈ**sta·tus sym·bol** símbolo *m* de estatus
stat·ute [ˈstætuːt] estatuto *m*
staunch [stɒːntʃ] *adj supporter* incondicional; *friend* fiel
stay [steɪ] **1** *n* estancia *f*, *L.Am.* estadía *f* **2** *v/i in a place* quedarse; *in a condition* permanecer; ***stay in a hotel*** alojarse en un hotel; ***stay right there!*** ¡quédate ahí!; ***stay put*** no moverse
◆ **stay away** *v/i*: ***tell the children to stay away*** diles a los niños que no se acerquen
◆ **stay away from** *v/t* no acercarse a
◆ **stay behind** *v/i* quedarse
◆ **stay up** *v/i* (*not go to bed*) quedarse levantado
stead·i·ly [ˈstedɪlɪ] *adv improve etc* constantemente
stead·y [ˈstedɪ] **1** *adj* (*not shaking*) firme; (*continuous*) continuo; *beat* regular; *boyfriend* estable **2** *adv*: ***they've been going steady for two years*** llevan saliendo dos años; ***steady on!*** ¡un momento! **3** *v/t* (*pret & pp* ***steadied***) afianzar; *voice* calmar
steak [steɪk] filete *m*
steal [stiːl] **1** *v/t* (*pret* ***stole***, *pp* ***stolen***) *money etc* robar **2** *v/i* (*pret* ***stole***, *pp* ***stolen***) (*be a thief*) robar; ***he stole into the bedroom*** entró furtivamente en la habitación
ˈ**stealth bomb·er** [stelθ] bombardero *m* invisible
stealth·y [ˈstelθɪ] *adj* sigiloso
steam [stiːm] **1** *n* vapor *m* **2** *v/t food* cocinar al vapor
◆ **steam up** *v/i of window* empañarse
steamed up [stiːmdˈʌp] *adj* F enojado, *Span* mosqueado F
steam·er [ˈstiːmər] *for cooking* olla *f* para cocinar al vapor
ˈ**steam i·ron** plancha *f* de vapor
steel [stiːl] **1** *n* acero *m* **2** *adj* (*made of steel*) de acero
ˈ**steel·work·er** trabajador(a) *m(f)* del acero
ˈ**steel·works** acería *f*
steep¹ [stiːp] *adj hill etc* empinado; F: *prices* caro
steep² [stiːp] *v/t* (*soak*) poner en remojo
stee·ple [ˈstiːpl] torre *f*
ˈ**stee·ple·chase** *in athletics* carrera *f* de obstáculos
steep·ly [ˈstiːplɪ] *adv*: ***climb steeply*** *of path* subir pronunciadamente; *of prices* dispararse
steer¹ [stɪr] *n animal* buey *m*
steer² [stɪr] *v/t car* conducir, *L.Am.* manejar; *boat* gobernar; *person* guiar; *conversation* llevar
steer·ing [ˈstɪrɪŋ] *n* MOT dirección *f*
ˈ**steer·ing wheel** volante *m*, *S. Am.* timón *m*
stem¹ [stem] *n of plant* tallo *m*; *of glass* pie *m*; *of pipe* tubo *m*; *of word* raíz *f*
◆ **stem from** *v/t* (*pret & pp* ***stemmed***) derivarse de
stem² [stem] *v/t* (*block*) contener
ˈ**stem·ware** [ˈstemwer] cristalería *f*
stench [stentʃ] peste *f*, hedor *m*
sten·cil [ˈstensɪl] **1** *n* plantilla *f* **2** *v/t* (*pret & pp* ***stenciled***, *Br* ***stencilled***) *pattern* estarcir
step [step] **1** *n* (*pace*) paso *m*; (*stair*) escalón *m*; (*measure*) medida *f*; ***step by step*** paso a paso **2** *v/i* (*pret & pp* ***stepped***): ***step on sth*** pisar algo; ***step into a pud-***

dle pisar un charco; ***I stepped back*** di un paso atrás; ***step forward*** dar un paso adelante
◆ **step down** *v/i from post etc* dimitir
◆ **step up** *v/t* (*increase*) incrementar
'**step·broth·er** hermanastro *m*
'**step·daugh·ter** hijastra *f*
'**step·fa·ther** padrastro *m*
'**step·lad·der** escalera *f* de tijera
'**step·moth·er** madrastra *f*
step·ping stone ['stepɪŋ] pasadera *f*; *fig* trampolín *m*
'**step·sis·ter** hermanastra *f*
'**step·son** hijastro *m*
ster·e·o ['sterɪoʊ] *n* (*sound system*) equipo *m* de música
ster·e·o·type ['sterɪoʊtaɪp] *n* estereotipo *m*
ster·ile ['sterəl] *adj* estéril
ster·il·ize ['sterəlaɪz] *v/t woman* esterilizar; *equipment* esterilizar
ster·ling ['stɜːrlɪŋ] *n* FIN libra *f* esterlina
stern[1] [stɜːrn] *adj* severo
stern[2] [stɜːrn] *n* NAUT popa *f*
stern·ly ['stɜːrnlɪ] *adv* con severidad
ster·oids ['sterɔɪdz] *npl* esteroides *mpl*
steth·o·scope ['steθəskoʊp] fonendoscopio *m*, estetoscopio *m*
Stet·son® ['stetsn] sombrero *m* de vaquero
ste·ve·dore ['stiːvədɔːr] estibador(a) *m(f)*
stew [stuː] *n* guiso *m*
stew·ard ['stuːərd] *n on plane* auxiliar *m* de vuelo; *on ship* camarero *m*; *at demonstration*, *meeting* miembro *m* de la organización
stew·ard·ess [stuːər'des] *on plane* auxiliar *f* de vuelo; *on ship* camarera *f*
stewed [stuːd] *adj apples*, *plums* en compota
stick[1] [stɪk] *n* palo *m*; *of policeman* porra *f*; (*walking stick*) bastón *m*; ***live out in the sticks*** F vivir en el quinto pino F, vivir en el campo
stick[2] [stɪk] **1** *v/t* (*pret & pp* **stuck**) *with adhesive* pegar; F (*put*) meter **2** *v/i* (*pret & pp* **stuck**) (*jam*) atascarse; (*adhere*) pegarse
◆ **stick around** *v/i* F quedarse
◆ **stick by** *v/t* F apoyar, no abandonar
◆ **stick out** *v/i* (*protrude*) sobresalir; (*be noticeable*) destacar; ***his ears stick out*** tiene las orejas salidas
◆ **stick to** *v/t* (*adhere to*) pegarse a; F (*keep to*) seguir; F (*follow*) pegarse a F
◆ **stick together** *v/i* mantenerse unidos
◆ **stick up** *v/t poster*, *leaflet* pegar
◆ **stick up for** *v/t* F defender

stick·er ['stɪkər] pegatina *f*
'**stick-in-the-mud** F aburrido(-a) *m(f)* F, soso(-a) *m(f)*
stick·y ['stɪkɪ] *adj hands*, *surface* pegajoso; *label* adhesivo
stiff [stɪf] **1** *adj cardboard*, *manner* rígido; *brush*, *penalty*, *competition* duro; *muscle*, *body* agarrotado; *mixture*, *paste* consistente; *drink* cargado **2** *adv*: ***be scared stiff*** F estar muerto de miedo F; ***be bored stiff*** F aburrirse como una ostra F
stiff·en ['stɪfn] *v/i of person* agarrotarse
◆ **stiffen up** *v/i of muscle* agarrotarse
stiff·ly ['stɪflɪ] *adv* con rigidez; *fig* forzadamente
stiff·ness ['stɪfnəs] *of muscles* agarrotamiento *m*; *fig*: *of manner* rigidez *f*
sti·fle ['staɪfl] *v/t yawn*, *laugh* reprimir, contener; *criticism*, *debate* reprimir
sti·fling ['staɪflɪŋ] *adj* sofocante; ***it's stifling in here*** hace un calor sofocante aquí dentro
stig·ma ['stɪgmə] estigma *m*
sti·let·tos [stɪ'letoʊz] *npl shoes* zapatos *mpl* de tacón de aguja
still[1] [stɪl] **1** *adj* (*not moving*) quieto; *with no wind* sin viento; ***it was very still*** *no wind* no soplaba nada de viento **2** *adv*: ***keep still!*** ¡estáte quieto!; ***stand still!*** ¡no te muevas!
still[2] [stɪl] *adv* (*yet*) todavía, aún; (*nevertheless*) de todas formas; ***do you still want it?*** ¿todavía *or* aún lo quieres?; ***she still hasn't finished*** todavía *or* aún no ha acabado; ***I still don't understand*** sigo sin entenderlo; ***she might still come*** puede que aún venga; ***they are still my parents*** siguen siendo mis padres; ***still more*** (*even more*) todavía más
'**still·born** *adj*: ***be stillborn*** nacer muerto
still 'life naturaleza *f* muerta, bodegón *m*
stilt·ed ['stɪltɪd] *adj* forzado
stim·u·lant ['stɪmjʊlənt] estimulante *m*
stim·u·late ['stɪmjʊleɪt] *v/t person* estimular; *growth*, *demand* estimular, provocar
stim·u·lat·ing ['stɪmjʊleɪtɪŋ] *adj* estimulante
stim·u·la·tion [stɪmjʊ'leɪʃn] estimulación *f*
stim·u·lus ['stɪmjʊləs] (*incentive*) estímulo *m*
sting [stɪŋ] **1** *n from bee*, *jellyfish* picadura *f* **2** *v/t* (*pret & pp* **stung**) *of bee*, *jellyfish* picar **3** *v/i* (*pret & pp* **stung**) *of eyes*, *scratch* escocer
sting·ing ['stɪŋɪŋ] *adj remark*, *criticism* punzante
sting·y ['stɪndʒɪ] *adj* F agarrado F, rácano

F

stink [stɪŋk] **1** *n* (*bad smell*) peste *f*, hedor *m*; F (*fuss*) escándalo F; ***kick up a stink*** F armar un escándalo F **2** *v/i* (*pret* ***stank***, *pp* ***stunk***) (*smell bad*) apestar; F (*be very bad*) dar asco

stint [stɪnt] *n* temporada *f*; ***do a stint in the army*** pasar una temporada en el ejército

◆ **stint on** *v/t* F racanear F

stip·u·late ['stɪpjʊleɪt] *v/t* estipular

stip·u·la·tion [stɪpjʊ'leɪʃn] estipulación *f*

stir [stɜːr] **1** *n*: ***give the soup a stir*** darle vueltas a la sopa; ***cause a stir*** causar revuelo **2** *v/t* (*pret & pp* ***stirred***) remover, dar vueltas a **3** *v/i* (*pret & pp* ***stirred***) *of sleeping person* moverse

◆ **stir up** *v/t crowd* agitar; *bad memories* traer a la memoria

stir-'cra·zy *adj* F majareta F

'stir-fry *v/t* (*pret & pp* ***stir-fried***) freír rápidamente y dando vueltas

stir·ring ['stɜːrɪŋ] *adj music, speech* conmovedor

stir·rup ['stɪrəp] estribo *m*

stitch [stɪʧ] **1** *n in sewing* puntada *f*; *in knitting* punto *m*; ***stitches*** MED puntos *mpl*; ***be in stitches*** *laughing* partirse de risa; ***have a stitch*** tener flato **2** *v/t sew* coser

◆ **stitch up** *v/t wound* coser, suturar

stitch·ing ['stɪʧɪŋ] (*stitches*) cosido *m*

stock [stɑːk] **1** *n* (*reserves*) reservas *fpl*; COM *of store* existencias *fpl*; (*animals*) ganado *m*; FIN acciones *mpl*; *for soup etc* caldo *m*; ***in stock*** en existencias; ***out of stock*** agotado; ***take stock*** hacer balance **2** *v/t* COM (*have*) tener en existencias; COM (*sell*) vender

◆ **stock up on** *v/t* aprovisionarse de

'stock·breed·er ganadero(-a) *m*(*f*)

'stock·brok·er corredor(a) *m*(*f*) de bolsa

'stock cube pastilla *f* de caldo concentrado

'stock ex·change bolsa *f* (de valores)

'stock·hold·er accionista *m*/*f*

stock·ing ['stɑːkɪŋ] media *f*

stock·ist ['stɑːkɪst] distribuidor(a) *m*(*f*)

'stock mar·ket mercado *m* de valores

'stock·mar·ket crash crack *m* bursátil

'stock·pile 1 *n of food, weapons* reservas *fpl* **2** *v/t* acumular

'stock·room almacén *m*

stock-'still *adv*: ***stand stock-still*** quedarse inmóvil

'stock·tak·ing inventario *m*

'stock·y ['stɑːkɪ] *adj* bajo y robusto

stodg·y ['stɑːdʒɪ] *adj food* pesado

sto·i·cal ['stoʊɪkl] *adj* estoico

sto·i·cism ['stoʊɪsɪzm] estoicismo *m*

stole [stoʊl] *pret* → ***steal***

stol·en ['stoʊlən] *pp* → ***steal***

stom·ach ['stʌmək] **1** *n* estómago *m*, tripa *f* **2** *v/t* (*tolerate*) soportar

'stom·ach·ache dolor *m* de estómago

stone [stoʊn] *n* piedra *f*; *in fruit* hueso *m*

stoned [stoʊnd] *adj* F (*on drugs*) colocado F

stone-'deaf *adj*: ***be stone-deaf*** estar más sordo que una tapia

'stone·wall *v/i* F andarse con evasivas

ston·y ['stoʊnɪ] *adj ground, path* pedregoso

stood [stuːd] *pret & pp* → ***stand***

stool [stuːl] (*seat*) taburete *m*

stoop[1] [stuːp] **1** *n*: ***have a stoop*** estar encorvado **2** *v/i* (*bend down*) agacharse

stoop[2] [stuːp] *n* (*porch*) porche *m*

stop [stɑːp] **1** *n for train, bus* parada *f*; ***come to a stop*** detenerse; ***put a stop to*** poner fin a **2** *v/t* (*pret & pp* ***stopped***) (*put an end to*) poner fin a; (*prevent*) impedir; (*cease*) parar; *person in street* parar; *car, bus, train, etc*: *of driver* detener; *check* bloquear; ***stop doing sth*** dejar de hacer algo; ***it has stopped raining*** ha parado *or* dejado de llover; ***I stopped her from leaving*** impedí que se fuera **3** *v/i* (*pret & pp* ***stopped***) (*come to a halt*) pararse, detenerse; *in a particular place*: *of bus, train* parar

◆ **stop by** *v/i* (*visit*) pasarse

◆ **stop off** *v/i* hacer una parada

◆ **stop over** *v/i* hacer escala

◆ **stop up** *v/t sink* atascar

'stop·gap solución *f* intermedia

'stop·light (*traffic light*) semáforo *m*; (*brake light*) luz *m* de freno

'stop·o·ver *n* parada *f*; *in air travel* escala *f*

stop·per ['stɑːpər] *for bath, bottle* tapón *m*

stop·ping ['stɑːpɪŋ]: ***no stopping*** *sign* prohibido estacionar

'stop sign (señal *f* de) stop *m*

'stop·watch cronómetro *m*

stor·age ['stɔːrɪdʒ] almacenamiento *m*; ***put sth in storage*** almacenar algo; ***be in storage*** estar almacenado

'stor·age ca·pac·i·ty COMPUT capacidad *f* de almacenamiento

'stor·age space espacio *m* para guardar cosas

store [stɔːr] **1** *n* tienda *f*; (*stock*) reserva *f*; (*storehouse*) almacén *m* **2** *v/t* almacenar; COMPUT guardar

'store·front fachada *f* de tienda

'store·house almacén *m*

S

'store·keep·er tendero(-a) *m(f)*
'store·room almacén *m*
sto·rey *Br* → ***story²***
stork [stɔːrk] cigüeña *f*
storm [stɔːrm] *n* tormenta *f*
'storm drain canal *m* de desagüe
'storm warn·ing aviso *m* de tormenta
storm 'win·dow contraventana *f*
storm·y ['stɔːrmɪ] *adj weather, relationship* tormentoso
sto·ry¹ ['stɔːrɪ] (*tale*) cuento *m*; (*account*) historia *f*; (*newspaper article*) artículo *m*; F (*lie*) cuento *m*
sto·ry² ['stɔːrɪ] *of building* piso *m*, planta *f*
stout [staʊt] *adj person* relleno, corpulento; *boots* resistente; *defender* valiente
stove [stoʊv] *for cooking* cocina *f*, *Col, Mex, Ven* estufa *f*; *for heating* estufa *f*
stow [stoʊ] *v/t* guardar
◆ **stow away** *v/i* viajar de polizón
'stow·a·way *n* polizón *m*
straggler ['stræglər] rezagado(-a) *m(f)*
straight [streɪt] **1** *adj line, back* recto; *hair* liso; (*honest, direct*) franco; *whisky* solo; (*tidy*) en orden; (*conservative*) serio; (*not homosexual*) heterosexual; ***be a straight A student*** sacar sobresaliente en todas las asignaturas; ***keep a straight face*** contener la risa **2** *adv* (*in a straight line*) recto; (*directly, immediately*) directamente; (*clearly*) con claridad; ***stand up straight!*** ¡ponte recto!; ***look s.o. straight in the eye*** mirar a los ojos de alguien; ***go straight*** F *of criminal* reformarse; ***give it to me straight*** F dímelo sin rodeos; ***straight ahead*** *be situated* todo derecho; *walk, drive* todo recto; *look* hacia delante; ***carry straight on*** *of driver etc* seguir recto; ***straight away, straight off*** en seguida; ***straight out*** directamente; ***straight up*** *without ice* solo
straight·en ['streɪtn] *v/t* enderezar
◆ **straighten out** **1** *v/t situation* resolver; F *person* poner por el buen camino **2** *v/i of road* hacerse recto
◆ **straighten up** *v/i* ponerse derecho
straight'for·ward *adj* (*honest, direct*) franco; (*simple*) simple
strain¹ [streɪn] **1** *n on rope* tensión *f*; *on engine, heart* esfuerzo *m*; *on person* agobio *m* **2** *v/t fig*: *finances, budget* crear presión en; ***strain one's back*** hacerse daño en la espalda; ***strain one's eyes*** forzar la vista
strain² [streɪn] *v/t vegetables* escurrir; *oil, fat etc* colar
strain³ [streɪn] *n of virus* cepa *f*
strained [streɪnd] *adj relations* tirante
strain·er ['streɪnər] *for vegetables etc* colador *m*
strait [streɪt] estrecho *m*
strait·laced [streɪt'leɪst] *adj* mojigato
strand¹ [strænd] *n of wool, thread* hebra *f*; ***a strand of hair*** un pelo
strand² [strænd] *v/t* abandonar; ***be stranded*** quedarse atrapado *or* tirado
strange [streɪndʒ] *adj* (*odd, curious*) extraño, raro; (*unknown, foreign*) extraño
strange·ly ['streɪndʒlɪ] *adv* (*oddly*) de manera extraña; ***strangely enough*** aunque parezca extraño
strang·er ['streɪndʒər] (*person you don't know*) extraño(-a) *m(f)*, desconocido(-a) *m(f)*; ***I'm a stranger here myself*** yo tampoco soy de aquí
stran·gle ['stræŋgl] *v/t person* estrangular
strap [stræp] *n of purse, watch* correa *f*; *of brassiere, dress* tirante *m*; *of shoe* tira *f*
◆ **strap in** *v/t* (*pret & pp* ***strapped***) poner el cinturón de seguridad a
◆ **strap on** *v/t* ponerse
strap·less ['stræplɪs] *adj* sin tirantes
stra·te·gic [strə'tiːdʒɪk] *adj* estratégico
strat·e·gy ['strætədʒɪ] estrategia *f*
straw¹ [strɒː] *material* paja *f*; ***that's the last straw!*** ¡es la gota que colma el vaso!
straw² [strɒː] *for drink* pajita *f*
straw·ber·ry ['strɒːberɪ] *fruit* fresa *f*, *S. Am.* frutilla *f*
stray [streɪ] **1** *adj animal* callejero; *bullet* perdido **2** *n dog* perro *m* callejero; *cat* gato *m* callejero **3** *v/i of animal, child* extraviarse, perderse; *fig*: *of eyes, thoughts* desviarse
streak [striːk] **1** *n of dirt, paint* raya *f*; *in hair* mechón *m*; *fig*: *of nastiness etc* vena *f* **2** *v/i move quickly* pasar disparado
streak·y ['striːkɪ] *adj* veteado
stream [striːm] **1** *n* riachuelo *m*; *fig*: *of people, complaints* oleada *f*; ***come on stream*** entrar en funcionamiento **2** *v/i*: ***there were tears streaming down my face*** me bajaban ríos de lágrimas por la cara; ***people streamed out of the building*** la gente salía en masa
stream·er ['striːmər] serpentina *f*
'stream·line *v/t fig* racionalizar
'stream·lined *adj car, plane* aerodinámico; *fig*: *organization* racionalizado
street [striːt] calle *f*
'street·car tranvía *f*
'street·light farola *f*
'street peo·ple *npl* los sin techo
'street value *of drugs* valor *m* en la calle
'street·walk·er F prostituta *f*
'street·wise *adj* espabilado
strength [streŋθ] fuerza *f*; (*fig*: *strong*

point) punto *m* fuerte; *of friendship etc* solidez *f*; *of emotion* intensidad *f*; *of currency* fortaleza *f*
strength·en ['streŋθn] **1** *v/t muscles, currency* fortalecer; *bridge* reforzar; *country, ties, relationship* consolidar **2** *v/i of bonds, ties* consolidarse; *of currency* fortalecerse
stren·u·ous ['strenjʊəs] *adj* agotador
stren·u·ous·ly ['strenjʊəslɪ] *adv deny* tajantemente
stress [stres] **1** *n* (*emphasis*) énfasis *m*; (*tension*) estrés *m*; *on syllable* acento *m*; ***be under stress*** estar estresado **2** *v/t* (*emphasize*: *syllable*) acentuar; *importance etc* hacer hincapié en; ***I must stress that ...*** quiero hacer hincapié en que ...
stressed 'out [strest] *adj* F estresado
stress·ful ['stresfəl] *adj* estresante
stretch [stretʃ] **1** *n of land, water* extensión *m*; *of road* tramo *m*; ***at a stretch*** (*non-stop*) de un tirón **2** *adj fabric* elástico **3** *v/t material, income* estirar; F *rules* ser flexible con; ***he stretched out his hand*** estiró la mano; ***my job stretches me*** mi trabajo me obliga a esforzarme **4** *v/i to relax muscles, reach sth* estirarse; (*spread*) extenderse; *of fabric* estirarse, dar de sí
stretch·er ['stretʃər] camilla *f*
strict [strɪkt] *adj* estricto
strict·ly ['strɪktlɪ] *adv* con rigor; ***it is strictly forbidden*** está terminantemente prohibido
strid·den ['strɪdn] *pp* → ***stride***
stride [straɪd] **1** *n* zancada *f*; ***take sth in one's stride*** tomarse algo con tranquilidad; ***make great strides*** *fig* avanzar a pasos agigantados **2** *v/i* (*pret* ***strode***, *pp* ***stridden***) caminar dando zancadas
stri·dent ['straɪdnt] *adj also fig* estridente
strike [straɪk] **1** *n of workers* huelga *f*; *in baseball* strike *m*; *of oil* descubrimiento *m*; ***be on strike*** estar en huelga; ***go on strike*** ir a la huelga **2** *v/i* (*pret & pp* ***struck***) *of workers* hacer huelga; (*attack*) atacar; *of disaster* sobrevenir; *of clock* dar las horas; ***the clock struck three*** el reloj dio las tres **3** *v/t* (*pret & pp* ***struck***) (*hit*) golpear; *fig*: *of disaster* sacudir; *match* encender; *oil* descubrir; ***didn't it ever strike you that ...?*** ¿no se te ocurrió que ...?; ***she struck me as being ...*** me dio la impresión de ser ...
◆ **strike out 1** *v/t* tachar; *in baseball* eliminar a, *L.Am.* ponchar **2** *v/i in baseball* quedar eliminado, *L.Am.* poncharse
'strike·break·er esquirol(a) *m*(*f*)
strik·er ['straɪkər] (*person on strike*) huelguista *m/f*; *in soccer* delantero(-a) *m*(*f*)
strik·ing ['straɪkɪŋ] *adj* (*marked*) sorprendente, llamativo; (*eye-catching*) deslumbrante
string [strɪŋ] *n also of violin, racket etc* cuerda *f*; ***strings*** *musicians* la sección de cuerda; ***pull strings*** mover hilos; ***a string of*** (*series*) una serie de
◆ **string along 1** *v/i* (*pret & pp* ***strung***) F apuntarse F **2** *v/t* (*pret & pp* ***strung***) F: ***string s.o. along*** dar falsas esperanzas a alguien
◆ **string up** *v/t* F colgar
stringed 'in·stru·ment [strɪŋd] instrumento *m* de cuerda
strin·gent ['strɪndʒnt] *adj* riguroso
'string play·er instrumentista *m/f* de cuerda
strip [strɪp] **1** *n of land* franja *f*; *of cloth* tira *f*; (*comic strip*) tira *f* cómica **2** *v/t* (*pret & pp* ***stripped***) (*remove*) quitar; (*undress*) desnudar; ***strip s.o. of sth*** despojar a alguien de algo **3** *v/i* (*pret & pp* ***stripped***) (*undress*) desnudarse; *of stripper* hacer striptease
'strip club club *m* de striptease
stripe [straɪp] raya *f*; *indicating rank* galón *m*
striped [straɪpt] *adj* a rayas
'strip joint F → ***strip club***
strip·per ['strɪpər] artista *m/f* de striptease; ***male stripper*** artista *m* de striptease
'strip show espectáculo *m* de striptease
strip'tease striptease *m*
strive [straɪv] *v/i* (*pret* ***strove***, *pp* ***striven***) esforzarse; ***strive to do sth*** esforzarse por hacer algo; ***strive for*** luchar por
striv·en ['strɪvn] *pp* → ***strive***
strobe (light) [stroʊb] luz *f* estroboscópica
strode [stroʊd] *pret* → ***stride***
stroke [stroʊk] **1** *n* MED derrame *m* cerebral; *when writing* trazo *m*; *when painting* pincelada *f*; (*style of swimming*) estilo *m*; ***stroke of luck*** golpe de suerte; ***she never does a stroke (of work)*** no pega ni golpe **2** *v/t* acariciar
stroll [stroʊl] **1** *n* paseo *m* **2** *v/i* caminar
stroll·er ['stroʊlər] *for baby* silla *f* de paseo
strong [strɒːŋ] *adj* fuerte; *structure* resistente; *candidate* claro, con muchos posibilidades; *support, supporter, views, objection* firme; *tea, coffee* cargado, fuerte
'strong·hold *fig* baluarte *m*
strong·ly ['strɒːŋlɪ] *adv* fuertemente, ro-

tundamente
strong-mind·ed [strɒːŋ'maɪndɪd] *adj* decidido
'strong point (punto *m*) fuerte *m*
'strong·room cámara *f* acorazada
strong-willed [strɒːŋ'wɪld] *adj* tenaz
strove [stroʊv] *pret* → ***strive***
struck [strʌk] *pret & pp* → ***strike***
struc·tur·al ['strʌktʃərl] *adj* estructural
struc·ture ['strʌktʃər] **1** *n* (*something built*) construcción *f*; *of novel, society etc* estructura *f* **2** *v/t* estructurar
strug·gle ['strʌgl] **1** *n* lucha *f* **2** *v/i with a person* forcejear; (*have a hard time*) luchar; ***they struggled for the gun*** forcejearon por conseguir la pistola; ***he was struggling with the door*** tenía problemas para abrir la puerta; ***struggle to do sth*** luchar por hacer algo
strum [strʌm] *v/t* (*pret & pp* ***strummed***) *guitar* rasguear
strung [strʌŋ] *pret & pp* → ***string***
strut [strʌt] *v/i* (*pret & pp* ***strutted***) pavonearse
stub [stʌb] **1** *n of cigarette* colilla *f*; *of check* matriz *f*; *of ticket* resguardo *m* **2** *v/t* (*pret & pp* ***stubbed***): ***stub one's toe*** darse un golpe en el dedo (del pie)
◆ **stub out** *v/t* apagar (apretando)
stub·ble ['stʌbl] *on man's face* barba *f* incipiente
stub·born ['stʌbərn] *adj person* testarudo, terco; *defense, refusal, denial* tenaz, pertinaz
stub·by ['stʌbɪ] *adj* regordete
stuck [stʌk] **1** *pret & pp* → ***stick²*** **2** *adj* F: ***be stuck on s.o.*** estar colado por alguien F
stuck-'up *adj* F engreído
stu·dent ['stuːdnt] *at high school* alumno(-a) *m*(*f*); *at college, university* estudiante *m/f*
stu·dent 'nurse estudiante *m/f* de enfermería
stu·dent 'teach·er profesor(a) *m*(*f*) en prácticas
stu·di·o ['stuːdɪoʊ] *of artist, sculptor* estudio *m*; (*film studio*, TV *studio*) estudio *m*, plató *m*
stu·di·ous ['stuːdɪəs] *adj* estudioso
stud·y ['stʌdɪ] **1** *n* estudio *m*; (*room*) (cuarto *m* de) estudio *m* **2** *v/t & v/i* (*pret & pp* ***studied***) estudiar
stuff [stʌf] **1** *n* (*things*) cosas *fpl* **2** *v/t turkey* rellenar; ***stuff sth into sth*** meter algo dentro de algo
stuffed 'toy [stʌft] muñeco *m* de peluche
stuff·ing ['stʌfɪŋ] relleno *m*
stuff·y ['stʌfɪ] *adj room* cargado; *person* anticuado, estirado
stum·ble ['stʌmbl] *v/i* tropezar
◆ **stumble across** *v/t* toparse con
◆ **stumble over** *v/t* tropezar con; *words* trastrabillarse con
stum·bling-block ['stʌmblɪŋ] escollo *m*
stump [stʌmp] **1** *n of tree* tocón *m* **2** *v/t of question, questioner* dejar perplejo
◆ **stump up** *v/t* F aflojar, *Span* apoquinar F
stun [stʌn] *v/t* (*pret & pp* ***stunned***) *of blow* dejar sin sentido; *of news* dejar atonito *or* de piedra
stung [stʌŋ] *pret & pp* → ***sting***
stunk [stʌŋk] *pp* → ***stink***
stun·ning ['stʌnɪŋ] *adj* (*amazing*) increíble, sorprendente; (*very beautiful*) imponente
stunt [stʌnt] *n for publicity* truco *m*; *in movie* escena *f* peligrosa
'stunt·man *in movie* doble *m*, especialista *m*
stu·pe·fy ['stuːpɪfaɪ] *v/t* (*pret & pp* ***stupefied***) dejar perplejo
stu·pen·dous [stuː'pendəs] *adj* extraordinario
stu·pid ['stuːpɪd] *adj* estúpido; ***what a stupid thing to say / do!*** ¡qué estupidez!
stu·pid·i·ty [stuː'pɪdətɪ] estupidez *f*
stu·por ['stuːpər] aturdimiento *m*
stur·dy ['stɜːrdɪ] *adj person* robusto; *table, plant* resistente
stut·ter ['stʌtər] *v/i* tartamudear
sty [staɪ] *for pig* pocilga *f*
style [staɪl] *n* estilo *m*; (*fashion*) moda *f*; ***go out of style*** pasarse de moda
styl·ish ['staɪlɪʃ] *adj* elegante
styl·ist ['staɪlɪst] (*hair stylist*) estilista *m/f*
sub·com·mit·tee ['sʌbkəmɪtɪ] subcomité *m*
sub·com·pact (car) [sʌb'kɑːmpækt] *utilitario de pequeño tamaño*
sub·con·scious [sʌb'kɑːnʃəs] *adj* subconsciente; ***the subconscious (mind)*** el subconsciente
sub·con·scious·ly [sʌb'kɑːnʃəslɪ] *adv* inconscientemente
sub·con·tract [sʌbkɑːn'trækt] *v/t* subcontratar
sub·con·trac·tor [sʌbkɑːn'træktər] subcontratista *m/f*
sub·di·vide [sʌbdɪ'vaɪd] *v/t* subdividir
sub·due [səb'duː] *v/t rebellion, mob* someter, contener
sub·dued [səb'duːd] *adj* apagado
sub·head·ing ['sʌbhedɪŋ] subtítulo *m*
sub·hu·man [sʌb'hjuːmən] *adj* inhumano
sub·ject **1** *n* ['sʌbdʒɪkt] (*topic*) tema *m*; (*branch of learning*) asignatura *f*, mate-

S

ria *f*; GRAM sujeto *m*; *of monarch* súbdito(-a) *m(f)*; ***change the subject*** cambiar de tema **2** *adj* ['sʌbdʒɪkt]: ***be subject to*** *have tendency to* ser propenso a; *be regulated by* estar sujeto a; ***subject to availability*** *of goods* promoción válida hasta fin de existencias **3** *v/t* [səb'dʒekt] someter
sub·jec·tive [səb'dʒektɪv] *adj* subjetivo
sub·junc·tive [səb'dʒʌŋktɪv] *n* GRAM subjuntivo *m*
sub·let ['sʌblet] *v/t* (*pret & pp* ***sublet***) realquilar
sub·ma'chine gun metralleta *f*
sub·ma·rine ['sʌbməriːn] submarino *m*
sub·merge [səb'mɜːrdʒ] **1** *v/t* sumergir **2** *v/i of submarine* sumergirse
sub·mis·sion [səb'mɪʃn] (*surrender*) sumisión *f*; *to committee etc* propuesta *f*
sub·mis·sive [səb'mɪsɪv] *adj* sumiso
sub·mit [səb'mɪt] **1** *v/t* (*pret & pp* ***submitted***) *plan, proposal* presentar **2** *v/i* (*pret & pp* ***submitted***) someterse
sub·or·di·nate [sə'bɔːrdɪneɪt] **1** *adj employee, position* subordinado **2** *n* subordinado(-a) *m(f)*
sub·poe·na [sə'piːnə] **1** *n* citación *f* **2** *v/t person* citar
◆ **sub·scribe to** [səb'skraɪb] *v/t magazine etc* suscribirse a; *theory* suscribir
sub·scrib·er [səb'skraɪbər] *to magazine* suscriptor(a) *m(f)*
sub·scrip·tion [səb'skrɪpʃn] suscripción *f*
sub·se·quent ['sʌbsɪkwənt] *adj* posterior
sub·se·quent·ly ['sʌbsɪkwəntlɪ] *adv* posteriormente
sub·side [səb'saɪd] *v/i of flood waters* bajar; *of high winds* amainar; *of building* hundirse; *of fears, panic* calmarse
sub·sid·i·a·ry [səb'sɪdɪerɪ] *n* filial *f*
sub·si·dize ['sʌbsɪdaɪz] *v/t* subvencionar
sub·si·dy ['sʌbsɪdɪ] subvención *f*
◆ **sub·sist on** *v/t* subsistir a base de
sub·sis·tence 'farm·er [səb'sɪstəns] agricultor(a) *m(f)* de subsistencia
sub'sis·tence lev·el nivel *m* mínimo de subsistencia
sub·stance ['sʌbstəns] (*matter*) sustancia *f*
sub·stan·dard [sʌb'stændərd] *adj performance* deficiente; *shoes, clothes* con tara
sub·stan·tial [səb'stænʃl] *adj* sustancial, considerable
sub·stan·tial·ly [səb'stænʃlɪ] *adv* (*considerably*) considerablemente; (*in essence*) sustancialmente, esencialmente
sub·stan·ti·ate [səb'stænʃɪeɪt] *v/t* probar
sub·stan·tive [səb'stæntɪv] *adj* significativo
sub·sti·tute ['sʌbstɪtuːt] **1** *n for person* sustituto(-a) *m(f)*; *for commodity* sustituto *m*; SP suplente *m/f* **2** *v/t* sustituir, reemplazar; ***substitute X for Y*** sustituir Y por X **3** *v/i*: ***substitute for s.o.*** sustituir a alguien
sub·sti·tu·tion [sʌbstɪ'tuːʃn] (*act*) sustitución *f*; ***make a substitution*** SP hacer un cambio *or* sustitución
sub·ti·tle ['sʌbtaɪtl] *n* subtítulo *m*
sub·tle ['sʌtl] *adj* sutil
sub·tract [səb'trækt] *v/t number* restar
sub·urb ['sʌbɜːrb] zona *f* residencial de la periferia
sub·ur·ban [sə'bɜːrbən] *adj housing* de la periferia; *attitudes, lifestyle* aburguesado
sub·ver·sive [səb'vɜːrsɪv] **1** *adj* subversivo **2** *n* subversivo(-a) *m(f)*
sub·way ['sʌbweɪ] metro *m*
sub 'ze·ro *adj* bajo cero
suc·ceed [sək'siːd] **1** *v/i* (*be successful*) tener éxito; *to throne* suceder en el trono; ***succeed in doing sth*** conseguir hacer algo **2** *v/t* (*come after*) suceder
suc·ceed·ing [sək'siːdɪŋ] *adj* siguiente
suc·cess [sək'ses] éxito *m*; ***be a success*** *of book, play, idea* ser un éxito; *of person* tener éxito
suc·cess·ful [sək'sesfəl] *adj person* con éxito; ***be successful in business*** tener éxito en los negocios; ***be successful in doing sth*** lograr hacer algo
suc·cess·ful·ly [sək'sesfəlɪ] *adv* con éxito
suc·ces·sion [sək'seʃn] sucesión *f*; ***three days in succession*** tres días seguidos
suc·ces·sive [sək'sesɪv] *adj* sucesivo
suc·ces·sor [sək'sesər] sucesor(a) *m(f)*
suc·cinct [sək'sɪŋkt] *adj* sucinto
suc·cu·lent ['ʃʌkjʊlənt] *meat, fruit* suculento
suc·cumb [sə'kʌm] *v/i* (*give in*) sucumbir
such [sʌʧ] **1** *adj* (*of that kind*) tal; ***such men are dangerous*** los hombres así son peligrosos; ***I know of many such cases*** conozco muchos casos así; ***don't make such a fuss*** no armes tanto alboroto; ***I never thought it would be such a success*** nunca imaginé que sería un éxito tal; ***such as*** como; ***there is no such word as …*** no existe la palabra … **2** *adv* tan; ***as such*** como tal
suck [sʌk] **1** *v/t candy etc* chupar; ***suck one's thumb*** chuparse el dedo **2** *v/i* P: ***it sucks*** (*is awful*) es una mierda P
◆ **suck up 1** *v/t* absorber **2** *v/i* F: ***suck up to s.o.*** hacer la pelota a alguien
suck·er ['sʌkər] F (*person*) primo(-a) *m/f* F, ingenuo(-a) *m/f*; F (*lollipop*) piruleta *f*

S

suc·tion ['sʌkʃn] succión *f*
sud·den ['sʌdn] *adj* repentino; ***all of a sudden*** de repente
sud·den·ly ['sʌdnlɪ] *adv* de repente
suds [sʌdz] *npl* (*soap suds*) espuma *f*
sue [suː] *v/t* demandar
suede [sweɪd] *n* ante *m*
suf·fer ['sʌfər] **1** *v/i* (*be in great pain*) sufrir; (*deteriorate*) deteriorarse; ***be suffering from*** sufrir **2** *v/t loss*, *setback*, *heart attack* sufrir
suf·fer·ing ['sʌfərɪŋ] *n* sufrimiento *m*
suf·fi·cient [sə'fɪʃnt] *adj* suficiente
suf·fi·cient·ly [sə'fɪʃntlɪ] *adv* suficientemente
suf·fo·cate ['sʌfəkeɪt] **1** *v/i* asfixiarse **2** *v/t* asfixiar
suf·fo·ca·tion [sʌfə'keɪʃn] asfixia *f*
sug·ar ['ʃʊgər] **1** *n* azúcar *m or f*; ***how many sugars?*** ¿cuántas cucharadas de azúcar? **2** *v/t* echar azúcar a; ***is it sugared?*** ¿lleva azúcar?
'**sug·ar bowl** azucarero *m*
'**sug·ar cane** caña *f* de azúcar
sug·gest [sə'dʒest] *v/t* sugerir; ***I suggest that we stop now*** sugiero que paremos ahora
sug·ges·tion [sə'dʒestʃən] sugerencia *f*
su·i·cide ['suːɪsaɪd] suicidio *m*; ***commit suicide*** suicidarse
suit [suːt] **1** *n* traje *m*; *in cards* palo *m* **2** *v/t of clothes*, *color* sentar bien a; ***suit yourself!*** F ¡haz lo que quieras!; ***be suited for sth*** estar hecho para algo
sui·ta·ble ['suːtəbl] *adj partner*, *words*, *clothing* apropiado, adecuado; *time* apropiado
sui·ta·bly ['suːtəblɪ] *adv* apropiadamente, adecuadamente
'**suit·case** maleta *f*, *L.Am.* valija *f*
suite [swiːt] *of rooms*, MUS suite *f*; *furniture* tresillo *m*
sul·fur ['sʌlfər] azufre *m*
sul·fur·ic acid [sʌl'fjuːrɪk] ácido *m* sulfúrico
sulk [sʌlk] *v/i* enfurruñarse; ***be sulking*** estar enfurruñado
sulk·y ['sʌlkɪ] *adj* enfurruñado
sul·len ['sʌlən] *adj* malhumorado, huraño
sul·phur *etc Br* → ***sulfur*** *etc*
sul·try ['sʌltrɪ] *adj climate* sofocante, bochornoso; *sexually* sensual
sum [sʌm] (*total*) total *m*, suma *f*; (*amount*) cantidad *f*; *in arithmetic* suma *f*; ***a large sum of money*** una gran cantidad de dinero; ***sum insured*** suma *f* asegurada; ***the sum total of his efforts*** la suma de sus esfuerzos
◆ **sum up 1** *v/t* (*pret & pp* ***summed***) (*summarize*) resumir; (*assess*) catalogar **2** *v/i* (*pret & pp* ***summed***) LAW recapitular
sum·mar·ize ['sʌməraɪz] *v/t* resumir
sum·ma·ry ['sʌmərɪ] *n* resumen *m*
sum·mer ['sʌmər] verano *m*
sum·mit ['sʌmɪt] *of mountain* cumbre *f*, cima *f*; POL cumbre *f*
'**sum·mit meet·ing** → ***summit***
sum·mon ['sʌmən] *v/t staff*, *ministers* llamar; *meeting* convocar
◆ **summon up** *v/t*: ***he summoned up his strength*** hizo acopio de fuerzas
sum·mons ['sʌmənz] *nsg* LAW citación *f*
sump [sʌmp] *for oil* cárter *m*
sun [sʌn] sol *m*; ***in the sun*** al sol; ***out of the sun*** a la sombra; ***he has had too much sun*** le ha dado demasiado el sol
'**sun·bathe** *v/i* tomar el sol
'**sun·bed** cama *f* de rayos UVA
'**sun·block** crema *f* solar de alta protección
'**sun·burn** quemadura *f* (del sol)
'**sun·burnt** *adj* quemado (por el sol)
Sun·day ['sʌndeɪ] domingo *m*
'**sun·dial** reloj *m* de sol
sun·dries ['sʌndrɪz] *npl* varios *mpl*
sung [sʌŋ] *pp* → ***sing***
'**sun·glass·es** *npl* gafas *fpl or L.Am.* anteojos *mpl* de sol
sunk [sʌŋk] *pp* → ***sink***
sunk·en ['sʌŋkn] *adj ship*, *cheeks* hundido
sun·ny ['sʌnɪ] *adj day* soleado; *disposition* radiante; ***it is sunny*** hace sol
'**sun·rise** amanecer *m*
'**sun·set** atardecer *m*, puesta *f* de sol
'**sun·shade** sombrilla *f*
'**sun·shine** sol *m*
'**sun·stroke** insolación *f*
'**sun·tan** bronceado *m*; ***get a suntan*** broncearse
su·per ['suːpər] **1** *adj* F genial F, estupendo F **2** *n* (*janitor*) portero(-a) *m*(*f*)
su·perb [sʊ'pɜːrb] *adj* excelente
su·per·fi·cial [suːpər'fɪʃl] *adj* superficial
su·per·flu·ous [sʊ'pɜːrflʊəs] *adj* superfluo
su·per'hu·man *adj efforts* sobrehumano
su·per·in·tend·ent [suːpərɪn'tendənt] *of apartment block* portero(-a) *m*(*f*); *Br of police* inspector(a) *m*(*f*) jefe
su·pe·ri·or [suː'pɪrɪər] **1** *adj* (*better*) superior; *pej*: *attitude* arrogante **2** *n in organization* superior *m*
su·per·la·tive [suː'pɜːrlətɪv] **1** *adj superb* excelente **2** *n* GRAM superlativo *m*
'**su·per·mar·ket** supermercado *m*
su·per'nat·u·ral 1 *adj powers* sobrenatur-

S

al **2** *n*: ***the supernatural*** lo sobrenatural

'su·per·pow·er POL superpotencia *f*

su·per·son·ic [suːpər'sɑːnɪk] *adj flight, aircraft* supersónico

su·per·sti·tion [suːpər'stɪʃn] superstición *f*

su·per·sti·tious [suːpər'stɪʃəs] *adj person* supersticioso

su·per·vise ['suːpərvaɪz] *v/t class* vigilar; *workers* supervisar; *activities* dirigir

su·per·vi·sor ['suːpərvaɪzər] *at work* supervisor(a) *m(f)*

sup·per ['sʌpər] cena *f, L.Am.* comida *f*

sup·ple ['sʌpl] *adj person* ágil; *limbs, material* flexible

sup·ple·ment ['sʌplɪmənt] (*extra payment*) suplemento *m*

sup·pli·er [sə'plaɪər] COM proveedor *m*

sup·ply [sə'plaɪ] **1** *n* suministro *m*, abastecimiento *m*; ***supply and demand*** la oferta y la demanda; ***supplies*** *of food* provisiones *fpl*; ***office supplies*** material *f* de oficina **2** *v/t* (*pret & pp* ***supplied***) *goods* suministrar; ***supply s.o. with sth*** suministrar algo a alguien; ***be supplied with …*** venir con …

sup·port [sə'pɔːrt] **1** *n for structure* soporte *m*; (*backing*) apoyo *m* **2** *v/t building, structure* soportar, sostener; *financially* mantener; (*back*) apoyar

sup·port·er [sə'pɔːrtər] partidario(-a) *m(f)*; *of football team etc* seguidor(a) *m(f)*

sup·port·ive [sə'pɔːrtɪv] *adj* comprensivo; ***be supportive*** apoyar (***toward, of*** a)

sup·pose [sə'poʊz] *v/t* (*imagine*) suponer; ***I suppose so*** supongo (que sí); ***you are not supposed to …*** (*not allowed to*) no deberías …; ***it is supposed to be delivered today*** (*be meant to*) se supone que lo van a entregar hoy; ***it's supposed to be very beautiful*** *is said to be* se supone que es hermosísimo

sup·pos·ed·ly [sə'poʊzɪdlɪ] *adv* supuestamente

sup·pos·i·to·ry [sə'pɑːzɪtɔːrɪ] MED supositorio *m*

sup·press [sə'pres] *v/t rebellion etc* reprimir, sofocar

sup·pres·sion [sə'preʃn] represión *f*

su·prem·a·cy [suː'preməsɪ] supremacía *f*

su·preme [suː'priːm] *adj* supremo

sur·charge ['sɜːrtʃɑːrdʒ] *n* recargo *m*

sure [ʃʊr] **1** *adj* seguro; ***I'm not sure*** no estoy seguro; ***be sure about sth*** estar seguro de algo; ***make sure that …*** asegurarse de que … **2** *adv*: ***sure enough*** efectivamente; ***it sure is hot today*** F vaya calor que hace F; ***sure!*** F ¡claro!

sure·ly ['ʃʊrlɪ] *adv* (*gladly*) claro que sí; ***surely you don't mean that!*** ¡ no lo dirás en serio!; ***surely somebody knows*** alguien tiene que saberlo

sur·e·ty ['ʃʊrətɪ] *for loan* fianza *f*, depósito *m*

surf [sɜːrf] **1** *n on sea* surf *m* **2** *v/t*: ***surf the Net*** navegar por Internet

sur·face ['sɜːrfɪs] **1** *n of table, object, water* superficie *f*; ***on the surface*** *fig* a primera vista **2** *v/i of swimmer, submarine* salir a la superficie; (*appear*) aparecer

'sur·face mail correo *m* terrestre

'surf·board tabla *f* de surf

surf·er ['sɜːrfər] *on sea* surfista *m/f*

surf·ing ['sɜːrfɪŋ] surf *m*; ***go surfing*** ir a hacer surf

surge [sɜːrdʒ] *n in electric current* sobrecarga *f*; *in demand etc* incremento *m* repentino

◆ **surge forward** *v/i of crowd* avanzar atropelladamente

sur·geon ['sɜːrdʒən] cirujano(-a) *m(f)*

sur·ge·ry ['sɜːrdʒərɪ] cirugía *f*; ***undergo surgery*** ser intervenido quirúrgicamente

sur·gi·cal ['sɜːrdʒɪkl] *adj* quirúrgico

sur·gi·cal·ly ['sɜːrdʒɪklɪ] *adv* quirúrgicamente

sur·ly ['sɜːrlɪ] *adj* arisco, hosco

sur·mount [sər'maʊnt] *v/t difficulties* superar

sur·name ['sɜːrneɪm] apellido *m*

sur·pass [sər'pæs] *v/t* superar

sur·plus ['sɜːrpləs] **1** *n* excedente *m* **2** *adj* excedente

sur·prise [sər'praɪz] **1** *n* sorpresa *f*; ***it came as no surprise*** no me sorprendió **2** *v/t* sorprender; ***be / look surprised*** estar / parecer sorprendido

sur·pris·ing [sər'praɪzɪŋ] *adj* sorprendente; ***it's not surprising that …*** no me sorprende que …

sur·pris·ing·ly [sər'praɪzɪŋlɪ] *adv* sorprendentemente

sur·ren·der [sə'rendər] **1** *v/i of army* rendirse **2** *v/t* (*hand in: weapons etc*) entregar **3** *n* rendición *f*; (*handing in*) entrega *f*

sur·ro·gate 'moth·er ['sʌrəgət] madre *f* de alquiler

sur·round [sə'raʊnd] **1** *v/t* rodear; ***surrounded by*** rodeado de *or* por **2** *n of picture etc* marco *m*

sur·round·ing [sə'raʊndɪŋ] *adj* circundante

sur·round·ings [sə'raʊndɪŋz] *npl of village* alrededores *mpl*; (*environment*) entorno *m*

sur·vey ['sɜːrveɪ] **1** *n* ['sɜːrveɪ] *of modern*

S

literature etc estudio *m*; *of building* tasación *f*, peritaje; *poll* encuesta *f* **2** *v/t* [sər'veɪ] (*look at*) contemplar; *building* tasar, peritar

sur·vey·or [sɜːr'veɪr] tasador(a) *m(f) or* perito (-a) *m(f)* de la propiedad

sur·viv·al [sər'vaɪvl] supervivencia *f*

sur·vive [sər'vaɪv] **1** *v/i* sobrevivir; ***how are you? - I'm surviving*** ¿cómo estás? - voy tirando; ***his two surviving daughters*** las dos hijas que aún viven **2** *v/t accident, operation* sobrevivir a; (*outlive*) sobrevivir

sur·vi·vor [sər'vaɪvər] superviviente *m/f*; ***he's a survivor*** *fig* es incombustible

sus·cep·ti·ble [sə'septəbl] *adj emotionally* sensible, susceptible; ***be susceptible to the cold / heat*** ser sensible al frío / calor

sus·pect **1** *n* ['sʌspekt] sospechoso(-a) *m(f)* **2** *v/t* [sə'spekt] *person* sospechar de; (*suppose*) sospechar

sus·pected [sə'spektɪd] *adj murderer* presunto; *cause, heart attack etc* supuesto

sus·pend [sə'spend] *v/t* (*hang*) colgar; *from office, duties* suspender

sus·pend·ers [sə'spendərz] *npl for pants* tirantes *mpl*, *S. Am.* suspensores *mpl*

sus·pense [sə'spens] *Span* suspense *m*, *L.Am.* suspenso *m*

sus·pen·sion [sə'spenʃn] MOT, *from duty* suspensión *f*

sus'pen·sion bridge puente *m* colgante

sus·pi·cion [sə'spɪʃn] sospecha *f*

sus·pi·cious [sə'spɪʃəs] *adj* (*causing suspicion*) sospechoso; (*feeling suspicion*) receloso, desconfiado; ***be suspicious of*** sospechar de

sus·pi·cious·ly [sə'spɪʃəslɪ] *adv behave* de manera sospechosa; *ask* con recelo *or* desconfianza

sus·tain [sə'steɪn] *v/t* sostener

sus·tain·able [sə'steɪnəbl] *adj* sostenible

swab [swɑːb] *material* torunda *f*; *test* muestra *f*

S

swag·ger ['swægər] *n*: ***walk with a swagger*** caminar pavoneándose

swal·low¹ ['swɑːloʊ] **1** *v/t liquid, food* tragar, tragarse **2** *v/i* tragar

swal·low² ['swɑːloʊ] *n bird* golondrina *f*

swam [swæm] *pret* → ***swim***

swamp [swɑːmp] **1** *n* pantano *m* **2** *v/t*: ***be swamped with*** estar inundado de

swamp·y ['swɑːmpɪ] *adj* pantanoso

swan [swɑːn] cisne *m*

swap [swɑːp] **1** *v/t* (*pret & pp* ***swapped***) cambiar; ***swap sth for sth*** cambiar algo por algo **2** *v/i* (*pret & pp* ***swapped***) hacer un cambio

swarm [swɔːrm] **1** *n of bees* enjambre *m* **2** *v/i*: ***the town was swarming with ...*** la ciudad estaba abarrotada de ...

swar·thy ['swɔːrðɪ] *adj face, complexion* moreno

swat [swɑːt] *v/t* (*pret & pp* ***swatted***) *insect, fly* aplastar, matar

sway [sweɪ] **1** *n* (*influence, power*) dominio *m* **2** *v/i* tambalearse

swear [swer] **1** *v/i* (*pret* ***swore***, *pp* ***sworn***) (*use swearword*) decir palabrotas *or* tacos; ***swear at s.o.*** insultar a alguien; ***I swear*** lo juro **2** *v/t* (*pret* ***swore***, *pp* ***sworn***) (*promise*), LAW jurar

◆ **swear in** *v/t witnesses etc* tomar juramento a

'swear·word palabrota *f*, taco *m*

sweat [swet] **1** *n* sudor *m*; ***covered in sweat*** empapado de sudor **2** *v/i* sudar

'sweat·band banda *f* (en la frente); *on wrist* muñequera *f*

sweat·er ['swetər] suéter *m*, *Span* jersey *m*

'sweat·shirt sudadera *f*

sweat·y ['swetɪ] *adj hands* sudoroso

Swede [swiːd] sueco(-a) *m(f)*

Swe·den ['swiːdn] Suecia

Swe·dish ['swiːdɪʃ] **1** *adj* sueco **2** *n* sueco *m*

sweep [swiːp] **1** *v/t* (*pret & pp* ***swept***) *floor, leaves* barrer **2** *n* (*long curve*) curva *f*

◆ **sweep up** *v/t mess, crumbs* barrer

sweep·ing ['swiːpɪŋ] *adj statement* demasiado generalizado; *changes* radical

sweet [swiːt] *adj taste, tea* dulce; F (*kind*) amable; F (*cute*) mono

sweet and 'sour *adj* agridulce

'sweet·corn maíz *m*, *S. Am.* choclo *m*

sweet·en ['swiːtn] *v/t drink, food* endulzar

sweet·en·er ['swiːtnər] *for drink* edulcorante *m*

'sweet·heart novio(-a) *m(f)*

swell [swel] **1** *v/i of wound, limb* hincharse **2** *adj* F (*good*) genial F, fenomenal F **3** *n of the sea* oleaje *m*

swell·ing ['swelɪŋ] *n* MED hinchazón *f*

swel·ter·ing ['sweltərɪŋ] *adj heat, day* sofocante

swept [swept] *pret & pp* → ***sweep***

swerve [swɜːrv] *v/i of driver, car* girar bruscamente, dar un volantazo

swift [swɪft] *adj* rápido

swim [swɪm] **1** *v/i* (*pret* ***swam***, *pp* ***swum***) nadar; ***go swimming*** ir a nadar; ***my head is swimming*** me da vueltas la cabeza **2** *n* baño *m*; ***go for a swim*** ir a darse un baño

swim·mer ['swɪmər] nadador(a) *m(f)*
swim·ming ['swɪmɪŋ] natación *f*
'**swim·ming cos·tume** traje *m* de baño, bañador *m*
'**swim·ming pool** piscina *f*, *Mex* alberca *f*, *Rpl* pileta *f*
swin·dle ['swɪndl] **1** *n* timo *m*, estafa *f* **2** *v/t* timar, estafar; ***swindle s.o. out of sth*** estafar algo a alguien
swine [swaɪn] F (*person*) cerdo(-a) *m(f)* F
swing [swɪŋ] **1** *n* oscilación *f*; *for child* columpio *m*; ***swing to the Democrats*** giro favorable a los Demócratas **2** *v/t* (*pret & pp* **swung**) balancear; *hips* menear **3** *v/i* (*pret & pp* **swung**) balancearse; (*turn*) girar; *of public opinion etc* cambiar
swing-'door puerta *f* basculante *or* de vaivén
Swiss [swɪs] **1** *adj* suizo **2** *n person* suizo(-a) *m(f)*; ***the Swiss*** los suizos
switch [swɪʧ] **1** *n for light* interruptor *m*; (*change*) cambio *m* **2** *v/t* (*change*) cambiar de **3** *v/i* (*change*) cambiar
◆ **switch off** *v/t lights, engine, PC,* TV apagar
◆ **switch on** *v/t lights, engine, PC,* TV encender, *L.Am.* prender
'**switch·board** centralita *f*, *L.Am.* conmutador
'**switch·o·ver** *to new system* cambio *m* (**to** a)
Swit·zer·land ['swɪtsərlənd] Suiza
swiv·el ['swɪvl] *v/i* (*pret & pp* **swiveled**, *Br* **swivelled**) *of chair, monitor* girar
swol·len ['swoʊlən] *adj* hinchado
swoop [swuːp] *v/i of bird* volar en picado
◆ **swoop down on** *v/t prey* caer en picado sobre
◆ **swoop on** *v/t of police etc* hacer una redada contra
sword [sɔːrd] espada *f*
'**sword·fish** pez *f* espada
swore [swɔːr] *pret* → **swear**
sworn [swɔːrn] *pp* → **swear**
swum [swʌm] *pp* → **swim**
swung [swʌŋ] *pret & pp* → **swing**
syc·a·more ['sɪkəmɔːr] plátano *m* (árbol)
syl·la·ble ['sɪləbl] sílaba *f*
syl·la·bus ['sɪləbəs] plan *m* de estudios
sym·bol ['sɪmbəl] símbolo *m*
sym·bol·ic [sɪm'bɑːlɪk] *adj* simbólico
sym·bol·ism ['sɪmbəlɪzm] simbolismo *m*
sym·bol·ist ['sɪmbəlɪst] simbolista *m/f*
sym·bol·ize ['sɪmbəlaɪz] *v/t* simbolizar
sym·met·ri·c(al) [sɪ'metrɪkl] *adj* simétrico
sym·me·try ['sɪmətrɪ] simetría *f*
sym·pa·thet·ic [sɪmpə'θetɪk] *adj* (*showing pity*) compasivo; (*understanding*) comprensivo; ***be sympathetic toward a person / an idea*** simpatizar con una persona / idea
◆ **sym·pa·thize with** ['sɪmpəθaɪz] *v/t person, views* comprender
sym·pa·thiz·er ['sɪmpəθaɪzər] POL simpatizante *m/f*
sym·pa·thy ['sɪmpəθɪ] (*pity*) compasión *f*; (*understanding*) comprensión *f*; ***don't expect any sympathy from me!*** no esperes que te compadezca
sym·pho·ny ['sɪmfənɪ] sinfonía *f*
'**sym·pho·ny or·ches·tra** orquesta *f* sinfónica
symp·tom ['sɪmptəm] *also fig* síntoma *f*
symp·to·mat·ic [sɪmptə'mætɪk] *adj*: ***be symptomatic of*** *fig* ser sintomático de
syn·chro·nize ['sɪŋkrənaɪz] *v/t* sincronizar
syn·o·nym ['sɪnənɪm] sinónimo *m*
sy·non·y·mous [sɪ'nɑːnɪməs] *adj* sinónimo; ***be synonymous with*** *fig* ser sinónimo de
syn·tax ['sɪntæks] sintaxis *f inv*
syn·the·siz·er ['sɪnθəsaɪzər] MUS sintetizador *m*
syn·thet·ic [sɪn'θetɪk] *adj* sintético
syph·i·lis ['sɪfɪlɪs] sífilis *f*
Syr·i·a ['sɪrɪə] Siria
Syr·i·an ['sɪrɪən] **1** *adj* sirio **2** *n* sirio(-a) *m(f)*
sy·ringe [sɪ'rɪndʒ] *n* jeringuilla *f*
syr·up ['sɪrəp] almíbar *m*
sys·tem ['sɪstəm] *also* COMPUT sistema *f*; ***the braking system*** el sistema de frenado; ***the digestive system*** el aparato digestivo
sys·te·mat·ic [sɪstə'mætɪk] *adj* sistemático
sys·tem·at·i·cal·ly [sɪstə'mætɪklɪ] *adv* sistemáticamente
sys·tems 'an·a·lyst ['sɪstəmz] COMPUT analista *m/f* de sistemas

T

tab [tæb] *n for pulling* lengüeta *f*; *in text* tabulador *m*; *bill* cuenta *f*; ***pick up the tab*** pagar (la cuenta)
ta·ble ['teɪbl] *n* mesa *f*; *of figures* cuadro *m*
'ta·ble·cloth mantel *m*
'table lamp lámpara *f* de mesa
table of 'con·tents índice *m* (de contenidos)
'ta·ble·spoon *object* cuchara *f* grande; *quantity* cucharada *f* grande
ta·blet ['tæblɪt] MED pastilla *f*
'ta·ble ten·nis tenis *m* de mesa
tab·loid ['tæblɔɪd] *n newspaper* periódico *m* sensacionalista (*de tamaño tabloide*)
ta·boo [tə'buː] *adj* tabú *inv*
ta·cit ['tæsɪt] *adj* tácito
ta·ci·turn ['tæsɪtɜːrn] *adj* taciturno
tack [tæk] **1** *n* (*nail*) tachuela *f* **2** *v/t* (*sew*) hilvanar **3** *v/i of yacht* dar bordadas
tack·le ['tækl] **1** *n* (*equipment*) equipo *m*; SP entrada *f*; ***fishing tackle*** aparejos *mpl* de pesca **2** *v/t* SP entrar a; *problem* abordar; *intruder* hacer frente a
tack·y ['tækɪ] *adj paint, glue* pegajoso; F (*cheap, poor quality*) chabacano, *Span* hortera F; *behavior* impresentable
tact [tækt] tacto *m*
tact·ful ['tæktfəl] *adj* diplomático
tact·ful·ly ['tæktfəlɪ] *adv* diplomáticamente
tac·tic·al ['tæktɪkl] *adj* táctico
tac·tics ['tæktɪks] *npl* táctica *f*
tact·less ['tæktlɪs] *adj* indiscreto
tad·pole ['tædpoʊl] renacuajo *m*
tag [tæg] *n* (*label*) etiqueta *f*
◆ **tag along** *v/i* (*pret & pp* ***tagged***) pegarse
tail [teɪl] *n of bird, fish* cola *f*; *of mammal* cola *f*, rabo *m*
'tail·back *Br* caravana *f*
'tail light luz *f* trasera
tai·lor ['teɪlər] *n* sastre *m*
tai·lor-made [teɪlər'meɪd] *adj suit, solution* hecho a medida
'tail·pipe *of car* tubo *m* de escape
'tail·wind viento *m* de cola
taint·ed ['teɪntɪd] *adj food* contaminado; *reputation* empañado
Tai·wan [taɪ'wɑn] Taiwán
Tai·wan·ese [taɪwɑn'iːz] **1** *adj* taiwanés **2** *n* taiwanés(-esa) *m*(*f*); *dialect* taiwanés *m*
take [teɪk] *v/t* (*pret* ***took***, *pp* ***taken***) (*remove*) llevarse; *Span* coger; (*steal*) llevarse; (*transport, accompany*) llevar; (*accept: money, gift, credit cards*) aceptar; (*study: maths, French*) hacer, estudiar; *photograph, photocopy* hacer, sacar; *exam, degree* hacer; *shower* darse; *stroll* dar; *medicine, s.o.'s temperature, taxi* tomar; (*endure*) aguantar; ***how long does it take?*** ¿cuánto tiempo lleva?; ***I'll take it*** *when shopping* me lo llevo; ***it takes a lot of courage*** se necesita mucho valor
◆ **take after** *v/t* parecerse a
◆ **take apart** *v/t* (*dismantle*) desmontar; F (*criticize*) hacer pedazos; F (*reprimand*) echar una bronca a F; F *in physical fight* machacar F
◆ **take away** *v/t pain* hacer desaparecer; (*remove: object*) quitar; MATH restar; ***take sth away from s.o.*** quitar algo a alguien
◆ **take back** *v/t* (*return: object*) devolver; *person* llevar de vuelta; (*accept back: husband etc*) dejar volver; ***that takes me back*** *of music, thought etc* me trae recuerdos
◆ **take down** *v/t from shelf* bajar; *scaffolding* desmontar; *trousers* bajarse; (*write down*) anotar, apuntar
◆ **take in** *v/t* (*take indoors*) recoger; (*give accommodation to*) acoger; (*make narrower*) meter; (*deceive*) engañar; (*include*) incluir
◆ **take off 1** *v/t clothes, hat* quitarse; *10% etc* descontar; (*mimic*) imitar; (*cut off*) cortar; ***take a day / week off*** tomarse un día / una semana de vacaciones **2** *v/i of airplane* despegar, *L.Am.* decolar; (*become popular*) empezar a cuajar
◆ **take on** *v/t job* aceptar; *staff* contratar
◆ **take out** *v/t from bag, pocket* sacar; *tooth* sacar, extraer; *word from text* quitar, borrar; *money from bank* sacar; *insurance policy* suscribir; ***he took her out to dinner*** la llevó a cenar; ***take the dog out*** sacar al perro a pasear; ***take the kids out to the park*** llevar a los niños al parque; ***don't take it out on me!*** ¡no la pagues conmigo!
◆ **take over 1** *v/t company etc* absorber, adquirir; ***tourists took over the town*** los turistas invadieron la ciudad **2** *v/i of new management etc* asumir el cargo; *of new government* asumir el poder; (*do sth in s.o.'s place*) tomar el relevo
◆ **take to** *v/t* (*like*): ***how did they take to***

the new idea? ¿qué les pareció la nueva idea?; ***I immediately took to him*** me cayó bien de inmediato; ***he has taken to getting up early*** le ha dado por levantarse temprano; ***she took to drink*** se dio a la bebida

◆ **take up** *v/t carpet etc* levantar; (*carry up*) subir; (*shorten*: *dress etc*) acortar; *hobby* empezar a hacer; *subject* empezar a estudiar; *offer* aceptar; *new job* comenzar; *space, time* ocupar; ***I'll take you up on your offer*** aceptaré tu oferta

'take-home pay salario *m* neto

'take·off *of airplane* despegue *m, L.Am.* decolaje *m*; (*impersonation*) imitación *f*

'take·o·ver COM absorción *f*, adquisición *f*

'take·o·ver bid oferta *f* pública de adquisición, OPA *f*

tak·en ['teɪkən] *pp* → ***take***

ta·kings ['teɪkɪŋz] *npl* recaudación *f*

tal·cum pow·der ['tælkəmpaʊdər] polvos *mpl* de talco

tale [teɪl] cuento *m*, historia *f*

tal·ent ['tælənt] talento *m*

tal·ent·ed ['tæləntɪd] *adj* con talento; ***she's very talented*** tiene mucho talento

'tal·ent scout cazatalentos *m inv*

talk [tɒːk] **1** *v/i* hablar; ***can I talk to ...?*** ¿podría hablar con ...?; ***I'll talk to him about it*** hablaré del tema con él **2** *v/t English etc* hablar; ***talk business / politics*** hablar de negocios / de política; ***talk s.o. into sth*** persuadir a alguien para que haga algo **3** *n* (*conversation*) charla *f, C.Am., Mex* plática *f*; (*lecture*) conferencia *f*, ***give a talk on sth*** dar una conferencia sobre algo; charla *f*; ***talks*** negociaciones *fpl*; ***he's all talk*** *pej* habla mucho y no hace nada

◆ **talk back** *v/i* responder, contestar

◆ **talk down to** *v/t* hablar con aires de superioridad a

◆ **talk over** *v/t* hablar de, discutir

talk·a·tive ['tɒːkətɪv] *adj* hablador

talk·ing-to ['tɒːkɪŋtuː] sermón *m*, rapapolvo *m*; ***give s.o. a good talking-to*** echar a alguien un buen sermón *or* rapapolvo

'talk show programa *m* de entrevistas

tall [tɒːl] *adj* alto; ***it is ten meters tall*** mide diez metros de alto

tall 'or·der: ***that's a tall order*** eso es muy difícil

tall 'sto·ry cuento *m* chino

tal·ly ['tælɪ] **1** *n* cuenta *f* **2** *v/i* (*pret & pp* ***tallied***) cuadrar, encajar

◆ **tally with** *v/t* cuadrar con, encajar con

tame [teɪm] *adj animal* manso, domesticado; *joke etc* soso

◆ **tam·per with** ['tæmpər] *v/t lock* intentar forzar; *brakes* tocar

tam·pon ['tæmpɑːn] tampón *m*

tan [tæn] **1** *n from sun* bronceado *m*; ***get a tan*** ponerse moreno; (*color*) marrón *m* claro **2** *v/i* (*pret & pp* ***tanned***) *in sun* broncearse **3** *v/t* (*pret & pp* ***tanned***) *leather* curtir

tan·dem ['tændəm] (*bike*) tándem *m*

tan·gent ['tændʒənt] MATH tangente *f*

tan·ge·rine [tændʒə'riːn] mandarina *f*

tan·gi·ble ['tændʒɪbl] *adj* tangible

tan·gle ['tæŋgl] *n* lío *m*, maraña *f*

◆ **tangle up**: ***get tangled up*** *of string etc* quedarse enredado

tan·go ['tæŋgoʊ] *n* tango *m*

tank [tæŋk] *for water* depósito *m*, tanque *m*; *for fish* pecera *f*; MOT depósito *m*; MIL, *for skin diver* tanque *m*

tank·er ['tæŋkər] *truck* camión *m* cisterna; *ship* buque *m* cisterna; *for oil* petrolero *m*

'tank top camiseta *f* sin mangas

tan·ned [tænd] *adj* moreno, bronceado

Tan·noy® ['tænɔɪ] megafonía *f*

tan·ta·liz·ing ['tæntəlaɪzɪŋ] *adj* sugerente

tan·ta·mount ['tæntəmaʊnt] *adj*: ***be tantamount to*** equivaler a

tan·trum ['tæntrəm] rabieta *f*

tap [tæp] **1** *n* grifo *m, L.Am.* llave *f* **2** *v/t* (*pret & pp* ***tapped***) (*knock*) dar un golpecito en; *phone* intervenir

◆ **tap into** *v/t resources* explotar

'tap dance *n* claqué *m*

tape [teɪp] **1** *n* cinta *f* **2** *v/t conversation etc* grabar; *with sticky tape* pegar con cinta adhesiva

'tape deck pletina *f*

'tape drive COMPUT unidad *f* de cinta

'tape meas·ure cinta *f* métrica

tap·er ['teɪpər] *v/i* estrecharse

◆ **taper off** *v/i of production, figures* disminuir

'tape re·cor·der magnetofón *m, L.Am.* grabador *m*

'tape re·cor·ding grabación *f* (magnetofónica)

ta·pes·try ['tæpɪstrɪ] *cloth* tapiz *m*; *art* tapicería *f*

'tape·worm tenia *f*, solitaria *f*

tar [tɑːr] *n* alquitrán *m*

tar·dy ['tɑːrdɪ] *adj* tardío

tar·get ['tɑːrgɪt] **1** *n in shooting* blanco *m*; *for sales, production* objetivo *m* **2** *v/t market* apuntar a

tar·get 'au·di·ence audiencia *f* a la que está orientado el programa

'tar·get date fecha *f* fijada

tar·get 'fig·ure cifra *f* objetivo

'**tar·get group** COM grupo *m* estratégico
'**tar·get mar·ket** mercado *m* objetivo
tar·iff ['tærɪf] (*price*) tarifa *f*; (*tax*) arancel *m*
tar·mac ['tɑːrmæk] *for road surface* asfalto *m*; *at airport* pista *f*
tar·nish ['tɑːrnɪʃ] *v/t metal* deslucir, deslustrar; *reputation* empañar
tar·pau·lin [tɑːr'pɒːlɪn] lona *f* (*impermeable*)
tart¹ [tɑːrt] *n* tarta *f*, pastel *m*
tart² [tɑːrt] *n* F *woman* fulana *f* F
tar·tan ['tɑːrtn] tartán *m*
task [tæsk] tarea *f*
'**task force** *for a special job* equipo *m* de trabajo; MIL destacamento
tas·sel ['tæsl] borla *f*
taste [teɪst] **1** *n* gusto *m*; *of food etc* sabor *m*; ***he has no taste*** tiene mal gusto **2** *v/t also fig* probar
taste·ful ['teɪstfəl] *adj* de buen gusto
taste·ful·ly ['teɪstfəlɪ] *adv* con buen gusto
taste·less ['teɪstlɪs] *adj food* insípido; *remark* de mal gusto
tast·ing ['teɪstɪŋ] *of wine* cata *f*, degustación *f*
tast·y ['teɪstɪ] *adj* sabroso, rico
tat·tered ['tætərd] *adj clothes* andrajoso; *book* destrozado
tat·ters ['tætərz]: ***in tatters*** *clothes* hecho jirones; *reputation*, *career* arruinado
tat·too [tə'tuː] *n* tatuaje *m*
tat·ty ['tætɪ] *adj* sobado, gastado
taught [tɒːt] *pret & pp* → **teach**
taunt [tɒːnt] **1** *n* pulla *f* **2** *v/t* mofarse de
Taur·us ['tɔːrəs] ASTR Tauro *m/f inv*
taut [tɒːt] *adj* tenso
taw·dry ['tɒːdrɪ] *adj* barato, cursi
tax [tæks] **1** *n* impuesto *m*; ***before / after tax*** sin descontar / descontando impuestos **2** *v/t people* cobrar impuestos a; *product* gravar
tax·a·ble '**in·come** ingresos *mpl* gravables
ta·x·ation [tæk'seɪʃn] (*act of taxing*) imposición *f* de impuestos; (*taxes*) fiscalidad *f*, impuestos *mpl*
'**tax avoid·ance** elusión *f* legal de impuestos
'**tax brack·et** banda *f* impositiva
'**tax de·duct·i·ble** *adj* desgravable
'**tax eva·sion** evasión *f* fiscal
'**tax free** *adj* libre de impuestos
'**tax haven** paraíso *m* fiscal
tax·i ['tæksɪ] *n* taxi *m*
'**tax·i dri·ver** taxista *m/f*
tax·ing ['tæksɪŋ] *adj* difícil, arduo
'**tax in·spect·or** inspector(a) *m*(*f*) de Hacienda
'**tax·i rank**, **tax·i stand** parada *f* de taxis
'**tax ·pay·er** contribuyente *m/f*
'**tax re·turn** *form* declaración *f* de la renta
'**tax year** año *m* fiscal
TB [tiː'biː] *abbr* (= **tuberculosis**) tuberculosis *f*
tea [tiː] *drink* té *m*; *meal* merienda *f*
tea·bag ['tiːbæg] bolsita *f* de té
teach [tiːʧ] **1** *v/t* (*pret & pp* **taught**) *person*, *subject* enseñar; ***teach s.o. to do sth*** enseñar a alguien a hacer algo **2** *v/i* (*pret & pp* **taught**): ***I taught at that school*** di clases en ese colegio; ***he always wanted to teach*** siempre quiso ser profesor
tea·cher ['tiːʧər] *at primary school* maestro(-a) *m*(*f*); *at secondary school*, *university* profesor(a) *m*(*f*)
tea·cher '**train·ing** formación *f* pedagógica, magisterio *m*
tea·ching ['tiːʧɪŋ] *profession* enseñanza *f*, docencia *f*
'**tea·ching aid** material *m* didáctico
'**tea cloth** paño *m* de cocina
'**tea·cup** taza *f* de té
'**tea drink·er** bebedor(a) *m*(*f*) de té
teak [tiːk] teca *f*
'**tea leaf** hoja *f* de té
team [tiːm] equipo *m*
'**team-mate** compañero(-a) *m*(*f*) de equipo
team '**spirit** espíritu *m* de equipo
team·ster ['tiːmstər] camionero(-a) *m*(*f*)
'**team·work** trabajo *m* en equipo
'**tea·pot** tetera *f*
tear¹ [ter] **1** *n in cloth etc* desgarrón *m*, rotura *f* **2** *v/t* (*pret* **tore**, *pp* **torn**) *paper*, *cloth* rasgar; ***be torn between two alternatives*** debatirse entre dos alternativas **3** *v/i* (*pret* **tore**, *pp* **torn**) (*run fast*, *drive fast*) ir a toda velocidad
◆ **tear down** *v/t poster* arrancar; *building* derribar
◆ **tear out** *v/t* arrancar
◆ **tear up** *v/t paper* romper, rasgar; *agreement* romper
tear² [tɪr] *in eye* lágrima *f*; ***burst into tears*** echarse a llorar; ***be in tears*** estar llorando
tear·drop ['tɪrdrɑːp] lágrima *f*
tear·ful ['tɪrfəl] *adj* lloroso
'**tear gas** gas *m* lacrimógeno
tease [tiːz] *v/t person* tomar el pelo a, burlarse de; *animal* hacer rabiar
'**tea serv·ice**, '**tea set** servicio *m* de té
'**tea·spoon** *object* cucharilla *f*; *quantity* cucharadita *f*
'**tea strain·er** colador *m* de té
teat [tiːt] teta *f*
'**tea to·wel** *Br* paño *m* de cocina

tech·ni·cal ['teknɪkl] *adj* técnico
tech·ni·cal·i·ty [teknɪ'kælətɪ] (*technical nature*) tecnicismo *m*; LAW detalle *m* técnico
tech·ni·cal·ly ['teknɪklɪ] *adv* técnicamente
tech·ni·cian [tek'nɪʃn] técnico(-a) *m*(*f*)
tech·nique [tek'niːk] técnica *f*
tech·no·log·i·cal [teknə'lɑːdʒɪkl] *adj* tecnológico
tech·no·lo·gy [tek'nɑːlədʒɪ] tecnología *f*
tech·no·phob·i·a [teknə'foʊbɪə] rechazo *m* de las nuevas tecnologías
ted·dy bear ['tedɪber] osito *m* de peluche
te·di·ous ['tiːdɪəs] *adj* tedioso
tee [tiː] *n in golf* tee *m*
teem [tiːm] *v/i*: ***be teeming with rain*** llover a cántaros; ***be teeming with tourists / ants*** estar abarrotado de turistas / lleno de hormigas
teen·age ['tiːneɪdʒ] *adj fashions* adolescente, juvenil; ***teenage boy / girl*** un adolescente / una adolescente
teen·ag·er ['tiːneɪdʒər] adolescente *m/f*
teens [tiːnz] *npl* adolescencia *f*; ***be in one's teens*** ser un adolescente; ***reach one's teens*** alcanzar la adolescencia
tee·ny ['tiːnɪ] *adj* F chiquitín F
teeth [tiːθ] *pl* → ***tooth***
teethe [tiːð] *v/i* echar los dientes
'**teething problems** *npl* problemas *fpl* iniciales
tee·to·tal [tiː'toʊtl] *adj person* abstemio
tee·to·tal·er [tiː'toʊtlər] abstemio(-a) *m*(*f*)
tel·e·com·mu·ni·ca·tions [telɪkəmjuːnɪ'keɪʃnz] telecomunicaciones *fpl*
tel·e·gram ['telɪgræm] telegrama *m*
tel·e·graph pole ['telɪgræf] poste *m* telegráfico
tel·e·path·ic [telɪ'pæθɪk] *adj* telepático; ***you must be telepathic!*** ¡debes tener telepatía!
te·lep·a·thy [tɪ'lepəθɪ] telepatía *f*
tel·e·phone ['telɪfoʊn] **1** *n* teléfono *m*; ***be on the telephone*** (*be speaking*) estar hablando por teléfono; (*possess a phone*) tener teléfono **2** *v/t person* telefonear, llamar por teléfono a **3** *v/i* telefonear, llamar por teléfono
'**tel·e·phone bill** factura *f* del teléfono
'**tel·e·phone book** guía *f* telefónica, listín *m* telefónico
'**tel·e·phone booth** cabina *f* telefónica
'**tel·e·phone call** llamada *f* telefónica
'**tel·e·phone con·ver·sa·tion** conversación *f* por teléfono *or* telefónica
'**tel·e·phone di·rec·to·ry** guía *f* telefónica, listín *m* telefónico
'**tel·e·phone ex·change** central *f* telefónica, centralita *f*
'**tel·e·phone mes·sage** mensaje *m* telefónico
'**tel·e·phone num·ber** número *m* de teléfono
tel·e·pho·to lens [telɪ'foʊtoʊlenz] teleobjetivo *m*
tel·e·sales ['telɪseɪlz] televentas *fpl*
tel·e·scope ['telɪskoʊp] telescopio n
tel·e·thon ['telɪθɑːn] maratón *m* benéfico televisivo
tel·e·vise ['telɪvaɪz] *v/t* televisar
tel·e·vi·sion ['telɪvɪʒn] televisión *f*; *set* televisión *f*, televisor *m*; ***on television*** en *or* por (la) televisión; ***watch television*** ver la televisión
'**tel·e·vi·sion au·di·ence** audiencia *f* televisiva
'**tel·e·vision pro·gram** programa *m* televisivo
'**tel·e·vision set** televisión *f*, televisor *m*
'**tel·e·vision stu·di·o** estudio *m* de televisión
tell [tel] **1** *v/t* (*pret & pp* ***told***) *story* contar; *lie* decir, contar; ***I can't tell the difference*** no veo la diferencia; ***tell s.o. sth*** decir algo a alguien; ***don't tell Mom*** no se lo digas a mamá; ***could you tell me the way to …?*** ¿me podría decir por dónde se va a …?; ***tell s.o. to do sth*** decir a alguien que haga algo; ***you're telling me!*** F ¡a mí me lo vas a contar! **2** *v/i* (*pret & pp* ***told***) (*have effect*) hacerse notar; ***the heat is telling on him*** el calor está empezando a afectarle; ***time will tell*** el tiempo lo dirá
tell·er ['telər] cajero(-a) *m*(*f*)
tell·ing ['telɪŋ] *adj* contundente
tell·ing 'off regañina *f*
tell·tale ['telteɪl] **1** *adj signs* revelador **2** *n* chivato(-a) *m*(*f*)
temp [temp] **1** *n employee* trabajador(a) *m*(*f*) temporal **2** *v/i* hacer trabajo temporal
tem·per ['tempər] (*bad temper*) mal *humor m*; ***be in a temper*** estar de mal *humor*; ***keep one's temper*** mantener la calma; ***lose one's temper*** perder los estribos
tem·pe·ra·ment ['temprəmənt] temperamento *m*
tem·pe·ra·men·tal [temprə'mentl] *adj* (*moody*) temperamental
tem·pe·rate ['tempərət] *adj* templado
tem·pe·ra·ture ['temprətʃər] temperatura *f*; (*fever*) fiebre *f*; ***have a temperature*** tener fiebre
tem·ple[1] ['templ] REL templo *m*

T

tem·ple² ['templ] ANAT sien *f*
tem·po ['tempou] tempo *m*
tem·po·rar·i·ly [tempə'rerılı] *adv* temporalmente
tem·po·ra·ry ['tempərerı] *adj* temporal
tempt [tempt] *v/t* tentar
temp·ta·tion [temp'teıʃn] tentación *f*
tempt·ing ['temptıŋ] *adj* tentador
ten [ten] diez
te·na·cious [tı'neıʃəs] *adj* tenaz
te·nac·i·ty [tı'næsıtı] tenacidad *f*
ten·ant ['tenənt] *of building* inquilino(-a) *m(f)*; *of farm, land* arrendatario *m*
tend¹ [tend] *v/t* (*look after*) cuidar (de)
tend² [tend]: ***tend to do sth*** soler hacer algo; ***tend toward sth*** tender hacia algo
ten·den·cy ['tendənsı] tendencia *f*
ten·der¹ ['tendər] *adj* (*sore*) sensible, delicado; (*affectionate*) cariñoso, tierno; *steak* tierno
ten·der² ['tendər] *n* COM oferta *f*
ten·der·ness ['tendərnıs] (*soreness*) dolor *m*; *of kiss etc* cariño *m*, ternura *f*
ten·don ['tendən] tendón *m*
ten·nis ['tenıs] tenis *m*
'ten·nis ball pelota *f* de tenis
'ten·nis court pista *f* de tenis; cancha *f* de tenis
'ten·nis pla·yer tenista *m/f*
'ten·nis rack·et raqueta *f* de tenis
ten·or ['tenər] MUS tenor *m*
tense¹ [tens] *n* GRAM tiempo *m*
tense² [tens] *adj muscle, moment* tenso; *voice, person* tenso, nervioso
◆ **tense up** *v/i* ponerse tenso
ten·sion ['tenʃn] *of rope* tensión *f*; *in atmosphere, voice* tensión *f*, tirantez *f*; *in film, novel* tensión *f*
tent [tent] tienda *f*
ten·ta·cle ['tentəkl] tentáculo *m*
ten·ta·tive ['tentətıv] *adj move, offer* provisional
ten·ter·hooks ['tentərhuks]: ***be on tenterhooks*** estar sobre ascuas
tenth [tenθ] **1** *adj* décimo **2** *n* décimo *m*, décima parte *f*; *of second, degree* décima *f*
tep·id ['tepıd] *adj water, reaction* tibio
term [tɜːrm] *in office etc* mandato *m*; EDU trimestre *m*; (*condition*) término *m*, condición *f*; (*word*) término *m*; ***be on good / bad terms with s.o.*** llevarse bien / mal con alguien; ***in the long / short term*** a largo / corto plazo; ***come to terms with sth*** llegar a aceptar algo
ter·mi·nal ['tɜːrmınl] **1** *n at airport, for buses, for containers* terminal *f*; ELEC, COMPUT terminal *m*; *of battery* polo *m* **2** *adj illness* terminal
ter·mi·nal·ly ['tɜːrmınəlı] *adv*: ***terminally ill*** en la fase terminal de una enfermedad
ter·mi·nate ['tɜːrmıneıt] **1** *v/t contract* rescindir; *pregnancy* interrumpir **2** *v/i* finalizar
ter·mi·na·tion [tɜːrmı'neıʃn] *of contract* rescisión *f*; *of pregnancy* interrupción *f*
ter·mi·nol·o·gy [tɜːrmı'nɑːlədʒı] terminología *f*
ter·mi·nus ['tɜːrmınəs] *for buses* final *m* de trayecto; *for trains* estación *f* terminal
ter·race ['terəs] terraza *f*
ter·ra cot·ta [terə'kɑːtə] *adj* de terracota
ter·rain [te'reın] terreno *m*
ter·res·tri·al [te'restrıəl] **1** *n* terrestre *m* **2** *adj television* por vía terrestre
ter·ri·ble ['terəbl] *adj* terrible, horrible
ter·ri·bly ['terəblı] *adv* (*very*) tremendamente
ter·rif·ic [tə'rıfık] *adj* estupendo
ter·rif·i·cal·ly [tə'rıfıklı] *adv* (*very*) tremendamente
ter·ri·fy ['terıfaı] *v/t* (*pret & pp* ***terrified***) aterrorizar; ***be terrified*** estar aterrorizado
ter·ri·fy·ing ['terıfaııŋ] *adj* aterrador
ter·ri·to·ri·al [terı'tɔːrıəl] *adj* territorial
ter·ri·to·ri·al 'wa·ters *npl* aguas *fpl* territoriales
ter·ri·to·ry ['terıtɔːrı] territorio *m*; *fig* ámbito *m*, territorio *m*
ter·ror ['terər] terror *m*
ter·ror·ism ['terərızm] terrorismo *m*
ter·ror·ist ['terərıst] terrorista *m*
'ter·ror·ist at·tack atentado *m* terrorista
'ter·ror·ist or·gan·i·za·tion organización *f* terrorista
ter·ror·ize ['terəraız] *v/t* aterrorizar
terse [tɜːrs] *adj* tajante, seco
test [test] **1** *n* prueba *f*; *academic, for driving* examen *m* **2** *v/t* probar, poner a prueba
tes·ta·ment ['testəmənt] *to s.o.'s life etc* testimonio *m*; ***Old / New Testament*** REL Viejo / Nuevo Testamento *m*
'test-drive *v/t* (*pret* ***test-drove***, *pp* ***test-driven***) *car* probar en carretera
tes·ti·cle ['testıkl] testículo *m*
tes·ti·fy ['testıfaı] *v/i* (*pret & pp* ***testified***) LAW testificar, prestar declaración
tes·ti·mo·ni·al [testı'mounıəl] *n* referencias *fpl*
tes·ti·mo·ny ['testımənı] LAW testimonio *m*
'test tube tubo *m* de ensayo, probeta *f*
'test-tube ba·by niño(-a) *m(f)* probeta
tes·ty ['testı] *adj* irritable
te·ta·nus ['tetənəs] tétanos *m*
teth·er ['teðər] **1** *v/t horse* atar **2** *n* correa

T

f; ***be at the end of one's tether*** estar al a punto de perder la paciencia
text [tekst] texto *m*
'text·book libro *m* de texto
tex·tile ['tekstəl] textil
tex·ture ['tekstʃər] textura *f*
Thai [taɪ] **1** *adj* tailandés **2** *n person* tailandés(-esa) *m(f)*; *language* tailandés *m*
Thai·land ['taɪlænd] Tailandia
than [ðæn] *adv* que; ***bigger / faster than me*** más grande / más rápido que yo; ***more than 50*** más de 50
thank [θæŋk] *v/t* dar las gracias a; ***thank you*** gracias; ***no thank you*** no, gracias
thank·ful ['θæŋkfəl] *adj* agradecido; ***we have to be thankful that …*** tenemos que dar gracias de que …
thank·ful·ly ['θæŋkfəlɪ] *adv* (*luckily*) afortunadamente
thank·less ['θæŋklɪs] *adj task* ingrato
thanks [θæŋks] *npl* gracias *fpl*; ***thanks!*** ¡gracias!; ***thanks to*** gracias a
Thanks·giv·ing (Day) [θæŋks'gɪvɪŋdeɪ] Día *m* de Acción de Gracias
that [ðæt] **1** *adj* ese *m*, esa *f*; *more remote* aquel *m*, aquella; ***that one*** ése **2** *pron* ése *m*, ésa; *more remote* aquél *m*, aquella *f*; ***what is that?*** ¿qué es eso?; ***who is that?*** ¿quién es ése?; ***that's mine*** ése es mío; ***that's tea*** es té; ***that's very kind*** qué amable; ***I think that …*** creo que …; ***the person / car that you see*** el coche / la persona que ves **3** *adv* (*so*) tan; ***that big / expensive*** tan grande / caro
thaw [θɒː] *v/i of snow* derretirse, fundirse; *of frozen food* descongelarse
the [ðə] el, la; *plural* los, las; ***the sooner the better*** cuanto antes, mejor
the·a·ter ['θɪətər] teatro *m*
'the·a·ter crit·ic crítico *m* teatral
the·a·tre *Br* → ***theater***
the·at·ri·cal [θɪ'ætrɪkl] *also fig* teatral
theft [θeft] robo *m*
their [ðer] *adj* su; (*his or her*) su; ***their brother*** su hermano; ***their books*** sus libros
theirs [ðerz] *pron* el suyo, la suya; ***theirs are red*** los suyos son rojos; ***that book is theirs*** ese libro es suyo; ***a friend of theirs*** un amigo suyo
them [ðem] *pron direct object* los *mpl*, las *fpl*; *indirect object* les; *after prep* ellos *mpl*, ellas *fpl*; ***I know them*** los / las conozco; ***I gave them the keys*** les di las llaves; ***I sold it to them*** se lo vendí; ***he lives with them*** vive con ellos / ellas; ***if a person asks for help, you should help them*** *him / her* si una persona pide ayuda, hay que ayudarla
theme [θiːm] tema *m*
'theme park parque *m* temático
'theme song tema *m* musical
them·selves [ðem'selvz] *pron reflexive* se; *emphatic* ellos mismos *mpl*, ellas mismas *fpl*; ***they hurt themselves*** se hicieron daño; ***when they saw themselves in the mirror*** cuando se vieron en el espejo; ***they saw it themselves*** lo vieron ellos mismos; ***by themselves*** (*alone*) solos; (*without help*) ellos solos, ellos mismos
then [ðen] *adv* (*at that time*) entonces; (*after that*) luego, después; *deducing* entonces; ***by then*** para entonces
the·o·lo·gian [θɪə'loʊdʒɪən] teólogo *m*
the·ol·o·gy [θɪ'ɑːlədʒɪ] teología *f*
the·o·ret·i·cal [θɪə'retɪkl] *adj* teórico
the·o·ret·i·cal·ly [θɪə'retɪklɪ] *adv* en teoría
the·o·ry ['θɪrɪ] teoría *f*; ***in theory*** en teoría
ther·a·peu·tic [θerə'pjuːtɪk] *adj* terapéutico
ther·a·pist ['θerəpɪst] terapeuta *m/f*
ther·a·py ['θerəpɪ] terapia *f*
there [ðer] *adv* allí, ahí, allá; ***over there*** allí, ahí, allá; ***down there*** allí *or* ahí *or* allá abajo; ***there is / are …*** hay …; ***there is / are not …*** no hay …; ***there you are*** *giving sth* aquí tienes; *finding sth* aquí está; *completing sth* ya está; ***there and back*** ida y vuelta; ***it's 5 miles there and back*** entre ida y vuelta hay cinco millas; ***there he is!*** ¡ahí está!; ***there, there!*** ¡venga!
there·a·bouts [ðerə'baʊts] *adv* aproximadamente
there·fore [ðerfɔːr] *adv* por (lo) tanto
ther·mom·e·ter [θər'mɑːmɪtər] termómetro *m*
ther·mos flask ['θɜːrməs] termo *m*
ther·mo·stat ['θɜːrməstæt] termostato *m*
these [ðiːz] **1** *adj* estos(-as) **2** *pron* éstos *mpl*, éstas *fpl*
the·sis ['θiːsɪs] (*pl* ***theses*** ['θiːsiːz]) tesis *f inv*
they [ðeɪ] *pron* ellos *mpl*, ellas *fpl*; ***they are Mexican*** son mexicanos; ***they're going, but we're not*** ellos van, pero nosotros no; ***if anyone looks at this, they will see that …*** si alguien mira esto, verá que …; ***they say that …*** dicen que …; ***they are going to change the law*** van a cambiar la ley
thick [θɪk] *adj soup* espeso; *fog* denso; *wall, book* grueso; *hair* poblado; *crowd* compacto; F (*stupid*) corto; ***it's 3 cm thick*** tiene 3 cm de grosor
thick·en ['θɪkən] *v/t sauce* espesar

thick·set ['θɪkset] *adj* fornido
thick·skinned [θɪk'skɪnd] *adj fig* insensible
thief [θiːf] (*pl* ***thieves*** [θiːvz]) ladrón(-ona) *m(f)*
thigh [θaɪ] muslo *m*
thim·ble ['θɪmbl] dedal *m*
thin [θɪn] *adj person* delgado; *hair* ralo, escaso; *soup* claro; *coat*, *line* fino
thing [θɪŋ] cosa *f*; ***things*** (*belongings*) cosas *fpl*; ***how are things?*** ¿cómo te va?; ***it's a good thing you told me*** menos mal que me lo dijiste; ***what a thing to do / say!*** ¡qué barbaridad!
thing·um·a·jig ['θɪŋʌmədʒɪg] F *object* chisme *m*; *person* fulanito *m*
think [θɪŋk] *v/t & v/i* (*pret & pp* ***thought***) pensar; *hold an opinion* pensar, creer; ***I think so*** creo que sí; ***I don't think so*** creo que no; ***I think so too*** pienso lo mismo; ***what do you think?*** ¿qué piensas o crees?; ***what do you think of it?*** ¿qué te parece?; ***I can't think of anything more*** no se me ocurre nada más; ***think hard!*** ¡piensa más!; ***I'm thinking about emigrating*** estoy pensando en emigrar
◆ **think over** *v/t* reflexionar sobre
◆ **think through** *v/t* pensar bien
◆ **think up** *v/t plan* idear
'**think tank** grupo *m* de expertos
thin-skinned [θɪn'skɪnd] *adj* sensible
third [θɜːrd] **1** *adj* tercero **2** *n* tercero(a) *m(f)*; *fraction* tercio *m*, tercera parte *f*
third·ly ['θɜːrdlɪ] *adv* en tercer lugar
third 'par·ty tercero *m*
third-par·ty in'sur·ance seguro *m* a terceros
third 'per·son GRAM tercera persona *f*
'**third-rate** *adj* de tercera, de pacotilla F
Third 'World Tercer Mundo *m*
thirst [θɜːrst] sed *f*
thirst·y ['θɜːrstɪ] *adj* sediento; ***be thirsty*** tener sed
thir·teen [θɜːr'tiːn] trece
thir·teenth [θɜːr'tiːnθ] *n & adj* decimotercero
thir·ti·eth ['θɜːrtɪɪθ] *n & adj* trigésimo
thir·ty ['θɜːrtɪ] treinta
this [ðɪs] **1** *adj* este *m*, esta *f*; ***this one*** éste **2** *pron* esto *m*, esta *f*; ***this is good*** esto es bueno; ***this is ...*** *introducing s.o.* éste / ésta es ...; TELEC soy ... **3** *adv*: ***this big / high*** así de grande / de alto
thorn [θɔːrn] espina *f*
thorn·y ['θɔːrnɪ] *adj also fig* espinoso
thor·ough ['θɜːroʊ] *adj search* minucioso; *knowledge* profundo; *person* concienzudo
thor·ough·bred ['θɜːroʊbred] *horse* purasangre *m*
thor·ough·ly ['θɜːroʊlɪ] *adv* completamente; *clean up* a fondo; *search* minuciosamente; ***I'm thoroughly ashamed*** estoy avergonzadísimo
those [ðoʊz] **1** *adj* esos *mpl*, esas *fpl*; *more remote* aquellos *mpl*, aquellas *fpl* **2** *pron* ésos *mpl*, ésas *fpl*; aquéllos *mpl*, aquéllas *mpl*
though [ðoʊ] **1** *conj* (*although*) aunque; ***as though*** como si **2** *adv* sin embargo; ***it's not finished though*** pero no está acabado
thought[1] [θɒːt] *single* idea *f*; *collective* pensamiento *m*
thought[2] [θɒːt] *pret & pp* → ***think***
thought·ful ['θɒːtfəl] *adj* pensativo; *book* serio; (*considerate*) atento
thought·less ['θɒːtlɪs] *adj* desconsiderado
thou·sand ['θaʊznd] mil *m*; ***thousands of*** miles de; ***a thousand and ten*** mil diez
thou·sandth ['θaʊzndθ] *n & adj* milésimo
thrash [θræʃ] *v/t* golpear, dar una paliza a; SP dar una paliza a
◆ **thrash about** *v/i with arms etc* revolverse
◆ **thrash out** *v/t solution* alcanzar
thrash·ing ['θræʃɪŋ] *also* SP paliza *f*
thread [θred] **1** *n* hilo *m*; *of screw* rosca *f* **2** *v/t needle* enhebrar; *beads* ensartar
thread·bare ['θredber] *adj* raído
threat [θret] amenaza *f*
threat·en ['θretn] *v/t* amenazar
threat·en·ing ['θretnɪŋ] *adj* amenazador
three [θriː] tres
three-'quart·ers tres cuartos *mpl*
thresh [θreʃ] *v/t corn* trillar
thresh·old ['θreʃhoʊld] *of house*, *new age* umbral *m*; ***on the threshold of*** en el umbral *or* en puertas de
threw [θruː] *pret* → ***throw***
thrift [θrɪft] ahorro *m*
thrift·y ['θrɪftɪ] *adj* ahorrativo
thrill [θrɪl] **1** *n* emoción *f*, estremecimiento *m* **2** *v/t*: ***be thrilled*** estar entusiasmado
thrill·er ['θrɪlər] *movie* película *f* de *Span* suspense *or L.Am.* suspenso; *novel* novela *f* de *Span* suspense *or L.Am.* suspenso
thrill·ing ['θrɪlɪŋ] *adj* emocionante
thrive [θraɪv] *v/i of plant* medrar, crecer bien; *of business*, *economy* prosperar
throat [θroʊt] garganta *f*
'**throat loz·enge** pastilla *f* para la garganta
throb [θrɑːb] **1** *n of heart* latido *m*; *of music* zumbido *m* **2** *v/i* (*pret & pp* ***throbbed***) *of heart* latir; *of music* zumbar

throm·bo·sis [θrɑːmˈboʊsɪs] trombosis *f*
throne [θroʊn] trono *m*
throng [θrɑːŋ] *n* muchedumbre *f*
throt·tle [ˈθrɑːtl] **1** *n on motorbike* acelerador *m*; *on boat* palanca *f* del gas; *on motorbike* mango *m* del gas **2** *v/t* (*strangle*) estrangular
◆ **throttle back** *v/i* desacelerar
through [θruː] **1** *prep* ◇ (*across*) a través de; ***go through the city*** atravesar la ciudad
◇ (*during*) durante; ***through the winter / summer*** durante el invierno / verano; ***Monday through Friday*** de lunes a viernes
◇ (*by means of*)a través de, por medio de; ***arranged through him*** acordado por él **2** *adv*: ***wet through*** completamente mojado; ***watch a film through*** ver una película de principio a fin; ***read a book through*** leerse un libro de principio a fin **3** *adj*: ***be through*** *of couple* haber terminado; (*have arrived*: *of news etc*) haber llegado; ***you're through*** TELEC ya puede hablar; ***I'm through with …*** (*finished with*) he terminado con …
ˈ**through flight** vuelo *m* directo
through·out [θruːˈaʊt] **1** *prep* durante, a lo largo de **2** *adv* (*in all parts*) en su totalidad
ˈ**through train** tren *m* directo
throw [θroʊ] **1** *v/t* (*pret* ***threw***, *pp* ***thrown***) tirar; *of horse* tirar, desmontar; (*disconcert*) desconcertar; *party* dar **2** *n* lanzamiento *m*; ***it's your throw*** te toca tirar
◆ **throw away** *v/t* tirar, *L.Am.* botar
◆ **throw off** *v/t jacket etc* quitarse rápidamente; *cold etc* deshacerse de
◆ **throw on** *v/t clothes* ponerse rápidamente
◆ **throw out** *v/t old things* tirar, *L.Am.* botar; *from bar, job, home* echar; *from country* expulsar; *plan* rechazar
◆ **throw up 1** *v/t ball* lanzar hacia arriba; ***throw up one's hands*** echarse las manos a la cabeza **2** *v/i* (*vomit*) vomitar
ˈ**throw-a·way** *adj remark* insustancial, pasajero; (*disposable*) desechable
ˈ**throw-in** SP saque *m* de banda
thrown [θroʊn] *pp* → ***throw***
thru [θruː] → ***through***
thrush [θrʌʃ] *bird* zorzal *m*
thrust [θrʌst] *v/t* (*pret & pp* ***thrust***) (*push hard*) empujar; *knife* hundir; ***thrust sth into s.o.'s hands*** poner algo en las manos de alguien; ***thrust one's way through the crowd*** abrirse paso a empujones entre la multitud
thud [θʌd] *n* golpe *m* sordo
thug [θʌg] matón *m*
thumb [θʌm] **1** *n* pulgar *m* **2** *v/t*: ***thumb a ride*** hacer autoestop
thumb·tack [ˈθʌmtæk] chincheta *f*
thump [θʌmp] **1** *n blow* porrazo *m*; *noise* golpe *m* sordo **2** *v/t person* dar un porrazo a; ***thump one's fist on the table*** pegar un puñetazo en la mesa **3** *v/i of heart* latir con fuerza; ***thump on the door*** aporrear la puerta
thun·der [ˈθʌndər] *n* truenos *mpl*
thun·der·ous [ˈθʌndərəs] *adj applause* tormenta *f*
thun·der·storm [ˈθʌndərstɔːrm] tormenta *f* (*con truenos*)
ˈ**thun·der·struck** *adj* atónito
thun·der·y [ˈθʌndərɪ] *adj weather* tormentoso
Thurs·day [ˈθɜːrzdeɪ] jueves *m inv*
thus [ðʌs] *adv* (*in this way*) así
thwart [θwɔːrt] *v/t person, plans* frustrar
thyme [taɪm] tomillo *m*
thy·roid gland [ˈθaɪrɔɪdglænd] (glándula *f*) tiroides *m inv*
tick [tɪk] **1** *n of clock* tictac *m*; *in text* señal *f* de visto bueno **2** *v/i of clock* hacer tictac
tick·et [ˈtɪkɪt] *for bus, train, lottery* billete *m*, *L.Am.* boleto *m*; *for airplane* billete *m*, *L.Am.* pasaje *m*; for *theater, concert, museum* entrada *f*, *L.Am.* boleto *m*; *for speeding etc* multa *f*
ˈ**ti·cket col·lec·tor** revisor(a) *m*(*f*)
ˈ**ti·cket in·spec·tor** revisor(a) *m*(*f*)
ˈ**ti·cket ma·chine** máquina *f* expendedora de billetes
ˈ**ti·cket of·fice** *at station* mostrador *m* de venta de billetes; THEA taquilla *f*, *L.Am.* boletería *f*
tick·ing [ˈtɪkɪŋ] *noise* tictac *m*
tick·le [ˈtɪkl] **1** *v/t person* hacer cosquillas a **2** *v/i of material* hacer cosquillas; ***stop that, you're tickling!*** ¡para ya, me haces cosquillas!
tickl·ish [ˈtɪklɪʃ] *adj person* tener cosquillas
ti·dal wave [ˈtaɪdlweɪv] maremoto *m* (*ola*)
tide [taɪd] marea *f*; ***high tide*** marea alta; ***low tide*** marea baja; ***the tide is in / out*** la marea está alta / baja
◆ **tide over** *v/t*: ***20 dollars will tide me over*** 20 dólares me bastarán
ti·di·ness [ˈtaɪdɪnɪs] orden *m*
ti·dy [ˈtaɪdɪ] *adj* ordenado
◆ **tidy away** *v/t* (*pret & pp* ***tidied***) guardar
◆ **tidy up 1** *v/t room, shelves* ordenar; ***tidy o.s. up*** arreglarse **2** *v/i* recoger
tie [taɪ] **1** *n* (*necktie*) corbata *f*; SP (*even result*) empate *m*; ***he doesn't have any***

T

ties no está atado a nada **2** *v/t knot* hacer, atar; *hands* atar; ***tie two ropes together*** atar dos cuerdas **3** *v/i* SP empatar

◆ **tie down** *v/t also fig* atar

◆ **tie up** *v/t person, laces* atar; *boat* amarrar; *hair* recoger; ***I'm tied up tomorrow*** (*busy*) mañana estaré muy ocupado

tier [tɪr] *of hierarchy* nivel *m*; *in stadium* grada *f*

ti·ger ['taɪgər] tigre *m*

tight [taɪt] **1** *adj clothes* ajustado, estrecho; *security* estricto; (*hard to move*) apretado; (*properly shut*) cerrado; (*not leaving much time*) justo de tiempo; F (*drunk*) como una cuba F **2** *adv hold* fuerte; *shut* bien

tight·en ['taɪtn] *v/t screw* apretar; *control* endurecer; *security* intensificar; ***tighten one's grip on sth*** *on rope etc* asir algo con más fuerza; *on power etc* incrementar el control sobre algo

◆ **tighten up** *v/i in discipline, security* ser más estricto

tight-fist·ed [taɪt'fɪstɪd] *adj* agarrado

tight·ly ['taɪtlɪ] *adv* → ***tight***

tight·rope ['taɪtroʊp] cuerda *f* floja

tights [taɪts] *npl Br* medias *fpl*, pantis *mpl*

tile [taɪl] *on floor* baldosa *f*; *on wall* azulejo *m*; *on roof* teja *f*

till[1] [tɪl] → ***until***

till[2] [tɪl] *n* (*cash register*) caja *f* (registradora)

till[3] [tɪl] *v/t soil* labrar

tilt [tɪlt] **1** *v/t* inclinar **2** *v/i* inclinarse

tim·ber ['tɪmbər] madera *f* (de construcción)

time [taɪm] tiempo *m*; (*occasion*) vez *f*; ***time is up*** se acabó (el tiempo); ***for the time being*** por ahora, por el momento; ***have a good time*** pasarlo bien; ***have a good time!*** ¡que lo paséis bien!; ***what's the time?, do you have the time?*** ¿qué hora es?; ***the first time*** la primera vez; ***four times*** cuatro veces; ***time and again*** una y otra vez; ***all the time*** todo el rato; ***two / three at a time*** de dos en dos / de tres en tres; ***at the same time*** *speak, reply etc* a la vez; (*however*) al mismo tiempo; ***in time*** con tiempo; ***on time*** puntual; ***in no time*** en un santiamén

'**time bomb** bomba *f* de relojería

'**time clock** *in factory* reloj *m* registrador

'**time-con·sum·ing** *adj* que lleva mucho tiempo

'**time dif·fer·ence** diferencia *f* horaria

'**time-lag** intervalo *m*

'**time lim·it** plazo *m*

time·ly ['taɪmlɪ] *adj* oportuno

time out SP tiempo *m* muerto

tim·er ['taɪmər] *device* temporizador *m*; *person* cronometrador *m*

'**time·sav·ing** *n* ahorro *m* de tiempo

'**time·scale** *of project* plazo *m* (de tiempo)

'**time switch** temporizador *m*

'**time·warp** salto *m* en el tiempo

'**time zone** huso *m* horario

tim·id ['tɪmɪd] *adj* tímido

tim·ing ['taɪmɪŋ] *of dancer* sincronización *f*; *of actor* utilización *f* de las pausas y del ritmo; ***the timing of the announcement was perfect*** el anuncio due realizado en el momento perfecto

tin [tɪn] *metal* estaño *m*; *Br* (*can*) lata *f*

tin·foil ['tɪnfɔɪl] papel *m* de aluminio

tinge [tɪndʒ] *n of color, sadness* matiz *m*

tin·gle ['tɪŋgl] *n* hormigueo *m*

◆ **tin·ker with** ['tɪŋkər] *v/t* enredar con

tin·kle ['tɪŋkl] *n of bell* tintineo *m*

tin·sel ['tɪnsl] espumillón *m*

tint [tɪnt] **1** *n of color* matiz *m*; *in hair* tinte *m* **2** *v/t hair* teñir

tint·ed ['tɪntɪd] *glasses* con un tinte; *paper* coloreado

ti·ny ['taɪnɪ] *adj* diminuto, minúsculo

tip[1] [tɪp] *n of stick, finger* punta *f*; *of mountain* cumbre *f*; *of cigarette* filtro *m*

tip[2] [tɪp] **1** *n advice* consejo *m*; *money* propina *f* **2** *v/t* (*pret & pp* ***tipped***) *waiter etc* dar propina a

◆ **tip off** *v/t* avisar

◆ **tip over** *v/t jug* volcar; *liquid* derramar; ***he tipped water all over me*** derramó agua encima mío

'**tip-off** soplo *m*

tipped [tɪpt] *adj cigarettes* con filtro

Tipp-Ex® *n* Tipp-Ex *m*

tip·py-toe ['tɪpɪtoʊ]: ***on tippy-toe*** de puntillas

tip·sy ['tɪpsɪ] *adj* achispado

tire[1] [taɪr] *n* neumático *m*, *L.Am.* llanta *f*

tire[2] [taɪr] **1** *v/t* cansar, fatigar **2** *v/i* cansarse, fatigarse; ***he never tires of telling the story*** nunca se cansa de contar la historia

tired [taɪrd] *adj* cansado, fatigado; ***be tired of s.o./sth*** estar cansado de algo / de alguien

tired·ness ['taɪrdnɪs] cansancio *m*, fatiga *f*

tire·less ['taɪrlɪs] *adj efforts* incansable, infatigable

tire·some ['taɪrsəm] *adj* (*annoying*) pesado

tir·ing ['taɪrɪŋ] *adj* agotador

tis·sue ['tɪʃuː] ANAT tejido *m*; (*handkerchief*) pañuelo *m* de papel, Kleenex® *m*

'**tis·sue pa·per** papel *m* de seda

tit[1] [tɪt] *bird* herrerillo *m*

tit² [tɪt]: ***give s.o. tit for tat*** pagar a alguien con la misma moneda
tit³ [tɪt] V (*breast*) teta *f* V
ti·tle ['taɪtl] *of novel, person etc* título *m*; LAW título *m* de propiedad
'ti·tle·hold·er SP campeón(-ona) *m(f)*
tit·ter ['tɪtər] *v/i* reírse tontamente
to [tuː] *unstressed* [tə] **1** *prep* a; ***to Japan / Chicago*** a Japón / Chicago; ***let's go to my place*** vamos a mi casa; ***walk to the station*** camina a la estación; ***to the north / south of …*** al norte / sur de …; ***give sth to s.o.*** dar algo a alguien; ***from Monday to Wednesday*** de lunes a miércoles; ***from 10 to 15 people*** de 10 a 15 personas **2** *with verbs*: ***to speak, to shout*** hablar, chillar; ***learn to swim*** aprender a nadar; ***nice to eat*** sabroso; ***too heavy to carry*** demasiado pesado para llevarlo; ***to be honest with you …*** para ser sincero … **3** *adv*: ***to and fro*** de un lado para otro
toad [toʊd] sapo *m*
toad·stool ['toʊdstuːl] seta *f* venenosa
toast [toʊst] **1** *n* pan *m* tostado; *drinking* brindis *m inv*; ***propose a toast to s.o.*** proponer un brindis en honor de alguien **2** *v/t drinking* brindar por
toast·er ['toʊstər] tostador(a) *m(f)*
to·bac·co [tə'bækoʊ] tabaco *m*
to·bog·gan [tə'bɑːgən] *n* tobogán *m*
to·day [tə'deɪ] hoy
tod·dle ['tɑːdl] *v/i of child* dar los primeros pasos
tod·dler ['tɑːdlər] niño *m* pequeño
to-do [tə'duː] F revuelo *m*
toe [toʊ] **1** *n* dedo *m* del pie; *of shoe* puntera *f* **2** *v/t*: ***toe the line*** acatar la disciplina
toe·nail ['toʊneɪl] uña *f* del pie
to·geth·er [tə'geðər] *adv* juntos(-as); ***mix two drinks together*** mezclar dos bebidas; ***don't all talk together*** no hablen todos a la vez
toil [tɔɪl] *n* esfuerzo *m*
toi·let ['tɔɪlɪt] *place* cuarto *m* de baño, servicio *m*; *equipment* retrete *m*; ***go to the toilet*** ir al baño
'toil·et pa·per papel *m* higiénico
toil·et·ries ['tɔɪlɪtrɪz] *npl* artículos *mpl* de tocador
'toi·let roll rollo *m* de papel higiénico
to·ken ['toʊkən] (*sign*) muestra *f*; *for gambling* ficha *f*; (*gift token*) vale *m*
told [toʊld] *pret & pp* → ***tell***
tol·e·ra·ble ['tɑːlərəbl] *adj pain etc* soportable; (*quite good*) aceptable
tol·e·rance ['tɑːlərəns] tolerancia *f*
tol·e·rant ['tɑːlərənt] *adj* tolerante
tol·e·rate ['tɑːləreɪt] *v/t noise, person* tolerar; ***I won't tolerate it!*** ¡no lo toleraré!
toll¹ [toʊl] *v/i of bell* tañer
toll² [toʊl] *n* (*deaths*) mortandad *f*, número *m* de víctimas
toll³ [toʊl] *n for bridge, road* peaje *m*; TELEC tarifa *f*
'toll booth cabina *f* de peaje
'toll-free *adj* TELEC gratuito
'toll road carretera *f* de peaje
to·ma·to [tə'meɪtoʊ] tomate *m*, *Mex* jitomate *m*
to·ma·to 'ketch·up ketchup *m*
to·ma·to 'sauce *for pasta etc* salsa *f* de tomate
tomb [tuːm] tumba *f*
tom·boy ['tɑːmbɔɪ] niña *f* poco femenina
tomb·stone ['tuːmstoʊn] lápida *f*
tom·cat ['tɑːmkæt] gato *m*
to·mor·row [tə'mɔːroʊ] mañana; ***the day after tomorrow*** pasado mañana; ***tomorrow morning*** mañana por la mañana
ton [tʌn] tonelada *f* (*907 kg*)
tone [toʊn] *of color, conversation* tono *m*; *of musical instrument* timbre *m*; *of neighborhood* nivel *m*; ***tone of voice*** tono *m* de voz
◆ **tone down** *v/t demands, criticism* bajar el tono de
ton·er ['toʊnər] tóner *m*
tongs [tɑːŋz] *npl* tenazas *fpl*; *for hair* tenacillas *fpl* de rizar
tongue [tʌŋ] *n* lengua *f*
ton·ic ['tɑːnɪk] MED tónico *m*
'ton·ic (wa·ter) (agua *f*) tónica *f*
to·night [tə'naɪt] esta noche
ton·sil ['tɑːnsl] amígdala *f*
ton·sil·li·tis [tɑːnsə'laɪtɪs] amigdalitis *f*
too [tuː] *adv* (*also*) también; (*excessively*) demasiado; ***me too*** yo también; ***too big / hot*** demasiado grande / caliente; ***too much rice*** demasiado arroz; ***eat too much*** comer demasiado
took [tʊk] *pret* → ***take***
tool [tuːl] herramienta *f*
toot [tuːt] *v/t* F tocar
tooth [tuːθ] (*pl* ***teeth*** [tiːθ]) diente *m*
'tooth·ache dolor *m* de muelas
'tooth·brush cepillo *m* de dientes
tooth·less ['tuːθlɪs] *adj* desdentado
'tooth·paste pasta *f* de dientes, dentífrico *m*
'tooth·pick palillo *m*
top [tɑːp] **1** *n of mountain* cima *f*; *of tree* copa *f*; *of wall, screen, page* parte *f* superior; (*lid*: *of bottle etc*) tapón *m*; *of pen* capucha *f*; *clothing* camiseta *f*, top *m*; (MOT: *gear*) directa *f*; ***on top of*** encima de, sobre; ***at the top of the page*** en la

parte superior de la página; ***at the top of the mountain*** en la cumbre; ***the top of the class / league*** *person, team* ser el primero de la clase / de la liga; ***get to the top*** *of company, mountain* llegar a la cumbre; *of mountain*; ***be over the top*** (*exaggerated*) ser una exageración **2** *adj branches* superior; *floor* de arriba, último; *management, official* alto; *player* mejor; *speed, note* máximo **3** *v/t* (*pret & pp* ***topped***): ***topped with ...*** *of cake etc* con una capa de ... por encima
◆ **top up** *v/t glass, tank* llenar
top 'hat sombrero *m* de copa
top 'heav·y *adj* sobrecargado en la parte superior
top·ic ['tɑːpɪk] tema *m*
top·ic·al ['tɑːpɪkl] *adj* de actualidad
top·less ['tɑːplɪs] *adj* en topless
top·most ['tɑːpmoʊst] *adj branches, floor* superior
top·ping ['tɑːpɪŋ] *on pizza* ingrediente *m*
top·ple ['tɑːpl] **1** *v/i* derrumbarse **2** *v/t government* derrocar
top 'se·cret *adj* altamente confidencial
top·sy-tur·vy [tɑːpsɪ'tɜːrvɪ] *adj* (*in disorder*) desordenado; *world* al revés
torch [tɔːrtʃ] *with flame* antorcha *f*
tore [tɔːr] *pret* → ***tear***[1]
tor·ment 1 *n* ['tɔːrment] tormento *m* **2** *v/t* [tɔːr'ment] *person, animal* atormentar; ***tormented by doubt*** atormentado por la duda
torn [tɔːrn] *pp* → ***tear***[1]
tor·na·do [tɔːr'neɪdoʊ] tornado *m*
tor·pe·do [tɔːr'piːdoʊ] **1** *n* torpedo *m* **2** *v/t also fig* torpedear
tor·rent ['tɑːrənt] *also fig* torrente *m*; *of lava* colada *f*
tor·ren·tial [tə'renʃl] *adj rain* torrencial
tor·toise ['tɔːrtəs] tortuga *f*
tor·ture ['tɔːrtʃər] **1** *n* tortura *f* **2** *v/t* torturar
toss [tɑːs] **1** *v/t ball* lanzar, echar; *rider* desmontar; *salad* remover; ***toss a coin*** echar a cara o cruz **2** *v/i*: ***toss and turn*** dar vueltas
to·tal ['toʊtl] **1** *n* total *m* **2** *adj sum, amount* total; *disaster* rotundo, completo; *idiot* de tomo y lomo; *stranger* completo **3** *v/t* F *car* cargarse F; ***the truck was totaled*** el camión quedó destrozado
to·tal·i·tar·i·an [toʊtælɪ'terɪən] *adj* totalitario
to·tal·ly ['toʊtəlɪ] *adv* totalmente
tote bag ['toʊtbæg] bolsa *f* grande
tot·ter ['tɑːtər] *v/i of person* tambalearse
touch [tʌtʃ] **1** *n* toque *m*; *sense* tacto *m*; ***lose touch with s.o.*** perder el contacto con alguien; ***keep in touch with s.o.*** mantenerse en contacto con alguien; ***we kept in touch*** seguimos en contacto; ***be out of touch*** no estar al corriente; ***the leader was out of touch with the people*** el líder estaba desconectado de lo que pensaba la gente; ***in touch*** SP fuera **2** *v/t* tocar; *emotionally* conmover **3** *v/i* tocar; *of two lines etc* tocarse
◆ **touch down** *v/i of airplane* aterrizar; SP marca un ensayo
◆ **touch on** *v/t* (*mention*) tocar, mencionar
◆ **touch up** *v/t photo* retocar; *sexually* manosear
touch·down ['tʌtʃdaʊn] *of airplane* aterrizaje *m*; SP touchdown *m*, ensayo *m*
touch·ing ['tʌtʃɪŋ] *adj* conmovedor
touch·line ['tʌtʃlaɪn] SP línea *f* de banda
'touch screen pantalla *f* tactíl
touch·y ['tʌtʃɪ] *adj person* susceptible
tough [tʌf] *adj person, meat, punishment* duro; *question, exam* difícil; *material* resistente, fuerte
◆ **tough·en up** ['tʌfn] *v/t person* hacer más fuerte
'tough guy F tipo *m* duro F
tour [tʊr] **1** *n of museum etc* recorrido *m*; *of area* viaje *m* (**of** por); *of band ecc* gira *f* **2** *v/t area* recorrer **3** *v/i of band etc* estar de gira
'tour guide guía *m/f* turístico(-a)
tour·i·sm ['tʊrɪzm] turismo *m*
tour·i·st ['tʊrɪst] turista *m/f*
'tour·ist at·trac·tion atracción *f* turística
'tour·ist in·dus·try industria *f* turística
'tour·i·st (in·for'ma·tion) of·fice oficina *f* de turismo
'tour·ist sea·son temporada *f* turística
tour·na·ment ['tʊrnəmənt] torneo *m*
'tour op·er·a·tor operador *m* turístico
tous·led ['taʊzld] *adj hair* revuelto
tow [toʊ] **1** *v/t car, boat* remolcar **2** *n*: ***give s.o. a tow*** remolcar a alguien
◆ **tow away** *v/t car* llevarse
to·ward [tɔːrd] *prep* hacia; ***we are working toward a solution*** estamos intentando encontrar una solución
tow·el ['taʊəl] toalla *f*
tow·er ['taʊər] *n* torre *m*
◆ **tower over** *v/t of building* elevarse por encima de; *of person* ser mucho más alto que
town [taʊn] ciudad *f*
town 'cen·ter centro *m* de la ciudad / del pueblo
town 'coun·cil ayuntamiento *m*
town 'hall ayuntamiento *m*
'tow·rope cuerda *f* para remolcar

tox·ic ['tɑːksɪk] *adj* tóxico
tox·ic 'waste residuos *mpl* tóxicos
tox·in ['tɑːksɪn] BIO toxina *f*
toy [tɔɪ] juguete *m*
'toy store juguetería *f*, tienda *f* de juguetes
◆ **toy with** *v/t object* juguetear con; *idea* darle vueltas a
trace [treɪs] **1** *n of substance* resto *m* **2** *v/t* (*find*) localizar; (*follow: footsteps of*) seguir el rastro a; (*draw*) trazar
track [træk] *n* (*path*) senda *f*, camino; *for horses* hipódromo *m*; *for dogs* canódromo *m*; *for cars* circuito *m*; *for athletics* pista *f*; *on CD* canción *f*, corte *m*; RAIL vía *f*; ***track 10*** RAIL via 10; ***keep track of sth*** llevar la cuenta de algo
◆ **track down** *v/t* localizar
'track·suit chándal *m*
trac·tor ['træktər] tractor *m*
trade [treɪd] **1** *n* (*commerce*) comercio *m*; (*profession, craft*) oficio *m* **2** *v/i* (*do business*) comerciar; ***trade in sth*** comerciar en algo **3** *v/t* (*exchange*) intercambiar; ***trade sth for sth*** intercambiar algo por algo
◆ **trade in** *v/t when buying* entregar como parte del pago
'trade fair feria *f* de muestras
'trade·mark marca *f* registrada
'trade mis·sion misión *f* comercial
trad·er ['treɪdər] comerciante *m*
trade 'se·cret secreto *m* de la casa, secreto *m* comercial
trades·man ['treɪdzmən] (*plumber etc*) *electricista, fontanero / plomero etc*
tra·di·tion [trə'dɪʃn] tradición *f*
tra·di·tion·al [trə'dɪʃnl] *adj* tradicional
tra·di·tion·al·ly [trə'dɪʃnlɪ] *adv* tradicionalmente
traf·fic ['træfɪk] *n on roads, in drugs* tráfico *m*
◆ **traffic in** *v/t* (*pret & pp* ***trafficked***) *drugs* traficar con
'traf·fic cir·cle rotonda *f*, *Span* glorieta
'traf·fic cop F poli *m* de tráfico F
'traf·fic is·land isleta *f*
'traf·fic jam atasco *m*
'traf·fic light semáforo *m*
'traf·fic po·lice policía *f* de tráfico
'traf·fic sign señal *f* de tráfico
tra·ge·dy ['trædʒədɪ] tragedia *f*
tra·gic ['trædʒɪk] *adj* tragico
trail [treɪl] **1** *n* (*path*) camino *m*, senda *f*; *of blood* rastro *m* **2** *v/t* (*follow*) seguir la pista de; (*tow*) arrastrar **3** *v/i* (*lag behind*) ir a la zaga
trail·er ['treɪlər] *pulled by vehicle* remolque *m*; (*mobile home*) caravana *f*; *of film* avance *m*, tráiler *m*
train¹ [treɪn] *n* tren *m*; ***go by train*** ir en tren
train² [treɪn] **1** *v/t team, athlete* entrenar; *employee* formar; *dog* adiestrar **2** *v/i of team, athlete* entrenarse; *of teacher etc* formarse
train·ee [treɪ'niː] aprendiz(a) *m*(*f*)
train·er ['treɪnər] SP entrenador(a) *m*(*f*); *of dog* adiestrador(a) *m*(*f*)
train·ers ['treɪnərz] *npl Br shoes* zapatillas *fpl* de deporte
train·ing [treɪnɪŋ] *of new staff* formación *f*; SP entrenamiento *m*; ***be in training*** SP estar entrenándose; ***be out of training*** SP estar desentrenado
'train·ing course cursillo *m* de formación
'train·ing scheme plan *m* de formación
'train sta·tion estación *f* de tren
trait [treɪt] rasgo *m*
trai·tor ['treɪtər] traidor(a) *m*(*f*)
tramp [træmp] **1** *n* (*vagabond*) vagabundo(-a) *m*(*f*) **2** *v/i* caminar con pasos pesados
tram·ple ['træmpl] *v/t* pisotear; ***be trampled to death*** morir pisoteado; ***be trampled underfoot*** ser pisoteado
◆ **trample on** *v/t person, object* pisotear
tram·po·line ['træmpəliːn] cama *f* elástica
trance [træns] trance *m*; ***go into a trance*** entrar en trance
tran·quil ['træŋkwɪl] *adj* tranquilo
tran·quil·i·ty [træŋ'kwɪlətɪ] tranquilidad *f*
tran·quil·iz·er ['træŋkwɪlaɪzər] tranquilizante *m*
trans·act [træn'zækt] *v/t deal* negociar
trans·ac·tion [træn'zækʃn] *action* transacción *f*; *deal* negociación *f*
trans·at·lan·tic [trænzət'læntɪk] *adj* transatlántico
tran·scen·den·tal [trænsen'dentl] *adj* trascendental
tran·script ['trænskrɪpt] transcripción *f*
trans·fer **1** *v/t* [træns'fɜːr] (*pret & pp* ***transferred***) transferir **2** *v/i* (*pret & pp* ***transferred***) *in traveling* hacer transbordo; *from one language to another* pasar **3** *n* ['trænsfɜːr] transferencia *f*; *in travel* transbordo *m*; *of money* transferencia *f*
trans·fer·a·ble [træns'fɜːrəbl] *adj ticket* transferible
'trans·fer fee *for football player* traspaso *m*
trans·form [træns'fɔːrm] *v/t* transformar
trans·form·a·tion [trænsfər'meɪʃn] transformación *f*
trans·form·er [træns'fɔːrmər] ELEC transformador *m*
trans·fu·sion [træns'fjuːʒn] transfusión *f*

tran·sis·tor [træn'zɪstər] transistor *m*; (*radio*) transistor *m*, radio *m* transistor
tran·sit ['trænzɪt]: ***in transit*** en tránsito
tran·si·tion [træn'sɪʒn] transición *f*
tran·si·tion·al [træn'sɪʒnl] *adj* de transición
'**tran·sit lounge** *at airport* sala *f* de tránsito
'**trans·it pas·sen·ger** pasajero *m* en tránsito
trans·late [træns'leɪt] *v/t & v/i* traducir
trans·la·tion [træns'leɪʃn] traducción *f*
trans·la·tor [træns'leɪtər] traductor(a) *m*(*f*)
trans·mis·sion [trænz'mɪʃn] *of news, program* emisión *f*; *of disease* transmisión *f*; MOT transmisión *f*
trans·mit [trænz'mɪt] *v/t* (*pret & pp* ***transmitted***) *news, program* emitir; *disease* transmitir
trans·mit·ter [trænz'mɪtər] *for radio*, TV emisora *f*
trans·par·en·cy [træns'pærənsɪ] PHOT diapositiva *f*
trans·par·ent [træns'pærənt] *adj* transparente; (*obvious*) obvio
trans·plant 1 *v/t* [træns'plænt] MED transplantar **2** *n* ['trænsplænt] MED transplante *m*
trans·port 1 *v/t* [træn'spɔːrt] *goods, people* transportar **2** *n* ['trænspɔːrt] *of goods, people* transporte *m*
trans·por·ta·tion [trænspɔːr'teɪʃn] *of goods, people* transporte *m*; ***means of transportation*** medio *m* de transporte; ***public transportation*** transporte *m* público; ***Department of Transportation*** Ministerio *m* de Transporte
trans·ves·tite [træns'vestaɪt] travestí *m*, travestido *m*
trap [træp] **1** *n* trampa *f*; ***set a trap for s.o.*** tender una trampa a alguien **2** *v/t* (*pret & pp* ***trapped***) atrapar; ***be trapped*** *by enemy, flames, landslide etc* quedar atrapado
trap·door ['træpdɔːr] trampilla *f*
tra·peze [trə'piːz] trapecio *m*
trap·pings ['træpɪŋz] *npl of power* parafernalia *f*
trash [træʃ] (*garbage*) basura *f*; (*poor product*) bazofia *f*; (*despicable person*) escoria *f*
trash·can [træʃkæn] cubo *m* de la basura
trash·y [træʃɪ] *adj goods, novel* barato
trau·mat·ic [trə'mætɪk] *adj* traumático
trau·ma·tize ['traʊmətaɪz] *v/t* traumatizar
trav·el ['trævl] **1** *n* viajes *mpl*; ***do you like travel?*** ¿te gusta viajar?; ***on my travels*** en mis viajes **2** *v/i* (*pret & pp* ***traveled***, *Br* ***travelled***) viajar **3** *v/t miles* viajar, recorrer
'**trav·el a·gen·cy** agencia *f* de viajes
'**trav·el a·gent** agente *m* de viajes
'**trav·el bag** bolsa *f* de viaje
trav·el·er, *Br* **trav·el·ler** ['trævələr] viajero(-a) *m*(*f*)
'**trav·el·er's check**, *Br* '**trav·el·ler's cheque** cheque *m* de viaje
'**trav·el ex·penses** *npl* gastos *mpl* de viaje
'**trav·el in·sur·ance** seguro *m* de asistencia en viaje
'**trav·el pro·gram**, *Br* '**trav·el programme** *on* TV *etc* programa *m* de viajes
'**trav·el·sick** *adj* mareado
trawl·er ['trɒːlər] (barco *m*) arrastrero *m*
tray [treɪ] bandeja *f*
treach·er·ous ['tretʃərəs] *adj* traicionero
treach·er·y ['tretʃərɪ] traición *f*
tread [tred] **1** *n* pasos *mpl*; *of staircase* huella *f* (del peldaño); *of tyre* dibujo *m* **2** *v/i* (*pret* ***trod***, *pp* ***trodden***) andar; ***mind where you tread*** cuida dónde pisas
◆ **tread on** *v/t s.o.'s foot* pisar
trea·son ['triːzn] traición *f*
trea·sure ['treʒər] **1** *n* tesoro *m*; *person* tesoro *m* **2** *v/t gift etc* apreciar mucho
trea·sur·er ['treʒərər] tesorero(-a) *m*(*f*)
Trea·sur·y De·part·ment ['treʒərɪ] Ministerio *m* de Hacienda
treat [triːt] **1** *n* placer; ***it was a real treat*** fue un auténtico placer; ***I have a treat for you*** tengo una sorpresa agradable para ti; ***it's my treat*** (*I'm paying*) yo invito **2** *v/t* tratar; ***treat s.o. to sth*** invitar a alguien a algo
treat·ment ['triːtmənt] tratamiento *m*
treat·y ['triːtɪ] tratado *m*
tre·ble[1] ['trebl] *n* MUS soprano *m*
tre·ble[2] ['trebl] **1** *adv*: ***treble the price*** el triple del precio **2** *v/i* triplicarse
tree [triː] árbol *m*
trem·ble ['trembl] *v/i* temblar
tre·men·dous [trɪ'mendəs] *adj* (*very good*) estupendo; (*enormous*) enorme
tre·men·dous·ly [trɪ'mendəslɪ] *adv* (*very*) tremendamente; (*a lot*) enormemente
trem·or ['tremər] *of earth* temblor *m*
trench [trentʃ] trinchera *f*
trend [trend] tendencia *f*; (*fashion*) moda *f*
trend·y ['trendɪ] *adj* de moda; *views* moderno
tres·pass ['trespæs] *v/i* entrar sin autorización; ***no trespassing*** prohibido el paso
◆ **trespass on** *v/t s.o.'s land* entrar sin autorización en; *s.o.'s privacy* entrometerse en

tres·pass·er ['trespæsər] intruso(-a) *m(f)*
tri·al ['traɪəl] LAW juicio *m*; *of equipment* prueba *f*; ***be on trial*** LAW estar siendo juzgado; ***have sth on trial*** *equipment* tener algo a prueba
tri·al 'pe·ri·od periodo *m* de prueba
tri·an·gle ['traɪæŋgl] triángulo *m*
tri·an·gu·lar [traɪ'æŋgjʊlər] *adj* triangular
tribe [traɪb] tribu *f*
tri·bu·nal [traɪ'bjuːnl] tribunal *m*
tri·bu·ta·ry ['trɪbjəterɪ] *of river* afluente *m*
trick [trɪk] **1** *n* (*to deceive*, *knack*) truco *m*; ***play a trick on s.o.*** gastar una broma a alguien **2** *v/t* engañar; ***trick s.o. into doing sth*** engañar a alguien para que haga algo
trick·e·ry ['trɪkərɪ] engaños *mpl*
trick·le ['trɪkl] **1** *n* hilo *m*, reguero *m*; *fig*: *of money* goteo *m* **2** *v/i* gotear, escurrir
trick·ster ['trɪkstər] embaucador(a) *m(f)*
trick·y ['trɪkɪ] *adj* (*difficult*) difícil
tri·cy·cle ['traɪsɪkl] triciclo *m*
tri·fle ['traɪfl] *n* (*triviality*) nadería *f*
tri·fling ['traɪflɪŋ] *adj* insignificante
trig·ger ['trɪgər] *n on gun* gatillo *m*; *on camcorder* disparador *m*
◆ **trigger off** *v/t* desencadenar
trim [trɪm] **1** *adj* (*neat*) muy cuidado; *figure* delgado **2** *v/t* (*pret & pp* ***trimmed***) *hair, hedge* recortar; *budget, costs* recortar, reducir; (*decorate*: *dress*) adornar **3** *n* (*light cut*) recorte *m*; ***just a trim, please*** *to hairdresser* corte sólo las puntas, por favor; ***in good trim*** en buenas condiciones
trim·ming ['trɪmɪŋ] *on clothes* adorno *m*; ***with all the trimmings*** *dish* con la guarnición clásica; *car* con todos los extras
trin·ket ['trɪŋkɪt] baratija *f*
tri·o ['triːoʊ] MUS trío *m*
trip [trɪp] **1** *n* (*journey*) viaje *m* **2** *v/i* (*pret & pp* ***tripped***) (*stumble*) tropezar **3** *v/t* (*pret & pp* ***tripped***) (*make fall*) poner la zancadilla a
◆ **trip up 1** *v/t* (*make fall*) poner la zancadilla a; (*cause to go wrong*) confundir **2** *v/i* (*stumble*) tropezar; (*make a mistake*) equivocarse
tripe [traɪp] mondongo *m*, *Span* callos *mpl*
trip·le ['trɪpl] → ***treble***[2]
trip·lets ['trɪplɪts] *npl* trillizos *mpl*
tri·pod ['traɪpɑːd] PHOT trípode *m*
trite [traɪt] *adj* manido
tri·umph ['traɪʌmf] *n* triunfo *m*
triv·i·al ['trɪvɪəl] *adj* trivial
triv·i·al·i·ty [trɪvɪ'ælətɪ] trivialidad *f*
trod [trɑːd] *pret* → ***tread***
trod·den ['trɑːdn] *pp* → ***tread***
trol·ley ['trɑːlɪ] (*streetcar*) tranvía *f*
trol·ley·bus ['trɑːlɪbʌs] trolebús *m*
trom·bone [trɑːm'boʊn] trombón *m*
troops [truːps] *npl* tropas *fpl*
tro·phy ['troʊfɪ] trofeo *m*
tro·pic ['trɑːpɪk] trópico *m*
trop·i·cal ['trɑːpɪkl] *adj* tropical
trop·ics ['trɑːpɪks] *npl* trópicos *mpl*
trot [trɑːt] *v/i* (*pret & pp* ***trotted***) trotar
trou·ble ['trʌbl] **1** *n* (*difficulties*) problema *m*, problemas *mpl*; (*inconvenience*) molestia *f*; (*disturbance*) conflicto *m*, desorden *m*; ***go to a lot of trouble to do sth*** complicarse mucho la vida para hacer algo; ***no trouble!*** no es molestia; ***get into trouble*** meterse en líos **2** *v/t* (*worry*) preocupar, inquietar; (*bother, disturb*) molestar
'trou·ble-free *adj* sin complicaciones
'trou·ble·mak·er alborotador(a) *m(f)*
'trou·ble·shoot·er (*mediator*) *persona encargada de resolver problemas*
'trou·ble·shoot·ing resolución *f* de problemas
trou·ble·some ['trʌblsəm] *adj* problemático
trou·sers ['traʊzərz] *npl* pantalones *mpl*
trout [traʊt] (*pl* ***trout***) trucha *f*
tru·ant ['truːənt]: ***play truant*** hacer novillos, *Mex* irse de pinta, *S. Am.* hacerse la rabona
truce [truːs] tregua *f*
truck [trʌk] camión *m*
'truck driv·er camionero(-a) *m(f)*
'truck farm huerta *f*
'truck farm·er horticultor(a) *m(f)*
'truck stop restaurante *m* de carretera
trudge [trʌdʒ] **1** *v/i* caminar fatigosamente **2** *n* caminata *f*
true [truː] *adj* verdadero, cierto; *friend, American* auténtico; ***come true*** *of hopes, dream* hacerse realidad
trul·y ['truːlɪ] *adv* verdaderamente, realmente; ***Yours truly*** le saluda muy atentamente
trum·pet ['trʌmpɪt] trompeta *f*
trum·pet·er ['trʌmpɪtər] trompetista *m/f*
trunk [trʌŋk] *of tree, body* tronco *m*; *of elephant* trompa *f*; (*large case*) baúl *m*; *of car* maletero *m*, *C.Am.*, *Mex* cajuela *f*, *Rpl* baúl *m*
trunks [trʌŋks] *npl Br for swimming* bañador *m*
trust [trʌst] **1** *n* confianza *f*; FIN fondo *m* de inversión **2** *v/t* confiar en
trusted ['trʌstɪd] *adj* de confianza
trust·ee [trʌs'tiː] fideicomisario(-a) *m(f)*

T

trust·ful, trust·ing ['trʌstfʊl, 'trʌstɪŋ] *adj* confiado
trust·wor·thy ['trʌstwɜːrðɪ] *adj* de confianza
truth [truːθ] verdad *f*
truth·ful ['truːθfəl] *adj person* sincero; *account* verdadero
try [traɪ] **1** *v/t* (*pret & pp* ***tried***) probar; LAW juzgar; ***try to do sth*** intentar hacer algo, tratar de hacer algo **2** *v/i* (*pret & pp* ***tried***): ***he didn't even try*** ni siquiera lo intentó; ***you must try harder*** debes esforzarte más **3** *n* intento *m*; ***can I have a try?*** *of food* ¿puedo probar?; *at doing sth* ¿puedo intentarlo?
◆ **try on** *v/t clothes* probar
◆ **try out** *v/t new machine, new method* probar
try·ing ['traɪɪŋ] *adj* (*annoying*) molesto, duro
T-shirt ['tiːʃɜːrt] camiseta *f*
tub [tʌb] (*bath*) bañera *f*, *L.Am.* tina *f*; *for liquid* cuba *f*; *for yoghurt, ice cream* envase *m*
tub·by ['tʌbɪ] *adj* rechoncho
tube [tuːb] tubo *m*
tube·less ['tuːblɪs] *adj tire* sin cámara de aire
tu·ber·cu·lo·sis [tuːbɜːrkjə'loʊsɪs] tuberculosis *f*
tuck [tʌk] **1** *n in dress* pinza *f* **2** *v/t* (*put*) meter
◆ **tuck away** *v/t* (*put away*) guardar; F (*eat quickly*) zamparse F
◆ **tuck in 1** *v/t children* arropar; *sheets* remeter **2** *v/i* (*start eating*) ponerse a comer
◆ **tuck up** *v/t sleeves etc* remangar; ***tuck s.o. up in bed*** meter a alguien en la cama
Tues·day ['tuːzdeɪ] martes *m inv*
tuft [tʌft] *of hair* mechón *m*; *of grass* mata *f*
tug [tʌg] **1** *n* (*pull*) tirón *m*; NAUT remolcador *m* **2** *v/t* (*pret & pp* ***tugged***) (*pull*) tirar de
tu·i·tion [tuː'ɪsn] clases *fpl*
tu·lip ['tuːlɪp] tulipán *m*
tum·ble ['tʌmbl] *v/i* caer, caerse
tum·ble·down ['tʌmbldaʊn] *adj* destartalado
tum·ble-dry·er ['tʌmbldraɪr] secadora *f*
tum·bler ['tʌmblər] *for drink* vaso *m*; *in circus* acróbata *m/f*
tum·my ['tʌmɪ] F tripa *f* F, barriga *f* F
'tum·my ache dolor *m* de tripa *or* barriga
tu·mor ['tuːmər] tumor *m*
tu·mult ['tuːmʌlt] tumulto *m*
tu·mul·tu·ous [tuː'mʌltʃʊəs] *adj* tumultuoso
tu·na ['tuːnə] atún *m*

T

tune [tuːn] **1** *n* melodía *f*; ***be in tune*** *of instrument* estar afinado; ***sing in tune*** cantar sin desafinar; ***be out of tune*** *of singer* desafinar; *of instrument* estar desafinado **2** *v/t instrument* afinar
◆ **tune in** *v/i Radio*, TV sintonizar
◆ **tune in to** *v/t Radio*, TV sintonizar (con)
◆ **tune up 1** *v/i of orchestra, players* afinar **2** *v/t engine* poner a punto
tune·ful ['tuːnfəl] *adj* melodioso
tun·er ['tuːnər] *hi-fi* sintonizador *m*
tune-up ['tuːnʌp] *of engine* puesta *f* a punto
tun·nel ['tʌnl] *n* túnel *m*
tur·bine ['tɜːrbaɪn] turbina *f*
tur·bu·lence ['tɜːrbjələns] *in air travel* turbulencia *f*
tur·bu·lent ['tɜːrbjələnt] *adj* turbulento
turf [tɜːrf] césped *m*; *piece* tepe *m*
Turk [tɜːrk] turco(-a) *m*(*f*)
Tur·key ['tɜːrkɪ] Turquía
tur·key ['tɜːrkɪ] pavo *m*
Turk·ish ['tɜːrkɪʃ] **1** *adj* turco **2** *n language* turco *m*
tur·moil ['tɜːrmɔɪl] desorden *m*, agitación *f*
turn [tɜːrn] **1** *n* (*rotation*) vuelta *f*; *in road* curva *f*; *junction* giro *m*; *in vaudeville* número *m*; ***take turns in doing sth*** turnarse para hacer algo; ***it's my turn*** me toca a mí; ***it's not your turn yet*** no te toca todavía; ***take a turn at the wheel*** turnarse para conducir *or L.Am.* manejar; ***do s.o. a good turn*** hacer un favor a alguien **2** *v/t wheel* girar; *corner* dar la vuelta a; ***turn one's back on s.o.*** dar la espalda a alguien **3** *v/i of driver, car, wheel* girar; *of person*: *turn around* volverse; ***turn left / right here*** gira aquí a la izquierda/a la derecha; ***it has turned sour / cold*** se ha cortado / enfriado; ***it turned blue*** se volvió *or* puso azul; ***he has turned 40*** ha cumplido cuarenta años
◆ **turn around 1** *v/t object* dar la vuelta a; *company* dar un vuelco a; (COM: *deal with*) procesar, preparar **2** *v/i of person* volverse, darse la vuelta; *of driver* dar la vuelta
◆ **turn away 1** *v/t* (*send away*) rechazar; ***the doorman turned us away*** el portero no nos dejó entrar **2** *v/i* (*walk away*) marcharse; (*look away*) desviar la mirada
◆ **turn back 1** *v/t edges, sheets* doblar **2** *v/i of walkers etc* volver; *in course of action* echarse atrás
◆ **turn down** *v/t offer, invitation* rechazar; *volume*, TV, *heating* bajar; *edge, collar* doblar

◆ **turn in 1** *v/i* (*go to bed*) irse a dormir **2** *v/t to police* entregar
◆ **turn off 1** *v/t* TV, *engine* apagar; *tap* cerrar; *heater* apagar; ***it turns me off*** F *sexually* me quita las ganas F **2** *v/i of car, driver* doblar
◆ **turn on 1** *v/t* TV, *engine*, *heating* encender, *L.Am.* prender; *tap* abrir; F *sexually* excitar F **2** *v/i of machine* encenderse, *L.Am.* prenderse
◆ **turn out 1** *v/t lights* apagar **2** *v/i*: ***it turned out well*** salió bien; ***as it turned out*** al final; ***he turned out to be …*** resultó ser …
◆ **turn over 1** *v/i in bed* darse la vuelta; *of vehicle* volcar, dar una vuelta de campana **2** *v/t* (*put upside down*) dar la vuelta a; *page* pasar; FIN facturar
◆ **turn up 1** *v/t collar* subirse; *volume, heating* subir **2** *v/i* (*arrive*) aparecer
turn·ing ['tɜːrnɪŋ] giro *m*
'**turn·ing point** punto *m* de inflexión
tur·nip ['tɜːrnɪp] nabo *m*
'**turn·out** *of people* asistencia *f*
'**turn·o·ver** FIN facturación *f*; ***staff turnover*** rotación *f* de personal
'**turn·pike** autopista *f* de peaje
'**turn sig·nal** *on car* intermitente *m*
'**turn·stile** torniquete *m* (*de entrada*)
'**turn·ta·ble** *of record player* plato *m*,
tur·quoise ['tɜːrkwɔɪz] *adj* turquesa
tur·ret ['tʌrɪt] *of castle* torrecilla *f*; *of tank* torreta *f*
tur·tle ['tɜːrtl] tortuga *f* (marina)
tur·tle·neck 'sweater suéter *m* de cuello alto
tusk [tʌsk] colmillo *m*
tu·tor ['tuːtər] *at university* tutor *m*; ***(private) tutor*** profesor(a) *m*(*f*) particular
tu·xe·do [tʌk'siːdoʊ] esmoquin *m*
TV [tiː'viː] televisión *f*; ***on TV*** en la televisión
T'V din·ner menú *m* precocinado
T'V guide guía *f* televisiva
T'V pro·gram programa *m* de televisión
twang [twæŋ] **1** *n in voice* entonación *f* nasal **2** *v/t guitar string* puntear
tweez·ers ['twiːzərz] *npl* pinzas *fpl*
twelfth [twelfθ] *n & adj* duodécimo
twelve [twelv] doce
twen·ti·eth ['twentɪɪθ] *n & adj* vigésimo
twen·ty ['twentɪ] veinte
twice [twaɪs] *adv* dos veces; ***twice as much*** el doble
twid·dle ['twɪdl] *v/t* dar vueltas a; ***twiddle one's thumbs*** holgazanear
twig [twɪg] *n* ramita *f*
twi·light ['twaɪlaɪt] crepúsculo *m*
twin [twɪn] gemelo *m*
'**twin beds** *npl* camas *fpl* gemelas
twinge [twɪndʒ] *of pain* punzada *f*
twin·kle ['twɪŋkl] *v/i of stars* parpadeo *m*; *of eyes* brillo *m*
twin 'room habitación *f* con camas gemelas
'**twin town** ciudad *f* hermana
twirl [twɜːrl] **1** *v/t* hacer girar **2** *n of cream etc* voluta *f*
twist [twɪst] **1** *v/t* retorcer; ***twist one's ankle*** torcerse el tobillo **2** *v/i of road, river* serpentear **3** *n in rope, road* vuelta *f*; *in plot, story* giro *m* inesperado
twist·y ['twɪstɪ] *adj road* serpenteante
twit [twɪt] F memo(-a) *m*(*f*) F
twitch [twɪʧ] **1** *n nervous* tic *m* **2** *v/i* (*jerk*) moverse (ligeramente)
twit·ter ['twɪtər] *v/i of birds* gorjear
two [tuː] dos; ***the two of them*** los dos, ambos
two-faced ['tuːfeɪst] *adj* falso
'**two-piece** (*woman's suit*) traje *m*
'**two-stroke** *adj engine* de dos tiempos
two-way 'traf·fic tráfico *m* en dos direcciones
ty·coon [taɪ'kuːn] magnate *m*
type [taɪp] **1** *n* (*sort*) tipo *m*, clase *f*; ***what type of …?*** ¿qué tipo *or* clase de …? **2** *v/i* (*use a keyboard*) escribir a máquina **3** *v/t with a typewriter* mecanografiar, escribir a máquina
type·writ·er ['taɪpraɪtər] máquina *f* de escribir
ty·phoid ['taɪfɔɪd] fiebre *f* tifoidea
ty·phoon [taɪ'fuːn] tifón *m*
ty·phus ['taɪfəs] tifus *m*
typ·i·cal ['tɪpɪkl] *adj* típico; ***that's typical of you / him!*** ¡típico tuyo / de él!
typ·i·cal·ly ['tɪpɪklɪ] *adv* típicamente; ***typically American*** típicamente americano
typ·ist ['taɪpɪst] mecanógrafo(-a) *m*(*f*)
ty·ran·ni·cal [tɪ'rænɪkl] *adj* tiránico
ty·ran·nize ['tɪrənaɪz] *v/t* tiranizar
ty·ran·ny ['tɪrənɪ] tiranía *f*
ty·rant ['taɪrənt] tirano(-a) *m*(*f*)
tyre *Br* → ***tire***[1]

U

ug·ly ['ʌglɪ] *adj* feo

UK [juː'keɪ] *abbr* (= ***United Kingdom***) RU *m* (= Reino *m* Unido)

ul·cer ['ʌlsər] úlcera *f*; *in mouth* llaga *f*

ul·ti·mate ['ʌltɪmət] *adj* (*final*) final; (*basic*) esencial; ***the ultimate car*** (*best, definitive*) lo último en coches

ul·ti·mate·ly ['ʌltɪmətlɪ] *adv* (*in the end*) en última instancia

ul·ti·ma·tum [ʌltɪ'meɪtəm] ultimátum *m*

ul·tra·sound ['ʌltrəsaʊnd] MED ultrasonido *m*; (*scan*) ecografía *f*

ul·travi·o·let [ʌltrə'vaɪələt] *adj* ultravioleta

um·bil·i·cal cord [ʌm'bɪlɪkl] cordón *m* umbilical

um·brel·la [ʌm'brelə] paraguas *m inv*

um·pire ['ʌmpaɪr] *n* árbitro *m*; *in tennis* juez *m/f* de silla

ump·teen [ʌmp'tiːn] *adj* F miles de F

UN [juː'en] *abbr* (= ***United Nations***) ONU *f* (= Organización *f* de las Naciones Unidas)

un·a·ble [ʌn'eɪbl] *adj*: ***be unable to do sth*** (*not know how to*) no saber hacer algo; (*not be in a position to*) no poder hacer algo

un·ac·cept·a·ble [ʌnək'septəbl] *adj* inaceptable; ***it is unacceptable that*** es inaceptable que

un·ac·count·a·ble [ʌnə'kaʊntəbl] *adj* inexplicable

un·ac·cus·tomed [ʌnə'kʌstəmd] *adj*: ***be unaccustomed to sth*** no estar acostumbrado a algo

un·a·dul·ter·at·ed [ʌnə'dʌltəreɪtɪd] *adj* (*fig: absolute*) absoluto

un-A·mer·i·can [ʌnə'merɪkən] *adj* poco americano; *activities* antiamericano

u·nan·i·mous [juː'nænɪməs] *adj verdict* unánime; ***be unanimous on*** ser unánime respecto a

u·nan·i·mous·ly [juː'nænɪməslɪ] *adv vote, decide* unánimemente

un·ap·proach·a·ble [ʌnə'proʊʧəbl] *adj person* inaccesible

un·armed [ʌn'ɑːrmd] *adj person* desarmado; ***unarmed combat*** combate *m* sin armas

un·as·sum·ing [ʌnə'suːmɪŋ] *adj* sin pretensiones

un·at·tached [ʌnə'tæʧt] *adj* (*without a partner*) sin compromiso, sin pareja

un·at·tend·ed [ʌnə'tendɪd] *adj* desatendido; ***leave sth unattended*** dejar algo desatendido

un·au·thor·ized [ʌn'ɒːθəraɪzd] *adj* no autorizado

un·a·void·a·ble [ʌnə'vɔɪdəbl] *adj* inevitable

un·a·void·a·bly [ʌnə'vɔɪdəblɪ] *adv*: ***be unavoidably detained*** entretenerse sin poder evitarlo

un·a·ware [ʌnə'wer] *adj*: ***be unaware of*** no ser consciente de

un·a·wares [ʌnə'werz] *adv* desprevenido; ***catch s.o. unawares*** agarrar *or Span* coger a alguien desprevenido

un·bal·anced [ʌn'bælənst] *adj also* PSYCH desequilibrado

un·bear·a·ble [ʌn'berəbl] *adj* insoportable

un·beat·a·ble [ʌn'biːtəbl] *adj team* invencible; *quality* insuperable

un·beat·en [ʌn'biːtn] *adj team* invicto

un·be·knownst [ʌnbɪ'noʊnst] *adj*: ***unbeknownst to her*** sin que ella lo supiera

un·be·lie·va·ble [ʌnbɪ'liːvəbl] *adj also* F increíble; ***he's unbelievable*** F (*very good / bad*) es increíble

un·bi·as(s)ed [ʌn'baɪəst] *adj* imparcial

un·block [ʌn'blɑːk] *v/t pipe* desatascar

un·born [ʌn'bɔːrn] *adj* no nacido

un·break·a·ble [ʌn'breɪkəbl] *adj plates* irrompible; *world record* inalcanzable

un·but·ton [ʌn'bʌtn] *v/t* desabotonar

un·called-for [ʌn'kɒːldfɔːr] *adj*: ***be uncalled-for*** estar fuera de lugar

un·can·ny [ʌn'kænɪ] *adj resemblance* increíble, asombroso; *skill* inexplicable; (*worrying: feeling*) extraño, raro

un·ceas·ing [ʌn'siːsɪŋ] *adj* incesante

un·cer·tain [ʌn'sɜːrtn] *adj future, origins* incierto; ***be uncertain about sth*** no estar seguro de algo; ***what will happen? - it's uncertain*** ¿qué ocurrirá? - no se sabe

un·cer·tain·ty [ʌn'sɜːrtntɪ] incertidumbre *f*; ***there is still uncertainty about his health*** todavía hay incertidumbre en torno a su estado de salud

un·checked [ʌn'ʧekt] *adj*: ***let sth go unchecked*** no controlar algo

un·cle ['ʌŋkl] tío *m*

un·com·for·ta·ble [ʌn'kʌmftəbl] *adj chair, hotel* incómodo; ***feel uncomfortable about sth*** *about decision etc* sentirse incómodo con algo; ***I feel uncomfortable with him*** me siento incómodo con él

un·com·mon [ʌn'kɑːmən] *adj* poco corriente, raro; ***it's not uncommon*** no es raro *or* extraño

un·com·pro·mis·ing [ʌn'kɑːmprəmaɪzɪŋ] *adj* inflexible

un·con·cerned [ʌnkən'sɜːrnd] *adj* indiferente; ***be unconcerned about s.o./sth*** no preocuparse por alguien / algo

un·con·di·tion·al [ʌnkən'dɪʃnl] *adj* incondicional

un·con·scious [ʌn'kɑːnʃəs] *adj* MED, PSYCH inconsciente; ***knock unconscious*** dejar inconsciente; ***be unconscious of sth*** (*not aware*) no ser consciente de algo

un·con·trol·la·ble [ʌnkən'troʊləbl] *adj anger, children* incontrolable; *desire* incontrolable, irresistible

un·con·ven·tion·al [ʌnkən'venʃnl] *adj* poco convencional

un·co·op·er·a·tive [ʌnkoʊ'ɑːpərətɪv] *adj*: ***be uncooperative*** no estar dispuesto a colaborar

un·cork [ʌn'kɔːrk] *v/t bottle* descorchar

un·cov·er [ʌn'kʌvər] *v/t remove cover from* destapar; *plot, ancient remains* descubrir

un·dam·aged [ʌn'dæmɪdʒd] *adj* intacto

un·daunt·ed [ʌn'dɒːntɪd] *adj* impertérrito; ***carry on undaunted*** seguir impertérrito

un·de·cid·ed [ʌndɪ'saɪdɪd] *adj question* sin resolver; ***be undecided about s.o./sth*** estar indeciso sobre alguien / algo

un·de·ni·a·ble [ʌndɪ'naɪəbl] *adj* innegable

un·de·ni·a·bly [ʌndɪ'naɪəblɪ] *adv* innegablemente

un·der ['ʌndər] **1** *prep* (*beneath*) debajo de, bajo; (*less than*) menos de; ***under the water*** bajo el agua; ***it is under review / investigation*** está siendo revisado / investigado **2** *adv* (*anesthetized*) anestesiado

un·der'age *adj*: ***underage drinking*** el consumo de alcohol por menores de edad

'un·der·arm *adv*: ***throw a ball underarm*** lanzar una pelota soltándola por debajo de la altura del hombro

'un·der·car·riage tren *m* de aterrizaje

'un·der·cov·er *adj agent* secreto

un·der'cut *v/t* (*pret & pp* ***undercut***) COM vender más barato que

'un·der·dog *n*: ***support the underdog*** apoyar al más débil

un·der'done *adj meat* poco hecho

un·der'es·ti·mate *v/t* subestimar

un·der·ex'posed *adj* PHOT subexpuesto

un·der'fed *adj* malnutrido

un·der'go *v/t* (*pret* ***underwent***, *pp* ***undergone***) *surgery, treatment* ser sometido a; *experiences* sufrir; ***the hotel is undergoing refurbishment*** se están efectuando renovaciones en el hotel

un·der'grad·u·ate *Br* estudiante *m/f* universitario(-a) (*todavía no licenciado*(*a*))

'un·der·ground **1** *adj passages etc* subterráneo; POL *resistance, newpaper etc* clandestino **2** *adv work* bajo tierra; ***go underground*** POL pasar a la clandestinidad

'un·der·growth maleza *f*

un·der'hand *adj* (*devious*) poco honrado

un·der'lie *v/t* (*pret* ***underlay***, *pp* ***underlain***) (*form basis of*) sostentar

un·der'line *v/t text* subrayar

un·der'ly·ing *adj causes, problems* subyacente

un·der'mine *v/t s.o.'s position, theory* minar, socavar

un·der·neath [ʌndər'niːθ] **1** *prep* debajo de, bajo **2** *adv* debajo

'un·der·pants *npl* calzoncillos *mpl*

'un·der·pass *for pedestrians* paso *m* subterráneo

un·der·priv·i·leged [ʌndər'prɪvɪlɪdʒd] *adj* desfavorecido

un·der'rate *v/t* subestimar, infravalorar

'un·der·shirt camiseta *f*

un·der·sized [ʌndər'saɪzd] *adj* demasiado pequeño

'un·der·skirt enaguas *fpl*

un·der·staffed [ʌndər'stæft] *adj* sin suficiente personal

un·der·stand [ʌndər'stænd] **1** *v/t* (*pret & pp* ***understood***) entender, comprender; *language* entender; ***I understand that you …*** tengo entendido que …; ***they are understood to be in Canada*** se cree que están en Canadá **2** *v/i* (*pret & pp* ***understood***) entender, comprender

un·der·stand·able [ʌndər'stændəbl] *adj* comprensible

un·der·stand·ably [ʌndər'stændəblɪ] *adv* comprensiblemente

un·der·stand·ing [ʌndər'stændɪŋ] **1** *adj person* comprensivo **2** *n of problem, situation* interpretación *f*; (*agreement*) acuerdo *m*; ***on the understanding that …*** (*condition*) a condición de que …

'un·der·state·ment *n*: ***that's an understatement*** ¡y te quedas corto!

un·der'take *v/t* (*pret* ***undertook***, *pp* ***undertaken***) *task* emprender; ***undertake to do sth*** (*agree to*) encargarse de hacer algo

U

un·der·tak·er ['ʌndər'teɪkər] *Br* encargado *m* de una funeraria
'un·der·tak·ing (*enterprise*) proyecto *m*, empresa *f*; ***give an undertaking to do sth*** compreterse a hacer algo
un·der'val·ue *v/t* infravalorar
'un·der·wear ropa *f* interior
un·der'weight *adj*: ***be underweight*** pesar menos de lo normal
'un·de·rworld *criminal* hampa *f*; *in mythology* Hades *m*
un·der'write *v/t* (*pret* ***underwrote***, *pp* ***underwritten***) FIN asegurar, garantizar
un·de·served [ʌndɪ'zɜːrvd] *adj* inmerecido
un·de·sir·a·ble [ʌndɪ'zaɪrəbl] *adj features*, *changes* no deseado; *person* indeseable; ***undesirable element*** *person* persona *f* problemática
un·dis·put·ed [ʌndɪ'spjuːtɪd] *adj champion*, *leader* indiscutible
un·do [ʌn'duː] *v/t* (*pret* ***undid***, *pp* ***undone***) *parcel*, *wrapping* abrir; *buttons*, *shirt* desabrochar; *shoelaces* desatar; *s.o. else's work* deshacer
un·doubt·ed·ly [ʌn'daʊtɪdlɪ] *adv* indudablemente
un·dreamt-of [ʌn'dremtəv] *adj riches* inimaginable
un·dress [ʌn'dres] **1** *v/t* desvestir, desnudar; ***get undressed*** desvestirse, desnudarse **2** *v/i* desvestirse, desnudarse
un·due [ʌn'duː] *adj* (*excessive*) excesivo
un·du·ly [ʌn'duːlɪ] *adv punished*, *blamed* injustamente; (*excessively*) excesivamente
un·earth [ʌn'ɜːrθ] *v/t* descubrir; *ancient remains* desenterrar
un·earth·ly [ʌn'ɜːrθlɪ] *adv*: ***at this unearthly hour*** a esta hora intempestiva
un·eas·y [ʌn'iːzɪ] *adj relationship*, *peace* tenso; ***feel uneasy about*** estar inquieto por
un·eat·a·ble [ʌn'iːtəbl] *adj* incomible
un·e·co·nom·ic [ʌniːkə'nɑːmɪk] *adj* antieconómico, no rentable
un·ed·u·cat·ed [ʌn'edʒəkeɪtɪd] *adj* inculto, sin educación
un·em·ployed [ʌnɪm'plɔɪd] *adj* desempleado, *Span* parado
un·em·ploy·ment [ʌnɪm'plɔɪmənt] desempleo *m*, *Span* paro *m*
un·end·ing [ʌn'endɪŋ] *adj* interminable
un·e·qual [ʌn'iːkwəl] *adj* desigual; ***be unequal to the task*** no estar a la altura de lo que requiere el trabajo
un·er·ring [ʌn'erɪŋ] *adj judgment*, *instinct* infalible
un·e·ven [ʌn'iːvn] *adj quality* desigual; *surface*, *ground* irregular
un·e·ven·ly [ʌn'iːvnlɪ] *adv distributed*, *applied* de forma desigual; ***be unevenly matched*** *of two contestants* no estar en igualdad de condiciones
un·e·vent·ful [ʌnɪ'ventfəl] *adj day*, *journey* sin incidentes
un·ex·pec·ted [ʌnɪk'spektɪd] *adj* inesperado
un·ex·pec·ted·ly [ʌnɪk'spektɪdlɪ] *adv* inesperadamente, de forma inesperada
un·fair [ʌn'fer] *adj* injusto; ***that's unfair*** eso no es justo
un·faith·ful [ʌn'feɪθfəl] *adj husband*, *wife* infiel; ***be unfaithful to s.o.*** ser infiel a alguien
un·fa·mil·i·ar [ʌnfə'mɪljər] *adj* desconocido, extraño; ***be unfamiliar with sth*** desconocer algo
un·fas·ten [ʌn'fæsn] *v/t belt* desabrochar
un·fa·vo·ra·ble, *Br* **un·fa·vou·ra·ble** [ʌn'feɪvərəbl] *adj* desfavorable
un·feel·ing [ʌn'fiːlɪŋ] *adj person* insensible
un·fin·ished [ʌn'fɪnɪʃt] *adj* inacabado; ***leave sth unfinished*** dejar algo sin acabar
un·fit [ʌn'fɪt] *adj*: ***be unfit*** *physically* estar en baja forma; ***be unfit to eat*** no ser apto para el consumo; ***be unfit to drink*** no ser potable; ***he's unfit to be a parent*** no tiene lo que se necesita para ser padre
un·fix [ʌn'fɪks] *v/t part* soltar, desmontar
un·flap·pa·ble [ʌn'flæpəbl] *adj* F impasible
un·fold [ʌn'foʊld] **1** *v/t sheets*, *letter* desdoblar; *one's arms* descruzar **2** *v/i of story etc* desarrollarse; *of view* abrirse
un·fore·seen [ʌnfɔːr'siːn] *adj* imprevisto
un·for·get·ta·ble [ʌnfər'getəbl] *adj* inolvidable
un·for·giv·a·ble [ʌnfər'gɪvəbl] *adj* imperdonable; ***that was unforgivable of you*** eso ha sido imperdonable
un·for·tu·nate [ʌn'fɔːrʧənət] *adj people* desafortunado; *event* desgraciado; *choice of words* desafortunado, desacertado; ***that's unfortunate for you*** has tenido muy mala suerte
un·for·tu·nate·ly [ʌn'fɔːrʧənətlɪ] *adv* desgraciadamente
un·found·ed [ʌn'faʊndɪd] *adj* infundado
un·friend·ly [ʌn'frendlɪ] *adj person* antipático; *place* desagradable; *welcome* hostil; *software* de difícil manejo
un·fur·nished [ʌn'fɜːrnɪʃt] *adj* sin amueblar
un·god·ly [ʌn'gɑːdlɪ] *adj*: ***at this ungodly hour*** a esta hora intempestiva

un·grate·ful [ʌn'greɪtfəl] *adj* desagradecido
un·hap·pi·ness [ʌn'hæpɪnɪs] infelicidad *f*
un·hap·py [ʌn'hæpɪ] *adj person, look* infeliz; *day* triste; *customer etc* descontento
un·harmed [ʌn'hɑːrmd] *adj* ileso; ***be unharmed*** salir ileso
un·health·y [ʌn'helθɪ] *adj person* enfermizo; *conditions, food, economy* poco saludable
un·heard-of [ʌn'hɜːrdəv] *adj* inaudito
un·hurt [ʌn'hɜːrt] *adj*: ***be unhurt*** salir ileso
un·hy·gi·en·ic [ʌnhaɪ'dʒiːnɪk] *adj* antihigiénico
u·ni·fi·ca·tion [juːnɪfɪ'keɪʃn] unificación *f*
u·ni·form ['juːnɪfɔːrm] **1** *n* uniforme *m* **2** *adj* uniforme
u·ni·fy ['juːnɪfaɪ] *v/t* (*pret & pp* ***unified***) unificar
u·ni·lat·e·ral [juːnɪ'lætərəl] *adj* unilateral
un·i·ma·gi·na·ble [ʌnɪ'mædʒɪnəbl] *adj* inimaginable
un·i·ma·gi·na·tive [ʌnɪ'mædʒɪnətɪv] *adj* sin imaginación
un·im·por·tant [ʌnɪm'pɔːrtənt] *adj* poco importante
un·in·hab·i·ta·ble [ʌnɪn'hæbɪtəbl] *adj* inhabitable
un·in·hab·it·ed [ʌnɪn'hæbɪtɪd] *adj building* deshabitado; *region* desierto
un·in·jured [ʌn'ɪndʒərd] *adj*: ***be uninjured*** salir ileso
un·in·tel·li·gi·ble [ʌnɪn'telɪdʒəbl] *adj* ininteligible
un·in·ten·tion·al [ʌnɪn'tenʃnl] *adj* no intencionado; ***sorry, that was unintentional*** lo siento, ha sido sin querer
un·in·ten·tion·al·ly [ʌnɪn'tenʃnlɪ] *adv* sin querer
un·in·te·rest·ing [ʌn'ɪntrəstɪŋ] *adj* sin interés
un·in·ter·rupt·ed [ʌnɪntə'rʌptɪd] *adj sleep, two hours' work* ininterrumpido
u·nion ['juːnjən] POL unión *f*; (*labor union*) sindicato *m*
u·nique [juː'niːk] *adj* único
u·nit ['juːnɪt] unidad *f*; ***unit of measurement*** unidad *f* de medida; ***power unit*** fuente *f* de alimentación
u·nit 'cost COM costo *m or Span* coste *m* unitario *or* por unidad
u·nite [juː'naɪt] **1** *v/t* unir **2** *v/i* unirse
u·nit·ed [juː'naɪtɪd] *adj* unido
U·nit·ed 'King·dom Reino *m* Unido
U·nit·ed 'Na·tions Naciones *fpl* Unidas
U·nit·ed 'States (of A'mer·i·ca) Estados *mpl* Unidos (de *América*)
u·ni·ty ['juːnətɪ] unidad *f*
u·ni·ver·sal [juːnɪ'vɜːrsl] *adj* universal
u·ni·ver·sal·ly [juːnɪ'vɜːrsəlɪ] *adv* universalmente
u·ni·verse ['juːnɪvɜːrs] universo *m*
u·ni·ver·si·ty [juːnɪ'vɜːrsətɪ] **1** *n* universidad *f*; ***he is at university*** está en la universidad **2** *adj* universitario
un·just [ʌn'dʒʌst] *adj* injusto
un·kempt [ʌn'kempt] *adj appearance* descuidado; *hair* revuelto
un·kind [ʌn'kaɪnd] *adj* desgradable, cruel
un·known [ʌn'noʊn] **1** *adj* desconocido **2** *n*: ***a journey into the unknown*** un viaje hacia lo desconocido
un·lead·ed [ʌn'ledɪd] *adj* sin plomo
un·less [ən'les] *conj* a menos que, a no ser que; ***don't say anything unless you're sure*** no digas nada a menos que *or* a no ser que estés seguro
un·like [ʌn'laɪk] *prep* (*not similar to*) diferente de; ***it's unlike him to drink so much*** él no suele beber tanto; ***that photograph is so unlike you*** has salido completamente diferente en esa fotografía
un·like·ly [ʌn'laɪklɪ] *adj* (*improbable*) improbable; *explanation* inverosímil; ***he is unlikely to win*** es improbable *or* poco probable que gane
un·lim·it·ed [ʌn'lɪmɪtɪd] *adj* ilimitado
un·list·ed [ʌn'lɪstɪd] *adj*: ***be unlisted*** no aparecer en la guía telefónica
un·load [ʌn'loʊd] *v/t* descargar
un·lock [ʌn'lɑːk] *v/t* abrir
un·luck·i·ly [ʌn'lʌkɪlɪ] *adv* desgraciadamente, por desgracia
un·luck·y [ʌn'lʌkɪ] *adj day, choice* aciago, funesto; *person* sin suerte; ***that was so unlucky for you!*** ¡qué mala suerte tuviste!
un·manned [ʌn'mænd] *adj spacecraft* no tripulado
un·mar·ried [ʌn'mærɪd] *adj* soltero
un·mis·ta·ka·ble [ʌnmɪ'steɪkəbl] *adj* inconfundible
un·moved [ʌn'muːvd] *adj*: ***he was unmoved by her tears*** sus lágrimas no lo conmovieron
un·mu·si·cal [ʌn'mjuːzɪkl] *adj person* sin talento musical; *sounds* estridente
un·nat·u·ral [ʌn'nætʃrəl] *adj* anormal; ***it's not unnatural to be annoyed*** es normal estar enfadado
un·ne·ces·sa·ry [ʌn'nesəserɪ] *adj* innecesario
un·nerv·ing [ʌn'nɜːrvɪŋ] *adj* desconcertante
un·no·ticed [ʌn'noʊtɪst] *adj*: ***it went un-***

noticed pasó desapercibido

un·ob·tain·a·ble [ʌnəb'teɪnəbl] *adj goods* no disponible; TELEC desconectado

un·ob·tru·sive [ʌnəb'truːsɪv] *adj* discreto

un·oc·cu·pied [ʌn'ɑːkjʊpaɪd] *adj building, house* desocupado; *post* vacante

un·of·fi·cial [ʌnə'fɪʃl] *adj* no oficial; ***this is still unofficial but …*** esto todavía no es oficial, pero …

un·of·fi·cial·ly [ʌnə'fɪʃlɪ] *adv* extraoficialmente

un·or·tho·dox [ʌn'ɔːrθədɑːks] *adj* poco ortodoxo

un·pack [ʌn'pæk] **1** *v/t* deshacer **2** *v/i* deshacer el equipaje

un·paid [ʌn'peɪd] *adj work* no remunerado

un·pleas·ant [ʌn'pleznt] *adj* desagradable; ***he was very unpleasant to her*** fue muy desagradable con ella

un·plug [ʌn'plʌg] *v/t* (*pret & pp* ***unplugged***) TV, *computer* desenchufar

un·pop·u·lar [ʌn'pɑːpjələr] *adj* impopular

un·pre·ce·den·ted [ʌn'presɪdentɪd] *adj* sin precedentes; ***it was unprecedented for a woman to …*** no tenía precedentes que una mujer …

un·pre·dict·a·ble [ʌnprɪ'dɪktəbl] *adj person, weather* imprevisible, impredecible

un·pre·ten·tious [ʌnprɪ'tenʃəs] *adj person, style, hotel* modesto, sin pretensiones

un·prin·ci·pled [ʌn'prɪnsɪpld] *adj* sin principios

un·pro·duc·tive [ʌnprə'dʌktɪv] *adj meeting, discussion* infructuoso; *soil* improductivo

un·pro·fes·sion·al [ʌnprə'feʃnl] *adj* poco profesional

un·prof·i·ta·ble [ʌn'prɑːfɪtəbl] *adj* no rentable

un·pro·nounce·a·ble [ʌnprə'naʊnsəbl] *adj* impronunciable

un·pro·tect·ed [ʌnprə'tektɪd] *adj borders* desprotegido, sin protección; ***unprotected sex*** sexo *m* sin preservativos

un·pro·voked [ʌnprə'voʊkt] *adj attack* no provocado

un·qual·i·fied [ʌn'kwɑːlɪfaɪd] *adj worker, doctor etc* sin titulación

un·ques·tio·na·bly [ʌn'kwestʃnəblɪ] *adv* (*without doubt*) indiscutiblemente

un·ques·tion·ing [ʌn'kwestʃnɪŋ] *adj attitude, loyalty* incondicional

un·rav·el [ʌn'rævl] *v/t* (*pret & pp* ***unraveled***, *Br* ***unravelled***) *string, knitting* desenredar; *mystery, complexities* desentrañar

un·rea·da·ble [ʌn'riːdəbl] *adj book* ilegible

un·re·al [ʌn'rɪəl] *adj* irreal; ***this is unreal!*** F ¡esto es increíble! F

un·rea·lis·tic [ʌnrɪə'lɪstɪk] *adj* poco realista

un·rea·so·na·ble [ʌn'riːznəbl] *adj person* poco razonable, irrazonable; *demand, expectation* excesivo, irrazonable; ***you're being unreasonable*** no estás siendo razonable

un·re·lat·ed [ʌnrɪ'leɪtɪd] *adj issues* no relacionado; *people* no emparentado

un·re·lent·ing [ʌnrɪ'lentɪŋ] *adj* implacable

un·rel·i·a·ble [ʌnrɪ'laɪəbl] *adj car, machine* poco fiable; *person* informal

un·rest [ʌn'rest] malestar *m*; (*rioting*) disturbios *mpl*

un·re·strained [ʌnrɪ'streɪnd] *adj emotions* incontrolado

un·road·wor·thy [ʌn'roʊdwɜːrðɪ] *adj* que no está en condiciones de circular

un·roll [ʌn'roʊl] *v/t carpet, scroll* desenrollar

un·ru·ly [ʌn'ruːlɪ] *adj* revoltoso

un·safe [ʌn'seɪf] *adj* peligroso; ***it's unsafe to drink / eat*** no se puede beber / comer

un·san·i·tar·y [ʌn'sænɪterɪ] *adj conditions, drains* insalubre

un·sat·is·fac·to·ry [ʌnsætɪs'fæktərɪ] *adj* insatisfactorio

un·sa·vo·ry [ʌn'seɪvərɪ] *adj person, reputation* indeseable; *district* desagradable

un·scathed [ʌn'skeɪðd] *adj* (*not injured*) ileso; (*not damaged*) intacto

un·screw [ʌn'skruː] *v/t top* desenroscar; *shelves, hooks* desatornillar

un·scru·pu·lous [ʌn'skruːpjələs] *adj* sin escrúpulos

un·self·ish [ʌn'selfɪʃ] *adj* generoso

un·set·tled [ʌn'setld] *adj issue* sin decidir; *weather, stock market, lifestyle* inestable; *bills* sin pagar

un·shav·en [ʌn'ʃeɪvn] *adj* sin afeitar

un·sight·ly [ʌn'saɪtlɪ] *adj* horrible, feo

un·skilled [ʌn'skɪld] *adj* no cualificado

un·so·cia·ble [ʌn'soʊʃəbl] *adj* insociable

un·so·phis·ti·cat·ed [ʌnsə'fɪstɪkeɪtɪd] *adj person, beliefs* sencillo; *equipment* simple

un·sta·ble [ʌn'steɪbl] *adj* inestable

un·stead·y [ʌn'stedɪ] *adj hand* tembloroso; *ladder* inestable; ***be unsteady on one's feet*** tamblearse

un·stint·ing [ʌn'stɪntɪŋ] *adj* generoso; ***be unstinting in one's efforts / generosity*** no escatimar esfuerzos / generosidad

un·stuck [ʌn'stʌk] *adj*: ***come unstuck*** F *of plan etc* irse al garete F

un·suc·cess·ful [ʌnsək'sesfəl] *adj writer etc* fracasado; *candidate* perdedor; *party, attempt* fallido; ***he tried but was unsuccessful*** lo intentó sin éxito

un·suc·cess·ful·ly [ʌnsək'sesfəlɪ] *adv try, apply* sin éxito

un·suit·a·ble [ʌn'suːtəbl] *adj partner, film, clothing* inadecuado; *thing to say* inoportuno

un·sus·pect·ing [ʌnsəs'pektɪŋ] *adj* confiado

un·swerv·ing [ʌn'swɜːrvɪŋ] *adj loyalty, devotion* inquebrantable

un·think·a·ble [ʌn'θɪŋkəbl] *adj* impensable

un·ti·dy [ʌn'taɪdɪ] *adj room, desk* desordenado; *hair* revuelto

un·tie [ʌn'taɪ] *v/t knot, laces, prisoner* desatar

un·til [ən'tɪl] **1** *prep* hasta; ***from Monday until Friday*** desde el lunes hasta el viernes; ***I can wait until tomorrow*** puedo esperar hasta mañana; ***not until Friday*** no antes del viernes; ***it won't be finished until July*** no estará acabado hasta julio **2** *conj* hasta que; ***can you wait until I'm ready?*** ¿puedes esperar hasta que esté listo?; ***they won't do anything until you say so*** no harán nada hasta que (no) se lo digas

un·time·ly [ʌn'taɪmlɪ] *adj death* prematuro

un·tir·ing [ʌn'taɪrɪŋ] *adj efforts* incansable

un·told [ʌn'toʊld] *adj suffering* indecible; *riches* inconmensurable; *story* nunca contado

un·trans·lat·a·ble [ʌntræns'leɪtəbl] *adj* intraducible

un·true [ʌn'truː] *adj* falso

un·used[1] [ʌn'juːzd] *adj goods* sin usar

un·used[2] [ʌn'juːst] *adj*: ***be unused to sth*** no estar acostumbrado a algo; ***be unused to doing sth*** no estar acostumbrado a hacer algo

un·u·su·al [ʌn'juːʒl] *adj* poco corriente; ***it is unusual ...*** es raro *or* extraño ...

un·u·su·al·ly [ʌn'juːʒəlɪ] *adv* inusitadamente; ***the weather's unusually cold*** hace un frío inusual

un·veil [ʌn'veɪl] *v/t memorial, statue etc* desvelar

un·well [ʌn'wel] *adj* indispuesto, mal; ***be unwell*** sentirse indispuesto *or* mal

un·will·ing [ʌn'wɪlɪŋ] *adj* poco dispuesto, reacio; ***be unwilling to do sth*** no estar dispuesto a hacer algo, ser reacio a hacer algo

un·will·ing·ly [ʌn'wɪlɪŋlɪ] *adv* de mala gana, a regañadientes

un·wind [ʌn'waɪnd] **1** *v/t* (*pret & pp* ***unwound***) *tape* desenrollar **2** *v/i* (*pret & pp* ***unwound***) *of tape* desenrollarse; *of story* irse desarrollando; F (*relax*) relajarse

un·wise [ʌn'waɪz] *adj* imprudente

un·wrap [ʌn'ræp] *v/t* (*pret & pp* ***unwrapped***) *gift* desenvolver

un·writ·ten [ʌn'rɪtn] *adj law, rule* no escrito

un·zip [ʌn'zɪp] *v/t* (*pret & pp* ***unzipped***) *dress etc* abrir la cremallera de; COMPUT descomprimir

up [ʌp] **1** *adv position* arriba; *movement* hacia arriba; ***up in the sky / up on the roof*** (arriba) en el cielo / tejado; ***up here / there*** aquí / allí arriba; ***be up*** (*out of bed*) estar levantado; *of sun* haber salido; (*be built*) haber sido construido, estar acabado; *of shelves* estar montado; *of prices, temperature* haber subido; (*have expired*) haberse acabado; ***what's up?*** F ¿qué pasa?; ***up to the year 1989*** hasta el año 1989; ***he came up to me*** se me acercó; ***what are you up to these days?*** ¿qué es de tu vida?; ***what are those kids up to?*** ¿qué están tramando esos niños?; ***be up to something*** (***bad***) estar tramando algo; ***I don't feel up to it*** no me siento en condiciones de hacerlo; ***it's up to you*** tú decides; ***it is up to them to solve it*** (*their duty*) les corresponde a ellos resolverlo; ***be up and about*** *after illness* estar recuperado **2** *prep*: ***further up the mountain*** más arriba de la montaña; ***he climbed up a tree*** se subió a un árbol; ***they ran up the street*** corrieron por la calle; ***the water goes up this pipe*** el agua sube por esta tubería; ***we traveled up to Chicago*** subimos hasta Chicago **3** *n*: ***ups and downs*** altibajos *mpl*

'up·bring·ing educación *f*

'up·com·ing *adj* (*forthcoming*) próximo

up'date[1] *v/t file, records* actualizar; ***update s.o. on sth*** poner a alguien al corriente de algo

'up·date[2] *n* actualización *f*; ***can you give me an update on the situation?*** ¿me puedes poner al corriente de la situación?

up'grade *v/t computers etc* actualizar; (*replace with new versions*) modernizar; *product* modernizar; ***upgrade s.o. to business class*** cambiar a alguien a clase ejecutiva

up·heav·al [ʌp'hiːvl] *emotional* conmo-

U

ción *m*; *physical* trastorno *m*; *political*, *social* sacudida *f*

up·hill 1 *adv* [ʌp'hɪl] *walk* cuesta arriba **2** *adj* ['ʌphɪl] *struggle* arduo, difícil

up'hold *v/t* (*pret & pp* ***upheld***) *traditions*, *rights* defender, conservar; (*vindicate*) confirmar

up·hol·ster·y [ʌp'hoʊlstərɪ] (*coverings of chairs*) tapicería *f*; (*padding of chairs*) relleno *m*

'up·keep *of buildings*, *parks etc* mantenimiento *m*

'up·load *v/t* COMPUT cargar

up'mar·ket *adj restaurant*, *hotel* de categoría

up·on [ə'pɑːn] *prep* → ***on***

up·per ['ʌpər] *adj part of sth* superior; *stretches of a river* alto; *deck* superior, de arriba

up·per 'class *adj accent*, *family* de clase alta

up·per 'clas·ses *npl* clases *fpl* altas

'up·right 1 *adj citizen* honrado **2** *adv sit* derecho

up·right ('pi·an·o) piano *m* vertical

'up·ris·ing levantamiento *m*

'up·roar (*loud noise*) alboroto *m*; (*protest*) tumulto *m*

up'set 1 *v/t* (*pret & pp* ***upset***) *drink*, *glass* tirar; *emotionally* disgustar **2** *adj emotionally* disgustado; ***get upset about sth*** disgustarse por algo; ***have an upset stomach*** tener el estómago mal

up'set·ting *adj* triste

'up·shot (*result*, *outcome*) resultado *m*

up·side 'down *adv* boca abajo; ***turn sth upside down*** *box etc* poner algo al revés *or* boca abajo

up'stairs 1 *adv* arriba **2** *adj room* de arriba

'up·start advenedizo(-a) *m*(*f*)

up'stream *adv* río arriba

'up·take FIN respuesta *f* (***of*** a); ***be quick / slow on the uptake*** F ser / no ser muy espabilado F

up'tight *adj* F (*nervous*) tenso; (*inhibited*) estrecho

up-to-'date *adj information* actualizado; *fashions* moderno

'up turn *in economy* mejora *f*

up·ward ['ʌpwərd] *adv fly*, *move* hacia arriba; ***upward of 10,000*** más de 10.000

u·ra·ni·um [jʊ'reɪnɪəm] uranio *m*

ur·ban ['ɜːrbən] *adj* urbano

ur·ban·i·za·tion [ɜːrbənaɪ'zeɪʃn] urbanización *f*

ur·chin ['ɜːrʧɪn] golfillo(-a) *m*(*f*)

urge [ɜːrdʒ] **1** *n* impulso *m*; ***I felt an urge to hit her*** me entraron ganas de pegarle; ***I have an urge to do something new*** siento la necesidad de hacer algo nuevo **2** *v/t*: ***urge s.o. to do sth*** rogar a alguien que haga algo

◆ **urge on** *v/t* (*encourage*) animar

ur·gen·cy ['ɜːrdʒənsɪ] *of situation* urgencia *f*

ur·gent ['ɜːrdʒənt] *adj job*, *letter* urgente; ***be in urgent need of sth*** necesitar algo urgentemente; ***is it urgent?*** ¿es urgente?

u·ri·nate ['jʊrəneɪt] *v/i* orinar

u·rine ['jʊrɪn] orina *f*

urn [ɜːrn] urna *f*

U·ru·guay ['jʊrəgwaɪ] *n* Uruguay

U·ru·guay·an [jʊrə'gwaɪən] **1** *adj* uruguayo **2** *n* uruguayo(-a) *m*(*f*)

us [ʌs] *pron* nos; *after prep* nosotros(-as); ***they love us*** nos quieren; ***she gave us the keys*** nos dio las llaves; ***he sold it to us*** nos lo vendió; ***that's for us*** eso es para nosotros; ***who's that? - it's us*** ¿quién es? - ¡somos nosotros!

US [juː'es] *abbr* (= ***United States***) EE.UU. *mpl* (= Estados *mpl* Unidos)

USA [juːes'eɪ] *abbr* (= ***United States of America***) EE.UU. (= Estados Unidos)

us·a·ble ['juːzəbl] *adj* utilizable; ***it's not usable*** no se puede utilizar

us·age ['juːzɪdʒ] uso *m*

use 1 *v/t* [juːz] *tool*, *word* utilizar, usar; *skills*, *knowledge*, *car* usar; *a lot of gas* consumir; *pej*: *person* utilizar; ***I could use a drink*** F no me vendría mal una copa **2** *n* [juːs] uso *m*, utilización *f*; ***be of great use to s.o.*** ser de gran utilidad para alguien; ***it's of no use to me*** no me sirve; ***is that of any use?*** ¿eso sirve para algo?; ***it's no use*** no sirve de nada; ***it's no use trying / waiting*** no sirve de nada intentarlo / esperar

◆ **use up** *v/t* agotar

used[1] [juːzd] *adj car etc* de segunda mano

used[2] [juːst] *adj*: ***be used to s.o./sth*** estar acostumbrado a alguien / algo; ***get used to s.o./sth*** acostumbrarse a alguien / algo; ***be used to doing sth*** estar acostumbrado a hacer algo; ***get used to doing sth*** acostumbrarse a hacer algo

used[3] [juːst]: ***I used to like him*** antes me gustaba; ***they used to meet every Saturday*** solían verse todos los sábados

use·ful ['juːsfəl] *adj* útil

use·ful·ness ['juːsfʊlnɪs] utilidad *f*

use·less ['juːslɪs] *adj* inútil; *machine*, *computer* inservible; ***be useless*** F *person* ser un inútil F; ***it's useless trying*** (*there's no point*) no vale la pena intentarlo

us·er ['juːzər] *of product* usuario
us·er-'friend·ly *adj software, device* de fácil manejo
ush·er ['ʌʃər] *n (at wedding) persona que se encarga de indicar a los asistentes dónde se deben sentar*
◆ **usher in** *v/t new era* anunciar
ush·er·ette [ʌʃə'ret] acomodadora *f*
u·su·al ['juːʒl] *adj* habitual, acostumbrado; ***as usual*** como de costumbre; ***the usual, please*** lo de siempre, por favor
u·su·al·ly ['juːʒəlɪ] *adv* normalmente; ***I usually start at 9*** suelo empezar a las 9
u·ten·sil [juː'tensl] utensilio *m*
u·te·rus ['juːtərəs] útero *m*
u·til·i·ty [juː'tɪlətɪ] (*usefulness*) utilidad *f*; ***public utilities*** servicios *mpl* públicos
u·til·ize ['juːtɪlaɪz] *v/t* utilizar
ut·most ['ʌtmoʊst] **1** *adj* sumo **2** *n*: ***do one's utmost*** hacer todo lo posible
ut·ter ['ʌtər] **1** *adj* completo, total **2** *v/t sound* decir, pronunciar
ut·ter·ly ['ʌtərlɪ] *adv* completamente, totalmente
U-turn ['juːtɜːrn] cambio *m* de sentido; ***do a U-turn*** *fig*: *in policy etc* dar un giro de 180 grados

V

va·can·cy ['veɪkənsɪ] *at work* puesto *m* vacante
va·cant ['veɪkənt] *adj building* vacío; *position* vacante; *look, expression* vago, distraído
va·cant·ly ['veɪkəntlɪ] *adv* distraídamente
va·cate [veɪ'keɪt] *v/t room* desalojar
va·ca·tion [veɪ'keɪʃn] *n* vacaciones *fpl*; ***be on vacation*** estar de vacaciones; ***go to ... on vacation*** ir de vacaciones a ...
va·ca·tion·er [veɪ'keɪʃənər] turista *m/f*; *in summer* veraneante *m/f*
vac·cin·ate ['væksɪneɪt] *v/t* vacunar; ***be vaccinated against ...*** estar vacunado contra ...
vac·cin·a·tion [væksɪ'neɪʃn] *action* vacunación *f*; (*vaccine*) vacuna *f*
vac·cine ['væksiːn] vacuna *f*
vac·u·um ['vækjʊəm] **1** *n* PHYS, *fig* vacío *m* **2** *v/t floors* pasar el aspirador por, aspirar
'vac·u·um clean·er aspirador *m*, aspiradora *f*
'vac·u·um flask termo *m*
vac·u·um-'packed *adj* envasado al vacío
vag·a·bond ['vægəbɑːnd] vagabundo(-a) *m(f)*
va·gi·na [və'dʒaɪnə] vagina *f*
va·gi·nal ['vædʒɪnl] *adj* vaginal
va·grant ['veɪgrənt] vagabundo(-a) *m(f)*
vague [veɪg] *adj* vago; ***he was very vague about it*** no fue muy preciso
vague·ly ['veɪglɪ] *adv answer*, (*slightly*) vagamente; *possible* muy poco
vain [veɪn] **1** *adj person* vanidoso; *hope* vano **2** *n*: ***in vain*** en vano; ***their efforts were in vain*** sus esfuerzos fueron en vano
val·en·tine ['væləntaɪn] *card* tarjeta *f* del día de San Valentín; ***Valentine's Day*** día de San Valentín *or* de los enamorados
val·et **1** *n* ['væleɪ] *person* mozo *m* **2** *v/t* ['vælət] *car* lavar y limpiar
'val·et ser·vice *for clothes* servicio *m* de planchado; *for cars* servicio *m* de lavado y limpiado
val·iant ['væljənt] *adj* valiente, valeroso
val·iant·ly ['væljəntlɪ] *adv* valientemente, valerosamente
val·id ['vælɪd] *adj* válido
val·i·date ['vælɪdeɪt] *v/t with official stamp* sellar; *s.o.'s alibi* dar validez a
va·lid·i·ty [və'lɪdətɪ] validez *f*
val·ley ['vælɪ] valle *m*
val·u·a·ble ['væljʊbl] **1** *adj* valioso **2** *n*: ***valuables*** objetos *mpl* de valor
val·u·a·tion [væljʊ'eɪʃn] tasación *f*, valoración *f*
val·ue ['væljuː] **1** *n* valor *m*; ***be good value*** ofrecer buena relación calidad-precio; ***get value for money*** recibir una buena relación calidad-precio; ***rise / fall in value*** aumentar / disminuir de valor **2** *v/t s.o.'s friendship, one's freedom* valorar; ***I value your advice*** valoro tus consejos; ***have an object valued*** pedir la valoración *or* tasación de un objeto
valve [vælv] válvula *f*
van [væn] camioneta *f*, furgoneta *f*

van·dal ['vændl] vándalo *m*, gamberro(-a) *m(f)*
van·dal·ism ['vændəlɪzm] vandalismo *m*
van·dal·ize ['vændəlaɪz] *v/t* destrozar (*intencionadamente*)
van·guard ['væŋgɑːrd] vanguardia *f*; ***be in the vanguard of*** *fig* estar a la vanguardia de
va·nil·la [və'nɪlə] **1** *n* vainilla *f* **2** *adj* de vainilla
van·ish ['vænɪʃ] *v/i* desaparecer
van·i·ty ['vænətɪ] *of person* vanidad *f*
'van·i·ty case neceser *m*
van·tage point ['væntɪdʒ] *on hill etc* posición *f* aventajada
va·por ['veɪpər] vapor *m*
va·por·ize ['veɪpəraɪz] *v/t of atomic bomb, explosion* vaporizar
'va·por trail *of airplane* estela *f*
va·pour *Br* → ***vapor***
var·i·a·ble ['verɪəbl] **1** *adj* variable **2** *n* MATH, COMPUT variable *f*
var·i·ant ['verɪənt] *n* variante *f*
var·i·a·tion [verɪ'eɪʃn] variación *f*
var·i·cose 'vein ['værɪkoʊs] variz *f*
var·ied ['verɪd] *adj* variado
va·ri·e·ty [və'raɪətɪ] (*variedness, type*) variedad *f*; ***a variety of things to do*** (*range, mixture*) muchas cosas para hacer
var·i·ous ['verɪəs] *adj* (*several*) varios; (*different*) diversos
var·nish ['vɑːrnɪʃ] **1** *n for wood* barniz *m*; *for fingernails* esmalte *m* **2** *v/t wood* barnizar; *fingernails* poner esmalte a, pintar
var·y ['verɪ] **1** *v/i* (*pret & pp* ***varied***) variar; ***it varies*** depende **2** *v/t* (*pret & pp* ***varied***) variar
vase [veɪz] jarrón *m*
vas·ec·to·my [və'sektəmɪ] vasectomía *f*
vast [væst] *adj desert, knowledge* vasto; *number, improvement* enorme
vast·ly ['væstlɪ] *adv* enormemente
VAT [viːeɪ'tiː, væt] *Br abbr* (= ***value-added tax***) IVA *m* (= impuesto *m* sobre el valor añanido)
Vat·i·can ['vætɪkən]: ***the Vatican*** el Vaticano
vau·de·ville ['vɒːdvɪl] *adj* vodevil *m*
vault[1] [vɒːlt] *n in roof* bóveda *f*; ***vaults*** (*cellar*) sótano *m*; *of bank* cámara *f* acorazada
vault[2] [vɒːlt] **1** *n* SP salto *m* **2** *v/t beam etc* saltar
VCR [viːsiː'ɑːr] *abbr* (= ***video cassette recorder***) aparato *m* de *Span* vídeo *or L.Am.* video
VDU [viːdiː'juː] *abbr* (= ***visual display unit***) monitor *m*
veal [viːl] ternera *f*
veer [vɪr] *v/i* girar, torcer
ve·gan ['viːgn] **1** *n* vegetariano(-a) *m(f)* estricto (-a) (*que no come ningún producto de origen animal*) **2** *adj* vegetariano estricto
vege·ta·ble ['vedʒtəbl] hortaliza *f*; ***vegetables*** verduras *fpl*
ve·ge·tar·i·an [vedʒɪ'terɪən] **1** *n* vegetariano(-a) *m(f)* **2** *adj* vegetariano
ve·ge·tar·i·an·ism [vedʒɪ'terɪənɪzm] vegetarianismo *m*
veg·e·ta·tion [vedʒɪ'teɪʃn] vegetación *f*
ve·he·mence ['viːəməns] vehemencia *f*
ve·he·ment ['viːəmənt] *adj* vehemente
ve·he·ment·ly ['viːəməntlɪ] *adv* vehementemente
ve·hi·cle ['viːɪkl] *also fig* vehículo *m*
veil [veɪl] **1** *n* velo *m* **2** *v/t* cubrir con un velo
vein [veɪn] ANAT vena *f*; ***in this vein*** *fig* en este tono
Vel·cro® ['velkroʊ] velcro *m*
ve·loc·i·ty [vɪ'lɑːsətɪ] velocidad *f*
vel·vet ['velvɪt] *n* terciopelo *m*
vel·vet·y ['velvɪtɪ] *adj* aterciopelado
ven·det·ta [ven'detə] vendetta *f*
vend·ing ma·chine ['vendɪŋ] máquina *f* expendedora
vend·or ['vendər] LAW parte *f* vendedora
ve·neer [və'nɪr] *on wood* chapa *f*; *of politeness etc* apariencia *f*, fachada
ven·e·ra·ble ['venərəbl] *adj* venerable
ven·e·rate ['venəreɪt] *v/t* venerar
ven·e·ra·tion [venə'reɪʃn] veneración *f*
ven·e·re·al dis·ease [vɪ'nɪrɪəl] enfermedad *f* venérea
ve·ne·tian 'blind persiana *f* veneciana
Ven·e·zue·la [venɪz'weɪlə] *n* Venezuela
Ven·e·zue·lan [venɪz'weɪlən] **1** *adj* venezolano **2** *n* venezolano(-a) *m(f)*
ven·geance ['vendʒəns] venganza *f*; ***with a vengeance*** con ganas
ven·i·son ['venɪsn] venado *m*
ven·om ['venəm] *also fig* veneno *m*
ven·om·ous ['venəməs] *adj snake* venenoso; *fig* envenenado
vent [vent] *n for air* respiradero *m*; ***give vent to*** *feelings* dar rienda suelta a
ven·ti·late ['ventɪleɪt] *v/t* ventilar
ven·ti·la·tion [ventɪ'leɪʃn] ventilación *f*
ven·ti'la·tion shaft pozo *m* de ventilación
ven·ti·la·tor ['ventɪleɪtər] ventilador *m*; MED respirador *m*
ven·tril·o·quist [ven'trɪləkwɪst] ventrilocuo(-a) *m(f)*
ven·ture ['ventʃər] **1** *n* (*undertaking*) iniciativa *f*; COM empresa *f* **2** *v/i* aventurarse
ven·ue ['venjuː] *for meeting* lugar *m*; *for concert* local *m*, sala *f*

V

ve·ran·da [və'rændə] porche *m*
verb [vɜːrb] verbo *m*
verb·al ['vɜːrbl] *adj* (*spoken*) verbal
verb·al·ly ['vɜːrbəlɪ] *adv* de palabra
ver·ba·tim [vɜːr'beɪtɪm] *adv* literalmente
ver·dict ['vɜːrdɪkt] LAW veredicto *m*; ***what's your verdict?*** ¿qué te parece?, ¿qué opinas?
verge [vɜːrdʒ] *n of road* arcén *m*; ***be on the verge of*** *ruin* estar al borde de; *tears* estar a punto de
◆ **verge on** *v/t* rayar en
ver·i·fi·ca·tion [verɪfɪ'keɪʃn] (*checking*) verificación *f*; (*confirmation*) confirmación *f*
ver·i·fy ['verɪfaɪ] *v/t* (*pret & pp* ***verified***) (*check*) verificar; (*confirm*) confirmar
ver·mi·cel·li [vɜːrmɪ'tʃelɪ] *nsg* fideos *mpl*
ver·min ['vɜːrmɪn] *npl* bichos *mpl*, alimañas *fpl*
ver·mouth [vɜːr'muːθ] vermut *m*
ver·nac·u·lar [vər'nækjələr] *n* lenguaje *m* de la calle
ver·sa·tile ['vɜːrsətəl] *adj* polifacético, versátil
ver·sa·til·i·ty [vɜːrsə'tɪlətɪ] polivalencia *f*, versatilidad *f*
verse [vɜːrs] verso *m*
versed [vɜːrst] *adj*: ***be well versed in a subject*** estar muy versado en una materia
ver·sion ['vɜːrʃn] versión *f*
ver·sus ['vɜːrsəs] *prep* SP, LAW contra
ver·te·bra ['vɜːrtɪbrə] vértebra *f*
ver·te·brate ['vɜːrtɪbreɪt] *n* vertebrado(-a) *m*(*f*)
ver·ti·cal ['vɜːrtɪkl] *adj* vertical
ver·ti·go ['vɜːrtɪgoʊ] vértigo *m*
ver·y ['verɪ] **1** *adv* muy; ***was it cold? - not very*** ¿hizo frío? - no mucho; ***the very best*** el mejor de todos **2** *adj*: ***at that very moment*** en ese mismo momento; ***that's the very thing I need*** (*exact*) eso es precisamente lo que necesito; ***the very thought*** (*mere*) sólo de pensar en; ***right at the very top / bottom*** arriba / al fondo del todo
ves·sel ['vesl] NAUT buque *m*
vest [vest] chaleco *m*
ves·tige ['vestɪdʒ] vestigio *m*; vestigio *m*
vet[1] [vet] *n* (*veterinary surgeon*) veterinario(-a) *m*(*f*)
vet[2] [vet] *v/t* (*pret & pp* ***vetted***) *applicants etc* examinar, investigar
vet[3] [vet] MIL veterano(-a) *m*(*f*)
vet·e·ran ['vetərən] **1** *n* veterano(-a) *m*(*f*) **2** *adj* veterano
vet·e·ri·nar·i·an [vetərə'nerɪən] veterinario(-a) *m*(*f*)
ve·to ['viːtoʊ] **1** *n* veto *m* **2** *v/t* vetar
vex [veks] *v/t* (*concern, worry*) molestar, irritar
vexed [vekst] *adj* (*worried*) molesto, irritado; ***the vexed question of*** la polémica cuestión de
vi·a ['vaɪə] *prep* vía
vi·a·ble ['vaɪəbl] *adj* viable
vi·brate [vaɪ'breɪt] *v/i* vibrar
vi·bra·tion [vaɪ'breɪʃn] vibración *f*
vic·ar ['vɪkər] vicario *m*
vic·ar·age ['vɪkərɪdʒ] vicaría *f*
vice[1] [vaɪs] vicio *m*; ***the problem of vice*** el problema del vicio
vice[2] *Br* → ***vise***
vice 'pres·i·dent vicepresidente(-a) *m*(*f*)
'vice squad brigada *f* antivicio
vi·ce ver·sa [vaɪs'vɜːrsə] *adv* viceversa
vi·cin·i·ty [vɪ'sɪnətɪ] zona *f*; ***in the vicinity of ...*** *the church etc* en las cercanías de ...; *$500 etc* rondando ...
vi·cious ['vɪʃəs] *adj dog* fiero; *attack, temper, criticism* feroz
vi·cious 'cir·cle círculo *m* vicioso
vi·cious·ly ['vɪʃəslɪ] *adv* con brutalidad
vic·tim ['vɪktɪm] víctima *f*
vic·tim·ize ['vɪktɪmaɪz] *v/t* tratar injustamente
vic·tor ['vɪktər] vencedor(a) *m*(*f*)
vic·to·ri·ous [vɪk'tɔːrɪəs] *adj* victorioso
vic·to·ry ['vɪktərɪ] victoria *f*; ***win a victory over ...*** obtener una victoria sobre ...
vid·e·o ['vɪdɪoʊ] **1** *n Span* vídeo *m*, *L.Am.* video *m*; ***have X on video*** tener a X en *Span* vídeo *or L.Am.* video **2** *v/t* grabar en *Span* vídeo *or L.Am.* video
'vid·e·o cam·e·ra videocámara *f*
vid·e·o cas'sette videocasete *m*
'vid·e·o con·fer·ence TELEC videoconferencia *f*
'vid·e·o game videojuego *m*
'vid·e·o·phone videoteléfono *m*
'vid·e·o re·cord·er aparato *m* de *Span* vídeo *or L.Am.* video
'vid·e·o re·cord·ing grabación *f* en *Span* vídeo *or L.Am.* video
'vid·e·o·tape cinta *f* de *Span* vídeo *or L.Am.* video
vie [vaɪ] *v/i* competir
Vi·et·nam [vɪet'nɑːm] Vietnam
Vi·et·nam·ese [vɪetnə'miːz] **1** *adj* vietnamita **2** *n* vietnamita *m/f*; *language* vietnamita *m*
view [vjuː] **1** *n* vista *f*; *of situation* opinión *f*; ***in view of*** teniendo en cuenta; ***be on view*** *of paintings* estar expuesto al público; ***with a view to*** con vistas a **2** *v/t events, situation* ver, considerar; TV *pro-*

gram, *house* ver **3** *v/i* (*watch* TV) ver la televisión
view·er ['vjuːər] TV telespectador(a) *m(f)*
'**view·find·er** PHOT visor *m*
'**view·point** punto *m* de vista
vig·or ['vɪgər] (*energy*) vigor *m*
vig·or·ous ['vɪgərəs] *adj shake* vigoroso; *person* enérgico; *denial* rotundo
vig·or·ous·ly ['vɪgərəslɪ] *adv shake* con vigor; *deny*, *defend* rotundamente
vig·our *Br* → ***vigor***
vile [vaɪl] *adj smell* asqueroso; *thing to do* vil
vil·la ['vɪlə] chalet *m*; *in the country* villa *f*
vil·lage ['vɪlɪdʒ] pueblo *m*
vil·lag·er ['vɪlɪdʒər] aldeano(-a) *m(f)*
vil·lain ['vɪlən] malo(a) *m(f)*
vin·di·cate ['vɪndɪkeɪt] *v/t* (*show to be correct*) dar la razón a; (*show to be innocent*) vindicar; ***I feel vindicated*** los hechos me dan ahora la razón
vin·dic·tive [vɪn'dɪktɪv] *adj* vengativo
vin·dic·tive·ly [vɪn'dɪktɪvlɪ] *adv* vengativamente
vine [vaɪn] vid *f*
vin·e·gar ['vɪnɪgər] vinagre *m*
vine·yard ['vɪnjɑːrd] viñedo *m*
vin·tage ['vɪntɪdʒ] **1** *n of wine* cosecha *f* **2** *adj* (*classic*) clásico *m*
vi·o·la [vɪ'oʊlə] MUS viola *f*
vi·o·late ['vaɪəleɪt] *v/t* violar
vi·o·la·tion [vaɪə'leɪʃn] violación *f*; (*traffic violation*) infracción *f*
vi·o·lence ['vaɪələns] violencia *f*; ***outbreak of violence*** estallido de violencia
vi·o·lent ['vaɪələnt] *adj* violento; ***have a violent temper*** tener muy mal genio
vi·o·lent·ly ['vaɪələntlɪ] *adv react* violentamente; *object* rotundamente; ***fall violently in love with s.o.*** enamorarse perdidamente de alguien
vi·o·let ['vaɪələt] *n color*, *plant* violeta *m*
vi·o·lin [vaɪə'lɪn] violín *m*
vi·o·lin·ist [vaɪə'lɪnɪst] violinista *m/f*
VIP [viːaɪ'piː] *abbr* (= ***very important person***) VIP *m*
vi·per ['vaɪpər] *snake* víbora *f*
vi·ral ['vaɪrəl] *adj infection* vírico, viral
vir·gin ['vɜːrdʒɪn] virgen *m/f*
vir·gin·i·ty [vɜːr'dʒɪnətɪ] virginidad *f*; ***lose one's virginity*** perder la virginidad
Vir·go ['vɜːrgoʊ] ASTR Virgo *m/f inv*
vir·ile ['vɪrəl] *adj man* viril; *prose* vigoroso
vi·ril·i·ty [vɪ'rɪlətɪ] virilidad *f*
vir·tu·al ['vɜːrtʃʊəl] *adj* virtual
vir·tu·al·ly ['vɜːrtʃʊəlɪ] *adv* (*almost*) virtualmente, casi
vir·tu·al re'al·i·ty realidad *f* virtual
vir·tue ['vɜːrʃtuː] virtud *f*; ***in virtue of*** en virtud de
vir·tu·o·so [vɜːrtʃuː'oʊzoʊ] MUS virtuoso(-a) *m(f)*
vir·tu·ous ['vɜːrtʃʊəs] *adj* virtuoso
vir·u·lent ['vɪrʊlənt] *adj* virulento
vi·rus ['vaɪrəs] MED, COMPUT virus *m inv*
vi·sa ['viːzə] visa *f*, visado *m*
vise [vaɪs] torno *m* de banco
vis·i·bil·i·ty [vɪzə'bɪlətɪ] visibilidad *f*
vis·i·ble ['vɪzəbl] *adj object*, *difference* visible; *anger* evidente; ***not visible to the naked eye*** no ser visible a simple vista
vis·i·bly ['vɪzəblɪ] *adv different* visiblemente; ***he was visibly moved*** estaba visiblemente conmovido
vi·sion ['vɪʒn] *also* REL visión *f*
vis·it ['vɪzɪt] **1** *n* visita *f*; ***pay a visit to the doctor / dentist*** visitar al doctor / dentista; ***pay s.o. a visit*** hacer una visita a alguien **2** *v/t* visitar
vis·it·ing card ['vɪzɪtɪŋ] tarjeta *f* de visita
'**vis·it·ing hours** *npl at hospital* horas *fpl* de visita
vis·it·or ['vɪzɪtər] (*guest*) visita *f*; (*tourist*), *to museum etc* visitante *m/f*
vi·sor ['vaɪzər] visera *f*
vis·u·al ['vɪʒʊəl] *adj* visual
vis·u·al 'aid medio *m* visuale
vis·u·al dis'play u·nit monitor *m*
vis·u·al·ize ['vɪʒʊəlaɪz] *v/t* visualizar; (*foresee*) prever
vis·u·al·ly ['vɪʒʊlɪ] *adv* visualmente
vis·u·al·ly im'paired *adj* con discapacidad visual
vi·tal ['vaɪtl] *adj* (*essential*) vital; ***it is vital that …*** es vital que …
vi·tal·i·ty [vaɪ'tælətɪ] *of person*, *city etc* vitalidad *f*
vi·tal·ly ['vaɪtəlɪ] *adv*: ***vitally important*** de importancia vital
vi·tal 'or·gans *npl* órganos *mpl* vitales
vi·tal sta'tis·tics *npl of woman* medidas *fpl*
vit·a·min ['vaɪtəmɪn] vitamina *f*
'**vit·a·min pill** pastilla *f* vitamínica
vit·ri·ol·ic [vɪtrɪ'ɑːlɪk] *adj* virulento
vi·va·cious [vɪ'veɪʃəs] *adj* vivaz
vi·vac·i·ty [vɪ'væsətɪ] vivacidad *f*
viv·id ['vɪvɪd] *adj color* vivo; *memory*, *imagination* vívido
viv·id·ly ['vɪvɪdlɪ] *adv* (*brightly*) vivamente; (*clearly*) vívidamente
V-neck ['viːnek] cuello *m* de pico
vo·cab·u·la·ry [voʊ'kæbjʊlərɪ] vocabulario *m*
vo·cal ['voʊkl] *adj to do with the voice* vocal; *expressing opinions* ruidoso; ***a vocal opponent*** un declarado adversario

'**vo·cal cords** *npl* cuerdas *fpl* vocales
'**vo·cal group** MUS grupo *m* vocal
vo·cal·ist ['voʊkəlɪst] MUS vocalista *m/f*
vo·ca·tion [və'keɪʃn] (*calling*) vocación *f*; (*profession*) profesión *f*
vo·ca·tion·al [və'keɪʃnl] *adj guidance* profesional
vod·ka ['vɑːdkə] vodka *m*
vogue [voʊg] moda *f*; ***be in vogue*** estar en boga
voice [vɔɪs] **1** *n* voz *f* **2** *v/t opinions* expresar
'**voice mail** correo *m* de voz
void [vɔɪd] **1** *n* vacío *m* **2** *adj*: ***void of*** carente de
vol·a·tile ['vɑːlətəl] *adj personality, moods* cambiante; *markets* inestable
vol·ca·no [vɑːl'keɪnoʊ] volcán *m*
vol·ley ['vɑːlɪ] *n of shots* ráfaga *f*; *in tennis* volea *f*
'**vol·ley·ball** voleibol *m*, balonvolea *m*
volt [voʊlt] voltio *m*
volt·age ['voʊltɪdʒ] voltaje *m*
vol·ume ['vɑːljəm] volumen *m*; *of container* capacidad *f*; *of book* volumen *m*, tomo *m*
vol·ume con'trol control *m* del volumen
vol·un·tar·i·ly [vɑːlən'terɪlɪ] *adv* voluntariamente
vol·un·ta·ry ['vɑːlənterɪ] *adj* voluntario
vol·un·teer [vɑːlən'tɪr] **1** *n* voluntario(-a) *m(f)* **2** *v/i* ofrecerse voluntariamente
vo·lup·tu·ous [və'lʌptʃʊəs] *adj woman, figure* voluptuoso
vom·it ['vɑːmət] **1** *n* vómito *m* **2** *v/i* vomitar
◆ **vomit up** *v/t* vomitar
vo·ra·cious [və'reɪʃəs] *adj appetite* voraz
vo·ra·cious·ly [və'reɪʃəslɪ] *also fig* vorazmente
vote [voʊt] **1** *n* voto *m*; ***have the vote*** (*be entitled to vote*) tener el derecho al voto **2** *v/i* POL votar; ***vote for / against*** votar a favor / en contra **3** *v/t*: ***they voted him President*** lo votaron presidente; ***they voted to stay behind*** votaron (a favor de) quedarse atrás
◆ **vote in** *v/t new member* elegir en votación
◆ **vote on** *v/t issue* someter a votación
◆ **vote out** *v/t of office* rechazar en votación
vot·er ['voʊtər] POL votante *m/f*
vot·ing ['voʊtɪŋ] POL votación *f*
'**vot·ing booth** cabina *f* electoral
◆ **vouch for** [vaʊtʃ] *v/t truth of sth* dar fe de; *person* responder por
vouch·er ['vaʊtʃər] vale *m*
vow [vaʊ] **1** *n* voto *m* **2** *v/t*: ***vow to do sth*** prometer hacer algo
vow·el [vaʊl] vocal *f*
voy·age ['vɔɪɪdʒ] *n* viaje *m*
vul·gar ['vʌlgər] *adj person, language* vulgar, grosero
vul·ne·ra·ble ['vʌlnərəbl] *adj to attack, criticism* vulnerable
vul·ture ['vʌltʃər] buitre *m*

W

wad [wɑːd] *n of paper, absorbent cotton etc* bola *f*; ***a wad of $100 bills*** un fajo de billetes de 100 dólares
wad·dle ['wɑːdl] *v/i of duck* caminar; *of person* anadear
wade [weɪd] *v/i* caminar en el agua
◆ **wade through** *v/t book, documents* leerse
wa·fer ['weɪfər] *cookie* barquillo *m*; REL hostia *f*
'**wa·fer-thin** *adj* muy fino
waf·fle[1] ['wɑːfl] *n to eat* gofre *m*
waf·fle[2] ['wɑːfl] *v/i* andarse con rodeos
wag [wæg] **1** *v/t* (*pret & pp* ***wagged***) *tail, finger* menear **2** *v/i* (*pret & pp* ***wagged***) *of tail* menearse
wage[1] [weɪdʒ] *v/t*: ***wage war*** hacer la guerra
wage[2] [weɪdʒ] *n* salario *m*, sueldo *m*; ***wages*** salario *m*, sueldo *m*
'**wage earn·er** asalariado(-a) *m(f)*
'**wage freeze** congelación *f* salarial
'**wage ne·go·ti·a·tions** *npl* negociación *f* salarial
'**wage pack·et** *fig* salario *m*, sueldo *m*
wag·gle ['wægl] *v/t hips* menear; *ears, loose screw etc* mover
wag·gon, *Br* **wag·on** ['wægən] RAIL vagón *m*; ***be on the wagon*** F haber dejado la bebida

wail [weɪl] **1** *n of person, baby* gemido *m*; *of siren* sonido *m*, aullido *m* **2** *v/i of person, baby* gemir; *of siren* sonar, aullar
waist [weɪst] cintura *f*
'**waist·coat** *Br* chaleco *m*
'**waist·line** cintura *f*
wait [weɪt] **1** *n* espera *f*; ***I had a long wait for a train*** esperé mucho rato el tren **2** *v/i* esperar; ***have you been waiting long?*** ¿llevan mucho rato esperando? **2** *v/t*: ***don't wait supper for me*** no me esperéis a cenar; ***wait table*** trabajar de camarero
◆ **wait for** *v/t* esperar; ***wait for me!*** ¡esperadme!
◆ **wait on** *v/t* (*serve*) servir; (*wait for*) esperar
◆ **wait up** *v/i* esperar levantado
wait·er ['weɪtər] camarero *m*
wait·ing ['weɪtɪŋ] *n* espera *f*; ***no waiting sign*** señal *f* de prohibido estacionar
'**wait·ing list** lista *f* de espera
'**wait·ing room** sala *f* de espera
wait·ress ['weɪtrɪs] camarera *f*
waive [weɪv] *v/t right* renunciar; *requirement* no aplicar
wake[1] [weɪk] **1** *v/i* (*pret* **woke**, *pp* **woken**): ***wake (up)*** despertarse **2** *v/t* (*pret* **woke**, *pp* **woken**): ***wake (up)*** despertar
wake[2] [weɪk] *n of ship* estela *f*; ***in the wake of*** *fig* tras; ***missionaries followed in the wake of the explorers*** a los exploradores siguieron los misioneros
'**wake-up call**: ***could I have a wake-up call at 6.30?*** ¿me podrían despertar a las 6.30?
Wales [weɪlz] *n* Gales
walk [wɒːk] **1** *n* paseo *m*; *longer* caminata *f*; (*path*) camino *m*; ***it's a long / short walk to the office*** hay una caminata / un paseo hasta la oficina; ***go for a walk*** salir a dar un paseo, salir de paseo; ***it's a five-minute walk*** está a cinco minutos a pie **2** *v/i* caminar, andar; ***she walked over to the window*** se acercó a la ventana; ***I walked over to her place*** fui a su casa **3** *v/t dog* sacar a pasear; ***walk the streets*** (*walk around*) caminar por las calles
◆ **walk out** *v/i of spouse* marcharse; *from theater etc* salir; (*go on strike*) declararse en huelga
◆ **walk out on** *v/t*: ***walk out on s.o.*** abandonar a alguien
walk·er ['wɒːkər] (*hiker*) excursionista *m/f*; *for baby, old person* andador *m*; ***be a slow / fast walker*** caminar *or* andar despacio / rápido
walk·ie-'talk·ie [wɒːkɪ'tɒːkɪ] walkie-talkie *m*
walk-in 'clos·et vestidor *m*, armario *m* empotrado
walk·ing ['wɒːkɪŋ] *n* (*hiking*) excursionismo *m*; ***walking is one of the best forms of exercise*** caminar es uno de los mejores ejercicios; ***it's within walking distance*** se puede ir caminando *or* andando
'**walk·ing stick** bastón *m*
'**walk·ing tour** visita *f* a pie
'**Walk·man®** walkman *m*
'**walk·out** *n* (*strike*) huelga *f*
'**walk·over** (*easy win*) paseo *m*
'**walk-up** *n apartamento en un edificio sin ascensor*
wall [wɒːl] *external, fig* muro *m*; *of room* pared *m*; ***go to the wall*** *of company* quebrar; ***drive s.o. up the wall*** F hacer que alguien se suba por las paredes
wal·let ['wɑːlɪt] cartera *f*
wal·lop ['wɑːləp] **1** *n* F *blow* tortazo *m* F, galletazo *m* F **2** *v/t* F dar un golpetazo a F; *opponent* dar una paliza a F
'**wall·pa·per 1** *n* papel *m* pintado **2** *v/t* empapelar
wall-to-wall 'car·pet *Span* moqueta *f*, *L.Am.* alfombra *f*
wal·nut ['wɒːlnʌt] nuez *f*; *tree, wood* nogal *m*
waltz [wɒːlts] *n* vals *m*
wan [wɑːn] *adj face* pálido *m*
wand·er ['wɑːndər] *v/i* (*roam*) vagar, deambular; (*stray*) extraviarse; ***my attention began to wander*** empecé a distraerme
◆ **wander around** *v/i* deambular, pasear
wane [weɪn] *v/i of interest, enthusiasm* decaer, menguar
wan·gle ['wæŋgl] *v/t* F agenciarse F
want [wɑːnt] **1** *n*: ***for want of*** por falta de **2** *v/t* querer; (*need*) necesitar; ***want to do sth*** querer hacer algo; ***I want to stay here*** quiero quedarme aquí; ***do you want to come too? - no, I don't want to*** ¿quieres venir tú también? - no, no quiero; ***you can have whatever you want*** toma lo que quieras; ***it's not what I wanted*** no es lo que quería; ***she wants you to go back*** quiere que vuelvas; ***he wants a haircut*** necesita un corte de pelo **3** *v/i*: ***he wants for nothing*** no le falta nada
'**want ad** anuncio *m* por palabras (*buscando algo*)
want·ed ['wɑːntɪd] *adj by police* buscado por la policía
want·ing ['wɑːntɪŋ] *adj*: ***the team is wanting in experience*** al equipo le falta experiencia
wan·ton ['wɑːntən] *adj* gratuito

W

war [wɔːr] *n also fig* guerra *f*; ***be at war*** estar en guerra
war·ble ['wɔːrbl] *v/i of bird* trinar
ward [wɔːrd] *n in hospital* sala *f*; *child* pupilo(-a) *m(f)*
◆ **ward off** *v/t blow* parar; *attacker* rechazar; *cold* evitar
war·den ['wɔːrdn] *of prison* director(-a) *m(f)*, alcaide(sa) *m(f)*; *Br of hostel* vigilante *m/f*
'**ward·robe** *for clothes* armario *m*; (*clothes*) guardarropa *m*
ware·house ['werhaʊs] almacén *m*
'**war·fare** guerra *f*
'**war·head** ojiva *f*
war·i·ly ['werɪlɪ] *adv* cautelosamente
warm [wɔːrm] **1** *adj hands, room, water* caliente; *weather, welcome* cálido; *coat* de abrigo; ***it's warmer than yesterday*** hace más calor que ayer **2** *v/t* → ***warm up***
◆ **warm up 1** *v/t* calentar **2** *v/i* calentarse; *of athlete etc* calentar
warm·heart·ed ['wɔːrmhɑːrtɪd] *adj* cariñoso, simpático
warm·ly ['wɔːrmlɪ] *adv welcome, smile* calurosamente; ***warmly dressed*** abrigado
warmth [wɔːrmθ] calor *m*; *of welcome, smile* calor *m*, calidez *m*
'**warm-up** SP calentamiento *m*
warn [wɔːrn] *v/t* advertir, avisar
warn·ing ['wɔːrnɪŋ] *n* advertencia *f*, aviso *m*; ***without warning*** sin previo aviso
warp [wɔːrp] **1** *v/t wood* combar; *character* corromper **2** *v/i of wood* combarse
warped [wɔːrpt] *adj fig* retorcido
'**war·plane** avión *m* de guerra
war·rant ['wɔːrənt] **1** *n* orden *f* judicial **2** *v/t* (*deserve, call for*) justificar
war·ran·ty ['wɔːrəntɪ] (*guarantee*) garantía *f*; ***be under warranty*** estar en garantía
war·ri·or ['wɔːrɪər] guerrero(-a) *m(f)*
'**war·ship** buque *m* de guerra
wart [wɔːrt] verruga *f*
'**war·time** tiempos *mpl* de guerra
war·y ['werɪ] *adj* cauto, precavido; ***be wary of*** desconfiar de
was [wʌz] *pret* → ***be***
wash [wɑːʃ] **1** *n* lavado *m*; ***have a wash*** lavarse; ***that shirt needs a wash*** hay que lavar esa camisa **2** *v/t* lavar **3** *v/i* lavarse
◆ **wash up** *v/i* (*wash one's hands and face*) lavarse
wash·a·ble ['wɑːʃəbl] *adj* lavable
'**wash·ba·sin**, '**wash·bowl** lavabo *m*
'**wash·cloth** toallita *f*
washed out [wɑːʃt'aʊt] *adj* agotado
wash·er ['wɑːʃər] *for faucet etc* arandela *f*; → ***washing machine***
wash·ing ['wɑːʃɪŋ] (*clothes washed*) ropa *f* limpia; (*dirty clothes*) ropa *f* sucia; ***do the washing*** lavar la ropa, hacer la colada
'**wash·ing ma·chine** lavadora *f*
wash·ing-'up liq·uid *Br* lavavajillas *m inv*
'**wash·room** lavabo *m*, aseo *m*
wasp [wɑːsp] *insect* avispa *f*
waste [weɪst] **1** *n* desperdicio *m*; *from industrial process* desechos *mpl*; ***it's a waste of time / money*** es una pérdida de tiempo / dinero **2** *adj* residual; ***waste land*** erial *m* **3** *v/t* derrochar; *money* gastar; *time* perder
◆ **waste away** *v/i* consumirse
'**waste dis·pos·al (unit)** trituradora *f* de basuras
waste·ful ['weɪstfəl] *adj* despilfarrador, derrochador
'**waste·land** erial *m*
waste·'pa·per papel *m* usado
waste·pa·per 'bas·ket papelera *f*
'**waste pipe** tubería *f* de desagüe
'**waste prod·uct** desecho *m*
watch [wɑːtʃ] **1** *n timepiece* reloj *m*; ***keep watch*** hacer la guardia, vigilar **2** *v/t film*, TV ver; (*look after*) vigilar **3** *v/i* mirar, observar
◆ **watch for** *v/t* esperar
◆ **watch out** *v/i* tener cuidado; ***watch out!*** ¡cuidado!
◆ **watch out for** *v/t* tener cuidado con
watch·ful ['wɑːtʃfəl] *adj* vigilante
'**watch·mak·er** relojero(-a) *m(f)*
wa·ter ['wɒːtər] **1** *n* agua *f*; ***waters*** NAUT aguas *fpl* **2** *v/t plant* regar **3** *v/i*: ***my eyes are watering*** me lloran los ojos; ***my mouth is watering*** se me hace la boca agua
◆ **water down** *v/t drink* aguar, diluir
'**water can·non** cañón *m* de agua
'**wa·ter·col·or**, *Br* '**wa·ter·col·our** acuarela *f*
'**wa·ter·cress** berro *m*
watered 'down ['wɒːtərd] *adj fig* dulcificado
'**wa·ter·fall** cascada *f*, catarata *f*
wa·ter·ing can ['wɒːtərɪŋ] regadera *f*
'**wa·ter·ing hole** *hum* bar *m*
'**wa·ter lev·el** nivel *m* del agua
'**wa·ter lil·y** nenúfar *m*
'**wa·ter·line** línea *f* de flotación
wa·ter·logged ['wɒːtərlɑːgd] *adj earth, field* anegado; *boat* lleno de agua
'**wa·ter main** tubería *f* principal
'**wa·ter·mark** filigrana *f*
'**wa·ter mel·on** sandía *f*
'**wa·ter pol·lu·tion** contaminación *f* del agua

W

ˈ**wa·ter po·lo** waterpolo *m*

ˈ**wa·ter·proof** *adj* impermeable

ˈ**wa·ter·shed** *fig* momento *m* clave

ˈ**wa·ter·side** *n* orilla *f*; ***at the waterside*** en la orilla

ˈ**wa·ter·ski·ing** esquí *m* acuático

ˈ**wa·ter·tight** *adj compartment* estanco; *fig* irrefutable

ˈ**wa·ter·way** curso *m* de agua navegable

ˈ**wa·ter·wings** *npl* flotadores *mpl* (*para los brazos*)

wa·ter·works F: ***turn on the waterworks*** ponerse a llorar como una magdalena F

wa·ter·y [ˈwɒːtərɪ] *adj* aguado

watt [wɑːt] vatio *m*

wave[1] [weɪv] *n in sea* ola *f*

wave[2] [weɪv] **1** *n of hand* saludo *m* **2** *v/i with hand* saludar con la mano; ***wave to s.o.*** saludar con la mano a alguien **3** *v/t flag etc* agitar

ˈ**wave·length** RAD longitud *f* de onda; ***be on the same wavelength*** *fig* estar en la misma onda

wa·ver [ˈweɪvər] *v/i* vacilar, titubear

wav·y [ˈweɪvɪ] *adj hair, line* ondulado

wax [wæks] *n for floor, furniture* cera *f*; *in ear* cera *f*, cerumen

way [weɪ] **1** *n* (*method*) manera *f*, forma *f*; (*manner*) manera *f*, modo *m*; (*route*) camino *m*; ***I don't like the way he behaves*** no me gusta cómo se comporta; ***can you tell me the way to ...?*** ¿me podría decir cómo se va a ...?; ***this way*** (*like this*) así; (*in this direction*) por aquí; ***by the way*** (*incidentally*) por cierto, a propósito; ***by way of*** (*via*) por; (*in the form of*) a modo de; ***in a way*** (*in certain respects*) en cierto sentido; ***be under way*** haber comenzado, estar en marcha; ***give way*** MOT ceder el paso; (*collapse*) ceder; ***give way to*** (*be replaced by*) ser reemplazado por; ***have one's (own) way*** salirse con la suya; ***OK, we'll do it your way*** de acuerdo, lo haremos a tu manera; ***lead the way*** abrir (el) camino; *fig* marcar la pauta; ***lose one's way*** perderse; ***be in the way*** (*be an obstruction*) estar en medio; ***it's on the way to the station*** está camino de la estación; ***I was on my way to the station*** iba camino de la estación; ***no way!*** ¡ni hablar!, ¡de ninguna manera!; ***there's no way he can do it*** es imposible que lo haga **2** *adv* F (*much*): ***it's way too soon to decide*** es demasiado pronto como para decidir; ***they are way behind with their work*** van atrasadísimos en el trabajo

way ˈ**in** entrada *f*

way of ˈ**life** modo *m* de vida

way ˈ**out** *n* salida *f*; *fig*: *from situation* salida *f*

we [wiː] *pron* nosotros *mpl*, nosotras *fpl*; ***we are the best*** somos los mejores; ***they're going, but we're not*** ellos van, pero nosotros no

weak [wiːk] *adj* débil; *tea, coffee* poco cargado

weak·en [ˈwiːkn] **1** *v/t* debilitar **2** *v/i* debilitarse

weak·ling [ˈwiːklɪŋ] *morally* cobarde *m/f*; *physically* enclenque *m/f*

weak·ness [ˈwiːknɪs] debilidad *f*; ***have a weakness for sth*** (*liking*) sentir debilidad por algo

wealth [welθ] riqueza *f*; ***a wealth of*** abundancia de

wealth·y [ˈwelθɪ] *adj* rico

wean [wiːn] *v/t* destetar

weap·on [ˈwepən] arma *f*

wear [wer] **1** *n*: ***wear (and tear)*** desgaste *m*; ***clothes for everyday / evening wear*** ropa *f* de diario / de noche **2** *v/t* (*pret* ***wore***, *pp* ***worn***) (*have on*) llevar; (*damage*) desgastar **3** *v/i* (*pret* ***wore***, *pp* ***worn***) (*wear out*) desgastarse; (*last*) durar

◆ **wear away 1** *v/i* desgastarse **2** *v/t* desgastar

◆ **wear down** *v/t* agotar

◆ **wear off** *v/i of effect, feeling* pasar

◆ **wear out 1** *v/t* (*tire*) agotar; *shoes* desgastar **2** *v/i of shoes, carpet* desgastarse

wea·ri·ly [ˈwɪrɪlɪ] *adv* cansinamente

wear·ing [ˈwerɪŋ] *adj* (*tiring*) agotador

wear·y [ˈwɪrɪ] *adj* cansado

weath·er [ˈweðər] **1** *n* tiempo *m*; ***what's the weather like?*** ¿qué tiempo hace?; ***be feeling under the weather*** estar pachucho **2** *v/t crisis* capear, superar

ˈ**weath·er-beat·en** *adj* curtido

ˈ**weath·er chart** mapa *m* del tiempo

ˈ**weath·er fore·cast** pronóstico *m* del tiempo

ˈ**weath·er·man** hombre *m* del tiempo

weave [wiːv] **1** *v/t* (*pret* ***wove***, *pp* ***woven***) tejer **2** *v/i* (*pret* ***wove***, *pp* ***woven***) *move* zigzaguear

web [web] *of spider* tela *f*; ***the Web*** COMPUT la Web

webbed ˈ**feet** patas *fpl* palmeadas

ˈ**web page** página *f* web

ˈ**web site** sitio *m* web

wed·ding [ˈwedɪŋ] boda *f*

ˈ**wed·ding an·ni·ver·sa·ry** aniversario *m* de boda

ˈ**wed·ding cake** pastel *m or* tarta *f* de boda

ˈ**wed·ding day** día *f* de la boda

ˈ**wed·ding dress** vestido *m* de boda *or*

W

novia
'wed·ding ring anillo *m* de boda
wedge [wedʒ] **1** *n to hold sth in place* cuña *f*; *of cheese etc* trozo *m* **2** *v/t*: ***wedge a door open*** calzar una puerta para que se quede abierta
Wed·nes·day ['wenzdeɪ] miércoles *m inv*
weed [wiːd] **1** *n* mala hierba **2** *v/t* escardar
◆ **weed out** *v/t* (*remove*) eliminar; *candidates* descartar
'weed-kill·er herbicida *m*
weed·y ['wiːdɪ] *adj* F esmirriado, enclenque
week [wiːk] semana *f*; ***a week tomorrow*** dentro de una semana
'week·day día *m* de la semana
week'end fin *m* de semana; ***on the weekend*** el fin de semana
week·ly ['wiːklɪ] **1** *adj* semanal **2** *n magazine* semanario *m* **3** *adv* semanalmente
weep [wiːp] *v/i* (*pret & pp* **wept**) llorar
'weep·ing wil·low sauce *m* llorón
weep·y ['wiːpɪ] *adj*: ***be weepy*** estar lloroso
wee-wee 1 *n* F pipí *m*; ***do a wee-wee*** hacer pipí **2** *v/i* F hacer pipí
weigh¹ [weɪ] **1** *v/t* pesar **2** *v/i* pesar; ***how much do you weigh?*** ¿cuánto pesas?
weigh² [weɪ] *v/t*: ***weigh anchor*** levar anclas
◆ **weigh down** *v/t* cargar; ***be weighed down with*** *bags* ir cargado con; *worries* estar abrumado por
◆ **weigh on** *v/t* preocupar
◆ **weigh up** *v/t* (*assess*) sopesar
weight [weɪt] peso *m*; ***put on weight*** engordar, ganar peso; ***lose weight*** adelgazar, perder peso
◆ **weight down** *v/t* sujetar (*con pesos*)
'weight·less ['weɪtləs] *adj* ingrávido
'weight·less·ness ['weɪtləsnəs] ingravidez *f*
'weight·lift·er levantador(a) *m*(*f*) de pesas
'weight·lift·ing halterofilia *f*, levantamiento *m* de pesas
weight·y ['weɪtɪ] *adj* (*fig*: *important*) serio
weir [wɪr] presa *f* (*rebasadero*)
weird [wɪrd] *adj* extraño, raro
weird·ly ['wɪrdlɪ] *adv* extrañamente
weird·o ['wɪrdoʊ] *n* F bicho *m* raro F
wel·come ['welkəm] **1** *adj* bienvenido; ***you're welcome!*** ¡de nada!; ***you're welcome to try some*** prueba algunos, por favor **2** *n* bienvenida *f* **3** *v/t guests etc* dar la bienvenida a; *fig*: *decision etc* acoger positivamente
weld [weld] *v/t* soldar
weld·er ['weldər] soldador(a) *m*(*f*)
wel·fare ['welfer] bienestar *m*; *financial assistance* subsidio *m* estatal; ***be on welfare*** estar recibiendo subsidios del Estado
'wel·fare check *cheque con el importe del subsidio estatal*
wel·fare 'state estado *m* del bienestar
'wel·fare work trabajo *m* social
'wel·fare work·er asistente *m/f* social
well¹ [wel] *n for water, oil* pozo *m*
well² 1 *adv* bien; ***as well*** (*too*) también; ***as well as*** (*in addition to*) así como; ***it's just as well you told me*** menos mal que me lo dijiste; ***very well*** muy bien; ***well, well!*** *surprise* ¡caramba!; ***well …*** *uncertainty, thinking* bueno …; ***you might as well spend the night here*** ya puestos quédate a pasar la noche aquí; ***you might as well throw it out*** yo de ti lo tiraría **2** *adj*: ***be well*** estar bien; ***how are you? - I'm very well*** ¿cómo estás? - muy bien; ***feel well*** sentirse bien; ***get well soon!*** ¡ponte bueno!, ¡que te mejores!
well-'bal·anced *adj person, diet* equilibrado
well-be'haved *adj* educado
well-'be·ing bienestar *m*
well-'built *adj also euph* fornido
well-'done *adj meat* muy hecho
well-'dressed *adj* bien vestido
well-'earned *adj* merecido
well-'heeled *adj* F adinerado, *Span* con pasta F
well-in'formed *adj* bien informado
well-'known *adj fact* conocido; *person* conocido, famoso
well-'made *adj* bien hecho
well-'man·nered *adj* educado
well-'mean·ing *adj* bienintencionado
well-'off *adj* acomodado
well-'paid *adj* bien pagado
well-'read *adj*: ***be well-read*** haber leído mucho
well-'timed *adj* oportuno
well-to-'do *adj* acomodado
'well-wish·er admirador(a) *m*(*f*)
well-'worn *adj* gastado
Welsh [welʃ] **1** *adj* galés **2** *n language* galés; ***the Welsh*** los galeses
went [went] *pret* → ***go***
wept [wept] *pret & pp* → ***weep***
were [wer] *pret* → ***be***
west [west] **1** *n* oeste *m*; ***the West*** (*Western nations*) Occidente *m*; (*western part of a country*) el oeste **2** *adj* del oeste; ***west Africa*** África occidental **3** *adv travel* hacia el oeste; ***west of*** al oeste de
West 'Coast *of USA* Costa *f* Oeste

West 'In·di·an 1 *adj* antillano **2** *n* antillano(-a) *m(f)*
West In·dies ['ɪndiːz] *npl*: ***the West Indies*** las Antillas
west·er·ly ['westərlɪ] *adj wind* del oeste; *direction* hacia el oeste
west·ern ['westərn] **1** *adj* occidental; ***Western*** occidental **2** *n movie* western *m*, película *f* del oeste
West·ern·er ['westərnər] occidental *m/f*
west·ern·ized ['westərnaɪzd] *adj* occidentalizado
west·ward ['westwərd] *adv* hacia el oeste
wet [wet] *adj* mojado; (*damp*) húmedo; (*rainy*) lluvioso; ***get wet*** mojarse; ***wet paint*** *as sign* recién pintado; ***be wet through*** estar empapado
wet 'blan·ket F aguafiestas *m/f inv*
'wet suit *for diving* traje *m* de neopreno
whack [wæk] **1** *n* F (*blow*) porrazo *m* F; F (*share*) parte *f* **2** *v/t* F dar un porrazo a F
whacked [wækt] *adj* F hecho polvo F
whale [weɪl] ballena *f*
whal·ing ['weɪlɪŋ] caza *f* de ballenas
wharf [wɔːrf] *n* embarcadero *m*
what [wɑːt] **1** *pron* qué; ***what is that?*** ¿qué es eso?; ***what is it?*** (*what do you want*) ¿qué quieres?; ***what?*** (*what do you want*) ¿qué?; (*what did you say*) ¿qué?, ¿cómo?; *astonishment* ¿qué?; ***what about some dinner?*** ¿os apetece cenar?; ***what about heading home?*** ¿y si nos fuéramos a casa?; ***what for?*** (*why*) ¿para qué?; ***so what?*** ¿y qué?; ***what is the book about?*** ¿de qué trata el libro?; ***take what you need*** toma lo que te haga falta **2** *adj* qué; ***what university are you at?*** ¿en qué universidad estás?; ***what color is the car?*** ¿de qué color es el coche?
what·ev·er [wɑːt'evər] **1** *pron*: ***I'll do whatever you want*** haré lo que quieras; ***whatever gave you that idea?*** ¿se puede saber qué te ha dado esa idea?; ***whatever the season*** en cualquier estación; ***whatever people say*** diga lo que diga la gente **2** *adj* cualquier; ***you have no reason whatever to worry*** no tienes por qué preocuparte en absoluto
wheat [wiːt] trigo *m*
whee·dle ['wiːdl] *v/t*: ***wheedle sth out of s.o.*** camelar algo a alguien
wheel [wiːl] **1** *n* rueda *f*; (*steering wheel*) volante *m* **2** *v/t bicycle* empujar **3** *v/i of birds* volar en círculo
◆ **wheel around** *v/i* darse la vuelta
'wheel·bar·row carretilla *f*
'wheel·chair silla *f* de ruedas
'wheel clamp cepo *m*
wheeze [wiːz] *n* resoplido *m*
when [wen] **1** *adv* cuándo; ***when do you open?*** ¿a qué hora abren? **2** *conj* cuando; ***when I was a child*** cuando era niño
when·ev·er [wen'evər] *adv* (*each time*) cada vez que; ***call me whenever you like*** llámame cuando quieras; ***I go to Paris whenever I can afford it*** voy a París siempre que me lo puedo permitir
where [wer] **1** *adv* dónde; ***where from?*** ¿de dónde?; ***where to?*** ¿a dónde? **2** *conj* donde; ***this is where I used to live*** aquí es donde vivía antes
where·a·bouts [werə'baʊts] **1** *adv* dónde **2** *npl* ***nothing is known of his whereabouts*** está en paradero desconocido
where·as *conj* mientras que
wher·ev·er [wer'evər] **1** *conj* dondequiera que; ***sit wherever you like*** siéntate donde prefieras **2** *adv* dónde
whet [wet] *v/t* (*pret & pp* ***whetted***) *appetite* abrir
wheth·er ['weðər] *conj* si; ***I don't know whether to tell him or not*** no sé si decírselo o no; ***whether you approve or not*** te parezca bien o no
which [wɪʧ] **1** *adj* qué; ***which one is yours?*** ¿cuál es tuyo? **2** *pron interrogative* cuál; *relative* que; ***take one, it doesn't matter which*** toma uno, no importa cuál
which·ev·er [wɪʧ'evər] **1** *adj*: ***whichever color you choose*** elijas el color que elijas **2** *pron*: ***whichever you like*** el que quieras; ***use whichever of the methods you prefer*** utiliza el método que prefieras
whiff [wɪf] (*smell*) olorcillo *m*
while [waɪl] **1** *conj* mientras; (*although*) si bien **2** *n* rato *m*; ***a long while*** un rato largo; ***for a while*** durante un tiempo; ***I lived in Tokyo for a while*** viví en Tokio una temporada; ***I'll wait a while longer*** esperaré un rato más
◆ **while away** *v/t* pasar
whim [wɪm] capricho *m*
whim·per ['wɪmpər] **1** *n* gimoteo *m* **2** *v/i* gimotear
whine [waɪn] *v/i of dog* gimotear; F (*complain*) quejarse
whip [wɪp] **1** *n* látigo *m* **2** *v/t* (*pret & pp* ***whipped***) (*beat*) azotar; *cream* batir, montar; F (*defeat*) dar una paliza a F
◆ **whip out** *v/t* F sacar rápidamente
◆ **whip up** *v/t* (*arouse*) agitar; F *meal* improvisar
'whipped cream [wɪpt] nata *f* montada
whip·ping ['wɪpɪŋ] (*beating*) azotes *mpl*; F (*defeat*) paliza *f* F

'whip·round F colecta *f*; ***have a whip-round*** hacer una colecta
whirl [wɜːrl] **1** *n*: ***my mind is in a whirl*** me da vueltas la cabeza **2** *v/i* dar vueltas
'whirl·pool *in river* remolino *m*; *for relaxation* bañera *f* de hidromasaje
whirr [wɜːr] *v/i* zumbar
whisk [wɪsk] **1** *n kitchen implement* **2** *v/t eggs* batir
◆ **whisk away** *v/t* retirar rápidamente
whis·kers ['wɪskərz] *npl of man* patillas *fpl*; *of animal* bigotes *mpl*
whis·key, whis·ky ['wɪskɪ] whisky *m*
whis·per ['wɪspər] **1** *n* susurro *m*; (*rumor*) rumor *m* **2** *v/i* susurrar **3** *v/t* susurrar
whis·tle ['wɪsl] **1** *n sound* silbido *m*; *device* silbato *m* **2** *v/t & v/i* silbar
white [waɪt] **1** *n color* blanco *m*; *of egg* clara *f*; *person* blanco(-a) *m*(*f*) **2** *adj* blanco; ***her face went white*** se puso blanca
white 'Christ·mas Navidades *fpl* blancas
white 'cof·fee *Br* café *m* con leche
white-col·lar 'work·er *persona que trabaja en una oficina*
'White House Casa *f* Blanca
white 'lie mentira *f* piadosa
white 'meat carne *f* blanca
'white·wash 1 *n* cal *f*; *fig* encubrimiento *m* **2** *v/t* encalar
white 'wine vino *m* blanco
whit·tle ['wɪtl] *v/t wood* tallar
◆ **whittle down** *v/t* reducir
whiz(z) [wɪz] *n*: ***be a whiz(z) at*** F ser un genio de
◆ **whizz by, whizz past** *v/i of time, car* pasar zumbando
'whizz·kid F joven *m/f* prodigio
who [huː] *pron interrogative* ¿quién?; *relative* que; ***who do you want to speak to?*** ¿con quién quieres hablar?; ***I don't know who to believe?*** no sé a quién creer
who·dun·(n)it [huː'dʌnɪt] *libro o película centrados en la resolución de un caso*
who·ev·er [huː'evər] *pron* quienquiera; ***whoever can that be calling at this time of night?*** ¿pero quién llama a estas horas de la noche?
whole [hoʊl] **1** *adj* entero; ***the whole town / country*** toda la ciudad / todo el país; ***he drank / ate the whole lot*** se lo bebió / comió todo; ***it's a whole lot easier / better*** es mucho más fácil / mucho mejor **2** *n* totalidad *f*; ***the whole of the United States*** la totalidad de los Estados Unidos; ***on the whole*** en general
whole-heart·ed [hoʊl'hɑːrtɪd] *adj* incondicional
whole-heart·ed·ly [hoʊl'hɑːrtɪdlɪ] *adv* incondicionalmente
whole·meal 'bread pan *m* integral
'whole·sale 1 *adj* al por mayor; *fig* indiscriminado **2** *adv* al por mayor
whole·sal·er ['hoʊlseɪlər] mayorista *m/f*
whole·some ['hoʊlsəm] *adj* saludable, sano
whol·ly ['hoʊlɪ] *adv* completamente
whol·ly owned 'sub·sid·i·ar·y subsidiaria *f* en propiedad absoluta
whom [huːm] *pron fml* quién; ***whom did you see?*** ¿a quién vio?; ***the person to whom I was speaking*** la persona con la que estaba hablando
whoop·ing cough ['huːpɪŋ] tos *f* ferina
whop·ping ['wɑːpɪŋ] *adj* F enorme
whore [hɔːr] *n* prostituta *f*
whose [huːz] **1** *pron interrogative* de quién; *relative* cuyo(-a); ***whose is this?*** ¿de quién es esto?; ***a country whose economy is booming*** un país cuya economía está experimentando un boom **2** *adj* de quién; ***whose bike is that?*** ¿de quién es esa bici?
why [waɪ] *adv interrogative* por qué; *relative* por qué; ***that's why*** por eso; ***why not?*** ¿por qué no?
wick [wɪk] pabilo *m*
wick·ed ['wɪkɪd] *adj* malvado, perverso
wick·er ['wɪkər] *adj* de mimbre
wick·er 'chair silla *f* de mimbre
wick·et ['wɪkɪt] *in station, bank etc* ventanilla *f*
wide [waɪd] *adj* ancho; *experience, range* amplio; ***be 12 feet wide*** tener 12 pies de ancho
wide a'wake *adj* completamente despierto
wide·ly ['waɪdlɪ] *adv used, known* ampliamente
wid·en ['waɪdn] **1** *v/t* ensanchar **2** *v/i* ensancharse
wide-'o·pen *adj* abierto de par en par
wide-'rang·ing *adj* amplio
'wide·spread *adj* extendido, muy difundido
wid·ow ['wɪdoʊ] *n* viuda *f*
wid·ow·er ['wɪdoʊər] viudo *m*
width [wɪdθ] anchura *f*, ancho *m*
wield [wiːld] *v/t weapon* empuñar; *power* detentar
wife [waɪf] (*pl* ***wives*** [waɪvz]) mujer *f*, esposa *f*
wig [wɪg] peluca *f*
wig·gle ['wɪgl] *v/t* menear
wild [waɪld] **1** *adj animal* salvaje; *flower* silvestre; *teenager, party* descontrolado; (*crazy: scheme*) descabellado; *applause*

arrebatado; ***be wild about …*** (*keen on*) estar loco por …; ***go wild*** (*express enthusiasm*) volverse loco; (*become angry*) ponerse hecho una furia; ***run wild*** *of children* descontrolarse **2** *n*: ***the wilds*** los parajes remotos

wil·der·ness ['wɪldərnɪs] (*empty place*) desierto *m*, yermo *m*; (*fig*: *garden etc*) jungla *f*

'wild·fire: ***spread like wildfire*** extenderse como un reguero de pólvora

wild-'goose chase búsqueda *f* infructuosa

'wild·life flora *f* y fauna; ***wildlife program*** TV documental *f* sobre la naturaleza

wild·ly ['waɪldlɪ] *adv applaud* enfervorizadamente; ***I'm not wildly enthusiastic about the idea*** la idea no me emociona demasiado

wil·ful *Br* → ***willful***

will[1] [wɪl] *n* LAW testamento *m*

will[2] [wɪl] *n* (*willpower*) voluntad *f*

will[3] [wɪl] *v/aux*: ***I will let you know tomorrow*** te lo diré mañana; ***will you be there?*** ¿estarás allí?; ***I won't be back until late*** volveré tarde; ***you will call me, won't you?*** me llamarás, ¿verdad?; ***I'll pay for this - no you won't*** esto lo pago yo - no, ni hablar; ***the car won't start*** el coche no arranca; ***will you tell her that …?*** ¿le quieres decir que …?; ***will you have some more tea?*** ¿quiere más té?; ***will you stop that!*** ¡basta ya!

will·ful ['wɪlfəl] *adj person* tozudo, obstinado; *action* deliberado, intencionado

will·ing ['wɪlɪŋ] *adj* dispuesto

will·ing·ly ['wɪlɪŋlɪ] *adv* gustosamente

will·ing·ness ['wɪlɪŋnɪs] buena disposición *f*

wil·low ['wɪloʊ] sauce *m*

'will·pow·er fuerza *f* de voluntad

wil·ly-nil·ly [wɪlɪ'nɪlɪ] *adv* (*at random*) a la buena de Dios

wilt [wɪlt] *v/i of plant* marchitarse

wi·ly ['waɪlɪ] *adj* astuto

wimp [wɪmp] F enclenque *m/f* F, blandengue *m/f* F

win [wɪn] **1** *n* victoria *f*, triunfo *m* **2** *v/t & v/i* (*pret & pp* **won**) ganar

◆ **win back** *v/t* recuperar

wince [wɪns] *v/i* hacer una mueca de dolor

winch [wɪntʃ] *n* torno *m*, cabestrante *m*

wind[1] [wɪnd] **1** *n* viento *m*; (*flatulence*) gases *mpl*; ***get wind of …*** enterarse de … **2** *v/t*: ***be winded*** quedarse sin respiración

wind[2] [waɪnd] **1** *v/i* (*pret & pp* **wound**) zigzaguear; serpentear; ***wind around*** enrollarse en **2** *v/t* (*pret & pp* **wound**) enrollar

◆ **wind down 1** *v/i of party etc* ir finalizando **2** *v/t car window* bajar, abrir; *business* ir reduciendo

◆ **wind up 1** *v/t clock* dar cuerda a; *car window* subir, cerrar; *speech, presentation* finalizar; *business, affairs* concluir; *company* cerrar **2** *v/i* (*finish*) concluir; ***wind up in hospital*** acabar en el hospital

'wind-bag F cotorra *f* F

'wind·fall *fig* dinero *m* inesperado

wind·ing ['waɪndɪŋ] *adj* zigzagueante, serpenteante

'wind in·stru·ment instrumento *m* de viento

'wind·mill molino *m* de viento

win·dow ['wɪndoʊ] *also* COMPUT ventana *f*; *of car* ventana *f*, ventanilla *f*; ***in the window*** *of store* en el escaparate *or L.Am.* la vidriera

'win·dow box jardinera *f*

'win·dow clean·er *person* limpiacristales *m/f inv*

'win·dow·pane cristal *f* (*de una ventana*)

'win·dow seat *on plane, train* asiento *m* de ventana

'win·dow-shop *v/i* (*pret & pp* **window-shopped**): ***go window-shopping*** ir de escaparates *or L.Am.* vidrieras

win·dow·sill ['wɪndoʊsɪl] alféizar *m*

'wind·pipe tráquea *f*

'wind·screen *Br*, **'wind·shield** parabrisas *m inv*

'wind·shield wip·er limpiaparabrisas *m inv*

'wind·surf·er *person* windsurfista *m/f*; *board* tabla *f* de windsurf

'wind·surf·ing el windsurf

wind·y ['wɪndɪ] *adj* ventoso; ***a windy day*** un día de mucho viento; ***it's very windy today*** hoy hace mucho viento; ***it's getting windy*** está empezando a soplar el viento

wine [waɪn] vino *m*

'wine bar *bar especializado en vinos*

'wine cel·lar bodega *f*

'wine glass copa *f* de vino

'wine list lista *f* de vinos

'wine mak·er viticultor(a) *m(f)*

'wine mer·chant comerciante *m/f* de vinos

win·ery ['waɪnərɪ] bodega *f*

wing [wɪŋ] *n* ala *f*; SP lateral *m/f*, extremo *m/f*

'wing·span envergadura *f*

wink [wɪŋk] **1** *n* guiño *m*; ***I didn't sleep a wink*** F no pegué ojo **2** *v/i of person* gui-

ñar, hacer un guiño; ***wink at s.o.*** guiñar *or* hacer un guiño a alguien
win·ner ['wɪnər] ganador(a) *m(f)*, vencedor(a) *m(f)*; *of lottery* acertante *m/f*
win·ning ['wɪnɪŋ] *adj* ganador
'win·ning post meta *f*
win·nings ['wɪnɪŋz] *npl* ganancias *fpl*
win·ter ['wɪntər] *n* invierno *m*
win·ter 'sports *npl* deportes *mpl* de invierno
win·try ['wɪntrɪ] *adj* invernal
wipe [waɪp] *v/t* limpiar; *tape* borrar
◆ **wipe out** *v/t* (*kill, destroy*) eliminar; *debt* saldar
wip·er ['waɪpər] → ***windshield wiper***
wire [waɪr] *n* alambre *m*; ELEC cable *m*
wire·less ['waɪrlɪs] radio *f*
wire 'net·ting tela *f* metálica
wir·ing ['waɪrɪŋ] *n* ELEC cableado *m*
wir·y ['waɪrɪ] *adj person* fibroso
wis·dom ['wɪzdəm] *of person* sabiduría *f*; *of action* prudencia *f*, sensatez *f*
'wis·dom tooth muela *f* del juicio
wise [waɪz] *adj* sabio; *action, decision* prudente, sensato
'wise·crack *n* F chiste *m*, comentario *m* gracioso
'wise guy *pej* sabelotodo *m*
wise·ly ['waɪzlɪ] *adv act* prudentemente, sensatamente
wish [wɪʃ] **1** *n* deseo *m*; ***best wishes*** un saludo cordial; ***make a wish*** pedir un deseo **2** *v/t* desear; ***I wish that you could stay*** ojalá te pudieras quedar; ***wish s.o. well*** desear a alguien lo mejor; ***I wished him good luck*** le deseé buena suerte **3** *v/i*: ***wish for*** desear
'wish·bone espoleta *f*
wish·ful 'think·ing ['wɪʃfəl] ilusiones *fpl*; ***that's wishful thinking on her part*** que no se haga ilusiones
wish·y-wash·y ['wɪʃɪwɑːʃɪ] *adj person* anodino; *color* pálido
wisp [wɪsp] *of hair* mechón *m*; *of smoke* voluta *f*
wist·ful ['wɪstfəl] *adj* nostálgico
wist·ful·ly ['wɪstfəlɪ] *adv* con nostalgia
wit [wɪt] (*humor*) ingenio *m*; *person* ingenioso(-a) *m(f)*; ***be at one's wits' end*** estar desesperado; ***keep one's wits about one*** mantener la calma; ***be scared out of one's wits*** estar aterrorizado
witch [wɪʧ] bruja *f*
'witch·hunt *fig* caza *f* de brujas
with [wɪð] *prep* con; ***shivering with fear*** temblando de miedo; ***a girl with brown eyes*** una chica de ojos castaños; ***are you with me?*** (*do you understand*) ¿me sigues?; ***with no money*** sin dinero
with·draw [wɪð'drɒː] **1** *v/t* (*pret* ***withdrew***, *pp* ***withdrawn***) *complaint, money, troops* retirar **2** *v/i* (*pret* ***withdrew***, *pp* ***withdrawn***) *of competitor, troops* retirarse
with·draw·al [wɪð'drɒːəl] *of complaint, application, troops* retirada *f*; *of money* reintegro *m*
with'draw·al symp·toms *npl* síndrome *m* de abstinencia
with·drawn [wɪð'drɒːn] *adj person* retraído
with·er ['wɪðər] *v/i* marchitarse
with'hold *v/t* (*pret & pp* ***withheld***) *information* ocultar; *payment* retener; *consent* negar
with'in *prep* (*inside*) dentro de; *in expressions of time* en menos de; ***within five miles of home*** a cinco millas de casa; ***we kept within the budget*** no superamos el presupuesto; ***it is well within your capabilities*** lo puedes conseguir perfectamente; ***within reach*** al alcance de la mano
with'out *prep* sin; ***without looking / asking*** sin mirar / preguntar
with'stand *v/t* (*pret & pp* ***withstood***) resistir, soportar
wit·ness ['wɪtnɪs] **1** *n* testigo *m/f* **2** *v/t accident, crime* ser testigo de; *signature* firmar en calidad de testigo
'wit·ness stand estrado *m* del testigo
wit·ti·cism ['wɪtɪsɪzm] comentario *m* gracioso *or* agudo
wit·ty ['wɪtɪ] *adj* ingenioso, agudo
wob·ble ['wɑːbl] *v/i* tambalearse
wob·bly ['wɑːblɪ] *adj* tambaleante
wok [wɑːk] wok *m, sartén típica de la cocina china*
woke [woʊk] *pret* → ***wake***[1]
wok·en ['woʊkn] *pp* → ***wake***[1]
wolf [wʊlf] **1** *n* (*pl* ***wolves*** [wʊlvz]) *animal* lobo *m*; (*fig: womanizer*) don juan *m* **2** *v/t*: ***wolf*** (***down***) engullir
'wolf whis·tle *n* silbido *m*
'wolf-whis·tle *v/i*: ***wolf-whistle at s.o.*** silbar a alguien (*como piropo*)
wom·an ['wʊmən] (*pl* ***women*** ['wɪmɪn]) mujer *f*
wom·an 'doc·tor médica *f*
wom·an 'driv·er conductora *f*
wom·an·iz·er ['wʊmənaɪzər] mujeriego(-a) *m(f)*
wom·an·ly ['wʊmənlɪ] *adj* femenino
wom·an 'priest mujer *f* sacerdote
womb [wuːm] matriz *f*, útero *m*
wom·en [wɪmɪn] *pl* → ***woman***
wom·en's lib [wɪmɪnz'lɪb] la liberación de la mujer
wom·en's lib·ber [wɪmɪnz'lɪbər] parti-

dario(-a) *m(f)* de la liberación de la mujer
won [wʌn] *pret & pp* → ***win***
won·der ['wʌndər] **1** *n* (*amazement*) asombro *m*; ***no wonder!*** ¡no me sorprende!; ***it's a wonder that ...*** es increíble que ... **2** *v/i* preguntarse; ***I've often wondered about that*** me he preguntado eso a menudo **3** *v/t* preguntarse; ***I wonder if you could help*** ¿le importaría ayudarme?
won·der·ful ['wʌndərfəl] *adj* maravilloso
won·der·ful·ly ['wʌndərfəlɪ] *adv* (*extremely*) maravillosamente
won't [woʊnt] → ***will³***
wood [wʊd] *n* madera *f*; *for fire* leña *f*; (*forest*) bosque *m*
wood·ed ['wʊdɪd] *adj* arbolado
wood·en ['wʊdn] *adj* (*made of wood*) de madera
wood·peck·er ['wʊdpekər] pájaro *m* carpintero
'wood·wind MUS sección *f* de viento de madera
'wood·work carpintería *f*
wool [wʊl] lana *f*
wool·en, *Br* **wool·len** ['wʊlən] **1** *adj* de lana **2** *n* prenda *f* de lana
word [wɜːrd] **1** *n* palabra *f*; ***I didn't understand a word of what she said*** no entendí nada de lo que dijo; ***is there any word from ...?*** ¿se sabe algo de ...?; ***I've had word from my daughter*** (*news*) he recibido noticias de mi hija; ***you have my word*** tienes mi palabra; ***have words*** (*argue*) discutir; ***have a word with s.o.*** hablar con alguien; ***the words*** *of song* la letra **2** *v/t article, letter* redactar
word·ing ['wɜːrdɪŋ]: ***the wording of a letter*** la redacción de una carta
word 'pro·cess·ing procesamiento *m* de textos
word 'pro·ces·sor *software* procesador *m* de textos
wore [wɔːr] *pret* → ***wear***
work [wɜːrk] **1** *n* (*job*) trabajo *m*; (*employment*) trabajo *m*, empleo *m*; ***out of work*** desempleado, *Span* en el paro; ***be at work*** estar en el trabajo; ***I go to work by bus*** voy al trabajo en autobús **2** *v/i of person* trabajar; *of machine*, (*succeed*) funcionar; ***how does it work?*** *of device* ¿cómo funciona? **3** *v/t employee* hacer trabajar; *machine* hacer funcionar, utilizar
◆ **work off** *v/t bad mood, anger* desahogarse de; *flab* perder haciendo ejercicio
◆ **work out 1** *v/t problem, puzzle* resolver; *solution* encontrar, hallar **2** *v/i at gym* hacer ejercicios; *of relationship etc* funcionar, ir bien
◆ **work out to** *v/t* (*add up to*) sumar
◆ **work up** *v/t appetite* abrir; ***work up enthusiasm*** entusiasmarse; ***get worked up*** (*get angry*) alterarse; (*get nervous*) ponerse nervioso
work·a·ble ['wɜːrkəbl] *adj solution* viable
work·a·hol·ic [wɜːrkə'hɑːlɪk] *n* F *persona obsesionada con el trabajo*
work·er ['wɜːrkər] trabajador(a) *m(f)*; ***she's a good worker*** trabaja bien
'work·day (*hours of work*) jornada *f* laboral; (*not a holiday*) día *m* de trabajo
'work·force trabajadores *mpl*
'work hours *npl* horas *fpl* de trabajo
work·ing ['wɜːrkɪŋ] *n* funcionamiento *m*
'work·ing class clase *f* trabajadora
'work·ing-class *adj* de clase trabajadora
'work·ing con·di·tions *npl* condiciones *fpl* de trabajo
work·ing 'day → ***workday***
'work·ing hours → ***work hours***
work·ing 'knowledge conocimientos *mpl* básicos
work·ing 'moth·er madre *f* que trabaja
'work·load cantidad *f* de trabajo
'work·man obrero *m*
'work·man·like *adj* competente
'work·man·ship factura *f*, confección *f*
work of 'art obra *f* de arte
'work·out sesión *f* de ejercicios
'work per·mit permiso *m* de trabajo
'work·shop (*also seminar*) taller *m*
'work sta·tion estación *f* de trabajo
'work·top encimera *f*
world [wɜːrld] mundo *m*; ***the world of computers / the theater*** el mundo de la informática / del teatro; ***out of this world*** F sensacional
World 'Cup Mundial *m*, Copa *f* del Mundo
world·ly ['wɜːrldlɪ] *adj* mundano
world-'class *adj* de categoría mundial
world-'fa·mous *adj* mundialmente famoso
world 'pow·er potencia *f* mundial
world 're·cord récord *m* mundial *or* del mundo
world 'war guerra *f* mundial
'world·wide 1 *adj* mundial **2** *adv* en todo el mundo
worm [wɜːrm] *n* gusano *m*
worn [wɔːrn] *pp* → ***wear***
worn-'out *adj shoes, carpet, part* gastado; *person* agotado
wor·ried ['wʌrɪd] *adj* preocupado
wor·ried·ly ['wʌrɪdlɪ] *adv* con preocupa-

ción

wor·ry ['wʌrɪ] **1** *n* preocupación *f* **2** *v/t* (*pret & pp* ***worried***) preocupar **3** *v/i* (*pret & pp* ***worried***) preocuparse; ***don't worry, I'll get it!*** ¡no te molestes, ya respondo yo!

wor·ry·ing ['wʌrɪɪŋ] *adj* preocupante

worse [wɜːrs] **1** *adj* peor; ***get worse*** empeorar **2** *adv* peor

wors·en ['wɜːrsn] *v/i* empeorar

wor·ship ['wɜːrʃɪp] **1** *n* culto *m* **2** *v/t* (*pret & pp* ***worshipped***) adorar, rendir culto a; *fig* adorar

worst [wɜːrst] **1** *adj & adv* peor **2** *n*: ***the worst*** lo peor; ***if the worst comes to the worst*** en el peor de los casos

worst-case scen'a·ri·o el peor de los casos

worth [wɜːrθ] *adj*: ***$20 worth of gas*** 20 dólares de gasolina; ***be worth …*** *in monetary terms* valer …; ***the book's worth reading*** valer la pena leer el libro; ***be worth it*** valer la pena

worth·less ['wɜːrθlɪs] *adj person* inútil; ***be worthless*** *of object* no valer nada

worth'while *adj* que vale la pena; ***be worthwhile*** valer la pena

worth·y ['wɜːrðɪ] *adj* digno; *cause* justo; ***be worthy of*** (*deserve*) merecer

would [wʊd] *v/aux*: ***I would help if I could*** te ayudaría si pudiera; ***I said that I would go*** dije que iría; ***I told him I would not leave unless ….*** le dije que no me iría a no ser que …; ***would you like to go to the movies?*** ¿te gustaría ir al cine?; ***would you mind if I smoked?*** ¿le importa si fumo?; ***would you tell her that …?*** ¿le podrías decir que …?; ***would you close the door?*** ¿podrías cerrar la puerta?; ***I would have told you but …*** te lo habría dicho pero …; ***I would not have been so angry if …*** no me habría enfadado tanto si …

wound¹ [wuːnd] **1** *n* herida *f* **2** *v/t with weapon, remark* herir

wound² [waʊnd] *pret & pp* → ***wind²***

wove [woʊv] *pret* → ***weave***

wov·en ['woʊvn] *pp* → ***weave***

wow [waʊ] *int* ¡hala!

wrap [ræp] *v/t* (*pret & pp* ***wrapped***) *parcel, gift* envolver; ***he wrapped a scarf around his neck*** se puso una bufanda al cuello

◆ **wrap up** *v/i against the cold* abrigarse

wrap·per ['ræpər] envoltorio *m*

wrap·ping ['ræpɪŋ] envoltorio *m*

'wrap·ping pa·per papel *m* de envolver

wrath [ræθ] ira *f*

wreath [riːθ] corona *f* de flores

wreck [rek] **1** *n* restos *mpl*; ***be a nervous wreck*** ser un manojo de nervios **2** *v/t ship* hundir; *car* destrozar; *plans, marriage* arruinar

wreck·age ['rekɪdʒ] *of car, plane* restos *mpl*; *of marriage, career* ruina *f*

wreck·er ['rekər] grúa *f*

wreck·ing com·pa·ny ['rekɪŋ] empresa *f* de auxilio en carretera

wrench [rentʃ] **1** *n tool* llave *f* **2** *v/t* (*pull*) arrebatar; ***wrench one's wrist*** hacerse un esguince en la muñeca

wres·tle ['resl] *v/i* luchar

◆ **wrestle with** *v/t problems* combatir

wres·tler ['reslər] luchador(a) *m(f)* (de lucha libre)

wrest·ling ['reslɪŋ] lucha *f* libre

'wres·tling match combate *m* de lucha libre

wrig·gle ['rɪgl] *v/i* (*squirm*) menearse; *along the ground* arrastrarse; *into small space* escurrirse

◆ **wriggle out of** *v/t* librarse de

◆ **wring out** *v/t* (*pret & pp* ***wrung***) *cloth* escurrir

wrin·kle ['rɪŋkl] **1** *n* arruga *f* **2** *v/t clothes* arrugar **3** *v/i of clothes* arrugarse

wrist [rɪst] muñeca *f*

'wrist watch reloj *m* de pulsera

writ [rɪt] LAW mandato *m* judicial

write [raɪt] **1** *v/t* (*pret* ***wrote***, *pp* ***written***) escribir; *check* extender **2** *v/i* (*pret* ***wrote***, *pp* ***written***) escribir

◆ **write down** *v/t* escribir, tomar nota de

◆ **write off** *v/t debt* cancelar, anular; *car* destrozar

writ·er ['raɪtər] escritor(a) *m(f)*; *of book, song* autor(a) *m(f)*

'write-up reseña *f*

writhe [raɪð] *v/i* retorcerse

writ·ing ['raɪtɪŋ] *words, text* escritura *f*; (*hand-writing*) letra *f*; ***in writing*** por escrito

'writ·ing desk escritorio *m*

'writ·ing pa·per papel *m* de escribir

writ·ten ['rɪtn] *pp* → ***write***

wrong [rɒːŋ] **1** *adj answer, information* equivocado; *decision, choice* erróneo; ***be wrong*** *of person* estar equivocado; *of answer* ser incorrecto; *morally* ser injusto; ***what's wrong?*** ¿qué pasa?; ***there is something wrong with the car*** al coche le pasa algo; ***you have the wrong number*** TELEC se ha equivocado **2** *adv* mal; ***go wrong*** *of person* equivocarse; *of marriage, plan etc* fallar **3** *n* mal *m*; ***right a wrong*** deshacer un entuerto; ***he knows right from wrong*** sabe distinguir entre el bien y el mal; ***be in the***

wrong tener la culpa
wrong·ful ['rɒːŋfəl] *adj* ilegal
wrong·ly ['rɒːŋlɪ] *adv* erróneamente
wrote [roʊt] *pret* → ***write***
wrought 'i·ron [rɔːt] hierro *m* forjado
wrung [rʌŋ] *pret & pp* → ***wring***
wry [raɪ] *adj* socarrón

X, Y

xen·o·pho·bi·a [zenoʊ'foʊbɪə] xenofobia *f*
X-ray ['eksreɪ] **1** *n* rayo *m* X; *picture* radiografía *f* **2** *v/t* radiografiar, sacar un radiografía de
xy·lo·phone [zaɪlə'foʊn] xilofón *m*
yacht [jɑːt] yate *m*
yacht·ing ['jɑːtɪŋ] vela *f*
yachts·man ['jɑːtsmən] navegante *m/f* (*en embarcación de vela*)
Yank [jæŋk] F yanqui *m/f*
yank [jæŋk] *v/t* tirar de
yap [jæp] *v/i* (*pret & pp* ***yapped***) *of small dog* ladrar (*con ladridos agudos*); F (*talk a lot*) parlotear F, largar F
yard[1] [jɑːrd] *of prison, institution etc* patio *m*; *behind house* jardín *m*; *for storage* almacén *m* (*al aire libre*)
yard[2] [jɑːrd] *measurement* yarda *f*
'yard·stick patrón *m*
yarn [jɑːrn] *n* (*thread*) hilo *m*; F (*story*) batallita *f* F
yawn [jɒːn] **1** *n* bostezo *m* **2** *v/i* bostezar
year [jɪr] año *m*; ***I've know her for years*** la conozco desde hace años; ***we were in the same year*** *at school* éramos del mismo curso; ***be six years old*** tener seis años (de edad)
year·ly ['jɪrlɪ] **1** *adj* anual **2** *adv* anualmente
yearn [jɜːrn] *v/i* anhelar
◆ **yearn for** *v/t* ansiar
yearn·ing ['jɜːrnɪŋ] *n* anhelo *m*
yeast [jiːst] levadura *f*
yell [jel] **1** *n* grito *m* **2** *v/i* gritar **3** *v/t* gritar
yel·low ['jeloʊ] **1** *n* amarillo *m* **2** *adj* amarillo
yel·low 'pag·es *npl* páginas *fpl* amarillas
yelp [jelp] **1** *n* aullido *m* **2** *v/i* aullar
yes [jes] *int* sí; ***she said yes*** dijo que sí
'yes·man *pej* pelotillero *m*
yes·ter·day ['jestərdeɪ] **1** *adv* ayer; ***the day before yesterday*** anteayer; ***yesterday afternoon*** ayer por la tarde **2** *n* ayer *m*
yet [jet] **1** *adv* todavía, aún; ***as yet*** aún, todavía; ***have you finished yet?*** ¿has acabado ya?; ***he hasn't arrived yet*** todavía *or* aún no ha llegado; ***is he here yet? - not yet*** ¿ha llegado ya? - todavía *or* aún no; ***yet bigger / longer*** aún más grande / largo; ***the fastest one yet*** el más rápido hasta el momento **2** *conj* sin embargo; ***yet I'm not sure*** sin embargo no estoy seguro
yield [jiːld] **1** *n from fields etc* cosecha *f*; *from investment* rendimiento *m* **2** *v/t fruit, good harvest* proporcionar; *interest* rendir, devengar **3** *v/i* (*give way*) ceder; *of driver* ceder el paso
yo·ga ['joʊgə] yoga *m*
yog·hurt ['joʊgərt] yogur *m*
yolk [joʊk] yema *f*
you [juː] *pron singular* tú, *L.Am.* usted, *Rpl*, *C.Am.* vos; *formal* usted; *plural*: *Span* vosotros, vosotras, *L.Am.* ustedes; *formal* ustedes; ***you are clever*** eres / es inteligente; ***do you know him?*** ¿lo conoces / conoce?; ***you go, I'll stay*** tú ve / usted vaya, yo me quedo; ***never know*** nunca se sabe; ***you have to pay*** hay que pagar; ***exercise is good for you*** es bueno hacer ejercicio
young [jʌŋ] *adj* joven
young·ster ['jʌŋstər] joven *m/f*
your [jʊr] *adj singular*: tu, *L.Am.* su; *formal* su; *plural*: *Span* vuestro, *L.Am.* su; *formal* su; ***your house*** tu / su casa; ***your books*** tus / sus libros
yours [jʊrz] *pron singular* el tuyo, la tuya, *L.Am.* el suyo, la suya; *formal* el suyo, la suya; *plural* el vuestro, la vuestra, *L.Am.* el suyo, la suya; *formal* el suyo, la suya; ***a friend of yours*** un amigo tuyo / suyo / vuestro; ***yours ...*** *at end of letter* un saludo
your·self [jʊr'self] *pron reflexive* te, *L.Am.* se; *formal* se; *emphatic* tú mismo *m*, tú misma *f*, *L.Am.* usted mismo, usted misma; *Rpl*, *C.Am.* vos mismo, vos mis-

ma; *formal* usted mismo, usted misma; ***did you hurt yourself?*** ¿te hiciste / se hizo daño?; ***when you see yourself in the mirror*** cuando te ves / se ve en el espejo; ***by yourself*** (*alone*) solo; (*without help*) tú solo, tú mismo, *Rpl, C.Am.* vos solo, vos mismo, *Am* usted solo, usted mismo; *formal* usted solo, usted mismo

your·selves [jʊr'selvz] *pron reflexive* os, *L.Am.* se; *formal* se; *emphatic* vosotros mismos *mpl*, vosotras mismas *fpl*, *Am* ustedes mismos, ustedes mismas; *formal* ustedes mismos, ustedes mismas; ***did you hurt yourselves?*** ¿os hicisteis / se hicieron daño?; ***when you see yourselves in the mirror*** cuando os veis / se ven en el espejo; ***by yourselves*** (*alone*) solos; (*without help*) vosotros solos, *Am* ustedes solos, ustedes mismos; *formal* ustedes solos, ustedes mismos

youth [juːθ] *n* juventud *f*; (*young man*) joven *m/f*

'youth club club *m* juvenil

youth·ful ['juːθfəl] *adj* joven; *fashion, idealism* juvenil

'youth hos·tel albergue *m* juvenil

Yu·go·sla·vi·a [juːgə'slɑːvɪə] Yugoslavia

Yu·go·sla·vi·an [juːgə'slɑːvɪən] **1** *adj* yugoslavo **2** *n* yugoslavo(-a) *m(f)*

yup·pie ['jʌpɪ] F yupi *m/f*

Z

zap [zæp] *v/t* (*pret & pp* ***zapped***) F (COMPUT: *delete*) borrar; (*kill*) liquidar F; (*hit*) golpear; (*send*) enviar

◆ **zap along** *v/i* F (*move fast*) volar F

zapped [zæpt] *adj* F (*exhausted*) hecho polvo F

zap·per ['zæpər] *for changing* TV *channels* telemando *m*, mando *m* a distancia

zap·py ['zæpɪ] *adj* F *car, pace* rápido; (*lively, energetic*) vivo

zeal [ziːl] celo *m*

ze·bra ['zebrə] cebra *f*

ze·ro ['zɪroʊ] cero *m*; ***10 degrees below zero*** 10 bajo cero

ze·ro 'growth crecimiento *m* cero

◆ **zero in on** *v/t* (*identify*) centrarse en

zest [zest] entusiasmo *m*

zig·zag ['zɪgzæg] **1** *n* zigzag *m* **2** *v/i* (*pret & pp* ***zigzagged***) zigzaguear

zilch [zɪltʃ] F nada de nada

zinc [zɪŋk] cinc *m*

zip [zɪp] *Br* cremallera *f*

◆ **zip up** *v/t* (*pret & pp* ***zipped***) *dress, jacket* cerrar la cremallera de; COMPUT compactar

'zip code código *m* postal

zip·per ['zɪpər] cremallera *f*

zit [zɪt] F *on face* grano *m*

zo·di·ac ['zoʊdɪæk] zodiaco *m*; ***signs of the zodiac*** signos *mpl* del zodiaco

zom·bie ['zɑːmbɪ] F (*idiot*) estúpido(-a) *m(f)* F; ***feel like a zombie*** (*exhausted*) sentirse como un zombi

zone [zoʊn] zona *f*

zonked [zɑːŋkt] *adj* P (*exhausted*) molido P

zoo [zuː] zoo *m*

zo·o·log·i·cal [zuːə'lɑːdʒɪkl] *adj* zoológico

zo·ol·o·gist [zuː'ɑːlədʒɪst] zoólogo(-a) *m(f)*

zo·ol·o·gy [zuː'ɑːlədʒɪ] zoología *f*

zoom [zuːm] *v/i* F (*move fast*) ir zumbando F

◆ **zoom in on** *v/t* PHOT hacer un zoom sobre

zoom 'lens zoom *m*

zuc·chi·ni [zuː'kiːnɪ] calabacín *m*

APPENDIX

Spanish verb conjugations

In the following conjugation patterns verb stems are shown in normal type and verb endings in *italic* type. Irregular forms are indicated by **bold** type.

Notes on the formation of tenses.

The following stems can be used to generate derived forms.

Stem forms	Derived forms
I. From the **Present indicative**, *3rd pers sg* (mand*a*, vend*e*, recib*e*)	**Imperative** *2nd pers. sg* (¡mand*a*! ¡vend*e*! ¡recib*e*!)
II. From the **Present subjunctive**, *2nd* and *3rd pers sg* and all plural forms (mand*es*, mand*e*, mand*emos*, mand*éis*, mand*en* - vend*as*, vend*a*, vend*amos*, vend*áis*, vend*an* - recib*as*, recib*a*, recib*amos*, recib*áis*, recib*an*)	**Imperative** *1st pers pl*, *3rd pers sg* and *pl* as well as the negative imperative of the *2nd pers sg* and *pl* (no mand*es*, mand*e* Vd., mand*emos*, no mand*éis*, mand*en* Vds. - no vend*as*, vend*a* Vd., vend*amos*, no vend*áis*, vend*an* Vds. - no recib*as etc*)
III. From the **Preterite**, *3rd pers pl* (mand*aron*, vend*ieron*, recib*ieron*)	**a)** **Imperfect Subjunctive I** by changing …ron to …*ra* (mand*ara*, vend*iera*, recib*iera*) **b)** **Imperfect Subjunctive II** by changing …ron to …*se* (mand*ase*, vend*iese*, recib*iese*) **c)** **Future Subjunctive** by changing …ron to …*re* (mand*are*, vend*iere*, recib*iere*)
IV. From the **Infinitive** (mand*ar*, vend*er*, recib*ir*)	**a)** **Imperative** *2nd pers pl* by changing …r to …*d* (manda*d*, vende*d*, recibi*d*) **b)** **Present participle by** changing …ar to …*ando*, …er and …ir to …*iendo* (or sometimes …*yendo*) (mand*ando*, vend*iendo*, recib*iendo*) **c)** **Future** by adding the *Present* tense endings of ***haber*** (mand*aré*, vend*eré*, recib*iré*) **d)** **Conditional** by adding the *Imperfect* endings of ***haber*** (mand*aría*, vend*ería*, recib*iría*)

V. From the **Past participle** (mand*ado*, vend*ido*, recib*ido*)	all **compound tenses** by placing a form of ***haber*** or ***ser*** in front of the participle.

First Conjugation

⟨**1a**⟩ **mandar.** No change to the written or spoken form of the stem.

Simple tenses

Indicative

	Present	**Imperfect**	**Preterite**
sg	mand*o*	mand*aba*	mand*é*
	mand*as*	mand*abas*	mand*aste*
	mand*a*	mand*aba*	mand*ó*
pl	mand*amos*	mand*ábamos*	mand*amos*
	mand*áis*	mand*abais*	mand*asteis*
	mand*an*	mand*aban*	mand*aron*

	Future	**Conditional**
sg	mand*aré*	mand*aría*
	mand*arás*	mand*arías*
	mand*ará*	mand*aría*
pl	mand*aremos*	mand*aríamos*
	mand*aréis*	mand*aríais*
	mand*arán*	mand*arían*

Subjunctive

Present		**Imperfect I**	**Imperfect II**
sg	mand*e*	mand*ara*	mand*ase*
	mand*es*	mand*aras*	mand*ases*
	mand*e*	mand*ara*	mand*ase*
pl	mand*emos*	mand*áramos*	mand*ásemos*
	mand*éis*	mand*arais*	mand*aseis*
	mand*en*	mand*aran*	mand*asen*

	Future	**Imperative**
sg	mand*are*	—
	mand*ares*	mand*a* (no mand*es*)
	mand*are*	mand*e* Vd.
pl	mand*áremos*	mand*emos*
	mand*areis*	mand*ad* (no mand*éis*)
	mand*aren*	mand*en* Vds.

Infinitive: mand*ar*
Present participle: mand*ando*
Past participle: mand*ado*

Compound tenses

1. **Active forms:** the conjugated form of ***haber*** is placed before the *Past participle* (which does not change):

Indicative

Perfect	*he* mand*ado*	**Future perfect**	*habré* mand*ado*
Pluperfect	*había* mand*ado*	**Past conditional**	*habría* mand*ado*
Past anterior	*hube* mand*ado*		
Past infinitive	*haber* mand*ado*	**Past gerundive**	*habiendo* mand*ado*

Subjunctive

Perfect	*haya* mand*ado*	**Future perfect**	*hubiere* mand*ado*
Pluperfect	*hubiera* mand*ado* *hubiese* mand*ado*		

2. **Passive forms:** the conjugated form of ***ser*** (or ***haber***) is placed before the *Past participle* (which does not change):

Indicative

Present	*soy* mand*ado*	**Past anterior**	*hube sido* mand*ado*
Imperfect	*era* mand*ado*	**Future**	*seré* mand*ado*
Preterite	*fui* mand*ado*	**Future perfect**	*habré sido* mand*ado*
Perfect	*he sido* mand*ado*	**Conditional**	*sería* mand*ado*
Pluperfect	*había sido* mand*ado*	**Past conditional**	*habría sido* mand*ado*

Infinitive		**Gerundive**	
Present	*ser* mand*ado etc*	**Present**	*siendo* mand*ado*
Past	*haber sido* mand*ado*	**Past**	*habiendo sido* mand*ado*

Subjunctive

Present	*sea* mand*ado*	**Pluperfect**	*hubiera sido* man-dado *hubiese sido* mand*ado*
Imperfect	*fuera* mand*ado* *fuese mandado*		
Future	*fuere mandado*	**Future perfect**	*hubiere sido mandado*
Past	*haya sido mandado*		

	Infinitive	Present Indicative	Present Subjunctive	Preterite
⟨**1b**⟩	**cambiar.** Model for all …*iar* verbs, unless formed like *variar* ⟨1c⟩.			
		cambi*o*	cambi*e*	cambi*é*
		cambi*as*	cambi*es*	cambi*aste*
		cambi*a*	cambi*e*	cambi*ó*
		cambi*amos*	cambi*emos*	cambi*amos*
		cambi*áis*	cambi*éis*	cambi*asteis*
		cambi*an*	cambi*en*	cambi*aron*
⟨**1c**⟩	**variar.** *i* becomes *í* when the stem is stressed.			
		var**í***o*	var**í***e*	vari*é*
		var**í***as*	var**í***es*	vari*aste*
		var**í***a*	var**í***e*	vari*ó*
		vari*amos*	vari*emos*	vari*amos*
		vari*áis*	vari*éis*	vari*asteis*
		var**í***an*	var**í***en*	vari*aron*
⟨**1d**⟩	**evacuar.** Model for all …*uar* verbs, unless formed like *acentuar* ⟨1e⟩.			
		evac*uo*	evac*ue*	evac*ué*
		evac*uas*	evac*ues*	evac*uaste*
		evac*ua*	evac*ue*	evac*uó*
		evac*uamos*	evac*uemos*	evac*uamos*
		evac*uáis*	evac*uéis*	evac*uasteis*
		evac*uan*	evac*uen*	evac*uaron*
⟨**1e**⟩	**acentuar.** *u* becomes *ú* when the stem is stressed.			
		acent**ú***o*	acent**ú***e*	acentu*é*
		acent**ú***as*	acent**ú***es*	acentu*aste*
		acent**ú***a*	acent**ú***e*	acentu*ó*
		acentu*amos*	acentu*emos*	acentu*amos*
		acentu*áis*	acentu*éis*	acentu*asteis*
		acent**ú***an*	acent**ú***en*	acentu*aron*
⟨**1f**⟩	**cruzar.** Final *z* in the stem becomes *c* before *e*. Model for all …*zar* verbs.			
		cruz*o*	cru**c***e*	cruc*é*
		cruz*as*	cru**c***es*	cruz*aste*
		cruz*a*	cru**c***e*	cruz*ó*
		cruz*amos*	cru**c***emos*	cruz*amos*
		cruz*áis*	cru**c***éis*	cruz*asteis*
		cruz*an*	cru**c***en*	cruz*aron*

	Infinitive	Present Indicative	Present Subjunctive	Preterite
⟨**1g**⟩	**tocar.** Final *c* in the stem becomes *qu* before *e*. Model for all *...car* verbs.			
		toc*o*	toqu*e*	toqu*é*
		toc*as*	to**qu***es*	toc*aste*
		toc*a*	to**qu***e*	toc*ó*
		toc*amos*	to**qu***emos*	toc*amos*
		toc*áis*	to**qu***éis*	toc*asteis*
		toc*an*	to**qu***en*	toc*aron*
⟨**1h**⟩	**pagar.** Final *g* in the stem becomes *gu* (*u* is silent) before *e*. Model for all *...gar* verbs.			
		pag*o*	pagu*e*	pagu*é*
		pag*as*	pa**gu***es*	pag*aste*
		pag*a*	pa**gu***e*	pag*ó*
		pag*amos*	pa**gu***emos*	pag*amos*
		pag*áis*	pa**gu***éis*	pag*asteis*
		pag*an*	pa**gu***en*	pag*aron*
⟨**1i**⟩	**fraguar.** Final *gu* in the stem becomes *gü* before *e* (*u* with dieresis is pronounced). Model for all *...guar* verbs.			
		fragu*o*	fragü*e*	fragü*é*
		fragu*as*	fra**gü***es*	fragu*aste*
		fragu*a*	fra**gü***e*	fragu*ó*
		fragu*amos*	fra**gü***emos*	fragu*amos*
		fragu*áis*	fra**gü***éis*	fragu*asteis*
		fragu*an*	fra**gü***en*	fragu*aron*
⟨**1k**⟩	**pensar.** Stressed *e* in the stem becomes *ie*.			
		piens*o*	**pien**s*e*	pens*é*
		piens*as*	**pien**s*es*	pens*aste*
		piens*a*	**pien**s*e*	pens*ó*
		pens*amos*	pens*emos*	pens*amos*
		pens*áis*	pens*éis*	pens*asteis*
		piens*an*	**pien**s*en*	pens*aron*
⟨**1l**⟩	**errar.** Stressed *e* in the stem becomes *ye* (because it comes at the beginning of the word).			
		yerr*o*	**ye**rr*e*	err*é*
		yerr*as*	**ye**rr*es*	err*aste*
		yerr*a*	**ye**rr*e*	err*ó*
		err*amos*	err*emos*	err*amos*
		err*áis*	err*éis*	err*asteis*
		yerr*an*	**ye**rr*en*	err*aron*

Infinitive	Present Indicative	Present Subjunctive	Preterite
⟨**1m**⟩ **contar.** Stressed *o* of the stem becomes *ue* (*u* is pronounced).			
	cuent*o*	**cue**nt*e*	cont*é*
	cuent*as*	**cue**nt*es*	cont*aste*
	cuent*a*	**cue**nt*e*	cont*ó*
	cont*amos*	cont*emos*	cont*amos*
	cont*áis*	cont*éis*	cont*asteis*
	cuent*an*	**cue**nt*en*	cont*aron*
⟨**1n**⟩ **agorar.** Stressed *o* of the stem becomes *üe* (*u* with dieresis is pronounced).			
	ag**üe**r*o*	ag**üe**r*e*	agor*é*
	ag**üe**r*as*	ag**üe**r*es*	agor*aste*
	ag**üe**r*a*	ag**üe**r*e*	agor*ó*
	agor*amos*	agor*emos*	agor*amos*
	agor*áis*	agor*éis*	agor*asteis*
	ag**üe**r*an*	ag**üe**r*en*	agor*aron*
⟨**1o**⟩ **jugar.** Stressed *u* in the stem becomes *ue*; final *g* of the stem becomes *gu* before *e*: (*see* ⟨1h⟩); *conjugar*, *enjugar* and *enjugarse* are regular.			
	jueg*o*	**jue**g**u***e*	jug**u***é*
	jueg*as*	**jue**g**u***es*	jug*aste*
	jueg*a*	**jue**g**u***e*	jug*ó*
	jug*amos*	jug**u***emos*	jug*amos*
	jug*áis*	jug**u***éis*	jug*asteis*
	jueg*an*	**jue**g**u***en*	jug*aron*
⟨**1p**⟩ **estar.** *Present indicative 1st pers sg* in …*oy*, otherwise regular, but note the stressed *a*; the *Present subjunctive* has a stress on the *e* in the endings (apart from *1st pers pl*); *Preterite etc* as ⟨21⟩. Otherwise regular.			
	esto**y**	est**é**	est**uve**
	est**á***s*	est**é***s*	est**uvi***ste*
	est**á**	est**é**	est**uvo**
	est*amos*	est*emos*	est**uvi***mos*
	est*áis*	est**é***is*	est**uvi***steis*
	est*án*	est**é***n*	est**uvie***ron*
⟨**1q**⟩ **andar.** *Preterite* and derived forms like *estar* as in ⟨21⟩. Otherwise regular.			
	and*o*	and*e*	and**uve**
	and*as*	and*es*	and**uvi***ste*
	and*a*	and*e*	and**uvo**
	and*amos*	and*emos*	and**uvi***mos*
	and*áis*	and*éis*	and**uvi***steis*
	and*an*	and*en*	and**uvie***ron*

	Infinitive	Present Indicative	Present Subjunctive	Preterite

⟨**1r**⟩ **dar.** *Present indicative 1st pers sg* in *…oy*, otherwise regular. *Present subjunctive 1st* and *3rd pers sg* takes an accent. *Preterite etc* follow the regular second conjugation. Otherwise regular.

		do**y**	**dé**	**di**
		d*as*	d*es*	**di***ste*
		d*a*	**dé**	**di***o*
		d*amos*	d*emos*	**di***mos*
		d*áis*	d*eis*	**di***steis*
		d*an*	d*en*	**die***ron*

Second Conjugation

⟨**2a**⟩ **vender.** No change to the written or spoken form of the stem.

Simple tenses

Indicative

	Present	**Imperfect**	**Preterite**
sg	vend*o*	vend*ía*	vend*í*
	vend*es*	vend*ías*	vend*iste*
	vend*e*	vend*ía*	vendi*ó*
pl	vend*emos*	vend*íamos*	vend*imos*
	vend*éis*	vend*íais*	vend*isteis*
	vend*en*	vend*ían*	vend*ieron*

	Future	**Conditional**
sg	vender*é*	vender*ía*
	vender*ás*	vender*ías*
	vender*á*	vender*ía*
pl	vender*emos*	vender*íamos*
	vender*éis*	vender*íais*
	vender*án*	vender*ían*

Subjunctive

	Present	**Imperfect I**	**Imperfect II**
sg	vend*a*	vend*iera*	vend*iese*
	vend*as*	vend*ieras*	vend*ieses*
	vend*a*	vend*iera*	vend*iese*
pl	vend*amos*	vend*iéramos*	vend*iésemos*
	vend*áis*	vend*ierais*	vend*ieseis*
	vend*an*	vend*ieran*	vend*iesen*

	Future	**Imperative**
sg	vend*iere*	—
	vend*ieres*	vend*e* (no vend*as*)
	vend*iere*	vend*a* Vd.
pl	vend*iéremos*	vend*amos*
	vend*iereis*	vend*ed* (no vend*áis*)
	vend*ieren*	vend*an* Vds.

Infinitive: vend*er*
Present participle: vend*iendo*
Past participle: vend*ido*

Compound tenses

Formed with the *Past participle* together with ***haber*** and ***ser***, see ⟨1a⟩.

Infinitive	Present Indicative	Present Subjunctive	Preterite
⟨2b⟩ **vencer.** Final *c* of the stem becomes *z* bevore *a* and *o*. Model for all ...*cer* verbs where the ...*cer* is proceded by a consonant.			
	ven**z**o	ven**z**a	vencí
	vences	ven**z**as	venciste
	vence	ven**z**a	venció
	vencemos	ven**z**amos	vencimos
	vencéis	ven**z**áis	vencisteis
	vencen	ven**z**an	vencieron
⟨2c⟩ **coger.** Final *g* of the stem becomes *j* before *a* and *o*. Model for all …*ger* verbs.			
	co**j**o	co**j**a	cogí
	coges	co**j**as	cogiste
	coge	co**j**a	cogió
	cogemos	co**j**amos	cogimos
	cogéis	co**j**áis	cogisteis
	cogen	co**j**an	cogieron
⟨2d⟩ **merecer.** Final *c* of the stem becomes *zc* before *a* and *o*.			
	mere**zc**o	mere**zc**a	merecí
	mereces	mere**zc**as	mereciste
	merece	mere**zc**a	mereció
	merecemos	mere**zc**amos	merecimos
	merecéis	mere**zc**áis	merecisteis
	merecen	mere**zc**an	merecieron
⟨2e⟩ **creer.** Unstressed *i* between two vowels becomes *y*. Past participle: *creído*. Present participle: *creyendo*.			
	creo	crea	creí
	crees	creas	creíste
	cree	crca	cre**y**ó
	creemos	creamos	creímos
	creéis	creáis	creísteis
	creen	crean	cre**y**eron
⟨2f⟩ **tañer.** Unstressed *i* is omitted after *ñ* and *ll*; compare ⟨3h⟩ Present participle: *tañendo*.			
	taño	taña	tañí
	tañes	tañas	tañiste
	tañe	taña	ta**ño**
	tañemos	tañamos	tañimos
	tañéis	tañáis	tañisteis
	tañen	tañan	ta**ñe**ron

	Infinitive	Present Indicative	Present Subjunctive	Preterite
⟨2g⟩	**perder.** Stressed *e* in the stem becomes *ie*; model for many other verbs.			
		pierdo	pierda	perdí
		pierdes	pierdas	perdiste
		pierde	pierda	perdió
		perdemos	perdamos	perdimos
		perdéis	perdáis	perdisteis
		pierden	pierdan	perdieron
⟨2h⟩	**mover.** Stressed *o* in the stem becomes *ue*. *…olver* verbs form their *Past participle* with *…uelto*.			
		muevo	mueva	moví
		mueves	muevas	moviste
		mueve	mueva	movió
		movemos	movamos	movimos
		movéis	mováis	movisteis
		mueven	muevan	movieron
⟨2i⟩	**oler.** Stressed *o* in the stem becomes *hue…* (when it comes at the beginning of the word).			
		huelo	huela	olí
		hueles	huelas	oliste
		huele	huela	olió
		olemos	olamos	olimos
		oléis	oláis	olisteis
		huelen	huelan	olieron
⟨2k⟩	**haber.** Many irregular forms. In the *Future* and *Conditional* the *e* after the stem *hab…* is dropped. Future: *habré*. Imperative *2nd pers sg*: *he*.			
		he	haya	hube
		has	hayas	hubiste
		ha	haya	hubo
		hemos	hayamos	hubimos
		habéis	hayáis	hubisteis
		han	hayan	hubieron
⟨2l⟩	**tener.** Irregular in most forms. In the *Future* and *Conditional* the *e* coming after the stem is dropped and a *d* is inserted. Future: *tendré*. Imperative *2nd pers sg*: *ten*.			
		tengo	tenga	tuve
		tienes	tengas	tuviste
		tiene	tenga	tuvo
		tenemos	tengamos	tuvimos
		tenéis	tengáis	tuvisteis
		tienen	tengan	tuvieron

	Infinitive	Present Indicative	Present Subjunctive	Preterite
⟨2m⟩	**caber.** Irregular in many forms. In the *Future* and *Conditional* the *e* coming after the stem is dropped. Future: *cabré*.			
		quep*o*	**quep***a*	**cupe**
		cab*es*	**quep***as*	**cup***iste*
		cab*e*	**quep***a*	**cupo**
		cab*emos*	**quep***amos*	**cup***imos*
		cab*éis*	**quep***áis*	**cup***isteis*
		cab*en*	**quep***an*	**cup***ieron*
⟨2n⟩	**saber.** Irregular in many forms. In the *Future* and *Conditional* the *e* coming after the stem is dropped. Future: *sabré*.			
		sé	**sep***a*	**supe**
		sab*es*	**sep***as*	**sup***iste*
		sab*e*	**sep***a*	**supo**
		sab*emos*	**sep***amos*	**sup***imos*
		sab*éis*	**sep***áis*	**sup***isteis*
		sab*en*	**sep***an*	**sup***ieron*
⟨2o⟩	**caer.** In the *Present …ig…* is inserted after the stem. Unstressed *i* between vowels changes to *y* as with ⟨2e⟩. Past participle: *caído*. Present participle: *cayendo*.			
		ca**ig***o*	cai**g***a*	ca*í*
		ca*es*	cai**g***as*	ca*íste*
		ca*e*	cai**g***a*	ca**y***ó*
		ca*emos*	cai**g***amos*	ca*ímos*
		ca*éis*	cai**g***áis*	ca*ísteis*
		ca*en*	cai**g***an*	ca**y***eron*
⟨2p⟩	**traer.** In the *Present …ig…* is inserted after the stem. The *Preterite* ends in *…je*. In the *Present participle i* changes to *y*. Past participle: *traído*. Present participle: *trayendo*.			
		tra**ig***o*	trai**g***a*	tra**je**
		tra*es*	trai**g***as*	tra**j***iste*
		tra*e*	trai**g***a*	tra**jo**
		tra*emos*	trai**g***amos*	tra**j***imos*
		tra*éis*	trai**g***áis*	tra**j***isteis*
		tra*en*	trai**g***an*	tra**j***eron*

Infinitive	Present Indicative	Present Subjunctive	Preterite

⟨2q⟩ **valer.** In the *Present …g…* is inserted after the stem. In the *Future* and *Conditional* the *e* coming after the stem is dropped and a *…d…* inserted. Future: *valdré*.

	Present Indicative	Present Subjunctive	Preterite
	valgo	valga	valí
	vales	valgas	valiste
	vale	valga	valió
	valemos	valgamos	valimos
	valéis	valgáis	valisteis
	valen	valgan	valieron

⟨2r⟩ **poner.** *…g…* is inserted in the *Present*. Irregular in the *Preterite* and *Past participle*. In the *Future* and *Conditional* the *e* coming after the stem is dropped and a *…d…* inserted. Future: *pondré*. Past participle: *puesto*. Imperative *2nd pers sg*: *pon*.

	Present Indicative	Present Subjunctive	Preterite
	pongo	ponga	puse
	pones	pongas	pusiste
	pone	ponga	puso
	ponemos	pongamos	pusimos
	ponéis	pongáis	pusisteis
	ponen	pongan	pusieron

⟨2s⟩ **hacer.** In the *1st* person of the *Present Indicative* and *Subjunctive g* replaces *c*. Irregular in the *Preterite* and *Past participle*. In the *Future* and *Conditional* the *ce* is dropped. In the *Imperative sg* just the stem is used with *…c* changing to *…z*. Future: *haré*. Imperative *2nd pers sg*: *haz*. Past participle: *hecho*.

	Present Indicative	Present Subjunctive	Preterite
	hago	haga	hice
	haces	hagas	hiciste
	hace	haga	hizo
	hacemos	hagamos	hicimos
	hacéis	hagáis	hicisteis
	hacen	hagan	hicieron

⟨2t⟩ **poder.** Stressed *o* in the stem changes to *…ue…* in the *Present* and the *Imperative*. Irregular in the *Preterite* and *Present participle*. In the *Future* and *Conditional* the *e* coming after the stem is dropped. Future: *podré*. Present participle: *pudiendo*.

	Present Indicative	Present Subjunctive	Preterite
	puedo	pueda	pude
	puedes	puedas	pudiste
	puede	pueda	pudo
	podemos	podamos	pudimos
	podéis	podáis	pudisteis
	pueden	puedan	pudieron

	Infinitive	Present Indicative	Present Subjunctive	Preterite
⟨2u⟩	**querer.** Stressed *e* in the stem changes to *ie* in the *Present* and *Imperative*. Irregular in the *Preterite*. In the *Future* and *Conditional* the *e* coming after the stem is dropped. Future: *querré*.			
		quier*o*	**quier***a*	qu**ise**
		quier*es*	**quier***as*	qu**is***iste*
		quier*e*	**quier***a*	qu**iso**
		quer*emos*	quer*amos*	qu**is***imos*
		quer*éis*	quer*áis*	qu**is***isteis*
		quier*en*	**quier***an*	qu**is***ieron*
⟨2v⟩	**ver.** *Present indicative 1st pers sg*, *Present subjunctive* and *Imperfect* are formed on the stem *ve*..., otherwise formation is regular using the shortened stem *v*... Irregular in the *Past participle*. Past participle: *visto*.			
		ve*o*	**ve***a*	v**i**
		v*es*	**ve***as*	v*iste*
		v*e*	**ve***a*	v*io*
		v*emos*	**ve***amos*	v*imos*
		v*eis*	**ve***áis*	v*isteis*
		v*en*	**ve***an*	v*ieron*

	Infinitive	Present Indicative	Present Subjunctive	Imperfect Indicative	Preterite

⟨**2w**⟩ **ser.** Totally irregular with several different stems being used. Past participle: *sido*. Imperative *2nd pers sg*: *sé*. *2nd pers pl*: *sed*.

	so**y**	se*a*	er*a*	**fu***i*
	er*es*	se*as*	er*as*	**fu***iste*
	es	se*a*	er*a*	**fue**
	so*mos*	se*amos*	**ér***amos*	**fu***imos*
	so*is*	se*áis*	er*ais*	**fu***isteis*
	so*n*	se*an*	er*an*	**fu***eron*

⟨**2x**⟩ **placer.** Used almost exclusively in the *3rd pers sg*. Irregular forms: *Present subjunctive pl***eg***a* and *pl***egue** egue as well as *plazca*; *Preterite pl***ugo** (or *plació*), *pl***ugu***ieron* (or *placieron*); *Imperfect subjunctive pl***u**-**g***uiera*, *pl***ugu***iese* (or *placiera*, *placiese*); *Future subjunctive pl***ugu***iere* (or *placiere*).

⟨**2y**⟩ **yacer.** Used mainly on gravestones and so used primarily in the *3rd pers*. The *Present indicative 1st pers sg* and *Present subjunctive* have three forms. The *Imperative* is regular; just the stem with *c* changing to *z*. *Present indicative*: *ya***zc***o*, *ya***zg***o*, *ya***g***o*, *yaces* etc; *Present subjunctive*: *ya***zc***a*, *ya***zg***a*, *ya***g***a* etc; *Imperative yace* and *ya***z**.

⟨**2z**⟩ **raer.** The regular forms of the *Present indicative 1st pers sg* and *Present subjunctive* are less common than the forms with inserted *…ig…* as in ⟨2o⟩: *ra***ig***o*, *ra***ig***a*; but also *ra***y***o*, *ra***y***a* (less common). Otherwise regular.

⟨**2za**⟩ **roer.** As well as their regular forms the *Present indicative 1st pers sg* and *Present subjunctive* have the less common forms: *ro***ig***o*, *ro***ig***a*, *ro***y***o*, *ro***y***a*.

Third Conjugation

⟨**3a**⟩ **recibir.** No change to the written or spoken form of the stem.

Simple tenses

Indicative

	Present	**Imperfect**	**Preterite**
sg	recib*o*	recib*ía*	recib*í*
	recib*es*	recib*ías*	recib*iste*
	recib*e*	recib*ía*	recib*ió*
pl	recib*imos*	recib*íamos*	recib*imos*
	recib*ís*	recib*íais*	recib*isteis*
	recib*en*	recib*ían*	recib*ieron*

	Future	**Conditional**
sg	recib*iré*	recib*iría*
	recib*irás*	recib*irías*
	recib*irá*	recib*iría*
pl	recib*iremos*	recib*iríamos*
	recib*iréis*	recib*iríais*
	recib*irán*	recib*irían*

Subjunctive

	Present	**Imperfect I**	**Imperfect II**
sg	recib*a*	recib*iera*	recib*iese*
	recib*as*	recib*ieras*	recib*ieses*
	recib*a*	recib*iera*	recib*iese*
pl	recib*amos*	recib*iéramos*	recib*iésemos*
	recib*áis*	recib*ierais*	recib*ieseis*
	recib*an*	recib*ieran*	recib*iesen*

	Future	**Imperative**
sg	recib*iere*	—
	recib*ieres*	recib*e* (no recib*as*)
	recib*iere*	recib*a* Vd.
pl	recib*iéremos*	recib*amos*
	recib*iereis*	recib*id* (no recib*áis*)
	recib*ieren*	recib*an* Vds.

Infinitive: recib*ir*
Present participle: recib*iendo*
Past participle: recib*ido*

Compound tenses

Formed with the *Past participle* together with ***haber*** and ***ser***, see ⟨1a⟩.

	Infinitive	Present Indicative	Present Subjunctive	Preterite
⟨3b⟩	**esparcir.** Final *c* of the stem becomes *z* before *a* and *o*.			
		espar**z***o*	espar**z***a*	esparc*í*
		esparc*es*	espar**z***as*	esparc*iste*
		esparc*e*	espar**z***a*	esparc*ió*
		esparc*imos*	espar**z***amos*	esparc*imos*
		esparc*ís*	espar**z***áis*	esparc*isteis*
		esparc*en*	espar**z***an*	esparc*ieron*
⟨3c⟩	**dirigir.** Final *g* of the stem becomes *j* before *a* and *o*.			
		diri**j***o*	diri**j***a*	dirig*í*
		dirig*es*	diri**j***as*	dirig*iste*
		dirig*e*	diri**j***a*	dirig*ió*
		dirig*imos*	diri**j***amos*	dirig*imos*
		dirig*ís*	diri**j***áis*	dirig*isteis*
		dirig*en*	diri**j***an*	dirig*ieron*
⟨3d⟩	**distinguir.** Final *gu* of the stem becomes *g* before *a* and *o*.			
		distin**g***o*	distin**g***a*	distingu*í*
		distingu*es*	distin**g***as*	distingu*iste*
		distingu*e*	distin**g***a*	distingu*ió*
		distingu*imos*	distin**g***amos*	distingu*imos*
		distingu*ís*	distin**g***áis*	distingu*isteis*
		distingu*en*	distin**g***an*	distingu*ieron*
⟨3e⟩	**delinquir.** Final *qu* of the stem becomes *c* before *a* and *o*.			
		delin**c***o*	delin**c***a*	delinqu*í*
		delinqu*es*	delin**c***as*	delinqu*iste*
		delinqu*e*	delin**c***a*	delinqu*ió*
		delinqu*imos*	delin**c***amos*	delinqu*imos*
		delinqu*ís*	delin**c***áis*	delinqu*isteis*
		delinqu*en*	delin**c***an*	delinqu*ieron*
⟨3f⟩	**lucir.** Final *c* of the stem becomes *zc* before *a* and *o*.			
		lu**zc***o*	lu**zc***a*	luc*í*
		luc*es*	lu**zc***as*	luc*iste*
		luc*e*	lu**zc***a*	luc*ió*
		luc*imos*	lu**zc***amos*	luc*imos*
		luc*ís*	lu**zc***áis*	luc*isteis*
		luc*en*	lu**zc***an*	luc*ieron*

	Infinitive	Present Indicative	Present Subjunctive	Preterite
⟨3g⟩	**concluir.** A *y* is inserted after the stem unless the ending begins with *i*. Past participle: *concluido*. Present participle: *concluyendo*.			
		conclu**y***o*	conclu**y***a*	conclu*í*
		conclu**y***es*	conclu**y***as*	conclu*iste*
		conclu**y***e*	conclu**y***a*	conclu**y***ó*
		conclu*imos*	conclu**y***amos*	conclu*imos*
		conclu*ís*	conclu**y***áis*	conclu*isteis*
		conclu**y***en*	conclu**y***an*	conclu**y***eron*
⟨3h⟩	**gruñir.** Unstressed *i* is dropped after *ñ*, *ll* and *ch*. Likewise *mullir*: *mu-lló*, *mulleron*, *mullendo*; *henchir*: *hinchó*, *hincheron*, *hinchendo* Present participle: *gruñendo*.			
		gruñ*o*	gruñ*es*	gruñ*e*
		gruñ*imos*	gruñ*ís*	gruñ*en*
		gruñ*a*	gruñ*í*	gruñ*as*
		gruñ*iste*	gruñ*a*	**gruñó**
		gruñ*amos*	gruñ*imos*	gruñ*áis*
		gruñ*isteis*	gruñ*an*	gru**ñe***ron*
⟨3i⟩	**sentir.** Stressed *e* of the stem becomes *ie*; unstressed *e* remains unchanged before endings starting with *i*, but before other endings it changes to *…i…*; likewise *adquirir*: stressed *i* of the stem becomes *ie*; unstressed *i* remains unchanged in all forms. Present participle: *sintiendo*.			
		sient*o*	**sien**t*a*	sent*í*
		sient*es*	**sien**t*as*	sent*iste*
		sient*e*	**sien**t*a*	**sin**t*ió*
		sent*imos*	**sin**t*amos*	sent*imos*
		sent*ís*	**sin**t*áis*	sent*isteis*
		sient*en*	**sien**t*an*	**sin**t*ieron*
⟨3k⟩	**dormir.** Stressed *o* of the stem becomes *ue*; unstressed *o* is unchanged when the ending starts with *i*; otherwise it changes to *…u…* Present participle: *durmiendo*.			
		d**ue**rm*o*	d**ue**rm*a*	dorm*í*
		d**ue**rm*es*	d**ue**rm*as*	dorm*iste*
		d**ue**rm*e*	d**ue**rm*a*	d**u**rm*ió*
		dorm*imos*	d**u**rm*amos*	dorm*imos*
		dorm*ís*	d**u**rm*áis*	dorm*isteis*
		d**ue**rm*en*	d**ue**rm*an*	d**u**rm*ieron*

	Infinitive	Present Indicative	Present Subjunctive	Preterite
⟨3l⟩	**medir.** The *e* of the stem is kept if the ending contains an *i.* Otherwise it changes to *…i…* whether stressed or unstressed. Present participle: *midiendo.*			
		m**i**d*o*	m**i**d*a*	med*í*
		m**i**d*es*	m**i**d*as*	med*iste*
		m**i**d*e*	m**i**d*a*	m**i**d*ió*
		med*imos*	m**i**d*amos*	med*imos*
		med*ís*	m**i**d*áis*	med*isteis*
		m**i**d*en*	m**i**d*an*	m**i**d*ieron*
⟨3m⟩	**reír.** As *medir* ⟨3l⟩; when *e* changes to *i* any second *i* belonging to the ending is dropped. Past participle: *reído.* Present participle: *riendo.*			
		r**í***o*	r**í***a*	re*í*
		r**í***es*	r**í***as*	re*íste*
		r**í***e*	r**í***a*	r**i***ó*
		re*imos*	r**i***amos*	re*ímos*
		re*ís*	r**i***áis*	re*ísteis*
		r**í***en*	r**í***an*	r**i***eron*
⟨3n⟩	**erguir.** As *medir* in the *Present indicative*, *Subjunctive* and *Imperative.* Other forms follow *sentir* with initial *ie…* changing to *ye…* Present participle: *irguiendo.* Imperative: *irgue*, *yergue.*			
		irg*o*, **yerg***o*	**irg***a*, **yerg***a*	*erguí*
		irgu*es*, **ye**rgu*es*	**irg***as*, **yerg***as*	ergu*iste*
		irgu*e*, **ye**rgu*e*	**irg***a*, **yerg***a*	**i**rgu*ió*
		ergu*imos*	**irg***amos*, **yerg***amos*	ergu*imos*
		ergu*ís*	**irg***áis*, **yerg***áis*	ergu*isteis*
		irgu*en*, **ye**rgu*en*	**irg***an*, **yerg***an*	**i**rgu*ieron*
⟨3o⟩	**conducir.** Final *c* of the stem, as with *lucir* ⟨3f⟩, becomes *zc* before *a* and *o*. *Preterite* is irregular with *…je.*			
		condu**zc***o*	condu**zc***a*	condu**je**
		conduc*es*	condu**zc***as*	condu**j***iste*
		conduc*e*	condu**zc***a*	condu**jo**
		conduc*imos*	condu**zc***amos*	condu**j***imos*
		conduc*ís*	condu**zc***áis*	condu**j***isteis*
		conduc*en*	condu**zc***an*	condu**je***ron*

Infinitive	Present Indicative	Present Subjunctive	Preterite

⟨**3p**⟩ **decir.** In the *Present* and *Imperative e* and *i* are changed, as with *medir*; in the *Present indicative 1st pers sg* and in the *Present subjunctive c* becomes *g*. Irregular *Future* and *Conditional* based on a shortened *Infinitive*. *Preterite* has *je*. Future: *diré*. Past participle: *dicho*. Present participle: *diciendo*. Imperative *2nd pers sg*: *di*.

	Present Indicative	Present Subjunctive	Preterite
	digo	diga	dije
	dices	digas	dijiste
	dice	diga	dijo
	decimos	digamos	dijimos
	decís	digáis	dijisteis
	dicen	digan	dijeron

⟨**3q**⟩ **oír.** In the *Present indicative 1st pers sg* and *Present subjunctive …ig…* is inserted after the *o…* of the stem. Unstressed *…i…* changes to *…y…* when coming between two vowels. Past participle: *oído*. Present participle: *oyendo*.

	Present Indicative	Present Subjunctive	Preterite
	oigo	oiga	oí
	oyes	oigas	oíste
	oye	oiga	oyó
	oimos	oigamos	oímos
	oís	oigáis	oísteis
	oyen	oigan	oyeron

⟨**3rk**⟩ **salir.** In the *Present indicative 1st pers sg* and the *Present subjunctive* a *…g…* is inserted after the stem. In the *Future* and *Conditional* the *i* is replaced by *d*. Future: *saldré*. Imperative: *2nd pers sg*: *sal*.

	Present Indicative	Present Subjunctive	Preterite
	salgo	salga	salí
	sales	salgas	saliste
	sale	salga	salió
	salimos	salgamos	salimos
	salís	salgáis	salisteis
	salen	salgan	salieron

	Infinitive	Present Indicative	Present Subjunctive	Imperfect Indicative	Preterite

⟨**3s**⟩ **venir.** In the *Present* two changes: either a …*g*… is inserted after the stem or *e*, *ie* and *i* follow the same changes as *sentir*. In the *Future* and *Conditional* the *i* is dropped and replaced by *d*. Future: *vendré*. Present participle: *viniendo*. Imperative *2nd pers sg*: *ven*.

Present Indicative	Present Subjunctive	Imperfect Indicative	Preterite
ven**g***o*	ven**g***a*	ven*ía*	**vine**
v**ie**n*es*	ven**g***s*	ven*ías*	v**i**n*iste*
v**ie**n*e*	ven**g***a*	ven*ía*	**vino**
ven*imos*	ven**g***amos*	ven*íamos*	v**i**n*imos*
ven*ís*	ven**g***áis*	ven*íais*	v**i**n*isteis*
v**ie**n*en*	ven**g***an*	ven*ían*	v**i**n*ieron*

⟨**3t**⟩ **ir.** Totally irregular with several different stems being used. Present participle: *yendo*

Present Indicative	Present Subjunctive	Imperfect Indicative	Preterite
voy	**vay***a*	**ib***a*	**fui**
va*s*	**vay***as*	**ib***as*	**fu***iste*
va	**vay***a*	**ib***a*	**fue**
va*mos*	**vay***amos*	**íb***amos*	**fu***imos*
vai*s*	**vay***áis*	**ib***ais*	**fu***isteis*
va*n*	**vay***an*	**ib***an*	**fue***ron*

Imperative: **ve** (no **vay***as*), **vay***a* Vd, **va***mos*, *id* (no **vay***áis*), **vay***an* Vds.

Notas sobre el verbo inglés

a) Conjugación

1. **El tiempo presente** tiene la misma forma que el infinitivo en todas las personas menos la **3ª** del singular; en ésta, se añade una *-s* al infinitivo, p.ej. *he brings*, o se añade *-es* si el infinitivo termina en sibilante (ch, sh, ss, zz), p.ej. *he passes*. Esta *s* tiene dos pronunciaciones distintas: tras consonante sorda se pronuncia sorda, p.ej. *he paints* [peɪnts]; tras consonante sonora se pronuncia sonora, *he sends* [sendz]; *-es* se pronuncia también sonora, sea la *e* parte de la desinencia o letra final del infinitivo, p.ej. *he washes* [wɑːʃɪz], *he urges* [ˈɜːrdʒɪz]. Los verbos que terminan en *-y* la cambian en *-ies* en la tercera persona, p.ej. *he worries*, *he tries*, pero son regulares los verbos que en el infinitivo tienen una vocal delante de la *-y*, p.ej. *he plays*. El verbo *to be* es irregular en todas las personas: *I am*, *you are*, *he is*, *we are*, *you are*, *they are*. Tres verbos más tienen forma especial para la tercera persona del singular: *do-he does*, *go-he goes*, *have-he has*.

   En los demás tiempos, todas las personas son iguales. **El pretérito y el participio del pasado** se forman añadiendo *-ed* al infinitivo, p.ej. *I passed*, *passed*, o añadiendo *-d* a los infinitivos que terminan en *-e*, p.ej. *I faced*, *faced*. (Hay muchos verbos irregulares: v. abajo). Esta *-(e)d* se pronuncia generalmente como [t]: *passed* [pæst], *faced* [feɪst]; pero cuando se añade a un infinitivo que termina en consonante sonora o en sonido consonántico sonoro o en *r*, se pronuncia como [d]: *warmed* [wɔːrmd], *moved* [muːvd], *feared* [fɪrd]. Si el infinitivo termina en *-d* o *-t*, la desinencia *-ed* se pronuncia [ɪd]. Si el infinitivo termina en *-y*, ésta se cambia en *-ie*, antes de añadirse la *-d*: *try-tried* [traɪd], *pity-pitied* [pɪtid]. **Los tiempos compuestos del pasado** se forman con el verbo auxiliar *have* y el participio del pasado, como en español: **perfecto** *I have faced*, **pluscuamperfecto** *I had faced*. Con el verbo auxiliar *will* (*shall*) y el infinitivo se forma **el futuro**, p.ej. *I shall face*; y con el verbo auxiliar *would* (*should*) y el infinitivo se forma **el condicional**, p.ej. *I should face*. En cada tiempo existe además una forma continua que se forma con el verbo *be* (= estar) y el participio del presente (v. abajo): *I am going*, *I was writing*, *I had been staying*, *I shall be waiting*, etc.

2. **El subjuntivo** ha dejado casi de existir en inglés, salvo en algún caso especial (*if I were you*, *so be it*, *it is proposed that a vote be taken*, etc.). En el presente, tiene en todas las personas la misma forma que el infinitivo, *that I go*, *that he go*, etc.

3. **El participo del presente** y **el gerundio** tienen la misma forma en inglés, añadiéndose al infinitivo la desinencia *-ing*: *painting*, *sending*. Pero **1**) Los verbos cuyo infinitivo termina en *-e* muda la pierden al añadir *-ing*, p.ej. *love-loving*, *write-writing* (excepciones que conservan la *-e*: *dye-dyeing*, *singe-singeing*); **2**) El participio del presente de los verbos *die*, *lie*, *vie*, etc. se escribe *dying*, *lying*, *vying*, etc.

4. Existe una clase de verbos ligeramente irregulares, que terminan en consonante simple precedida de vocal simple acentuada; en éstos, antes de añadir la desinencia *-ing* o *-ed*, se dobla la consonante:

lob	lob*bed*	lob*bing*	compel	compel*led*	compel*ling*
wed	wed*ded*	wed*ding*	control	control*led*	control*ling*
beg	beg*ged*	beg*ging*	bar	bar*red*	bar*ring*
step	step*ped*	step*ping*	stir	stir*red*	stir*ring*
quit	quit*ted*	quit*ting*			

Los verbos que terminan en *-l*, *-p*, aunque precedida de vocal átona, tienen doblada la consonante en los dos participios en el inglés escrito en Gran Bretaña, aunque no en el de Estados Unidos:

travel traveled, *Br* travel*led*, travel*ing*, *Br* travel*led*

Los verbos que terminan en *-c* la cambian en *-ck* al añadirse las desinencias *-ed*, *-ing*:

traffic traffi*cked* traffi*cking*

5. **La voz pasiva** se forma exactamente como en español, con el verbo *be* y el participio del pasado: *I am obliged*, *he was fined*, *they will be moved*, etc.

6. Cuando se dirige uno directamente a otra(s) persona(s) en inglés se emplea únicamente el pronombre *you*. *You* se traduce por el *tú*, *vosotros*, *usted* y *ustedes* del español.

b) Los verbos irregulares ingleses

Se citan las tres partes principales de cada verbo: infinitivo, pretérito, participio del pasado.

alight - alighted, alit - alighted, alit
arise - arose - arisen
awake - awoke - awoken, awaked
be (am, is, are) - was (were) been
bear - bore - borne
beat - beat - beaten
become - became - become
begin - began - begun
behold - beheld - beheld
bend - bent - bent
beseech - besought, beseeched - besought, beseeched
bet - bet, betted - bet, betted
bid - bid - bid
bind - bound - bound
bite - bit - bitten
bleed - bled - bled
blow - blew - blown
break - broke - broken
breed - bred - bred
bring - brought - brought
broadcast - broadcast - broadcast
build - built - built
burn - burnt, burned - burnt, burned
burst - burst - burst
bust - bust(ed) - bust(ed)
buy - bought - bought
cast - cast - cast
catch - caught - caught
choose - chose - chosen
cleave (*cut*) - clove, cleft - cloven, cleft
cleave (*adhere*) - cleaved - cleaved
cling - clung - clung

come - came - come
cost (*v/i*) - cost - cost
creep - crept - crept
crow - crowed, crew - crowed
cut - cut - cut
deal - dealt - dealt
dig - dug - dug
do - did - done
draw - drew - drawn
dream - dreamt, dreamed - dreamt, dreamed
drink - drank - drunk
drive - drove - driven
dwell - dwelt, dwelled - dwelt, dwelled
eat - ate - eaten
fall - fell - fallen
feed - fed - fed
feel - felt - felt
fight - fought - fought
find - found - found
flee - fled - fled
fling - flung - flung
fly - flew - flown
forbear - forbore - forborne
forbid - forbad(e) - forbidden
forecast - forecast(ed) - forecast(ed)
forget - forgot - forgotten
forgive - forgave - forgiven
forsake - forsook - forsaken
freeze - froze - frozen
get - got - got, gotten
give - gave - given
go - went - gone
grind - ground - ground
grow - grew - grown
hang - hung, (*v/t*) hanged - hung, (*v/t*) hanged
have - had - had
hear - heard - heard
heave - heaved, NAUT hove heaved, NAUT hove
hew - hewed - hewed, hewn
hide - hid - hidden
hit - hit - hit
hold - held - held
hurt - hurt - hurt
keep - kept - kept
kneel - knelt, kneeled - knelt, kneeled
know - knew - known
lay - laid - laid
lead - led - led
lean - leaned, leant - leaned, leant
leap - leaped, leapt - leaped, leapt
learn - learned, learnt - learned, learnt
leave - left - left
lend - lent - lent
let - let - let
lie - lay - lain
light - lighted, lit - lighted, lit
lose - lost - lost
make - made - made
mean - meant - meant
meet - met - met
mow - mowed - mowed, mown
pay - paid - paid
plead - pleaded, pled - pleaded, pled
prove - proved - proved, proven
put - put - put
quit - quit(ted) - quit(ted)
read - read [red] - read [red]
rend - rent - rent
rid - rid - rid
ride - rode - ridden
ring - rang - rung
rise - rose - risen
run - ran - run
saw - sawed - sawn, sawed
say - said - said
see - saw - seen
seek - sought - sought
sell - sold - sold
send - sent - sent
set - set - set
sew - sewed - sewed, sewn
shake - shook - shaken
shear - sheared - sheared, shorn
shed - shed - shed
shine - shone - shone
shit - shit(ted), shat - shit(ted), shat
shoe - shod - shod
shoot - shot - shot
show - showed - shown
shrink - shrank - shrunk

shut - shut - shut
sing - sang - sung
sink - sank - sunk
sit - sat - sat
slay - slew - slain
sleep - slept - slept
slide - slid - slid
sling - slung - slung
slink - slunk - slunk
slit - slit - slit
smell - smelt, smelled - smelt, smelled
smite - smote - smitten
sow - sowed - sown, sowed
speak - spoke - spoken
speed - sped, speeded - sped, speeded
spell - spelt, spelled - spelt, spelled
spend - spent - spent
spill - spilt, spilled - spilt, spilled
spin - spun, span - spun
spit - spat - spat
split - split - split
spoil - spoiled, spoilt - spoiled, spoilt
spread - spread - spread
spring - sprang, sprung - sprung
stand - stood - stood
stave - staved, stove - staved, stove
steal - stole - stolen
stick - stuck - stuck
sting - stung - stung
stink - stunk, stank - stunk
strew - strewed - strewed, strewn
stride - strode - stridden
strike - struck - struck
string - strung - strung
strive - strove - striven
swear - swore - sworn
sweep - swept - swept
swell - swelled - swollen
swim - swam - swum
swing - swung - swung
take - took - taken
teach - taught - taught
tear - tore - torn
tell - told - told
think - thought - thought
thrive - throve - thriven
throw - threw - thrown
thrust - thrust - thrust
tread - trod - trodden
understand - understood - understood
wake - woke, waked - woken, waked
wear - wore - worn
weave - wove - woven
wed - wed(ded) - wed(ded)
weep - wept - wept
wet - wet(ted) - wet(ted)
win - won - won
wind - wound - wound
wring - wrung - wrung
write - wrote - written

Numbers – Numerales

Cardinal Numbers – Números cardinales

0 *zero, Br tb nought* cero
1 *one* uno, una
2 *two* dos
3 *three* tres
4 *four* cuatro
5 *five* cinco
6 *six* seis
7 *seven* siete
8 *eight* ocho
9 *nine* nueve
10 *ten* diez
11 *eleven* once
12 *twelve* doce
13 *thirteen* trece
14 *fourteen* catorce
15 *fifteen* quince
16 *sixteen* dieciséis
17 *seventeen* diecisiete
18 *eighteen* dieciocho
19 *nineteen* diecinueve
20 *twenty* veinte
21 *twenty-one* veintiuno
22 *twenty-two* veintidós
30 *thirty* treinta
31 *thirty-one* treinta y uno
40 *forty* cuarenta
50 *fifty* cincuenta
60 *sixty* sesenta
70 *seventy* setenta
80 *eighty* ochenta
90 *ninety* noventa
100 *a hundred, one hundred* cien(to)
101 *a hundred and one* ciento uno
110 *a hundred and ten* ciento diez
200 *two hundred* doscientos, *-as*
300 *three hundred* trescientos, -as
400 *four hundred* cuatrocientos, -as
500 *five hundred* quinientos, *-as*
600 *six hundred* seiscientos, -as
700 *seven hundred* setecientos, -as
800 *eight hundred* ochocientos, *-as*
900 *nine hundred* novecientos, -as
1000 *a thousand, one thousand* mil
1959 *one thousand nine hundred and fifty-nine* mil novecientos cincuenta y nueve
2000 *two thousand* dos mil
1 000 000 *a million, one million* un millón
2 000 000 *two million* dos millones

Notas:

i) In Spanish numbers a comma is used for decimals:

1.25 **one point two five** una coma veinticinco

ii) A period is used where, in English, we would use a comma:

1.000.000 = 1,000,000

Numbers like this can also be written using a space instead of a comma:

1 000 000 = 1,000,000

Ordinal Numbers – Números ordinales

1st	*first*	**1°**	primero
2nd	*second*	**2°**	segundo
3rd	*third*	**3°**	tercero
4th	*fourth*	**4°**	cuarto
5th	*fifth*	**5°**	quinto
6th	*sixth*	**6°**	sexto
7th	*seventh*	**7°**	séptimo
8th	*eighth*	**8°**	octavo
9th	*ninth*	**9°**	noveno, nono
10th	*tenth*	**10°**	décimo
11th	*eleventh*	**11°**	undécimo
12th	*twelfth*	**12°**	duodécimo
13th	*thirteenth*	**13°**	decimotercero
14th	*fourteenth*	**14°**	decimocuarto
15th	*fifteenth*	**15°**	decimoquinto
16th	*sixteenth*	**16°**	decimosexto
17th	*seventeenth*	**17°**	decimoséptimo
18th	*eighteenth*	**18°**	decimoctavo
19th	*nineteenth*	**19°**	decimonoveno, decimonono
20th	*twentieth*	**20°**	vigésimo
21st	*twenty-first*	**21°**	vigésimo prim(er)o
22nd	*twenty-second*	**22°**	vigésimo segundo
30th	*thirtieth*	**30°**	trigésimo
31st	*thirty-first*	**31°**	trigésimo prim(er)o
40th	*fortieth*	**40°**	cuadragésimo
50th	*fiftieth*	**50°**	quincuagésimo
60th	*sixtieth*	**60°**	sexagésimo
70th	*seventieth*	**70°**	septuagésimo
80th	*eightieth*	**80°**	octogésimo
90th	*ninetieth*	**90°**	nonagésimo
100th	*hundredth*	**100°**	centésimo
101st	*hundred and first*	**101°**	centésimo primero
110th	*hundred and tenth*	**110°**	centésimo décimo
200th	*two hundredth*	**200°**	ducentésimo
300th	*three hundredth*	**300°**	trecentésimo
400th	*four hundredth*	**400°**	cuadringentésimo
500th	*five hundredth*	**500°**	quingentésimo
600th	*six hundredth*	**600°**	sexcentésimo
700th	*seven hundredth*	**700°**	septingentésimo
800th	*eight hundredth*	**800°**	octingentésimo
900th	*nine hundredth*	**900°**	noningentésimo
1000th	*thousandth*	**1000°**	milésimo
2000th	*two thousandth*	**2000°**	dos milésimo
1,000,100th	*millionth*	**1 000 100°**	millonésimo
2,000,000th	*two millionth*	**2 000 000°**	dos millonésimo

Fractions and other Numerals – Números quebrados y otros

$^{1}/_{2}$	*one half, a half*	medio, media
$1^{1}/_{2}$	*one and a half*	uno y medio
$2^{1}/_{2}$	*two and a half*	dos y medio
$^{1}/_{3}$	*one third, a third*	un tercio, la tercera parte
$^{2}/_{3}$	*two thirds*	dos tercios, las dos terceras partes
$^{1}/_{4}$	*one quarter, a quarter*	un cuarto, la cuarta parte
$^{3}/_{4}$	*three quarters*	tres cuartos, las tres cuartas partes
$^{1}/_{5}$	*one fifth, a fifth*	un quinto
$3^{4}/_{5}$	*three and four fifths*	tres y cuatro quintos
$^{1}/_{11}$	*one eleventh, an eleventh*	un onzavo
$^{5}/_{12}$	*five twelfths*	cinco dozavos
$^{1}/_{1000}$	*one thousandth, a thousandth*	un milésimo
	seven times as big, seven times bigger	siete veces más grande
	twelve times more	doce veces más
	first(ly)	en primer lugar
	second(ly) etc	en segundo lugar
7 + 8 = 15	*seven and (or plus) eight are (or is) fifteen*	siete y (*or* más) ocho son quince
10 – 3 = 7	*ten minus three is seven, three from ten leaves seven*	diez menos tres resta siete, de tres a diez van siete
2 × 3 = 6	*two times three is six*	dos por tres son seis
20 4 = 5	*twenty divided by four is five*	veinte dividido por cuatro es cinco

Dates – Fechas

1996	*nineteen ninety-six*	mil novecientos noventa y seis
2005	*two thousand (and) five*	dos mil cinco

the 10th of November, November 10 (ten)
el diez de noviembre, el 10 de noviembre

the 1st of March, March 1 (first)
el uno de marzo, *L.Am.* **el primero de marzo, el 1o de marzo**